June 22–25, 2015
Hangzhou, China

Association for
Computing Machinery

Advancing Computing as a Science & Profession

MobiHoc'15

Proceedings of the 16th ACM International Symposium on
Mobile Ad Hoc Networking and Computing

Sponsored by:

ACM SIGMOBILE

Supported by:

Microsoft Research, Zhejiang University, Datang Group, NSF, and Zhejiang Gongshang Uinversity

Association for
Computing Machinery

Advancing Computing as a Science & Profession

The Association for Computing Machinery
2 Penn Plaza, Suite 701
New York, New York 10121-0701

ISBN: 978-1-4503-3489-1

Additional copies may be ordered prepaid from:

ACM Order Department
PO Box 30777
New York, NY 10087-0777, USA

Phone: 1-800-342-6626 (USA and Canada)
+1-212-626-0500 (Global)
Fax: +1-212-944-1318
E-mail: acmhelp@acm.org
Hours of Operation: 8:30 am – 4:30 pm ET

ACM Order Number: 533155

Printed in the USA

Greetings from General Chairs

On behalf of the organizing committee, we are pleased to invite you to the ACM MobiHoc 2015, which will be held in Hangzhou, China on June 22-25, 2015. ACM MobiHoc is a premier international annual conference with a highly selective single-track technical program dedicated to addressing the challenges emerging from wireless networking and computing. It will also feature three prominent invited keynote speakers: Professor Ness B. Shroff from the Ohio State University, USA, Professor Andrea Goldsmith from Stanford University, USA, and Professor Wen Gao from NSF China and Peking University. In addition, it will showcase workshops, posters, and demos.

We would like to express our sincere thanks and appreciation to all the organizing committee members, the technical program chairs, the technical program committee members and reviewers for their great efforts and contributions to the conference. We would also like to thanks all the authors for submitting their papers to the conference.

We are very grateful to the sponsorship from Microsoft Research Asia, Zhejiang University, National Science Foundation, USA, Datang Group, China, and Zhejiang Gongshang University. The conference venue is at the Hangzhou Jinxi Hotel which is right on the West Lake. The gardens and scenery are mutually attractive and reflect the tranquility of the South China home. We look forward to welcoming you all in Hangzhou, China to experience the wonderful ACM MobiHoc 2015 and to enjoy the spectacular city.

General Chairs

Xuemin (Sherman) Shen
Professor and University Research Chair
University of Waterloo, Canada

Youxian Sun
Professor and Academician of the Chinese Academy of Engineering.
Zhejiang University, China

Vice General Chair

Jiming Chen
Professor
Zhejiang University, China

Technical Program Chairs' Welcome Message

Dear colleagues,

On behalf of the Technical Program Committee, we would like to welcome you to ACM MobiHoc 2015 in Hangzhou, China.

ACM MobiHoc is the premier international symposium dedicated to addressing challenges emerging from wireless networking and computing. The highly selective technical program has traditionally brought together a unique blend of researchers and practitioners, thereby influencing the direction of a wide range of wireless networking research areas. We hope that you will find the conference intellectually stimulating.

We are delighted to report that this year's program continues the tradition of excellence set by this conference over the years. We received 250 submissions, which has made it extremely challenging to select only 37 papers for presentation and inclusion in the proceedings. At such a selective acceptance rate (14.8%) many of the papers that we could not accept are of high quality and we are certain that many of them will appear in the near future at other top-tier conferences.

The paper selection process was handled by the Technical Program Committee (TPC). The TPC included 65 excellent members with expertise spanning all the major areas relevant to the conference scope. In particular, the TPC was composed of members from 16 countries and included 11 members from research labs and industry.

The 250 submitted papers went through a first phase of reviews followed by a very active online discussion phase. Then, several papers went through a second review phase. The reviews were provided by the TPC members and, when needed, a few reviews were provided by external expert reviewers. At the end of this process and based on the results of the online discussion, 12 papers were accepted and 46 papers were further discussed at the TPC meeting that was held on Feb. 28, 2015 at Columbia University in New York. Following the discussions at the meeting, 25 additional papers were accepted. Ten of the accepted papers were assigned shepherds who volunteered to assist the authors during the process of preparing the final version. The work of the TPC was outstanding and we thank all the members for the time and efforts they dedicated to the paper selection process and to attending the meeting. These efforts make this wonderful conference possible.

We are pleased with the strong technical program of the conference, represented by the papers in these proceedings. The conference program covers a wide range of topics, including routing, scheduling, algorithms, performance evaluation, dynamic spectrum access, cellular networks, sensor networks, mobile applications and crowdsensing, security, and wireless systems.

This year's program is preceded by a set of seven workshops. It continues the tradition of having keynote talks from outstanding leaders in the field, and it includes a poster/demo session. The keynote speakers are Prof. Ness B. Shroff, the Ohio Eminent Scholar in Networking and Communications at The Ohio State University, Prof. Wen Gao, Vice President of the NSF of China, and Prof. Andrea Goldsmith, the Stephen Harris Professor in the School of Engineering, Professor of Electrical Engineering at Stanford University.

Finally, we would like to thank many people who contributed to the success of ACM MobiHoc 2015: Prof. Sherman Shen and Prof. Youxian Sun, who provided leadership and continuous support as general chairs; members of steering committee and, in particular, Prof. P. R. Kumar who provided valuable advice on several organizational issues; Dr. Lei Yang and Dr. Donghoon Shin who have been the Webmasters; Dr. Minghui Shi who took care of various aspects related to EDAS; Dr. Xianghui Cao, Dr. Guy Grebla, and Prof. Kai Xing who have been the publicity chairs, Prof. Sangheon Pack and Prof. Zhaoyang Zhang who tirelessly took care of various aspects of the proceedings production; and Prof. Javad Ghaderi, Dr. Guy Grebla, and Prof. Lei Ying, who organized an exciting pre-TPC meeting workshop.

Best wishes for another great ACM MobiHoc conference experience!

ACM MobiHoc 2015 Technical Program Committee Co-Chairs

Junshan Zhang, *Arizona State University*

Gil Zussman, *Columbia University*

Table of Contents

Session: Security, Censorship, and RFID

Session: Wireless Systems and Applications

Session: Cellular and MU-MIMO

Session: Wireless Sensor Networks

Poster Session

Demo Session

ACM MobiHoc 2015 Symposium Organization

General Chairs:	Sherman Shen *(University of Waterloo, Canada)* Youxian Sun *(Zhejiang University, China)*
Vice General Chair:	Jiming Chen *(Zhejiang University, China)*
Program Chairs:	Junshan Zhang *(Arizona State University, USA)* Gil Zussman *(Columbia University, USA)*
Steering Committee Chair:	P. R. Kumar *(Texas A&M University, USA)*
Steering Committee:	Mario Gerla *(University of California Los Angeles, USA)* Jean-Pierre Hubaux *(EPFL, Switzerland)* Joseph Macker *(Naval Research Lab, USA)* Sergio Palazzo *(University of Catania, Italy)* Charles Perkins *(WiChorus, USA)* Martha Steenstrup *(Stow Research L.L.C, USA)*
Workshop Co-Chairs:	Randall Berry *(Northwestern University, USA)* Xiuzhen Cheng *(George Washington University, USA)*
Panel Co-Chairs:	Nei Kato *(Tohoku University, Japan)* Zhisheng Niu *(Tshinghua University, China)*
Local Arrangements Co-Chairs:	Peng Cheng *(Zhejiang University, China)* Guiyi Wei *(Zhejiang Gongshang University, China)*
EDAS Chair:	Minghui Shi *(CIPO, Industry Canada)*
Student Travel Grants Co-Chairs:	Xinbing Wang *(Shanghai Jiangtong University, China)* Yingying Chen *(Stevens Institute of Technology, USA)*
Web Co-Chairs:	Lei Yang *(Arizona State University, USA)* Donghoon Shin *(Arizona State University, USA)*
Poster Co-Chairs:	Catherine Rosenberg *(University of Waterloo, Canada)* Xiaodong Lin *(UOIT, Canada)*
Demo Co-Chairs:	Satyajayant Misra *(New Mexico State University, USA)* Yu Cheng *(IIT, USA)*
Registration and Finance Chair:	Shibo He *(Zhejiang University, China)*

Publicity Co-Chairs: Guy Grebla *(Columbia University, USA)*
Xianghui Cao *(IIT, USA)*
Kai Xing *(USTC, China)*

Publication Co-Chairs: Sangheon Pack *(Korean University, Korea)*
Zhaoyang Zhang *(Zhejiang University, China)*

Pre-TPC Meeting Workshop Organizers: Javad Ghaderi *(Columbia University, USA)*
Guy Gerbla *(Columbia University, USA)*
Lei Ying *(Arizona State University, USA)*

Technical Program Committee: Alhussein Abouzeid *(Rensselaer Polytechnic Institute, USA)*
Vaneet Aggarwal *(AT&T Labs - Research, USA)*
Matthew Andrews *(Bell Labs, Alcatel-Lucent, USA)*
Yigal Bejerano *(Bell-Labs, Alcatel-Lucent, USA)*
Randall Berry *(Northwestern University, USA)*
Sem Borst *(Alcatel-Lucent, Bell Labs, USA)*
Zhipeng Cai *(Georgia State University, USA)*
Jiming Chen *(Zhejiang University, China)*
Xu Chen *(University of Goettingen, Germany)*
Xiuzhen Cheng *(George Washington Univ, USA)*
Carla-Fabiana Chiasserini *(Politecnico di Torino, Italy)*
Florin Ciucu *(University of Warwick, England)*
Reuven Cohen *(Technion, Israel)*
Anthony Ephremides *(University of Maryland, USA)*
Atilla Eryilmaz *(Ohio State University, USA)*
Do Young Eun *(North Carolina State University, USA)*
Massimo Franceschetti *(University of California at San Diego, USA)*
Jie Gao *(Stony Brook University, USA)*
Javad Ghaderi *(Columbia University, USA)*
Seth Gilbert *(National University of Singapore, Singapore)*
Guy Grebla *(Columbia University, USA)*
Omer Gurewitz *(Ben Gurion University, Israel)*
Magnús Halldórsson *(Reykjavik University, Iceland)*
Stephen Hanly *(Macquarie University, Australia)*
David Hay *(The Hebrew University of Jerusalem, Israel)*
I-Hong Hou *(Texas A&M University, USA)*
Krishna Jagannathan *(Indian Institute of Technology Madras, India)*
Tara Javidi *(University of California, San Diego, USA)*
Koushik Kar *(Rensselaer Polytechnic Institute, USA)*
Fabian Kuhn *(Albert-Ludwigs-Universität, Germany)*

Technical Program Committee (continued):

T.V. Lakshman *(Bell Labs, Alcatel-Lucent, USA)*
Emilio Leonardi *(Politecnico di Torino, Italy)*
Ilias Leontiadis *(Telefonica I+D, Spain)*
Xiaojun Lin *(Purdue University, USA)*
Mingyan Liu *(University of Michigan, USA)*
Wenjing Lou *(Virginia Tech, USA)*
John Chi Shing Lui *(Chinese University of Hong Kong, China)*
Armand Makowski *(University of Maryland, USA)*
Peter Marbach *(University of Toronto, Canada)*
Athina Markopoulou, (*University of California, USA*)
Ravi Mazumdar, (*University of Waterloo, Canada*)
Tommaso Melodia *(Northeastern University, USA)*
Ruben Merz, Swisscom *(Group Strategy & Innovation, Switzerland)*
Vishal Misra *(Columbia University, USA)*
Eytan Modiano *(MIT, USA)*
Aradhana Narula-Tam *(MIT Lincoln Laboratory, USA)*
Ariel Orda *(Technion, Israel)*
Panagiotis (Panos) Papadimitratos *(KTH, Sweden)*
Chiara Petrioli *(University of Rome "La Sapienza", Italy)*
Alexandre Proutiere *(KTH, Sweden)*
Lili Qiu *(The University of Texas at Austin, USA)*
Bozidar Radunovic *(Microsoft Research, UK)*
Souvik Sen *(HP Labs, USA)*
Srinivas Shakkottai *(Texas A&M University, USA)*
Ness Shroff *(Ohio State University, USA)*
Vijay Subramanian *(University of Michigan, USA)*
Peter van de Ven *(IBM Thomas J. Watson Research Center, USA)*
Peng-Jun Wan *(Illinois Institute of Technology, USA)*
Xinbing Wang *(Shanghai Jiaotong University, China)*
Guoliang Xue *(Arizona State University, USA)*
Roy Yates *(Rutgers University, USA)*
Yung Yi *(KAIST, South Korea)*
Lei Ying *(Arizona State University, USA)*
Yanchao Zhang *(Arizona State University, USA)*
Zhi-Li Zhang *(University of Minnesota, USA)*

Additional Reviewers:

Erez Biton
Angelo Capossele
Tingjun Chen
Asaf Cohen
Lorenzo Coviello
Dibakar Das
Changlai Du
Alon Efrat
Marco Fiore
Radha Krishna Ganti
Petrika Gjanci
Minas Gjoka
Xiaowen Gong
Varun Gupta
Craig Gutterman
Raziel Haimi-Cohen
Benjamin Hamilton
Shibo He
Martin Hoefer
Xin Jin
Mehrdad Khaledi
Yaron Koral
Gregory Kuperman
Min Li
Yanhua Li
Chunshan Liu
Andreas Loukas
Francesco Malandrino
Jelena Marasevic
Robert Margolies
Jayakrishnan Nair
Arvind Narayanan
Brian Proulx
Gaurav Raina
Pedro Santacruz
Dong-Hoon Shin
Rakesh Sinha
Saleh Soltan
Dora Spenza
Rahul Vaze
Bing Wang
Weina Wang
Xiaohua Xu
Lei Yang
Jiemin Zeng
Kai Zeng
Mengyuan Zhang
Yin Zhang
Zhengyu Zhang

ACM MobiHoc 2015 Sponsor & Supporters

Sponsor:

Supporters:

Keynote

Fast Data Retrieval in Cloud Storage Systems

Ness B. Shroff
Ohio Eminent Scholar in Networking and Communications
Chaired Professor of ECE and CSE
The Ohio State University
2015 Neil Avenue, Columbus, OH 43210
shroff.11@osu.edu

ABSTRACT

We are in the midst of a major data revolution. The total data generated by humans from the dawn of civilization until the turn of the new millennium is now being generated every two days. Driven by a wide range of data-intensive devices and applications, this growth is expected to continue its astonishing march, and fuel the development of new and larger data centers. In order to exploit the low-cost services offered by these resource-rich data centers, application developers are pushing computing and storage away from the end-devices and instead deeper into the data-centers. Hence, the end-users' experience is now dependent on the performance of the algorithms used for data retrieval, and job scheduling within the data-centers. In particular, providing low-latency services are critically important to the end-user experience for a wide variety of applications. Our goal has been to develop the analytical foundations and methodologies to enable cloud storage and computing solutions that result in low-latency services. In this talk, I will overview some of the recent research efforts at fast data retrieval in these large-scale data center systems. Specifically, our focus will be on the new tools and techniques required to address these complex issues, the progress made, and the open challenges that remain.

Bio

Ness B. Shroff received his Ph.D. degree in Electrical Engineering from Columbia University in 1994. He joined Purdue university immediately thereafter as an Assistant Professor in the school of ECE. At Purdue, he became Full Professor of ECE in 2003 and director of CWSA in 2004, a university-wide center on wireless systems and applications. In July 2007, he joined The Ohio State University, where he holds the Ohio Eminent Scholar endowed chair in Networking and Communications, in the departments of ECE and CSE. From 2009-2012, he served as a Guest Chaired professor of Wireless Communications at Tsinghua University, Beijing, China, and currently holds honorary Guest professorships at Shanghai Jiaotong University in China, and the Indian Institute of Technology, Mumbai. His research interests span the areas of communication, social, and cyberphysical networks. He is especially interested in fundamental problems in the design, control, performance, pricing, and security of these networks.

Dr. Shroff is currently an editor at large of IEEE/ACM Trans. on Networking, and on the editorial board of IEEE Transactions on Control of Networked Systems and the IEEE Networks Magazine. He has chaired various conferences and workshops, and co-organized workshops for the NSF to chart the future of communication networks. Dr. Shroff is a Fellow of the IEEE and an NSF CAREER awardee. He has received numerous best paper awards for his research, e.g., at IEEE INFOCOM 2008, IEEE INFOCOM 2006, Journal of Communication and Networking 2005, Computer Networks 2003 (two of his papers also received runner-up awards at IEEE INFOCOM 2005 and INFOCOM 2013), and also student best paper awards (from all papers whose first author is a student) at IEEE WiOPT 2013, IEEE WiOPT 2012 and IEEE IWQoS 2006.

He received the IEEE INFOCOM achievement award for seminal contributions to scheduling and resource allocation in wireless networks, and is noted on the Thomson Reuters ISI list of highly cited researchers, and in Thomson Reuters Book on The World's Most Influential Scientific Minds in 2014.

MobiHoc'15, June 22-25, 2015, Hangzhou, China
ACM 978-1-4503-3489-1/15/06.
http://dx.doi.org/10.1145/2746285.2746323

Keynote

Mobile Visual Search

Wen Gao
NSFC Vice President
Professor of EE and CS
Peking University
Beijing 100871, China
gaowen@nsfc.gov.cn

ABSTRACT

Current mobile search is mainly based on keyword or text, with limited capability in describing real-world objects. In many cases, a query in image taken by the smart phone is simply more descriptive. Mobile devices have shown great potential for visual search, Emerging applications include landmark search, dress product search, book search, location recognition, and scene retrieval, etc. The challenge for mobile visual search is how to cost down the task with high speed searching. In addition, a practical issue remains open on how to make visual search applications compatible across a broad range of devices and platforms. In this talk, I will discuss the key research efforts on CDVS by many teams from academia, and reviewing the standardization activity took by ISO/IEC MPEG working group. A competitive and collaborative platform to evaluate the state-of-the-art visual search techniques and solutions will be given as well, where learning techniques have been shown to be the most promising approach to improve the performance and efficiency of mobile visual search.

MobiHoc'15, June 22-25, 2015, Hangzhou, China
ACM 978-1-4503-3489-1/15/06.
http://dx.doi.org/10.1145/2746285.2767183

Bio

Wen Gao received his Ph.D. degree in electronics engineering from the University of Tokyo in 1991. He is a professor of computer science at the Peking University since 2006. He joined with the Harbin Institute of Technology from 1991 to 1995, as professor, department head of computer science. He was with Institute of Computing Technology (ICT), Chinese Academy of Sciences (CAS) from 1996 to 2005. During his career in CAS, he served as the managing director of ICT from 1998 to 1999, the executive vice president of Graduate School of CAS from 2000 to 2004, the vice president of University of Science and Technology China from 2000 to 2003. Dr. Gao is working at the areas of video coding, video processing, computer vision, and multimedia. He is a Member of Chinese Academy of Engineering, a Fellow of IEEE, and a Fellow of ACM.

Keynote

The Road Ahead for Wireless Technology: Dreams and Challenges

Adrea Goldsmith
The Stephen Harris Professor in the School of Engineering
Professor of Electrical Engineering
Stanford University
Stanford, CA 94305-9515
andrea@ee.stanford.edu

ABSTRACT

Wireless technology has enormous potential to change the way we live, work, and play. Future wireless networks will support Gigabit per second multimedia communication between people and devices with high reliability and uniform coverage indoors and out. Software will create a virtual wireless network cloud, enabling resource management, seamless connectivity, and roaming across heterogeneous access networks, including WiFi and cellular systems. Wireless technology will also enable smart and energy-efficient homes and buildings, automated highways and skyways, and in-body networks for analysis and treatment of medical conditions. The shortage of spectrum will be alleviated by advances in cognitive radios, and breakthrough energy-efficiency algorithms and hardware will be employed to make wireless systems "green". There are many technical challenges that must be overcome in order to make this vision a reality. This talk will describe what the wireless future might look like and some of the innovations and breakthroughs that are required to realize this vision.

Bio

Andrea Goldsmith is the Stephen Harris professor in the School of Engineering and a professor of Electrical Engineering at Stanford University. She was previously on the faculty of Electrical Engineering at Caltech. Dr. Goldsmith co-founded and served as CTO for two wireless companies: Accelera, Inc., which develops software-defined wireless network technology for cloud-based management of WiFi access points, and Quantenna Communications, Inc., which develops high-performance WiFi chipsets. She has previously held industry positions at Maxim Technologies, Memorylink Corporation, and AT&T Bell Laboratories. She is a Fellow of the IEEE and of Stanford, and has received several awards for her work, including the IEEE ComSoc Armstrong Technical Achievement Award, the National Academy of Engineering Gilbreth Lecture Award, the IEEE ComSoc and Information Theory Society joint paper award, the IEEE ComSoc Best Tutorial Paper Award, the Alfred P. Sloan Fellowship, and the Silicon Valley/San Jose Business Journal's Women of Influence Award. She is author of the book ``Wireless Communications" and co-author of the books ``MIMO Wireless Communications" and "Principles of Cognitive Radio," all published by Cambridge University Press. Dr. Goldsmith has authored over 100 journal and 300 conference papers, has a Google Scholar h-index of 78, and is an ISI Highly Cited Researcher. She is also an inventor on 28 patents. She received the B.S., M.S. and Ph.D. degrees in Electrical Engineering from U.C. Berkeley.

Dr. Goldsmith has served as editor for the IEEE Transactions on Information Theory, the Journal on Foundations and Trends in Communications and Information Theory and in Networks, the IEEE Transactions on Communications, and the IEEE Wireless Communications Magazine as well as on the Steering Committee for the IEEE Transactions on Wireless Communications. She participates actively in committees and conference organization for the IEEE Information Theory and Communications Societies and has served on the Board of Governors for both societies. She has also been a Distinguished Lecturer for both societies, served as President of the IEEE Information Theory Society in 2009, founded and chaired the Student Committee of the IEEE Information Theory Society, and chaired the Emerging Technology Committee of the IEEE Communications Society. At Stanford she received the inaugural University Postdoc Mentoring Award, served as Chair of Stanford's Faculty Senate in 2009, and currently serves on its Faculty Senate, Budget Group, and Task Force on Women and Leadership.

MobiHoc'15, June 22-25, 2015, Hangzhou, China
ACM 978-1-4503-3489-1/15/06.
http://dx.doi.org/10.1145/2746285.2746324

WATCH: WiFi in Active TV Channels

Xu Zhang and Edward W. Knightly
Rice University, Houston, Texas, USA
{Xu.Zhang,knightly}@rice.edu

Abstract

Today's "white space" model of spectrum sharing applied in the UHF TV band allows channels that are not being used regionally by a TV broadcaster to be re-purposed for unlicensed-style secondary access in 24 hour increments. Unfortunately, populated areas have few unused channels for white space usage. Nonetheless, from the UHF TV viewer's perspective, Nielsen data show severe *under-utilization* of this spectrum, with vast regions that are in range of TV transmitters having no active TV receivers on multiple channels even at peak TV viewing times. In this paper, we present the design, implementation, and experimental evaluation of WATCH (WiFi in Active TV CHannels), the first system to enable secondary WiFi transmission even in the presence of kilowatt-scale TV transmitters, while simultaneously protecting TV receivers when they are active. To protect active TV receivers, WATCH includes a smartphone-based TV remote or an Internet-connected TV to inform the WATCH controller of TV receivers' spatial-spectral requirements. To enable WiFi transmission in UHF bands, we design WATCH-IC (Interference Cancellation) and CAT (Constructive Addition Transmission) to *(i)* exploit the unique environment of asynchronous WiFi transmission in the presence of a strong streaming interferer, and *(ii)* require no coordination with legacy TV transmitters. With FCC permission to test our implementation, we show that WATCH can provide at least 6 times the total achievable rate to 4 watt secondary devices compared to current TV white space systems, while limiting the increase in TV channel switching time to less than 5%.

Categories and Subject Descriptors

C.2.1 [**COMPUTER-COMMUNICATION NETWORKS**]: Network Architecture and Design—*Wireless communication*

General Terms

Design, Experimentation, Performance, Reliability

MobiHoc'15, June 22–25, 2015, Hangzhou, China.

http://dx.doi.org/10.1145/2746285.2746313.

Keywords

Spectrum Re-use; TV White Space; Database Controller; TV Receiver Feedback; Interference Cancellation; Transmit Beamforming

1. INTRODUCTION

The UHF band of 400 MHz to 700 MHz is often termed the "beach front property" of spectrum due to its superior range and penetration compared to higher frequency bands. Globally, this band is typically licensed to TV broadcasters, which can be considered as primary transmitters (or primary users, PU) because they have the highest priority to access the spectrum as protected incumbents. When a geographical region has no primary broadcaster on a particular channel, that channel is said to be "TV white space (TVWS)," which is available for transmission by secondary users (SU) under today's regulatory frameworks, e.g., in the U.S. [9] and U.K. [15]. Unfortunately, the large number of over-the-air TV broadcasters in many populated areas yields extremely limited white space availability [13]. Nonetheless, in practice, the number of viewers watching TV via UHF is dwarfed by those watching via satellite or cable. For example, in the U.S., only 7% to 10% of all TV households rely on over-the-air UHF broadcast for TV programming [5,20].

In this paper, we design, implement and evaluate WATCH, the first system that enables secondary WiFi transmission in *active* TV channels. WATCH exploits the property that few households are *receiving* UHF-band TV programming in a given channel, time, and location. Because TV transmitters cannot be rapidly power-cycled even if they temporarily have no receivers (due to high transmit power associated capacitance), nor can they direct their energy only towards active TV receivers, WATCH comprises the following three contributions.

First, we propose a new spectrum sharing model and obtain an FCC license for its testing.[1] To date, TVWS models calculate exclusion zones (areas where secondary transmissions are not allowed/transmit power is set to zero) based on transmitting TV channels and their corresponding tower locations [9]. In contrast, we propose a dynamically computed exclusion zone characterized as the union of locations where secondary user transmit power must be reduced in order to protect *active TV receivers*. By exploiting that the receiver-based exclusion zone has a much smaller footprint

[1]FCC experimental license call sign WH9XHJ and file number 0121-EX-ST-2014.

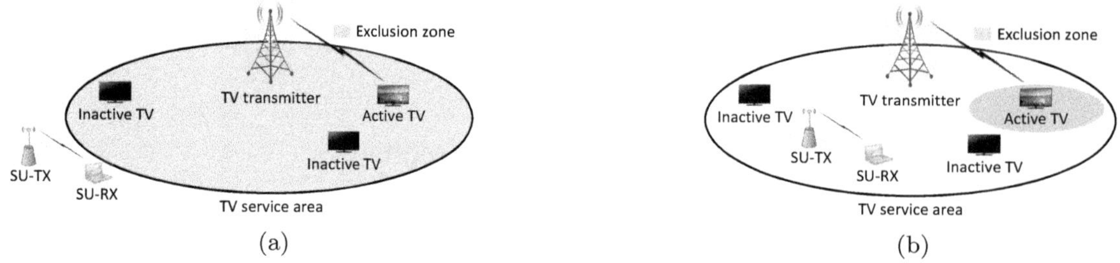

Figure 1: The exclusion zone is computed with (a) TV transmitters in TVWS systems and (b) active TV receivers in WATCH.

than the transmitter-based exclusion zone, WATCH enables vastly increasing secondary spectrum re-use.

Second, to protect *active TV receivers* from secondary transmissions, we introduce two mechanisms to dynamically control the exclusion zone: *(i)* By generalizing the functionality of the spectrum database controller in standards such as IEEE 802.11af [10], we design the WATCH spectrum database controller to collect information of active TV receivers and accordingly coordinate secondary transmissions. Namely, with active TV receiver channel usage and location information, the WATCH controller dynamically determines the maximum transmit power for SU's. *(ii)* We design a WATCH TV receiver that can inform the controller of TV viewing. We introduce two complimentary feedback mechanisms to allow use with legacy TV systems: first, we propose a smart remote control coupled with a legacy TV, e.g., via a smartphone. Upon switching the TV channel via infrared, the enhanced remote also informs the WATCH controller of the new selection. Second, we propose a smart TV coupled with a legacy remote, in which the Internet-connected TV informs the WATCH controller of the new selection.

Third, we design a novel secondary transmit-receive architecture that enables secondary WiFi transmission even when the kilowatt-scale TV transmitters are broadcasting. For secondary *reception*, we design an interference cancellation (IC) technique, WATCH-IC, which exploits the fact that TV signals are always being broadcasted, unlike IC in non-streaming-broadcast systems such as cellular or WiFi. In particular, our design cancels TV signals without requiring their preambles to be known a priori such that WATCH is compatible with any broadcast technology and is not specific to a regional TV coding scheme. For secondary *transmission*, we design CAT, a Constructive Addition Transmission scheme for secondary WiFi transmitters. CAT precodes transmissions and computes beam weights of the secondary transmitting antenna array to ensure that secondary signals add constructively *after WATCH-IC*. It addresses the problem of inadvertent cancellation of secondary signals without coordination with legacy TV systems. Moreover, we employ selective feedback to reduce CAT's overhead. Compared to transmit beamforming in IEEE 802.11n, CAT adapts to continuous and strong interference.

Finally, we implement the key components of WATCH and experimentally evaluate their performance with FCC permission and have the following outcomes.

Protecting active TV receivers: Without WATCH, off-the-shelf TV tuners incur an average delay of 1.86 seconds to switch between UHF channels (the time between receiving the command from the remote and displaying the new channel content on the screen). We show that WATCH's TV receiver feedback process adds no more than 5% to the above channel switching time.

Secondary WiFi transmission in active TV channels: We build two-antenna secondary transceivers using WARP [25] and its UHF-band radio boards [1] and implement both WATCH-IC and CAT. We provide the first demonstration of secondary transmission in active TV channels, including under interference of the strongest DTV signals in our lab location in Houston. With 16-QAM and no channel coding, WATCH-IC alone enables an average BER of 2.4×10^{-3} for secondary transmission at 2 dB secondary signal SINR in a typical indoor environment. CAT further doubles the percentage of zero-BER packets from fewer than 40% to more than 90%. In the same setup, legacy IEEE 802.11af techniques cannot decode *any* secondary packets. We also show that larger sub-carrier density is needed in WATCH for secondary transmission compared to current TVWS systems [10] in order to cancel long-distance TV interference.

Urban scale analysis: We provide an urban-scale data-driven analysis of WATCH with UHF spectrum usage data of a U.S. major city (Houston) [24], TV viewing data from Nielsen [19–21], and WATCH parameters from our implementation. We find that with 1% active TV receivers (among all TV households) per UHF channel, WATCH can provide 6 times the total achievable rate to 4 watt secondary devices compared to current TVWS systems. This represents 42% of the total achievable rate if all TV transmitters were turned off.

The remainder of this paper is organized as follows. Sec. 2 compares legacy spectrum sharing with WATCH spectrum sharing. Sec. 3 and Sec. 4 introduce how active TV receivers are protected and how secondary transmissions are enabled, respectively. Our implementation and evaluations are in Sec. 5. Sec. 6 discusses the related work. Finally, Sec. 7 concludes the paper.

2. WATCH ARCHITECTURE

2.1 Legacy Spectrum Sharing

Current TVWS regulations target exclusion of secondary re-use based on locations where TV broadcast services are available. A typical scenario is shown in Fig. 1a: the secondary transmitter (SU-TX) and the secondary receiver (SU-RX) can only communicate outside the TV service area. In order to calculate the exclusion zone, information of all TV transmitters is stored in a database. SU's are required to query the database periodically for updated information of their operational parameters, e.g., per location re-usable frequencies [10].

Different methods are employed to compute the exclusion zone. According to the FCC, the exclusion zone is an area where the TV signal strength exceeds a pre-defined value, which is calculated by the TV service threshold, SU antenna height, etc. Outside this area, fixed secondary devices are allowed to transmit at up to 4 W EIRP (Effective Isotropic Radiation Power/transmit power including antenna gains), while personal/portable secondary devices are restricted to 100 mW EIRP, or 40 mW EIRP if there are TV transmitters occupying at least one of the two adjacent UHF channels [9]. In comparison, Ofcom divides space into 100 m×100 m blocks with each one having a calculated maximum SU EIRP [15].

2.2 WATCH Spectrum Sharing

Legacy spectrum sharing models (e.g., TVWS) protect a region determined by TV transmitter. However, because the percentage of active TV receivers relying on over-the-air UHF broadcasts is very small [5,20], we can re-purpose spectrum even within the TV service area: *(i) Spectrum in the spatial gaps:* In-between active TV receivers, we allow secondary transmissions without interfering with TV receivers. *(ii) Spectrum in the temporal gaps:* When a TV receiver is not tuned into a particular TV channel, we allow secondary transmissions in that channel and in the region around the TV receiver.

While current TVWS systems cannot re-use both of the above spectrum opportunities, WATCH enables re-use by dynamically deciding the per-channel exclusion zone based on protection of only *active TV receivers*. As illustrated in Fig. 1b, the TV transmitter location is now irrelevant to WATCH, because only *active TV receivers* can trigger secondary exclusion. The exclusion zone for each channel is also dynamic and adapted each time a TV *receiver* is tuned in or out of that channel.

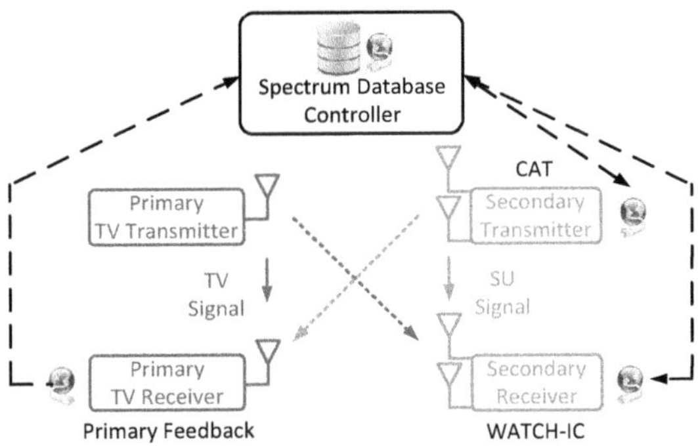

Figure 2: WATCH system overview.

To realize the new spectrum sharing model, WATCH comprises the following components as shown in Fig. 2: a spectrum database controller adapted to receive primary receiver feedback and compute active-TV-receiver-based exclusion zones, legacy TV receivers enhanced with the capability to provide feedback to the database controller, and multiple-antenna SU's. For the PU part, because spectrum sensing cannot detect activity of TV *receivers*, WATCH employs primary feedback to collect information (current channel reception and location) when a TV receiver is tuned into a UHF channel and accordingly triggers secondary exclusion. For the SU part, WATCH multiple-antenna SU's employ WATCH-IC and CAT to enable secondary transmission under TV interference. These subsystems are described separately in the following sections.

3. PROTECTING ACTIVE TV RECEIVERS

In this section, we describe mechanisms to protect broadcast reception quality of active TV receivers. We present the design of the WATCH spectrum database controller, and the functions and realization of primary feedback.

3.1 Spectrum Database Controller

The WATCH database controller computes the operational parameters of SU's based on *active TV receivers* coupled with implicitly determined exclusion zones. In particular, WATCH does not explicitly disallow secondary transmissions in certain areas. Instead, we divide the region into blocks and compute the maximum SU EIRP for each block. Secondary transmission requests are disallowed only in blocks where the maximum SU EIRP is zero. Current TVWS database already has the information of transmit power and location of TV transmitters. We further require that WATCH database also collects the location and channel reception of active TV receivers. Therefore, the maximum SU EIRP for each block can be computed with various pathloss models.

Whenever a TV receiver i becomes active in channel c, the WATCH controller updates the maximum SU EIRP $S_{c,j}^{SU}$ for channel c and each block j that is within distance d^c from TV receiver i. d^c is only related to the channel and can be computed as follows: In WATCH, we limit the maximum SU EIRP to S_{max}^{SU}. We also obtain the minimum required TV signal strength $S_{service\_min}^{PU}$ and TV signal SINR Δ_{TV_SINR} within the TV service area from legacy standards, e.g., the ATSC DTV standard. Denote $h(\cdot)$ as the pathloss of secondary signals, which does not need to be isotropical. $h_{max}(\cdot)$ is the maximum pathloss over a certain distance. d^c is selected to satisfy

$$\Delta_{TV\_SINR} + \Delta_{redundency} = \frac{S_{service\_min}^{PU}}{S_{max}^{SU} \cdot h_{max}(d^c)}, \quad (1)$$

where an additional $\Delta_{redundency}$ is added to represent the aggregate interference from multiple SU's. When updating $S_{c,j}^{SU}$, WATCH ensures that

$$S_{c,j}^{SU} \leq \frac{S_{c,i}^{PU}}{(\Delta_{TV\_SINR} + \Delta_{redundency}) \cdot h(d_{i,j}^c)}, \quad (2)$$

where $S_{c,i}^{PU}$ denotes the mean TV signal strength at TV receiver i in channel c, which can be computed by the Longley-Rice irregular terrain model (currently used by FCC [18]). When TV receiver i is turned off or switched to another channel, all $S_{c,j}^{SU}$ within d^c distance are updated again by the WATCH controller: either to a larger value restricted by another active TV receiver i' or to S_{max}^{SU}.

All SU's are required to provide their infomation to the spectrum database controller in order to acquire the transmission parameters, exactly as in current TVWS systems.

3.2 Primary Receiver Feedback

WATCH employs primary feedback to connect active TV receivers to the spectrum database controller and dynamically determine the exclusion zone. The main functions of primary feedback are to inform the controller of TV channel changes and to act as a fail-safe mechanism.

In WATCH, the in-block maximum SU EIRP $S_{c,j}^{SU}$ is dynamically set with different active TV receivers. For block j, if all TV receivers within d^c are switched to channels other than c or turned off, $S_{c,j}^{SU}$ is reset to S_{max}^{SU} (for either a TV receiver i or a block j, calculations are limited to SU's or PU's within distance d^c). However, channel changes of TV receivers cannot be detected by external techniques such as spectrum sensing. Therefore, we require active TV receivers to inform the database controller of the channel changes through primary feedback.

After a TV receiver informs the controller that it is tuned into a particular UHF channel c, the controller updates all $S_{c,j}^{SU}$ within d^c. However, if the active TV receiver is nonetheless incurring excessive interference due to the errors in either the collected data, (errors in locations of PU's/SU's, errors in pathloss estimates, etc.), WATCH employs the following fail-safe mechanism: If a TV receiver infers that there is excessive interference, the WATCH controller will gradually increase $\Delta_{redundency}$, grow the exclusion zone, and recalculate $S_{c,j}^{SU}$, until that the TV receiver can successfully decode the TV programming. If $\Delta_{redundency}$ exceeds a predefined threshold $\Delta_{redundancy}^{max}$ and the TV receiver still infers being interfered, WATCH controller will consider that the excessive interference is due to poor channel quality of TV signals instead of SU interference.

3.3 Primary Feedback Subsystem

While the broadcasting TV signals and the secondary data are sent in the UHF band, primary feedback can be transmitted out-of-band via WiFi, cellular, or wired connections such as DSL, or in-band via a UHF feedback channel. We propose two methods to implement primary feedback with minimum modifications to legacy TV systems: *(i) Smart remote:* Smartphones can control TVs via infrared, e.g., Samsung Galaxy S5 and HTC One M8.[2] Consequently, smartphones can be used as combined feedback and remote devices. *(ii) Smart TV:* Feedback can be sent via the TV's Internet access.

The required feedback in the previous discussion considers all channels (TV channels, UHF channels) as identical. However, in practice, channels are divided into two types: a physical channel which occupies 6 MHz bandwidth and a virtual channel which contains TV programming. Each physical channel can comprise several virtual channels. Therefore, when an active TV receiver is switched between virtual channels but stays in the same physical channel, it does not need to contact the controller. Feedback is required only when the TV receiver is switched between physical channels. According to [8], TV viewers switch among virtual channels with an average of 2.3-2.7 times per hour. The rate of physical channel switch cannot be larger, which indicates that the primary feedback of channel switch will not be sent very frequently. For the fail-safe mechanism, the value of $\Delta_{redundency}$ determines how well active TV receivers can be protected. A large initial $\Delta_{redundency}$ reduces the amount of feedback to trigger the fail-safe mechanism, whereas in the meantime increases the possibility to excessively limit the SU EIRP.

In order to analyze the quality degradation of broadcast video reception that occurs immediately following a physical channel switch, we denote t_{legacy} as the time that a legacy TV receiver takes to switch between physical channels, which includes physical signal decode, transport stream demultiplexing and video data decode. WATCH increases t_{legacy} to t_{WATCH} by adding an additional delay used by the TV receiver to send the primary feedback and the WATCH controller to update $S_{c,j}^{SU}$ and contact SU's. A comparison between t_{legacy} and t_{WATCH} will be given in Sec. 5.

One concern of this subsystem is that some TVs lack the ability to locate themselves. However, since a TV receiver usually has a fixed location, we can register that location once and use it for subsequent primary feedback. Registration of TV location is already required in some countries, e.g., in Norway [8]. Moreover, even if a TV receiver cannot use the above two methods to provide real-time feedback, we can use its previously stored location to determine a quasi-static protection zone and only update it occasionally. Another concern is the privacy of TV receivers. One solution is to use data with larger granularity at the controller, e.g. grouping nearby TV receivers and using larger time slot when updating activeness.

[2]`http://en.wikipedia.org/wiki/Infrared_blaster`

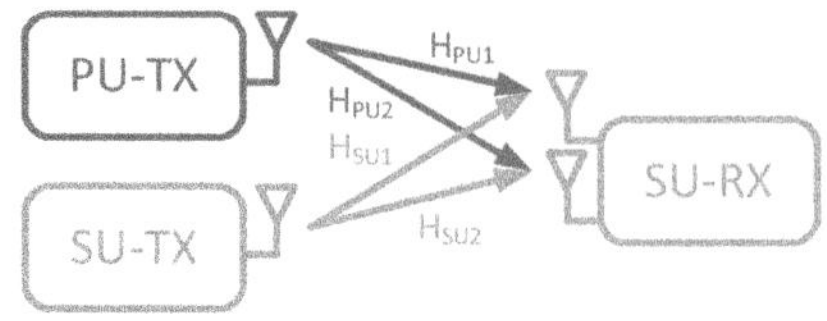

Figure 3: WATCH employs two-antenna SU-RX to cancel TV signals.

4. SECONDARY NETWORKS IN RANGE OF TV BROADCASTS

After a SU is given permission by the WATCH controller to transmit, it can freely access the channel. However, new mechanisms are needed to enable communication in the presence of TV transmitters, since TV transmitters cannot be rapidly power cycled or adapt their energy footprint. Moreover, the maximum EIRP of a 30 m-high secondary device is 4 W over 1000 kW for a 200 m-high TV transmitter. In this section, we show how WATCH exploits the unique properties of continuous TV interference to cancel TV signals at the SU-RX and precode secondary transmission at SU-TX.

4.1 WATCH-IC: Cancellation of TV Signals

Receive beamforming uses multiple antennas to project received signals onto the direction that is orthogonal to the interference. When the interference is relatively strong, receive beamforming can lead to large SINR increase after canceling most of the interfering signals.

A typical scenario of receive beamforming with a two-antenna SU-RX is shown in Fig. 3. WATCH does not require more than two antennas since there will only be signals from a single TV transmitter per UHF channel requiring cancellation. Denote X_{PU} and X_{SU} to be the primary and secondary signals, respectively. The two signals Y_1 and Y_2 at the two receiving antennas are

$$\begin{aligned} Y_1 &= H_{PU1}X_{PU} + H_{SU1}X_{SU}, \\ Y_2 &= H_{PU2}X_{PU} + H_{SU2}X_{SU}. \end{aligned} \tag{3}$$

If the SU-RX could receive a clean (uninterfered) preamble of TV signals, it could estimate the primary channel state information (CSI) H_{PU1} and H_{PU2}, and therefore cancel X_{PU}. However, this method cannot be applied to WATCH due to the vast system-level heterogeneity between the primary and the secondary system (while the analysis hereafter is focused on DTV signals, WATCH techniques can also be applied to analog TV signals): *(i)* The ATSC DTV stan-

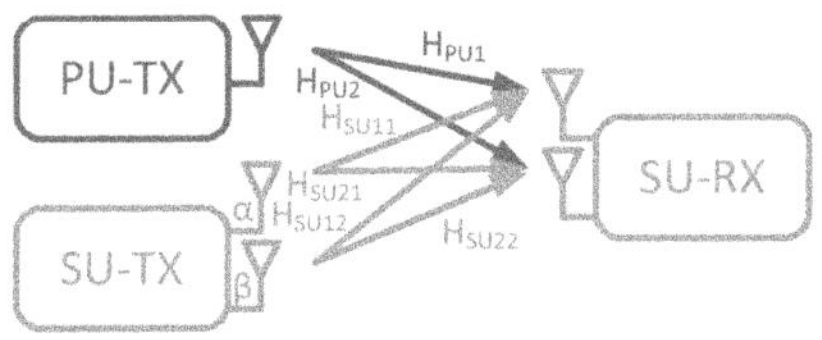

Figure 4: WATCH employs CAT to improve the performance of WATCH-IC.

dard [2] uses single-carrier transmission. Its preambles (field synchronized signals) are only defined for in-phase components. In contrast, the secondary system uses multi-carrier OFDM transmission, for which preambles are defined for in-phase/quadrature components. Moreover, for some sub-carriers, there may be no preambles for estimating the CSI of TV signals. *(ii)* Secondary signals may use different bandwidth from the 6 MHz DTV signals, e.g., a wider bandwidth through channel bonding or occupying only part of the 6 MHz channel. *(iii)* Preambles of DTV signals are sent only every 24.2 ms, which is inconvenient for the SU to use.

As a result, WATCH cancels TV signals without estimating H_{PU1} and H_{PU2}. Instead, we estimate $\frac{H_{PU1}}{H_{PU2}}$, which does not need to use preambles of TV signals and therefore does not require synchronization between the primary and the secondary system. That is, the SU network operates fully asynchronously. In particular, we exploit that *the TV transmitter is always transmitting whereas SU-TX transmits intermittently*. Consequently, when SU-TX is not sending data and $X_{SU} = 0$, SU-RX can estimate

$$H'_{PU/SU-RX} = \frac{Y_1}{Y_2} = \frac{H_{PU1}}{H_{PU2}}. \tag{4}$$

When SU-TX is sending data, TV signals can be canceled at SU-RX by computing $Y = Y_1 - H'_{PU/SU-RX}Y_2$. To realize the receiver signal processing, we can use ZF (zero-forcing) IC by Eq. (4) [11]. We can also use MMSE (minimum mean square error) IC by computing $H'_{PU/SU-RX} = C_{Y_1Y_2}C^{-1}_{Y_2Y_2}$ when $X_{SU} = 0$, where C is the covariance matrix.

To generalize, M antennas at SU-RX can cancel N_1 TV signals and support N_2 secondary data streams as long as $N_1 + N_2 \leq M$. In practice, N_1 usually equals 1 due to the deployment of broadcasting TV systems.

4.2 CAT: Constructive Addition Transmission of Secondary Signals

Transmit beamforming is a method that adapts transmitter antennas' gains and phases to focus signal energy onto the receiver. Unfortunately, this technique alone would provide little benefit to WATCH due to the strong interference from TV transmitters. Consequently, we design CAT, a Constructive Addition Transmission scheme that maximizes secondary signal SINR at SU-RX after accounting for the channels from the TV transmitter to SU-RX.

Namely, without CAT, when WATCH cancels TV signals, secondary signals may be inadvertently canceled as well in some sub-carriers. This effect can be severer when the sub-carrier density for secondary transmission becomes large and when TV signals cannot be completely canceled. Indeed, our experiments in Sec. 5 show that most bit errors of secondary transmissions are focused in several sub-carriers. To address this problem, CAT leverages multiple antennas at SU-TX to rotate the secondary signals at SU-RX to maximize the strength of its effective channel, which is $|H'_{SU}|$ and it includes the WATCH-IC process.

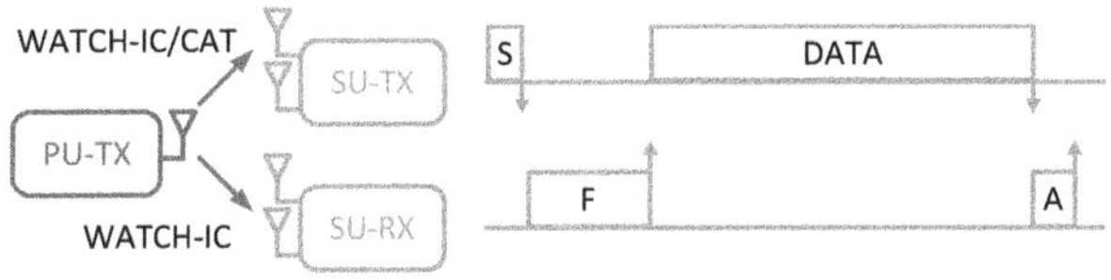

Figure 5: CAT's timeline.

As shown in Fig. 4, $\alpha = \cos\theta$ and $\beta = e^{j\phi}\sin\theta$ are the two beam weights. Different from Eq. (3), the two receiving signals Y_1 and Y_2 now become

$$\begin{aligned} Y_1 &= H_{PU1}X_{PU} + (\alpha H_{SU11} + \beta H_{SU12})X_{SU}, \\ Y_2 &= H_{PU2}X_{PU} + (\alpha H_{SU21} + \beta H_{SU22})X_{SU}. \end{aligned} \tag{5}$$

After WATCH-IC, H'_{SU} can be calculated as

$$\begin{aligned} H'_{SU} = \; & (\alpha H_{SU11} + \beta H_{SU12}) - \\ & H'_{PU/SU-RX}(\alpha H_{SU21} + \beta H_{SU22}). \end{aligned} \tag{6}$$

If all the CSI in Eq. (6) are known, we can calculate the optimal $\hat{\alpha}$ and $\hat{\beta}$ to maximize $|H'_{SU}|$. However, to estimate the CSI, SU-RX needs to receive clean preambles of secondary signals, which is impossible in WATCH due to the continuous and strong TV signals.

To solve this problem, we define

$$\begin{aligned} H_1 &= H_{SU11} - H'_{PU/SU-RX}H_{SU21}, \\ H_2 &= H_{SU12} - H'_{PU/SU-RX}H_{SU22}. \end{aligned} \tag{7}$$

Observe that $H'_{SU} = \alpha H_1 + \beta H_2$. Since there are only two unknowns H_1 and H_2, we can obtain their values by using two sets of α and β.

An illustrative timeline of CAT is shown in Fig. 5:

(i) First, a sounding packet which contains training sequences with two different (α, β) sets is sent from SU-TX to SU-RX.

(ii) At SU-RX, after TV signals are canceled, we can estimate H'_{SU} and compute H_1 and H_2. Then the optimal $\hat{\phi}$ and $\hat{\theta}$ for $\hat{\alpha}$ and $\hat{\beta}$ can be calculated as

$$\begin{aligned} \hat{\phi} &= \arg H_1 - \arg H_2, \\ \hat{\theta} &= \tfrac{\pi}{2} - \arccos \frac{|H_2|}{\sqrt{|H_1|^2 + |H_2|^2}}. \end{aligned} \tag{8}$$

(iii) The values of $\hat{\phi}$ and $\hat{\theta}$ are sent from SU-RX to SU-TX. Similar to Eq. (4), at SU-TX $H'_{PU/SU-TX}$ is estimated. TV signals are canceled before the secondary feedback data are decoded.

(iv) SU-TX uses $\hat{\phi}$ and $\hat{\theta}$ for precoding. At SU-RX, WATCH-IC is used to cancel the TV signals.

4.3 Selective Sub-carrier Feedback

While CAT reduces BER, it also requires overhead. As shown in Fig. 5, explicit sounding and feedback packets need to be sent before CAT SU data transmission.

One way to reduce overhead in obtaining the CSI at the transmitter is to use implicit sounding, which does not require feedback packets: Instead, SU-TX overhears packets from SU-RX and employs channel reciprocity to estimate $\hat{\phi}$ and $\hat{\theta}$. Unfortunately, implicit sounding cannot be used in WATCH due to TV interference. Namely, TV signals are different at SU-RX and SU-TX. With different $H'_{PU/SU-RX}$ and $H'_{PU/SU-TX}$, SU-TX cannot estimate H'_{SU} (at SU-RX), which is required by CAT.

Therefore, WATCH employs an alternative to reduce the overhead of collecting CSI. Generally, the feedback packets account for most of the additional overhead, because the coded information of $\hat{\phi}$ and $\hat{\theta}$ of every sub-carrier need to be sent to the SU-TX. Since secondary signals are not inadver-

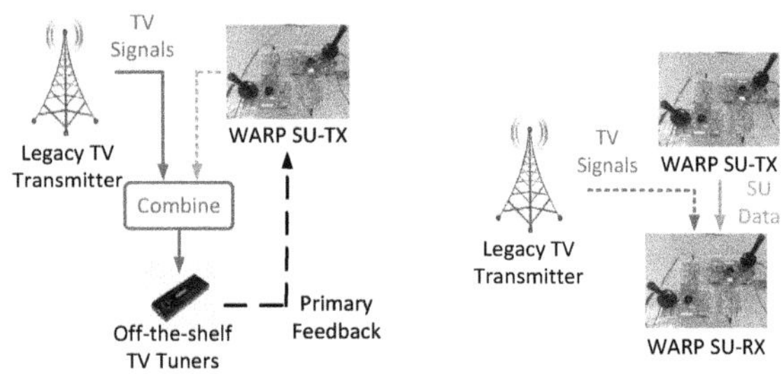

(a) PU sub-system (b) SU sub-system

Figure 6: Implementation of WATCH.

tently canceled in every sub-carrier, CAT need only send selective $\hat{\phi}$ and $\hat{\theta}$ of those sub-carriers where secondary signals are canceled, after which bit errors of secondary transmissions can still be largely reduced. Evaluations of CAT with selective feedback are shown in Sec. 5.

5. IMPLEMENTATION AND EVALUATION

To evaluate the performance of WATCH, we build a small scale indoor testbed and perform over-the-air experiments with FCC permission. Moreover, with UHF spectrum usage and TV viewing data, we characterize WATCH's performance on an urban scale.

5.1 Testbed Implementation

We implement the key components of WATCH and configure a testbed as follows: *(i)* The DTV systems are urban scale DTV broadcasters and the DTV receivers are off-the-shelf TV tuners.[3,4] *(ii)* We implement all aforementioned SU functionality on the software-defined radio platform WARP [25]. To enable UHF transmission and reception, we replace the default 2.4/5 GHz radio boards with UHF-band radio boards designed by [1].

PU system. As shown in Fig. 6a, we combine over-the-air DTV signals with secondary signals generated by WARP and feed them into the TV tuners, which output TV programing to a laptop through the USB interface. To emulate the latency of primary feedback, we set a timer when the channel switching command is sent to the TV tuners, and stop WARP transmission by disabling the transmitting chain after the timer expires.

SU system. As shown in Fig. 6b, we synchronize two WARP boards to build a two-antenna secondary transceiver, and construct a secondary link between secondary transceivers with 10 m separation. To download/upload signal samples to/from WARP, we use the WARPLab 7 framework. At SU-TX, we generate secondary packets according to the IEEE 802.11a standard, including preambles, pilots and data. The SU-RX collects signals in a special format as shown in Fig. 7. The first part only contain TV signals with SU-TX not transmitting. We employ them to calculate $H'_{PU/SU-RX}$ for WATCH-IC. The second part contain both TV signals and header and payload of the secondary packet. We first cancel TV signals with $H'_{PU/SU-RX}$. Then we correct the timing and frequency offset of the secondary packet before decode. Secondary signal SINR before WATCH-IC is calculated as

$$SINR = \frac{E\{S_{PUSU}\} - E\{S_{PU}\}}{E\{S_{PU}\}}. \tag{9}$$

[3]DIAMOND ATI Theater HD 750 tuner
[4]Hauppauge WinTV-HVR-950Q tuner

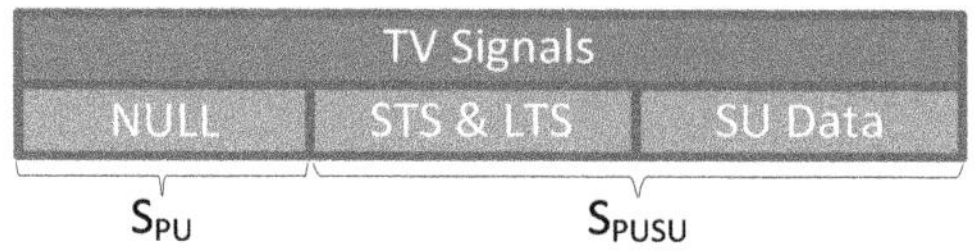

Figure 7: Collected data format at SU-RX.

5.2 Timing Requirement of Primary Feedback

Experiment Setup. To evaluate the interaction between the primary and the secondary system in WATCH, we measure the channel switching time of off-the-shelf TV tuners with different latencies of primary feedback. The channel switching time is defined as the duration between when the channel switching command is sent and when the new TV programming is displayed. Our experiments address two issues: *(i)* How much latency can primary feedback have so that WATCH's increase in channel switching time is overwhelmed by the inherent TV tuner's channel switching time? *(ii)* Can TV receivers begin the tuning process even when the SU-TX is sending data?

To characterize the degradation of broadcast video reception quality, we define $\Delta = (t_{WATCH} - t_{legacy})/t_{legacy}$, with t_{legacy} and t_{WATCH} defined in Sec. 3. Three channels with strong DTV signals are used in the experiments: 19 (503 MHz), 35 (599 MHz), and 42 (641 MHz). For the TV tuners, we find that there is a very narrow transition zone of TV signal SINR between perfect TV programming displaying without errors and undecodable TV signals. We set the WARP transmit power sufficiently high to create strong SU interference, so that TV signals cannot be decoded if a SU is transmitting.

Experiment Results. We vary the control-loop latency of feedback between TV remote channel change indication and notification to SU to vacate the corresponding channel. For each latency, we perform repeated experiments with both TV tuners and different channel pairs and measure the corresponding channel switching time for the TV tuner. The results are depicted in Fig. 8: the x-axis shows the feedback latency and the blue bars depict the measured average channel switching time, e.g., for zero feedback latency it is 1.86 s. The red line shows the sum of the zero-latency case result and the feedback latency as depicted on the x-axis (i.e. 1.86 + x) to provide a baseline for comparison. We only display *average* channel switching time since results are close for different TV tuners and channel pairs.

We make several observations: First, channel switch alone is quite lengthy at 1.86 seconds even without WATCH. This is because highly compressed TV programming results in long initial decoding delay. Moreover, the TV tuner must adapt to the new frequency and a potentially new TV signal SINR. Second, the measured channel switching time with WATCH (the blue bars) is smaller than the calculated sum with feedback latency (the red line). This indicates that even if the secondary signals are initially too strong to prevent the decode of TV signals, the TV tuner can begin the tuning process while the SU is still transmitting.

To estimate the latency of the primary feedback with a smartphone-based remote, we consider an LTE scenario: According to [16, 26], the round-trip delay time (RTT) including both the access and core networks is approximately 35 ms. Such time can be divided into the uplink delay from the smart remote to the database controller and the downlink delay from the database controller to SU's. Further measurements over LTE including end-to-end server response

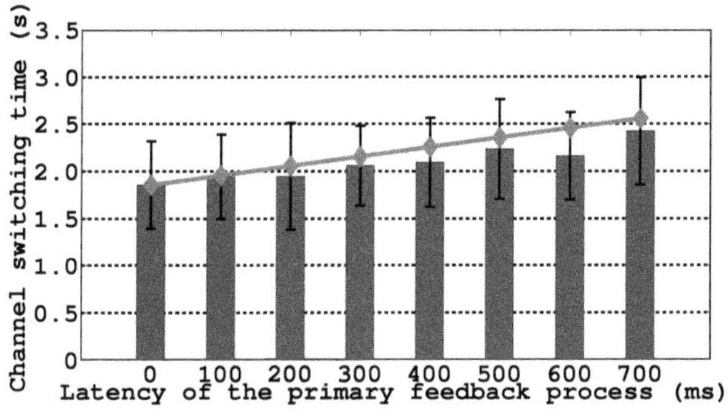

Figure 8: Measured channel switching time with different primary feedback latencies.

delay to a large database server report about 80 ms average RTT.[5] *Finding: In a full-scale system, the expected primary feedback latency of WATCH will be less than 100 ms, which leads to an additional channel switching time of TV's with* $\Delta < 5\%$. *Use of a wire-connected Smart TV can further reduce* Δ *due to smaller RTT.*

5.3 Cancellation of TV Signals

To evaluate WATCH under the most adversarial conditions, we sweep all UHF channels and select the one with the strongest DTV signal, which is channel 26 (545 MHz) in our lab location at Rice University. According to [24], the TV transmitter of channel 26 is approximately 17 km away from our lab and it can broadcast at a maximum of 1300 kW EIRP. In TVWS systems, this channel is clearly excluded from secondary transmission. Consequently, we received an experimental license from the FCC to conduct the first experiments of secondary transmission in active TV channels. Since channel 26 contains the strongest DTV signals, our analysis shows the lower-bound performance of WATCH in our lab. For evaluation, we separately evaluate WATCH-IC and CAT, with this sub-section considering WATCH-IC without CAT.

Experiment Setup. Because the primary (single-carrier) and the secondary (multi-carrier) system use different modulation, it is important to determine the sub-carrier density (number of sub-carriers in certain bandwidth) for secondary transmission required by WATCH in diverse primary/secondary environments. SU transmissions in our experiments use 5 MHz bandwidth, 16-QAM and no channel coding. For different secondary signal SINR, we vary the transmit power at SU-TX. We also change the sub-carrier density of SU transmission from 64 to 512. The sampling rate and buffer size of WARP limit that we can use at most 512 sub-carriers for 5 MHz bandwidth.

Experiment Results. The results are shown in Fig. 9. The x-axis is the maximum SINR of secondary signals at the two receiving antennas before WATCH-IC (we do not use average SINR since BER is more related to one of the two receiving signals that has larger SINR). The y-axis is the average BER of secondary signals. There are five curves in the figure: The upper dashed curve shows the BER before WATCH-IC, whereas the bottom four solid curves show the BER after WATCH-IC.

Without WATCH-IC, the BER is near 0.5 (random guessing) indicating a complete failure if legacy systems are used.

[5]`http://www.fiercewireless.com/special-reports/3g4g-wireless-network-latency-how-did-verizon-att-sprint-and-t-mobile-compa-3`

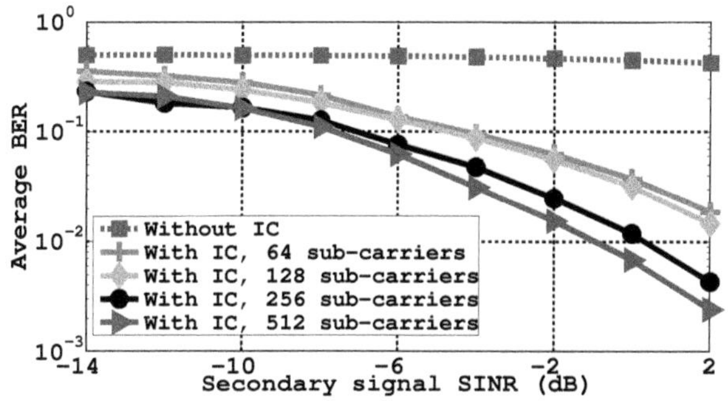

Figure 9: Impact of sub-carrier density on MMSE WATCH-IC.

However, after WATCH cancels the TV signals, the BER decreases, with larger sub-carrier density having a more rapid decreasing rate (indicating better cancellation). At 2 dB secondary signal SINR, the BER for 64 and 512 sub-carriers is 1.9×10^{-2} and 2.4×10^{-3} respectively. In the experiments, while the increase of secondary signal strength after WATCH-IC is similar, the cancellation degree of TV signals vary significantly with different sub-carrier densities.

Generally, the required sub-carrier density is governed by the delay spread (coherence bandwidth) of the signals, so that channel fading can be considered flat over an OFDM sub-carrier. However, in WATCH, the required sub-carrier density of secondary signals is dominated by the delay spread of *TV signals*. In our experiments, the distance from the SU-TX to the SU-RX is only 10 m, whereas the distance from the TV transmitter to the SU-RX is 17 km. According to [17], the delay spread of the UHF band for indoor WLANs is smaller than 1 μs, while that for tower-to-home environments with tens of kilometers of distance is 11 to 25 μs. Therefore, even for short range secondary transmission, in order to sufficiently cancel TV signals, a large sub-carrier density is required. This sharply contrasts with the TVWS standard: In IEEE 802.11af, SU's only use 144 sub-carriers for 6 MHz bandwidth (equivalent to 120 sub-carriers for 5 MHz bandwidth) [10]. *Finding: To sufficiently cancel TV signals with large delay spread, WATCH requires high sub-carrier density even for short range secondary transmission.*

We analyze the impact of other operational parameters of the secondary system in [32] due to space limitations.

5.4 Constructive Addition Transmission of Secondary Signals

In the following, we evaluate the performance of CAT coupled with WATCH-IC.

Experiment Setup. For repeatable experiments, we collect over-the-air channel traces and evaluate CAT with TV signals received in channel 26. We use channel 29 (563 MHz) to collect the CSI between SU-TX and SU-RX. According to Google Spectrum Database, there are no co-channel TV signals in channel 29 in our lab, so that we can collect the secondary CSI without TV interference. For trace post-processing, 5 MHz secondary signals are generated with 512 sub-carriers, 16-QAM and no channel coding. The signals are transmitted through secondary channels first and then mixed with TV signals.

Out of the 512 sub-carriers, only 396 are used to transmit data/pilots (non-silent sub-carriers). To evaluate selective feedback, we only send $\hat{\phi}$ and $\hat{\theta}$ of $N\%$ of the 396 non-silent sub-carriers to the SU-TX. As shown in Sec. 4.2,

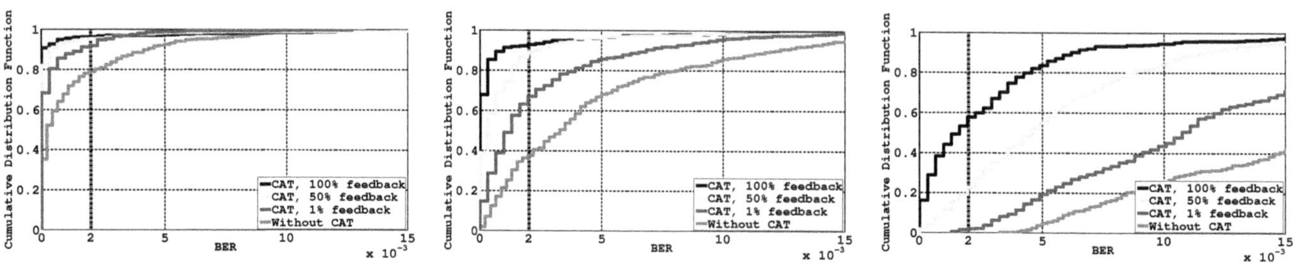

(a) (b) (c)

Figure 10: Cumulative distribution functions of the BER of secondary packets at (a) 2 dB, (b) -2 dB, and (c) -6 dB secondary signal SINR.

the SU-RX can estimate the current value of $|H'_{SU}|$, which is $|H'_{SU-current}|$. It can also calculate the optimal beam weights for the SU-TX and thereby the maximum value of $|H'_{SU}|$, which is $|H'_{SU-max}|$. Therefore, SU-RX, we can compute

$$\gamma = \frac{|H'_{SU-max}|}{|H'_{SU-current}|} \quad (10)$$

for each non-silent sub-carrier. These γ's are sorted and the top $N\%$ sub-carriers with the largest γ are selected. Because feedback accounts for most of the overhead, $N\%$ feedback can be coarsely regarded as reducing the overhead to $N\%$. Note that both data and pilot sub-carriers are considered for selective feedback. This is because pilots help to correct phase offset. Therefore, inadvertently canceled pilots have significant impact on signal decoding. We consider values of N including 100 (all non-silent sub-carriers), 50 (the top half), and 1 (top 1%).

Experiment Results. The cumulative distribution functions of secondary packet BER at different secondary signal SINR are shown in Fig. 10. For Fig. 10a, 10b, and 10c, the secondary signal SINR is 2 dB, -2 dB, and -6 dB, respectively. There is a vertical line of 2×10^{-3} BER in each figure. In practical systems, forward error correction coding can reduce 2×10^{-3} BER to below 2×10^{-16} [14]. Therefore, we approximately view all the secondary packets with BER smaller than 2×10^{-3} as largely error-free packets.

In Fig. 10, the red curves show the results when CAT is not applied, while the black curves show the results when CAT is applied with feedback of all sub-carriers. The results indicate that CAT significantly increases the percentage of error-free secondary packets. At 2 dB, -2 dB, and -6 dB secondary signal SINR, it is increased from 79.0% to 96.2%, 37.7% to 92.9%, and 0.0% to 57.8%, respectively. In Fig. 10a, the percentage of packets with zero BER also increases from 35.2% to 90.8%. However, even with CAT, some SU packets still have relative large BER. There are mainly two reasons: *(i)* When the residual TV signals are relatively strong compared to both $|H_1|$ and $|H_2|$ in Eq. (7), CAT cannot provide significant gain. This is because even if the secondary signals add constructively, the increase of the secondary signal SINR is small. *(ii)* When channels vary rapidly, the calculation of CAT may be stale.

There are two other curves showing the performance of CAT with 50% (yellow curve) and 1% (blue curve) feedback. Note that with 1% feedback, we only send the beam weights of 4 sub-carriers. At 2 dB secondary signal SINR, 50% feedback leads to 95.4% error-free packets, which is very close to that of 100% feedback. Even with 1% feedback, 91.9% packets are error free. However, when the secondary

Table 1: Percentage of bit errors of the top $M\%$ data sub-carriers with highest BER.

SINR (dB)	2	-2	-6	-10	-14	-18
$M = 1$	50.0%	40.8%	19.2%	9.5%	5.5%	4.0%
$M = 10$	99.4%	98.9%	91.1%	58.2%	38.4%	28.8%
$M = 50$	100%	100%	100%	100%	99.6%	87.9%

signal SINR decreases, the improvement by selective feedback also decreases. At -6 dB secondary signal SINR, the percentage of error-free packets with 50% and 1% feedback is only 22.6% and 2.0%, respectively. Both of them have a large difference from the 57.8% error-free rate with 100% feedback. The reason is shown in Table 1. M denotes the percentage of data sub-carriers with highest BER (which is different from N in Fig. 10 that considers data/pilot sub-carriers). When the secondary signal SINR increases, bit errors are more focused on the several sub-carriers. This is because when the secondary signal SINR is large, most bit errors are caused by inadvertent cancellation of secondary signals in certain sub-carriers. However, when the secondary signal SINR becomes smaller, more bit errors are caused by residual TV signals.

Finding: (i) *CAT significantly improves the performance of secondary transmission even after WATCH-IC.* (ii) *For cases of relatively high secondary signal SINR, CAT requires feedback of only 1% non-silent sub-carriers.* (iii) *The improvement of CAT's selective feedback is diminished when the secondary signal SINR decreases, mainly because more bit errors are caused by residual TV signals instead of inadvertent cancellation of secondary signals.*

5.5 Urban Scale Analysis

Finally, we couple the in-lab measurements with UHF spectrum usage and TV viewing data to estimate the performance of an urban scale deployment.

Setup. We collect TV signal strength of 20 strong UHF channels in Houston (4th largest U.S. city) from TVFool [24]. Moreover, we use data of the total TV households in that city [21], the percentage of TV households that rely on broadcasts in the U.S. [20], and the percentage of TV households that are watching a certain TV programming among all TV households at peak TV viewing time in the U.S. [19].

In the data-driven simulation, we first divide the city into blocks of 10 m×10 m. Active TV receivers are randomly placed according to the calculated density. The maximum EIRP of SU's in each block is computed so that for all TV receivers that can originally decode the TV programming (TV signal strength larger than the TV service threshold), the TV signal SINR is still above the TV SINR threshold. If a PU and a SU are in the same block, we assume that

Table 2: Parameters for urban scale analysis.

MAX SU EIRP [9] - S^{SU}_{max}	4 W
SU-TX, SU-RX/PU-RX Antenna Height	3/10 m
TV SINR Threshold - Δ_{TV_SINR} [9]+$\Delta_{redundency}$	23+10 dB
TV Service Threshold [9] - $S^{PU}_{service\_min}$	-84 dBm/6 MHz
Noise Floor [9,31]	-114 dBm/6 MHz
SU-SU/SU-PU Reference Distance	10/5 m

there is a SU-PU reference distance between them. We also assume that SU-TX and SU-RX are separated by a SU-SU reference distance. For the secondary signal pathloss, we employ the Extended-Hata and Hata-SRD model [7]. Even though here the coverage of each SU-TX is a sphere, in practice WATCH can be used with any non-isotropical pathloss models. The achievable rates of secondary links in all the blocks are calculated with Shannon equation, which are then averaged over the whole urban area yielding spatial-spectral efficiency results with unit $bits/sec/Hz/m^2$. Table 2 summarizes the parameters.

Results. Fig. 11 depicts the average spatial-spectral efficiency for all SU's in one UHF channel. In particular, we compute average $bits/sec/Hz/m^2$ for each UHF channel and present average values of the 20 channels normalized to the achievable rate of a UHF channel that has no TV transmitters nor TV receivers. In other words, the normalization baseline, 1, is the average achievable rate for SU's in an unused UHF channel by current TV white space regulations. There are two groups of bars in Fig. 11: the left one shows the results when WATCH-IC and CAT are not applied, while the right one shows the results when WATCH-IC and CAT are both applied. According to our experiments, combined WATCH-IC and CAT can lead to approximately 20 dB increase of secondary signal SINR (for 512-sub-carrier SU transmission). Within each group, the three bars from left to right represent 0%, 1%, and 5% TV active (among all TV households) in each UHF channel, respectively. The case of 0% provides a baseline in which only the TV transmitter is on but no TV receivers are viewing the channel. In this case, the secondary system is only constrained by TV interference and not by the need to avoid interfering with active TV receivers.

When WATCH-IC and CAT are not employed, the average achievable rate for SU's is only 0.23 per UHF channel in the case of 0% TV active rate. WATCH-IC and CAT can almost double the achievable rate to 0.42 by increasing the SINR of secondary signals. When there are TVs viewing the channel, the spatial-spectral efficiency of the secondary system decreases due to the protection of active TV receivers. When WATCH-IC and CAT are not applied (applied), compared to 0% TV active rate, 1% TV active rate results in 22.2% (12.7%) decrease of SU achievable rate, while 5% TV active rate results in 46.6% (28.2%) decrease of SU achievable rate. However, while the number of active TV receivers has a large influence on WATCH's performance, in practice, there cannot be an average of 5% TVs active in each UHF channel since each household can view only a single channel at a time. Therefore, the operational limit of WATCH is primarily from strong TV signals (interference) rather than protecting active TV receivers. Moreover, because TV signal strengths are different in different UHF channels, the corresponding per channel achievable rate for SU's are also different.

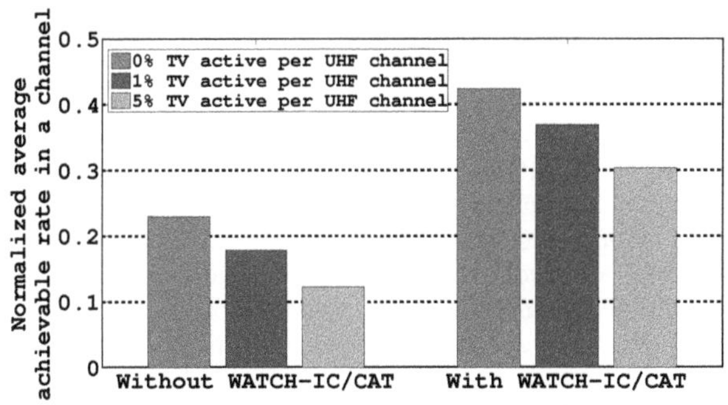

Figure 11: Normalized average achievable rates that WATCH provides to SU's in one UHF channel

Considering the case of 1% TV per-channel activity, the corresponding average achievable rate for SU's is 0.37 per UHF channel. According to Google Spectrum Database, Houston has only 3.26 out of the 47 UHF channels that can be used by TVWS systems (spatially averaged), which leads to a total normalized average achievable rate for SU's of 3.26. Compared to that, WATCH provides $0.37 \times (47 - 3.26) + 3.26 = 19.44$ total achievable rate of all the 47 UHF channels. As an upper bound, if all TV transmitters were turned off, the total achievable rate for SU's would be 47 (1 per channel). Therefore, WATCH provides at least 6.0 times the total achievable rate to SU's compared to current TVWS systems, which is also over 42% of the maximum value if all TV transmitters were turned off.

Finding: (i) *WATCH can provide at least 6.0 times the total achievable rate to SU's compared to current TV white space systems in Houston (typical of a large U.S. city).* (ii) *The operational limit of WATCH is dominated by strong TV signals, and not by the need to protect active TV receivers as TV viewers have low viewing rates and only view one channel at a time when active.*

6. RELATED WORK

Re-use of UHF channels. Most prior work on secondary re-use of UHF band employed the TVWS model, in which TV transmitters determine the exclusion zone and only "idle" channels can be re-purposed [3, 18, 30, 31]. Other work attempts to reduce the exclusion zone by excluding indoor environments where thick walls can largely attenuate interference both from TV system to SU's and from secondary system to TV receivers [4, 28]. Ellingsaeter et al. proposed to use TV receiver information to increase SU spectrum re-use and estimated the resulting increase in spectrum availability (in Hz) for several Norwegian cities [8]. In contrast, we realize the design, implementation, and experimental evaluation of WATCH to cancel TV signals at SU-RX's and protect dynamically active TV receivers from secondary transmissions. Therefore, WATCH targets both indoor and outdoor environments.

Interference cancellation. Previous IC work focused on 2.4/5 GHz ISM bands [11, 23, 27]. Tan et al. decoded overlapping WiFi packets [23]. Gollakota et al. proposed to cancel interference without the help of preambles [11]. Based on that, Yan et al. decode a WiFi packet and an overlapping ZigBee packet [27]. In comparison, we design IC mechanisms under the constraint of a streaming kilowatt-scale interferer in the UHF band.

Constructive addition transmission. Transmit beamforming is employed in IEEE 802.11n and combined transmit beamforming (interference alignment) and receive beamforming (interference cancellation) have been proposed for WiFi bands [6, 12, 29]. However, such techniques require coordination among different access points/clients. In contrast, TV transmitters are non-adaptive to the secondary system in our scenario. CAT also operates under continuous and strong interfering TV signals.

Noam et al. proposed to send secondary signals in the null-space of the interference channel of primary signals at the primary receiver, so that interference to the primary receiver is minimized [22]. However, this technique requires multiple-antenna PU and SU, with the primary transmitter adaptively beamforming to the primary receiver according to interference and channel conditions. In comparison, CAT is compatible with legacy single-antenna broadcast TV systems. The purpose of CAT is also different, which is to avoid inadvertent cancellation of secondary signals.

7. CONCLUSION

In this paper, we propose WATCH, the first system to enable secondary WiFi transmission during active TV broadcasts. WATCH utilizes primary receiver feedback to protect incumbent TV reception. We also design WATCH-IC and CAT to enable secondary WiFi transmission under interference from streaming kilowatt-scale TV transmitters. We build a testbed and evaluate WATCH with FCC permission and show that in a typical U.S. major city, WATCH can provide at least 6 times the total achievable rate to SU's compared to current TVWS regulatory models, while at the same time only increasing TV channel switching time by less than 5%.

8. ACKNOWLEDGMENTS

The authors would like to thank Narendra Anand and Ryan Guerra for their assistance in performing the experiments. This research was supported by Cisco Systems, Intel, the Keck Foundation, and by NSF grants CNS-1444056, CNS-1126478 and CNS-1012831.

9. REFERENCES

[1] N. Anand, R. Guerra, and E. Knightly. The Case for UHF-Band MU-MIMO. In *Proc. of ACM MobiCom*, 2014.

[2] ATSC. ATSC Digital Television Standard – Part 2: RF/Transmission System Characteristics, 2011.

[3] P. Bahl, R. Chandra, T. Moscibroda, R. Murty, and M. Welsh. White Space Networking with Wi-Fi Like Connectivity. In *Proc. of ACM SIGCOMM*, 2009.

[4] L. Bedogni, A. Achtzehn, M. Petrova, and P. Mähönen. Smart Meters with TV Gray Spaces Connectivity: A Feasibility Study for Two Reference Network Topologies. In *Proc. of IEEE SECON*, 2014.

[5] CEA. U.S. Household Television Usage Update. `http://store.ce.org/Default.aspx?TabID=251&productId=328850`, 2013.

[6] L. Ching-Ju, S. Gollakota, and D. Katabi. Random Access Heterogeneous MIMO Networks. In *Proc. of ACM SIGCOMM*, 2011.

[7] CPTE. Extended Hata and Hata-SRD Models. `http://tractool.seamcat.org/wiki/Manual/PropagationModels/ExtendedHata`.

[8] B. Ellingsaeter, H. Bezabih, J. Noll, and T. Maseng. Using TV Receiver Information to Increase Cognitive White Space Spectrum. In *Proc. of IEEE DYSPAN*, 2012.

[9] FCC. Second Report and Order and Memorandum Opinion and Order in the Matter of Unlicensed Operation in the TV Broadcast Bands Additional Spectrum for Unlicensed Devices below 900 MHz and in the 3 GHz Band, 2008.

[10] A. Flores, R. Guerra, E. Knightly, P. Ecclesine, and S. Pandey. IEEE 802.11af: A Standard for TV White Space Spectrum Sharing. *IEEE Communications Magazine*, 51(10):92–100, 2013.

[11] S. Gollakota, F. Adib, D. Katabi, and S. Seshan. Clearing the RF Smog: Making 802.11n Robust to Cross-Technology Interference. In *Proc. of ACM SIGCOMM*, 2011.

[12] S. Gollakota, S. Perli, and D. Katabi. Interference Alignment and Cancellation. In *Proc. of ACM SIGCOMM*, 2009.

[13] K. Harrison, S. Mishra, and A. Sahai. How Much White-Space Capacity Is There? In *Proc. of IEEE DYSPAN*, 2010.

[14] ITU. ITU-T Recommendation G.975.1. `http://www.itu.int/rec/T-REC-G.975.1`, 2004.

[15] H. Karimi. A Framework for Calculation of TV White Space Availability Subject to the Protection of DTT and PMSE. In *Proc. of IEEE PIMRC*, 2013.

[16] M. Laner, P. Svoboda, P. Romirer-Maierhofer, N. Nikaein, F. Ricciato, and M. Rupp. A Comparison between One-Way Delays in Operating HSPA and LTE Networks. In *Proc. of IEEE WiOpt*, 2012.

[17] D. Lekomtcev and R. Maršálek. Comparison of 802.11 af and 802.22 Standards – Physical Layer and Cognitive Functionality. *Elektro Revue*, 3(2):12–18, 2012.

[18] R. Murty, R. Chandra, T. Moscibroda, and P. Bahl. Senseless: A Database-Driven White Spaces Network. In *Proc. of IEEE DYSPAN*, 2011.

[19] Nielsen. Nielsen Top 10 List. `http://www.nielsen.com/content/corporate/us/en/top10s.html`.

[20] Nielsen. Cross-Platform Report. `http://www.nielsen.com/us/en/insights/reports/2014/shifts-in-viewing-the-cross-platform-report-q2-2014.html`, 2014.

[21] Nielsen. Local Television Market Universe Estimates. `http://www.nielsen.com/content/dam/corporate/us/en/docs/solutions/measurement/television/2013-2014-DMA-Ranks.pdf`, 2014.

[22] Y. Noam and A. Goldsmith. Blind Null-Space Learning for MIMO Underlay Cognitive Radio with Primary User Interference Adaptation. *IEEE Transactions on Wireless Communications*, 12(4):1722–1734, 2013.

[23] K. Tan, H. Liu, J. Fang, W. Wang, J. Zhang, M. Chen, and G. Voelker. SAM: Enabling Practical Spatial Multiple Access in Wireless LAN. In *Proc. of ACM MobiCom*, 2009.

[24] TVFOOL. `http://www.tvfool.com/`.

[25] WARP. `http://mangocomm.com/`.

[26] M. Wylie-Green and T. Svensson. Throughput, Capacity, Handover and Latency Performance in a 3GPP LTE FDD Field Trial. In *Proc. of IEEE GLOBECOM*, 2010.

[27] Y. Yan, P. Yang, X. Li, Y. Tao, L. Zhang, and L. You. ZIMO: Building Cross-technology MIMO to Harmonize ZigBee Smog with WiFi Flash Without Intervention. In *Proc. of ACM MobiCom*, 2013.

[28] X. Ying, J. Zhang, L. Yan, G. Zhang, M. Chen, and R. Chandra. Exploring Indoor White Spaces in Metropolises. In *Proc. of ACM MobiCom*, 2013.

[29] H. Yu, O. Bejarano, and L. Zhong. Combating Inter-cell Interference in 802.11ac-based Multi-user MIMO Networks. In *Proc. of ACM MobiCom*, 2014.

[30] Y. Yuan, P. Bahl, R. Chandra, P. A. Chou, I. Ferrell, T. Moscibroda, S. Narlanka, and Y. Wu. KNOWS: Kognitiv Networking Over White Spaces. In *Proc. of IEEE DYSPAN*, 2007.

[31] T. Zhang, N. Leng, and S. Banerjee. A Vehicle-based Measurement Framework for Enhancing Whitespace Spectrum Databases. In *Proc. of ACM MobiCom*, 2014.

[32] X. Zhang. WATCH: WiFi in Active TV Channels (Master Thesis), Rice University, Houston, Texas.

FIWEX: Compressive Sensing Based Cost-Efficient Indoor White Space Exploration*

Dongxin Liu†, Zhihao Wu†, Fan Wu‡ Yuan Zhang§, and Guihai Chen†
†Shanghai Key Laboratory of Scalable Computing and Systems, Shanghai Jiao Tong University, China
§Department of Computer Science and Technology, Nanjing University, China
{liu-dx,sjtu_wuzhihao,wu-fan}@sjtu.edu.cn, zhangyuan@nju.edu.cn, gchen@cs.sjtu.edu.cn

ABSTRACT

Exploring the utilization of white spaces (vacant VHF and UHF TV channels) is a promising way to satisfy the rapid growth of the radio frequency (RF) demand. Although a few outdoor white space exploration methods have been proposed in the past few years, researches that focus on indoor white space exploration just emerge recently. In this paper, we propose a novel cost-efficient indoor white space exploration method by exploiting the location dependence and channel dependence of TV channels' signal strength in indoor environments. We measure the UHF TV channels in a building, and study the temporal and spatial features of indoor white spaces. Based on the extracted features, we design a cost-e**F**ficient **I**ndoor **W**hite space **EX**ploration mechanism, namely FIWEX. Furthermore, we build a prototype of FIWEX and extensively evaluate its performance in real world environments. The evaluation results show that FIWEX can identify 47.8% more indoor white spaces with 38.4% less false alarms compared with the best known existing solution.

Categories and Subject Descriptors

C.2.1 [**Computer-Communication Networks**]: Network Architecture and Design – *Wireless Communication*

Keywords

White Space, Compressive Sensing

†F. Wu is the corresponding author.

*This work was supported in part by the State Key Development Program for Basic Research of China (973 project 2014CB340303), in part by China NSF grant 61422208, 61402223, 61472252, 61272443, and 61133006, in part by CCF-Intel Young Faculty Researcher Program and CCF-Tencent Open Fund, in part by the Scientific Research Foundation for the Returned Overseas Chinese Scholars, and in part by Jiangsu Future Network Research Project No. BY2013095-1-10. The opinions, findings, conclusions, and recommendations expressed in this paper are those of the authors and do not necessarily reflect the views of the funding agencies or the government.

MobiHoc'15, June 22–25, 2015, Hangzhou, China.

http://dx.doi.org/10.1145/2746285.2746298.

1. INTRODUCTION

The growth of wireless networks are currently facing an increasing shortage of available radio frequency spectrums, since the number of mobile devices and their related applications is raising rapidly. However, the amount of unlicensed spectrums that are free to use is very limited. To deal with this problem, the concept of Dynamic Spectrum Access (DSA) that aims at exploring the opportunity of sharing and utilization of licensed spectrums among both licensed users and unlicensed users is proposed and has been applied to several applications [30, 31].

In 2008, FCC (Federal Communications Commission) issued a historic ruling that allowed unlicensed devices to use the TV spectrum that is not locally occupied by licensed devices. (The unoccupied TV spectrum is often referred to as TV white spaces or simply white spaces). After that, the TV white spaces receive more and more attentions from DSA developers. Although white spaces are open for unlicensed use now, FCC also required that unlicensed white space devices should not interfere with the licensed devices (TV broadcasts). Therefore, it is essential for all user devices (especially the unlicensed ones) to find out whether a spectrum band is available before using it in communications.

To explore white spaces, there are mainly two approaches: spectrum sensing approach and geo-location database approach. The spectrum sensing approach, which is less widely used, relies on the user devices to perform spectrum sensing. Thus, it requires the devices to be equipped with proper sensing hardware and to have enough power for sensing and signal analysis. On the contrary, the geo-location database approach that is currently used by most white space user devices and standards does not need the user devices to sense and thus saves their power. Instead, a user device gets to know the availability of white spaces by querying an online geo-location database that stores a "white space availability map" indicating spectrum's availability information at different locations.

For the geo-location database approach, the map of white space availability is vital. In this paper, we study how to efficiently construct a "white space availability map", which is used by the geo-location database approach in indoor environments. Most prior works [26–28] on white space exploration only focus on outdoor scenarios. Since there is relatively few obstructions in outdoor environments, existing works use signal propagation models to infer whether a spectrum band at a specific location is available or not. However, if we directly apply these approaches to indoor environments, which generally have many man-made obstacles, it is likely that we would get results that are overly conservative.

To solve the problem of indoor white space exploration, we propose a cost-eFficient Indoor White space EXploration mechanism, called FIWEX. Intuitively, one can always solve the problem by deploying a large number of RF-sensors that cover the entire floor in a building. However, this could incur a large amount of expense on the sensors. By strategically deploying only a limited number of sensors, FIWEX is able to reconstruct the white space availability map of the entire floor with a small number of RF sensors at high accuracy. Due to the innovative utilizations of 1) the existence of *strong channel*, 2) the *location dependence* as well as *channel dependence* of channels' signal strength in indoor environments, 3) the compressive sensing technique, and 4) a well designed *k-medoids*-based sensor deployment method, FIWEX features a promising efficiency on the total number of sensors deployed and reconstruction accuracy.

The main contributions of this paper are as follows.

- We perform indoor white space measurements in a building for two weeks. The measurement results confirm that (1) there exists strong channels whose signal strength is at least 5dB greater than the white space threshold. (2) indoor white spaces' signal strength has both location dependence and channel dependence. These two key characteristics allow us to efficiently explore indoor white spaces without making a very dense deployment of RF-sensors over the entire building.

- We propose FIWEX, a cost-efficient indoor white space exploration mechanism that does not require user devices to sense the spectrum by themselves. By taking strong channels, location dependence, and channel dependence into consideration, we propose a novel data reconstruction algorithm based on compressive sensing technique to reduce the number of sensors needed for detection. In addition, we design an innovative sensor deployment method to improve the reconstruction accuracy.

- We have built a prototype of FIWEX, and evaluated its performance with real-world experiments. First, we evaluate FIWEX's performance compared to WISER, the best indoor white space identification system so far. In average, FIWEX can identify 47.8% more indoor white spaces with 38.4% less false alarms compared to WISER. Then, we studied the performance versus the number of indoor sensors.

The remainder of the paper is organized as follows. We introduce our indoor white space measurement experiments in Section 2. We describe system model of FIWEX in Section 3. In Section 4, we provide detailed algorithms of FIWEX, including compressive sensing based data reconstruction and the sensor deployment method. In Section 5, we present evaluation results. Related work and conclusions are in Section 6 and Section 7, respectively.

2. INDOOR WHITE SPACE AVAILABILITY MEASUREMENT

We perform our indoor white space measurement in the third floor of a building. The purpose of the indoor white space measurement is exploring strong channels and location-channel dependence of indoor white spaces. These features will be utilized in designing the indoor white space exploration mechanism in Section 3.

2.1 Measurement Setup

The measurement device (Figure 1) we used consists of a USRP N210, an omni-directional receive antenna, a laptop and a uninterrupted power supply (UPS). The daughterboard of our USRP is SBX with 5-10 dBm noise figure. We

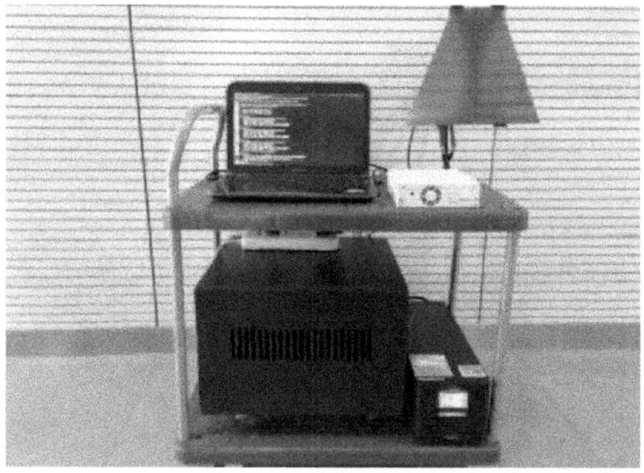

Figure 1: The measurement device.

calibrate the device using a RF signal generator to get the accurate signal strength. As suggested by FCC [1], the gain of the antenna is also taken into consideration during the calibration process.

A number of different methods were proposed for identifying the presence of signal transmissions, such as energy detection, waveform-based sensing, and matched-filtering [18]. Here, we choose energy detection, since it is the most common way with low computation and implementation complexities. In our measurements, we judge whether a TV channel is vacant by comparing the channel's signal strength with a threshold, which depends on the noise floor [19]. If the signal strength of a TV channel is greater than the threshold, we label this channel as locally occupied, otherwise the channel is labeled as vacant. We measure the digital TV channels between 470 MHz - 566 MHZ and 606 MHz - 870 MHz with 8 MHz channel bandwidth, and use the same threshold -84.5 dBm/8 MHz as [2] for digital TV signals. Due to the hardware limitations, the vacant channels determined using the above mentioned threshold may be not safe to use, but the observations drawn from the measurement are general, and our mechanism is not limited to any specific threshold. We believe that if the sensitivity of the measurement hardware can support a threshold of -114 dBm as suggested by FCC [1], our mechanism can be safely used in practice.

We implement the energy detector with a bin size of 1024 and sampling rate 4 MHz. We calculate the power of a channel using the average value of all corresponding bins. During the indoor white space measurement experiment, we measure 45 channels in total.

Our measurement is divided into two parts, namely *long-time sensing* and *short-time sensing*.

2.2 Long-Time Sensing

In long-time sensing, we randomly choose 20 rooms and deploy a USRP coupled with a laptop in every room. The absolute signal strength for all 45 TV channels is measured for 87.5 hours in total. For the convenience of comparisons, we convert absolute power to relative power by subtracting the white space threshold from the absolute power. Devices in different rooms are synchronized using "crontab" of Ubuntu 12.04, and the spectrum sensing programs of different computers run synchronously every half an hour.

We have the following observations from long-time sensing results. First, as shown in Figure 2(a), there exists strong channels whose relative signal strength is obviously greater than 0 during most of the time. For example, we observe 3 channels with >5dB relative signal strength during the

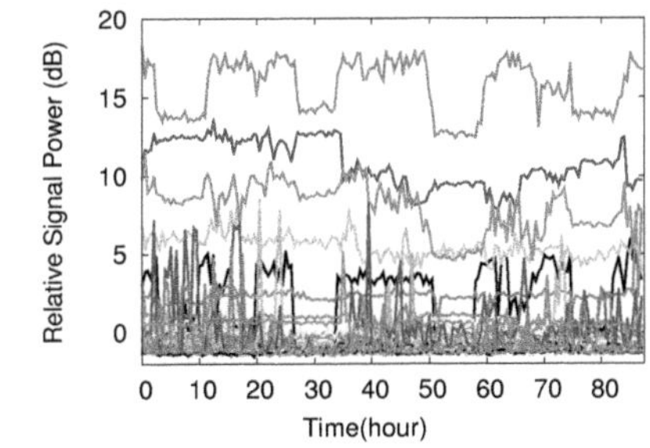

(a) Relative signal strength for 45 TV channels of room 11 in a 87.5-hour window.

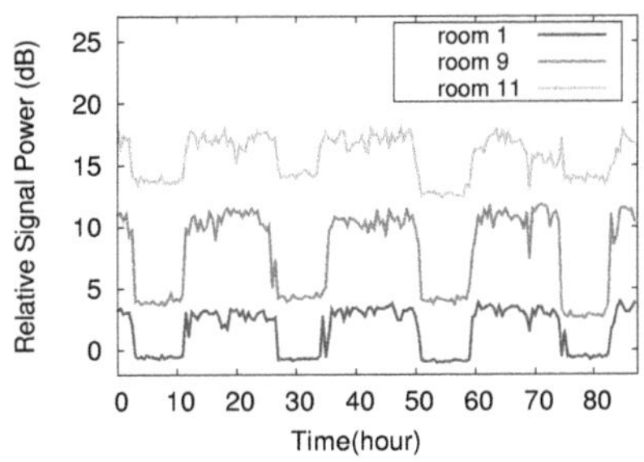

(b) TV channel 13 in room (1, 9 ,11)

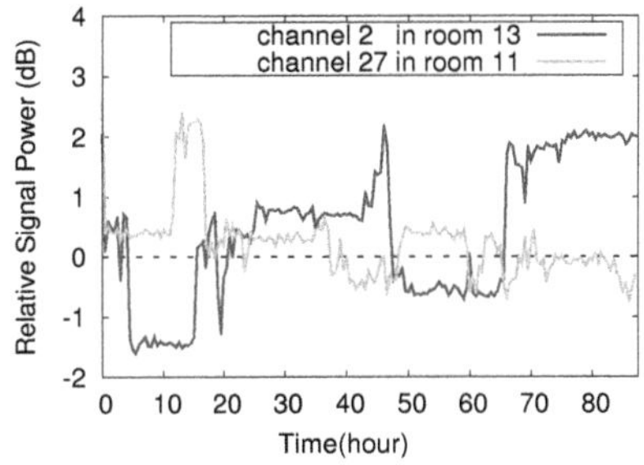

(c) Two short term occupied channels

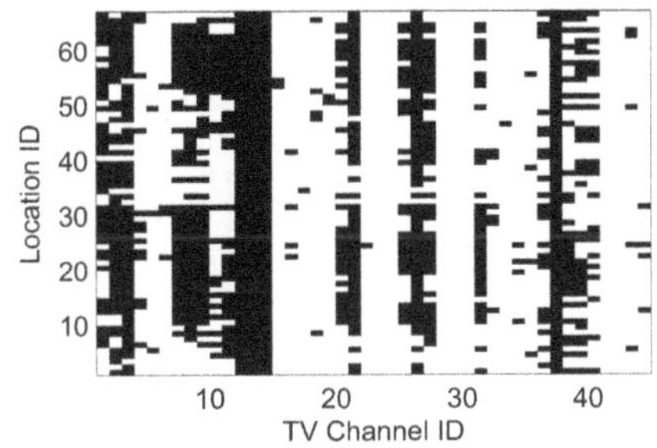

(d) Indoor white space availability map

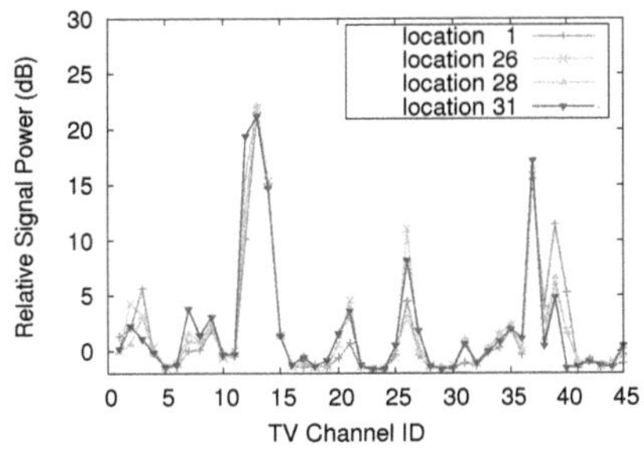

(e) Location dependence

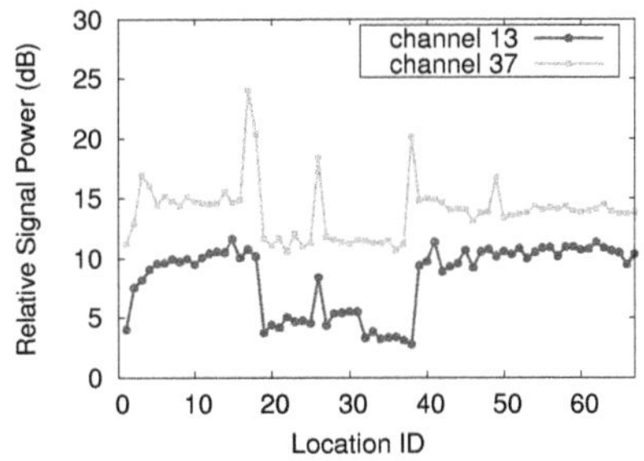

(f) Channel dependence

Figure 2: Results of indoor white space measurement

whole 87.5 hours interval. That means these three channels are long time occupied in room 11.

Second, we observe that a channel may have different signal strengths in different locations. As shown in Figure 2(b), the relative signal strength of channel 13 in room 11 is greater than 5 dB during the whole measurement period; in room 9, the channel's relative signal strength moves up and down around 5 dB; in room 1 it is always below 5 dB.

Finally, short term occupied channels exist. We refer a channel which is occupied for some periods of time and vacant for the rest of time as a short term occupied channel. Figure 2(c) shows two short term occupied channels (channel 2 in room 13 and channel 27 in room 11) whose relative signal strength moves up and down around 0.

Long-time sensing experiment results show the existence of strong channels and short term occupied channels. If we find strong channels and consider them always strong in the future, then we can pay our attention to the short term occupied channels, and in this way, the resources (e.g., RF-sensors, energy) can be more efficiently utilized. Actually, there exists weak channels whose signal strength is lower than the white space threshold in our measurement experiments, but we don't consider them as always weak in order to protect the licensed user.

2.3 Short-Time Sensing

Indoor short-time sensing experiments collect the spatial-channel features of indoor white space. Our indoor white space exploration mechanism was designed based on the data collected during this process.

We choose 67 typical locations labeled as location 1 to location 67, and measure all 45 TV channels at every location and record the received signal strength using our movable device (a cart with a USRP, an antenna, a laptop, and a UPS). After each round of short-time sensing, we get a *Measurement Matrix (MM)*, which is a 67×45 matrix denoted by M. M contains the absolute signal strength for 45 channels at 67 locations, each row/column of which represents a location/channel. We perform 14 rounds of short-time sensing in a period of two weeks and get 14 measurement matrices in total. From the short-time sensing, we have the following observations.

First, Figure 2(d) shows the indoor white space availability map where white blocks represent white spaces and black blocks represent occupied channels. We observed that the signal strength of a channel at different locations could be different (a channel could be occupied at some locations while be vacant at others). This is mainly caused by the complex indoor signal attenuation patterns due to obstructions (e.g., walls). If we directly use the outdoor white space exploration approaches to indoor scenarios, we will lose a lot of white spaces.

Second, in Figure 2(e), the relative signal strength of all channels is similar at four different locations (1, 26, 28, 31). Prior work [2] described this kind of relationship between different locations according to locations' similarity. They treat the correlated locations as a group and represents the white space availability of all locations in this group using only one of them. It is indeed a creative way to utilize the similarity relationship between locations. However, in our mechanism, we consider not only the similarity relationship but also the linear dependence between locations. *Location dependence* represents the linear dependence between different locations, that means any row of M can be approximately represented as a linear function of some of the other rows. Assume that M_i is ith row of M (M_i is a 1×45 row vector containing the signal strength of 45 channels at location i), we can approximate M_i as

$$M_i \approx a_0 M_0 + a_1 M_{i_1} + a_2 M_{i_2} + ... + a_k M_{i_k},$$

where M_0 is a 1×45 row vector equals to $(1, 1, ..., 1)$ and $M_{i_1}, M_{i_2}, ..., M_{i_k}$ $(i_1, i_2, ..., i_k \neq i)$ are the i_1th, i_2th, ..., i_kth rows of MM, and $a_0, ..., a_k$ are the weight parameters. Similar to location dependence, we define *channel dependence* as the linear dependence of channels. As shown in Figure 2(f), although the similar relationship is not suitable here as the signal strength of channel 13 and channel 37 are not close, our linear dependence relationship works well since the difference of them is almost fixed in different locations. According to the definition of relative location-channel matrix X (Section 3.1), we got that location-channel dependence also exists in X, since $M - X$ is a constant matrix. In Section 4.3, we introduce a novel way to draw the location-channel dependence.

2.4 Summary

The indoor white space measurements give us a better understanding about the characteristics of indoor white spaces. Below we summarize guidelines for designing FIWEX.

- Strong channels are occupied for most of time, thus we can neglect these channels once we spot them.
- Location dependence and channel dependence allow us to infer a channel's signal strength or status based on its correlated channels or locations.

In next section, we will show how to use these guidelines to make FIWEX cost-efficient and accurate.

3. SYSTEM MODEL

FIWEX aims to accurately identify indoor white spaces with a small number of RF sensors deployed. As shown in Figure 3, FIWEX is mainly composed of two parts: central server and real time sensing module. The central server receives the real-time sensing results reported by the indoor sensors, and maintains the historical sensing records. Upon receiving a query for availability of the white space at a certain location from a user, the central server calculates the up-to-date indoor white space availability map, and make a respond.

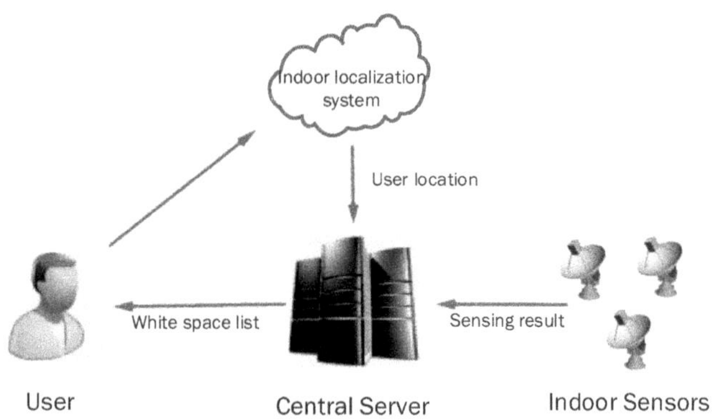

Figure 3: System architecture of FIWEX.

3.1 Real Time Sensing Module

We describe the real time sensing module using our test building with 67 locations as an example. The real time sensing module's job is choosing a part of these 67 locations, placing a sensor at each chosen location, performing a "partial sensing" (since not all 67 locations have sensors deployed), and sending the data to the central server.

If the real time sensing module deploys sensors at all 67 locations, clearly the central server can get complete short-time sensing data. However, due to the cost considerations, real time sensing module aims to use less number of sensors to get complete sensing data.

For ease of presentation, we define the following matrices:

- **Relative Location-Channel Matrix (RLCM)**: is a 67×45 matrix recording channels' relative signal strength. RLCM is denoted by X, where $X(i, j)$ is the relative signal strength of channel j at location i.

$$X(i, j) = M(i, j) - TH,$$

where TH is the white space threshold. If $X(i, j) < 0$, then channel j is vacant at location i, otherwise occupied.

- **Binary Index Matrix (BM)**: is a 67×45 matrix, which indicates where the sensors are deployed. BM is denoted by B, and for any channel j between 1 and 45

$$B(i, j) = \begin{cases} 0 & \text{if no sensor is deployed at location } i, \\ 1 & \text{otherwise.} \end{cases}$$

- **Direct Sensory Matrix (DM)**: is a 67×45 matrix, which records the relative signal strength at locations with sensors deployed. For locations without a sensor, the corresponding rows in DM contain 45 0s. DM is denoted by D:

$$D(i, j) = \begin{cases} X(i, j) & \text{if } B(i, j) = 1, \\ 0 & \text{if } B(i, j) = 0. \end{cases}$$

This means $D = B \circ X$, where $\circ$ refers to the Hadamard product. ($D = B \circ X$ means $D(i, j) = B(i, j)X(i, j)$).

Given a specific number of sensors, different deployments of these sensors lead to different performance of FIWEX. (We will discuss our indoor sensor deployment method in Section 4.5). Once a sensor deployment is determined, B is fixed. Sensors deployed at different locations collect absolute signal strength in real time and the corresponding relative ones are recorded in D. After that, real time sensing module submits matrix D to the central server at regular intervals.

3.2 Central Server:

The central server of FIWEX consists of two parts: *data reconstruction* and *white space database*.

In data reconstruction part, a complete relative location-channel matrix is reconstructed based on the direct sensory matrix (D). We define the reconstructed matrix as follows:

- **Reconstructed Matrix (RM)** : is a 67×45 matrix generated by interpolating the missing values in D. RM is denoted by $\tilde{X}$.

Data reconstruction part aims to find $\tilde{X}$ that approximates X as accurate as possible.

Strong channels can be utilized to improve the accuracy of data reconstruction. In contrast to existing works, observations in Section 2.2 (Figure 2(b)) show that different locations may have different strong channels. Based on this observation, we define the strong channel matrix as follows:

- **Strong Channel Matrix (SCM)** : is a 67×45 matrix that indicates strong channels in different locations. SCM is denoted by

$$S(i, j) = \begin{cases} 1 & \text{channel } j \text{ is a strong channel at location } i, \\ 0 & \text{otherwise.} \end{cases}$$

Given D, B and S as inputs, the central server performs data reconstruction based on compressive sensing. We will present the details of this process in Section 4.

White space database receives the result of data reconstruction $\tilde{X}$, and produces the up-to-date indoor white space availability map according to $\tilde{X}$. In order to avoid interference with licensed users, we compare $\tilde{X}(i,j)$ with PR (instead of 0) to decide whether channel j at location i is vacant. We define the reconstructed indoor white space availability map as

$$MAP(i,j) = \begin{cases} 1 & \text{if } \tilde{X}(i,j) < PR, \\ 0 & \text{if } \tilde{X}(i,j) \geq PR, \end{cases}$$

where PR is the protection range ($PR = -0.7$ by default). Hence, MAP approximately denotes the availability (1 for vacant and 0 for occupied) of indoor white spaces with a low false alarm rate.

Users submit their indoor positions to the central server through an indoor localization system [20, 21]. Given the indoor position of a user, the database first finds one of the 67 profiled locations which is the nearest to the user, and then returns the white space list of this profiled location to the user after considering the interference with neighbors. Here for simplicity, FIWEX assumes the white space availability of a non-profiled location is the same as the availability of the nearest profiled one. We leave the case where these two availability results are not equal to our future work. We have to note that our approach proposed in the paper is to efficiently identify indoor white spaces. A closely related problem on how to utilize the identified indoor white spaces without interfering is our another future work.

4. DATA RECONSTRUCTION AND SENSOR DEPLOYMENT

In this section, we present our compressive sensing based indoor white space reconstruction algorithm, and propose a cost-efficient sensor deployment method.

Compressive sensing is a generic data reconstruction technique based on the structure and redundancy of real-world signals or datasets [3–6]. So far, compressive sensing has been widely applied to different realms [7–11]. However, indoor white spaces have unique strong channels and location-channel dependence. Consequently, we cannot directly apply the traditional compressive sensing technique to the relative location-channel matrix recovery. To deal with this issue, we introduce strong channels and location-channel dependence to compressive sensing, and solve the problem using alternative least square method. Compressive sensing based data reconstruction algorithms perform very differently given different data loss patterns [8], and thus different sensor deployments may lead to different performance of FIWEX. In order to find appropriate locations to deploy sensors, we propose a *k-medoids* [13] based sensor deployment method.

4.1 Compressive Sensing

Given D, B and S, compressive sensing can help us to approximately reconstruct X. According to the theory of compressive sensing, matrices with low-rank feature can be reconstructed with a high accuracy. When the vector containing all singular values of a matrix is sparse, the matrix is low-rank. In Figure 4, we illustrate the distribution of singular values in 7 of the 14 relative location-channel matrices we got in the short time sensing experiments. The X-axis presents the i-th singular values, and the Y-axis presents the normalized values of i-th singular value. This figure suggests that the energy is always contributed by the top several singular values in X. In average, the top 25% singular values contribute most of the energy in this graph. This phenomenon reveals that X exhibits approximate low-rank structure. The followings are the details about our compressive sensing algorithm.

We begin with the Singular Value Decomposition (SVD) using the similar methodology as [7]. SVD is a kind of factorization of a matrix, and it is a useful tool for creating low-rank matrix approximation. Here, we generalize the discussion of the relative location-channel matrix (X) to an $m \times n$ matrix. For the $m \times n$ matrix X, there exists a factorization of the form

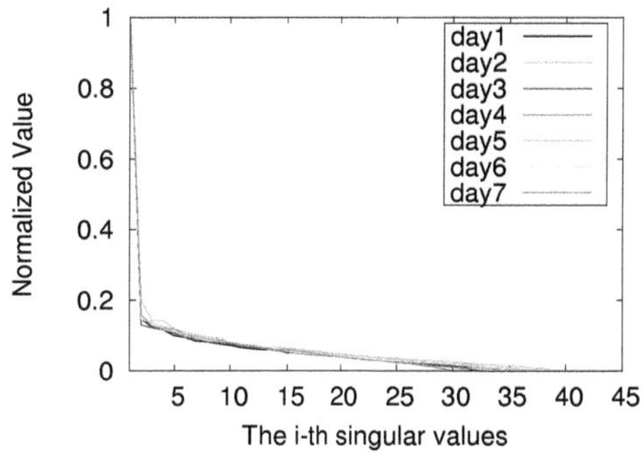

Figure 4: Low-rank feature of X.

$$X = U\Sigma V^T = \sum_{i=1}^{min(m,n)} \sigma_i \mathbf{u}_i \mathbf{v}_i^T, \tag{1}$$

where U is an $m \times m$ unitary matrix (*i.e.*, $UU^T = U^T U = I$), V^T is the transpose of an $n \times n$ unitary matrix, Σ is an $m \times n$ diagonal matrix with the singular value σ_i of X on the main diagonal, where $\sigma_i \geq \sigma_{i+1}$. Here $\mathbf{u}_i$ and $\mathbf{v}_i$ are the ith columns of U and V, respectively. As we mentioned before, the top 25% singular values of X contribute most of the sum of all singular values, and this means that

$$\sum_{i=1}^{r} \sigma_i \approx \sum_{i=1}^{min(m,n)} \sigma_i \tag{2}$$

and

$$\sum_{i=1}^{r} \sigma_i \mathbf{u}_i \mathbf{v}_i^T \approx \sum_{i=1}^{min(m,n)} \sigma_i \mathbf{u}_i \mathbf{v}_i^T, \tag{3}$$

where $r \ll min(m,n)$. Hence we can approximately represent X as

$$\tilde{X} = \sum_{i=1}^{r} \sigma_i \mathbf{u}_i \mathbf{v}_i^T, \tag{4}$$

where r is the rank of $\tilde{X}$. Actually, $\tilde{X}$ is the best r-rank approximation that minimize the Frobenius norm $\|\cdot\|_F$ between X and $\tilde{X}$. That is, $\tilde{X}$ is the solution to:

$$\begin{aligned} \text{Minimize} \quad & \|X - \tilde{X}\|_F, \\ \text{Subject to} \quad & \text{rank}(\tilde{X}) \leq \text{r}. \end{aligned} \tag{5}$$

In the indoor white space exploration, we are given D and required to estimate X. Then, we can judge whether a channel is busy or not at a given location. It is impossible to directly solve (5), since we do not know the value of original matrix and the proper rank. Instead, we use $B \circ X = D$ as the constraint. Considering the low rank property of X, we can alternatively solve the following rank minimization problem:

$$\begin{aligned} \text{Minimize} \quad & rank(X), \\ \text{Subject to} \quad & B \circ X = D. \end{aligned} \tag{6}$$

However, it is also difficult to solve this rank minimization problem as it is non-convex. So, we transform it to the nuclear norm minimization problem in help of the SVD-like factorization of X:

$$X = U\Sigma V^T = LR^T, \tag{7}$$

where $L = U\Sigma^{1/2}$, $R = V\Sigma^{1/2}$.

According to the compressive sensing theory [3, 4], we can perform the rank minimization by solving the nuclear norm minimization problem for the low rank matrix LR^T, if the isometry property [4] holds on binary index matrix B. Therefore we just need to minimize the sum of L and R's Frobenius norms:

$$\begin{aligned} \text{Minimize} \quad & \|L\|_F^2 + \|R\|_F^2, \\ \text{Subject to} \quad & B \circ (LR^T) = D. \end{aligned} \tag{8}$$

It is usually difficult to find L and R that strictly satisfy (8), because (i) the direct sensory matrix D contains noise, (ii) X is just approximately low-rank in the real world, and the rank of X may be largely different in different indoor environments. Thus, we use Lagrange multiplier method to solve (8):

$$\text{Minimize} \quad \|B \circ (LR^T) - D\|_F^2 + \lambda(\|L\|_F^2 + \|R\|_F^2). \tag{9}$$

In this way, the constraint $B \circ (LR^T) = D$ is not strictly enforced, and we use the Lagrange multiplier λ to control the tradeoff between the precise fit to the measurement and the rank minimization.

The compressive sensing approach (9) finds the global low-rank structure in matrix X. We can further improve the accuracy in two ways: strong channel improvement and location-channel dependence improvement.

4.2 Introducing Strong Channel

Performance of the compressive sensing based indoor white space reconstruction can be improved by taking strong channels into consideration. In contrast to most prior works, which just define a single set of strong channels shared by all indoor locations, we argue that different locations have different strong channels as shown in Section 2. Based on this observation, we define strong channel matrix S in Section 3.2 to describe the spatial variance of strong channels.

In short-time sensing experiment, we obtain 14 short-time sensing data (MMs) in total and we use 7 of them as the training set while the other 7 are used for evaluation. If the signal strength of channel j at location i are at least 5dB higher than the white space threshold in all 7 training MMs, then channel j is a strong channel at location i and $S(i,j) = 1$; otherwise, $S(i,j) = 0$. We simply consider strong channels as always busy because channels that carry strong signals are normally used for TV broadcast and TV broadcasting arrangement is normally in long term (e.g., years). Hence, S can be used in FIWEX.

To combine compressive sensing and strong channels' feature, we define new Binary Index Matrix B_s and Direct Sensory Matrix D_s considering the influence of S:

$$B_s(i,j) = \begin{cases} 1 & \text{if } S(i,j) = 1, \\ B(i,j) & \text{otherwise.} \end{cases}$$

$$D_s(i,j) = \begin{cases} ave_{ij} & \text{if } S(i,j) = 1, \\ D(i,j) & \text{otherwise.} \end{cases}$$

Here ave_{ij} is the average relative signal strength of channel j at location i in the training set. In this way, formula (9) can be rewritten as

$$\text{Minimize} \quad \|B_s \circ (LR^T) - D_s\|_F^2 + \lambda(\|L\|_F^2 + \|R\|_F^2). \tag{10}$$

4.3 Introducing Location-Channel Dependence

The channel dependence and location dependence (Section 2) represent the channel/location structure of indoor white spaces, and can be utilized to improve the performance of FIWEX. Taking compressive sensing, strong channels, channel dependence and location dependence into consideration, we expand (10) as follows:

$$\begin{aligned} \text{Minimize } & \|B_s \circ (LR^T) - D_s\|_F^2 + \lambda(\|L\|_F^2 + \|R\|_F^2) \\ & + \|P(LR^T) - P_0\|_F^2 + \|(LR^T)C - C_0\|_F^2, \end{aligned} \tag{11}$$

where P and P_0 are the location dependence constraint matrices, while C and C_0 represent the channel dependence constraint matrices. Since different choices of P, P_0, C, and C_0 yield different performance of FIWEX, we discuss how to choose these matrices in the following section.

4.3.1 Choice of location-channel dependence constraint matrices

Choice of $P_{(67\times67)}$ and $P_{0(67\times45)}$: Matrix P and P_0 represent the location dependence in relative location-channel matrix (X) and express the linear relationship between different rows of $X_{(67\times45)}$. We propose an innovative way to find appropriate P and P_0. For each row X_i of X, location dependence means that we can approximate X_i as a linear function of other K most correlated rows $X_{i_k}(k = 1, 2, ..., K$ and $i_k \neq i)$ of X_i. We will discuss the proper value of K in Section 4.3.2. The correlation between different rows is measured by the sum of *Pearson product-moment correlation coefficient* [32]. Then we perform multivariate linear regression to find a set of weights w_{i_k}, such that X_i can be best approximated by a linear function of X_{i_k}:

$$X_i \approx w_{i_0} X_0 + \sum_{k=1}^{K} w_{i_k} X_{i_k}, \tag{12}$$

where X_0 is a row vector (1×45) equals to $(1, 1, 1, ..., 1)$. Initially, every element of P is set to be 0. For the i-th row of P, we set $P(i,i) = 1$, $P(i, i_k) = -w_{i_k}$, for $k = 1, 2, ..., K$. We also set $P_0(i,j) = w_{i_0}$ for $j = 1, 2, ..., 45$. In this way,

$$P(LR^T) - P_0 = \begin{bmatrix} X_1 - \sum_{k=1}^{K} w_{1_k} X_{1_k} - w_{1_0} X_0 \\ X_2 - \sum_{k=1}^{K} w_{2_k} X_{2_k} - w_{2_0} X_0 \\ \cdots \\ \cdots \\ X_{67} - \sum_{k=1}^{K} w_{67_k} X_{67_k} - w_{67_0} X_0 \end{bmatrix},$$

and it describes the difference between each row and its linear representation. Since $X_i \approx w_{i_0} X_0 + \sum_{k=1}^{K} w_{i_k} X_{i_k}$, the value of $\|P(LR^T) - P_0\|_F^2$ is expected to be small. Therefore, the existence of $\|P(LR^T) - P_0\|_F^2$ in minimizing (11) guarantees the location dependence in X and this really improve the reconstruction accuracy.

Choice of $C_{(45\times45)}$ and $C_{0(67\times45)}$: Matrix C and C_0 represent the channel dependence in relative location-channel matrix (X), and express the linear relationship between different columns of $X_{(67\times45)}$. Actually, the way to find C and C_0 is almost the same as that of finding P and P_0, except that C and C_0 consider the columns of X instead of rows. In this way, the channel dependence in X is guaranteed by $\|(LR^T)C - C_0\|_F^2$ in (11).

4.3.2 Stability of location-channel dependence

In this part, we study the stability of the location-channel dependence based on the short-time indoor sensing results, and then find the proper value of K. In Section 2.3, a total of 14 short-time sensing data sets were collected and we can get 14 relative location-channel matrices (RLCM) $X^{(1)}$,

$X^{(2)}$, ..., $X^{(14)}$. We calculate P, P_O, C, and C_O based on one of these 14 RLCMs. If the location dependence and channel dependence are stable over time, then P, P_O, C, and C_O we get can approximately represent the location dependence and channel dependence of other 13 RLCMs.

We calculate P, P_O, C, and C_O based on $X^{(1)}$ in the way described in Section 4.3.1. As we mentioned before, the value of $\|PX^{(1)} - P_O\|_F^2$ and $\|X^{(1)}C - C_O\|_F^2$ is expected to be small. If the value of $\|PX^{(i)} - P_O\|_F^2(\|X^{(i)}C - C_O\|_F^2)$ $(i = 2, 3, ..., 14)$ is close to $\|PX^{(1)} - P_O\|_F^2(\|X^{(1)}C - C_O\|_F^2)$, then the four matrices (P, P_O, C, C_O) can approximately represent the location-channel dependence in $X^{(i)}$ $(i = 2, 3, ..., 14)$. As a result, the location dependence and channel dependence are stable over time.

We compare $\|PX^{(1)} - P_O\|_F^2$ and the average of $\|PX^{(i)} - P_O\|_F^2$ $(i = 2, 3, ..., 14)$, and set

$$DIFF_P = \frac{[\frac{1}{13}\sum_{i=2}^{14}\|PX^{(i)} - P_O\|_F^2] - \|PX^{(1)} - P_O\|_F^2}{\|PX^{(1)} - P_O\|_F^2}.$$

Similarly, we set

$$DIFF_C = \frac{[\frac{1}{13}\sum_{i=2}^{14}\|X^{(i)}C - C_O\|_F^2] - \|X^{(1)}C - C_O\|_F^2}{\|X^{(1)}C - C_O\|_F^2}.$$

If the values of $DIFF_P$ and $DIFF_C$ are small, then the location dependence and channel dependence are stable. Figure 5 shows the value of $DIFF_P$ and $DIFF_C$, when K varies from 1 to 30. $DIFF_P$ gets its minimum value (1.54) when $K = 1$ and $DIFF_C$ gets its minimum value (1.28) when $K = 2$. It means that we would obtain very similar P, P_O, C, and C_O using different $X^{(i)}$ as input, indicating that the location-channel dependence is consistent across different days. Since $DIFF_P$ and $DIFF_C$ get their minimum value when $K = 1$ and $K = 2$, respectively, we set $K = 1$ when calculating P and P_O and $K = 2$ when calculating C and C_O.

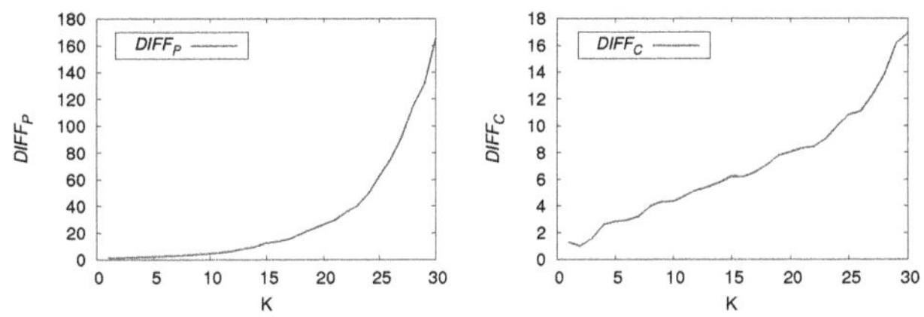

(a) Location dependence (b) Channel dependence

Figure 5: Stability of location dependence and channel dependence

4.4 Data Reconstruction Algorithm

Data reconstruction part aims to find $\tilde{X} = \tilde{L}\tilde{R}^T$ that optimize (11). We design an algorithm to get $\tilde{L}$ and $\tilde{R}$ based on alternating least squares method. Before solving (11), we should scale P, P_O, C, and C_O so that $\|P(LR^T) - P_O\|_F^2$, $\|(LR^T)C - C_O\|_F^2$ and $\|B_s \circ (LR^T) - D_s\|_F^2$ in (11) are of similar order of magnitude, otherwise they may overshadow each other during the optimization process [7].

As shown in Algorithm 1, L is randomly initialized. Then we fix L and find proper R to optimize (11) by finding its derivative with respect to R^T and making the derivative be equal to zero. Next we fix R and find the proper L in a similar way. We repeat this process until convergence. In Algorithm 1, we repeat for t times ($t = 100$ by default).

We now explain the alternating least squares method in detail. First, we assume that L is fixed and find proper R

Algorithm 1 Compressive sensing

Input:
D_s: DM with strong channels, B_s: BM with strong channels, λ: Lagrange multiplier, t: iteration times, r: rank bound, $\tilde{v}$: initially a sufficiently large number.
Output:
$\tilde{X}$: estimation matrix

1: $L \leftarrow random\_matrix(67, r)$
2: **for** 1 to t **do**
3: $R \leftarrow$ findDer$(B_s, D_s, L, \lambda, r)$;
4: $L \leftarrow$ findDer$(B_s^T, D_s^T, R, \lambda, r)$;
5: $v \leftarrow \|B_s \circ (LR^T) - D_s\|_F^2 + \lambda(\|L\|_F^2 + \|R\|_F^2) + \|P(LR^T) - P_O\|_F^2 + \|(LR^T)C - C_O\|_F^2$
6: **if** $v < \tilde{v}$ **do**
7: $\tilde{L} \leftarrow L; \tilde{R} \leftarrow R; \tilde{v} \leftarrow v$
8: **end if**
9: **end for**
10: $\tilde{X} \leftarrow \tilde{L}\tilde{R}^T$
11: return $\tilde{X}$;

to minimize (11). It seems that we should set the derivative of (11) with respect to R^T to 0, but it's difficult to directly find this derivative. Thus, we try another way to solve this problem. We alternatively use (10) as the objective function and $\|P(LR^T) - P_O\|_F^2$, $\|(LR^T)C - C_O\|_F^2$ as constraints just like [8]. That means in every iteration, we find the L and R through making the derivative of (10) to be 0 (line 3-4 in Algorithm 1), then we compare the new value of (11) (v) to the current smallest value ($\tilde{v}$). If $v < \tilde{v}$, we update $\tilde{L}$ and $\tilde{R}$, otherwise, we do nothing (line 5-8 in Algorithm 1). The evaluation results in Section 5 show that Algorithm 1 really performs well.

Algorithm 2 describes the detailed derivation process. Let

$$f(L, R^T) = \|B_s \circ (LR^T) - D_s\|_F^2 + \lambda(\|L\|_F^2 + \|R^T\|_F^2),$$

and L be fixed. The value of R can be obtained by solving: $\frac{\partial f}{\partial R^T} = \mathbf{0}$. Let $\Theta = R^T$, we have

$$\begin{aligned}\frac{\partial f(L,\Theta)}{\partial\Theta} &= \frac{\partial(\|B_s\circ(L\Theta)-D_s\|_F^2+\lambda(\|L\|_F^2+\|\Theta\|_F^2))}{\partial\Theta} \\ &= \frac{\partial(\sum_{j=1}^{45}\|Diag(\boldsymbol{b_j})L\boldsymbol{\theta_j}-\boldsymbol{d_j}\|_F^2+\lambda\|\boldsymbol{\theta_j}\|_F^2)}{\partial\Theta}\end{aligned} \quad (13)$$

where $\boldsymbol{b_j}$, $\boldsymbol{d_j}$, and $\boldsymbol{\theta_j}$ represent the jth column of B_s, D_s and Θ, respectively, and $Diag(\boldsymbol{b_j})$ refers to a diagonal matrix with elements of $\boldsymbol{b_j}$ on its main diagonal. $\frac{\partial f(L,\Theta)}{\partial\Theta} = \mathbf{0}$ is equal to that for every j from 1 to 45

$$\frac{\partial f(L,\Theta)}{\partial\theta_j} = \mathbf{0},$$

which means

$$\frac{\partial(\|Diag(\boldsymbol{b_j})L\boldsymbol{\theta_j} - \boldsymbol{d_j}\|_F^2 + \lambda\|\boldsymbol{\theta_j}\|_F^2)}{\partial\boldsymbol{\theta_j}} = \mathbf{0}. \quad (14)$$

Equation (14) is a linear least squares problem and we have

$$\boldsymbol{\theta_j} = (Q_j^TQ_j + \lambda I_r)^{-1}(Q_j^T\boldsymbol{d_j}),$$

where $Q_j = Diag(\boldsymbol{b_j})L$. At last, the value of R can be calculated by $R = \Theta^T$. When R is fixed, L can be found in a similar way.

4.5 Sensor Deployment

As mentioned before, different deployments of sensors lead to different performance of FIWEX. Although brute-force

We first run FIWEX and WISER using two different num-

Algorithm 2 Derivation

Θ^T=**findDer**(B_s,D_s,L,λ,r)
1: $[m, n]$ =size(B_s);
2: **for** $j = 1$ to n **do**;
3: $\quad Q_j \leftarrow Diag(\mathbf{b_j})L$;
4: $\quad \boldsymbol{\theta_j} = (Q_j^T Q_j + \lambda I_r)^{-1}(Q_j^T \mathbf{d_j})$;
5: **end for**
6: **return** Θ^T;

enumeration of indoor locations can find the best deployment solution, the computation overhead is unacceptable ($C_{67}^N - 1$ comparisons are needed given N sensors). In this section, we propose a novel sensor deployment method based on location dependence and the clustering technique.

As we mentioned in Section 2, there exists linear dependences between different locations. In section 4.3, we utilize the location dependence to improve the performance of FIWEX by representing the channels strength at one location in form of the linear combination of those at other K most correlated locations. Given N sensors, FIWEX can collect the channels strength of N locations, and then reconstruct channels strength of all locations based on them. Furthermore, if the channels strength in every location can be approximated by the combination of these N locations, the reconstruction accuracy would be high. Hence, deploying sensors at "independent" locations is a good choice as every one of them can represents a set of correlated locations.

Clustering is a useful method to deploy sensors at "independent" locations. Our sensor deployment algorithm can be briefly divided into two steps: (i) Cluster all locations into N groups (N is the number of sensors here). (ii) Deploy one sensor in each center of these N groups. In particular, we choose *k-mediod* [13] technology to do the clustering and use the sum of Pearson product-moment correlation coefficients of one row as the similarity metric. In Algorithm 3 line 2, kmedoids(X, N) divides the rows of X into N clusters, the centers of which are stored in SL. v stores the sum of all distances between every row and the center of cluster it belongs to, and a smaller v means a better clustering result. Considering the truth that *k-medoids* clustering algorithm may find the local optimization, we run kmedoids for 100 times and select the best result. Then we deploy N sensors in the N cluster centers.

At last, we consider the stability of the clustering results. In Section 4.3.2, we show that the location dependence is stable over time, as a result, the clustering algorithm based on location dependence is also stable. That means, if we deploy sensors according to different relative location-channel matrices, the results would be similar.

Algorithm 3 Sensor deployment

Input:
X: relative location-channel matrix
N: the number of given sensors
v_{opt}: initially a sufficiently large number.
Output:
SL_{opt}: a list of sensor locations
1: **for** 1 to 100 **do**
2: $\quad [SL, v]$ = kmedoids(X, N);
3: $\quad$**if** $v < v_{opt}$ **do**
4: $\quad\quad SL_{opt} = SL; v_{opt} = v$;
5: $\quad$**end if**
6: **end for**
7: return SL_{opt};

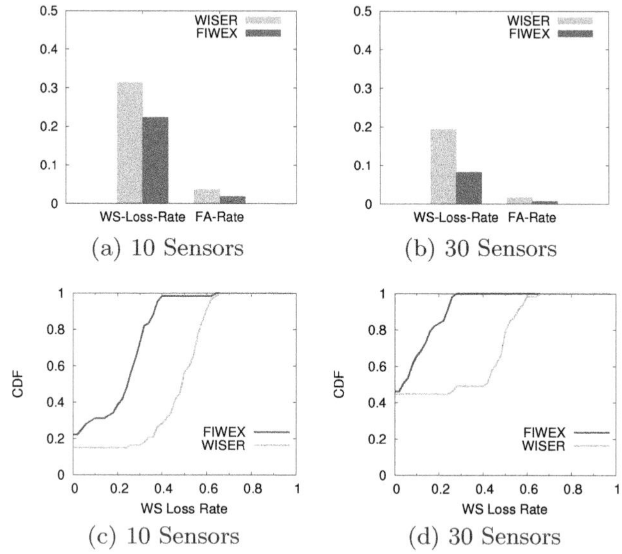

(a) 10 Sensors (b) 30 Sensors (c) 10 Sensors (d) 30 Sensors

Figure 6: Average FA rate, WS Loss Rate and CDF curves.

5. PERFORMANCE EVALUATION

In this section, we perform experiments to evaluate the performance of FIWEX. To the best of our knowledge, WISER is the most efficient indoor white space exploration system till now, and we examine the cost-efficiency of FIWEX by comparing it to WISER. First, we evaluate the performance of FIWEX and WISER in the scenarios of 10 sensors and 30 sensors. Then we compare the FA Rates and WS Loss Rates of FIWEX and WISER in different number of sensors, and we calculate the ratio of extra white spaces identified by FIWEX. The evaluation results show that FIWEX is better than WISER.

5.1 Methodology

To evaluate FIWEX's performance, we build a prototype of it on the third floor of a building. We set the white space threshold to be -84.5dBm/8 MHz as WISER does, and a total of 14 short-time sensing data sets were collected. We divide these 14 data sets into two parts: one part of 7 data sets for training FIWEX, the other part for evaluations. From the training set, we get 7 relative location-channel matrices, and we use the average of these 7 relative location-channel matrices to find P, P_0, C, C_0 and to deploy sensors. Then we evaluate the performance of FIWEX based on the other 7 datasets. We choose FA Rate and WS Loss Rate as the metrics of system's performance. Their definitions are as follows.

- **False Alarm Rate (FA Rate)**: the ratio between the number of channels that a system mis-identifies as vacant and the total number of vacant channels identified by the system.
- **White Space Loss Rate (WS Loss Rate)**: the ratio between the number of channels that a system mis-identifies as occupied and the total number of actually-vacant channels.

Since we use 7 datasets for evaluation, we get 7 sets of FA Rates and WS Loss Rate, then we use their average in the following part of evaluation.

5.2 Performance Comparison With WISER

We first run FIWEX and WISER using two different numbers of sensors: 10 and 30, and compare their FA Rates and

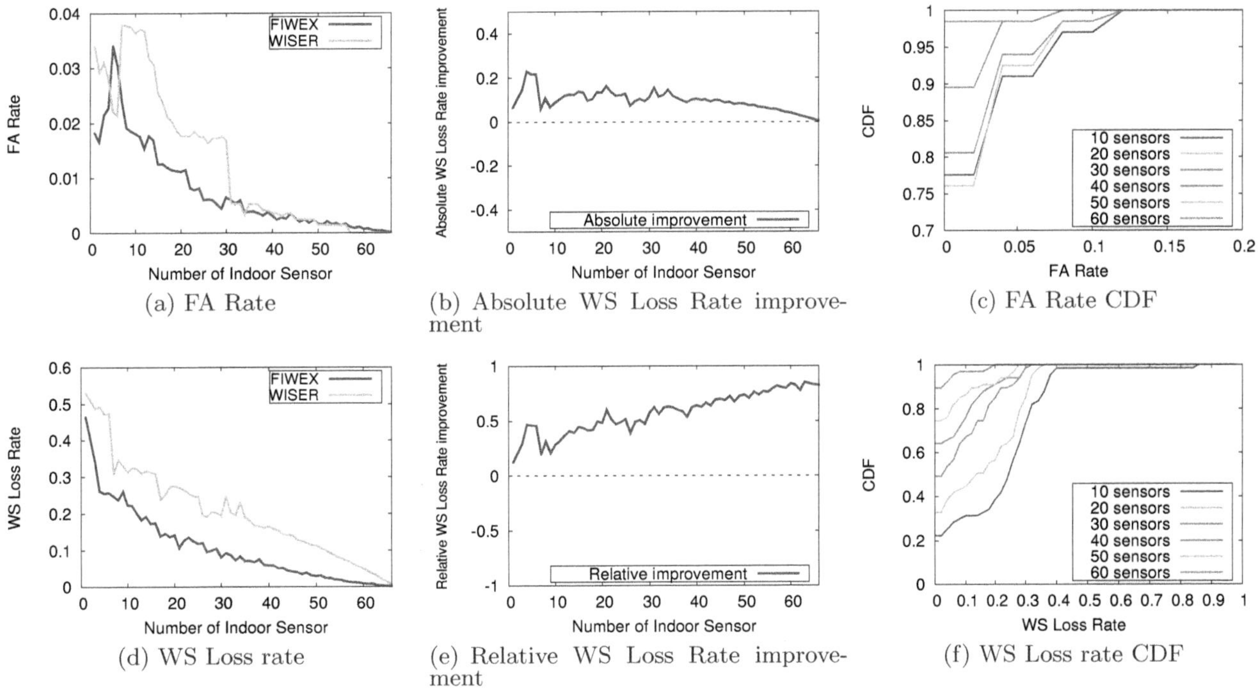

(a) FA Rate

(b) Absolute WS Loss Rate improvement

(c) FA Rate CDF

(d) WS Loss rate

(e) Relative WS Loss Rate improvement

(f) WS Loss rate CDF

Figure 7: Evaluation results on the number of indoor sensors

WS Loss Rates. As shown in Figure 6(a), when there are 10 sensors, the FA Rate and WS Loss rate of FIWEX are 1.8% and 22.3% while WISER performs an FA rate 3.6% and a WS Loss Rate 31.3%. The result shows that FIWEX has lower or better FA Rate and WS Loss Rate compared with WISER when 10 sensors are used. We also depict the CDF (Cumulative Distribution Function) curves of WS Loss Rate after calculating the WS Loss Rate for each location. Figure 6(c) shows the CDF curves of WS Loss Rate of FIWEX and WISER with 10 sensors. In WISER, 83.6% locations suffer a WS Loss Rate that is higher than 30%. The number is 26.9% in FIWEX. In WISER, 71.6% locations suffer a WS Loss Rate which is higher than 40% while the number is only 1.5% in FIWEX. Figure 6(b) shows the FA Rates and WS Loss Rates in the scenario of 30 sensors and the corresponding CDF curves are shown in Figure 6(d). These two figures shows that FIWEX also outperforms WISER in 30 sensors scenario.

5.3 Performance on The Number of Indoor Sensors

In a general indoor scenario, there exists a tradeoff between system performance and the number of indoor sensors that are deployed. To understand this tradeoff, we vary the number of sensors from 1 to 66 (when there are 67 sensors, FA Rate and WS Loss Rate of FIWEX and WISER are both 0), and evaluate the performance of FIWEX and WISER. In this experiment, we define the following four metrics to describe the FIWEX's performance improvement compared to WISER.

- **Absolute FA Rate improvement:** the difference between FA Rates of WISER and FIWEX.
- **Relative FA Rate improvement:** the ratio between absolute FA Rate improvement and the corresponding FA rate of WISER. (If the FA Rate of WISER is 0 while the absolute FA Rate improvement is not 0, we set the relative FA Rate improvement to be -1.)
- **Absolute WS Loss Rate improvement:** the difference between WS Loss Rates of WISER and FIWEX.
- **Relative WS Loss Rate improvement:** the ratio between absolute WS Loss Rate improvement and the corresponding WS Loss rate of WISER. (If the WS Loss Rate of WISER is 0 while the absolute WS Loss Rate improvement is not 0, we set the relative WS Loss Rate improvement to be -1.)

In Figure 7(a), we compare the FA Rates. It is clear that the FA Rates of FIWEX are lower than those of WISER in most cases. Actually, the average FA rate (from 1 sensor to 66 sensors) of WISER is 1.25% while this number is 0.77% for FIWEX. FIWEX has an average absolute FA Rate improvement of 0.48% and an average relative FA Rate improvement of 38.4% compared with WISER.

Figure 7(d) shows the WS Loss Rate of FIWEX and WISER with different number of indoor sensors. The average WS Loss Rate (from 1 sensor to 66 sensors) of WISER is 20.3% and for FIWEX, this number is 10.6%. FIWEX has an average absolute WS Loss Rate improvement of 9.7% and an average relative WS Loss Rate improvement of 47.8% compared to WISER. Figure 7(b) and Figure 7(e) show the absolute and relative WS Loss Rate improvement versus the number of indoor sensors, respectively, and they demonstrate the amount of extra white spaces FIWEX can identify compared with WISER.

We depict the CDF curves of FIWEX regarding to the FA Rates and WS Loss Rates of all locations. Figure 7(c) shows the 6 CDF curves (10,20,...,60 sensors) about FA rate, and considering the attributes of FA rate (the value of FA rate is small), we change the range of axes to [0:0.2] and [0.7:1]. The CDF curve is "higher" when more sensors are used, and this means that the number of locations with high FA Rates decreases as the increasing number of sensors. In addition, 50 sensors and 60 sensors share the same CDF curve, so we can only find 5 CDF curves in Figure 7(c). The CDF curves of WS Loss rate of different number of sensors are shown in Figure 7(f).

6. RELATED WORK

Most of the existing works on TV white space focus on outdoor scenarios. For example, in [24], the authors design a Wi-Fi like AP system constructed on top of UHF white spaces and a dynamic spectrum allocation network system is proposed in [25]. Spectrum sensing and geo-location database are two main approaches for white space exploration, and have been widely studied these years [26, 27, 29].

The outdoor white space exploration methods cannot be directly applied to indoor scenarios because of the complicated indoor environment. In [2], the authors propose the first indoor white space identification system, called WISER. WISER utilized the channel-location clustering based algorithm to explore indoor white spaces, and obtained great improvement compared to the baseline approaches. However, the property that different locations have different strong channels and the linear dependence of locations and channels are not considered by the authors. Based on these observations, we present FIWEX, a compressive sensing based cost-efficient indoor white space exploration mechanism.

These years, compressive sensing theory has been widely studied and utilized in a lot of fields. For instance, [6] proposed the robust network compressive sensing and proved its efficiency based on a large amount of evaluation, and compressive sensing technology has been utilized for network traffic estimation [7], localization in mobile networks [9], soil moisture sensing [10] and data gathering [11, 12]. In FIWEX, we combine compressive sensing with indoor white space exploration in an innovative way and efficiently explore indoor white spaces with a high accuracy.

7. CONCLUSIONS

In this paper, we performed indoor white space measurements in a real building to study the characteristics of indoor white spaces. The measurement results confirmed the existence of strong channels and location-channel dependence. Motivated by these observations, we proposed a cost-efficient indoor white space exploration mechanism, called FIWEX. Given the same number of sensors, FIWEX can identify more indoor white spaces with an average less false alarms compared to the existing indoor white space exploration systems.

References

[1] Second Memorandum Option And Order. https://apps.fcc.gov/edocs_public/attachmatch/FCC-10-174A1.pdf

[2] X. Ying, J. Zhang, L. Yan, G. Zhang, M. Chen, and R. Chandra, "Exploring indoor white spaces in metropolises," In *Proc. of ACM MOBICOM*, 2013.

[3] D. Donoho, "Compressed sensing," *IEEE Trans. on Information Theory*, 52(4): 1289-1306, 2006.

[4] B. Recht, M. Fazel, and P. Parrilo, "Guaranteed Minimum-Rank Solutions of Linear Matrix Equations via Nuclear Norm Minimization," *SIAM Review*, 52(3): 1289-1306, 2007.

[5] E. Candes, J. Romberg, and T. Tao, "Robust Uncertainty Principles: Exact Signal Reconstruction from Highly Incomplete Frequency Information," *IEEE Trans. on Information Theory*, 52(2): 489-509, 2006.

[6] Y. Chen, L. Qiu, Y. Zhang, G. Xue and Z. Hu, "Robust Network Compressive Sensing," In *Proc. of ACM MOBICOM*, 2014.

[7] Y. Zhang, M. Roughan, W. Willinger, and L. Qiu, "Spatio-Temporal Compressive Sensing and Internet Traffic Matrices," In *Proc. of ACM SIGCOMM*, 2009.

[8] L. Kong, M. Xia, X. Liu, M. Wu and X. Liu, "Data Loss and Reconstruction in Sensor Networks," In *Proc. of IEEE INFOCOM*, 2013.

[9] S. Rallapalli, L. Qiu, Y. Zhang, and Y. Chen, "Exploiting Temporal Stability and Low-Rank Structure for Localization in Mobile Networks," In *Proc. of ACM MOBICOM*, 2010.

[10] X. Wu and M. Liu, "In-situ Soil Moisture Sensing: Measurement Scheduling and Estimation using Compressive Sensing," In *Proc. of ACM IPSN* 2012.

[11] H. Zheng, S. Xiao, X. Wang and X. Tian, "Energy and Latency Analysis for In-network Computation with Compressive Sensing in Wireless Sensor Networks," In *Proc. of IEEE INFOCOM*, 2012.

[12] C. Luo, F. Wu, J. Sun, and C. Chen, "Compressive data gathering for large-scale wireless sensor networks," In *Proc. of ACM MOBICOM* 2009.

[13] H.S. Park and C.H. Jun, "A simple and fast algorithm for K-medoids clustering," *Expert Systems with Applications*, 36(2): 3336-3341, 2009.

[14] M. McHenry, P. Tenhula and D. McCloskey, "Chicago Spectrum Occupancy Measurements & Analysis and A Long-term Studies Proposal" In *Proc. of ACM TAPAS*, 2006.

[15] D. Gurney, G. Buchwald, L. Ecklund, S. Kuffner and J. Grosspietsch, "Geo-location Database Techniques for Incumbent Protection in the TV White Space", In *Proc. of IEEE DySPAN*, 2008.

[16] N. Klepeis, W. Nelson, W. Ott, J.Robinson, A. Tsang, P. Switzer, J. Behar, S. Hern and W. Engelmann, "The national human activity pattern survey (nhaps): A resource for assessing exposure to environmental pollutants", *Journal of Exposure Analysis and Environmental Epidemiology*, 11(3): 231-252, 2001.

[17] V. Chandrasekhar, J. Andrews, and A. Gatherer, "Femtocell networks: a survey," *Communications Magazine, IEEE*, 46(9):59-67, 2008

[18] Yucek, Tevfik, and H. Arslan, "A survey of spectrum sensing algorithms for cognitive radio applications," *Communications Surveys & Tutorials, IEEE*, 11(1): 116-130, 2009.

[19] H. Urkowitz, "Energy detection of unknown deterministic signals," *Proceedings of the IEEE*, 55(4): 523-531, 1967.

[20] M. Vossiek, L. Wiebking, P. Gulden, J. Wiehardt, C. Hoffmann, and P. Heide, "Wireless Local Positioning", *IEEE Microwave Magazine*, 4(4): 77-86 2003.

[21] S. Kumar, S. Gil, D. Katabi and D. Rus, "Accurate Indoor Localization With Zero Start-up Cost," In *Proc. of ACM MOBICOM*, 2014.

[22] E. Candes and B.Recht, "Exact Matrix Completion via Convex Optimization," *Foundations of Computational mathematics* 9(6): 717-772, 2009.

[23] B. Recht, W. Xu, and B. Hassibi, "Necessary and sufficient conditions for success of the nuclear norm heuristic for rank minimization," In *Proc. of IEEE CDC*, 2008.

[24] P. Bahl, R. Chandra, T. Moscibroda, R. Murty and M. Welsh, "White space networking with Wi-Fi like connectivity," In *Proc. of ACM SIGCOMM*, 2009.

[25] S. Deb, V. Srinivasan, and R. Maheshwari, "Dynamic spectrum access in DTV whitespaces: design rules, architecture and algorithms," In *Proc. of ACM MOBICOM*, 2009.

[26] R. Balamurthi, H. Joshi, C. Nguyen, A. Sadek, S. Shellhammer and C. Shen, "A TV white space spectrum sensing prototype," In *Proc. of IEEE DySPAN*, 2011.

[27] T. Zhang, N. Leng and S. Banerjee, "A Vehicle-based Measurement Framework for Enhancing Whitespace Spectrum Databases," In *Proc. of ACM MOBICOM*, 2014.

[28] R. Ahuja, R. Corke, and A. Bok, "Cognitive radio system using IEEE 802.11a over UHF TVWS," In *Proc. of IEEE DySPAN*, 2008.

[29] D. Gurney, G. Buchwald, L. Ecklund, S. Kuffner and J. Grosspieetsch, "Geo-location database techniques for incumbent protection in the TV white space," In *Proc. of IEEE DySPAN*, 2008.

[30] Ian F. Akyildiz, W. Lee, et al, "NeXt generation/ dynamic spectrum access/cognitive radio wireless networks: a survey," *Computer Networks* 50(13): 2127-2159, 2006.

[31] Y. Xing, R. chandramouli, S. Mangold and S. Shankar, "Dynamic spectrum access in open spectrum wireless networks," *Selected Areas in Communications, IEEE Journal* 24(3): 626-637, 2006.

[32] J. Rodgers, Joseph, and W. Alan Nicewander, "Thirteen ways to look at the correlation coefficient," *The American Statistician* 42(1): 59-66, 1988.

ALETHEIA: Robust Large-Scale Spectrum Auctions against False-name Bids

Qinhui Wang [†♯], Baoliu Ye[†*], Bin Tang[†], Tianyin Xu[‡], Song Guo[¶], Sanglu Lu[†], and Weihua Zhuang[§]
[†]National Key Laboratory for Novel Software Technology, Nanjing University, China
[♯]Department of Military Management, Army Command College, China
[‡]Department of Computer Science and Engineering, U.C. San Diego, USA
[¶]School of Computer Science and Engineering, The University of Aizu, Japan
[§]Department of Electrical and Computer Engineering, University of Waterloo, Canada
qhwang@dislab.nju.edu.cn, {yebl,tb, sanglu}@nju.edu.cn, tixu@cs.ucsd.edu, sguo@u-aizu.ac.jp, wzhuang@bbcr.uwaterloo.ca

ABSTRACT

Auction is a promising approach for dynamic spectrum access in Cognitive Radio Networks. Existing auction mechanisms are mainly proposed to be *strategy-proof* to stimulate bidders to reveal their valuations of spectrum truthfully. However, they would suffer significantly from a new cheating pattern named *false-name bids*, where a bidder can manipulate the auction by submitting bids under multiple fictitious names. We show such false-name bid cheating is easy to make but hard to be detected in dynamic spectrum auctions. To resolve this issue, we propose ALETHEIA, a novel *flexible, false-name-proof* auction framework for large-scale dynamic spectrum access. ALETHEIA has the following important features: (1) it not only guarantees strategy-proofness but also resists false-name bids, (2) it enables spectrum reuse across a large number of bidders, (3) it provides the bidders the flexibility of diverse demand formats, and (4) it incurs low computational overhead. Simulation results show that ALETHEIA achieves both high spectrum redistribution efficiency and auction efficiency.

Categories and Subject Descriptors

C.2.1 [**Computer-Communication Networks**]: Network Architecture and Design

*B. Ye is the corresponding author.

[†]This work was partially supported by NSFC Grants (No. 61170069, 61373014, 91218302 and 61321491); Science and Technology Pillar Program (Industry) of Jiangsu Province Grant (No. BE2013116); Collaborative Innovation Center of Novel Software Technology and Industrialization; EU FP7 IRSES MobileCloud Project Grant (No. 612212).

MobiHoc'15, June 22–25, 2015, Hangzhou, China.

http://dx.doi.org/10.1145/2746285.2746307.

Keywords

Spectrum auctions, false-name-proofness, cognitive radio networks

1. INTRODUCTION

1.1 Motivation

Radio spectrum is a critical but scarce resource for wireless communication. With the rapid growth of wireless services and devices, the limited spectrum is draining away, while most licensed spectrum bands (e.g., TV channels) are under-utilized as reported in [2,14]. To address this dilemma, dynamic spectrum access (DSA) has been proposed based on the advance of cognitive radio (CR) techniques [2], where primary users with licenses can gain financial benefits by leasing their idle spectrum to secondary users without licenses to access, i.e., a win-win situation.

Auctions are the well recognized and *de facto* mechanisms for redistributing spectrum in DSA that can achieve both fairness and allocation efficiency [10]. In auction-based DSA, the spectrum is divided into multiple channels, then the secondary users (referred to as bidders) submit their bids for channels based on the valuation of their short-term local usage, and finally the auction mechanism performed by the primary user (referred to as auctioneer) determines winners as well as their channel allocation and payment. In order to achieve fairness and maximize spectrum utilization, existing spectrum auction designs (e.g., [3,9,20,24]) mainly aim to i) exploit *spectrum reusability*, i.e., a channel can be allocated to multiple bidders as long as these bidders do not interfere with each other, and ii) guarantee *strategy-proofness* (a.k.a. *truthfulness*), i.e., no bidder can improve its own utility by cheating with false valuation, so that each bidder is encouraged to tell the auctioneer its true valuation.

However, the auction manipulation by the bidders could go beyond the cheating with false valuations. As demonstrated in recent studies [5,7,16], it is fairly easy for a CR user to generate multiple "names" identified by service-set identifiers (SSIDs). For example, the Atheros chipset supports up to 64 identifiers for one physical device [1]. This can lead to a new cheating pattern named *false-name bids*, i.e., a bidder can submit bids using multiple fictitious names to manipulate the auction results. Unfortunately, due to the open, mobile and ubiquitous nature of CR users, it is prohibitively difficult to detect false identifiers, even using the state-of-the-art authentication methods [5,7,16]. A series of questions then naturally arise. What are the consequences of false-name bids for existing spectrum auction mechanisms? Can we design efficient auction mechanisms that are *false-name-proof*, so that each bidder cannot improve its utility by using false-name bids?

1.2 Our results

To answer the first question, we conduct a broad and deep investigation on several typical strategy-proof spectrum auction mechanisms. For example, we use simulation experiments to examine the effect of false-name cheating to VERITAS [24], a state-of-the-art strategy-proof spectrum auction design. The results show that even a simple pattern of false-name cheating can substantially improve the utilities of cheating bidders and reduce the revenue of the auctioneer by 40%. This highlights the importance of providing false-name-proofness in spectrum auction designs. While prior studies have enforced false-name-proofness in auctions for traditional goods (e.g., books and paintings) [11,17], we show that existing false-name-proof designs fail when spectrum reusability is embraced. Moreover, it usually results in a low spectrum efficiency.

The above pessimistic results lead us to develop a completely new spectrum auction to resist false-name-bids robustly. In this paper, we propose ALETHEIA, the *first* false-name-proof seal-bid spectrum auction framework for the emerging large-scale DSAs. It is implemented in a price oriented fashion, where the prices of bidders are computed first while winners are then determined independently based on these prices and get corresponding channels in a sequential manner. In this way, it is then ensured that the price of buying a bundle of channels is no larger than the sum of prices for buying these channels separately using multiple fictitious names. In summary, ALETHEIA provides the following advantages:

- As the primary feature, both strategy-proofness and false-name-proofness are guaranteed.
- It exploits the spectrum reusability substantially, to significantly improve spectrum utilization.
- It provides the bidders the flexibility of diverse demand formats, i.e., either an exact number of or a range of channels to be asked.
- It incurs a low computational overhead, making it more applicable to real-time spectrum auction in large-scale DSA. For instance, when each bidder requests an exact number of channels, it has the same time complexity as VERITAS at order of $O(N \log N + NKE)$, where N, K, E are the number of bidders, channels, and pairs of conflicting bidders (i.e., they cannot access the same channel simultaneously), respectively.
- It achieves both high spectrum redistribution efficiency and auction efficiency, as demonstrated by extensive simulation results.

2. PRELIMINARIES

2.1 System Model

We consider a cognitive radio network where spectrum is divided into K identical channels, denoted as $\mathcal{K} = \{1, \ldots, K\}$ and to be auctioned to N secondary users, denoted as $\mathcal{N} = \{1, \ldots, N\}$. We assume that each bidder $i \in \mathcal{N}$ requests $d_i (0 < d_i \leq K)$ channels, and it has a *valuation* function $v_i : \mathcal{K} \to \mathbb{R}^+$ which calculates the true valuation (a non-negative value) for the requested channels. Each bidder submits its bid valuation b_i to the auctioneer, with a per-channel bid valuation t_i ($t_i = b_i/d_i$). Note that the bid valuation b_i does not have to be equal to the true valuation $v_i(d_i)$ if manipulation on b_i can make profit.

After collecting all bids and requests that are submitted by all bidders simultaneously, the auctioneer determines the winners from the bidders based on the predefined allocation rules. It then charges each bidder i with a payment denoted as $p_i(b_i, \mathbf{b}_{-i})$, where $\mathbf{b}_{-i}$ denotes the vector including all the bids from b_1 to b_N except b_i. Note that no payment applies to loser i, i.e., $p_i(b_i, \mathbf{b}_{-i}) = 0$. The *utility* of bidder i, denoted by $u_i(b_i, \mathbf{b}_{-i})$, is then defined as the difference between valuation and payment, *i.e.*, $u_i(b_i, \mathbf{b}_{-i}) = v_i(d_i) - p_i(b_i, \mathbf{b}_{-i})$. We simplify the notations $v_i(d_i)$, $p_i(b_i, \mathbf{b}_{-i})$, and $u_i(b_i, \mathbf{b}_{-i})$ as v_i, p_i, and u_i respectively, if no confusion is incurred.

Same as [8,19,24,25], we use the conflict graph $G(\mathcal{N}, \mathcal{E})$ [8] to capture the interference among bidders, where $\mathcal{N}$ is the set of bidders and $\mathcal{E}$ is the collection of all edges. An edge $(i, j) \in \mathcal{E}$ iff bidders i and j conflict with each other when they use a same channel simultaneously. Therefore, a channel can be allocated to multiple bidders as long as no edge exists between any pair of these bidders, which is referred to as *spatial reusability*. Without loss of generality, we assume that the conflict graph is a connected graph. Otherwise, we can perform the auction in each connected component.

When a bidder uses multiple names to submit bids, the auctioneer takes them as if they are from a group of bidders, called *virtual bidders* in this paper. These virtual bidders have the same interference condition of the real bidder, *i.e.*, the real bidder's conflicting neighbors still conflict with these virtual bidders. This is because when a bidder generates multiple names, its geographic information does not change. Moreover, to obtain different channels for real use, these bidders conflict with each other, *i.e.*, the subgraph consisting of these virtual bidders is a clique.

2.2 Design Targets

The basic target of our auction design is to satisfy *allocation feasibility*.

Definition 1 (Allocation Feasibility). *An allocation $\} = (\mathcal{A}_1, \ldots, \mathcal{A}_N)$, where $\mathcal{A}_i \subset \mathcal{K}$ denotes the set of channels allocated to bidder i, is feasible if $\mathcal{A}_i \cap \mathcal{A}_j = \emptyset$ holds for any $(i, j) \in \mathcal{E}$.*

More importantly, we need to ensure strategy-proofness and false-name-proofness that are the primary design targets of the auction mechanisms proposed in this paper.

Definition 2 (Strategy-proofness [13,15]). *An auction mechanism is strategy-proof (or truthful) if for any bidder i and $\mathbf{b}_{-i}$, $u_i(v_i, \mathbf{b}_{-i}) \geq u_i(b_i, \mathbf{b}_{-i})$ holds for any $b_i \neq v_i$.*

DEFINITION 3 (FALSE-NAME-PROOFNESS [18, 22]). *An auction mechanism is false-name-proof if for any bidder i using m false identifiers $i_1, \ldots, i_m$ to participate the auction and any $\mathbf{b}_{-i}$,*

$$u_i(v_i, \mathbf{b}_{-i}) \geq \sum_{j=1}^{m} u_{i_j}(b_{i_j}, \mathbf{b}_{-i} \cup I_{-j}^m)$$

where $I_{-j}^m = \{b_{i_l} : l \in \{1, \ldots, m\}, l \neq j\}$.

Generally speaking, strategy-proofness prohibits improved utility from cheating on bid valuation, while false-name-proofness not only prohibits such a cheating but also discourages bidders to submit false-name bids. Note that false-name-proofness generalizes the concept of strategy-proofness (the case when $m = 1$). In other words, false-name-proofness is a sufficient but in general not a necessary condition of strategy-proofness.

3. FALSE-NAME BID CHEATING IN SPECTRUM AUCTIONS

In this section, we study the formation and the impact of false-name cheating in the emerging dynamic spectrum auctions. We demonstrate that *a simple form of false-name cheating can effectively raise the cheating bidders' utility and thus degrade the auctioneer's revenue (i.e., the sum of payments of the winners).*

3.1 Methodology

We start by demonstrating that it could be fairly easy to design a false-name cheating pattern in existing strategy-proof spectrum auctions that can raise bidder's utility effectively. Then conduct simulation-based experiments to examine how this pattern of cheating impacts the auction outcomes.

Since a cheating pattern is specific to the auction design, we select VERITAS [24], a most famous strategy-proof spectrum auction mechanism, for our case study. Similar works are also done to some other mechanisms, e.g., SMALL [20], which lead to very similar results as in this paper, so we omit the details for saving space. For the sake of completeness, we briefly introduce how VERITAS works. In VERITAS, bidders are considered in the descending order of per-channel bid, and if there are enough available channels for a bidder, the bidder will get the requested number of channels with smallest indices. A channel is available to a bidder if it has not been assigned to any other neighboring bidders. To charge a winner i, VERITAS finds its critical neighbor, the first rejected neighboring bidder j who would win if i do not participate the auction, and then charges i with $d_i \cdot t_j$. If no such a neighbor exists, then charge 0.

3.2 A Cheating Pattern

We first introduce a very simple false-name cheating pattern in VERITAS named Real-Fake (RF) cheating. It works as follows. A bidder i uses two identifiers, Real and Fake, to bid. Then Real and Fake bid x $(0 < x < d_i)$ and $d_i - x$ channels, respectively, with the same per-channel bid t_i. If bidder i can win using a single identifier, it is straightforward to check that it can also win using RF cheating, and achieve the same or higher utility. Figure 1 shows such an example where higher utility is obtained via RF cheating, where 3 bidders (A,B,C) competing for 3 channels. When bidding via a single name, bidder A obtains a utility of 3 with bidder B as its critical neighbor. However, when bidder A uses two identifiers (A_1 and A_2) to bid, bidder A achieves an improved utility $u_A = u_{A_1} + u_{A_2}$=2+3=5 since A_1's critical neighbor is B while A_2 does not have a critical neighbor.

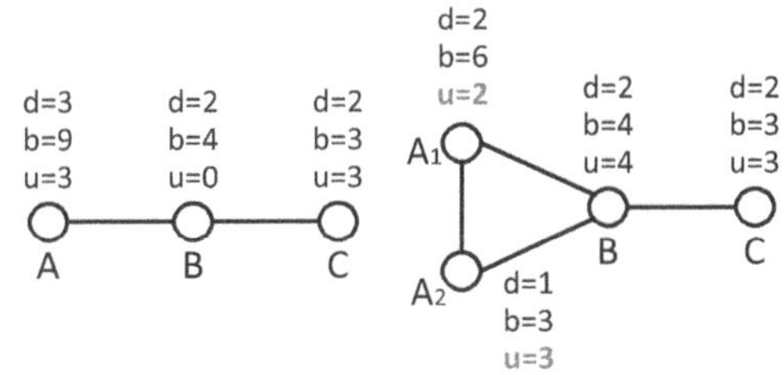

Figure 1: An example of RF cheating in VERITAS. When bidder A uses two names (A_1 and A_2) to bid, it increases its utility by getting the same number of channels but paying less.

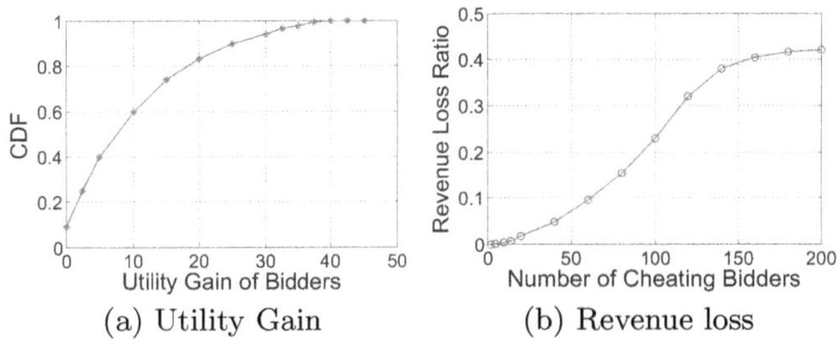

Figure 2: RF cheating is effective in large-scale spectrum auctions like VERITAS [24]. (a) It can effectively improve bidder utility, giving bidders incentive to cheat. (b) It can significantly impair the revenue when a number of bidders choose to cheat.

3.3 Impacts of False-name Cheating

We further conduct simulations to examine how RF cheating impairs the auction outcomes. We simulate 1000 bidders competing 10 channels in the auction. These bidders are positioned in a 100×100 square and the interference range is set as 1, where each bidder has about 3 conflict neighbors on average, and thus a high degree of spectrum reuse could be exploited. The request and per-channel bid of each bidder are randomly chosen from integers in $[1, 6]$ and $[1, 10]$, respectively. For RF cheating, the value x is also uniformly chosen at random from all possible values.

We run the experiment 100 times. Figure 2(a) plots the utility gain of each RF cheating bidder. We observe that over 80% cheating bidders can gain profit by submitting false-name bids. Figure 2(b) plots the revenue loss ratio where the number of cheating bidders varies. From this figure, we can see that the revenue loss depends heavily on the number of cheating bidders. When the number of cheating bidders is small, the revenue loss ratio is low. This is because the effect of each RF cheating has a local feature which is inherited from the pricing method of VERITAS. When the number of RF cheating grows, the revenue decreases quickly, and the loss ratio can achieve 35% -40% when more than 150 bidders perform RF cheating.

The above results confirm that the unique requirement of spectrum reuse and the resulting local competition make traditional mechanisms vulnerable to false-name bids. Even simple RF cheating can significantly impair the auction revenue and fairness. This motivates us to design new mechanisms that are robust to the false-name cheating.

4. CHALLENGES

In this section, we discuss the challenges to design false-name-proof spectrum auction mechanisms. We first analyze the classic false-name-proof auctions and articulate their limitations when spectrum reusability is exploited. Then we introduce a simple false-name-proof design with fairly low spectrum reuse, which serves as a baseline for performance comparison.

4.1 False-name-proofness vs. Spatial Reusability

We first study two classic false-name-proof designs, GAL [17] and IR [11] for conventional goods auctions and show that they cannot even guarantee truthfulness and thus lose false-name-proofness when spatial reuse is enabled in spectrum auctions. One basic rule for extension here is to guarantee that the extended mechanism is equivalent to the original one if all bidders conflict with each other, *i.e.*, the conflict graph is a complete graph.

4.1.1 GAL Auction Design

GAL [17] is a false-name-proof multi-unit auction design using greedy allocation. It can be extended for spectrum auctions, with the following allocation and pricing methods.

Allocations:

1. Sort bidders in a descending order by the per-channel bid and set each bidder's available channel set as $\mathcal{K}$.
2. Check these sorted bidders one by one. For each bidder i, if there are at least d_i channels in its available-channel set, it wins and is allocated with the first d_i channels with the lowest indices, each of which is then removed from the available-channel sets of the neighbors of i. Otherwise, bidder i loses.

Pricing: For each winner i, find the first rejected conflicting neighbor j with a rank behind i. If such neighbor exists, then charge $d_i \cdot t_j$. Otherwise, charge 0.

We prove that this auction is not false-name-proof using a counter example, in which five bidders (A, B, ąd' ąd' ąd' , E) compete for two channels, as show in Figure 3. We find out that bidder E will lose with a utility of 0 under truthful bidding, while increasing its utility to 1 if it cheats by raising its bid to 4. In the latter case, bidder E will obtain a channel with a charge of 0. Hence, this mechanism is not strategy-proof and thus not false-name-proof.

4.1.2 IR Auction Design

Iterative Reducing (IR) [11] is another false-name-proof multi-unit mechanism where bidders with largest requests will be considered firstly. We extend IR by following this idea while considering spatial reuse, leading to the following auction design.

Allocation:

1. Group bidders by their requests d_i and sort these groups in a descending order by d_i. In each group, all bidders are sorted in a descending order by per-channel bid t_i. Initial each bidder's available channel set as $\mathcal{K}$.
2. Sequentially check the ordered groups. For a group, channels are allocated to the bidders sequentially until all bidders in the group win or a bidder loses. In the former case, we continue to check the next group. In the latter case, all the remaining bidders in the group lose and the allocation terminates.

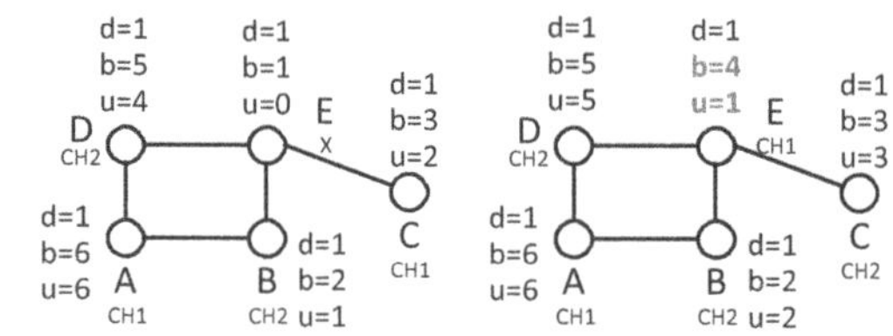

Figure 3: An illustrative example shows extended GAL is not false-name-proof, because bidder E can improve its utility by raising its bid.

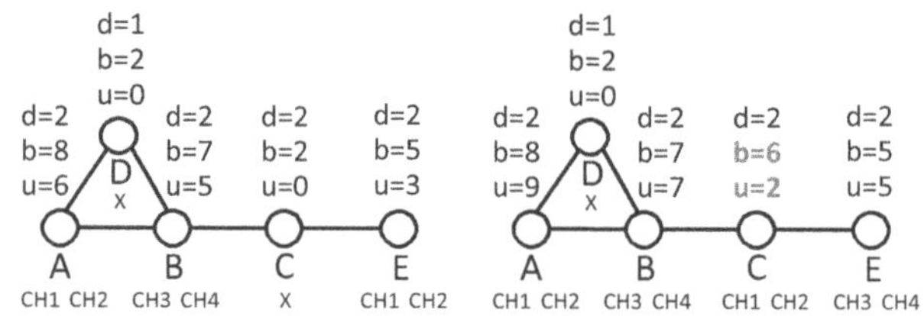

Figure 4: An illustrative example shows extended IR is not false-name-proof, where bidder C can improve its utility by raising its bid.

Pricing: If all bidders in a same group win, then these bidders are charged 0. Otherwise, each winner i in this group is charged by $d_i * t_j$, where j is the first rejected bidder in the group.

Again, we prove the above mechanism is not false-name-proof, using a counter example given in Fig. 4, where 5 bidders $A, B, \cdots, E$ are competing 4 channels. By the grouping method, bidders A, B, C and E are in group g_1, and bidder D constitutes group g_2. Consider g_1. Bidder C loses and its utility is 0. However, if C cheats by bidding 6, all bidders in g_1 win and thus are charged 0. Therefore, C improves its utility to 2, breaking the strategy-proofness and thus the false-name-proofness.

4.2 A False-name-proof Spectrum Auction

The spectrum utilization would be significantly impaired when existing false-name-proof designs are directly applied to spectrum auctions. The mechanism works as follows.

- Plane Division and Coloring. Divide the plane into boxes with length of the maximal interference radius, and proceed to uniformly color these boxes using 4 colors. The coloring guarantees: i) each pair of bidders in the same box interfere with each other, ii) bidders in different co-colored boxes do not interfere with each other. See Figure 5 for an illustration.
- Allocation in Each Box. Split all K channels into 4 subsets, each with $K/4$ channels. Allocate these sub-

1-A	2-B	1-A	2-B
3-C	4-D	3-C	4-D
1-A	2-B	1-A	2-B

Figure 5: The plane is divided into boxes and colored using 4 colors (indexed from 1 to 4). The channels are divided into 4 subsets (indexed from A to D). Allocation rule is one color relates one subset.

sets to the boxes, one color relating to an independent subset. In each box, apply the GAL mechanism.

Since the false-name-proofness is guaranteed within each box by the GAL, when a bidder in a box submits false-name bids, the created virtual bidders are all in the same box and thus cannot improve its utility by the GAL. Therefore, the above mechanism is false-name-proof. Nevertheless, the static partition of spectrum among the boxes could result in a significant spectrum degradation of a factor up to 4.

Algorithm 1: ALETHEIA-Prices(B, i)

```
1  p_i ← 0; A_N(i) ← ∅;
2  for i ∈ 𝒩 do
3      Avai(i) ← 𝒦;
4  B' ← B\{i};
5  while B' ≠ φ do
6      j ← Top(B');
7      if |Avai(j)| ≥ d_j then
8          Let C be the set of d_j channels with lowest
           indices in Avai(j);
9          if j ∉ N(i) || (j ∈ N(i)&&|C ∪ A_N(i)| + d_i ≤ K)
           then
10             A_i ← C;
11             for k ∈ N(j) do
12                 Avai(k) ← Avai(k) − C;
13     B' ← B'\{j};
14 for j ∈ N(i) do
15     if A_j = ∅ then
16         temp ← d_i * b_j/d_j;
17         p_i ← max(p_i, temp);
18 return p_i;
```

5. ALETHEIA

Motivated by the findings in previous Sections, we design ALETHEIA, a novel false-name-proof mechanism for large-scale dynamic spectrum auctions. In this section, we introduce the basic design of ALETHEIA, where bidders are assumed to be *single-minded* [11, 17, 24], i.e., a bidder i that requests d_i channels only accepts either all d_i channels or nothing. The extension of ALETHEIA to support range-based requests where bidder i accepts any number of channels between 0 and d_i is deferred to the next section.

5.1 Auction Design

ALETHEIA consists of three steps: (1) order the bidders into a bidder list (§5.1.1), (2) compute the price for each bidder (§5.1.2), and (3) determine the winners according to the finely computed prices (§5.1.3). One example is given in §5.1.4 to show how ALETHEIA works.

5.1.1 Bidder Ordering

A fixed order of bidders is critical to satisfying the interference constraints and makes it easier to design an bid-independent pricing rule. To maximize spectrum reusability, we present a novel ordering algorithm based on the Breadth-First-Search (BFS) procedure.

The ordered bidder list B is built via constructing a tree described as follows. (1) The bidder with the largest per-channel bid is selected as the root node, and all its conflicting neighbors become its child nodes. (2) For each leaf node, from the one with largest per-channel bid to the lowest one, we add its unincluded conflicting neighbors as its child nodes. The second step iteratively proceeds until all bidders are included in the tree. Note that a bidder's child nodes are ordered in a descending order of per-channel bid from the left to the right.

Finally, list B is obtained by walking through the tree layer by layer from the root node and from left to right on each layer. In particular, whenever we visit a new node, we append it at the tail of a FIFO list. The resulting list is B, after we search the whole tree.

5.1.2 Pricing Scheme

With the sorted bidder list B, we use the pricing algorithm (Algorithm 1) to compute the price for each bidder. The price for each bidder i is its request d_i multiplied by the per-channel bid of its *critical bidder*, denoted as $c(i)$. Generally speaking, a bidder i will win when bidding higher than its critical bidder $c(i)$ (*i.e.*, $t_i > t_{c(i)}$), and it will lose when bidding lower than that.

[Find Critical Bidder] To find the critical bidder for i, we first suppose that d_i channels have been allocated to bidder i, to reserve d_i channels for bidder i. It proceeds to allocate channels to other bidders sequentially, and find its all neighboring bidders that cannot be allocated. The losing neighboring bidder with the largest per-channel bid is i's critical bidder. If all of its neighbors win, then the critical bidder is a *null* bidder, whose per-channel bid equals 0.

The pricing algorithm, described in Algorithm 1 where $\mathcal{A}_{\mathbb{N}(i)}$ represents the set of channels that have been allocated to i's neighbors, *i.e.*, $\mathcal{A}_{\mathbb{N}(i)} = \cup_{j \in \mathbb{N}(i)} \mathcal{A}_j$, sequentially examine each bidder j ($j \neq i$). When there are enough channels for j (line 7), there are two cases to be considered (line 9). Case 1: If j does not belong to $\mathbb{N}(i)$, we assign the d_j channels with the **lowest indices** in $Avai(j)$ to bidder j. Case 2: If j conflicts with i, since we have to reserve d_i channels for i, we thus need to check whether j's allocation would cause i's request cannot be satisfied. In other words, we need to ensure the equation $|\mathcal{C} \cup \mathcal{A}_{\mathbb{N}(i)}| + d_i \leq K$ holds when allocating $\mathcal{C}$ to bidder j, where $\mathcal{C}$ denotes the channels pre-allocated to bidder j. After all bidders except i have been considered, we find the losing neighbor j with largest per-channel bid, and compute the price as $d_i * t_j$ (line 14-17).

5.1.3 Allocation Rule

Channel allocation is made by applying Algorithm 2 that sequentially checks all bidders. For each bidder i, the algorithm examines whether its bid valuation is greater than its computed price. If so, we assign d_i channels **with lowest indices** in its available channel set $Avai(i)$ to bidder i.

Algorithm 2: ALETHEIA-Allocation(B)

```
for i ∈ 𝒩 do
    Avai(i) ← 𝒦;
while B ≠ φ do
    i ← Top(B);
    if b_i > p_i then
        Set 𝒜_i as the set of channels with lowest indices in Avai(i);
        Assign 𝒜_i to bidder i;
        for j ∈ ℕ(i) do
            Avai(j) ← Avai(j) − 𝒜_i;
    B ← B\{i};
```

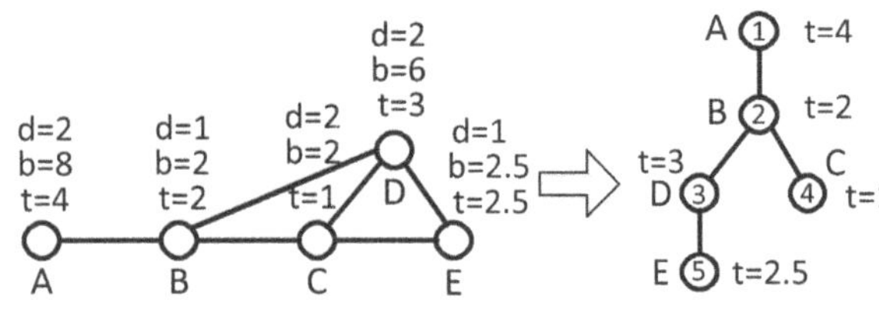

Figure 6: An illustrative example of ALETHEIA, where 3 channels (CH1, CH2 and CH3) are auctioned: (left) the conflict graph; (right) the corresponding BFS tree. The index of each bidder in list B is given in the node circle.

Otherwise, bidder i loses with no charge. In this way, we ensure that no bidders would be charged more than its bid valuation, to incentivize bidders to participate the auction.

5.1.4 *All Together in One Example*

Consider an example shown in Figure 6(left), where 5 bidders compete for 3 channels. The ordered bidder list is shown in Figure 6(right). We use bidder D as an example to find its critical bidder. We sequentially allocate channels to other bidders by reserving 2 channels for bidder D. Then bidder C and bidder E lose. Since E has higher per-channel bid, it becomes D's critical bidder. Similarly, we can find that *null*, C, D and C are the critical bidders of A, B, C and E, respectively. Therefore, we know bidder C loses and other bidders win by the allocation rule. Bidders A and D win CH1 and CH2, and bidders B and E win CH3.

5.2 Properties

Now we introduce the key properties of ALETHEIA. The proofs are deferred to the next subsection. The basic property regarding the correctness of ALETHEIA is that it can always produce a feasible allocation.

THEOREM 1. *ALETHEIA satisfies allocation feasibility, i.e., for any bidder $i \in \mathcal{N}$ with $b_i > p_i$, its request will be satisfied without causing conflicts.*

The key feature of ALETHEIA is its false-name-proofness, given in the following theorem.

THEOREM 2. *ALETHEIA is false-name-proof.*

Another property of ALETHEIA is that it incurs a low computational overhead.

THEOREM 3. *ALETHEIA runs in $O(N \log N + E + NKE)$, where N, K and E are the number of bidders, auctioned channels and edges in the conflict graph, respectively.*

5.3 Proofs

5.3.1 *Proof of Theorem 1*

One key observation is that, during the allocation process of ALETHEIA, the allocated channels always satisfy the conflict constraints. Therefore, it is sufficient for us to show for a bidder i with $b_i > p_i$, there are sufficient available channels for allocation to i. In the following, we prove this property by induction on N, the number of bidders.

Base Case. $N = 1$. In this case, the root node is the first node, and its request is less than (or equal to) K, can be allocated and thus the theorem holds.

Induction Step. Now suppose the theorem holds when $N < m$, we show that it still holds when $N = m$.

We prove this by contradiction. Since the bidders are considered in a sequential manner, according to the induction hypothesis, it is straightforward to show that for any bidder $i < m$ such that $b_i > p_i$, bidder i can get enough channels. So we only need to consider bidder m and $b_m > p_m$. By contradiction, we assume that bidder m with $b_m > p_m$ cannot be allocated. According to the allocation algorithm, bidder m's request to be rejected only happens when those channels have been allocated to its neighbors, i.e.,

$$|\cup_{j \in \mathbb{N}(m)} \mathcal{A}_j| + d_m > K. \quad (1)$$

Consider the pricing procedure for bidder m, if we first reserve d_m channels for bidder m, the above inequality indicates that there must exist a bidder $j \in \mathbb{N}(m)$, who originally wins, but cannot be allocated any more. Now two cases need to be considered. **Case I:** $t_m \le t_j$. Since bidder j is m's losing neighbor and thus the price for m is no less than $d_m \cdot t_j$, *i.e.*, $p_m \ge d_m \cdot t_j$. This contradicts with $b_m > p_m$. **Case II:** $t_m > t_j$. Consider the computing of the price for bidder j. After reserving d_j channels for bidder j, bidder m would lose according to (1) and thus the price for j is no less than $d_j \cdot t_m$. By the inductive hypothesis, we know that bidder j is a winner, i.e., $b_j > p_j$. Combining the above results, we obtain $b_j > d_j \cdot t_m$ which contradicts with $t_m > t_j$. Therefore, Theorem 1 holds for $N = m$. The proof is accomplished.

5.3.2 *Proof of Theorem 2*

We first show that a bidder cannot increase its utility by using multiple identifiers.

LEMMA 1. *A bidder cannot increase its utility by submitting false-name bids, provided that all other bidders and their bids are same.*

PROOF. Suppose a bidder i uses two names i_1 and i_2 to participate the auction, and obtains x and y channels under the names i_1 and i_2, respectively. We show bidder i using a single identifier can obtain a total of $z = x + y$ channels with a utility that is no less than the sum of that obtained by i_1 and i_2.

[Case I: When names i_1 and i_2 are used.] We prove that their critical bidders have the same per-channel bid price, *i.e.*, $t_{c(i_1)} = t_{c(i_2)}$. The fundamental basis is that they both win and have the same conflicting neighbors except themselves. The claim holds when $c(i_1) = c(i_2)$. Otherwise, w.l.o.g., we assume $c(i_1) < c(i_2)$. For bidder i_1, by the procedure of finding critical bidder, we know i_1's allocation would cause $c(i_1)$ to lose, *i.e.*, $|\cup_{j \in \mathbb{N}(i_1), j \leq c(i_1)} \mathcal{A}_j| + x > K$. Since $c(i_2) \in \mathbb{N}(i_1)$ and $c(i_1) < c(i_2)$, we obtain $|\cup_{j \in \mathbb{N}(i_1), j < c(i_2)} \mathcal{A}_j| + x > K$ which means i_1's allocation would cause $c(i_2)$ to lose. Therefore, we have $t_{c(i_1)} = max(t_{c(i_1)}, t_{c(i_2)})$.

Now consider computing price for bidder i_2, reserving y channels would cause $c(i_2)$ loses, but i_1 is i_2's winning neighbor since both i_1 and i_2 win. By the above deduction, i_1's allocation would cause $c(i_1)$ to lose and thus we have $t_{c(i_2)} = max(t_{c(i_1)}, t_{c(i_2)})$.

[Case II: When a single name i is used.] Since the requested channels in both cases are the same (*i.e.*, $z = x + y$) and i has the same conflict conditions as i_1 and i_2, i.e., satisfying i's request would cause $c(i_1)$ and $c(i_2)$ to lose , leading to $t_{c(i)} = max(t_{c(i_1)}, t_{c(i_2)})$.

Finally, we achieve that the bidder has the same utility in both cases. Similarly, when a bidder uses multiple names, the same deduction still holds. □

Then we prove that a bidder cannot increase its utility by submitting a cheating bid when using a single name.

LEMMA 2. *A bidder, using a single name, cannot increase its utility by submitting a cheating bid. (provided that all other bidders and bids are same)*

PROOF. Assume that bidder i's true valuation is v_i, which is different from its bid b_i, *i.e.*, $b_i \neq v_i$. We consider the following cases.

- Case I: Bidder i loses by bidding b_i and wins by bidding v_i. We have $u_i(v_i) > 0 = u_i(b_i)$.
- Case II: Bidder i loses by bidding both b_i and v_i, we have $u_i(v_i) = u_i(b_i) = 0$.
- Case III: Bidder i wins by bidding b_i and loses by bidding v_i. This case only happens when $t_{c(i)} > t_i$, and thus we have $u_i(v_i) = 0 > u_i(b_i)$.
- Case IV: Bidder i wins by bidding both b_i and v_i. Recall that the critical bidder of bidder i only depends on its demands and other bidders' demands. Since these parameters do no change when its bid changes and thus the critical bidders are the same for both cases. Therefore, we get $u_i(v_i) = u_i(b_i)$.

In summary, we have $u_i(v_i) \geq u_i(b_i)$ in all cases, which completes the proof. □

Finally, the false-name-proofness of ALETHEIA follows by Lemma 1 and Lemma 2 immediately.

5.3.3 *Proof of Theorem 3*

In the first step (§5.1.1), ALETHEIA uses a BFS procedure to construct the bidder list which takes $O(N + E)$ and also sorts each bidder's neighbor nodes with a complexity of $O(N \log N)$ in the worst case. Therefore this step takes $O(N + E + N \log N)$ time. In the second step (§5.1.2), for each bidder, ALETHEIA-Prices takes $2KE$ (each edge is updated at most 2 times) to update the available channel information of all bidders' neighboring bidders. Therefore it takes $O(NKE)$ time to compute the prices for all bidders. In the last step (§5.1.3), ALETHEIA-Allocation uses $O(N)$ to allocate channels to bidders and uses $2KE$ to update the availability of each bidder's channel, and hence its complexity is $O(N + KE)$. By summing up the cost of all three steps, the theorem holds directly.

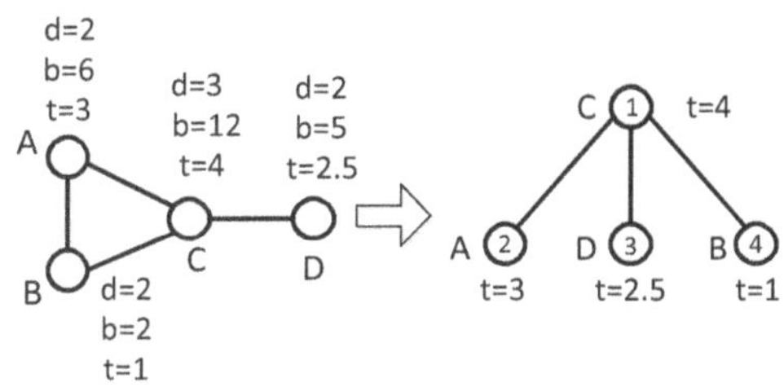

Figure 7: An illustration of demand reduction cheating, where bidder C can improve its utility when cheating by requesting 2 channels.

6. ALETHEIA EXTENSION

To make ALETHEIA more flexible and practical, we extend the basic ALETHEIA design, which only supports all-or-none requests, by enabling range-based requests. We name the enhanced design as ALETHEIA-RG, in which, bidders do not need to be single-minded. A bidder i can request d_i channels, and accepts any number of channels from 0 to d_i.

6.1 Valuation for Partial Satisfaction

Since requests of bidders are allowed to be partially satisfied, we need to rethink the corresponding valuation function. We make the following assumptions for the valuation function based on the fact that bidders are *rational.*

First, for each bidder i who requests d_i channels with true valuation $v(d_i)$, we assume that the valuation function satisfies *free disposal* [4]: for any $d_i' \geq d_i$, we have $v(d_i) = v(d_i')$. Free disposal indicates that when i's request is completely satisfied, allocating more channels will not improve its utility.

Second, we assume that the valuation function satisfies *super-additive* [4]: for any d' and d'', such that $d' + d'' \leq d_i$ we have

$$v_i(d' + d'') \geq v(d') + v(d'). \qquad (2)$$

Super-addition implies that a bidder would have higher utility when its request is closer to be fulfilled completely. Note that the above assumptions include the single-mind request as a special case.

6.2 New Cheating Pattern

When the requests can be partially satisfied, another cheating pattern, named *demand-reduction cheating* [6] arises, which may break the false-name-proofness of ALETHEIA. To see this, we introduce Figure 7 as an example. In this example, there are 4 bidders (A, B, C, and D) attend the auction to compete $K = 4$ channels. Their bids and demands, together with the conflict graph, are shown at the left side of Figure 7. According to ALETHEIA, bidder C wins and other bidders lose. Bidder C's critical bidder is A, and thus its utility is computed as $12 - 3 * 3 = 3$. Now we consider bidder C cheats on demand, by submitting $b_i = 8$ to request $d_i = 2$ channels, while other bidders stay unchanged. Now by the ALETHEIA, we know only bidder B loses and other bidders win, and C's critical bidder becomes bidder B. In this case, the utility of C is $8 - 1 * 2 = 6$. That is to say, bidder C can improve its own utility by reducing the demand.

Algorithm 3: Procedure *PreventDR*()

for $i = 1$ *to* N **do**
  if *i is a winner* **then**
    for *each* $< b_{i'}, d_{i'} > \in \mathcal{L}$ **do**
      $\mathcal{N} = \mathcal{N} \backslash \{i\} \cup \{i'\}$;
      $p_{i'}$ = ALETHEIA-Prices(i');
      $u_{i'} = v_{i'} - p_{i'}$;
      if $u_{i'} > u_i$ **then**
        $u_i = u_{i'}$;
        Re-allocate $d_{i'}$ channels to i.

6.3 Design of ALETHEIA-RG

To prevent demand reduction cheating, ALETHEIA-RG introduces a new component named PreventDR (Algorithm 3) besides the basic design ALETHEIA. In particular, after finding out the winners by running ALETHEIA, ALETHEIA-RG runs PreventDR for each winner to find the possible maximum utility when the winner reduces its channel demand to ensure the false-name-proofness.

PreventDR traverses all possible demand reduction cheatings, denoted as $d_i' \in \{1, 2, \ldots, d_i\}$, in order to find the maximal utility for each winner i in ALETHEIA. We denote $\mathcal{L} = \{\langle v_i(d_i), d_i\rangle, \langle v_i(d_i - 1), d_i - 1\rangle, \ldots, \langle v_i(1), 1\rangle\}$ as the cheating set. To ease the description, we use i' to denote the bidder i with cheating demand. For each possible cheating $\langle b_{i'}, d_{i'}\rangle \in \mathcal{L}$, we re-run ALETHEIA-prices by substituting i with i' to compute its new utility $u_{i'}$. If the newly obtained utility is greater than the obtained utility that i bids b_i for d_i channels, then Algorithm 3 withdraws previous allocation of i and reallocate $d_{i'}$ to i. Note that, the remaining channels $(d_i - d_{i'})$ will not be allocated to other bidders.

6.4 Properties with Proofs

THEOREM 4. *ALETHEIA-RG satisfies allocation feasibility.*

PROOF. Since ALETHEIA-RG is based on the results of ALETHEIA and it only decreases the number of allocated channels of each winner in ALETHEIA. Thus, ALETHEIA-RG does not violate the allocation feasibility property. □

THEOREM 5. *ALETHEIA-RG is false-name-proof.*

PROOF. The proof is very similar to the one for Theorem 2, and also consists of two parts. We thus only describe the differences between them.

For the first part (similar to Lemma 1), consider that bidder i uses two false names i_1 and i_2. The only differences coming from ALETHEIA-RG are that i_1 and i_2 may choose demand reduction cheating. Assume that the utility of bidder i_1 is maximized when bidding $b_{i_1'}$ for $d_{i_1'}$, and thus its utility is $u_{i_1'} = v_i(d_{i_1'}) - d_{i_1'} \cdot t_{c(i_1')}$. Similarly, we get the utility of i_2 as $u_{i_2'} = v_i(d_{i_2'}) - d_{i_2'} * t_{c(i_2')}$. Now we consider the same auction except that bidder i participates under a single name. If i chooses to lie on its demand, we have $d_{i'} \geq d_{i_1'}$ and $d_{i'} \geq d_{i_2'}$. Larger demands mean that we need to reserve more channels when computing the charging price, and thus more of its neighbors cannot be allocated, leading to $t_{c(i')} \geq t_{c(i_1')}$ and $t_{c(i')} \geq t_{c(i_2')}$. Moreover, by Eq. (2), we get $v_i(d_{i_1'} + d_{i_2'}) \geq v_i(d_{i_1'}) + v_i(d_{i_2'})$. Combining these above equations, we obtain

$$u_{i'} = v(d_{i_1'} + d_{i_2'}) - (d_{i_1'} + d_{i_2'}) \cdot t_{c(i')} \geq u_{i_1'} + u_{i_2'}. \quad (3)$$

In other words, if demand reduction cheating is profitable for bidder i, our claim holds by equation (3). If demand reduction cheating is not profitable for bidder i, we have $u_i \geq u_{i'} \geq u_{i_1'} + u_{i_2'}$, again our claim holds.

For the second part (similar to Lemma 2), the differences also come from the case that bidder i chooses to make demand reduction cheating. Such cheating only happens when i is a winner, and its payment is irrelevant to b_i and v_i $(b_i \neq v_i)$. Thus it achieves the same utility no matter whether it cheats on the demand or not. Therefore, we conclude that a bidder using a single name cannot increase its utility by cheating on bids. □

THEOREM 6. *ALETHEIA-RG runs in polynomial complexity of* $O(N^2 K \log N + N^2 K^2 E)$.

PROOF. For each winner i, we need to run ALETHEIA-prices at most d_i times and thus the prevent demand reduction lie procedure takes $N \cdot d_i \cdot O(N \log N + NKE)$ for all winners. Therefore, the ALETHEIA-RG runs in complexity less than $O(N^2 K \log N + N^2 K^2 E)$. □

7. EVALUATION

7.1 Simulation Setup

We randomly deploy bidders in a 100×100 square area, and set the interference range as 10. If the distance between any two bidders is less than 10, they interfere with each other when accessing the same channel at the same time. The per-channel bids of bidders are randomly distributed in the range of [0, 1]. We run the simulation 100 times and average the results to get rid of the randomness and observe the general patterns.

7.2 Performance

We use the *revenue* and *spectrum utilization* as our performance metrics, which are defined as the total payments and numbers of allocated channels of all winners, respectively. We compare ALETHEIA with the simple strawman approach proposed in §4.2. For ease description, we name it as SIMPLE.

We compare them in two scenarios. First, we set the number of bidders as $N = 300$ and vary the number of auctioned channels. Each bidder requests either 1 or 2 channels. The results are plotted in Figure 8. ALETHEIA and SIMPLE achieve similar peak revenue when 4 and 8 channels are used, respectively, as illustrated in Figure 8(a). Figure Figure 8(b) shows that ALETHEIA significantly improves spectrum utilizations compared to SIMPLE under any number of auctioned channels. Figure 8(c) plots revenue as a function of spectrum utilization. Again, ALETHEIA performs much better. Second, we compare them by varying the number of bidders, setting the default number of auctioned channels as $K = 4$, and the request of each bidder is randomly draw from set $\{1, 2, 3, 4\}$. The results are shown in Figure 10. In this case, ALETHEIA significantly improves revenue and spectrum utilization compared to SIMPLE by up to 300%. This is because SIMPLE sacrifices spectrum reuse to maintain false-name-proofness. When the number of bidders grows, the number of allocated bidders in each partitioned

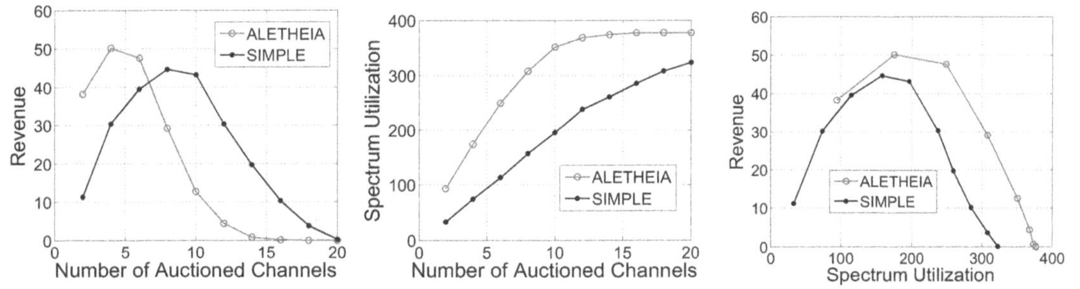

(a) Revenue (b) Spectrum Utilization (c) Revenue vs. Spectrum Utilization

Figure 8: Compare ALETHEIA with SIMPLE by varying the number of auctioned channels.

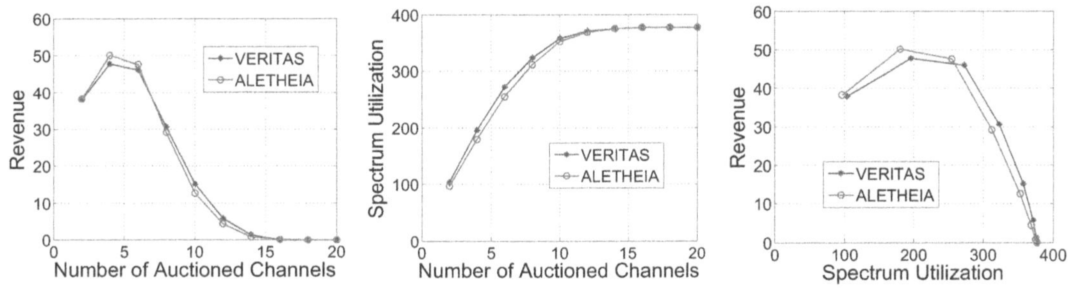

(a) Revenue (b) Spectrum Utilization (c) Revenue vs. Spectrum Utilization

Figure 9: Compare ALETHEIA with VERITAS by varying the number of auctioned channels.

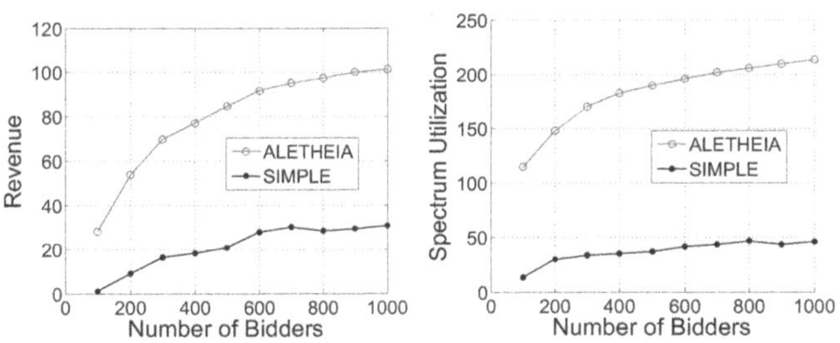

(a) Revenue (b) Spectrum Utilization

Figure 10: Compare ALETHEIA with SIMPLE by varying the number of bidders.

box in SIMPLE is nearly constant. In contrast, ALETHEIA can accommodate more bidders, i.e., achieving much higher spectrum reuse.

7.3 Cost of False-name-proofness

We also compare ALETHEIA with VERITAS to evaluate the cost of false-name-proofness. Specifically, we try to answer the question: how much performance would ALETHEIA lose if no bidders submit false-name bids?

We compare them by vary the number of auctioned channels from 2 to 20 and set the number bidders as 300. Each bidder's request is either 1 or 2. The results are shown in Figure 9. We can see that ALETHEIA has very similar performance, in terms of both revenue and utilization, as VERITAS. In order to guarantee false-name-proofness, ALETHEIA sacrifices part of bidders who have no critical neighbors in VERITAS (as shown in Section 3.1) and thus it performs slightly worse than VERITAS. On other hands, when the competition between bidders is high (i.e., when the number of auctioned channels is small), ALETHEIA performs slightly better than VERITAS in terms of revenue. This is because ALETHEIA charges by the highest losing neighbor's per-channel bid while VERITAS charges by that of the first losing neighbor.

8. RELATED WORK

Spectrum allocation mechanisms have been extensively studied in recent years. A number of auction designs have been proposed to improve spectrum utilization and allocation efficiency. VERITAS [24] is one of the pioneer auction designs with strategy-proofness that exploits the spectrum reusability in radio spectrum. Later, the work is extended to consider double spectrum auctions [25]. Jia *et al.* [9] and Al-Ayyoub *et al.* [3] design spectrum auctions to maximize the expected revenue by assuming that the bids of the secondary users follow certain distributions. SMALL [20] is designed for the scenario where the primary user sets a reserved price for each channel. TRUMP [19] allocates spectrum access rights on the basis of QoS demands. The aforementioned work achieve strategy-proofness under the assumption that each bidder is associated with a unique name. As a result, none of them can resist false-name bid cheating where bidders can improve their utilities by submitting multiple false-name bids simultaneously. Another group of work (e.g., [21, 26]) study the collusion issue among bidders in spectrum auctions. Compared with collusion, while a bidder has to seek out and persuade other bidders to join in collusion, a false-name bid is easier to make since it can be done alone.

With the popularity and success of Internet auctions, false-name bid cheating has attracted more and more research interests. The effects of false-name bids on combinatorial auctions are analyzed in [23]. Following that, a series of false-name-proof mechanisms have been developed for a variety of scenarios. For example, Yokoo *et al.* [12] designed a leveled division set based mechanism for multi-item single-unit auctions and prove its false-name-proofness. In [11,17], false-name-proof mechanisms have been proposed to address the multi-unit single-item settings. Unfortunately, all these designs are for traditional goods (e.g., books or paintings). They do not consider the spectrum reusability and cannot deal with the complex inference constraints in spectrum auctions. As a result, when being applied to spectrum auctions, these designs either lose false-name-proofness or create excess interference, as discussed in Section 4.

Different from the previous studies, ALETHEIA not only provides strategy-proofness but also resists false-name bid cheating. To the best of our knowledge, ALETHEIA is the first spectrum auction design that can achieve false-name-proofness.

9. CONCLUSIONS

In this paper, we studied the new type of cheating named false-name bids, in large-scale spectrum auctions. We demonstrated that false-name bid cheating is easy to form in existing strategy-proof spectrum auctions and can severely impair the auction revenue. We further devised ALETHEIA, the first false-name-proof design for spectrum auction that nullifies the possibility of increasing profits by submitting false-name bids. It achieves high spectrum redistribution efficiency and low computational overhead, and is very flexible to support diverse request formats of bidders.

10. REFERENCES

[1] http://www.atheros.com.

[2] I. Akyildiz, W. Y. Lee, M. Vuran, and S. Mohanty. Next generation/dynamic spectrum access/cognitive radio wireless networks: a survey. *Computer Networks*, 50(13):2127–2159, 2006.

[3] M. Al-Ayyoub and H. Gupta. Truthful spectrum auctions with approximate revenue. In *Proc. of INFOCOM.* IEEE, 2011.

[4] Y. Bartal, R. Gonen, and N. Nisan. Incentive compatible multi unit combinatorial auctions. In *Proc. of TARK*, 2003.

[5] T. Clancy and N. Goergen. Security in cognitive radio networks: Threats and mitigation. In *Proc. of CrownCom.* IEEE, 2008.

[6] R. Engelbrecht-Wiggans, J. List, and D. Reiley. Demand reduction in multi-unit auctions with varying numbers of bidders: Theory and field experiments. *Inernational Economic Review*, 47(1):203–231, 2006.

[7] K. Ezirim, E. Troja, and S. Sengupta. Sustenance against rl-based sybil attacks in cognitive radio networks using dynamic reputation systems. In *Proc. of MILCOM.* IEEE, 2013.

[8] K. Jain, J. Padhye, V. N. Padmanabhan, and L. Qiu. Impact of interference on multi-hop wireless network performance. In *Proc. of MOBICOM.* ACM, 2003.

[9] J. Jia, Q. Zhang, Q. Zhang, and M. Liu. Revenue generation for truthful spectrum auction in dynamic spectrum access. In *Proc. of MOBIHOC.* ACM, 2009.

[10] P. Klemperer. *Auctions, theory and practice.* Princeton University Press, USA, 2004.

[11] S. M. M. Yokoo, Y. Sakurai. Robust multi-unit auction protocol against false-name bids. In *Proc. of IJCAI.* IEEE, 2001.

[12] S. M. M. Yokoo, Y. Sakurai. Robust combinatorial auction protocol against false-name bids. *Artificial Intelligence*, 130(1):167–181, 2002.

[13] A. Mas-Colell, M. D. Whinston, and J. R. Green. *Microeconomic Theory.* Oxford Press, USA, 1995.

[14] M. McHenry, P. Tenhula, D. McCloskey, D. Roberson, and C. Hood. Chicago spectrum occupancy measurements & analysis and a long-term studies proposal. In *Proc. of TAPAS*, 2006.

[15] M. J. Osborne and A. Rubenstein. *A Course in Game Theory.* MIT Press, USA, 1994.

[16] Y. Tan, S. Sengupta, and K. Subbalakshmi. Spectrum stealing via sybil attacks in dsa networks: implementation and defense. In *Proc. of ICC.* IEEE, 2011.

[17] K. Terada and M. Yokoo. False-name-proof multi-unit auction protocol utilizing greedy allocation based on approximate evaluation values. In *Proc. of AAMAS*, 2003.

[18] T. Todo, A. Iwasaki, M. Yokoo, and Y. Sakurai. Characterizing false-name-proof allocation rules in combinatorial auctions. In *Proc. of AAMAS*, 2009.

[19] Q. Wang, B. Ye, S. Lu, and S. Guo. A truthful qos-aware spectrum auction with spatial reuse for large-scale networks. *TPDS*, 46(1):2499–2508, 2014.

[20] F. Wu and N. Vaidya. Small: A strategy-proof mechanism for radio spectrum allocation. In *Proc. of INFOCOM.* IEEE, 2011.

[21] Y. Wu, B. Wang, K. Liu, and T. Clancy. A scalable collusion-resistant multi-winner cognitive spectrum auction game. *Transactions on Communications*, 57(12):3805 – 3816, 2009.

[22] M. Yokoo, Y. Sakurai, and S. Matsubara. The effect of false-name declarations in mechanism design: Towards collective decision making on the internet. In *Proc. of ICDCS.* IEEE, 2000.

[23] M. Yokoo, Y. Sakurai, and S. Matsubara. The effect of false-name bids in combinatorial auctions: New fraud in internet auctions. *Games and Economic Behavior*, 46(1):174–188, 2004.

[24] X. Zhou, S. Gandhi, S. Suri, and H. Zheng. ebay in the sky: Strategy-proof wireless spectrum auctions. In *Proc. of MOBICOM.* ACM, 2008.

[25] X. Zhou and H. Zheng. Trust: A general framework for truthful double spectrum auctions. In *Proc. of INFOCOM.* IEEE, 2009.

[26] X. Zhou and H. Zheng. Breaking bidder collusion in large-scale spectrum auctions. In *Proc. of MOBIHOC.* ACM, 2010.

Turning Waste into Wealth: Enabling Communication in Guardband Whitespace

Jiansong Zhang*, Jin Zhang‡, Kun Tan*, Lin Yang†, Qian Zhang†, and Yongguang Zhang*
Microsoft Research Asia*
CSE, Hong Kong University of Science and Technology†
South University of Science and Technology of China‡
{jiazhang, kuntan, ygz}@microsoft.com* {lyangab, qianzh}@cse.ust.hk† zhang.j4@sustc.edu.cn‡

Abstract

Similar to TV bands, the guardband frequencies are not occupied therefore are whitespace that potentially allows additional communication activities. Considering the difference to TV whitespace, we propose independent communication for guardband whitespace. In this paper, we present the Pilotfish system which realizes independent communication and turns guardband whitespace into new communication channels. To address the big challenges of interference mitigation, we employ novel PHY design which includes specially customized FBMC and an Nulled Decoding technique to null the strong background signal in guardbands. We implemented Pilotfish using software radio system. Empirical evaluation results validate the Pilotfish design in both PHY and MAC.

Categories and Subject Descriptors

C.3 [**Special-Purpose and Application-Based Systems**]: ; C.2.1 [**Computer-Communication Networks**]: Network Architecture and Design—*Wireless communication*

General Terms

System, Design, Experimentation, Measurement

Keywords

Wireless; Guardband Whitespace; Independent Communication; Filtering; Nulled Decoding

1. INTRODUCTION

Spectrum resource for wireless communication has become scarce. Existing communication bands are being overwhelmed with the rapid growth of broadband access needs, which therefore has driven governments to seek for innovative use of spectrum and turn more spectrum from other purposes to wireless communications [2].

However, despite this spectrum scarcity, there is a counterintuitive fact in today's communication systems that some of the available spetrum is NOT utilized to transmit bits – a substantial part of the communication spectrum, called *guardbands*, is left unused.

MobiHoc'15, June 22–25, 2015, Hangzhou, China.

http://dx.doi.org/10.1145/2746285.2746299.

As shown in Figure 1, guardbands reside in two sides of every communication channel and occupy roughly 10% of spectrum in major communication systems like LTE [20] and Wi-Fi [5]. Taking Wi-Fi with 20MHz channels as an example, guardbands cause 2.2MHz-wide wasted spectrum between every two adjacent channels.

Actually, the design of guardband is not purely a waste of resource. The purpose is to insulate transmissions on adjacent frequencies to prevent mutual interference. For example, in LTE and Wi-Fi, the transmitted OFDM signal spreads quite a lot of energy into nearby frequencies, thus requires a large size of guardbands to mitigate its effect. Although guardbands could be reduced or even eliminated in theory, *i.e.* if communication systems running in adjacent frequencies can be tightly coordinated [8,22] or even OFDMA can be applied [18], in practice, fine-grained coordination between these separated systems requires complicated mechanism which is hardly fulfilled in general[1] .

In this paper, we borrow a definition which treats guardbands as a special type of whitespace [4] and address the following question: *Is it possible to utilize the "wasted" guardband frequencies for communications?* Similar to the efforts spent on TV whitespace [12], we aim for utilizing guardbands to create new communication channels that can provide meaningful capacity but do not add burden to the incumbents (*i.e.*, existing systems which occupy the communication spectrum). We expect these new channels will bring significant value, because communication spectrum is quite expensive today. For example, according to US Federal Communications Commission, the average price calculated from recent spectrum auctions is $1.5 per MHz-pop [1], meaning every megahertz has costed service providers $0.5 billion just for license [2].

The problem of designing communication system in guardband whitespace is fundamentally different from in TV whitespace. In TV whitespace, TV stations transmit in a sparse and predictable manner [12], therefore the "transmitting if idle" strategy is suitable and possible to realize with the help of TV-station database or channel sensing [12]. But in guardband whitespace, incumbents transmit in an either persistent (*e.g.*, LTE) or highly dynamic (*e.g.*, Wi-Fi) manner therefore makes database or sensing useless. In this paper, we propose *independent communication* for guardband whitespace, means communications could be conducted anytime no matter incumbents are active or not, anywhere no matter incumbents are close or far away.

Independent communication represents an ambitious design goal. It is possible to achieve because the frequencies of guardbands are

[1]OFDMA can be realized in limited cases, *e.g.* downlink of LTE inside a cell [20]. However, LTE still relies on guardbands to insulate adjacent cells that are on adjacent frequenies.

[2]given the over 300 million population in US today

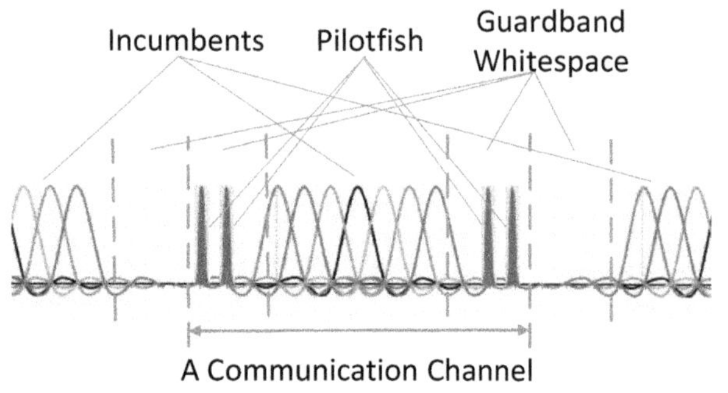

Figure 1: Pilotfish in guardband whitespace. Pilotfish works with all OFDM based incumbents and enables independent communication in the wasted guardband frequencies.

not directly occupied. However, designing a system to realize independent communication is non-trivial because we need to address two important concerns: First, since guardband is very close to incumbent's frequency, the guardband system should suppress its out-of-band emission extremely well, otherwise it could destructively affect incumbents. The requirement on sidelobe suppression is at least -60dB, which is much higher than any existing communication system. Second, OFDM based incumbents generate strong out-of-band emission which severely polluts the guardbands. For example, our measurements of the signal-to-interference-and-noise ratio (SINR) in guardbands was usually less than 0dB and as low as -30dB, meaning close to zero capacity conventionally.

Our solutions for these challenges are two-fold. First, we choose *Filter Bank Multi-Carrier* (FBMC) [13] as our physical layer (PHY) structure, which has been proved much more efficient in suppressing out-of-band emission than both single carrier PHY (*e.g.* DSSS) and OFDM. Second, we develop the *Nulled Decoding* technique which nulls incumbents' OFDM signal while decoding the guardband transmission, thereby significantly improving the SINR in guardbands and making decoding possible.

In this paper, we present the Pilotfish system which employs these techniques to realize independent communication. As shown in Figure 1, Pilotfish works with all OFDM based incumbents – Pilotfish devices communicate using the guardband frequencies on two sides of an incumbent band. Pilotfish achieves a spectrum efficiency comparable to or better than typical narrow-band communication systems, such as Zigbee, Z-Wave, BLE, *etc.*. Still using Wi-Fi with 20MHz channels as an example, Pilotfish creates 1.22Mbps independent communication channels using the 2.2MHz guardband frequencies. Moreover, Pilotfish brings the benefit of new communication channels without causing interference to incumbents or requiring modification to incumbents. Benefitting from its advanced PHY techniques, Pilotfish also does not require synchronization between Pilotfish transmitters and incumbent transmitters or being sensitive to the frequency offset between the transmitters.

We have built a prototype of Pilotfish using the Sora software radio system [19]. As transmitting in LTE bands requires license, we only built the prototype for Wi-Fi in unlicensed band, though the Pilotfish design can be applied to both. We evaluated both PHY and MAC based on the prototype. Experimental results validated the Pilotfish design. Specifically, 1) we prove that Pilotfish transmissions do not interfere with incumbent transmissions. 2) We show Nulled Decoding is able to greatly improve SINR in guardband and therefore enable the decoding in guardband whitespace. The SINR improvement is not affected by clock phase noise, frequency offset or multipath channel. 3) We prove the Pilotfish MAC is effective.

To demonstrate the benefits that Pilotfish brings, we also propose two applications of Pilotfish.

In summary, we make the following contributions: 1) We propose independent communication in guardband whitespace, which creates new communication channels without requiring spectrum resource. 2) We propose the Pilotfish system which employs advanced PHY techniques to address the uncommon challenges in guardband whitespace. 3) We implemented Pilotfish using software radio and verified the Pilotfish design through experiments.

2. Pilotfish OVERVIEW

This section provides an overview of Pilotfish. First we discuss the widely adopted guardband design as the background of this paper. Then we describe our *independent communication* strategy for transmissions in guardband as well as the challenges to realize this strategy. Finally we briefly introduce filter bank multicarrier to explain why we choose it for Pilotfish's PHY structure.

2.1 Guardband in Communication Systems

Guandband is a widely adopted design in wireless systems. The purpose is to protect the systems that are in adjacent frequency bands by insulating them from mutual interference, where the systems could be designed for either the same or different purposes (*e.g.*, communication *vs.* radar or TV broadcast), or used in either the same or different manners (*e.g.* exclusive in licensed bands *vs.* shared in unlicensed bands). The guardband design is also commonly used for systems inside a frequency band, for example, to insulate adjacent Wi-Fi channels in 5GHz ISM band [5] or insulate adjacent LTE channels in LTE band number 41 [20].

The guardband design leaves a substantial portion of the precious spectrum resource unused. For example, according to the IEEE 802.11 standards [5], 2.2 $\sim$3.4 MHz of a Wi-Fi channel is left as guardband, which results in more than 10% waste for 20 MHz channels. The number in LTE is similar [20]. The size of guardband highly depends on frequency domain characteristics of the transmitted signal. Majority of the advanced communication systems, including Wi-Fi and LTE, employ OFDM as their PHY design for high spectrum efficiency and low complexity [15]. The problem of OFDM is that it spouts quite a lot of energy into adjacent channels, therefore requires a large guardband size.

2.2 Independent Communication in Guardband Whitespace

Similar to the TV whitespace, we can potentially conduct communication using the unused frequencies in guardbands. In this paper, we adopt an existing definition [4] to term it *guardband whitespace*. The goal of this paper is to develop techniques to conduct communication effectively and efficiently in guardband whitespace.

Similar to the communication in TV whitespace, communication in guardband whitespace should also avoid generating interference to incumbents and prevent themselves from being interfered by incumbents. However, the strategies for communication are totally different because the behaviors of incumbents are different. In TV whitespace, the communication systems try to utilize the frequencies which were allocated for TV broadcasting because some frequencies are rarely used in some regions. Usually, the schedule of TV broadcasting is available in advance and the location of TV stations is fixed. Therefore, the strategy of "transmitting if idle" is necessary to prevent incumbents and sufficient to prevent themselves. However, in guardband whitespace, the same strategy will be neither necessary nor sufficient. Since guardband is not directly occupied, it is possible that the communication does not generate noticeable interference to the incumbents (*i.e.* existing wireless systems). Since the incumbents could have unpredictable behavior, it will be very difficult to determine an idle time. For example, in LTE bands, the incumbents (base stations) transmit persistently, in Wi-Fi bands, the incumbents (APs and stations) transmit in a highly dynamic manner (on per-packet basis).

In this paper, we propose *Independent Communication* as our strategy for guardband whitespace, which means communication does not depends on the status of incumbents, *i.e.* no matter they are active or silent, no matter they are close or far away. Independent communication represents an ambitious design goal that if achieved, the communication system will be possible to be inserted in any existing wireless systems' guardband. With independent communication, we remove the burden of additional database or channel sensing as in TV whitespace, but need to rely on advanced PHY techniques to protect both the guardband communication system and incumbents. The requirement for PHY design is actually very high because we need to address two uncommon challenges in communication system design as follows.

First, the guardband system should suppress its out-of-band emission extremely well. Different from exisiting narrow band systems (*e.g.* Zigbee, Z-wave and bluetooth) in which both a system itself and its adjacent system are based on spread spectrum PHY (*e.g.* DSSS)[3], the guardband system in our design must handle adjacent systems based on OFDM. Spread spectrum systems have a nice property that OFDM systems do not have, *i.e.* resistant to cross-interference because of the employed spreading code (*e.g.* CDMA) [16]. Therefore the requirement on out-of-band suppression is reduced. However, to protect OFDM based incumbents, we must suppress guardband system's out-of-band emission much better. We set our goal as a emitted energy level comparable to noise floor, meaning $60dB$ to $80dB$ sidelobe suppression.

Second, since the guardband system is designed to work concurrently and independently with incumbents, the guardband system must handle potentially very strong background signal emitted by incumbents. As characterized with transmit power mask [5, 20], OFDM based incumbents emit a energy level merely $20dB$ less in guardband than in their center frequency. To obtain a rough understanding of the SINR in guardband, we set up a 9-node test-bed with commodity Wi-Fi cards, in which every node can hear from all the other nodes. We recorded received signal strength indicator (RSSI) on every link, then calculated SINR in guardband using a model with three nodes: one node as guardband transmitter, one as guardband receiver and one as incumbent transmitter. In this caclulation, we assumed the same transmit power density of guardband transmitter as incumbent transmitter, and derived the RSSI in guardband from transmit power mask. Results are shown in Figure 2. We exclude the cases that guardband transmitter is stronger than incumbent transmitter because they are trivial to handle. We can see in many cases, the SINR in guardband was less than $0dB$. In some cases, the SINR was even as low as $-30dB$. Conventionally, this SINR level means impossible for meaningful transmission, or as low as 1 bit per Wi-Fi packet with 20MHz channel [17].

2.3 Filter Bank Multi-Carrier

In this paper, we propose the Pilotfish system to realize independent communication in guardband whitespace. To address the uncommon challenges mentioned in above subsection, we propose a novel PHY design in Pilotfish. As the basis, we choose *Filter Bank Multi-Carrier* (FBMC) [13] as Pilotfish's PHY structure. In this subsection, we briefly introduce the advantages of FBMC to facilite the detailed discuss of Pilotfish's PHY in next section.

[3]These systems only consider intra-protocol interference in their design. Cross-protocol interference is still an research problem.

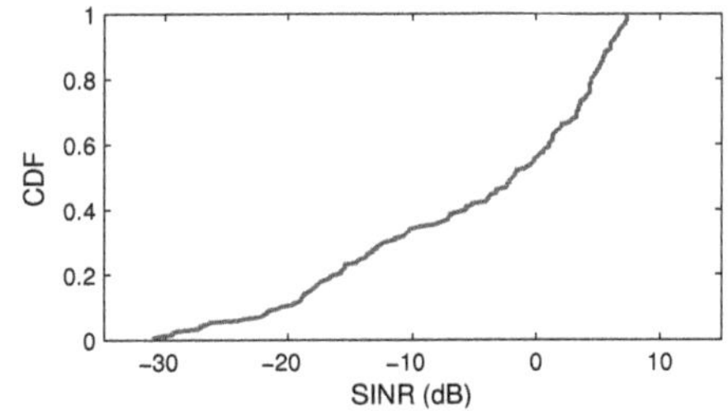

Figure 2: Measured guardband SINR from a 9-node test-bed.

FBMC, as the same as OFDM, is a form of multi-carrier modulation that contains a set of narrow subcarriers. It therefore enjoys the advantages of multi-carrier modulation, *e.g.* high spectrum efficiency, immunity to multi-path fading and impulse noise, enhanced immunity to inter-symbol interference, *etc.* [16]. However, different from OFDM which causes strong out-of-band emission because of the employed time-domain window function as subcarrier filter, FBMC can suppress out-of-band emission arbitrarily well because of its flexible choice of subcarrier filter. Therefore, FBMC is a good choice for Pilotfish. FBMC also has another advantage that it does not require symbol synchronization as OFDM, because it can insulate subcarriers with properly designed subcarrier filter. Therefore FBMC based scheme could be a better choice for multiple access than OFDM based scheme (*i.e.* OFDMA) when symbol synchronization among multiple transmitters is difficult.

3. PILOTFISH DESIGN

This paper presents Pilotfish[4], a system that realizes independent communication in guardband whitespace. Pilotfish represents a novel communication system design which addresses the uncommon challenges mentioned in above section using advanced PHY techniques. Specifically, Pilotfish employs FBMC as its PHY structure for the purpose of better suppressing its out-of-band emission. In §3.1 we will discuss the filter design in details as well as its impact. We also develop the *Nulled Decoding* technique to enable decoding under the extremely low SINR in guardband. Nulled Decoding leverages the orthogonality property of OFDM to null the emitted signal from incumbents. In §3.2 we will elaborate Nulled Decoding. Finally, in §3.3 we will discuss additional design considerations for truely independent guardband transmission with incumbent transmission.

For the sake of simplicity, we choose CSMA as Pilotfish's MAC. We leave other choices, *e.g.* frequency domain multiple access, as our future work which may be a better choice in centrally controlled wireless systems such as cellular networks.

3.1 Filter Design

The first requirement of Pilotfish is extremely well out-of-band emission suppression. This is achieved by applying a carefully designed filter in Pilotfish's FBMC PHY. In the following, we will first discuss the requirement of such a filter, and then we describe how we can design a digital filter that satisfies the requirement.

Figure 3 shows a simple prototype filter that divides the response of the filter into three parts: a pass-band, a stop-band, and a transition-band [6]. The stop-band rejection is defined as the ratio of the signal strength at the stop-band to that in the pass-band (in dB), *i.e.*, how much signal has been suppressed by the filter. The goal of our filter design is that the signal leakage at the stop-band would be as low as noise floor (*i.e.*, -90dBm), and thus the interference to nearby

[4]We name the system after a cute family of fish that usually lives around big sharks or sea turtles, which is a metaphor for guardband communication system that works concurrently with incumbents.

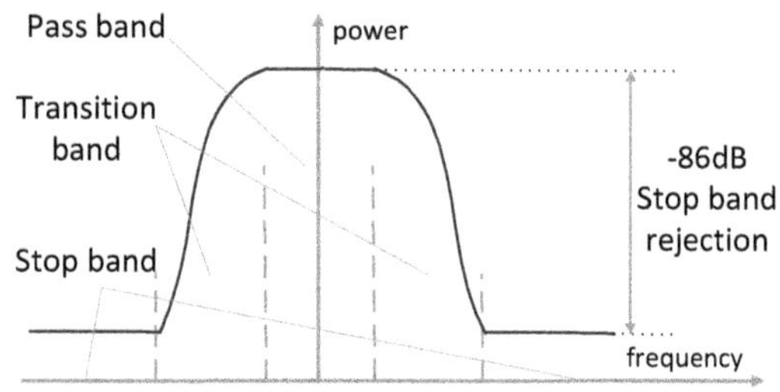

Figure 3: Prototype filter used in Pilotfish.

data communication can be neglected. Assuming the transmission power at the guardband channel is the same as Wi-Fi, *i.e.*, 20dBm, a receiver that is 1 foot apart would sense the signal strength as -30dBm – the path loss is about 50dB [17]. Therefore, in order to suppress the signal at the stop-band to noise floor, the stop band rejection should be at least -60dB.

Such a high rejection is very difficult to be implemented with conventional *finite impulse response* (FIR) filter as it may require a very long taps that incurs prohibitive computation overhead. To overcome this issue, in Pilotfish, we choose to use an *infinite impulse response* (IIR) filter. Specifically, we choose Type I Chebyshev filter [11] as the ripples in stop-band is very small. The implementation of such a filter is actually simple. It requires only 20 additions and 26 multiplications per symbol, which is comparable to a 26 taps FIR, therefore can be easily handled by modern digital signal processing (DSP) units. The stop-band rejection of our filter is actually -86dB and the transition-to-pass band ratio is 2.

The downside of such an IIR filter, however, is that the signal will spread out in the time domain. Therefore, it is not an ISI-free filter. ISI is generally considered harmful in communication as this self-interference caps the SINR of the channel, no matter how high the transmission power is. However, this SINR bound, 12 dB in our design, is not truely a critical issue for Pilotfish, because the SINR in guardband is far lower in many cases as shown in §2.2. Moreover, the application based on Pilotfish (§6) may only require broadcasting which is transmitted in low modulation rate anyway for reliability.

3.2 Nulled Decoding

While the filter prevents guardband transmission from interfering with incumbents, the incumbents, however, still spill significantly amount of energy into guardband (§2.2). Fortunately, the incumbents are mostly based on OFDM, which has a unique signal structure that we can explore to remove the interference.

Figure 4 illustrates the signal structure of an OFDM symbol. OFDM divides a channel into many small and partially overlapping subcarriers. The central frequencies of these subcarriers are carefully chosen so that they are "orthogonal" to one another, meaning that cross-talk of all other subcarriers sums up to zero at the central frequency of any subcarrier. Similarly, we can also find such points in guardbands where interference from all data subcarriers also sums to zero. These points are called *nulling points*. If we can just "take samples" of the guardband transmission at these nulling points, the data transmissions actually do not interfere with the guardband communication – as all interference is nulled at this "sampling point" (in frequency domain). Therefore, we call this technique as *Nulled Decoding*. Taking samples in frequency domain is realized using FFT, which is a basic building block of both OFDM receivers and Nulled Decoding based receivers. At the end of this section, we provide simple mathematics to describe the orthogonality of OFDM and Nulled Decoding in more detail.

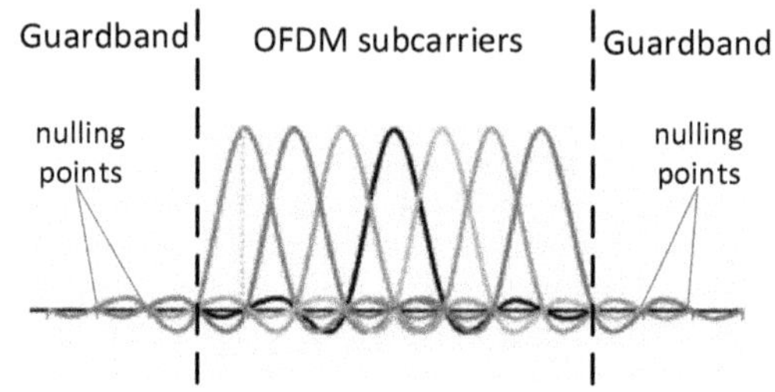

Figure 4: Multiple nulling points in guardband.

To find these nulling points in guardbands is actually simple. Imaging that if we fill the guardband with additional OFDM subcarriers, then the central frequencies of the added subcarriers are the nulling points in guardbands. For example, in Wi-Fi with 20MHz channel and HT mode, as defined in the standard [5], subcarrier -32∼-29 and 29∼31 are located in guardbands, and their central frequencies form the nulling points. Since Nulled Decoding takes samples from nulling points, Pilotfish aligns the subchannels of its FBMC PHY[5] with these nulling points. Specifically, around each nulling point, we place a Pilotfish subchannel, which has a width roughly the half of an incumbent OFDM subcarrier (125 KHz wide for Wi-Fi). To provide further isolation from incumbents, Pilotfish explicitly leaves the two nulling points adjacent to incumbent unused. Therefore, using Wi-Fi with 20MHz channel as an example, we can have 9 (non-HT mode) or 5 (HT mode) Pilotfish subchannels, respectively.

Same as OFDM subcarriers, the frequency separation between two Pilotfish subchannels is 312.5 KHz. According to the filter design in §3.1, one subchannel lies in the stop-band of the other. Therefore, the interference between subchannels is minor. In other words, Pilotfish satisfies the requirement of a FBMC PHY with its filter design and its subchannel separation.

The Pilotfish receiver then "takes samples" for the subchannels at these nulling points. It is achieved by simply performing FFT on the received signal, and the FFT outputs with the corresponding indexes are picked up. In this case, FFT can be regarded as a matched filter at the receiver side, and only samples on these nulling frequencies are retained. To enable this simple sampling, the major requirement for Pilotfish receiver is to determine symbol boundaries according to the symbols of incumbent's transmission.

To summarize the PHY design of Pilotfish, we first carefully choose parameters of the filter and locations of the subchannels to construct the FBMC PHY, then we use OFDM-like receiver to decode the FBMC transmissions. Pilotfish represents an uncommon *hybrid* PHY design, which therefore can solve the two uncommon challenges for communication in guardband whitespace. In the following, we discuss two practical issues of the Pilotfish PHY.

One issue is frequency offset. As shown in Figure 5, since there may be certain frequency offset between Pilotfish transmitter and incumbent transmitter, the Pilotfish receiver will not be able to *synchronize* its frequency[6] to both of them. In our design, we choose to synchronize to incumbent transmitter, *i.e.* to "take samples" from the nulling point instead of central frequency of the subchannel. The purpose is to optimize the performance of interference nulling. In this case, Pilotfish receiver must handle a slight non-compensatable frequency offset to Pilotfish transmitter. Therefore,

[5]Although subchannel and subcarrier could be used interchangeably, in this paper we only use "OFDM subcarrier" and "Pilotfish/FBMC subchannel" to differentiate two PHY structures.

[6]usually through frequency compensation algorithms

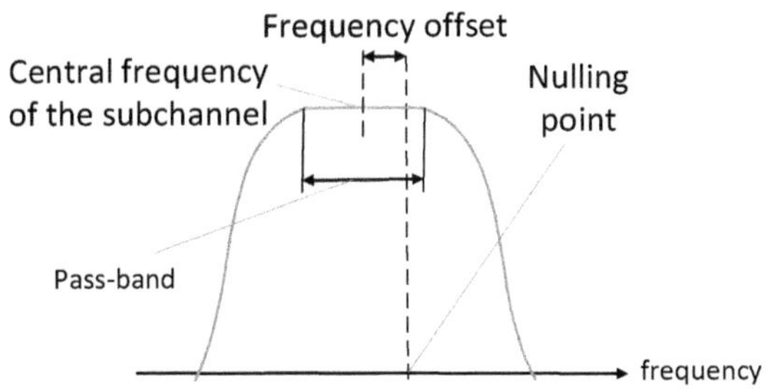

Figure 5: Frequency offset between Pilotfish transmitter and incumbent transmitter causes mis-alignment between Pilotfish subchannel and the nulling point. We choose to "take samples" from the nulling point to optimize nulling performance. SNR loss due to this mis-alignment will be small as long as the frequency offset is within pass-band of the Pilotfish filter.

we always use differential modulation for Pilotfish to address this frequency offset, as the same consideration in some DSSS PHYs. We notice that this slight frequency offset still causes loss in signal strength because the samples are not taken from central frequency of a subchannel. However, since the filter has a flat shape near its center, this SNR loss will be small as long as the frequency offset is within pass-band of the filter (125/2 KHz in case of Wi-Fi).

The other issue is the emitted energy from the incumbent in adjacent channel. It cannot be nulled because Pilotfish receiver is not able to align symbol boundary simultaneously to multiple unaligned incumbents in adjacent channels. We handle this issue with following three approaches: 1) As shown in Figure 1, the spectrum hole between two adjacent incumbents are divided into two equal parts that each part is associated with the closer incumbent. In this way, we still reserve a half-sized guardband between Pilotfish and the adjacent incumbent. 2) Considering the same power limit of devices, Pilotfish can use high power density than incumbents because of the narrower bandwidth, therefore provides additional gain. 3) We use a strong channel code to protect Pilotfish transmissions. As we will show later (§5), Pilotfish is more reliable than incumbents to the same interference from adjacent channel.

The Orthogonality of OFDM and Nulled Decoding. We provide simple mathematics as follows. Basically, the time-domain waveform $Y = [y_1, y_2, \cdots, y_N]^T$ of an OFDM symbol is generated using the linear equation:

$$Y = W \cdot X \tag{1}$$

where the vector $X = [x_1, x_2, \cdots, x_N]^T$ is the frequency-domain representation of the symbol which is generated by mapping information bits into signals using constellation maps, and the matrix $W = [w_1^T, w_2^T, \cdots, w_N^T]^T$ is the inverse Discrete Fourier Transform (IDFT) matrix which consists of a set of DFT vectors. DFT vectors have the property that they are orthogonal to each other, *i.e.*

$$w_p \cdot w_q^* = \{ \begin{array}{l} 1, ifp = q \\ 0, ifp \neq q \end{array} \tag{2}$$

where w_q^* is the conjugate transpose of w_q. Benefiting from this orthogonality property, we can easily recover each signal x_k from Y that we multiplying Y by the conjugate transpose of the corresponding DFT vector w_k, *i.e.*

$$w_k^* \cdot Y = w_k^* \cdot [w_1^T, w_2^T, \cdots, w_N^T]^T \cdot X = x_k, \tag{3}$$

In practice, Equation (1) is realized using IFFT (Inverse Fast Fourier Transform) and Equation (3) is realized using FFT (Fast Fourier Transform).

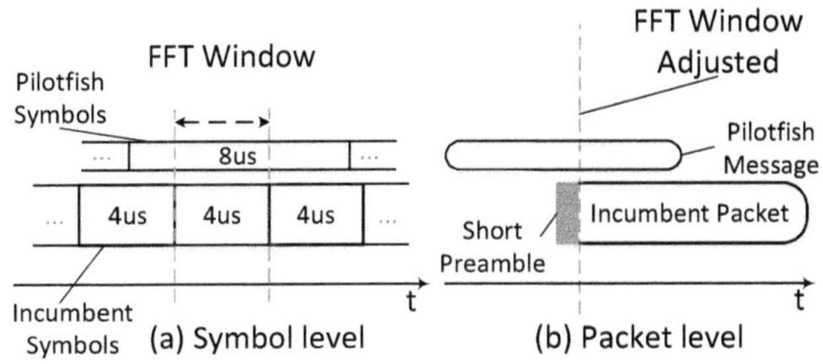

Figure 6: (a) Larger (2x) Pilotfish symbol size enables truely independent transmissions. (b) FFT window is adjusted upon a new short preamble.

The idea of the Nulled Decoding technique is to leverage the fact that some elements of the frequency-domain symbol X are left as zero for the purpose of constructing the guardbands. Therefore, at the receiving side, if we pick the FFT outputs (*i.e.* take samples) corresponding to these elements, the received OFDM symbol will be entirely nulled.

3.3 Independent Pilotfish Transmissions

As mentioned above, the Nulled Decoding technique requires Pilotfish receiver to perform FFT within the same FFT windows of an OFDM symbol in incumbent transmissions. Otherwise, the orthogonality property will be lost and interference will increase. However, if Pilotfish transmission is independent to incumbent transmission, their symbol boundaries will not be aligned.

Instead of explicitly aligning Pilotfish symbols to incumbent symbols, we prefer truely independent transmissions. Therefore, in our design we set Pilotfish's symbol size to be twice of the incumbent symbol, as shown in Figure 6(a). In this way, we ensure that we can always find a good FFT window from every two incumbent symbols that is perfect for both nulling and sampling. Considering Wi-Fi that an OFDM symbol is $4\mu s$, the symbol size of Pilotfish will be 8 μs accordingly. We further notice that twice the symbol size also means half the Pilotfish subchannel width of incumbent subcarrier, as mentioned above.

Considering asynchronous incumbent transmissions such as Wi-Fi, the FFT window should be adjusted for every incumbent packet, because successive packets are unaligned in symbol boundaries. In our design, this FFT window adjustment is performed right after the symbol boundary determination from a newly received short preamble (*i.e.* Short Training Sequence or STS), as shown in Figure 6(b).

Summary. We have described the techniques we used in Pilotfish to enable independent communication in guardband whitespace without introducing additional interference to incumbents. The Pilotfish PHY is based on FBMC which comprises a group of subchannels, each of which is aligned to a nulling point in guardband. We employ a digital Chebyshev filter to suppress the out-of-band energy emissions to be as low as $-86dB$. The Pilotfish receiver uses Nulled Decoding to null out the interference from incumbents and therefore obtains a reasonably high SINR to support communication. We estimate the overall capacity of the Pilotfish design for Wi-Fi guardbands as follows. As mentioned earlier, the SINR in a Pilotfish subchannel is capped at 12 dB due to ISI. This is enough to support 16QAM 1/2 coded frames. Taken the symbol rate 125 KHz, the overall capacity of one subchannel is

$$C_{sc} = 125K * 4bit/2 = 250Kbps.$$

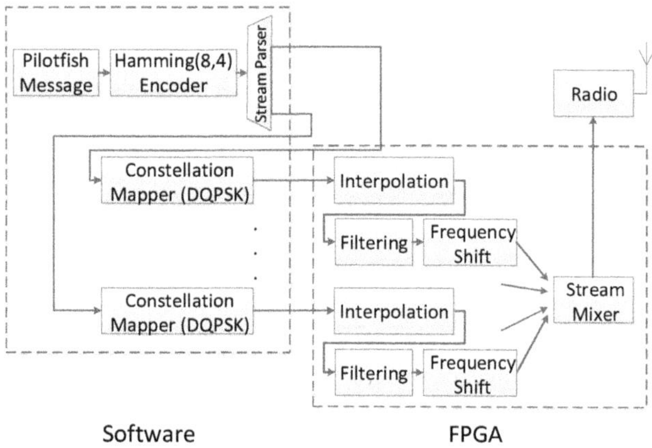

Figure 7: Pilotfish transmitter. It contains multiple streams for multiple subchannels. Multiple instances of the filter are implemented in FPGA to accelerate the computation.

So, in case of Wi-Fi HT mode with 20MHz, we can have up to 5 such subchannels. Therefore, the aggregate capacity of Pilotfish is 1.22M bps. In general, this gives a meaningful capacity that is comparable to existing narrow band systems (Zigbee, *etc.*).

3.4 Discussion

We now briefly touch upon some practical issues in the design.

Mobility. Device mobility brings Doppler effect and additional frequency offset, thereby introducing an additional challenge. According to our experience, device mobility associated with human movement can be easily handled by modern OFDM based wireless systems. This level of mobility also does not add problem to Pilotfish as Pilotfish shares the same principle with OFDM systems.

Requirements on the Pilotfish receiver. The Pilotfish receiver should be able to entirely receive incumbent's signal, estimate and compensate frequency offset, and calculate DFT outputs on the nulling points. Since these requirements are already fulfilled by the incumbent receiver, we can leverage the incumbent receiver to simplify the implementation of Pilotfish (such as our implementation) if the device is designed to have both functions. However, the Pilotfish receiver also can be implemented independently.

Varying channel width and overlapping channels. In some cases, the guardband may be overlapped with some other incumbent systems. For example, in 5GHz band, the Wi-Fi channel-width is varying, in 2.4GHz band, not only the channel width is varying, but also the channels are overlapping. In these cases, the Pilotfish transmitter relies on carrier-sensing to avoid conflicting with incumbents.

4. IMPLEMENTATION

As transmitting in LTE's bands requires license, we built the Pilotfish prototype only for Wi-Fi which uses unlicensed bands. We implemented the prototype using Sora [19] software radio system. The incumbent Wi-Fi was the SoftWiFi implementation on Sora which has been proven compatible with commodity Wi-Fi card.

4.1 Pilotfish Transmitter

For the sake of simplicity, we chose Hamming(8,4) code with 1/2 coding rate, DQPSK, and four Pilotfish subchannels that every two are on a side of a Wi-Fi channel. Therefore, each byte of Pilotfish message is encoded into two symbols carried in four parallel streams (subchannels). As a result, the data rate is 500kbps.

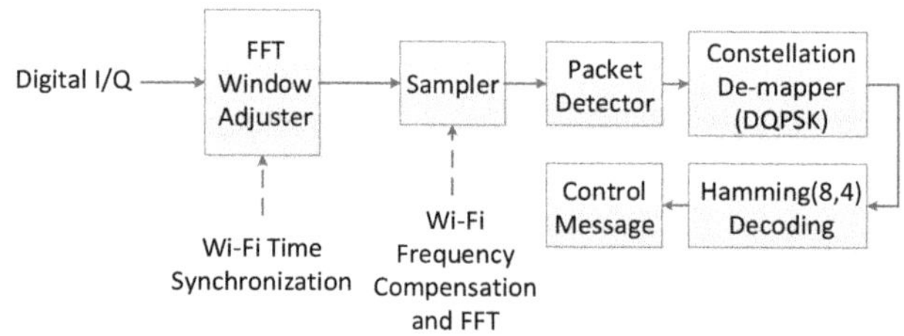

Figure 8: Pilotfish control decoder. It takes advantage of time synchronization, frequency compensation and FFT calculation of Wi-Fi decoder.

Figure 7 presents the modules of Pilotfish transmitter. As shown in the figure, a Pilotfish message is first encoded by Hamming(8,4) encoder. Then coded bits are divided into four streams by stream parser. Each bit stream is mapped to constellation points (I/Q) independently by DQPSK modulator. After that, each modulated I/Q stream is interpolated from 125KSPS to 40MSPS to match sampling rate of DAC. Digital IIR filtering is performed on 40MSPS samples for every stream, after which filtered streams are shifted to corresponding nulling points. Finally, four signal streams are mixed together to generate the final waveform.

The digital IIR filter is computationally intensive for software radio. Comparing to the 37-tap FIR shaping filter implemented in SoftWiFi 802.11b [19], Pilotfish's four steams need four filter instances which summing up requires approximately 3x computation as 802.11b's filter. In order to accelarate the computation, we implement the filters in the FPGA of Sora radio adapter board (RAB). To avoid crossing software/FPGA interface multiple times, we also implement interpolater, freuqency shifter and stream mixer in FPGA. Other modules, *e.g.* Hamming encoder, stream parser and constellation mapper, are implemented in software using Sora UMX API [3].

4.2 Pilotfish Receiver

Figure 8 presents the modules of Pilotfish receiver. For the sake of simplicity, we continuously perform FFT and take Pilotfish samples on received digital I/Q, no matter there is any Pilotfish transmission or incumbent transmission. Then, packet detection, constellation de-mapping and Hamming decoding are performed based on these samples output from FFT. We notice that this implementation is not optimal in terms of power efficiency. To improve, we could use a Zigbee-like narrow band receiver while there is no incumbent transmission. We leave this optimization for our future work. As discussed in §3.3, the FFT window should be adjusted upon a new incumbent packet. The window adjuster is triggered by SoftWiFi's time synchronization module. To save computation, we reuse the FFT calculation in Wi-Fi decoder to take Pilotfish samples. Moreover, SoftWiFi performs frequency compensation to mitigate frequency offset between Wi-Fi transmitter and Wi-Fi receiver. We also reuse this frequency compensation for Pilotfish receiver. Finally, we notice that all modules of Pilotfish receiver are implemented in software.

5. EVALUATION

In this section, we present the empirical evaluation for the Pilotfish design. We set up a small test-bed to conduct the experiments. The basic setting consists of three nodes, *i.e.* one 20MHz-wide Wi-Fi transmitter, one Pilotfish transmitter and one receiver which is capable for both Wi-Fi decoding and Pilotfish decoding. The Pilotfish transmitter and Wi-Fi transmitter always transmit simultaneously. We adjust the power received at the receiver to assess

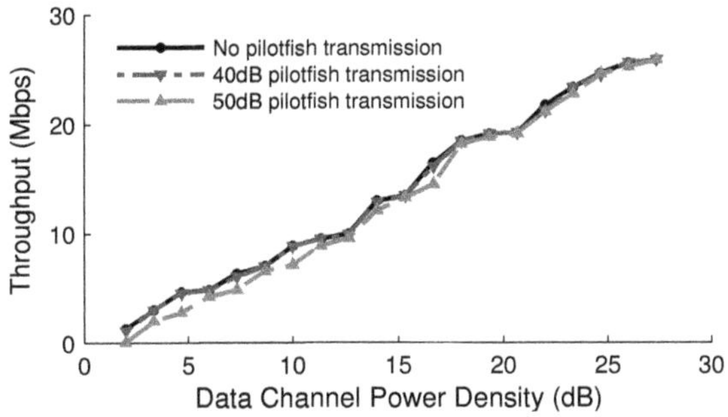

Figure 9: The Pilotfish filter suppresses its out-of-band emission very well. As a result, the strong Pilotfish transmissions with 50dB power density generate neglectable interference to incumbent Wi-Fi transmissions.

various building blocks in Pilotfish. In general, we always evaluate the most challenging stituations. For example, we evaluate the Pilotfish filter while the transmitting power of Pilotfish is high and the power of Wi-Fi is low. Also, we evaluate Nulled Decoding while Wi-Fi power is high and Pilotfish power is low. For Pilotfish, we also evaluate the affect of clock phase noise, frequency offset, multipath channel and adjacent channel interference. In order to create the adjacent channel interference, we add a fourth node transmitting in adjacent Wi-Fi channel.

In order to fairly compare the power in Wi-Fi channel and Pilotfish channel, we should use power density (*i.e.* dBm/Hz) instead of power (*i.e.* dBm) because the channel widths are largely different. For the sake of simplicity, we use relative power density over noise instead of absolute power density. Specifically, we assume the power density of noise is identical in Wi-Fi channel and guardband. Then, we use *signal to noise ratio* (SNR) to indicate relative power density. For example, we indicate the power density of a signal as 50dB if power density of the signal is 50dB higher than noise in its occupied band. We notice that this SNR calculation is equivalent to the SNR calculated using absolute power as long as the signal is flat, which is the case in both Wi-Fi channel and Pilotfish channel.

5.1 Out-of-band Emission Suppressing

The purpose of the Pilotfish filter is to suppress out-of-band emission so that Pilotfish transmission does not generate interference to incumbent transmissions. To assess the performance in challenging cases, we set up a strong Pilotfish transmitter to check whether it interferes with Wi-Fi transmissions. To make the experiment repeatable, we use cables and power combiner to connect three nodes, then manually add attenuator or tune transmission power to adjust received power.

We tried two high values of transmitting power for Pilotfish, *i.e.* 40dB and 50dB, which means, if the 50dB Pilotfish transmissions do not interfere with Wi-Fi transmissions, the effective stop-band rejection is at least -50dB. In order to check whether Wi-Fi transmissions are interfered, we first disable Pilotfish transmitter and measure Wi-Fi throughput under different Wi-Fi channel power density (*i.e.* SNR) using broadcast packets. We also disable rate adaptation and manually find the best rate. Then, we enable Pilotfish transmitter by broadcasting back-to-back messages, and measure Wi-Fi throughput again.

In Figure 9, we plot two throughput curves together for side-by-side comparision. As shown, the 40dB Pilotfish transmissions lead to exactly the same throughput curve as Pilotfish transmissions are disabled, means no interference is introduced. The 50dB Pilotfish transmission generate slightly degraded throughput curve, means slight interference is introduced. We further check the power spectrum density of transmitted Pilotfish signal and find that the interference is not caused by out-of-band emission but induced by nolinear effect of the radio, where harmonic components of Pilotfish signal appears in the Wi-Fi frequencies. Similar obseravtion has been discussed in [7].

We notice that in real networks a 40dB power density is already extreme which means Pilotfish transmitter is very close to the Wi-Fi receiver. Therefore, we conclude that the Pilotfish filter has effectively suppressed its out-of-band emission.

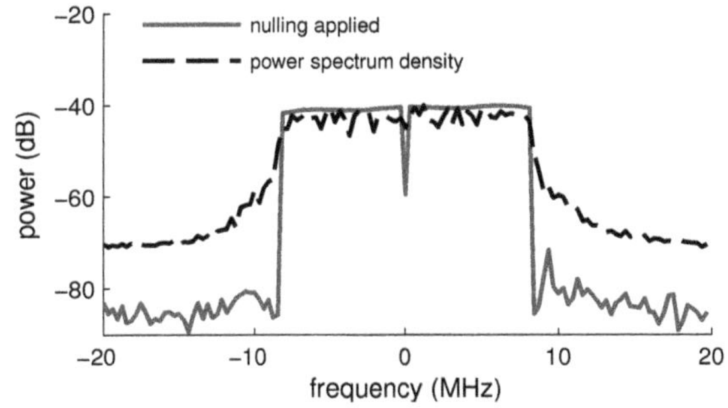

Figure 10: Nulling illustration. Two curves reflect the received signal w/ and w/o nulling. The nulling technique nulls out the emitted signal from incumbent transmissions, thereby enabling the decoding of a weak Pilotfish transmission with extremely low (-20dB) SINR (the litte spike on the right side).

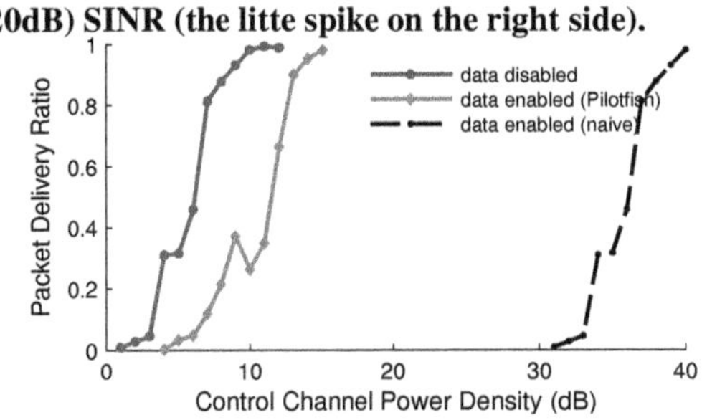

Figure 11: Pilotfish effectively nulls out 25dB of a 30dB emitted signal, remains only 5dB residual interference. This experiment uses three Sora nodes.

5.2 Nulled Decoding

We first use Figure 10 to qualitatively illustrate how the nulling technique works. For the sake of clear demonstration, we only transmit Pilotfish signal in one subchannel. The power spectrum density of received signal shows that incumbent transmissions spill out a lot of energy to guardband. In this example, since the received Pilotfish signal is relatively weak, *i.e.* the SINR in guardband control channel is as low as -20dB, the Pilotfish signal is inundated in the emitted signal from incumbent transmissions, therefore is not detectable. When we apply Nulled Decoding by taking Pilotfish samples from the FFT output calculated on FFT windows, the emitted signal is nulled out as shown in the figure. As a result, the SINR in guardband increases dramatically.

In following of this subsections, we quantitatively evaluate the effectiveness of Nulled Decoding. In our experiments, we consider frequency offset, clock phase noise and multipath channel as the factors that potentially affect the effectiveness of Nulled Decoding. We also evaluate the robustness of Pilotfish decoding when interference from adjacent incumbent channel exists.

5.2.1 Basic Case

As a basic use case, we set up three nodes, including one Wi-Fi transmitter, one Pilotfish transmitter and one receiver capable of receiving both transmissions. We focus our evaluation on the most challenging case that the Wi-Fi transmissions are very strong.

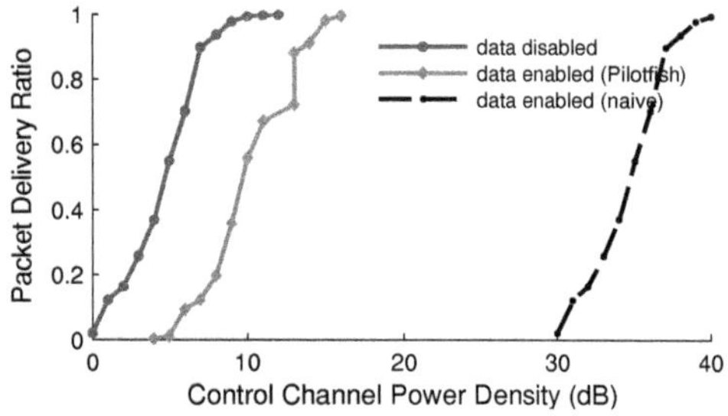

Figure 12: Eliminating frequency offset does not remove residual interference, therefore frequency offset is not the cause. This experiment uses one Sora MIMO node.

Specifically, we fix the power density of Wi-Fi signal to 50dB. This strong signal generates 30dB interference in guardband. We manually add/remove attenuators to set different power density in Pilotfish channel and measure packet delivery ratio (PDR) of Pilotfish messages in various settings. To make the experiment controllable and repeatable, we use cables and power combiner to connect three radios. In subsection 5.2.4, we will present results using antennas.

We broadcast 24-bit messages in Pilotfish channel. We compare the PDR while Wi-Fi transmissions are disabled and enabled. When Wi-Fi transmissions are enabled, we broadcast 1500-byte back-to-back packets. The result is shown in Figure 11. We can see that when Wi-Fi transmissions are enabled, the PDR curve is shifted by roughly 5dB. Comparing to a naive method which treats interference as noise therefore should shift the curve by 30dB, Pilotfish equivalently nulls out 25dB interference.

Therefore, we conclude that Nulled Decoding is effective on real radio devices. However, the nulling is not perfect in the experiment that roughly 5dB residual interference still remains. In order to figure out the cause, in following subsections, we further study several potential factors.

5.2.2 *Frequency Offset*

The first factor to study is frequency offset. Every Sora device equips a cheap 20MHz *temperature compensated crystal oscillator* (TCXO) as reference clock for both carrier frequency and sampling clock. The TCXO has frequency accuracy of 10^{-6}, which causes roughly 10kHz carrier frequency offset and 100Hz sampling frequency offset between devices. We take a exclusion method for the study. Specifically, we use a Sora MIMO device to replace the three Sora devices mentioned above, by which we can emulate three devices using three radios of the Sora MIMO device. In this way, we eliminate the frequency offset between nodes because the radios share a common TCXO.

We repeat the above experiment. Result is shown in Figure 12. The result is very similar to Figure 11. Therefore, we conclude that frequency offset is not the cause of residual interference. This result is not out of expectation, because Wi-Fi decoder already contains a frequency offset compensation module. Specifically, the frequency offset is estimated from long training sequency of preamble. We find the estimation result provided by SoftWiFi is quite accurate that error is always with 1kHz. Moreover, sampling frequency offset also does not cause degradation as long as symbol boundary is correctly determined.

5.2.3 *Clock Phase Noise*

The next factor to study is clock phase noise which introduces noise to the signal. We still take the exclusion method. Specifically, we replace the TCXO on the Sora MIMO device with a much more accurate *oven controlled crystal oscillator* (OCXO). The OCXO has frequency accuracy of 10^{-9} and number of magnitudes lower

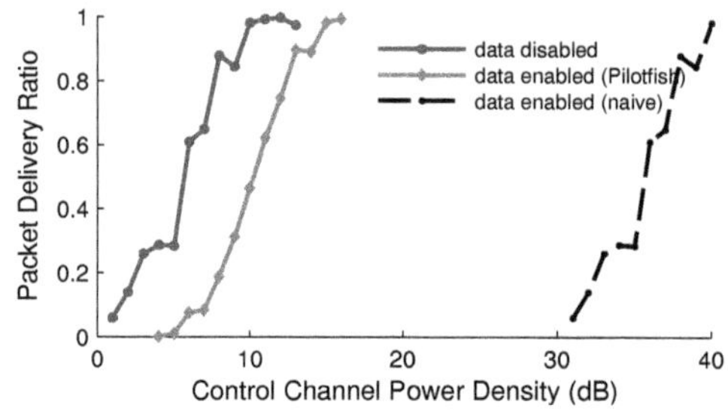

Figure 13: Replacing TCXO with OCXO does not remove residual interference, therefore clock phase noise is not the cause.

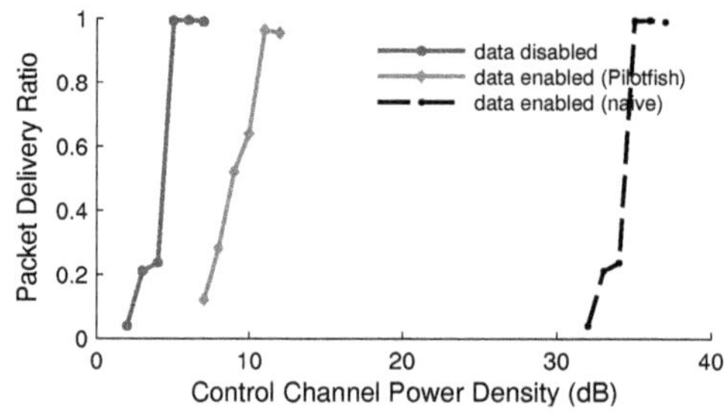

Figure 14: Multipath channel does not degrade the effectiveness of Nulled Decoding. In this experiment we use antennas instead of RF cables.

phase noise. We repeat the experiment again. Result is presented in Figure 13. The result is also very similar to Figure 11. Therefore, we conclude that clock phase noise is not the cause of residual interference.

Our hypothesis is that the residual interference is caused by imperfection of the RF front end. The imperfection usually contains non-linear effect that linear signal processing technique like Pilotfish is not able to handle. Solving this problem requires non-linear signal processing technique [7] or better engineered RF font end. We leave handling residual interference as our future work.

5.2.4 *Multipath Channel*

Since our experiments above are conducted using cables, a remaining concern is whether multipath wireless channel degrades the effectiveness of Nulled Decoding. To study this issue, we conduct a simple experiment by replacing cables with antennas. In order to set up a 50dB high receiving power in Wi-Fi channel, we place the antenna of Wi-Fi transmitter close to the antenna of receiver. The result is shown in Figure 14. We can see the result is similar to above. This is not out of expectation because in general OFDM handles multipath very well because of the design of cyclic prefix. Therefore, we conclude multipath channel does not degrade Nulled Decoding.

5.2.5 *Robustness under Cross-Channel Interference*

As discussed in §3.2, Pilotfish does not null out the interference from adjacent incumbent, therefore we carefully design Pilotfish's physical layer to ensure its robustness.

We conduct experiment to evaluate the robustness. Besides three Pilotfish nodes used above, we add another node to transmit in adjacent Wi-Fi channel by broadcasting 1500-byte back-to-back packets. The received power density measured in the adjacent Wi-Fi channel is 40dB. The interference in guardband and the data channel is 10$\sim$20dB. We compare the robustness of Pilotfish transmissions to Wi-Fi transmissions in incumbent channel. For the sake of fair comparison, we present the result using bit error rate (BER) instead of PDR. We also assume the Wi-Fi transmissions in incumbent channel use the lowest data rate, which is therefore the most

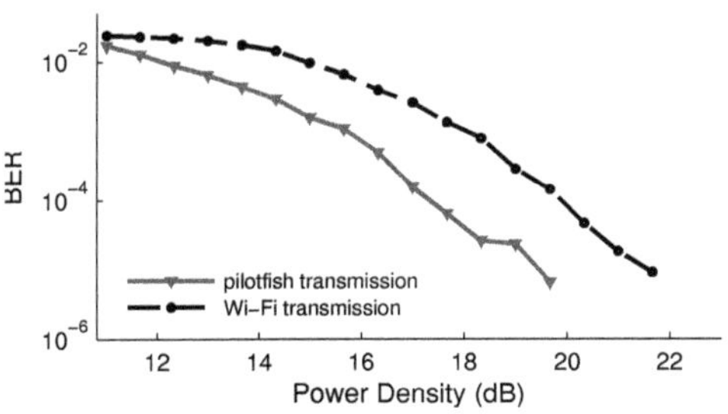

Figure 15: Pilotfish transmissions in guardband control channel are slightly more robust than Wi-Fi transmissions when cross-channel interference exists.

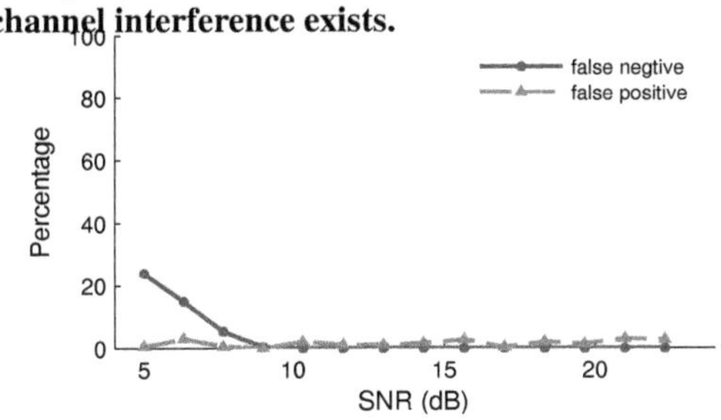

Figure 16: CCA performance of Pilotfish MAC.

robust. Figure 15 shows the result. We can see the transmission in Pilotfish channel is slightly (2dB) more robust. The gain mainly comes from placing control subchannels to both sides of a incumbent channel.

Therefore, we conclude that Pilotfish transmissions in guardband are more robust than Wi-Fi transmissions in incumbent channel when cross-channel interference exists.

5.3 Pilotfish MAC

Clear Channel Assessment (CCA) is the basis of CSMA based protocol. To verify the feasibility of Pilotfish MAC, we conduct experiments to evaluate the CCA performance. We still use cables to set up controlled environment as above. We measured both false negtive and false positive rate with various SNR values. Figure 16 shows that the false rates are very low with $10dB$ or higher SNR. Only when the SNR approachs to marginal value, *e.g.* $5dB$, the false negtive rate increases a little to 20%. Thus, we conclude that the CCA for Pilotfish MAC is robust.

5.4 Minor Issues

We also verified some minor issues using experiments, for example, device mobility and higher modulation density of incumbents.

Our test-bed has a limitation that it is not easy to move the whole Sora system around. Therefore, we connected the antennas and the radios using 2-meter long cables. The experiments were conducted by moving the antennas. We repeated the experiments in above subsections. Since we only moved the antenna in limited space, we only obtained results for a subset of the SNR values. The results were similar to above subsections therefore we do not include them in the paper. This experiments validated that the mobility associated with human movement does not cause problem to Pilotfish.

Finally, we also tried high-density modulation, *i.e.* 16-QAM, for the Wi-Fi transmitters. The high-density modulation lead to a nonflat spectrum of the incumbent signal. However, we validated that it does not make any difference to Pilotfish.

6. Pilotfish APPLICATIONS

In this section, we briefly discuss two applications that Pilotfish can enable to demonstrate the value of Pilotfish.

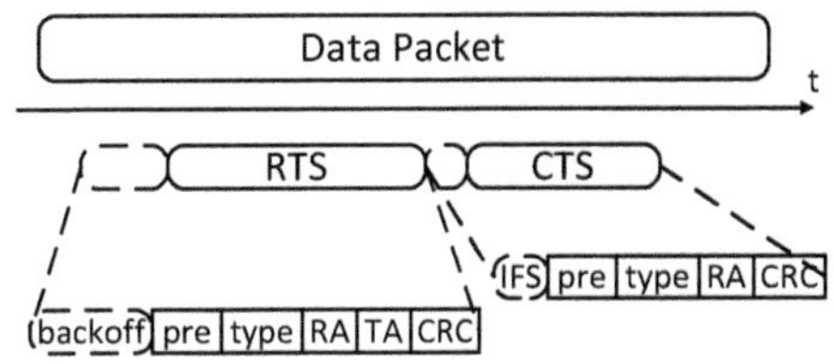

Figure 17: Illustration of control channel RTS/CTS.

6.1 Decoupled Control Channel

The first application is to convey Wi-Fi control messages using Pilotfish. In this subsection, we use a simple example to demonstrate the benefits of a decoupled control channel enabled by Pilotfish. As already discussed in [10], in enterprise Wi-Fi networks where downlink scheduling is possible, a decoupled control channel can add important functionality to uplink thereby enabling a lot of interesting applications, such as spectrum efficiency improvement, power efficiency improvement, quality of service, seamless roaming, *etc.*.

In this section, we discuss a simple augment to Wi-Fi's distributed control function (DCF), which is enabled by Pilotfish. The idea is to move RTS/CTS exchange from data channel to control channel, as shown in Figure 17. We call this protocol as control channel RTS/CTS (CCRC). The benefits of CCRC are in multi-folds. First, a successful exchange of RTS/CTS reserves a transmission opportunity. The winning sender can transmit its packet immediately after current data packet, without waiting for the backoff slots. Therefore, the overhead of backoff can be largely saved. Second, benefit from the capability of making reservation, many packet transmissions do not need to rely on random backoff, collisions caused by choosing the same backoff time can be largely reduced. Third, the broadcasting RTS/CTS can mitigate hidden terminal. This feature is usually disabled due to large overhead of RTS/CTS performed in data channel. Fourth, CCRC is backwards compatible with Wi-Fi. We remain the existing control schemes of Wi-Fi in CCRC, therefore CCRC capable devices seamlessly work with legacy Wi-Fi devices, though CCRC capable devices may take advantage of the reservation to get more transmission opportunities.

Simulation Results.

In order to study the benefit of CCRC in larger scale, we conduct NS-3 based simulation. The simulated network includes multiple APs and a varying number of clients that are randomly and uniformly distribted on a 100×100 grid. We simulate a congested network that every node is trying to schedule a large amount of traffic.

Figure 18 shows the throughput gain of CCRC. When RTS/CTS is disabled, CSMA/CA suffers from collisions due to hidden terminals. When RTS/CTS is enabled in data channel, it causes much overhead. CCRC enables RTS/CTS without overhead, therefore consistently outperform both schemes. As the number of nodes increases, CCRC achieves more throughput gain because it mitigates more hidden terminals as well as reduces more contention overhead. As a result, CCRC's throughput gain is up to $3.3\times$ over CSMA/CA and $3.7\times$ over RTS/CTS.

6.2 Interference-Free Zigbee

The other application is using Pilotfish to realize an interference-free Zigbee system in 2.4GHz unlicensed band. As mainly working in the shared unlicensed band, Zigbee suffers a lot from Wi-Fi interference. With the help of Pilotfish's Nulled Decoding technique, we will be able to develop a new Zigbee system that nulls Wi-Fi interference.

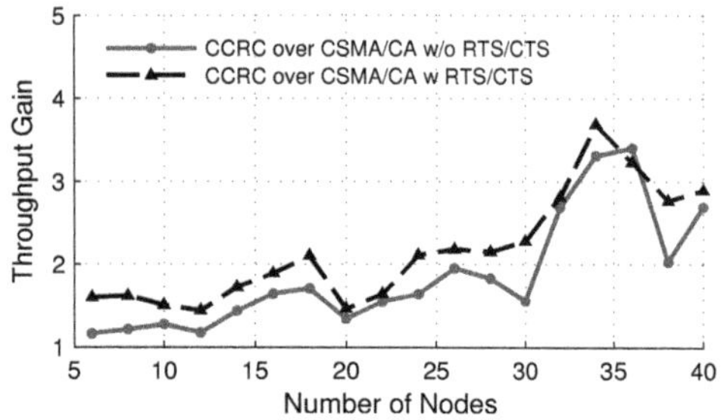

Figure 18: Simulation study. The throughput gain of CCRC over CSMA/CA with and without RTS/CTS.

7. RELATED WORK

The guardband and adjacent channel interference has been extensively studied by Yang, *et. al.* [22] where the observation is that the current fixed guardband does not entirely solve the adjacent channel interference problem. Therefore a variable size guardband is proposed. Chintalapudi, *et. al.* [9] proposes to apply sharp filter on data channel and largely reduces guardband size. The filtered data channel is totally different from the current OFDM PHY in Wi-Fi, therefore is not a target for our work.

Explicit control channels have been proposed in literatures [10, 14,21,23]. Kyasanur, *et. al.* [14] proposes the similar idea as CCRC by allocating a control channel in a distant frequency of $900MHz$ ISM band. Although significant improvement has been shown as the same as CCRC, it is difficult to deploy in practice since the freqency is not specified in Wi-Fi. Zhang, *et. al.* [23], exploits a feedback control to send symbol-level acknowledgement to improve the error recovery performance on lossy wireless links, it also faces the problem of finding an additional frequency band for the control channel. In-band control channels [10, 21] does not require additional spectrum, but they introduce interference to the data channel which eventually causes packet loss.

8. CONCLUSION

In this paper, we present the Pilotfish system which realizes independent communication in guardband whitespace. Empirical results based on a prototype validated the design and techniques. Since Pilotfish turns the wasted guardband frequencies into new commmunication channels, we believe it will bring great value given spectrum resource is so scarce and expensive today.

Acknowledgement

We would like to thank our shepherd, Prof. Vijay Subramanian for his help with the final version. We also thank the W&N group members of MSRA and the anonymous reviewers for their insightful and constructive comments.

9. REFERENCES

[1] Estimated potential auction compensation. *http://wireless.fcc.gov/incentiveauctions/learn-program/docs/compensation-charts.pdf.*

[2] Presidential memorandum: Unleashing the wireless broadband revolution. *http://www.whitehouse.gov/the-press-office/presidential-memorandum-unleashing-wireless-broadband-revolution.*

[3] The sora manual version 1.5. *http://research.microsoft.com/apps/pubs/?id=144847.*

[4] White space (radio). *http://en.wikipedia.org/wiki/White spaces (radio).*

[5] *ANSI/IEEE Std 802.11-2012, Part 11: Wireless LAN Medium Access Control (MAC) and Physical Layer (PHY) Specification.* IEEE Press, 2012.

[6] A. Antoniou. *Digital Signal Processing: Signals, Systems and Filters.* McGraw-Hill, 2006.

[7] D. Bharadia, E. McMilin, and S. Katti. Full duplex radios. In *Proceedings of the ACM SIGCOMM 2013 conference on SIGCOMM*, pages 375–386. ACM, 2013.

[8] W. Chen, G. Cui, J. Duan, W. Wang, and Y. Zhang. Research on utilizing guard band in lte uplink co-existence based on uncoordinated deployment scenario. In *ICCTA '11*, Oct 2011.

[9] K. Chintalapudi, B. Radunovic, V. Balan, M. Buettener, S. Yerramalli, V. Navda, and R. Ramjee. Wifi-nc: Wifi over narrow channels. In *NSDI'12*, Berkeley, CA, USA, 2012. USENIX Association.

[10] A. Cidon, K. Nagaraj, S. Katti, and P. Viswanath. Flashback: decoupled lightweight wireless control. In *SIGCOMM '12*, New York, NY, USA, 2012. ACM.

[11] S. Darlington. Filters with chebyshev stopbands, flat passbands, and impulse responses of finite duration. *Circuits and Systems, IEEE Transactions on*, 25(12):966 – 975, dec 1978.

[12] S. Deb, V. Srinivasan, and R. Maheshwari. Dynamic spectrum access in dtv whitespaces: Design rules, architecture and algorithms. In *MobiCom '09*, New York, NY, USA, 2009. ACM.

[13] B. Farhang-Boroujeny. Ofdm versus filter bank multicarrier. *Signal Processing Magazine, IEEE*, 28(3):92–112, 2011.

[14] P. Kyasanur, J. Padhye, and P. Bahl. On the efficacy of separating control and data into different frequency bands. In *Broadband Networks, 2005*, oct. 2005.

[15] R. v. Nee and R. Prasad. *OFDM for Wireless Multimedia Communications.* Artech House, Inc., Norwood, MA, USA, 1st edition, 2000.

[16] T. S. Rappaport et al. *Wireless communications: principles and practice*, volume 2. prentice hall PTR New Jersey, 1996.

[17] S. Sen, R. Choudhury, and S. Nelakuditi. Csma/cn: Carrier sense multiple access with collision notification. *Networking, IEEE/ACM Transactions on*, 20(2):544–556, April.

[18] K. Tan, J. Fang, Y. Zhang, S. Chen, L. Shi, J. Zhang, and Y. Zhang. Fine-grained channel access in wireless lan. In *SIGCOMM '10*, New York, NY, USA, 2010. ACM.

[19] K. Tan, J. Zhang, J. Fang, H. Liu, Y. Ye, S. Wang, Y. Zhang, H. Wu, W. Wang, and G. M. Voelker. Sora: High performance software radio using general purpose multi-core processors. In *NSDI '09*.

[20] G. T. . V7.1.0. *Physical layer aspect for evolved Universal Terrestrial Radio Access (UTRA).* T-ech. Spec.n Group RAN Rel.7, 2006.

[21] K. Wu, H. Tan, Y. Liu, J. Zhang, Q. Zhang, and L. Ni. Side channel: bits over interference. In *MobiCom '10*, New York, NY, USA, 2010. ACM.

[22] L. Yang, B. Y. Zhao, and H. Zheng. The spaces between us: setting and maintaining boundaries in wireless spectrum access. In *MobiCom '10*, New York, NY, USA, 2010. ACM.

[23] J. Zhang, H. Shen, K. Tan, R. Chandra, Y. Zhang, and Q. Zhang. Frame retransmissions considered harmful: improving spectrum efficiency using micro-acks. In *Mobicom '12*, New York, NY, USA, 2012. ACM.

Asynchronous Neighbor Discovery on Duty-cycled Mobile Devices: Integer and Non-Integer Schedules

Sixia Chen
Central Connecticut State University
schen@ccsu.edu

Alexander Russell
University of Connecticut
acr@cse.uconn.edu

Ruofan Jin
University of Connecticut
ruofan@uconn.edu

Yanyuan Qin
University of Connecticut
yanyuan.qin@uconn.edu

Bing Wang
University of Connecticut
bing@engr.uconn.edu

Sudarshan Vasudevan
Palo Alto Networks
svasudevan@paloaltonetworks.com

ABSTRACT

Neighbor discovery is a fundamental problem in wireless networks. In this paper, we study asynchronous neighbor discovery between duty-cycled mobile devices. Each node is duty-cycled, i.e., its radio may only be active for a small fraction of the time. The duty cycles of the nodes can be the same or different, leading to symmetric or asymmetric cases of the neighbor discovery problem. In addition, the setting is asynchronous, i.e., clocks of different nodes may not be synchronized. Most existing studies assume an integer model (where time proceeds in discrete steps); two recent studies break away from this assumption, which allows them to develop significantly more efficient schemes. Our study improves the state-of-the-art in three main fronts. Firstly, we develop a generalized non-integer model (where time is continuous) that permits unified treatment of the assumptions in existing studies. We also provide a reduction that transforms any schedule in the basic integer model to a corresponding schedule in the generalized non-integer model while improving the performance by a factor of two. Applying this reduction, an optimal schedule in the integer model becomes an optimal schedule in the non-integer model. Thirdly, we establish a new family of lower bounds for the best achievable latency guarantee in the non-integer model. They are applicable to both symmetric and asymmetric settings, and encompass the lower bounds for the integer model as special cases. Finally, we develop a novel optimal construction based on Sidon sets for the symmetric setting. Our approach differs from the approaches taken by all existing studies, and provides a new direction for constructing neighbor discovery schedules.

Categories and Subject Descriptors

C.2.1 [**Computer-Communication Networks**]: Network Architecture and Design—*Wireless Communication*; F.2.2 [**Analysis of Algorithms and Problem Complexity**]: Nonnumerical Algorithms and Performance

MobiHoc'15, June 22–25, 2015, Hangzhou, China.

http://dx.doi.org/10.1145/2746285.2746297.

General Terms

Algorithm, Design, Performance, Theory

Keywords

Neighbor discovery, deterministic algorithms, Sidon set, difference set

1. INTRODUCTION

Neighbor discovery is a fundamental problem in wireless networks. Specifically, the proliferation of mobile devices, e.g., smartphones, PDAs, and sensors, has fueled many novel applications that utilize opportunistic localized device-to-device communication, including mobile social networking [14, 22, 18, 19], proximity-based services [1, 26], media sharing [16], traffic uploading [6], asset management [20], emergency rescue [8], tracking encountering pattern of migrating animals [13], and many more. These applications require mobile devices to rendezvous as they move into each other's transmission range. On the other hand, limited battery sources often mandate these devices to be duty-cycled, making them unable to discover other nodes while being asleep. In addition, in practice, nodes typically have no means of coordination (e.g., through a shared server or dedicated control channel), their clocks may not be synchronized, and they cannot act depending on individual "identities" (since the identities are not known before rendezvous).

We broadly refer to the above problem as *asynchronous* neighbor discovery on *duty-cycled* mobile devices. The duty cycles of the nodes can be the same or different, resulting in *symmetric* or *asymmetric* neighbor discovery, respectively. In such settings, it is possible to construct simple and powerful randomized algorithms (e.g., [15]); however, these schemes do not provide a bound on worst-case discovery latency and—rather remarkably—deterministic schemes can achieve better performance, even when compared with the "average case" performance of randomized algorithms. In this paper, we focus on *deterministic* algorithms, where the schedules of the nodes are determined beforehand and the worst-case discovery latency is bounded.

Most existing studies [5, 9, 11, 24, 7] develop *integer* schedules where time proceeds in discrete slots of length Δ, and a node is either awake for an entire slot or asleep for an entire slot. Two recent studies [3, 17] break away from integer schedules by allowing "overflow" of active slots (i.e., an active slot is slightly lengthened to intersect the previous or subsequent slot), and demonstrate that the slight overflow can provide significant improvement.

In this paper, we improve the state-of-the-art on three main fronts: (i) we develop a generalized *non-integer* model that permits unified treatment of existing studies, and demonstrate that *any* integer schedule can be converted into a non-integer schedule while improving the performance by a factor of two, (ii) we derive a family of lower bounds in the generalized non-integer model, and (iii) we develop a novel optimal construction for the symmetric setting.

Our main contributions are as follows:

- We develop a generalized non-integer model motivated by the observation that the integer model needlessly constrains switching to occur on integer boundaries and, additionally, does not reflect an important constraint that arises in practice. In our proposed non-integer model, time is continuous: nodes may become active or inactive at any point in time, subject to a few constraints. In addition to switching latency Δ, we also introduce a *required meeting time* δ: to discover one another, two nodes must be simultaneously awake for a continuous interval of duration at least δ. This generalized non-integer model permits unified treatment of the assumptions in existing studies: the basic integer model used in most existing studies arises as when $\delta = \Delta/2$; the model of [3, 17] arises when $\delta \ll \Delta$.
- We provide a general reduction that can transform *any* schedule in the basic integer model to a corresponding schedule in the generalized non-integer model. The reduction reduces the duty cycles of the nodes by a factor of two while preserving the discovery latency. Applying this reduction, an optimal schedule in the integer model becomes an optimal schedule in the non-integer model.
- We derive a family of lower bounds on the best achievable latency guarantees in the non-integer model (they reduce to lower bounds for the integer model when $\delta = \Delta/2$). These are the first lower bounds that are characterized by both Δ and δ, and the first lower bounds that are applicable to both symmetric and asymmetric settings. The two existing lower bounds derived in [30] and [17] are only for the symmetric setting; they are special cases of our lower bounds by taking $\Delta = 1$, $\delta = \Delta/2$ ([30]) and $\delta \ll \Delta$ ([17]).
- We propose a novel optimal construction based on the theory of *Sidon sets* for the symmetric setting. All existing optimal schemes [30, 11, 17] are based on Singer difference sets. Our construction uses a different approach, and provides a new direction for constructing neighbor discovery schedules.

Our optimal scheme based on Sidon sets is directly applicable in practice (in fact, we have implemented it on smartphones). The non-integer schedules are particularly important for mobile devices with $\delta \ll \Delta$ (e.g., current smartphones where Δ is one or two seconds while δ is in milliseconds) since they require significantly lower duty cycle for the same discovery latency (or lead to much faster discovery under the same duty cycle) compared to integer schedules. Using our reduction, all integer schedules in the literature can be directly converted into their corresponding non-integer schedules.

The rest of the paper is organized as follows. Section 2 briefly describes related work. Section 3 introduces the non-integer model and proposes a general reduction to transform any schedule in the integer model to a schedule in the non-integer model. Section 4 presents a family of lower bounds for the non-integer model. Section 5 presents the Sidon sets construction. Finally, Section 6 concludes the paper and describes future work.

2. RELATED WORK

Neighbor discovery has been studied extensively in the literature (e.g., [15, 4, 10, 25]). In the following, we only briefly review the studies that are closest to ours, specifically, those that develop deterministic schedules for asynchronous neighbor discovery on duty-cycled mobile devices.

Most existing studies develop integer schedules. Zheng et al. [30] derive a lower bound for the symmetric setting, and show the existence of optimal schedules through *Singer* difference sets [21]. Lai et al. [11] expand the idea of cyclic quorum systems [24, 7], and propose a scheme, CQS-pair, that is also based on Singer difference sets. The construction for CQS-pair, however, takes exponential time, and hence is only practical for very large duty cycles. The general lower bound derived in our study encompasses the lower bound in [30] as a special case. We also provide a polynomial-time construction for Singer difference set based on the existence proof in [21]. In addition, we propose a novel optimal scheme based on Sidon sets for the symmetric setting; it is the first optimal scheme that does not rely on Singer difference sets.

Two other existing integer schedules are Disco [5] and U-connect [9]. In Disco, for duty cycle d, a node selects two different primes p_1, p_2 so that $1/p_1 + 1/p_2 \approx d$ and wakes up in the slots that are multiples of p_1 or p_2. Suppose node i has duty cycle d_i and chooses two primes, $p_{i1} < p_{i2}$, such that $1/p_{i1} + 1/p_{i2} \approx d_i$, $i = 1, 2$. Then by virtue of the Chinese Remainder Theorem, the two nodes can discover each other with the worst-case discovery latency of $p_{11}p_{21}$, which is on the order of $c/(d_1 d_2)$, c being a constant. In U-Connect, a node uses a single prime, p. It wakes up in the first $(p+1)/2$ slots as well as the slots that are multiples of p in every p^2 slots. For duty cycle d, the prime, p, is chosen so that $(3p+1)/(2p^2) \leq d$. Suppose node i has duty cycle d_i and chooses a prime p_i, $i = 1, 2$. Then the two nodes can discover each other with the worst-case latency of $1/(p_1 p_2) \approx 2.25/(d_1 d_2)$. Both Disco and U-Connect provide integer schedules that are applicable to both symmetric and asymmetric settings. We propose a general reduction that can convert these integer schedules to their corresponding non-integer schedules while reducing the worst-case discovery latency by a factor of two.

The first study that breaks away from integer schedules is [3]. Specifically, Bakht et al. design a simple probing based approach, Searchlight, by leveraging the constant offset between periodic awake slots. The authors propose both integer and non-integer variants of Searchlight, and show that the non-integer variant significantly outperforms the integer variant. In our study, we propose a generalized non-integer model that encompasses the assumptions in [3] and provide a reduction that transforms any integer schedule to a corresponding non-integer schedule. This reduction can transform the integer variant of Searchlight to a non-integer version, and achieves the same performance as the non-integer variant of Searchlight (see Section 3.4).

A recent study [17] adopts the same non-integer assumption in [3]. The authors derive a new lower bound for the symmetric setting as well as an optimal scheme, Diff-Codes, that is based on Singer difference sets (they also provide a greedy heuristic technique to deal with the cases when prime numbers are sparse, which leads to sub-optimal schedules for those cases). The general lower bound that we derive is applicable to both symmetric and asymmetric settings, encompassing the lower in bound [17] as a special case. In addition, applying our reduction to an optimal integer schedule based on Singer difference sets leads to a family of optimal non-integer schedules for the symmetric setting; Diff-Codes (the optimal schedules that are based on Singer difference sets) is a special instance. In addition, we also develop a novel optimal scheme based on Sidon sets; the first optimal scheme that does not use Singer difference sets.

As other related work, the studies in [28, 27] propose schemes that are based upon an existing asynchronous neighbor discovery scheme to further reduce energy consumption. Two recent studies [29, 12] propose neighbor discovery schemes on mobile duty-cycled devices. Both of them however require clock synchronization, and hence are not applicable to asynchronous settings.

3. INTEGER AND NON-INTEGER MODELS

In this section, we briefly describe the integer model that is adopted by most existing studies. We then present an intersection property that holds for any valid schedule in the integer model and use it to motivate the definition of the *generalized non-integer model.* We then establish a general reduction that transforms any schedule in the integer model to a corresponding schedule in the non-integer model; the reduction *reduces duty cycle by a factor of two while preserving the discovery latency.*

3.1 Integer Model

In this model, time is discretized into slots of width Δ, a hardware-dependent parameter that we refer to as the *switching interval.* Specifically, Δ is the time required by nodes to change their states (from asleep to awake and vice versa). On certain mobile devices, Δ may be on the order of milliseconds [5, 9] or even a fraction of a millisecond [20], while it can be over a second for other mobile devices (e.g., Δ is one or two seconds on current smartphones due to limitation of the hardware [3]).

A schedule may then be described by calling for a node to be *awake* during some of these slots and *asleep* during the others. Indexing the slots with the natural numbers $0, 1, 2, \ldots$, a schedule is simply determined by a subset S of $\mathbb{N}$; such a schedule we call an *integer schedule.* We shall typically constrain nodes to adopt schedules with bounded *duty cycles*: they must be awake for no more than a bounded fraction of the time. Formally, we say that an integer schedule $S \subset \{0, 1, \ldots\}$ has duty cycle d if there is an infinite sequence of times $\tau_1 < \tau_2 < \cdots$ so that

$$\frac{|S \cap \{0, 1, \ldots, \tau_i - 1\}|}{\tau_i} \leq d\,.$$

Consider two nodes, A_1 and A_2, each with a fixed *duty cycle*, denoted $d_i < 1$. We may determine the behavior of these nodes by associating with each of them an integer schedule $S_i \subset \{0, 1, 2, \ldots\}$ meeting the duty cycle constraint; then the node A_i is awake only during those slots indexed by the schedule S_i. In general, we do not assume that the clocks of the two nodes are synchronized and so must entertain the possibility of arbitrary (even non-integer) shifts of the nodes' schedules. For this reason, it is convenient to treat the schedules S_i as subsets of the real numbers $\mathbb{R}$ in the obvious way: associate the integer s with the interval $[s\Delta, (s+1)\Delta)$. (We use the notation $[a, b)$ to denote the "half open" interval $\{x \mid a \leq x < b\}$.) Then, for the integer schedule S we define

$$S^{\Delta} = \bigcup_{s \in S} [s\Delta, (s+1)\Delta) \subset \mathbb{R}.$$

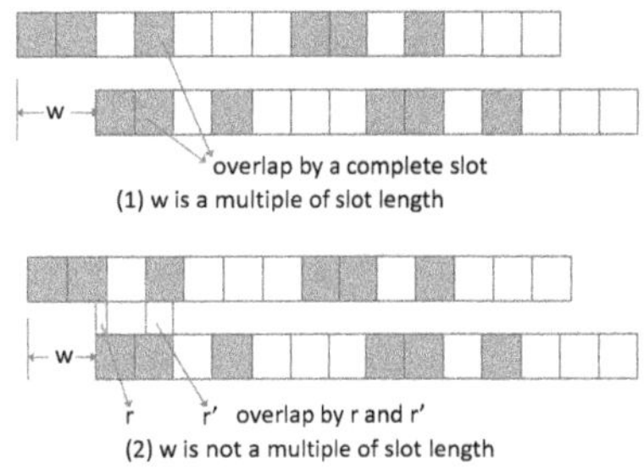

Figure 1: Illustration of the intersection property in the basic integer model.

Consider the circumstances where the nodes A_1 and A_2 come into each other's range at the moment when A_1's clock reads t_1 and A_2's clock reads t_2. The time to discovery for these particular shifts is then given by the smallest t for which both nodes are awake: $t_1 + t \in S_1$ and $t_2 + t \in S_2$. We write this quantity as

$$L(S_1, S_2; t_1, t_2) = \min\{t \mid t_1 + t \in S_1 \text{ and } t_2 + t \in S_2\}\,.$$

For two schedules S_1 and S_2, then, this motivates the following definition of *discovery latency*, the worst case time to discovery taken over all shifts:

$$L(S_1, S_2) = \max_{t_1, t_2 > 0} L(S_1, S_2; t_1, t_2)\,.$$

We remark that—in general—this quantity may not even be well-defined (that is, there may be shifts for which the schedules never overlap). The basic problem is to construct schedules S_i, satisfying the duty-cycle constraints, that minimize the discovery latency $L(S_1, S_2)$.

Periodic schedules. One natural way to define an integer schedule is to fix a finite-length schedule and periodically repeat this sequence. More specifically, fixing a subset $\check{S} \subset \mathbb{Z}_n$ of the integers modulo n, one can define an integer schedule $S = \{z \mid z \bmod n \in \check{S}\} \subset \mathbb{Z}$. One advantage of schedules S defined in this way is that their duty cycle can be determined as the simple ratio $|\check{S}|/n$. As a matter of notation, we blur the distinction between $\check{S}$ and S, referring to the finite set $\check{S}$ as a schedule.

3.2 Motivation for Non-Integer Model

We next show any valid schedule in the basic integer model has the following property:

PROPERTY 1. *Consider two nodes using a schedule in the basic integer model for neighbor discovery. Suppose the schedule guarantees discovery in time n. Let w denote the relative time shift of the two nodes. Then, for any w, we find one of two possible cases:*

- *The shift w is an integer, and there exists an entire time slot during which both nodes are awake.*
- *The shift w is non-integral, and there exist two time periods (among the first n) during which both nodes are awake; furthermore, the durations of these time periods, r and r', sum to Δ. Hence either r or r' is longer than $\Delta/2$.*

This property is illustrated in Fig. 1. The first case in the above property is straightforward. We therefore only describe why the second property holds. For ease of exposition, we assume $\Delta = 1$ (when $\Delta \neq 1$, we just need to divide time by Δ and the explanation below applies similarly). Since w is non-integral, consider w as a fractional number between two integers z and $z+1$. We shall show that the schedules of the two nodes, denoted as S_1 and S_2, have (at least) two overlaps, one of which has length $w-z$ and the other has length $z+1-w$. We know that if S_2 started at z, then there would be a complete time slot (say s_1 in the schedule of S_2) so that S_1 and S_2 overlap. Since now S_2 starts at w, they will just overlap for part of s_1 which has length $(1-(w-z)) = z+1-w$. Similarly, if S_2 started at $z+1$, there would be a complete time slot (say s_2 in the schedule of S_2 which is different from s_1) that S_1 and S_2 overlapped. Since the real case is to shift S_2 to the left by length $z+1-w$, the overlap is actually part of s_2 that is with length $1-(z+1-w) = w-z$. It is clear that the sum of the two overlapping portions is one, and one of them has length at least half, as desired.

The above property prompts us to define a further hardware-dependent parameter, the *required meeting time* $\delta > 0$: This is the minimum amount of time required by two devices to discover each other when they are both active. The basic integer model implicitly assumes that $\delta = \Delta/2$. While this assumption is reasonable for some wireless devices that have compatible δ and Δ (e.g., both in a few milliseconds or less than one millisecond [5, 9, 20]), it can be quite pessimistic for other wireless devices where $\delta \ll \Delta/2$ (for instance, Δ is one or two seconds while δ is in milliseconds on current smartphones [3]). We therefore propose a generalized model that considers both δ and Δ. This model provides a unified setting that accommodates the characteristics of a diverse range of wireless devices. It meaningfully considers continuous time, which is less restrictive than the integer model. When $\delta = \Delta/2$, it reduces to the basic integer model.

3.3 Non-Integer Model

Fix Δ and δ as above. As we have relaxed the assumption that schedules adhere to integer boundaries, we may consider arbitrary schedules of the form $S \subset \mathbb{R}$; we assume, however, that each schedule S consists of a set of disjoint intervals, $S = \bigcup_\ell [a_\ell, b_\ell)$, and that each $b_\ell - a_\ell \geq \Delta$ so that the schedule satisfies the Δ switching constraint. We refer to such schedules as *non-integer* schedules. The quantity δ then determines the discovery latency as follows. Consider a pair of schedules S_i and a pair of shifts $t_1, t_2 \geq 0$ $(i = 1, 2)$. For these two shifts, we define the time to discovery to be the smallest time at which the two schedules overlap at an interval of width at least δ:

$$L(S_1, S_2; t_1, t_2) = \min \left\{ t \;\middle|\; \begin{array}{l} [t+t_1-\delta, t+t_1) \subset S_1 \text{ and} \\ [t+t_2-\delta, t+t_2) \subset S_2 \end{array} \right\}.$$

As above, we define the *discovery latency* for such a pair of schedules to be the worst case over all shifts:

$$L(S_1, S_2) = \min_{t_1, t_2 \geq 0} L(S_1, S_2; t_1, t_2).$$

As above we may consider periodic schedules. Specifically, if the schedule S repeats with period $n \in \mathbb{R}$ it can be represented as a subset $\check{S} \subset [0, n)$. We say that such a periodic schedule has duty cycle d if $|\check{S}|/n \leq d$, where $|\check{S}| = \sum_\ell (b_\ell - a_\ell)$. As above, we notationally blur the distiction between S and the "finite length" schedule $\check{S}$, which describes one "period" of S. Again the goal is, given duty cycles d_i, to design periodic schedules $S_i \subset [0, n_i)$ (so that S_i has period n_i), that minimize the resulting discovery latency.

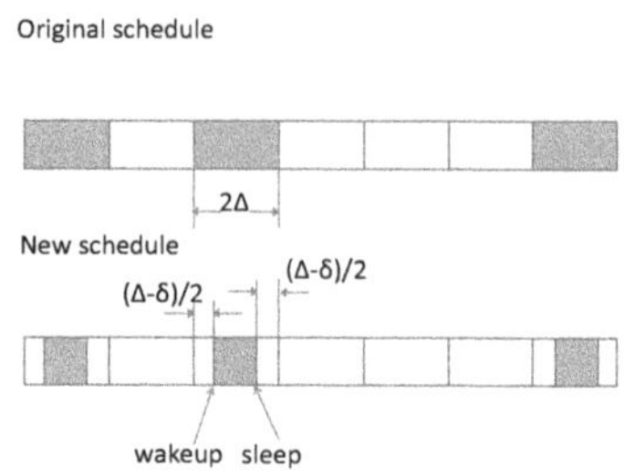

Figure 2: Illustration of the reduction that converts an integer schedule to a corresponding non-integer schedule.

3.4 General Reduction from Integer Schedules to Non-integer Schedules

We propose a general reduction that can be applied to any integer schedule to obtain a corresponding (lower duty-cycle) non-integer schedule. The reduction is motivated by the following observation. Consider an integer schedule with slot length Δ. We can construct a new schedule by "trimming" the amount of time that a node is awake in an active slot from Δ to $\Delta/2 + \delta$. The new schedule still guarantees that two nodes can discover each other. This is because, by Property 1, if the two nodes discover each other by time n according to the original schedule, then there exists a time interval of at least $\Delta/2$, during which both of them are awake. After "trimming", since the amount of time a node is awake in an active slot is $\Delta/2 + \delta$, the new schedule can still guarantee at least δ amount of overlap while both nodes are awake, which is sufficient for neighbor discovery. The above construction significantly reduces the duty cycle: in the new schedule, the duty cycle is $d_i(\Delta/2 + \delta)/\Delta$, approximately half of d_i when $\delta \ll \Delta$, where d_i is the original duty cycle of node i, $i = 1, 2$. The new schedule, however, violates the switching interval constraint (since the amount of awake time, $\Delta/2 + \delta$, in a slot is less than Δ). This violation can be easily fixed by assuming that the original integer schedule uses slot length of 2Δ (instead of Δ); the "trimming" reduces the amount of time that a node is awake in an active slot from Δ to $\Delta/2+\delta$. Fig. 2 illustrates the "trimming" procedure. In the figure, the "trimming" is by removing $(\Delta - \delta)/2$ on each end of an active slot. In general, the "trimming" only needs to ensure that there remains a continuous length of $\Delta/2+\delta$ awake time in an active slot. Besides the example shown in Fig. 2, there are many other ways of "trimming", e.g., removing $(\Delta - \delta)$ at the beginning or end of an active slot.

The above reduction converts an integer schedule to a non-integer schedule while preserving the discovery latency and reducing the duty cycle by (approximately) a factor of two. We next describe how to obtain a non-integer schedule from an integer schedule so that the duty cycle remains to be the same while the discovery latency is significantly reduced. Suppose the duty cycle is d. The new non-integer schedule is constructed as follows. We first construct an integer schedule with duty cycle of $d(2\Delta)/(\Delta + \delta)$ and slot length of 2Δ. We then apply the above "trimming" procedure (see Fig. 2) so that the duty cycle is reduced to d, as desired. For two nodes with duty cycles d_1 and d_2, if the worst-case discovery latency of the original integer schedule is $c/(d_1 d_2) \cdot \Delta$, where c is a constant (many existing schedules have this property; and as we shall see, optimal schedules also have this property), then the discovery latency of the new non-integer schedule is $c/(4d_1d_2) \cdot 2\Delta = c/(2d_1d_2) \cdot \Delta$, only half of the original value.

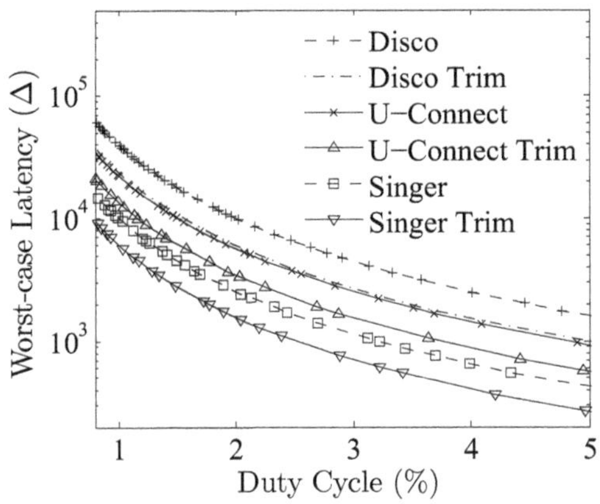

Figure 3: Performance of integer schedules and their corresponding non-integer schedules (symmetric case).

The above reduction can be applied to *any* integer schedule. We next illustrate it using three existing schemes, Disco [5] U-Connect [9], and schemes using Singer difference sets [30, 11], that provide integer schedules. Using the above reduction, we convert the integer schedules to their corresponding non-integer schedules. Fig. 3 plots the worst-case discovery latency versus duty cycle for these three schemes in the symmetric case. The results of both the original integer schedules and the "trimmed" non-integer schedules are plotted in the figure. We observe that for all three schemes, the worst-case discovery latency of the non-integer schedule is only half of that of the integer schedule. When "trimming" Singer sets based integer schedules using our reduction, the performance of the resultant non-integer schedules coincides with that of Diff-Codes [17] (for the schedules of duty cycles that are constructed using Singer sets). This is because Diff-Codes expands each slot in the schedule from Singer sets to two consecutive slots, an active slot followed by a sleeping slot, and a sleeping slot followed by another sleeping slot. When overflowing an active slot to its subsequent slot, it coincides with a special form of "trimming" (i.e., by "trimming" an amount $\Delta - \delta$ at the end of a 2Δ slot).

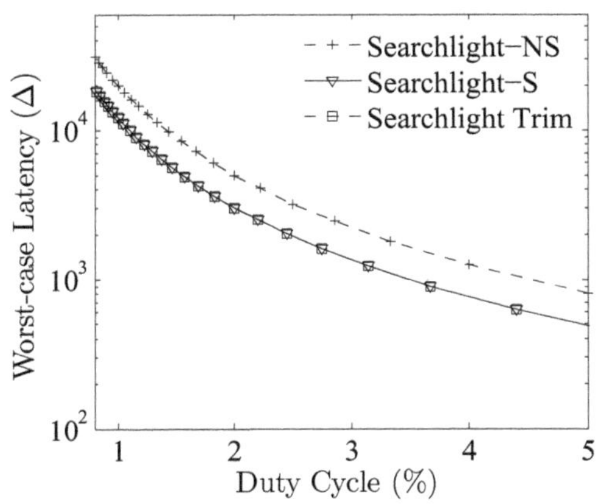

Figure 4: Performance of the integer and non-integer schedules for Searchlight (symmetric case).

The study in [3] proposes both integer and non-integer variants of Searchlight, referred to as Searchlight-NS (no striped probing) and Searchlight-S (with striped probing), respectively. We can convert Searchlight-NS to a non-integer schedule, referred to as "Searchlight trim," following our proposed reduction. Fig. 4 plots the worst-case discovery latency versus duty cycle for these three schemes for symmetric duty cycles. We observe the performance of "Searchlight trim" overlaps with that of Searchlight-S, both reducing the worst-case discovery latency of Searchlight-NS by a factor of two.

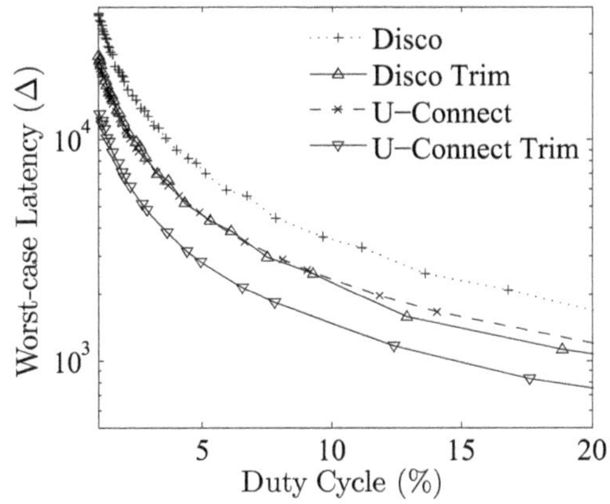

Figure 5: Performance of integer schedules and their corresponding non-integer schedules (asymmetric case).

The above examples illustrate applying the reduction in the symmetric case. The reduction also works for the asymmetric case. One example is shown in Fig. 5, where we plot the performance of Disco [5] and U-Connect [9], and their corresponding non-integer schedules under asymmetric duty cycles. The duty cycle of one node is fixed to be 1% while the duty cycle of the other node varies from 1% to 20%. We again observe the non-integer schedule reduces the worst-case discovery latency of the integer schedule by a factor of two.

4. LOWER BOUNDS

We next develop a general lower bound in the non-integer model. This lower bound is characterized by both Δ (switching time) and δ (required meeting time). It is for the general case where two nodes have duty cycles, d_1 and d_2, which can be the same or different. As we remark at the end, this lower bound leads to a family of lower bounds for both symmetric and asymmetric settings.

THEOREM 2. *Consider two schedules S_1, S_2 in the non-integer model with parameters Δ, δ. Assume that S_1, S_2 have duty cycles d_1, d_2 and, furthermore, $L(S_1, S_2) \le n$, i.e., they guarantee discovery within time n. Then $d_1d_2 \ge \Delta^2/(2n(\Delta-\delta))$. Conversely, the discovery latency is at least $\Delta^2/(2d_1d_2(\Delta-\delta))$.*

PROOF. Consider two schedules $S_1 \subset \mathbb{R}^+$ and $S_2 \subset \mathbb{R}^+$ with duty cycles d_1 and d_2, respectively. We suppose that these schedules achieve discovery latency n, and proceed to prove that we must then have

$$n \ge \frac{\Delta^2}{2d_1d_2(\Delta-\delta)}\,. \tag{1}$$

Select two large times $T_1, T_2 \gg n$ for which $T_j + n \notin S_j$ (for each $j = 1, 2$) and

$$\big|S_1 \cap [0, T_1 + n)\big| \le d_1(T_1 + n)\,, \text{and}$$
$$\big|S_2 \cap [0, T_2 + n)\big| \le d_2(T_2 + n)\,.$$

(Recall that if $A = \bigcup_i [\alpha_i, \beta_i)$ is a disjoint union of half-open intervals, we define $|A| = \sum_i (\beta_i - \alpha_i)$.) We may express each of these "prefixes" of the schedules $S_j \cap [0, T_j + n)$ as a disjoint union of some (maximal) intervals:

$$S_1 \cap [0, T_1 + n) = \bigcup_{i=1}^{k_1} B_i^{(1)}\,, \qquad S_2 \cap [0, T_2 + n) = \bigcup_{i=1}^{k_2} B_i^{(2)}\,,$$

where each $B_i^{(j)}$ has the form $[\alpha, \beta)$. Let $\ell_i^{(j)} = |B_i^{(j)}|$, the length of the ith interval appearing in S_j; then, for each node j,

$$|S_j \cap [0, T_j + n)| = \sum_i \ell_i^{(j)} \le d_j(T_j + n)\,.$$

We pause briefly to introduce some further notation. For a subset $S \subset \mathbb{R}$ and an element $r \in \mathbb{R}$, we let $S + r = \{s + r \mid s \in S\}$ (and likewise define $S - r$). We also extend the notation $|A|$, defined above for subsets $A \subset \mathbb{R}$, to subsets of $\mathbb{R} \times \mathbb{R}$. Specifically, if $A = [\alpha^{(1)}, \beta^{(1)}) \times [\alpha^{(2)}, \beta^{(2)})$, we define $|A| = (\beta^{(1)} - \alpha^{(1)}) \cdot (\beta^{(2)} - \alpha^{(2)})$. If A is a disjoint union $\bigcup_i A_i$, where each A_i is such a product of intervals, we define $|A| = \sum_i |A_i|$.

As S_1 and S_2 achieve discovery latency n, for any $(t_1, t_2) \in [0, T_1) \times [0, T_2)$ the intersection of $(S_1 - t_1) \cap [0, n)$ and $(S_2 - t_2) \cap [0, n)$ must contain an interval of width at least δ. Fixing the position of a particular interval $B_i^{(1)}$, observe that the interval $B_{i'}^{(2)}$ overlaps with $B_i^{(1)}$ at an interval of width δ for a collection of times of length $\ell_i^{(1)} + \ell_{i'}^{(2)} - 2\delta$ (see Fig. 6). It follows that

$$\left|\left\{ (t_1, t_2) \;\middle|\; \begin{array}{l} B_i^{(1)} - t_1 \text{ meets } B_{i'}^{(2)} - t_2 \\ \text{at an interval of width } \delta \\ \text{in } [0, n) \end{array} \right\}\right| \le n(\ell_i^{(i)} + \ell_{i'}^{(2)} - 2\delta)\,.$$

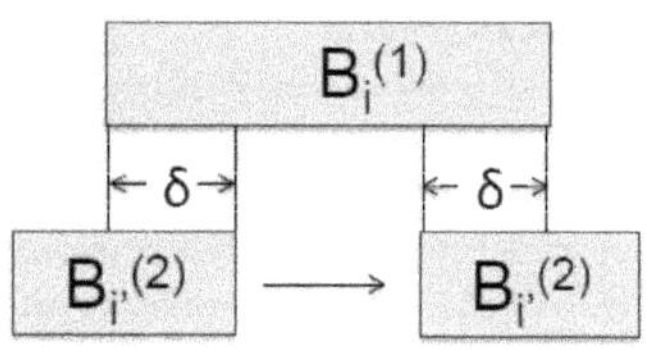

Figure 6: Overlap occurrences from a pair of intervals.

As every pair $(t_1, t_2) \in [0, T_1) \times [0, T_2)$ must be covered by some pair of intervals as above, we have

$$\begin{aligned} T_1 T_2 &\le \sum_{i,i'} n\left(\ell_i^{(1)} + \ell_{i'}^{(2)} - 2\delta\right) \\ &= n\left(k_1 \sum_{i'} \ell_{i'}^{(2)} + k_2 \sum_i \ell_i^{(1)} - 2k_1 k_2 \delta\right) \\ &\le n(k_1 d_2(T_2 + n) + k_2 d_1(T_1 + n) - 2k_1 k_2 \delta)\,. \end{aligned}$$

We conclude that

$$n \ge \frac{T_1 T_2}{k_1 d_2(T_2 + n) + k_2 d_1(T_1 + n) - 2k_1 k_2 \delta}\,. \tag{2}$$

Additionally, we recall that any interval of activity must have width Δ, and hence

$$k_1 \Delta \le d_1(T_1 + n) \quad \text{and} \quad k_2 \Delta \le d_2(T_2 + n)\,. \tag{3}$$

To complete the proof, we establish an upper bound on the denominator of (2)

$$\phi(k_1, k_2) \triangleq k_1 d_2(T_2 + n) + k_2 d_1(T_1 + n) - 2k_1 k_2 \delta$$

subject to the constraints (3). Note that, assuming k_2 satisfies (3),

$$\begin{aligned} \frac{\partial}{\partial k_1} \phi(k_1, k_2) &= d_2(T_2 + n) - 2\delta k_2 \\ &\ge d_2(T_2 + n) - 2\delta \frac{d_2(T_2 + n)}{\Delta} \\ &= d_2(T_2 + n)\left(1 - \frac{2\delta}{\Delta}\right) \ge 0\,. \end{aligned}$$

(Recall that $2\delta/\Delta \le 1$). It follows that for any choice of k_2 consistent with (3), the function ϕ is maximized by taking k_1 as large as possible—that is, so that the constraint (3) for k_1 is tight. An analogous computation of $\partial\phi/\partial k_2$ establishes the corresponding statement for k_2: In particular, $\phi(k_1, k_2)$ is maximized when the constraints (3) are tight. We conclude that

$$\phi(k_1, k_2) \le 2d_1 d_2 (T_1 + n)(T_2 + n)\frac{\Delta - \delta}{\Delta^2}$$

Finally, in light of (2), we conclude that

$$n \ge \frac{\Delta^2}{2d_1 d_2(\Delta - \delta)} \cdot \frac{T_1 T_2}{(T_1 + n)(T_2 + n)}\,.$$

As we are free to select T_j as large as we wish, the inequality (1) follows, as desired. □

A few remarks area in order.

- When $\delta = \Delta/2$, the lower bound becomes the lower bound for the basic integer model. We see when $\delta \ll \Delta$ (the assumptions in [3, 17]), the lower bound is a factor 2 less than the lower bound for the integer model, showing the significant benefits of non-integer schedules. In the rest of the paper, non-integer model assumes $\delta \ll \Delta$.

- When $d_1 = d_2$, the lower bound on discovery latency becomes $\Delta/\sqrt{2n(\Delta - \delta)}$. When $\Delta = 1$ and $\delta \ll \Delta$, it reduces to the lower bound of $1/\sqrt{2n}$ in a recent study [17]. The derivation of [17] only considers symmetric settings. Our lower bound applies to both symmetric and asymmetric settings, and permits a quite general model, characterized by the two parameters Δ and δ that account for practical constraints.

- When $d_1 = d_2$ and $\delta = \Delta/2$, the lower bound on discovery latency is Δ/d^2, which coincides with the lower bound for integer schedules in the symmetric case [30]. When $d_1 \neq d_2$ and $\delta = \Delta/2$, the lower bound on discovery latency is $\Delta/(d_1 d_2)$, which is, to be best of our knowledge, the first lower bound for integer schedules in the asymmetric case.

5. OPTIMAL SCHEDULES

In this section, we first demonstrate that the reduction in Section 3.4 converts an optimal integer schedule to an optimal non-integer schedule. We then discuss optimal schedules for symmetric and asymmetric settings, respectively. Our focus is on periodic schedules, as in most existing studies.

5.1 Optimal Integer and Non-integer Schedules

Consider an optimal integer schedule. Suppose two nodes have cycles d_1 and d_2. When the slot length is 2Δ, based on the lower bound in Section 4, for the two nodes to discover each other in time n, we must have

$$d_1 d_2 \geq \frac{2\Delta}{n}. \tag{4}$$

Under the reduction in Section 3.4, the duty cycle of a node in the non-integer schedule, denoted as d_i', satisfies

$$d_i' = d_i \frac{\Delta + \delta}{2\Delta}, i = 1, 2, \tag{5}$$

$$d_1' d_2' = d_1 d_2 \left(\frac{\Delta + \delta}{2\Delta} \right)^2 \tag{6}$$

Substituting (4) into (6) yields

$$d_1' d_2' \geq \frac{2\Delta}{n} \left(\frac{\Delta + \delta}{2\Delta} \right)^2 = \frac{(\Delta + \delta)^2}{2n\Delta} \approx \frac{\Delta^2}{2n(\Delta - \delta)},$$

where the last approximation holds since $\delta \ll \Delta$ (we only consider the non-integer model with $\delta \ll \Delta$, see remarks in Section 4). The new non-integer schedule therefore meets the lower bound for the non-integer model, and hence is an optimal non-integer schedule.

In fact, we can use a more exact reduction (see Fig. 7), which divides time into slots of length $2(\Delta - \delta)$ and "trim" a total amount of $\Delta - 2\delta$ in each active slot. This reduction still ensures discovery since the length of the awake time in an active slot is Δ while the ensured overlap is at least $2(\Delta - \delta)/2 = \Delta - \delta$. Repeating the above derivation, we have

$$d_1 d_2 \geq \frac{2(\Delta - \delta)}{n},$$

$$d_i' = d_i \frac{\Delta}{2(\Delta - \delta)}, i = 1, 2,$$

$$d_1' d_2' \geq \frac{2(\Delta - \delta)}{n} \left(\frac{\Delta}{2(\Delta - \delta)} \right)^2 = \frac{\Delta^2}{2n(\Delta - \delta)}.$$

That is, the constructed non-integer schedule matches the lower bound in the non-integer model exactly, and hence is optimal.

5.2 Symmetric Case

Our discussion below only considers optimal integer schedules; using the reduction in Section 3.4, they can be readily converted to optimal non-integer schedules.

While existing studies [30, 11, 17] show optimal schedules can be achieved through Singer difference sets, the only explicit construction [11] in the networking community that we are aware of requires exponential running time. In the appendix, we describe an efficient polynomial-time construction based on the existence proof in [21]. In the following, we present a novel optimal construction that is based on the theory of *Sidon sets* (see, e.g., [23] for a detailed description of the theory). It is the first polynomial-time optimal algorithm that does not rely on Singer difference sets.

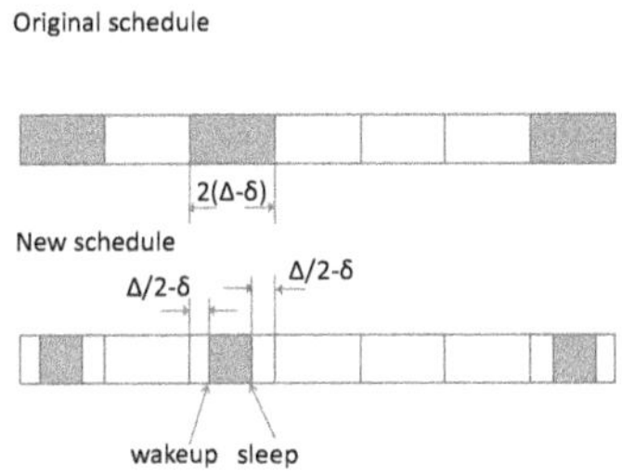

Figure 7: Illustration of an optimal reduction that converts an integer schedule to a corresponding non-integer schedule.

In the following, for ease of exposition, we regard the step length, Δ, as one unit of time and approach the dual problem: fixing a period n, how can one schedule a node's wake-up slots so that the schedule intersects with every rotation of the schedule and, furthermore, minimizes the duty cycle, d (determined by the number of active slots)? A solution to the dual problem can be immediately converted to a schedule for the original problem, i.e., for a given duty cycle, scheduling the wake-up times so that the discovery latency is minimized. Let S represent the schedule. Let $L(S) = L(S, S)$ represent the worst-case discovery latency.

Let $\mathbb{Z}_n$ denote the residue classes of the integers modulo n. We wish to construct a set $S \subseteq \mathbb{Z}_n$ of size $|S| \approx \sqrt{n}$ such that for any $\alpha, \beta \in \mathbb{Z}_n$,

$$|(\alpha + S) \cap (\beta + S)| \neq 0,$$

where $\alpha + S$ denotes the set $\{\alpha + s \mid s \in S\}$. Note that using this set S to define a periodic schedule immediately results in $L(S) \leq n$ (and $d = |S|/n$). To simplify our requirements on the set S, we observe the following:

LEMMA 3. *$|(\alpha + S) \cap (\beta + S)| \neq 0$ for any $\alpha, \beta \in \mathbb{Z}_n$ if and only if $\mathbb{Z}_n \subseteq S - S$, where $S - S$ denotes the set of differences $\{s_1 - s_2 \mid s_1, s_2 \in S\}$.*

PROOF. It is easy to see the statement that $|(\alpha + S) \cap (\beta + S)| \neq 0$ for any $\alpha, \beta \in \mathbb{Z}_n$ is equivalent with $|(\alpha + S) \cap S| \neq 0$ for any $\alpha \in \mathbb{Z}_n$. If $|(\alpha + S) \cap S| \neq 0$ for any $\alpha \in \mathbb{Z}_n$, then there exist two elements $s_1, s_2 \in S$ such that $\alpha + s_1 = s_2$; thus $\alpha = s_2 - s_1 \in S$, which proves one direction of the lemma. For the other direction, as $\mathbb{Z}_n \subseteq S - S$ for any $\alpha \in \mathbb{Z}_n$, we can find two elements $s_1, s_2 \in S$ such that $\alpha = s_2 - s_1$. Therefore $\alpha + s_1 = s_2 \in (\alpha + S) \cap S$, as desired. □

This allows us to focus our efforts on construction of *saturated difference sets* in $\mathbb{Z}_n$. Specifically, we say that a subset $S \subset \mathbb{Z}_n$ is a saturated difference set if $S - S \triangleq \{s_1 - s_2 \mid s_1, s_2 \in S\}$ contains every element of $\mathbb{Z}_n$.

The Sidon set construction. Consider a prime number p and let ϑ be a generator of the *multiplicative* group $\mathbb{Z}_p^* = \{1, \ldots, p-1\}$ of units modulo p. Then the map $t \mapsto \vartheta^t$ is an isomorphism between $\mathbb{Z}_{p-1}$, the integers modulo $p-1$ under addition, and $\mathbb{Z}_p^*$, the multiplicative group of units modulo p. Consider the set

$$S_0 = \{(t, \vartheta^t) \mid t \in \mathbb{Z}_{p-1}\} \subset \mathbb{Z}_{p-1} \oplus \mathbb{Z}_p.$$

While the set S_0 is defined using the multiplicative structure of the ring of integers modulo p, our goal is to establish additive properties of the set (as a subset of the additive group $\mathbb{Z}_{p-1} \oplus \mathbb{Z}_p$).

LEMMA 4. $\{(a,b) \mid a,b \neq 0\} \cup \{(0,0)\} \subset S_0 - S_0$.

PROOF. It is easy to see that $(0,0) \in S_0 - S_0$. For a pair $(a,b) \in \mathbb{Z}_{p-1} \times \mathbb{Z}_p$ for which $a,b \neq 0$, consider the differences

$$(a+\ell, \vartheta^{a+\ell}) - (\ell, \vartheta^{\ell}) = (a, \vartheta^{\ell}(\vartheta^a - 1))$$

for $\ell \in \mathbb{Z}_{p-1}$. As $a \neq 0$, the sum $\vartheta^a - 1 \neq 0$ and it follows that $b \in \{\vartheta^{\ell}(\vartheta^a - 1) \mid \ell \in \mathbb{Z}_{p-1}\} = \mathbb{Z}_p^*$ as ϑ is a multiplicative generator. In particular, by choosing ℓ to be $\log_{\vartheta}(b/(\vartheta^a - 1))$ we find that $(a,b) = (a+\ell, \vartheta^{a+\ell}) - (a, \vartheta^a)$, as desired. (Here the notation $\log_{\vartheta} x$ denotes the unique exponent in the set $\{1,\ldots,p-1\}$ for which $\vartheta^{\alpha} = x$.) □

Observe that since p and $p-1$ are relatively prime, $\mathbb{Z}_{p-1} \oplus \mathbb{Z}_p \cong \mathbb{Z}_{p(p-1)}$ by the Chinese remainder theorem, and a saturated difference set in $\mathbb{Z}_{p-1} \oplus \mathbb{Z}_p$ immediately yields a saturated difference set in the cyclic group $\mathbb{Z}_{p(p-1)}$. However, the set S_0 above is *not* saturated: differences of elements of the set miss a few evasive "slices" of $\mathbb{Z}_{p-1} \oplus \mathbb{Z}_p \cong \mathbb{Z}_{p(p-1)}$: the elements (a,b) where $a = 0$ or $b = 0$.

To complete the construction, we can apply an existing scheme in these small "slices." We recall here the basic details of U-Connect [9], which we adapt for this purpose. For a given $k > 0$, consider the set $A_k = \{k, 2k, \ldots, k^2\} \cup \{0,1,2,\ldots,k-1\} \subset \mathbb{Z}$. Observe that $\{-k^2,\ldots,k^2\} \subset A_k - A_k$ and hence that $A_k - A_k$ contains an element from every equivalence class of the integers modulo $2k^2+1$. To be precise, defining $A_{k,n} = \{a \bmod n \mid a \in A_k\}$ it follows immediately that $\mathbb{Z}_n \subset A_{k,n} - A_{k,n}$ so long as $n \leq 2k^2+1$.

To summarize, for the integer n, define $k_n = \lceil\sqrt{(n-1)/2}\rceil$ and $D_n = A_{k_n,n}$. By the discussion above, D_n is a saturated difference set in $\mathbb{Z}_n$ of size $2k_n$. As a function of n, this yields a saturated difference set of size $2\lceil\sqrt{(n-1)/2}\rceil \leq \sqrt{2n}+2 = \sqrt{2n}+O(1)$.

Returning to our construction, define $S_a = \{(0,b) \mid b \in D_p\}$ and $S_b = \{(a,0) \mid a \in D_{p-1}\}$ (where D_n is as defined above), and observe now that the set $S \triangleq S_0 \cup S_a \cup S_b$ clearly has the property that $Z_{p-1} \oplus Z_p \subset S - S$. To summarize, this construction yields a saturated difference set in $Z_{p(p-1)} \cong Z_{p-1} \oplus Z_p$ of size no more than

$$\begin{aligned} & p-1+\sqrt{2p}+\sqrt{2(p-1)} \\ \leq\ & \sqrt{p(p-1)}+\sqrt{2p}+\sqrt{2(p-1)} \\ \leq\ & \sqrt{p(p-1)}+3\sqrt[4]{p(p-1)}, \end{aligned}$$

as $p > 2$. (The fact that $\sqrt{2p}+\sqrt{2(p-1)} \leq 3\sqrt[4]{p(p-1)}$ for $p \geq 2$ follows immediately by expanding the fourth power of both sides.)

We record the results of this construction in the following theorem.

THEOREM 5. *For any n of the form $p(p-1)$ with $p > 2$, there is an explicit saturated difference set in $\mathbb{Z}_n$ of size no more than $\sqrt{n}+3\sqrt[4]{n}$. For such a set, defining $d = |S|/n$, we have $L(S) \leq |S| = (1+o(1))/d^2$.*

We use the word *explicit* in the above theorem to indicate that one can efficiently compute, given p, the elements of the difference set. The construction requires generating the elements of S_0, S_a, and S_b, which is straightforward given a generator ϑ of the cyclic group $\mathbb{Z}_p^*$. Such a generator can be found very quickly with randomization; deterministically, one can simply check the first $\sqrt{p}$ elements of $\mathbb{Z}_p$ to find one with the property that $x^{p-1} \equiv 1$ but $x^{(p-1)/r} \not\equiv 1$ for each prime r dividing $p-1$. See [2] for details.

It remains, of course, to represent the set S inside $\mathbb{Z}_{p(p-1)}$ via the isomorphism promised by the Chinese remainder theorem. For this purpose, note that

$$\begin{aligned} p &\equiv 1 \mod p-1 \qquad & (p-1)^2 &\equiv 0 \mod p-1 \\ p &\equiv 0 \mod p \qquad & (p-1)^2 &\equiv 1 \mod p. \end{aligned}$$

It follows immediately that the element $(a,b) \in \mathbb{Z}_{p-1} \oplus \mathbb{Z}_p$ is carried to the element $a \cdot p + b(p-1)^2 \mod p(p-1)$ in $\mathbb{Z}_{p(p-1)}$. As arithmetic in $\mathbb{Z}_p$, $\mathbb{Z}_{p-1}$ and $\mathbb{Z}_{p(p-1)}$ can be carried out in time poly$(\log p)$, we conclude that the entire set S can be computed in time $p \cdot \text{poly}(\log p)$.

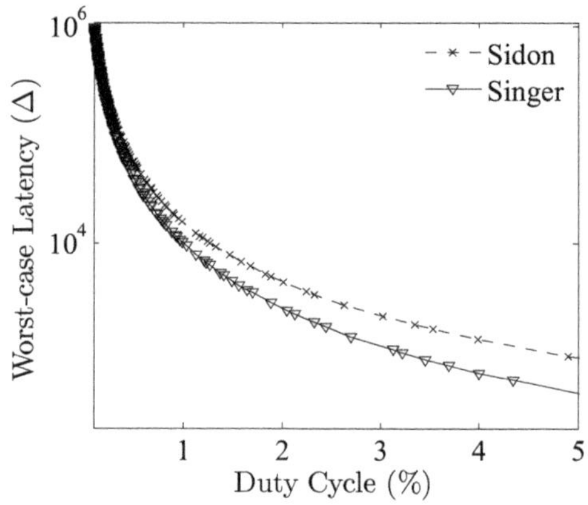

Figure 8: The worst case discovery latency of two optimal schemes (based on Singer and Sidon difference sets) for symmetric duty cycles.

Fig. 8 compares the performance of the two optimal constructions based on Singer and Sidon difference sets, respectively. The performance of Sidon set construction is very close to that of the Singer set construction for small duty cycles. The deviation under larger duty cycles is because the lower order terms in Sidon set construction, which can be improved using more efficient construction when filling the small "slices." We remark that like the other known constructions that achieve asymptotic optimality, this Sidon set construction requires n (and hence d) to have particular number-theoretic properties.

5.3 Asymmetric Case

In the asymmetric case, we again only consider optimal integer schedules for the same reason as described earlier. For two nodes with duty cycles d_1 and d_2, $d_1 \neq d_2$, the lower bound of discovery latency is $1/(d_1 d_2)$ (see Theorem 2). A simple optimal schedule is as follows. Each node picks the closest prime number, p_i, so that $p_i \leq 1/d_i$ and $p_1 \neq p_2$. Then a node wakes up in the slots that are the multiples of p_i. By the Chinese Remainder Theorem, since $p_1 \neq p_2$, for any time shift between these two nodes, they can meet in time $p_1 p_2 \approx 1/(d_1 d_2)$. This simple optimal schedule, however, only works when $p_1 \neq p_2$. Hence it does not work for the symmetric setting or when two nodes have similar duty cycles (which leads to $p_1 = p_2$). In practice, we need a scheme that works for both asymmetric and symmetric settings since the nodes do not know whether they have the same or different duty cycles beforehand.

Existing schemes that are based on prime numbers overcome the limitation in the above simple scheme through adding mechanisms. Specifically, in Disco [5], each node uses two prime numbers instead of one prime number; in

U-Connect [9], each node uses one prime, but is awake for a continuous period of time in addition to the multiples of the prime numbers. Neither of them is optimal. The asymmetric schedules in [3, 17] are not optimal either. Finding a schedule that is optimal in the asymmetric setting while also applicable (or even optimal) for the symmetric setting remains an open question that is left as future work.

6. CONCLUSION AND FUTURE WORK

In this paper, we first developed a generalized non-integer model for asynchronous neighbor discovery on duty-cycled mobile devices. This generalized model permits unified treatment of the assumptions in existing studies, and allows us to place various existing results into a single setting. We then provided a reduction that transforms any schedule in the basic integer model to a corresponding schedule in the generalized non-integer model while improving the performance by a factor of two. After that, we established a new family of lower bounds for the best achievable latency guarantee in the non-integer model. Last, we developed a novel optimal construction based on Sidon sets for the symmetric setting.

Our work motivates two directions of further work. The first is to develop optimal schedules for general duty cycles, d, in the symmetric setting. (As mentioned above, known constructions—including the new construction presented here—only provide control for a particular set of d.) One way to achieve this is through padding, in which case the analysis of the worst-case performance requires detailed analysis of the density of the relevant d. The second is to develop practical (close-to) optimal schedules for the asymmetric setting.

Acknowledgements

We gratefully acknowledge support from the National Science Foundation under grant 0835735, CAREER award 0746841, and grants 1117427 and 1407205. Any opinions, findings, and conclusions or recommendations expressed in this material are those of the authors and do not necessarily reflect the views of the funding agencies. We would like to thank the anonymous reviewers for their insightful comments.

7. REFERENCES

[1] L. Aalto, N. Göthlin, J. Korhonen, and T. Ojala. Bluetooth and WAP push based location-aware mobile advertising system. In *Proc. of MobiSys*, June 2004.

[2] E. Bach and J. Shallit. *Algorithmic Number Theory, Volume 1: Efficient Algorithms*. Foundations of Computing. MIT Press, 1996.

[3] M. Bakht, M. Trower, and R. H. Kravets. Searchlight: Won't you be my neighbor? In *Proc. of ACM MobiCom*, 2012.

[4] S. A. Borbash, A. Ephremides, and M. J. McGlynn. An asynchronous neighbor discovery algorithm for wireless sensor networks. *Ad Hoc Networks*, 5(7):998–1016, 2007.

[5] P. Dutta and D. Culler. Practical asynchronous neighbor discovery and rendezvous for mobile sensing applications. In *Proc. of ACM SenSys*, 2008.

[6] B. Han, P. Hui, V. Kumar, M. Marathe, J. Shao, and A. Srinivasan. Mobile data offloading through opportunistic communications and social participation. *IEEE Transactions on Mobile Computing*, 11(5):821–834, 2012.

[7] C. S. Hsu, J. R. Jiang, Y. C. Tseng, and T. H. Lai. Quorum-based asynchronous power-saving protocols for ieee 802.11 and hoc networks. *ACM Journal on Mobile Networks and Applications (MONET)*, 10(1-2):169–181, 2005.

[8] J.-H. Huang, S. Amjad, and S. Mishra. CenWits: a sensor-based loosely coupled search and rescue system using witnesses. In *Proc. of ACM SenSys*, 2005.

[9] A. Kandhalu, K. Lakshmanan, and R. R. Rajkumar. U-Connect: a low-latency energy-efficient asynchronous neighbor discovery protocol. In *Proc. of IPSN*, 2010.

[10] A. Keshavarzian, E. Uysal-Biyikoglu, F. Herrmann, and A. Manjeshwar. Energy-efficient link assessment in wireless sensor networks. In *Proc. of IEEE INFOCOM*, March 2004.

[11] S. Lai, B. Zhang, B. Ravindran, and H. Cho. CQS-Pair: Cyclic quorum system pair for wakeup scheduling in wireless sensor networks. In *Proc. of Principles of Distributed Systems*, 2008.

[12] D. Li and P. Sinha. RBTP: low-power mobile discovery protocol through recursive binary time partitioning. *IEEE Transactions on Mobile Computing*, 13(2):263–273, 2014.

[13] T. Liu, C. M. Sadler, P. Zhang, and M. Martonosi. Implementing software on resource-constrained mobile sensors: experiences with Impala and ZebraNet. In *Proc. of ACM MobiSys*, 2004.

[14] Locast. `http://www.lokast.com`.

[15] M. J. McGlynn and S. A. Borbash. Birthday protocols for low energy deployment and flexible neighbor discovery in ad hoc wireless networks. In *Proc. of ACM MobiHoc*, October 2001.

[16] L. McNamara, C. Mascolo, and L. Capra. Media sharing based on colocation prediction in urban transport. In *Proc. of ACM MobiCom*, September 2008.

[17] T. Meng, F. Wu, and G. Chen. On designing neighbor discovery protocols: A code-based approach. In *Proc. of IEEE INFOCOM*, 2014.

[18] M. Motani, V. Srinivasan, and P. S. Nuggehalli. PeopleNet: engineering a wireless virtual social network. In *Proc. of ACM MobiCom*, 2005.

[19] A. K. Pietiläinen, E. Oliver, J. Lebrun, G. Varghese, and C. Diot. MobiClique: middleware for mobile social networking. In *Proc. of ACM Workshop on Online Social Networks*, August 2009.

[20] A. Purohit, N. Priyantha, and J. Liu. WiFlock: collaborative group discovery and maintenance in mobile sensor networks. In *Proc. of IPSN*, 2011.

[21] D. R. Stinson. Combinatorial designs: Constructions and analysis. *Springer Verlag*, 2003.

[22] Nintendo 3ds's streetpass. `http://www.nintendo.com/3ds/features`.

[23] T. Tao and V. Vu. *Additive Combinatorics*. Number 105 in Cambridge Studies in Advanced Mathematics. Cambridge University Press, 2006.

[24] Y.-C. Tseng, C.-S. Hsu, and T.-Y. Hsieh. Power-saving protocols for IEEE 802.11-based multi-hop ad hoc networks. In *Proc. of IEEE INFOCOM*, 2002.

[25] S. Vasudevan, M. Adler, D. Goeckel, and D. Towsley. Efficient algorithms for neighbor discovery in wireless networks. *IEEE/ACM Transactions on Networking*. To Appear.

[26] Z. Yang, B. Zhang, J. Dai, A. Champion, D. Xuan, and D. Li. E-SmallTalker: A distributed mobile system for

social networking in physical proximity. In *Proc. of IEEE ICDCS*, June 2010.

[27] D. Zhang, T. He, Y. Liu, Y. Gu, F. Ye, R. K. Ganti, and H. Lei. Acc: generic on-demand accelerations for neighbor discovery in mobile applications. In *Proc. ACM SenSys*, 2012.

[28] D. Zhang, T. He, F. Ye, R. K. Ganti, and H. Lei. EQS: neighbor discovery and rendezvous maintenance with extended quorum system for mobile sensing applications. In *Proc. of IEEE ICDCS*, 2011.

[29] L. Zhang and D. Guo. Neighbor discovery in wireless networks using compressed sensing with Reed-Muller codes. In *Proc. of WiOpt*, 2011.

[30] R. Zheng, J. C. Hou, and L. Sha. Asynchronous wakeup for ad hoc networks. In *Proc. of ACM MobiHoc*, 2003.

APPENDIX

The Singer Difference Set Construction

DEFINITION 6. *A subset $D \subseteq \mathbb{Z}_v$ is called a $(v, k, 1)$-difference set if $|D| = k$ and, for any $g \in \mathbb{Z}_v \backslash \{0\}$, there exists exactly one pair $(x, y) \in D \times D$ such that $g \equiv x - y \mod v$.*

For a given v, the Singer difference set [21] has $k^2 + k + 1 = v$ and $k - 1$ is a prime power. It is the minimal difference set whose size, k, approximates the lower bound $\sqrt{v}$, i.e., $k \approx \sqrt{v}$. It can be directly used to construct an optimal neighbor discovery schedule for the symmetric setting. In the following, for completeness, we first prove the existence of Singer difference sets (the proof is adapted from that in [21]). We then describe an explicit polynomial time construction.

THEOREM 7. *Let q be a prime power. Then there exists an explicit $(q^2 + q + 1, q + 1, 1)$-difference set in $\mathbb{Z}_{q^2+q+1}$.*

PROOF. The finite field $\mathbb{F}_{q^3}$ is a three-dimensional vector space over $\mathbb{F}_q$ for any prime power q. Let $\mathcal{V}_1$ denote the collection of all one-dimensional subspaces of $\mathbb{F}_{q^3}$ and $\mathcal{V}_2$ denote the collection of all two-dimensional subspaces of $\mathbb{F}_{q^3}$. For each $B \in \mathcal{V}_2$, let $A_B \triangleq \{C \in \mathcal{V}_1 \mid C \subset B\}$. It is easy to check that $|\mathcal{V}_1| = q^2 + q + 1$, a quantity we call ℓ throughout the construction; furthermore $|\mathcal{V}_2| = |\mathcal{V}_1|$, as every two-dimensional space is dual to a unique one-dimension space under the bilinear map $\langle x, y\rangle = \mathrm{Tr}_{\mathbb{F}_{q^3}/\mathbb{F}_q}(xy) = (xy)^{q^2} + (xy)^q + xy$. It is also easy to check that $|A_B| = q + 1$ for each $B \in \mathcal{V}_2$ and that any distinct pair $(C_1, C_2) \in \mathcal{V}_1 \times \mathcal{V}_1$ is contained exactly in one two-dimensional space $B \in \mathcal{V}_2$.

Let ω denote a primitive element of $\mathbb{F}_{q^3}$ (that is, a generator for the multiplicative group $\mathbb{F}^*_{q^3}$). Define a mapping $\alpha : \mathbb{F}_{q^3} \to \mathbb{F}_{q^3}$ by $\alpha(x) = \omega x$. Note that α is $\mathbb{F}_q$-linear (and clearly bijective): it carries subspaces to subspaces. It is not difficult to show that α permutes the elements in $\mathcal{V}_1$ in a single cycle of length ℓ. Fixing a particular one-dimensional space C_0, we write $\mathcal{V}_1 = \{C_0, C_1, \cdots C_{\ell-1}\}$ with the convention that $\alpha(C_i) = C_{i+1 \bmod \ell}$ and, hence, $C_i = \omega^i C_0$. (Note that this is well-defined because α^ℓ, corresponding to left-multiplication by ω^ℓ, has the identity action on the C_i.) Rather remarkably, it can be proved that α also permutes the elements in $\mathcal{V}_2$ in a single cycle of length ℓ.

Let B_0 denote a fixed two-dimensional subspace and define $D \triangleq \{i \mid C_i \subset B_0\} \subset \mathbb{Z}_\ell$. To see that D is a difference set, consider an element $g \in \mathbb{Z}_\ell$, $g \neq 0$. Now, the pair (C_0, C_g) is contained in exactly one two-dimensional subspace B; let i have the property that $\alpha^i B_0 = B$. Now it follows that $\alpha^{-i} B = B_0$ and both C_{-i} and C_{g-i} are contained in B_0; hence $-i$ and $g-i$ are both in D, with $g-i-(-i) \equiv g \mod \ell$. Uniqueness follows similarly. Thus D is a $(q^2+q+1, q+1, 1)$-difference set in $\mathbb{Z}_{q^2+q+1}$. □

Construction: For a prime power p, $\mathbb{F}_{p^3}$ can be realized as $\mathbb{F}_p[x]/(g(x))$ where $g(x) \in \mathbb{F}_p[x]$ is an irreducible polynomial of degree 3. Then the elements of $\mathbb{F}_{p^3}$ can be represented as polynomials in $\mathbb{F}_p[x]$ having degree at most 2. We may choose $C_0 = \mathbb{F}_p$, the constant polynomials; we then choose $B_0 \in \mathcal{V}_2$ to be $\mathrm{span}(1, x) = \{i + jx \mid i, j \in \mathbb{F}_p\}$. This yields the difference set

$$D = \{y \in \mathbb{Z}_{p^2+p+1} \mid \omega^y = ax + b \text{ for some } a, b \in \mathbb{F}_q\},$$

where ω is a primitive element of $\mathbb{F}_{p^3}$.

The remaining work is to find a irreducible polynomial $g(x)$ and a primitive element ω. It turns out that we can do both at once. Initially, factor $p^3 - 1$ such that $p^3 - 1 = p_1^{n_1} \cdots p_k^{n_k}$, where each p_i is a prime number. It suffices to identify a polynomial $g(x) = x^3 + bx^2 + cx + d$ (where $b, c, d \in \mathbb{F}_p$) so that: (i.) $x^{p^3-1} \equiv 1 \mod g(x)$, and (ii.) $x^{(p^3-1)/p_i} \not\equiv 1 \mod g(x)$ for each i. Such $g(x)$ is irreducible in $\mathbb{F}_p[x]$ and guarantees that x is a primitive element of $\mathbb{F}_{p^3}$. As such g are known to be sufficiently dense (in fact, they have density $\phi(p^3 - 1)/(3p^3)$, where ϕ is the Euler totient function), this can be carried out very quickly with a randomized algorithm; see [2]. As construction of the set S will take time polynomial in p anyway, it is also possible to carry out this search over all triples a, b and c. In either case, so long as fast modular exponentiation is used to compute the powers x^v, the construction can be carried out in time $p^3 \,\mathrm{poly}(\log p)$, as desired.

This construction can be applied as well for prime powers of the form $q = p^k$. The only new complication is that one must first construct the field $\mathbb{F}_q$, which can be accomplished using the same technique as described above: specifically, one chooses an irreducible polynomial $h(x) \in \mathbb{F}_p[x]$ of degree k and uses the set $\mathbb{F}_p[x]/(h(x))$ as a representation of $\mathbb{F}_q$, where addition is simply addition of polynomimals, and multiplication is given by polynomial multiplcation modulo the polynomial $h(x)$. The remainder of the construction proceeds as above.

The Value-of-Information in Matching with Queues

Longbo Huang
longbohuang@tsinghua.edu.cn
IIIS, Tsinghua University

ABSTRACT

We consider the problem of *optimal matching with queues* in dynamic systems and investigate the value-of-information. In such systems, the operators match tasks and resources stored in queues, with the objective of maximizing the system utility of the matching reward profile, minus the average matching cost. This problem appears in many practical systems and the main challenges are the no-underflow constraints, and the lack of matching-reward information and system dynamics statistics. We develop two online matching algorithms: Learning-aided Reward optimAl Matching (`LRAM`) and Dual-`LRAM` (`DRAM`) to effectively resolve both challenges. Both algorithms are equipped with a learning module for estimating the matching-reward information, while `DRAM` incorporates an additional module for learning the system dynamics. We show that both algorithms achieve an $O(\epsilon+\delta_r)$ close-to-optimal utility performance for any $\epsilon > 0$, while `DRAM` achieves a faster convergence speed and a better delay compared to `LRAM`, i.e., $O(\delta_z/\epsilon + \log(1/\epsilon)^2))$ delay and $O(\delta_z/\epsilon)$ convergence under `DRAM` compared to $O(1/\epsilon)$ delay and convergence under `LRAM` (δ_r and δ_z are maximum estimation errors for reward and system dynamics). Our results reveal that information of different system components can play very different roles in algorithm performance and provide a systematic way for designing joint learning-control algorithms for dynamic systems.

1. INTRODUCTION

Matching is a fundamental problem that appears in resource allocation in various systems across different areas. For instance, network switch scheduling [1], online advertising [2], crowdsourcing [3], ride sharing [4], cloud computing [5], and inventory control [6]. Hence, efficient matching algorithms are of great importance to system control.

In this paper, we study the problem of optimal matching with queues in a dynamic environment with unknown matching reward statistics. Specifically, we consider a system consists of a set of *task queues* and a set of *resource queues*, which store different types of workload and different types of resources that come into the system according to some random processes. At every time, the system operator decides how to match the resources to the pending workload. Each matching incurs a *cost* that depends on the resource allocated and random factors in the system, e.g., changing channel conditions in a downlink system, time-varying prices in inventory control, or fluctuating payment requirements in crowdsourcing. On the other hand, the matching also generates a *reward*, which is random with an unknown distribution determined by the amount of tasks resolved and the system condition. The objective is to design a matching strategy that carefully manages the resources and tasks, so as to achieve optimal system utility, which is a function of the achieved reward profile, subject to the constraint that all tasks are fulfilled timely.

This is a general problem and models the aforementioned application scenarios. However, it is very challenging to solve. First, the system utility is a function of the matching reward, which means that it is affected by when and how much resource is actually matched to the tasks and is only indirectly related to the traffic rates. This differs significantly from traditional flow utility optimization problems [7], [8], and requires both careful admission control to avoid instability and appropriate matching to achieve good utility. Second, since each matching action is rewarded based on the actual amount of tasks resolved, the matching scheme must ensure that there are nonzero tasks and nonzero resources in the queues, i.e., *no-underflow*. This constraint is complex and is mostly tackled with dynamic programming, which can have high computational complexity. Third, the system is dynamic and the statistics of system conditions and reward functions are unknown beforehand. This requires that the matching scheme can efficiently learn the sufficient statistics of the randomness and adapt to the changing environment.

In addition to resolving the above challenges, we also take one step further and try to investigate the *value-of-information* in such matching systems with queues, by explicitly considering the impact of information on algorithm performance. Existing works on stochastic system control either focus on systems with perfect a-prior information, e.g., [9], [10], or rely on stochastic approximation techniques that do not require such information, e.g., [11], [12]. While the proposed solutions are effective, they do not capture how information affects algorithm design and performance, and do not provide interfaces for integrating the fast-developing "data science" tools, e.g., data collecting methods and machine learning algorithms, [13], [14], into system control.

MobiHoc'15, June 22–25, 2015, Hangzhou, China.

http://dx.doi.org/10.1145/2746285.2746316.

To provide a rigorous quantification of the value of information, we first introduce an abstract notion of a *learning module*, which represents a general information learning algorithm and features a learning accuracy level δ (maximum error), a learning time T_δ, and the probability of learning accuracy guarantee P_δ. We then design two online matching algorithms: Learning-aided Reward optimAl Matching (LRAM) and Dual-LRAM (DRAM). LRAM utilizes a single $(T_{\delta_r}, \delta_r, P_{\delta_r})$ learning module for estimating the reward statistics and achieves an $O(\epsilon + \delta_r)$ system utility, for any $\epsilon > 0$, while ensuring an $O(1/\epsilon)$ delay bound and an $O(1/\epsilon)$ algorithm convergence time, defined to be the time taken for the algorithm to enter the optimal control state. DRAM incorporates an additional $(T_{\delta_z}, \delta_z, P_{\delta_z})$ learning module for the random system state distribution and guarantees a similar $O(\epsilon + \delta_r)$ system utility. Moreover, DRAM is able to achieve an $O(\delta_z/\epsilon + \log(1/\epsilon)^2)$ delay bound and an $O(\delta_z/\epsilon)$ algorithm convergence time, which can be significantly faster compared to LRAM.

Our results reveal an interesting fact that the reward information largely determines the utility performance, while the system dynamics information greatly affects delay and algorithm convergence. This indicates that *information of different system components can have different impacts on algorithm performance, and may require different learning power for achieving a desired goal.* Closest to our paper is the recent work [15], which considers joint learning and control. Our framework allows much more general learning methods and resolves the no-underflow constraints. We also quantify the values of different system information.

We summarize the main contributions as follows:

1. We propose a matching queueing system model, which can model general resource-task matching problems in stochastic systems. To explicitly quantify the value of information in such systems, we introduce an abstract notion of a $(T_\delta, \delta, P_\delta)$-*learning module* that captures key characteristics of general learning algorithms and provides interfaces for bringing the information learning aspect into system control.
2. We design two learning-aided matching algorithms LRAM and DRAM. We show that with a single $(T_{\delta_r}, \delta_r, P_{\delta_r})$-module for learning reward statistics, LRAM achieves an $O(\epsilon+\delta_r)$ utility, while ensuring an $O(1/\epsilon)$ delay bound and an $O(1/\epsilon)$ algorithm convergence time. DRAM adopts an additional $(T_{\delta_z}, \delta_z, P_{\delta_z})$-module for learning the system state distribution, and guarantees a similar $O(\epsilon + \delta_r)$ system utility, while achieving an $O(\delta_z/\epsilon+\log(1/\epsilon)^2)$ delay and an $O(\delta_z/\epsilon)$ convergence time. We also construct two $(O(1/\epsilon^c), O(\epsilon^{c/2}), 1-O(\epsilon^{\log(1/\epsilon)}))$ online learning modules based on sampling ($c > 0$). Combining them with DRAM, one achieves a fast $O(1/\epsilon^{1-c/2}+1/\epsilon^c)$ convergence time with $c < 1$ (existing algorithms require $\Theta(1/\epsilon)$).
3. Our algorithm design approach provides a low-complexity way to tackle multiple simultaneous no-underflow constraints in systems and jointly optimize utilities that are not defined on flow rates. The development of DRAM also demonstrates how general learning algorithms can be combined with queue-based control (stochastic approximation) to achieve superior delay performance and accelerate algorithm convergence speed.

The rest of the paper is organized as follows. We first list a few motivating examples in Section 2. We then present the matching system model in Section 3. The algorithm design approach and the two algorithms LRAM and DRAM are presented in Section 4. Analysis is carried out in Section 5 and simulation results are presented in Section 6. We then conclude the paper in Section 7.

2. MOTIVATING EXAMPLES

Crowdsourcing: In a crowdsourcing application, e.g., crowdsourcing query search [3] or ride-sharing [4], tasks of different types (task) arrive at the server and are assigned to workers (resource). The workers then carry out the tasks. Depending on the workers' qualifications, the types of jobs, and the instantaneous system condition (state), e.g., whether a query requestor is in a hurry due to weather, the requestors receives certain reward, e.g., satisfaction, and the workers receive payments. The objective of the system is to design a matching scheme, so as to maximize the system utility, which is a function of the achieved requestor reward profile.

Energy Harvesting Networks: In an energy harvesting network, e.g., [16], [17], nodes are responsible for transmitting data (task) and can harvest energy (resource) from the environment. At every time, each node decides how much energy to allocate for transmission and determines traffic scheduling. Depending on the time-varying channel condition (state), the amount of energy enables certain processing results. The objective is to design a joint energy management and scheduling algorithm, so as to maximize traffic utility and ensure that no energy outage happens.

Online Advertisement: In an online advertising system, [2], [18], advertisers deposit money (task) into their accounts at the advertising platform. Queries (resource) for different keywords arrive in the system and the server decides which advertiser's ads to show, based on their relevance to the keywords and the available budget of the advertisers. Depending on the chosen ad and the user's condition (state), e.g., location or mood, a business transaction may take place. The goal of the system is to design an ad matching scheme, so as to maximize the system's utility, which is a function of the average income profile from advertisers.

Cloud Computing: In a cloud computing platform, e.g., [5], computing resources (resource), e.g., CPU, memory, are assigned to virtual machine instances (task) for processing arriving job requests. The quality of experience of a requestor depends on the job completion quality, which is affected by system conditions such as background task level (state) and the user status. The objective here is to design a resource allocation policy, such that the overall quality of service is maximized.

In all these examples, the underlying problem is indeed matching with queues. Below, we present the general model.

3. SYSTEM MODEL

We consider a discrete-time system shown in Fig. 1. In this system, there are two sets of queues, *task queues* and *resource queues*, and a central server (called operator below), which coordinates resource allocation and scheduling in the system. Time is divided into unit-size slots, i.e., $t \in \{0, 1, ...\}$.

3.1 Tasks and Resources

The task queues store jobs that come into the system and are waiting to be served by the server. We assume there

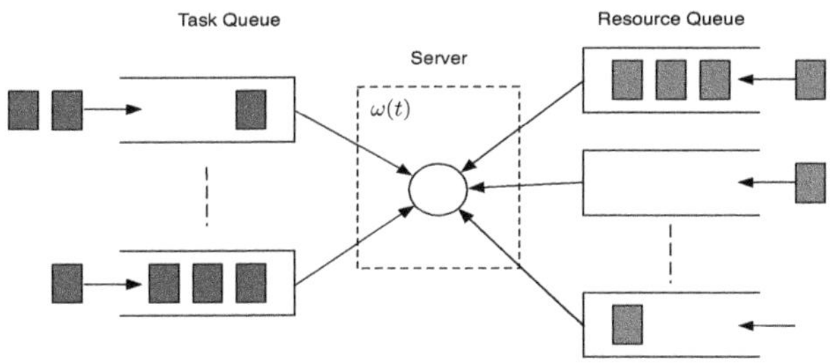

Figure 1: The matching queueing system.

are N types of tasks and denote the set of task queues by $\mathcal{Q} = \{\mathcal{Q}_1, ..., \mathcal{Q}_N\}$. We use $A_n(t)$ to denote the amount of new tasks arrivaling at $\mathcal{Q}_n$ at time t and assume that $0 \leq A_n(t) \leq A_{\max}$. We then define the arrival vector $\boldsymbol{A}(t) = (A_1(t), ..., A_N(t))$. In many systems, arrivals to the system may not always all be admitted due to congestion control, e.g., when all servers are busy. We model this by using $0 \leq R_n(t) \leq A_n(t)$ to denote the actual admitted traffic to $\mathcal{Q}_n$ at time t. We then use $Q_n(t)$ to denote the amount of tasks stored at $\mathcal{Q}_n$ at time t and denote $\boldsymbol{Q}(t) = (Q_1(t), ..., Q_N(t))$ the task queue vector.

The resource queues, on the other hand, hold the resources the system collects over time. There are M types of system resources and we denote the resource queues by $\mathcal{H} = \{\mathcal{H}_1, ..., \mathcal{H}_M\}$. We similarly let $e_m(t)$ be the amount of new resource arriving at $\mathcal{H}_m$ with $0 \leq e_m(t) \leq h_{\max}$. We also use $H_m(t)$ to denote the amount of resource m the system current holds and denote $\boldsymbol{H}(t) = (H_1(t), ..., H_M(t))$ the resource queue vector.

In many systems, it is feasible (and sometimes necessary) to control the amount of resources in the system, e.g., to avoid too many workers waiting in crowdsourcing. We model this decision by using $h_m(t) \in [0, e_m(t)]$ to denote the actual amount of type m resource admitted. For now, it is also convenient to temporarily assume that the queues are all of unlimited sizes. We will later show that our algorithms ensure that finite buffer sizes are sufficient.

3.2 System State and Resource allocation

We assume that the system has a time-varying condition, e.g., the channel conditions in a downlink system, or the expected happiness measures of human users in a crowdsourcing system. We call this condition the *system state* and model it by a random state variable $\omega(t)$. Note that $\omega(t)$ represents the *aggregate* system condition.

Denote $\boldsymbol{z}(t) = (\boldsymbol{A}(t), \boldsymbol{e}(t), \omega(t))$. In this paper, we assume that $\boldsymbol{z}(t)$ is i.i.d. and takes values in $\mathcal{Z} = \{\boldsymbol{z}_1, ..., \boldsymbol{z}_K\}$. We then denote $\pi_k = \Pr\{\boldsymbol{z}(t) = \boldsymbol{z}_k\}$. Note that this allows arbitrary dependency among $\boldsymbol{A}(t)$, $\boldsymbol{e}(t)$, and $\omega(t)$.

At every time t, the system operator determines the amount of resource to allocate to serving each queue. We denote this decision by a *matching matrix* $\boldsymbol{b}(t) = (b_{mn}(t), m, n)$, where $b_{mn}(t)$ denotes the type m resource allocated to queue n. When $\boldsymbol{z}(t) = \boldsymbol{z}_k$, $\boldsymbol{b}(t)$ takes values from a finite discrete set $\mathcal{B}_k \subset \mathbb{R}_+^N$.[1] We define $b_{\max} \triangleq \max_{\boldsymbol{b} \in \mathcal{B}_k, k} \|\boldsymbol{b}\|_\infty$ the maximum amount of resource allocated to any queue at any time. It is clear that at any time t, we must have:

$$\sum_n b_{mn}(t) \leq H_m(t), \quad \forall m. \tag{1}$$

This is because one cannot spent more resource than what is available. In the following, we call (1) the *no-underflow* constraint. Depending on the system state and the resource allocation decision, each task queue gets a service rate $\mu_n(t) \triangleq \mu_n(\boldsymbol{z}(t), \boldsymbol{b}(t))$. We assume $\mu_n(\boldsymbol{z}(t), \boldsymbol{b}(t)) \in [0, \mu_{\max}]$ for all $\boldsymbol{z}(t)$ and $\boldsymbol{b}(t)$ and that $\{\mu_n(\boldsymbol{z}(t), \boldsymbol{b}(t))\}_{n \in \mathcal{N}}$ are known to the operator. Also, they satisfy that $\mu_n(\boldsymbol{z}(t), \boldsymbol{0}) = 0$ for all $\boldsymbol{z}(t)$, and if $\mu_n(\boldsymbol{z}(t), \boldsymbol{b}) > 0$, then

$$\mu_n(\boldsymbol{z}(t), \boldsymbol{b}) \geq \beta_\mu^l \min_{m: b_{mn} > 0} b_{mn}, \tag{2}$$

for some $\beta_\mu^l > 0$. Moreover, if two vectors $\boldsymbol{b}$ and $\boldsymbol{b}'$ are such that $\boldsymbol{b}'$ is obtained by setting b_{mn} in $\boldsymbol{b}$ to zero, then,

$$\mu_n(\boldsymbol{z}, \boldsymbol{b}) \leq \mu_n(\boldsymbol{z}, \boldsymbol{b}') + \beta_\mu^u b_{mn}, \forall n. \tag{3}$$

Note that (2) and (3) are not restrictive. They simply require that nonzero resource is needed for getting a positive service rate, and that a positive rate is upper and lower bounded by linear functions of the resources allocated.

3.3 Matching Cost and Reward

In every time slot, due to resource expenditure, there is a *matching cost* associated with the resource allocation decision. We model this by denoting $c(t) = c(\boldsymbol{z}(t), \boldsymbol{b}(t))$ the cost for choosing the resource vector $\boldsymbol{b}(t)$. This cost can represent, e.g., cost for purchasing raw materials in inventory control, or payments to workers in a crowdsourcing application. One example is $c(\boldsymbol{z}(t), \boldsymbol{b}(t)) = \sum_{nm} c_m(\boldsymbol{z}(t)) b_{nm}(t)$, where $c_m(\boldsymbol{z}(t))$ denotes the per-unit resource price for type m resource under state $\boldsymbol{z}(t)$. We assume that $c(\boldsymbol{z}(t), \boldsymbol{b}(t)) \in [0, c_{\max}]$ for all time and it is known to the system operator. Also, if $\boldsymbol{0} \preceq \boldsymbol{b}_1 \preceq \boldsymbol{b}_2$ (entrywise-less), when $c(\boldsymbol{z}(t), \boldsymbol{b}_1) \leq c(\boldsymbol{z}(t), \boldsymbol{b}_2)$.

Every time a matching is completed, the operator collects a *matching reward*, e.g., a customer conversion due to an ad, or user satisfaction due to job completion. We model this by denoting the reward collected at time t from type n tasks by $\kappa_n(t)$. We assume that $\kappa_n(t) \in [0, r_{\max}]$ is an i.i.d. random variable given $\boldsymbol{z}(t)$ and $\boldsymbol{b}(t)$, and its mean is determined by the reward function $r_n(\boldsymbol{z}(t), \tilde{\mu}_n(t)) \triangleq \mathbb{E}\{\kappa_n(t) \mid \boldsymbol{z}(t), \boldsymbol{b}(t), \boldsymbol{Q}(t)\}$, where $\tilde{\mu}_n(t) = \min[Q_n(t), \mu_n(t)]$ denotes the *actual* amount of tasks completed. We assume that $r_n(\boldsymbol{z}(t), \tilde{\mu}_n(t))$ satisfies:

$$r_n(\boldsymbol{z}(t), \mu) \leq r_n(\boldsymbol{z}(t), \mu'), \text{ if } \mu \leq \mu', \tag{4}$$

and denote $\boldsymbol{r} = \{r_n(\boldsymbol{z}, \mu_n(\boldsymbol{z}, \boldsymbol{b}_z)), \boldsymbol{z} \in \mathcal{Z}, \boldsymbol{b}_z \in \mathcal{B}_{\boldsymbol{z}}\}$ the reward matrix. Since each $\mathcal{B}_{\boldsymbol{z}}$ is finite, $\boldsymbol{r}$ is also finite.

Different from existing works, e.g., [18], [19], we do not assume any prior knowledge of the functions $r(\boldsymbol{z}(t), \mu)$.[2] This is quite common in practice. For example, in crowdsourcing applications, it is often unknown a-prior how qualified a worker is for a certain type of tasks; or in online advertising, one often does not know the conversion probabilities beforehand.

[1] This assumption is made to simplify the learning algorithm description (Section 4.2). Our results can likely be extended to the case when $\{\mathcal{B}_k, k\}$ are general compact sets in $\mathbb{R}_+^N$.

[2] This is different from the $\boldsymbol{\mu}$ functions, which measure how much resources are spent and can typically be observed by the system controller.

3.4 Queueing

From the above, we see that the queue vectors $\boldsymbol{Q}(t)$ and $\boldsymbol{H}(t)$ evolve according to:

$$Q_n(t+1) = \max[Q_n(t) - \mu_n(t), 0] + R_n(t), \forall n, \quad (5)$$
$$H_m(t+1) = H_m(t) - \sum_n b_{mn}(t) + h_m(t), \forall m. \quad (6)$$

Notice that there is no $\max[\cdot,\cdot]$ operator in (6). This is due to the no-underflow constraint (1). In our paper, we say that a queue vector process $\boldsymbol{x}(t) \in \mathbb{R}_+^d$ is stable if it satisfies: [3]

$$x_{\text{av}} \triangleq \lim_{t\to\infty} \frac{1}{t} \sum_{\tau=0}^{t} \sum_{n=1}^{d} \mathbb{E}\{x_n(\tau)\} < \infty. \quad (7)$$

3.5 Utility Optimization

The system's utility is determined by a function of the average matching reward profile. Specifically, define $\overline{r}_n \triangleq \lim_{t\to\infty} \frac{1}{t} \sum_{\tau=0}^{t-1} \mathbb{E}\{r_n(\tau)\}$. The system utility is given by:

$$U_{\text{total}}(\overline{\boldsymbol{r}}) \triangleq \sum_n U_n(\overline{r}_n). \quad (8)$$

Here each $U_n(r)$ is an increasing concave function with $U_n(0) = 0$ and $U'(0) < \infty$. We denote $\beta \triangleq \max_{n,r}(U_n(r))'$ the maximum first derivative of the utility functions. We also define the following system cost due to resource expenditure:

$$C_{\text{total}} \triangleq \lim_{t\to\infty} \frac{1}{t} \sum_{\tau=0}^{t-1} \mathbb{E}\{c(\tau)\}. \quad (9)$$

We say that a matching algorithm Π is feasible if for all time t, it selects $0 \preceq \boldsymbol{R}(t) \preceq \boldsymbol{A}(t)$, $0 \preceq \boldsymbol{h}(t) \preceq \boldsymbol{e}(t)$, and $\boldsymbol{b}(t) \in \mathcal{B}_{\boldsymbol{z}(t)}$, and it ensures constraint (1) for all time. Our objective is to design a feasible policy Π, so as to:

$$\max: \quad f_{\text{av}} \triangleq U_{\text{total}}(\overline{\boldsymbol{r}}) - C_{\text{total}} \quad (10)$$
$$\text{s.t.} \quad Q_{\text{av}} < \infty, H_{\text{av}} < \infty. \quad (11)$$

We denote the optimal solution value as f_{av}^*. Here the queue stability constraints are to ensure that the tasks and resources do not stay in the queue forever. This is important in many cases. For instance, in an energy harvesting network, it is important to ensure timely packet delivery, or in a crowdsourcing system, it is desirable to keep the worker waiting time short.

3.6 Discussion on the Model

Due to the general matching reward function, our problem is different from a flow utility maximization problem, e.g., [7], which is a special case when $r_n(t) = \tilde{\mu}_n(t)$. By tuning the parameters of the model, our model can model all the examples in Section 2. For example, by choosing $U_{\text{total}} = \sum_n \alpha_n \overline{r}_n$, the system models the revenue maximziation problem in online advertisement systems. By choosing $\mu_n(t) = 1_{[b_1(t) > b_1^{\min}]} 1_{[b_2(t) > b_2^{\min}]}$, our model can represent a cloud computing system, where a computing task requires two types of resources.

Problem (10) is very challenging. First of all, the no-underflow constraint (1) requires a very careful selection of control actions, because actions in a slot can affect action feasibility in later slots. Problems of this kind are often tackled with dynamic programming, whose computational complexity can be extremely high when the action space is large. Secondly, the reward function $r_n(\boldsymbol{z}(t), \tilde{\mu}_n(t))$ is unknown and is dependent on $\boldsymbol{Q}_n(t)$. This makes the problem very different from existing utility maximization works, e.g., [7], [8]. Thirdly, due to the more and more stringent user requirements on service quality, it is more desirable to ensure small queueing delay.

[3]In this paper, we assume that all limits exist with probability 1. Our results can be extended to more general cases with lim inf or lim sup arguments.

4. OPTIMAL MATCHING

In this section, we present our matching algorithms. We will first present an ideal algorithm, which assumes full knowledge of the reward functions $r_n(\boldsymbol{z}(t), \mu)$ and will serve as a basic building block. Even in this case, we will see that the problem is highly nontrivial due to the existence of the no-underflow constraint (1) and the dependency of $r_n(t)$ on $\boldsymbol{Q}(t)$.

4.1 With Full Reward Information

To start, we first introduce an auxiliary variable $\gamma_n(t) \in [0, r_{\max}]$ and create for each n a *deficit queue* $d_n(t)$ that evolves as follows:

$$d_n(t+1) = \max[d_n(t) - \kappa_n(t), 0] + \gamma_n(t), \quad (12)$$

with $\boldsymbol{d}(0) = \boldsymbol{0}$. Note that the input into $d_n(t)$ is $\kappa_n(t)$ instead of $r_n(t)$. The deficit queue $d_n(t)$ measures how much the actual reward profile is currently lagging behind the target value (due to randomness).

Then, we denote $f(t) \triangleq \sum_n U_n(\gamma_n(t)) - c(t)$ the instantaneous system utility minus cost and denote $\boldsymbol{y}(t) \triangleq (\boldsymbol{Q}(t), \boldsymbol{H}(t), \boldsymbol{d}(t))$. We also define a Lyapunov function as follows:

$$L(t) = \frac{1}{2}\|\boldsymbol{Q}(t) - \boldsymbol{\theta}_1\|^2 + \frac{1}{2}\|\boldsymbol{H}(t) - \boldsymbol{\theta}_2\|^2 + \frac{1}{2}\|\boldsymbol{d}(t)\|^2, \quad (13)$$

where $\|\cdot\|$ is the euclidean norm and $\boldsymbol{\theta}_1 = \theta_1 \cdot \boldsymbol{1}^N$ and $\boldsymbol{\theta}_2 = \theta_2 \cdot \boldsymbol{1}^M$ with $\boldsymbol{1}^k \in \mathbb{R}^k$ being the vector with all components being 1, and θ_1 and θ_2 are constants that will be specified later. We define the one-slot utility-based conditional Lyapunov drift $\Delta_V(t) \triangleq \mathbb{E}\{L(t+1) - L(t) - Vf(t) \mid \boldsymbol{y}(t)\}$. Using the queueing dynamics (5), (6), and (12), we obtain the following lemma, in which $V \geq 1$ is a tunable parameter introduced for controlling the tradeoff between system utility and service delay (explained later).

Lemma 1. *Under any feasible policy, we have:*

$$\begin{aligned}\Delta_V(t) \leq\ & G - V \sum_n \mathbb{E}\{U_n(\gamma_n(t)) - d_n(t)\gamma_n(t) \mid \boldsymbol{y}(t)\} \quad (14)\\ & + \sum_n (Q_n(t) - \theta_1)\mathbb{E}\{R_n(t) \mid \boldsymbol{y}(t)\}\\ & + \sum_m (H_m(t) - \theta_2)\mathbb{E}\{h_m(t) \mid \boldsymbol{y}(t)\}\\ & + \mathbb{E}\{Vc(t) - \sum_m (H_m(t) - \theta_2) \sum_n b_{mn}(t)\\ & - \sum_n (Q_n(t) - \theta_1)\mu_n(t) - \sum_n d_n(t) r_n(t) \mid \boldsymbol{y}(t)\}.\end{aligned}$$

Here $G \triangleq N(A_{\max}^2 + \mu_{\max}^2 + 2r_{\max}^2) + Mh_{\max}^2 + MN^2 b_{\max}^2$ does not depend on V, and the expectations are taken over the randomness in the system as well as in the policy. $\diamond$

PROOF. See Appendix A. □

We now construct our algorithm by minimizing the right-hand-side (RHS) of the drift (14).

Reward optimAl Matching (RAM): At every time t, observe $\boldsymbol{z}(t)$ and $\boldsymbol{y}(t)$. Do:

1. **Quota:** For each n, choose $\gamma_n(t)$ by solving:

$$\max: \ VU_n(\gamma_n(t)) - d_n(t)\gamma_n(t), \ \text{s.t. } 0 \le \gamma_n(t) \le r_{\max}. \quad (15)$$

2. **Admission:** For each n, if $Q_n(t) < \theta_1$, let $R_n(t) = A_n(t)$; otherwise $R_n(t) = 0$. Similarly, for each m, if $H_m(t) < \theta_2$, let $h_m(t) = e_m(t)$; otherwise $h_m(t) = 0$.
3. **Resource:** Choose the resource allocation vector $\boldsymbol{b}(t)$ by solving:

$$\begin{aligned}\min: \quad & \Psi_r(\boldsymbol{b}) \triangleq Vc(\boldsymbol{z}, \boldsymbol{b}) - \sum_m (H_m(t) - \theta_2) \sum_n b_{mn} \quad (16)\\ & - \sum_n (Q_n(t) - \theta_1)\mu_n(\boldsymbol{z}(t), \boldsymbol{b})\\ & - \sum_n d_n(t) r_n(\boldsymbol{z}(t), \mu_n(\boldsymbol{z}(t), \boldsymbol{b}))\\ \text{s.t.} \quad & \boldsymbol{b} \in \mathcal{B}_{\boldsymbol{z}(t)}, \text{Constraint (1)} \quad (17)\end{aligned}$$

4. **Queueing:** Update $\boldsymbol{Q}(t)$, $\boldsymbol{H}(t)$, and $\boldsymbol{d}(t)$, according to (5), (6), and (12), respectively. ◇

Note that in (16) we have used $r_n(\boldsymbol{z}(t), \mu_n(t))$ instead of $r_n(\boldsymbol{z}(t), \tilde{\mu}_n(t))$. We will see in our later analysis that our algorithm automatically guarantees $\tilde{\mu}_n(t) = \mu_n(t)$. This is very useful, for otherwise the algorithm performance will be very hard to analyze. We also emphasize here that the introduction of θ_1 and θ_2 are important. It can be seen in the admission step here that if $\theta_1 = \theta_2 = 0$, i.e., without θ_1 and θ_2, no task or resource will be admitted at the first place and the algorithm will not even proceed!

4.2 With Reward Information Learning

Here we consider the case when one does not have full reward information and provide an algorithm that can integrate general learning methods for estimating $\boldsymbol{r}$.

To also investigate the impact of learning on algorithm design and performance, we first define learning capability. Specifically, for any general matrix $\boldsymbol{W}$ and a learning algorithm Γ that outputs an estimation $\hat{\boldsymbol{W}}$, we denote its maximum estimation error by:

$$\delta_w \triangleq \|\hat{\boldsymbol{W}} - \boldsymbol{W}\|_{\max}, \quad (18)$$

where $\|\boldsymbol{x}\|_{\max} \triangleq \max_{ij} |x_{ij}|$. Then, the formal definition of a *learning module* is as follows.

Definition 1. *An algorithm Γ is called a $(T_\delta, P_\delta, \delta)$-learning module, if (i) it completes learning in T_δ time, (ii) it guarantees that $Pr\{\delta_w < \delta\} \ge P_\delta$, and (iii) for any $T \ge 0$, P_δ does not decrease if the algorithm is run for $T_\delta + T$ time.* ◇

Here T_δ can be both random or deterministic depending on the termination rules. This definition is general and captures key features of learning algorithms. With this definition, having perfect knowledge at the beginning can be viewed as having an $(0, 1, 0)$-learning module.

We now present an optimal matching algorithm for general systems that do not possess perfect knowledge of $\boldsymbol{r}$ and need to rely on some learning algorithms for estimation. In the algorithm, we use $\beta_{\hat{r}}$ to denote the maximum "derivative" of the estimated $\hat{\boldsymbol{r}}$ with respect to any b_{mn}. Specifically, we assume that if $\boldsymbol{b}$ and $\boldsymbol{b}'$ are such that $\boldsymbol{b}'$ is obtained by setting one b_{mn} in $\boldsymbol{b}$ to zero. Then,

$$\hat{r}_n(\boldsymbol{z}, \mu_n(\boldsymbol{z}, \boldsymbol{b})) \ \le \ \hat{r}_n(\boldsymbol{z}, \mu_n(\boldsymbol{z}, \boldsymbol{b}')) + \beta_{\hat{r}} b_{mn}, \forall n. \quad (19)$$

Since both $\mathcal{Z}$ and $\{\mathcal{B}_{\boldsymbol{z}}\}$ are finite, we see that $\beta_{\hat{r}}$ exists and is $\Theta(1)$ (possibly depends on $\hat{\boldsymbol{r}}$).

Learning-aided Reward OptimAl Matching (LRAM):

1. (**Learning**) Apply any $(T_{\delta_r}, P_{\delta_r}, \delta_r)$-learning module Γ_r. Terminate at $t = T_{\delta_r}$ and output $\hat{\boldsymbol{r}}$.
2. (**Matching**) Set $\boldsymbol{Q}(T_{\delta_r}+1) = 0$, $\boldsymbol{H}(T_{\delta_r}+1) = 0$, and $\boldsymbol{d}(T_{\delta_r}+1) = 0$. Choose θ_1 and θ_2 according to:

$$\begin{aligned}\theta_1 &= (h_{\max} + (V\beta + r_{\max})\beta_{\hat{r}})/\beta_\mu^l + \mu_{\max} \quad (20)\\ \theta_2 &= (V\beta + r_{\max})\beta_{\hat{r}} + r_{\max}\beta_\mu^u + Nb_{\max}. \quad (21)\end{aligned}$$

Run RAM with $\hat{\boldsymbol{r}}$. ◇

In LRAM, we explicitly separate the algorithm into two disjoint phases. This is chosen to facilitate presentation and analysis. Doing so also does not change the order of the overall algorithm convergence time and performance. We can also transform LRAM and DRAM below into continuous-learning versions, e.g., [15], and update estimations from time to time, e.g., using sliding-window estimation or frame-based estimation. It is also worth noting that θ_1 and θ_2 can be computed beforehand easily. This is a feature useful for implementation.

4.3 With System State Information Learning

In the previous section, we describe how the estimated reward information $\hat{\boldsymbol{r}}$ can be naturally integrated into a matching algorithm. Here we consider the case when a learning module is also applied to learning the statistics of the system state $\boldsymbol{z}(t)$. Our result here generalizes the dual-learning approach proposed in [15] to handle underflow and to allow general learning methods.

To start, we define the following optimization problem:

$$\begin{aligned}\max: \quad & \Phi \triangleq V[\sum_n U_n(\gamma_n) - Cost] \quad (22)\\ \text{s.t.} \quad & \gamma_n \le r_n \triangleq \sum_k \pi_k r_n(\boldsymbol{z}_k, \mu_n(\boldsymbol{z}_k, \boldsymbol{b}^k)) \quad (23)\\ & Cost \triangleq \sum_k \pi_k c(\boldsymbol{z}_k, \boldsymbol{b}^k) \quad (24)\\ & \sum_k \pi_k R_n^k = \sum_k \pi_k \mu_n(\boldsymbol{z}_k, \boldsymbol{b}^k), \forall n \quad (25)\\ & \sum_k \pi_k \sum_n b_{mn}^k = \sum_k \pi_k h_m^k, \forall m \quad (26)\\ & 0 \le \gamma_n \le r_{\max}, \boldsymbol{b}^k \in \mathcal{B}_k \quad (27)\\ & 0 \preceq \boldsymbol{R}^k \preceq \boldsymbol{A}^k, 0 \preceq \boldsymbol{h}^k \preceq \boldsymbol{e}^k. \quad (28)\end{aligned}$$

Problem (22) can intuitively be viewed as a way to solve our matching problem. The equalities in (25) and (26) are due to fact that only tasks that are actually served generate reward and the no-underflow constraint (1). However, a scheme obtained by solving (22) may not be implementable due to (i) it ignores the no-underflow constraint, and (ii) it assumes that all resources allocated are fully utilized, i.e., using $\mu_n(z_k, \boldsymbol{b}^k)$ in (23). We will also see later that, it requires a much larger learning time for such a scheme to have the right statistics for achieving a performance comparable to ours.

We now obtain the dual problem for (22) as follows.

$$\min: \quad g(\boldsymbol{\alpha}^d, \boldsymbol{\alpha}^q, \boldsymbol{\alpha}^h) \text{ s.t. } \boldsymbol{\alpha}^d \succeq \mathbf{0}, \boldsymbol{\alpha}^q \in \mathbb{R}^N, \boldsymbol{\alpha}^h \in \mathbb{R}^M, \quad (29)$$

where $g(\boldsymbol{\alpha}^d, \boldsymbol{\alpha}^q, \boldsymbol{\alpha}^h) = \sum_k \pi_k g_k(\boldsymbol{\alpha}^d, \boldsymbol{\alpha}^q, \boldsymbol{\alpha}^h)$ is the dual function, and $g_k(\boldsymbol{\alpha}^d, \boldsymbol{\alpha}^q, \boldsymbol{\alpha}^h)$ is defined as:

$$g_k(\boldsymbol{\alpha}^d, \boldsymbol{\alpha}^q, \boldsymbol{\alpha}^h) = \sup_{\boldsymbol{R},\boldsymbol{\gamma},\boldsymbol{b},\boldsymbol{h}} \Big\{ V[\sum_n U_n(\gamma_n) - Cost] \quad (30)$$
$$- \sum_n \alpha_n^d [r_n(\boldsymbol{z}_k, \mu_n(z_k, \boldsymbol{b})) - \gamma_n]$$
$$- \sum_n \alpha_n^q [R_n - \mu_n(\boldsymbol{z}_k, \boldsymbol{b})] - \sum_m \alpha_m^h [\sum_n b_{mn} - h_n] \Big\}.$$

Note that $g_k(\boldsymbol{\alpha}^d, \boldsymbol{\alpha}^q, \boldsymbol{\alpha}^h)$ is indeed the dual function for state $\boldsymbol{z}_k$. With (29), we now present our algorithm, which integrates system state information learning into control.

<u>Dual learning-aided Reward optimAl Matching (DRAM):</u>

1. (**Learning**) Apply any $(T_{\delta_r}, P_{\delta_r}, \delta_r)$-learning module Γ_r for $\boldsymbol{r}$ and any $(T_{\delta_z}, P_{\delta_z}, \delta_z)$-learning module Γ_z for $\boldsymbol{z}$. Terminate at $T_L = \max(T_{\delta_r}, T_{\delta_z})$ and output $\hat{\boldsymbol{r}}$ and $\hat{\boldsymbol{\pi}}$. Choose θ_1 and θ_2 according to:
$$\theta_1 = (h_{\max} + (V\beta + r_{\max})\beta_{\hat{r}})/\beta_\mu^l + \mu_{\max} \quad (31)$$
$$\theta_2 = (V\beta + r_{\max})\beta_{\hat{r}} + r_{\max}\beta_\mu^u + N b_{\max}. \quad (32)$$

2. (**Dual learning**) Solve the *empirical dual problem*:
$$\min: \quad \sum_k \hat{\pi}_k \hat{g}_k(\boldsymbol{\alpha}^d, \boldsymbol{\alpha}^q - \boldsymbol{\theta}_1, \boldsymbol{\alpha}^h - \boldsymbol{\theta}_2) \quad (33)$$
$$\text{s.t.} \quad \boldsymbol{\alpha}^d \succeq \mathbf{0}, \boldsymbol{\alpha}^q \in \mathbb{R}^N, \boldsymbol{\alpha}^h \in \mathbb{R}^M.$$
Here $\hat{g}_k(\boldsymbol{\alpha}^d, \boldsymbol{\alpha}^q - \boldsymbol{\theta}_1, \boldsymbol{\alpha}^h - \boldsymbol{\theta}_2)$ is defined in (30) with $\hat{\boldsymbol{r}}$. Denote the optimal solution as $\hat{\boldsymbol{\alpha}}^* = (\hat{\boldsymbol{\alpha}}^{d*}, \hat{\boldsymbol{\alpha}}^{q*}, \hat{\boldsymbol{\alpha}}^{h*})$.

3. (**Matching**) Set $\boldsymbol{Q}(T_L + 1) = 0$, $\boldsymbol{H}(T_L + 1) = 0$, and $\boldsymbol{d}(T_L + 1) = 0$. For all $t \geq T_L + 1$, define:
$$\hat{\boldsymbol{Q}}(t) = \boldsymbol{Q}(t) + \hat{\boldsymbol{\alpha}}^{q*} - \boldsymbol{\zeta}_N \quad (34)$$
$$\hat{\boldsymbol{H}}(t) = \boldsymbol{H}(t) + \hat{\boldsymbol{\alpha}}^{h*} - \boldsymbol{\zeta}_M \quad (35)$$
$$\hat{\boldsymbol{d}}(t) = \boldsymbol{d}(t) + \hat{\boldsymbol{\alpha}}^{d*} - \boldsymbol{\zeta}_N. \quad (36)$$
where $\boldsymbol{\zeta}_k$ is a vector in $\mathbb{R}^k$ with all elements being $\zeta \triangleq 2\max(\delta_z V \log(V)^2, \log(V)^2)$. Run RAM with $\hat{\boldsymbol{r}}$, $\hat{\boldsymbol{Q}}(t)$, $\hat{\boldsymbol{H}}(t)$, and $\hat{\boldsymbol{d}}(t)$. If the resulting $\boldsymbol{b}(t)$ from (16) violates (1) for some m, change $\{b_{mn}(t)\}_{n\in\mathcal{N}}$ to $\{\tilde{b}_{mn}(t)\}_{n\in\mathcal{N}}$ with $\sum_n \tilde{b}_{mn}(t) = h_m(t)$ and drop $\mu_n(\boldsymbol{z}(t), \boldsymbol{b}(t))$ tasks from each n that has $b_{mn}(t) > 0$. $\diamond$ [4]

DRAM first utilizes learning to obtain an empirical distribution, which is usually crude but fast at the beginning. Then, it transforms to queue-based control (or more generally, stochastic approximation), by obtaining an empirical optimal multiplier via dual learning. It then starts from the empirical multiplier and rely on queue-based control to learn the true optimal operation point. The procedure is shown in Fig. 2. This combination avoids the slow convergence regime of statistical learning and the slow start of stochastic approximation, and algorithms so developed can achieve much faster convergence and superior delay.

[4]In actual implementation, one can still serve the tasks with the actual allocated resource.

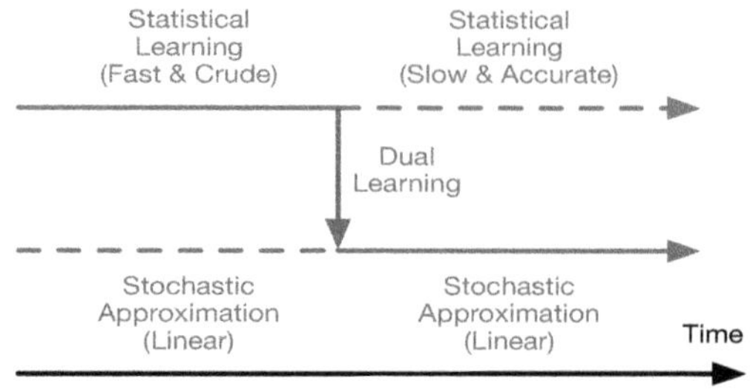

Figure 2: DRAM combines the fast regime of statistical learning and the smoothness of queue-based control (more generally, stochastic approximation).

Also note here that the dropping step is introduced to ensure zero underflow, by giving up the service rates and reward at that particular slot. We will see in later analysis and simulation that such an event almost never happens and hence does not affect performance.

4.4 Sampling-based Learning Module

Here we describe two sampling-based learning modules for estimating $\boldsymbol{r}$ and $\boldsymbol{\pi}$. We first describe a threshold-based sampling module for estimating $\boldsymbol{r}$. In the module, we use $s(\boldsymbol{z}, \boldsymbol{b}, t)$ to denote the number of times the pair $(\boldsymbol{z}, \boldsymbol{b})$ is sampled, i.e., adopt $\boldsymbol{b}$ when $\boldsymbol{z}(t) = \boldsymbol{z}$, up to time t. We also denote $s_{\min}(t) = \min_{(\boldsymbol{z},\boldsymbol{b})} s(\boldsymbol{z}, \boldsymbol{b}, t)$.

<u>Threshold-Based Sampling TBS(s_{th}):</u> Every time t, sample the resource allocation vector $\boldsymbol{b}^* \in \arg\min_{\boldsymbol{b}} s(\boldsymbol{z}(t), \boldsymbol{b}, t)$ until $s_{\min}(t) \geq s_{th}$. If terminate at T_{tbs}, output $\hat{r}_n(\boldsymbol{z}, \boldsymbol{b}) = \sum_{t=1}^{T_{tbs}} 1_{[\boldsymbol{z}(t)=\boldsymbol{z}, \boldsymbol{b}(t)=\boldsymbol{b}]} \kappa_n(t)/s(\boldsymbol{z}, \boldsymbol{b}, T_{tbs})$. $\diamond$

Here $1_{[x]}$ is the indication function of x. The learning module TBS(s_{th}) is very intuitive. It tries to balance the sampling frequencies of all $(\boldsymbol{z}, \boldsymbol{b})$ until every pair is sampled at least s_{th} times. In this case, the learning algorithm running time T_{tbs} is random. In the following, we look at a deterministic time sampler for estimating $\boldsymbol{\pi}$. This module sets a sampling time threshold T_{th}.

<u>Time-Limited Sampling TLS(T_{th}):</u> Observe $\boldsymbol{z}(t)$ for T_{th} slots. Output $\hat{\pi}_k = \sum_{t=1}^{T_{th}} 1_{[\boldsymbol{z}(t)=\boldsymbol{z}_k]}/T_{th}$ for all k. $\diamond$

The following lemma shows the performance of the two modules.

Lemma 2. *The two learning modules satisfy:*

(a) TBS(s_{th}): $\mathbb{E}\{T_{tbs}\} = \Theta(s_{th})$ *and with probability* $1 - O(e^{-\frac{s_{th}\log(s_{th})^2}{2(s_{th} r_{\max}^2 + r_{\max}\sqrt{s_{th}}/3)}})$, $\delta_r = \frac{\log(s_{th})}{\sqrt{s_{th}}}$.

(b) TLS(T_{th}): *With probability* $1 - O(e^{-\frac{T^{th}\log(T_{th})^2}{2(T_{th} + \sqrt{T_{th}}/3)}})$, $\delta_z = \frac{\log(T_{th})}{\sqrt{T_{th}}}$. $\diamond$

PROOF. See Appendix B. $\square$

By choosing $s_{th} = T_{th} = V^c$, we can guarantee $\delta_r = \delta_z = c\log(V)V^{-c/2}$ with P_{δ_r} and P_{δ_z} being $1 - O(V^{-\log(V)})$.

5. PERFORMANCE ANALYSIS

In this section, we present the performance results of LRAM and DRAM. We start with some definitions and assumptions.

For notation simplicity, we denote $\boldsymbol{\alpha} = (\boldsymbol{\alpha}^d, \boldsymbol{\alpha}^q, \boldsymbol{\alpha}^h)$ and write $\boldsymbol{\alpha} - \boldsymbol{\theta} = (\boldsymbol{\alpha}^d, \boldsymbol{\alpha}^q - \boldsymbol{\theta}_1, \boldsymbol{\alpha}^h - \boldsymbol{\theta}_2)$. Also, to indicate the different distributions and reward functions used, we use $\hat{g}(\boldsymbol{\alpha})$ to denote the dual function when $\boldsymbol{r}$ is replaced by $\hat{\boldsymbol{r}}$ in (30) and the distribution is given by $\boldsymbol{\pi}$. Then, we use $g^{\hat{\boldsymbol{\pi}}}(\boldsymbol{\alpha})$ and $\hat{g}^{\hat{\boldsymbol{\pi}}}(\boldsymbol{\alpha})$ to denote the dual function with distribution $\hat{\boldsymbol{\pi}}$ and $\boldsymbol{r}$, and with $\hat{\boldsymbol{\pi}}$ and $\hat{\boldsymbol{r}}$, respectively.

5.1 Preliminaries

We define the following polyhedral system structure:

Definition 2. *A system is polyhedral with parameter $\rho > 0$ if the dual function $g(\boldsymbol{\alpha})$ satisfies:*

$$g(\boldsymbol{\alpha}^*) \leq g(\boldsymbol{\alpha}) - \rho \|\boldsymbol{\alpha}^* - \boldsymbol{\alpha}\|. \tag{37}$$

Here $\boldsymbol{\alpha}^*$ is an optimal solution of (29). ◇

The polyhedral structure typically appears in practical systems, especially when the system action sets are discrete (see [20] for more discussions). Note that (37) holds for all V if it holds under any V, in particular $V = 1$.

In our analysis, we make the following assumptions.

Assumption 1. *There exist constants $\epsilon_r, \epsilon_z = \Theta(1) > 0$ such that for any valid state distribution $\hat{\boldsymbol{\pi}}$ and reward statistics $\hat{\boldsymbol{r}}$ with $\|\hat{\boldsymbol{\pi}} - \boldsymbol{\pi}\| \leq \epsilon_z$ and $\|\boldsymbol{r} - \hat{\boldsymbol{r}}\| \leq \epsilon_r$, there exist a set of actions $\{\boldsymbol{\gamma}^k\}_{k=1,\dots,|\mathcal{Z}|}$, $\{\boldsymbol{R}_i^k\}_{k=1,\dots,|\mathcal{Z}|}^{i=1,2,\dots,\infty}$, $\{\boldsymbol{b}_i^k\}_{k=1,\dots,|\mathcal{Z}|}^{i=1,2,\dots,\infty}$, and $\{\boldsymbol{h}_i^k\}_{k=1,\dots,|\mathcal{Z}|}^{i=1,2,\dots,\infty}$, and variables $\lambda_i^k \geq 0$ with $\sum_i \lambda_i^k = 1$ for all k (possibly depending on $\hat{\boldsymbol{\pi}}$ and $\hat{\boldsymbol{r}}$), such that:*

$$\gamma_n - \sum_k \hat{\pi}_k \sum_i \lambda_i^k \hat{r}_n(\boldsymbol{z}_k, \mu_n(z_k, \boldsymbol{b}_i^k)) \leq -\eta_0, \tag{38}$$

where $\eta_0 = \Theta(1) > 0$ is independent of $\hat{\boldsymbol{\pi}}$ and $\hat{\boldsymbol{r}}$, and that

$$\sum_k \hat{\pi}_k \sum_i \lambda_i^k R_{in}^k = \sum_k \hat{\pi}_k \sum_i \lambda_i^k \mu_n(\boldsymbol{z}_k, \boldsymbol{b}_i^k) \tag{39}$$

$$\sum_k \hat{\pi}_k \sum_i \lambda_i^k \sum_n b_{imn}^k = \sum_k \hat{\pi}_k \sum_i \lambda_i^k h_{im}^k \tag{40}$$

where $0 < \sum_k \hat{\pi}_k \sum_i \lambda_i^k R_{in}^k < \mathbb{E}_{\hat{\boldsymbol{\pi}}}\{A_n(t)\}$ as well as $0 < \sum_k \hat{\pi}_k \sum_i \lambda_i^k h_{im}^k < \mathbb{E}_{\hat{\boldsymbol{\pi}}}\{e_m(t)\}$. ◇

Assumption 2. *For any $\hat{\boldsymbol{\pi}}$ and $\hat{\boldsymbol{r}}$ with $\|\hat{\boldsymbol{\pi}} - \boldsymbol{\pi}\| \leq \epsilon_z$ and $\|\hat{\boldsymbol{r}} - \boldsymbol{r}\| \leq \epsilon_r$, if $g(\boldsymbol{\alpha})$ is polyhedral with parameter ρ, then $\hat{g}^{\hat{\boldsymbol{\pi}}}(\boldsymbol{\alpha})$ is also polyhedral with parameter ρ.* ◇

Assumption 3. *For any $\hat{\boldsymbol{\pi}}$ and $\hat{\boldsymbol{r}}$ with $\|\hat{\boldsymbol{\pi}} - \boldsymbol{\pi}\| \leq \epsilon_z$ and $\|\hat{\boldsymbol{r}} - \boldsymbol{r}\| \leq \epsilon_r$, $\hat{g}^{\hat{\boldsymbol{\pi}}}(\boldsymbol{\alpha})$ has a unique optimal solution over $\mathbb{R}^{M+2N}$.* ◇

In the network optimization literature, e.g., [12], [21], Assumption 1 is commonly assumed with $\epsilon_r = \epsilon_z = 0$. By allowing $\epsilon_r, \epsilon_z > 0$, we assume that systems with similar statistics have similar stability regions. Assumption 2 assumes that systems with similar statistics share a similar dual structure. This is not restrictive. In fact, when action sets are discrete, it is often the case that $g_k(\boldsymbol{\alpha})$ is polyhedral, which usually leads to a polyhedral structure of $\hat{g}^{\hat{\boldsymbol{\pi}}}(\boldsymbol{\alpha})$. The uniqueness assumption is also often guaranteed by the utility maximization structure, e.g., [22].

5.2 Queue and Utility Performance

We first summarize the performance of `LRAM`.

Theorem 1. *Suppose $T_{\delta_r} < \infty$ with probability 1. Under* `LRAM`*, we have for all $t \geq T_{\delta_r} + 1$ that:*

$$d_n(t) \leq d_{\max} \triangleq V\beta + r_{\max}, \forall n \tag{41}$$

$$Q_n(t) \leq Q_{\max} \triangleq \theta_1 + r_{\max}, \forall n \tag{42}$$

$$H_m(t) \leq H_{\max} \triangleq \theta_2 + h_{\max}, \forall m. \tag{43}$$

Moreover, we have with probability P_{δ_r} that,

$$f_{av}^{\mathtt{LRAM}} \geq f_{av}^* - \frac{G + r_{\max}\delta_r}{V} - 2N\beta\delta_r. \diamond \tag{44}$$

Proof. Omitted due to space limitation. Please see our technical report [23]. □

The last term in (44) involves the estimation error δ_r. This can be viewed as the performance loss due to inaccurate reward information. We remark here that the deterministic queueing bounds are important for both algorithm implementation and performance guarantee. This is so because errors in reward function estimation will be amplified by the queue sizes when used in decision making, i.e., (16).

We now present the performance results for `DRAM`.

Theorem 2. *Suppose $\max(T_{\delta_r}, T_{\delta_z}) < \infty$ with probability 1. Suppose $g(\boldsymbol{\alpha})$ is polyhedral with $\rho = \Theta(1) > 0$, and that $\delta_z \leq \epsilon_z$ and $\delta_r \leq \epsilon_r$, and $\boldsymbol{\alpha}^* + \boldsymbol{\theta} \succ \mathbf{0}$. Then, with a sufficiently large V, we have with probability $P_{\delta_z} P_{\delta_r}$ that, under* `DRAM`*,*

$$f_{av}^{\mathtt{DRAM}} \geq f_{av}^* - \frac{G}{V} - O(1/V + \delta_r). \tag{45}$$

Also, the fraction of time dropping happens is $O(V^{-\log(V)})$. Moreover, for all queues, there exist $\Theta(1)$ constants D, K, a such that:

$$Pr\{d_n(t) \geq \frac{3}{2}\zeta + D + \nu\} \leq ae^{-K\nu} \tag{46}$$

$$Pr\{Q_n(t) \geq \frac{3}{2}\zeta + D + \nu\} \leq ae^{-K\nu} \tag{47}$$

$$Pr\{H_m(t) \geq \frac{3}{2}\zeta + D + \nu\} \leq ae^{-K\nu}. \tag{48}$$

Thus, all queues are stable. ◇

Proof. Omitted due to space limitation. Please see our technical report [23]. □

Note that if we have $\delta_r = 0$ with $T_{\delta_r} = 0$ and $P_{\delta_r} = 1$, then Theorem 1 recovers the known $[O(1/V), O(V)]$ utility-delay tradeoff for stochastic network problems [12]. On the other hand, if we also have $\delta_z = 0$ with $T_{\delta_z} = 0$ and $P_{\delta_z} = 1$, then `DRAM` provides a new way for achieving the near-optimal $[O(1/V), O(\log(V)^2)]$ utility-delay tradeoff.

In both `LRAM` and `DRAM`, it is possible to continuously update the reward function estimations during the control steps. However, this does not automatically guarantee that we can always eliminate the effect of δ_r. This is so because the initial estimation $\hat{\boldsymbol{r}}$ may affect what options will be continuously updated later. On the other hand, the same performance results will hold if further updates do not increase δ_r.

5.3 Convergence time

Here we look at another important performance metric - algorithm convergence time, which characterizes the time it takes for the algorithm to enter the "steady state." Faster convergence implies better robustness against system statistics changes and higher efficiency in resource allocation, and is particularly important when system statistics can change. The formal definition of convergence time is as follows [15].

Definition 3. *For a given constant D, the D-convergence time of a control algorithm* Π*, denoted by* T_D^{Π}*, is the time it takes for the queue vector* $(\boldsymbol{d}(t), \boldsymbol{Q}(t), \boldsymbol{H}(t))$ *(*$(\hat{\boldsymbol{d}}(t), \hat{\boldsymbol{Q}}(t), \hat{\boldsymbol{H}}(t))$ *under* DRAM*) to get to within D distance of* $\boldsymbol{\alpha}^* + \boldsymbol{\theta}$*, i.e.,*

$$T_D^{\Pi} \triangleq \inf\{t \,|\, ||(\boldsymbol{d}(t), \boldsymbol{Q}(t), \boldsymbol{H}(t)) - (\boldsymbol{\alpha}^* + \boldsymbol{\theta})|| \leq D\}. \diamond \quad (49)$$

This definition of convergence time concerns about when an algorithm enters its "optimal state." It is different from the metrics considered in [24] and [25], which concern about the time it takes for the objective value and constraints to be within certain accuracy. With Definition 3, we have the following results:

Theorem 3. *Suppose* $g(\boldsymbol{\alpha})$ *is polyhedral with* $\rho = \Theta(1) > 0$*,* $\delta_z \leq \epsilon_z$ *and* $\delta_r \leq \epsilon_r$*, and* $\boldsymbol{\alpha}^* + \boldsymbol{\theta} \succ \boldsymbol{0}$*. Then, with a sufficiently large V, we have:*

$$\mathbb{E}\{T_{D_1}^{\texttt{LRAM}}\} = O(T_{\delta_r} + \Theta(V)) \ w.p. \ P_{\delta_r} \quad (50)$$

$$\mathbb{E}\{T_{D_2}^{\texttt{DRAM}}\} = O((T_l + \Theta(\delta_z V)) \ w.p. \ P_{\delta_r} P_{\delta_z}. \quad (51)$$

Here $T_l \triangleq \max(T_{\delta_r}, T_{\delta_z})$ *denotes the total learning time in* DRAM*,* $D_1 \triangleq \Theta(\delta_r V) + \Theta(1)$*, and* $D_2 \triangleq \Theta(\delta_r V) + \Theta(1)$*.* $\diamond$

Proof. Omitted due to space limitation. Please see our technical report [23]. □

Combining Theorems 1, 2, and 3, we see that δ_r largely affects the overall utility performance (reflected by D_1 and D_2), while δ_z can greatly improve the convergence time and delay! This indicates that information of different system components can play very different roles in algorithm performance and learning accuracies should be carefully chosen for meeting a desired performance goal.

5.4 Necessity in Controlling δ_r

Here we provide a simple example showing that it is necessary to control δ_r for good utility performance. Hence, it is important to learn the reward value for each matching option. Consider the case when $N = 2$ and $M = 1$. Suppose $e(t) = A_1(t) = A_2(t) = 1$ for all t. Also suppose $\boldsymbol{b}(t) \in \{(0,1), (1,0), (0,0)\}$, that is, at every time t, we can only allocate resource to one or zero queue. Suppose $c(t) = 0$, $\mu_n(t) = b_n(t)$, and $r_n(t) = \tilde{\mu}_n(t)$. Finally, assume that $U_1(r_1) = \log(1 + r_1)$ and $\log(1 + 2r_2)$.

In this case, the true optimal takes place at $\overline{r}_1 = 1/4$ and $\overline{r}_2 = 3/4$ with $U_{\text{total}} = 0.7828$. Now suppose we incorrectly estimate the rewards to be $r_n(t) = (1+\delta_n)\tilde{\mu}_n(t)$. Then, one can show that the optimal rewards become:

$$r_1 = \frac{2(1+\delta_1)(1+\delta_2) - 2(1+\delta_2) + (1+\delta_1)}{4(1+\delta_1)(1+\delta_2)} \quad (52)$$

$$r_2 = \frac{2(1+\delta_1)(1+\delta_2) + 2(1+\delta_2) - (1+\delta_1)}{4(1+\delta_1)(1+\delta_2)}, \quad (53)$$

which is roughly $r_1 \approx \frac{1}{4} + \frac{2\delta_1 - \delta_2}{4}$ and $r_2 \approx \frac{3}{4} - \frac{2\delta_1 - \delta_2}{4}$. Thus, the resulting optimal utility is given by:

$$U_{\text{total}} \approx 0.7828 - \frac{|2\delta_1| + |\delta_2|}{5}. \quad (54)$$

Therefore, in order to obtain an $O(1/V)$ close-to-optimal utility, it is necessary to ensure that $\max(|\delta_1|, |\delta_2|) = O(1/V)$.

6. SIMULATION

In this section, we present simulation results for our algorithms. We consider a system that has $N = 2$ and $M = 1$. We assume that $e(t)$ is 0 or 2 with equal probabilities. $A_1(t)$ is 0 or 2 with equal probabilities and $A_2(t)$ is 1 or 2 with equal probabilities. $\boldsymbol{b}(t) \in \{(0,1), (1,0), (0,0)\}$, i.e., at every time t, we allocate one unit resource to one or zero queue. We set $c(t) = b_1(t) + b_2(t)$ and $\mu_n(t) = b_n(t)$, and $\gamma_n(t) \in \{0, 1, 2\}$. There are two system states $\omega(t) \in \{1, 2\}$. In each state, the reward functions are given by $r_n(t) = w_n(\omega(t))\tilde{\mu}_n(t)$, where $w_1(1) = 0.8$ and $w_2(1) = 1$ and $w_1(2) = 1$ and $w_2(2) = 0.8$. Thus, the system state indicates which tasks are preferred under the specific condition. Every time the corresponding reward is either $0.5r_n(t)$ or $1.5r_n(t)$, with equal probabilities. Finally, we assume that $U_1(r_1) = 1.2\log(1 + 2r_1)$ and $U_2(r_2) = 1.2\log(1 + 4r_2)$.

From the definitions, we have that $\beta = 5$, $\beta_\mu^u = \beta_\mu^l = 1$ and $\beta_{\hat{r}} = \max_{\omega(t),n} \hat{r}_n(\omega(t))$. We also set $r_{\max} = 2$, $\mu_{\max} = 1$ and $b_{\max} = 1$, $h_{\max} = 2$. We simulate both LRAM and DRAM with $V = \{10, 20, 50, 80, 100\}$. According to (20) and (21), $\theta_1 = (5V + 2)\beta_{\hat{r}} + 4$ and $\theta_2 = (5V + 2)\beta_{\hat{r}} + 3$. In DRAM, we set $\zeta = \log(V)^2$. We use $\texttt{TBS}(s_{th})$ to estimate $\boldsymbol{r}$ and set $s_{th} = \log(V)^2$, and use $\texttt{TLS}(T_{th})$ to estimate $\boldsymbol{\pi}$ and set $T_{th} = T_{tbs}$. In LRAM, we randomly add or subtract the estimation error δ_r from the true values.

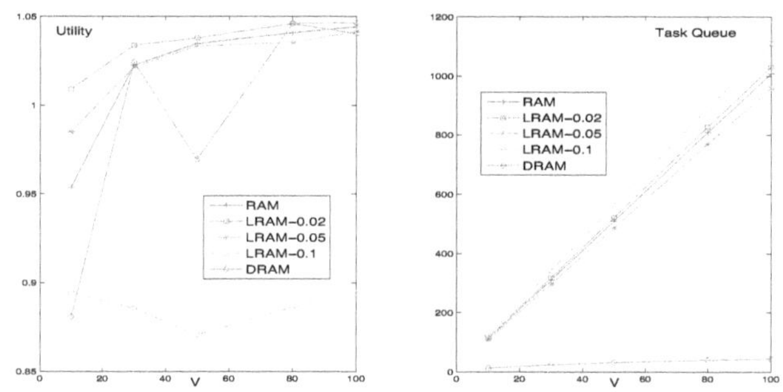

Figure 3: Utility performance and task queue size.

Fig. 3 first shows the utility performance and the task queue behavior of LRAM and DRAM, where the number after LRAM denotes δ_r. We see from the left plot that except for $\delta_r = 0.1$, LRAM performs very well under all other error values, suggesting that estimation error indeed plays an important role in system utility. We also see that DRAM performs very well starting from $V \geq 50$. The right plot shows the backlog (delay) performance under different schemes. It is evident that DRAM achieves an $O(\log(V)^2)$ delay in this case, while all other variants possess an $O(V)$ delay. This demonstrates the importance of incorporating system dynamics information into algorithm design.

Fig. 4 then shows the resource queue $H(t)$ and deficit queues $\boldsymbol{d}(t)$. We see that DRAM ensures an $O(\log(V)^2)$ average resource queue, while other algorithms result in an $O(V)$ queue size. This implies that DRAM ensures a very short stay in the system for the resource items! This feature is particularly useful if the resource items are human users, e.g., in crowdsourcing.

Finally, Fig. 5 shows the convergence behavior of the algorithms for $V = 100$. Here we show the resource queue value as its convergence time dominates the others. We see that RAM takes an $O(V)$ time to converge, which is expected. We also observe that $H(t)$ under LRAM-0.05 and LRAM-0.1 converge to values slightly above those under RAM. This ex-

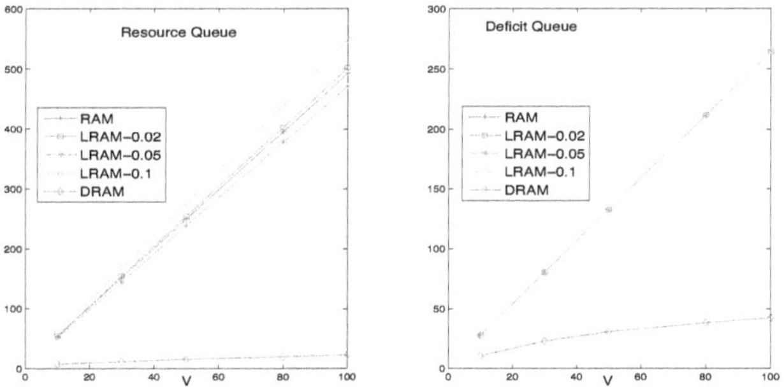

Figure 4: Resource queue and deficit queue sizes.

plains why their performance is slightly worse. On the other hand, we also see that DRAM converges quickly. The reason its steady state value is slightly above that under RAM is due to the inaccuracy of $\hat{\boldsymbol{r}}$. Even in this case, we see that there is a 2.5× convergence speedup (most of the learning time is due to sampling) and DRAM achieves very good performance. In the case when $\boldsymbol{r}$ can be obtained from other data source beforehand, which can commonly be done in practice, e.g., in online advertising, we see that DRAM (called state-only DRAM in this case) achieves a 10× convergence speedup (50 slots vs. 500 slots)!

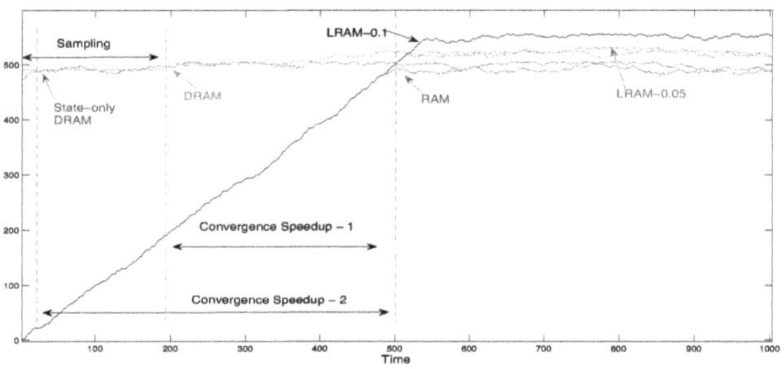

Figure 5: Convergence of LRAM and DRAM for $V = 100$.

We observe in all simulation instances that no dropping occurs. This demonstrates the effectiveness of the algorithms and validates Theorem 2.

7. CONCLUSION

In this paper, we study the problem of optimal matching with queues in dynamic systems. We develop two online learning-aided algorithms LRAM and DRAM for resolving the challenging underflow problem and to achieve near-optimality. We show that LRAM achieves an $O(\epsilon + \delta_r)$ system utility, for any $\epsilon > 0$, while ensuring an $O(1/\epsilon)$ delay bound and an $O(1/\epsilon)$ algorithm convergence time. DRAM, on the other hand, guarantees a similar $O(\epsilon + \delta_r)$ system utility, while achieving an $O(\delta_z/\epsilon + \log(1/\epsilon)^2)$ delay bound and an $O(\delta_z/\epsilon)$ algorithm convergence time, which can be significantly better compared to LRAM when δ_z is small. Our algorithms and results reveal the interesting fact that different system information can play very different roles in algorithm performance and provide insights into joint learning-control algorithm design for dynamic systems.

8. ACKNOWLEDGEMENT

This work was supported in part by the National Basic Research Program of China Grant 2011CBA00300, 2011CBA00301, the National Natural Science Foundation of China Grant 61033001, 61361136003, 61303195, Tsinghua Initiative Research Grant, and the China Youth 1000-talent Grant.

9. REFERENCES

[1] N. Mckeown, V. Anantharam, and J. Walrand. Achieving 100% throughput in an input-queued switch. *Proceedings of INFOCOM*, 1996.

[2] A. Mehta. *Online Matching and Ad Allocation.* Foundations and Trends in Theoretical Computer Science Vol. 8, no. 4, pp. 265-368, 2013.

[3] F. Alt, A. Shirazi, A. Schmidt, U. Kramer, and Z. Nawaz. Location-based crowdsourcing: Extending crowdsourcing to the real world.

[4] Uber. https://www.uber.com/.

[5] S. Maguluri, R. Srikant, and L. Ying. Stochastic models of load balancing and scheduling in cloud computing clusters. *Proceedings of INFOCOM*, 2012.

[6] M. J. Neely and L. Huang. Dynamic product assembly and inventory control for maximum profit. *IEEE Conference on Decision and Control (CDC), Atlanta, Georgia*, Dec. 2010.

[7] M. J. Neely. Super-fast delay tradeoffs for utility optimal fair scheduling in wireless networks. *IEEE Journal on Selected Areas in Communications (JSAC), Special Issue on Nonlinear Optimization of Communication Systems*, 24(8):1489–1501, Aug. 2006.

[8] Libin Jiang and Jean Walrand. A distributed csma algorithm for throughput and utility maximization in wireless networks. *IEEE/ACM Transactions on Networking, vol. 18, no.3, pp. 960 - 972*, Jun. 2010.

[9] C. W. Tan, D. P. Palomar, and M. Chiang. Energy-robustness tradeoff in cellular network power control. *IEEE/ACM Transactions on Networking, Vol. 17, No. 3, pp. 912-925*, 2009.

[10] X. Lin P. Huang and C. Wang. A low-complexity congestion control and scheduling algorithm for multihop wireless networks with order-optimal per-flow delay. *Proceedings of INFOCOM*, 2011.

[11] I. Hou and P.R. Kumar. Utility-optimal scheduling in time-varying wireless networks with delay constraints. *Proceedings of MobiHoc*, 2010.

[12] L. Georgiadis, M. J. Neely, and L. Tassiulas. *Resource Allocation and Cross-Layer Control in Wireless Networks.* Foundations and Trends in Networking Vol. 1, no. 1, pp. 1-144, 2006.

[13] Committee on the Analysis of Massive Data; Committee on Applied, Theoretical Statistics; Board on Mathematical Sciences, Their Applications; Division on Engineering, and Physical Sciences; National Research Council. *Frontiers in Massive Data Analysis.* 2013.

[14] C. Bishop. *Pattern Recognition and Machine Learning.* Springer, 2006.

[15] L. Huang, X. Liu, and X. Hao. The power of online learning in stochastic network optimization. *Proceedings of ACM Sigmetrics*, 2014.

[16] O. Simeone C. Tapparello and M. Rossi. Dynamic compression-transmission for energy-harvesting multihop networks with correlated sources. *IEEE/ACM Trans. on Networking*, 2014.

[17] S. Chen, P. Sinha, N. B. Shroff, and C. Joo. A simple asymptotically optimal joint energy allocation and

routing scheme in rechargeable sensor networks. *IEEE/ACM Trans. on Networking*, to appear.

[18] B. Tan and R. Srikant. Online advertisement, optimization and stochastic networks. *50th IEEE Conference on Decision and Control and European Control Conference (CDC-ECC) Orlando, FL, USA*, December 2011.

[19] L. Huang and M. J. Neely. The optimality of two prices: Maximizing revenue in a stochastic network. *IEEE/ACM Transactions on Networking*, 18(2):406–419, April 2010.

[20] L. Huang and M. J. Neely. Delay reduction via Lagrange multipliers in stochastic network optimization. *IEEE Trans. on Automatic Control*, 56(4):842–857, April 2011.

[21] T. Ji J. Ghaderi and R. Srikant. Flow-level stability of wireless networks: Separation of congestion control and scheduling.

[22] A. Eryilmaz and R. Srikant. Fair resource allocation in wireless networks using queue-length-based scheduling and congestion control. *IEEE/ACM Trans. Netw.*, 15(6):1333–1344, 2007.

[23] L. Huang. The value-of-information in matching with queues. *ArXiv Tech Report arXiv:1503.07975*, 2015.

[24] B. Li, A. Eryilmaz, and R. Li. Wireless scheduling for utility maximization with optimal convergence speed. *Proceedings of IEEE INFOCOM, Turin, Italy*, April 2013.

[25] M. Neely. Energy-aware wireless scheduling with near optimal backlog and convergence time tradeoffs. *Proceedings of INFOCOM*, 2015.

[26] F. Chung and L. Lu. Concentration inequalities and martingale inequalities - a survey. *Internet Math.*, 3 (2006-2007), 79–127.

Appendix A – Proof of Lemma 1

We prove Lemma 1 here.

PROOF. (Lemma 1) Using the queueing dynamics (5) and (6), we have:

$$(Q_n(t+1)-\theta_1)^2 \leq (Q_n(t)-\theta_1)^2 \\ -2(Q_n(t)-\theta_1)(\mu_n(t)-R_n(t)) + R_n(t)^2 + \mu_n(t)^2.$$

Similarly, we get:

$$(H_m(t+1)-\theta_2)^2 \leq (H_m(t)-\theta_2)^2 \\ -2(H_m(t)-\theta_2)(\sum_n b_{mn}(t)-h_m(t)) + (\sum_n b_{mn}(t))^2 + h_m(t)^2,$$

and that

$$d_n(t+1)^2 \leq d_n(t)^2 - 2d_n(t)(\kappa_n(t)-\gamma_n(t)) + \kappa_n(t)^2 + \gamma_n(t)^2.$$

Summing the above and using the definition of $L(t)$ and $\Delta_V(t)$, we get:

$$\begin{aligned} &L(t+1) - L(t) - Vf(t) \\ &\leq G - V(\sum_n U_n(\gamma_n(t)) - c(t)) \\ &\quad - \sum_n (Q_n(t)-\theta_1)(\mu_n(t)-R_n(t)) \\ &\quad - \sum_n d_n(t)(\kappa_n(t)-\gamma_n(t)) \\ &\quad - \sum_m (H_m(t)-\theta_2)(\sum_n b_{mn}(t)-h_m(t)). \end{aligned}$$

Here $G \triangleq N(A_{\max}^2 + \mu_{\max}^2 + 2r_{\max}^2) + Mh_{\max}^2 + MN^2b_{\max}^2$. Rearranging terms, we obtain:

$$\begin{aligned} &L(t+1) - L(t) - Vf(t) \\ &\leq G - V\sum_n [U_n(\gamma_n(t)) - d_n(t)\gamma_n(t)] \\ &\quad + \sum_n (Q_n(t)-\theta_1)R_n(t) + \sum_m (H_m(t)-\theta_2)h_m(t) \\ &\quad + \Big[Vc(t) - \sum_m (H_m(t)-\theta_2)\sum_n b_{mn}(t) \\ &\quad - \sum_n (Q_n(t)-\theta_1)\mu_n(t) - \sum_n d_n(t)\kappa_n(t)\Big]. \end{aligned}$$

Taking an expectations on both sides conditioning on $\boldsymbol{y}(t)$ and using the fact that $\kappa_n(t)$ is an i.i.d. random variable given $\boldsymbol{z}(t), \boldsymbol{b}(t), \boldsymbol{Q}(t)$, we see that the lemma follows. □

Appendix B – Proof of Lemma 2

We prove Lemma 2 here. In our proof, we will use the following theorem from [26].

Theorem 4. *[26] Suppose X_i are independent random variables satisfying $X_i \leq B$ for $1 \leq i \leq n$. Let $X = \sum_i X_i$ and $\|X\| = \sqrt{\sum_i \mathbb{E}\{X_i^2\}}$. Then we have:*

$$Pr\{X \leq \mathbb{E}\{X\} - b\} \leq e^{-\frac{b^2}{2(\|X\|^2 + Bb/3)}}. \diamond \tag{55}$$

PROOF. (Lemma 2) First of all, we show that $\mathbb{E}\{T_{tbs}\} = \Theta(\log(V)^2)$. To see this, notice that since each $\mathcal{B}_k$ is finite, if the state $\boldsymbol{z}(t) = k$ appears $|\mathcal{B}_k|s_{th}$ times, we must have sampled every $\boldsymbol{b} \in \mathcal{B}_k$ s_{th} times. Thus,

$$T_{tbs} \leq \sum_k T\{\text{visit } \boldsymbol{z}_k\ |\mathcal{B}_k|s_{th} \text{ times}\}. \tag{56}$$

Taking the expectations, we see that $\mathbb{E}\{T_{tbs}\} \leq s_{th}\sum_k \frac{|\mathcal{B}_k|}{\pi_k}$.

Then, we see that in $\hat{\boldsymbol{r}}$, each single value has been sampled s_{th} times. Using Theorem 4 and the fact that $\kappa_n(t) \leq r_{\max}$, we get:

$$\Pr\{\sum_{t=1}^{T_{tbs}} 1_{[\boldsymbol{z}(t)=\boldsymbol{z}, \boldsymbol{b}(t)=\boldsymbol{b}]}\kappa_n(t) \leq r_n(\boldsymbol{z},\boldsymbol{b})s(\boldsymbol{z},\boldsymbol{b},T_{tbs}) - b\} \\ \leq e^{-\frac{b^2}{2(s_{th}r_{\max}^2 + r_{\max}b/3)}}.$$

Choosing $b = \sqrt{s_{th}}\log(s_{th})$, dividing both sides of the inequality inside by $s(\boldsymbol{z},\boldsymbol{b},T_{tbs})$, and using $s(\boldsymbol{z},\boldsymbol{b},T_{tbs}) \geq s_{th}$, we get:

$$\Pr\{\hat{r}_n(\boldsymbol{z},\boldsymbol{b}) \leq r_n(\boldsymbol{z},\boldsymbol{b}) - \frac{\log(s_{th})}{\sqrt{s_{th}}}\} \leq e^{-\frac{s_{th}\log(s_{th})^2}{2(r_{\max}^2 s_{th} + r_{\max}\sqrt{s_{th}}/3)}}.$$

Using Theorem 4 with $-X$, we get a similar bound for the other side. Hence,

$$\Pr\{|\hat{r}_n(\boldsymbol{z},\boldsymbol{b}) - r_n(\boldsymbol{z},\boldsymbol{b})| \leq \frac{\log(s_{th})}{\sqrt{s_{th}}}\} \leq 2e^{-\frac{s_{th}\log(s_{th})^2}{2(r_{\max}^2 s_{th} + r_{\max}\sqrt{s_{th}}/3)}}.$$

Using the union bound, we see that Part (a) follows. Part (b) can be proven similarly. □

EarlyBird: Mobile Prefetching of Social Network Feeds via Content Preference Mining and Usage Pattern Analysis

Yichuan Wang
University of California, Davis
yichuan1118@gmail.com

Xin Liu
University of California, Davis
liu@cs.ucdavis.edu

David Chu
Microsoft Research
davidchu@microsoft.com

Yunxin Liu
Microsoft Research
yunliu@microsoft.com

ABSTRACT

Social networks are the most engaging applications on mobile devices, and they are becoming the main sources for users to consume content. However, content retrieval, especially for embedded links and multimedia, can often be too slow, too energy hungry or too expensive for on-the-go mobile users. To address these issues, we collect and analyze a large set of traces from over 6000 real-life users of a popular mobile Twitter client. Based on the unique challenges identified from our dataset, we present inference-based social network content prefetcher, EarlyBird. It uses the specific signals unique to social data in order to retrieve news feeds and associated links and multimedia ahead of users' usage. Our regression-based content prediction model is able to estimate a user's likely content interests 55% of the time. Second, we develop a prefetch scheduling scheme to maximize delay reduction under users' resource constraints. For validation, we apply Earlybird to our collected dataset. We show that on average users can reduce their delays by 62 % at the cost of no more than 3% battery and 40MB/month cellular data.

Categories and Subject Descriptors

C.2.1 [**Computer Communications Networks**]: Network Architecture and Design—*Wireless communication* ; H.2.8 [**Database Management**]: Database Applications—*Data mining*

General Terms

Performance

Keywords

Mobile prefetching; social network; user behavior

MobiHoc'15, June 22–25, 2015, Hangzhou, China.

http://dx.doi.org/10.1145/2746285.2746312.

1. INTRODUCTION

Mobile users spend an increasingly large amount of time on social applications. It is reported that 1/3 of mobile minutes are spent on Facebook and Twitter [2], and the time spent has been increasing 63% year-over-year [6]. Currently 55% of social networking consumption occurs on a mobile device [1].

Social posts have already become a mainstream channel for content consumption. Over 52% and 47% of the users get news from Twitter and Facebook respectively [3]. Whereas each post's text content is small (e.g. limited to 140 characters for Twitter and Weibo), embedded content — photos, videos and URL links — is often much larger. Additionally, emerging social networks such as Instagram (sharing photos) and Vine (sharing video cliplets) are placing greater emphasis on both mobile and multimedia. The increasing popularity and ubiquity of such content consumption calls for exceptional support from mobile devices.

However, the current experience of content consumption is far from satisfactory in terms of access delay and network availability. First, cellular network connection establishment and roundtrip times – at least 3 seconds [4] and often 10 seconds or more [13] – are excessive taxes to fluid and engaging social interaction, especially when users try to retrieve multimedia content from embedded URLs in social posts. Using a popular Android device and stable Wi-Fi connection, we crawled over 150000 links that mobile Twitter users clicked on. The average load time (not including rendering time) of a link is 16.71 seconds, and the median is 7.5 seconds. Compounding access latencies, mobile users often "snack" on social media in gap times such as while in elevators, on public transit, and in large gatherings (e.g., conferences, parties, and sporting events). Such scenarios often correlate to challenging network environments with weaker signals, congested networks, and moving devices. Lastly, the bandwidth cost of multimedia content, especially video, is high and intolerable for many cost-sensitive users on pay-per-bit data plans.

Unique features of mobile social content prefetching Existing work has carefully and extensively studied how to model, predict, and explore favorable network conditions for prefetching. However, social mobile content has its unique features. Consider the Twitter usage of a real-life user from our dataset, shown in Fig. 1. The bars show the numbers of tweets (we only concern about tweets with URL links) the user subscribed to, downloaded, and clicked during each hour of the day, averaged over 30 days. We observe that a user only download a subset of the tweets she subscribes to (about 40% on average in our dataset, see § *User Behavior*), and time of the day clearly matters. Among the downloaded tweets with URL links, a user clicks only a subset of the links (about 11% on average). Moreover, although not shown in the figure, freshness is critical - 70% of content consumed is within one hour of generation (in our dataset). Therefore, **when** and **what** to prefetch are tightly coupled difficult questions. Specifically, a user does not value his subscribed content equally and thus we need to judiciously decide what to prefetch. In addition, *when* not only includes the classic network-condition-driven prefetching issue, but also user's access pattern. Last, *when* will also affect *what* due to the time-sensitive nature of social content.

One might think that prefetch on WiFi and prefetch at application launch should work well. However when we take a look at representative Twitter users, we see that fresh content attracts most attention, and is largely missed by sparse WiFi connections. Simulation with real-life trace shows that WiFi-only approach can only reduce delay by 5% on average. Therefore, simply prefetch on WiFi does not work well. Also, notice that since WiFi is often not available when our users launch Twitter, prefetch at application launch can be costly in terms of data and battery usage. Therefore, simply prefetch at launch does not work as well.

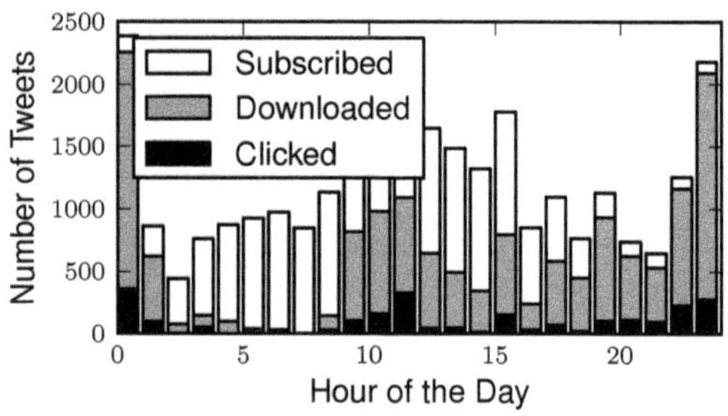

Figure 1: Twitter usage of a real-life user.

Earlybird To address such challenges, we present EarlyBird, a social network content prefetch system. Earlybird estimates user's potential interest in individual links base on history clicks. Such estimation, user access pattern, and dynamic network condition, will jointly decide when and how aggressively the content is prefetched.

First, we build a content access model to estimate a user's interests among the links she downloads. We employ a combination of content metadata, sender metadata, and receiver metadata in order to identify salient features that can be used in a prediction model. Real-life twitter click-through traces from 200 users show 55% accuracy of our prediction model.

Then, Earlybird jointly consider user's interests, access pattern, and dynamic network conditions to decide when and how aggressively the content is prefetched. Please note that, because a user on average only downloads 40% of the subscribed tweets, only using content prediction may result in high false positive, e.g., 2 a.m. to 9 a.m. for the user shown in Fig. 1.

Although prefetch-at-launch and prefetch-on-wifi do not perform well by themselves, integrating them with user's content preference, access pattern, and dynamic network condition, by leveraging the complementary the nature of the two, we can perform effective prefetch that adapt to users' diverse cellular data usage and battery consumption budgets.

Prefetch-at-launch caches URL content right after user launches the Twitter application. Tweets with high likelihood of click-through are prefetched in the reversed chronological order, from new to old. Prefetching at launch time helps filter out the unread tweets and increase the prefetching accuracy, but results in increased cellular data and energy usage. In particular, users tend to snack on social applications on public transport or elevators where network connection is poor or even disconnected.

To alleviate these issues, prefetch-on-wifi caches social content when the prefetching cost is low while taking into account user access pattern. In this regard, we can fully leverage the existing work on network-condition-based prefetching, using techniques including predicting favorable network conditions, using WiFi hotspots, and piggy-backing with other transmissions, etc [9, 27, 21].

By intelligently integrating these two approaches, we can optimize user experience (delay reduction) while accommodating users' different resource constraints, in terms of cellular data usage and battery consumption.

Data and Evaluation As a case study of EarlyBird, we collect user traces from Twidere [8], an Android Twitter client which has over 100,000 downloads and over 6,000 users having consented to reporting usage data to us (§*Data Collection and Statistics*). We then crawled over 30 million tweets in the data set using Twitter API. This provides a realistic evaluation of the practicality of the proposed approach and its corresponding challenges (§*Evaluation*). We show that, for example, on average users can reduce their delays by at least 62% at the cost of no more than 3% battery and 40MB/month cellular data consumption; or with 6% of battery and no extra cellular data consumption, which is a significant improvement over WiFi only approaches.

Contributions In this paper, we identify unique features in mobile social content prefetching, and develop a multi-dimensional approach, Earlybird, that leverages content preference, usage pattern, and dynamic network conditions to improve user experience, under their specific data and energy budgets.

- We build a regression-based content prediction model to estimate a user's potential interest in embedded mobile content.
- We develop a prefetch scheduling scheme that effectively integrates two complementary prefetching mechanisms to maximize delay reduction under users' resource constraints.
- We collect a large set of real-life mobile Twitter traces from over 6000 users, including Twitter application usage, link click, and network availability.
- We analyze the real-life user traces to identify the unique characteristics of Twitter user behavior on mobile devices, and their impact on prefetching.
- As a case study of EarlyBird, we comprehensively evaluate the performance of Earlybird using trace-driven emulations and simulations.

In this work, we use Twitter as a case study, however the techniques can be applied to other social network as well.

For example, Earlybird could benefit Weibo [5], a microblogging service similar to Twitter with 503 million registered users, with little changes. Using the same resource budget, multiple social networks would provide a larger pool of links to choose from, thus increase the prefetching performance of Earlybird.

2. PREFETCH ARCHITECTURE

Fig. 2 illustrates the architecture of EarlyBird. Prefetching is coordinated by a prefetch server, which retrieves all tweets for the given user as they are posted using the Twitter streaming API [7], and determines *what* embedded links in tweets and *when* should be prefetched at the user's mobile device.

The two primary components in EarlyBird architecture are *content prediction* and *prefetch scheduling*. Both components rely on the user profile that contains the historical social content accessed and network conditions encountered. Such information is collected and stored on the mobile device by the data collector, and is uploaded (daily) to the server only when the mobile device is both charging and on WiFi.

Based on the user profile, the content prediction model is trained to predict the likelihood the user will click the URL in a posted tweet if it is downloaded. Tweets are fed to the corresponding user's content prediction model to calculate the likelihood of click-through and are stored in the prefetch queue. Then, the scheduling model decides when to prefetch and which ones to prefetch from the queue, based on estimates regarding future network conditions, battery conditions, underlying network traffic pattern, and when the user will access social content. In addition, priority-based mechanisms, such as TCP-LP [19], can also be set up between the proxy and the mobile device to minimize the impact on other network traffic.

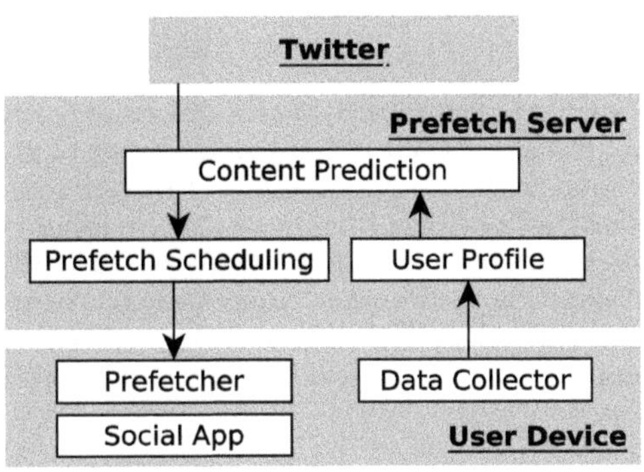

Figure 2: EarlyBird prefetch architecture.

3. DATA COLLECTION AND STATISTICS

To study the real life usage of social media on mobile devices, it is crucial to collect enough usage data from the general public. Although Twitter's tweets are publicly available, when and how users access Twitter is not. Therefore, we collected a large set of usage data from Twidere[1] users who agreed to provide this information to us. With the users' consent[2], we collect usage pattern, link click-through, and network availability. Because existing work has carefully studied the network-condition-based prefetching scheduling using fine-grained traces [27, 21], we focus our work and the corresponding data collection on the complementary components. Therefore, to limit the collection overhead and to avoid user burn out, we decide not to collect detailed network trace in a fine-grain manner, but only log the WiFi availability, which is a major leverage for prefetching. We note that existing traces and techniques for predicting and utilizing favorable network conditions apply here if needed when traces are available.

Data	Format
Launch Client	Timestamp
Download Tweets	Timestamp, Tweets ID list
Link Click	Timestamp, Tweet ID, Link URL
Image View	Timestamp, Tweet ID, Image URL
WiFi Connectivity	Timestamp, WiFi connection
Coarse Location	Timestamp, coordinates

Table 1: Data Collected

Table 1 lists the items collected. To minimize overhead, we only record the tweet IDs that users download and URLs clicked. We then download all the tweet content including links, which is publicly available, from Twitter API [7].

3.1 Data Statistics

In three months, we have collected data from over 6,000 users from all over the world with a diverse demographic composition. The users downloaded 300 million tweets written in 71 languages. The volume and diversity of data reflect the real-life behavior of the mobile social app users. Such realism in data is crucial for understanding and predicting mobile social application network traffic.

Tweets contain URL On average, 29.36% of tweets contain URL links. The percentage of links in tweets varies greatly among users due to their different followings on Twitter. In our prediction algorithm, we are primarily interested in tweets with links because tweets by themselves are simply short character strings. *Therefore, unless otherwise specified, we only consider tweets with embedded links, and only prefetch those links.*

3.2 User Behavior

Twitter access session Users access twitter frequently, but briefly. On average, users spend 17 minutes each time on twitter. However the median access session is only 16 seconds long.

Twitter inter-access time The Twitter inter-access time is the time between two adjacent Twitter accesses. The average inter-access time is more than 6 hours, while the median inter-access time is only 40 seconds. In such bursty accesses where users only access a small amount of content, the network setup and round trip time become a significant overhead. The long average inter-access time also means that

[1]Twidere is an Android Twitter client which has over 100,000 downloads[8].

[2]During the installation and update, the app discloses the information collected and we collect data only if the users choose to opt in. There are less than 15% of users choose to opt in, which indicates user privacy-awareness and the effectiveness of the privacy disclosure. In addition, we only keep a hashed user ID, which is not recoverable through a one-way hash function. Last, twitter contents and social graph are publicly available information.

a user will likely only access a portion of his subscriptions, i.e. tweets generated early during the inter-access time are likely ignored, which needs to be considered in prefetching.

Selective Content Consumption Users exhibit different behavior in terms of how many tweets they read as well as how many links they click on. On average a user downloads 829 tweets with a median of 278. On average, Twitter users only download about 40% of the tweets they subscribe to. Furthermore, users click 11% of the links in the tweet they download from their twitter stream on average, with a median of 6% and a standard deviation of 12.7%. Such selectivity brings challenges to *what* to prefetch.

Time-sensitivity Popular tweets attract interests quickly, then fade away just as fast. The life-span of links on social networks are less than three hours [12]. our data also validates this phenomena on Twitter. The time between posting and clicking of an URL link on Twitter is under one hour 70% of the time, and under 10 minutes 40% of the time. In another word, if prefetching is done one hour before the actual Twitter launch, it will miss at least 70% of the clicked links since they have not been posted yet at that time. Such time-sensitivity of content consumption along with its selective nature introduces great challenges in deciding *when* and *what* to prefetch.

Diurnal access pattern A subset of users show clear diurnal patterns, e.g., the user as shown in Fig. 1. Such diurnal patterns, significant in about 20% of users, can be leveraged to integrate *when* and *what* to prefetch.

4. SOCIAL CONTENT PREDICTION

In this section, we focus on the *what* component of prefetching. In the case of Twitter, the social content is embedded in the tweets as URL links, and we are interested in predicting whether a user will click the URL link *assuming the tweet is downloaded* (i.e., the black in the gray bar in Fig. 1). We build a personalized regression-based model to achieve the goal. First, we select a set of features to represent tweets with embedded links. Then, we use linear regression to build a social content *model* for each user to predict the likelihood of link click-through of the user's future links. This information is used in combination with the *when* component (§*Scheduling Prefetching*) for all possible prefetching.

We have tried several different machine learning algorithms. Regression-based methods are most suitable in our context because SVM methods are sensitive to kernel selection and decision trees are prone to overfitting. For regression based algorithms, linear regression slightly outperforms logistic regression (Fig. 3).

4.1 Initial Feature Set

The number of available features is relatively small in Twitter due to its short style. Therefore, we consider as many features as possible. The features we selected are from simple-to-extract metadata fields of a tweet, summarized in Table 2. There are two natural groups of features, one reflects the properties of a tweet, and the other reflects that of the author.

4.2 Regression-based Prediction

Given a set of k features, each tweet i with link is represented as a k-component feature vector f_i. We denote the binary target variable c_i as whether the user clicked the link in tweet i. We observe that c_i exhibits a coarse linear relationship with the feature vector f_i:

$$c_i = f_i \times W + e \qquad (1)$$

where W is the linear coefficient vector, and e is the noise vector.

Message Features	Author Features
Hashtags contained	Name
Other users mentioned	Ghostwriters allowed
Media embedded	Avatar customized
Link position within tweet	Liked tweets count
Geocoordinates if specified	Follower count
Recipient if specified	Following count
Adult maturity rating	Presence in public lists, if any
Retweet count	Total number of tweets
Message length	Verified account status

Table 2: Features selected for click-through prediction

Model Training W is derived using linear regression of the feature vectors of the historical tweets against the observed user clicks during model training. Specifically, we use an L1-norm regularized L2-norm minimization algorithm to calculate the feature coefficients using n historical tweets. Formally, we have:

$$\underset{W}{\text{minimize}} \; ||FW - C||_2^2 + ||W||_1 \qquad (2)$$

where L1-norm regularization, i.e., $||W||_1$, is used to prevent over-fitting. Each row of the feature matrix $F^{n\times k}$ is the feature vector of a historical tweet. $C^{n\times 1}$ is the click-through vector. The values of $C^{(i,1)}$ is 1 if the corresponding history tweet is clicked, and 0 otherwise. The coefficient vector for all features is denoted as $W^{1\times k}$. Solving Eq. (2) will give us the coefficient vector W.

Model Inference The product of feature vector f and coefficient vector W is a scalar value called click-through score S:

$$S = f \times W. \qquad (3)$$

Ideally, S should be 1 for clicked tweet links and 0 otherwise. In practice, S is a real value roughly in the range of $[0, 1]$, and is proportional to the likelihood of click-through. The click-through score is a critical component in deciding whether a link will be prefetched. It is compared to a threshold value that depends on the *when* component based on access pattern, the time of prefetching, and the cellular data and battery budget. The details will be discussed in §*Scheduling Prefetching.*

4.3 Sequential Forward Feature Selection

We select as many as possible features in the initial set to be comprehensive. However, for each individual user, features without good distinguish power introduce noise in the prediction. Because users are different, we need to select a personalized set of efficient features for each user. We employ a greedy Sequential Forward Selection (SFS) algorithm to select the efficient feature set.

SFS is an iterative algorithm for picking an efficient subset from our initial feature set. SFS starts with an empty set F. In every iteration, for each feature x that is not already in F, we evaluate the prediction performance of feature set $\{x\} \cup F$ using the regression-based algorithm we proposed in §*Regression-based Prediction* based on *balanced accuracy.*

Balanced accuracy is a wildly used metric in the data mining community [11], defined as the average of *sensitivity* (the percentage of correctly predicted tweets that are clicked), and *specificity* (the percentage of correctly predicted tweets that are not clicked). SFS selects the feature set $\{x\} \cup F$ that maximizes the balanced accuracy, and then adds x to F before starting the next iteration. The SFS algorithm stops iterating when the balanced accuracy stops to increase.

4.4 Performance Evaluation

In Table 3, we list the selected features of users using the sequential forward feature selection algorithm. A first look at the popular feature set may be somewhat surprising, e.g., why is Avatar a feature and author not. This highlights the importance of *data-driven* approach; i.e., such features are supported by data instead of assumptions on what should be important. A more careful look also suggests sophistication among features. For example, having a customized avatar attracts user attention, and clearly distinguish the account from new users and bots.

Top Features	User Selected
Media embedded	92%
Geocoordinates if specified	69%
Ghostwriters allowed	56%
Avatar customized	53%
Adult maturity rating	47%
Verified account status	35%
Hashtags contained	34%
Recipient if specified	33%

Table 3: Top features selected by SFS

Fig. 3 shows the overall balanced accuracy of the linear regression prediction algorithm using the efficient feature set selected by SFS for each user. We also implement the same prediction algorithm using the logistic regression for comparison, and find that linear regression achieves slightly better performance.

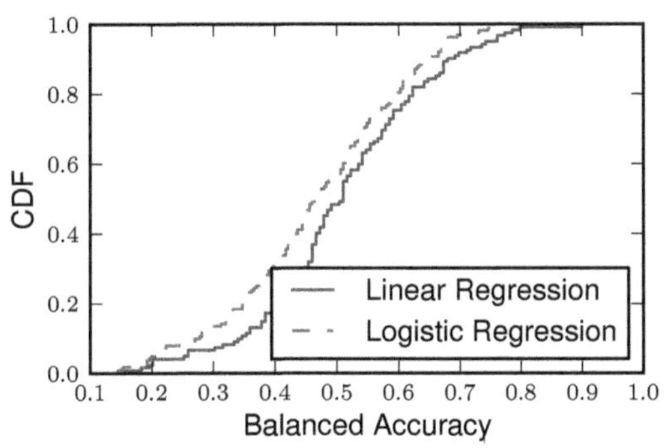

Figure 3: Balanced accuracy of linear regression and logistic regression.

5. SCHEDULING PREFETCHING

The unique features of social mobile content consumption brings interesting and challenging new dimensions in determining prefetch schedules. In particular, real trace analysis (§*Data Collection and Statistics*) suggests that social content consumption has 1) high selectiveness (partially addressed in §*Social Content Prediction*); 2) time-sensitivity; and 3) diverse access pattern. To address these issues, we present a systematic framework that integrates two complementary prefetching components, prefetch-at-launch and prefetch-on-wifi that best leverage content freshness and channel conditions. We adjust the two components to fit to *user-specific cellular data usage and battery consumption budgets*, as discussed in detail next.

Prefetch-at-launch The time-sensitivity of social mobile content suggests prefetch-at-launch, i.e., prefetch right after a user launches the Twitter application. This is the best time to fetch fresh content with high accuracy. However, prefetch-at-launch can be costly as it consumes additional cellular data and energy, and thus needs to be used judiciously. We achieve this goal by selecting an appropriate threshold and time-window. In particular, only links with a click-through score higher than the threshold (based on budget §*Tuning the Thresholds*) will be prefetched. In addition, we only prefetch links in posts within one hour. This time window is suggested by the data analysis in §*Data Collection and Statistics*, as 70% of click-through are generated within one hour. One can adjust these parameters if desired, for example, using different thresholds for different signal strength and using a different time-window. In this paper, we opt for the current simpler design. In addition to data and energy consumption, another challenge that prefetch-at-launch faces is channel condition. Users tend to snack on social applications on public transport or elevators where network connection is poor or even disconnected. This greatly deteriorates user experiences. To address these issues, we consider the following complementary component.

Prefetch-on-wifi Existing work has extensively studied network-condition-aware transmission/prefetching, based on techniques such as predicting and leveraging favorable network conditions, using WiFi hotspots, piggy-backing with other transmissions, and batching, e.g., in [22, 17, 31, 14, 24]. On the regard, we can fully leverage the existing results. In particular, based on earlier studies, we adopt two simple yet effective mechanisms: opportunistic prefetching on WiFi and piggy-backing/batching with existing transmissions. We choose these two for their effectiveness and low overhead, and note that other schemes can be equally adopted.

The main improvement on prefetch-on-wifi we make is to consider the user access pattern. In particular, we define P_t as the probability of a user accesses twitter at time (hour) t. Note that P_t varies significantly over time and across users, illustrated as in Fig. 1. We adjust how aggressive the prefetcher works based on the access probability: the click-through score for each tweet generated by content predictor (§*Social Content Prediction*) is weighted using P_t so that we prefetch more aggressively during active hours and vice versa.

Specifically, prefetch-on-wifi runs only when a WiFi network is available. It wakes up periodically (30 minutes in our setting) and waits for the next piggy-backing opportunity; i.e., transmissions initiated by other applications. Upon detecting such a transmission, the prefetcher checks-in with the prefetch server. The user device notifies the prefetch server with the links accessed by the user since the last check-in which are then removed from the user's queue. The click-through score of each tweet with links in the queue is weighted by $S' = S \times P_t$. The tweets with weighted click-through score S' higher than a threshold are then compressed and sent to the user device in one batch. Again, the threshold depends on energy budget, and is coupled with the threshold of prefetch-at-launch, which are determined in §*Tuning the Thresholds*.

Fig. 4 illustrates how Earlybird operates. The first timeline shows when the tweets with links (A to K) are posted. The second shows the Earlybird operations: an prefetch-on-wifi operation during WiFi and a prefetch-at-launch one when the user launches the app. Links in tweets C,F and I,J are prefetched by these two mechanisms respectively, with respect to their corresponding thresholds. The third timeline shows the user activity, where prefetched contents in tweets F and I are consumed.

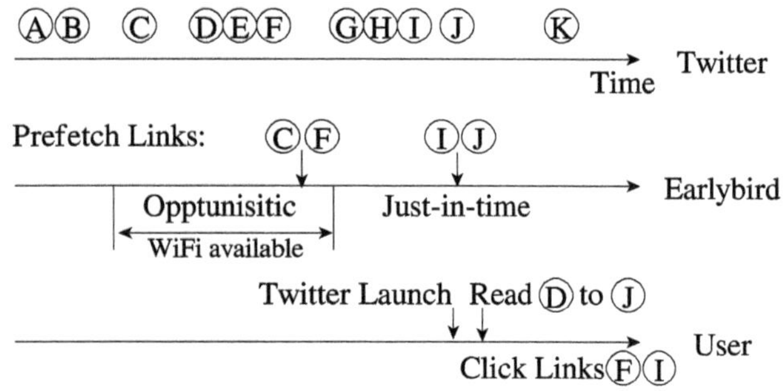

Figure 4: Earlybird operation.

5.1 Tuning the Thresholds

The two components of prefetching have complementary characteristics. Prefetch-at-launch consumes extra cellular data and battery; and prefetch-on-wifi reduces cellular data consumption, and may reduce or increase battery consumption depending on the accuracy of prefetching. Both cellular data and battery are precious resources on mobile devices, and thus must be considered in prefetching. Tuning the thresholds for the two components can adapt the prefetching to the user preference.

Threholds for fixed budget Our objective is to maximize the access delay reduction for each user under its specific cellular data budget and battery consumption constraints. Such constraints are set according to user preferences. In this paper, we take a data-driven approach to solve the above optimization problem. In particular, for each user, for each set of thresholds, we simulate Earlybird on the replay of the training data set. Based on the replay, we obtain the corresponding usage of energy and data, and the delay reduction. We then choose the appropriate threshold values based on the budgets. We note that this computation only needs to run once every few days, and can be done offline in a server, and thus do not impose heavy burdens on mobile.

Thresholds to maximize prefetching accuracy The above approach assumes that a user sets a cellular data and energy budget. Many users may not want to or know how to set such values. Therefore, an alternative way is for the system to select an appropriate threshold, e.g., a threshold that maximize the balanced accuracy in prefetching prediction, and report the cellular/energy consumption to users. As long as such consumptions are acceptable, the user does not need to do anything. We will present evaluation results on both in §*Evaluation*.

6. EVALUATION

In this section, we perform both emulation and simulation evaluations. Emulation evaluations allow us to study the behavior and randomness of users, networks, and batteries in a more realistic setting, including the current limited implementation of caching mechanisms. Trace-driven simulations allow us to evaluate a large variety of parameters and settings, and thus provide a more thorough understanding.

Emulation To realistically evaluate how Earlybird performs on an actual device and network, we run an emulation on an Android Nexus 5 for 60 long-term users from our dataset, each with at least 30 days of traces. They are also users who consumes URL links on Twitter, i.e. access more than 10% of the links in their Twitter streams. We choose these users because they have provided us with long and continuous traces to run statistically meaningful emulations.

We built the emulator as an Android application. The emulator runs on a Nexus 5 Android phone connected to T-Mobile 4G cellular network and also has access to a campus WiFi network. The emulator reads and replays the usage events collected from real-life users, including connecting to or disconnecting from WiFi networks, accessing Twitter, and opening URL links in Tweets. We run three emulations for each user, Earlybird, WiFi-Only, and On-Launch. In each emulation, the same user events are replayed, with the only difference of the caching strategies used. In Earlybird emulation, URL links are prefetched using the Earlybird algorithm. The threshold parameter used in the Earlybird algorithm is set to maximize the prefetching accuracy. In the WiFi-Only emulation, URL links are prefetched only when the phone is on WiFi. In the On-Launch emulation, the most recent 20 URL links are prefetched whenever the Twitter application is launched. The emulator opens URL links using the *WebView* provided by the Android framework. The WebView provides a notification when the web page has finished loading which is used by the emulator to calculate the loading delay of an URL link. We have observed that this notification is not precise, especially when there is dynamic content loaded using javascript in a web page. In most cases, the notification is delivered prematurely which leads to a conservative estimate of the loading delay. The emulator also relies on the Android WebView's caching mechanism to prefetch URL links. When prefetching a link, the emulator simply opens the link so that the content from the links can be cached by the WebView. We note that the implementation of WebView caching mechanism is limited. Ideally, when a user accesses the cached content is cached, the network traffic and network delay should reduce to zero. However, in the current implementation of WebView, we observe that 54.7% of network traffic for cached content. Therefore, when caching implementation improves, the benefit of prefetching would further increase.

Fig. 5 shows the delay reduction and total cellular data usage of each emulation. Without caching mechanism, users on average consume 1.1 MB per day on content. Earlybird reduces delay by 63.6 seconds per day and uses 1.25 MB per day on average, including both the necessary content network consumption and prefetch overhead. On-Launch reduces 84.3 seconds delay per day and uses 3.21 MB per day. WiFi-Only emulation reduces delay by 7 seconds by day, but due to its low prefetching accuracy, it still uses 0.7 MB data per day, which is 0.4 MB smaller than that without prefetching. Fig. 6 shows the prefetching accuracy, volume, and effectiveness. Earlybird has a significantly better prefetch hit ratio, 48.9% on average, WiFi-Only has only 6%, and On-Launch has 24%. One limitation of the Android platform is that it only provides battery usage at percentage level. It's difficult to account for the energy consumption of each user and link. Therefore, we report the aggregated behavior here. For all of the users in the emulations, Earlybird uses 4.2 times of the total battery of Nexus 5, WiFi-Only uses 2.1 times, and On-Launch uses 6.1 times.

Trace-driven Simulation To evaluate the algorithm on a larger data set, and under multiple budget constraints, we run a trace-driven evaluation for 224 long-term users from our dataset, each with at least 30 days of traces.

The network trace only shows network availability, i.e., WiFi or cellular. We measured the load time and total size of each link in the dataset using an Android crawler we wrote. We measured on both 3G and WiFi networks in our lab. The average load time (not including rendering time) for links is 16.71 second, and the median is 7.5 second.

We use the energy model presented in previous work [10] to calculate the energy consumption of prefetching each link base on the link size.

Baselines For comparison, we also consider three prefetching benchmarks: 1) WiFi-only: every 30 minutes if on WiFi is available; 2) On-launch: when the app launches. (This is the most aggressive version of prefetching, as done in many current app implementations, as well as the content prefetching part of [23, 25]); and 3) 30-min: every 30 minutes regardless of network (this is to emulate default settings in some email/news applications). We note that 1) and 2) can also be considered as special cases of EarlyBird where we set the thresholds to (0,∞) and (∞,0), respectively.

Under Budget Constraints We first evaluate the performance of Earlybird under three different budget constraints: (0.5%, 600MB), (3%, 300MB), (6%, 0MB), where the former is the percentage of battery allowed per day and the latter is the total cellular budget per month. These three sets of constraints represent different user preference on energy and cellular data consumption. We also compare with the three baseline schemes.

In Fig. 7, we show the CDFs of users in terms of delay reduction (per day), data usage (per month), and battery consumption (per day). Overall, Earlybird under (3%,300MB) and (6%,0MB) shows very good delay reduction, while operating within their corresponding resource budgets. The results of (6%,0MB) might be surprising at the first glance as it shows significant delay reduction. We note that this highlights the complementary nature of prefetch-at-launch and prefetch-on-wifi. Although the total data budget is zero, because prefetch-on-wifi reduces cellular reduction, which can be used for prefetch-at-launch, and thus jointly significantly reduce the access delay for many users. On the other hand, (0.5%,600MB) shows rather limited improvement - primarily due to the tight energy budget. The time between posting and clicking of an URL link on Twitter is under one hour 70% of the time, and under 10 minutes 40% of the time. WiFi-only scheme often misses the window of opportunity since it is restricted by when the device connects to WiFi.

In Fig. 8, we show the details of the prefetching algorithms. Clearly, on-launch shows the best prefetch hit ratio and effectiveness, as its timing is perfect. WiFi-only shows the lowest effectiveness, which explains its limited performance in delay reduction. We also note that (0.5%,600MB) caches a much smaller number of links per day due to its tight energy budget, and thus its limited delay reduction.

The impact of thresholds Next, we carefully evaluate the impact of prefetching threshold used in Earlybird. We do not include baselines here as they do not use thresholds. To show the tradeoff between energy, data, and delay, we compare the following click-through threshold: (0.1,0.1), (0.5,0.5), (0.9,0.9). Intuitively, a lower threshold allows the user device to prefetch more content. Fig. 9(a) shows the number of tweets prefetched, where each curve represents a different threshold. On average, we prefetch 89 links per day for each user. Fig. 9(b) shows the prefetch hit ratio, which is the percentage of the prefetched tweets that are actually clicked by the user. The prefetch hit ratio is 12.5% on average. Fig. 9(c) shows the percentage of link clicks that are prefetched. Clearly, a lower threshold allows more content to be prefetched and thus increases the percentage of link clicks that are prefetched, at the cost of lower hit ratio. This figure clearly demonstrates the trade-off between unprefetched ratio and hit ratio.

The corresponding effects on user experience are shown in Fig. 10. Fig. 10(a) shows the delay reduction per day enabled by prefetching. Fig. 10(b) shows the cellular data usage of different thresholds. At (0.5,0.5), prefetching only uses 43 MB cellular data every month on average for each user, where the average total data volume is 890 MB for all the links each user clicked. Last, Fig. 10(c) shows the additional battery used by prefetching. The average battery consumption ranges from 0.7% to 4.3%, corresponding to threshold (0.9, 0.9) to (0.1, 0.1). Clearly, a lower threshold more effectively reduces access delay and cellular data usage, at the cost of slightly higher energy consumption. It worths highlighting that the energy consumption is low in our scheme - this illustrates the importance of piggy-backing and leveraging better network conditions (i.e., WiFi in this evaluation) in conjunction with content prediction.

	Earlybird (0.5, 0.5)	**on-wifi**	**at-launch**
Delay Reduction (Seconds)	78.04	34.81	72.58
Delay Reduction (%)	62.04	30.21	59.11
Battery Used (%)	2.59	2.1	2.41
Extra Data (MB)	43.81	-2.71	57.99
Hit Ratio (%)	12.54	8.49	12.39
Prefetched Ratio (%)	39.77	15.65	37.04

Table 4: Effect of prefetch-on-wifi and prefetch-at-launch.

Interaction between prefetch-on-wifi and prefetch-at-launch The results summarized in Tab. 4 highlight the complementary nature of prefetch-at-launch and prefetch-on-wifi. We compare the average performance of Earlybird (0.5, 0.5) with that of prefetch-on-wifi only with threshold 0.5 (equivalent to Earlybird (0.5, ∞)), and prefetch-at-launch only with threshold 0.5 (equivalent to Earlybird (∞,

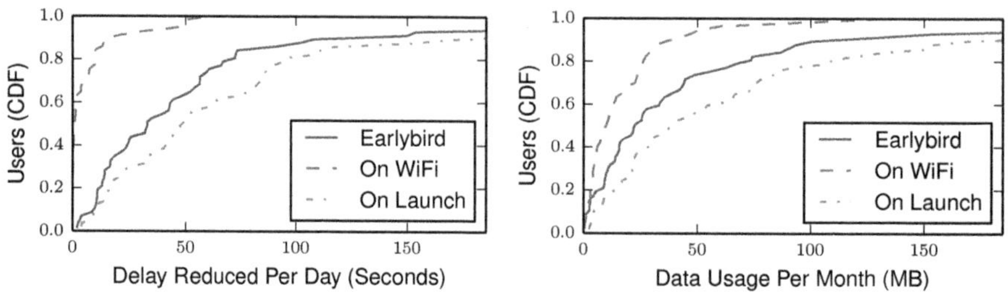

Figure 5: Prefetch emulation cost and benefit: delay reduction, cellular data usage.

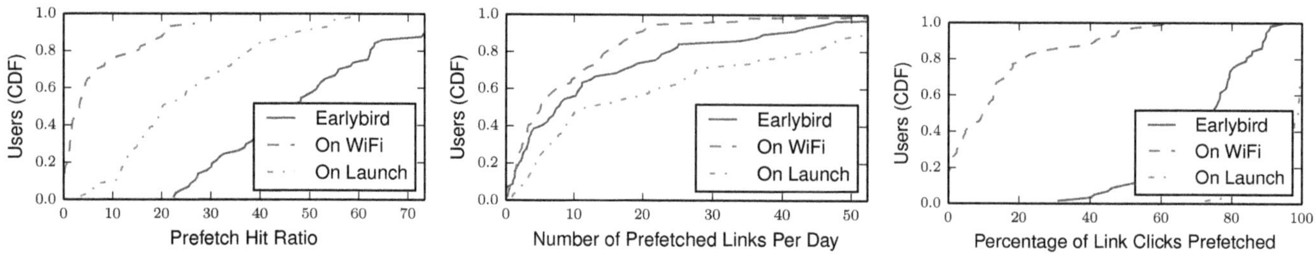

Figure 6: Prefetch emulation accuracy: efficiency, volume, and effectiveness.

0.5)) The combination of the two has higher hit ratio and prefetched ratio, and at the same time uses less data at the same time, comparing to either approach alone.

Impact of Training Set

In simulation, we use a subset of each user's data as the training set to build the prediction model and the scheduling policy, then use the others for performance evaluation.

First, we try several fixed sizes for the training set. Users download different amount of links per day, and only click a small portion of them. To avoid building a biased model, we make sure that the training set contains enough number of clicked links, and use the number of clicked links as the size of th training set. We tried the following training set sizes: 10, 50, 90, 130, 170.

We then compare the fixed training set with a rolling training set. For a rolling training set, the first training set contains 50 clicks is used in the beginning. The resulting model is used to predict the click-through of the following tweets, which is the test set, until we see 50 clicks in the test set. Then the previous model is discarded, and we use the test set, which also contains 50 clicks, to train a new model. This process is repeated until we processed all the tweets.

The average balanced accuracy increases from 71.9% to 77.4% as the training set size increase from 10 to 170. However, using a rolling training set of size 50, the average balanced accuracy is 80.8% which is higher than any fixed training set. The result indicated that user preferences do changes over time, using recent history data as training set yields higher training accuracy.

7. RELATED WORK

Prefetching on Mobile Systems In [15], the authors present an architecture for mobile prefetching where IMP (Informed Mobile Prefetching) is structured as a library to which any mobile application may link to. In IMP, it assumes that applications provide precise information on "what" to prefetch. We focus on the unique features of mobile social content, to address "what" and the interaction of "what" and "when". In [25], the authors show that inappropriate prefetching can be costly to users. They implement and evaluate Procastinator that decides prefetching based on a few factors including whether the user is on WiFi or cellular network, the status of the user's data plan, and whether the object is needed at the present time. The implementation achieves "zero-effort", i.e., it requires no developer effort, no source code, and no OS changes. The technique developed can be leveraged to in the implementation of Earlybird. In [23], the authors proposed an app prefetching algorithm, which predicts when and what application will be launched on mobile phone and prefetch applications accordingly. The content prefetching algorithm is similar to the prefetch-at-launch in this work, which is compared in §*Evaluation*.

Recently, CDN-based approaches have been proposed by researchers to increase QoE for web services, e.g. in [29, 26]. The authors propose to use social network relationships, read access patterns to efficiently distribute content geographically to lower bandwidth costs and increase QoE. Typically, CDN-based solutions do not deal with challenges that are special to wireless networks and personalized usage patterns.

Also relevant to our work is user profile and and how to leverage them for efficient transmission such as prefetching. Both Wiffler [9] and Bartendr [27] consider the setting of vehicular systems to offload cellular data traffic to either WiFi networks or to time-instants when signal strength is stronger. Breadcrumb [21] and smarttransfer [30] address the issue of predicting future network condition and user profile. We build upon such network-aware techniques while focusing on the unique properties of mobile social content.

Prefetching in general is well-studied under different context. In [22, 17], the authors explored user access prediction and prefetching for file systems and databases. [31, 14, 24] addressed the theoretical problem in prefetching such as cost benefit analysis.

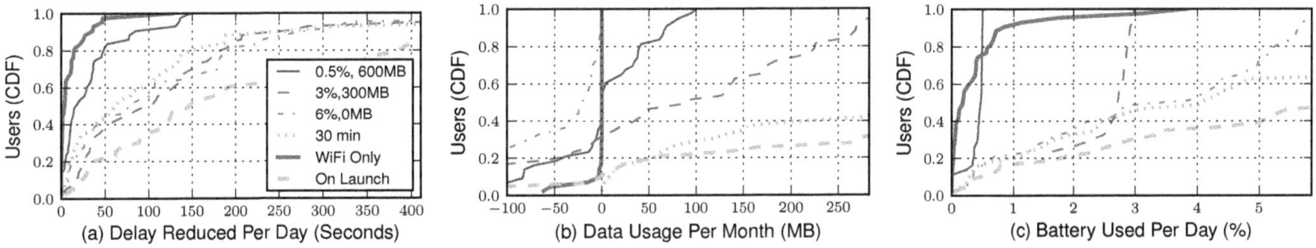

Figure 7: Prefetch cost and benefit: delay reduction, cellular data usage, and energy consumption.

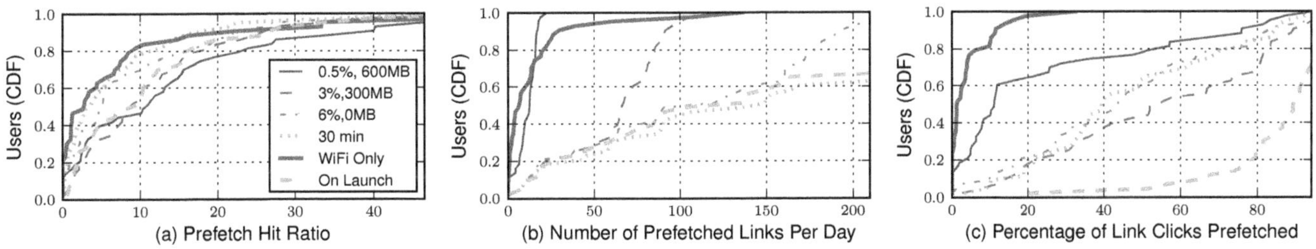

Figure 8: Prefetch accuracy: efficiency, volume, and effectiveness.

Twitter studies In [16, 20], the authors study the basic social graph such as following relationship, and statistics of Twitter, including number of user, posting and retweet. Factors that impact retweeting is also explored. Suh, et al. discussed the factors that affected the retweeting or retweetability of a tweet using PCA and generalized linear model [28]. Kunegis et al. also studied the likelihood of retweeting [18] based on content features. They only used 7 features to start with, and the effective features selected are quite different from us, showing that retweet and content access have very different models. We are the first to use the click-through dataset and build a content-prediction model for mobile networking.

8. CONCLUSION

Mobile users are consuming increasingly large amount of embedded content through social applications. Social content prefetching is a promising technique for improving user experience on mobile devices. By identifying the unique features of mobile social applications, we propose a unified mobile social prefetching framework, Earlybird, that jointly optimizes the *what* and *when* in prefetching, leveraging content preference, user behavior pattern, and dynamic network conditions. The proposed scheme can adapt to user-specific budget constraints in terms of (extra) energy and cellular data, with the objective of maximizing delay reduction. We use a data-driven approach to develop personalized content model and control variables (prefetching thresholds) to achieve this goal. Evaluation using real-life Twitter traces show promising performance of Earlybird. In addition to EarlyBird's immediate utility for Twitter users, we speculate that our approach of unifying social and network access patterns can be generalized to other social networks as well.

9. REFERENCES

[1] 2013 Mobile Future in Focus. `http://www.comscore.com/Insights/Presentations_and_Whitepapers/2013/2013_Mobile_Future_in_Focus`.

[2] Mobile apps: We interrupt this broadcast. http://blog.flurry.com/bid/92105/Mobile-Apps-We-Interrupt-This-Broadcast.

[3] News use across social media platforms. `http://www.journalism.org/2013/11/14/news-use-across-social-media-platforms/`.

[4] Public dataset: Google mobile network measurements. https://dev.twitter.com/.

[5] Sina weibo. `http://en.wikipedia.org/wiki/Sina_Weibo`.

[6] Social media report 2012: Social media comes of age. http://www.nielsen.com/us/en/newswire/2012/social-media-report-2012-social-media-comes-of-age.html.

[7] Twitter api. https://dev.twitter.com/.

[8] Twidere for twitter. `https://play.google.com/store/apps/details?id=org.mariotaku.twidere&hl=en`, 2013.

[9] A. Balasubramanian, R. Mahajan, and A. Venkataramani. Augmenting mobile 3G using WiFi. In *Proc. of ACM International Conference on Mobile Systems, Applications, and Services (MobiSys'10)*, pages 209–222, San Francisco, CA, June 2010.

[10] N. Balasubramanian, A. Balasubramanian, and A. Venkataramani. Energy consumption in mobile phones: A measurement study and implications for network applications. In *Proc. of ACM SIGCOMM Internet Measurement Workshop (IMC'09)*, pages 280–293, Chicago, IL, November 2009.

[11] P. Baldi, S. r. Brunak, Y. Chauvin, C. A. F. Andersen, and H. Nielsen. Bioinformatics review. 16(5):412–424, 2000.

[12] Bit.ly. You just shared a link. how long will people pay attention? `http://blog.bitly.com/post/9887686919/you-just-shared-a-link-how-long-will-people-pay`.

[13] D. Chu, A. Kansal, J. Liu, and F. Zhao. Mobile apps: it's time to move up to condos. In *Proceedings of the 13th USENIX conference on Hot topics in operating systems*, HotOS'13, 2011.

[14] V. de Nitto Personè, V. Grassi, and A. Morlupi. Modeling and evaluation of prefetching policies for context-aware information services. In *Proceedings of the 4th annual ACM/IEEE international conference*

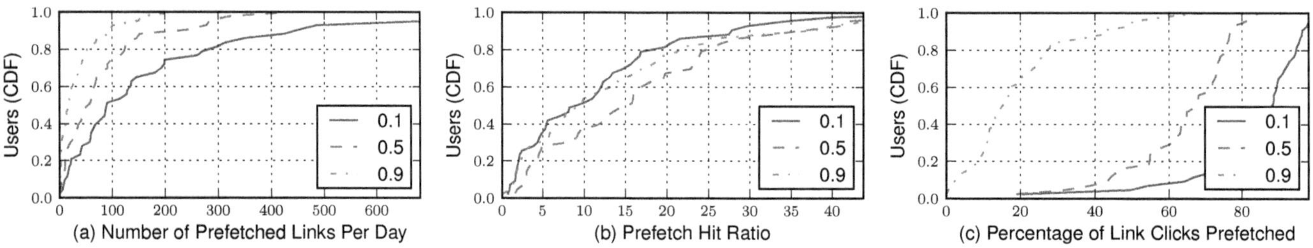

Figure 9: Prefetch accuracy: volume, efficiency, and effectiveness.

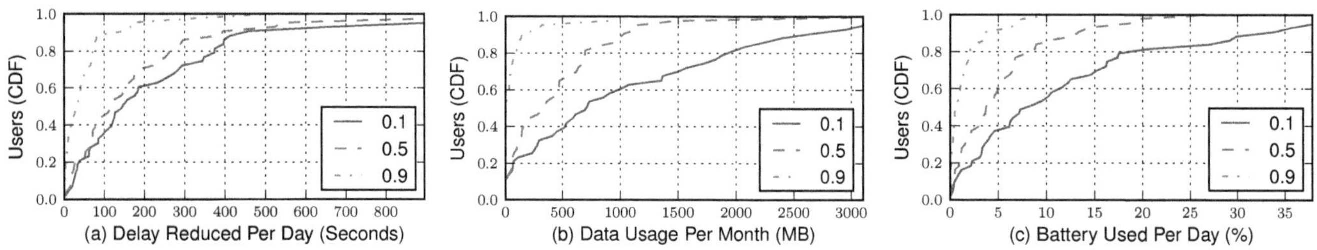

Figure 10: Prefetch cost and benefit: delay reduction, cellular data usage, and energy consumption.

on Mobile computing and networking, pages 55–65. ACM, 1998.

[15] B. D. Higgins, J. Flinn, T. J. Giuli, B. Noble, C. Peplin, and D. Watson. Informed mobile prefetching. In *Proceedings of the 10th international conference on Mobile systems, applications, and services*, MobiSys '12, pages 155–168, New York, NY, USA, 2012. ACM.

[16] A. Java, X. Song, T. Finin, and B. Tseng. Why we twitter: understanding microblogging usage and communities. In *Proceedings of the 9th WebKDD and 1st SNA-KDD 2007 workshop on Web mining and social network analysis*, pages 56–65. ACM, 2007.

[17] D. Kotz and C. S. Ellis. Practical prefetching techniques for parallel file systems. In *Parallel and Distributed Information Systems, 1991., Proceedings of the First International Conference on*, pages 182–189. IEEE, 1991.

[18] N. N. T. G. J. Kunegis and A. C. Alhadi. Bad news travel fast: A content-based analysis of interestingness on twitter. 2011.

[19] A. Kuzmanovic and E. W. Knightly. Tcp-lp: A distributed algorithm for low priority data transfer. In *INFOCOM 2003. Twenty-Second Annual Joint Conference of the IEEE Computer and Communications. IEEE Societies*, volume 3, pages 1691–1701. IEEE, 2003.

[20] H. Kwak, C. Lee, H. Park, and S. Moon. What is twitter, a social network or a news media? In *Proceedings of the 19th international conference on World wide web*, pages 591–600. ACM, 2010.

[21] A. J. Nicholson and B. D. Noble. Breadcrumbs: forecasting mobile connectivity. In *Proceedings of the 14th ACM international conference on Mobile computing and networking*, pages 46–57. ACM, 2008.

[22] M. Palmer and S. B. Zdonik. *Fido: A cache that learns to fetch.* Brown University, Department of Computer Science, 1991.

[23] A. Parate, M. Böhmer, D. Chu, D. Ganesan, and B. M. Marlin. Practical prediction and prefetch for faster access to applications on mobile phones. In *Proceedings of the 2013 ACM International Joint Conference on Pervasive and Ubiquitous Computing*, UbiComp '13, pages 275–284, New York, NY, USA, 2013. ACM.

[24] R. H. Patterson, G. A. Gibson, E. Ginting, D. Stodolsky, and J. Zelenka. *Informed prefetching and caching*, volume 29. ACM, 1995.

[25] L. Ravindranath, S. Agarwal, J. Padhye, and C. Riederer. Give in to procrastination and stop prefetching. In *ACM HotNets XII*, 2013.

[26] S. Scellato, C. Mascolo, M. Musolesi, and J. Crowcroft. Track globally, deliver locally: Improving content delivery networks by tracking geographic social cascades. In *Proceedings of the 20th International Conference on World Wide Web*, WWW '11, pages 457–466, New York, NY, USA, 2011. ACM.

[27] A. Schulman, V. Navda, R. Ramjee, N. Spring, P. Deshpande, C. Grunewald, K. Jain, and V. Padmanabhan. Bartendr: A practical approach to energy-aware cellular data scheduling. In *Proc. of ACM Annual International Conference on Mobile Computing and Networking (MobiCom'10)*, pages 85–96, Chicago, IL, September 2010.

[28] B. Suh, L. Hong, P. Pirolli, and E. H. Chi. Want to be retweeted? large scale analytics on factors impacting retweet in twitter network. In *Social Computing (SocialCom), 2010 IEEE Second International Conference on*, pages 177–184. IEEE, 2010.

[29] S. Traverso, K. Huguenin, I. Trestian, V. Erramilli, N. Laoutaris, and K. Papagiannaki. Tailgate: Handling long-tail content with a little help from friends. In *Proceedings of the 21st International Conference on World Wide Web*, WWW '12, pages 151–160, New York, NY, USA, 2012. ACM.

[30] Y. Wang, X. Liu, A. Nicoara, T.-A. Lin, and C.-H. Hsu. Smarttransfer: transferring your mobile multimedia contents at the right time. In *Proceedings of the 22nd international workshop on Network and Operating System Support for Digital Audio and Video*, pages 71–76. ACM, 2012.

[31] T. Watson. Application design for wireless computing. In *Mobile Computing*, pages 363–373. Springer, 1996.

Handoff Rate Analysis in Heterogeneous Wireless Networks with Poisson and Poisson Cluster Patterns

Wei Bao and Ben Liang
Department of Electrical and Computer Engineering, University of Toronto
Toronto, Ontario, Canada
wbao@comm.utoronto.ca, liang@comm.utoronto.ca

ABSTRACT

In multi-tier heterogeneous wireless networks (HWNs), both horizontal and vertical handoffs impact the signaling overhead and quality of service in the system. However, they are difficult to analyze due to the diverse and irregularly shaped cells in HWNs. The causes of this irregularity are three-fold: (1) small-cell base stations (BSs) tend to be deployed with a high level of spatial randomness; (2) BSs are likely to aggregate around highly populated geographical regions; (3) various transmission power levels in different tiers further create diverse cell sizes and shapes. In this work we present a new stochastic geometric analysis framework on user mobility in HWNs. Each tier of BSs is modeled as either a Poisson point process (PPP) or a Poisson cluster process (PCP), to capture their spatial randomness and their non-uniform and dependent aggregation in space. Flexible user association is also taken into consideration, such that various scales of cell sizes are accommodated. We derive analytical expressions for the rates of all handoff types experienced by an active user with arbitrary movement trajectory. We also demonstrate an example application of the proposed analysis, in optimizing the multi-tier BS selection by users, to balance the tradeoff between data rate and handoff overhead. Finally, extensive simulation is conducted to validate the correctness and usefulness of our analysis.

Categories and Subject Descriptors

C.2.1 [**Network Architecture and Design**]: Wireless communication

Keywords

Mobility; handoff; stochastic geometry; analytic geometry; Poisson cluster process

1. INTRODUCTION

Traditional single-tier macro-cellular networks provide wide coverage for mobile user equipments (UEs), but they are insufficient to satisfy the exploding demand for high bandwidth access driven by modern mobile traffic. One effective means to increase network capacity is to provide more serving stations within a geographical area, i.e., installing a diverse set of small-cells such as femtocells and WiFi hotspots, overlaying the macrocells, to form a multi-tier heterogeneous wireless network (HWN). Each small-cell is equipped with a shorter-range and lower-cost base station (BS) or access point (AP), to give nearby UEs higher-bandwidth network access with lower power usage, and to offload data traffic from macrocells.

In the presence of multiple tiers of cells, however, mobility management of the UEs becomes more challenging. In particular, HWNs introduce vertical handoffs, i.e., handoffs made between two BSs in different tiers [30]. Compared with horizontal handoffs, i.e., handoffs made between two BSs in the same tier, vertical handoffs impact both the UEs and the overall system in more complicated ways. For example, extra traffic latency and additional network signaling are incurred during channel setup and tear down when a vertical handoff is made; more UE power may be consumed due to simultaneously active network interface to multiple tiers; call drops or degraded quality of service (QoS) could also be experienced by UEs due to the lack of radio resource after handoff.

We define the handoff rate as the expected number of handoffs experienced by one UE per unit time. It is closely related to the signaling overhead in the system and the QoS of UEs. As a prerequisite to performance evaluation and system design in HWNs, it is essential to quantify the rates of different handoff types. However, the analysis on handoff rates in HWNs is complicated by the irregularly shaped multi-tier network topologies introduced by the small-cell structure. *First*, small-cell BSs are often installed incrementally and irregularly, with a high level of spatial randomness. *Second*, BSs are likely to aggregate around some highly populated geographical regions (e.g., urban areas, attractions, etc.), which further complicates the spatial pattern of the network. *Third*, different tiers of BSs communicate at different power levels, causing various scales of cell sizes, and non-polygon cell shapes. As a consequence, it is difficult to characterize the cell boundaries and to track boundary crossings made by UEs (i.e., handoffs) in the system. Fig. 1(a) shows an example topology with two tiers of BSs. Previously developed analytical techniques in the literature, using queueing theory [3, 5, 10, 13, 15, 21], regular grids [2, 17, 28], or homogeneous Poisson point processes (PPPs) [6, 9, 23],

MobiHoc'15, June 22–25, 2015, Hangzhou, China.

http://dx.doi.org/10.1145/2746285.2746317.

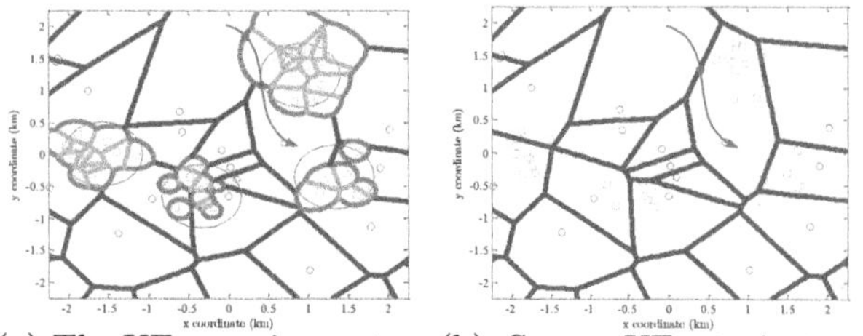

(a) The UE experiences two vertical handoffs. (b) Same UE trajectory with one horizontal handoff.

Figure 1: An example of a two-tier HWN. Tier-1 and 2 BSs are represented by "○" and "□" respectively. Tier-2 BSs are clustered in four disk regions. Blue, red, and green curves show cell boundaries within tier-1, between tier-1 and tier-2, and within tier-2, respectively. The magenta arrow represents the trajectory of an active UE.

are insufficient to accurately model the complex handoff patterns in HWNs.

In this work, we establish a new analytical framework to quantify the rates of horizontal and vertical handoffs in HWNs with more general cell topologies and general UE movement patterns. In order to capture the spatial randomness, conventional stochastic geometric analysis on HWNs usually models each tier of BSs as a homogeneous PPP. However, the PPP cannot capture the non-uniform and dependent aggregation of BSs in, for example, popular regions of the network where more BSs tend to be installed, as the positions of the points in PPP are independent of each other. Instead, we accommodate the non-uniform and dependent aggregation by modeling some BS tiers as Poisson cluster processes (PCPs) [32]. Each BS cluster includes multiple nearby BSs, and multiple BS clusters are randomly distributed in space. Furthermore, to model flexible scaling of cell sizes in different tiers, we consider the *biased user association* scheme (also called flexible user association) [7,20,29], in which each tier of BSs is assigned an association bias value, and a UE is associated with a BS that provides the largest biased received power. In this case, the resultant cell splitting is a tessellation generated by both PPPs and PCPs (see Fig. 1(a) for an example). Through our proposed stochastic and analytic geometric analysis, we derive exact expressions for the rates of all handoff types experienced by an active UE with arbitrary movement trajectory.

Our characterization of the handoff rates also provides important guidelines for system design. One example is the open problem of optimal tier selection. Consider the example in Fig. 1(a), where an active UE's trajectory is indicated by the magenta arrow. By choosing to access both tier-1 and tier-2 cells, the UE experiences two vertical handoffs. In contrast, as shown in Fig. 1(b), by choosing to access tier-1 cells only, it experiences one horizontal handoff only. However, in the latter case, the UE gives up the opportunity to access a tier-2 BS, which potentially has higher bandwidth and requires lower power consumption. Thus, a UE may choose to access small-cell BSs to improve data rate and power consumption, but this may also lead to more frequent vertical handoffs, which potentially deteriorates the service quality. The proposed handoff analysis can be used to provide design guidelines for optimal tier selection, where the handoff rate plays a key role.

The rest of this paper is organized as follows. In Section 2, we discuss the relation between our work and prior works. In Section 3, we describe the system model. In Section 4, we present theoretical analysis on different types of handoff rates. In Section 5, we study the optimal tier selection problem as an application scenario of handoff rate analysis. In Section 6, we validate our analysis with simulation. Finally, conclusions are given in Section 7.

2. RELATED WORKS

In this section, we survey the related prior works on mobility modeling and handoff analysis. We first summarize two categories of mobility modeling techniques, based on either abstract queueing formulations or actual geometric cell patterns. We then discuss relevant handoff and association decision algorithms in the literature.

2.1 Mobility Modeling with Queueing Systems

One classical category of mobility analysis techniques in cellular networks employ queueing formulation, without explicitly modeling the geometric patterns of cell shapes in the networks. In these works, cells are modeled as queues containing active users, and handoffs are modeled as unit transfers between queues. For example, Ghosh *et al.* [15] studied the single-cell scenario using an $M/G/\infty$ queue. Kirsal *et al.* [21] studied one WLAN cell overlaying one 3G cell, and a two-queue model was proposed accordingly. For more general multicell networks, queueing network models have been proposed and analyzed in [3,5,10,13]. In contrast, we explicitly model the cell geometry in this work.

2.2 Mobility Modeling with Cell Geometry

In mobility analysis techniques that consider cell geometry, non-random regular grids are commonly employed for mathematical convenience. Traditional one-tier cellular network is commonly modeled as a hexagonal grid [27]. For HWN analysis, Anpalagan and Katzela [2] studied a two-tier network by modeling small-cells as hexagons, and each macrocell as a cluster of neighbouring small-cells. Shenoy and Hartpence [28] studied a two-tier network by modeling WLAN small-cells as squares, and macrocells as larger squares, each covering 5×5 WLAN cells. Hasib and Fapojuwo [17] studied a two-tier cellular network including one hexagonal macrocell and a predetermined number of circular microcells.

To further capture the spatial randomness of network topologies, Lin *et al.* [23] conducted a pioneering study on the user mobility in a one-tier cellular network with randomly distributed BSs, where the BSs were modeled as a homogeneous PPP, and cell splitting was modeled as a standard Poisson Voronoi. In [6,9], we extended the above study to the multi-tier case, where each tier of BSs was modeled as a homogeneous PPP, and the resultant cell splitting was modeled as a weighted Poisson Voronoi. The studies in [6,9,23] follow conventional stochastic geometric analysis of HWNs, where the PPP is commonly used to model the distribution of BSs to capture their spatial randomness (e.g., [1,11,12]). However, in reality, often a higher density of BSs are installed in more populated regions. The PPP assumption does not apply in such a scenario. In order to resolve this issue, the PCP has been adopted as an alternative to capture the non-uniform and dependent aggregation of BSs [16, 19, 33]. We thus use the PCP model in our work. Note that previous studies [16, 19, 33] only focused on the average throughput and outage performance for randomly placed but stationary UEs. In contrast, in our work we consider moving UEs and their handoff between PCP BSs, which is essential to performance analysis in a mobile network but has not been addressed in the existing literature.

2.3 Handoff and Association Decisions

Orthogonal to the scope of our work, there is also a large body of previous works that study handoff timing algorithms, without considering the random geometric patterns of UEs and BSs. One type of handoff decision algorithms employ threshold comparison of one or several metrics (e.g., received signal strength, network loading, bandwidth, etc.) [22, 25, 26]. Another type uses dynamic programming [31] or artificial intelligence techniques [18] to improve the effectiveness of handoff procedures. In our work, we do not explicitly specify the handoff timing. Instead, we derive handoff rates and the corresponding optimal tier-selection decisions through stochastic geometric analysis.

The optimization of tier association in HWNs has been studied using stochastic geometric analysis [7, 20, 29]. These works assume that the UEs are randomly placed but stationary. They focus on average performance metrics such as the mean data throughput or outage probability. They ignore the movement of UEs and the effect of handoffs, which are the main focus of our work.

3. SYSTEM MODEL

In this section, we describe the multi-tier network under consideration, along with how the UEs are associated with BSs and are handed off between BSs as they move.

3.1 Multi-tier Network

We consider an HWN with randomly distributed K tiers of BSs. It includes K_P Poisson tiers (P-tiers) and K_C Poisson cluster tiers (C-tiers), so that $K = K_P + K_C$. Let $\mathcal{K}_P = \{1, \dots, K_P\}$ denote the set of P-tiers, and $\mathcal{K}_C = \{K_P + 1, \dots, K_P + K_C\}$ denote the set of C-tiers. Let $\mathcal{K} = \{1, \dots, K_P + K_C\}$.

Let Φ_k denote the point process representing the locations of tier-k BSs. If $k \in \mathcal{K}_P$, Φ_k is a homogeneous PPP with intensity of λ_k on the two dimensional space $\mathbb{R}^2$. If $k \in \mathcal{K}_C$, Φ_k is a PCP defined as follows: First, *cluster centers* are generated as a parent point process Θ_k, which is a homogeneous PPP with intensity μ_k on the two dimensional space $\mathbb{R}^2$. Second, for each parent point (cluster center) $\mathbf{x}$ in Θ_k, a cluster of BSs form a child point process $\Omega_k(\mathbf{x})$, which is a PPP with intensity ν_k in the region $\mathcal{B}(\mathbf{x}, R_k)$, where $\mathcal{B}(\mathbf{x}, R)$ is defined as the disk region centered at $\mathbf{x}$ with radius R throughout this paper. The overall PCP Φ_k is the union of all child point processes, i.e., $\Phi_k = \bigcup_{\mathbf{x}\in\Theta_k} \Omega_k(\mathbf{x})$. Note that Φ_k does *not* include parent points Θ_k. Given the location of some BS $\mathbf{x}_{\text{BS}}$ in a tier-k PCP, let $\mathcal{C}(\mathbf{x}_{\text{BS}})$ denote the cluster center of the BS. Thus $\Omega_k(\mathcal{C}(\mathbf{x}_{\text{BS}}))$ is the cluster it belongs to.

3.2 Biased User Association

Different tiers of BSs transmit at different power levels. Let P_k be the transmission power of tier-k BSs. These power levels are fixed and given. If $P_t(\mathbf{x})$ is the transmission power from a BS at location $\mathbf{x}$ and $P_r(\mathbf{y})$ is the received power at location $\mathbf{y}$, we have $P_r(\mathbf{y}) = \frac{P_t(\mathbf{x})}{|\mathbf{x}-\mathbf{y}|^\gamma}$, where $|\mathbf{x}-\mathbf{y}|^\gamma$ is the propagation loss function with $\gamma > 2$.

We consider a general biased user association rule as follows [20, 29]. Given that a UE is located at $\mathbf{y}$, it associates itself with the BS that provides the maximum *biased received power* as follows:

$$\mathcal{BS}(\mathbf{y}) = \arg \max_{\mathbf{x}\in\Phi_k, \forall k} B_k P_k |\mathbf{x}-\mathbf{y}|^{-\gamma}, \tag{1}$$

where $\mathcal{BS}(\mathbf{y})$ denotes the location of the BS chosen to serve the UE, $P_k|\mathbf{x}-\mathbf{y}|^{-\gamma}$ is the received power from a tier-k BS located at $\mathbf{x}$, and B_k is the association bias, indicating the power preference of UEs toward tier-k BSs.

As an example, the cell splitting resultant from biased user association is shown in Fig. 1(a) (a two-tier scenario including one P-tier and one C-tier). Let $\mathbf{T}^{(1)}$ denote the set of overall cell boundaries, and let $\mathbf{T}^{(1)}_{kj}$ denote the set of boundaries between tier-k cells and tier-j cells, which is also referred to as the set of *type k-j cell boundaries* in this paper. Note that $\mathbf{T}^{(1)}_{kj}$ and $\mathbf{T}^{(1)}_{jk}$ are equivalent.

Note that for $B_1, B_2, \dots, B_K$, their effects remain the same if we multiply all of them by the same positive constant. For presentation convenience, we define $\beta_{kj} = \left(\frac{P_k B_k}{P_j B_j}\right)^{1/\gamma}$. Clearly, $\beta_{kj} = \frac{1}{\beta_{jk}}$, and $\beta_{kk} = 1$.

3.3 UE Trajectory and Handoff Rate

We aim to study the rates of all handoff types of some active UE moving in the network. Let $\mathcal{T}_0$ denote the trajectory of the UE, which is of finite length. In this paper, a handoff made from a tier-k cell to a tier-j cell is called a *type k-j handoff*. The total number of type k-j handoffs along $\mathcal{T}_0$ is denoted by $\mathcal{N}_{kj}(\mathcal{T}_0, \mathbf{T}^{(1)}_{kj})$.

Note that if $j \neq k$, a type k-j (vertical) handoff is *not* equivalent to a type j-k handoff. When the UE crosses some type k-j boundary, either a type k-j or a type j-k handoff is made, depending on its direction of movement. Thus, the number of type k-j plus type j-k handoffs is equal to the number of intersections of $\mathcal{T}_0$ and $\mathbf{T}^{(1)}_{kj}$, which is denoted by $\mathcal{N}(\mathcal{T}_0, \mathbf{T}^{(1)}_{kj})$. In other words, we have $\mathcal{N}(\mathcal{T}_0, \mathbf{T}^{(1)}_{kj}) = \mathcal{N}_{kj}(\mathcal{T}_0, \mathbf{T}^{(1)}_{kj}) + \mathcal{N}_{jk}(\mathcal{T}_0, \mathbf{T}^{(1)}_{kj})$. If $j = k$, $\mathcal{N}(\mathcal{T}_0, \mathbf{T}^{(1)}_{kk}) = \mathcal{N}_{kk}(\mathcal{T}_0, \mathbf{T}^{(1)}_{kk})$ indicates the number of type k-k (horizontal) handoffs. We obtain the overall number of handoffs by adding the numbers of all types of handoffs.

4. HANDOFF RATE ANALYSIS

The proposed analysis of handoff rates consists of a progressive sequence of four components, which are described in the following subsections.

4.1 Length Intensity of Cell Boundaries

Handoffs occur at the intersections of the active UE's trajectory and cell boundaries. In order to track the number of intersections, we need to first study the length intensity of different types of cell boundaries $\mathbf{T}^{(1)}_{kj}$, which is defined as the expected length of $\mathbf{T}^{(1)}_{kj}$ in a unit square.

The set of cell boundaries $\mathbf{T}^{(1)}_{kj}$ is generated by all K tiers of BSs $\Phi_1, \Phi_2, \dots, \Phi_K$. It corresponds to the set of points on $\mathbb{R}^2$ where the same biased power level is received from a tier-k BS and a tier-j BS, and this biased received power level is greater than those from any other BS in all tiers. Mathematically, $\mathbf{T}_{kj}^{(1)}$ is expressed as

$$\mathbf{T}_{kj}^{(1)} = \left\{ \mathbf{x} \middle| \exists \mathbf{x}_1 \in \Phi_k, \mathbf{x}_2 \in \Phi_j, \mathbf{x}_1 \neq \mathbf{x}_2, \text{s.t. } P_r = \frac{P_k B_k}{|\mathbf{x}_1 - \mathbf{x}|^\gamma} = \frac{P_j B_j}{|\mathbf{x}_2 - \mathbf{x}|^\gamma}, \text{ and } \forall i \in \mathcal{K}, \mathbf{y} \in \Phi_i, P_r \geq \frac{P_i B_i}{|\mathbf{y} - \mathbf{x}|^\gamma} \right\}. \quad (2)$$

A main challenge in this work is in characterizing handoff rates across the highly irregular cell boundaries generated by BSs that form PCPs. If we consider the cell boundaries within tier-k, and tier-k is a C-tier (i.e., $k \in \mathcal{K}_C$), then we can further classify the set of cell boundaries $\mathbf{T}_{kk}^{(1)}$ into the set of intra-cluster cell boundaries (i.e., the two BSs that provide the largest biased received power belong to the same cluster), which is denoted by $\mathbf{T}_{kk,in}^{(1)}$, and the set of inter-cluster cell boundaries (i.e., the two BSs belong to two different clusters), which is denoted by $\mathbf{T}_{kk,out}^{(1)}$. We formally express

$$\mathbf{T}_{kk,in}^{(1)} = \left\{ \mathbf{x} \middle| \exists \mathbf{x}_1 \in \Phi_k, \mathbf{x}_2 \in \Phi_k, \mathbf{x}_1 \neq \mathbf{x}_2, \mathcal{C}(\mathbf{x}_1) = \mathcal{C}(\mathbf{x}_2), \text{ s.t. } P_r = \frac{P_k B_k}{|\mathbf{x}_1 - \mathbf{x}|^\gamma} = \frac{P_j B_j}{|\mathbf{x}_2 - \mathbf{x}|^\gamma}, \text{ and } \forall i \in \mathcal{K}, \mathbf{y} \in \Phi_i, P_r \geq \frac{P_i B_i}{|\mathbf{y} - \mathbf{x}|^\gamma} \right\}. \quad (3)$$

Similarly, by replacing $\mathcal{C}(\mathbf{x}_1) = \mathcal{C}(\mathbf{x}_2)$ by $\mathcal{C}(\mathbf{x}_1) \neq \mathcal{C}(\mathbf{x}_2)$ in (3), we have the expression of $\mathbf{T}_{kk,out}^{(1)}$.

Note that we have $\mathbf{T}_{kk}^{(1)} = \mathbf{T}_{kk,in}^{(1)} \bigcup \mathbf{T}_{kk,out}^{(1)}$. Also, if $k, j \in \mathcal{K}_C$ and $k \neq j$, we cannot classify $\mathbf{T}_{kj}^{(1)}$ in the same way, as the cell boundary is surely formed by two BSs in two different clusters in two different tiers.

Let $\mu_1(\mathbf{T}_{kj}^{(1)})$ denote the length intensity of $\mathbf{T}_{kj}^{(1)}$, which is the expected length of $\mathbf{T}_{kj}^{(1)}$ in a unit square. Because $\Phi_1, \ldots, \Phi_K$ are stationary, $\mathbf{T}_{kj}^{(1)}$ is also stationary, and thus the unit square could be arbitrarily picked on $\mathbb{R}^2$. Hence, we have

$$\mu_1(\mathbf{T}_{kj}^{(1)}) = \mathbb{E}\left(\left| \mathbf{T}_{kj}^{(1)} \bigcap [0,1)^2 \right|_1 \right), \quad (4)$$

where $|L|_1$ denotes the length of a collection of curves L (i.e., one-dimensional Lebesgue measure of L). Similarly, if $k \in \mathcal{K}_C$,

$$\mu_1(\mathbf{T}_{kk,x}^{(1)}) = \mathbb{E}\left(\left| \mathbf{T}_{kk,x}^{(1)} \bigcap [0,1)^2 \right|_1 \right), \quad (5)$$

where the subscript "x" indicates either "*in*" or "*out*". Note that $\mu_1(\mathbf{T}_{kk}^{(1)}) = \mu_1(\mathbf{T}_{kk,in}^{(1)}) + \mu_1(\mathbf{T}_{kk,out}^{(1)})$.

4.2 Δd-Extended Cell Boundaries

It is difficult to directly quantify the one-dimensional measures $\mu_1(\mathbf{T}_{kj}^{(1)})$, $\mu_1(\mathbf{T}_{kk,in}^{(1)})$, and $\mu_1(\mathbf{T}_{kk,out}^{(1)})$ on the two-dimensional plane. Instead, we first introduce the set of Δd-*extended cell boundaries*, which extends the one-dimensional measures to two-dimensional measures.

The Δd-extended cell boundaries of $\mathbf{T}_{kj}^{(1)}$, denoted by $\mathbf{T}_{kj}^{(2)}(\Delta d)$, is defined as

$$\mathbf{T}_{kj}^{(2)}(\Delta d) = \left\{ \mathbf{x} \middle| \exists \mathbf{y} \in \mathbf{T}_{kj}^{(1)}, \text{ s.t. } |\mathbf{x} - \mathbf{y}| < \Delta d \right\}. \quad (6)$$

In other words, $\mathbf{T}_{kj}^{(2)}(\Delta d)$ is the Δd-neighbourhood of $\mathbf{T}_{kj}^{(1)}$. A point is in $\mathbf{T}_{kj}^{(2)}(\Delta d)$ if and only if its (shortest) distance to $\mathbf{T}_{kj}^{(1)}$ is less than Δd. Similarly, $\mathbf{T}_{kk,in}^{(2)}(\Delta d)$ and $\mathbf{T}_{kk,out}^{(2)}(\Delta d)$ are defined as the Δd-neighbourhoods of $\mathbf{T}_{kk,in}^{(1)}$ and $\mathbf{T}_{kk,out}^{(1)}$ respectively.

The area intensity of $\mathbf{T}_{kj}^{(2)}(\Delta d)$ is defined as the expected area of $\mathbf{T}_{kj}^{(2)}(\Delta d)$ in a unit square:

$$\mu_2(\mathbf{T}_{kj}^{(2)}(\Delta d)) = \mathbb{E}\left(\left| \mathbf{T}_{kj}^{(2)}(\Delta d) \bigcap [0,1)^2 \right| \right), \quad (7)$$

where $|S|$ denotes the area of some region S (i.e., two-dimensional Lebesgue measure of S).

Because $\Phi_1, \Phi_2 \ldots, \Phi_K$ are stationary and isotropic, $\mathbf{T}_{kj}^{(2)}(\Delta d)$ is also stationary and isotropic. As a result, given a reference UE located at $\mathbf{0}$, the area intensity of $\mathbf{T}_{kj}^{(2)}(\Delta d)$ is equal to the probability that the reference UE at $\mathbf{0}$ is in $\mathbf{T}_{kj}^{(2)}(\Delta d)$.

$$\mu_2(\mathbf{T}_{kj}^{(2)}(\Delta d)) = \mathbb{P}(\mathbf{0} \in \mathbf{T}_{kj}^{(2)}(\Delta d)). \quad (8)$$

Similarly, if $k \in \mathcal{K}_C$,

$$\mu_2(\mathbf{T}_{kk,x}^{(2)}(\Delta d)) = \mathbb{P}(\mathbf{0} \in \mathbf{T}_{kk,x}^{(2)}(\Delta d)), \quad (9)$$

where the subscript "x" indicates either "*in*" or "*out*".

We observe that the probabilities in (8)-(9) are analytically tractable, which will be presented in the next subsection.

4.3 Derivation of Area Intensities

In this subsection, we present the derivation of $\mathbb{P}(\mathbf{0} \in \mathbf{T}_{kj}^{(2)}(\Delta d))$. It consists of a progressive sequence of four steps. In the first step, we recall a few important properties of two intersecting circles, which will be frequently used in the subsequent steps. In the second step, we study the distribution of the distance from the *reference UE* at $\mathbf{0}$ to the BS it is associated with, which is referred to as the *reference BS* throughout the rest of this paper. In the third step, we study the conditional probability of $\mathbf{0} \in \mathbf{T}_{kj}^{(2)}(\Delta d)$ given the distance from the reference UE to the reference BS. Based on step two and step three, we derive the unconditioned probability of $\mathbf{0} \in \mathbf{T}_{kj}^{(2)}(\Delta d)$ in the fourth step.

4.3.1 Geometric Patterns of Two Intersecting Circles

We first recall a few important properties of two intersecting circles (as shown in Fig. 2), which will be frequently used in the subsequent steps to derive $\mathbb{P}(\mathbf{0} \in \mathbf{T}_{kj}^{(2)}(\Delta d))$. Let r_1 and r_2 be the radii of these circles, and r be the distance between their centers. We assume $|r_1 - r_2| \leq r \leq r_1 + r_2$.

As labeled in Fig. 2, let $C(r_1, r_2, r)$ denote the area of the overlapping part of the two circles, $L(r_1, r_2, r)$ denote the arc length of circle 1 covered by circle 2, and $\theta_m(r_1, r_2, r)$ denote the half central angle corresponding to the arc. The expressions of $C(\cdot)$, $L(\cdot)$, and $\theta_m(\cdot)$ are all in closed form, which are shown in Appendix 8.1.

4.3.2 Distance Distribution of Reference UE-BS Pair

Let $\mathcal{R}_k$ denote the distance from $\mathbf{0}$ to the nearest tier-k BS. If $k \in \mathcal{K}_P$, i.e., Φ_k is a PPP, by the Markovian property

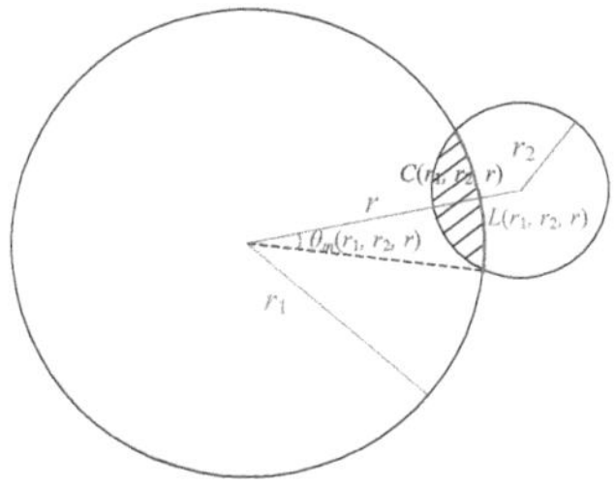

Figure 2: Geometric patterns of two intersecting circles.

of PPPs, it is straightforward to derive the complementary cumulative distribution function (ccdf) and probability density function (pdf) of $\mathcal{R}_k$:

$$\text{ccdf}_{\mathcal{R}_k}(R_0) = \mathbb{P}(\mathcal{R}_k > R_0) = \exp\left(-\pi R_0^2 \lambda_k\right), \tag{10}$$

$$\text{pdf}_{\mathcal{R}_k}(R_0) = 2\pi R_0 \lambda_k \left(-\pi R_0^2 \lambda_k\right). \tag{11}$$

If $k \in \mathcal{K}_C$, the ccdf of $\mathcal{R}_k$ is more complex due to the dependent and non-uniform aggregation of points in PCP. It can be shown that

$$\text{ccdf}_{\mathcal{R}_k}(R_0) \triangleq \mathbb{P}(\mathcal{R}_k > R_0) = \tag{12}$$

$$\begin{cases} \exp\Big[-\pi(R_0 - R_k)^2 \mu_k \left(1 - e^{-\pi R_k^2 \nu_k}\right) \\ \quad - \int_{R_0 - R_k}^{R_0 + R_k} 2\pi r \mu_k \left(1 - e^{-C(R_0, R_k, r)\nu_k}\right) \mathrm{d}r\Big], \\ \qquad \text{if } R_0 \geq R_k, \\ \exp\Big[-\pi(R_0 - R_k)^2 \mu_k \left(1 - e^{-\pi R_0^2 \nu_k}\right) \\ \quad - \int_{R_k - R_0}^{R_k + R_0} 2\pi r \mu_k \left(1 - e^{-C(R_0, R_k, r)\nu_k}\right) \mathrm{d}r\Big], \\ \qquad \text{if } R_0 < R_k. \end{cases}$$

By taking the first derivative, we find the pdf of $\mathcal{R}_k$ as

$$\text{d}_{\mathcal{R}_k}(R_0) = \tag{13}$$

$$\begin{cases} \text{ex}\Big[-\pi(R_0 - R_k)^2 \mu_k \left(1 - e^{-\pi R_k^2 \nu_k}\right) - \\ \quad \int_{R_0 - R_k}^{R_0 + R_k} 2\pi r \mu_k \left(1 - e^{-C(R_0, R_k, r)\nu_k}\right) \mathrm{d}r\Big] \\ \cdot \mu_k \int_{R_0 - R_k}^{R_0 + R_k} 2\pi r e^{-\nu_k C(R_0, R_k, r)} \nu_k L(R_0, R_k, r) \mathrm{d}r, \\ \qquad \text{i } R_0 \geq R_k, \\ \text{ex}\Big[-\pi(R_0 - R_k)^2 \mu_k \left(1 - e^{-\pi R_0^2 \nu_k}\right) - \\ \quad \int_{R_k - R_0}^{R_k + R_0} 2\pi r \mu_k \left(1 - e^{-C(R_0, R_k, r)\nu_k}\right) \mathrm{d}r\Big] \\ \cdot \mu_k \Big[2\pi^2 (R_k - R_0)^2 R_0 e^{-\pi R_0^2 \nu_k} \nu_k \\ + \int_{R_k - R_0}^{R_k + R_0} 2\pi r e^{-\nu_k C(R_0, R_k, r)} \nu_k L(R_0, R_k, r) \mathrm{d}r\Big], \\ \qquad \text{i } R_0 < R_k. \end{cases}$$

We note that the reference UE is placed at $\mathbf{0}$. Hence, $\mathcal{R}_k$ is also the distance from the reference UE to its nearest BS in tier-k. However, the reference UE is associated with the BS providing the largest biased received power (i.e., the reference BS), which may not be the nearest BS. Let $\mathcal{R}$ denote the distance between the reference UE and the reference BS. The probability that the reference BS is a tier-k BS and $\mathcal{R}$ is greater than some R_0 is derived as follows:

$$\mathbb{P}[\mathcal{R} > R_0, \text{tier} = k] = \mathbb{P}[\mathcal{R} > R_0 | \text{tier} = k]\mathbb{P}[\text{tier} = k]$$

$$= \int_{R_0}^{\infty} \prod_{i=1, i \neq k}^{K} \mathbb{P}[\mathcal{R}_i > \beta_{ik} r] \text{pdf}_{\mathcal{R}_k}(r) \mathrm{d}r. \tag{14}$$

The last equality reflects the fact that the biased received power from the nearest BSs in all other tiers should not exceed that from the reference BS.

Let $\text{pdf}_{\mathcal{R}|k}(R_0)$ denote the pdf of $\mathcal{R}$ given that the reference BS is in tier-k, and let $f_{\mathcal{R},k}(R_0) \triangleq \text{pdf}_{\mathcal{R}|k}(R_0)\mathbb{P}[\text{tier} = k]$, we have

$$f_{\mathcal{R},k}(R_0) = \prod_{i=1, i \neq k}^{K} \text{ccdf}_{\mathcal{R}_i}(\beta_{ik} R_0) \cdot \text{pdf}_{\mathcal{R}_k}(R_0). \tag{15}$$

4.3.3 *Conditional Probability of* $\mathbf{0} \in \mathbf{T}_{kj}^{(2)}(\Delta d)$

In this subsection, we study the conditional probabilities that the reference UE at $\mathbf{0}$ is in $\mathbf{T}_{kj}^{(2)}(\Delta d)$, given that it is associated with a tier-k BS (reference BS) at a distance of R_0 from it, which is denoted as $\mathbb{P}\left(\mathbf{0} \in \mathbf{T}_{kj}^{(2)}(\Delta d) | \mathcal{R} = R_0, \text{tier} = k\right)$. By employing both analytic geometric and stochastic geometric tools, we derive the probability in different cases, given in Theorems 1-4 below. We note that the handoff rates for P-tiers are already known in the literature (e.g., [6,9,23]). These theorems additionally address boundaries between P-tiers and C-tiers, boundaries between different C-tiers, and inter-cluster and intra-cluster boundaries within a C-tier.

For brevity, we define the following quantities that will be used extensively in the rest of this section:

$$\mathcal{F}(\beta) \triangleq \frac{1}{\beta^2} \int_0^{\pi} \sqrt{(\beta^2 + 1) - 2\beta \cos(\theta)}\, \mathrm{d}\theta, \tag{16}$$

and

$$\mathcal{H}_{kj}(R_0) \triangleq \frac{1}{\pi} \mathcal{F}(\beta_{kj}) \beta_{kj} \frac{\text{pdf}_{\mathcal{R}_j}(R_0 \beta_{jk})}{\text{ccdf}_{\mathcal{R}_j}(R_0 \beta_{jk})}. \tag{17}$$

THEOREM 1. *If tier-j is a P-tier, i.e., $j \in \mathcal{K}_P$, for all $k \in \mathcal{K}$ ($k = j$ is allowed), we have*

$$\mathbb{P}\left(\mathbf{0} \in \mathbf{T}_{kj}^{(2)}(\Delta d) | \mathcal{R} = R_0, \text{tier} = k\right)$$

$$= 2\lambda_j \Delta d R_0 \mathcal{F}(\beta_{kj}) + \mathcal{O}(\Delta d^2). \tag{18}$$

PROOF. See Appendix 8.2 for the proof. □

THEOREM 2. *If tier-j is a C-tier, i.e., $j \in \mathcal{K}_C$, for all $k \in \mathcal{K}$, $k \neq j$, we have*

$$\mathbb{P}\left(\mathbf{0} \in \mathbf{T}_{kj}^{(2)}(\Delta d) | \mathcal{R} = R_0, \text{tier} = k\right)$$

$$= \mathcal{H}_{kj}(R_0) \Delta d + \mathcal{O}(\Delta d^2). \tag{19}$$

PROOF. See Appendix 8.3 for the proof. □

THEOREM 3. *If tier-k is a C-tier, i.e., $k \in \mathcal{K}_C$, we have*

$$\mathbb{P}\left(\mathbf{0} \in \mathbf{T}_{kk,out}^{(2)}(\Delta d) | \mathcal{R} = R_0, \text{tier} = k\right)$$

$$= \mathcal{H}_{kk}(R_0) \Delta d + \mathcal{O}(\Delta d^2). \tag{20}$$

PROOF. Given the reference tier-k BS located at $\mathbf{x}_{\text{BS}}$, we know that $\mathbf{x}_{\text{BS}}$ belongs to some BS cluster $\Omega_k(\mathcal{C}(\mathbf{x}_{\text{BS}}))$. Because the point process of cluster centers Θ_k is a PPP, by the Slivnyak Theorem [4], the set of all cluster centers other than $\mathcal{C}(\mathbf{x}_{\text{BS}})$ remain a PPP with the same statistics as Θ_k. Consequently, if we denote the set of all tier-k BSs other than the cluster $\Omega_k(\mathcal{C}(\mathbf{x}_{\text{BS}}))$ as Φ'_k, then Φ'_k remains a PCP with the same statistics as Φ_k. Because the set of inter-cluster cell boundaries $\mathbf{T}_{kk,out}^{(2)}(\Delta d)$ is generated by $\mathbf{x}_{\text{BS}}$ and Φ'_k, and Φ'_k is still a PCP, the proof of Theorem 3 is the same as that of Theorem 2. □

The set of intra-cluster cell boundaries $\mathbf{T}^{(2)}_{kk,in}(\Delta d)$ is generated by $\mathbf{x}_{\mathrm{BS}}$ and $\Omega_k(\mathcal{C}(\mathbf{x}_{\mathrm{BS}}))\backslash\{\mathbf{x}_{\mathrm{BS}}\}$. We have the following theorem:

THEOREM 4. *If tier-k is a C-tier, i.e., $k \in \mathcal{K}_C$, we have* $\mathbb{P}\left(\mathbf{0} \in \mathbf{T}^{(2)}_{kk,in}(\Delta d)|\mathcal{R}=R_0, \text{tier}=k\right) = G_k(R_0)\Delta d + \mathcal{O}(\Delta d^2)$, *where $G_k(R_0)$ is expressed in (21) (shown on the next page).*

The proof is omitted due to the space limitation.

4.3.4 Unconditioned Probability of $\mathbf{0} \in \mathbf{T}^{(2)}_{kj}(\Delta d)$

Through deconditioning on $\mathcal{R}$, we derive the unconditioned probabilities that the reference UE at $\mathbf{0}$ is in $\mathbf{T}^{(2)}_{kj}(\Delta d)$. If $k \neq j$, we have

$$\begin{aligned}&\mathbb{P}(\mathbf{0} \in \mathbf{T}^{(2)}_{kj}(\Delta d)) \quad (22)\\ &= \int_0^\infty \mathbb{P}(\mathbf{0} \in \mathbf{T}^{(2)}_{kj}(\Delta d)|\mathcal{R}=R_0, \text{tier}=k) f_{\mathcal{R},k}(R_0)\mathrm{d}R_0\\ &+ \int_0^\infty \mathbb{P}(\mathbf{0} \in \mathbf{T}^{(2)}_{kj}(\Delta d)|\mathcal{R}=R_0, \text{tier}=j) f_{\mathcal{R},j}(R_0)\mathrm{d}R_0.\end{aligned}$$

If $k \in \mathcal{K}_P$, we have

$$\begin{aligned}&\mathbb{P}(\mathbf{0} \in \mathbf{T}^{(2)}_{kk}(\Delta d)) \quad (23)\\ &= \int_0^\infty \mathbb{P}(\mathbf{0} \in \mathbf{T}^{(2)}_{kk}(\Delta d)|\mathcal{R}=R_0, \text{tier}=k) f_{\mathcal{R},k}(R_0)\mathrm{d}R_0.\end{aligned}$$

If $k \in \mathcal{K}_C$, we have

$$\begin{aligned}&\mathbb{P}(\mathbf{0} \in \mathbf{T}^{(2)}_{kk,x}(\Delta d)) \quad (24)\\ &= \int_0^\infty \mathbb{P}(\mathbf{0} \in \mathbf{T}^{(2)}_{kk,x}(\Delta d)|\mathcal{R}=R_0, \text{tier}=k) f_{\mathcal{R},k}(R_0)\mathrm{d}R_0,\end{aligned}$$

where the subscript "x" indicates either "*in*" or "*out*".

4.4 From Area Intensities to Handoff Rates

Next, we compute the handoff rates using the area intensities derived in Section 4.3. This involves two steps: (1) from area intensities $\mu_2(\mathbf{T}^{(2)}_{kj}(\Delta d))$ to length intensities $\mu_1(\mathbf{T}^{(1)}_{kj})$, and (2) from length intensities to handoff rates.

In the first step, we derive the length intensity $\mu_1(\mathbf{T}^{(1)}_{kj})$ from the area intensity $\mu_2(\mathbf{T}^{(2)}_{kj}(\Delta d))$. Following Section 3.2 in [14], we have

$$\mu_1(\mathbf{T}^{(1)}_{y}) = \lim_{\Delta d \to 0} \frac{\mu_2(\mathbf{T}^{(2)}_{y}(\Delta d))}{2\Delta d}, \quad (25)$$

where the subscript "y" indicates "kj", "kk, in", or "kk, out".

Consequently, combining (15)-(25), we have

Case 1: If $k, j \in \mathcal{K}_P$ and $k \neq j$,

$$\begin{aligned}&\mu_1(\mathbf{T}^{(1)}_{kj}) \quad (26)\\ &= \int_0^\infty \prod_{i=1,i\neq k}^{K} \mathrm{ccdf}_{\mathcal{R}_i}(\beta_{ik}R_0)\mathrm{pdf}_{\mathcal{R}_k}(R_0)\lambda_j R_0 \mathcal{F}(\beta_{kj})\mathrm{d}R_0\\ &+ \int_0^\infty \prod_{i=1,i\neq j}^{K} \mathrm{ccdf}_{\mathcal{R}_i}(\beta_{ij}R_0)\mathrm{pdf}_{\mathcal{R}_j}(R_0)\lambda_k R_0 \mathcal{F}(\beta_{jk})\mathrm{d}R_0.\end{aligned}$$

Case 2: If $k \in \mathcal{K}_P$ we have

$$\begin{aligned}&\mu_1(\mathbf{T}^{(1)}_{kk}) \quad (27)\\ &= \int_0^\infty \prod_{i=1,i\neq k}^{K} \mathrm{ccdf}_{\mathcal{R}_i}(\beta_{ik}R_0)\mathrm{pdf}_{\mathcal{R}_k}(R_0)\lambda_k R_0 \mathcal{F}(1)\mathrm{d}R_0.\end{aligned}$$

Case 3: If $k \in \mathcal{K}_P$ and $j \in \mathcal{K}_C$, $\mu_1(\mathbf{T}^{(1)}_{kj})$ can be obtained by replacing the term $\lambda_j R_0 \mathcal{F}(\beta_{kj})$ with $\frac{1}{2}\mathcal{H}_{kj}(R_0)$ in (26).

Case 4: If $k, j \in \mathcal{K}_C$ and $k \neq j$, $\mu_1(\mathbf{T}^{(1)}_{kj})$ can be obtained by replacing the term $\lambda_j R_0 \mathcal{F}(\beta_{kj})$ with $\frac{1}{2}\mathcal{H}_{kj}(R_0)$ and the term $\lambda_k R_0 \mathcal{F}(\beta_{jk})$ with $\frac{1}{2}\mathcal{H}_{jk}(R_0)$ in (26).

Case 5: If $k \in \mathcal{K}_C$, by replacing the term $\lambda_k R_0 \mathcal{F}(1)$ with $\frac{1}{2}\mathcal{H}_{kk}(R_0)$ and $\frac{1}{2}G_k(R_0)$ in (27), we find the expressions of $\mu_1(\mathbf{T}^{(1)}_{kk,out})$ and $\mu_1(\mathbf{T}^{(1)}_{kk,in})$ respectively.

In the second step, we derive the expected number of handoffs of an active UE as follows:

THEOREM 5. *Let $\mathcal{T}_0$ denote an arbitrary UE's trajectory on $\mathbb{R}^2$ with length $|\mathcal{T}_0|_1$. Then, the expected number of intersections between $\mathcal{T}_0$ and $\mathbf{T}^{(1)}_{kj}$ is*

$$\mathbb{E}\left(\mathcal{N}(\mathcal{T}_0, \mathbf{T}^{(1)}_{kj})\right) = \frac{2}{\pi}\mu_1(\mathbf{T}^{(1)}_{kj})|\mathcal{T}_0|_1, \quad (28)$$

and the expected number of type k-j handoffs is

$$\mathbb{E}\left(\mathcal{N}_{kj}(\mathcal{T}_0, \mathbf{T}^{(1)}_{kj})\right) = \begin{cases}\frac{1}{2}\mathbb{E}\left(\mathcal{N}(\mathcal{T}_0, \mathbf{T}^{(1)}_{kj})\right), & \text{if } k \neq j,\\ \mathbb{E}\left(\mathcal{N}(\mathcal{T}_0, \mathbf{T}^{(1)}_{kj})\right), & \text{if } k = j.\end{cases} \quad (29)$$

PROOF. We note that $\mathbf{T}^{(1)}_{kj}$ is a stationary and isotropic fibre process with length intensity $\mu_1(\mathbf{T}^{(1)}_{kj})$. The proof follows the conclusions in Section 9.3 of [32]. □

Note that the expected number of type k-j handoffs is the same as the expected number of type j-k handoffs, both of which are equal to half of $\mathbb{E}\left(\mathcal{N}(\mathcal{T}_0, \mathbf{T}^{(1)}_{kj})\right)$.

Furthermore, let v denote the instantaneous velocity of an active UE, and $H_{kj}(v)$ denote its type k-j handoff rate. We have the following Corollary from Theorem 5:

COROLLARY 1.

$$H_{kj}(v) = \begin{cases}\frac{1}{\pi}\mu_1(\mathbf{T}^{(1)}_{kj})v, & \text{if } k \neq j,\\ \frac{2}{\pi}\mu_1(\mathbf{T}^{(1)}_{kj})v, & \text{if } k = j.\end{cases} \quad (30)$$

Note that the above handoff rates are instantaneous rates. Hence, our analysis allows time-varying velocity for the UEs, in which case the handoff rates are also time varying.

5. APPLICATION SCENARIO: OPTIMAL TIER SELECTION

In this section, we study the problem of optimal tier selection, as an application scenario for the handoff rate analysis above. Note that previous works focusing on biased user association in HWNs usually assumed stationary UEs [7–9,20,24,29]. In contrast, in this section, a UE's velocity is accommodated as one important factor for its tier-selection decision. The optimal tier selections are individualized for different UEs and can be adaptive to a UE's changing velocity over time.

Suppose that an active UE chooses to connect only to a set of tiers $\mathcal{S}$ that is a subset of $\mathcal{K}$ and ignore other tiers. We assume that $1 \in \mathcal{S}$ (i.e., the UE always includes tier-1 in its candidate set, which may correspond to macrocells in practice). Our goal is to derive the optimal selection of candidate tiers $\mathcal{S}$ among all subsets of $\mathcal{K}$.

Following (14), the probability that the active UE is associated with a tier-k BS, for $k \in \mathcal{S}$, is

$$A_{k,\mathcal{S}} = \mathbb{P}[\mathcal{R} > 0, \text{tier} = k]$$

$$G_k(R_O) = \begin{cases} \dfrac{\int_{R_O-R_k}^{R_O+R_k} r\nu_k R_O\cdot(16\theta_m(R_O,R_k,r)-16\sin\theta_m(R_O,R_k,r))\exp(-\nu_k C(R_O,R_k,r))\mathrm{d}r}{\int_{R_O-R_k}^{R_O+R_k} 2\theta_m(R_O,R_k,r)r\exp(-C(R_O,R_k,r)\nu_k)\mathrm{d}r}, & \text{i } R_O \geq R_k, \\ \dfrac{\pi(R_k-R_O)^2\exp(-\pi R_O^2\nu_k)\cdot 8\nu_k R_O+\int_{R_k-R_O}^{R_k+R_O} r\nu_k R_O\cdot(16\theta_m(R_O,R_k,r)-16\sin\theta_m(R_O,R_k,r))\exp(-\nu_k C(R_O,R_k,r))\mathrm{d}r}{\pi(R_k-R_O)^2\exp(-\pi R_O^2\nu_k)+\int_{R_k-R_O}^{R_k+R_O} 2\theta_m(R_O,R_k,r)r\exp(-C(R_O,R_k,r)\nu_k)\mathrm{d}r}, & \text{i } R_O < R_k. \end{cases} \quad (21)$$

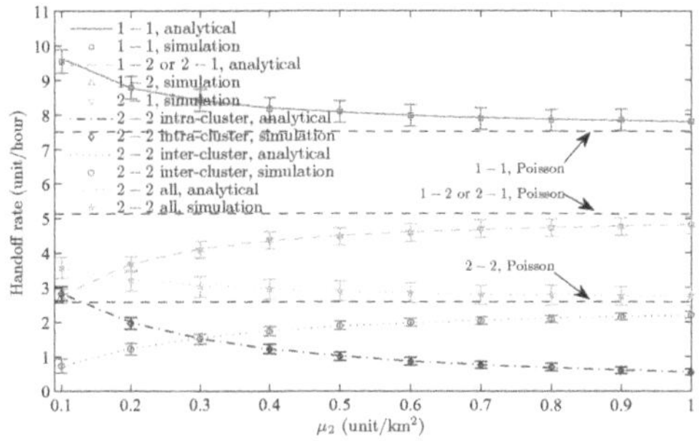

Figure 3: Accuracy of PCP handoff rate analysis under different μ_2 values, for $\mu_2 \cdot \nu_2 = 0.5$. For comparison, black dashed lines indicate analytical results assuming all PPP BSs.

$$= \int_0^\infty \prod_{i\in\mathcal{S}, i\neq k} \mathrm{ccdf}_{\mathcal{R}_i}(\beta_{ik}R_O)\cdot \mathrm{pdf}_{\mathcal{R}_k}(R_O)\mathrm{d}R_O. \quad (31)$$

We assume that the active UE is given some tier access benefit $\mathcal{U}_k$ per second if it is associated with a tier-k BS. For example, such benefit may represent data rate, power consumption, and service charge at the tier. If the active UE's tier selection is $\mathcal{S}$, its overall tier access utility (per second) is

$$U(\mathcal{S}) = \sum_{k\in\mathcal{S}} \mathcal{U}_k A_{k,\mathcal{S}}. \quad (32)$$

Let $\mathcal{E}_{kj}$ be the expense for each type k-j handoff. Such handoff expenses could be assigned arbitrarily. For example, the expense on a horizontal handoff $\mathcal{E}_{kk}$ is expected to be smaller than that of a vertical handoff $\mathcal{E}_{kj}$ ($k \neq j$). The average handoff expense (per second) given tier selection and velocity is computed as

$$E(v,\mathcal{S}) = \sum_{k,j\in\mathcal{S}} \mathcal{E}_{kj}H_{kj}(v,\mathcal{S}). \quad (33)$$

where $H_{kj}(v,\mathcal{S})$ are the handoff rates computed from (30) for the set of tiers $\mathcal{S}$.

Finally, the optimal tier selection under velocity v is

$$\mathcal{S}_{opt}(v) = \arg\max_{\mathcal{S}\in\mathbb{S}} U(\mathcal{S}) - E(v,\mathcal{S}), \quad (34)$$

where $\mathbb{S}$ is the set of all possible tier selections. Because the number of tiers K is usually not high in reality (i.e., $K \leq 5$), the cardinality of $\mathbb{S}$, 2^{K-1}, is not large. Therefore, $\mathcal{S}_{opt}$ can be derived through comparing all possible tier selections.

6. NUMERICAL STUDY

In this section, we present simulation studies in Matlab to validate the accuracy and usefulness of the proposed analytical framework. In each round of simulation, multiple tiers of BSs are generated on a 20 km × 20 km square. Then, we randomly generate 5 waypoints $\mathbf{X}_1, \mathbf{X}_2, \ldots, \mathbf{X}_5$ in

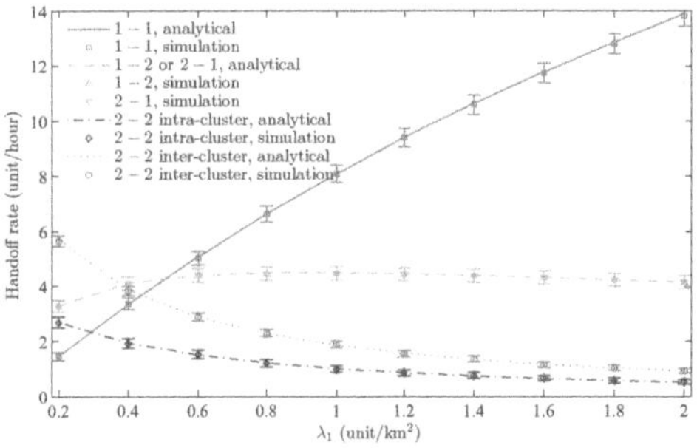

Figure 4: Handoff rates under different λ_1 values.

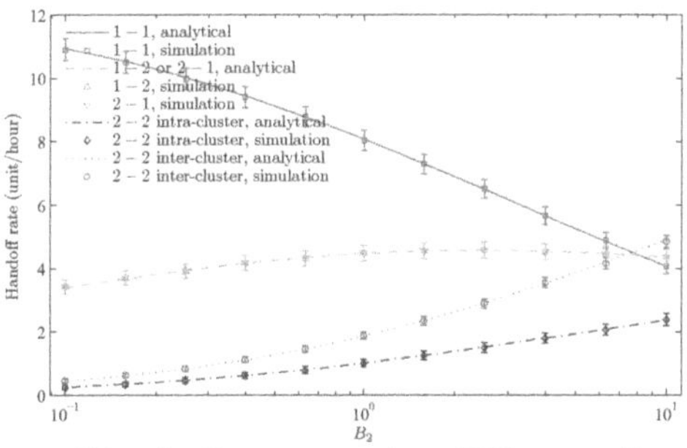

Figure 5: Handoff rates under different B_2 values.

the central 10 km × 10 km square. The four line segments $\mathbf{X}_1\mathbf{X}_2, \mathbf{X}_2\mathbf{X}_3, \ldots, \mathbf{X}_4\mathbf{X}_5$ form the trajectory of an active UE in one round of simulation. By tracking which BSs the UE is associated with along its trajectory, we can obtain its handoff rates in this round of simulation. Each simulation data point is averaged over 2000 simulation rounds. Error bars in the figures show the 95% confidence intervals for simulation results.

Comparison with Simple PPP Modeling. First, we focus on a two-tier HWN with one P-tier (representing macrocell BSs) and one C-tier (representing clustered femtocell BSs). Tier-1 is the P-tier, with $\lambda_1 = 1$ unit/km^2, $P_1 = 30$ dBm, and $B_1 = 1$; tier-2 is the C-tier, with $R_2 = 1$ km, $P_2 = 20$ dBm, and $B_2 = 1$; $\gamma = 3.5$; and $v = 10$ km/hour. In Fig. 3, we study the handoff rates under different μ_2 values while maintaining a constant $\mu_2\nu_2 = 0.5$ (i.e., the overall tier-2 BS intensity is a constant 0.5π unit/km^2). For reference, we also show the handoff rates (black dashed lines) if tier-2 is replaced by a P-tier with the same BS intensity of 0.5π unit/km^2. Fig. 3 shows that the actual handoff rates obtained from simulation match well with the proposed analysis, while they are far from the dashed lines when μ_2 is small (and ν_2 is large). This interesting observation suggests that using a simple PPP to model the BSs as in [6, 9, 23] can lead to substantial numerical errors in computing the handoff rates in HWNs with clustered BSs. The PPP model gives a close approximation only when the cluster intensities

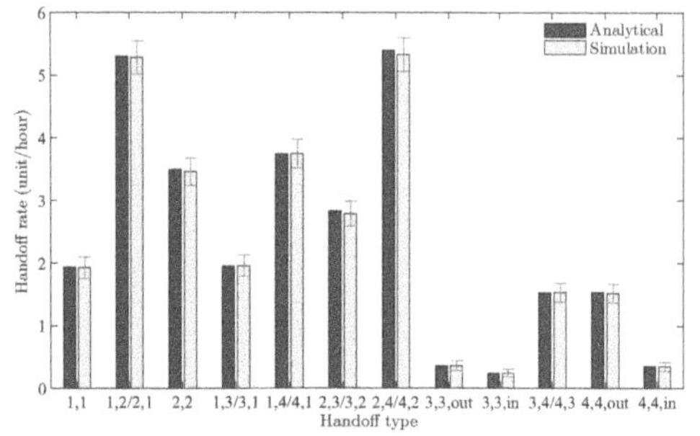

Figure 6: Handoff rates, two P-tiers and two C-tiers.

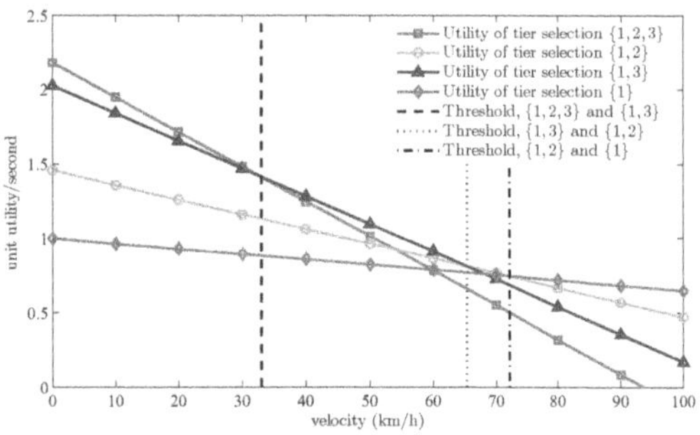

Figure 7: Optimal tier selection.

are high but per cluster BS intensities are low in the C-tier. In general, we observe that the actual handoff rates vary drastically as μ_2 and ν_2 change, which can be accounted for only by the proposed PCP analysis.

Effect of BS Densities and Association Bias Values. We further study the influence of different network parameters on the handoff rates. In Figs. 4 and 5, we consider a two-tier network with the same default parameter values as in Fig. 3, except $\mu_2 = 0.5$ unit/km^2 and $\nu_2 = 1$ unit/km^2.

Fig. 4 shows handoff rates under different tier-1 BS intensities λ_1. The figure illustrates that increasing λ_1 leads to a higher type 1-1 handoff rate but a lower type 2-2 handoff rate. Fig. 5 shows the handoff rates under different tier-2 association bias values B_2. We observe that increasing the association bias value of one tier has a similar effect as increasing the BS intensity of this tier, leading to a higher horizontal handoff rate within this tier, but lower handoff rates outside the tier. Moreover, both figures illustrate that the simulation results agree with the analytical results, demonstrating the correctness of our analysis for different types of handoff rates.

A More Complex Example. In Fig. 6, we study different types of handoff rates in a network with four tiers. The network parameters are as follows: Tier-1 and tier-2 are P-tiers, with $(\lambda_1, \lambda_2) = (1, 1)$ unit/km^2; tier-3 and tier-4 are C-tiers, with $(\mu_3, \mu_4) = (0.5, 1)$ unit/km^2, $(R_3, R_4) = (0.9, 1.1)$ unit/km^2, and $(\nu_3, \nu_4) = (1, 0.5)$ unit/km^2; $(P_1, P_2, P_3, P_4) = (30, 33, 20, 23)$ dBm; $(B_1, B_2, B_3, B_4) = (1, 1, 1, 1)$; $\gamma = 3.5$; and $v = 10$ km/hour. In order to avoid redundancy, we only show the sum rate of type k-j and type j-k ($k \neq j$) handoffs for easier inspection; the individual handoff rates are half of the sum handoff rate. We again observe that the simulation results agree with the analytical results, validating the correctness of our analysis. We further observe that the handoff rates of types 2-2, 2-3/3-2, and 2-4/4-2 are higher than those of 1-1, 1-3/3-1, and 1-4/4-1 respectively, due to the higher transmission power of tier-2 BSs compared with tier-1 BSs. The handoff rates of types 4-4, 1-4/4-1, and 2-4/4-2 are higher than those of 3-3, 1-3/3-1, and 2-3/3-2 respectively, due to the higher transmission power and higher intensity of tier-4 BSs, i.e., $\pi R_4^2 \mu_4 \nu_4$, compared with tier-3 BSs.

Tier Selection Optimization. Finally, we present an example of the optimal tier selection problem presented in Section 5. The network parameters are as follows: tier-1 is a P-tier, with $\lambda_1 = 1$ unit/km^2; tier-2 and tier-3 are C-tiers, with $(\mu_2, \mu_3) = (0.5, 1)$ unit/km^2, $(R_2, R_3) = (0.9, 1.1)$ unit/km^2, and $(\nu_2, \nu_3) = (1, 0.5)$ unit/km^2; $(P_1, P_2, P_3) = (30, 20, 23)$ dBm; $(B_1, B_2, B_3) = (1, 1, 1)$; and $\gamma = 3.5$. Tier access benefits are $(\mathcal{U}_1, \mathcal{U}_2, \mathcal{U}_3) = (1, 3, 3.5)$ unit utility/second. The horizontal handoff expenses are $(\mathcal{E}_{11}, \mathcal{E}_{22}, \mathcal{E}_{33}) = (10, 15, 15)$ unit utility per handoff, and the vertical handoff expenses are $(\mathcal{E}_{12}, \mathcal{E}_{21}, \mathcal{E}_{13}, \mathcal{E}_{31}, \mathcal{E}_{23}, \mathcal{E}_{32}) = (30, 30, 50, 50, 50, 50)$ unit utility per handoff.

Given a specific tier selection, the overall tier access benefit does not change with the UE's velocity, but the handoff expense increases linearly. Therefore, the overall utility linearly decreases with the UE's velocity. As shown in Fig. 7, when the UE's velocity is low, tier selection $\{1, 2, 3\}$ is preferred since the handoff expense is relatively low compared with its tier access benefit. When the UE's velocity is high, tier selection $\{1\}$ is preferred, because handoff expense dominates tier access benefit, and tier selection $\{1\}$ has the smallest handoff expense. Overall, the UE's velocity can be divided into four regions: tier selection $\{1, 2, 3\}$ is optimal when the velocity is in $[0, 33.00)$ km/hour; tier selection $\{1, 3\}$ is optimal when the velocity is in $[33.00, 65.27)$ km/hour; tier selection $\{1, 2\}$ is optimal when the velocity is in $[65.27, 72.10)$ km/hour; tier selection $\{1\}$ is optimal when the velocity is in $[72.10, \infty)$ km/hour.

7. CONCLUSIONS

In this work, we present a stochastic geometric framework to study user mobility in multi-tier HWNs. Each tier of BSs is modeled as either a PPP or a PCP. We are able to capture (1) the spatial randomness of BSs, (2) the non-uniform and dependent aggregation of BSs, and (3) the various scales of cell sizes. Theoretical expressions for all types of handoff rates experienced by an active UE with arbitrary movement trajectory are derived. Based on these results, optimal tier selection considering both the handoff expense and tier access benefit is studied. Finally, extensive simulations are conducted, validating the accuracy and usefulness of our analytical results.

8. APPENDIX

8.1 Expressions Related to Two Intersecting Circles

By applying basic analytical geometric tools, it can be shown that

$$C(r_1, r_2, r) = \arccos\left((r_1^2 + r^2 - r_2^2)/(2r_1 r)\right) \cdot r_1^2$$
$$+ \arccos\left((r_2^2 + r^2 - r_1^2)/(2r_2 r)\right) \cdot r_2^2$$
$$- 2\sqrt{((r_1 + r_2 + r)/2)\left((r_1 + r_2 + r)/2 - r_1\right)}$$

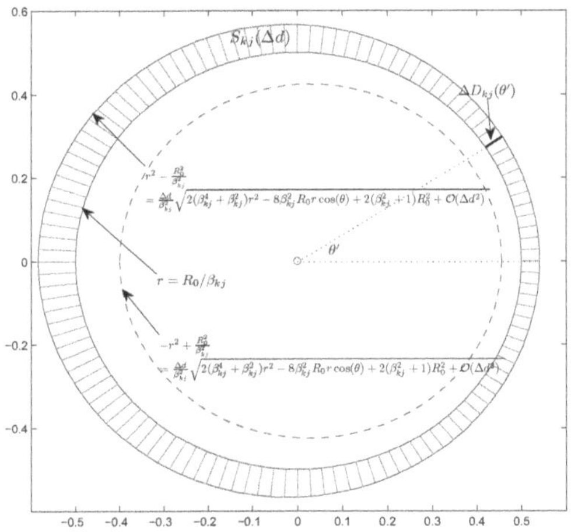

Figure 8: The region (shaded part) of $S_{kj}(\Delta d)$.

$$\cdot \sqrt{((r_1+r_2+r)/2-r_2)\left((r_1+r_2+r)/2-r\right)}, \tag{35}$$

$$L(r_1,r_2,r) = 2r_1 \arccos\left((r_1^2+r^2-r_2^2)/(2r_1 r)\right), \tag{36}$$

$$\theta_m(r_1,r_2,r) = \arccos\left((r_1^2+r^2-r_2^2)/(2r_1 r)\right). \tag{37}$$

8.2 Proof of Theorem 1

PROOF. We study the probability $\mathbb{P}\Big(\mathbf{0} \in \mathbf{T}_{kj}^{(2)}(\Delta d)|\mathcal{R} = R_0, \text{tier} = k\Big)$. Without loss of generality, we assume the reference BS is located at $\mathbf{R}_0 = (R_0, 0)$. Note that because the reference UE receives the highest biased power level from the reference BS, for all other tiers, there are no tier-j BSs located within $\mathcal{B}(\mathbf{0}, \frac{R_0}{\beta_{kj}})$.

Let $\mathbf{x}_0 = (x_0, y_0)$ denote the position of some tier-j BS (other than the reference BS if $j = k$). Let $\mathcal{T}(\mathbf{R}_0, \mathbf{x}_0, \beta_{kj})$ denote the curve satisfying the following condition:

$$\mathcal{T}(\mathbf{R}_0,\mathbf{x}_0,\beta_{kj}) = \left\{(x,y)\middle| \frac{P_k B_k}{((x-R_0)^2+y^2)^{\gamma/2}} = \frac{P_j B_j}{((x-x_0)^2+(y-y_0)^2)^{\gamma/2}}\right\}. \tag{38}$$

Note that $\mathbf{0} \in \mathbf{T}_{kj}^{(2)}(\Delta d)$ is equivalent to the event that the distance from $\mathbf{0}$ to $\mathcal{T}(\mathbf{R}_0, \mathbf{x}_0, \beta_{kj})$ is less than Δd.

In the following, we discuss three cases separately: $\beta_{kj} > 1$, $\beta_{kj} = 1$, and $\beta_{kj} < 1$.

Case 1: $\beta_{kj} > 1$. In this case, $\mathcal{T}(\mathbf{R}_0, \mathbf{x}_0, \beta_{kj})$ is a circle centered at $\left(\frac{\beta_{kj}^2 x_0 - R_0}{\beta_{kj}^2-1}, \frac{\beta_{kj}^2 y_0}{\beta_{kj}^2-1}\right)$ with radius $\frac{\beta_{kj}\sqrt{(R_0^2+x_0^2+y_0^2-2x_0R_0)}}{(\beta_{kj}^2-1)}$. Thus, the distance from $\mathbf{0}$ to $\mathcal{T}(\mathbf{R}_0, \mathbf{x}_0, \beta_{kj})$ is

$$d(\mathbf{R}_0,\mathbf{x}_0,\beta_{kj}) \tag{3 }$$
$$= \left|\frac{\sqrt{(\beta_{kj}^2 x_0 - R_0)^2 + (\beta_{kj}^2 y_0)^2} - \sqrt{\beta_{kj}^2 (R_0^2 + x_0^2 + y_0^2 - 2x_0R_0)}}{(\beta_{kj}^2-1)}\right|.$$

As a consequence, $\mathbf{0} \in \mathbf{T}_{kj}^{(2)}(\Delta d)$ iff $d(\mathbf{R}_0, \mathbf{x}_0, \beta_{kj}) < \Delta d$, or equivalently, $\mathbf{x}_0 \in \widetilde{S}_{kj}(\Delta d)$, where

$$\widetilde{S}_{kj}(\Delta d) = \left\{\mathbf{x}_0 \middle| d(\mathbf{R}_0,\mathbf{x}_0,\beta_{kj}) < \Delta d\right\}. \tag{40}$$

After mathematical manipulations on (40), and converting (x_0, y_0) into polar coordinates (r, θ), we have

$$\widetilde{S}_{kj}(\Delta d) = \left\{(r,\theta)\middle| \left|r^2 - \frac{R_0^2}{\beta_{kj}^2}\right| < \frac{\Delta d}{\beta_{kj}^2}\cdot \sqrt{2\left(\beta_{kj}^4+\beta_{kj}^2\right)r^2 - 8\beta_{kj}^2 R_0 r \;\text{o}\;(\theta) + 2(\beta_{kj}^2+1)R_0^2 + \mathcal{O}(\Delta d^2)}\right\}. \tag{41}$$

Note that there are no tier-j BSs located inside $\mathcal{B}(\mathbf{0}, \frac{R_0}{\beta_{kj}})$. Let $S_{kj}(\Delta d) = \widetilde{S}_{kj}(\Delta d) \bigcap \overline{\mathcal{B}(\mathbf{0}, R_0/\beta_{kj})}$, where $\overline{\mathcal{B}(\cdot)} \triangleq \mathbb{R}^2 \backslash \mathcal{B}(\cdot)$ is the complement of $\mathcal{B}(\cdot)$. As a result, $\mathbf{0} \in \mathbf{T}_{kj}^{(2)}(\Delta d)$ iff $\mathbf{x}_0 \in S_{kj}(\Delta d)$, where

$$S_{kj}(\Delta d) = \left\{(r,\theta)\middle| r \geq \frac{R_0}{\beta_{kj}} \text{ and } \left|r^2 - \frac{R_0^2}{\beta_{kj}^2}\right| < \frac{\Delta d}{\beta_{kj}^2}\cdot \sqrt{2\left(\beta_{kj}^4+\beta_{kj}^2\right)r^2 - 8\beta_{kj}^2 R_0 r \;\text{o}\;(\theta) + 2(\beta_{kj}^2+1)R_0^2 + \mathcal{O}(\Delta d^2)}\right\}. \tag{42}$$

According to (42), $S_{kj}(\Delta d)$ corresponds to a non-concentric "ring" region (shaded area) shown in Fig. 8. We can observe that $\forall(r,\theta) \in S_{kj}(\Delta d)$, $r = \frac{R_0}{\beta_{kj}} + \mathcal{O}(\Delta d)$. Substituting it into (42) gives

$$S_{kj}(\Delta d) = \left\{(r,\theta)\middle| r \geq \frac{R_0}{\beta_{kj}} \text{ and } \left|r^2 - \frac{R_0^2}{\beta_{kj}^2}\right| < \frac{2\Delta d R_0}{\beta_{kj}^2}\sqrt{\left(\beta_{kj}^2+1\right) - 2\beta_{kj}\;\text{o}\;(\theta) + \mathcal{O}(\Delta d^2)}\right\}. \tag{43}$$

The area of $S_{kj}(\Delta d)$ is

$$|S_{kj}(\Delta d)| = \frac{2\Delta d R_0}{\beta_{kj}^2}\int_0^{\pi} \sqrt{\left(\beta_{kj}^2+1\right) - 2\beta_{kj}\;\text{o}\;(\theta)}\mathrm{d}\theta + \mathcal{O}(\Delta d^2). \tag{44}$$

Given the reference UE and BS, it can be shown that Φ_j[1] is a PPP with intensity 0 in $\mathcal{B}\left(\mathbf{0}, \frac{R_0}{\beta_{kj}}\right)$ and intensity λ_j in $\overline{\mathcal{B}(\mathbf{0}, R_0/\beta_{kj})}$ [4]. Because $\mathbb{P}\Big(\mathbf{0} \in \mathbf{T}_{kj}^{(2)}(\Delta d)|\mathcal{R} = R_0, \text{tier} = k\Big)$ is equal to the probability that there is at least one point of Φ_j in $S_{kj}(\Delta d)$ (i.e., some $\mathbf{x}_0$ in $S_{kj}(\Delta d)$), we have

$$\begin{aligned}
&\mathbb{P}\left(\mathbf{0} \in \mathbf{T}_{kj}^{(2)}(\Delta d)|\mathcal{R} = R_0, \text{tier} = k\right)\\
=&1 - \text{ex}\;\left(-\lambda_j|S_{kj}(\Delta d)|\right)\\
=&1 - \text{ex}\;\left(-2\lambda_j \Delta d R_0 \mathcal{F}(\beta_{kj}) + \mathcal{O}(\Delta d^2)\right)\\
=&2\lambda_j \Delta d R_0 \mathcal{F}(\beta_{kj}) + \mathcal{O}(\Delta d^2),
\end{aligned} \tag{45}$$

which completes the proof of Case 1.

Case 2: $\beta_{kj} < 1$. The proof is similar to that of Case 1.

Case 3: $\beta_{kj} = 1$. The proof of this case is relatively simple, which is omitted due to space limitation. □

8.3 Proof of Theorem 2

PROOF. Similar to the proof of Theorem 1, $\mathbf{0} \in \mathbf{T}_{kj}^{(2)}(\Delta d)$ is equivalent to the event that there is at least one point of Φ_j in the region $S_{kj}(\Delta d)$, given that no point of Φ_j is in

[1]If $k = j$, it is the reduced Palm point process [20] corresponding to all tier-k BSs other than the reference BS.

$\mathcal{B}(\mathbf{0}, R_0/\beta_{kj})$. Note that $S_{kj}(\Delta d)$ here is still expressed in (43) and shown in Fig. 8.

As labeled in Fig. 8, we also define $\Delta D_{kj}(\theta)$ as the thickness of $S_{kj}(\Delta d)$ at angular coordinate θ. It can be shown that

$$
\begin{aligned}
&\Delta D_{kj}(\theta) \\
=&\sqrt{\frac{R_0^2}{\beta_{kj}^2} + \frac{2\Delta d R_0}{\beta_{kj}^2}\sqrt{\left(\beta_{kj}^2+1\right) - 2\beta_{kj}\ \ \mathrm{o}\ (\theta)} + \mathcal{O}(\Delta d^2)} - \frac{R_0}{\beta_{kj}} \\
=&\Delta d\frac{\sqrt{\beta_{kj}^2 + 1 - 2\beta_{kj}\ \ \mathrm{o}\ (\theta)}}{\beta_{kj}} + \mathcal{O}(\Delta d^2). \qquad (46)
\end{aligned}
$$

Then, we have

$$
\begin{aligned}
&\mathbb{P}\left(\mathbf{0} \in \mathbf{T}_{kj}^{(2)}(\Delta d) | \mathcal{R} = R_0, \text{tier} = k\right) \qquad (47) \\
=&\mathbb{P}\left(\Phi_j \bigcap S_{kj}(\Delta d) \neq \emptyset \middle| \Phi_j \bigcap \mathcal{B}(\mathbf{0}, R_0/\beta_{kj}) = \emptyset\right) \qquad (48) \\
=&\frac{1}{\pi}\int_0^{\pi} \frac{\mathrm{d}\ \ _{\mathcal{R}_j}\left(\frac{R_0}{\beta_{kj}}\right) - \ \mathrm{d}\ \ _{\mathcal{R}_j}\left(\frac{R_0}{\beta_{kj}} + \Delta D_{kj}(\theta)\right) + \mathcal{O}(\Delta d^2)}{\mathrm{d}\ \ _{\mathcal{R}_j}(R_0/\beta_{kj})}\mathrm{d}\theta \\
=&\frac{1}{\pi}\int_0^{\pi} \Delta D_{kj}(\theta)\mathrm{d}\theta \frac{\mathrm{d}\ \ _{\mathcal{R}_j}(R_0/\beta_{kj})}{\mathrm{d}\ \ _{\mathcal{R}_j}(R_0/\beta_{kj})} + \mathcal{O}(\Delta d^2) \qquad (4\ ) \\
=&\frac{1}{\pi}\int_0^{\pi} \Delta d \frac{\sqrt{\beta_{kj}^2 + 1 - 2\beta_{kj}\ \ \mathrm{o}\ (\theta)}}{\beta_{kj}}\mathrm{d}\theta \frac{\mathrm{d}\ \ _{\mathcal{R}_j}(R_0/\beta_{kj})}{\mathrm{d}\ \ _{\mathcal{R}_j}(R_0/\beta_{kj})} + \mathcal{O}(\Delta d^2) \\
=&\frac{1}{\pi}\mathcal{F}(\beta_{kj})\beta_{kj}\Delta d \frac{\mathrm{d}\ \ _{\mathcal{R}_j}(R_0\beta_{jk})}{\mathrm{d}\ \ _{\mathcal{R}_j}(R_0\beta_{jk})} + \mathcal{O}(\Delta d^2), \qquad (50)
\end{aligned}
$$

which completes the proof. □

9. REFERENCES

[1] J. G. Andrews, F. Baccelli, and R. Ganti. A tractable approach to coverage and rate in cellular networks. *IEEE Trans. on Communications*, 59(11):3122–3134, Nov. 2011.

[2] A. Anpalagan and I. Katzela. Overlaid cellular system design, with cell selection criteria for mobile wireless users. In *Proc. of IEEE Canadian Conference on Electrical and Computer Engineering*, Edmonton, Canada, May 1999.

[3] F. Ashtiani, J. Salehi, and M. Aref. Mobility modeling and analytical solution for spatial traffic distribution in wireless multimedia networks. *IEEE Journal on Selected Areas in Communications*, 21(10):1699 – 1709, Dec. 2003.

[4] F. Baccelli and B. Blaszczyszyn. Stochastic geometry and wireless networks, volume 1: Theory. *Foundations and Trends in Networking*, 3(3-4):249 – 449, 2009.

[5] W. Bao and B. Liang. Insensitivity of user distribution in multicell networks under general mobility and session patterns. *IEEE Trans. on Wireless Communications*, 12(12):6244–6254, Dec. 2013.

[6] W. Bao and B. Liang. Handoff rate analysis in heterogeneous cellular networks: a stochastic geometric approach. In *Proc. of ACM MSWiM*, Montreal, Canada, 2014.

[7] W. Bao and B. Liang. Structured spectrum allocation and user association in heterogeneous cellular networks. In *Proc. of IEEE INFOCOM*, Toronto, Canada, Apr. 2014.

[8] W. Bao and B. Liang. Radio resource allocation in heterogeneous wireless networks: a spatial-temporal perspective. In *Proc. of IEEE INFOCOM*, Hong Kong, China, Apr. 2015.

[9] W. Bao and B. Liang. Stochastic geometric analysis of user mobility in heterogeneous wireless networks. *IEEE Journal on Selected Areas in Communications, Special Issue on Recent Advances in Heterogeneous Cellular Networks*, 2015.

[10] Y. Chen, J. Kurose, and D. Towsley. A mixed queueing network model of mobility in a campus wireless network. In *Proc. of IEEE INFOCOM*, Orlando, FL, Mar. 2012.

[11] W. C. Cheung, T. Q. S. Quek, and M. Kountouris. Throughput optimization, spectrum allocation, and access control in two-tier femtocell networks. *IEEE Journal on Selected Areas in Communications*, 30(3):561–574, Apr. 2012.

[12] H. Dhillon, R. Ganti, F. Baccelli, and J. G. Andrews. Modeling and analysis of K-tier downlink heterogeneous cellular networks. *IEEE Journal on Selected Areas in Communications*, 30(3):550–560, Apr. 2012.

[13] A. Farbod and B. Liang. Structured admission control policies in heterogeneous wireless networks with mesh underlay. In *Proc. of IEEE INFOCOM*, Rio de Janeiro, Brazil, Apr. 2009.

[14] H. Federer. *Geometric Measure Theory*. Springer, 1969.

[15] A. Ghosh, R. Jana, V. Ramaswami, J. Rowland, and N. Shankaranarayanan. Modeling and characterization of large-scale Wi-Fi traffic in public hot-spots. In *Proc. of IEEE INFOCOM*, Shanghai, China, Apr. 2011.

[16] K. Gulati, B. Evans, J. Andrews, and K. Tinsley. Statistics of co-channel interference in a field of poisson and poisson-poisson clustered interferers. *IEEE Trans. on Signal Processing*, 58(12):6207–6222, Dec. 2010.

[17] A. Hasib and A. Fapojuwo. Mobility model for heterogeneous wireless networks and its application in common radio resource management. *IET Communications*, 2(9):1186–1195, Oct. 2008.

[18] J. Hou and D. O'brien. Vertical handover-decision-making algorithm using fuzzy logic for the integrated radio-and-OW system. *IEEE Trans. on Wireless Communications*, 5(1):176–185, Jan. 2006.

[19] Z. Jako and G. Jeney. Outage probability in poisson-cluster-based lte two-tier femtocell networks. *Wiley Wireless Communications and Mobile Computing*, Jun. 2014.

[20] H.-S. Jo, Y. J. Sang, P. Xia, and J. G. Andrews. Heterogeneous cellular networks with flexible cell association: A comprehensive downlink SINR analysis. *IEEE Trans. on Wireless Communications*, 11(10):3484–3495, Oct. 2012.

[21] Y. Kirsal, E. Gemikonakli, E. Ever, G. Mapp, and O. Gemikonakli. An analytical approach for performance analysis of handoffs in the next generation integrated cellular networks and WLANs. In *Proc. of International Conference on Computer Communications and Networks*, Zurich, Switzerland, Aug. 2010.

[22] C. W. Lee, L. M. Chen, M. C. Chen, and Y. S. Sun. A framework of handoffs in wireless overlay networks based on mobile IPv6. *IEEE Journal on Selected Areas in Communications*, 23(11):2118 – 2128, Nov. 2005.

[23] X. Lin, R. Ganti, P. Fleming, and J. Andrews. Towards understanding the fundamentals of mobility in cellular networks. *IEEE Trans. on Wireless Communications*, 12(4):1686–1698, Apr. 2013.

[24] Y. Lin, W. Bao, W. Yu, and B. Liang. Optimizing user association and spectrum allocation in HetNets: a utility perspective. *IEEE Journal on Selected Areas in Communications, Special Issue on Recent Advances in Heterogeneous Cellular Networks*, 2015.

[25] M. Liu, Z. Li, X. Guo, and E. Dutkiewicz. Performance analysis and optimization of handoff algorithms in heterogeneous wireless networks. *IEEE Trans. on Mobile Computing*, 7(7):846–857, Jul. 2008.

[26] G. Pollini. Trends in handover design. *IEEE Communications Magazine*, 34(3):82–90, Mar. 1996.

[27] T. S. Rappaport. *Wireless Communications: Principles and Practice.* Prentice Hall, second edition, 2002.

[28] N. Shenoy and B. Hartpence. A mobility model for cost analysis in integrated cellular/WLANs. In *Proc. of International Conference on Computer Communications and Networks*, Chicago, IL, Oct. 2004.

[29] S. Singh, H. Dhillon, and J. G. Andrews. Offloading in heterogeneous networks: Modeling, analysis, and design insights. *IEEE Trans. on Wireless Communications*, 12(5):2484–2497, May 2013.

[30] M. Stemm and R. H. Katz. Vertical handoffs in wireless overlay networks. *ACM/Springer Mobile Networks and Applications*, 3(4):335–350, Jan. 1998.

[31] E. Stevens-Navarro, Y. Lin, and V. Wong. An MDP-based vertical handoff decision algorithm for heterogeneous wireless networks. *IEEE Trans. on Vehicular Technology*, 57(2):1243–1254, Mar. 2008.

[32] D. Stoyan, W. Kendall, and J. Mecke. *Stochastic Geometry and Its Applications.* Wiley, second edition, 1995.

[33] Y. Zhong and W. Zhang. Multi-channel hybrid access femtocells: A stochastic geometric analysis. *IEEE Trans. on Communications*, 61(7):3016–3026, Jul. 2013.

Loop-Free Backpressure Routing Using Link-Reversal Algorithms

Anurag Rai
LIDS, MIT
Cambridge, MA, USA
rai@mit.edu

Chih-ping Li*
Qualcomm Research
San Diego, CA, USA
cpli@qti.qualcomm.com

Georgios Paschos†
Mathematical and Algorithmic Sciences Lab
France Research Center
Huawei Technologies Co., Ltd.
georgios.paschos@huawei.com

Eytan Modiano
LIDS,MIT
Cambridge, MA, USA
modiano@mit.edu

ABSTRACT

The backpressure routing policy is known to be a throughput optimal policy that supports any feasible traffic demand in data networks, but may have poor delay performance when packets traverse loops in the network. In this paper, we study loop-free backpressure routing policies that forward packets along directed acyclic graphs (DAGs) to avoid the looping problem. These policies use link reversal algorithms to improve the DAGs in order to support any achievable traffic demand.

For a network with a single commodity, we show that a DAG that supports a given traffic demand can be found after a finite number of iterations of the link-reversal process. We use this to develop a joint link-reversal and backpressure routing policy, called the loop free backpressure (LFBP) algorithm. This algorithm forwards packets on the DAG, while the DAG is dynamically updated based on the growth of the queue backlogs. We show by simulations that such a DAG-based policy improves the delay over the classical backpressure routing policy. We also propose a multicommodity version of the LFBP algorithm, and via simulation we show that its delay performance is better than that of backpressure.

This work was supported by NSF Grant CNS-1116209 and ONR Grant N00014-12-1-0064.

*The work of C.P.Li was done when he was a postdoctoral scholar at LIDS, MIT.

†The work of G. Paschos was done while he was at MIT and affiliated with CERTH-ITI. It was supported in part by the WiNC project of the Action: Supporting Postdoctoral Researchers, funded by national and community funds (European Social Fund).

MobiHoc'15, June 22–25, 2015, Hangzhou, China.

ACM 978-1-4503-3489-1/15/06 ...$15.00.
http://dx.doi.org/10.1145/2746285.2746304.

Categories and Subject Descriptors

C.2.2 [**Computer-Communication Networks**]: Network Protocols—*routing*

Keywords

loop free; backpressure; directed acyclic graph; link reversal

1. INTRODUCTION

Throughput and delay are the two major metrics used to evaluate the performance of communication networks. For networks that exhibit high variability, such as mobile ad hoc networks, the dynamic backpressure routing policy [1] is a highly desirable solution, known to maximize throughput in a wide range of settings. However, the delay performance of backpressure is poor [2]. The high delay is attributed to a property of backpressure that allows the packets to loop within the network instead of moving towards the destination. In this paper we improve the delay performance of backpressure routing by constraining the data routing along loop free paths.

To eliminate loops in the network, we assign directions to the links such that the network becomes a directed acyclic graph (DAG). Initially, we generate an arbitrary DAG and use backpressure routing over it. If the initial DAG has max-flow smaller than the traffic demand, parts of the network become overloaded. By reversing the direction of the links that point from non-overloaded to overloaded nodes a new DAG with a lower overload is obtained. Iterating over this process, our distributed algorithm gradually converges to a DAG that supports any traffic demand feasible in the network. Hence the loop-free property is achieved without the loss of throughput.

Prior work identifies looping as a main cause for high delays in backpressure routing and proposes delay-aware backpressure techniques. Backpressure enhanced with hop count bias is first proposed in [3] to drive packets through paths with smallest hop counts when the load is low. An alternative backpressure modification that utilizes shortest path information is proposed in [8]. A different line of works proposes to learn the network topology using backpressure and then use this information to enhance routing decisions. In [7] backpressure is constrained to a subgraph which is discovered by running unconstrained backpressure for a time period and computing the average number of packets routed over each link. Learning is effectively used in scheduling [9] and utility optimization [13] for wireless networks. In our work we aim to eliminate loops by restricting backpressure to a DAG, while we dynamically improve the DAG by reversing links.

The link-reversal algorithms were introduced in [4] as a means to maintain connectivity in networks with volatile links. These distributed algorithms react to any topological changes to obtain a DAG such that each node has a loop-free path to the destination. In [5], one of the link-reversal algorithms was used to design a routing protocol (called TORA) for multihop wireless networks. Although these algorithms provide loop free paths and guarantee connectivity from the nodes to the destination, they do not maximize throughput. Thus, the main goal of this paper is to create a new link-reversal algorithm and combine it with the backpressure algorithm to construct a distributed throughput optimal algorithm with improved delay performance.

The main contributions of this paper are as follows:

- For a DAG with a single commodity, we study the lexicographic optimization of the queue growth rate. We develop a novel link-reversal algorithm that reverses link direction based on overload conditions to form a new DAG with lexicographically smaller queue growth rates.
- We show that the queue backlog information from backpressure routing can be used to perform the link reversals. We develop loop free backpressure (LFBP) algorithm, a distributed routing scheme that eliminates loops and retains the throughput optimality property.
- Our simulation results of LFBP show a significant delay improvement over backpressure in static and dynamic networks.
- We extend the LFBP algorithm to networks with multiple commodities, and provide a simulation result to show its delay improvement over backpressure.

Due to space limitations, some of the lemmas and the proofs have been removed from this paper; we refer the readers to the technical report [15] for complete proofs.

2. SYSTEM MODEL AND DEFINITIONS

2.1 Network model

We consider the problem of routing single-commodity data packets in a network. The network is represented by a graph $G = (N, E)$, where N is the set of nodes and E is the set of undirected links $\{i, j\}$ with capacity c_{ij}. Packets arrive at the source node s at rate λ and are destined for a receiver node d. Let $f^{\max}$ denote the maximum flow from node s to d in the network G. The quantity $f^{\max}$ is the maximally achievable throughput at the destination node d.

To avoid unnecessary routing loops, we restrict forwarding along a directed acyclic graph (DAG) embedded in the graph G. An optimal DAG exists to support the max-flow $f^{\max}$ and can be found by: (i) computing a feasible flow allocation (f_{ij}) that yields the max-flow $f^{\max}$ in G (e.g. using [11]); (ii) trimming any positive flow on directed cycles; (iii) defining an embedded DAG by assigning a direction for each link $\{i, j\}$ according to the direction of the flow f_{ij} on that link. Since backpressure achieves the max-flow of a constrained graph [14], performing backpressure routing over the optimal DAG supports λ.

This centralized approach is unsuitable for mobile ad-hoc networks, which are based on wireless links with time-varying capacities and may undergo frequent topology changes. In such situations, the optimal embedded DAG also changes with time, which requires constantly repeating the above offline process. Instead, it is possible to use a distributed adaptive mechanism that reverses the direction of links until a DAG that supports the current traffic demand is found. In this paper we propose an algorithm that reacts to the traffic conditions by changing the directions of some links. To understand the properties of the link-reversing operations, we first study the fluid level behavior of a network under overload conditions.

2.2 Flow equations

Consider an embedded DAG $D_k = (N_k, E_k)$ in the network graph G, where $N_k = N$ is the set of network nodes and E_k is the set of directed links.[1] For each link $\{i, j\} \in E$, either (i, j) or (j, i) belongs to E_k (but not both). Each directed link (i, j) has the capacity of the undirected counterpart $\{i, j\}$, which is c_{ij}. Let $f_k^{\max}$ be the maximum flow of the DAG D_k from the source node s to the destination node d. Any embedded DAG has smaller or equal max-flow with respect to G, $f_k^{\max} \leq f^{\max}$.

For two disjoint subsets A and B of nodes in D_k, we define $\text{cap}_k(A, B)$ as the total capacity of the directed links going from A to B, i.e.,

$$\text{cap}_k(A, B) = \sum_{(i,j) \in E_k : i \in A,\, j \in B} c_{ij}. \quad (1)$$

A cut is a partition of nodes (A, A^c) such that $s \in A$ and $d \in A^c$. A cut (A_k, A_k^c) is a min-cut if it minimizes the expression $\text{cap}_k(A_k, A_k^c)$ over all cuts. By the max-flow min-cut theorem $f_k^{\max} = \text{cap}_k(A_k, A_k^c)$, where (A_k, A_k^c) is the min-cut of the DAG D_k. We remark that a cut in a DAG is also a cut in G or another DAG. However, the value of $\text{cap}_k(.,.)$ depends on the graph considered (see summation in (1)).

We consider the network as a time-slotted system, where slot t refers to the time interval $[t, t+1)$, $t \in \{0, 1, 2, \ldots\}$. Each network node n maintains a queue $Q_n(t)$, where $Q_n(t)$ also denotes the queue backlog at time t. We have $Q_d(t) = 0$ for all t since the destination node d does not buffer packets. Let $A(t)$ be the number of exogenous packets arriving at the source node s in slot t. Under a routing policy that forwards packets over the directed links defined by the DAG D_k, let $F_{ij}(t)$ be the number of packets that are transmitted over the directed link $(i, j) \in E_k$ in slot t; the link capacity constraint states that $F_{ij}(t) \leq c_{ij}$ for all t. The queues $Q_n(t), n \neq d$, are updated over slots according to

$$Q_n(t) = Q_n(t-1) + 1_{[n=s]} A(t) + \sum_{i:(i,n) \in E_k} F_{in}(t) - \sum_{j:(n,j) \in E_k} F_{nj}(t), \quad (2)$$

[1] The notation D_k of an embedded DAG is useful in the paper; it will denote the DAG that is formed after the kth iteration of the link-reversal algorithm.

where $1_{[\cdot]}$ is an indicator function.

To study the overload behavior of the system we define the queue overload (i.e., growth) rate at node n as

$$q_n = \lim_{t\to\infty} \frac{Q_n(t)}{t}. \quad (3)$$

Additionally, define the exogenous packet arrival rate λ and the flow f_{ij} over a directed link (i, j) as

$$\lambda = \lim_{t\to\infty} \frac{1}{t}\sum_{\tau=0}^{t-1} A(\tau), \quad f_{ij} = \lim_{t\to\infty} \frac{1}{t}\sum_{\tau=0}^{t-1} F_{ij}(\tau),$$

where the above limits are assumed to exist almost surely (see [6] for details). Using the recursion (2), taking time averages and letting $t \to \infty$, we have the fluid-level equation:

$$q_n = 1_{[n=s]}\lambda + \sum_{i:(i,n)\in E_k} f_{in} - \sum_{j:(n,j)\in E_k} f_{nj}, \ \forall n \in N\backslash\{d\} \quad (4)$$

$$0 \le f_{ij} \le c_{ij}, \ \forall(i, j) \in E_k. \quad (5)$$

Equations (4) and (5) are the flow conservation and link capacity constraints, respectively. A network node n is said to be overloaded if its queue growth rate q_n is positive, which implies that $Q_n(t) \to \infty$ as $t \to \infty$ (see (3) and [10]). Summing (4) over $n \in N$ yields

$$\sum_{n\in N\backslash\{d\}} q_n = \lambda - \sum_{i:(i,d)\in E_k} f_{id}, \quad (6)$$

where $\sum_{i:(i,d)\in E_k} f_{id}$ denotes the throughput received at the destination d. Therefore, equation (6) states that the received throughput is equal to the exogenous arrival rate λ less the sum of queue growth rates $\sum_{n\in N} q_n$ in the network.

2.3 Properties of queue overload vector

If the traffic arrival rate λ is strictly larger than the maximum flow $f_k^{\max}$ of the DAG D_k, then some network nodes will be overloaded. It is because, from (6), we have

$$\sum_{n\in N} q_n = \lambda - \sum_{i:(i,d)\in E_k} f_{id} \ge \lambda - f_k^{\max} > 0, \quad (7)$$

which implies that $q_n > 0$ for some node $n \in N$. Let $\boldsymbol{q} = (q_n)_{n\in N}$ be the queue overload vector. A queue overload vector $\boldsymbol{q}$ is feasible in the DAG D_k if there exist overload rates $(q_n)_{n\in N}$ and flow variables $(f_{ij})_{(i,j)\in E_k}$ that satisfy (4) and (5). Let $\mathcal{Q}_k$ be the set of all feasible queue overload vectors in D_k. We are interested in the *lexicographically smallest* queue overflow vector in set $\mathcal{Q}_k$. Formally, given a vector $\boldsymbol{u} = (u_1, \dots, u_N)$, let $\overline{u}_i$ be the ith maximal component of $\boldsymbol{u}$. We say that a vector $\boldsymbol{u}$ is *lexicographically smaller* than a vector $\boldsymbol{v}$, denoted by $\boldsymbol{u} <_{\text{lex}} \boldsymbol{v}$, if $\overline{u}_1 < \overline{v}_1$ or $\overline{u}_i = \overline{v}_i$ for all $i = 1, ..., (j-1)$ and $\overline{u}_j < \overline{v}_j$ for some $j = 2, \dots, N$. If $\overline{u}_i = \overline{v}_i$ for all i, then the two vectors are lexicographically equal, represented by $\boldsymbol{u} =_{\text{lex}} \boldsymbol{v}$.[2] The above-defined vector comparison induces a total order on the set $\mathcal{Q}_k$, and hence the existence of a lexicographically smallest vector is always guaranteed [12].

LEMMA 1 ([6]). *Let $\boldsymbol{q}_k^{min}$ be the lexicographically smallest vector in the queue overload region $\mathcal{Q}_k$ of the DAG D_k. We have the following properties:*

1. *The vector $\boldsymbol{q}_k^{min}$ exists and is unique in the set $\mathcal{Q}_k$.*
2. *The vector $\boldsymbol{q}_k^{min}$ minimizes the sum of queue overload rates, i.e., it is a solution to the optimization problem:*

$$\text{minimize} \sum_{n\in N} q_n, \ \text{subject to } \boldsymbol{q} \in \mathcal{Q}_k$$

(direct consequence of Theorem 1 in [6]). Due to (6), the corresponding throughput is maximized.

3. *A feasible flow allocation vector $(f_{ij})_{(i,j)\in E_k}$ induces $\boldsymbol{q}_k^{min}$ if and only if over each link $(i, j) \in E_k$ the following holds:*

$$\text{if } q_i < q_j, \text{ then } f_{ij} = 0, \quad (8)$$

$$\text{if } q_i > q_j, \text{ then } f_{ij} = c_{ij}. \quad (9)$$

In general, there are many flow allocations that yield the maximum throughput. Focusing on those that additionally induce $\boldsymbol{q}_k^{\min}$ has two advantages. First, as shown next, these allocations lead to link-reversal operations that improve the max-flow of the DAG D_k. Second, the backpressure algorithm can be used to preform the same reversals and improve the max-flow; we will use this observation in Section 4 to combine link-reversal algorithms with backpressure routing.

3. LINK-REVERSAL ALGORITHMS

The link-reversal algorithms given in [4] were designed to maintain a path from each node in the network to the destination. One algorithm relevant to this paper is the *full reversal method*. This algorithm is triggered when some nodes $n \neq d$ lose all of their outgoing links. At every iteration of the algorithm, nodes n, that have no outgoing link, reverse the direction of all their incoming links. This process is repeated until all the nodes other than the destination have at least one outgoing link. When the process stops these nodes are guaranteed to have a path to the destination. The example in Figure 1, taken from [4], illustrates this algorithm at work.

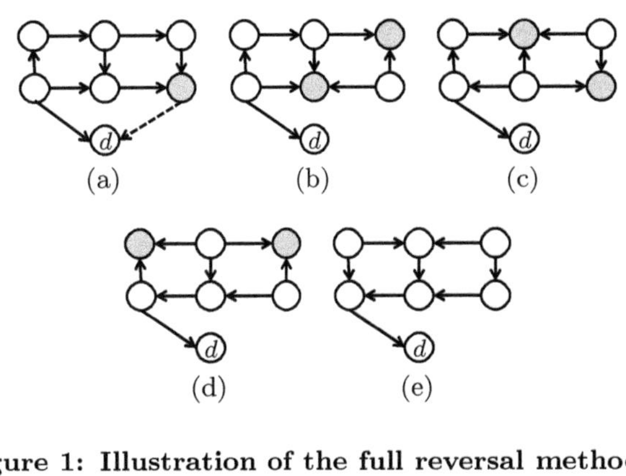

Figure 1: Illustration of the full reversal method of [4] when the dashed link in Figure 1(a) is lost. At every iteration, the algorithm reverses all the links incident to the nodes with no outgoing link.

Although the full reversal algorithm guarantees connectivity, the resulting throughput may be significantly lower than the maximum possible. Hence, in this paper we shift the focus from connectivity to maximum throughput. Specifically, we propose a novel link-reversal algorithm that pro-

[2]As an example, the two vectors $\boldsymbol{u} = (3, 2, 1, 2, 1)$ and $\boldsymbol{v} = (1, 2, 3, 2, 2)$ satisfy $\boldsymbol{u} <_{\text{lex}} \boldsymbol{v}$ because $\overline{u}_1 = \overline{v}_1 = 3$, $\overline{u}_2 = \overline{v}_2 = \overline{u}_3 = \overline{v}_3 = 2$, and $\overline{u}_4 = 1 < \overline{v}_4 = 2$.

duces a DAG which supports the traffic demand λ, assuming $\lambda \leq f^{\max}$. We do this by quickly constructing an initial DAG and improving upon it in multiple iterations.

3.1 Initial DAG

We assume that each node in the network has a unique ID. These IDs give a topological ordering to the nodes. So, the initial DAG can be created simply by directing each link to go from the node with the lower ID to the node with the higher ID. If the unique IDs are not available, the initial DAG can be created by using a strategy such as the one given in [5].

3.2 Overload detection

Given a DAG D_k, $k = 0, 1, 2, \ldots$, we suppose that there is a routing policy π that yields the lexicographically minimal queue overload vector $\boldsymbol{q}_k^{\min}$. [3] Then we use the vector $\boldsymbol{q}_k^{\min}$ to detect node overload and decide whether a link should be reversed.

If the data arrival rate λ is less than or equal to the maximum flow $f_k^{\max}$ of the DAG D_k, then there exists a flow allocation (f_{ij}) that supports the traffic demand and yields zero queue overload rates $q_n = 0$ at all nodes $n \in N$. By the second property of Lemma 1 and nonnegativity of the overload vector, the queue overload vector $\boldsymbol{q}_k^{\min}$ is zero. Thus, the throughput under policy π is λ according to (6), and the current DAG D_k supports λ; no link-reversal operations are needed.

On the other hand, if the arrival rate λ is strictly larger than the maximum flow $f_k^{\max}$, by the second property in Lemma 1 the maximum throughput is $f_k^{\max}$ and the queue overload vector $\boldsymbol{q}_k^{\min} = (q_{k,n}^{\min})_{n \in N}$ is nonzero because we have from (7) that

$$\sum_{n \in N} q_{k,n}^{\min} > \lambda - f_k^{\max} > 0.$$

We may therefore detect the event "DAG D_k supports λ" by testing whether the overload vector $\boldsymbol{q}_k^{\min}$ is zero or non-zero.

The next lemma shows that if DAG D_k does not support λ then it contains at least one under-utilized link (our link-reversal algorithm will reverse the direction of such links to improve network throughput).

LEMMA 2. *Suppose that the traffic demand λ satisfies*

$$f_k^{\max} < \lambda \leq f^{\max}.$$

where $f_k^{\max}$ is the max-flow of the DAG D_k and $f^{\max}$ is the max-flow of the undirected network G. Then there exists a link $(i, j) \in E_k$ such that $q_{k,i}^{\min} = 0$ and $q_{k,j}^{\min} > 0$.

PROOF OF LEMMA 2. Let A_k be the set of overloaded nodes under a flow allocation that induces the lexicographically minimal overload vector $\boldsymbol{q}_k^{\min}$ in the DAG D_k; the set A_k is nonempty due to $\lambda > f_k^{\max}$ and (7). It follows that the partition (A_k, A_k^c) is a min-cut of D_k (see Lemma 7 in the technical report [15]).[4] By the max-flow min-cut theorem, the capacity of the min-cut (A_k, A_k^c) in D_k satisfies $\text{cap}_k(A_k, A_k^c) = f_k^{\max} < f^{\max}$.

The proof is by contradiction. Let us assume that there is no directed link that goes from the set A_k^c to A_k in the DAG D_k. It follows that $\text{cap}_k(A_k, A_k^c)$ is the sum of capacities of all undirected links between the sets A_k and A_k^c, i.e.,

$$\text{cap}_k(A_k, A_k^c) = \sum_{i \in A_k, j \notin A_k} c_{ij},$$

which is equal to the value of the cut (A_k, A_k^c) in graph G. Since the value of any cut is larger or equal to the min-cut, applying the max-flow min-cut theorem on G we have

$$f^{\max} \leq \sum_{i \in A_k, j \notin A_k} c_{ij} = \text{cap}_k(A_k, A_k^c) = f_k^{\max},$$

which contradicts the assumption that $f_k^{\max} < \lambda \leq f^{\max}$. $\square$

3.3 Link reversal

Lemma 2 shows that if the DAG D_k has insufficient capacity to support the traffic demand $\lambda \leq f^{\max}$, then there exists a directed link from an underloaded node i to an overloaded one j under the lexicographically minimum overflow vector $\boldsymbol{q}_k^{\min}$. Because of property (8), we may infer that this link is not utilized. Next we show that reversing the direction of this link provides a strictly improved DAG.

We consider the link-reversal algorithm (Algorithm 1) that reverses all such links that satisfy the property in Lemma 2. This reversal yields a new directed graph $D_{k+1} = (N, E_{k+1})$.

Algorithm 1 Link-Reversal Algorithm

```
1: for all (i, j) ∈ E_k do
2:     if q^min_{k,i} = 0 and q^min_{k,j} > 0 then
3:         (j, i) ∈ E_{k+1}
4:     else
5:         (i, j) ∈ E_{k+1}
6:     end if
7: end for
```

LEMMA 3. *The directed graph D_{k+1} is acyclic.*

PROOF OF LEMMA 3. Recall that A_k is the set of overloaded nodes in the DAG D_k under the lexicographically minimum queue overload vector $\boldsymbol{q}_k^{\min}$. Let $L_k \subseteq E$ be the set of undirected links between A_k and A_k^c. Algorithm 1 changes the link direction in a subset of L_k. More precisely, it enforces the direction of all links in L_k to go from A_k to A_k^c.

We complete the proof by construction in two steps. First, we remove all links in L_k from the DAG D_k, resulting in two disconnected subgraphs that are DAGs themselves. Second, consider that we add a link in L_k back to the network with the direction going from A_k to A_k^c. This link addition does not create a cycle because there is no path from A_k^c to A_k, and the resulting graph remains to be a DAG. We can add the other links in L_k one-by-one back to the graph with the direction from A_k to A_k^c; similarly, these link additions do not create cycles. The final directed graph is D_{k+1}, and it is a DAG. See Fig. 2 for an illustration. $\square$

The next lemma shows that the new DAG D_{k+1} supports a lexicographically *smaller* optimal overload vector

[3]Such a policy π can simply solve an optimization problem offline to compute the required flow allocation. In Section 4, we develop a distributed algorithm using backpressure that does not require the computation of the lexicographically optimal overload vector. We use this vector only to prove the properties of our link-reversal algorithm.

[4]The set A_k^c contains the destination node d and is nonempty.

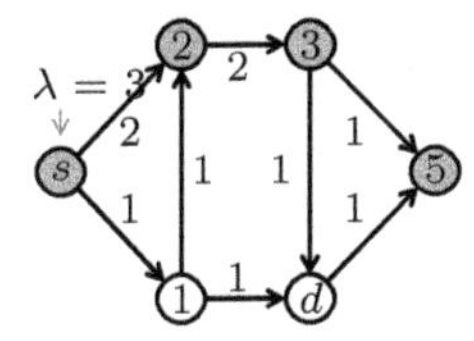

(a) The DAG D_k with $A_k = \{s, 2, 3, 5\}$.

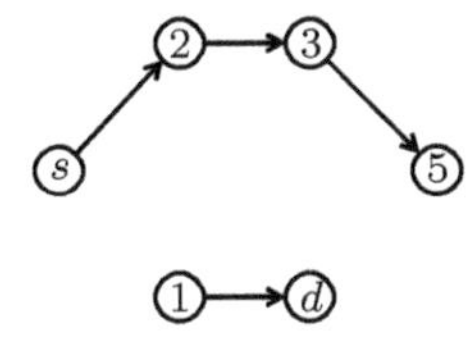

(b) Two disconnected DAGs formed by removing all links between A_k and A_k^c.

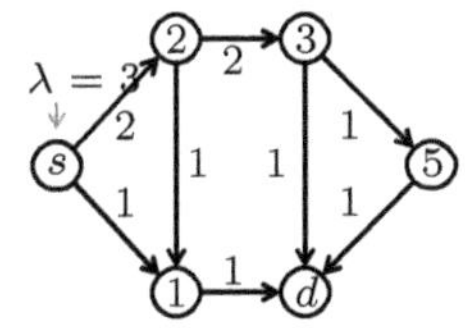

(c) The DAG D_{k+1} formed by adding all links in L_k back to the graph with the direction going from A_k to A_k^c.

Figure 2: Illustration for the proof of Lemma 3.

(and therefore potentially better throughput) than the DAG D_k.

LEMMA 4. *Let D_k be a DAG with the maximum flow $f_k^{\max} < \lambda \leq f^{\max}$. The DAG D_{k+1}, obtained by performing Algorithm 1 over D_k, has the lexicographically minimum queue overload vector satisfying $\boldsymbol{q}_{k+1}^{min} <_{\text{lex}} \boldsymbol{q}_k^{min}$.*

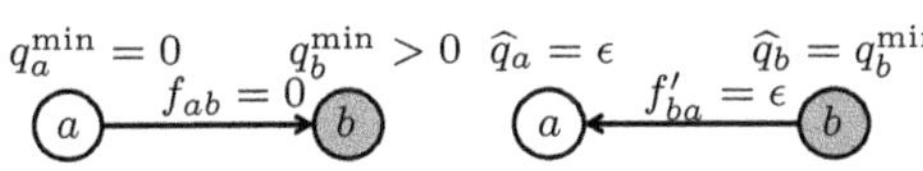

(a) Link (a, b) before the link reversal.
(b) Link (b, a) after the link reversal.

Figure 3: A link $\{a, b\}$ in the network in Fig. 2 before and after link reversal. Before the reversal, the flow f_{ab} is zero on (a, b). After the reversal, an ϵ flow can be sent over (b, a) so that $(\widehat{q}_a, \widehat{q}_b) <_{\text{lex}} (q_{k,a}^{\min}, q_{k,b}^{\min})$, while the rest of the flow allocation remains the same.

PROOF OF LEMMA 4. Consider a link $(a, b) \in E_k$ such that $q_{k,a}^{\min} = 0$ and $q_{k,b}^{\min} > 0$; this link exists by Lemma 2. From the property (8), any feasible flow allocation (f_{ij}) that yields the lexicographically minimum overload vector $\boldsymbol{q}_k^{\min}$ must have $f_{ab} = 0$ over link (a, b). The link-reversal algorithm reverses the link (a, b) so that $(b, a) \in E_{k+1}$ in the DAG D_{k+1}. Consider the following feasible flow allocation (f'_{ij}) on the DAG D_{k+1}:

$$f'_{ij} = \begin{cases} \epsilon & \text{if } (i,j) = (b,a) \\ 0 = f_{ji} & \text{if } (i,j) \neq (b,a) \text{ but } (j,i) \text{ is reversed} \\ f_{ij} & \text{if } (i,j) \text{ is not reversed} \end{cases}$$

where $\epsilon < q_{k,b}^{\min}$ is a sufficiently small value. In other words, the flow allocation (f'_{ij}) is formed by reversing links and keeping the previous flow allocation (f_{ij}) except that we forward an ϵ-amount of overload traffic from node b to a. Let $\widehat{\boldsymbol{q}} = (\widehat{q}_n)_{n \in N}$ be the resulting queue overload vector. We have

$$\widehat{q}_b = q_{k,b}^{\min} - \epsilon < q_{k,b}^{\min}, \; \widehat{q}_a = \epsilon > q_{k,a}^{\min} = 0, \text{ and}$$
$$\widehat{q}_n = q_{k,n}^{\min}, \; n \notin \{a, b\}.$$

Therefore, $\widehat{\boldsymbol{q}} <_{\text{lex}} \boldsymbol{q}_k^{\min}$ (see Fig. 3 for an illustration). Let $\boldsymbol{q}_{k+1}^{\min}$ be the lexicographically minimal overload vector in D_{k+1}. It follows that $\boldsymbol{q}_{k+1}^{\min} \leq_{\text{lex}} \widehat{\boldsymbol{q}} <_{\text{lex}} \boldsymbol{q}_k^{\min}$, completing the proof. □

THEOREM 1. *Suppose the traffic demand is feasible in G, i.e., $\lambda \leq f^{\max}$, and the routing policy induces the overload vector $\boldsymbol{q}_k^{\min}$ at every iteration k. Then, the link-reversal algorithm will find a DAG whose maximum flow supports λ in a finite number of iterations.*

PROOF OF THEOREM 1. The link-reversal algorithm creates a sequence of DAGs $\{D_0, D_1, D_2, \ldots\}$ in which a strict improvement in the lexicographically minimal overload vector is made after each iteration, i.e.,

$$\boldsymbol{q}_0^{\min} >_{\text{lex}} \boldsymbol{q}_1^{\min} >_{\text{lex}} \boldsymbol{q}_2^{\min} >_{\text{lex}} \cdots.$$

The lexicographically minimal overload vector is unique in a DAG by Lemma 1, the DAGs $\{D_0, D_1, D_2, \ldots\}$ must all be distinct. Since there are a finite number of unique DAGs in the network, the link-reversal algorithm will find a DAG D_{k^*} that has the lexicographically minimal overload vector $\boldsymbol{q}_{k^*}^{\min} = \mathbf{0}$ and the maximum flow $f_{k^*}^{\max} \geq \lambda$ in a finite number of iterations; this DAG D_{k^*} exists because the undirected graph G has the maximum flow $f^{\max} \geq \lambda$. □

3.4 Arrivals outside stability region

We show that even when $\lambda > f^{\max}$, the link reversal algorithm will stop reversing the links in a finite number of iterations, and it will obtain the DAG that supports the maximum throughput $f^{\max}$. We begin by examining the termination condition of our algorithm and show that if the algorithm stops at iteration k, then the DAG D_k supports the max-flow of the network.

LEMMA 5. *Consider the situation when $\lambda > f_k^{\max}$. If there is no link (i, j) such that $q_{k,i}^{\min} = 0$ and $q_{k,j}^{\min} > 0$, then $f^{\max} = f_k^{\max}$ and $\lambda > f^{\max}$. That is, if there are no links to reverse at iteration k, and $\mathbf{q}_k^{\min} > 0$, then the throughput of D_k is equal to $f^{\max}$.*

PROOF. Let A_k be the set of overloaded nodes under a flow allocation that induces the lexicographically minimal overload vector $\mathbf{q}_k^{\min}$ in the DAG D_k. We know that (A_k, A_k^c) is a min-cut of the network (see Lemma 7 in the technical report [15]), so

$$cap_k(A_k, A_k^c) = f_k^{\max}.$$

Suppose the link reversal algorithm stops after iteration k, i.e. at iteration k there are no links to reverse. In this situation, there is no link (i, j) such that $q_{k,i}^{\min} = 0$ and $q_{k,j}^{\min} > 0$, so by property (9), all the links between A_k and A_k^c go from A_k to A_k^c. The capacity of the cut (A_k, A_k^c) is given by

$$cap_k(A_k, A_k^c) = \sum_{i \in A_k, j \in A_k^c} c_{ij}.$$

This is equal to the capacity of the cut (A_k, A_k^c) in the undirected network G. So $f^{\max} \leq cap_k(A_k, A_k^c) = f_k^{\max}$. Because $f_{\max}^k$ cannot be greater than f^{max}, $f_{\max}^k = f^{\max}$. By assumption $\lambda > f_k^{\max}$, so $\lambda > f^{\max}$. $\square$

When $\lambda > f^{\max}$, this lemma shows that the link reversal algorithm stops only when the DAG achieves the maximum throughput of the network. Hence, if the DAG doesn't support the maximum throughput, then there exists a link that can be reversed. After each reversal, Lemma 3 holds, so the directed graph obtained after the reversal is acyclic. We can modify Lemma 4 to show that every reversal produces a DAG that supports an improved lexicographically optimal overload vector. We can combine these results to prove the following theorem.

THEOREM 2. *Suppose the traffic demand is not feasible in G, i.e., $\lambda > f^{\max}$, and the routing policy induces the overload vector $\mathbf{q}_k^{\min}$ at every iteration k. Then, the link-reversal algorithm will find a DAG whose maximum flow supports f^{max} in a finite number of iterations.*

4. DISTRIBUTED DYNAMIC ALGORITHM

In the previous sections we developed a link reversal algorithm based on the assumption that we had a routing policy that lexicographically minimized the overload vector $\mathbf{q}_k^{\min}$. The algorithm reversed all the links that went from the set of all the non-overloaded nodes A_k^c to the set of overloaded nodes A_k. We showed that repeating this process for some iterations results in a DAG that supports the arrival rate λ.

The goal of this paper is to develop a link reversal algorithm based on backpressure. To achieve this goal, we develop a threshold based algorithm that identifies the cut (A_k, A_k^c) using the queue backlog information of backpressure. We can use this cut to perform the same link reversals as in Section 3 without computing the lexicographically minimum overload vector. Hence, this algorithm generates the same sequence of DAGs as the link reversal algorithm described in the previous section. So, all the previous theorems hold, and the new algorithm will obtain the DAG that supports the arrival rate λ (when possible). We will call this algorithm the loop free backpressure (LFBP) algorithm.

We begin by creating an initial DAG D_0 using the method presented in Section 3.1. Then, we use the backpressure algorithm to route the packets from the source to the destination over D_0. Let $Q_n(t)$ be the queue length at node n in slot t. The backpressure algorithm can be written as in Algorithm 2. It simply sends packets on a link (i, j) if node i has more packets than j.

Algorithm 2 Backpressure algorithm (BP)

for all $(i, j) \in E_k$ **do**
    if $Q_i(t) > Q_j(t)$ **then**
        Transmit $\min\{c_{ij}, Q_i(t)\}$ packets from i to j
    end if
end for

Since backpressure is throughput optimal [1], if the arrival rate is less than $f_0^{\max}$, then all queues are stable. If the arrival rate is larger than $f_0^{\max}$, the system is unstable and the queue length grows at some nodes. In this case, the next lemma shows that if we were using a routing policy that produced the optimal overload vector $\mathbf{q}_k^{\min}$, the set of all the overloaded nodes A_k and the non-overloaded nodes A_k^c form the smallest min-cut of the DAG D_k.

DEFINITION 1. *We define the smallest min-cut (X^*, X^{*c}) in the DAG D_k as the min-cut with the smallest number of nodes in the source side of the cut, i.e., (X^*, X^{*c}) solves*

$$\text{minimize: } |X|$$
$$\text{subject to: } (X, X^c) \text{ is a min-cut of } D_k.$$

LEMMA 6. *Let A_k the set of overloaded nodes under a flow allocation (f_{ij}) that induces the lexicographically minimum overload vector in the DAG D_k. If $|A_k| > 0$, then (A_k, A_k^c) is the unique smallest min-cut in D_k.*

PROOF OF LEMMA 6. See the technical report [15]. $\square$

Essentially, at every iteration, the link reversal algorithm of Section 3 discovers the smallest min-cut (A_k, A_k^c) of the DAG D_k and reverses the links that go from A_k^c to A_k. Now the following theorem shows that the backpressure algorithm can be augmented with some thresholds to identify the smallest min-cut.

THEOREM 3. *Assume that (A_k, A_k^c) is the smallest min-cut for DAG D_k with a cut capacity of $f_k^{\max} = cap(A_k, A_k^c) < \lambda$. If packets are routed using the backpressure routing algorithm, then there exist finite constants T and R such that the following happens:*

1. *For some $t < T$, $Q_n(t) > R$ for all $n \in A_k$, and*
2. *For all t, $Q_n(t) < R$ for $n \in A_k^c$.*

PROOF. We will prove the two claims separately. To prove the first claim we will use the fact that the network is overloaded and bottlenecked at the cut (A_k, A_k^c). We will prove the second claim using the fact that the number of packets that arrive into A_k^c in each time-slot is upper-bounded by $f_k^{\max}$, and any cut in the network has a capacity larger than or equal to f_k^{max}. The detailed proofs for both claims are given in the technical report [15]. $\square$

Each node n has a threshold-based smallest min-cut detection mechanism. When we start using a particular DAG D_k, in each time-slot, we check whether the queue crosses a prespecified threshold R_k. Any queue that crosses the threshold gets marked as overloaded. After using the DAG D_k for T_k timeslots, all the nodes that have their queue marked overloaded form the set A_k. When the time T_k and threshold R_k are large enough, the cut (A_k, A_k^c) is the smallest min-cut as proven in Theorem 3. After determining the smallest min-cut, an individual node can perform a link reversal by comparing its queue's overload status with its neighbor's. All the links that go from a non-overloaded node to an overloaded node are reversed to obtain D_{k+1}. The complete LFBP algorithm is given in Algorithm 3.

COROLLARY 1. *Suppose the traffic demand is feasible in G, i.e., $\lambda \leq f^{\max}$. Then, the LFBP algorithm (Algorithm 3) will find a DAG, whose maximum flow supports λ, in a finite number of iterations.*

PROOF. Theorem 3 shows that LFBP identifies the smallest min-cut (A, A^c) for the DAG D_k. Lemma 6 shows that A is the set of overloaded nodes, and A^c is the set of non-overloaded nodes in a flow allocation that induces the lexicographically minimal overload vector. LFBP reverses the

Algorithm 3 LFBP (Executed by node n)

```
Input: sequences {T_k}, {R_k}, unique ID n
Generate initial DAG D_0 by directing each link {n, j}
  to (n, j) if n < j, to (j, n) if j > n.
Mark the queue Q_n as not overloaded
Initialize t ← 0, k ← 0
while true do
    Use BP to send/recive packets on all links of node n
    if (Q_n(t) > R_k) then
        Mark Q_n as overloaded.
    end if
    t ← t + 1

    T_k ← T_k − 1
    if T_k = 0 then
        Reverse all links (j, n) such that Q_j is not over-
  loaded and Q_n is overloaded.
        k ← k + 1
        Mark Q_n as not overloaded
    end if
end while
```

links going from A^c to A, which is also the reversals performed by the link reversal algorithm (Algorithm 1). Hence, by Theorem 1, LFBP obtains the DAG that supports λ. □

Good choices for the thresholds T_k and R_k are topology dependent. When the value of R_k is too small, nodes that are not overloaded might cross the threshold producing a false positive. If the value of R_k is large but T_k is small, the overloaded nodes might not have enough time to develop the backlog to cross R_k which produces false negatives. Hence, a good strategy is to choose a large R_k so that the non-overloaded nodes don't (or rarely) cross this threshold, then chose a large T_k such that the overloaded nodes have enough time to build the backlog to cross R_k. Optimizing these thresholds requires further research. Note that our algorithm performance degrades graciously with false positives/negatives. Even when it detects the smallest min-cut incorrectly, the actions of the algorithm preserve the acyclic structure. Thus, in the subsequent iterations the algorithm can improve the DAG again.

4.1 Algorithm modification for topology changes

In this section we consider networks with time-varying topologies, where several links of graph G may appear or disappear over time. Although the DAG that supports λ depends on the topology of G, our proposed policy LFBP can adapt to the topology changes and efficiently track the optimal solution.Additionally, the loop free structure of a DAG is preserved under link removals. Thus, if some of the links in the network disappear, we may continue using LFBP on the new network.

To handle the appearance of new links in the network smoothly, we will slightly extend LFBP to guarantee the loop free structure. For a DAG D_k, every node n stores a unique state $x_n(k)$ representing its position in the topological ordering of the DAG D_k. The states are maintained such that they are unique and all the links go from a node with the lower state to a node with the higher state. When a new link $\{i, j\}$ appears we can set its direction to go from i to j if $x_i(k) < x_j(k)$ and from j to i otherwise. Since this assignment of direction to the new link is in alignment with the existing links in the DAG, the loop-free property is preserved.

The state for each node n can be initialized using the unique node ID during the initial DAG creation, i.e. $x_n(0) = n$. Then whenever a reversal is performed the state of node n can be updated as follows:

$$x_n(k) = \begin{cases} x_n(k-1) - 2^k\Delta, & \text{if } n \text{ is overloaded,} \\ x_n(k-1), & \text{otherwise.} \end{cases}$$

Here, Δ is some constant chosen such that $\Delta > \max_{i,j \in N} x_i(0) - x_j(0)$. Note that this assignment of state is consistent with the way the link directions are assigned by the link reversal algorithm. The states for the non-overloaded nodes are unchanged, so the links between these nodes are unaffected. Also, the states for all the overloaded nodes are decreased by the same amount $2^k\Delta$, so the direction of the links between the overloaded nodes is also preserved. Furthermore, the quantity $-2^k\Delta$ is less than the lowest possible state before the kth iteration, so the overloaded nodes have a lower state than the non-overloaded nodes. Hence, the links between the overloaded and non-overloaded nodes go from the overloaded nodes to the non-overloaded nodes.

In this scheme, the states x_n decrease unboundedly as more reversals are preformed. In order to prevent this, after a certain number of reversals, we can rescale the states by dividing them by a large positive number. This decreases the value of the state while maintaining the topological ordering of the DAG. The number of reversals k can be reset to 0, and a new Δ can be chosen such that it is greater than the largest difference between the rescaled states.

5. COMPLEXITY ANALYSIS

To understand the number of iteration the link-reversal algorithm takes to obtain the optimal DAG, we analyze the time complexity of the algorithm.

THEOREM 4. *Let C be a vector of the capacities of all the links in E, and let I be the set of indices $1, 2, ..., |E|$. Define $\delta > 0$ to be the smallest positive difference between the capacity of any two cuts. Specifically, δ is the solution of the following optimization problem*

$$\min_{A,B \subseteq I} \sum_{a \in A} c_a - \sum_{b \in B} c_b$$

$$\textit{subject to: } \sum_{a \in A} c_a > \sum_{b \in B} c_b.$$

The number of iterations taken by the link reversal algorithm before it stops is upper bounded by $\lceil |N| \frac{f^{\max}}{\delta} \rceil$, where $f^{\max}$ is the max-flow of the undirected network.

PROOF. After each iteration of the link-reversal algorithm, either the max-flow of the DAG increases, or the max-flow stays the same and the number of nodes in the source side of the smallest min-cut increases (see Lemma 8 in the technical report [15]). We can bound the number of consecutive iterations such that there is no improvement in the max-flow. In particular, every such iteration will add at least one node to the source set. So, it is impossible to have more than $|N| - 2$ such iteration. Hence, every $|N|$ iterations we are guaranteed to have at least one increase in the max-flow.

Max-flow is equal to the min-cut capacity, and min-cut capacity is defined as the sum of link capacities. Say, the max-flow of DAG D_{k+1} is greater than that of D_k. Let A be the set of indices (in the capacity vector C) of the links in the min-cut of D_{k+1} , and B be the set of indices of the links in the min-cut of D_k. This choice of A and B forms a feasible solution to the optimization problem given in the theorem statement. Since the optimal solution δ lower bounds all the feasible solutions in the minimization problem, the increase in the max-flow must be greater than or equal to δ.

Every $|N|$ iteration the max-flow increases at least by δ. Hence, the DAG supporting the max-flow $f^{\max}$ is formed within $\lceil |N| f^{\max}/\delta \rceil$ iterations. $\square$

COROLLARY 2. *In a network where all the link capacities are rational with the least common denominator $\mathcal{D} \in \mathbb{N}$, the number of iterations is upper bounded by $(|N|\mathcal{D}f^{\max})$.*

PROOF. Since the capacities are rational we can write the capacity of the ith link as $c_i = \frac{\mathcal{N}_i}{\mathcal{D}}$, where $\mathcal{N}_i$ is a natural number. From the definition of δ in Theorem 4, we get δ to be the value of the following optimization problem:

$$\min_{A,B \subseteq I} \frac{1}{\mathcal{D}} \left(\sum_{a \in A} \mathcal{N}_a - \sum_{b \in B} \mathcal{N}_b \right)$$

$$\text{subject to: } \sum_{a \in A} \mathcal{N}_a > \sum_{b \in B} \mathcal{N}_b.$$

All the $\mathcal{N}_{(.)}$ are integers, so to satisfy the constraint we must have the difference $\sum_{a \in A} \mathcal{N}_a - \sum_{b \in B} \mathcal{N}_b \geq 1$. Hence $\delta \geq \frac{1}{\mathcal{D}}$. Using this value of δ in Theorem 4, we can see that the number of iterations is upper bounded by $(|N|\mathcal{D}f^{\max})$. $\square$

COROLLARY 3. *In a network with unit capacity links, the number of iterations the link-reversal algorithm takes to obtain the optimal DAG is upper bounded by $|N||E|$.*

PROOF. The max-flow $f^{\max} \leq |E|$. So, by Corollary 2, the number of iterations is upper bounded by $|N||E|$. $\square$

We conjecture that these upper bounds are not tight, and finding a tighter bound will be pursued in the future research. We simulated the link reversal algorithm in 50,000 different Erdos-Renyi networks ($p = 0.5$) of sizes 10 to 50 with randomly assigned link capacities. The link reversal algorithm started with a random initial DAG. We found that it took less than 2 iterations on average to find the optimal DAG.

A worst case lower bound for the number of iteration is $|N|$. This lower bound can be achieved in a line network where the initial DAG has all of its links in the wrong direction.

6. SIMULATION RESULTS

We compare the delay performance of the LFBP algorithm and the BP algorithm via simulations. We will see that the network with the LFBP routing has a smaller backlog on average under the same load. This shows that the LFBP algorithm has a better delay performance. We consider two types of networks for the simulations: a simple network with fixed topology, and a network with grid topology where the links appear and disappear randomly.

6.1 Fixed topology

We consider a network with the topology shown in Figure 4(a). The edge labels represent the link capacities. The undirected network has the maximum throughput of 15 packets per time slot. Figure 4(b) shows the initial DAG D_0. Instead of running the initial DAG algorithm of Section 3.1, here we choose a zero throughput DAG to test the worst-case performance of LFBP. The arrivals to the network are Poisson with rate $\lambda = 15\rho$, where we vary $\rho = .5, .55, ..., .95$. For the LFBP algorithm, we set the overload detection threshold to $R_k = 60$ for all n, k. To choose this parameter, we observed that the backlog buildup in normal operation rarely raises above 60. We also choose the detection period $T_1 = 150$ and $T_k = 50$ for all $k > 1$. This provides enough time for buildup, which improve the accuracy of the overload detection mechanism.

We simulate both algorithms for one million slots, using the same arrival process sample path. Figures 4(c) - 4(e) show the various DAGs that are formed by the LFBP algorithm at iterations $k = 1, 2, 3$. We can see that the nodes in the smallest min-cut get overloaded and the link reversals gradually improve the DAG until the throughput optimal DAG is reached.

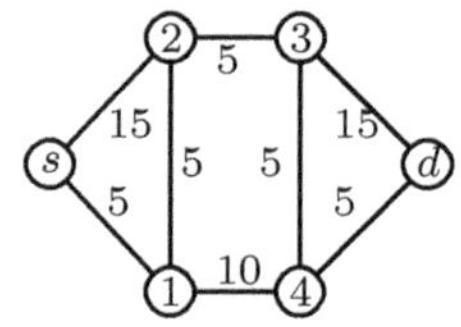

(a) Network topology.

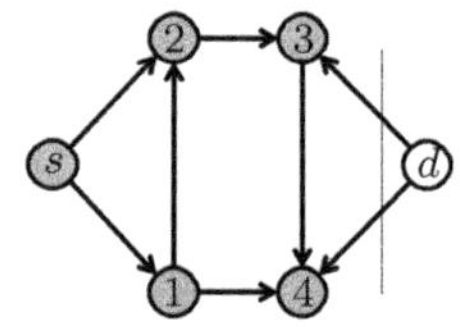

(b) The initial DAG chosen so that LFBP requires several iteration to reach the optimal.

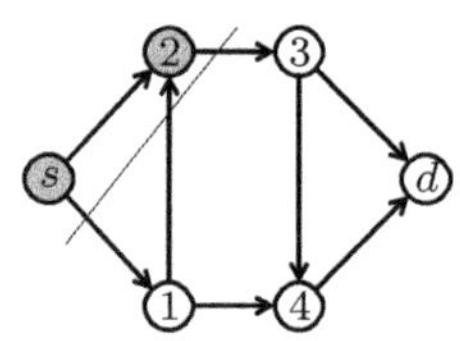

(c) After 1st reversal.

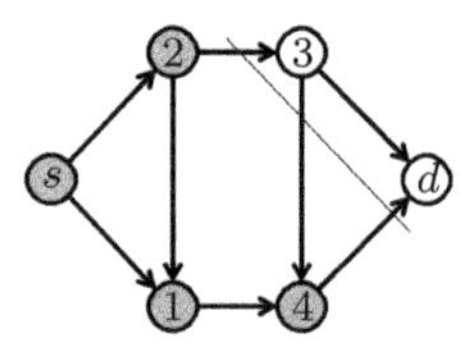

(d) After 2nd reversal.

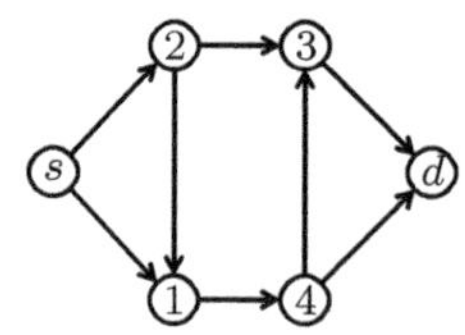

(e) The optimal DAG.

Figure 4: Figure (a) depicts the original network. Figures (b)-(e) are the various stages of the DAG. The red nodes represent the overloaded nodes, and the dashed line shows the boundary of the overloaded and the non-overloaded nodes.

Figure 5 compares the total average backlog in the network for BP and LFBP, which is indicative of the average delay. A significant delay improvement is achieved by LFBP, for example at load 0.5 the average delay is reduced by 66% We observe that the gain in the delay performance is more pronounced when the load is low. In low load situations, the network doesn't have enough "pressure" to drive the packets to the destination and so under BP the packets go in loops.

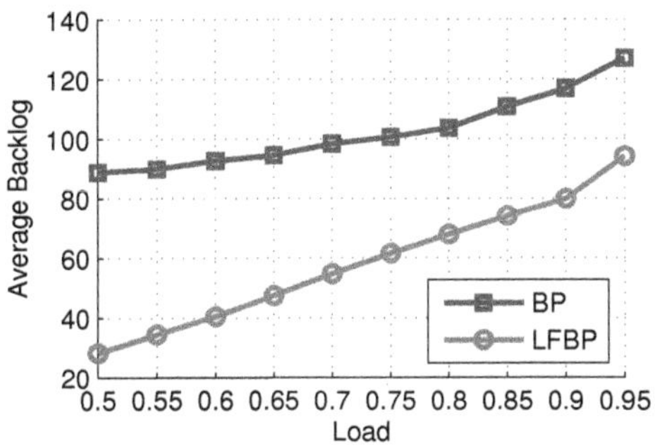

Figure 5: Average backlog in the network (Fig. 4(a)) with fixed topology for the Loop Free Backpressure (LFBP) and the Backpressure (BP) algorithms.

6.2 Randomly changing topology

To understand the delay performance of the LFBP algorithm on networks with randomly changing topology, we consider a network where 16 nodes are arranged in a 4×4 grid. All the links are taken to be of capacity six. For the LFBP algorithm, we choose a random initial DAG with zero throughput shown in Figure 6. The source is on the upper left corner (node 1) and the destination is on the bottom right (node 16).

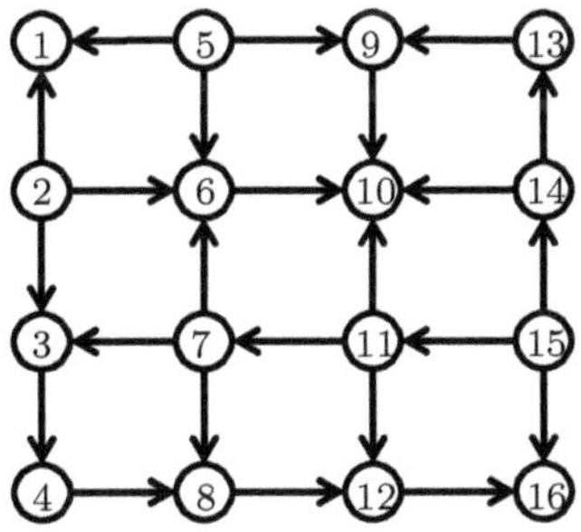

Figure 6: Initial DAG for the LFBP algorithm chosen so that the LFBP needs several iterations to reach the optimal DAG. All the links have capacity six.

In the beginning of the simulations all 24 network links are activated. At each time slot an active link fails with a probability 10^{-4} and an inactive link is activated with a probability 10^{-3}. The maximum throughput of the undirected network without any link failures is 12. Clearly on average, each link is "on" a fraction $\frac{10}{11}$ of the time, and thus the average maximum throughput of the undirected network with these link failure rates is $\frac{10}{11} \times 12 = 10.9$. The arrivals to the networks are Poisson with rate $\lambda = 10.9\rho$, where $\rho = .1, .2, ..., .6$. For the LFBP algorithm, the detection threshold is set to $R_k = 100$ and the detection period is $T_k = 30$ for all n, k. These parameters were chosen so that there are several reversals before a topology change occurs in the undirected network. The simulation was carried out for a million slots.

Figure 7 compares the average backlog of LFBP and BP. In the low load scenarios LFBP reduces delay significantly (by 85% for load = 0.1) even though the topology changes challenge the convergence of the link-reversal algorithm. As the load increases, both the algorithms begin to obtain a similar delay performance.

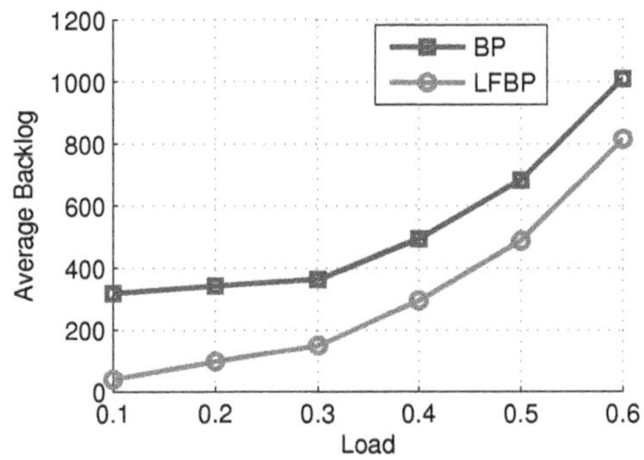

Figure 7: Average backlog in the network with random link failures (Fig. 6) for the Loop Free Backpressure algorithm and the Backpressure algorithm.

7. MULTICOMMODITY SIMULATION

We extend of the link reversal algorithm to the networks with multiple commodities. The multi-commodity algorithm is identical to the single commodity algorithm, with the exception that we now use the multicommodity backpressure of [1]. Each node n maintains a queue $Q_n^y(t)$ for each commodity y. Each commodity is assigned its own initial DAG. A pseudocode for the multicommodity LFBP that we used is given in Algorithm 4. An important direction for future research is to determine whether the claims proven for a single commodity in the previous sections extend to the multicommodity case.

For the simulation, we consider a network arranged in a 4×4 grid as shown in Figure 6. Each link has a capacity of 6 packets per time-slot. There are three commodities in the network defined by the source destination pairs (1,16), (4,13) and (5,8). For the LFBP algorithm, each commodity starts with the same initial DAG given in Figure 6.

We use the arrival rate vector $\lambda^{\max} = [7.18, 6.96, 9.86]$, which is a max-flow vector for this network computed by solving a linear program. We scale this vector by various load factors ρ ranging from 0.1 to 0.9. The arrivals for each commodity i is Poisson with rate $\rho\lambda_i^{\max}$. In the beginning of the LFBP simulation, $\lfloor 500/\rho \rfloor$ dummy packets are added to the source of each commodity. This is helpful in low load cases because it forces the algorithm to find a DAG with high throughput, and avoids stopping at a DAG that only supports the given (low) load. R_k was chosen to be 50 and $T_k = 50$ for all $k > 0$. The simulation was executed for 500,000 time-steps.

Figure 8 shows the average backlog in the network for different loads under backpressure and multicommodity LFBP. We can see that the LFBP algorithm has a significantly improved delay performance compared to backpressure.

8. CONCLUSION

Backpressure routing and link reversal algorithms have been separately proposed for mobile wireless networks applications. In this paper we show that these two distributed

Algorithm 4 Multicommodity LFBP (Executed by n)

Input: sequences $\{T_k\}, \{R_k\}$, unique ID n
For each commodity y, generate initial DAG D_0^y by directing $\{n, j\}$ to (n, j) if $n < j$, to (j, n) if $j > n$.
Mark all queues Q_n^y as not overloaded
Initialize $t \leftarrow 0$, $k \leftarrow 0$
while true **do**
    Use Multicommodity BP to send/recive packets on all links of node n
    for all y **do**
        if $(Q_n^y(t) > R_k)$ **then**
            Mark this Q_n^y as overloaded.
        end if
    end for
    $t \leftarrow t + 1$

    $T_k \leftarrow T_k - 1$
    if $T_k = 0$ **then**
        for all y **do**
            Reverse links (j, n) in D_k^y if Q_j^y is not overloaded and Q_n^y is overloaded.
        end for
        $k \leftarrow k + 1$
        Mark all queues as not overloaded
    end if
end while

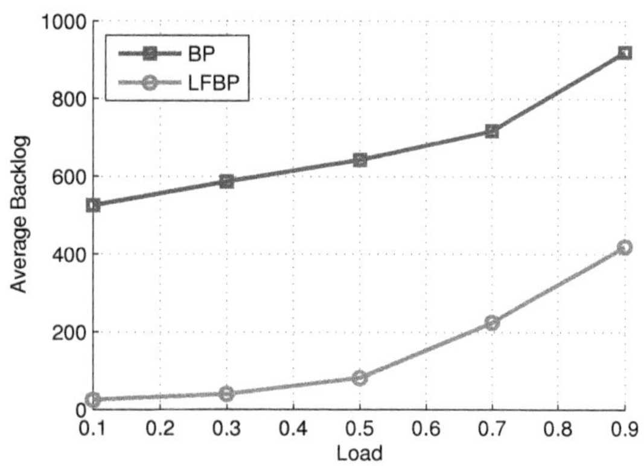

Figure 8: Average backlog in a multicommodity network with fixed topology for LFBP and BP algorithms.

schemes can be successfully combined to yield good throughput and delay performance.We develop the Loop-Free Backpressure Algorithm which jointly routes packets in a constrained DAG and reverses the links of the DAG to improve its throughput. We show that the algorithm ultimately results in a DAG that yields the maximum throughput. Additionally, by restricting the routing to this DAG we eliminate loops, thus reducing the average delay. Future investigations involve optimization of the overload detection parameters and studying the performance of the scheme on the networks with multiple commodities.

9. REFERENCES

[1] L. Tassiulas and A. Ephremides, "Stability properties of constrained queueing systems and scheduling for maximum throughput in multihop radio networks," *IEEE Transactions on Automatic Control*, vol. 37, no. 12, pp. 1936-1949, December 1992.

[2] L. X. Bui, R. Srikant and A. Stolyar, "A novel architecture for reduction of delay and queueing structure complexity in the back-pressure algorithm," *IEEE/ACM Transactions on Networking*, vol. 19, no. 6, pp. 1597-1609, December 2011.

[3] M. J. Neely, E. Modiano and C. E. Rohrs, "Dynamic power allocation and routing for time varying wireless networks," *IEEE Journal on Selected Areas in Communications*, Special Issue on Wireless Ad-hoc Networks, vol. 23, no. 1, pp. 89-103, January 2005.

[4] E. Gafni and D. Bertsekas, "Distributed algorithms for generating loop-free routes in networks with frequently changing topology," *IEEE Transactions on Communications*, vol. 29, no. 1, pp. 11-18, January 1981.

[5] V.D. Park and M.S. Corson, "A highly adaptive distributed routing algorithm for mobile wireless networks," INFOCOM, 1997.

[6] L. Georgiadis and L. Tassiulas, "Optimal overload response in sensor networks." *IEEE Transactions on Information Theory*, vol.52, no. 6, pp. 2684-2696, June 2006.

[7] H. Xiong, R. Li, A. Eryilmaz and E. Ekici, "Delay-aware cross-layer design for network utility maximization in multi-hop networks." *IEEE Journal on Selected Areas in Communications*, vol. 29, no. 5, pp. 951-959, May 2011.

[8] L. Ying, S. Shakkottai, A. Reddy and S. Liu, "On combining shortest-path and backpressure routing over multihop wireless networks," *IEEE/ACM Transactions on Networking*, vol. 19, no. 3, pp. 841-854, June 2011.

[9] P.-K. Huang, X. Lin, and C.-C. Wang, "A low-complexity congestion control and scheduling algorithm for multihop wireless networks with order-optimal per-flow delay," *IEEE/ACM Trans. on Networking*, vol. 21, no. 2, pp. 2588-2596, April 2013.

[10] M. J. Neely, "Stochastic network optimization with application to communication and queueing systems," Morgan & Claypool, 2010.

[11] L. R. Ford and D. R. Fulkerson, "Maximal flow through a network," *Canadian Journal of Mathematics*, 8: 399, 1956.

[12] L. Georgiadis, P. Georgatsos, K. Floros, and S. Sartzetakis, "Lexicographically optimal balanced networks," *IEEE/ACM Transactions on Networking*, vol. 10, no. 6, pp. 818-829, December 2002.

[13] L. Huang and M. J. Neely, "Delay reduction via Lagrange multipliers in stochastic network optimization," *IEEE Transactions on Automatic Control*, vol. 56, no. 4, pp. 842-857, April 2011.

[14] L. Georgiadis, M. J. Neely and L. Tassiulas, "Resource allocation and cross-layer control in wireless networks," Foundations and trends in networking, Now Publishers Inc, 2006.

[15] A. Rai, C.P. Li, G. Paschos, E. Modiano, "Loop-Free Backpressure Routing Using Link-Reversal Algorithms," `http://arxiv.org/abs/1503.06857`, Technical Report.

Face Routing on a Non-Planar Graph: Theory and Applications to Networks

Yuan-Po Cheng
Network Video System Department
Industrial Technology Research Institute
Hsinchu, Taiwan, ROC
goldmoun@itri.org.tw

Ming-Jer Tsai
Department of Computer Science
National Tsing Hua University
Hsinchu, Taiwan, ROC
mjtsai@cs.nthu.edu.tw

ABSTRACT

In geographic routing protocols, face forwarding is often used in helping a packet escape from the stuck state. To guarantee packet delivery, face forwarding usually routes a packet in a planar subgraph of the network, which might disable many edges in the network and, in turn, worsen the routing performance and reduce the link failure tolerance. In this paper, we aim to improve the connectivity of the graphs on which face forwarding can guarantee packet delivery. We present a sufficient condition for the packet delivery guarantee of GFG face forwarding, augment the graph used in face forwarding with selected disabled edges in the network, and propose a geographic routing protocol, termed GFG-NP, in which a packet escapes from the stuck state by performing GFG face forwarding on the augmented graph that might be non-planar. We show, using theoretical analysis, that GFG-NP guarantees packet delivery when performed on the augmented graphs of the partial Delaunay triangulation (PDT) and the CLDP-stable graph constructed by the cross-link detection protocol (CLDP), termed PDT- and CLDP-augmented graphs, respectively. In addition, simulations on network simulator NS-2 show that GFG-NP with face forwarding performed on PDT- and CLDP-augmented graphs outperforms GFG with face forwarding performed on PDT and the CLDP-stable graph, respectively, in terms of load balance, path length, routing latency, and packet delivery rate.

Categories and Subject Descriptors

C.2.2 [**Computer-Communication Networks**]: Network Protocols—*Routing protocols*

Keywords

Wireless ad hoc networks; routing protocol; face routing

1. INTRODUCTION

A wireless ad hoc network consists of wireless nodes that communicate with each other without the aid of a fixed infrastructure. There is a wide range of applications for wireless ad hoc networks, including disaster relief, environmental monitoring, forest fire detection, etc. Since routing is an important issue and the popularity of the global positioning system (GPS) facilitates the use of GPS in nodes, many geographic routing protocols have been proposed for wireless ad hoc networks. In this paper, we undertake the development of the geographic routing protocols with guaranteed packet delivery and low path stretch in wireless ad hoc networks.

There are many geographic routing protocols in UDG networks, where the unit disk graph (UDG) is employed as the node communication model. Usually, greedy forwarding is used to forward a packet from a node to the neighbor closest to the destination until the packet gets stuck at a node with no neighbor closer to the destination (concave node). To save a packet to escape from the stuck state, CR [12], GPSR [9], GFG [2], GOAFR+ [13], and GPVFR [14] use face forwarding to route a packet along the face boundary in a planar subgraph of the network by the right-hand rule until the packet reaches a node closer to the destination than the concave node.

Several algorithms have been proposed to construct the planar graphs used in face forwarding, such as the Gabriel graph (GG) [6], the relative neighborhood graph (RNG) [18], and the partial Delaunay triangulation (PDT) [15]. Among them, PDT has the most edges, which in turn improves the performance of face forwarding and withstands more link failures. GG, RNG, and PDT can be constructed using the node's 1-hop neighbor geographic locations. Using 2-hop neighbor geographic locations, the number of edges in PDT can be further increased [15]. In [5], GPSR and GPVFR are shown to guarantee packet delivery on GG, RNG, and PDT while CR, GFG, and GOAFR+ guarantee packet delivery on any planar graph. Since the transmission range of a node is not a perfect circle in our real life, the cross-link detection protocol (CLDP) [11] is proposed for non-UDG networks. CLDP disables all crossing edges, except for the ones whose removal disconnects the network, from the network such that GFG can guarantee packet delivery.

To guarantee packet delivery, many edges in the network are not allowed to be used in face forwarding, which might in turn worsen the routing performance and reduce the link failure tolerance. In this paper, our goal is to increase the number of edges in the graph on which face forwarding can guarantee packet delivery. Note that a planar graph can be used to guarantee packet delivery of GFG face forwarding (one kind of well-known face forwarding used in GFG) but not every face forwarding [5]. Hence, we concentrate on the improvement of the connectivity of the graphs on which GFG face forwarding can guarantee packet delivery. Remark that routing a packet in a planar graph is sufficient but not necessary to guarantee packet delivery of GFG face forwarding. We present a sufficient condition for the packet delivery guarantee of GFG face forward-

MobiHoc'15, June 22–25, 2015, Hangzhou, China.

ACM 978-1-4503-3489-1/15/06 ...$15.00.
http://dx.doi.org/10.1145/2746285.2746314.

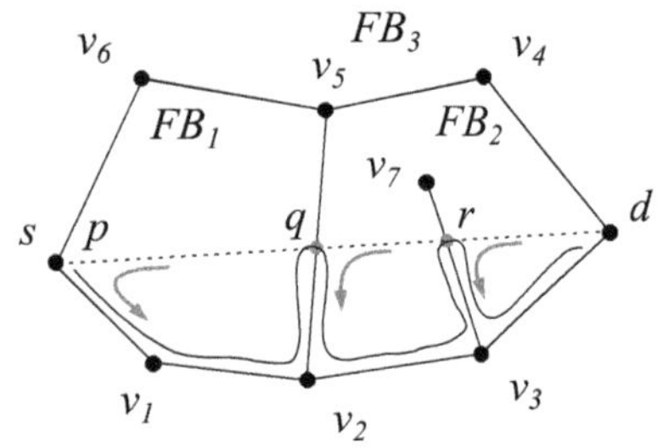

Figure 1: Illustration of GFG face forwarding. There are three boundaries of face in the graph: $FB_1(s, v_1, v_2, v_5, v_6, s)$, $FB_2(d, v_4, v_5, v_2, v_3, v_7, v_3, d)$, and the boundary of the outer face $FB_3(s, v_6, v_5, v_4, d, v_3, v_2, v_1, s)$.

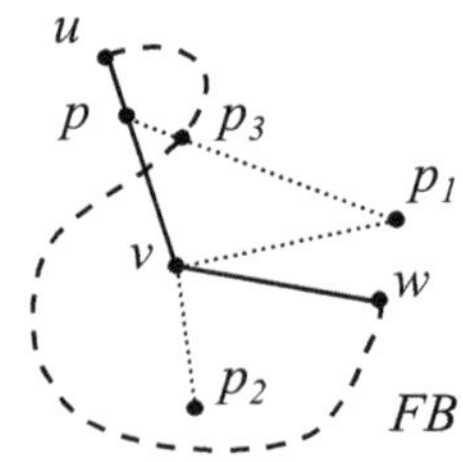

Figure 2: Illustrations of Definitions 1 and 2, where u, v, and w are successive nodes on a general face boundary, FB, traversed by the right-hand rule, point p lies on edge (u, v), and point p_3 lies on the intersection of FB and line segment $\overline{pp_1}$. The dashed lines denote all nodes and edges on FB except for (u, v) and (v, w), and the dotted lines indicate the line segments.

ing, augment the graph used in face forwarding with selected disabled edges in the network, and propose a geographic routing protocol, termed GFG-NP, in which a packet escapes from the stuck state by performing GFG face forwarding on the augmented graph that might be non-planar.

The remainder of this paper is organized as follows. In Section 2, we demonstrate GFG face forwarding. In Section 3, we present the sufficient condition, the rules for constructing an augmented graph, and GFG-NP. In Section 4, PDT and the CLDP-stable graph are augmented with edges, called PDT- and CLDP-augmented graphs, respectively. Using theoretical analysis, in Section 5, we show GFG-NP guarantees packet delivery if the protocol performs face forwarding on a PDT- or CLDP-augmented graph. We conduct simulations to evaluate the performance of GFG-NP with face forwarding performed on the PDT- and CLDP-augmented graphs in Section 6. Finally, we conclude this paper in Section 7.

2. PRELIMINARY

In GFG face forwarding, a packet traverses face boundaries one by one using the right-hand rule until the packet reaches the destination or a node closer to the destination than the stuck node, where the right-hand rule can be illustrated as placing the right hand on one edge on the face boundary and continuing to explore the edges by walking along the face boundary. The face boundary traversed by a packet changes when the packet encounters an edge intersecting with the line segment from the last intersection point (which is the stuck node at the beginning of GFG face forwarding) to the destination, in which case the face boundary traversed by the packet changes to the face boundary encountered after placing the right hand on the line segment from the destination to the new intersection point and walking from the destination to the new intersection point.

Example 1. *Take Fig. 1, for example, where a packet is routed from s to d using GFG face forwarding. Since the face boundary FB_1 is encountered after placing the right hand on $\overline{ds}$ and walking from d to s, the packet is routed along FB_1. As the packet encounters the edge (v_2, v_5) that intersects $\overline{sd}$ at q, the face boundary traversed by the packet changes to FB_2, the face boundary encountered after placing the right hand on $\overline{dq}$ and walking from d to q. The packet traverses nodes v_1, v_2, and v_3 during the transmission from s to d by GFG face forwarding.*

3. GFG-NP

We first show a sufficient condition for the packet delivery guarantee of GFG face forwarding in Section 3.1. Subsequently, we show the rules for constructing an augmented graph in Section 3.2. Finally, we propose GFG-NP in Section 3.3. In this paper, a general face boundary denotes a sequence of nodes and edges traversed by the right-hand rule, and we use "node" and "point" alternately since a node lies on the point with the geographic location of the node.

3.1 Sufficient Condition

The following notations are necessary for the sufficient condition for the packet delivery guarantee of GFG face forwarding.

Definition 1. *Let FB be a general face boundary, u and v be two successive nodes on FB traversed by the right-hand rule, and p be a point on the edge (u, v). Then, u (or v) is called the preceding (or succeeding) point of p with respect to (wrt) FB if node v (or u) lies on p; otherwise, u and v are called the preceding and succeeding points of p, respectively. In what follows, the preceding and succeeding points of p wrt FB are denoted by $p_{pre,FB}$ and $p_{suc,FB}$, respectively.*

Definition 2. *For a point, p, on a general face boundary FB, the point $t \neq p$ is said to be covered, wrt FB, by p if line segment $\overline{pt}$ is between line segments $\overline{pp_{pre,FB}}$ and $\overline{pp_{suc,FB}}$ in the clockwise direction and does not cross the general face boundary FB.*

Example 2. *Fig. 2 illustrates Definitions 1 and 2. According to Definition 1, u and w are the preceding and succeeding points of v wrt FB; u and v are the preceding and succeeding points of p wrt FB. That is, $v_{pre,FB} = p_{pre,FB} = u$, $v_{suc,FB} = w$, and $p_{suc,FB} = v$. Clearly, $\overline{vp_1}$ is between $\overline{vv_{pre,FB}}$ (i.e., $\overline{vu}$) and $\overline{vv_{suc,FB}}$ (i.e., $\overline{vw}$) in the clockwise direction, and $\overline{vp_1}$ does not cross FB. Thus, p_1 is covered, wrt FB, by v according to Definition 2. By contrast, p_2 is not covered, wrt FB, by v since $\overline{vp_2}$ is not between $\overline{vv_{pre,FB}}$ and $\overline{vv_{suc,FB}}$ in the clockwise direction. On the other hand, although $\overline{pp_1}$ is between $\overline{pp_{pre,FB}}$ (i.e., $\overline{pu}$) and $\overline{pp_{suc,FB}}$ (i.e., $\overline{pv}$) in the clockwise direction, p_1 is not covered, wrt FB, by p because $\overline{pp_1}$ crosses FB. On the contrary, p_3 is covered, wrt FB, by p since $\overline{pp_3}$ intersects but does not cross FB. In Fig. 1, $\overline{pd}$ (or $\overline{qd}$) is between $\overline{pp_{pre,FB_1}}$ (or $\overline{qq_{pre,FB_2}}$) and $\overline{pp_{suc,FB_1}}$ (or $\overline{qq_{suc,FB_2}}$) in the clockwise direction. In addition, wrt FB_2, d is covered by r but not covered by q, and, wrt FB_1, d is not covered by p. It is noteworthy that there is an* *intersection of $\overline{pd}$ and FB_1 and an intersection of $\overline{qd}$ and FB_2. This is why d is not covered, wrt FB_1, by p and not covered, wrt FB_2, by q.*

Intuitively, GFG face forwarding can guarantee packet delivery if a packet can always encounters an edge intersecting with the line segment from the last intersection point p to the destination d as the destination does not lie on the general face boundary FB along which the packet is routed. This requirement of guaranteeing packet delivery of GFG face forwarding can be satisfied if d is not covered, wrt FB, by p according to Definition 2. Thus, we have the following result.

THEOREM 1. *For any pair of nodes c and d, GFG face forwarding can always route a packet from c to d if the following condition is satisfied:*

$$\text{For any general face boundary } FB \text{ crossing the line segment } \overline{cd} \text{ but not containing } d, d \text{ is not covered, wrt } FB, \text{ by each intersection of } \overline{cd} \text{ and } FB. \quad (1)$$

PROOF. Let FB be the general face boundary along which the packet is routed after the packet encounters the intersection, p, of the routing path and $\overline{cd}$. Since GFG face forwarding is used, $\overline{pd}$ is between $\overline{pp_{pre,FB}}$ and $\overline{pp_{suc,FB}}$ in the clockwise direction. Clearly, if d lies on FB and is covered, wrt FB, by p, $\overline{pd}$ does not cross FB by Definition 2. Thus, the packet can reach d along FB. It suffices to show if d lies on FB but is not covered, wrt FB, by p or if d does not lie on FB, there exists an intersection, t, of $\overline{pd}$ and FB, $t \neq p$, so that the packet can reach t along FB. This is clearly true. Otherwise, d is covered, wrt FB, by p by Definition 2. □

3.2 Augmented Graph

We first introduce the concept of an sc-sat subgraph of a network in Definition 3. Then, we give the rules for obtaining an augmented graph from an sc-sat subgraph of the network in Definition 4.

DEFINITION 3. *Given a graph G, a spanning subgraph of G is called an sc-sat subgraph of G, denoted G_{sc}, if the sufficient condition in Eq.* (1) *is satisfied for any pair of nodes in G_{sc}.*

According to Definition 3, we have the following results. Corollaries 1 and 3 immediately follow Theorem 1 and Corollary 2, respectively.

COROLLARY 1. *GFG face forwarding can always route from a node, c, to another node, d, in any sc-sat subgraph of a given graph G.*

COROLLARY 2. *Let FB be a general face boundary traversed by the right-hand rule on a graph G, and let p be an arbitrary point on FB. If any point on a general face boundary rather than FB is not covered, wrt FB, by p, then G is an sc-sat subgraph.*

PROOF. Let c and d be an arbitrary pair of nodes in G. By Definition 3, we need to show the sufficient condition in Eq. (1) is satisfied for c and d. Let FB' be an arbitrary general face boundary crossing the line segment $\overline{cd}$ but not containing d, and p' an arbitrary intersection of $\overline{cd}$ and FB'. It suffices to show d is not covered, wrt FB', by p'. This must hold because d lies on a general face boundary rather than FB'. □

COROLLARY 3. *Any planar subgraph of G is an sc-sat subgraph.*

DEFINITION 4. *Given $G(V, E)$ and $G_{sc}(V, E_{sc})$, an edge (u, v) is called an augmented edge if (u, v) satisfies the following conditions:*

1. *There is a general face boundary, FB, in G_{sc} such that u and v lie on FB.*
2. *$(u, v) \in E - E_{sc}$.*
3. *(u, v) and the edges on FB form two general face boundaries FB_1 and FB_2.*
4. *All points on FB but not on FB_1 (or FB_2) are not covered by any point on FB_1 (or FB_2) wrt FB_1 (or FB_2).*
5. *For any point p on both FB_1 and FB_2 but not on (u, v), if p is covered, wrt FB_1 (or FB_2), by a point q on FB_1 (or FB_2) but not on (u, v), then q is covered, wrt FB_1 (or FB_2), by p.*

Furthermore, an augmented graph of G_{sc}, denoted G_a, is obtained from G_{sc} by adding augmented edges.

EXAMPLE 3. *An illustration of Definitions 3 and 4 is shown in Fig. 3. In G_{sc}, there are three general faces: $FB_1(v_1, v_2, v_{13}, v_3, v_{12}, v_{11}, v_{10}, v_9, v_8, v_7, v_6, v_5, v_4, v_3, v_{13}, v_2, v_1)$, $FB_2(v_3, v_4, v_{12}, v_3, v_{11}, v_{12}, v_{10}, v_{11}, v_4, v_{10}, v_{12}, v_4, v_{11}, v_3)$, and $FB_3(v_4, v_5, v_6, v_7, v_8, v_9, v_{10}, v_4)$. Note that, for any point p on FB_1 (or FB_2 or FB_3), only the points on FB_1 (or FB_2 or FB_3) is covered, wrt FB_1 (or FB_2 or FB_3), by p. Thus, G_{sc} is an sc-sat subgraph of the network in Fig. 3(a) by Corollary 2. In addition, since no general face boundary, FB, exists such that both v_1 and v_{10} lie on FB, (v_1, v_{10}) is not an augmented edge according to Definition 4. Although v_5 and v_8 both lie on FB_1 (or FB_3), (v_5, v_8) and the edges on FB_1 (or FB_3) cannot form two general face boundaries. Therefore, (v_5, v_8) is not an augmented edge. It is noteworthy that FB_1 and FB_3 are merged into one larger general face boundary after (v_5, v_8) is added; i.e., (v_5, v_8), the edges on FB_1, and the edges on FB_3 form a general face boundary. Also, (v_3, v_9) is not an augmented edge due to the argument analogous to that for (v_5, v_8). Moreover, v_5 and v_9 both lie on FB_3; meanwhile, (v_5, v_9) and the edges on FB_3 form two general face boundaries $FB_{3-1}(v_4, v_5, v_9, v_{10}, v_4)$ and $FB_{3-2}(v_5, v_6, v_7, v_8, v_9, v_5)$. However, (v_5, v_9) is still not an augmented edge because v_7, which lies on FB_3 but not on FB_{3-1}, is covered, wrt FB_{3-1}, by v_4, which lies on FB_{3-1}. Furthermore, (v_3, v_{10}) and the edges on FB_2 form two general face boundaries FB_{2-1} $(v_3, v_{10}, v_{12}, v_4, v_{11}, v_3)$ and FB_{2-2} $(v_4, v_{12}, v_3, v_{11}, v_{12}, v_{10}, v_{11}, v_4, v_{10}, v_3, v_4)$. In this situation, point p_1 lies on both FB_{2-1} and FB_{2-2}. Since p_1 is covered, wrt FB_{2-1}, by v_{12} but v_{12} is not covered, wrt FB_{2-1}, by p_1, condition 5 of Definition 4 is violated; therefore, (v_3, v_{10}) is not an augmented edge. It is worth mentioning that an augmented graph of G_{sc} does not need to contain every edge that satisfies five conditions described in Definition 4.*

3.3 The Algorithm

We propose GFG-NP in Algorithm 1, and show it guarantees packet delivery in Theorem 2. Like GFG, GFG-NP forwards a packet using greedy forwarding (step 1) and face forwarding (step 2) alternately. In the face forwarding, GFG face forwarding is performed on an augmented graph of an sc-sat subgraph of the network, G_a, with the removal of every augmented edge that crosses $\overline{sd}$. Definition 5 is necessary for the proof of Theorem 2.

DEFINITION 5. *Let c and d be the concave node and the destination node, respectively, and let FB be a general face boundary. A point p is called an FB node-intersection point if p lies on a*

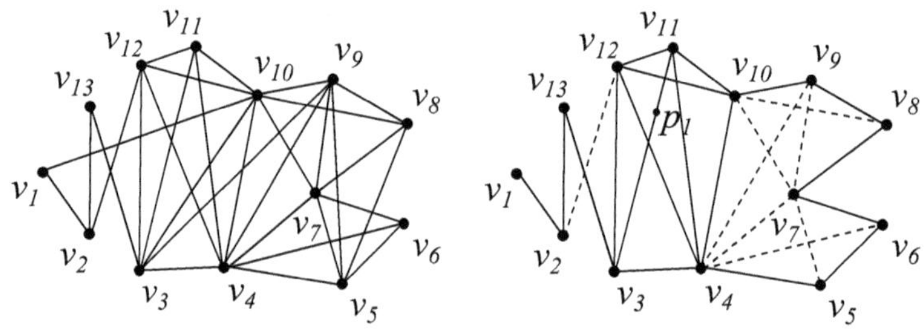

(a) (b)

Figure 3: Illustrations of Definitions 3 and 4. (a) The graph, G, denoting the sample network. (b) An sc-sat subgraph of G, G_{sc}, and its augmented graph, G_a, where the edges shown in solid lines are in both G_{sc} and G_a, and the edges shown in dashed lines are edges in $G_a - G_{sc}$ (the augmented edges).

Algorithm 1 GFG-NP

Require: G, G_a, the current node n

If n has a neighbor closer to d, then n forwards the packet using greedy forwarding in G.

Otherwise, n forwards the packet using GFG face forwarding in $G_a^{c,d} = G_a - \{(u, v) | (u, v) \notin E_{sc}$ and (u, v) intersects $\overline{cd}\}$, where c denotes the stuck node that starts this time GFG face forwarding.

node on FB or is an intersection of FB and $\overline{cd}$. In addition, an ordered list $(s_0, s_1, \cdots, s_n)$ is called an FB node-intersection point sequence if s_i is an FB node-intersection point for $0 \le i \le n$, s_i and s_{i+1} are two successive FB node-intersection points (i.e., no FB node-intersection point lies between s_i and s_{i+1}) for $0 \le i \le n-1$, and s_0 and s_n are the same FB node-intersection point. Moreover, an edge with endpoints s_i and s_j, (s_i, s_j), is called an FB augmented edge if s_i and s_j are FB node-intersection points, (s_i, s_j) is an augmented edge, and (s_i, s_j) is between $\overline{s_i s_{i_{pre,FB_0}}}$ and $\overline{s_i s_{i_{suc,FB_0}}}$ and between $\overline{s_j s_{j_{pre,FB_0}}}$ and $\overline{s_j s_{j_{suc,FB_0}}}$ in the clockwise direction.

Example 4. *An illustration of Definition 5 is shown in Fig. 4. According to Definition 5, $v_1, v_2, \cdots, v_9$, p, and p' are FB_0 node-intersection points. In Fig. 4(a), $(s_0, s_1, \cdots, s_{13})$ is an FB_0 node-intersection point sequence, where s_0 and s_{13} represent the point p. In Fig. 4(b), $(s_0, s_1, \cdots, s_{14})$ is an FB_0 node-intersection point sequence, where s_0 and s_{14} represent the point p, s_6 and s_{10} represent the point v_5, and s_7 and s_9 represent the point p'. In Fig. 4(a), (s_5, s_{10}) is not between $\overline{s_5 s_{5_{pre,FB_0}}}$ and $\overline{s_5 s_{5_{suc,FB_0}}}$ and between $\overline{s_{10} s_{10_{pre,FB_0}}}$ and $\overline{s_{10} s_{10_{suc,FB_0}}}$ in the clockwise direction; therefore, (s_5, s_{10}) cannot be an FB_0 augmented edge. Similarly, (s_5, s_{11}), (s_6, s_{10}), (s_6, s_{11}), and (s_6, s_{12}) cannot be FB_0 augmented edges. In addition, according to Definition 4, (s_5, s_{12}) cannot be an augmented edge due to the violation of condition 4, and (s_1, s_8), (s_2, s_8), and (s_3, s_8) cannot be augmented edges due to the violation of condition 3. This implies that (s_5, s_{12}), (s_1, s_8), (s_2, s_8), and (s_3, s_8) cannot be FB_0 augmented edges. Thus, an FB_0 augmented edge (s_i, s_j) not intersecting $\overline{cd}$ with $0 < i < 7$ and $7 < j < 13$ does not exist. That is, each FB_0 augmented edge (s_i, s_j) not intersecting $\overline{cd}$ must satisfy $0 < i, j < 7$ or $7 < i, j < 13$. According to the property of the right-hand rule, p' must lie on FB in $G_a^{c,d}$, where FB denotes the general face boundary in $G_a^{c,d}$ obtained from FB_0 by adding all the augmented edges not intersecting $\overline{cd}$. In Fig. 4(b), it can easily be verified that each FB_0 augmented edge (s_i, s_j) not intersecting $\overline{cd}$ also satisfies $0 < i, j < 9$ or $9 < i, j < 14$. In fact, for an arbitrary FB_0, there is an FB_0 node-intersection point, s_k, located at p' in $G_a^{c,d}$ such that each FB_0 augmented edge (s_i, s_j) satisfies $0 < i, j < k$ or $k < i, j < n$, which ensures that GFG face forwarding can always route the packet from c to d in $G_a^{c,d}$ and thus guarantees the packet delivery of GFG-NP, as demonstrated in the proof of Theorem 2.*

Theorem 2. *For any pair of nodes c and d, GFG-NP can always route a packet from c to d in a connected network G.*

Proof. By Theorem 1, we need only to show the sufficient condition in Eq. (1) is satisfied in $G_a^{c,d}$. Let FB be a general face boundary crossing $\overline{cd}$ but not containing d, and p an arbitrary intersection of $\overline{cd}$ and FB in $G_a^{c,d}$. Clearly, d is not covered, wrt FB, by p if $\overline{pd}$ is not between $\overline{pp_{pre,FB}}$ and $\overline{pp_{suc,FB}}$ in the clockwise direction by Definition 2. We need only to show:

d is not covered, wrt FB, by p in $G_a^{c,d}$, where FB denotes the general face boundary such that $\overline{pd}$ is between $\overline{pp_{pre,FB}}$ and $\overline{pp_{suc,FB}}$ in the clockwise direction. (2)

Note that if a node lies on p, edges $(p_{pre,FB}, p)$ and $(p, p_{suc,FB})$ are in G_{sc}; otherwise, edge $(p_{pre,FB}, p_{suc,FB})$ is in G_{sc}. This is because each edge in $G_a^{c,d} - G_{sc}$ does not intersects $\overline{cd}$. Thus, there is a general face boundary FB_0 containing edges $(p_{pre,FB}, p)$ and $(p, p_{suc,FB})$ (as a node lies on p) or edge $(p_{pre,FB}, p_{suc,FB})$ (as no node lies on p) such that $\overline{pd}$ is between $\overline{pp_{pre,FB}}$ and $\overline{pp_{suc,FB}}$ in the clockwise direction in G_{sc}. There are two cases:

c1) d is not covered, wrt FB_0, by p in G_{sc}.

c2) d is covered, wrt FB_0, by p in G_{sc}.

Proof for c1. By Definition 2, there exists an intersection, p', of $\overline{pd}$ and FB_0 such that p' is covered, wrt FB_0, by p in G_{sc}. To have (2), it suffices to show p' lies on FB in $G_a^{c,d}$. Let $s_0, s_1, \cdots, s_n$ be an FB_0 node-intersection point sequence, and let (s_i, s_j) be an FB_0 augmented edge, where s_0 and s_n are located at p. By the property of the right-hand rule, p' lies on FB in $G_a^{c,d}$ if there exists an FB_0 node-intersection point, s_k, located at p' such that each FB_0 augmented edge (s_i, s_j) satisfying that $0 < i, j < k$ or $k < i, j < n$. Therefore, we need only to show such point s_k exists.

Let s_{k1} be an FB_0 node-intersection point located at p'. We first show if s_{k1} is not the desired s_k, there exists another FB_0

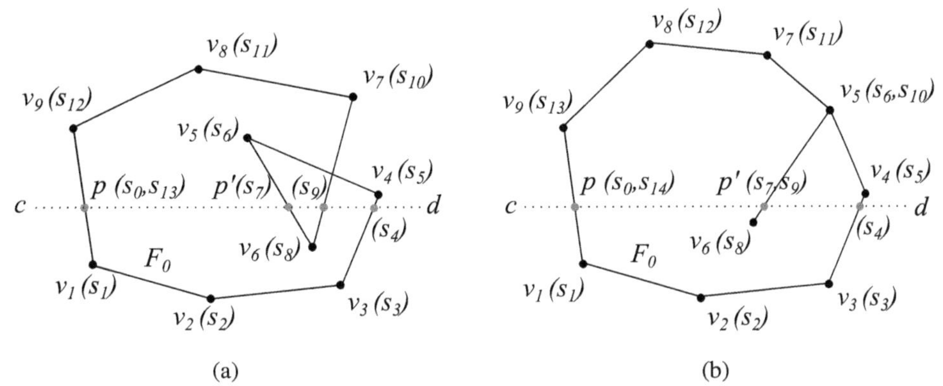

Figure 4: Illustration of Definition 5. FB_0 denotes the general face boundary in G_{sc} consisting of nodes $v_1, v_2, \cdots, v_9$ and the edges shown in solid lines; the dotted line denotes $\overline{cd}$; p and p' are two intersections of $\overline{cd}$ and FB_0. In (a) and (b), $(s_0, s_1, \cdots, s_{13})$ and $(s_0, s_1, \cdots, s_{14})$ are FB_0 node-intersection point sequences, respectively.

node-intersection point, s_{k2}, located at p' such that $\overline{pp'}$ is between $\overline{s_{k2}s_{k2_{pre,FB_0}}}$ and $\overline{s_{k2}s_{k2_{suc,FB_0}}}$ in the clockwise direction. Suppose that s_{k1} is not the desired s_k. Then, there is an FB_0 augmented edge (s_i, s_j) with $0 < i < k1$ and $k1 < j < n$ in $G_a^{c,d}$. By condition 3 of Definition 4, (s_i, s_j) and the edges on FB_0 form two general face boundaries $FB_{0\text{-}1}$ and $FB_{0\text{-}2}$. We assume, without loss of generality, s_0 and s_{k1} are $FB_{0\text{-}1}$ and $FB_{0\text{-}2}$ points, respectively. This means p and p' are on $FB_{0\text{-}1}$ and $FB_{0\text{-}2}$, respectively. Note that $\overline{pp'}$ is between $\overline{s_0s_{0_{pre,FB_0}}}$ and $\overline{s_0s_{0_{suc,FB_0}}}$ in the clockwise direction and thus between $\overline{s_0s_{0_{pre,FB_{0\text{-}1}}}}$ and $\overline{s_0s_{0_{suc,FB_{0\text{-}1}}}}$ in the clockwise direction. In addition, as described in algorithm 1, no augmented edge in $G_a^{c,d}$ intersects $\overline{pp'}$. Thus, p and p' is not on any augmented edge and p' is covered, wrt $FB_{0\text{-}1}$, by p according to Definition 2. By condition 4 of Definition 4, p' must be on $FB_{0\text{-}1}$. This impies p' is on both $FB_{0\text{-}1}$ and $FB_{0\text{-}2}$. By condition 5 of Definition 4, p is covered, wrt $FB_{0\text{-}1}$, by p'. Thus, there must exist an $FB_{0\text{-}1}$ point, s_{k2}, located at p' such that $\overline{p'p}$ is between $\overline{s_{k2}s_{k2_{pre,FB_{0\text{-}1}}}}$ and $\overline{s_{k2}s_{k2_{suc,FB_{0\text{-}1}}}}$ in the clockwise direction according to Definition 2. Clearly, s_{k2} is an FB_0 node-intersection point such that $\overline{pp'}$ is between $\overline{s_{k2}s_{k2_{pre,FB_0}}}$ and $\overline{s_{k2}s_{k2_{suc,FB_0}}}$ in the clockwise direction.

Next, we show s_{k2} is the desired s_k. Suppose that there exists an FB_0 augmented edge (s_i, s_j) with $0 < i < k2$ and $k2 < j < n$ in $G_a^{c,d}$. Using the argument just described, there exists another FB_0 node-intersection point, s_{k3}, such that $\overline{pp'}$ is between $\overline{s_{k3}s_{k3_{pre,FB_0}}}$ and $\overline{s_{k3}s_{k3_{suc,FB_0}}}$ in the clockwise direction. This constitutes a contradiction.

Proof for c2. By Definition 3, the sufficient condition in Eq. (1) is satisfied in G_{sc} for the pair of nodes c and d. This implies d lies on FB_0 in G_{sc}. Using the similar argument of c1 by regarding d as p', we have d lies on FB in $G_a^{c,d}$, a contradiction. This implies c2 does not exist. □

4. APPLICATIONS

We show how to augment PDT (the version using 2-hop neighbor geographic locations) and the CLDP-stable graph to construct the PDT- and CLDP-augmented graphs in Sections 4.1 and 4.2, respectively. In what follows, a UDG is used to construct PDT as in [15] and a general graph is used to construct CLDP-stable graph as in [11].

4.1 PDT-Augmented Graph

Algorithm 2 describes how nodes construct the PDT-augmented graph using 2-hop neighbor geographic locations in a distributed manner, where each edge in PDT is marked as a GG (or PDT) edge in step 1 (or 2), each edge not in PDT is marked as a GFG-NP edge if 2 conditions are satisfied in step 3, and the PDT-augmented graph is a spanning subgraph of the network G consisting of GG, PDT, and GFG-NP edges. The idea of Algorithm 2 is to augment PDT with edges that do not cross any GG or PDT edge. Condition a (or b) of step 3 prohibits a GFG-NP edge from crossing a GG (or PDT) edge, as proved in Theorem 3.

Algorithm 2 Construction of the PDT-augmented Graph

Require: The current node u, u's 2-hop neighbor geographic locations, and an incident edge, (u, v)

1: If no node is within the circle with diameter $\overline{uv}$, $C_{\overline{uv}}$, then (u, v) is marked as a GG edge.

2: Otherwise, if no node is within the half of $C_{\overline{uv}}$ not containing w, $C_{\triangle uvw}$ is within the union of the transmission regions of u and v, and no node is within $C_{\triangle uvw}$, then (u, v) is marked as a PDT edge, where w is the node within $C_{\overline{uv}}$ such that the size of the circumscribed circle, $C_{\triangle uvw}$, of the triangle consisting of u, v, and w, $\triangle uvw$, is maximum.

3: Otherwise, if no edge crosses (u, v) or each edge, (m, n), crossing (u, v) meets the following two conditions, then (u, v) is marked as a GFG-NP edge:
a) None of u's or v's neighbors is not within $C_{\overline{mn}}$.
b) None of u's or v's neighbors is not within the half of $C_{\overline{mn}}$ not containing w, $C_{\triangle mnw}$ is not within the union of the transmission regions of m and n, or none of u's or v's neighbors is not within $C_{\triangle mnw}$, where w is u's or v's neighbor within $C_{\overline{mn}}$ such that the size of $C_{\triangle mnw}$ is maximum.

EXAMPLE 5. *Fig. 5 illustrates the PDT-augmented graph constructed by Algorithm 2. By step 1, (v_1, v_2) is marked as a GG edge because there is no node within the circle $C_{\overline{v_1v_2}}$; in contrast, (v_1, v_3) and (v_1, v_4) are not marked as GG edges. By step 2, (v_1, v_3) is marked as a PDT edge; however, (v_1, v_4) is not marked as a PDT edge because $C_{\triangle v_1v_4v_3}$ is not within the union of the transmission regions of v_1 and v_4 (in which case v_3 is the denoted w). In addition, (v_1, v_4) is marked as a GFG-NP edge in step 3 since no edge crosses (v_1, v_4). Note that (v_2, v_4) is not marked as a GG and PDT*

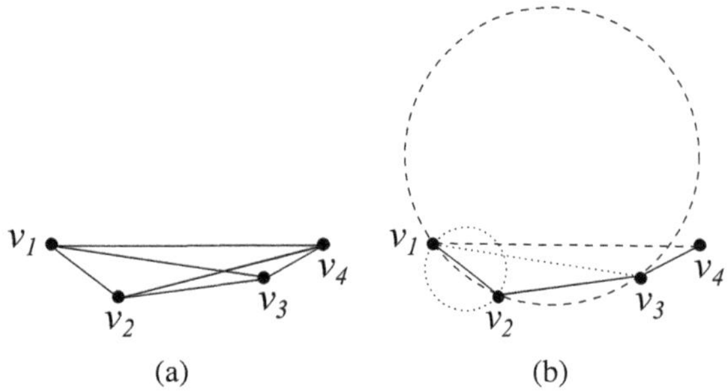

Figure 5: Construction of the PDT-augmented graph. (a) A network consisting of nodes v_1, v_2, v_3, and v_4 on $(0, 0.15R)$, $(0.2R, 0)$, $(0.6R, 0.05R)$, and $(0.8R, 0.15R)$, respectively, where R denotes the node transmission range. (b) The PDT-augmented graph, where the GG, PDT, and GFG-NP edges are shown in solid, dotted, and dashed lines, respectively. The dotted and dashed circles denote $C_{\overline{v_1 v_2}}$ and $C_{\triangle v_1 v_3 v_2}$, respectively.

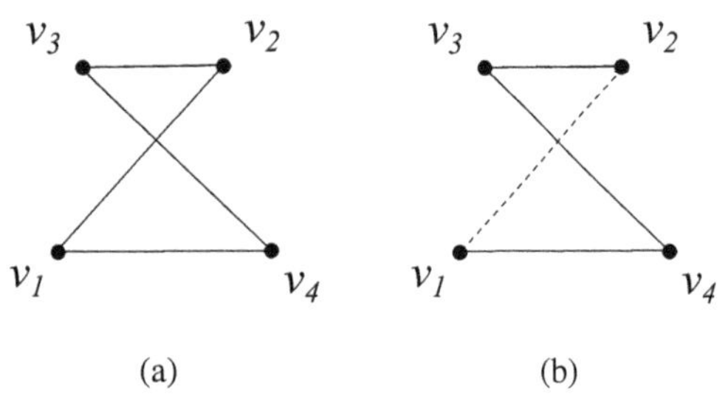

Figure 6: Construction of the CLDP-augmented graph. (a) A network consisting of nodes $v_1, \cdots, v_4$. (b) The CLDP-augmented graph, where the CLDP and GFG-NP edges are shown in solid and dashed lines, respectively.

edge in steps 1 and 2, respectively. Furthermore, (v_1, v_3) crosses (v_2, v_4) and $C_{\triangle v_1 v_3 v_2}$ is within the transmission region of v_1 and v_3; i.e., there is an edge crossing (v_2, v_4) such that the condition b of step 3 is violated. Thus, (v_2, v_4) is not marked as a GFG-NP edge in step 3.

4.2 CLDP-Augmented Graph

In CLDP, each node, u, generates a *probe* message to traverse the graph using the right-hand rule for each incident edge, (u, v). A *probe* message collects the geographic locations of the nodes on the general face boundary the message traverses. Once u receives its generated *probe* message, the node removes (u, v) from the network if (u, v) is traversed by the *probe* message once and (u, v) crosses at least one edge traversed by the *probe* message. Algorithm 3 describes the method for constructing an CLDP-augmented graph, where any edge in the CLDP-stable graph is marked as a CLDP edge in step 1, any non-CLDP edge satisfying the conditions in Definition 4 is marked as a GFG-NP edge in step 2, and the CLDP-augmented graph is a spanning subgraph of the network G consisting of CLDP and GFG-NP edges. Note that since a node, u, has the geographic locations of the nodes on the general face boundaries containing the incident edge, (u, v), u can verify if (u, v) satisfies the conditions in Definition 4.

Example 6. *Fig. 6 shows the CLDP-augmented graph constructed by Algorithm 3. Assume that v_1 first generates a probe message for (v_1, v_2) in the construction of the CLDP-stable graph. Using the right-hand rule, the probe message traverses the network along the path $(v_1, v_2, v_3, v_4, v_1)$. Since (v_1, v_2) is traversed by the probe message once and (v_1, v_2) crosses (v_3, v_4) traversed by the probe message, (v_1, v_2) is removed from the network in the construction of the CLDP-stable graph. All edges in the network except for (v_1, v_2) are contained in the CLDP-stable graph and, thus, marked as CLDP edges by step 1. After the CLDP edges are identified, v_1 verifies that (v_1, v_2) satisfies the five conditions in step 2 and marks (v_1, v_2) as a GFG-NP edge.*

Algorithm 3 Construction of the CLDP-augmented Graph

Require: The current node u and the geographic locations of the nodes on general face boundaries containing u

1: Each incident edge, (u, v), in the CLDP-stable graph is marked as a CLDP edge.

2: Each incident edge, (u, v), is marked as a GFG-NP edge if the following conditions are satisfied:

1. There is a general face boundary, FB, such that u and v lie on FB.
2. (u, v) is not marked as a CLDP edge.
3. (u, v) and the edges on FB form two general face boundaries FB_1 and FB_2.
4. All points on FB but not on FB_1 (or FB_2) are not covered by any point on FB_1 (or FB_2) wrt FB_1 (or FB_2).
5. For any point p on both FB_1 and FB_2 but not on (u, v) if p is covered, wrt FB_1 (or FB_2), by a point q on FB_1 (or FB_2) but not on (u, v), then q is covered, wrt FB_1 (or FB_2), by p.

5. ANALYSIS

In Sections 5.1 and 5.2, we show GFG-NP guarantees packet delivery if the protocol performs face forwarding on the PDT- and CLDP-augmented graphs constructed by Algorithms 2 and 3, respectively.

Lemma 1. *Let $G_p(V, E_p)$ be a planar subgraph of $G(V, E)$, and let (u, v) be an edge in $E - E_p$. If (u, v) does not cross any edge in G_p, then (u, v) is an augmented edge.*

Proof. Note that G_p is an sc-sat subgraph by Corollary 3. We need only to show (u, v) satisfies the five conditions in Definition 4. Clearly, (u, v) satisfies the condition 2. Besides, in a planar graph, a face denotes a maximal continuous region, and the face boundary is a special case of the general face boundary. Since (u, v) does not cross any edge in G_p, all points on (u, v) lie on a face in G_p and both u and v lie on the boundary of the face, satisfying the condition 1. Let u and v lie on the face boundary FB in G_p. Since (u, v) does not cross FB, the face surrounded by FB is divided into two faces, surrounded by, say, FB_1 and FB_2, implying that the condition 3 is satisfied. Furthermore, it is noted that the faces surrounded by FB_1 and FB_2 are closed regions. Thus, if a point p on FB_1 (or FB_2) is covered by a point q, wrt FB_1 (or FB_2), q is a point on FB_1 (or FB_2) and is covered by p, wrt FB_1 (or FB_2). This implies (u, v) satisfies the conditions 4 and 5. □

5.1 Correctness of PDT-augmented Graph

THEOREM 3. *GFG-NP guarantees packet delivery in a connected network if the protocol performs face forwarding on the PDT-augmented graph constructed by Algorithm 2.*

PROOF. By Theorem 2, we need only to show the PDT-augmented graph is a G_a, an augmented graph of an sc-sat subgraph of the network G. First note that PDT consisting of GG or PDT edges constructed in steps 1 and 2 is planar by [15], and thus, it is a G_{sc}, an sc-sat subgraph of G, by Corollary 3. By Lemma 1, it suffices to show any GFG-NP edge, (u, v), constructed in step 3 does not cross any GG or PDT edge, (m, n), in PDT. There are 2 cases: c1) (m, n) is a GG edge, and c2) (m, n) is a PDT edge. The proof of c1 is omitted due to its similarity to that of c2. Suppose that (u, v) crosses (m, n). Let w_1 be the node within $C_{\overline{mn}}$ such that the size of $C_{\triangle mnw_1}$ is maximum. Since (m, n) is a PDT edge, we have p1) no node is within the half of $C_{\overline{mn}}$ not containing w_1, p2) $C_{\triangle mnw_1}$ is within the union of the transmission regions of m and n, and p3) no node is within $C_{\triangle mnw_1}$, by step 2. Let w_2 be u's or v's neighbor within $C_{\overline{mn}}$ such that the size of $C_{\triangle mnw_2}$ is maximum. We claim that each of the following conditions does not hold: c2.1) none of u's or v's neighbors is not within the half of $C_{\overline{mn}}$ not containing w_2, c2.2) $C_{\triangle mnw_2}$ is not within the union of the transmission regions of m and n, and c2.3) none of u's or v's neighbors is not within $C_{\triangle mnw_2}$. By p1, w_2 must be within the half of $C_{\overline{mn}}$ containing w_1, and thus, none of u's or v's neighbors is within the half of $C_{\overline{mn}}$ not containing w_2. This implies c2.1 does not hold. It is easy to verify that $C_{\triangle mnw_2}$ is within the union of the regions of $C_{\triangle mnw_1}$ and $C_{\overline{mn}}$. This implies $C_{\triangle mnw_2}$ is within the union of the transmission regions of m and n by p2, and thus, c2.2 does not hold. Since no node is within $C_{\triangle mnw_1}$ by p3, none of u's or v's neighbors is within the intersection of the regions of $C_{\triangle mnw_1}$ and $C_{\triangle mnw_2}$. Note that if there exists 1 u's or v's neighbor, w_3, within the region of $C_{\triangle mnw_2}$ but not the region of $C_{\triangle mnw_1}$, the size of $C_{\triangle mnw_3}$ is larger than that of $C_{\triangle mnw_2}$ except that w_3 lies on $C_{\triangle mnw_2}$. This implies c2.3 does not hold. Thus, (m, n) does not satisfy condition b. This implies (u, v) is not a GFG-NP edge by step 3. This is a contradiction. □

5.2 Correctness of CLDP-augmented Graph

THEOREM 4. *GFG-NP guarantees packet delivery in a connected network if the protocol performs face forwarding on the CLDP-augmented graph constructed by Algorithm 3.*

PROOF. By Theorem 2, we need only to show the CLDP-augmented graph is a G_a. Since each edge marked as a GFG-NP edge in step 2 is an augmented edge by Definition 4, it suffices to show the CLDP-stable graph consisting of CLDP edges constructed in step 1 is a G_{sc}. Suppose that there is a source-destination pair s and d such that the sufficient condition in Eq. (1) is not satisfied. That is, there is an intersection, p, of $\overline{sd}$ and a general face boundary FB not containing d such that d is covered, wrt FB, by p. Then, using GFG face forwarding, the packet cannot be routed from p to d. This contradicts that GFG face forwarding never fails on the CLDP-stable graph shown in Theorem 5.2 of [10]. □

6. PERFORMANCE EVALUATION

We conducted simulations on NS-2 (version 2.35) to evaluate the performance of GFG-NP based on the PDT- and CLDP-augmented graphs using the synthetic and semisynthetic data in terms of edge saving, load balance, path length, routing latency, and packet delivery improvement factors. The edge saving improvement factor denoted the ratio of the number of disabled edges in the network to construct PDT or the CLDP-stable graph to that to construct the PDT- or CLDP-augmented graph, respectively. The load balance (resp. path length, resp. routing latency) improvement factor denoted the ratio of the maximum load (resp. path length, resp. routing latency) of GFG based on PDT or the CLDP-stable graph to that of GFG-NP based on the PDT- or CLDP-augmented graph, respectively. The packet delivery improvement factor denoted the ratio of the packet delivery rate of GFG-NP based on the PDT- or CLDP-augmented graph to that of GFG based on PDT or the CLDP-stable graph, respectively. A performance improvement (or deterioration) was indicated by an improvement factor greater (or smaller) than 1, and a greater performance improvement was indicated by a greater improvement factor. To generate the synthetic data, the UDG networks with network densities 8, 10, 12, 14, or 16 were produced to construct PDT and their augmented graphs by randomly deploying nodes in square regions with side length 10 times the node transmission range, where the network density denoted the number of neighbors per node. The non-UDG networks for constructing CLDP and its augmented graph were constructed by removing 20% edges from the UDG networks randomly. In addition, to generate the semisynthetic data, the UDG networks were constructed for the construction of PDT and its augmented graphs by the FlockLab testbed in [1], the ENL testbed in [8], and the UZL testbed in [3]. The non-UDG networks were constructed for the construction of CLDP and its augmented graph by 3 testbeds, MD 1F, MD 2F, and MD 3F in [19]. In all simulations, the empirical data were obtained by averaging data of 1000 source-destination pairs from 100 networks. In NS-2 settings, the packet generation rate was set to 10 packets/sec, the packet size 32 bytes, and the packet time to live (TTL) 5000. Figs. 7, 8, 9, 10, and 11 show the simulation results for the performance of GFG-NP based on the PDT- and CLDP-augmented graphs in terms of edge saving, load balance, path length, routing latency, and packet delivery improvement factors, respectively. The NS-2 settings were summarizes in Table 1.

Table 1: NS-2 Settings

MAC Layer	IEEE 802.11
Node Bandwidth	1 Mbps
Signal Propagation Model	Two-Ray Ground Reflection
Data Packet Generation Rate	10 packets/sec
Data Packet Size	32 bytes
Data Packet Time to Live (TTL)	5000

6.1 Edge Saving and Load Balance

Using synthetic data, the edge saving improvement factor of the PDT-augmented graph is close to 1. This results from the observations that almost all face boundaries in PDT are triangles.

Thus, disabled edges in the network are hard to satisfy the first condition of definition 4 and hard to be augmented edges. In CLDP-augmented graph, the edge saving improvement factor is about 1.4 which means that there is 1 in every 1.4 disabled edge can be marked as an augmented edge. The greater the network density, the greater the number of augmented edges in the CLDP-augmented graphs.

Compared to the simulation results using the synthetic data, the PDT-augmented graph has a greater edge saving improvement factor in the FlockLab testbed, and the CLDP-augmented graph has a smaller edge saving improvement factor in the MD 1F, MD 2F, and

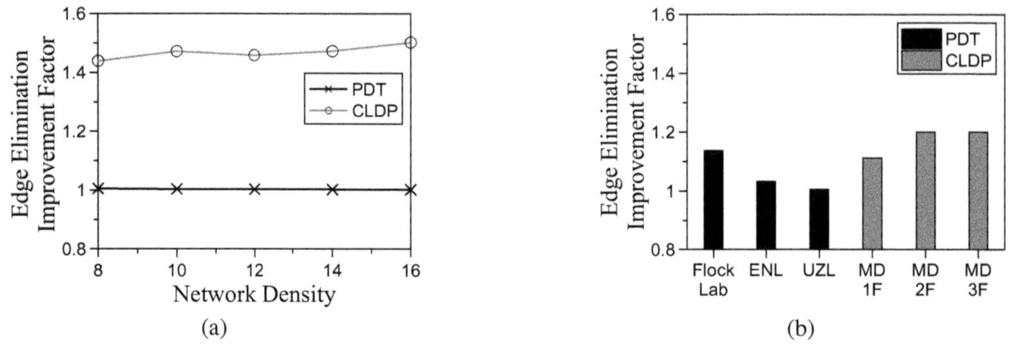

Figure 7: Edge saving improvement factors of the PDT- and CLDP-augmented graphs using (a) synthetic data and (b) semisynthetic data.

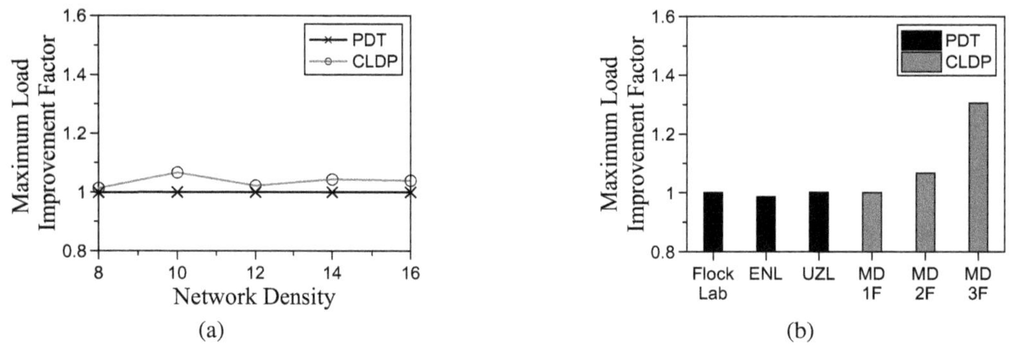

Figure 8: Load balance improvement factors of GFG-NP using (a) synthetic data and (b) semisynthetic data.

MD 3F testbeds. This is because the number of edges in the network in the FlockLab testbed is small. Thus, adding a small number of augmented edges results in a great edge saving improvement factor. In addition, the number of crossing edges in the network in the MD 1F, MD 2F, or MD 3F testbed is small, which in turn results in a small number of augmented edges. In general, the greater the edge saving improvement factor, the greater the load balance improvement factor.

6.2 Path Length and Routing Latency

Using synthetic data, the path length improvement factor of GFG-NP based on the PDT-augmented graph is smaller than that based on the CLDP-augmented graph because the PDT-augmented graph has a much smaller edge saving improvement factor than the CLDP-augmented graph. The path length improvement factor of GFG-NP based on the CLDP-augmented graph ranges from 1.09 to 1.19. The greater the network density, the greater the number of augmented edges in the CLDP-augmented graph. Therefore, as the network density increases from 8 to 10, the path length improvement factor of GFG-NP based on the CLDP-augmented graph increases. As the network density increases from 10 to 16, the path length improvement factor of GFG-NP based on the CLDP-augmented graph becomes smaller because the ratio of face forwarding decreases. The differences between the simulation results for the routing latency improvement factors and the path length improvement factors are negligible.

6.3 Packet Delivery

All packet delivery improvement factors of GFG-NP based on the PDT- and CLDP-augmented graphs are close to 1 using the synthetic and semisynthetic data since the packet delivery rates of GFG based on PDT and the CLDP-stable graph and the packet delivery rates of GFG-NP based on the PDT- and CLDP-augmented graphs all approach 1. In addition, as the routing latency increases, the packet has a greater probability of getting lost due to the collision. Since the routing latencies of GFG-NP based on the PDT- and CLDP-augmented graphs are smaller than those of GFG based on PDT and the CLDP-stable graph, the packet delivery rates of GFG-NP based on the PDT- and CLDP-augmented graphs are slightly better than those of GFG based on PDT and the CLDP-stable graph, respectively, in most cases.

7. CONCLUSION

In this paper, we first present a sufficient condition for the packet delivery guarantee of GFG face forwarding. With the help of the sufficient condition, we identify the rules for adding the disabled edges in the network to augment the graph used in GFG face forwarding, and propose a delivery-guaranteed geographic routing protocol, GFG-NP, in which it performs GFG face forwarding on the augmented graph. So far, to the best of our knowledge, PDT has more edges than any other existing planar graph constructed with a localized method and CLDP is the well-known protocol which disables a number of cross-links from the non-UDG networks to obtain the CLDP-stable graph on which GFG can guarantee packet delivery. Thus, we apply the identified rules to augment PDT and the CLDP-stable graph without additional message overhead costs. We conducted simulations on NS-2 to evaluate the performance of GFG-NP on the PDT- and CLDP-augmented graphs using the synthetic and semisynthetic data. Simulations show the number of

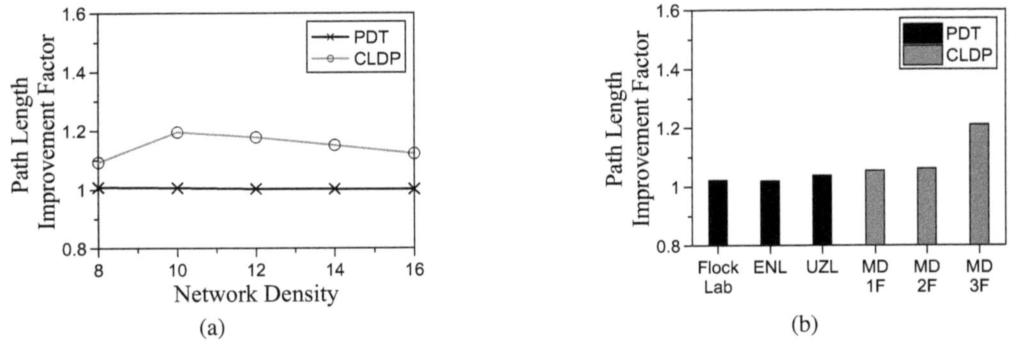

Figure 9: Path length improvement factors of GFG-NP using (a) synthetic data and (b) semisynthetic data.

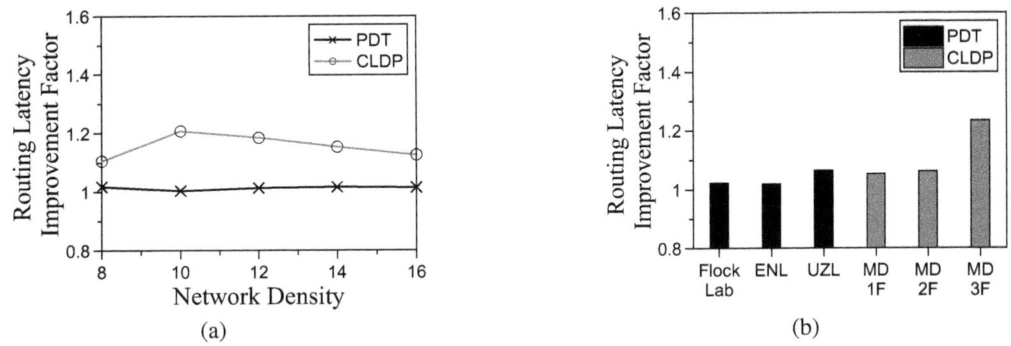

Figure 10: Routing latency improvement factors of GFG-NP using (a) synthetic data and (b) semisynthetic data.

augmented edges added to PDT is small because almost all face boundaries in PDT are triangles, in which case the disabled edges in the network are hard to be augmented edges. Thus, GFG-NP based on the PDT-augmented graph just slightly outperforms GFG based on PDT in terms of load balance, path length, and routing latency. In contrast, a great number of augmented edges are added to the CLDP-stable graph, and thus, GFG-NP based on the CLDP-augmented graphs significantly outperforms GFG based on the CLDP-stable graph, respectively, in terms of load balance, path length, routing latency, and packet delivery rate.

Recently, beaconless routing protocols [7, 16, 17] have received considerable attention because a local planar graph used in face forwarding is constructed without complete neighbor geographic locations. Future research includes the study of improving the performance of the beaconless routing protocols by incorporating the proposed sufficient condition with them. In addition, there exists a routing protocol that employs GFG to forward packets in the networks where the node location information is unavailable [4]. Another research direction is to study how to improve the performance of the location-free routing protocols by using the the proposed sufficient condition. Furthermore, there are some cases on which GFG face forwarding guarantees packet delivery although the proposed sufficient condition is not satisfied. We are also interested in finding the necessary and sufficient condition for the packet delivery guarantee of GFG face forwarding.

8. REFERENCES

[1] J. Beutel, R. Lim, A. Meier, L. Thiele, C. Walser, M. Woehrle, and M. Yuecel. The FlockLab testbed architecture. In *SenSys*, 2009.

[2] P. Bose, P. Morin, I. Stojmenovic, and J. Urrutia. Routing with guarantee delivery in ad hoc networks. *ACM Wireless Networks*, 7:609–616, 2001.

[3] I. Chatzigiannakis, S. Fischer, C. Koninis, G. Mylonas, and D. Pfisterer. WISEBED: An open large-scale wireless sensor network testbed. In *Sensor Applications, Experimentation, and Logistics*, 2010.

[4] Y.-P. Cheng, Y.-J. Tang, and M.-J. Tsai. LF-GFG: Location-free greedy-face-greedy routing with guaranteed delivery and lightweight maintenance cost in a wireless sensor network with changing topology. *IEEE Transactions on Wireless Communications*, 13:7025–7036, 2014.

[5] H. Frey and I. Stojmenovic. On delivery guarantees and worst-case forwarding bounds of elementary face routing components in ad hoc and sensor networks. *IEEE Transactions on Computers*, 59:1224–1238, 2010.

[6] K. R. Gabriel and R. R. Sokal. A new statistical approach to grographic variation analysis. *Systematic Zoology*, 18:259–287, 1969.

[7] M. Heissenbuettel, T. Braun, T. Bernoulli, and M. Waelchli. BLR: beacon-less routing algorithm for mobile ad hoc networks. *Elservier Computer Communications*, 27:1076–1086, 2004.

[8] K.-Y. Jang, M. Vieira, S. Rangwala, O. Gnawali, and R. Govindan. Tutornet: A tiered sensor network testbed. In *http://nsl.cs.usc.edu/Projects/Tutornet/*.

[9] B. Karp and H. T. Kung. GPSR: Greedy perimeter stateless routing for wireless networks. In *ACM MobiCom*, 2000.

[10] Y.-J. Kim, R. Govindan, B. Karp, and S. Shenker. Practical and robust geographic routing in wireless networks.

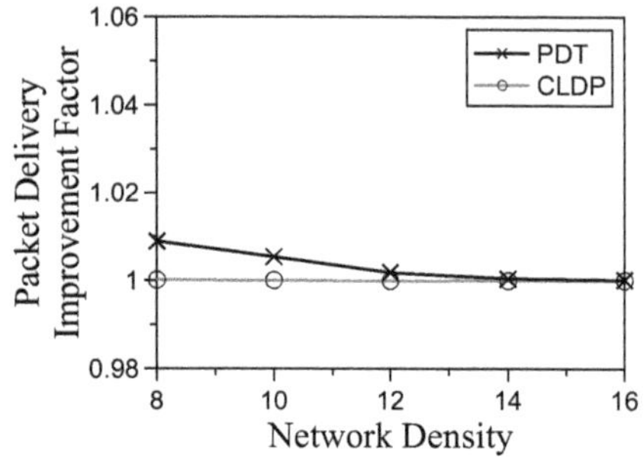

(a)

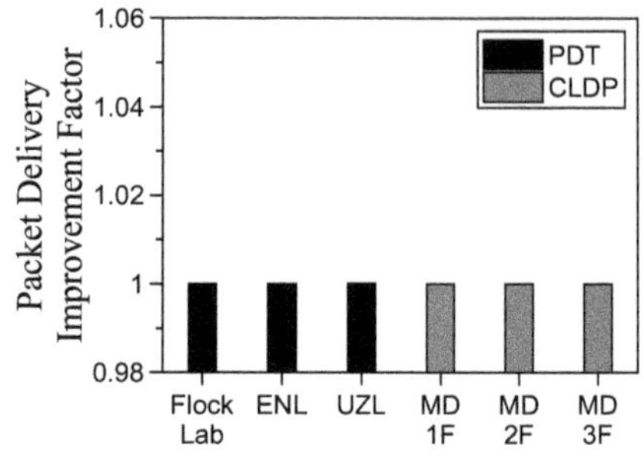

(b)

Figure 11: Packet delivery improvement factors of GFG-NP using (a) synthetic data and (b) semisynthetic data.

Technical Report 04-832, Department of Computer Science, University of Southern California, 2004.

[11] Y.-J. Kim, R. Govindan, B. Karp, and S. Shenker. Geographic routing made practical. In *NSDI*, 2005.

[12] E. Kranakis, H. Singh, and J. Urrutia. Compass routing on geometric networks. In *CCCG*, 1999.

[13] F. Kuhn, R. Wattenhofer, Y. Zhang, and A. Zollinger. Geometric ad-hoc routing: Of theory and practice. In *ACM PODC*, 2003.

[14] B. Leong, S. Mitra, and B. Liskov. Path vector face routing: Geographic routing with local face information. In *IEEE ICNP*, 2005.

[15] X.-Y. Li, I. Stojmenovic, and Y. Wang. Partial delaunay triangulation and degree limited localized bluetooth scatternet formation. *IEEE Transactions on Parallel and Distributed Systems*, 15:350 – 361, 2004.

[16] S. Rührup, H. Kalosha, A. Nayak, and I. Stojmenović. Message-efficient beaconless georouting with guaranteed delivery in wireless sensor, ad hoc, and actuator networks. *IEEE/ACM Transactions on Networking*, 18:95 – 108, 2010.

[17] S. Rührup and I. Stojmenović. Contention-based georouting with guaranteed delivery, minimal communication overhead, and shorter paths in wireless sensor networks. In *IEEE IPDPS*, 2010.

[18] K. J. Supowit. The relative neighborhood graph, with an application to minimum spanning trees. *Journal of the ACM*, 30:428–448, 1983.

[19] G. Werner-Allen, P. Swieskowski, and M. Welsh. MoteLab: a wireless sensor network testbed. In *IPSN*, 2005.

From Rateless to Hopless

Zhenjiang Li[1], Wan Du[1], Yuanqing Zheng[2], Mo Li[1], Dapeng Wu[3]
[1]School of Computer Engineering, Nanyang Technological University, Singapore
[2]Department of Computing, Hong Kong Polytechnic University, Hong Kong
[3]Department of Electrical & Computer Engineering, University of Florida, USA
{lzjiang, duwan, limo}@ntu.edu.sg, csyqzheng@comp.polyu.edu.hk, wu@ece.ufl.edu

ABSTRACT

This paper presents a hopless networking paradigm. Incorporating recent techniques of rateless codes, senders break packets into rateless information streams and each single stream automatically adapts to diverse channel qualities at all potential receivers, regardless of their hop distances. The receivers are capable of accumulating rateless information pieces from different senders and jointly decoding the packet, largely improving throughput. We develop a practical protocol, called HOPE, which instantiates the hopless networking paradigm. Compared with the existing opportunistic routing protocol family, HOPE best exploits the wireless channel diversity and takes full advantage of the wireless broadcast effect. HOPE incurs minimum protocol overhead and serves general networking applications. We extensively evaluate the performance of HOPE with indoor network traces collected from USRP N210s and Intel 5300 NICs. The results show that HOPE achieves 1.7x and 1.3x goodput gain over ExOR and MIXIT, respectively.

Categories and Subject Descriptors

C.2.1 [**Network Architecture and Design**]: Wireless Communication; C.2.2 [**Network Protocols**]: Routing protocols

Keywords

Rateless codes; wireless networks; routing

1. INTRODUCTION

Conventional multi-hop wireless networks route packets hop-by-hop along a path of favorable links from the source to the destination [1, 22, 6], e.g., $s \to n_1 \to n_2 \to d$ in Fig. 1(a). The validity of multi-hop routing is based on the belief that any other paths cannot provide higher throughput than the selected one. Instead of choosing a fixed path, *opportunistic routing* approaches delay the path selection and broadcast packets to a sub-set of nodes at each hop, exploiting the opportunities of the successful packet reception over the traditionally unfavorable links [2, 3, 14], e.g., $s \to n_2$, $s \to d$, and $n_1 \to d$ in Fig. 1(b). Nevertheless, wireless channels are still under utilized as opportunistic routing is usually packet-oriented, which turns only the intact packet opportunities into effective throughput.

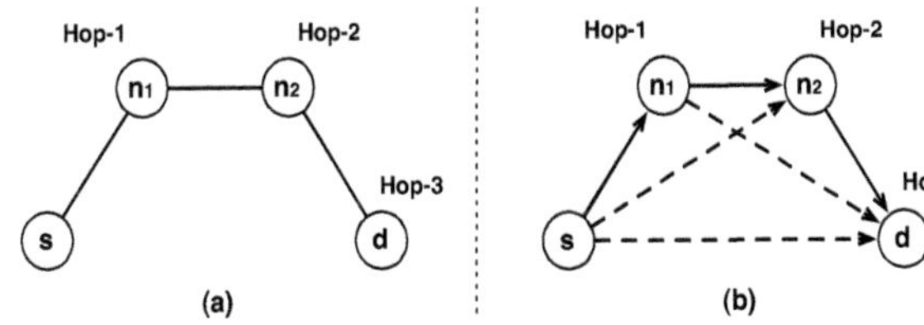

Figure 1: (a) A three-hop path in a wireless network. (b) Favorable and unfavorable links in the network.

This paper studies from an information-oriented perspective and observes that while the data packet is delivered in a hop-by-hop manner, e.g., s transmits packets to n_1 in Fig. 1(b), the information contained in the transmission is spread beyond each hop. All the network nodes are potential receivers and they have the opportunities to receive different amount of information from the sender, though the information may not be immediately adequate to be translated to an intact packet. In this paper, we apply recent rateless coding schemes and encode packets into rateless information streams. Rateless codes adapt each individual data transmission to multiple receivers, automatically synchronizing the effective data rate to the diverse channel qualities of all the wireless links. At the receiver side, channels from all the potential senders are viewed as a single joint information channel. Each node accumulates rateless information from the joint information channel regardless of hop distances, and jointly decodes the packet using the information pieces from multiple senders. We name such a networking paradigm *hopless networking*. Hopless networking breaks the hop-by-hop packet transmission into the hopless information accumulation. The applied rateless codes allow each node to best adapt to the information quality.

We develop a hopless data forwarding protocol, HOPE, to instantiate the hopless networking paradigm. HOPE entails a non-trivial design which concerns forward scheduling, role transition of nodes, protocol stack development, etc. At any time, HOPE selects a "best" candidate from the nodes possessing a packet to forward it in the network until another "better" candidate decodes the packet. To do so,

MobiHoc'15, June 22–25, 2015, Hangzhou, China.

http://dx.doi.org/10.1145/2746285.2746308.

HOPE prioritizes intermediate nodes by their channel qualities to the destination, and performs a distributed scheduling to delegate the forwarding "right" among the nodes. Each node switches its role between the information accumulator, delegated source, and destination in forwarding the data packet. All above operational logics are assembled in a hopless layer, which works with the link and network layers in the traditional protocol stack. The hopless layer can be further extended down to work with the recent physical layer rateless codes for higher throughput. We carefully address the practical challenges to incorporate the existing rateless codes with multiple senders and receivers in the hopless data packet forwarding. The joint rateless coding scheme efficiently aggregates information from multiple senders and decodes the original data packet without a central coordination. Compared with the existing opportunistic routing family, HOPE has the following advantages.

- HOPE accumulates the rateless information from multiple senders, and jointly decodes the packet to improve throughput over the packet-oriented approaches [1, 2, 3, 14]. In HOPE, the successful packet decoding and forwarding at all potential receivers are essentially asynchronous, involving small coordination overhead.
- Data forwarding in HOPE best adapts to the channel quality diversity and makes full use of the wireless broadcast effect. Recent studies (e.g., SPaC [9] and MIXIT [20]) cannot fit all potential receivers in one transmission and are thus suboptimal in utilizing the hopless information.
- Unlike the existing flow-based approaches built on intra-flow network coding (e.g., MIXIT [20], MORE [3], FUN [16]), HOPE does not feature the aggressive usage of the network bandwidth. HOPE smoothly works with the conventional CSMA, and performs well with the flow traffics and the intermittent traffics in the network.

We extensively evaluate HOPE with the indoor network traces collected from 19 USRP N210s and 19 Intel 5300 NICs. We compare HOPE with state-of-the-art opportunistic routing approaches. The results show that compared with ExOR [2] and MIXIT [20], HOPE improves average goodput by 1.7x and 1.3x respectively in both single- and multiple-flow scenarios.

In the rest of this paper: we introduce the motivation and the hopless networking in § 2. § 3 details the design of HOPE. In § 4, we conduct extensive performance evaluation. § 5 reviews related works and § 6 concludes this paper.

2. MOTIVATION

2.1 Packet-oriented v.s. information-oriented

Packet-oriented: We deploy 4 USRP software radios based on the topology of Fig. 1 and look into the detailed channel qualities when packets traverse from s to d. The USRP nodes are configured to operate on OFDM at 2.4GHz. The detailed experiment settings will be given in §7. We let s, n_1, and n_2 send 40 packets in sequence and measure the SNRs at downstream nodes. Fig. 2 depicts the measured SNRs of the packets "heard" over all 6 links in Fig. 1(b). The favorable links, $s{\to}n_1$, $n_1{\to}n_2$, and $n_2{\to}d$, selected in conventional multi-hop networks, experience good average SNR

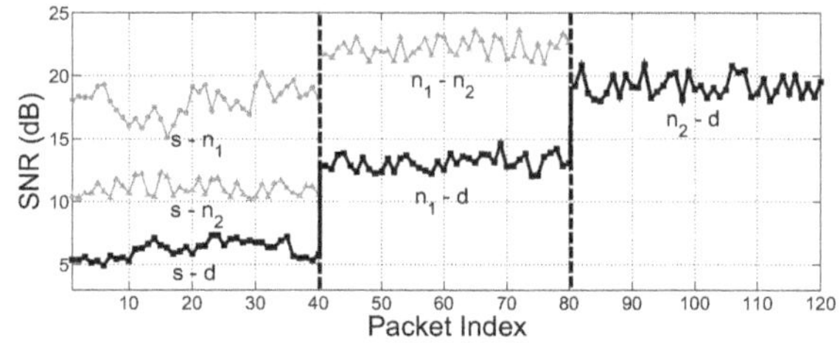

Figure 2: Channel SNRs across different links.

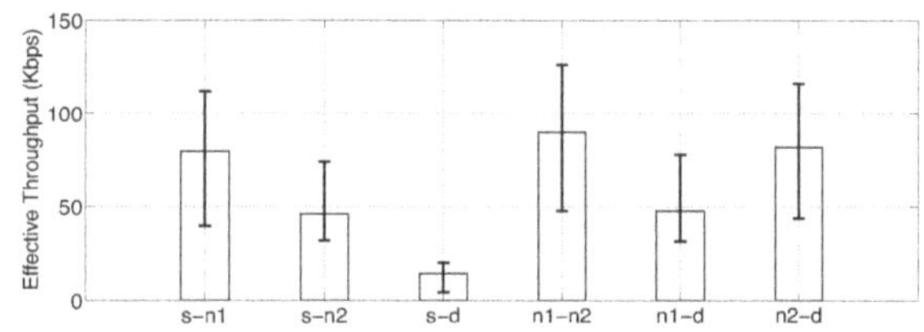

Figure 3: Effective throughput across different links.

($\geq$15dB). The traditionally unfavorable links, $s{\to}n_2$, $s{\to}d$, and $n_1{\to}d$, experience poorer SNR conditions. In conventional multi-hop networks, the information from unfavorable links is usually not utilized if it is not adequate to translate to a decoded packet. Being packet-oriented, the multi-hop networking keeps routing intact packets to a "better" relay at each hop until the packets reach the destination. Benefitting from the wireless broadcast effect, however, when one node sends a packet, all nodes have access to the transmitted signals though with distinct qualities.

Information-oriented: This paper studies from an information oriented perspective and aims at improving throughput with the previously underutilized information across multiple hops (which we call hopless information). We apply the recent rateless codes to encode the raw data packets into a stream of rateless units. Rateless codes allow the sender to incrementally reduce the effective data rate by sending more rateless units, which adaptively matches the channel condition to the receiver.

We experiment with the USRP testbed and quantify the potential gain of making use of the hopless information. We leverage Spinal codes [26] to perform rateless coding on the raw data packet. Spinal codes apply a pseudo-random hash function to the raw data bits to produce a sequence of coded symbols in a way that "*every achievable higher coding rate is a prefix of achievable lower rates*" [26]. A constant number of coded symbols are packed together to form each rateless unit, named Spinal "pass". Spinal codes allow a sender to gradually reduce the effective data rate by sending more Spinal "passes".

We let s keep transmitting Spinal "passes" for a L-bit packet. The three nodes n_1, n_2, and d simultaneously receive the "passes" from s. As the channel quality of $s{\to}n_1$ is better than $s{\to}n_2$ and $s{\to}d$, we expect that n_1 first decodes the packet with fewer "passes". During the time, n_2 and d accumulate the same number of "passes", but containing more symbol errors. We keep s sending the "passes" until n_2 and d are eventually able to decode the packet. We record the time t of each node in decoding the L-bit packet and derive the *effective throughput* $etp = L/t$. We repeat the experiment 100 times and obtain the effective throughput achieved on all $s \to n_1$, $s \to n_2$, and $s \to d$. We also do the same experiment for the rest 3 links. In Fig. 3, we observe that the effective throughputs on traditionally unfavorable links $s \to n_2$ and $s \to d$ are substantial, i.e., when n_1 decodes a packet from s, the hopless information accumulated at n_2 and d statistically corresponds to 56% and 18% of the packet. Link $n_1 \to d$ also has substantial effective throughput, e.g., 53% of $n_1 \to n_2$'s.

2.2 Hopless networking paradigm

We propose a hopless networking paradigm to incorporate the potential effective throughput gained from the hopless information. In hopless networking, a receiver decodes the packet using the rateless codes from multiple senders. From the receiver's point of view, however, it is unnecessary to identify the information pieces from each individual sender. Instead, the receiver may treat the entire network as a whole and view the channels from each sender as a single information channel, which is called *joint information channel* in this paper. The receiver then takes information from its joint information channel. The highlighted links $s \to d$, $n_1 \to d$ and $n_2 \to d$ in Fig. 2 compose the joint information channel for d. With the help of rateless codes, d is able to make the full use of hopless information from both the conventional favorable links $n_2 \to d$, and the complementary links $s \to d$ and $n_1 \to d$.

Fig. 4 depicts the general hopless networking paradigm, where each node n_i is connected to the network through its joint information channel. As adequate information is accumulated from the network, n_i is able to decode the packet. At this time, if n_i is the "best" candidate to forward the packet, it takes the place of the packet forwarding and injects the rateless codes of this packet to the network until another "better" candidate decodes it. With such a networking paradigm, whenever the information of a fresh packet is available in the network, any node can fully accumulate it through its own joint information channel. On the other hand, when any node transmits a packet, the rateless codes automatically adapt to the channel qualities of all potential receivers (explained below).

A natural question one may ask is: *Why the potential throughput gain revealed in hopless networking has kept being overlooked in previous multi-hop networks?*

Many existing studies tried to harvest such potential gains by aggressively capturing opportunistic packets from unfavorable links. Existing packet-oriented opportunistic routing schemes, e.g., ExOR [2] and MORE [3], however, cannot make the full use of those low-quality links. Only successfully decoded packets surviving from low quality links are utilized.

Some latest works [9, 20] notice similar gain of exploiting partial information from corrupted packets and value the "clean" bits or symbols from corrupted packets. By packet combinations or network coding schemes, they can make a better use of the low-quality links. Constrained by the unified data rate of each transmission from the sender, those works still cannot make the full advantage of wireless broadcast effect. For the example in Fig. 2, s usually sets a suitable data rate that matches the per-hop link quality of $s \to n_1$. The high data rate for the good link, however, would be too high for weak links like $s \to n_2$ and $s \to d$ to accept enough correct symbols or data bits. Thus, only when the weak links dramatically improve can intact pack-

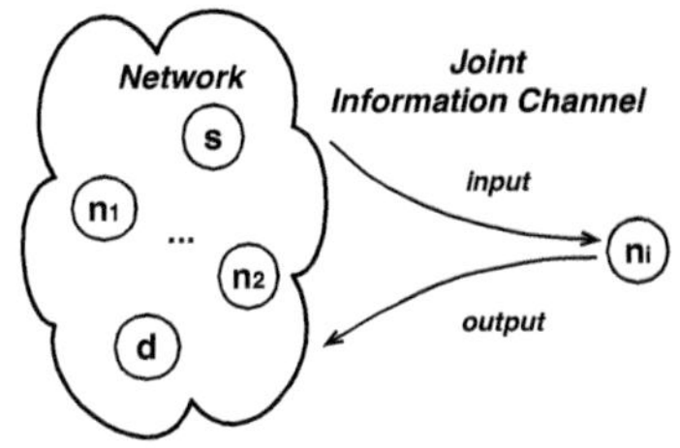

Figure 4: Hopless networking paradigm for an arbitrary node n_i.

ets and yield the opportunistic throughput gain. A low data rate helps to increase the opportunistic gain over weak links, but on the other hand, limits the throughput that can be achieved over good links. Similar problems also exist on $n_1 \to n_2$. In conventional multi-hop networks, a sender always faces the dilemma of adapting to an impossible best sending rate, which has long been considered an open problem in opportunistic routing [2, 3].

Hopless networking hence outperforms prior designs from two aspects: 1) Each *receiver* can adapt to the joint information channel and the success of packet decoding attributes to the rateless information from multiple senders; 2) Each *sender* can adapt to the joint information channel and produce rateless data streams that automatically adapt to all various links.

3. DESIGN

We instantiate the hopless networking paradigm and develop HOPE, a non-trivial design to coordinate the network and acquire full throughput gain in the hopless forwarding.

3.1 Design principle

In HOPE, each packet is rateless coded into a stream of units. Many existing rateless codes can be applied, including LT [24] and Raptor codes [30] for the link layer bit blocks or recent Strider [10] and Spinal codes [26] for the physical layer symbols. For each packet delivery, all nodes in the network play the roles of the source, the accumulator, or the destination to forward data. We elaborate the different roles and their interactions in HOPE. We aim at giving a high level behavior description and temporarily omit the technical details for the sake of a clear presentation. Details are introduced in §3.2.

The accumulator: In HOPE, all nodes work as accumulators. An accumulator listens to the network and accumulates rateless units for each undecoded packet until the packet can be decoded or the decoding is aborted.

The source: There are two types of sources in HOPE: *the original source* and *the delegated source.*

The original source initiates the packet transfer and sends out the stream of rateless data units. The source keeps sending until the packet gets ACKed.

A delegated source comes from an accumulator that successfully decodes a packet and is ready to forward it. Multiple accumulators may transit to delegated sources concurrently for the same packet. A priority list specifies the priority rank of all the accumulators, and HOPE leverages a priority based back-off scheme (§3.3) such that the delegated source with the highest priority is more likely to forward first

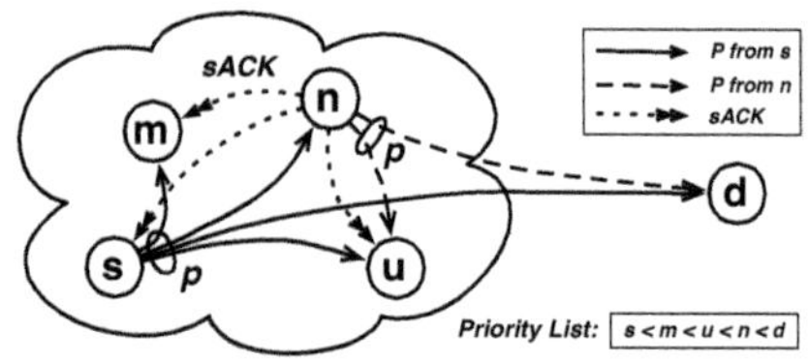

Figure 5: An example of packet transmissions.

and the potential duplicated forwardings from new delegated sources with lower priorities are prevented.

The destination: The destination behaves the same as an accumulator except that it does not further forward packets.

After decoding a packet, the destination or the new delegated source sends out an ACK (via broadcast) to stop the previous delegated source's transmission. The ACK contains the IDs of the ACKed packet (e.g., p) and the delegated source (e.g., n), which can also make accumulators with lower priorities than n abort the decoding of packet p (as a higher priority node n has already decoded p). In case of multiple delegated sources for the same packet, the ACK sent from a high priority delegated source prevents the duplicated forwarding from the lower priority delegated sources. Different from traditional per-hop ACKs, the purpose of ACKs in HOPE is to switch and control the data forwarding roles, so we denote them as sACKs.

Fig. 5 illustrates the interaction of different roles with an example scenario. The original source s starts sending a packet p to destination d. At the beginning, nodes n, m, u, and d all work as accumulators, among which nodes n and u first successfully decode the packet and become the delegated sources. Due to the priority based back-off (§3.3), node n sends out an sACK to stop s and u from forwarding, and aborts the decoding of packet p at m. On the other hand, d keeps accumulating the rateless units from n and tries to decode the packet with the stored rateless units from both s and n.

3.2 Hopless Layer

Although the design emphasis of HOPE is fundamentally different from the existing hop based paradigm, a complete redesign of existing protocol stack is less attractive. We seek to provide a clean abstraction of the hopless operations and integrate it with the current protocol stack. Fig. 6 depicts the architecture of HOPE. HOPE adds a *Hopless Layer*, primarily working with the link layer as follows.

To transmit a packet, the data payload is first delivered from upper layers to the *Role Transition Module* of the hopless Layer. The role transition module locally decides whether the transmission should be aborted if other higher priority nodes have already transmitted this packet to the network. The decision is made based on the *Priority list* and the *Packet list*. If the transmission can continue, the *Information Bucket* generates rateless units of the packet, and adds a hopless header in front of the rateless units. The rateless units with the hopless header are finally passed to the link layer and undergo CSMA before the transmission.

For receiving, the PHY layer loads the bits from a receiving buffer after detecting a preamble. It passes the bits to the link layer, which are further retrieved by the information bucket to perform the rateless decoding. In addition,

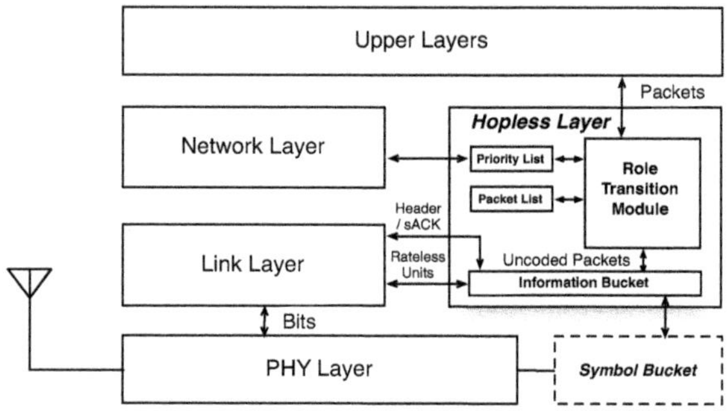

Figure 6: HOPE architecture.

the packet list is updated based on the hopless header of the received packet. If the rateless code requires to access PHY symbols, we extend the information bucket to the PHY layer and introduce a *Symbol Bucket* to substitute the function of the information bucket.

In the rest of this section, we present the detailed design of the hopless layer.

Information bucket. The hopless layer receives rateless units from the link layer. An information bucket is maintained to organize rateless units of all undecoded packets. For an incoming data packet p, a node n retrieves the original source, destination, and sequence number from its header, which uniquely identifies this packet. If the packet has not been locally decoded before (by looking up the packet list which will be detailed later), the node registers a unique piece of buffer to accumulate the rateless units of the packet. If p has already been registered, the rateless units are directed to the existing buffer of p. Node n performs rateless decoding for the packet whenever new rateless units are received. If decoding is successful, the decoded packet is passed to the state transition module and the buffer is released. If decoding fails, the buffer is maintained to accumulate more rateless units. The main functionality of the information bucket is to incorporate the rateless coding scheme in receiving packets from the joint information channel. The partial information of undecoded packets is stored orderly until the packets get decoded.

The information bucket can be extended down to work with the PHY layer. A symbol bucket can be included, which directly fetches PHY symbols and can perform recent physical rateless coding schemes. In our current design, we use Spinal codes as the default scheme. The symbol bucket accumulates the Spinal "passes" of symbols and performs rateless decoding for each packet. The symbol bucket substitutes the information bucket and preserves all operation logics. By performing the physical layer rateless codes, the capability of the information accumulation improves.

Priority list. A priority list is maintained for each destination in the network, which evaluates the data forwarding utilities of all nodes to the destination, based on which their forwarding priorities are ranked. Traditional routing metrics, e.g., the geographic distance [19], ETX [5], etc, characterize the packet-oriented transmissions, which do not truthfully evaluate the forwarding utilities atop the hopless networking. To this end, in HOPE, we propose the end-to-end effective throughput from the current node to the destination as the cost metric. A packet may be forwarded by arbitrary delegated sources from the current node n to the destination d. Suppose the packet length is L. The effective throughput from n to d, denoted as $etp_{n,d}$, can be approximated as:

$$etp_{n,d} = \max_{i \in N}\{\frac{L}{t_{n,i} + (L - t_{n,i} \times \frac{L}{t_{n,d}})/etp_{i,d}}\}, \quad (1)$$

where $t_{i,j}$ is the time required for node i to deliver a packet to node j with the best data rate, and N is the set of all nodes in the network. The variables $t_{n,i}$ and $t_{n,d}$ in Eq. (1) can be directly measured by n with probing packets. Probing packets are decoded directly from one sender each time, without the accumulation from other nodes. The $etp_{n,d}$ can thus be derived through the periodic channel estimation and iterative state exchange among nodes, similar to most existing routing protocols. Therefore, we reuse the original periodic channel estimation module in the network layer, but intercept probing packets and add the hopless header before releasing them to the link layer. Similar to existing routing protocols, e.g., [5, 31, 15, 25], the frequency to probe channels is set to be once every tens of minutes.

Based on the channel probing, the priority list for each destination d is then formed and maintained based on the descending rank of $etp_{i,d}$. As all the nodes in the network are ordered in the priority list, the conventional routing loop (oscillation between different delegated sources) will not occur in HOPE. In addition, HOPE also tolerates certain suboptimal selection of the delegated sources from the priority list because its rateless feature. Therefore, each node reports their updated $etp_{i,d}$ infrequently to reduce the communication overhead[1], e.g., with a long period length, or after the transmissions of several data batches from the source node. After collecting $etp_{i,d}$ from each node, the destination reorders the nodes in the network and distributes the updated priority list to all the nodes using the standard flooding technique. In our current implementation, the priority list is empirically updated every 30 minutes. Between two consecutive updates, the priority lists of each node are not changed.

Packet list. Each node in HOPE also maintains a packet list that reflects the packet possessions in the network, based on which the node can locally manage its actions and role transitions. An entry is maintained in the packet list for each packet according to its source ID, destination ID, and sequence number. Each packet entry records the highest priority node (based on the node's best local knowledge) that possesses the intact packet. Each node dynamically updates the packet list upon the reception of a data packet or an sACK. If the decoded packet or the sACKed packet is not in the list, the node creates a new entry. A packet entry thus does not necessarily indicate the packet decoded by the node. The node may only receive sACKs about this packet. Packet entries are periodically flushed to control the storage overhead. We adopt the same period length as the priority list update to flush the packet list since we do not observe the sojourn time of one data file packet greater than 30 minutes in our study.

Role transition. In HOPE, nodes transit between two roles, accumulator and delegated source. Initially, the original source directly acts as a delegated source and all other nodes start from accumulators. Destination is a special accumulator.

Being an accumulator, a node (e.g., n) waits for incoming units. The node tells different unit types based on a field in the header (UNIT_TYPE detailed in Fig. 7). If the incoming unit is an sACK, node n checks the entry about the sACKed packet in its packet list. If the recorded packet possessor in the list has lower priority, node n updates the entry with the possessor indicated in the sACK. If no entry is found about the sACKed packet, a new entry is created. A node remains as an accumulator after receiving an sACK. If the incoming unit is a rateless unit, node n accepts it in its information bucket. However, prior to decoding, the node refers to the packet and priority lists and takes the following possible actions:

Role transition: If the rateless unit sender has lower priority than node n, and a) the packet is not in the packet list or b) the packet is in the list but the recorded possessor has lower priority than node n, node n accumulates the rateless unit and performs rateless decoding in the information bucket. In case the decoding is successful, node n transits to a delegated source and updates the packet entry in the packet list with its own ID (If no such an entry, the node creates one); otherwise it remains as an accumulator and waits for new incoming units. Becoming a delegated source, node n first broadcasts an sACK after wining the channel contention. Prior to transmit rateless units, the node further refers to the packet and priority lists. If the packet list indicates that the data packet is owned by some higher priority node, the delegated source cancels the packet forwarding and then transits back to the accumulator (it happens when multiple accumulators become delegated sources concurrently and node n receives an sACK from a higher priority node); Otherwise, node n generates a stream of rateless units and sends them out. After sending a rateless unit, node n transits back to an accumulator for receiving possible sACKs. If no acknowledgement is received within a time interval, node n turns to the delegated source again and sends out another stream of rateless units.

sACK transmission without role transition: If node n has higher priority than the sender of the incoming rateless unit and has already decoded this packet, it transmits an sACK and stays as an accumulator. Another possibility of merely transmitting an sACK without role transition is that node n has not decoded the packet, but the packet entry already exists (due to a previous sACK). In this case, if the recorded possessor in the packet list has higher priority than the sender, node n transmits an sACK as well. The sACK is to inform the sender to stop transmitting and update its packet list.

No role transition and communication: If the sender of the incoming unit has higher priority than node n, node n takes no communication actions. It updates its packet list, if the sender has higher priority than the recorded one.

In summary, the knowledge about the packet possession is mainly updated through sACKs. An sACK is sent out when either a node decodes a new packet or detects a packet already decoded by a higher priority node while still transmitted by a lower priority node so as to prevent such an unnecessary forwarding. Each sACK is broadcasted once and not all nodes are ensured to receive it. As a result, multiple delegated sources may transmit the same packet concurrently. Since the knowledge about the packet possession is updated

[1]In HOPE, nodes explicitly report $etp_{i,d}$, instead of including it in data packets, because some nodes may not participate in the data delivery from a source to a destination.

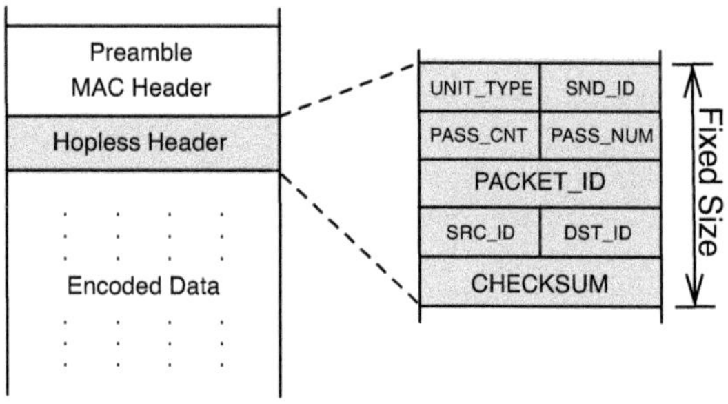

Figure 7: The format of HOPE units.

through sACKs as well as rateless units, a delegated source can immediately cancel the packet forwarding once it knows a higher priority node that possess this packet. HOPE tolerates such inconsistency. In §4, we experimentally examine the overhead due to duplicated transmissions and the result shows the cost is generally small, e.g., < 10% of the total throughput.

3.3 Practical Issues

To translate the HOPE design into a working protocol, we need to carefully address several practical issues, which are discussed in the following.

Design and format of rateless units. HOPE supplements a fixed length header for each rateless unit. Fig. 7 depicts the header format. UNIT_TYPE tells the current unit is a rateless data unit, sACK, or probing packet. The ID of the current sender is stored in the SND_ID field. The packet ID (PACKET_ID), the source ID (SRC_ID), and the destination ID (DST_ID), uniquely identify the packet that the current rateless unit belongs to. The PASS_CNT and PASS_NUM fields are two parameters related to the Spinal codes which will be explained later. A CHECK_SUM field is applied to protect the header. The total overhead of header is only 12 bytes in our current design.

In HOPE, the header contains meta information to distinguish different units. The rateless units of the same packet transmitted by different delegated sources have different headers, so the headers are not rateless coded. Following the design in 802.11, HOPE lets nodes transmit plain headers with the lowest bit rate (e.g., $6.5Mbps$ in 802.11n networks [34]) so as to lower the SNR requirement in acquiring the headers. This maximizes the range of candidate accumulators that can successfully retrieve the headers and accumulate the rateless units. According to our experimental results in §4, the slow rate header transmission can be decoded with as low as 5dB SNR. sACK is a special unit with preamble [13, 12, 29] and header only.

Rateless decoding from joint information channel. None of existing rateless codes consider jointly decoding data from different senders with different data qualities. HOPE extends Spinal codes to decode data "passes" from multiple senders, which can be similarly made to other rateless codes.

Pass numbering: In HOPE, the Spinal codes hash function H used across all nodes is the same. To maximize the information gain from the accumulated "passes", different delegated sources forward different "passes" for the same data packet. To make "passes" independent with each other, a delegated source transmits symbols following the latest "pass" received from the previous delegated source, e.g., if the latest "pass" received by node n_2 from n_1 is $pass_1$, n_2 can start transmitting from $pass_1 + 1$. To add some tolerance in accommodating more "passes" (n_1 may continue transmitting extra "passes" until sACKed, and those "passes" may be received and made use of by some accumulators), n_2 may skip a random number b "passes" and start from $pass_1 + b$. The start point is specified by PASS_NUM in the header for the receivers' decoding. On the other hand, each rateless unit can contain fixed number of Spinal "passes", e.g., PASS_CNT=1 in Fig. 7. It can also be set adaptively [23].

Weighted decoding: After a delegated source transmits the jth "pass" including N symbols, $\mathbf{X}_j(M) = [x_1, x_2, \ldots, x_N]$, for a data packet M, we denote received symbols as $\mathbf{Y}_j = [y_1, y_2, \ldots, y_N]$. In AWGN channels, a max-likelihood decoder requires to satisfy:

$$\max_M\{p(\mathbf{Y}_j|\mathbf{X}_j(M))\} = \max_M\{\prod_{i=1}^{N} \frac{1}{\sqrt{2\pi\sigma_{ij}^2}} e^{-\frac{(y_i-x_i)^2}{2\sigma_{ij}^2}}\},$$

where σ_{ij}^2 is the noise variance of the ith symbol in the jth "pass". Taking the natural logs and dropping terms that are not a function of M, we obtain:

$$\max_M\{\ln p(\mathbf{Y}_j|\mathbf{X}_j(M))\} \propto \min_M\{\sum_{i=1}^{N} \frac{(y_i - x_i)^2}{\sigma_{ij}^2}\}. \quad (2)$$

To maximize the decoding probability, Eq. (2) implies that the "passes" with lower SNRs should contribute less to decoding compared with those with higher SNRs. In the original Spinal codes, received symbols are viewed equally in decoding, as they are from the same sender over a relatively stable channel. We extend the Spinal decoder to $\min_M\{\sum_{i=1}^{N} \frac{(y_i-x_i)^2}{\sigma_j^2}\}$, where σ_j^2 is the SNR of the jth "pass" measured from the rateless unit preamble. One may further supplement a packet postamble to improve the SNR estimation as [18], e.g., measuring σ_j with a higher accuracy from both the preamble and the postamble.

Multiple access. In HOPE, each sender strictly follows CSMA for channel access. When accumulating information from one source, an accumulator always launches the preamble detection when it detects a sudden increase of RSS (Received Signal Strength). This is because the sudden increase of RSS usually indicates a new incoming unit with higher SNR and it is more beneficial for the receiver to accumulate the high-SNR information. The preambles or headers of the incoming unit may not be correctly detected if its RSS is not strong enough. In such a case, traditional networks cannot hook on the incoming data as well. Traditional packet collisions at the receiver translate to very low SNR rateless units received in HOPE, which are usually assigned negligible weights in the weighted decoding scheme in Eq. (2).

Multiple nodes may decode a same packet and send out sACKs simultaneously. In this case, collision occurs and the sender fails to be notified. To address such an issue, receivers conduct a priority based back-off before sending the sACK. Higher priority nodes are prone to have shorter back-off delays. In HOPE, the priority list is equally divided into m groups (the last group may contain fewer nodes). Nodes in group i performs back-off in $[0, 2^i - 1] \cdot 16\mu s$, where $16\mu s$ is the *SIFS* duration. Thus, the time interval for the delegated source to transmit the next round of rateless units equals to the maximum back-off latency plus an sACK transmission delay. In §4, the maximum back-off latency is set to $128\mu s$.

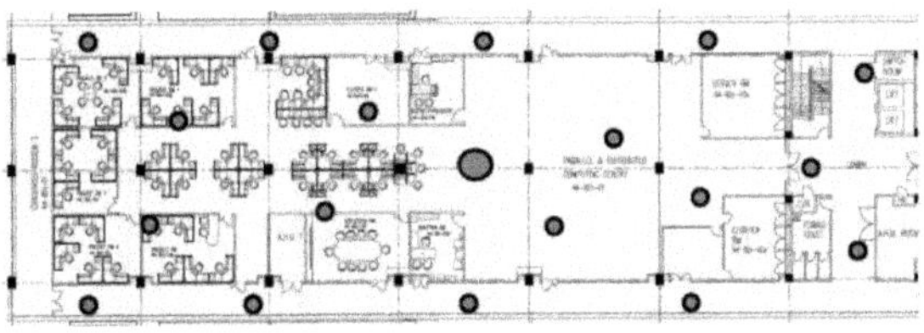

Figure 8: Traces are collected from 19 positions in a $800m^2$ office room.

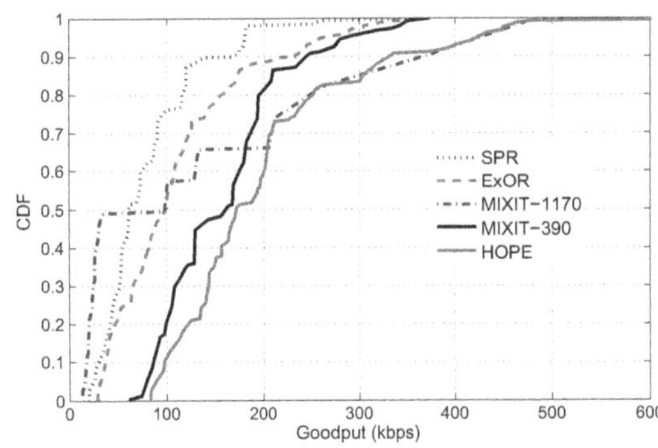

Figure 9: Goodputs of various approaches.

4. PERFORMANCE EVALUATION

We compare HOPE with: a EXT-based Single Path Routing protocol, SPR [5]; a classical opportunistic routing protocol, ExOR [2]; and a state-of-the-art symbol-level network coding based opportunistic routing protocol, MIXIT [20].

4.1 Experiment configuration

We conduct a trace driven evaluation with data traces collected from USRP N210 software defined radios mainly because HOPE adopts Spinal codes which require excessive decoding overhead for the general software radio platforms.

Experiment setup. With the Spinal codes, a (delegated) source first divides each raw data packet into k-bit blocks. Each k-bit block is hashed to a v-bit spine value, which is then used as a seed to generate c-bit random numbers. Every "pass" is a concatenation of a set of c-bit random numbers. In particular, the ith "pass" for a data packet consists of the ith c-bit random number generated from each block of the packet. A receiver uses maximum likelihood decoder to recover the k-bit message from c-bit numbers. Our implementation of Spinal codes is based on the codes provided by the authors of [26] and we configure $k = 3$, $c = 4$, $v = 32$, and $B = 256$.

Trace collection. *Trace from USRP N210.* Each USRP node is configured to operate on OFDM with 600KHz frequency band in the 2.4GHz range. Each node uses a USRP RFX2400 daughterboard as the RF frontend with the transmission power of 50mW (i.e., 17dbm) attached to an omnidirectional antenna with 3dBi gain. We connect each node to a laptop to collect PHY symbols. The PHY of 802.11n in the single input single output mode is implemented on the GNU Radio platform. We collect the pairwise packet transmission traces of all 342 links among 19 positions in Fig. 8. The links include direct line-of-sight paths as well as those blocked by objects. We perform the trace collection with 19 rounds. In each round, one USRP sender is placed at one of the 19 locations, broadcasts the packets from a fixed 5MB data file, and circulates all data rates to transmit the same file. The rest 18 USRP receivers record all the received packets as the packet-level trace at the rest 18 locations simultaneously (no matter packets are successfully decoded or not). The packet-level trace directly records the fate of each packet from the 5 MB data file which is used to evaluate the packet-oriented protocols, SPR and ExOR. The USRP receivers further compare the received symbols with the transmitted ones for all received packets at all rates and compose a symbol-level trace of errors, which is used to test MIXIT and HOPE. By doing so, a 19-node network with all possible running traffic flows is constructed.

Trace from Intel 5300 NICs. USRP N210 can directly record the symbol-level traces, but mainly works in the narrow band channels due to the hardware constraints. We further adopt the channel state information (CSI) tool developed on Intel 5300 NICs [11] to collect transmission traces and test HOPE in the wideband channels with frequency selective fading. We deploy Intel 5300 nodes, operating in 20 MHz channel, at the same positions in Fig. 8 and perform the trace collection in the same way as we do with USRP N210s. Intel 5300 is only able to report packet-level traces. The dispersion of each symbol cannot be directly measured. To obtain the symbol-level traces for evaluating MIXIT and HOPE, when one node transmits, we let other nodes measure the subcarrier-level SNRs to the transmitter. For each transceiver pair, we use the measured SNRs to generate the symbol-level dispersions [11].

We perform trace-driven emulations with the collected 19-node network traces. We build a custom emulator to evaluate HOPE compared with benchmarks. The emulator implements 802.11-like PHY (e.g., convolutional coding and modulations) and MAC. We first experiment with the USRP trace to investigate the detailed performance of different approaches, and then use Intel 5300 trace to evaluate the wideband performance.

4.2 Results

Goodput. We evaluate the goodput that refers to the actual data size transmitted over unit time. We consider goodput over throughput as different protocols incur different amounts of protocol overhead, and goodput can better reflect the data transmission efficiency and delay, i.e., a higher goodput indicates better efficiency and a shorter delay [33]. On the other hand, to understand the protocol overhead, we further evaluate the detailed breakdown of throughput for each protocol in this section.

Goodput comparison. We evaluate the goodput performance of different protocols. We randomly select one node pair and measure its end-to-end goodput. For all benchmark protocols SPR, ExOR and MIXIT, we test all possible 802.11n single-stream data rates in the USRP 600KHz frequency band and select their best performance. Both SPR and ExOR achieve the maximum goodput with 390Kbps data rate. MIXIT achieves a better average goodput at 1.17Mbps, but has some unique advantage at 390Kbps data rate, so we plot both MIXIT-1170 and MIXIT-390. We set the data rate 1.17Mbps for HOPE, which yields a gradually decreasing effective data rate when more Spinal "passes" are transmitted. We repeat the experiments 120 times by randomly selecting 120 node pairs in total. Fig. 9 depicts the

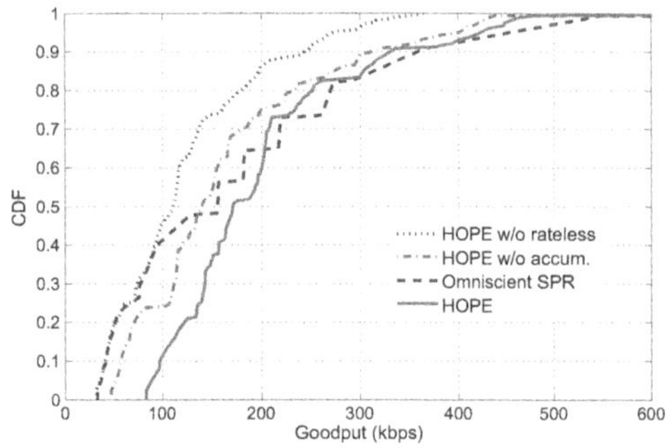

Figure 10: Goodput gain breakdown of HOPE.

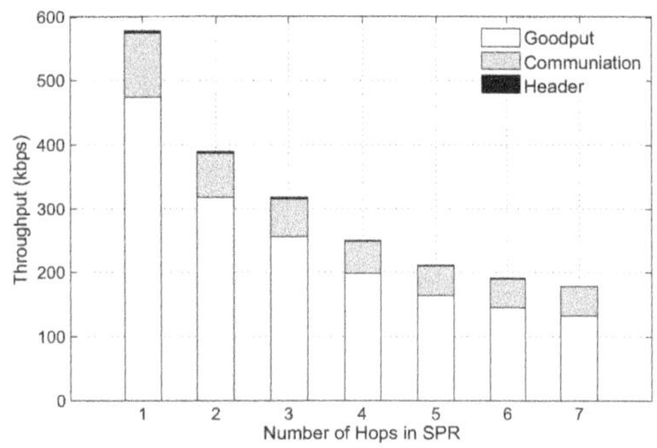

Figure 11: Overhead breakdown of HOPE.

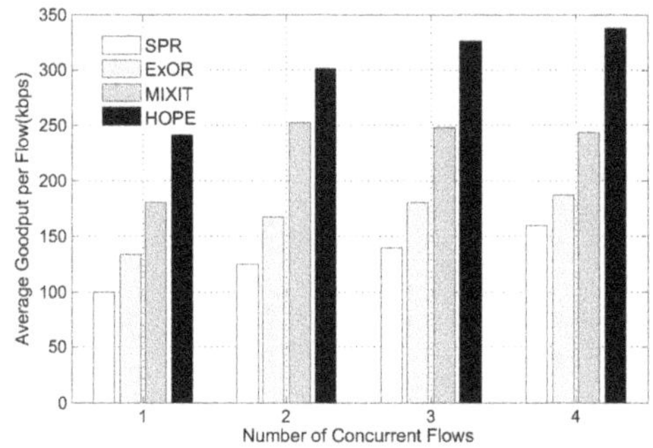

Figure 12: Goodputs in a multi-flow mesh network.

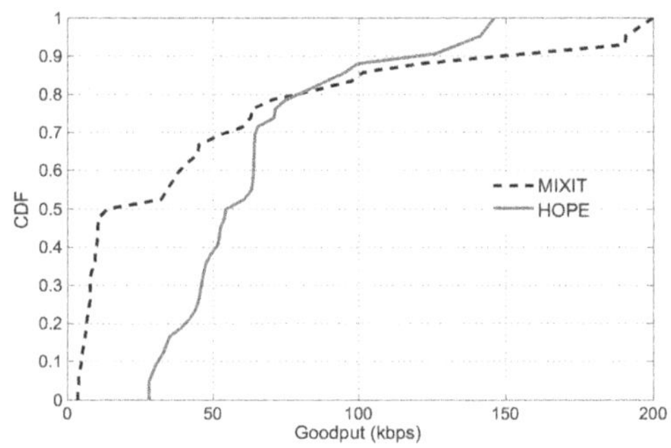

Figure 13: Goodputs in a multi-flow ad-hoc network.

CDF of the achieved goodput by different protocols. Generally HOPE achieves an average goodput gain of 2.4x over SPR, 1.7x over ExOR, 1.3x over MIXIT of both 1.17Mbps and 390Kbps, respectively. HOPE significantly outperforms SPR and ExOR primarily because HOPE allows each delegated source to adapt to all possible accumulators' channel conditions simultaneously and thus accumulators largely accelerate the packet decoding based on the cumulative information from multiple sources.

Along short paths or high quality links (mostly the right part of the figure), we see that both MIXIT-1170 and HOPE achieve high goodput because the channel condition supports their transmissions with full rates. Over long paths or weak links (mostly the left part of the figure), however, MIXIT-1170 suffers dramatic goodput drop. It is probably because MIXIT at 1.17Mbps data rate misses many low quality symbol transmissions and suffers high symbol error rate over weak links. The uncertain symbol errors may accumulate and propagate over long paths. If we set the data rate to 13Mbps on the other hand, MIXIT captures the symbol accumulation opportunities over weaker links, but cannot completely exploit good links with full rates. *Note that, as opportunistic routing protocols, e.g., MIXIT and ExOR, have no fixed receiver for each transmission. They cannot automatically adapt their own rates to different links of different qualities.*

Gain analysis. We test HOPE with three different settings to understand its goodput gain in detail. We first substitute the rateless codes of HOPE with a fixed data rate of 390Kbps, which degrades to capturing packet-level opportunities similar as ExOR (HOPE w/o rateless). We then enable rateless codes but disable the information accumulation of HOPE (HOPE w/o accum). Finally, we fully enable HOPE with both benefits. Fig. 10 depicts the performance of the three settings. With the rateless codes, HOPE harvests more than half of its full goodput gain. For good channel conditions (e.g., the goodput is higher than 240Kbps), the rateless codes play a critical role in acquiring the goodput. In Fig. 10, the goodput of HOPE w/o accum. is comparable to HOPE in this region. For the long paths or poor links, rateless codes also help in adapting different links and counteracting channel fluctuations. Enabling information accumulation allows HOPE to benefit more in the low goodput region. From Fig. 10 we see the main improvement of HOPE over HOPE w/o accum. when the goodput is lower than 240Kbps. This is because the cumulative information is more valuable for long paths and weaker links. In Fig. 10, we also examine omniscient SPR for comparison. Omniscient SPR always sets the optimal data rate for the packet transmission at each hop. HOPE achieves comparable goodput with omniscient SPR in the high goodput region due to the auto rate adaptation. For the long paths and weak links, HOPE outperforms omniscient SPR, as HOPE accumulates more overheard rateless units under such scenarios. We further find that HOPE can rapidly adapt to a better link when the channel condition varies while SPR lacks this flexibility.

Overhead. Fig. 11 examines the overhead of HOPE over paths of different hop counts. We separate the communication overhead and data header overhead from the goodput. The communication overhead consists of ACK transmissions, duplicate packet transmissions from different nodes, carrier sensing time, etc. The small and fixed-sized header in HOPE poses negligible overhead. The communication overhead is also small, $< 10\%$ of throughput, as HOPE does not have to spend time in arbitrating the next forwarder each time. According to the experiment results,

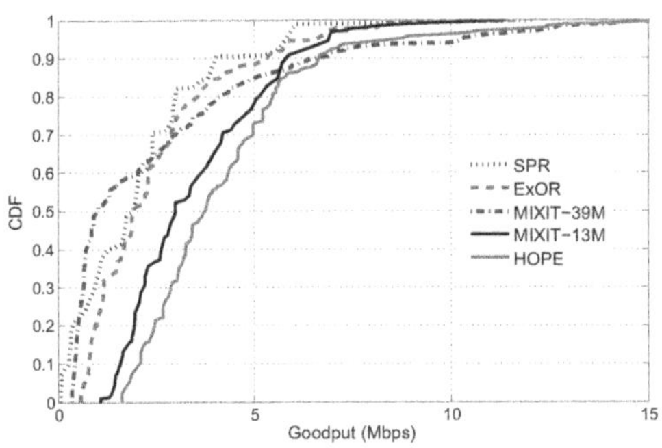

Figure 14: Goodputs in wideband channels.

we see that the fraction of overhead gradually increases as hop counts increase, which is mainly because the involved extra control overhead adds up every hop while the payload size stays constant at 1500bytes.

Multiple flows. We test the performance of SPR, ExOR, MIXIT and HOPE with multiple flows for mesh-like and ad-hoc-like networks. For MIXIT, we find that the 1.17Mbps rate outperforms the 390Kbps rate in this trial of experiments and thus only present its performance with the 1.17 Mbps rate. In Fig. 12, we examine the performance of each protocol in a mesh-like network with a gateway node (the highlighted node in Fig. 8) and other nodes incur the flow based traffic to the gateway. By setting different numbers of original sources, we can vary the number of flows in the network. Each original source incurs a traffic flow to the gateway for transmitting a 5MB file. Fig. 12 plots the total network goodput with varied numbers of flows. The network goodput increases towards the saturated capacity as the number of concurrent flows increases. HOPE, however, consistently outperforms benchmark protocols due to its best use of the wireless channel. According to statistics, HOPE achieves an average goodput gain of 2.3x over SPR, 1.7x over ExOR, 1.3x over MIXIT at 1.17Mbps.

We further evalaute HOPE and MIXIT (with highest goodput among benchmark schemes) in an ad-hoc network with intermittent traffics. All 19 nodes in Fig. 8 act as ad-hoc-like nodes and we configure 6 coexisting flows with different sender-destination pairs in the network but of randomly selected data volume ranging from 1.5-30K bytes. When one flow finishes, we immediately appoint a new flow between a random pair of nodes. We experiment 50 flows in total. Fig. 13 depicts the CDF of the goodput achieved by MIXIT and HOPE, respectively. In the high goodput region, MIXIT slightly performs better mainly because its congestion-aware scheme helps to approach the network capacity. The high control overhead and per-hop errors, however, limit the performance of MIXIT over longer paths. In the low goodput region HOPE achieves more efficient bandwidth utilization. Overall, HOPE achieves 1.4x average goodput gain.

HOPE on wideband channels. In this section, we experiment with the wideband traces collected from Intel 5300 NICs. We select one node pair and measure its end-to-end goodput. We repeat the experiments 120 times by randomly selecting 120 node pairs. To avoid long runs of consecutive errors in the coded bit sequences due to frequency selective fading, interleaving is implemented for each protocol. Fig. 14 shows the CDF of the achieved goodput of different protocols. Compared with the performance in narrowband channels (Fig. 9), the goodput gain achieved by HOPE is still substantial. In particular, HOPE achieves an average goodput gain of 2.0x over SPR, 1.6x over ExOR, 1.5x over MIXIT-39M, and 1.3x over MIXIT-13M. MIXIT-39M and MIXIT-13M represent MIXIT works at 39Mbps and 13Mbps and correspond to MIXIT-1170 and MIXIT-390 in Fig. 9, respectively. The gain achieved by HOPE over SPR and ExOR is preserved since it can still adapt to accumulators' channel conditions simultaneously even with frequency selective fading. Accumulators can thus leverage the cumulative information to accelerate packet decoding.

We also evaluate HOPE on low-power wireless networks. Due to the page limitation, the results can be found at [23].

5. RELATED WORKS

Rate adaptation and rateless codes. Rateless codes can achieve optimal rate adaptation [10, 26]. With rateless codes, a sender incrementally adapts to a suitable data rate by sending more coded data until the receiver decodes the data. Strider [10] presents a systematic design of automatic rate adaptation based on a layered rateless code with the linear combination of turbo codes. LT [24] and Raptor codes [30] can achieve Shannon capacity for binary erasure channels, but it remains unclear how close they are to the capacity over wireless channels. The authors in [8] further investigate how LT codes can be used to prolong the end-to-end communication range in low-power wireless networks. Departing from prior linear rateless codes, Spinal codes [26] use hash functions to produce infinite sequence of PHY symbols, achieving near optimal capacity over both erasure and wireless channels. Different from existing works, our design leverages rateless codes to adapt to joint information channels with hopless networking.

Opportunistic routing. ExOR [2] pioneers the opportunistic routing, which broadcasts packets without predetermined next hops and delays forwarding decisions to exploit channel diversity. MORE [3] obviates strict scheduling and enhances spatial reuse by leveraging network coding. Both ExOR and MORE can only make use of intact packets surviving over opportunistic links. SPaC [9] combines multiple corrupted packets in sensor networks to recover data. MIXIT [20] can forward clean symbols in corrupted packets and applies symbol-level network coding. The unified data rate of each transmission, however, limits the information utility of SPaC and MIXIT. In contrast, HOPE features rateless information dissemination and adapts to diverse channel conditions of all wireless links. MIXIT does study from a rateless perspective but relies on the end-to-end network coding to adapt to the network, which inevitably misses the full gain from internal channel diversities within the network. MIXIT requires an accurate network reliability prediction to avoid error propagation.

Cooperative communication. Our work is related to cooperative communication in which users coordinate to enhance communication quality [21, 28, 27, 32]. Laneman et. al [21] develop information-theoretic approaches to exploit wireless spatial diversity. Hunter *et al.* [17] propose to integrate cooperative communication with channel coding. Cover *et al.* [4] present the theoretical analysis on the capacity of relay channel. Draper *et al.* [7] design routing protocols for cooperative networks that perform mutual information accumulation. The major difference between [7] and HOPE is that the former study focuses on the optimization of the transmission order in theory, while our solution concentrates on addressing realistic challenges and designing a practical system incorporating the latest rateless codes, e.g., Spinal codes. In summary, existing researches mainly study cooperative communications from a theoretical perspective, e.g., gain analysis, schedule optimization, etc. In this paper, we propose a clean hopless networking abstraction from a system perspective, address a sequence of realistic design issues, and develop a practical solution using rateless codes to harvest cooperative diversity of autonomous wireless nodes which has never been done before.

6. CONCLUSION

This paper presents a novel hopless networking paradigm. The key idea is to break per-hop packet transmission to rateless information dissemination that adapts to diverse channel conditions of wireless links, taking the full advantage of wireless broadcast effect. We develop a practical protocol, HOPE, which instantiates the hopless networking. Experimental evaluation demonstrates that HOPE significantly improves network throughput over existing approaches. While the current HOPE design does not pursue the performance optimality, we point out several important future works, e.g., optimal rateless segmentation, better concurrency in multiple access, and flow-based optimization.

7. ACKNOWLEDGEMENTS

This work is supported by Singapore MOE AcRF Tier 2 Grant MOE2012-T2-1-070 and Singapore MOE AcRF Tier 1 grant MOE2013-T1-002-005. This work is also supported by the Singapore National Research Foundation under its Environment and Water Technologies Strategic Research Programme and administered by the Environment and Water Industry Programme Office (EWI) of the PUB on project 1002-IRIS-09, NSF CNS-1116970, and NSFC 61303233.

8. REFERENCES

[1] J. Bicket, D. Aguayo, S. Biswas, and R. Morris. Architecture and evaluation of an unplanned 802.11b mesh network. In *ACM MobiCom*, 2005.

[2] S. Biswas and R. Morris. ExOR: opportunistic multi-hop routing for wireless networks. In *ACM SIGCOMM*, 2005.

[3] S. Chachulski, M. Jennings, S. Katti, and D. Katabi. Trading structure for randomness in wireless opportunistic routing. In *ACM SIGCOMM*, 2007.

[4] T. Cover and A. E. Gamal. Capacity theorems for the relay channel. *IEEE Trans. on Information Theory*, 1979.

[5] D. S. J. De Couto, D. Aguayo, J. Bicket, and R. Morris. A high-throughput path metric for multi-hop wireless routing. In *ACM MobiCom*, 2003.

[6] W. Dong, Y. Liu, Y. He, and T. Zhu. Measurement and analysis on the packet delivery performance in a large scale sensor network. In *IEEE INFOCOM*, 2013.

[7] S. C. Draper, L. Liu, A. F. Molisch, and J. S. Yedidia. Cooperative transmission for wireless networks using mutual-information accumulation. *IEEE Trans. on Information Theory*, 2011.

[8] W. Du, Z. Li, J. C. Liando, and M. Li. From rateless to distanceless: Enabling sparse sensor network deployment in large areas. In *ACM SenSys*, 2014.

[9] H. Dubois-Ferrière, D. Estrin, and M. Vetterli. Packet combining in sensor networks. In *ACM SenSys*, 2005.

[10] A. Gudipati and S. Katti. Strider: automatic rate adaptation and collision handling. In *ACM SIGCOMM*, 2011.

[11] D. Halperin, W. Hu, A. Sheth, and D. Wetherall. Predictable 802.11 packet delivery from wireless channel measurements. In *ACM SIGCOMM*, 2010.

[12] J. Han, C. Qian, X. Wang, D. Ma, J. Zhao, P. Zhang, W. Xi, and Z. Jiang. Twins: Device-free object tracking using passive tags. In *IEEE INFOCOM*, 2014.

[13] J. Han, C. Qian, P. Yang, D. Ma, Z. Jiang, W. Xi, and J. Zhao. Geneprint: Generic and accurate physical-layer identification for UHF RFID tags. *IEEE Trans. on Networking*, 2015.

[14] M. K. Han, A. Bhartia, L. Qiu, and E. Rozner. O3: optimized overlay-based opportunistic routing. In *ACM MobiHoc*, 2011.

[15] L. He, L. Fu, L. Zheng, Y. Gu, P. Cheng, J. Chen, and J. Pan. Esync: An energy synchronized charging protocol for rechargeable wireless sensor networks. In *ACM MobiHoc*, 2014.

[16] Q. Huang, K. Sun, X. Li, and D. Wu. Just fun: A joint fountain coding and network coding approach to loss-tolerant information spreading. In *ACM MobiHoc*, 2014.

[17] T. E. Hunter and A. Nosratinia. Diversity through coded cooperation. *IEEE Trans. on Wireless Commununication*, 2006.

[18] K. Jamieson and H. Balakrishnan. PPR: Partial packet recovery for wireless networks. In *ACM SIGCOMM*, 2007.

[19] B. Karp and H. T. Kung. GPSR: greedy perimeter stateless routing for wireless networks. In *ACM MobiCom*, 2000.

[20] S. Katti, D. Katabi, H. Balakrishnan, and M. Medard. Symbol-level network coding for wireless mesh networks. In *ACM SIGCOMM*, 2008.

[21] J. N. Laneman, D. N. C. Tse, and G. W. Wornell. Cooperative diversity in wireless networks: Efficient protocols and outage behavior. *IEEE Trans. on Information Theory*, 2002.

[22] Y. Li, L. Qiu, Y. Zhang, R. Mahajan, and E. Rozner. Predictable performance optimization for wireless networks. In *ACM SIGCOMM*, 2008.

[23] Z. Li, W. Du, Y. Zheng, M. Li, and D. Wu. From rateless to hopless. In *Technical Report*, 2015.

[24] M. Luby. Lt codes. In *Proceedings of IEEE FOCS*, 2002.

[25] Q. Ma, K. Liu, X. Xiao, Z. Cao, and Y. Liu. Link scanner: Faulty link detection for wireless sensor networks. In *IEEE INFOCOM*, 2013.

[26] J. Perry, P. A. Iannucci, K. E. Fleming, H. Balakrishnan, and D. Shah. Spinal codes. In *ACM SIGCOMM*, 2012.

[27] A. Sendonaris, E. Erkip, and B. Aazhang. User cooperation diversity - part ii: Implementation aspects and performance analysis. *IEEE Trans. on Communications*, 2003.

[28] A. Sendonaris, E. Erkip, and B. Aazhang. User cooperation diversity: System description. *IEEE Trans. on Communications*, 2003.

[29] L. Shangguan, Z. Yang, L. Alex, and Y. Liu. Relative localization of rfid tags using spatial-temporal phase profiling. In *USENIX NSDI*, 2015.

[30] A. Shokrollahi. Raptor codes. *IEEE Trans. on Information Theory*, 2006.

[31] L. Wang, Y. He, Y. Liu, W. Liu, J. Wang, and N. Jing. It is not just a matter of time: oscillation-free emergency navigation with sensor networks. In *IEEE RTSS*, 2012.

[32] X. Wang, L. Fu, and C. Hu. Multicast performance with hierarchical cooperation. *IEEE/ACM Trans. on Networking*, 2012.

[33] X. Wang, W. Huang, S. Wang, J. Zhang, and C. Hu. Delay and capacity tradeoff analysis for motioncast. *IEEE/ACM Trans. on Networking*, 2011.

[34] C. Wu, Z. Yang, Z. Zhou, K. Qian, Y. Liu, and M. Liu. Phaseu: Real-time los identification with wifi. In *IEEE INFOCOM*, 2015.

SmartGuide: Towards Single-image Building Localization with Smartphone

Xi Xiong
School of Software and TNList
Tsinghua University, China
xiongxi08@gmail.com

Zheng Yang
School of Software and TNList
Tsinghua University, China
hmilyyz@gmail.com

Longfei Shangguan
CSE, Hong Kong University of Science and Technology
Hong Kong
lshangguan@cse.ust.hk

Yun Fei
Department of Computer Science
Columbia University, New York
fyun@acm.org

Milos Stojmenovic
Department of Informatics and Computing
Singidunum University, Serbia
mstojmenovic@singidunum.ac.rs

Yunhao Liu
School of Software and TNList
Tsinghua University, China
yunhao@greenorbs.com

ABSTRACT

We introduce SmartGuide, a light-weighted and efficient approach to localize and recognize a distant unknown building. Our approach relies on shooting only a single photo of a target building via a smartphone and a local 2D Google map. SmartGuide first extracts a partial top view contour of a building from its side-view photo by applying vanishing point and the Manhattan World Assumption, and then fetches a candidate building set from a local 2D Google map based on smartphone's GPS readings. Partial top view shape, orientation and distance relative to the camera are used as input parameters in a probability model, which adversely recognizes the best candidate building in the local map. Our model is developed based on kernel density estimation that helps reduce noise in the smartphone sensors, such as GPS readings and camera ray direction reported by noisy accelerometer and compass. Experimental results demonstrate that our approach recognizes buildings ranging from 20m to 520m and achieves 92.7% accuracy in downtown areas where the Manhattan World Assumption is applicable. In addition, the processing time is no more than 6 seconds for 87% of cases. Compared with existing building localization schemes, SmartGuide offers numerous advantages. Our method avoids taking multiple photos, intricate 3D reconstruction or any initial deployment cost of database construction, making it faster and less labor-intensive than existing solutions.

Categories and Subject Descriptors

H.3.4 [**Information Storage and Retrieval**]: Systems and Software

MobiHoc'15, June 22–25, 2015, Hangzhou, China.

http://dx.doi.org/10.1145/2746285.2746294.

General Terms

Algorithms, Design, Experimentation, Performance, Ubiquitous Computing

Keywords

Building Localization; Smartphone; Mobile Computing; Single Image

1. INTRODUCTION

In many cases, a mobile user may be interested in identifying and locating a remote building that appears in the viewfinder of his/her smartphone when s/he wants to know which building it is, how to arrive at the building, or what kinds of merchants (e.g., stores, restaurants, and companies) are located in the building. For instance, Bob is travelling in New York City, a metropolis famous for its grand architecture. Bob can easily recognize famous landmarks such as the Empire State Building or Freedom Tower. However, he also wants to know details about some attractive but less well-known buildings within his sight. These buildings of interest may be located in a distance very far from Bob, and Bob could resort to some non-technical solutions, such as asking local residents or searching a city map. However, such approaches have various disadvantages. The building information provided by local residents may be insufficient or inaccurate. Besides, the city map is sometimes unavailable or outdated. Moreover, Bob has to identify the specific building of interest from a massive crowd buildings in a city map, which can be troublesome or even annoying.

Object localization has recently received extensive research efforts in the community of mobile computing. Several approaches to this problem have been proposed. One solution is to take several pictures of the target object and calculate physical depth of the building from the camera [10, 21], which is sometimes cumbersome. For instance, OPS [10] requires a user to shoot an object from multiple distinct positions and reconstructs a 3D model of the object to estimate the distance between the user and the object. Nevertheless, it is more user-friendly for the user to take only a single photo to localize a target. However, a pre-available image database [14, 17, 23, 31], or prior knowledge of the target's true size [20, 26] are often required. For example, a queried image is matched against the GPS-tagged image data to find its accurate GPS location, which requires a prepared tree-indexing database [31].

Nevertheless, there are some disadvantages existing in those solutions when it comes to building localization. Taking multiple photos of the target may be troublesome; constructing the spatial relationship between objects could introduce significant computational cost and corresponsive delay; deploying an indexed database of building photos is labor-intensive; knowing the true size of the target building in advance can be impractical.

To address the problems mentioned above, we propose SmartGuide: a fast light-weighted single-image-based building localization system based on the *Manhattan World Assumption*. Our solution enables a user to localize and recognize a distant unknown building, using only one photo of a target building and a local 2D Google map, without any other prior knowledge. Compared with previous image-based object detection and localization schemes, our solution avoids intricate 3D reconstruction and any initial deployment cost of database construction, which makes it much faster. It can also handle noisy sensor data because our probability model is based on kernel density estimation. Its processing time is no more than 6 seconds for 87% cases. While it is viable to adopt object localization method [10] to localize the target building, 30-60 seconds are required for 3D reconstruction. Additionally, experiments show our system can localize the farmost building at a distance of 520m, which is more than twice longer distance than other database-free methods [10, 21, 26].

The main point of this paper is to extract the partial top view contour of a targeted building from a single captured photo, and use a probability model to match it to a building in a local online maps (2D Google Maps in this paper) obtained by smartphone's GPS. The 2D local map contains not only the top view of the target building but also other surrounding building top views. Thus, we shall find an optimal matching of partial top view contour in the local map along with the camera ray direction, which can be obtained by fusing sensor data of smartphone. Our system responds quickly using off-the-shelf smartphones.

This design leaves out the trouble of taking multiple photos of a building and the high computational cost caused by 3D reconstruction, as well as any initial deployment cost of database construction. Nevertheless, to implement it one must overcome several challenges. (1) Single image of a building provides some structural information but not enough details for us to reconstruct the partial top view of the building. Moreover, existing techniques on 3D reconstruction [5, 15, 18] cannot provide the acceptable performance in terms of accuracy and computational cost. (2) Even after we have acquired the building's partial top view, there may exist many other buildings that own similar partial top view contours with the building of interest in the map. How to distinguish the targeted building from other similar buildings remains an important issue. (3) The smartphone sensors, such as GPS, accelerometer, compass, and gyroscope, are themselves noisy, which can further decrease the accuracy of recognition.

For the first issue, SmartGuide leverages the Manhattan World Assumption [3] and vanishing points to generate a partial top view using only a single photograph. The Manhattan World Assumption assumes that the majority of man-made buildings share a common characteristic: all edges of buildings and windows lie in three orthogonal directions. Utilizing this very reasonable assumption, we can extract the partial top view of a target building much more efficiently than by using 3D-based methods while still maintaining the required accuracy. The extracted partial top view contour not only shows a partial overlooked shape of the building, but also contains the building's orientation relative to the camera. Different buildings do not only own different top view contour shapes, but also own different orientations and different distances from the camera (which can be calculated from the camera parameters and the real sizes of the buildings obtained from the map). Therefore, leveraging these features helps a lot in distinguishing the target building from other similar buildings, which solves the second issue. Lastly, we prepare a probability model based on kernel density estimation (KDE) [13] for the noisy sensor data.

We prototyped SmartGuide on Android smartphones, including LG Nexus 5, Samsung Galaxy Tab 10.1, and Samsung i9100, to collect building photos of different resolutions and qualities. Over fifty locations across four cities (Beijing, Wuxi, Hong Kong, and Shanghai) were evaluated in total. Under the Manhattan World Assumption, all photos are captured from the downtown area or universities where the shape of most buildings are constructed by straight line segments (see our examples below). The experimental results demonstrate that the systems can identify and locate buildings from 20m to 520m and achieve 92.7% identification accuracy in downtown areas where the Manhattan World Assumption is applicable. SmartGuide costs no more than 6 seconds for 87% cases and less than 9 seconds for all cases.

The key contributions of SmartGuide are summarized as follows.

1. **Identified the possibility of localizing a remote building via top view feature matching.** By analyzing top view features (shape, orientation and distance from camera) of the candidate buildings and the target building, we tried to localize the target building from a set of candidate buildings. Our method avoided taking multiple photos, intricate 3D reconstruction or any initial deployment of image databases.

2. **Introduced a kernel-based probability model to deal with the smartphone's sensor noises.** We took a scrutiny on the sensor data, handled it with rigid mathematical models and demonstrated the efficiency of our model.

3. **Implemented a prototype of our system with evaluation.** We prototyped SmartGuide and evaluated its performance in various settings. We demonstrated that our system worked in nearly real-time on off-the-shelf smartphones while also preserving or improving accuracy.

The rest of the paper is organized as follows. Section 2 describes the system overview and Section 3 provides preliminary techniques used in our systems. In Section 4, we dive into the design details. The prototype implementation and performance are evaluated in Section 5. We review the

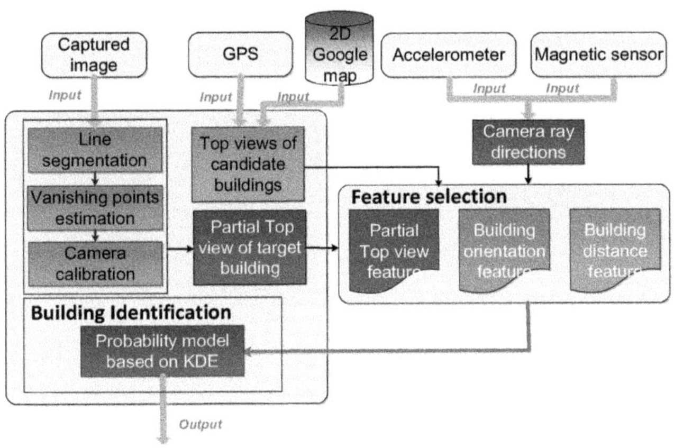

Figure 1: The pipeline of our system. Directions of the arrows indicate the latter consumes result from the former

related work in Section 6 and conclude this work in Section 7.

2. SYSTEM OVERVIEW

In this section, we introduce the basic components of SmartGuide and their work-flow. Fig. 1 portrays an overview of SmartGuide's architecture.

Once the user captures a photo of a target building with a smartphone, SmartGuide records the GPS of the smartphone and calculates the camera ray direction at the same time. SmartGuide detects line segments and classifies these line segments into three orthogonal directions to estimate three vanishing points. According to the positions of three vanishing points, intrinsic camera parameters are calibrated to transform the coordinates of points in 2D photo into the 3D world space. After that, we extract the line segments on the top of the target building and project them onto the ground plane to get the partial top view of the target building.

Simultaneously, SmartGuide fetches a local map via online map services according to the GPS reading. The buildings in the local map compose a candidate building set which contains the target building, and their partial top views are also extracted. Since these buildings present different partial top view shapes, different orientations relative to camera, and different distances from the camera, we evaluate these three features of candidate buildings according to the partial top view, orientation, and size in photo of the target building. At last, we establish a probability model based on kernel density estimation (KDE), whose parameters are calculated according to the above three features, to identify the target building from a number of candidates.

3. PRELIMINARIES

We briefly review some techniques behind our system, and clarify their necessity for our purpose in this section.

Pinhole Camera: We use the classical Pinhole Camera model to simplify the process for acquiring the camera parameters [27]. In this model, 3D points in the real world and their projected points in the image plane construct an ideal pinhole camera, where its aperture is described as a point and no lenses are used for focusing light. In this way, we can ignore geometric distortions and unfocused blurring caused by lenses and finite sized apertures. In the pinhole camera model, all lines that are parallel in reality, such as edges of buildings and windows, are projected to a group of straight lines that converge to *vanishing points* in a image plane, which are crucial for us to extract the partial top view from a single image. Based on this model, we can achieve the focal length, the size and center of the image plane from the smartphone's camera parameters, which are essential factors for building identification.

Manhattan World Assumption: Most man-made scenes follow the Manhattan World Assumption [3], where Cartesian coordinate system is used as a Manhattan grid. All lines in a photo image are assumed parallel to three directions. The lines in one direction are extrapolated to converge to a vanishing point. Accordingly, we can categorize all lines (corresponding to edges of buildings and windows) appearing in the image into three perpendicular directions. Hence the top view contour can be extracted from the categorized lines from a single image.

Kernel Density Estimation (KDE): Let $x_1, x_2, ..., x_n$ be independent and identically distributed samples drawn from some distribution with an unknown density function. We can estimate the unknown density function by kernel density estimation (KDE) as following [13]:

$$\hat{f}(x,h) = \frac{1}{nh}\sum_{i=1}^{n} K_i(\frac{x-x_i}{h}). \qquad (1)$$

$K_i(\frac{x-x_i}{h})$ is the kernel function of the sample x_i, a non-negative function that integrates to one and has mean zero, where h is a smoothing parameter called bandwidth. Fundamentally, KDE is a data smoothing method used to infer data probability distribution based on finite data samples. Since the shooting position is unknown because of noisy GPS readings, the KDE is a powerful tool for us to estimate probability distribution of the shooting position given a finite set of candidate buildings in a 2D local map.

Hu's Seven Moment Invariants: Moment theory is well established and widely applied in a number of digital image areas because image moments are important statistical properties of an image. The raw image moment is a weighted average of pixels' intensities in the image, usually defined as

$$M_{ij} = \sum_x \sum_y x^i y^j I(x,y), \qquad (2)$$

where $I(x, y)$ is the pixel intensity at (x, y).

Hu et al. [7] proved theoretically that an image can be summarized with seven functions that are various combinations of the raw moments M_{ij}. Furthermore, these seven functions are invariant under translation, scaling, as well as rotation, which makes them appropriate for comparing the similarity between different shapes [8].

4. SYSTEM DESIGN

SmartGuide consists of four components: (1) partial top view extraction from a single image, (2) candidate building set acquisition, (3) candidate building feature selection, (4) building identification. In this section, we detail the design challenges and implementations of each module.

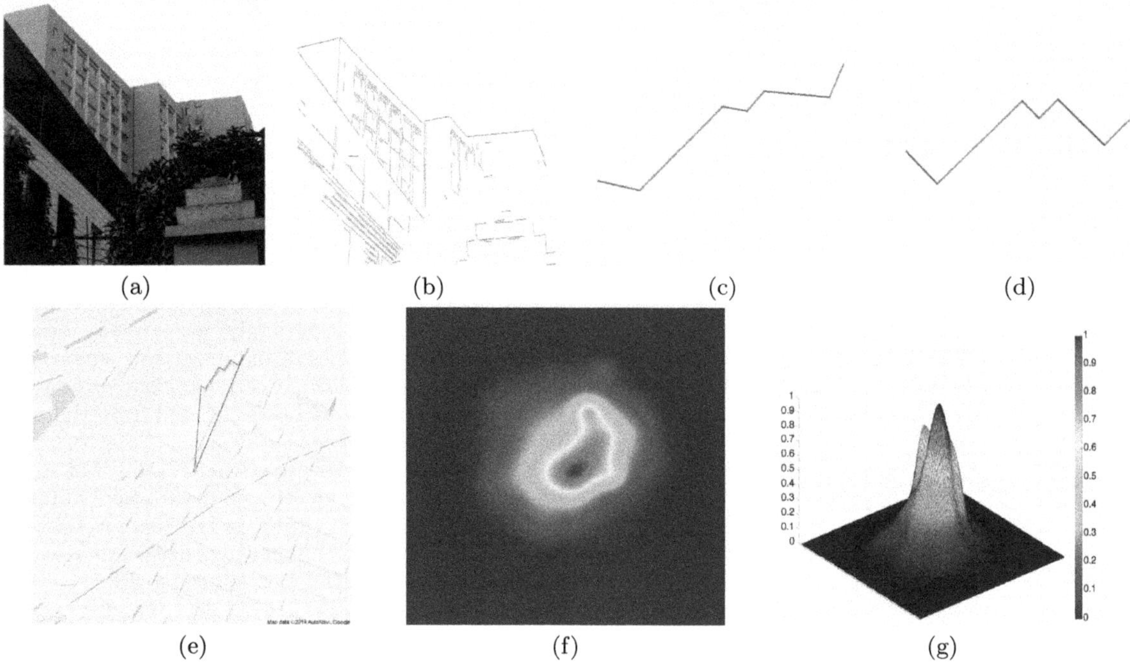

Figure 2: The intermediate results corresponding to each step of the pipeline: a) the captured image of a target building; b) the extracted line segments; c) the partial top view contour before angle adjusting; d) the final extracted partial top view contour; e) the local map provided by online maps service, whose center corresponds to GPS readings of smartphone; f) the color-mapped probability model based on KDE, presenting the probability distribution of estimated shooting position; g) the corresponding 3D view of the probability model based on KDE.

4.1 Partial Top View Extraction from a Single Image

On online maps, buildings are typically drawn in line segments of their top views. Therefore, matching buildings can be converted to the matching building's top view contours. However, in practice, users seldom take a photo from the top of a building, instead they take photos of the facades of a building. Hence, a critical problem is how to extract the top view contour from a side-view photo. We propose a novel approach in which one single image suffices to enable user-friendly and power-saving partial top view extraction on smartphones. These benefits come from the following observations in practical circumstances.

Vanishing Point Estimation: Since we are using the Manhattan World Assumption, we need to estimate the positions of three vanishing points before the contour extraction. Our method refers to a state-of-the-art technique proposed by Nieto and Salgado [11]. After obtaining three vanishing points, we group the input line segments based on their orientation towards three vanishing points. As a result, we can infer the geometrical relationships of these line segments. This is crucial for the following steps.

Estimation of the Smartphone Camera Parameters: We construct a camera matrix K that contains intrinsic and extrinsic camera parameters [5]. In this step we leave out skew parameters caused by the perspective transform.

Given the three vanishing points, we can compute a matrix Q, which equals KK^T [12], thus K can be computed from the Cholesky factorization of Q. The matrix K transforms a point from world space to perspective space. Hence, K^{-1} helps us convert the coordinate system of every 2D line in the perspective image space into world space.

Generating Top View Line Segments: In the context of SmartGuide, we introduce a simple and fast method for the extraction of partial top view contour. The rationale behind is twofold. Firstly, if a line segment is on the top view of a building, it must also lie on the upper part of the photo. Secondly, based on the Manhattan World Assumption, we know if one segment has directions different from its neighbor segments, the angles between them can only be $\pi/2$ or $-\pi/2$. Based on these observations we design the algorithm as follows:

1. Line segments are extracted from the photo with Line Segment Detector [24].

2. From the top of image, we find the highest segment of the building, using the first vertex as the root of the following procedures.

3. From the root we search for the segments next to it. For a vertex, we extract all the segments within its neighborhood. If the number of segments are below some expected threshold, we expand our searching

area. We then store the found segments into two bins according to their inclination to the vanishing points.

4. One or two new segments are created from the segments in the bins: the direction of a new segment is the averaged direction of the segments in one bin, and the length of that new segment is the maximal length of the segments in that bin.

5. The created segments are linked to the root. For each created segment, we treat its far end as the new root; repeat from Step 3 until no new segments are found around the root.

After this step, a linked-list of line segments is built. Then we demonstrate how to construct the partial top view contour from these selected line segments.

Each vertex in the linked-list and its two segment neighbors (or one for the last vertex) construct a hinge. From the Manhattan World Assumption we know the angle of each hinge can be either $\pi/2$ or $-\pi/2$, or 0. We use the following function to determine the angle ω_i of each hinge made from the i-th and $i+1$-th segments (the current angle is denoted as ϖ_i):

$$\omega_i = \begin{cases} \pi/2 & \text{if } v_i \neq v_{i+1}, |\varpi_i - \pi/2| < |\varpi_i + \pi/2| \\ -\pi/2 & \text{if } v_i \neq v_{i+1}, |\varpi_i - \pi/2| \geq |\varpi_i + \pi/2| \\ 0 & \text{if } v_i = v_{i+1} \end{cases}, \quad (3)$$

where v_i is the vanishing point to which the i-the segment points. For each hinge adjustment we calculate its corresponding rotation matrix R_i. Then we apply them onto each line segment, i.e., for the i-th segments, its rotation matrix is computed as $\prod_{k=0}^{i} R_{k,k+1}$.

4.2 Candidate Building Set Acquisition

SmartGuide relies on online map services for building identification. In this section, we explain in detail how SmartGuide acquires a candidate set of buildings from the commercial map service.

Local Map fetching: Once a user takes a photo of a target building, it automatically triggers the GPS to acquire the world coordinate of the user. Based on the world coordinate, SmartGuide fetches a Google Map image (containing the candidate buildings) where the user lies in the center via standard Google map API. Fig. 2e gives a concrete example of a Google map image.

Candidate Building Top View Detection: After downloading the static Google map, the next step is to extract the top view contour of each building on this static map. Here we adopt a state-of-the-art method [22] to extract the borders of each building on the map. Since the contours of most buildings on the map are geometric polygons, it is thus unnecessary to store all the coordinates along each straight line. Therefore we further apply the Ramer-Douglas-Peucker (RDP) algorithm [9] to remove redundant coordinates along a straight line. After this process, each contour is represented by a vector of corner points, which are arranged counter clockwise.

4.3 Candidate Building Features Selection

It is understandable that every building possesses a unique top view contour, orientation relative to the camera ray direction, and distance from the camera. Therefore, after acquiring the candidate building set from the Google Map image, the next step is to match the targeting building to its actual location by comparing top view contours, orientation, and distance from the camera.

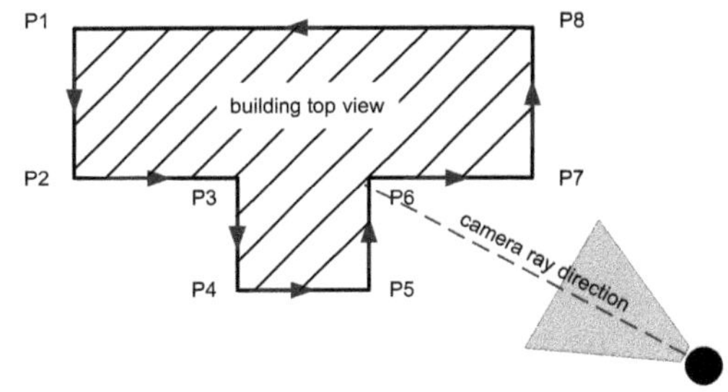

Figure 3: Only the part of building top view that faces the camera ray direction can be captured in photo.

Camera Direction Vector: In the standard sensor coordinate system of a smartphone, X and Y axes lie in the plane of the surface of the device and the Z axis points toward the outside of the screen face, so that the vector of camera ray direction is $(0, 0, -1)$. To obtain the camera direction in the world coordinate system (where X axis is tangential to the ground pointing East and Y axis is tangential to the ground pointing toward the geomagnetic North Pole), we need to learn the rotation matrix between the two coordinate systems. The rotation matrix can be inferred by fusing accelerometer and magnetometer data from the smartphone, which are used to find the orientation relative to the vector of gravity and the vector of north direction respectively. Given the rotation matrix R:

$$R = \begin{bmatrix} r_{00} & r_{01} & r_{02} \\ r_{10} & r_{11} & r_{12} \\ r_{20} & r_{21} & r_{22} \end{bmatrix}, \quad (4)$$

The camera ray direction in world coordinate system is calculated by $R(0, 0, -1)^T = (-r_{02}, -r_{12}, -r_{22})^T$. Thus vector $\vec{D} = (-r_{02}, -r_{12})$ represents the camera ray direction projected onto a horizontal plane, where the X axis points to the East and the Y axis points to the North.

Partial Top View Shape Feature Evaluation: We have extracted the partial top view of the target building and full top views of the candidate buildings in the previous sections. In order to evaluate candidate buildings' top view shapes, we should extract the part of candidate buildings' top view contours that are facing the camera ray direction. Fig. 3 illustrates such a case where the camera shoots the building from the front and only covers partial corner points $\langle \mathbf{p}_4, \mathbf{p}_5, \mathbf{p}_6, \mathbf{p}_7, \mathbf{p}_8 \rangle$.

For convenience we define the direction of our contour to be counter-clockwise. To detect the line segments that face the camera, we first determine whether a line segment is inward or outward by using the outer product between the camera ray direction $\vec{D}$ with the line segment: if the outer product between them is negative, they are in the opposite direction, otherwise they are in the same direction. Hence if the line segment is facing the camera we know the outer product between it and the camera direction should be negative.

More intuitively, in a sequence of segments which faces the camera, every segment should face the camera. Therefore, the outer product of camera ray direction $\vec{D}$ with the sequence of segments should be all negative. For instance, $\vec{D} \times \overrightarrow{\mathbf{p}_2\mathbf{p}_3} < 0$ but $\vec{D} \times \overrightarrow{\mathbf{p}_3\mathbf{p}_4} > 0$, thus contour $\langle \mathbf{p}_2, \mathbf{p}_3, \mathbf{p}_4 \rangle$ is not all facing to the camera.

However, one building can own several different visible partial contours that face the camera. For instance, visible corner points $\langle \mathbf{p}_4, \mathbf{p}_5, \mathbf{p}_6, \mathbf{p}_7, \mathbf{p}_8 \rangle$ can form 6 different contours, namely $\langle \mathbf{p}_4, \mathbf{p}_5, \mathbf{p}_6 \rangle$, $\langle \mathbf{p}_5, \mathbf{p}_6, \mathbf{p}_7 \rangle$, $\langle \mathbf{p}_6, \mathbf{p}_7, \mathbf{p}_8 \rangle$, $\langle \mathbf{p}_4, \mathbf{p}_5, \mathbf{p}_6, \mathbf{p}_7 \rangle$, $\langle \mathbf{p}_5, \mathbf{p}_6, \mathbf{p}_7, \mathbf{p}_8 \rangle$, and $\langle \mathbf{p}_4, \mathbf{p}_5, \mathbf{p}_6, \mathbf{p}_7, \mathbf{p}_8 \rangle$. Therefore, we need to find the one whose shape is the most similar with the partial top view contour extracted from photo.

Shape comparison should not be affected by translation, scaling and rotation, thus we adopt the aforementioned Hu's seven moment invariants and an empirical formulae to compare two contour shapes as following:

$$I(A, B) = \sum_{i=1...7} |m_i^A - m_i^B|, \tag{5}$$

where

$$m_i^A = sign(h_i^A) \cdot \log h_i^A, m_i^B = sign(h_i^B) \cdot \log h_i^B, \tag{6}$$

and h_i^A, h_i^B are the Hu moment invariants of contour A and B. The more similar A and B are, the smaller $I(A, B)$ is.

To conclude, we compare the shapes of all partial visible contours with the partial top view contours extracted from the photo, and assume that the most similar one, which owns the smallest difference, as actual part that have been captured into the camera. The specific details are presented in Algorithm 1. In other words, for a candidate building contour C_i, we can get the best matching partial contour $\tilde{C}_i$ in the photo and take its corresponding shape matching score as the candidate building shape score s_i. The better they match with each other, the lower s_i is.

Input: a candidate building contour $C_i = \langle \mathbf{p}_1, \mathbf{p}_2, ..., \mathbf{p}_{a_i} \rangle$, target building contour C, and camera ray direction $\vec{D}$
Output: partial visible contour $\tilde{C}_i$, s_i
float s_i = MAXVALUE;
for $m = 1; m \leq a_i; m++$ **do**
  if $\vec{D} \times \overrightarrow{\mathbf{p}_m\mathbf{p}_{m+1}} > 0$ **then**
    continue;
  end
  for $n = 2; n < a_i; n++$ **do**
    if $\vec{D} \times \overrightarrow{\mathbf{p}_{(m+n-1)\%a_i}\mathbf{p}_{(m+n)\%a_i}} > 0$ **then**
      break;
    end
    let $temptC = \langle \mathbf{p}_m, \mathbf{p}_{m+1}, ..., \mathbf{p}_{(m+n)\%a_i} \rangle$;
    if $I(\tilde{C}_i, C) < s_i$ **then**
      $s_i = I(\tilde{C}_i, C)$;
      $\tilde{C}_i = temptC$;
    end
  end
end
return $\tilde{C}_i$, s_i;

Algorithm 1: extractPartialVisibleContour

Building Orientation Feature Evaluation: Different buildings also own different orientations relative to the camera ray direction. Based on the camera ray direction and the positions of three vanishing points, which correspond to three orthogonal directions, from the photo, we can calculate the target building orientation in world coordinates. In addition, we can get each candidate building orientation from the Google Map. Therefore the orientation error δ_i between the i-th candidate building orientation and the target building orientation can be obtained.

Building Depth Feature: Given the camera parameters such as focal length F and CCD width W_{ccd}, physical building size c_m in meters computed from the map, and building size c_p in pixels in photo, we can estimate the averaged camera-to-building distance as following:

$$d = \frac{FW_p}{W_{ccd}} \cdot \frac{c_m}{c_p}, \tag{7}$$

where W_p is the width of the photo.

Therefore, given the location of candidate building on the map, the distance from camera to candidate building and the camera ray direction, we can infer the estimated shooting position (ESP) $\mathbf{e}_i$ of i-th candidate building.

4.4 Building Identification

Probability Model based on KDE: From the previous steps, we have obtained the shape matching score s_i, the building orientation error δ_i, and an estimated shooting position (ESP) $\mathbf{e}_i$ for the i-th candidate building. Given shooting position $\mathbf{o}$ estimated by GPS, a naive method is directly taking the i-th candidate building which owns the smallest distance from $\mathbf{e}_i$ to $\mathbf{o}$ as the target building. However, we know that $\mathbf{o}$ may not be accurate since there can be significant error in the GPS data. Moreover, since smartphone sensors are noisy, the camera ray direction inferred by accelerometer and magnetometer data also has random errors, which results in an inaccurate $\mathbf{e}_i$. In addition, the naive method does not take the shape matching score and the building orientation error into consideration. Hence, the result from this direct method can be problematic and unstable.

Since we do not know which building is captured in the photo, as well as the exact shooting position, we propose the probability distribution of the shooting position as the joint probability distribution of the probability distribution of all candidate buildings' shooting positions and the probability distribution of the GPS coordinate. First, we model the distribution of the i-th candidate building's shooting position as a normal distribution. The probability density function (PDF) at each pixel $\mathbf{x}$ is:

$$f_i(\mathbf{x}) = \frac{1}{\sqrt{2\pi}\sigma_i} e^{-\frac{\|\mathbf{x}-\mathbf{e}_i\|^2}{2\sigma_i^2}}, \tag{8}$$

where $\mathbf{e}_i$ is the ESP of i-th candidate building, σ_i is the standard deviation of the ESP, and $\|\cdot\|$ is the 2-norm distance.

The σ_i depends on the shape matching score s_i and the candidate building's orientation error δ_i. We observe that the higher s_i is and the higher δ_i is, the less possible the shooting position of i-th building concentrates on $\mathbf{e}_i$. Hence we model σ_i proportional to s_i. However, how to evaluate the candidate building's orientation error δ_i remains another issue.

The candidate building's orientation error δ_i is introduced by two parts: the actual orientation deviation between i-th candidate building's orientation and the target building's

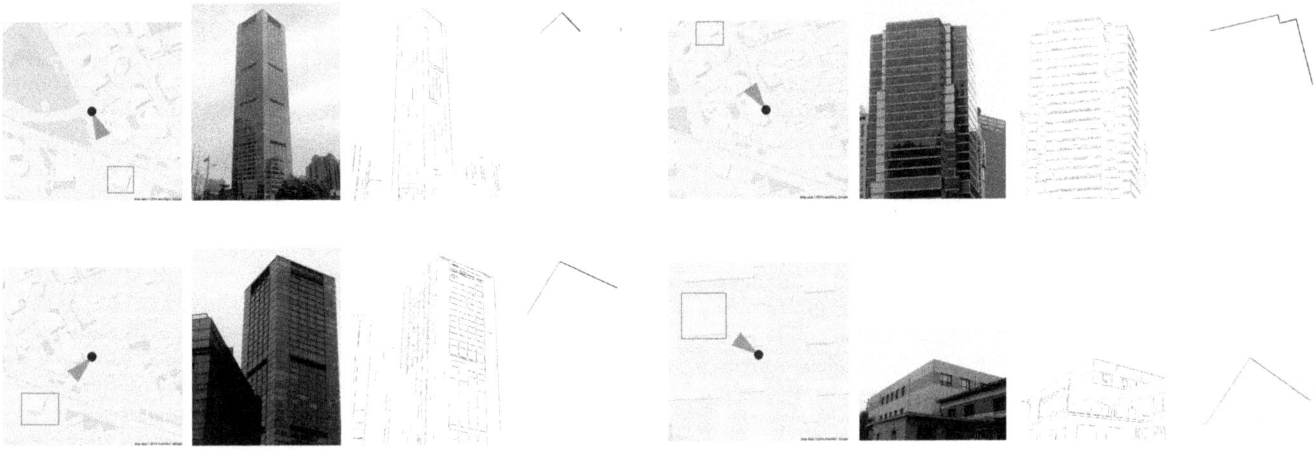

Figure 4: Partial Top View Extraction

orientation; the camera ray direction error caused by noisy smartphone's sensor data. To evaluate camera ray direction error, we captured photos of different buildings at different locations, and recorded the computed camera ray directions multiple times. Compared with the true direction, we observe that the distribution of the camera ray direction error follows a homogeneous normal distribution. Hence we compute a score α_i for the direction error as

$$\alpha_i = e^{-\frac{\delta_i^2}{\sigma_\delta^2}}, \tag{9}$$

where σ_δ is the standard deviation of camera ray direction. The less the orientation error δ_i is, the higher the score α_i is.

Therefore, we define σ_i is proportional to shape matching score s_i and inversely proportional to building orientation error score α_i:

$$\sigma_i = \frac{\epsilon s_i}{\alpha_i}. \tag{10}$$

where ϵ is a constant scaling coefficient.

Since the probability distributions of every candidate building's shooting position are mutually independent, the total probability density function (PDF) $\hat{f}$ can be estimated by using kernel density estimation (KDE), as following:

$$\hat{f}(\mathbf{x}) = \frac{1}{n}\sum_{i}^{n} f_i(\mathbf{x}) \tag{11}$$

There is another issue we should take into consideration: we have the GPS of smartphone, however, the distribution of GPS location is not perfectly Gaussian since it is determined by the shape and acceleration of satellites, as well as the atmosphere turbulence. Fortunately, its error can be estimated and bounded by a Gaussian distribution [6, 16]. In this way, the final probability distribution of the shooting position is the joint distribution of 1) the distribution of all candidate buildings' shooting positions, and 2) the distribution of GPS. Therefore, we modulate $\hat{f}(\mathbf{x})$ with a Gaussian distribution whose center is located at the captured GPS location:

$$\begin{aligned}\hat{f}_{final}(\mathbf{x}) &= \frac{1}{\sqrt{2\pi}\epsilon_G} e^{-\frac{\|\mathbf{x}-\mathbf{o}\|^2}{2\epsilon_G^2}} \hat{f}(\mathbf{x}) \\ &= \frac{1}{n\sqrt{2\pi}\epsilon_G} e^{-\frac{\|\mathbf{x}-\mathbf{o}\|^2}{2\epsilon_G^2}} \sum_{i}^{n} \frac{\alpha_i}{\sqrt{2\pi} s_i \epsilon} e^{-\frac{\alpha_i^2\|\mathbf{x}-\mathbf{e}_i\|^2}{2 s_i^2 \epsilon^2}},\end{aligned} \tag{12}$$

with GPS's standard deviation denoted as ϵ_G

According to Eqn. 12, we treat the location $\mathbf{x}$ which owns the highest $\hat{f}_{final}(\mathbf{x})$ as the most possible shooting position. Since we have obtained the shooting position and probability distribution of every candidate building's shooting position, the candidate building, whose probability distribution of shooting position contributes most probability value in Eqn. 11, is identified as the target building in photo.

5. SYSTEM EVALUATION

In this section, we present the experimental evaluation of SmartGuide from several aspects. First, we will introduce its implementation details.

5.1 Implementation

All the functional components of SmartGuide are implemented on the Android platform (version 4.4). We evaluate its performance on an LG Nexus5 with a 2.3GHz CPU and 2GB RAM. Nearly 9k lines of Java implementation is involved in the functional structure (Fig. 1). We adopt OpenCV for Android SDK (version 2.4.9) [1] to implement the contour detection and calculate Hu's invariant moments to match the top view shapes. Since we can expect the phone to be roughly static when the user is capturing photos, we use the immediate sensor output before the capturing to calculate the camera ray direction and GPS location.

To demonstrate the ubiquity of SmartGuide, over fifty locations across four cities (Beijing, Wuxi, Hong Kong, and Shanghai) were evaluated in total and the shooting distance spans from 20m to 520m. Moreover, we adopt various smartphones, including LG Nexus5, Samsung Galaxy Tab 10.1 and Samsung i9100, to collect building photos of different resolutions and qualities.

5.2 Evaluation

In the following, we first show the results of partial top view extraction with different buildings as input, and then verify the Gaussian distribution of the camera ray direction. Then we measure the overall identification accuracy and the time delay of SmartGuide.

Partial Top View Contour Extraction: Fig. 4 presents the results of partial top view extraction, whose inputs are four different buildings. The first three photos are captured in some downtown areas at a relatively remote distance $\approx$ 300 meters and the last photo is captured in a campus at close distance. For better presentation we also show their corresponding locations (marked by red rectangles) on the Google Map. The four buildings own different shapes and orientations (relative to the camera), which can be revealed in our results of partial top view extraction. Even though there are some trees or other buildings occluding the target building in the photo, our algorithm can still extract the correct partial top view contour of the building.

Camera Ray Direction PDF: To demonstrate that the probability distribution of the camera ray direction follows Gaussian distribution, we collected the camera ray direction data at different locations multiple times. The histogram of camera ray direction in Fig. 5 approximates the Gaussian distribution shape. Fig. 6 displays a quantile-quantile plot of the sample quantiles of camera ray direction versus theoretical quantiles from a normal distribution. If the distribution of camera ray direction is normal, the plot will be close to linear.

Accuracy of Building Identification: We tested SmartGuide at more than 50 locations across four cities. The closest and the farmost buildings we can identify are 20m away and 520m away respectively. The farmost distance of previous works on object localization without leveraging prepared image database is no more than 250m [10, 21]. This distance range is caused by two reasons. First, if the distance is too short, it is hard to include a whole building into one photo, which hinders the partial top view extraction. Also it is usually unnecessary to identify a building which is very close to the user's location. Next, the further the building, the less clear the photo is. When the image is blurry, the detection of line segments may be incorrect, which results in distorted top view extraction and exceptions in building identification.

The SmartGuide can achieve 92.7% accuracy in downtown areas where the Manhattan World Assumption is applicable. To evaluate SmartGuide's performance with varied photo qualities, we downsample full-resolution photos to different levels of resolution. Fig. 7 shows the accuracy of identification suffers when the levels of resolution are below 640×480. Moreover, we compare the accuracy of SmartGuide with the method that does not apply our probability model based on KDE but only the i-th candidate building which owns the smallest distance from the estimated shooting position $\mathbf{e}_i$ to the GPS measurement $\mathbf{o}$ as the target building. Fig. 7 demonstrates that the latter method performs much worse than SmartGuide.

In Fig. 8 we analyze SmartGuide's accuracy based on different distances of the buildings from the shooting place. The target buildings within 100 meters are all correctly mapped. Two buildings within 100-300 meters and two buildings within 300-500 meters are wrongly identified. Thus we can infer that near buildings are more likely to be identified correctly than remote buildings due to their higher sharpness and smaller candidate building set.

Time Delay: We analyze the time cost of three functional components: partial top view extraction from a single photo, feature selection of candidate buildings and building identification. We leave out the time cost of candidate building set acquisition since Google Map API limits the maximal map size to be 30KB, so that we can download the local google map synchronously while extracting target building top view to reduce the time cost.The time cost of partial top view extraction is influenced by the photo resolution. Since using 640×480 resolution can achieve the same performance as higher resolution, thus we resize every photo into 640×480 for the evaluation.

In the building identification phase, we use an image with the same size as the map to represent the final PDF. For each pixel we fill it with a probability value according to its world-space location. A naive solution to compute $\hat{f}_{final}(\mathbf{x})$ is gathering the PDF values computed from each building for each location $\mathbf{x}$ on the map, which can be very inefficient. However, we notice the probability where $\mathbf{x}$ is far from $\mathbf{e}_i$ is extremely low in practice. Hence we may approximate the result by ignoring the locations where $\|\mathbf{e}_i - \mathbf{x}\| > r$. In this way the performance can be largely improved since we only need to consider a small neighborhood around $\mathbf{e}_i$.

We ran SmartGuide 70 times and compare the time cost of different functional components in Fig. 9. It can be seen that the phase for partial top view extraction is the major factor influencing the total time consumption. The variation of the time cost for partial top view extraction is caused by the various line segment numbers detected in different photos. Besides, the time cost for feature selection is stable, and is small enough to be ignored. Furthermore, the time spent on location mapping is affected by the densities of buildings in the map. More buildings in a map take more time to calculate the probability distributions of candidate buildings' shooting positions.

Fig. 10 presents the cumulative distribution function of total time cost. It takes at most 9 seconds for SmartGuide to calculate the target building location after taking the photo, and in 87% cases it takes no more than 6 seconds to get the result. By providing this interactivity, SmartGuide is rather efficient compared with the most relevant previous image-based localization method, which requires 30 $\sim$ 60 seconds [10].

6. RELATED WORK

In this section, we broadly review two categories of research directly related to our work.

Image based localization: Many recent works leverage computer vision techniques (e.g., STERO and SfM) for object localization [4, 17, 10, 23, 31]. Sattler et al. [17] proposed an 2D-3D matching method for object localization. Such method relies on multiple photos of the targeting object with various shooting angles. In [23], Laere et al. used SIFT features to match a query image against a set of reference images with known GPS coordinates. In [20, 26], the true size of the target is needed to localize the remote target. OPS [10] is the most relevant work to us. It requires a user to shoot an object from multiple distinct views and then uses SfM technique to reconstruct the 3D model of this object on the cloud end. After the 3D reconstruction, the distance between the user and this object will be

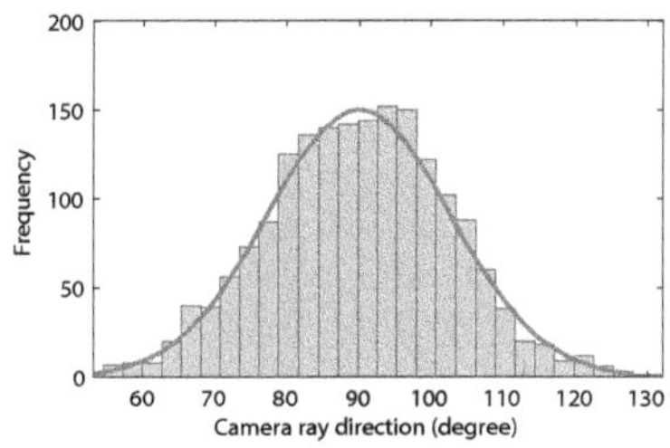

Figure 5: Camera Ray Direction PDF

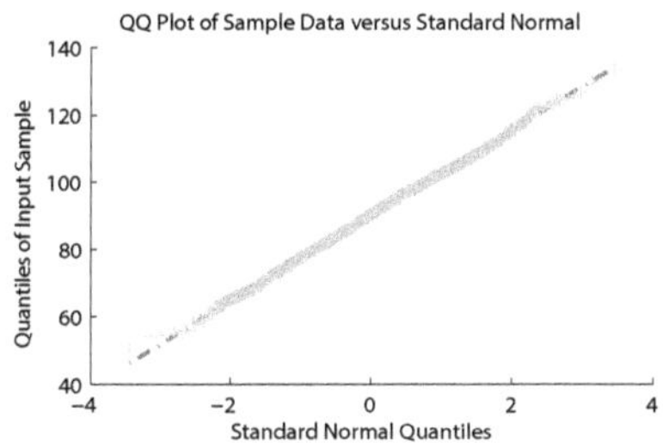

Figure 6: QQ-plot

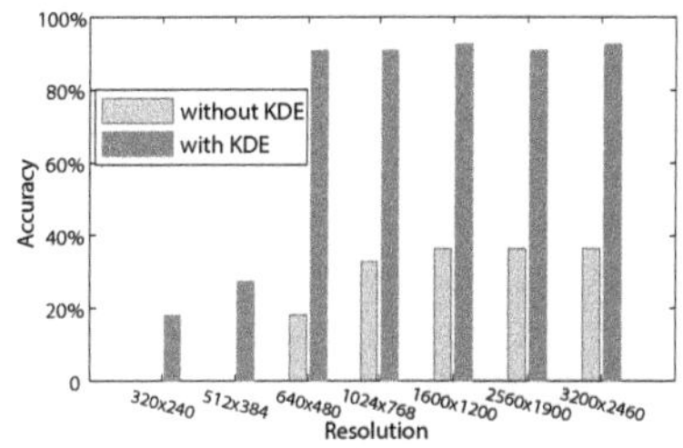

Figure 7: Accuracy of Building Identification

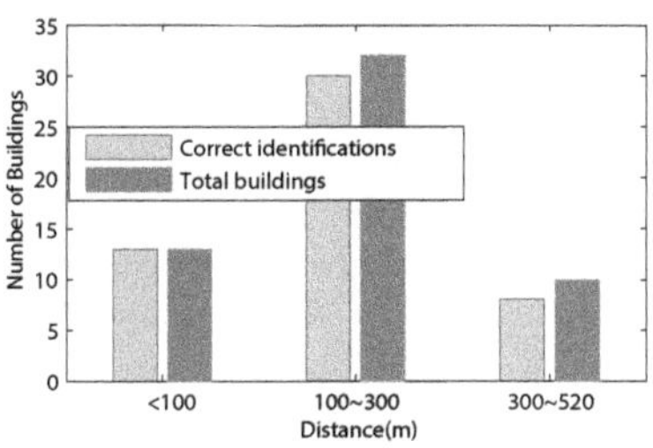

Figure 8: Accuracy vs. Distance

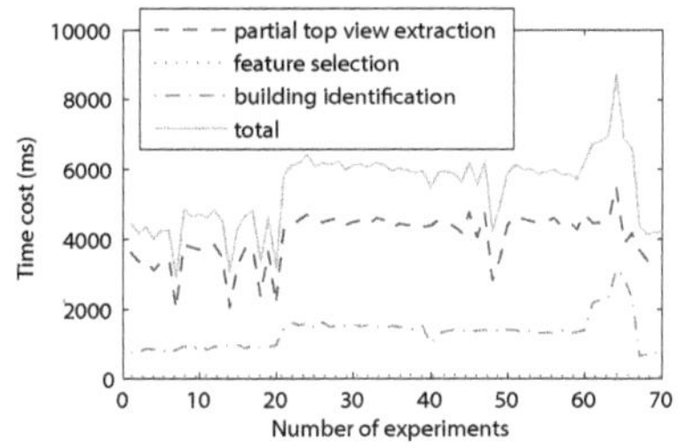

Figure 9: Time Cost of Functional Components

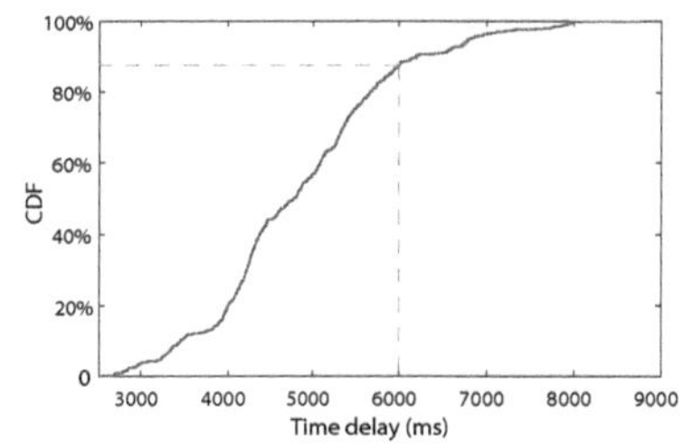

Figure 10: CDF of Time Cost

returned to the user end, based on which the user could locate the geo-location of this object. Different from this method, SmartGuide requires the user to shoot the target only once and can immediately know its exact location and semantic information without a prepared image database or knowledge of the size of the target.

Smartphone based localization: Recent advances in embedding sensors of smarthpones open new research opportunities for pervasive localization services [2, 19, 25, 28, 29, 30]. WILL [28] designed an indoor localization technique which leverages user mobility and WiFi signal profiles for room-level human localization. UnLoc [25] proposed an sensor-fusion based localization technique which localizes/tracks the user's location/trace while avoiding war-driving or fingerprints. Sen et al. [19] explored the frequency diversity of WiFi signals to characterize the fine-grained location of the user in an indoor environment. Escort [2] obtains cues from social encounters and leverages an audio beacon to guide the user to find a desired person. These systems mainly focus on how to identify the people's location, with the help of existing infrastructure such as WiFi access points and GSM towers. While our work addresses localizing the remote building with a smartphone in quick and responsive manner, which tackles with another branch of localization issues.

View Extraction from Single Image: The methods that reconstruct a specific view from a single photo have been widely studied. A branch of these methods use deep learning. Markov random field, trained via supervised learning, is used to infer the 3D location and 3D orientation of every patch [18]. Another branch closer to our method use vanishing points, orthogonal structure and linear programming to reconstruct the 3D arrangement of lines extracted from a single image [15]. However, previous methods either require a large database for deep learning, or demand for high computational costs, which are not quite suitable in our scenario.

7. CONCLUSION

In this paper, we introduced SmartGuide, a fast system for accurate building localization with smartphones. We experimented on using a single image to locate the building in the map without any prior knowledge, which provided promising results for future research. It still has several limitations: it inherits the limitations of other works based on the Manhattan World Assumption, and for very complicated building structures, it can hardly recover the partial top view accurately, which can significantly decrease the efficiency of our algorithm. However, as 3D online maps services become increasingly mature, the height of a building also can be take into consideration to improve localization accuracy, which can be an attractive research direction.

8. ACKNOWLEDGEMENTS

We would like to thank the anonymous reviewers for providing valuable comments. This work is supported in part by the NSFC Major Program 61190110, NSFC under Grant 61171067, 61332004, 61303209, NSFC Distinguished Young Scholars Program under Grant 61125202, and Beijing Nova Program.

9. REFERENCES

[1] Developers Android. Opencv, 2014. `http://opencv.org/platforms/android.html`.

[2] Ionut Constandache, Xuan Bao, Martin Azizyan, and Romit Roy Choudhury. Did you see bob?: human localization using mobile phones. In *Proceedings of the MobiCom 2010*, pages 149–160, 2010.

[3] James M Coughlan and Alan L Yuille. Manhattan world: Compass direction from a single image by bayesian inference. In *Proceedings of the ICCV 1999*, volume 2, pages 941–947, 1999.

[4] Gerald Friedland, Jaeyoung Choi, Howard Lei, and Adam Janin. Multimodal location estimation on flickr

videos. In *Proceedings of SIGMM 2011*, pages 23–28, 2011.

[5] Richard Hartley and Andrew Zisserman. *Multiple view geometry in computer vision.* Cambridge university press, 2003.

[6] Jeffrey Hightower and Gaetano Borriello. Location systems for ubiquitous computing. *Computer*, 34(8):57–66, 2001.

[7] Ming-Kuei Hu. Visual pattern recognition by moment invariants. *IRE Transactions on Information Theory*, 8(2):179–187, 1962.

[8] Zhihu Huang and Jinsong Leng. Analysis of hu's moment invariants on image scaling and rotation. In *Proceedings of the ICCET 2010*, volume 7, pages V7–476, 2010.

[9] David P Luebke. A developer's survey of polygonal simplification algorithms. *Computer Graphics and Applications*, 21(3):24–35, 2001.

[10] Justin Gregory Manweiler, Puneet Jain, and Romit Roy Choudhury. Satellites in our pockets: an object positioning system using smartphones. In *Proceedings of the MobiSys 2012*, pages 211–224, 2012.

[11] Marcos Nieto and Luis Salgado. Non-linear optimization for robust estimation of vanishing points. In *Proceedings of the ICIP 2010*, pages 1885–1888, 2010.

[12] Radu Orghidan, Joaquim Salvi, Mihaela Gordan, and Bogdan Orza. Camera calibration using two or three vanishing points. In *Proceedings of the FedCSIS 2012*, pages 123–130, 2012.

[13] Emanuel Parzen. On estimation of a probability density function and mode. *The annals of mathematical statistics*, pages 1065–1076, 1962.

[14] Arun Qamra and Edward Y Chang. Scalable landmark recognition using extent. *Multimedia tools and Applications*, 38(2):187–208, 2008.

[15] Srikumar Ramalingam and Matthew Brand. Lifting 3d manhattan lines from a single image. In *Proceedings of the ICCV 2013*, pages 497–504, 2013.

[16] Jason Rife, Sam Pullen, Boris Pervan, and Per Enge. Paired overbounding and application to gps augmentation. In *Proceedings of the PLANS 2004*, pages 439–446, 2004.

[17] Torsten Sattler, Bastian Leibe, and Leif Kobbelt. Fast image-based localization using direct 2d-to-3d matching. In *Proceedings of ICCV 2011*, pages 667–674, 2011.

[18] Ashutosh Saxena, Min Sun, and Andrew Y Ng. Make3d: Learning 3d scene structure from a single still image. *IEEE Transactions on Pattern Analysis and Machine Intelligence*, 31(5):824–840, 2009.

[19] Souvik Sen, Romit Roy Choudhury, Bozidar Radunovic, and Tom Minka. Precise indoor localization using phy layer information. In *Proceedings of the 10th ACM Workshop on Hot Topics in Networks*, page 18, 2011.

[20] Yi Shang, Wenjun Zeng, Dominic K Ho, Dan Wang, Qia Wang, Yue Wang, Tiancheng Zhuang, Aleksandre Lobzhanidze, and Liyang Rui. Nest: Networked smartphones for target localization. In *Consumer Communications and Networking Conference (CCNC), 2012 IEEE*, pages 732–736. IEEE, 2012.

[21] Longfei Shangguan, Zimu Zhou, Zheng Yang, Kebin Liu, Zhenjiang Li, Xibin Zhao, and Yunhao Liu. Towards accurate object localization with smartphones. *IEEE Transactions on Parallel and Distributed Systems*, 25(10):2731–2742, 2014.

[22] Satoshi Suzuki et al. Topological structural analysis of digitized binary images by border following. *Computer Vision, Graphics, and Image Processing*, 30(1):32–46, 1985.

[23] Olivier Van Laere, Steven Schockaert, and Bart Dhoedt. Finding locations of flickr resources using language models and similarity search. In *Proceedings of the ICMR 2011*, page 48, 2011.

[24] R Grompone Von Gioi, Jeremie Jakubowicz, Jean-Michel Morel, and Gregory Randall. Lsd: A fast line segment detector with a false detection control. *IEEE Transactions on Pattern Analysis and Machine Intelligence*, 32(4):722–732, 2010.

[25] He Wang, Souvik Sen, Ahmed Elgohary, Moustafa Farid, Moustafa Youssef, and Romit Roy Choudhury. No need to war-drive: unsupervised indoor localization. In *Proceedings of the MobiSys 2012*, pages 197–210, 2012.

[26] Qia Wang, Alex Lobzhanidze, Suman Deb Roy, Wenjun Zeng, and Yi Shang. Positionit: an image-based remote target localization system on smartphones. In *Proceedings of the 19th ACM international conference on Multimedia*, pages 821–822. ACM, 2011.

[27] Wikipedia. Pin hole camera model, 2008. `http://en.wikipedia.org/wiki/Pinhole_camera_model`.

[28] Chenshu Wu, Zheng Yang, Yunhao Liu, and Wei Xi. Will: Wireless indoor localization without site survey. *IEEE Transactions on Parallel and Distributed Systems*, 24(4):839–848, 2013.

[29] Zheng Yang, Chenshu Wu, and Yunhao Liu. Locating in fingerprint space: wireless indoor localization with little human intervention. In *Proceedings of the 18th annual international conference on Mobile computing and networking*, pages 269–280. ACM, 2012.

[30] Zheng Yang, Zimu Zhou, and Yunhao Liu. From rssi to csi: Indoor localization via channel response. *ACM Computing Surveys (CSUR)*, 46(2):25, 2013.

[31] Amir Roshan Zamir and Mubarak Shah. Accurate image localization based on google maps street view. In *Computer Vision–ECCV 2010*, pages 255–268. Springer, 2010.

Distributed Caching and Small Cell Cooperation for Fast Content Delivery

Weng Chon Ao
University of Southern California
wao@usc.edu

Konstantinos Psounis*
University of Southern California
kpsounis@usc.edu

ABSTRACT

Modern wireless devices such as tablets and smartphones are pushing the demand for higher and higher wireless data rates. The vast majority of this demand comes from media content. In this paper we propose to combine two recent ideas, distributed caching of content in small cells, and, cooperative transmissions from nearby base stations/BSs (generally known as coordinated multi-point), to achieve unprecedented content delivery speeds while reducing backhaul cost and delay. A key characteristic of our architecture is the interdependence between the caching strategy and the PHY/MAC layer coordination. Specifically, the caching strategy may cache different content in nearby BSs to maximize the hit ratio, or cache the same content in multiple nearby BSs such that the corresponding BSs can transmit concurrently, e.g. to multiple users using zero force beamforming, and achieve multiplexing gains. With this in mind, given the popularity distribution of the content, the available cache size, and the network topology, we devise optimal strategies of caching such that the throughput of the system is maximized. Our analytical and simulation results show that our system yields significantly faster content delivery, which, under realistic scenarios and assumptions can be one order of magnitude faster than that of legacy systems.

Categories and Subject Descriptors

C.2 [**Computer-Communication Networks**]: Wireless Communication

General Terms

Performance, Theory

Keywords

Heterogeneous cellular networks, Caching, Coordinated Multi-Point, Multi-user MIMO, Diversity, Multiplexing

*This work was supported by NSF grant ECCS-1444060.

MobiHoc'15, June 22–25, 2015, Hangzhou, China.

http://dx.doi.org/10.1145/2746285.2746300.

1. INTRODUCTION

The proliferation of advanced mobile devices such as smart phones and tablets together with the popularity of video streaming are causing a tremendous growth of data traffic in cellular networks. To address this challenge the cellular industry is advocating the deployment of small cells (via the use of low power nodes like micro-BSs, pico-BSs and femto-BSs) together with traditional macro-BSs in a heterogeneous networking architecture [6,10]. These low power nodes provide short-range localized communication links resulting in a higher density of spatial reuse of radio recourses and thus in higher overall network throughput.

Deploying a dense network of low power nodes comes with its own challenges. One such challenge that service providers consistently rank high is the deployment cost associated with connecting all the small cells to the backbone with fast links. Motivated by this, there is a growing interest to cache popular content to those low power nodes in a distributed manner, effectively trading off fast backhaul capacity with storage capacity. Specifically, the authors in [12, 13, 24] have introduced the concept of FemtoCaching, which is the idea of embedding femto-BSs with high storage capacity to store popular video files. When a user requests a video file, the user may be served by a nearby femto-BS that has the requested file in its cache over a high rate short-range wireless link. If the requested file is not in the cache of any nearby femto-BS, the user will be served directly by the macro-BS over a low rate long-range wireless link. Since the popularity distribution of video files changes at a much slower pace than that of user requests, cache updates (downloading popular video files via backhaul into the caches) can be done at off-peak hours, which results in a significant reduction of backhaul cost and delay while maintaining the performance benefits of a dense deployment of low power BSs.

A dense deployment of low power BSs yields even higher throughput when multiple neighboring BSs coordinate their data transmissions such that they aggregate constructively, see, for example, two recent tutorial-style papers [16, 18] and [2,3,23] where real-world testbeds have been created and tested using software defined radios. As a matter of fact, in the absence of such BS coordination, interference between nearby BSs may cancel the performance gains of dense deployments, and service providers consistently rank the technological challenges related to this issue as yet another major challenge in the deployment of small cells. There are many schemes for BS coordination, and in this paper we will consider the two most basic/popular ones: Maximum Ratio Transmission (MRT) and Zero-Forcing BeamForming

(ZFBF) [25]. Consider that low power BSs form cooperation clusters. Then, under MRT, each BS in the cooperation cluster beamforms to a user such that the signals from the neighboring BSs are coherently combined resulting in a diversity gain [4]. Under ZFBF, the BSs in the cluster are simultaneously transmitting multiple data streams to multiple users [3,9], resulting in a multiplexing gain. Note that in the absence of offline cache updates, both MRT and ZFBF would further increase the cost and delay associated with backhaul, as they require multiple copies of the same files to be distributed to multiple BSs.

In this paper, we propose to combine FemtoCaching and femto-BS cooperation. The proposed cooperation scheme is cache/data-driven in the sense that if a typical user makes a request of a video file, only the neighboring femto-BSs that have the requested video file in their caches will participate in the cooperative transmission. In other words, the cluster of cooperating femto-BSs is dynamically formed on a per-request basis. An important aspect of our framework is the joint optimization of the cache allocation (content placement) in the application layer and the cooperative transmission techniques (MRT for diversity and ZFBF for multiplexing) in the physical layer. We jointly optimize these aspects of the system because caching different content in nearby caches increases hit ratio, but caching the same content increases the chances to get diversity and multiplexing gains. In general, the optimal cache allocation depends on a number of parameters, including the file popularity distribution, the cache size, the number of neighboring femto-BSs, and the transmission rate of the macro-BS in comparison to that of a femto-BS.

The remainder of this paper is organized as follows. We present related work in Section 2. Section 3 describes the setup, the caching strategies, and the cache-driven cooperation policies. In Section 4 we derive analytical formulas for the achieved rates under a variety of scenarios considering both background noise and co-channel interference. In Section 5 we present numerical results for a number of real-world scenarios, highlighting the rate gains from our framework. Notably, our schemes can increase the speed of content delivery by an order of magnitude without requiring fast backhaul speeds. Last, Section 6 discusses practical considerations and Section 7 concludes the paper.

2. PRIOR WORK AND CONTRIBUTIONS

This work touches upon a number of prior lines of work. The setup is that of heterogeneous networks, formed by distributing multi-tier low power nodes (e.g., micro-BSs and femto-BSs) in macro-cellular networks, see, for example, two recent tutorial-style papers and references therein [6, 10]. It is building upon prior work on BS cooperation, more generally known as Coordinated Multi-Point (CoMP), and FemtoCaching. There is a long line of research in CoMP, see, for example, [16, 18]. FemtoCaching has been recently introduced to trade off backhaul capacity with cache capacity [12, 13, 24] and can be further applied to device-to-device communication networks [11,17] and to coded caching [21, 22]. FemtoCaching itself is building up upon prior work on distributed caching, content placement schemes and content distribution networks, see, for example, [5].

In addition to using standard analytical tools like convex and integer optimization, combinatorics, and Shannon rate formulas, we also use stochastic geometry [14] to take into account co-channel interference in the context of heterogeneous networks, see, for example, the relevant analysis in [7].

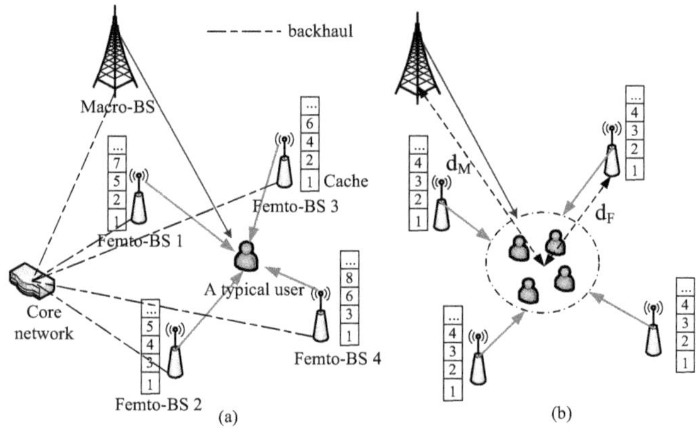

Figure 1: System model for cache-driven femto-BS cooperation: (a) randomized caching and MRT (b) threshold-based caching and ZFBF.

Directly related to this work is [19, 20] where the authors use a coding scheme to introduce redundancy in caches and create CoMP opportunities for cooperative transmissions. A fundamental difference between this prior work and our paper is that we consider the effect of cache misses, since any type of redundancy decreases the number of distinct files that can be stored in finite size caches. To optimize the system performance, we appropriately control the stored redundancy for each individual file and dynamically (per-request basis) form a cluster of cooperating femto-BSs.

Our contributions are as follows: We combine the concepts of FemtoCaching and BS cooperation to propose a novel, high-performing system architecture. We derive analytical expressions for the user rates and jointly optimize the caching strategy and the PHY layer cooperation. We devise efficient caching strategies for providing diversity gains under MRT, multiplexing gains under ZFBF, and the optimal diversity-multiplexing tradeoff. Last, we study the performance of our schemes under practical scenarios and address deployment considerations.

3. SYSTEM MODEL

3.1 Topology

Consider a typical user in a macrocell. Suppose there are N femto-BSs and another $K-1$ users in the neighborhood of the typical user. We denote by $d_{0,k}$, $1 \leq k \leq K$, and $d_{j,k}$, $1 \leq j \leq N$, $1 \leq k \leq K$, the distance between the macro-BS and the kth user, and the jth femto-BS and the kth user respectively. Let these K co-located users be associated with the same N neighboring femto-BSs and the macro-BS. These N neighboring femto-BSs are candidates for cooperative transmissions, see Fig. 1a for a scenario where femto-BSs transmit the same content (say, file 1) to one user, and Fig. 1b for a scenario where femto-BSs transmit concurrently to multiple users (say, to four users four different files, namely file 1, 2, 3, and 4).

In a typical real-world scenario one may have tens or hundreds of femto-BSs inside a macrocell and hundreds or thousands of users. Thus, femto-BSs would be grouped into clusters of nearby femto-BSs which can concurrently serve a number of users. For example, one may have one such clus-

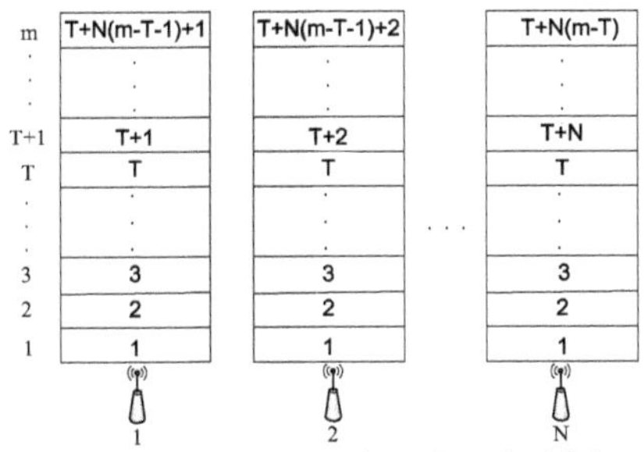

Figure 2: Caching strategy under threshold-based caching and ZFBF.

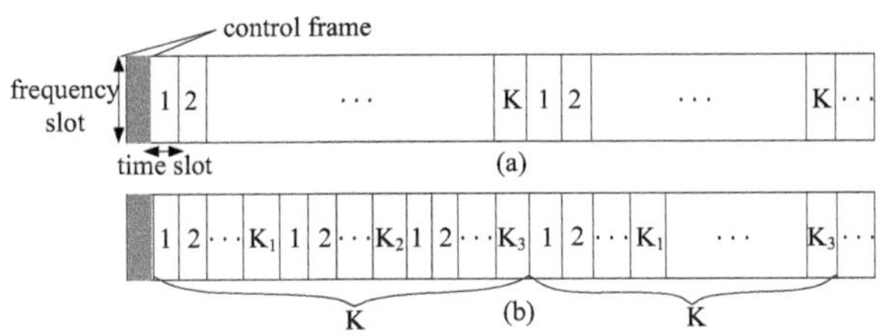

Figure 3: Control and data frames under (a) randomized caching and MRT, (b) threshold-based caching and ZFBF.

ter per floor on a large building or one cluster per building. In the rest of this paper we will focus on one such cluster of co-located femto-BSs and users.

In general, the users, the macro-BS, and the femto-BSs would be assigned different time-frequency slots (resource blocks) for data transmissions. We will only focus on the downlink, and thus on transmissions towards the K users. Also, for simplicity and without loss of generality, we will focus on a single frequency slot which the macro-BS and the femto-BSs may use to transmit to the users. In some of the physical layer schemes that we study, one time slot can be used for a single user only, e.g. MRT, while in others it can be used for multiple users concurrently, e.g. ZFBF. Depending on whether a user is served by the macro-BS, a single femto-BS, or multiple femto-BSs using MRT or ZFBF, the data rate that it will receive during this time slot will vary. Last, a control frame will be used to collect requests from the users at the macro-BS, and then the users will be served in subsequent time slots (see Fig. 3). Since a request for a media file corresponds to multiple data packets, such control frames will be infrequent.

3.2 Caching Strategies and Cache-driven Cooperation policies

Suppose that there is a library of M video files which are ordered according to their (normalized) popularity p_i, $1 \leq i \leq M$, $p_1 \geq p_2 \geq \cdots \geq p_M$, $\sum_{i=1}^{M} p_i = 1$. In other words, a typical user would request the ith file with probability p_i. The macro-BS stores (or has access to) all of the M files, while each femto-BS has a cache that can store on average up to m files with $m < M$. We have the following two different caching and cooperation strategies aiming at providing diversity gain and multiplexing gain.

3.2.1 *Providing a diversity gain by randomized caching and MRT*

For each femto-BS the caching strategy caches the ith file with probability q_i, $0 \leq q_i \leq 1$, $i = 1, \cdots, M$, subject to the probabilistic cache size constraint $\sum_{i=1}^{M} q_i \leq m$. (To simplify the analytical exposition and without loss of generality, here we have assumed that all files have the same size, the unit of storage/size is a file, and the average cache size is m.) Note that q_i, $i = 1, \cdots, M$ are design parameters.

Then, the cooperation policy dictates that for a request of the ith file, generated by a typical user according to the popularity distribution law p_i, the request will be jointly served by the femto-BSs that have the requested file in their caches. Thus, no data file exchanges are needed for the cooperation.[1] Under MRT, each femto-BS that has the requested file in its cache beamforms its signal to the typical user so that the signals (from the cooperating femto-BSs) are coherently combined at the receiver, producing a diversity gain for the desired signal. If none of the femto-BSs have the requested file, the request will be served by the macro-BS. For example, in Fig. 1a, if a user requests the 2nd file, then femto-BSs 1 and 3 will beamform to the user. Fig. 3a shows a typical sequence of time slots under MRT, where each of the K users receives its data at one of K time slots.

3.2.2 *Providing a multiplexing gain by threshold-based caching and ZFBF*

Aiming at providing multiplexing gain we consider the following caching strategy. We first choose a threshold T, where $0 \leq T \leq m$, which is a design parameter (we will generalize to the case with multiple thresholds in Section 4.3). We cache the files 1 to T in all of the femto-BSs, and cache the files $T+1$ to $T+N(m-T)$ in exactly one of the femto-BSs. That is, we have N copies for each of the most popular files 1 to T, one copy of the files $T+1$ to $T+N(m-T)$, and the remaining files $T+N(m-T)+1$ to M can be downloaded only by the macro-BS (see Fig. 2).

We associate the K users with K different time slots as in Fig. 3b. The K users can be partitioned into three groups according to their requests: The first group consists of users with requests of files between 1 and T, i.e., for files that are cached in all femto-BSs (the group size is denoted as K_1), the second group consists of users with requests of files between $T+1$ and $T+N(m-T)$, i.e., for files that are cached in only one femto-BS (the group size is K_2), and the third group consists of users with requests of files between $T+N(m-T)+1$ and M, i.e., for files that can be fetched only by the macro-BS (the group size is $K_3 = K - K_1 - K_2$). Since all the femto-BSs cache the files requested by users of the first group, the N femto-BSs can coordinate their transmissions when serving these K_1 users. Specifically, the N femto-BSs can simultaneously serve these K_1 users ($K_1 \leq N$) during K_1 time slots using ZFBF producing a multiplexing gain of order K_1.[2] No cooperative transmission is used for serving a user of the second (third) group because only a single femto-BS (the macro-BS) has the user's requested file. Note that if one desires all users to receive similar rates, one may assign less than K_1 slots to the users of the first group, e.g. one may simply assign a single slot. Our analysis in the next section can be easily extended to model any desirable

[1] Note that control signals such as channel state information may be required to be distributed among the femto-BSs in the cooperation cluster.

[2] By using ZFBF, suppose there are N transmitters and K receivers ($K \leq N$), the N transmitters can transmit K independent (non-interfering or spatially isolated) streams to the K receivers simultaneously, each with a diversity of order 1.

Table 1: Main notation

Number of femto-BSs	N
Distance between a typical user and a macro(femto)BS	d_M (d_F)
Number of video files	M
Cache size in a femto-BS	m
Number of users	K
File popularity distribution	p_i (cdf v_i)
Probability of caching the ith file for MRT	q_i
Caching threshold for ZFBF	T
Bandwidth of a frequency slot	W
Transmit power of macro(femto)-BS	P_M (P_F)
Data rate of macro(femto)-BS	R_M (R_F)
Effective data rate of macro(femto)-BS	$\tilde{R}_M$ ($\tilde{R}_F/\tilde{R}_F^{(j)}$)
Path loss exponent	α
Noise power spectral density	N_0
Density of interfering macro(femto)-BSs	λ_M (λ_F)
Average effective data rate with MRT(ZFBF)	R_{MRT} (R_{ZFBF})
Average effective data rate with MRT–ZFBF	$R_{\text{MRT-ZFBF}}$

fairness among users and the associated user scheduling in different time slots.

4. PERFORMANCE ANALYSIS

For simplicity, we assume that the distances between the co-located users and the N neighboring femto-BSs (the macro-BS) are the same, i.e., $d_{j,k} \triangleq d_F$ ($d_{0,k} \triangleq d_M$), see Fig. 1b for a pictorial representation. Also, we assume that the macro-BS, the femto-BSs, and the users are all equipped with a single antenna, and we consider quasi-static Rayleigh flat-fading channels with unit mean power. We denote the transmit power of a macro-BS and a femto-BS by P_M and P_F, and the data rates of a macro-BS and a femto-BS by R_M and R_F. The bandwidth of the frequency slot is denoted by W, the path loss exponent by α, and the noise power spectral density by N_0.

To simplify the notation in the following derivations, we also define the effective data rate as the data rate multiplied by the non-outage (transmission success) probability (i.e., the probability that the channel can support the data rate [25]). Thus, for a macro-BS the effective data rate equals $\tilde{R}_M \triangleq R_M \cdot \Pr(W\log(1+\frac{P_M S_{\Gamma(1)} d_M^{-\alpha}}{N_0 W}) > R_M)$ and for a femto-BS cluster with a diversity of order j it equals $\tilde{R}_F^{(j)} \triangleq R_F \cdot \Pr(W\log(1+\frac{P_F S_{\Gamma(j)} d_F^{-\alpha}}{N_0 W}) > R_F)$, where $S_{\Gamma(1)}$ is an exponential random variable with unit mean (Rayleigh fading), and $S_{\Gamma(j)}$ is the sum of j i.i.d. exponential random variables with unit mean due to the coherent combining of the signals from j femto-BSs. Note that for further simplicity, when $j=1$ we denote $\tilde{R}_F^{(j)}$ as $\tilde{R}_F$. Table 1 summarizes the main notation used in the paper.

In the following, convex optimization is used in the performance analysis of randomized caching and MRT, while integer optimization is used in the performance analysis of threshold-based caching and ZFBF. Also, in Sections 4.1-4.4, we consider background noise without co-channel interference, and Section 4.5 extends the results in the presence of co-channel interference.

4.1 Randomized caching and MRT

We aim to maximize the average effective data rate of a typical user (denoted as R_{MRT}) with respect to the randomized caching parameters subject to the cache size constraint. We have the following optimization problem:

$$\max_{q_1,\cdots,q_M} \sum_{i=1}^{M} p_i U(q_i) \triangleq R_{\text{MRT}}$$
$$\text{subject to } 0 \le q_i \le 1,\ \forall i = 1,\cdots,M$$
$$\sum_{i=1}^{M} q_i \le m,$$

where p_i is the file popularity distribution (i.e., the probability that the typical user requests the ith file), q_i is the probability that the ith file is cached in a femto-BS and $U(q_i)$ is the effective data rate for the transmission of the ith file. (See Section 3.2.1 for a detailed description of the caching strategy.) Since we have N femto-BSs, the number of copies of the ith file in the femto-BSs is a binomial random variable with mean Nq_i. Thus, the number of cooperating femto-BSs for the transmission of the ith file (denoted as C_i) follows the law

$$\Pr(C_i = j) = \binom{N}{j} q_i^j (1-q_i)^{N-j},\ j = 0, 1, \cdots, N.$$

The effective data rate for the transmission of the ith file, $U(q_i)$, can be computed as

$$U(q_i) = \Pr(C_i = 0) R_M \Pr(\text{transmission success with macro-BS})$$
$$+ \sum_{j=1}^{N} \Pr(C_i = j) R_F \Pr(\text{trans. success with } j \text{ femto-BSs jointly})$$
$$= (1-q_i)^N \tilde{R}_M + \sum_{j=1}^{N} \binom{N}{j} q_i^j (1-q_i)^{N-j} \tilde{R}_F^{(j)}. \qquad (1)$$

Since we have assumed Rayleigh fading, we can rewrite the effective data rates as $\tilde{R}_M = R_M e^{-\eta_M}$ and $\tilde{R}_F = R_F e^{-\eta_F}$ where $\eta_M = (2^{R_M/W}-1) N_0 W d_M^{\alpha}/P_M$ and $\eta_F = (2^{R_F/W} - 1) N_0 W d_F^{\alpha}/P_F$. We have the following theorem.

THEOREM 1. *If $R_M e^{-\eta_M} \le R_F e^{-\eta_F}(1-\eta_F)$, then $U(q_i)$ is concave and thus $R_{MRT}(q_1,\cdots,q_M)$ is concave in the domain $0 \le q_i \le 1$, $i = 1,\cdots,M$.*

PROOF. The proof is provided in the Appendix. □

The condition $R_M e^{-\eta_M} \le R_F e^{-\eta_F}(1-\eta_F)$ implies that the marginal rate gain of including one more femto-BS into the cluster to perform cooperative transmission is decreasing and is smaller than the marginal gain of using a femto-BS instead of the macro-BS (see the appendix for a detailed discussion). These conditions usually hold in practice[3].

For the maximization problem with concave objective and linear constraints, we can find the optimal q_i^* by the KKT conditions. We have:

$$q_i^* = \left[U'^{-1}\left(\frac{\lambda}{p_i}\right)\right]_0^1,\ i = 1,\cdots,M;\ \sum_{i=1}^{M} q_i^* = m, \qquad (2)$$

where λ is the Lagrange multiplier, $U'^{-1}(\cdot)$ is the inverse function of $U'(\cdot)$, which exists since $U'(\cdot)$ is monotonic (see Lemma 1 in the Appendix), and $[x]_0^1 \triangleq \min(\max(0,x),1)$. We also note that $U'^{-1}(\cdot)$ is a decreasing function. So, q_i^* increases as p_i increases, i.e., we have a higher probability to cache a more popular file, which makes sense intuitively.

[3]When these assumptions do not hold, one can still solve the optimization problem using non-convex optimization techniques.

4.2 Threshold-based caching and ZFBF

Here we aim to maximize the average effective data rate of the K users (denoted as $R_{\mathrm{ZFBF}}(T)$), where T is the caching threshold in the threshold-based caching and ZFBF. To keep the exposition simple, we start by assuming that the number of users K is smaller than the number of femto-BSs N ($K \le N$). We extend the analysis to the practical case with $K > N$ in the end of the section. Last, we define the cdf of the file popularity distribution as $v_j = \sum_{i=1}^{j} p_i$, $j = 1, \cdots, M$.

Since each of the K users generates a request in an i.i.d. manner, a user would be in the first group, the second group, and the third group with probability v_T, $v_{T+N(m-T)} - v_T$, and $1 - v_{T+N(m-T)}$, respectively. (See Section 3.2.2 for the definition of these three groups.) So, the probability that there are $K_1 = i$ users in the first group, $K_2 = j$ users in the second group, and $K_3 = K - K_1 - K_2 = K - i - j$ users in the third group is $\frac{K!}{i!j!(K-i-j)!} v_T^i (v_{T+N(m-T)} - v_T)^j (1 - v_{T+N(m-T)})^{K-i-j}$.

As shown in Fig. 3b, we associate the K users with K different time slots. The requested file of a user of the third group (with group size $K_3 = K - i - j$) only appears in the macro-BS and it is served by the macro-BS with rate $\tilde{R}_M$ in this user's dedicated time slot. The resulting group sum rate is $(K - i - j)\tilde{R}_M$. For a user of the second group (with group size $K_2 = j$), its requested file only appears in a single femto-BS and it is served by that femto-BS with rate $\tilde{R}_F$ in this user's dedicated time slot. Thus, the resulting group sum rate is $j\tilde{R}_F$. For each user of the first group (with group size $K_1 = i$), its requested file appears in all N femto-BSs. By using ZFBF we create i spatially isolated channels (i.e., all i users can be served simultaneously with rate $\tilde{R}_F$ without seeing interference from each other), achieving a multiplexing gain of order i. Simultaneous transmissions can occur in their i dedicated time slots, so each user of the first group achieves an i-fold increase in rate, $i\tilde{R}_F$. The resulting group sum rate is $i \cdot i\tilde{R}_F$.

The average effective data rate $R_{\mathrm{ZFBF}}(T)$ of the K users in the three groups can be computed as

$$\begin{aligned} R_{\mathrm{ZFBF}}(T) &= \frac{1}{K}\Bigg\{\sum_{i=0}^{K}\sum_{j=0}^{K-i} \frac{K!}{i!j!(K-i-j)!} \\ &\cdot v_T^i (v_{T+N(m-T)} - v_T)^j (1 - v_{T+N(m-T)})^{K-i-j} \\ &\cdot \Big[i \cdot i\tilde{R}_F + j\tilde{R}_F + (K-i-j)\tilde{R}_M\Big]\Bigg\} \\ &= \frac{1}{K}\Big\{(\mathbb{E}[K_1^2] + \mathbb{E}[K_2])\tilde{R}_F + \mathbb{E}[K_3]\tilde{R}_M\Big\} \qquad (3) \\ &= [v_{T+N(m-T)} + (K-1)v_T^2]\tilde{R}_F + (1 - v_{T+N(m-T)})\tilde{R}_M. \end{aligned}$$

Note that with the averaging $\frac{1}{K}\{\cdot\}$ in R_{ZFBF}, both R_{ZFBF} and R_{MRT} are consistently defined with respect to a unit time slot. We can find the optimal caching threshold T^* by enumeration of the solution space $T = 0, 1, \cdots, m$, which is linear in the cache size m and thus easy to compute in practice. Fig. 6 in Section 5 shows the resulting data rate under various threshold values for practical scenarios.

Example: We consider two special cases.

- When $T = m$, we cache the most popular m files in all N femto-BSs and we have $R_{\mathrm{ZFBF}}(m) = [v_m + (K-1)v_m^2]\tilde{R}_F + (1 - v_m)\tilde{R}_M$. If $v_m \approx 1$, that is, we almost always request one of the m most popular files, we have $R_{\mathrm{ZFBF}}(m) \approx K\tilde{R}_F$.
- When $T = 0$, we cache only one copy of the most popular Nm files in femto-BSs and we have $R_{\mathrm{ZFBF}}(0) = v_{Nm}\tilde{R}_F + (1 - v_{Nm})\tilde{R}_M$. If $v_{Nm} \approx 1$, we have $R_{\mathrm{ZFBF}}(0) \approx \tilde{R}_F$.
- We can see that for very skewed popularity distribution satisfying $v_m \approx 1$, the rate R_{ZFBF} with threshold $T = m$ is K times higher than that with threshold $T = 0$, where K is the maximum multiplexing gain.

We now discuss how to extend the above results for the case where the number of users K is larger than the number of femto-BSs N. When $K > N$ and there are $K_1 = i > N$ users in the first group, the maximum multiplexing gain that can be achieved in a time slot is N, limited by the number of neighboring femto-BSs. It is easy to see that with time sharing between $\binom{i}{N}$ subsets of users of the first group (i.e., we arbitrarily choose N users out of i users to form a subset and a time slot is divided for analytical purposes into $\binom{i}{N}$ sub-slots to time share between the $\binom{i}{N}$ subsets), each user would be served with rate $\binom{i-1}{N-1}\tilde{R}_F / \binom{i}{N}$ in a time slot (since a user belongs to exactly $\binom{i-1}{N-1}$ subsets). Simultaneous transmissions with ZFBF can occur in total $K_1 = i$ dedicated time slots, so each user of the first group achieves the rate $i\binom{i-1}{N-1}\tilde{R}_F / \binom{i}{N} = N\tilde{R}_F$. The resulting group sum rate is $i \cdot N\tilde{R}_F$. The average effective data rate can be written as

$$\begin{aligned} R_{\mathrm{ZFBF}}(T) &= \frac{1}{K}\sum_{i=0}^{K}\sum_{j=0}^{K-i} \frac{K!}{i!j!(K-i-j)!} \\ &\cdot v_T^i (v_{T+N(m-T)} - v_T)^j (1 - v_{T+N(m-T)})^{K-i-j} \\ &\cdot \Big[i \cdot \min\{i, N\}\tilde{R}_F + j\tilde{R}_F + (K-i-j)\tilde{R}_M\Big]. \end{aligned}$$

Remark: It is evident that there is a tradeoff associated with the value of the design parameter T. When T is large, we benefit from the multiplexing gain but more redundant files are held in the caches, resulting in an increasing amount of requests towards the low-rate macro-BS (cache misses). When T is small, we lose the multiplexing gain but most of the files are in the caches of the femto-BSs, generating fewer requests towards the macro-BS. The optimal choice of T depends on the file popularity distribution.

4.3 Multiple thresholds

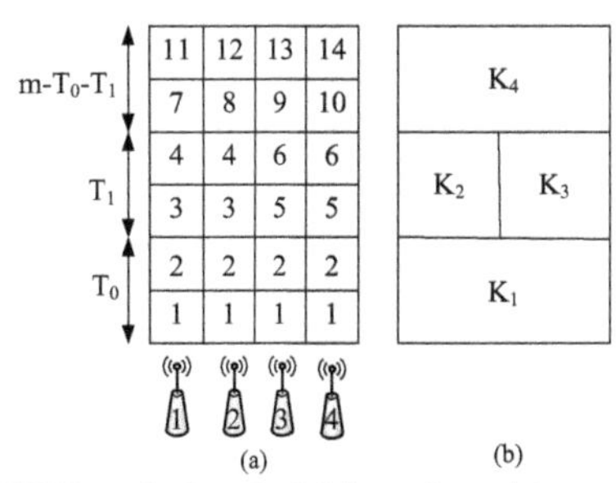

Figure 4: ZFBF and threshold-based caching with multiple thresholds ($m = 6$, $T_0 = 2$, $T_1 = 2$).

The above threshold-based caching scheme can be generalized to one with multiple thresholds where the basic idea is that the more popular a file is, the larger the number of copies of the file in the caches. Without loss of generality, assume that the number of neighboring femto-BSs is $N = 2^n$ and define n thresholds $T_0, T_1, \cdots, T_{n-1}$, which are design parameters. The T_0 most popular files will be stored in all 2^n femto-BSs like before (2^n copies each), the next $2T_1$ most popular files will have 2^{n-1} copies each, and in general, the threshold T_i means that we allocate $2^n T_i$ storage units to cache $2^i T_i$ files, each with 2^{n-i} copies. Fig. 4a shows an example with $n = 2$ ($N = 4$).

In addition, the K users are divided into $2^n + 1$ groups according to their requests, where the size of the jth group is denoted as K_j, $j = 1, \cdots, 2^n$ (see Fig. 4b) and $K_{2^n+1} = K - K_1 - \cdots - K_{2^n}$ (the 2^n+1st group consists of users whose requested files only appear in the macro-BS). For example, in Fig. 4, if a user requests file "5", then the user belongs to group "3". Note that above we have defined more groups than thresholds, because different femto-BSs will store different files having the same number of copies, and thus they cannot simultaneously transmit any such set of files. For example, among files with two copies, only the sets (file "3", file "4") and (file "5", file "6") can be simultaneously transmitted, the former by femto-BSs "1" and "2" and the later by femto-BSs "3" and "4", thus the need to distinguish users in group "2" from those in group "3".

The probability that there are $K_j = k_j$, $j = 1, \cdots, 2^n + 1$, users in the jth group is

$$\Pr(K_1 = k_1, \cdots, K_{2^n+1} = k_{2^n+1} = K - k_1 - \cdots - k_{2^n})$$
$$= \frac{K!}{k_1! k_2! \cdots k_{2^n+1}!} \prod_{l=0}^{n-1} \prod_{j=0}^{2^l-1} a_{2^l+j}^{k_{2^l+j}} a_{2^n}^{k_{2^n}} a_{2^n+1}^{k_{2^n+1}},$$

where a_g is the probability that a user belongs to the g-th group. For example, a_{2^l+j} is the probability that a user belongs to the $2^l + j$-th group, i.e., the user requests a file in the range of $\sum_{t=0}^{l-1} 2^t T_t + jT_l + 1$ to $\sum_{t=0}^{l-1} 2^t T_t + (j+1)T_l$, and thus $a_{2^l+j} = \sum_{i=\sum_{t=0}^{l-1} 2^t T_t + jT_l + 1}^{\sum_{t=0}^{l-1} 2^t T_t + (j+1)T_l} p_i$. Similarly, $a_{2^n} = \sum_{i=\sum_{t=0}^{n-1} 2^t T_t + 1}^{\sum_{t=0}^{n-1} 2^t T_t + 2^n(m - \sum_{t=0}^{n-1} T_t)} p_i$, and $a_{2^n+1} = 1 - a_1 - \cdots - a_{2^n}$. As a numerical example, in Fig. 4 the probability that a user belongs to group "3" is simply $p_5 + p_6$.

The average effective data rate can be computed as

$$R_{\text{ZFBF}}^{\text{multi}}(T_0, \cdots, T_{n-1}) = \frac{1}{K} \sum_{k_1=0}^{K} \sum_{k_2=0}^{K-k_1} \cdots \sum_{k_{2^n}=0}^{K-k_1-\cdots-k_{2^n-1}}$$
$$\cdot \Pr(K_1 = k_1, K_2 = k_2, \cdots, K_{2^n} = k_{2^n}, K_{2^n+1} = k_{2^n+1})$$
$$\cdot \left[\sum_{l=0}^{n-1} \sum_{j=0}^{2^l-1} k_{2^l+j} \min\{k_{2^l+j}, 2^{n-l}\} \tilde{R}_F + k_{2^n} \tilde{R}_F + k_{2^n+1} \tilde{R}_M \right],$$

where the multiplexing gain that can be achieved in a time slot for the users in the $2^l + j$-th group is $\min\{k_{2^l+j}, 2^{n-l}\}$. To maximize $R_{\text{ZFBF}}^{\text{multi}}$, the optimal caching thresholds $T_i^*, i = 0, \cdots, n-1$ can be found by enumeration of the solution space $0 \le T_i \le m$, $i = 0, \cdots, n-1$, $\sum_{i=0}^{n-1} T_i \le m$, which is of size m^n. While this complexity is exponential in n, it is not very large in practice since the number of caching thresholds is quite small ($n = \log_2 N$). For example, even for relatively large clusters with, say, 8 cooperating femto-BSs there are at most 3 thresholds.

4.4 Joint MRT–ZFBF

We can achieve both diversity and multiplexing gain with a careful design of the ZFBF precoding [26]. Suppose there are N transmitters and K receivers ($K \le N$). Then, the N transmitters can transmit K independent (non-interfering or spatially isolated) streams to the K receivers simultaneously, each with a diversity of order $N - K + 1$ [26]. We will refer to this scheme as the MRT–ZFBF scheme. Assuming the (single) threshold-based caching and following the analysis in Section 4.2, the average effective date rate (denoted as $R_{\text{MRT-ZFBF}}(T)$) can be computed as

$$R_{\text{MRT-ZFBF}}(T) = \frac{1}{K} \sum_{i=0}^{K} \sum_{j=0}^{K-i} \frac{K!}{i! j! (K-i-j)!}$$
$$\cdot v_T^i (v_{T+N(m-T)} - v_T)^j (1 - v_{T+N(m-T)})^{K-i-j} \tag{4}$$
$$\cdot \left[i \cdot \min\{i, N\} \tilde{R}_F^{(N - \min\{i,N\}+1)} + j\tilde{R}_F + (K-i-j)\tilde{R}_M \right].$$

When the number of users in the first group $K_1 = i < N$, each user of the first group can achieve the rate $\tilde{R}_F^{(N-i+1)}$ in a time slot with a diversity of order $N - i + 1$.

4.5 Noise and co-channel interference

We extend the analytical model to take into account co-channel interference from other macro-BSs and other femto-BSs outside the cooperation cluster using the same frequency slot at the same time with the typical user under study (i.e., the same resource block is spatially reused). We can approximate the spatial distribution of the interfering macro-BSs (outside the circle centered at the typical user with radius d_M, denoted as $B(0, d_M)$) as a Poisson point process Φ with density λ_M [7]. The co-channel interference from the interfering macro-BSs is denoted as I_M, $I_M = \sum_{x \in \Phi \setminus B(0,d_M)} P_M S_{x,\Gamma(1)} D_x^{-\alpha}$, where $S_{x,\Gamma(1)}$ denotes the fading gain of the interfering link from the xth interfering macro-BS to the typical user, which is exponentially distributed with unit mean (Rayleigh fading) and D_x is the distance between the xth interfering macro-BS and the typical user.

Similarly, we can approximate the spatial distribution of the interfering femto-BSs (outside the circle centered at the typical user with radius d_F, denoted as $B(0, d_F)$) as a Poisson point process Ψ with density λ_F. The co-channel interference from the interfering femto-BSs is denoted as I_F, $I_F = \sum_{y \in \Psi \setminus B(0,d_F)} P_F S_{y,\Gamma(1)} D_y^{-\alpha}$, where $S_{y,\Gamma(1)}$ and D_y are similarly defined.

Following the derivations in [15], the success (non-outage) probability of the transmission between the typical user and its serving macro-BS can be computed as

$$\Pr(W \log(1 + \frac{P_M S_{\Gamma(1)} d_M^{-\alpha}}{I_M + I_F + N_0 W}) > R_M)$$
$$= \exp\left(-\tau_M N_0 W d_M^{\alpha} P_M^{-1}\right) \exp\Big\{-\lambda_M \pi d_M^2$$
$$\cdot \left(\tau_M^{\delta} \mathbb{E}_S[S^{\delta} \gamma(1-\delta, \tau_M S)] - \mathbb{E}_S[1 - \exp(-\tau_M S)]\right)\Big\}$$
$$\cdot \exp\Big\{-\lambda_F \pi d_F^2 \big(\tau_M^{\delta} \xi^{\delta} \mathbb{E}_S[S^{\delta} \gamma(1-\delta, \tau_M \xi S)]$$
$$- \mathbb{E}_S[1 - \exp(-\tau_M \xi S)]\big)\Big\},$$

where $\tau_M = 2^{R_M/W} - 1$, $\delta = 2/\alpha$, $\xi = (\frac{d_M}{d_F})^{\alpha} \frac{P_F}{P_M}$, S is an exponential random variable with unit mean, and $\gamma(a, z) = \int_0^z \exp(-t) t^{a-1} dt$ is the lower incomplete gamma function.

In addition, the success probability of the transmission between the typical user and a cluster of j femto-BSs is

$$\Pr(W\log(1+\frac{P_F S_{\Gamma(j)} d_F^{-\alpha}}{I_M+I_F+N_0W}) > R_F) = \sum_{k=0}^{j-1}\frac{1}{k!}(-1)^k\frac{d^k}{dt^k}V(t)\Big|_{t=1}$$

where $V(t)$ is

$$V(t) = \exp\left(-\tau_F N_0 W d_F^{\alpha} t P_F^{-1}\right)\exp\Big\{-\lambda_F\pi d_F^2 \cdot\Big(\tau_F^{\delta} t^{\delta}\mathbb{E}_S[S^{\delta}\gamma(1-\delta,\tau_F tS)] - \mathbb{E}_S[1-\exp(-\tau_F tS)]\Big)\Big\} \cdot\exp\Big\{-\lambda_M\pi d_M^2\Big(\tau_F^{\delta} t^{\delta}\xi^{-\delta}\mathbb{E}_S[S^{\delta}\gamma(1-\delta,\tau_F t\xi^{-1}S)] - \mathbb{E}_S[1-\exp(-\tau_F t\xi^{-1}S)]\Big)\Big\}$$

and $\tau_F = 2^{R_F/W}-1$. With these expressions, we can compute the effective data rates following the same steps as we did in Sections 4.1-4.4.

5. NUMERICAL RESULTS

In this section we present performance results by numerically solving our analytical model in a number of practical scenarios. We assume that there is a library of $M = 1000$ video files, and the file popularity distribution follows the Zipf distribution with parameter s, i.e., $p_i = c_{M,s}/i^s$, $i = 1,\dots,M$, where $c_{M,s}$ is the so called normalization constant.

Without loss of generality, consider a macro-BS with transmission range 4000m and a number of femto-BSs each with transmission range 200m deployed inside the macro-BS cell. Note that these are typical transmission ranges for a macro cell and for low-power BSs, see, for example, the capabilities of picocells, metrocells, and microcells defined in [1]. The number of femto-BSs inside a cluster (N), that is, the number of femto-BSs that a typical user can receive useful signal from, depends on the density of the femto-BSs and varies in the scenarios that we study. The data rate of the macro-BS is assumed to be $R_M = 2$ Mbps and the data rate of the femto-BSs is assumed to be $R_F = 10$ Mbps, again in line with industry practice. The transmit power of the macro-BS equals $P_M = 20$ W and of the femto-BSs equals $P_F = 20$ mW, as has been assumed in prior works as well [6].

Without loss of generality, consider a cluster of femto-BSs covering an area of radius 200m at distance 2000m from the macro-BS. Then, the distance of the typical user from a femto-BS of the cluster is assumed to lie between 0 and 200m, and the distance from the macro-BS lies between 1800 and 2200m. We assume that the path loss exponent equals $\alpha = 4$ and consider quasi-static Rayleigh flat-fading channels with unit mean power. In addition, the bandwidth of the frequency slot is $W = 5$ MHz and the noise power spectral density varies from $N_0 = 4\times10^{-19}$ W/Hz to $N_0 = 8\times10^{-20}$ W/Hz. As a result, by substituting these numerical values into the formulas of Section 4, the transmission success (non-outage) probability for the macro- and the femto-BSs with a unit diversity varies from 0.6 to 0.9, and the effective data rate of the macro- and femto-BSs with a unit diversity varies from $\tilde{R}_M = 2\times0.6 = 1.2$ to 1.8 Mbps and from $\tilde{R}_F = 10\times0.6 = 6$ to 9 Mbps, respectively.

5.1 Data rates under diversity gains

We study the rate of a user under MRT achieved at an arbitrary time slot. To highlight the effect of diversity gains to the data rate, we show results when the success (non-outage) probability with a unit diversity equals 0.6. We later show results when the outage probability is smaller.

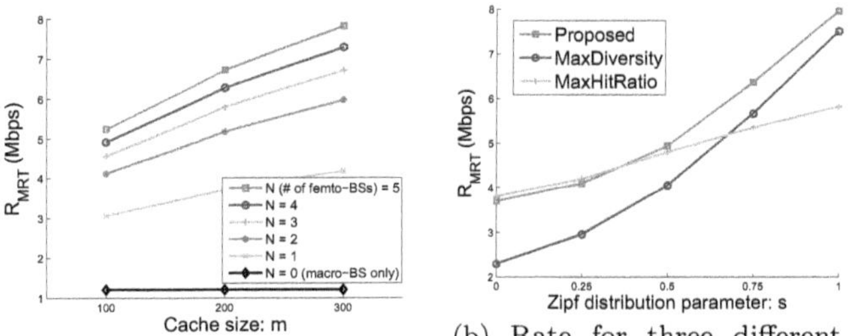

(a) Rate as a function of the cache size m for a cluster of N femto-BSs, $s = 0.56$.

(b) Rate for three different caching approaches for different degrees of popularity skewness, $N = 5$, $m = 100$.

Figure 5: Performance of the system under MRT.

In Fig. 5a we plot the rate as a function of the cache size (m) and the number of nearby femto-BSs (N) for a popularity distribution with a typical parameter $s = 0.56$ [24, 27]. As expected, the rate R_{MRT} increases with the cache size and the number of neighboring femto-BSs, the later because as N increases we have a larger diversity that reduces the transmission link failure (outage) probability. In this plot we also show the achieved rate when no femto-BSs are used. It is evident that using femto-BSs improves rates by 2-3x and adding MRT results in an additional gain of 2-3x. Last, note that for a fixed cache size and as we increase the number of femto-BSs, the marginal gain decreases since the outage probability has already been reduced to a very small value.

In Fig. 5b we plot the rate as a function of the Zipf distribution parameter s. We vary s from 0 (uniform distribution) to 1 (quite skewed distribution) and compare our scheme with the following two basic schemes: a "MaxDiversity" caching scheme and a "MaxHitRatio" caching scheme, to investigate how well our system adapts to changing levels of popularity. In the "MaxDiversity" scheme, we cache the most popular files 1 to m in every femto-BS so that we have a diversity of order N for all these files. Intuitively, this scheme would perform well for a skewed distribution with a large s. On the other hand, in the "MaxHitRatio" scheme we cache in the femto-BSs the most popular files 1 to mN, each with a single copy. This scheme would perform well for a near-flat (uniform) popularity distribution with a small s. As shown in Fig. 5b, our proposed cross-layer optimization scheme adapts to the popularity distribution and controls the diversity gain (equivalently, the number of copies of a file in the caches of the femto-BSs) for each individual file, attending a good performance in the whole range of s.

5.2 Data rates under multiplexing gains

We study the rate under ZFBF achieved at an arbitrary time slot.

Fig. 6 plots the rate $R_{\mathrm{ZFBF}}(T)$ as a function of the caching threshold T, $0 \le T \le m$. We assume that the cluster of neighboring femto-BSs consists of $N = 5$ femto-BSs, the cache size of each of those femto-BSs is $m = 100$, and we consider three values for the Zipf distribution parameter, $s = 0$, 0.56 and 1.5. In practice, a cluster of $N = 5$ femto-BSs may serve tens to hundreds of users. In our study we are focusing on the users who receive transmissions from the macro- and femto-BSs at a single resource (time-frequency) block and thus vary their number from $K = 1$ to 10.

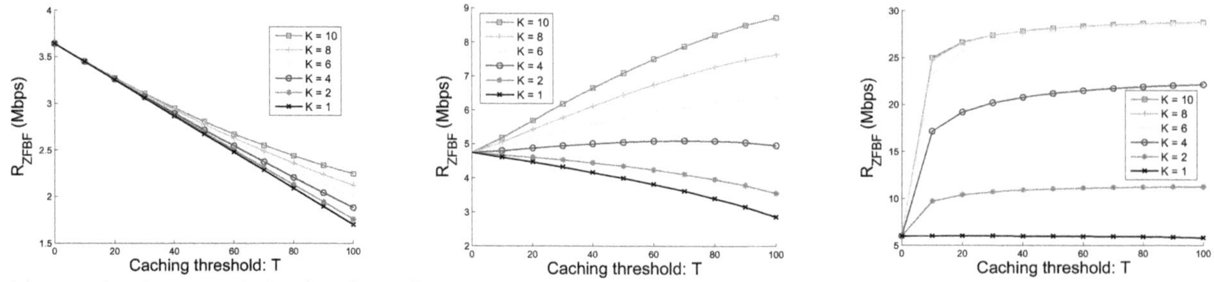

(a) $s = 0$ (uniform popularity distribution) (b) $s = 0.56$ (moderately skewed) (c) $s = 1.5$ (very skewed)

Figure 6: Performance of the system under ZFBF, $N = 5$, $m = 100$.

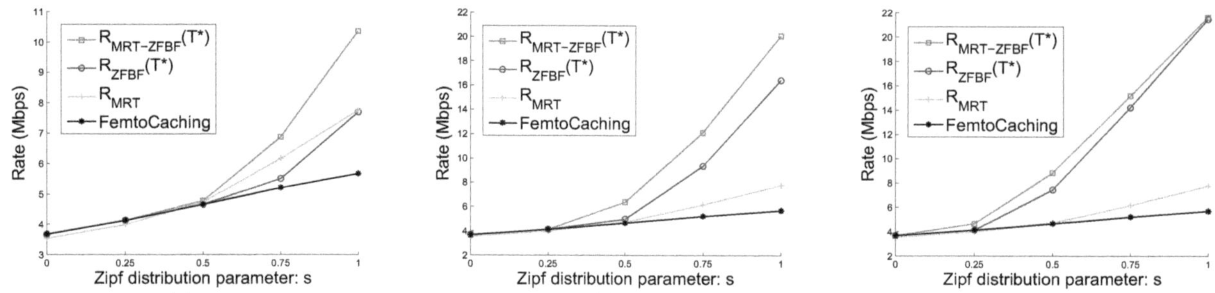

(a) $K = 2$ (b) $K = 5$ (c) $K = 10$

Figure 7: Performance of the system under FemtoCaching only, MRT, ZFBF, and MRT–ZFBF, $N = 5$, $m = 100$.

From Fig. 6a we observe that for a uniform popularity distribution ($s = 0$) the optimal threshold is $T^* = 0$, i.e., we prefer to have only a single copy of a file in the caches to reduce cache misses and choose not to have a multiplexing gain. On the other hand, in Fig. 6c, for the very skewed popularity distribution ($s = 1.5$), the optimal threshold is $T^* = m = 100$ (for $K > 2$), i.e., we prefer to have multiple copies of the most popular files in the caches of femto-BSs, achieving a larger multiplexing gain. Note that for the very skewed distribution, we have $v_m \approx 1$ (v_m is the probability a user requests one of the m most popular files) and $R_{\text{ZFBF}}(m) \approx \min\{K, N\}\tilde{R}_F$, where the multiplexing gain is $\min\{K, N\}$. For a moderately skewed distribution, as shown in Fig. 6b with $s = 0.56$, the optimal threshold lies somewhere in the middle and depends on K (e.g., for $K = 4$, $T^* = 71$). Thus, our caching scheme can adapt to the file popularity distribution by properly setting the value of the caching threshold. Last, note that the rate gain from using ZFBF on the femto-BSs can be very substantial, reaching 10-20x in the case of skewed distributions.

5.3 Data rates using joint MRT–ZFBF

Fig. 7a-c compare the rates for $K = 2$, 5, and 10 users with "FemtoCaching only", MRT (R_{MRT}), ZFBF ($R_{\text{ZFBF}}(T^*)$), and MRT–ZFBF ($R_{\text{MRT-ZFBF}}(T^*)$), where in the latter two cases the rates are evaluated at their optimal caching thresholds, respectively. In the "FemtoCaching only" scheme, we cache in the femto-BSs the most popular files 1 to mN, each with a single copy, and there is no cooperative transmission among the femto-BSs.

The MRT–ZFBF scheme outperforms the ZFBF scheme for smaller values of K because there is some probability that the number of users in the first group K_1 is less than the number of femto-BSs N reducing the multiplexing gain. As a matter of fact, for $K = 2$ ZFBF performs worse than even plain MRT. This is because MRT/MRT–ZFBF achieves a diversity of order $N - K_1 + 1 \geq 2$ for all the users in the first group (see Eq. (4)) increasing the transmission success (non-outage) probability from 0.6 to more than 0.9 (equality for a diversity of 2), which, in turn, increases the effective data rate. Of course, when the number of users is large (e.g. $K = 10$) and thus $K_1 \geq N$ with high probability, ZFBF performs almost as well as MRT–ZFBF.

The results above are generated when the success (non-outage) probability with a unit diversity equals 0.6. For a larger success probability, e.g. 0.9, MRT is expected to perform relatively worse, and the ZFBF scheme is expected to be very close to MRT–ZFBF. Fig. 8 confirms the above. As a matter of fact, since the caching strategy under MRT caches files in a probabilistic fashion, when the file popularity is not very skewed it sometimes caches multiple copies of not so popular files which results in worse performance than even plain FemtoCaching (because the loss from the lower hit ratio is larger than the small gain from the diversity gain).

5.4 Single threshold vs. multiple thresholds

Fig. 9 plots the rate with ZFBF when two thresholds are used ($R^{\text{multi}}_{\text{ZFBF}}(T^*_0, T^*_1)$), over the rate when one threshold is used ($R_{\text{ZFBF}}(T^*)$) in a setup with 4 femto-BSs ($N = 4$). We observe that when the number of users is small (e.g. $K = 2$), the caching scheme with multiple thresholds is beneficial in the regime of skewed popularity (large s) because to get the maximum multiplexing gain it is sufficient to store 2 copies of the same file, which is possible under the multiple thresholds scheme. On the other hand, when K is large (e.g. $K = 8$) multiple thresholds are beneficial in the regime of near-flat popularity (small s). This is because for large s both schemes achieve the maximum multiplexing gain, whereas for small s multiple thresholds provide a finer granularity for controlling the trade-off between cache hit ratio and spatial multiplexing. Nevertheless, we can see

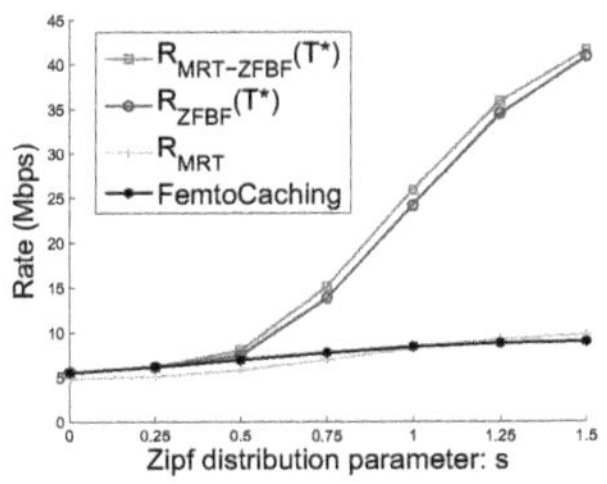

Figure 8: Performance of the system with a low outage probability of 0.1, $K = 5$, $N = 5$, $m = 100$.

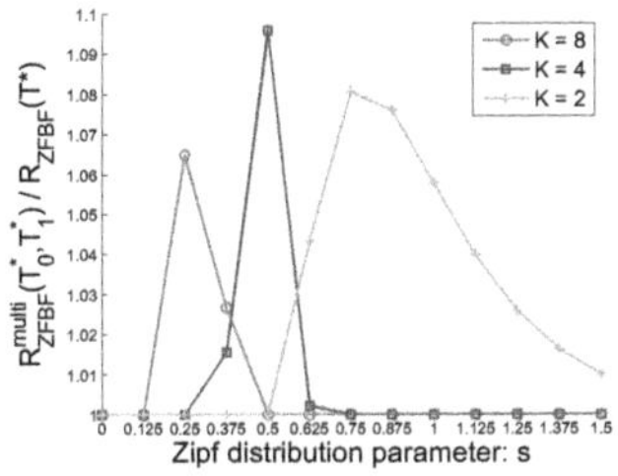

Figure 9: Performance of the system under ZFBF with single and multi-thresholds, $N = 4$, $m = 100$.

that $R^{\text{multi}}_{\text{ZFBF}}(T_0^*, T_1^*)$ is at most 10% larger than $R_{\text{ZFBF}}(T^*)$ across the whole range of file popularity distributions (s). Thus, the use of a single threshold appears to be enough to get most of the rate gains.

6. PRACTICAL CONSIDERATIONS

Updating the parameters of the caching strategy: The parameters of the caching strategy depend on the file popularity distribution p_i, e.g. q_i in Eq. (2) for MRT and the threshold T in Eq. (3) for ZFBF. The file popularity distribution can be estimated by user requests, see, for example, [8]. The complexity of computing the caching strategy parameter q_i in randomized caching under MRT is low since q_i's can be obtained efficiently by solving a convex optimization problem, see Theorem 1. The complexity of computing T in threshold-based caching is also tractable since the size of the solution space is linear in the cache size for the single threshold case. For the multi-threshold case the solution space is exponential in the number of thresholds, but (i) even for large cluster sizes, e.g. 8 femto-BSs, the number of thresholds is as small as 3, and (ii) as we have shown in Section 5.4 the use of a single threshold is enough to get most of the rate gains thus we do not anticipate the use of multiple thresholds in the majority of cases. The right place to perform the above computations is the macro-BS as it can keep track of all file requests and thus of the file popularity distribution, and it has more than enough computation power to compute the caching strategy parameters. Upon computing the parameters, the macro-BS will send their values to the femto-BSs. Last, since the time scale of significant changes in the file popularity distribution is in the order of a day or longer, updating the caching strategy parameters will happen infrequently.

Cache content update: Macro-BS and femto-BSs coordinate the cache content update (downloading popular video files via backhaul into caches in femto-BSs) according to updates in the caching strategy parameters. This can be done at off-peak hours because the time scale of significant changes in the file popularity distribution (e.g. days) is much larger than the time scale of receiving users' requests (e.g. seconds) [13]. Note also that only significant changes in the file popularity will result in a cache content update, while small changes in the file popularity will only result in re-ordering (relabeling) files in the caches.

The effect of asynchronous user requests: In the presence of many femto-BSs large rates occur when many users are served concurrently taking advantage of multiplexing gains. In practice this would occur when the system is highly loaded, which is the most relevant case since it is under high loads that it is a challenge to provide high rates. Under medium/low loads, the asynchronous nature of user requests poses the dilemma to wait till enough requests are collected to concurrently serve many users (which may result in extra delays) or to immediately serve less users resulting in a smaller multiplexing gain. Specifically, to get a multiplexing gain of i under threshold-based caching and ZFBF (see Section 4.2) there has to be i users that request anyone of the T most popular files "right now". While it is part of future work to fully investigate the effect of the asynchronous nature of user requests to performance, simply collecting requests for these most popular files while serving the users in the second and third groups (during time slots $1, \cdots, K_2$ and $1, \cdots, K_3$ in Fig. 3b), yields enough requests/users in the first group to achieve very large multiplexing gains (during the subsequent $1, \cdots, K_1$ time slots) without having to wait for any more requests. For typical system setup parameters, this achieved multiplexing gain is within 10% or closer to the maximum possible.

7. CONCLUSION

In this paper we proposed to jointly use and optimize distributed caching in femto-BSs and femto-BS cooperative transmissions. Our analytical and simulation results show that our system achieves an order of magnitude faster content delivery than legacy systems. The gains are particularly pronounced for skewed popularity distributions where caching multiple copies of popular files across multiple femto-BSs yields particularly large diversity and multiplexing gains without sizeably increasing cache misses. Given that content popularity is well known to be heavily skewed, our approach is expected to have a large impact in real-world setups.

8. REFERENCES

[1] http://www.smallcellforum.org/.

[2] H. V. Balan, R. Rogalin, A. Michaloliakos, K. Psounis, and G. Caire. Achieving high data rates in a distributed MIMO system. In *Proc. ACM MOBICOM*, Aug. 2012.

[3] H. V. Balan, R. Rogalin, A. Michaloliakos, K. Psounis, and G. Caire. Airsync: Enabling distributed multiuser MIMO with full spatial multiplexing. *IEEE/ACM Transactions on Networking*, Dec. 2013.

[4] D. Ben Cheikh, J. M. Kelif, M. Coupechoux, and P. Godlewski. Analytical joint processing multi-point cooperation performance in Rayleigh fading. *IEEE Wireless Commun. Lett.*, Aug. 2012.

[5] S. Borst, V. Gupta, and A. Walid. Distributed caching algorithms for content distribution networks. In *Proc. IEEE INFOCOM*, 2010.

[6] V. Chandrasekhar, J. G. Andrews, and A. Gatherer. Femtocell networks: a survey. *IEEE Commun. Mag.*, 46(9):59–67, Sept. 2008.

[7] H. S. Dhillon, R. K. Ganti, F. Baccelli, and J. G. Andrews. Modeling and analysis of k-tier downlink heterogeneous cellular networks. *IEEE J. Sel. Areas Commun.*, 30(3):550–560, Apr. 2012.

[8] F. Figueiredo, F. Benevenuto, and J. M. Almeida. The tube over time: characterizing popularity growth of YouTube videos. In *Proc. ACM WSDM*, 2011.

[9] D. Gesbert, S. Hanly, H. Huang, S. Shitz, O. Simeone, and W. Yu. Multi-cell MIMO cooperative networks: A new look at interference. *IEEE J. Sel. Areas Commun.*, 28(9):1380–1408, Dec. 2010.

[10] A. Ghosh, N. Mangalvedhe, R. Ratasuk, B. Mondal, M. Cudak, E. Visotsky, T. A. Thomas, J. G. Andrews, P. Xia, H. S. Jo, H. S. Dhillon, and T. D. Novlan. Heterogeneous cellular networks: From theory to practice. *IEEE Commun. Mag.*, 50(6):54–64, June 2012.

[11] N. Golrezaei, A. Dimakis, and A. Molisch. Scaling behavior for device-to-device communications with distributed caching. *IEEE Trans. Inf. Theory*, 2014.

[12] N. Golrezaei, A. F. Molisch, A. G. Dimakis, and G. Caire. Femtocaching and device-to-device collaboration: A new architecture for wireless video distribution. *IEEE Commun. Mag.*, Apr. 2013.

[13] N. Golrezaei, K. Shanmugam, A. G. Dimakis, A. F. Molisch, and G. Caire. Femtocaching: Wireless video content delivery through distributed caching helpers. In *Proc. IEEE INFOCOM*, Mar. 2012.

[14] M. Haenggi, J. G. Andrews, F. Baccelli, O. Dousse, and M. Franceschetti. Stochastic geometry and random graphs for the analysis and design of wireless networks. *IEEE J. Sel. Areas Commun.*, 27(7):1029–1046, Sept. 2009.

[15] M. Haenggi and R. K. Ganti. Interference in large wireless networks. *Found. Trends Netw.*, 2009.

[16] R. Irmer, H. Droste, P. Marsch, M. Grieger, G. Fettweis, S. Brueck, H. P. Mayer, L. Thiele, and V. Jungnickel. Coordinated multipoint: Concepts, performance, and field trial results. *IEEE Commun. Mag.*, Feb. 2011.

[17] M. Ji, G. Caire, and A. F. Molisch. Fundamental limits of distributed caching in D2D wireless networks. In *Proc. IEEE ITW*, 2013.

[18] D. Lee, H. Seo, B. Clerckx, E. Hardouin, D. Mazzarese, S. Nagata, and K. Sayana. Coordinated multipoint transmission and reception in LTE-advanced: deployment scenarios and operational challenges. *IEEE Commun. Mag.*, Feb. 2012.

[19] A. Liu and V. K. N. Lau. Mixed-timescale precoding and cache control in cached MIMO interference network. *IEEE Trans. Signal Process.*, Dec. 2013.

[20] A. Liu and V. K. N. Lau. Cache-enabled opportunistic cooperative MIMO for video streaming in wireless systems. *IEEE Trans. Signal Process.*, Jan. 2014.

[21] M. A. Maddah-Ali and U. Niesen. Decentralized coded caching attains order-optimal memory-rate tradeoff. *IEEE/ACM Trans. Netw.*, 2014.

[22] M. A. Maddah-Ali and U. Niesen. Fundamental limits of caching. *IEEE Trans. Inf. Theory*, May 2014.

[23] H. S. Rahul, S. Kumar, and D. Katabi. JMB: Scaling wireless capacity with user demands. In *Proc. ACM SIGCOMM*, Aug. 2012.

[24] K. Shanmugam, N. Golrezaei, A. G. Dimakis, A. F. Molisch, and G. Caire. Femtocaching: Wireless content delivery through distributed caching helpers. *IEEE Trans. Inf. Theory*, Dec. 2013.

[25] D. Tse and P. Viswanath. *Fundamentals of Wireless Communication.* Cambridge University Press, 2005.

[26] K.-K. Wong and Z. Pan. Array gain and diversity order of multiuser miso antenna systems. *Int. J. Wireless Inf. Networks*, 2008.

[27] M. Zink, K. Suh, Y. Gu, and J. Kurose. Characteristics of YouTube network traffic at a campus network - measurements, models, and implications. *Comput. Netw.*, Mar. 2009.

Appendix: Proof of Theorem 1

First, let us define the function

$$G(q) \triangleq \sum_{j=0}^{N} \binom{N}{j} q^j (1-q)^{N-j} w_j, \; 0 \le q \le 1, \tag{5}$$

where $w_j \ge 0$, $\forall j = 0, \cdots, N$. We have the following lemma.

LEMMA 1. *If $w_j \ge w_{j-1}$, $\forall j = 1, \cdots, N$, then $G(q)$ is a non-decreasing function. Furthermore, if $w_{j+1} - w_j \le w_j - w_{j-1}$, $\forall j = 1, \cdots, N-1$, then $G(q)$ is concave.*

PROOF. Using basic analysis, the first derivative of $G(q)$ can be computed as

$$G'(q) = \sum_{j=1}^{N} \frac{N!}{(j-1)!(N-j)!} q^{j-1} (1-q)^{N-j} (w_j - w_{j-1}) \ge 0,$$

where for the inequality we use the conditions $w_j \ge w_{j-1}$, $\forall j = 1, \cdots, N$. So, $G(q)$ is non-decreasing.

Similarly, the second derivative of $G(q)$ is computed as

$$G''(q) = \sum_{j=1}^{N-1} \frac{N!}{(j-1)!(N-j-1)!} q^{j-1} (1-q)^{N-j-1} \cdot [(w_{j+1} - w_j) - (w_j - w_{j-1})] \le 0,$$

where for the inequality we use the conditions $w_{j+1} - w_j \le w_j - w_{j-1}$, $\forall j = 1, \cdots, N-1$. So, $G(q)$ is concave. □

Let w_0 represent the effective data rate of a macro-BS ($w_0 = \tilde{R}_M$) and w_j represent the effective data rate of a femto-BS cluster with a diversity of order j ($w_j = \tilde{R}_F^{(j)}$), $j = 1, \cdots, N$. From (1) and (5), we have $U(q_i) = \sum_{j=0}^{N} \binom{N}{j} q_i^j (1-q_i)^{N-j} w_j = G(q_i)$. In addition, since the ccdf of $S_{\Gamma(j)}$ is $\bar{F}_{S_{\Gamma(j)}}(z) = \sum_{n=0}^{j-1} \frac{1}{n!} e^{-z} z^n$, we obtain

$$\begin{aligned} w_{j+1} - w_j &= R_F \sum_{n=0}^{j} \frac{1}{n!} e^{-\eta_F} \eta_F^n - R_F \sum_{n=0}^{j-1} \frac{1}{n!} e^{-\eta_F} \eta_F^n \\ &= R_F \frac{1}{j!} e^{-\eta_F} \eta_F^j, \; \forall j = 1, \cdots, N-1; \\ w_1 - w_0 &= R_F e^{-\eta_F} - R_M e^{-\eta_M}. \end{aligned}$$

We note that the conditions $w_{j+1} \ge w_j$, $j \ge 0$ are equivalent to $R_F e^{-\eta_F} \ge R_M e^{-\eta_M}$. Also, the conditions $w_{j+1} - w_j \le w_j - w_{j-1}$, $j \ge 2$ (the marginal rate gain of including one more femto-BS into the cluster to perform cooperative transmission is decreasing) are equivalent to $\eta_F \le 2$. Moreover, the condition $w_2 - w_1 \le w_1 - w_0$ (the aforementioned marginal gain is smaller than the marginal gain of using femto-BS instead of macro-BS) is equivalent to $R_M e^{-\eta_M} \le R_F e^{-\eta_F}(1 - \eta_F)$. As a result, by Lemma 1 and combining the above conditions, we conclude that if $R_M e^{-\eta_M} \le R_F e^{-\eta_F}(1 - \eta_F)$ holds, $U(q_i)$ is concave and thus $R_{\mathrm{MRT}}(q_1, \cdots, q_M) = \sum_{i=1}^{M} p_i U(q_i)$ is concave.

Multi-view Wireless Video Streaming Based on Compressed Sensing: Architecture and Network Optimization

Nan Cen[†], Zhangyu Guan[†‡], Tommaso Melodia[†]
[†]Department of Electrical and Computer Engineering
Northeastern University, Boston, MA 02115
[‡]Department of Electrical Engineering
State University of New York at Buffalo, Buffalo, NY 14226
{ncen, zguan, melodia}@ece.neu.edu

ABSTRACT

Multi-view wireless video streaming has the potential to enable a new generation of efficient and low-power pervasive surveillance systems that can capture scenes of interest from multiple perspectives, at higher resolution, and with lower energy consumption. However, state-of-the-art multi-view coding architectures require relatively complex predictive encoders, thus resulting in high processing complexity and power requirements. To address these challenges, we consider a wireless video surveillance scenario and propose a new encoding and decoding architecture for multi-view video systems based on Compressed Sensing (CS) principles, composed of cooperative sparsity-aware block-level rate-adaptive encoders, feedback channels and independent decoders. The proposed architecture leverages the properties of CS to overcome many limitations of traditional encoding techniques, specifically massive storage requirements and high computational complexity. It also uses estimates of image sparsity to perform efficient rate adaptation and effectively exploit inter-view correlation at the encoder side.

Based on the proposed encoding/decoding architecture, we further develop a CS-based end-to-end rate distortion model by considering the effect of packet losses on the perceived video quality. We then introduce a modeling framework to design network optimization problems in a multi-hop wireless sensor network. Extensive performance evaluation results show that the proposed coding framework and power-minimizing delivery scheme are able to transmit multi-view streams with guaranteed video quality at low power consumption.

Categories and Subject Descriptors

C.2.1 [**Computer-Communication Networks**]: Network Architecture and Design—*Wireless communication*

Keywords

Compressed sensing; Multi-view video streaming; Network optimization.

MobiHoc'15, June 22–25, 2015, Hangzhou, China.
Copyright 2015 ACM 978-1-4503-3489-1/15/06...$15.00.
http://dx.doi.org/10.1145/2746285.2746309.

1. INTRODUCTION

Low-power wireless video monitoring and surveillance systems (sometimes referred to as wireless multimedia sensor networks (WMSNs) [1]) have the potential to enable new generations of monitoring and surveillance systems, e.g., multi-view surveillance networks composed of wirelessly interconnected low-power and low-complexity sensing devices equipped with audio and visual information collection modules that are able to ubiquitously capture multimedia content from environments of interest. In wireless multi-view video streaming systems, arrays of miniature camera sensors simultaneously capture scenes from different perspectives [2] and then deliver the captured video data to the decoder through wireless links. This often comes with large storage requirements and intense processing loads.

While there has been intense research and considerable progress in wireless video sensing systems, *how to enable real-time quality-aware power-efficient multi-view video streaming in large-scale, possibly multi-hop, wireless networks of battery-powered embedded devices is still a substantially open problem.* State-of-the-art Multi-view Video Coding (MVC) technologies such as MVC H.264/AVC [3,4] are mainly based on predictive encoding techniques, i.e., selecting one frame (referred to as reference frame) in one view (referred to as reference view), based on which they perform motion compensation and disparity compensation to predict other intra-view and inter-view frames, respectively. As a consequence, they are characterized by the following fundamental limitations when applied to multi-view streaming in multi-hop wireless sensor networks:

Large storage space, high power consumption and encoder complexity on embedded devices. State-of-the-art MVC technologies incorporating inter-view and intra-view prediction require extra storage space for reference views and frames. They also induce intensive computational complexity at the encoder, which further results in high processing load or additional cost for specialized processors (to perform operations such as motion estimation and compensation) and high power consumption.

Prediction-based encoding techniques are vulnerable to channel errors. In predictive encoding approaches, errors in independently encoded frames can lead to error propagation on the predictively encoded frames, which is especially detrimental in wireless networks with lossy links, where best-effort delivery scheme with simple error detection schemes such as UDP are usually adopted [5]. Therefore, to guarantee multi-view video streaming quality, a desirable

MVC framework should allow graceful degradation of video quality as the channel quality decreases.

Recently, so-called compressed sensing (CS) techniques have been proposed that are able to reconstruct image or video signals from a relatively "small" number of (random or deterministic) linear combinations of original image pixels, referred to as measurements, *without collecting the entire frame* [6,7], thereby offering a promising alternative to traditional video encoders by *acquiring and compressing video or images simultaneously at very low computational complexity for encoders* [8]. This attractive feature motivated a number of works that have applied CS to video streaming in low-power wireless surveillance scenarios. For example, [9–11] mainly concentrate on single-view CS-based video compression, by exploiting temporal correlation among successive video frames [9, 10] or considering energy-efficient rate allocation in WMSNs with traditional CS reconstruction methods [11]. In [12], we showed that CS-based wireless video streaming can deliver surveillance-grade video for a fraction of the energy consumption of traditional systems based on predictive video encoding such as H.264. In addition, [11] illustrated and evaluated the *error-resilience* property of CS-based video streaming, which results in graceful quality degradation in wireless lossy links. A few recent contributions [13–15] have proposed CS-based multi-view video streaming techniques, primarily focusing on an independent-encoder and joint-decoder paradigm, which exploits the implicit correlation among multiple views at the decoder side to improve the resulting video quality using complex joint reconstruction algorithms.

From a systems perspective, how to allocate power-efficient rates to different views for a required level of video quality is another important open problem in wirelessly networked multi-view video streaming systems. Very few algorithms have been reported in the literature to address this issue. For example, [16] and [17] have looked at this problem by considering traditional encoding paradigms, e.g., H.264 or MPEG4; these contributions focus on video transmission in single-hop wireless networks and provide a framework to improve power efficiency by adjusting encoding parameters such as quantization step (QS) size to adapt the resulting rate.

To bridge the aforementioned gaps, in this paper we first propose a novel CS-based multi-view coding and decoding architecture composed of cooperative encoders and independent decoders. Unlike existing works [13–15], the proposed system is based on independent encoding and independent decoding procedures with limited channel feedback information and negligible content sharing among camera sensors. Furthermore, we propose a power-efficient quality-guaranteed rate allocation algorithm based on a compressive Rate-Distortion (R-D) model for multi-view video streaming in multi-path multi-hop wireless sensor networks with lossy links. Our work makes the following contributions:

CS-based multi-view video coding architecture with independent encoders and independent decoders. Different from state-of-the-art multi-view coding architectures, that are either based on joint encoding or on joint decoding, we propose a new CS-based sparsity-aware independent encoding and decoding multi-view structure, that relies on lightweight feedback and inter-camera cooperation.

- *Sparsity estimation.* We develop a novel adaptive approach to estimate block sparsity based on the reconstructed frame at the decoder. The estimated sparsity is then used to calculate the block-level measurement rate to be allocated with respect to a given frame-level rate. Next, the resulting block-level rates are transmitted back to the encoder through the feedback channel. The encoder that is selected to receive the feedback information, referred to as reference view (R-view), shares the content with other non-reference views (NR-views) nearby.

- *Block-level rate adaptive multi-view encoders.* R-view and NR-views perform the block-level CS encoding independently based on the shared block-level measurement rate information. The objective is to not only implicitly leverage the considerable correlation among views, but also to adaptively balance the number of measurements among blocks with different sparsity levels. Our experimental results show that the proposed method outperforms state-of-the-art CS-based encoders with equal block-level measurement rate by up to 5 dB.

Modeling framework for CS-based multi-view video streaming in multi-path multi-hop wireless sensor networks. We consider a rate-distortion model of the proposed streaming system that captures packet losses caused by unreliable links and playout deadline violations. Based on this model, we propose a two-fold (frame-level and path-level) rate control algorithm designed to minimize the network power consumption under constraints on the minimum required video quality for multi-path multi-hop multi-view video streaming scenarios.

The rest of the paper is organized as follows. In Section 2, we review a few preliminary notions. In Section 3, we introduce the proposed CS-based multi-view video encoding/decoding architecture. In Section 4, we discuss the modified R-D model, and in Section 5 we present a modeling framework to design optimization problems of multi-view streaming in multi-hop sensor networks based on the end-to-end R-D model. Finally, simulation results are presented in Section 6, while in Section 7 we draw the main conclusions and discuss future work.

2. PRELIMINARIES

2.1 Compressed Sensing Basics

We first briefly review basic concepts of CS for signal acquisition and recovery, especially as applied to CS-based video streaming. We consider an image signal vectorized and then represented as $\mathbf{x} \in \mathbb{R}^N$, where $N = H \times W$ is the number of pixels in the image, and H and W represent the dimensions of the captured scene. Each element x_i denotes the ith pixel in the vectorized image signal representation. Most natural images are known to be very nearly sparse when represented using some transformation basis $\boldsymbol{\Psi} \in \mathbb{R}^{N \times N}$, e.g., Discrete Wavelet Transform (DWT) or Discrete Cosine Transform (DCT), denoted as $\mathbf{x} = \boldsymbol{\Psi}\mathbf{s}$, where $\mathbf{s} \in \mathbb{R}^N$ is sparse representation of $\mathbf{x}$. If $\mathbf{s}$ has at most K nonzero components, we call $\mathbf{x}$ a K-sparse signal with respect to $\boldsymbol{\Psi}$.

In CS-based imaging system, sampling and compression are executed simultaneously through a linear measurement matrix $\boldsymbol{\Phi} \in \mathbb{R}^{M \times N}$, with $M \ll N$, as

$$\mathbf{y} = \boldsymbol{\Phi}\mathbf{x} = \boldsymbol{\Phi}\boldsymbol{\Psi}\mathbf{s}, \tag{1}$$

with $\mathbf{y} \in \mathbb{R}^M$ representing the resulting sampled and compressed vector.

It was proven in [6] that if $\mathbf{A} \triangleq \mathbf{\Phi\Psi}$ satisfies the following Restricted Isometry Property (RIP) of order K,

$$(1-\delta_k)||\mathbf{s}||_{l_2}^2 \leq ||\mathbf{A}\mathbf{s}||_{l_2}^2 \leq (1+\delta_k)||\mathbf{s}||_{l_2}^2, \quad (2)$$

with $0 < \delta_k < 1$ being a small "isometry" constant, then we can recover the optimal sparse representation $\mathbf{s}^*$ of $\mathbf{x}$ by solving the following optimization problem

$$\begin{aligned} \mathrm{P}_1: \quad & \text{Minimize} \quad ||\mathbf{s}||_0 \\ & \text{Subject to:} \quad \mathbf{y} = \mathbf{\Phi\Psi s} \end{aligned} \quad (3)$$

by taking only

$$M = c \cdot K\log(N/K) \quad (4)$$

measurements, where c is some predefined constant. Afterwards, $\mathbf{x}$ can be obtained by

$$\hat{\mathbf{x}} = \mathbf{\Psi s}^*. \quad (5)$$

However, problem P_1 is NP-hard in general, and in most practical cases, measurements $\mathbf{y}$ may be corrupted by noise, e.g., channel noise or quantization noise. Then, most state-of-the-art work relies on l_1 minimization with relaxed constraints in the form

$$\begin{aligned} \mathrm{P}_2: \quad & \text{Minimize} \quad ||\mathbf{s}||_1 \\ & \text{Subject to:} \quad ||\mathbf{y} - \mathbf{\Phi\Psi s}||_2 \leq \epsilon \end{aligned} \quad (6)$$

to recover $\mathbf{s}$. Note that P_2 is a convex optimization problem. Researchers in sparse signal reconstruction have developed various solvers [18–20]. For example, the Least Absolute Shrinkage and Selection Operator (LASSO) solver [19] can solve problem P_2 with computational complexity $\mathcal{O}(M^2N)$. We consider a Gaussian random measurement matrix $\mathbf{\Phi}$ in this paper.

2.2 Rate-Distortion Model for Compressive Imaging

Throughout this paper, end-to-end video distortion is measured as mean squared error (MSE). Since Peak Signal-to-Noise Ratio (PSNR) is a more common metric in the video coding community, we use PSNR $= 10\log_{10}(255^2/\mathrm{MSE})$ to illustrate simulation results. The distortion at the decoder D_{dec} in general includes two terms, i.e., D_{enc}, distortion introduced by the encoder (e.g., not enough measurements and quantization); and D_{loss}, distortion caused by packet losses due to unreliable wireless links and violating playout deadlines because of bandwidth fluctuations. Therefore,

$$D_{\mathrm{dec}} = D_{\mathrm{enc}} + D_{\mathrm{loss}}. \quad (7)$$

To the best of our knowledge, there are only a few works [11] that have investigated rate-distortion models for compressive video streaming, but without considering losses. For example, [11] expands the distortion model in [21] to CS video transmission as

$$D(R) = D_0 + \frac{\theta}{R - R_0}, \quad (8)$$

where D_0, θ and R_0 are image- or video-dependent constants that can be determined by linear least squares fitting techniques; $R = \frac{M}{N}$ is the user-controlled measurement rate of each video frame.

3. CS-BASED MULTI-VIEW CODING ARCHITECTURE DESIGN

In this section, we introduce a novel encoding/decoding architecture design for CS multi-view video streaming. The proposed framework is based on three main components: (i) cooperative sparsity-aware block-level rate adaptive encoder, (ii) independent decoder, and (iii) a centralized controller located at the decoder. As illustrated in Fig. 1, considering a two-view example, camera sensors acquire a scene of interest with adaptive block-level rates and transmit sampled measurements to the base station/controller through a multi-path multi-hop wireless sensor network. Then, the centralized controller calculates the relevant information and feeds it back to the selected R-view. The R-view then shares the limited feedback information with the other one - NR-view. The architecture can be easily extended to $V \geq 2$ views.

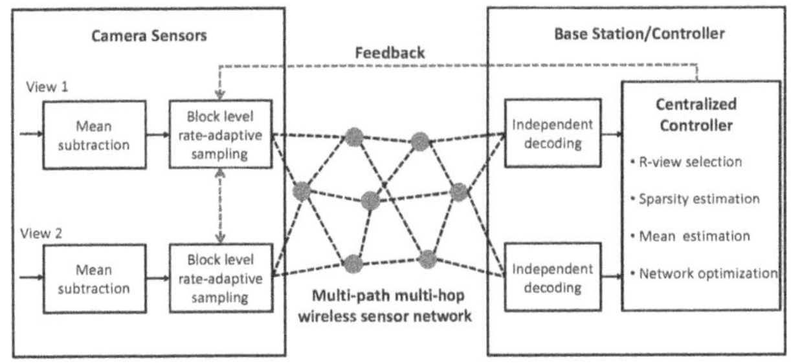

Figure 1: Encoding/decoding architecture for multi-hop CS-based multi-view video streaming.

Different from existing compressive encoders with equal block measurement rate [10, 11], the objective of the proposed framework is to improve the reconstruction quality by leveraging each block's sparsity as a guideline to adapt the block-level measurement rate. We next describe how to implement the proposed paradigm by discussing each component in detail.

3.1 Cooperative Block-level Rate-adaptive Encoder

To reduce the computational burden at encoders embedded in power-constrained devices, most state-of-the-art multi-view proposals focus on developing complex joint reconstruction algorithms to improve the reconstruction quality. Differently, in our architecture we obtain improved quality only through sparsity-aware encoders.

To illustrate the idea, Figure 2(b) depicts the sparse representation of Fig. 2(a) with respect to block-based DCT transformation. We can observe that sparsity differs among blocks, e.g., the blocks within the coat area are more sparse than others. According to basic compressed sensing theory in Section 2.1, (4) indicates that the number of required measurements is inversely proportional to the sparsity K. Therefore, we propose to adapt the measurement rate at the block level according to sparsity information, i.e., more measurements will be allocated to less-sparse blocks, and vice versa.

In our work, the number of required measurements M_{vf}^i for block i in frame f of view v, $1 \leq i \leq B$, is calculated based on the sparsity estimated at the centralized controller and sent back via a feedback channel. Here, $B = \frac{N}{N_b}$ denotes

(a) (b)

Figure 2: Block Sparsity: (a) Original image, (b) Block-based DCT coefficients of (a).

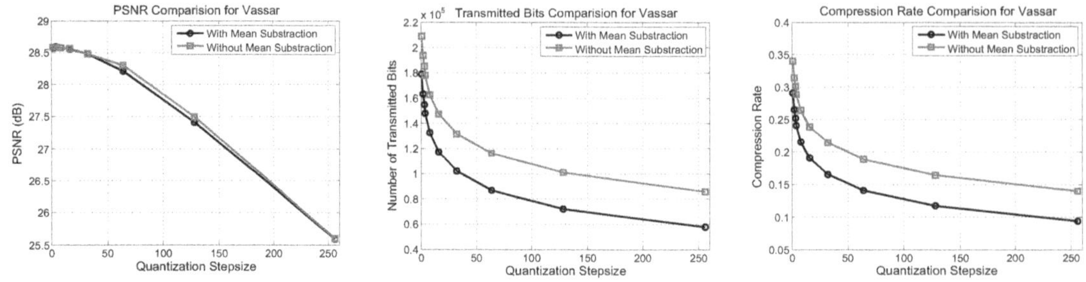

(a) (b) (c)

Figure 3: Comparison of (a) PSNR, (b) the number of transmitted bits, and (c) the compression rate between approaches with and without mean subtraction.

the total number of blocks in one frame with N and N_b being the total number of pixels in one frame and block, respectively. Assume that we have received $\{M_{vf}^i\}_{i=1}^B$. Then, the encoding process is similar to (1), described as

$$\mathbf{y}_{vf}^i = \mathbf{\Phi}_{vf}^i \mathbf{x}_{vf}^i, \quad (9)$$

where $\mathbf{y}_{vf}^i \in \mathbb{R}^{M_{vf}^i}$ and $\mathbf{\Phi}_{vf}^i \in \mathbb{R}^{M_{vf}^i \times N_b}$ are the measurement vector and measurement matrix for block i in frame f of view v, respectively; $\mathbf{x}_{vf}^i \in \mathbb{R}^{N_b}$ represents the original pixel vector of block i. From (9), we can see that M_{vf}^i varies among blocks from 1 to N_b, thereby implementing block-level rate adaptation. In Section 6, the simulation results will show that this approach can improve the quality by up to 5 dB.

Mean value subtraction. The CS-based imaging system acquires and compresses each frame simultaneously through simple linear operations as in (1). Therefore, it can help reduce the energy consumption compared with traditional signal acquisition and encoding approaches (e.g., H.264/AVC) that are based on complicated motion estimation and motion compensation operations. However, the compression rate of CS is not as high as traditional encoding schemes [12]. To compensate for this, we perform *mean value subtraction*, which can further help reduce the number of transmitted bits. How to obtain the mean value $\bar{m}$ will be discussed in Section 3.3. Since the original pixels are not available at the compressive encoder, we perform the *mean value subtraction in the measurement domain.* First, we establish a mean value vector $\mathbf{m} \in \mathbb{R}^{N_b}$ with dimensions the same as $\mathbf{x}_{vf}^i$, and where each element is equal to $\bar{m}$. Then, we use the same block-level measurement matrix $\mathbf{\Phi}_{vf}^i$ to sample $\mathbf{m}$ and then subtract the result from $\mathbf{y}_{vf}^i$ as

$$\tilde{\mathbf{y}}_{vf}^i = \mathbf{y}_{vf}^i - \mathbf{\Phi}_{vf}^i \mathbf{m} = \mathbf{\Phi}_{vf}^i(\mathbf{x}_{vf}^i - \mathbf{m}). \quad (10)$$

After sampling, $\tilde{\mathbf{y}}_{vf}^i$ is transmitted to the decoder. From (10), we can see that the proposed mean value subtraction in the measurement domain is equivalent to subtraction in the pixel domain.

Next, to validate the effectiveness of mean value subtraction, we take the *Vassar* sequence as an example. We select a uniform quantization method. The forward quantization stage and the reconstruction stage can be expressed as $q = \mathrm{sgn}(x) \cdot \lfloor \frac{|x|}{\Delta} + \frac{1}{2} \rfloor$ and $\hat{q} = \Delta \cdot q$, respectively. Here, x, q, $\hat{q}$ and Δ represent original signal, quantized signal, de-quantized signal and quantization step size, respectively. Figure 3 shows a comparison of PSNR, the number of transmitted bits and the compression rate with and without mean subtraction, where a measurement rate 0.2 is used, and the total bits in the original frame are $320 \times 240 \times 8 = 614400$ bits. Quantization step sizes from the set $\{1, 2, 3, 4, 8, 16, 32, 64, 128, 256\}$ are selected. From Fig. 3(a), we can observe that mean subtraction has a negligible effect on the reconstruction quality and there is no significant quality degradation when the quantization step size is less than 32. This is because the value of measurement is up to thousand and tens of thousand compared to original pixel value with maximum 255. Figures 3(b) and (c) illustrate that with mean subtraction the total number of bits transmitted for one frame is significantly reduced by up to 30 kbits compared to not using mean subtraction, which corresponds to an improvement in compression rate from 0.2391 to 0.1902.

Cooperation via sparsity pattern sharing. Multi-view video streaming is based on reducing the redundancy among views captured by arrays of camera sensors that are assumed to be close enough to each other. Most state-of-the-art literature adopts the concept of distributed system coding architecture [22, 23], where a reference view transmits more measurements than other non-reference views and then the receiver jointly decodes by exploiting the implicit correlation among views. Instead, we allow the encoders to explicitly cooperate to a certain extent. For example, the R-view selected by the centralized controller will periodically receive feedback information, i.e., $\{M_i\}_{i=1}^B$ and $\bar{m}$, and then share it with the NR-views in the same group. Since camera sensors in the same group are assumed to be close enough to each other, the block sparsity among views will be correlated. By using the same sparsity information, we can directly exploit multi-view correlation at the encoders, thus resulting in a clean-slate compressive multi-view coding framework with simple encoders and simple decoders but with improved reconstruction quality.

3.2 Independent Decoder

As mentioned above, the proposed framework results in relatively simple decoders. At each decoder, the received $\hat{\mathbf{y}}_{vf}^i$, distorted version of $\tilde{\mathbf{y}}_{vf}^i$ because of the joint effects of quantization, transmission errors, and packet drops, will be independently decoded. The optimal solution $\mathbf{s}_{vf}^{i,\star}$ can be obtained by solving

$$\begin{array}{lll} \mathrm{P}_3: & \text{Minimize} & \|\mathbf{s}_{vf}^i\|_1 \\ & \text{Subject to:} & \|\hat{\mathbf{y}}_{vf}^i - \mathbf{\Phi}_{\mathbf{vf}}^{\mathbf{i}} \mathbf{\Psi}_b \mathbf{s}_{vf}^i\|_2 \leq \epsilon, \end{array} \quad (11)$$

where $\mathbf{\Psi}_b \in \mathbb{R}^{N_b \times N_b}$ represents the sparsifying matrix (2-D DCT in this work). We then use (5) to obtain the reconstructed block-level image $\hat{\mathbf{x}}_{vf}^i$, by solving $\hat{\mathbf{x}}_{vf}^i = \mathbf{\Psi}_b \mathbf{s}_{vf}^{i,\star}$. Afterward, $\{\hat{\mathbf{x}}_{vf}^i\}_{i=1}^B$ can be simply reorganized to obtain the reconstructed frame $\hat{\mathbf{x}}_{vf}$.

3.3 Centralized Controller

The centralized controller is the key component at the receiver, which is mainly in charge of selecting the R-view and estimating sparsity and mean value required to be sent back to the transmitter. Additionally, the controller is also responsible for implementing the power-efficient multi-path rate allocation algorithm discussed in Section 5. Next, we introduce the three key functions executed at the controller in sequence, i.e., *R-view selection, sparsity estimation, and mean value estimation.*

R-view selection. The controller selects a view to be used as reference view (R-view) among views in the same group and then sends feedback information to the selected R-view. For this purpose, the controller first calculates the Pearson correlation coefficients among the measurement vectors of any two views as

$$\rho_{mn} = \text{corr}(\hat{\mathbf{y}}_{mf}, \hat{\mathbf{y}}_{nf}),\ \forall m \neq n,\ m,n = 1,\dots,V, \quad (12)$$

where $\hat{\mathbf{y}}_{mf}$ is the simple cascaded version of all $\hat{\mathbf{y}}^i_{mf}$ and $\text{corr}(\hat{\mathbf{y}}_{mf}, \hat{\mathbf{y}}_{nf}) \triangleq \frac{\text{cov}(\hat{\mathbf{y}}_{mf}, \hat{\mathbf{y}}_{nf})}{\sigma_{mf}\sigma_{nf}}$. Then, view $m^\star$, referred to as R-view, is selected by solving

$$m^\star = \underset{m=1,\dots,V}{\text{argmax}}\, \tilde{\rho}_m, \quad (13)$$

where $\tilde{\rho}_m \triangleq \frac{1}{V-1}\sum_{n\neq m} \rho_{mn}$. The reconstructed frame $\hat{\mathbf{x}}_{vf}$ of the R-view is then used to estimate the block sparsity K^i and the frame mean value $\bar{m}$ for block i.

Next, we take the *Vassar* 5-view scenarios as an example, Table 1 shows the calculated $\tilde{\rho}_m$. We can see that the average Pearson correlation coefficient of view 3 is the largest. Therefore, view 3 is selected as R-view. Moreover, to elaborate how much quality gain we can obtain if the other views except view 3 are selected as R-view, we also set them as R-view and calculate the average improved PSNR, respectively, as shown in Table 2. We can observe that the improved average PSNR is proportional to $\tilde{\rho_m}$, where selecting view 3 as R-view results in the highest improved average PSNR gain, i.e., 1.6674 dB. For this case, because the *Vassar* multi-view sequences used here is captured by parallel-deployed cameras with equal spacing, we obtain the same result, i.e., view 3 as R-view, as if we were to choose simply the most central sensor. However, for scenarios with cameras that are not parallel-deployed with unequal spacing, selecting the most central sensor is not necessarily a good choice.

Table 1: Average Pearson correlation coefficient for *Vassar* five views.

	View 1	View 2	View 3	View 4	View 5
$\tilde{\rho}_m$	0.8184	0.8988	0.9243	0.8973	0.8435

Table 2: Improved average PSNR (dB) when selecting different *Vassar* views as R-view.

R-view	View 1	View 2	View 3	View 4	View 5
PSNR (dB)	1.2312	1.6241	1.6674	1.6167	1.3833

Sparsity estimation. Since the original frame in the pixel domain is not available, we propose to estimate sparsity based on the reconstructed frame $\hat{\mathbf{x}}_{vf}$ as follows. By solving the optimization problem P_3 in (11), we can obtain the block sparse representation $\mathbf{s}^{i,\star}_{vf}$ and then reorganize $\{\mathbf{s}^{i,\star}_{vf}\}^B_{i=1}$ to get the frame sparse representation $\mathbf{s}^\star_{vf}$ periodically. The sparsity coefficient K^i is defined as the number of non-zero entries of $\mathbf{s}^\star_{vf}$. However, natural pictures in general are not exactly sparse in the transform domain. Hence, we introduce a predefined percentile p_s, and assume that the frame can be perfectly recovered with $N \cdot p_s$ measurements. Based on this, one can adaptively find a threshold T above which transform-domain coefficients are considered as non-zero entries. The threshold can be found by solving

$$\frac{||\max(|s^\star_{vf}| - T, 0)||_0}{N} = p_s. \quad (14)$$

Then, we apply T to each block i to estimate the block sparsity K^i as

$$K^i = ||\max(|s^{i,\star}_{vf}| - T, 0)||_0. \quad (15)$$

According to (4) and given the frame measurement rate R, M^i_{vf} can then be obtained as

$$M^i_{vf} = \frac{K^i \log_{10}(\frac{N_b}{K_i})}{\sum_{i=1}^B K^i \log_{10}(\frac{N_b}{K_i})} NR. \quad (16)$$

Mean value estimation. Finally, the mean value $\bar{m}$ can be estimated from $\hat{\mathbf{x}}_{vf}$ as

$$\bar{m} = \frac{1}{N}\sum_{i=1}^{N} \hat{\mathbf{x}}_{vf}(i). \quad (17)$$

With limited feedback and lightweight information sharing, implementing block-level rate adaptation at the encoder without adding computational complexity can improve the reconstruction performance of our proposed encoding/decoding paradigm. This claim will be validated in Section 6 in terms of Peak Signal-to-Noise Ratio (PSNR) and Structure Similarity (SSIM) [24].

4. END-TO-END RATE-DISTORTION MODEL

To handle CS-based multi-view video streaming with guaranteed quality, a rate-distortion model to measure the end-to-end distortion that jointly captures the effects of encoder distortion and transmission distortion as stated in (7) is needed. To this end, we modify the R-D model (8) proposed in [11] by adding a packet loss term to jointly account for compression loss and packet loss in compressive video wireless streaming systems. In traditional predictive-encoding based imaging systems, the importance of packets is not equal (i.e., I-frame packets have higher impact than P-frame and B-frame packets on the reconstructed quality). Instead, each packet in CS-based imaging systems has the same importance, i.e., it contributes equally to the reconstruction quality. Therefore, the packet loss probability p_{loss} can be converted into a measurement rate reduction through a conversion parameter κ and considered into the rate-distortion performance, described as

$$D_{\text{dec}} = D_{\text{enc}} + D_{\text{loss}} = D_0 - \frac{\theta}{R - \kappa p_{\text{loss}} - R_0}. \quad (18)$$

However, how to derive captured-scene-dependent constants D_0, θ, and R_0 in (18) is not trivial. The reasons are listed as follows:

1) Packet loss rate plays a fundamental role in the modified R-D model. In multi-view video streaming in multi-path multi-hop wireless network, how to model the packet loss rate as accurately as possible is still an open problem. In Section 5, we describe our proposed packet loss probability model in detail.

2) The original pixel values are not available at the receiver

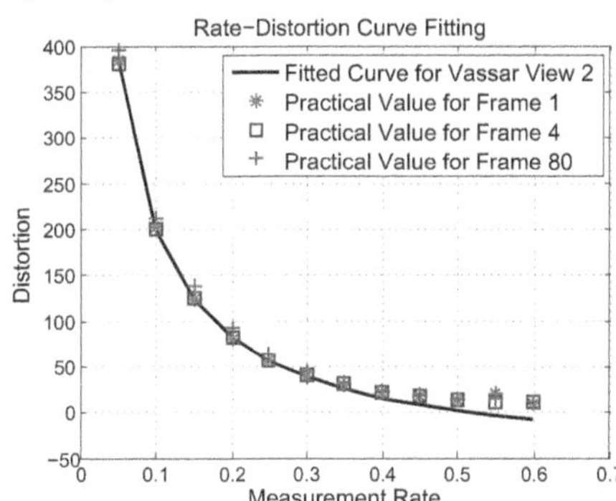

Figure 4: Rate-Distortion curve fitting for *Vassar* view 2 sequence.

end and even not available at the transmitter side in compressive multi-view streaming systems. To address this challenge, we develop a simple but very effective online estimation approach to obtain these three fitting parameters. We let the R-view periodically transmit a frame at a higher measurement rate, e.g., 60% measurement, and after reconstruction at the decoder side, the reconstructed frame is considered as the original image in the pixel domain. We then resample it at different measurement rates and perform the reconstruction procedure again. Finally, approximate distortion in terms of MSE can be calculated between the reconstructed frame at lower measurement rates and the reconstructed frame with 60% measurements.

We take the *Vassar* view 2 sequence as example. According to the above-mentioned online rate-distortion estimation approach, a measurement rate of 0.6 is selected.. Figure 4 illustrates the simulation results, where the black solid line is the rate-distortion curve fitted through a linear least-square approach. To evaluate this approach, we calculate the distortion value for frames 1, 4 and 80 at different measurement rates and then compare them with the estimated rate-distortion curve, where ground-truth distortion values are depicted as red pentagrams, blue squares and green pluses compared to the black line (estimated rate-distortion curve), respectively. We can observe that model (18) matches well the ground-truth distortion values.

Next, in Section 5 we further validate the effectiveness of the R-D model by applying it to the design of a modeling framework for compressive multi-path wireless video streaming, where a power-efficient problem is presented as an example.

5. NETWORK MODELING FRAMEWORK

We consider compressive wireless video streaming over multi-path multi-hop wireless multimedia sensor networks (WMSNs). Based on the R-D model developed in Section 4, we first formulate a video-quality-assured power minimization problem, and then solve the resulting nonlinear nonconvex optimization problem by proposing an online solution algorithm with low computational complexity.

Network model. In the considered WMSN there are a set $\mathcal{V}$ of camera sensors at the transmitter side, with each camera capturing a video sequence of the same scene of interest, and then sending the sequence to the server side through a set $\mathcal{Z}$ of pre-established multi-hop paths. Denote $\mathcal{L}^z$ as the set of hops belonging to path $z \in \mathcal{Z}$, with $d^{z,l}$ being the hop distance of the lth hop in $\mathcal{L}^z$. Let $V = |\mathcal{V}|$, $Z = |\mathcal{Z}|$, and $L^z = |\mathcal{L}^z|$ represent cardinality of sets $\mathcal{V}$, $\mathcal{Z}$ and $\mathcal{L}^z$, respectively. The following three assumptions are considered:

- *Pre-established routing*, i.e., the set of multi-hop paths $\mathcal{Z}$ is established in advance through a given routing protocol (e.g., AODV [25]) and does not change during the video streaming session.
- *Orthogonal channel access*, i.e., there exists a pre-established orthogonal channel access, e.g., based on TDMA, FDMA, or CDMA, and hence concurrent transmissions do not interfere with each other [26].
- *Time division duplexing*, i.e., each node cannot transmit and receive simultaneously, implying that only half of the total air-time is used for transmission or reception.

At the receiver side, the video server concurrently and independently decodes each view of the received video sequences, and based on the reconstructed video sequences it then computes the rate control information and sends the information back to camera sensors for actual rate control. For this purpose, we define two types of video frames, Reference Frame (referred to as *R-frame*) and Non-Reference Frame (referred to as *NR-frame*). An R-frame is periodically transmitted by the R-view; all other frames sent out by the R-view and all frames transmitted by the NR-views are categorized as NR-frames. Compared to an NR-frame, an R-frame is encoded with equal or higher sampling rate and then sent to the receiver side with much lower transmission delay. Hence, an R-frame can be reconstructed with equal or higher video quality and used to estimate sparsity pattern information, which is then fed back to video cameras for rate control in encoding the following NR-frames. For the R-view, we consider a periodic frame pattern, meaning that the R-view camera encodes its captured video frames as R-frames periodically, e.g., one every 30 consecutive frames.

In the above setting, our objective is to minimize the average power consumption of all cameras and communication sensors in the network with guaranteed reconstructed video quality for each view, by jointly controlling video encoding rate and allocating the rate among candidate paths. To formalize this minimization problem, next we first derive the packet loss probability p_{loss} in (18).

Packet loss probability. According to the proposed modified R-D model (18), packet losses affect the video reconstruction quality because they introduce an effective measurement rate reduction. Therefore, effective estimation of packet loss probability at the receiver side has significant impact on frame-level measurement rate control.

In real-time wireless video streaming systems, a video packet can be lost primarily for two reasons: i) the packet fails to pass a parity check due to transmission errors introduced by unreliable wireless links, and ii) it takes too long for the packet to arrive at the receiver side, hence violating the maximum playout delay constraint. Denoting the corresponding packet loss probability as p_{per} and p_{dly}, respectively, the total packet loss rate p_{loss} can then be written as

$$p_{\text{loss}} = p_{\text{per}} + p_{\text{dly}}. \tag{19}$$

In the case of multi-path routing as considered above, p_{per} and p_{dly} in (19) can be further expressed as

$$p_{\text{per}} = \sum_{z \in \mathcal{Z}} \frac{b^z}{b} p^z_{\text{per}}, \tag{20}$$

$$p_{\text{dly}} = \sum_{z \in \mathcal{Z}} \frac{b^z}{b} p^z_{\text{dly}}, \tag{21}$$

where p^z_{per} and p^z_{dly} represent the packet loss rate for path $z \in \mathcal{Z}$ due to transmission error and delay constraint violation, respectively; b and b^z represent total video rate and the rate allocated to path $z \in \mathcal{Z}$, respectively.

Since each path $z \in \mathcal{Z}$ may have one or multiple hops, to derive the expressions for p^z_{per} and p^z_{dly} in (20) and (21), we need to derive the resulting packet error rate and delay violation probability at each hop l of path $z \in \mathcal{Z}$, denoted as $p^{z,l}_{\text{per}}$ and $p^{z,l}_{\text{dly}}$, respectively. For this purpose, we first express the feasible transmission rate achievable at each hop. For each hop $l \in \mathcal{L}^z$ along path $z \in \mathcal{Z}$, let $G^{z,l}$ and $N^{z,l}$ represent the channel gain that accounts for both path loss and fading, and the additive white Gaussian noise (AWGN) power currently measured by hop l, respectively. Denoting

$P^{z,l}$ as the transmission power of the sender of hop l, then the attainable transmission rate for the hop, denoted by $C^{z,l}(P^{z,l})$, can be expressed as [27]

$$C^{z,l}(P^{z,l}) = \frac{W}{2}\log_2\left(1 + K\frac{P^{z,l}G^{z,l}}{N^{z,l}}\right), \quad (22)$$

where W is channel bandwidth in Hz, calibration factor K is defined as

$$K = \frac{-\phi_1}{\log(\phi_2 p_{\text{ber}})}, \quad (23)$$

with ϕ_1, ϕ_2 being constants depending on available set of channel coding and modulation schemes, and p_{ber} is the predefined maximum residual bit error rate (BER). Then, if path $z \in \mathcal{Z}$ is allocated video rate b^z, for each hop $l \in \mathcal{L}^z$, the average attainable transmission rate should be equal to or higher than b^z, i.e.,

$$\text{E}[C^{z,l}(P^{z,l})] \geq b^z, \quad (24)$$

with $\text{E}[C^{z,l}(P^{z,l})]$ defined by averaging $C^{z,l}(P^{z,l})$ over all possible channel gains $G^{z,l}$ in (22).

Based on the above setting, we can now express the single hop packet error rate $p_{\text{per}}^{z,l}$ for each hop $l \in \mathcal{L}^z$ of path $z \in \mathcal{Z}$ as,

$$p_{\text{per}}^{z,l} = 1 - (1 - p_{\text{ber}})^L, \quad (25)$$

where L is the predefined packet length in bits. Further, we characterize the queueing behavior at each wireless hop as in [28] using a M/M/1 model to capture the effects of channel-state-dependent transmission rate (22) single-hop queueing delay. Denoting $T^{z,l}$ as the delay budget tolerable at each hop $l \in \mathcal{L}^z$ of path $z \in \mathcal{Z}$, the resulting packet drop rate due to delay constraint violation can then be given as [29]

$$p_{\text{dly}}^{z,l} = e^{-(\text{E}[C^{z,l}(P^{z,l})] - b^z)\frac{T^{z,l}}{L}}, \quad (26)$$

with $\text{E}[C^{z,l}(P^{z,l})]$ defined in (24). For each path $z \in \mathcal{Z}$, the maximum tolerable end-to-end delay $T^{\max}$ can be assigned to each hop in different ways, e.g., equal assignment or distance-proportional assignment [30]. We adopt the same delay budget assignment scheme as in [30].

Finally, given $p_{\text{per}}^{z,l}$ and $p_{\text{dly}}^{z,l}$ in (25) and (26), we can express the end-to-end packet error rate p_{per}^{z} and delay violation probability p_{dly}^{z} in (20) and (21) as, for each path $z \in \mathcal{Z}$,

$$p_{\text{per}}^{z} = \sum_{l \in \mathcal{L}^z} p_{\text{per}}^{z,l}, \ \forall z \in \mathcal{Z}, \quad (27)$$

$$p_{\text{dly}}^{z} = \sum_{l \in \mathcal{L}^z} p_{\text{dly}}^{z,l}, \ \forall z \in \mathcal{Z}, \quad (28)$$

by neglecting the second and higher order product of $p_{\text{per}}^{z,l}$ and of $p_{\text{dly}}^{z,l}$. The resulting p_{per}^{z} and p_{dly}^{z} provide an upper bound on the real end-to-end packet error rate and delay constraint violation probability. The approximation error is negligible if packet loss rate at each wireless hop is low or moderate. Note that it is also possible to derive a lower bound on the end-to-end packet loss rate, e.g., by applying the Chernoff Bound [31].

Packet loss to measurement rate. After having modeled p_{loss}, we now concentrate on determining κ to convert p_{loss} to measurement rate reduction (referred to as $R_d = \kappa \cdot p_{\text{loss}}$). First, parameter $\tau = \frac{1}{QN}$ is defined to convert the amount of transmitted bits of each frame to its measurement rate R used in the (18), with Q being the bit-depth for each measurement. We assume that b is equally distributed among F frames within 1 second for all V views, i.e., the transmitted bits for each frame is $b/F/V$. Thus, measurement rate R for each frame of each view is equal and defined as $R = \tau b/F/V$. Then, we can define κ as

$$\kappa = \tau L \lceil \frac{b/F/V}{L} \rceil, \quad (29)$$

and rewrite (18) as

$$D_{\text{dec}} = D_0 - \frac{\theta}{\tau b/F/V - \kappa p_{\text{loss}} - R_0}. \quad (30)$$

Problem formulation. Based on (30), we formulate, as an example of applicability of the proposed framework, the problem of power consumption minimization for quality-assured compressive multi-view video streaming over multi-hop wireless sensor networks, by jointly determining the optimal frame-level encoding rate and allocating transmission rate among multiple paths, i.e.,

$$\text{P}_4: \underset{P^{z,l}, b^z, l \in \mathcal{L}^z, \forall z \in \mathcal{Z}}{\text{Minimize}} \sum_{z \in \mathcal{Z}} \sum_{l \in \mathcal{L}^z} P^{z,l} \quad (31)$$

$$\text{Subject to:} \quad b = \sum_{z \in \mathcal{Z}} b^z \quad (32)$$

$$D_{\text{dec}} \leq D_{\text{t}} \quad (33)$$

$$0 < \tau b/F/V - \kappa p_{\text{loss}} \leq 1 \quad (34)$$

$$0 \leq P^{z,l} \leq P_{\max}, \ \forall l \in \mathcal{L}^z, z \in \mathcal{Z}, \quad (35)$$

where D_{t} and $P_{\max}$ represent the constraints upon distortion and power consumption, respectively. Here, (33) and (34) are the constraints for required video quality level and total measurement rate not lower than 0 and higher than 1, respectively. In fact, the optimization problem P_4 is non-convex because the distortion constraint is non-convex. In Section 6, we adopt a solution algorithm to solve problem P_4 and demonstrate the reduction of the power saving by applying it based on the modeling framework.

6. PERFORMANCE EVALUATION

The topology includes a certain number V camera sensors and pre-established paths with random number of hops between camera sensors and the receiver. The frame rate is $F = 30$ fps, and the R-view periodically sends the R-frame every second. At the sparsity-aware CS independent encoder side, each frame is partitioned into 16×16 non-overlapped blocks implying $N_d = 256$. A measurement matrix $\mathbf{\Phi}_{vf}^i$ with elements drawn from independent and identically distributed (i.i.d) Gaussian random variables is considered, where the random seed is fixed for all experiments to make sure that $\mathbf{\Phi}_{vf}^i$ is drawn from the same matrix. The elements of the measurement vector $\tilde{\mathbf{y}}_{vf}^i$ are quantized individually by an 8-bit uniform scalar quantizer and then transmitted to the decoder. At the independent decoder end, we use $\mathbf{\Psi}_b$ composed of DCT transform basis as sparsifying matrix and choose the LASSO algorithm for reconstruction motivated by its low-complexity and excellent recovery performance characteristics. We consider two test multi-view sequences, *Exit* and *Vassar*, which are made publicly available [32]. In the sequences considered, the optical axis of each camera is parallel to the ground, and each camera is 19.5 cm away from its left and right neighbors. A spatial resolution of $(H = 240) \times (W = 320)$ is considered. *Exit* and *Vassar* are indoor surveillance and outdoor surveillance videos, respectively. The texture change of *Exit* is faster

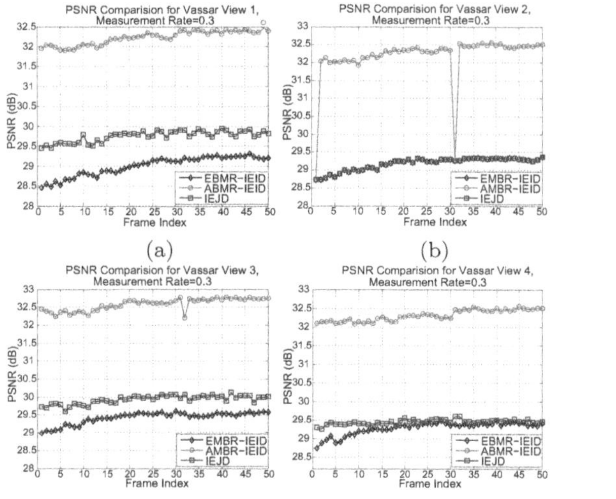

Figure 5: PSNR against frame index for (a) view 1, (b) view 2 (R-view), (c) view 3, and (d) view 4 of sequence *Vassar*.

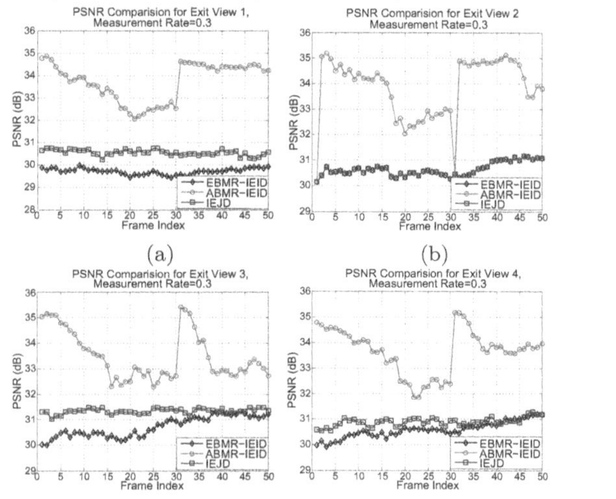

Figure 6: PSNR against frame index for (a) view 1, (b) view 2 (R-view), (c) view 3, and (d) view 4 of sequence *Exit*.

than that of *Vassar*, i.e., the block sparsity of *Exit* changes more quickly.

6.1 Evaluation of CS-based Multi-view Encoding/Decoding Architecture

We first experimentally study the performance of the proposed CS-based multi-view encoding/decoding architecture by evaluating the PSNR (as well as SSIM) of the reconstructed video sequences. Experiments are carried out only on the luminance component. Next, we illustrate the performance comparisons among (i) traditional Equal-Block-Measurement-Rate Independently Encoding and Independently Decoding approach (referred to as EBMR-IEID), (ii) the proposed sparsity-aware Adaptive-Block-Measurement-Rate Independently Encoding and Independently Decoding approach (referred to as ABMR-IEID) and (iii) Independently Encoding and Jointly Decoding (referred to as IEJD) proposed in [15] which selects one view as reference view reconstructed by traditional CS recovery method, while other views are jointly reconstructed by using reference frame.

Figures 5 and 6 show the PSNR comparisons of 50 frames for views 1, 2, 3 and 4 of *Vassar* and *Exit* multi-view sequences, where a 0.3 measurement rate for each view of

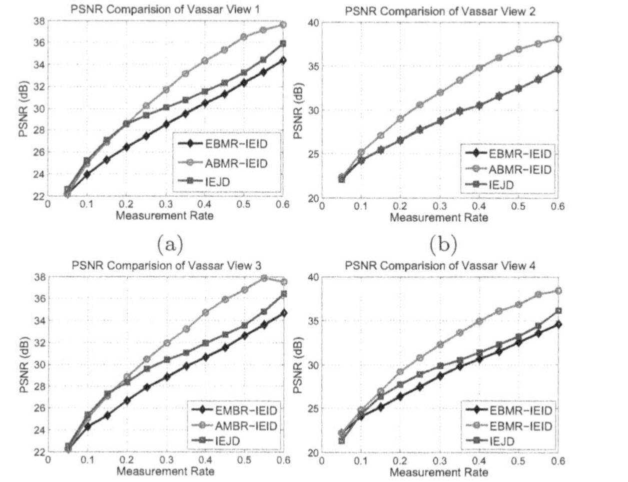

Figure 7: Rate-distortion comparison for frame 75 of *Vassar* sequences: (a) view 1, (b) view 2, (c) view 3, and (d) view 4.

ABMR-IEID and EBMR-IEID is selected. To assure fair comparison, the measurement rate of each view in IEJD is also set to 0.3. Besides, according to the R-view selection algorithm, view 2 is chosen as the R-view for this scenario. Since the R-view transmits the R-frame periodically, i.e., per second, and for the first frame of each period, the encoder will not encode them based on sparsity pattern, therefore we can observe drops occurred periodically in Fig. 5(b) and Fig. 6(b). For the *Vassar* sequences, as illustrated in Fig. 5, we can see that the proposed method ABMR-IEID outperforms the traditional approach EBMR-IEID and IEJD by up to 3.5 dB and 2.5 dB in terms of PSNR,respectively. For the *Exit* sequences, Figure 6 shows improvement in the reconstruction quality of ABMR-IEID compared with EBMR-IEID and IEJD fluctuates more than that of *Vassar* video, with increased PSNR varying from 5 dB to 2 dB and from 4 dB to 1 dB, respectively. This phenomenon occurs because of the video-based features, i.e., the texture of *Exit* changes faster than in *Vassar*. In other words, the proposed scheme is more robust in surveillance scenarios where the changes of texture are less severe. However, we can eliminate this phenomenon by transmitting R-frames more frequently. Figures 5 and 6 also depict performance improvement on NR-views (views 1, 3 and 4 here), i.e., by sharing the sparsity information between R-view and NR-views, correlation among views is implicitly exploited to improve the reconstruction quality.

We then illustrate the rate-distortion characteristics of ABMR-IEID, EBMR-IEID and IEJD. Figure 7 shows the comparisons of 4-view scenario, where the 75th frame of *Vassar* is taken as example. Evidently, ABMR-IEID outperforms significantly EBMR-IEID and IEJD, especially as the number of measurements increases. We can observe that at measurement rate 0.4, ABMR-IEID can improve PSNR by up to 4.4 dB and 2.4 dB, not only on R-view but also on NR-views. In the experiments, as the number of views increases, ABMR-IEID can still obtain significant PSNR gain compared to EBMR-IEID; while the performance of IEJD degrades faster as the distance to R-view increases, which can be apparently observed from Figs. 5, 6 and 7 where view 4 has distance 2 to R-view but with relatively lower PSNR gain compared to views 1 and 3.

Figure 8: Reconstructed frame 25 of view 3 by (a) ABMR-IEID, (b) EBMR-IEID, (c) IEJD, and reconstructed frame 25 of view 7 by (d) ABMR-IEID, (e) EBMR-IEID, and (f) IEJD.

Table 3: PSNR and SSIM comparison for *Vassar* eight views.

View #	ABMR-IEID		EBMR-IEID		IEJD	
	PSNR (dB)	SSIM	PSNR (dB)	SSIM	PSNR (dB)	SSIM
1	33.6675	0.8648	30.0883	0.8215	30.2717	0.7887
2	33.7768	0.8686	30.3459	0.8262	30.3355	0.7902
3	34.1934	0.8771	30.6265	0.8323	30.9214	0.8106
4	33.5766	0.8696	30.4168	0.8294	30.4168	0.8294
5	33.3030	0.8624	30.1011	0.8169	30.3641	0.7909
6	34.2191	0.8846	30.6803	0.8382	30.7265	0.8059
7	32.9924	0.8575	29.8250	0.8162	29.6648	0.7772
8	32.3376	0.8472	29.3713	0.8054	29.5466	0.7742

Next, we extend the scenario to 8 views on *Vassar*, where view 4 is selected as R-view, and the measurement rate is set to 0.35 for all views. Figure 8 shows the specific reconstructed image comparison, where the left column illustrates the reconstructed frame 25 of view 3 and view 7 by ABMR-IEID, respectively. The milldle column shows the reconstructed images by EBMR-IEID, and the left columns shows the results obtained by using IEJD. We can observe that the quality of images located in the left column is much better than that in the right two columns (e.g., the curtain in the 2nd floor and person in the scene, and etc.). Furthermore, Table 3 shows the detailed PSNR and SSIM value comparison between ABMR-IEID and EBMR-IEID and IEJD for frame 25 of 8 views. From Fig. 8 and Table 3, we can see that ABMR-IEID also works well on 8 views compared to ABMR-IEID and EBMR-IEID, with PSNR and SSIM improvement up to 3.5 dB and 0.05, respectively. However, the IEJD method proposed in [15] does not perform well on 8 views, where the gain is almost negligible.

6.2 Evaluation of Power-efficient Compressive Video Streaming

The following network topology is considered: 2-path scenario with 2-hop path 1 and 1-hop path 2. We assume bandwidth $W = 1$ MHz for each channel. The maximum transmission power at each node is set to 1 W and the target distortion in MSE is 50. We also assume the maximum end-to-end delay is $T^{\max} = 0.5$s assigned to each hop proportional to the hop distance. To evaluate PE-CVS (referred to as the proposed power-efficient compressive video streaming algorithm), we compare it with an algorithm (referred to as ER-CVS) that equally splits the frame-level rate calculated by PE-CVS onto different paths.

Figure 9 illustrates the total power consumption comparison between PE-CVS and ER-CVS and the saved power by PE-CVS compared to ER-CVS. From Fig. 9(a), we see that PE-CVS (depicted in red line) results in less power consumption than ER-CVS (black dash line). At some points, the total power consumption of PE-CVS and ER-CVS is almost the same. This occurs because the path-level bit rates calculated by PE-CVS are equal to each other. Since ER-CVS uses frame-level rate obtained from PE-CVS and equally allocates it to each path, thereby resulting in the same power consumption. As shown in Fig. 9(b), the histogram apparently shows that PE-CVS saves more power than ER-CVS, up to 170 mW.

7. CONCLUSIONS

We have proposed a novel compressive multi-view video coding/decoding architecture - cooperative sparsity-aware independent encoder and independent decoder. We also introduced a central controller to do the sparsity pattern estimation, R-view selection, mean value estimation and implement network optimization algorithms. By introducing limited channel feedback and enabling lightweight sparsity information sharing between R-view and NR-views, the encoders independently encode the video sequences with sparsity awareness and exploit multi-view correlation to improve

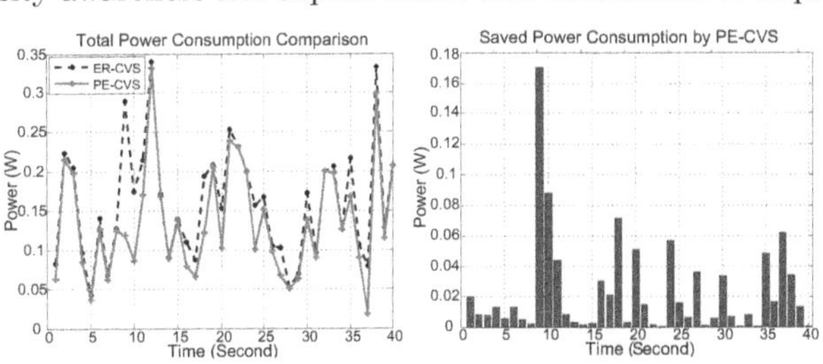

Figure 9: 2-path Scenario: (a) Total power consumption comparison, (b) Saved power consumption by PE-CVS compared to ER-CVS.

the reconstruction quality of NR-views. Based on the proposed encoding/decoding architecture, we developed an R-D model that considers the packet loss effect in CS video streaming in WSNs. Then, we studied a modeling framework to design network optimization algorithms, where packet loss rate for a multi-hop multi-path sensor network and the conversion from packet loss rate to the measurement rate reduction are derived. Finally, we presented a power-efficient algorithm. Extensive simulation results showed that the designed compressive multi-view framework can considerably improve the video reconstruction quality with minimal power consumption.

8. ACKNOWLEDGMENTS

This paper is based upon work supported in part by the US National Science Foundation under grants CNS1117121 and CNS1218717 and by the Office of Naval Research under grant N00014-11-1-0848. Zhangyu Guan was also supported in part by the Shandong Doctoral Foundation under grant 2012BSE27052.

9. REFERENCES

[1] I. F. Akyildiz, T. Melodia, and K. R. Chowdhury. A Survey on Wireless Multimedia Sensor Networks. *Computer Networks*, 51(4):921–960, March 2007.

[2] Z. Guan and T. Melodia. Cloud-Assisted Smart Camera Networks for Energy-Efficient 3D Video Streaming. *IEEE Computer*, 47(5):60–66, May 2014.

[3] M. M. Hannuksela, D. Rusanovskyy, W. Su, L. Chen, R. Li, P. Aflaki, D. Lan, M. Joachimiak, H. Li, and M. Gabbouj. Multiview-Video-Plus-Depth Coding Based on the Advanced Video Coding Standard. *IEEE Transactions on Image Processing*, 22(9):3449–3458, September, 2013.

[4] A. Vetro, T. Wiegand, and G. J. Sullivan. Overview of the Stereo and Multiview Video Coding Extensions of the H.264/MPEG-4 AVC Standard. *Proceedings of the IEEE*, 99(4):626–642, April 2011.

[5] S. Pudlewski, N. Cen, Z. Guan, and T. Melodia. Video Transmission over Lossy Wireless Networks: A Cross-layer Perspective. *IEEE Journal of Selected Topics in Signal Processing*, 9(1):6–22, February 2015.

[6] E. J. Candes and M. B. Wakin. An Introduction to Compressive Sampling. *IEEE Signal Processing Magazine*, 25(2):21–30, March 2008.

[7] D. L. Donoho. Compressed Sensing. *IEEE Trans. on Information Theory*, 52(4):1289–1306, April 2006.

[8] S. Pudlewski and T. Melodia. A Tutorial on Encoding and Wireless Transmission of Compressively Sampled Videos. *IEEE Communications Surveys & Tutorials*, 15(2):754–767, Second Quarter 2013.

[9] H. Chen, L. Kang, and C. Lu. Dynamic measurement rate allocation for distributed compressive video sensing. In *Proc. IEEE/SPIE Visual Communications and Image Processing (VCIP)*, Huangshan, China, July 2010.

[10] Y. Liu, M. Li, and D. A. Pados. Motion-aware Decoding of Compressed-sensed Video. *IEEE Trans. on Circuits System Video Technology*, 23(3):438–444, March 2013.

[11] S. Pudlewski, T. Melodia, and A. Prasanna. Compressed-Sensing-Enabled Video Streaming for Wireless Multimedia Sensor Networks. *IEEE Trans. on Mobile Computing*, 11(6):1060–1072, June 2012.

[12] S. Pudlewski and T. Melodia. Compressive Video Streaming: Design and Rate-Energy-Distortion Analysis. *IEEE Transactions on Multimedia*, 15(8):2072–2086, December 2013.

[13] X. Chen and P. Frossard. Joint Reconstruction of Compressed Multi-view Images. In *Proc. IEEE International Conf. on Acoustics, Speech and Signal Processing (ICASSP)*, Taipei, Taiwan, April 2009.

[14] M. Trocan, T. Maugey, E. W. Tramel, J. E. Fowler, and B. Pesquet-Popescu. Compressed Sensing of Multiview Images Using Disparity Compensation. In *Proc. Intern. Conf. on Image Processing (ICIP)*, Hong Kong, September 2010.

[15] N. Cen, Z. Guan, and T. Melodia. Joint Decoding of Independently Encoded Compressive Multi-view Video Streams. In *Proc. of Picture Coding Symposium (PCS)*, San Jose, CA, December 2013.

[16] C. Li, D. Wu, and H. Xiong. Delay-Power-Rate-Distortion Model for Wireless Video Communication Under Delay and Energy Constraints. *IEEE Transactions on Circuits and Systems for Video Technology*, 24(7):1170–1183, July 2014.

[17] Z. He, Y. Liang, L. Chen, I. Ahmad, and D. Wu. Power-rate-distortion Analysis for Wireless Video Communication under Energy Constraints. *IEEE Transactions on Circuits and Systems for Video Technology*, 15(5):645–658, May 2005.

[18] M. A. T. Figueiredo, R. D. Nowak, and S. J. Wright. Gradient Projection for Sparse Reconstruction: Application to Compressed Sensing and Other Inverse Problems. *IEEE Journal on Selected Topics in Signal Processing*, 1(4):586–598, December 2007.

[19] R. Tibshirani. Regression Shrinkage and Selection Via the Lasso. *Journal of the Royal Statistical Society, Series B*, 58:267–288, 1996.

[20] D. L. Donoho, M. Elad, and V. N. Temlyakov. Stable Recovery of Sparse Overcomplete Representations in the Presence of Noise. *IEEE Transactions on Information Theory*, 52(1):6–18, January 2006.

[21] K. Stuhlmuller, N. Farber, M. Link, and B. Girod. Analysis of Video Transmission over Lossy Channels. *IEEE Journal on Selected Areas in Communications*, 18(6):1012–1032, June 2000.

[22] D. Slepian and J. K. Wolf. Noiseless Coding of Correlated Information Sources. *IEEE Transactions on Information Theory*, 19(4):471–480, July 1973.

[23] A. D. Wyner and J. Ziv. The Rate-distortion Function for Source Coding with Side-information at the Decoder. *IEEE Transactions on Information Theory*, 22(1):1–10, January 1976.

[24] Z. Wang, A. Bovik, H. Sheikh, and E. Simoncelli. Image Quality Assessment: From Error Visibility to Structural Similarity. *IEEE Transactions on Image Processing*, 13(4):600–612, April 2004.

[25] Charles E. Perkins and Elizabeth M. Royer. Ad hoc On-Demand Distance Vector (AODV) Routing. *RFC 3561*, July 2003.

[26] Y. Shi, S. Sharma, Y. T. Hou, and S. Kompella. Optimal Relay Assignment for Cooperative Communications. In *Proc. ACM Intern. Symp. on Mobile Ad Hoc Networking and Computing (MobiHoc)*, Hong Kong, China, May 2008.

[27] A. Goldsmith. *Wireless Communications*. Cambridge University Press, New York, NY, USA, 2005.

[28] X. Zhu, E. Setton, and B. Girod. Congestion-distortion Optimized Video Transmission over Ad Hoc Networks. *EURASIP Journal of Signal Processing: Image Communications*, 20:773–783, 2005.

[29] D. Bertsekas and R. Gallager. *Data Networks*. Prentice Hall, USA, 2000.

[30] T. Melodia and I. D. Akyildiz. Cross-layer Quality of Service Support for UWB Wireless Multimedia Sensor Networks. In *Proc. of IEEE Conference on Computer Communications (INFOCOM)*, Phoenix, AZ, April 2008.

[31] H. Chernoff. A Measure of Asymptotic Efficiency for Tests of a Hypothesis Based on The Sum of Observations. *Ann. Math. Statist.*, 23(4):493–507, December 1952.

[32] Mitsubishi Electric Research Laboratories. MERL Multi-view Video Sequences. [Available] ftp://ftp.merl.com/pub/avetro/mvc-testseq.

When Network Effect Meets Congestion Effect: Leveraging Social Services for Wireless Services

Xiaowen Gong
School of Electrical, Computer and Energy Engeering
Arizona State University
Tempe, AZ 85287, USA
xgong9@asu.edu

Lingjie Duan
Engineering Systems and Design Pillar
Singapore University of Technology and Design
Singapore 487372, Singapore
lingjie_duan@sutd.edu.sg

Xu Chen*
Institute of Computer Science
University of Goettingen
Goettingen 37073, Germany
xu.chen@cs.uni-goettingen.de

ABSTRACT

The recent development of social services tightens wireless users' social relationships and encourages them to generate more data traffic under network effect. This boosts the demand for wireless services yet may challenge the limited wireless capacity. To fully exploit this opportunity, we study mobile users' data usage behaviors by jointly considering the network effect based on their social relationships in the social domain and the congestion effect in the physical wireless domain. Accordingly, we develop a Stackelberg game for problem formulation: In Stage I, a wireless provider first decides the data pricing to all users to maximize its revenue, and then in Stage II users observe the price and decide data usage subject to mutual interactions under both network and congestion effects. We analyze the two-stage game using backward induction. For Stage II, we first show the existence and uniqueness of a user demand equilibrium (UDE). Then we propose a distributed update algorithm for users to reach the UDE. Furthermore, we investigate the impacts of different parameters on the UDE. For Stage I, we develop an optimal pricing algorithm to maximize the wireless provider's revenue. We evaluate the performance of our proposed algorithms by numerical studies using real data, and thereby draw useful engineering insights for the operation of wireless providers.

Categories and Subject Descriptors

C.2.1 [**Computer-Communication Networks**]: Network Architecture and Design—*Wireless communication*

*The corresponding author is Xu Chen.

MobiHoc'15, June 22–25, 2015, Hangzhou, China.

http://dx.doi.org/10.1145/2746285.2746315.

Keywords

Mobile social network, wireless data usage, network effect, congestion effect

1. INTRODUCTION

The past few years have witnessed pervasive penetration of mobile devices in people's daily life, thanks to the wireless technology advances. Motivated by many social applications on mobile platforms (e.g., WeChat, WhatsApp [1, 2]), mobile users' data usage behaviors have been increasingly influenced by their social relationships. In 2014, the number of online social media users on mobile platforms has reached 1.6 billion, accounting for 44% of mobile users and 80% of online social media users [3].

The popularity of social services on mobile platforms also gives opportunities to wireless service providers who operate the mobile networks. Intuitively, social services can encourage mobile users to demand more data usage by stimulating their interactions with each other through these services (e.g., online social gaming and blogging). When a user increases its activity in a social service, its social friends would also increase their activities. Therefore, users' data usage levels for social services present network effect to others [4]. This demand increase provides a great potential for wireless providers' revenue increase.

However, this potential benefit is subject to the limited wireless capacity in physical communication networks (e.g., spectrum). As users increase their data usage, they also experience more congestion (e.g., service delays), which discourages them to use more. The increasing congestion poses a significant challenge for wireless providers to increase their revenues.

As a result, mobile users' data usage behaviors are not only subject to congestion effect in the physical network, but also network effect in the social network (as illustrated in Fig. 1), which has been largely overlooked by traditional wireless providers. To fully exploit the potential benefit brought by social services, it is necessary to investigate users' data usage behaviors in these two domains, so that a wireless provider can take the best strategy in favor of its revenue. With this insight, we not only analyze users' interactions

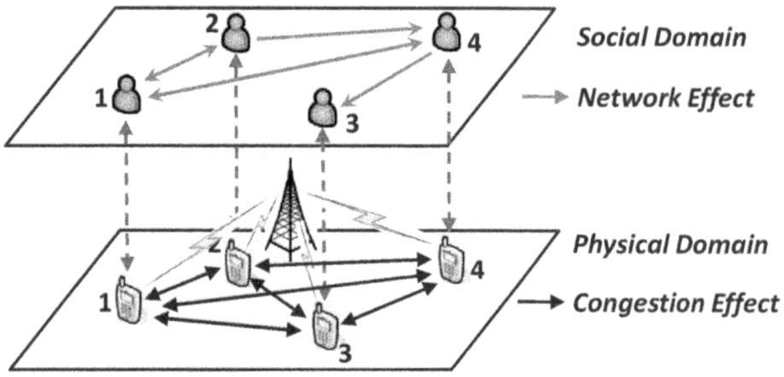

Figure 1: Mobile users experience network effect in the social network and congestion effect in the physical network.

subject to both network and congestion effects, but also study the optimal pricing strategy for the wireless provider.

The main contributions of this paper can be summarized as follows.

- *Stackelberg game formulation:* By jointly considering users' social relationships and the wireless network's congestion, we formulate the interaction between the wireless provider and mobile users as a Stackelberg game: In Stage I, the wireless provider chooses a price to maximize its revenue; in Stage II, mobile users choose their data usage levels based on the price to maximize their socially-aware payoffs.

- *Equilibrium analysis for user demands in Stage II:* We first give a general condition under which there exists a user demand equilibrium (UDE), and then we show that under a further general condition the game is a concave game and thus admits a unique UDE. We also propose a distributed algorithm for users to achieve the UDE. Next we show that a user's usage can increase when price increases. We further show that if the social network is symmetric, the total usage always increases when a user's parameter (e.g., social tie) improves.

- *Provider's optimal pricing in Stage I:* Finally, by taking into account users' equilibrium demands, we develop an optimal pricing algorithm to maximize the revenue of the wireless provider. We evaluate the performance of total usage and revenue by simulations, and draws useful engineering insights for the wireless provider's operation.

The rest of this paper is organized as follows. In Section 2, we formulate the Stackelberg game between the wireless provider and mobile users. Section 3 studies users' demand equilibrium in Stage II. Section 4 studies the provider's optimal pricing strategy in Stage I. Simulation results and discussions are given in Section 5. Related work are reviewed in Section 6. Section 7 concludes this paper.

2. SYSTEM MODEL

2.1 Socially-aware Wireless Service

Consider a set of users $\mathcal{N} \triangleq \{1, \dots, N\}$ participating in a wireless service provided by a wireless operator (e.g., AT&T). Each user $i \in \mathcal{N}$ consumes an amount of data usage in the wireless service, denoted by x_i where $x_i \in [0, \infty)$. Let $\mathbf{x} \triangleq (x_1, \dots, x_N)$ denote the usage profile of all the users and $\mathbf{x}_{-i}$ denote the the usage profile without user i. Affected by the other users' usage subject to congestion effect due to the limited resources in the wireless network, the payoff of user i by consuming data usage x_i is

$$v_i(x_i, \mathbf{x}_{-i}, p) = a_i x_i - \frac{1}{2} b_i x_i^2 - \frac{1}{2} c(\sum_{j \in \mathcal{N}} x_j)^2 - p x_i,$$

where $a_i > 0$ and $b_i > 0$ are the *internal utility coefficients* that capture the intrinsic value of the wireless service to user i, $c > 0$ is the *congestion coefficient* that is determined by the resource constraints of the wireless network, and p is the usage-based price charged by the wireless provider[1]. As in [5], the quadratic form of the internal utility function not only allows for tractable analysis, but also serves as a good second-order approximation for a broad class of concave utility functions. In particular, a_i models the maximum internal demand rate, and b_i models the internal demand elasticity factor. For the congestion model, the quadratic sum form reflects that a user's congestion experience is affected by all the users, and the marginal cost of congestion increases as the total usage increases.

Traditional wireless providers' operation does not take into account the fact that social services encourage mobile users to demand more data usage. We thus account for this effect in our model. Then user i's payoff includes the addition of social utility, i.e.,

$$u_i(x_i, \mathbf{x}_{-i}, p) = a_i x_i - \frac{1}{2} b_i x_i^2 + \sum_{j \neq i} g_{ij} x_i x_j - \frac{1}{2} c(\sum_{j \in \mathcal{N}} x_j)^2 - p x_i \quad (1)$$

where $g_{ij} \geq 0$ is the *social tie* that quantifies the social influence from user j to user i. As in [5], the product form $g_{ij} x_i x_j$ of the social utility function captures that a user derives more utility by increasing its usage in social services, and the marginal gain of social utility increases as its social friends increase their usage. Therefore, social services bring in network effect among users and can increase their utilities.

2.2 Stackelberg Game Formulation

We model the interaction between the wireless provider and mobile users for the socially-aware wireless service as a two-stage Stackelberg game.

DEFINITION 1 (TWO-STAGE PRICING-USAGE GAME).

- Stage I (Pricing): *The wireless provider chooses price p to maximize its revenue:*

$$p^* = \arg \max_{p \in [0, \infty)} t(\mathbf{x}) p$$

where $t(\mathbf{x}) \triangleq \sum_{i \in \mathcal{N}} x_i$ denotes the total usage under strategy profile $\mathbf{x}$;

- Stage II (Usage): *Each user $i \in \mathcal{N}$ chooses its data usage level x_i to maximize its payoff given the price p and the usage levels of the other users $\mathbf{x}_{-i}$:*

$$x_i^* = \arg \max_{x_i \in [0, \infty)} u_i(x_i, \mathbf{x}_{-i}, p).$$

We study the two-stage pricing-usage game by backward induction [6]. For Stage II, given a price chosen by the wireless provider in Stage I, we are interested in the existence of

[1]Usage-based pricing is widely used in practice by wireless operators to control the demand. Here the price is the same for all users to ensure fairness.

a stable outcome of users' interactions at which no user will deviate. This leads to the concept of user equilibrium.

Definition 2 (User Demand Equilibrium). *For any price p given in Stage I, the user demand equilibrium (UDE) in Stage II is a strategy profile $\mathbf{x}^*$ such that no user can improve its payoff by unilaterally changing its usage, i.e.,*

$$x_i^* = \arg \max_{x_i \in [0,\infty)} u_i(x_i, \mathbf{x}_{-i}^*, p), \ \forall i.$$

Given the UDE in Stage II, we will study the optimal pricing strategy for the wireless provider in Stage I.

3. STAGE II: USER DEMAND EQUILIBRIUM

In this section, we study users' demands in Stage II.

Using the concave payoff function (1), by setting the derivative $\frac{\partial u_i(x_i, \mathbf{x}_{-i})}{\partial x_i} = 0$ as the first-order condition, we obtain the *best response function* of user i as

$$r_i(\mathbf{x}_{-i}) = \max \left\{ 0, \ \frac{a_i - p}{b_i + c} + \sum_{j \neq i} \frac{g_{ij} - c}{b_i + c} x_j \right\}. \tag{2}$$

According to (2), each user i's usage demand consists of two parts: *internal demand* $\frac{a_i - p}{b_i + c}$ that is independent of the other users, and *external demand* $\sum_{j \neq i} \frac{g_{ij}-c}{b_i+c} x_j$ that depends on the other users. The coefficient $\frac{g_{ij}-c}{b_i+c}$ represents the marginal increase or decrease of user i's demand when user j's usage increases: when $g_{ij} > c$, user j's influence to user i is dominated by network effect; when $g_{ij} < c$, it is dominated by congestion effect.

3.1 Existence and Uniqueness of UDE

We first investigate the existence of UDE in Stage II. We make the following assumption.

Assumption 1. $\sum_{j \neq i} \frac{|g_{ij} - c|}{b_i + c} < 1, \ \forall i.$

This assumption is for analysis tractability. It is an important condition to guarantee the existence of UDE, as there can exist no UDE when it does not hold (as illustrated by an example in Fig. 2). According to the best response function (2), Assumption 1 implies that any user's absolute external demand $|\sum_{j \neq i} \frac{g_{ij}-c}{b_i+c} x_j|$ is less than the maximum usage $\max_{j \neq i} x_j$ among all the other users. This is a mild condition as the aggregate effect experienced by a user from all the other users would be less than the largest effect the user can experience from an individual of the other users. A similar assumption is made in [5] for similar considerations.

Now we can show that there always exists a UDE in Stage II.

Theorem 1. *Under Assumption 1, the Stage II game admits a UDE.*

The proof is given in Appendix and the main idea is to show that the game has an equivalent game which admits a UDE.

Next we give another general technical condition under which the game admits a unique UDE.

Theorem 2. *Under Assumption 1, the Stage II game admits a unique UDE if $\sum_{j \neq i} \frac{|g_{ji} - c|}{b_i + c} < 1, \ \forall i.$*

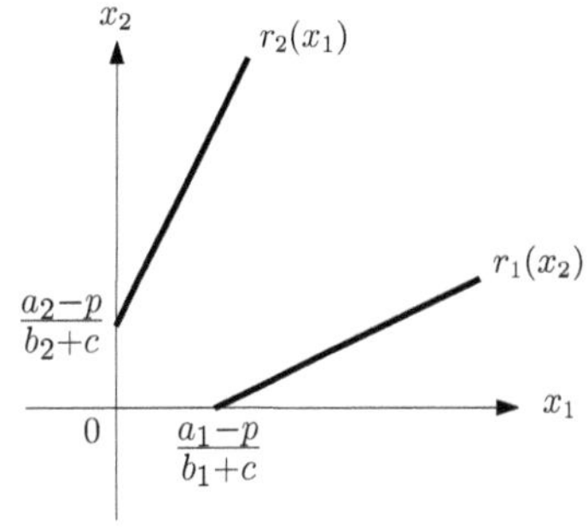

Figure 2: For Stage II for two users, when $\frac{g_{12}-c}{b_1+c} > 1$ and $\frac{g_{21}-c}{b_2+c} > 1$, there does not exist a UDE. The bold lines are the best response functions and do not intersect.

The proof is given in Appendix and the main idea is is to show that the game is a concave game [7], and thus admits a unique UDE.

Remark: According to Theorem 2, it is worth noting that the Stage II game admits a unique UDE when users' social ties are symmetric (i.e., $g_{ij} = g_{ji}, \forall i \neq j$). The symmetric setting of social networks is of great interests. Motivated by the idea of social reciprocity [8], a user's social behavior to another is likely to imitate the latter's behavior to the former. As a result, two users' social ties to each other tend to be the same.

3.2 Computing and Achieving UDE

As we have showed the existence of UDE, we then design an algorithm to compute the UDE, as described in Algorithm 1. The algorithm iteratively updates users' strategies based on their best response functions (2) and converges to the UDE.

Algorithm 1: Compute the UDE in Stage II

```
input: precision threshold ε;
x_i^(0) ← 0, ∀i ∈ N; t ← 1;
repeat
    foreach i ∈ N;
    do
        x_i^(t+1) = max{0, (a_i − p)/(b_i + c) + Σ_{j≠i} (g_ij − c)/(b_i + c) x_j^(t)};
    end
    t ← t + 1;
until ||x^(t) − x^(t−1)|| ≤ ε;
return x^(t);
```

Theorem 3. *Algorithm 1 computes the UDE in Stage II.*

The proof is given in Appendix and the main idea is to show that the best response updates in the algorithm result in a contraction mapping and hence converges to a fixed point.

It is desirable for users to reach the UDE in a distributed manner. We then propose a distributed update algorithm based on Algorithm 1, as described in Algorithm 2.

Note that the usage update in Algorithm 2 is equivalent to the best response update in Algorithm 1. Each user i chooses its best response usage based on the usage of its

Algorithm 2: Distributed algorithm to achieve the UDE in Stage II

each user $i \in \mathcal{N}$ **chooses** an initial usage $x_i^{(0)} \geq 0$;
loop at each time interval $t = 1, 2, \ldots$
each user $i \in \mathcal{N}$ in parallel:
updates its usage by

$$\max\left\{0, \frac{a_i - p}{b_i + c} + \frac{1}{b_i + c}\sum_{j \neq i, g_{ij} > 0} g_{ij} x_j^{(t)} - \frac{c}{b_i + c}\sum_{j \neq i} x_j^{(t)}\right\}$$

end loop

social friends who have social influences to it (i.e., each user j with $g_{ij} > 0$), which can be obtained from the social friends, and the total usage of all users, which can be obtained from the wireless provider. The correctness of Algorithm 2 follows from that of Algorithm 1 and is thus omitted.

PROPOSITION 1. *Algorithm 2 achieves the UDE in Stage II.*

3.3 Parameter Analysis at UDE

We first investigate the impact of price on the UDE. To draw clean insights, we start with the case for two users. Without loss of generality, assume that $a_1 \geq a_2$.

PROPOSITION 2. *For Stage II for two users, there exists a price threshold $p_{th} \in [0, a_1]$ where*

$$p_{th} = \frac{a_2(b_1 + c) - a_1(c - g_{21})}{b_1 + g_{21}} \quad (3)$$

such that the UDE $\mathbf{x}^*$ is given as follows, depending on the price p:

- High price regime: *When $p \geq a_1$, $x_1^* = x_2^* = 0$;*
- Medium price regime: *When $p_{th} \leq p < a_1$, $x_1^* = \frac{a_1 - p}{b_1 + c}$ and $x_2^* = 0$;*
- Low price regime: *When $0 \leq p < p_{th}$, $x_1^* = \frac{(a_1-p)(b_2+c)-(a_2-p)(c-g_{12})}{b_1 b_2 - g_{12} g_{21} + c(b_1+b_2+g_{12}+g_{21})}$ and $x_2^* = \frac{(a_2-p)(b_1+c)-(a_1-p)(c-g_{21})}{b_1 b_2 - g_{12} g_{21} + c(b_1+b_2+g_{12}+g_{21})}$.*

Due to space limitation, the proof is given in our online technical report [9]. According to (3), there are three cases of the threshold p_{th} depending on which effect dominates user 2's experience from user 1 (as illustrated in Fig. 3).

1. *Neither effect:* When $g_{21} = c$, we have $p_{th} = a_2$. As network effect and congestion effect cancel each other, user 2 experiences neither effect from user 1. Then user 2's usage demand is equal to its internal demand, and it reaches 0 when $p = a_2$.
2. *Congestion effect:* When $g_{21} < c$, we have $p_{th} < a_2$. As user 2 experiences congestion effect from user 1, even when p is less than a_2 such that user 2 has a positive internal demand, its external demand can be sufficiently negative such that user 2's usage demand is negative. In particular, when $\frac{a_1}{a_2} \geq \frac{b_1 + c}{c - g_{21}}$, user 2's usage is 0 even when the price is 0.
3. *Network effect:* When $g_{21} > c$, we have $p_{th} > a_2$. As user 2 experiences network effect from user 1, even when p is greater than a_2 such that user 2 has a negative internal demand, its external demand can be sufficiently positive such that user 2's usage demand is positive.

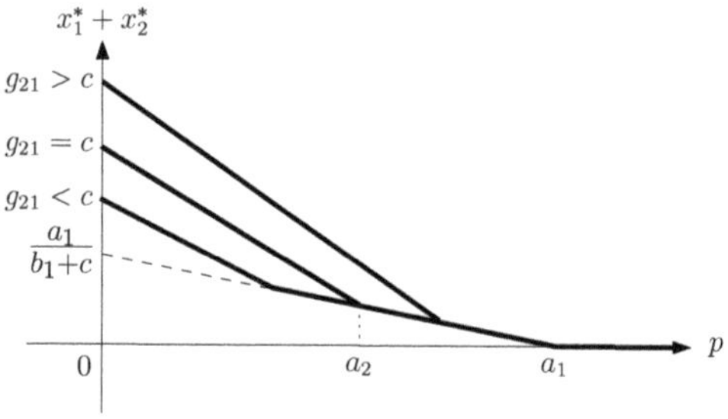

Figure 3: Total usage at the UDE in Stage II for two users.

Next we study the general case for any number of users. For convenience, let us define

$$B = \begin{bmatrix} b_1 + c & c & \cdots & c \\ c & b_2 + c & \cdots & c \\ \vdots & \vdots & \ddots & \vdots \\ c & c & \cdots & b_N + c \end{bmatrix}, G = \begin{bmatrix} 0 & g_{12} & \cdots & g_{1N} \\ g_{21} & 0 & \cdots & g_{2N} \\ \vdots & \vdots & \ddots & \vdots \\ g_{N1} & g_{N2} & \cdots & 0 \end{bmatrix}.$$

Also define C as the $N \times N$ matrix with each entry being c. For a UDE $\mathbf{x}^*$, let $\mathcal{S}$ be the set of users with positive usage in $\mathbf{x}^*$ (i.e., $x_i^* > 0$, $\forall i \in \mathcal{S}$ and $x_i^* = 0$, $\forall i \notin \mathcal{S}$). For convenience, let $\mathbf{v}_\mathcal{S}$ denote the $|\mathcal{S}| \times 1$ vector comprised of the entries of a vector $\mathbf{v}$ with indices in $\mathcal{S}$, $M_\mathcal{S}$ denote the $|\mathcal{S}| \times |\mathcal{S}|$ matrix comprised of the entries of a matrix M with indices in $\mathcal{S} \times \mathcal{S}$, and $[M]_{i,\mathcal{S}}$ denote the $1 \times |\mathcal{S}|$ vector comprised of the entries of the ith row of a matrix M with column indices in $\mathcal{S}$. According to the best response function (2), $\mathbf{x}_\mathcal{S}^*$ is the solution to the system of equations

$$B_\mathcal{S}\mathbf{x}_\mathcal{S} = \mathbf{a}_\mathcal{S} - p\mathbf{1}_\mathcal{S} + G_\mathcal{S}\mathbf{x}_\mathcal{S}$$

where $\mathbf{1}$ denotes the $N \times 1$ vector of 1s. We need the following lemma:

LEMMA 1. *Under Assumption 1, $(B_\mathcal{S} - G_\mathcal{S})$ is invertible for any set $\mathcal{S} \subseteq \mathcal{N}$.*

The proof is given in [9]. Thus we have

$$\mathbf{x}_\mathcal{S}^* = (B_\mathcal{S} - G_\mathcal{S})^{-1}(\mathbf{a}_\mathcal{S} - p\mathbf{1}_\mathcal{S}). \quad (4)$$

When users have the same internal coefficient a_i, we can show that the same set of users have positive equilibrium usage at different prices.

PROPOSITION 3. *For Stage II, when $a_i = a$, $\forall i$, the UDE $\mathbf{x}^*$ is given as follows, depending on the price p:*

- *When $p > a$, $x_i^* = 0$, $\forall i$;*
- *When $0 \leq p \leq a$, there exists a set $\mathcal{S} \subseteq \mathcal{N}$ such that for any $p \in [0, a)$,*

  $$x_i^* = [(B_\mathcal{S} - G_\mathcal{S})^{-1}(\mathbf{a}_\mathcal{S} - p\mathbf{1}_\mathcal{S})]_i > 0, \forall i \in \mathcal{S},$$

  and $x_i^* = 0$, $\forall i \notin \mathcal{S}$, where $[M]_i$ denotes the ith row of matrix M.

The proof is given in Appendix. Proposition 3 shows that the set of users with positive equilibrium usage (if they exist)

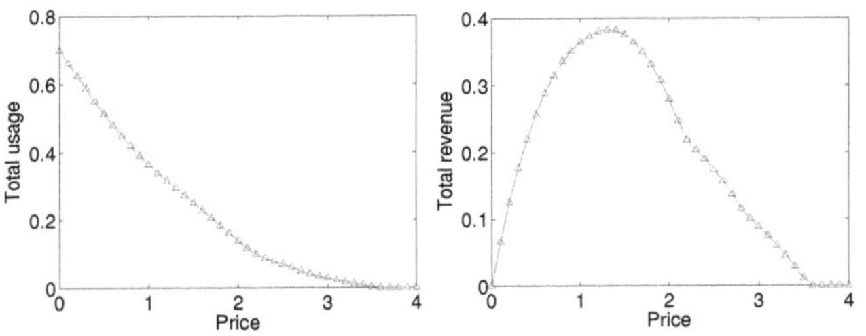

(a) Total usage vs. price p. (b) Total revenue vs. price p.

Figure 4: (a) Total usage at the UDE is a piece-wise linear function of price; (b) Total revenue at the UDE is a piece-wise quadratic function of price.

does not change with price, and each user's positive usage decreases when price increases.

We then show by a counterexample that if users have different internal coefficients a_i, a user's equilibrium usage can increase when price increases. Consider a case for three users where $a_1 = 2$, $a_2 = a_3 = 1.5$, $b_i = 3, \forall i$, $c = 2$, $p = 0.4$, and $g_{23} = g_{32} = 4$, $g_{ij} = 0, \forall \{i,j\} \neq \{2,3\}$[2]. We can show that there exists a unique UDE $\mathbf{x}^*$ and it is the solution to the system of equations below:

$$5x_1 + 2x_2 + 2x_3 = 1.6$$
$$5x_2 + 2x_1 - 2x_3 = 1.1$$
$$5x_3 - 2x_2 + 2x_1 = 1.1.$$

Solving these equations, we have $x_1^* = 0.0571$, $x_2^* = 0.3286$, $x_3^* = 0.3286$. When price p increases to 0.5, the new UDE is the solution to

$$5x_1 + 2x_2 + 2x_3 = 1.5$$
$$5x_2 + 2x_1 - 2x_3 = 1$$
$$5x_3 - 2x_2 + 2x_1 = 1$$

which is $x_1^* = 0.0714 > 0.0571$, $x_2^* = 0.2857$, $x_3^* = 0.2857$. Thus the usage of user 1 increases.

Remark: Intuitively, when the price increases, the usage of both user 2 and 3 decrease and the internal demand of user 1 decreases. However, as user 1 experiences strong congestion effect from both user 2 and 3, user 1's external demand increases due to the decrease of congestion effect, and it increases faster than the decrease of user 1's internal demand as price increases, such that the total of internal and external demand increases. In addition, a larger internal coefficient a_1 of user 1 than that of user 2 and 3 allows user 1 to have a positive equilibrium usage $x_1^* = 0.0714$ even when its external demand is negative due to the strong congestion effect. Indeed, if user 1 has the same internal coefficient $a_1 = 1.5$ as user 2 and 3, then we can show that its equilibrium usage is 0.

Furthermore, when users have different internal coefficients a_i, we have the following result.

PROPOSITION 4. *For Stage II, the UDE $\mathbf{x}^*$ is given as follows, depending on the price p:*

- *When $p > \max_{i \in \mathcal{N}} a_i$, $x_i^* = 0, \forall i$;*
- *When $0 \leq p \leq \max_{i \in \mathcal{N}} a_i$, there is a set of prices $p_0 \triangleq 0 < p_1 < \cdots < p_M < p_{M+1} \triangleq \max_{i \in \mathcal{N}} a_i$, and for each $k \in \{0, \ldots, M\}$, there exists a set $\mathcal{S}_k \subseteq \mathcal{N}$ such that for any $p \in [p_k, p_{k+1}]$,*
$$x_i^* = [(B_{\mathcal{S}_k} - G_{\mathcal{S}_k})^{-1}(\mathbf{a}_{\mathcal{S}_k} - p\mathbf{1}_{\mathcal{S}_k})]_i > 0, \forall i \in \mathcal{S}_k$$
and $x_i^* = 0$, $\forall i \notin \mathcal{S}_k$.

[2]Note that Assumption 1 holds under this setting.

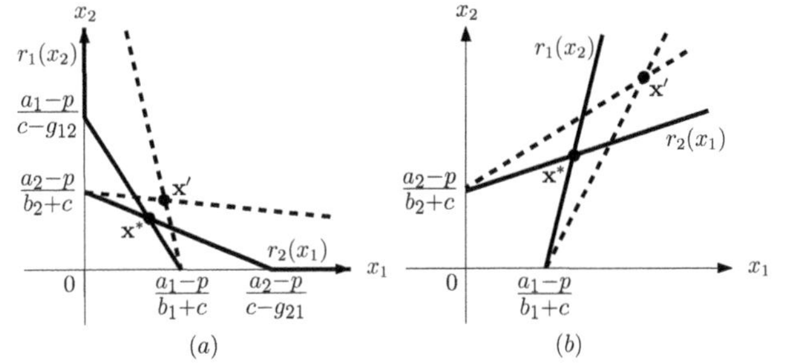

Figure 5: For Stage II for two users, the unique UDE $\mathbf{x}^*$ is achieved at the intersection of the best response functions (bold lines): (a) $\frac{g_{12}-c}{b_1+c} \in (-1, 0)$, $\frac{g_{21}-c}{b_2+c} \in (-1, 0)$; (b) $\frac{g_{12}-c}{b_1+c} \in (0, 1)$, $\frac{g_{21}-c}{b_2+c} \in (0, 1)$. When $g_{12} = g_{21}$ increases, the UDE $\mathbf{x}^*$ moves to $\mathbf{x}'$.

The proof is given in [9]. Proposition 4 shows that each user's equilibrium usage is a piece-wise linear function of price: within each price interval $[p_k, p_{k+1}]$, the equilibrium usage is a linear function of price p.

Next we investigate the impacts of other parameters on the UDE. We show that the total usage always increases when a user's parameter improves, under the condition that users' social network is symmetric. For tractable analysis, we assume that users have the same internal coefficient a_i[3].

PROPOSITION 5. *For Stage II, when $a_i = a$, $\forall i$ and social ties are symmetric (i.e., $g_{ij} = g_{ji}$, $\forall i \neq j$), the total equilibrium usage increases when a or any g_{ij} increases, or any b_i or c decreases.*

The proof is given in Appendix. We illustrate Proposition 5 by an example in Fig. 5. As mentioned before, users' social ties tend to be symmetric in practice due to social reciprocity [8]. In Section 5, simulation results will show that the performance under asymmetric social ties is very close to that under symmetric social ties.

4. STAGE I: OPTIMAL PRICING

In the previous section, we have investigated the UDE in Stage II given a price chosen by the wireless provider. In this section, we study the optimal pricing of the provider in Stage I.

We first observe from Proposition 4 that the total usage is a piece-wise linear function of price (as illustrated in Fig. 4(a)). As a result, the total revenue is a piece-wise quadratic function of price (as illustrated in Fig. 4(b)). Based on this observation, we develop an algorithm that computes the optimal price to maximize the provider's revenue, as described in Algorithm 3. The basic idea is to first

[3]Users can still have different b_i.

Algorithm 3: Compute the optimal price that maximizes revenue in Stage I

```
compute the UDE x* at price 0 using Algorithm 1;
p_ ← 0; p* ← 0; r* ← 0; S ← ∅;
foreach i ∈ N do
    if x*_i > 0 then
        S ← S ∪ {i};
    end
end
while p_ ≤ max_{i∈N} a_i and S ≠ ∅ do
    S' ← ∅; S'' ← ∅;
    foreach i ∈ S do
        if [(B_S − G_S)^{-1}]_i 1_S > 0 then
            S' ← S' ∪ {i}; p̃_i ← [(B_S − G_S)^{-1}]_i a_S / [(B_S − G_S)^{-1}]_i 1_S;
        end
    end
    foreach i ∉ S do
        if [G − C]_{i,S}(B_S − G_S)^{-1} 1_S < −1 then
            S'' ← S'' ∪ {i};
            p̃_i ← ([G − C]_{i,S}(B_S − G_S)^{-1} a_S + a_i) / ([G − C]_{i,S}(B_S − G_S)^{-1} 1_S + 1);
        end
    end
    p¯ ← min_{i∈S'∪S''} p̃_i; k ← arg min_{i∈S'∪S''} p̃_i;
    p̂ ← 1_S^T (B_S − G_S)^{-1} a_S / (2 1_S^T (B_S − G_S)^{-1} 1_S);
    if p̂ ∈ [p_, p¯] then
        p' ← p̂;
        else
            if p̂ < p_ then
                p' ← p_;
                else
                    p' ← p¯;
                end
            end
        end
    end
    r' ← p' 1_S^T (B_S − G_S)^{-1}(a_S − p' 1_S);
    if r' > r* then
        p* ← p'; r* ← r';
    end
    p_ ← p¯;
    if k ∈ S then
        S ← S \ {k};
        else
            S ← S ∪ {k};
        end
    end
end
return p*, r*;
```

determine the price intervals that characterize the piece-wise structure, such that within each price interval, the set of users with positive usage is the same at any price. Then we find the optimal price within each interval that maximizes the revenue. Thus we can find the optimal price with the maximum revenue among all the intervals.

In particular, Algorithm 3 starts with computing the set of users $\mathcal{S}$ with positive usage at price 0 by using Algorithm 1. Then this set $\mathcal{S}$ serves as the initial condition for the following steps. As the price p increases from 0 to $\max_{i\in\mathcal{N}} a_i$ (which is the largest possible value of the optimal price according to Theorem 4), it iteratively finds the critical prices at which the set $\mathcal{S}$ changes. In each iteration, given the current critical price $\underline{p}$, the next critical price $\overline{p}$ is the minimum price greater than $\underline{p}$ at which some user $i \in \mathcal{S}$ with positive usage decreases its usage to 0, or some user $i \notin \mathcal{S}$ with usage 0 increases its usage to a positive value[4]. Within each price interval $[\underline{p}, \overline{p}]$, as the revenue R is a quadratic function of price p, the optimal price in $[\underline{p}, \overline{p}]$ that maximizes the revenue is the price $\hat{p}$ such that $\frac{\partial R(p)}{\partial p}|_{p=\hat{p}} = 0$, if $\hat{p}$ is in $[\underline{p}, \overline{p}]$; otherwise, the optimal price is one of the endpoints $\underline{p}$ and $\overline{p}$. By comparing the maximum revenues at the optimal prices for all the price intervals, the algorithm finds the optimal price in the entire range of price.

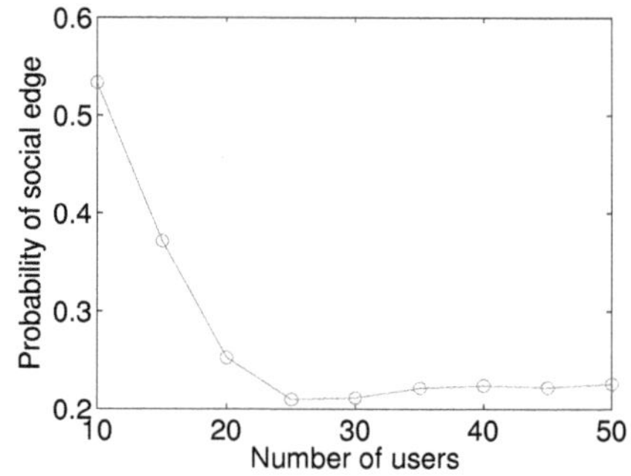

Figure 6: Probability of social edge vs. number of users in real data trace [10].

THEOREM 4. *Algorithm 3 computes the optimal price in Stage I.*

The proof is given in [9]. In the next section, numerical results will show that the computational complexity of Algorithm 3 is linear in the number of users.

5. PERFORMANCE EVALUATION

In this section, we first use simulation results to evaluate the performance of the two-stage game for the mobile users and the wireless provider. Then we discuss the engineering insights that can be drawn from the simulation results.

5.1 Simulation Setup

To illustrate the impacts of different parameters of mobile social networks on the performance, we consider a random setting as follows. We simulate the social graph G using the Erdős-Rényi (ER) graph model [11], where a social edge exists between each pair of users with probability P_S. If a social edge exists, the social tie follows a normal distribution $N(\mu_G, 2)$ (with mean μ_G and variance 2). We assume that each a_i follows a normal distribution $N(\mu_A, 2)$, and each b_i follows a normal distribution $N(\mu_B, 2)$. We set default parameter values as follows: $N = 10$, $P_s = 0.8$, $\mu_A = 4$, $\mu_B = 10$, $\mu_G = 4$, $c = 4$. To evaluate the performance in practice, we also simulate the social graph according to

[4]Recall that some user's equilibrium usage can increase when price increases as illustrated by the example in Section 3.

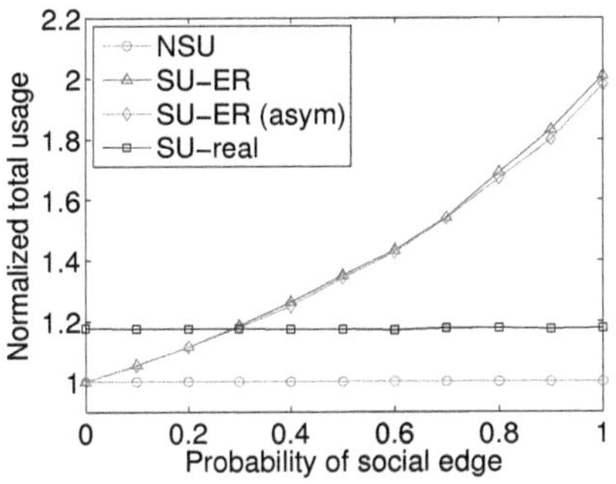

Figure 7: Normalized total usage vs. probability of social edge P_S.

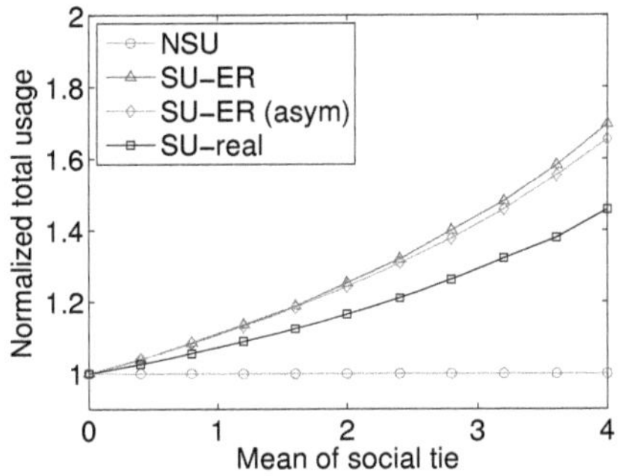

Figure 8: Normalized total usage vs. mean of social tie μ_G.

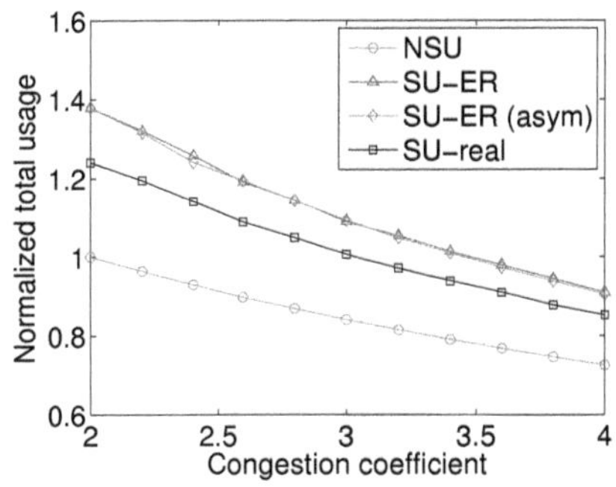

Figure 9: Normalized total usage vs. congestion coefficient c.

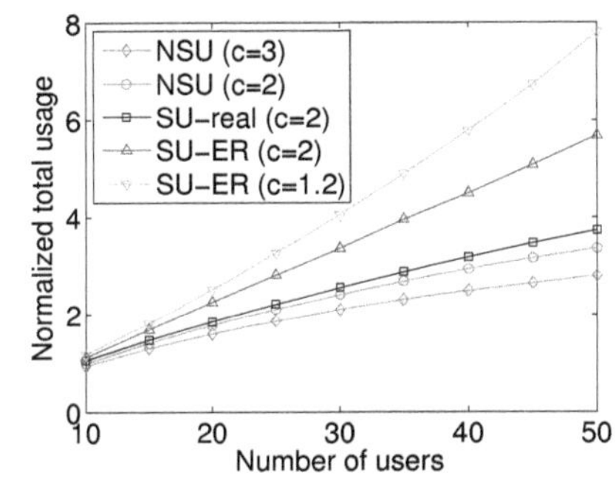

Figure 10: Normalized total usage vs. number of users N.

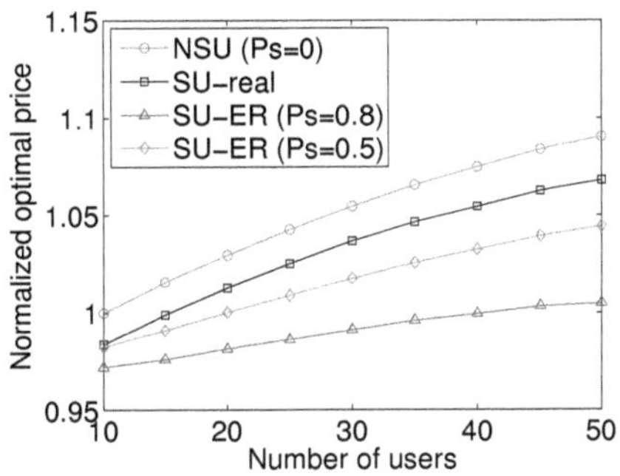

Figure 11: Normalized optimal price vs. number of users N.

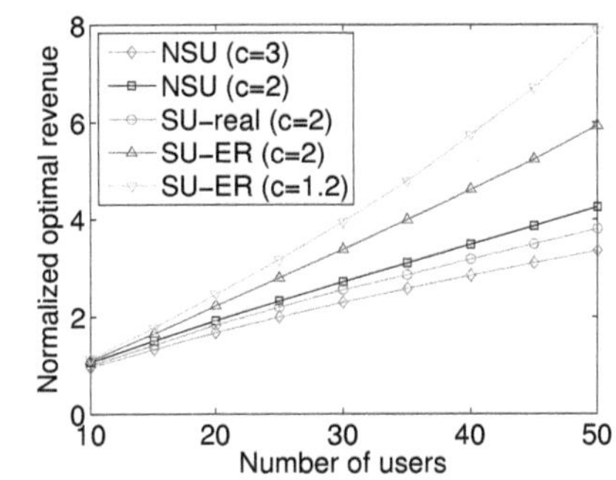

Figure 12: Normalized optimal revenue vs. number of users N.

the real data trace from Brightkite [10], which is a social friendship network based on mobile phones. For this data trace, we plot the average number of social ties between two users versus the number of users in Fig. 6. If a social edge exists based on the real data, the social tie also follows a normal distribution $N(\mu_G, 2)$.

As a benchmark, we evaluate the performance when users demand non-socially-aware usage (NSU) in comparison to our proposed socially-aware usage (SU). Since NSU is a special case of SU with all social ties being 0, the UDE and optimal pricing for NSU can be computed as for SU. To highlight the performance comparison, we normalize the results with respect to NSU. We also compare the performance under SU with ER model based social graph (SU-ER) and with real data based social graph (SU-real).

5.2 Simulation Results

5.2.1 *Total Usage in Stage II*

We first evaluate the performance of total usage in Stage II.

We illustrate the impacts of P_S, μ_G, c on total usage in Figs. 7-9, respectively. As expected, we observe from all these figures that SU always dominates NSU, and can perform significantly better than NSU. From Figs. 7-8, we can see that the performance gain of SU over NSU increases as P_S or μ_G increases, and the marginal gain is also increasing. Similarly, we can see from Fig. 9 that the performance gain of SU over NSU increases as congestion coefficient c decreases, and the marginal gain is also increasing. We also evaluate the performance under SU with ER model based the asymmetric social graph. We observe that its performance is very close to that with the symmetric social graph.

Fig. 10 illustrates the impact of N on total usage. As expected, we observe that the total usage always increases with the number of users. However, for the case of NSU and SU-real, the marginal gain of total usage decreases with the number of users, while for the case of SU-ER, the marginal gain increases. Intuitively, in the former case, when a new user joins the network, as the new user's social ties with the existing users are weak, the congestion effect between the new user and the existing users outweighs the network effect between them. Furthermore, as more users exist in the network, the weight difference between the congestion effect and the network effect increases, and thus the marginal gain of total usage by adding a user decreases. In the latter case, as the new user's social ties with the existing users are strong, the roles of the congestion effect and network effect are switched.

5.2.2 *Optimal Price in Stage I*

Next we evaluate the performance of the optimal price and optimal revenue in Stage I.

Fig. 11 illustrates the optimal price as the number of users increases. We observe that the optimal price always decreases with the number of users. Intuitively, this is because as the number of users increases, more users have higher internal demands, so that increasing the price does not result in significant decrease in total usage. Comparing different curves, we can also see that the optimal price decreases as P_S increases from 0 to 0.3 and then to 0.8. Intuitively, this is because that when network effect is strong, a low price

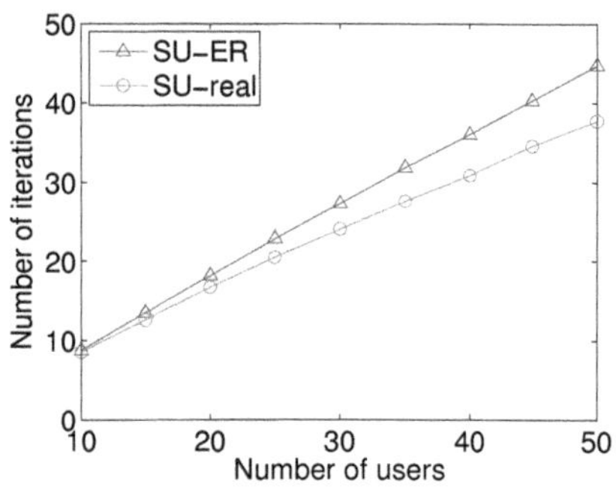

Figure 13: Computational complexity of Algorithm 3 vs. number of users N.

is desirable, since it encourages users' internal usage which further stimulate significantly more usage by the network effect; when congestion effect is strong, a high price is desirable, since decreasing the price cannot encourage significantly more usage due to the congestion effect.

Fig. 12 illustrates the optimal revenue achieved at the optimal price as the number of users increases. As expected, we can make similar observations as for Fig. 10: when network effect dominates congestion effect, the marginal gain of optimal revenue by adding more users is increasing; otherwise, the marginal gain is decreasing.

Fig. 13 illustrates the computational complexity of Algorithm 3 as the number of users increases. The number of iterations is equal to the number of price intervals that determine the piece-wise structure of total usage and revenue as a function of price. We observe that the complexity is $O(N)$.

5.3 Further Discussions

Based on the simulation results, we can draw the following engineering insights for the operation of wireless providers.

- The observations from Figs. 7-9 suggest that as users' social ties become stronger (which can be promoted by social services), the wireless provider can receive an increasing total usage and thus revenue, and also an increasing marginal gain. In addition, the wireless provider can also receive an increasing marginal return by incorporating more resources for the wireless service to mitigate congestion.

- The observations from Figs. 10 and 12 suggest that the wireless provider should be aware of whether the network effect determined by users' social ties dominates the congestion effect. If the network effect dominates, it receives an increasing marginal gain by taking in more users; otherwise, the marginal gain is decreasing and the total usage will saturate when the number of users is sufficiently large.

- The observations from Figs. 11 suggest that the wireless provider should set a low price when users' social ties are strong (evidenced by the popularity of social services), as the decrease of price will be outweighed by the increase of total usage resulted from the network effect, so that the total revenue increases. Otherwise, the wireless provider should set a high price, as cutting the price cannot stimulate sufficiently more usage due to the congestion effect to compensate the price decrease.

6. RELATED WORK

There have been many studies on users' behaviors and the provider's pricing strategy when either network effect (also known as positive externality) or congestion effect is present, respectively [5,12,13]. In [5], different pricing strategies of a provider have been studied where users' behaviors are only subject to network effect. When users experience both network effect and congestion effect as considered in this paper, the coupling among users is very different and more complex than when only network effect is present as in [5]. Very few work have studied the case where both network effect and congestion effect are present. [14] has studied users' behaviors when they experience both network effect and congestion effect. However, it assumes that the network effect is the same for all users, which does not capture the fact that users experience different levels of network effect based on their diverse social ties as considered in this paper.

The social aspect of mobile networking is an emerging paradigm for network design and optimization. Social contact patterns have been exploited for efficient data forwarding and dissemination in delay tolerant networks [15,16]. Social trust and social reciprocity have been leveraged in [17] to enhance cooperative D2D communication based on a coalitional game. A social group utility maximization (SGUM) framework has been recently studied in [18–20], which captures the impact of mobile users' diverse social ties on the interactions of their mobile devices subject to diverse physical relationships.

7. CONCLUSION

In this paper, we have formulated the interaction between mobile users and a wireless provider as a Stackelberg game, by jointly considering the network effect in the social domain and the congestion effect in the physical wireless domain. For Stage II, we have analyzed users' demand equilibrium given a price chosen by the wireless provider. For Stage I, we have developed an algorithm to compute the optimal price to maximize the wireless provider's revenue. We have also conducted simulations using real data to evaluate the performance, and drawn useful engineering insights for the operation of wireless providers.

For future work, we can examine other utility functions, e.g., a logarithmic function for internal utility, yet the major engineering insights should remain the same. Another interesting direction is to study the provider's pricing strategy when it is allowed to differentiate the price for different users. In this case, the price offered to each user will depend on its social influences to others based on the social network.

ACKNOWLEDGEMENT

The work of Xiaowen Gong was supported in part by the U.S. NSF grants CNS-1422277, ECCS-1408409, CNS-1117462, DTRA grant HDTRA1-13-1-0029. The work of Lingjie Duan was supported in part by SUTD-ZJU Research Collaboration Grant (Project no. SUTD-ZJU/RES/03/2014). The work of Xu Chen was supported in part by the funding from Alexander von Humboldt Foundation.

8. REFERENCES

[1] "WeChat: The new way to connect." [Online]. Available: http://www.wechat.com/

[2] "WhatsApp: Simple. Personal. Real time messaging." [Online]. Available: http://www.whatsapp.com/

[3] "Global Digital Statistics." [Online]. Available: http://wearesocial.net/tag/sdmw/

[4] B. Briscoe, A. Odlyzko, and B. Tilly, "Metcalfe's law is wrong-communications networks increase in value as they add members-but by how much?" *IEEE Spectrum*, vol. 43, no. 7, pp. 34–39, 2006.

[5] O. Candogan, K. Bimpikis, and A. Ozdaglar, "Optimal pricing in networks with externalities," *INFORMS Operation Research*, vol. 60, no. 4, pp. 883–905, 2012.

[6] D. Fudenberg and J. Tirole, *Game Theory.* MIT Press, 1991.

[7] J. B. Rosen, "Existence and uniqueness of equilibrium points for concave N-person games," *Econometrica*, vol. 33, no. 3, pp. 520–534, 1965.

[8] F. Ernst and S. Gächter, "Fairness and retaliation: The economics of reciprocity," *Journal of Economic Perspectives*, vol. 14, no. 3, pp. 159–181, 2000.

[9] X. Gong, L. Duan, and X. Chen, "When network effect meets congestion effect: Leveraging social services for wireless services," Technical Report. [Online]. Available: http://informationnet.asu.edu/pub/social-wireless-mobihoc15-TR.pdf

[10] "SNAP: Network datasets: Brightkite." [Online]. Available: http://snap.stanford.edu/data/loc-brightkite.html

[11] P. Erdos and A. Renyi, "On the evolution of random graphs," *Publications of the Mathematical Institute of the Hungarian Academy of Sciences*, pp. 17–61, 1960.

[12] J. Nair, A. Wierman, and B. Zwart, "Exploiting network effects in the provisioning of large scale systems," in *Proc. of IFIP Performance 2011.*

[13] W. Wu, T. B. Ma, and C. S. Lui, "Exploring bundling sale strategy in online service markets with network effects," in *Proc. of IEEE INFOCOM 2014.*

[14] R. Johari and S. Kumar, "Congestible services and network effects," in *Proc. ACM Conference on Electronic Commerce 2010.*

[15] P. Costa, C. Mascolo, M. Musolesi, and G. P. Picco, "Socially-aware routing for publish-subscribe in delay-tolerant mobile ad hoc networks," *IEEE JSAC*, vol. 26, no. 5, pp. 748–760, 2008.

[16] W. Gao, Q. Li, B. Zhao, and G. Cao, "Multicasting in delay tolerant networks: a social network perspective," in *ACM MOBIHOC*, 2009.

[17] X. Chen, B. Proulx, X. Gong, and J. Zhang, "Social trust and social reciprocity based cooperative D2D communications," in *Proc. ACM MOBIHOC 2013.*

[18] X. Gong, X. Chen, and J. Zhang, "Social group utility maximization game with applications in mobile social networks," in *Proc. IEEE Allerton Conference on Communication, Control, and Computing 2013.*

[19] X. Chen, X. Gong, L. Yang, and J. Zhang, "A social group utility maximization framework with applications in database assisted spectrum access," in *Proc. IEEE INFOCOM 2014.*

[20] X. Gong, X. Chen, K. Xing, D.-H. Shin, M. Zhang, and J. Zhang, "Personalized location privacy in mobile networks: A social group utility approach," in *Proc. IEEE INFOCOM 2015.*

[21] B. Debreu, "A social equilibrium existence theorem," *Proceedings of the National Academy of Sciences of the United States of America*, vol. 38, no. 10, pp. 886–893, 1952.

[22] I. Glicksberg, "A further generalization of the Kakutani fixed point theorem, with application to Nash equilibrium," *Proceedings of the American Mathematical Society*, vol. 3, no. 1, pp. 170–174, 1952.

[23] K. Fan, "Fixed-point and minimax theorems in locally convex topological linear spaces," *Proceedings of the National Academy of Sciences of the United States of America*, vol. 38, no. 2, pp. 121–126, 1952.

[24] R. Horn and C. Johnson, *Matrix Analysis.* Cambridge University Press, 1985.

APPENDIX

Proof of Theorem 1

To show the existence of UDE, we make use of the following lemma, which shows that the Stage II game with unbounded usage range is equivalent to that with bounded usage range.

LEMMA 2. *Under Assumption 1, the Stage II game* $\mathcal{G} \triangleq \{\mathcal{N}, \{u_i\}_{i\in\mathcal{N}}, [0,\infty)^N\}$ *admits the same set of UDEs as the game* $\mathcal{G}' \triangleq \{\mathcal{N}, \{u_i\}_{i\in\mathcal{N}}, [0,\bar{x}]^N\}$, *where* $\bar{x}$ *is any number that satisfies* $\bar{x} > \max_{i\in\mathcal{N}} |a_i - p|/(b_i + c - \sum_{j\neq i} |g_{ij} - c|)$.

Proof: Let $\mathbf{x}^*$ be any UDE of game $\mathcal{G}$ and x_i^* be the largest in $\mathbf{x}^*$, i.e., $x_i^* \geq x_j^*$, $\forall i \neq j$. If $x_i^* > 0$, using the best response function (2), we have

$$x_i^* = \frac{a_i - p}{b_i + c} + \sum_{j\neq i} \frac{g_{ij} - c}{b_i + c} x_j^* \leq \frac{|a_i - p|}{b_i + c} + \sum_{j\neq i} \frac{|g_{ij} - c|}{b_i + c} x_i^*. \tag{5}$$

Using Assumption 1, it follows from (5) that

$$x_i^* \leq |a_i - p|/(b_i + c - \sum_{j\neq i} |g_{ij} - c|) < \bar{x}.$$

Since x_i^* is the largest in $\mathbf{x}^*$, we have $x_j^* \in [0,\bar{x}]$, $\forall j \in \mathcal{N}$, and thus $\mathbf{x}^* \in [0,\bar{x}]^N$. Therefore, as game $\mathcal{G}$ and game $\mathcal{G}'$ have the same set of payoff functions and the strategy spaces in both games contain $[0,\bar{x}]^N$, they have the same set of UDEs. □

Using a celebrated result in [21–23], the infinite game $\mathcal{G}'$ admits a UDE if the strategy space $[0,\bar{x}]^N$ is compact and convex, the payoff function $u_i(x_i, \mathbf{x}_{-i})$ is continuous in x_i and $\mathbf{x}_{-i}$, and the payoff function $u_i(x_i, \mathbf{x}_{-i})$ is concave in x_i. It is easy to check that all these conditions hold, and thus the game $\mathcal{G}'$ admits a UDE. Then it follows from Lemma 2 that the Stage II game $\mathcal{G}$ admits a UDE.

Proof of Theorem 2

We will show that the UDE is unique by showing that the game $\mathcal{G}'$ defined in Lemma 2 is a concave game. The Jacobian matrix $\nabla u(\mathbf{x})$ of the payoff function profile $u(\mathbf{x}) \triangleq$

$(u_1(\mathbf{x}), \ldots, u_N(\mathbf{x}))$ of game $\mathcal{G}'$ is given by

$$\nabla u(\mathbf{x}) = \begin{bmatrix} \frac{\partial^2 u_1(\mathbf{x})}{\partial x_1^2} & \frac{\partial^2 u_1(\mathbf{x})}{\partial x_1 \partial x_2} & \cdots & \frac{\partial^2 u_1(\mathbf{x})}{\partial x_1 \partial x_N} \\ \frac{\partial^2 u_2(\mathbf{x})}{\partial x_2 \partial x_1} & \frac{\partial^2 u_2(\mathbf{x})}{\partial x_2^2} & \cdots & \frac{\partial^2 u_2(\mathbf{x})}{\partial x_2 \partial x_N} \\ \vdots & \vdots & \ddots & \vdots \\ \frac{\partial^2 u_N(\mathbf{x})}{\partial x_N \partial x_1} & \frac{\partial^2 u_N(\mathbf{x})}{\partial x_N \partial x_2} & \cdots & \frac{\partial^2 u_N(\mathbf{x})}{\partial x_N^2} \end{bmatrix}$$
$$= \begin{bmatrix} -b_1 - c & g_{12} - c & \cdots & g_{1N} - c \\ g_{21} - c & -b_2 - c & \cdots & g_{2N} - c \\ \vdots & \vdots & \ddots & \vdots \\ g_{N1} - c & g_{N2} - c & \cdots & -b_N - c \end{bmatrix}$$
$$= -(B - G).$$

Using Assumption 1, it follows that

$$[B - G]_{ii} \geq \sum_{j \neq i} |[B - G]_{ij}|, \ \forall i$$

where $[M]_{ij}$ denotes the entry in the ith row and jth column of matrix M. Therefore, $B - G$ is strictly diagonal dominant [24]. It follows from the condition $\sum_{j \neq i} \frac{|g_{ji} - c|}{b_i + c} < 1, \forall i$ that $(B - G)^T$ is also strictly diagonal dominant. Then we have that

$$\nabla u(\mathbf{x}) + \nabla u(\mathbf{x})^T = -(B - G) - (B - G)^T$$

is strictly diagonal dominant. Also observe that it is symmetric. It is known that a symmetric matrix that is strictly diagonally dominant with real nonnegative diagonal entries is positive definite [24]. Therefore, $\nabla u(\mathbf{x}) + \nabla u(\mathbf{x})^T$ is negative definite. It follows from [7, Theorem 6] that $u(\mathbf{x})$ is diagonally strictly concave. Therefore, using [7, Theorem 2], game $\mathcal{G}'$ has a unique UDE.

Proof of Theorem 3

Let $\Delta x_i^{(t)} \triangleq x_i^{(t)} - x_i^*, \forall i$. For any $i \in \mathcal{N}$, according to step 6 in Algorithm 1, we have

$$|\Delta x_i^{(t+1)}| \leq |\sum_{j \neq i} \frac{g_{ij} - c}{b_i + c} \Delta x_j^{(t)}| \leq \sum_{j \neq i} \frac{|g_{ij} - c|}{b_i + c} |\Delta x_j^{(t)}|. \quad (6)$$

Let $\|\Delta \mathbf{x}^{(t)}\|_\infty$ be the l_∞-norm of vector $(\Delta x_i^{(t)}, \ldots, \Delta x_N^{(t)})$, i.e.,

$$\|\Delta \mathbf{x}^{(t)}\|_\infty \triangleq \max_{i \in \mathcal{N}} |\Delta x_i^{(t)}|.$$

Then, using Assumption 1 and (6), we have

$$\begin{aligned} \|\Delta \mathbf{x}^{(t+1)}\|_\infty &\leq \max_{i \in \mathcal{N}} \left(\sum_{j \neq i} \frac{|g_{ij} - c|}{b_i + c} |\Delta x_j^{(t)}| \right) \\ &\leq \left(\max_{i \in \mathcal{N}} \sum_{j \neq i} \frac{|g_{ij} - c|}{b_i + c} \right) \left(\max_{i \in \mathcal{N}} |\Delta x_j^{(t)}| \right) \\ &= \left(\max_{i \in \mathcal{N}} \sum_{j \neq i} \frac{|g_{ij} - c|}{b_i + c} \right) \|\Delta \mathbf{x}^{(t)}\|_\infty. \end{aligned}$$

According to Assumption 1, we have $\max_{i \in \mathcal{N}} \sum_{j \neq i} \frac{|g_{ij} - c|}{b_i + c} < 1$. Then it follows that the algorithm results in a contraction mapping of $|\Delta x_i^{(t)}|$, and thus converges to the UDE.

Proof of Proposition 3

We first show part 1). Suppose $p > a$ and $x_i^* > 0$ is the largest in $\mathbf{x}^*$, i.e., $x_i^* \geq x_j^*, \forall i \neq j$. Using the best response function (2), we have

$$x_i^* = \frac{a - p}{b_i + c} + \sum_{j \neq i} \frac{g_{ij} - c}{b_i + c} x_j^* \leq \sum_{j \neq i} \frac{|g_{ij} - c|}{b_i + c} x_i^* < x_i^*$$

where the last inequality follows from Assumption 1. This shows a contradiction. Thus we have $x_i^* = 0, \forall i$.

Next we show part 2). Let $\mathcal{S}$ be the set of users with positive usage in $\mathbf{x}^*$ at price 0. For any $i \notin \mathcal{S}$, using (2), we have

$$x_i^* = 0 \geq \frac{a}{b_i + c} + \frac{a}{b_i + c} [G - C]_{i,\mathcal{S}} (B_\mathcal{S} - G_\mathcal{S})^{-1} \mathbf{1}_\mathcal{S}. \quad (7)$$

For any $p \in (0, a]$, we next show that $\mathbf{x}'$ with $\mathbf{x}'_\mathcal{S} = (a - p)(B_\mathcal{S} - G_\mathcal{S})^{-1} \mathbf{1}_\mathcal{S}$ and $x'_i = 0, \forall i \notin \mathcal{S}$ is the UDE at price p. We observe that for any $i \in \mathcal{S}$, x'_i is its best response at $\mathbf{x}'$. For any $i \notin \mathcal{S}$, using (7), we have

$$\frac{a - p}{b_i + c} + \frac{a - p}{b_i + c} [G - C]_{i,\mathcal{S}} (B_\mathcal{S} - G_\mathcal{S})^{-1} \mathbf{1}_\mathcal{S} \leq 0 = x_i^*,$$

and thus is user i's best response at $\mathbf{x}'$.

Proof of Proposition 5

We only prove the case when any g_{ij} increases, since the cases when a increases, any b_i decreases, or c increases can be proved similarly. Then it suffices to prove the case when any g_{ij} increases by any small amount. Let G be a symmetric matrix. Let $\mathbf{x}^*$ be the UDE under G and $\mathcal{S}$ be the set of users with positive usage in $\mathbf{x}^*$. It is easy to check that the UDE is a continuous function of the matrix G. Then we can always find a symmetric matrix G' with $[G']_{ij} \geq [G]_{ij}$, $\forall i, j$ and at least one strict inequality, such that the set of users with positive usage at the UDE $\mathbf{x}'$ under G' is also $\mathcal{S}$. Therefore, using the best response functions (2), we have

$$B_\mathcal{S} \mathbf{x}_\mathcal{S}^* = (a - p) \mathbf{1}_\mathcal{S} + G_\mathcal{S} \mathbf{x}_\mathcal{S}^* \quad (8)$$
$$B_\mathcal{S} \mathbf{x}'_\mathcal{S} = (a - p) \mathbf{1}_\mathcal{S} + G'_\mathcal{S} \mathbf{x}'_\mathcal{S}. \quad (9)$$

Subtracting (8) from (9), we have

$$B_\mathcal{S} (\mathbf{x}'_\mathcal{S} - \mathbf{x}_\mathcal{S}^*) = G_\mathcal{S} (\mathbf{x}'_\mathcal{S} - \mathbf{x}_\mathcal{S}^*) + \Delta G_\mathcal{S} \mathbf{x}'_\mathcal{S} \quad (10)$$

where $\Delta G_\mathcal{S} \triangleq G'_\mathcal{S} - G_\mathcal{S}$. According to Lemma 1, $B_\mathcal{S} - G_\mathcal{S}$ is invertible. Then it follows from (10) that

$$\mathbf{x}'_\mathcal{S} - \mathbf{x}_\mathcal{S}^* = (B_\mathcal{S} - G_\mathcal{S})^{-1} \Delta G_\mathcal{S} \mathbf{x}'_\mathcal{S}. \quad (11)$$

On the other hand, it follows from (8) that

$$\mathbf{x}_\mathcal{S}^* = (a - p)(B_\mathcal{S} - G_\mathcal{S})^{-1} \mathbf{1}_\mathcal{S}. \quad (12)$$

Using (11) and (12), we have

$$\begin{aligned} t(\mathbf{x}') - t(\mathbf{x}^*) &= \mathbf{1}_\mathcal{S}^T (\mathbf{x}'_\mathcal{S} - \mathbf{x}_\mathcal{S}^*) \\ &= \mathbf{1}_\mathcal{S}^T (B_\mathcal{S} - G_\mathcal{S})^{-1} \Delta G_\mathcal{S} \mathbf{x}'_\mathcal{S} \\ &= [(B_\mathcal{S} - G_\mathcal{S})^{-1} \mathbf{1}_\mathcal{S}]^T \Delta G_\mathcal{S} \mathbf{x}'_\mathcal{S} \\ &= \frac{1}{a - p} (\mathbf{x}_\mathcal{S}^*)^T \Delta G_\mathcal{S} \mathbf{x}'_\mathcal{S} \end{aligned}$$

where the third equality is due to the fact that $(B_\mathcal{S} - G_\mathcal{S})^{-1}$ is symmetric since $B_\mathcal{S} - G_\mathcal{S}$ is symmetric. Since $a > p$ and $\mathbf{x}_\mathcal{S}^*$, ΔG, $\mathbf{x}'_\mathcal{S}$ only have nonnegative entries, it follows that $t(\mathbf{x}') \geq t(\mathbf{x}^*)$.

Distributed Time-Sensitive Task Selection in Mobile Crowdsensing

Man Hon Cheung*#, Richard Southwell#, Fen Hou*, and Jianwei Huang#
*Department of Electrical and Computer Engineering, University of Macau, Macau
#Department of Information Engineering, The Chinese University of Hong Kong, Hong Kong, China
mhcheung@ie.cuhk.edu.hk, richardsouthwell254@gmail.com, fenhou@umac.mo,
jwhuang@ie.cuhk.edu.hk

ABSTRACT

With the rich set of embedded sensors installed in smartphones and the large number of mobile users, we witness the emergence of many innovative commercial mobile crowdsensing applications that combine the power of mobile technology with crowdsourcing to deliver time-sensitive and location-dependent information to their customers. Motivated by these real-world applications, we consider the task selection problem for heterogeneous users with different initial locations, movement costs, movement speeds, and reputation levels. Computing the social surplus maximization task allocation turns out to be an NP-hard problem. Hence we focus on the distributed case, and propose an asynchronous and distributed task selection (ADTS) algorithm to help the users plan their task selections on their own. We prove the convergence of the algorithm, and further characterize the computation time for users' updates in the algorithm. Simulation results suggest that the ADTS scheme achieves the highest Jain's fairness index and coverage comparing with several benchmark algorithms, while yielding similar user payoff to a greedy centralized benchmark. Finally, we illustrate how mobile users coordinate under the ADTS scheme based on some practical movement time data derived from Google Maps.

Categories and Subject Descriptors

C.2.4 [**Computer-Communication Networks**]: Distributed Systems—*Distributed applications*

Keywords

Mobile crowdsensing; crowdsourcing; game theory

1. INTRODUCTION

Today's smartphones and wearable devices have embedded a rich set of sensors, such as cameras, microphones, global positioning systems (GPS), thermometers, and accelerometers [5,6,12]. Thanks to the large number of mobile users and their inherent mobility, we are witnessing the rise of *mobile crowdsensing* (MCS), where individuals use their mobile devices to collectively extract and share information related to some phenomenon of interest. Applications of MCS include traffic jam alerts, wireless indoor localization, and small cell network monitoring.

Recently, commercial MCS platforms, such as Gigwalk [8] and Field Agent [4], combine the power of mobile technology with crowdsourcing to provide their customers with *time-sensitive* and *location-dependent* information related to their stores and products. For example, in Field Agent [4], there are two types of *tasks*, namely audit and research. An audit task mainly involves fact finding and data gathering (such as checking on-shelf availability and prices), while a research task mainly involves the collection of users' opinions and insights (such as surveys and shop-alongs). For a location-dependent and time-sensitive sensing task, such as checking the on-shelf availability of Coca-Cola in a convenience store on Main Street at 9am, the users need to collect the data at the *precise* time and location. With this information, a district manager can reduce the cost of taking inventories, while maintaining the proper stock levels at different stores. Currently, several well-known brands and retailers (such as Coca-Cola and Johnson & Johnson) are among the customers of Gigwalk and Field Agent. This suggests that the collection of location-dependent and time-sensitive data using MCS is a practice of growing importance.

A key question for MCS platforms is *how to find users to complete tasks, while accounting for the users' different initial locations, movement costs, movement speeds, and reputation levels?* A number of recent results have focused on the *centralized* task allocation in MCS, with the objectives of either improving the energy efficiency or maximizing the social surplus. For example, Sheng *et al.* in [15] considered opportunistic energy-efficient collaborative sensing. Given a set of roads, mobile devices, and their trajectories, the objective is to find a sensing schedule that minimizes the total energy consumption by reducing redundancy in sensing. Zhao *et al.* in [16] considered fair and energy-efficient task allocation in MCS, and solved a min-max aggregate sensing time problem. He *et al.* in [9] considered social surplus maximization for location-dependent task scheduling in MCS. They formulated a task scheduling problem, where the objective is to maximize the overall net reward of all the users, subject to the time budget of each user and the sensing redundancy constraint of each sensing task.

Different from the above literature, which focuses on the collection of location-dependent data *without* any time con-

MobiHoc'15, June 22–25, 2015, Hangzhou, China.

http://dx.doi.org/10.1145/2746285.2746293.

straints in a *centralized* fashion, we consider the case where the service provider aims to collect *time-sensitive* and location-dependent information for its customers through *distributed* decisions of mobile users. The solution of such a problem needs to balance the rewards and movement costs of the users for completing tasks. The consideration along both space and time dimensions makes the design of a good solution very challenging. The distributed nature of the solution that is required by the current commercial platform such as Gigwalk and Field Agent further complicates the analysis.

In this paper, we focus on solving the distributed time-sensitive and location-dependent task selection problem, where users are heterogeneous in their initial locations, movement costs, movement speeds, and reputation levels. We formulate the interactions among users as a non-cooperative task selection game (TSG), and propose an asynchronous and distributed task selection (ADTS) algorithm for each user to compute her task selection and mobility plan. Each user only requires limited information on the aggregate task choices of all users, which is publicly available in many of today's crowdsourcing platforms, such as Amazon Mechanical Turk (MTurk) [1], Gigwalk [8], and Field Agent [4].

As a *performance benchmark* on the social surplus, we formulate a centralized task allocation (CTA) problem, assuming that all users are controlled by the service provider, and show that it is an NP-hard problem. We propose a heuristic greedy centralized algorithm that computes the approximate centralized solution with a lower complexity.

To the best of our knowledge, this is the first paper that considers distributed time-sensitive and location-dependent data collection in MCS motivated by real-life commercial applications. To summarize, the contributions of our work are as follows:

- *Practical MCS modeling*: Motivated by commercial MCS applications, we consider the collection of time-sensitive and location-dependent sensing data by multiple users. We assume that the users are heterogeneous in their initial locations, movement costs, movement speeds, and reputation levels.
- *Asynchronous and distributed task selection algorithm*: We propose a distributed algorithm that helps the users determine their task selections and mobility plans. Each user only needs to know limited information on the aggregate task choices readily available in the MCS mobile apps.
- *Convergence guaranteed*: We show that the task selection game has the finite improvement property, which means that users' asynchronous best response updates globally converge to a Nash equilibrium. We also show that each best response update can be computed in polynomial time.
- *Balanced performance*: Simulation results suggest that the proposed asynchronous and distributed task selection scheme achieves the best performance in terms of fairness and coverage comparing with various benchmark algorithms.

2. SYSTEM MODEL

We consider a mobile crowdsensing (MCS) platform that involves the collection of *time-sensitive* and *location-dependent*

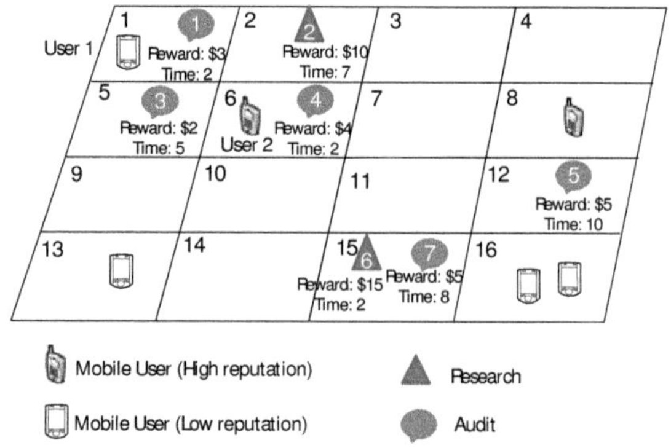

Figure 1: In a MCS platform, we assume that the service provider collects location-dependent time-sensitive information with the help of the users. Through the mobile app interface, the service provider would announce the rewards, locations, and execution times of the tasks to the users. Each user then decides how to move and which tasks to work on over the coming time slots.

information in the form of photos, video, audio, data, opinions, and feedback. In the platform, once a user has installed the mobile app on her smartphone, she will be able to use the built-in map to check the available tasks, together with the task attributes including locations, execution times, and rewards, as shown in Fig. 1.

More specifically, let $\mathcal{L} = \{1, \ldots, L\}$ be the set of *locations*, such as buildings, landmarks, or fields. Let $\mathcal{T} = \{1, \ldots, T\}$ be the set of *time slots*. Let $\mathcal{K} = \{1, \ldots, K\}$ be the set of *tasks*. We describe the attributes related to a task as follows.

DEFINITION 1. (Task Attributes) Each task $k \in \mathcal{K}$ is associated with:

- A location $l[k] \in \mathcal{L}$ *where* the task must be performed.
- A time $t[k] \in \mathcal{T}$ *when* the task must be executed.
- A *reward* amount $\rho[k] \geq 0$ for performing the task. In the case where multiple users perform the same task, the reward is shared evenly among them [3].

For example, for task 5 in Fig. 1, we have $l[5] = 12$, $t[5] = 10$, and $\rho[5] = \$5$. Notice that there can be multiple tasks at the same location, such as $l[6] = l[7] = 15$.

Let $\mathcal{I} = \{1, \ldots, I\}$ be the set of users, who can move through space and perform tasks. Given a user's initial location, the set of tasks that she chooses to work on is influenced by her *movement time*, *movement cost*, and *reputation*. Formally, we define a user's attributes as follows.

DEFINITION 2. (User Attributes) Each user $i \in \mathcal{I}$ is associated with:

- An *initial location* $l_i^{\text{init}} \in \mathcal{L}$. (For example, we have $l_2^{\text{init}} = 6$ in Fig. 1.)
- An (integer valued) *movement time* $\Delta_i^{l,l'} \geq 1$, which equals the number of time slots it takes user i to move from location l to location l'.
- A (real valued) *movement cost* $c_i^{l,l'} \geq 0$ for user i to move from location l to location l'.

- A non-empty set $\mathcal{K}_i \subseteq \mathcal{K}$ of tasks that user i is eligible for.

If a user has specified her mode of transportation (e.g., walking, cycling, driving, or taking the bus), then her mobile device can retrieve data from Google Maps and local public transportation databases to compute her movement time and movement cost. For example, user i may have a zero cost (i.e., $c_i^{l,l'} = 0$) for walking, and a linear cost for driving.

The set of eligible tasks $\mathcal{K}_i$ often relates to the *reputation* of user i. Reputation mechanisms are commonly found in crowdsensing applications, such as Gigwalk [8] and MTurk [1], to allocate tasks based on users' past performance. A service provider can reserve the more complicated but higher paying tasks (e.g., research tasks) for users with higher reputations. For example, in Fig. 1, the lower reputation user 1 can only work on the audit tasks, so $\mathcal{K}_1 = \{1, 3, 4, 5, 7\}$; whereas the higher reputation user 2 can work on both the audit and research tasks, so $\mathcal{K}_2 = \{1, \ldots, 7\}$.

Given the rewards, locations, and execution times of different tasks, each user needs to decide how she should move and which tasks she should select in order to maximize her total profit (i.e., reward minus movement cost). In Section 3, we formulate the task selection of multiple users as a task selection game, and propose an ADTS algorithm. In Section 4, we establish a performance benchmark under the ideal centralized task allocation scenario. We use simulations to evaluate the performance of our proposed algorithms in Section 5, and draw conclusions in Section 6.

3. DISTRIBUTED TASK SELECTION GAMES

In this section, we formulate the users' task selection problem as a *task selection game (TSG)*, where each user aims to maximize her own payoff. We also study the equilibria and convergence properties of the game.

3.1 Task-Time Routing

A user's decision making includes two aspects. First, she must choose which locations to visit over the T time slots (i.e., selecting a route through space-time). Second, she must choose which tasks to do along that route. However, since each task k is only identified with a single location $l[k]$ and time $t[k]$, we can simplify the modeling by just considering how the users select different tasks at different times (i.e., choosing a route through *task-time*).

Since a user may choose not to work on any task, for each user i we define an initial virtual task $k_i^{\text{init}} \in \mathcal{K}_i$, which occurs at time slot $t[k_i^{\text{init}}] \in \mathcal{T}$ and at location $l[k_i^{\text{init}}] = l_i^{\text{init}}$ (user i's initial location) with a zero reward (i.e., $\rho[k_i^{\text{init}}] = 0$).

To clearly describe the task-time routing decision problem, we use a sequences of task-time points, described in Definition 3, to represent a user's task-time route. We say that a task-time route is available to a user when it is physically possible for her to visit the corresponding locations over the time slots, and she is eligible to perform the tasks on the route based on her reputation.

DEFINITION 3. (Available Task-Time Route) An *available task-time route for a user i is a sequence*

$$r_i = \left((k_i^1, t_i^1), (k_i^2, t_i^2), \ldots, (k_i^n, t_i^n)\right) \in (\mathcal{K} \times \mathcal{T})^n \quad (1)$$

of n task-time points (for some $n \geq 1$) which satisfies the following conditions:

1. *Time increases:* $1 = t_i^1 < t_i^2 < \ldots < t_i^n \leq T$.
2. *The user is eligible for the tasks:* $k_i^1, k_i^2, \ldots, k_i^n \in \mathcal{K}_i$.
3. *Sequence starts at the initial virtual task:* $k_i^1 = k_i^{\text{init}}$.
4. *Sequence accounts for movement time:* $t_i^{a+1} - t_i^a = \Delta_i^{l[k_i^a], l[k_i^{a+1}]}$, for each $a \in \{1, \ldots, n-1\}$.

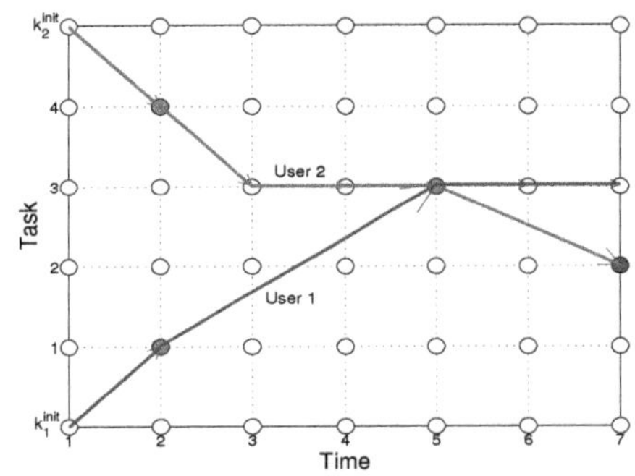

Figure 2: Task-time routes chosen by two users with audit (red circles) and research (blue circle) tasks.

Condition 1 accounts for the fact that time is always increasing. Condition 2 ensures that the users are eligible to perform each of their chosen tasks. Condition 3 ensures that the user begins at her initial location. Condition 4 ensures that the time difference between successive elements in the sequence of task-time elements is equal to the movement time between the locations of the corresponding tasks. (In other words, it ensures that the movement time is indeed the time they spend moving.) When a user does not move, we define $\Delta_i^{l,l} = 1, \forall i \in \mathcal{I}, l \in \mathcal{L}$ to represent the fact that the user stays at the same location after one time slot.

Based on the example in Fig. 1 by considering task 1 to task 4, we show an example of the task-time routes of two users in Fig. 2. Here the solid and empty circles represent task-time points with and without positive rewards, respectively. When a user's route passes through a solid circle, it means that the user works on the task (e.g., user 2 works on task 3 at time 5). On the other hand, when a user's route passes through an empty circle, it means that the user is only physically present at the location of a task, but she is not working on the task (e.g., user 2 is at location $l[3]$ at time 3). In this way, a user can move to the location of a task before the actual execution time of that task (e.g., user 2 arrives at location of task 3 at time 3, while the execution time of task 3 is at time 5).

In Fig. 2, we suppose that a low reputation user 1 has movement times $\Delta_1^{l_1^{\text{init}}, l[1]} = 1$ and $\Delta_1^{l[1], l[3]} = 3$, while a high reputation user 2 has movement times $\Delta_2^{l_2^{\text{init}}, l[4]} = 1$, $\Delta_2^{l[4], l[3]} = 1$, and $\Delta_2^{l[3], l[2]} = 2$. The purple and green curves represent the two task-time routes: $r_1 = \left((k_1^{\text{init}}, 1), (1, 2), (3, 5), (3, 6), (3, 7)\right)$ and $r_2 = \left((k_2^{\text{init}}, 1), (4, 2), (3, 3), (3, 4), (3, 5), (2, 7)\right)$.

3.2 Task Selection Game

Based on the discussion aforementioned, we can formulate the users' task selection problem as a TSG, where users act as players that choose available task-time routes.

In the task-time routing framework, changing tasks will often involve changing locations and hence will involve movement costs. To allow a user to move to the location of a task before its execution time, we define the *time-dependent reward* $\rho^*[k,t']$ for task $k \in \mathcal{K}$ and time $t' \in \mathcal{T}$ as

$$\rho^*[k,t'] = \begin{cases} \rho[k], & \text{if } t' = t[k], \\ 0, & \text{otherwise.} \end{cases}$$

For example, in Fig. 2, the rewards for task-time points $(3,3)$ and $(3,5)$ are $\rho^*[3,3] = 0$ and $\rho^*[3,5] = \rho[3] = \$2$, respectively. We assume that the reward $\rho^*[k,t']$ is evenly shared among all the users who have chosen to work on task k at time t' (i.e., the task-time point (k,t').)

DEFINITION 4. (Task-time points) Let us define the *task-time points* of a task-time route r_i in (1) to be the set $\mathbb{V}(r_i) = \{(k_i^1, t_i^1), (k_i^2, t_i^2), \ldots, (k_i^n, t_i^n)\}$, of all task-time points visited by the route $r_i \in \mathcal{R}_i$, where $\mathcal{R}_i$ denotes the set of all available task-time routes of user i.

The *payoff* $U_i(\boldsymbol{r})$ that user i gets for choosing route r_i in (1) in a strategy profile $\boldsymbol{r} = (r_1, \ldots, r_I) \in \mathcal{R}_1 \times \ldots \times \mathcal{R}_I$ is equal to

$$U_i(\boldsymbol{r}) = \left(\sum_{a=1}^{n} \frac{\rho^*[k_i^a, t_i^a]}{m^{(k_i^a, t_i^a)}(\boldsymbol{r})} \right) - \sum_{a=1}^{n-1} c_i^{l[k_i^a], l[k_i^{a+1}]}, \quad (2)$$

where $m^{(k,t)}(\boldsymbol{r}) = |\{j \in \mathcal{I} : (k,t) \in \mathbb{V}(r_j)\}|$ is the number of routes that pass through task-time point (k,t). The first term in (2) corresponds to the total reward that user i obtains (taking into account how the reward is shared evenly when multiple users perform the same task). The second term in (2) corresponds to the total movement cost, which user i spends in order to travel to the locations of the selected tasks.

DEFINITION 5. (Task selection game) A *task selection game* $\Omega = (\mathcal{I}, \mathcal{L}, \mathcal{K}, \mathcal{T}, (\rho^*[k,t])_{k\in\mathcal{K}, t\in\mathcal{T}}, (c_i^{l,l'}, \Delta_i^{l,l'})_{i\in\mathcal{I}, l,l'\in\mathcal{L}})$, involves each user (player) i choosing an available task-time route (strategy) $r_i \in \mathcal{R}_i$ and receiving the payoff in (2).

DEFINITION 6. (Task-time point pairs) The *task-time point pairs* of a task-time route r_i in (1) is defined as the set $\mathbb{E}(r_i) = \left\{ [(k_i^a, t_i^a), (k_i^{a+1}, t_i^{a+1})] : a = 1, \ldots, n-1 \right\}$ of task-time point pairs subsequently visited by the route r_i.

Let $g_i\Big([(k_i^a, t_i^a), (k_i^{a+1}, t_i^{a+1})] \Big) = c_i^{l[k_i^a], l[k_i^{a+1}]}$ be the movement cost between two adjacent task-time points of user i. The payoff of user i in (2) can be rewritten as

$$U_i(\boldsymbol{r}) = \left(\sum_{(k,t)\in\mathbb{V}(r_i)} \frac{\rho^*[k,t]}{m^{(k,t)}(\boldsymbol{r})} \right) - \sum_{e\in\mathbb{E}(r_i)} g_i(e). \quad (3)$$

3.3 Equilibrium Existence and Convergence Analysis

Before analyzing the task selection games, let us recall some commonly used definitions from game theory. Let $\boldsymbol{r}_{-i} = (r_1, \ldots, r_{i-1}, r_{i+1}, \ldots, r_I)$ denote the strategies of all the users except user i. A strategy profile can be written as $\boldsymbol{r} = (r_i, \boldsymbol{r}_{-i})$.

DEFINITION 7. (Better and best response updates) A *better response update*, starting from some strategy $\boldsymbol{r} = (r_i, \boldsymbol{r}_{-i})$, is an event where a single user i changes to another strategy, $r_i' \in \mathcal{R}_i$, and increases her payoff as a result, i.e., $U_i(r_i', \boldsymbol{r}_{-i}) > U_i(r_i, \boldsymbol{r}_{-i})$.

A *best response update* is a special type of better response update, where the newly selected strategy r_i' maximizes user i's payoff among user i's all possible better response updates.

DEFINITION 8. (Pure Nash equilibrium) A *pure Nash equilibrium (NE)* is a strategy profile $\boldsymbol{r}^*$, where no user can perform a better response update unilaterally.

DEFINITION 9. (Finite improvement property) A game possesses the *finite improvement property* (FIP) when asynchronous better response updates always converge to a pure NE within a finite number of steps, irrespective of the initial strategy profile or the users' updating order.

Existence of the finite improvement property implies that better response updating always leads to pure Nash equilibria, which implies the existence of pure Nash equilibria.

THEOREM 1. *Every task selection game possesses the finite improvement property.*

A proof sketch of Theorem 1 is given in Appendix A. We then proceed to study how long it takes for a strategy profile to converge to a pure NE. Theorem 2 ensures that each best response update can be computed in polynomial time.

THEOREM 2. *A best response update can be computed in* $\mathcal{O}(K^3T^3)$ *time.*

The proof of Theorem 2 is given in Appendix B. The proof is constructive, as it allows us to compute best response updates in polynomial time. Simulations suggest that the number of best response updates required to reach a pure Nash equilibrium grows linearly with the number of users in a wide variety of scenarios, although a theoretical proof is quite challenging to obtain.

3.4 Asynchronous and Distributed Task Selection Algorithm

Theorems 1 and 2 guarantee the convergence of our asynchronous and distributed task selection (ADTS) algorithm (Algorithm 1). To initialize the algorithm, a user inputs her private information on the movement cost (line 2), checks the task descriptions (line 3), and then computes her movement time from Google Maps data based on her speed (line 4).

With the aggregate information on the total number of users working on different tasks (line 9) provided by the service provider in Algorithm 2, each user performs a best response update (lines 11 and 12), and claims the tasks by sending her updated task selection $\boldsymbol{q}_i = (q_i^{(k,t)}, \forall (k,t) \in$

Algorithm 1 *Asynchronous and distributed task selection (ADTS) algorithm for user $i \in \mathcal{I}$.*

```
1: Initialization
2: User Input: Movement cost c_i^{l,l'} ∀ l, l' ∈ L.
3: Check the task description, location l[k], time t[k], and reward
   ρ[k] for all task k ∈ K on the mobile app interface.
4: Calculate movement time Δ_i^{l,l'}, ∀ l, l' ∈ L using Google Maps
   data based on movement speed ν_i.
5: Planning Phase: Task Selection Game
6: repeat
7:    Check clock timer τ on the mobile app.
8:    if τ ∈ Γ_i
9:       Check the mobile app for the number of participants
         q^(k,t) for all (k,t) ∈ H.
10:      Calculate the number of participants excluding user i
         itself: q_{-i}^(k,t) := q^(k,t) - q_i^(k,t), ∀ (k,t) ∈ H.
11:      Perform a best response update: Find a route r_i ∈ R_i
         that maximizes user i's payoff:
```

$$U_i(r_i, \boldsymbol{r}_{-i}) := \left(\sum_{(k,t)\in\mathbb{V}(r_i)} \frac{\rho^*[k,t]}{q_{-i}^{(k,t)}+1} \right) - \sum_{e\in\mathbb{E}(r_i)} g_i(e).$$

```
12:      Update the task selection decision:
```

$$q_i^{(k,t)} := \begin{cases} 1, & \text{if } (k,t) \in \mathbb{V}(r_i), \\ 0, & \text{otherwise,} \end{cases} \quad \forall (k,t) \in \mathcal{H}. \qquad (4)$$

```
13:      Report q_i := (q_i^(k,t), ∀ (k,t) ∈ H) to the service provider.
14:   end if
15: until τ ≥ τ^max.
16: Data Collection and Sensing Phase
17: for each user i ∈ I
18:    Move and complete the sensing task in each time slot t
       based on the task selection plan r_i.
19: end for
```

$\mathcal{H}$) to the service provider. Here, $\mathcal{H} = \{(k,t) \in \mathcal{K} \times \mathcal{T} : \rho^*[k,t] > 0\}$ is the set of task-time points that provide a positive reward.

Notice that users only need to claim the tasks that they are interested in working on, and do not need to reveal their movement plans to the service provider. This will preserve the privacy of users. Let Γ_i be the set of iterations during which user i updates her task selection strategy. We assume that each user updates her strategy distributively and asynchronously until a predefined iteration limit $\tau^{\max}$. We set $\tau^{\max}$ to be a large enough value such that the ADTS can converge. Simulations suggest it is enough to set $\tau^{\max} \geq 5$ when $I \leq 30$ and $K \leq 10$.

In the data collection and sensing phase of Algorithm 1, each user moves around and completes her claimed sensing tasks. The service provider would only pay a user, if the user has claimed the task in the planning phase, and has completed the task with an acceptable quality. As in Field Agent [4], for quality control, the service provider can employ techniques such as GPS marking (for location verification), time stamping (for time verification), and photo/video confirmation. Except the user input (line 2) and sensing execution (lines 16-19), all the other computation, communication, and information checking from maps can be done by the mobile app on behalf of the users.

4. CENTRALIZED TASK ALLOCATION

In this section, we consider the benchmark centralized task allocation (CTA) problem, where the service provider

Algorithm 2 *Information Update Algorithm for the Service Provider.*

```
Initialization
Announce the task description, location l[k], time t[k], and
   reward ρ[k] for all task k ∈ K on the mobile app interface.
Allocate memory for q_i^(k,t), ∀ i ∈ I, (k,t) ∈ H.
Initialize clock timer τ := 1 on the mobile app interface.
Information Update for Task Selection Game in Algorithm 1
repeat
   if task selection update message q_i is received from user i
      Calculate the number of participants for all (k,t) ∈ H:
         q^(k,t) := Σ_{i∈I} q_i^(k,t), ∀ (k,t) ∈ H.
      Update q^(k,t), ∀ (k,t) ∈ H on the mobile app interface.
   end if
   Set τ := τ + 1.
until τ ≥ τ^max.
```

seeks to maximize the social surplus in the TSG. We prove that the CTA problem is NP-hard. Due to the high complexity of finding the optimal solution, we propose a heuristic greedy centralized algorithm, which turns out to have close-to-optimal performance in our simulations.

4.1 Centralized Task Allocation Problem

In the CTA benchmark problem, the service provider allocates tasks to the users in order to maximize the social surplus (i.e., users' total rewards minus total movement costs). The social surplus represents the maximum total profit that the service provider can generate, under the ideal case that all the users are under its direct control.

For user i's given strategy (task-time route choice) r_i in (1), we use $y_i^k(r_i) = 1$ to denote that user i works on task k under strategy r_i, and $y_i^k(r_i) = 0$ otherwise. That is,

$$y_i^k(r_i) = \begin{cases} 1, & \text{if } (k, t[k]) \in r_i, \\ 0, & \text{otherwise.} \end{cases} \qquad (5)$$

Given the users' strategy profile $\boldsymbol{r}$, the social surplus is

$$\text{surplus}(\boldsymbol{r}) = \text{reward}(\boldsymbol{r}) - \text{cost}(\boldsymbol{r}), \qquad (6)$$

where reward($\boldsymbol{r}$) is the total rewards received by all users, and cost($\boldsymbol{r}$) is the total movement costs of all users. Since the reward $\rho[k]$ is equally shared among all the users working on task k, reward($\boldsymbol{r}$) equals the total reward of those tasks that have at least one assigned user. So we have

$$\text{reward}(\boldsymbol{r}) = \sum_{k\in\mathcal{K}} \mathbf{1}_{\{\sum_{i\in\mathcal{I}} y_i^k(r_i) \geq 1\}} \rho[k], \qquad (7)$$

where $\mathbf{1}_{\{.\}}$ is the indicator function. Moreover, we have

$$\text{cost}(\boldsymbol{r}) = \sum_{i\in\mathcal{I}} \text{cost}_i(r_i) = \sum_{i\in\mathcal{I}} \sum_{a=1}^{n-1} c_i^{l[k_i^a], l[k_i^{a+1}]}, \qquad (8)$$

where $\text{cost}_i(r_i) = \sum_{a=1}^{n-1} c_i^{l[k_i^a], l[k_i^{a+1}]}$ is the movement cost of user i.

In practice, it is reasonable to assume that the total movement cost of a user is non-decreasing in the number of locations she visited. That is,

$$c_i^{l,l'} + c_i^{l',l''} \geq c_i^{l,l''}, \forall i \in \mathcal{I}, l, l', l'' \in \mathcal{L}. \qquad (9)$$

With this assumption, we can show that there always exists an optimal task allocation where each task is allocated to at most one user.

Algorithm 3 *Greedy Centralized (GC) Algorithm for Task Allocation.*

1: Initialization
2: Obtain movement costs, speeds, and initial locations from all the users: $c_i^{l,l'}$, $\forall\, l, l' \in \mathcal{L}, i \in \mathcal{I}$, ν_i and l_i^{init}, $\forall\, i \in \mathcal{I}$.
3: Initialize the next available time and current location of the users: $\phi_i := 1$ and $l_i := l_i^{\text{init}}$, $\forall\, i \in \mathcal{I}$.
4: Initialize the optimization variables $y_i^k := 0$, $\forall\, i \in \mathcal{I}, k \in \mathcal{K}$.
5: Greedy Centralized Task Allocation
6: Sort the tasks in set $\mathcal{K}$ in the ascending order of the execution time $t[k]$.
7: **for** $k = 1$ to K
8: Set $flag := 0$.
9: Sort the users in set $\mathcal{I}$ in the ascending order of $c_i^{l_i, l[k]}$.
10: Set $i := 1$.
11: **while** $i \leq I$ **and** $flag = 0$
12: **if** $k \in \mathcal{K}_i$ **and** $t[k] - \phi_i \geq \Delta_i^{l_i, l[k]}$ **and** $\rho[k] \geq c_i^{l_i, l[k]}$
13: Update user i's next available time $\phi_i := t[k]$ and current location $l_i := l[k]$.
14: Indicate the task allocation $y_i^k := 1$ and set $flag := 1$.
15: **end if**
16: Set $i := i + 1$.
17: **end while**
18: **end for**
19: **for** $i \in \mathcal{I}$
20: Inform user i the task allocation $(y_i^k, \forall\, k \in \mathcal{K})$.
21: **end for**
22: Data Collection and Sensing Phase
23: **for** each user $i \in \mathcal{I}$
24: Move and complete the sensing tasks based on the task allocation $(y_i^k, \forall\, k \in \mathcal{K})$.
25: **end for**

LEMMA 1. *There always exists a social surplus maximizing (optimal) task assignment* $\boldsymbol{r}^* = \underset{\boldsymbol{r}\in\mathcal{R}_1\times\ldots\times\mathcal{R}_I}{\arg\max}\ surplus(\boldsymbol{r})$ *such that* $\sum_{i\in\mathcal{I}} y_i^k(r_i^*) \leq 1, \forall\, k \in \mathcal{K}$.

The proof of Lemma 1 is given in Appendix C. With this lemma, we can establish the NP-hardness of the CTA benchmark.

THEOREM 3. *The problem of finding the social surplus maximization solution of the TSG is NP-hard.*

The proof sketch of Theorem 3 is given in Appendix D. Theorem 3 motivates us to consider a greedy heuristic algorithm to solve the CTA problem.

4.2 Greedy Centralized Task Allocation Algorithm

We propose a low complexity greedy centralized (GC) algorithm (Algorithm 3), which computes an approximate solution to the social surplus maximization problem. The key idea is that the service provider sorts the tasks in ascending order of the execution time, and then allocates one user to each task sequentially in a greedy manner. Specifically, in line 6, the service provider first serves tasks with the earliest execution time. In line 9, the service provider sorts users in the order of an increasing movement costs (from the users' current locations to the location of the current task k). Line 12 indicates that a user i will be chosen if it is eligible to perform the task ($i : k \in \mathcal{K}_i$), can reach the task location on time ($t[k] - \phi_i \geq \Delta_i^{l_i, l[k]}$), and has the incentive to perform the task ($\rho[k] \geq c_i^{l_i, l[k]}$) (line 12). Here ϕ_i is the first time slot of user i after finishing any existing allocating task. It is possible that some task k may not be allocated to any users (i.e., $y_i^k = 0, \forall\, i \in \mathcal{I}$).

Table 1: Simulation Parameters

Parameters	Values
Number of tasks K	10
Number of time slots T	15
Rewards for three levels of tasks	\$10, \$15, \$20
Duration of a time slot δ	1 minute
Movement speed ν	0.1 km/min

LEMMA 2. *Algorithm 3 has a computational complexity of* $\mathcal{O}(KI \log I)$.

The proof of Lemma 2 is given in Appendix E.

5. PERFORMANCE EVALUATIONS

In this section, we evaluate the performance of our proposed ADTS scheme by comparing with the CTA benchmark, the GC scheme, and a greedy distributed (GD) scheme. We study the impact of various system parameters on the average user payoff, fairness, coverage, and average reward per measurement on different schemes. We also present an example using real movement time data from Google Maps. Our simulations involve the following schemes:

- ADTS scheme: Algorithms 1 and 2.
- CTA benchmark: Global optimal solution of the social surplus maximization problem.
- GC scheme: Algorithm 3 that approximately solves the social surplus maximization problem.
- GD scheme: Each user chooses to work on the earliest feasible task without coordinating with other users. Like the GC scheme, user i should be eligible for the task (i.e., $i : k \in \mathcal{K}_i$), can arrive on time to perform the task (i.e., when $t[k] - \phi_i \geq \Delta_i^{l_i, l[k]}$ given that user i is at location l_i), and has an incentive to perform sensing assuming no other users share the reward of that task (i.e., $\rho[k] \geq c_i^{l_i, l[k]}$). If there is more than one feasible task with the same execution time, then the user will choose the task with the highest reward.

For each set of system parameter choices, we run the simulations 1000 times with randomized initial user locations, and randomized locations and times for the tasks, and show the average value. Unless specified otherwise, we assume that the locations of the K tasks and I users are randomly placed in a 1 km $\times$ 1 km region. Each user is randomly allocated one of three reputation levels, and each task is randomly assigned a threshold. A user is eligible to perform a task when her reputation exceeds the threshold of the task. Each user i moves at constant speed ν_i, and the movement time from location $l \in \mathcal{L}$ to location $l' \in \mathcal{L}$ is $\Delta_i^{l,l'} = \left\lceil \frac{\text{dist}(l,l')}{\nu_i \delta} \right\rceil$, where $\text{dist}(l,l')$ is the traveling distance on the road between locations l and l', δ is the length of a time slot, and $\lceil\cdot\rceil$ is the ceiling function. We assume that the movement cost of user i is linearly proportional to the distance between two locations in the form $c_i^{l,l'} = c_i^{\text{move}}\text{dist}(l,l')$. For simplicity, we assume that all the

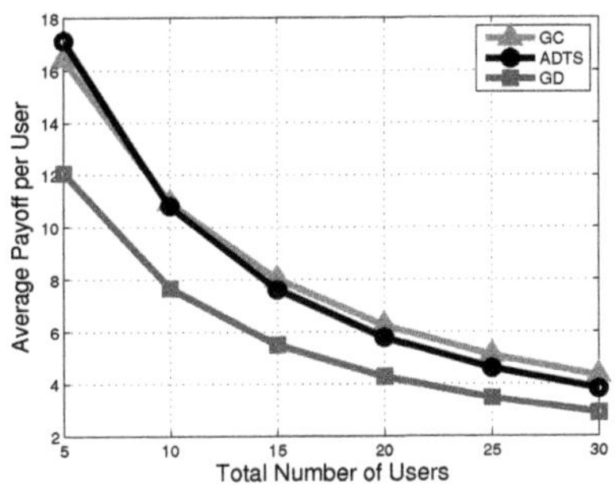

Figure 3: The average user payoff versus the total number of users I for $K = 10$ and $c^{\text{move}} = 0.1$.

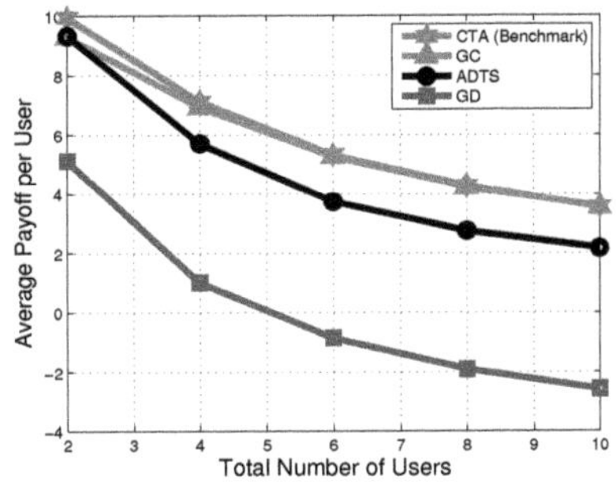

Figure 4: The average user payoff versus the total number of users I for $K = 5$ and $c^{\text{move}} = 1$.

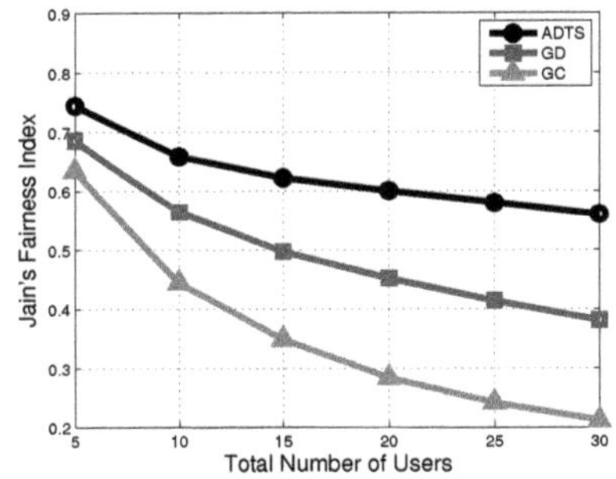

Figure 5: Jain's fairness index versus the total number of users I for $K = 10$ and $c^{\text{move}} = 0.1$.

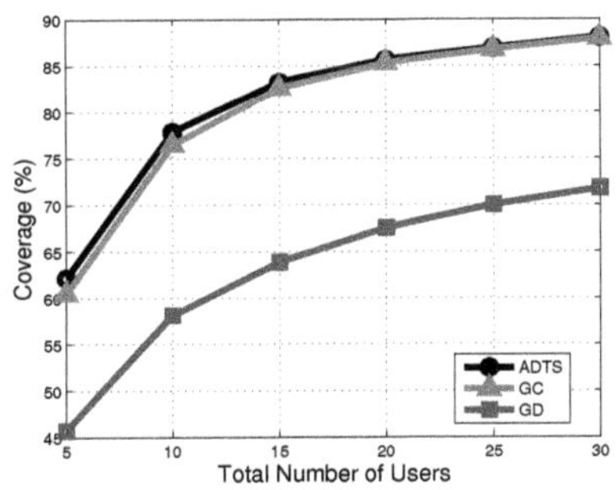

Figure 6: The coverage versus the total number of users I for $K = 10$ and $c^{\text{move}} = 0.1$.

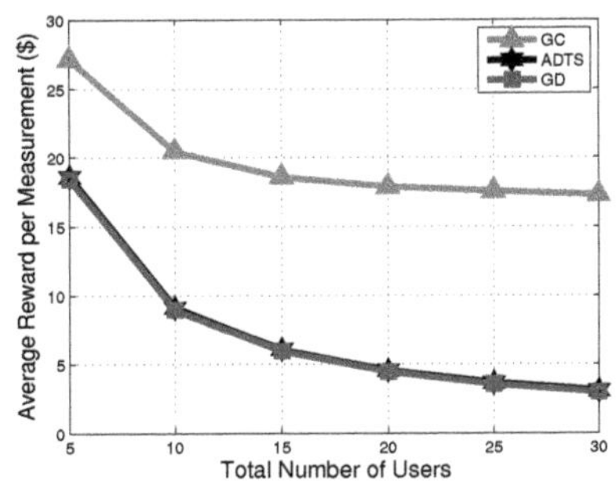

Figure 7: The average reward per measurement versus the total number of users I for $K = 10$ and $c^{\text{move}} = 0.1$.

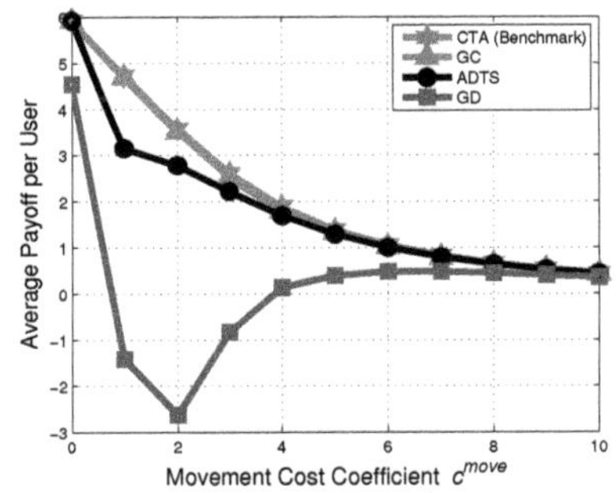

Figure 8: The average user payoff versus the movement cost coefficient c^{move} for $I = 7$ and $K = 5$.

users have the same movement cost coefficient $c_i^{\text{move}} = c^{\text{move}}$ and the same movement speed $\nu_i = \nu$. Other simulation parameters are listed in Table 1.

5.1 Average User Payoff and Fairness

Impact of user number on user payoff: In Fig. 3, we plot the average user payoff against the number of users I, with $K = 10$ tasks and movement cost coefficient $c^{\text{move}} = 0.1$. The average user payoff decreases with I under all three schemes, due to the increased competition with the increasing number of users. The ADTS scheme achieves a similar average user payoff as the GC scheme.

Comparison with centralized optimal solution: In Fig. 4, we plot the average user payoff against I in a smaller scale, with $K = 5$ and $c^{\text{move}} = 1$, so that we can evaluate the CTA benchmark as well. Note that GC achieves a similar payoff to the benchmark, especially when I is large.

Fairness: In Fig. 5, we study how the payoffs are distributed among the users by plotting Jain's fairness index [10] (defined as $\left(\sum_{i\in\mathcal{I}} U_i(\boldsymbol{r})\right)^2/\left(I\sum_{i\in\mathcal{I}} U_i(\boldsymbol{r})^2\right)$) against I, with $K = 10$ and $c^{\text{move}} = 0.1$. The ADTS scheme has the highest fairness index, as each user has an equal chance to update her strategy profile in ADTS in Algorithm 1. On the other hand, the GC scheme has the lowest fairness index, as it allocates K tasks to at most K users. As a result, when I increases, the number of users not allocated any task increases, so the fairness decreases.

5.2 Coverage and Reward Per Measurement

We examine the coverage and average reward per measurement under the three schemes, with $K = 10$ tasks and $c^{\text{move}} = 0.1$. The coverage is defined as the percentage of tasks with at least one measurement received.

Impact of user number on coverage: In Fig. 6, we plot the coverage against I. When I increases, we see the coverage under all the schemes increases, as there are more users to work on the tasks. The ADTS scheme has a slightly higher coverage than the GC scheme, as users try to avoid too much overlapping with each other in ADTS. The large difference between the coverage of the ADTS and GD schemes is due to the lack of coordination in the GD scheme.

Average reward per measurement: Fig. 7 shows the average reward per measurement against I. We can see that the ADTS and GD schemes have the same smaller average reward per measurement than the centralized scheme GC. From a service provider's point of view, with the same amount of total reward, lower average reward per measurement means that more sensing data can be collected, which is beneficial for the service provider.

5.3 Impact of Moving Cost and Speed

Impact of movement cost on user payoff: In Fig. 8, we plot the average user payoff against c^{move} with $I = 7$ and $K = 5$. As c^{move} increases, the payoffs for collecting measurements under CTA, ADTS, and GC decrease. Moreover, since users under CTA, ADTS, and GC are aware of

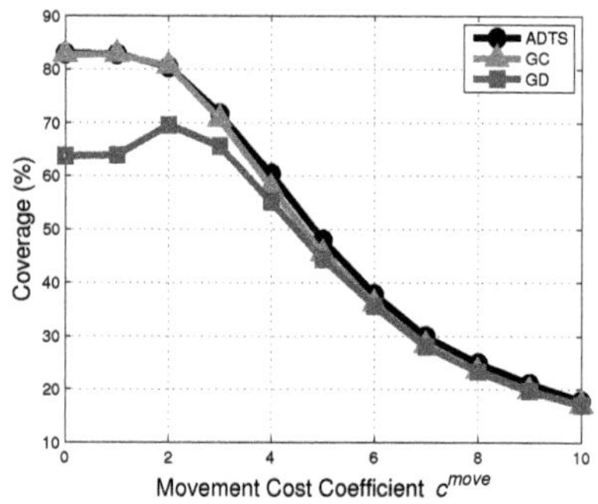

Figure 9: The coverage versus the movement cost coefficient c^{move} for $I = 10$ and $K = 10$.

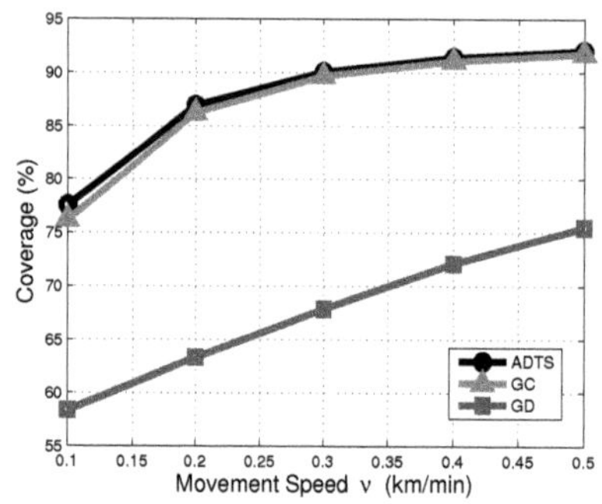

Figure 10: The coverage versus the movement speed ν for $I = 10$ and $K = 10$.

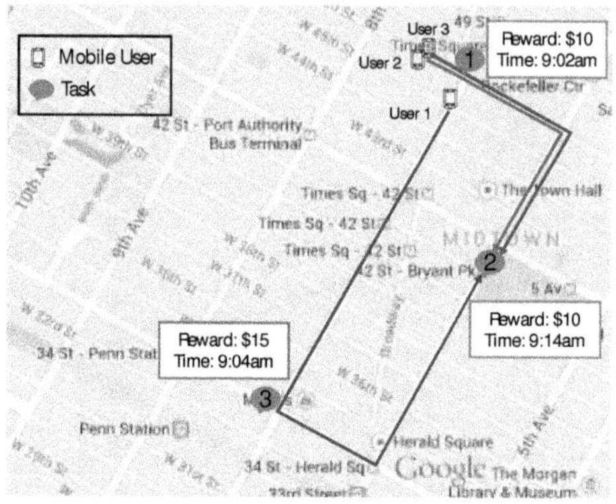

Figure 11: An illustration on the task selection and mobility plans of the users on the map under the ADTS scheme.

Table 2: Movement Time Data from Google Maps

Drive/Walk (min)	Location 1	Location 2	Location 3
Location 1	0 / 0	3 / 11	4 / 15
Location 2	3 / 11	0 / 0	2 / 6
Location 3	4 / 15	2 / 6	0 / 0

the actual reward that they can receive (after sharing with other users), the users would not receive a negative payoff for collecting data. However, for the GD scheme without any user coordination, a user makes decisions with the belief that she will gain the full reward $\rho[k]$ for task k, rather than the actual reward she can achieve (after sharing with other users). When $c^{\text{move}} \leq 4$, users become overly aggressive in GD, and it becomes common that multiple users work on the same task. As a result, the actual reward per user is much less than the full reward of the task, which results in the decrease of the average payoff (even to a negative value) in GD. However, when c^{move} increases beyond 4, users are less likely to work on the same task in GD, so the evaluation of the reward is more accurate, and the average user payoff in GD gradually converges to a non-negative value, similar to those under the ADTS and GC schemes.

Impact of movement cost on coverage: In Fig. 9, we plot the coverage against the movement cost coefficient c^{move} with $I = 10$ and $K = 10$. As c^{move} increases, the coverage decreases in general, because the users are less willing to perform sensing. The slight increase in coverage in GD for $c^{\text{move}} \leq 2$ is due to the inaccurate reward estimation mentioned in the previous paragraph.

Impact of movement speed on coverage: In Fig. 10, we plot the coverage against the movement speed ν for $I = 10$ and $K = 10$. As ν increases, the coverages under all three schemes increases. The ADTS scheme has a slightly larger coverage than the GC scheme.

5.4 A Real-World Example Using Google Maps

To better illustrate the schemes, we next introduce a more concrete example based on the neighborhood map in New York City with real data from Google Maps. We consider $I = 3$ users and $K = 3$ tasks. The locations of the users, tasks, the execution times, and rewards are shown in Fig. 11.

Table 3: Summary of Performance in the Real-world Example

	ADTS	GC and CTA benchmark	GD
Average user payoff	\$10.33	\$11	\$7
Jain's fairness index	0.93	0.64	0.93
Coverage	100%	100%	66.67%

We assume that user 1 prefers driving, while users 2 and 3 prefer walking. We compute the movement time of driving and walking between different locations through Google Maps, as shown in Table 2. For the movement cost, we assume that driving between any two different locations costs \$2 and walking is free.

Fig. 11 shows the task selection plans of three users (i.e., the blue, red, and purple broken lines with arrows) under the ADTS scheme. As we can see, user 1 takes the task selection plan of task 3 $\rightarrow$ task 2, while users 2 and 3 take the task selection plan of task 1 $\rightarrow$ task 2. The intuition is that as users 2 and 3 are pedestrians, who do not have enough time to go to the far away location 3 from their initial locations. As a result, user 1, who is driving, prefers to take task 3 with the minimum competition, and enjoys a higher reward. After finishing their first chosen task, all three users have enough time to work on task 2, and share the reward of \$10. In contrast, under both the GC scheme and CTA benchmark (not shown in the figure), user 1 works on task 3, user 2 works on both tasks 1 and 2, and user 3 does not have any task to work on. For the GD scheme (not shown in the figure), since the initial locations of all the users are nearby, their task selection plans are identical: task 1 $\rightarrow$ task 2, as everyone chooses to pursue the earliest task without any coordination. The performance of the three schemes are summarized in Table 3. We can see that the ADTS scheme achieves a high level of fairness, coverage, and user payoff.

6. CONCLUSION

Motivated by commercial mobile crowdsensing applications, such as Gigwalk and Field Agent, we studied the distributed time-sensitive and location-dependent task selection problem in this paper. We examined the problem from the perspectives of both noncooperative game and centralized optimization. We proposed an asynchronous and distributed task selection (ADTS) algorithm to help users determine their task selection and mobility plans in a distributed fashion, based on limited information on users' aggregate task choices. We proved that finding the social surplus maximization solution is NP-hard. Simulation results showed that the ADTS scheme achieves the highest Jain's fairness index and coverage as compared with two heuristic schemes. In this paper, we focus on the distributed task selections of a fixed set of users. In the future work, we will consider the case a changing user population, where users can dynamically join and leave the system.

7. ACKNOWLEDGMENT

This work is supported by University of Macau Grant MYRG2014-00140-FST. This work is also supported by the General Research Funds (Project Number CUHK 412713 and 14202814) established under the University Grant Committee of the Hong Kong Special Administrative Region, China.

APPENDIX

A. PROOF SKETCH OF THEOREM 1

The key idea is to show that the mapping

$$\Phi(\boldsymbol{r}) = \left(\sum_{(k,t)\in\mathcal{K}\times\mathcal{T}} \sum_{q=1}^{m^{(k,t)}(\boldsymbol{r})} \frac{\rho^*[k,t]}{q} \right) - \sum_{i\in\mathcal{I}} \sum_{e\in\mathbb{E}(r_i)} g_i(e)$$

is a *potential function* [13] of the TSG (where $\mathbb{E}(r_i)$ is defined in Definition 6). This means that for each strategy profile $\boldsymbol{r} = (r_1, \ldots, r_I) \in \mathcal{R}_1 \times \ldots \times \mathcal{R}_I$, each user $i \in \mathcal{I}$, and each strategy $r_i' \in \mathcal{R}_i$ available to user i, we have $\Phi(r_i', \boldsymbol{r}_{-i}) - \Phi(\boldsymbol{r}) = U_i(r_i', \boldsymbol{r}_{-i}) - U_i(\boldsymbol{r})$. In [13], the authors prove that every finite game with a potential function has the FIP. Since the TSG is a finite game, we prove the statement in Theorem 1. Full details of the proof can be found in [2]. ∎

B. PROOF OF THEOREM 2

The key proof idea is to show that the problem of a generic user j finding a best response strategy in a strategy profile $\boldsymbol{r}$ can be reformulated as the problem of finding a longest path in a weighted directed acyclic graph $\mathcal{G}^*$, which can be solved in polynomial time.

To construct such a graph $\mathcal{G}^*$, we construct a weighted directed graph $\mathcal{G} = (\mathcal{V}, \mathcal{E})$. Recall that $\mathbb{V}$ is defined in Definition 4 and $\mathbb{E}$ is defined in Definition 6. The vertex set $\mathcal{V} = \bigcup_{s\in\mathcal{R}_j} \mathbb{V}(s)$ corresponds to the set of task-time points (k,t), which lie on routes which are feasible for user j. The directed edge set $\mathcal{E} = \bigcup_{s\in\mathcal{R}_j} \mathbb{E}(s)$ corresponds to the set of all pairs $[(k,t),(k',t')] \in \mathbb{E}(s)$ such that user j can move between. Each directed edge $e = [(k,t),(k',t')]$ of the graph $\mathcal{G}$ is associated with an edge weight $w(e) = -g_j(e) = -c_j^{l[k],l[k']}$. Each vertex (k,t) is associated with a value

$$\theta((k,t)) = \frac{\rho^*[k,t]}{|\{i\in\mathcal{I} : i \neq j, (k,t) \in \mathbb{V}(r_i)\}| + 1}, \tag{10}$$

where $|\{i\in\mathcal{I} : i \neq j, (k,t) \in \mathbb{V}(r_i)\}|$ equals the number of users other than j which have selected task-time routes that pass through (k,t) in the strategy profile $\boldsymbol{r}$. Notice that $\theta((k,t))$ equals the reward that user j would get for visiting task-time point (k,t).

A path in a directed graph is a sequence of vertices, where each vertex is linked to its successor in the sequence. A best response for user j corresponds to a path in the graph $\mathcal{G}$, which starts at the task-time point $(k_j^{\text{init}}, 1)$, and maximizes the sum of the weights of the edges, and the values of the vertices along the path.

Starting from graph $\mathcal{G}$ defined above, we form a new graph $\mathcal{G}^* = (\mathcal{V}^*, \mathcal{E}^*)$, by replacing each vertex (k,t) in $\mathcal{G}$ with a pair of new vertices $(k,t,0)$ and $(k,t,1)$. These two new vertices are linked by a new directed edge $[(k,t,0),(k,t,1)]$, which has an edge weight $w^*([(k,t,0),(k,t,1)]) = \theta((k,t))$ as in (10), equal to the value of the original vertex (k,t).

As a result, graph $\mathcal{G}^*$ has a vertex set

$$\mathcal{V}^* = \{(k,t,\gamma) : (k,t) \in \mathcal{V}, \gamma \in \{0,1\}\},$$

and an edge set $\mathcal{E}^* = \mathcal{E}_1^* \cup \mathcal{E}_2^*$. Here set

$$\mathcal{E}_1^* = \left\{ [(k,t,1),(k',t',0)] : [(k,t),(k',t')] \in \mathcal{E} \right\},$$

and each edge $[(k,t,1),(k',t',0)] \in \mathcal{E}_1^*$ has a weight

$$w^*\left([(k,t,1),(k',t',0)]\right) = w\left([(k,t),(k',t')]\right),$$

with the right hand side being the weight of the edge originally in graph $\mathcal{G}$. Also set $\mathcal{E}_2^* = \{[(k,t,0),(k,t,1)] : (k,t) \in \mathcal{V}\}$, and each edge $[(k,t,0),(k,t,1)] \in \mathcal{E}_2^*$ has a weight

$$w^*\left([(k,t,1),(k',t',0)]\right) = \theta((k,t)),$$

where the right hand side follows (10).

By considering the weights of all edges in $\mathcal{G}^*$ as lengths, one can see that a best response for user j in strategy profile $\boldsymbol{r}$ corresponds to a longest path in $\mathcal{G}^*$ that starts at the vertex $(k_j^{init}, t, 0)$. Such a longest path can be computed in $\mathcal{O}(|\mathcal{V}^*| \times |\mathcal{E}^*|) = \mathcal{O}(K^3T^3)$ time using the algorithm described in [14], because $\mathcal{G}^*$ is a directed acyclic graph. Since $\mathcal{G}^*$ itself can be constructed in $\mathcal{O}(K^2T^2)$ time based on the previous discussions, the entire process for a user to compute the best response has a complexity of $\mathcal{O}(K^3T^3)$. ∎

C. PROOF OF LEMMA 1

We prove the lemma by contradiction. Assume that for any optimal solution $\boldsymbol{r}^*$, we can always find a task $q \in \mathcal{K}$ such that $\sum_{i\in\mathcal{I}} y_i^q(r_i^*) > 1$. Let us focus on a particular user $j \in \mathcal{I}$ that is assigned to work on task q (i.e., $y_j^q(r_j^*) = 1$). We can define another strategy profile $\boldsymbol{r}$, which is the same as $\boldsymbol{r}^*$ for the task allocation of all users, except that task q is not allocated to user j. That is,

$$y_i^k(r_i) = \begin{cases} 0, & \text{if } k = q \text{ and } i = j, \\ y_i^k(r_i^*), & \text{otherwise.} \end{cases} \tag{11}$$

Since the coverage of the tasks under $\boldsymbol{r}$ is the same as $\boldsymbol{r}^*$, where $\sum_{i\in\mathcal{I}} y_i^k(r_i) \geq 1$ and $\sum_{i\in\mathcal{I}} y_i^k(r_i^*) \geq 1$ for each task $k \in \mathcal{K}$, we have from (7) that

$$\text{reward}(\boldsymbol{r}) = \text{reward}(\boldsymbol{r}^*). \tag{12}$$

Since user j works on one task less in r_j than in r_j^*, from (9), we have

$$\text{cost}_j(r_j) \leq \text{cost}_j(r_j^*). \tag{13}$$

However, the movement costs of other users remain the same such that

$$\text{cost}_i(r_i) = \text{cost}_i(r_i^*), \forall i \in \mathcal{I}\backslash\{j\}. \tag{14}$$

Overall, substituting (12), (13), and (14) into (6), we have

$$\text{surplus}(\boldsymbol{r}^*) \leq \text{surplus}(\boldsymbol{r}), \tag{15}$$

which means that strategy profile $\boldsymbol{r}$ is also an optimal solution. This leads to a contradiction. ■

D. PROOF SKETCH OF THEOREM 3

We prove the NP-hardness by *restriction* [7]: We show that finding the social surplus maximization solution in a special case of a TSG can be transformed into a 3-dimensional matching decision problem, which is NP-complete [7, 11].

DEFINITION 10. (3-dimensional matching) Let $\mathcal{X}$, $\mathcal{Y}$, and $\mathcal{Z}$ be three finite disjoint sets. Let $\mathcal{R} \subseteq \mathcal{X} \times \mathcal{Y} \times \mathcal{Z}$ be a set of ordered triples, i.e., $\mathcal{R} = \{(x, y, z) : x \in \mathcal{X}, y \in \mathcal{Y}, z \in \mathcal{Z}\}$. $\mathcal{R}' \subseteq \mathcal{R}$ is a *3-dimensional matching* if for any two different triples $(x_1, y_1, z_1) \in \mathcal{R}'$ and $(x_2, y_2, z_2) \in \mathcal{R}'$, we have $x_1 \neq x_2$, $y_1 \neq y_2$, and $z_1 \neq z_2$.

DEFINITION 11. (3-dimensional matching decision problem) Suppose $|\mathcal{X}| = |\mathcal{Y}| = |\mathcal{Z}| = M$. Given an input $\mathcal{R}$ with $|\mathcal{R}| \geq M$, decide whether there exists a 3-dimensional matching $\mathcal{R}' \subseteq \mathcal{R}$ with the maximum size $|\mathcal{R}'| = M$.

Consider a restricted TSG, which is a special case of a TSG, which we place the following restrictions:

(a) Tasks and time slots: There are $T = 3$ time slots, and there are M tasks in each time slot (hence a total of $3M$ tasks in 3 time slots). Sets $\mathcal{X}$, $\mathcal{Y}$, and $\mathcal{Z}$ represent the sets of available tasks in the three time slots, where $|\mathcal{X}| = |\mathcal{Y}| = |\mathcal{Z}| = M$.

(b) Task-time route: Set $\mathcal{R}$ represents the set of available task-time routes of all the users. Assume that each user i can only choose one particular available task-time route $r_i \in \mathcal{R}$. We assume that I is large enough, such that the task-time routes of all the users cover all the tasks in $\mathcal{X} \cup \mathcal{Y} \cup \mathcal{Z}$, so $|\mathcal{R}| = I \geq M$. $\mathcal{R}' \subseteq \mathcal{R}$ in Definition 11 represents a feasible task allocation. We assume that a user, whose route is not chosen in $\mathcal{R}'$, will not work on any real task.

(c) Large reward: The reward of a task is larger than the movement cost to work on the task, i.e., $\rho[k] > c_i^{l[k'],l[k]}$ for each user $i \in \mathcal{I}$ and all tasks $k, k' \in \mathcal{K}$.

(d) User-independent movement cost: The movement cost only depends on its destination location and is independent of its initial location, such that $c_i^{l,l'} = c[l'], \forall i \in \mathcal{I}, l, l' \in \mathcal{L}$, where $c[l']$ is the movement cost of destination $l' \in \mathcal{L}$.

In the restricted TSG, first, restrictions (c) and (d) imply that we can maximize the social surplus by covering *all* the tasks with *any* available users. Second, Lemma 1 implies that we can focus on an optimal solution, where each task should be allocated to *at most one* user. So the optimal task allocation should not contain any overlapping components (i.e., multiple users working on the same task) as defined in Definition 10. Putting the above discussions together, we know that in the social surplus maximization solution, *every* element of $\mathcal{X} \times \mathcal{Y} \times \mathcal{Z}$ (i.e., every task) should be contained in *exactly one* of the triples (i.e., the task-time routes) in $\mathcal{R}'$. In other words, $\mathcal{R}' \subseteq \mathcal{R}$ is the optimal task allocation. So the surplus maximization problem can be transformed to a 3-dimensional matching decision problem, which is NP-complete [7, 11]. By restriction, we establish that the problem of finding the social surplus maximization solution of the TSG is NP-hard. Full details of the proof can be found in [2]. ■

E. PROOF OF LEMMA 2

The sorting of execution time in line 6 takes $\mathcal{O}(K \log K)$ time [11]. For each task, besides some simple computations, most of the time is consumed for sorting the movement costs of the users in line 9, and it takes a running time of $\mathcal{O}(I \log I)$. Since we generally have more users than tasks, i.e., $I \log I > \log K$, the total run time with K tasks is $\mathcal{O}(KI \log I)$. ■

F. REFERENCES

[1] Amazon Mechanical Turk. https://www.mturk.com/mturk/.

[2] M. H. Cheung, R. Southwell, F. Hou, and J. Huang. Distributed time-sensitive task selection in mobile crowdsensing. `http://arxiv.org/abs/1503.06007`, 2015.

[3] L. Duan, T. Kubo, K. Sugiyama, J. Huang, T. Hasegawa, and J. Walrand. Motivating smartphone collaboration in data acquisition and distributed computing. *IEEE Trans. on Mobile Computing*, 13(10):2320–2333, Oct. 2014.

[4] Field Agent. http://www.fieldagent.net/.

[5] R. K. Ganti, F. Ye, and H. Lei. Mobile crowdsensing: Current state and future challenges. *IEEE Communications Magazine*, 49(11):32–39, Nov. 2011.

[6] L. Gao, F. Hou, and J. Huang. Providing long-term participation incentive in participatory sensing. In *Proc. of IEEE INFOCOM*, Hong Kong, China, Apr. 2015.

[7] M. R. Garey and D. S. Johnson. *Computers and Intractability: A Guide to the Theory of NP-Completeness*. Freeman, San Francisco, CA, first edition, 1979.

[8] Gigwalk. http://gigwalk.com/.

[9] S. He, D. Shin, J. Zhang, and J. Chen. Towards optimal allocation of location dependent tasks in crowdsensing. In *Proc. of IEEE INFOCOM*, Toronto, Canada, Apr. 2014.

[10] R. K. Jain, D. Chiu, and W. R. Hawe. A quantitative measure of fairness and discrimination for resource allocation in shared computer systems. Tech. Report DEC-TR-301, Eastern Research Lab, Sept. 1984.

[11] J. Kleinberg and E. Tardos. *Algorithm Design*. Addison-Wesley, Boston, MA, first edition, 2005.

[12] N. D. Lane, E. Miluzzo, H. Lu, D. Peebles, T. Choudhury, and A. T. Campbell. A survey of mobile phone sensing. *IEEE Communications Magazine*, 48(9):140–150, Sept. 2010.

[13] D. Monderer and L. S. Shapley. Potential games. *Games and Economic Behavior*, 14(1):124–143, May 1996.

[14] R. Sedgewick and K. Wayne. *Algorithms*. Pearson Education, 2011.

[15] X. Sheng, J. Tang, and W. Zhang. Energy-efficient collaborative sensing with mobile phones. In *Proc. of IEEE INFOCOM*, Orlando, FL, Mar. 2012.

[16] Q. Zhao, Y. Zhu, H. Zhu, J. Cao, G. Xue, and B. Li. Fair energy-efficient sensing task allocation in participatory sensing with smartphones. In *Proc. of IEEE INFOCOM*, Toronto, Canada, Apr. 2014.

Quality of Information Aware Incentive Mechanisms for Mobile Crowd Sensing Systems*

Haiming Jin† Lu Su§ Danyang Chen§ Klara Nahrstedt† Jinhui Xu§
†Department of Computer Science, University of Illinois at Urbana-Champaign, IL, USA
§Department of Computer Science and Engineering, State University of New York at Buffalo, NY, USA
hjin8@illinois.edu, {lusu, danyangc}@buffalo.edu, klara@illinois.edu, jinhui@buffalo.edu

ABSTRACT

Recent years have witnessed the emergence of mobile crowd sensing (MCS) systems, which leverage the public crowd equipped with various mobile devices for large scale sensing tasks. In this paper, we study a critical problem in MCS systems, namely, incentivizing user participation. Different from existing work, we incorporate a crucial metric, called users' *quality of information (QoI)*, into our incentive mechanisms for MCS systems. Due to various factors (e.g., sensor quality, noise, etc.) the quality of the sensory data contributed by individual users varies significantly. Obtaining high quality data with little expense is always the ideal of MCS platforms. Technically, we design incentive mechanisms based on reverse combinatorial auctions. We investigate both the single-minded and multi-minded combinatorial auction models. For the former, we design a truthful, individual rational and computationally efficient mechanism that approximately maximizes the social welfare with a guaranteed approximation ratio. For the latter, we design an iterative descending mechanism that achieves close-to-optimal social welfare while satisfying individual rationality and computational efficiency. Through extensive simulations, we validate our theoretical analysis about the close-to-optimal social welfare and fast running time of our mechanisms.

Categories and Subject Descriptors

C.2.1 [**Computer-Communication Networks**]: Network Architecture and Design

General Terms

Algorithm, Design, Economics

Keywords

Crowd Sensing, Incentive Mechanism, Quality of Information

*This work was supported in part by the National Science Foundation under award numbers CNS-1329686, 1329737, 1330142, and 1330491.

†The first two authors contribute equally to this paper.

MobiHoc'15, June 22–25, 2015, Hangzhou, China.

http://dx.doi.org/10.1145/2746285.2746310.

1. INTRODUCTION

The ubiquity of human-carried mobile devices (e.g., smartphones, tablets, etc.) with a plethora of on-board and portable sensors (e.g., accelerometer, compass, camera, etc.) has given rise to the emergence of various people-centric *mobile crowd sensing (MCS)* systems [1–3]. In a typical MCS system, a cloud-based platform aggregates and analyzes the sensory data provided by the public crowd instead of professionals and dedicatedly deployed sensors. The mobile devices of participating users collect and may process in certain level the data before submitting them to the platform.

Such MCS systems hold a wide spectrum of applications including healthcare, ambient environment monitoring, smart transportation, indoor localization, etc. For example, MedWatcher [2] is a US FDA advocated MCS system for post-market medical device surveillance. Participating users upload photos of their medical devices to a cloud-based platform using the MedWatcher mobile application, which help identify visible problems with the devices. The platform aggregates and analyzes the user-provided information, sends reports to the FDA and alerts users about medical device problems. Such a crowdsourcing paradigm enables easier detection of device safety issues and faster propagation of alerts to device users compared to traditional reporting methods such as mail or telephone. Moreover, air quality monitoring [3] is another area where MCS systems obtain their recent popularity. In such systems, crowdsourced air quality data are aggregated from a large number of people using air quality sensors ported to their smartphones, which help estimate the city or district level air quality.

Participating in such crowd sensing tasks is usually a costly procedure for individual users. On one hand, it consumes users' resources, such as computing power, battery and so forth. On the other hand, a considerable portion of sensing tasks require the submission of some types of users' sensitive private information, which causes privacy leakage for participating users. For example, by uploading the photos of their medical devices, users reveal the types of their illnesses. By submitting air quality estimation samples, users usually reveal information about their locations. Therefore, without satisfactory rewards that compensate participating costs, users will be reluctant to carry out the sensing tasks. However, most of the existing MCS systems are based on voluntary user participation or lack effective incentive mechanisms.

Aware of the paramount importance of stimulating user participation, the research community has recently developed some game-theoretic incentive mechanisms for MCS systems [4–18]. However, most of the existing mechanisms fail to incorporate one important aspect, that is users' *quality of information (QoI)*, into their designs. The meaning of QoI varies for different applications. For example, in the aforementioned MedWatcher system [2] QoI refers to the quality (e.g., resolution, contrast, sharpness, etc.) of uploaded photos. Higher quality ones will help the platform better identify visible device problems. In air quality monitoring MCS systems [3], QoI means a user's estimation accuracy of air quality. The QoI of every user could be affected by various factors, including poor sensor quality, noise, lack of sensor calibration and so forth.

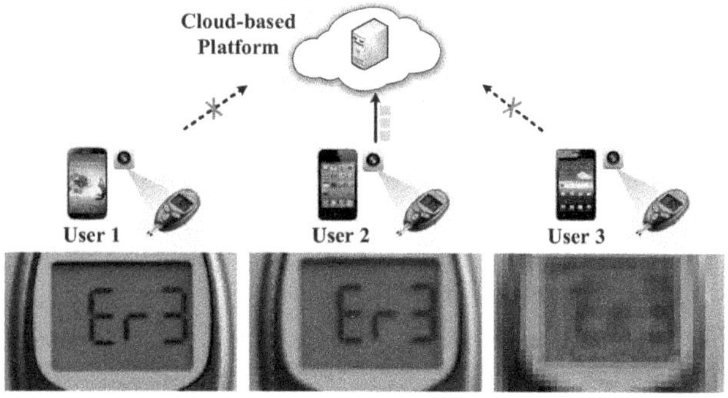

Figure 1: A MedWatcher MCS system example (3 users try to upload the photos of the error message "Er3" on the screens of their blood glucose meters to the MedWatcher platform. The prices that the 3 users ask for cost compensation are 100\$, 10\$ and 1\$ respectively.)

To compensate the cost of each user's participation, existing incentive mechanisms have used the user's bidding price as an important metric to allocate sensing tasks. However, as shown in the example in Figure 1, QoI is also a major factor that should be considered together with bidding price. Although user 1 has the highest quality photo, her high price prohibits the platform from requesting her data. Furthermore, despite user 3's low price the platform will not be interested in her data either, because her low quality photo could hardly contribute to identifying the error message "Er3". By jointly considering price and QoI, the platform will select user 2 with medium price and acceptable photo quality as the data provider. Therefore, our goal is to *design QoI aware incentive mechanisms for MCS systems.*

Considering users' *strategic* behaviors and the combinatorial nature of the tasks that every user executes, we design incentive mechanisms based on *reverse combinatorial auctions*, where the platform acts as the auctioneer that purchases the data from participating users. Not only do we study the *single-minded* scenario where every user is willing to execute one subset of tasks, but also we investigate the *multi-minded* case in which any user might be interested in executing multiple subsets of tasks. Similar to the traditional VCG mechanisms [19, 20], our mechanisms also aim to maximize the social welfare. Mechanism design for combinatorial auctions is typically challenging in that usually we aim to design a computationally efficient mechanism with close-to-optimal social welfare in the presence of an NP-hard winner determination problem, which meanwhile satisfies *truthfulness* and *individual rationality*. Addressing all these challenges, our paper has the following contributions.

- Different from most of the previous work, we design *QoI aware* incentive mechanisms for MCS systems.
- We use reverse combinatorial auction to design a truthful, individual rational and computationally efficient incentive mechanism that approximately maximizes the social welfare with a guaranteed approximation ratio for the single-minded case.
- For the multi-minded reverse combinatorial auction, we design an iterative descending mechanism that achieves close-to-optimal social welfare with a guaranteed approximation ratio while satisfying individual rationality and computational efficiency.

2. RELATED WORK

Game theory has been widely utilized to tackle networking problems such as spectrum sharing [21–25], cooperative communication [26, 27], channel and bandwidth allocation [28, 29] and so forth. Similar to many other problems, when it comes to incentive mechanism design in MCS systems, game theoretic models are also frequently adopted by researchers due to their ability to capture and tackle users' strategic behaviors.

Yang *et al.* [4] design incentive mechanisms using auction and Stackelberg game for both user-centric and platform-centric models. Their auction-based mechanism, however, does not consider users' untruthful behaviors about bidding task sets. Duan *et al.* [5] propose a Stackelberg game-based incentive mechanism which is similar to [4] but able to deal with the asymmetrically incomplete information between users and the platform. Faltings *et al.* [6] design an incentive mechanism to ensure the truthfulness of reported data without considering users' strategic behaviors about bidding prices and task sets. Zhang *et al.* [30] design an incentive mechanism specifically for binary crowd labelling systems. Furthermore, [7, 8] design social cost minimizing incentive mechanisms.

[9–11] study crowdsourcing systems with multiple task requesters and workers. Zhang *et al.* [9] propose a reputation-based incentive protocol for crowdsourcing applications and use repeated gift-giving game to model the interaction between task requesters and workers. In [10, 11], the authors integrate the effort and skill levels of workers into their mechanisms. Another series of work [12–14] utilize online auctions to design incentive mechanisms in crowdsourcing systems where users arrive sequentially.

A common feature of the aforementioned results is that they do not consider QoI in their mechanism designs. This is the major difference with our mechanisms.

In [15], He *et al.* aim to ensure that every task is executed by enough number of users, which implies that users have identical quality of their sensory data. In contrast, our mechanisms have the ability to handle not only this case, but also the more general case in which users may have heterogeneous QoIs. Authors in [16, 17] design incentive mechanisms based on the assumption of known prior information about the distribution of users' task execution costs. However, we do not assume the availability of such prior knowledge. Furthermore, the QoI aware dynamic participant selection protocol proposed in [18] does not utilize game theoretic frameworks. Hence, it cannot handle users' strategic behaviors as our mechanisms.

3. PRELIMINARIES

In this section, we present an overview of MCS systems, our auction model and design objectives.

3.1 System Overview

The MCS system model considered in this paper consists of a platform residing in the cloud and a set of N users, denoted as $\mathcal{N} = \{1, \cdots, N\}$. The users execute a set of M sensing tasks, denoted as $\mathcal{T} = \{\tau_1, \cdots, \tau_M\}$ and send their sensory data to the platform. The workflow of the system is described as follows.

1. Firstly, the platform announces the set of sensing tasks, $\mathcal{T}$, to users.
2. Then, the platform and users enter the auctioning stage in which the platform acts as the auctioneer that purchases the

sensory data collected by individual users. Every user $i \in \mathcal{N}$ submits her bid, which is a tuple (Γ_i, b_i) consisting of the set of tasks $\Gamma_i \subseteq \mathcal{T}$ she wants to execute and her bidding price b_i for executing these tasks.

3. Based on users' bids, the platform determines the set of winners, denoted as $\mathcal{S} \subseteq \mathcal{N}$ and the payment to all users, denoted as $\overrightarrow{p} = \{p_1, \cdots, p_N\}$. Specifically, a loser does not execute any task and receives zero payment.

4. After the platform receives winners' sensory data, it gives the payment to the corresponding winners.

One major difference between this paper and most of the previous work is that we integrate the quality of information (QoI) corresponding to every user, denoted as $\overrightarrow{q} = \{q_1, \cdots, q_N\}$, into our incentive mechanisms. Generally speaking, QoI indicates the quality of users' sensory data. The definition of QoI varies for different applications. For example, in the MedWatcher system [2], QoI refers to the quality (e.g., resolution, contrast, sharpness, etc.) of uploaded photos. Photos with higher quality will help the platform better identify visible problems with medical devices. In air quality monitoring MCS systems [3], QoI refers to a user's estimation accuracy of air quality. We assume that the platform maintains a historical record of users' QoI profile $\overrightarrow{q}$ used as inputs for winner and payment determination. There are many methods for the platform to calculate users' QoIs. Intuitively, in the cases where the platform has adequate amount of ground truth data, QoIs can be obtained by directly calculating the deviation of users' data from the ground truths. However, even without ground truths, QoIs can still be effectively inferred from users' data by utilizing algorithms such as those proposed in [31–34]. Alternatively in many applications, QoIs can be inferred from other factors (e.g., the price of a user's sensors, her experience and reputation of executing specific sensing tasks, etc.) using methods proposed in previous studies such as [35]. The problem of which method the platform adopts to calculate users' QoIs is application dependent and out of the scope of this paper. Typically, users might know some of the factors that affect their QoIs. However, users usually do not know exactly how QoIs are calculated by the platform. Hence, they do not know the exact values of their QoIs.

3.2 Auction Model

In this paper, we consider *strategic* and *selfish* users that aim to maximize their own utilities. The fact that users bid on subsets of tasks motivates us to use *reverse combinatorial auction* to model the problem. In the rest of the paper, we use *bundle* to refer to any subset of tasks of $\mathcal{T}$. Different from traditional *forward combinatorial auction* [36, 37], we formally define the concept of reverse combinatorial auction for our problem setting in Definition 1.

Definition 1 (RC Auction). *In a reverse combinatorial auction (RC auction), each user $i \in \mathcal{N}$ is interested in a set of $K_i \geq 1$ bundles, denoted as $\mathcal{T}_i = \{\Gamma_i^1, \cdots, \Gamma_i^{K_i}\}$. For any bundle $\Gamma \subseteq \mathcal{T}$, the user has a cost function defined in Equation 1.*

$$C_i(\Gamma) = \begin{cases} c_i, & \text{if } \exists \Gamma_i^j \in \mathcal{T}_i \text{ s.t. } \Gamma \subseteq \Gamma_i^j \\ +\infty, & \text{otherwise} \end{cases}. \tag{1}$$

Both $\mathcal{T}_i$ and the cost function $C_i(\cdot)$ are user i's private information. If $K_i = 1$ for every user, then the auction is defined as a single-minded reverse combinatorial auction (SRC auction). And it is defined as a multi-minded reverse combinatorial auction (MRC auction), if $K_i > 1$ for at least one user.

In an SRC auction, $\mathcal{T}_i$ contains only user i's *maximum executable task set* $\overline{\Gamma}_i$. That is, $\overline{\Gamma}_i$ consists of all the sensing tasks that user i is able to execute. Since she is not capable to carry out tasks beyond $\overline{\Gamma}_i$, her cost for any bundle $\Gamma \not\subseteq \overline{\Gamma}_i$ can be equivalently viewed as $+\infty$. Similarly in an MRC auction, the union of all the bundles in $\mathcal{T}_i$ is $\overline{\Gamma}_i$. That is, $\bigcup_{j=1}^{K_i} \Gamma_i^j = \overline{\Gamma}_i$. If user i is a winner of the RC auction, she will be paid p_i for executing the corresponding set of sensing tasks. In contrast, she will not be allocated any sensing task and will receive zero payment if she is a loser. We present the definitions of the utility of a user and the profit of the platform formally in Definition 2 and 3.

Definition 2 (A User's Utility). *The utility of any user $i \in \mathcal{N}$ is*

$$u_i = \begin{cases} p_i - c_i, & \text{if } i \in \mathcal{S} \\ 0, & \text{otherwise} \end{cases}. \tag{2}$$

Definition 3 (Platform's Profit). *The profit of the platform given users' QoI profile $\overrightarrow{q}$ is*

$$u_0 = V_{\overrightarrow{q}}(\mathcal{S}) - \sum_{i \in \mathcal{S}} p_i, \tag{3}$$

where the value function $V_{\overrightarrow{q}}(\cdot) : 2^{\mathcal{N}} \to \mathbb{R}^+$ maps the winner set $\mathcal{S}$ to the value that the winners bring to the platform. Furthermore, $V_{\overrightarrow{q}}(\cdot)$ is monotonic in $\overrightarrow{q}$. That is, for any $\overrightarrow{q} = \{q_1, \cdots, q_N\}$ and $\overrightarrow{q}' = \{q_1', \cdots, q_N'\}$ such that $q_i \geq q_i'$ holds $\forall i \in \mathcal{N}$, we have $V_{\overrightarrow{q}}(\mathcal{S}) \geq V_{\overrightarrow{q}'}(\mathcal{S})$.

Similar to the traditional VCG mechanism design [19, 20], we aim to design mechanisms that maximize the social welfare, which is formally defined in Definition 4.

Definition 4 (Social Welfare). *The social welfare of the whole MCS system is*

$$u_{social} = u_0 + \sum_{i \in \mathcal{N}} u_i = V_{\overrightarrow{q}}(\mathcal{S}) - \sum_{i \in \mathcal{S}} c_i. \tag{4}$$

3.3 Design Objective

In this paper, we aim to design *dominant-strategy mechanisms* in which for every user there exists a dominant strategy [38] defined in Definition 5.

Definition 5 (Dominant Strategy). *A strategy st_i is the dominant strategy for user i if and only if for any other strategy st_i' and any strategy profile of the other users, denoted as st_{-i}, the property $u_i(st_i, st_{-i}) \geq u_i(st_i', st_{-i})$ holds.*

In our SRC auction, each user submits to the platform a bid (Γ_i, b_i) consisting of her declared interested bundle Γ_i and the bidding price b_i. Since users are strategic, it is possible that she declares a bid that deviates from the true value $(\overline{\Gamma}_i, c_i)$. However, one of our goals for the SRC auction is to design a *truthful* mechanism defined in Definition 6.

Definition 6 (Truthfulness). *An SRC auction is truthful if and only if it is the dominant strategy for every user $i \in \mathcal{N}$ to bid her true value $(\overline{\Gamma}_i, c_i)$.*

Noticed from Definition 6 that we aim to ensure the truthfulness of both the cost c_i and bundle $\overline{\Gamma}_i$. Besides truthfulness, another design objective for the SRC auction is to ensure that every user receives non-negative utility from participating. Such property is critical in incentive mechanisms because it ensures that users will not be disincentivized to participate for receiving negative utilities. This property is defined as *individual rationality* in Definition 7.

Definition 7 (Individual Rationality). *A mechanism is individual rational (IR) if and only if $u_i \geq 0$ is satisfied for every user $i \in \mathcal{N}$.*

As mentioned in Section 3.2, our mechanism aims to maximize the social welfare. However, as will be proved in Section 4, the problem of maximizing the social welfare in the SRC auction is NP-hard. Hence, we aim to design a *polynomial-time* mechanism that gives us approximately optimal social welfare with a *guaranteed approximation ratio*.

Model	Dominant Strategy	Truthful	IR	Approx. Ratio	Complexity
SRC	√	√	√	Guaranteed	Polynomial
MRC	√	×	√	Guaranteed	Polynomial

Table 1: Summary of design objectives

In the domain of multi-minded combinatorial auction, requiring truthfulness limits the family of mechanisms that can be used, as pointed out in [39]. Hence, in our MRC auction, we aim to design a dominant-strategy mechanism that can still yield a *guaranteed approximation ratio* to the optimal social welfare without ensuring truthfulness. In fact, as mentioned in [37], the requirement of truthfulness is only to obtain close-to-optimal social welfare with strategic user behaviors, but not the real essence. Therefore, as long as the approximation ratio is guaranteed when users play their dominant strategies, it is justifiable for us to relax the truthfulness requirement. Additionally, we also require our mechanism to be *individual rational* and have a *polynomial* computational complexity.

Authors in [37, 40] address the issue of mechanism design for multi-minded forward combinatorial auctions. Their mechanisms cannot ensure that users have dominant strategies and cannot be applied to reverse combinatorial auctions. However, in contrast, we are able to design a dominant-strategy incentive mechanism for the MRC auction in this paper. We summarize our design objectives for both the SRC and MRC auctions in Table 1.

4. SRC AUCTION

In this section, we introduce the mathematical formulation, mechanism design, an intuitive walk-though example and the corresponding analysis for the SRC auction.

4.1 Mathematical Formulation

In our SRC auction, each user's bid (Γ_i, b_i) consists of her declared interested bundle Γ_i and the bidding price b_i. Although our model is valid for any general value function $V_{\vec{q}}(\cdot)$ that satisfies Definition 3, to simplify our analysis we assume that $V_{\vec{q}}(\cdot)$ is the sum of the value, v_i, contributed by every winner $i \in \mathcal{S}$. Furthermore, we assume that v_i is proportional to the total QoI provided by this user. Given users' bidding bundle profile $\vec{\Gamma} = \{\Gamma_1, \cdots, \Gamma_N\}$ and the winner set $\mathcal{S}$, the platform's value function $V_{\vec{q}}(\cdot)$ can be represented by Equation 5.

$$V_{\vec{q}}(\mathcal{S}) = \sum_{i\in\mathcal{S}} v_i = \sum_{i\in\mathcal{S}} \alpha q_i|\Gamma_i|, \tag{5}$$

where α is a coefficient that transforms QoI to monetary reward.

Another aspect that distinguishes our paper from previous work is that we consider *QoI coverage* in the SRC auction. For the task that none of the users capable to execute it has adequately high QoI, collective efforts of multiple users are necessary to ensure sensing quality. We use $Q_{\tau_j,\vec{q}}(\mathcal{S})$ to denote the total QoI that all winners have on task $\tau_j \in \mathcal{T}$. Furthermore, we approximate $Q_{\tau_j,\vec{q}}(\mathcal{S})$ as the sum of the QoIs of the winners that execute this task. Therefore, QoI coverage is equivalent to guaranteeing that every task is executed by users with sufficient amount of QoI in total. Based on this additive assumption of QoI, $Q_{\tau_j,\vec{q}}(\mathcal{S})$ can be represented by Equation 6.

$$Q_{\tau_j,\vec{q}}(\mathcal{S}) = \sum_{i:\tau_j\in\Gamma_i, i\in\mathcal{S}} q_i. \tag{6}$$

Since we aim to maximize the social welfare given in Definition 4, the winner determination and pricing can be decoupled into two separate problems. We formulate the SRC auction winner determination (SRC-WD) problem as the following integer linear program.

SRC-WD Problem:

$$\max \sum_{i\in\mathcal{N}} (\alpha q_i|\Gamma_i| - b_i)x_i \tag{7}$$

$$\text{s.t.} \sum_{i:\tau_j\in\Gamma_i, i\in\mathcal{N}} q_i x_i \ge Q_j, \quad \forall \tau_j \in \mathcal{T} \tag{8}$$

$$x_i \in \{0,1\}, \quad \forall i \in \mathcal{N} \tag{9}$$

Constants. The SRC-WD problem takes as input constants α, users' bid profile $\{(\Gamma_1, b_1), \cdots, (\Gamma_N, b_N)\}$, users' QoI profile $\vec{q}$ and tasks' QoI requirement profile $\vec{Q} = \{Q_1, \cdots, Q_M\}$.

Variables. In the SRC-WD problem, we have a set of binary variables $\{x_1, \cdots, x_N\}$ for every user $i \in \mathcal{N}$. If user i is in the winner set $\mathcal{S}$, then $x_i = 1$. Otherwise, $x_i = 0$.

Objective function. Since the platform does not know the true values of users' interested bundles and the corresponding costs, $\{(\overline{\Gamma}_1, c_1), \cdots, (\overline{\Gamma}_N, c_N)\}$, the objective function that it directly tries to maximize is the social welfare based on users' bid profile $\{(\Gamma_1, b_1), \cdots, (\Gamma_N, b_N)\}$. We use $\vec{w} = \{w_1, \cdots, w_N\}$, in which $w_i = \alpha q_i|\Gamma_i| - b_i$, to denote the marginal social welfare profile of all users based on users' bids. Then, we have the objective function $\sum_{i\in\mathcal{S}} w_i = \sum_{i\in\mathcal{S}}(\alpha q_i|\Gamma_i| - b_i) = \sum_{i\in\mathcal{N}}(\alpha q_i|\Gamma_i| - b_i)x_i$. Later in Section 4.4, we will show that in our mechanism every user in fact bids truthfully. Hence, the objective function is equivalent to the actual social welfare.

Constraints. Constraint 8 represents the QoI coverage for every task $\tau_j \in \mathcal{T}$, which ensures that the total QoI of all the winners for this task, calculated as $Q_{\tau_j,\vec{q}}(\mathcal{S}) = \sum_{i:\tau_j\in\Gamma_i, i\in\mathcal{S}} q_i = \sum_{i:\tau_j\in\Gamma_i, i\in\mathcal{N}} q_i x_i$, is no less than the QoI requirement Q_j.

Next, we prove the NP-hardness of the SRC-WD problem.

Theorem 1. *The SRC-WD problem is NP-hard.*

Proof. In this proof, we demonstrate that the NP-complete minimum weight set cover (MWSC) problem is polynomial-time reducible to the SRC-WD problem. The reduction starts with an instance of the MWSC problem consisting of a universe of elements $\mathcal{U} = \{\tau_1, \cdots, \tau_M\}$ and a set of N sets $\mathcal{O} = \{\Gamma_1, \cdots, \Gamma_N\}$ whose union equals $\mathcal{U}$. Every set $\Gamma_i \in \mathcal{O}$ is associated with a non-negative weight w_i. The MWSC problem is to find the subset of $\mathcal{O}$ with the minimum total weight whose union contains all the elements in $\mathcal{U}$.

Based on the instance of the MWSC problem, we construct an instance of the SRC-WD problem. Firstly, we transform Γ_i into Γ'_i such that for every element in Γ_i there exist $l_i \in \mathbb{Z}^+$ copies of the same element in Γ'_i. We require that every element $\tau_j \in \mathcal{U}$ is covered for at least $L_j \in \mathbb{Z}^+$ times. After the reduction, we obtain an instance of the SRC-WD problem in which users' QoI profile is $\vec{q} = \{l_1, \cdots, l_N\}$, users' bidding bundle profile is $\vec{\Gamma} = \{\Gamma_1, \cdots, \Gamma_N\}$, users' marginal social welfare profile is $\vec{w} = \{-w_1, \cdots, -w_N\}$ and tasks' QoI requirement profile is $\vec{Q} = \{L_1, \cdots, L_M\}$. Noticed that the SRC-WD problem represents a richer family of problems in which any user i's QoI, q_i, and any task j's QoI requirement, Q_j, could take any value in $\mathbb{R}^+$. Furthermore, the marginal social welfare can take any value in $\mathbb{R}$. Hence, every instance of the MWSC problem is polynomial-time reducible to an instance of the SRC-WD problem. The SRC-WD problem is NP-hard. □

4.2 Mechanism Design

Because of the NP-hardness of the SRC-WD problem, it is impossible to compute the set of winners that maximize the social welfare in polynomial time unless P = NP. As a result, we cannot use the off-the-shelf VCG mechanism [19, 20] since the truthfulness of VCG mechanism requires that the social welfare is exactly maximized. Therefore, as mentioned in Section 3.3, we aim to design a mechanism that approximately maximizes the social welfare while guaranteeing truthfulness.

Algorithm 1: QoI-SRC Auction Winner Determination

Input: $\mathcal{T}, \mathcal{N}, \overrightarrow{w}, \overrightarrow{q}, \overrightarrow{Q}, \overrightarrow{\Gamma}$;
Output: $\mathcal{S}$;
`// Initialization`
1 $\mathcal{N}^- \leftarrow \emptyset, \mathcal{S} \leftarrow \emptyset$;
`// Select non-negative marginal social welfare users`
2 **foreach** i *s.t.* $w_i \geq 0$ **do**
3 $\quad \mathcal{S} \leftarrow \mathcal{S} \cup \{i\}$;
4 $\mathcal{N}^- \leftarrow \mathcal{N} \setminus \mathcal{S}$;
`// Calculate residual QoI requirement`
5 **foreach** j *s.t.* $\tau_j \in \mathcal{T}$ **do**
6 $\quad Q'_j \leftarrow Q_j - \min\{Q_j, \sum_{i:\tau_j \in \Gamma_i, i \in \mathcal{S}} q_i\}$;
`// Main loop`
7 **while** $\sum_{j:\tau_j \in \mathcal{T}} Q'_j \neq 0$ **do**
$\quad$ `// Find the user with the minimum marginal social welfare effectiveness`
8 $\quad l = \arg\min_{i \in \mathcal{N}^-} \frac{|w_i|}{\sum_{j:\tau_j \in \Gamma_i} \min\{Q'_j, q_i\}}$;
9 $\quad \mathcal{S} \leftarrow \mathcal{S} \cup \{l\}$;
10 $\quad \mathcal{N}^- \leftarrow \mathcal{N}^- \setminus \{l\}$;
$\quad$ `// Update residual requirement`
11 $\quad$ **foreach** j *s.t.* $\tau_j \in \mathcal{T}$ **do**
12 $\quad\quad Q'_j \leftarrow Q'_j - \min\{Q'_j, q_l\}$;
13 **return** $\mathcal{S}$;

Myerson's characterizations of truthfulness for single-parameter auctions [41] are not directly applicable in our scenario, because our SRC auction is a double-parameter auction that considers both bundle and cost truthfulness. Moreover, different from the characterizations of truthfulness for single-minded forward combinatorial auctions proposed in [36], we describe and prove the necessary and sufficient conditions for a truthful SRC auction in Lemma 1.

Lemma 1. *An SRC auction is truthful if and only if the following two properties hold:*

- ***Monotonicity**. Any user i who wins by bidding (Γ_i, b_i) still wins by bidding any $b'_i < b_i$ and any $\Gamma'_i \supset \Gamma_i$ given that other users' bids are fixed.*
- ***Critical payment**. Any winner i with bid (Γ_i, b_i) is paid the supremum of all bidding prices b'_i such that bidding (Γ_i, b'_i) still wins, which is defined as user i's critical payment.*

Proof. It is easily verifiable that a truthful bidder will never receive negative utility. If user i's any untruthful bid (Γ_i, b_i) is losing or $\Gamma_i \not\subseteq \overline{\Gamma}_i$, her utility from bidding (Γ_i, b_i) will be non-positive. Therefore, we only need to consider the case in which (Γ_i, b_i) is winning and $\Gamma_i \subseteq \overline{\Gamma}_i$.

- Because of the property of monotonicity, $(\overline{\Gamma}_i, b_i)$ is also a winning bid. Suppose the payment for bid (Γ_i, b_i) is p and that for bid $(\overline{\Gamma}_i, b_i)$ is $\overline{p}$. Every bid $(\overline{\Gamma}_i, b'_i)$ with $b'_i > \overline{p}$ is losing because $\overline{p}$ is the user i's critical payment given bundle $\overline{\Gamma}_i$. From monotonicity, bidding (Γ_i, b'_i) is also losing. Therefore, the critical payment for (Γ_i, b_i) is at most that for $(\overline{\Gamma}_i, b_i)$, which means $p \leq \overline{p}$. Hence, the user will not increase her utility by bidding (Γ_i, b_i) instead of $(\overline{\Gamma}_i, b_i)$.
- Then, we consider the case in which bidding truthfully $(\overline{\Gamma}_i, c_i)$ wins. This bid earns the same payment $\overline{p}$ as $(\overline{\Gamma}_i, b_i)$. Then her utilities from these two bids will be the same. If bidding $(\overline{\Gamma}_i, c_i)$ loses, then we have $c_i > \overline{p} \geq b_i$. Hence, bidding $(\overline{\Gamma}_i, b_i)$ will receive negative utility. Therefore, $(\overline{\Gamma}_i, b_i)$ will also not increase her utility compared to $(\overline{\Gamma}_i, c_i)$.

Thus, we conclude that an SRC auction is truthful if and only if the monotonicity and critical payment properties hold. □

Algorithm 2: QoI-SRC Auction Pricing

Input: $\mathcal{S}, \alpha, \overrightarrow{q}, \overrightarrow{w}, \overrightarrow{\Gamma}$;
Output: $\overrightarrow{p}$;
`// Initialization`
1 $\mathcal{N}^+ \leftarrow \emptyset, \overrightarrow{p} \leftarrow \{0, \cdots, 0\}$;
`// Find non-negative marginal welfare users`
2 **foreach** i *s.t.* $w_i \geq 0$ **do**
3 $\quad \mathcal{N}^+ \leftarrow \mathcal{N}^+ \cup \{i\}$;
`// Main loop`
4 **foreach** $i \in \mathcal{S}$ **do**
5 $\quad$ run Algorithm 1 on $\mathcal{N} \setminus \{i\}$ until $\sum_{j:\tau_j \in \Gamma_i} Q'_j = 0$;
6 $\quad \mathcal{S}' \leftarrow$ the winner set when step 5 stops;
$\quad$ `// Calculate payment`
7 $\quad$ **if** $|\mathcal{S}'| < |\mathcal{N}^+|$ **then**
8 $\quad\quad p_i \leftarrow \alpha q_i |\Gamma_i|$;
9 $\quad$ **else**
10 $\quad\quad$ **foreach** $k \in \mathcal{S}' \setminus \mathcal{N}^+$ **do**
11 $\quad\quad\quad \overrightarrow{Q}' \leftarrow$ tasks' residual QoI requirement profile when winner k is selected;
12 $\quad\quad\quad p_i \leftarrow \max\left\{p_i, \alpha q_i |\Gamma_i| - w_k \frac{\sum_{j:\tau_j \in \Gamma_i} \min\{Q'_j, q_i\}}{\sum_{j:\tau_j \in \Gamma_k} \min\{Q'_j, q_k\}}\right\}$;
13 **return** $\overrightarrow{p}$;

We utilize the rationale provided in Lemma 1 to design a *quality of information aware SRC (QoI-SRC) auction.* Specifically, we present the winner determination and pricing mechanisms of the QoI-SRC auction respectively in Algorithm 1 and 2.

The platform calculates users' marginal social welfare profile $\overrightarrow{w}$ using users' bids $\{(\Gamma_1, b_1), \cdots, (\Gamma_N, b_N)\}$ and utilizes $\overrightarrow{w}$ as input to the winner determination algorithm shown in Algorithm 1. Firstly, the platform includes all users with non-negative marginal social welfare into the winner set $\mathcal{S}$ (line 2-3). By removing the current winners from $\mathcal{N}$, the platform gets the set of users $\mathcal{N}^-$ with negative marginal social welfare (line 4). Then, the platform calculates tasks' residual QoI requirement profile $\overrightarrow{Q}'$ by subtracting from $\overrightarrow{Q}$ the QoI provided by the currently selected winners (line 5-6). The main loop (line 7-12) is executed until every task's QoI requirement is satisfied. In the main loop, winner selection is based on *marginal social welfare effectiveness (MSWE)*, defined as the ratio between the absolute value of user i's marginal social welfare $|w_i|$ and her effective QoI contribution $\sum_{j:\tau_j \in \Gamma_i} \min\{Q'_j, q_i\}$. In every iteration, the user with the minimum MSWE among the remaining users in $\mathcal{N}^-$ is included into $\mathcal{S}$ (line 8-9). After that, the platform updates $\mathcal{N}^-$ and tasks' residual QoI requirement profile $\overrightarrow{Q}'$ (line 10-12).

Algorithm 2 describes the corresponding pricing mechanism. It takes the winner set $\mathcal{S}$ as input and outputs the payment profile $\overrightarrow{p}$. Firstly, $\overrightarrow{p}$ is initialized as a zero vector (line 1). Then, the platform includes all users with non-negative marginal social welfare into $\mathcal{N}^+$ (line 2-3). The main loop (line 4-12) calculates the platform's payment to every winner. For every winner $i \in \mathcal{S}$, the winner determination mechanism in Algorithm 1 is executed with all users except user i until the QoI requirement of every task in Γ_i has been fully satisfied (line 5). We reach the point such that it is impossible for user i to be selected as a winner in future iterations of Algorithm 1. Then, the platform gets the current winner set $\mathcal{S}'$ (line 6) and calculates p_i differently in the following two cases.

- **Case 1** (line 7-8). Any winner i belonging to case 1 has $w_i \geq 0$. Hence, this user's critical payment is the bidding price b'_i that satisfies $w'_i = \alpha q_i |\Gamma_i| - b'_i = 0$. That is, $p_i = \alpha q_i |\Gamma_i|$.
- **Case 2** (line 10-11). For any winner i belonging to case 2, we go through every user $k \in \mathcal{S}' \setminus \mathcal{N}^+$. We calculate user

i's maximum bidding price b'_i to be able to substitute user k as the winner. That is, b'_i satisfies Equation 10.

$$\frac{b'_i - \alpha q_i|\Gamma_i|}{\sum_{j:\tau_j\in\Gamma_i}\min\{Q'_j, q_i\}} = \frac{|w_k|}{\sum_{j:\tau_j\in\Gamma_k}\min\{Q'_j, q_k\}}. \quad (10)$$

This means

$$b'_i = \alpha q_i|\Gamma_i| - w_k\frac{\sum_{j:\tau_j\in\Gamma_i}\min\{Q'_j, q_i\}}{\sum_{j:\tau_j\in\Gamma_k}\min\{Q'_j, q_k\}}. \quad (11)$$

Finally, the maximum value among all b'_i's is used as the payment to user i.

4.3 A Walk-through Example

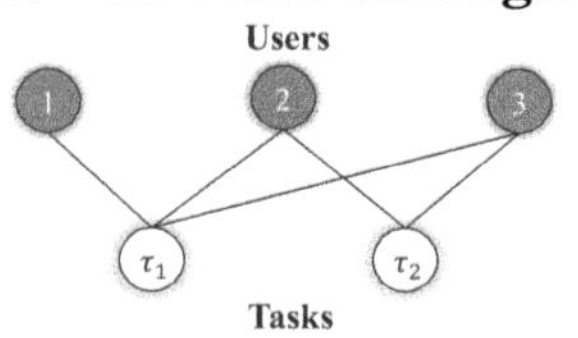

Figure 2: Bidding graph

Parameters	Value
α	0.1
$\vec{q}$	$\{0.8, 1.2, 1.2\}$
$\vec{b}$	$\{0.2, 2.6, 2.7\}$
$\vec{Q}$	$\{1.1, 0.8\}$
$\vec{w}$	$\{0.4, -0.2, -0.3\}$

Table 2: Parameter setting

We use a simple toy example to illustrate how the QoI-SRC auction works. In this example, there are 3 users $\mathcal{N} = \{1,2,3\}$ and 2 tasks $\mathcal{T} = \{\tau_1, \tau_2\}$. In Figure 2, an edge between a user i and a task τ_j indicates that $\tau_j \in \Gamma_i$. That is, users' bidding bundles are $\Gamma_1 = \{\tau_1\}$, $\Gamma_2 = \{\tau_1, \tau_2\}$ and $\Gamma_3 = \{\tau_1, \tau_2\}$. Other parameters are shown in Table 2. The process of the QoI-SRC winner determination is shown in Table 3. We show the corresponding pricing process in Table 4.

$\mathcal{S}$	$\vec{Q}'$	New Winner	Reason
$\emptyset$	$\{1.1, 0.8\}$	$\{1\}$	$w_1 > 0$
$\{1\}$	$\{0.3, 0.8\}$	$\{2\}$	$\text{MSWE}_{\text{user }2} = \frac{0.2}{1.1} < \text{MSWE}_{\text{user }3} = \frac{0.3}{1.1}$
$\{1, 2\}$	$\{0, 0\}$	$\emptyset$	$Q'_1 = Q'_2 = 0$ and $w_3 < 0$

Table 3: The QoI-SRC auction winner determination

Winner	$\mathcal{S}'$	Payment
1	$\{2\}$	$p_1 = 0.1 \times 0.8 \times 1 + 0.2 \times \frac{0.8}{1.9} \approx 0.164$
2	$\{1, 3\}$	$p_2 = 0.1 \times 1.2 \times 2 + 0.3 \times \frac{1.1}{1.1} \approx 0.540$

Table 4: The QoI-SRC auction pricing

4.4 Analysis

Firstly, we analyze the truthfulness and individual rationality of the QoI-SRC auction in Theorem 2 and 3.

Theorem 2. *The QoI-SRC auction is truthful.*

Proof. Suppose user i wins by bidding (Γ_i, b_i). We consider user i's any other bid (Γ'_i, b'_i) such that $b'_i < b_i$ or $\Gamma'_i \supset \Gamma_i$.

- **Case 1** ($w_i \geq 0$). The marginal social welfare for bidding (Γ'_i, b'_i) is $w'_i = \alpha q_i|\Gamma'_i| - b'_i > \alpha q_i|\Gamma_i| - b_i \geq 0$.
- **Case 2** ($w_i < 0$). Bidding (Γ'_i, b'_i) will make $w'_i \geq 0$ or decrease the value of user i's MSWE.

Hence, user i is still a winner by bidding (Γ'_i, b'_i) and the QoI-SRC auction winner determination algorithm satisfies both bidding bundle and price monotonicity. Furthermore, it is easily verifiable that the pricing mechanism in Algorithm 2 uses the supremum of bidding prices b'_i such that bidding (Γ_i, b'_i) still wins. Hence, from Lemma 1 we conclude that the QoI-SRC auction is truthful. □

Theorem 3. *The QoI-SRC auction is individual rational.*

Proof. From Theorem 2, we have proved that users bid truthfully in our QoI-SRC auction. Hence, any user i bids its true cost c_i. Since every winner i is paid the supremum of bidding prices given the bundle Γ_i, we have $p_i \geq c_i$ for every winner. Apparently, losers have zero utilities in our QoI-SRC auction. Therefore, the utility for every user i satisfies $u_i \geq 0$ and the QoI-SRC auction is individual rational. □

Then, we analyze the algorithmic properties of the QoI-SRC auction including its computational complexity and approximation ratio to the optimal social welfare in Theorem 4 and 5.

Theorem 4. *The computational complexity of the QoI-SRC auction is $O(N^2M)$.*

Proof. The computational complexity of Algorithm 1 is dominated by the main loop, which terminates after N iterations in the worst case. In every iteration, the algorithm goes through every task $\tau_j \in \mathcal{T}$. Hence, the computational complexity of Algorithm 1 is $O(NM)$. Similarly, we have that the computational complexity of Algorithm 2 is $O(N^2M)$. Therefore, we conclude that computational complexity of the QoI-SRC auction is $O(N^2M)$. □

Then, we provide our analysis about the approximation ratio of the QoI-SRC auction using the method similar to the one proposed by Rajagopalan *et al.* [42]. In our following analysis, we use $\mathcal{N}^-$ to denote all users $i \in \mathcal{N}$ with negative w_i and $\vec{Q}^- = \{Q_1^-, \cdots, Q_M^-\}$ to denote tasks' residual QoI requirement profile after Algorithm 1 includes all users with $w_i \geq 0$ into the winner set. Then, we normalize the w_i for every user $i \in \mathcal{N}^-$, such that the normalized marginal social welfare $w'_i = \frac{w_i}{\max_{n\in\mathcal{N}^-} w_n} > 0$. Thus, with only a multiplicative factor change to the objective function, we formulate the linear program relaxation of the residual SRC-WD problem defined on user set $\mathcal{N}^-$ as the normalized primal linear program **P**. The dual program is formulated in program **D**.

$$\mathbf{P}: \min \sum_{i\in\mathcal{N}^-} w'_i x_i \quad (12)$$

$$\text{s.t.} \sum_{i:\tau_j\in\Gamma_i, i\in\mathcal{N}^-} q_i x_i \geq Q_j^-, \quad \forall \tau_j \in \mathcal{T} \quad (13)$$

$$0 \leq x_i \leq 1, \quad \forall i \in \mathcal{N}^- \quad (14)$$

$$\mathbf{D}: \max \sum_{j:\tau_j\in\mathcal{T}} Q_j^- y_j - \sum_{i\in\mathcal{N}^-} z_i \quad (15)$$

$$\text{s.t.} \sum_{j:\tau_j\in\Gamma_i} q_i y_j - z_i \leq w'_i, \quad \forall i \in \mathcal{N}^- \quad (16)$$

$$y_j \geq 0, \quad \forall \tau_j \in \mathcal{T} \quad (17)$$

$$z_i \geq 0, \quad \forall i \in \mathcal{N}^- \quad (18)$$

It is easily verifiable that the $|\max_{i\in\mathcal{N}^-} w_i|$ multiplicative factor difference between the objective functions of **P** and the SRC-WD problem does not affect the approximation ratio of Algorithm 1. Next, we introduce several notations and concepts utilized in our following analysis.

We define any task $\tau_j \in \mathcal{T}$ as *alive* at any particular iteration of the main loop in Algorithm 1 if its QoI requirement is not fully satisfied. Furthermore, we define that task τ_j is *covered* by Γ_i if $\tau_j \in \Gamma_i$ and τ_j is alive when user i is selected. The coverage relationship is represented as $\tau_j \preceq \Gamma_i$. Then, we define the minimum measure of QoI as Δq, the *unit QoI*. Suppose when user i is about to be selected, the residual QoI requirement profile is $\vec{Q}' = \{Q'_1, \cdots, Q'_M\}$ and Γ_i is the i_jth set that covers τ_j, the corresponding normalized MSWE in terms of unit QoI can be represented in Equation 19.

$$W(\tau_j, i_j) = \frac{w'_i \Delta q}{\sum_{j:\tau_j\in\Gamma_i}\min\{Q'_j, q_i\}}. \quad (19)$$

We assume that τ_j is covered by k_j sets and we have $W(\tau_j, 1) \leq \cdots \leq W(\tau_j, k_j)$ from Equation 19. Then, we define constants $\theta = \max_{i,j} q_i|\Gamma_i|w'_j$ and $m = \frac{1}{\Delta q}\sum_{j:\tau_j\in\mathcal{T}} Q_j^-$ that are used in the presentation of the following Lemma 2.

Lemma 2. *The following assignments of y_j and z_i for $\forall \tau_j \in \mathcal{T}$ and $\forall i \in \mathcal{N}^-$ are feasible to* **D**.

$$y_j = \frac{W(\tau_j, k_j)}{2\theta H_m \Delta q}, \; \forall \tau_j \in \mathcal{T},$$

$$z_i = \begin{cases} \frac{\sum_{j:\tau_j \preceq \Gamma_i}\left(\min\{Q'_j, q_i\}(W(\tau_j,k_j) - W(\tau_j,i_j))\right)}{2\theta H_m \Delta q}, & i \in \mathcal{S}. \\ 0, \; i \notin \mathcal{S} \end{cases}$$

Proof. Suppose for any user $i \in \mathcal{N}^-$, there are t_i tasks in bundle Γ_i. We reorder these tasks in the order in which they are fully covered.

If user i is not selected as a winner in $\mathcal{S}$, then we have $z_i = 0$. Suppose when the last unit QoI of τ_j is about to be covered, the residual QoI requirement profile is $\overrightarrow{Q}'' = \{Q''_1, \cdots, Q''_M\}$, then the total residual QoI of alive tasks contained by Γ_i is represented as $\sum_{h=j}^{t_i} \min\{Q''_h, q_i\}$. We have

$$W(\tau_j, k_j) \leq \frac{w'_i \Delta q}{\sum_{h=j}^{t_i} \min\{Q''_h, q_i\}}.$$

Therefore, we have

$$\begin{aligned}\sum_{j=1}^{t_i} q_i y_j - z_i &\leq \sum_{j=1}^{t_i} \frac{w'_i q_i}{2\theta H_m \sum_{h=j}^{t_i} \min\{Q''_h, q_i\}} - 0 \\ &\leq \frac{w'_i}{H_m}\left(1 + \frac{1}{2} + \cdots + \frac{1}{m}\right) \\ &\leq w'_i\end{aligned}$$

If user $i \in \mathcal{S}$, then we assume that when user i is selected as a winner, t'_i tasks in Γ_i have already been fully covered. We have

$$\begin{aligned}&\sum_{j=1}^{t_i} q_i y_j - z_i \\ =&\frac{\sum_{j=1}^{t_i} q_i W(\tau_j,k_j)}{2\theta H_m \Delta q} - \frac{\sum_{j=t'_i+1}^{t_i} \min\{Q'_j, q_i\}(W(\tau_j,k_j) - W(\tau_j,i_j))}{2\theta H_m \Delta q} \\ =&\frac{\sum_{j=1}^{t'_i} q_i W(\tau_j,k_j)}{2\theta H_m \Delta q} + \frac{\sum_{j=t'_i+1}^{t_i} \min\{Q'_j, q_i\} W(\tau_j,i_j)}{2\theta H_m \Delta q} \\ &+ \frac{\sum_{j=t'_i+1}^{t_i} (q_i - \min\{Q'_j, q_i\}) W(\tau_j,k_j)}{2\theta H_m \Delta q} \\ \leq& \frac{\sum_{j=1}^{t'_i} \frac{q_i w'_i}{\sum_{h=j}^{t_i} \min\{Q'_h, q_i\}}}{2\theta H_m} + \frac{w'_i}{2\theta H_m} + \frac{\theta}{2\theta H_m} \\ \leq& w'_i\end{aligned}$$

Therefore, we arrive at the conclusion that the assignments of y_j and z_i in Lemma 2 are feasible to **D**. □

Then in Theorem 5, we present our result regarding the approximation ratio of Algorithm 1.

Theorem 5. *Algorithm 1 is a $2\theta H_m$-approximation algorithm for the residual SRC-WD problem defined on user set $\mathcal{N}^-$.*

Proof. By substituting the dual assignments given in Lemma 2 into the objective function 15, we have

$$\begin{aligned}&\sum_{j:\tau_j \in \mathcal{T}} Q_j^- y_j - \sum_{i \in \mathcal{N}^-} z_i \\ =&\frac{\sum_{i \in \mathcal{N}^- \cap \mathcal{S}} \sum_{j:\tau_j \preceq \Gamma_i}\left(\min\{Q'_j, q_i\}(W(\tau_j,i_j) - W(\tau_j,k_j))\right)}{2\theta H_m \Delta q} \\ &+ \frac{\sum_{j:\tau_j \in \mathcal{T}} Q_j^- W(\tau_j,k_j)}{2\theta H_m \Delta q} \\ =&\frac{\sum_{i \in \mathcal{N}^- \cap \mathcal{S}} \sum_{j:\tau_j \preceq \Gamma_i} \min\{Q'_j, q_i\} \frac{w'_i \Delta q}{\sum_{j:\tau_j \in \Gamma_i} \min\{Q'_j, q_i\}}}{2\theta H_m \Delta q} \\ =&\frac{\sum_{i \in \mathcal{N}^- \cap \mathcal{S}} w'_i}{2\theta H_m}\end{aligned}$$

Because **D** is the dual program of **P**, we have

$$\frac{\sum_{i \in \mathcal{N}^- \cap \mathcal{S}} w'_i}{2\theta H_m} \leq \text{OPT}_{\mathbf{D}} \leq \text{OPT}_{\mathbf{P}} \leq \text{OPT}_{\text{SRC-WD}}.$$

Therefore, Algorithm 1 is a $2\theta H_m$-approximation algorithm for the residual SRC-WD problem defined on user set $\mathcal{N}^-$. □

5. MRC AUCTION

In this section, we present the mathematical formulation, mechanism design and the corresponding analysis for the MRC auction.

5.1 Mathematical Formulation

In the MRC auction, we also use the form of the platform's value function $V_{\overrightarrow{q}}(\cdot)$ given in Equation 5. If the platform is given users' cost function profile, denote as $\overrightarrow{C} = \{C_1(\cdot), \cdots, C_N(\cdot)\}$, the MRC auction winner determination (MRC-WD) problem can be formulated as follows.

MRC-WD Problem:

$$\max \sum_{i \in \mathcal{N}} \left(\alpha q_i |\Gamma_i| - C_i(\Gamma_i)\right) x_i \tag{20}$$

$$\text{s.t. } \Gamma_i \subseteq \Gamma_i^j, \; \exists \Gamma_i^j \in \mathcal{T}_i, \qquad \forall i \in \mathcal{N} \tag{21}$$

$$x_i \in \{0,1\}, \qquad \forall i \in \mathcal{N} \tag{22}$$

The MRC-WD problem takes the parameter α, users' QoI profile $\overrightarrow{q}$ and users' cost function profile $\overrightarrow{C}$ as input. It has a set of binary variables $\{x_1, \cdots, x_n\}$ indicating whether user i is selected in the winner set $\mathcal{S}$. That is, if $i \in \mathcal{S}$, then $x_i = 1$. Otherwise, $x_i = 0$.

Furthermore, for every user i, we have a variable Γ_i indicating the set of sensing tasks that the platform allocates to this user. Constraint 21 ensures that Γ_i is the subset of at least one bundle $\Gamma_i^j \in \mathcal{T}_i$. Therefore, the MRC-WD problem aims to find the set of winners $\mathcal{S}$ and the corresponding task allocation profile denoted as $\overrightarrow{\Gamma} = \{\Gamma_1, \cdots, \Gamma_N\}$ that maximize the social welfare represented by the objective function. We use $\Gamma_{\max}^i$ to denote the bundle with the maximum cardinality in $\mathcal{T}_i$ and $w_{\max}^i = \alpha q_i |\Gamma_{\max}^i| - c_i$ to denote user i's marginal social welfare for $\Gamma_{\max}^i$. The maximum social welfare is achieved by selecting all users with positive $w_{\max}^i$ as winners and allocating to every winner i the set of tasks $\Gamma_{\max}^i$.

However, the challenge is that cost function profile $\overrightarrow{C}$ is not known by the platform and we still aim to design a mechanism that approximately maximizes the social welfare with a guaranteed approximation ratio. Then, we present the design of our mechanism in Section 5.2 that achieves this objective while ensuring individual rationality and polynomial computational complexity.

5.2 Mechanism Design

Requiring truthfulness in multi-minded combinatorial auctions limits the family of mechanisms that can be used, as mentioned in [39]. As long as the mechanism can achieve close-to-optimal social welfare with a guaranteed approximation ratio, it is justifiable for us to relax the truthfulness requirement, as pointed out in [37]. In Algorithm 3 we describe our design of the iterative descending dominant-strategy *quality of information aware MRC (QoI-MRC)* auction which is different from the mechanisms designed for multi-minded forward combinatorial auctions proposed in [37, 40].

The QoI-MRC auction described in Algorithm 3 consists of a winner determination phase (line 1-18) and a pricing phase (line 19). Every winner $i \in \mathcal{S}$ will be allocated her bidding bundle Γ_i and be paid her bidding price b_i of the final iteration of the winner determination phase. We assume that the platform has the information about the upper bound and lower bound of users' costs denoted as $c_{\max}$ and $c_{\min}$ respectively. The platform initializes every user i's bidding bundle and bidding price as $\Gamma_i = \emptyset$ and $b_{\max} \geq c_{\max}$ (line 2). Moreover, the input parameters $\beta > 1$ and $\epsilon \in (0, c_{\min}]$.

The main loop (line 3-17) is executed until every user is either a winner or a loser. In every iteration of the main loop, every user i such that $\alpha q_i |\Gamma_i| - b_i \geq \epsilon$ is included in the winner set $\mathcal{S}$ (line

Algorithm 3: QoI-MRC Auction

Input: $\mathcal{N}$, $b_{\max}$, ϵ, α, β, $\overrightarrow{q}$;
Output: $\mathcal{S}$, $\overrightarrow{p}$, $\overrightarrow{\Gamma}$;
`// Winner determination`
`// Initialize winner and loser sets`
1 $\mathcal{S} \leftarrow \emptyset$, $\mathcal{L} \leftarrow \emptyset$;
`// Initialize bidding bundles and prices`
2 $\overrightarrow{\Gamma} \leftarrow \{\emptyset, \cdots, \emptyset\}$, $\overrightarrow{\Gamma}' \leftarrow \overrightarrow{\Gamma}$, $\overrightarrow{b} \leftarrow \{b_{\max}, \cdots, b_{\max}\}$;
`// Main loop`
3 **while** $\mathcal{S} \cup \mathcal{L} \neq \mathcal{N}$ **do**
4   **foreach** $i \in \mathcal{N} \setminus (\mathcal{S} \cup \mathcal{L})$ **do**
5   **if** $\alpha q_i|\Gamma_i| - b_i \geq \epsilon$ **then**
6       $\mathcal{S} \leftarrow \mathcal{S} \cup \{i\}$;
7   **else**
      `// Give user i the option to enlarge her bidding bundle`
8   allow user i to enlarge Γ_i to any Γ_i' s.t. $\Gamma_i' \supseteq \Gamma_i$;
      `// Update bidding bundle`
9   **if** $\Gamma_i \neq \Gamma_i'$ **then**
10         $\Gamma_i \leftarrow \Gamma_i'$;
11   **if** $\alpha q_i|\Gamma_i| - b_i \geq \epsilon$ **then**
12         $\mathcal{S} \leftarrow \mathcal{S} \cup \{i\}$;
13   **foreach** $i \in \mathcal{N} \setminus (\mathcal{S} \cup \mathcal{L})$ **do**
    `// Give user i two options`
14   option 1: $b_i \leftarrow \frac{b_i}{\beta}$;
15   option 2: $b_i \leftarrow 0$;
16   **if** $b_i = 0$ **then**
17       $\mathcal{L} \leftarrow \mathcal{L} \cup \{i\}$;
18 $\overrightarrow{\Gamma} \leftarrow \{\Gamma_i \in \overrightarrow{\Gamma} | i \in \mathcal{S}\}$;
`// Pricing`
19 $\overrightarrow{p} \leftarrow \overrightarrow{b}$;
20 **return** $\mathcal{S}$, $\overrightarrow{p}$, $\overrightarrow{\Gamma}$;

5-6). For any user i that is neither a winner nor a loser in the current iteration, the Algorithm gives her an option to choose whether she will enlarge her current bidding bundle Γ_i to any bundle Γ_i' that contains Γ_i (line 5). If after the bundle enlarging $\alpha q_i|\Gamma_i'| - b_i \geq \epsilon$ holds, this user is included in the winner set (line 11-12). Otherwise, she is given the following two options to choose from.

- **Option 1** (line 14). By choosing option 1, user i divides her bidding price b_i by β. As long as she is fully rational, she will choose option 1 rather than option 2 to drop out of the auction, if $\frac{b_i}{\beta} > c_i$ hold. By doing so, she keeps herself in the auction and makes it still possible for her to win in one of the future iterations to receive positive utility.
- **Option 2** (line 15). By choosing option 2, the user i drops out of the auction. If $\frac{b_i}{\beta} \leq c_i$, any rational user i will choose option 2 because it is impossible for her to obtain positive utility even though she remains in the auction in this case.

Finally, every winner i is allocated her bidding bundle Γ_i (line 18) and be paid her bidding price b_i (line 19) of the final iteration of the winner determination phase.

5.3 Analysis

Although the QoI-MRC auction cannot guarantee truthfulness because users' bidding prices when Algorithm 3 terminates will possibly not be equal to users' true costs, we show in the following Theorem 6 that every user still has a dominant strategy.

Theorem 6. *Every user $i \in \mathcal{N}$ has the following dominant strategy in the QoI-MRC auction.*

- *User i enlarges bundle Γ_i to $\Gamma_{\max}^i$ in the first iteration.*
- *When user i is given the options to divide her bidding price b_i by β or drop out of the auction, she will always choose the former as long as $\frac{b_i}{\beta} > c_i$ and the latter if $\frac{b_i}{\beta} \leq c_i$.*

Proof. Obviously, any rational user i will choose to divide her current bidding price b_i by β as long as $\frac{b_i}{\beta} > c_i$ when she is given the two options. By doing so, it is still possible for her to win the auction and be paid $p_i > c_i$. If $\frac{b_i}{\beta} \leq c_i$, then even if she wins the auction the payment p_i will not be larger than c_i. Hence, she will drop out in this case.

Then, we study whether any user i will enlarge her bundle to some $\Gamma_i' \neq \Gamma_{\max}^i$ in the first iteration.

- **Case 1** ($\alpha q_i|\Gamma_{\max}^i| - b_{\max} > \alpha q_i|\Gamma_i'| - b_{\max} \geq \epsilon$). Both $\Gamma_{\max}^i$ and Γ_i' will make the user win the auction in the first iteration and be paid b_{max}. We have $u(\Gamma_{\max}^i) = u(\Gamma_i')$.
- **Case 2** ($\alpha q_i|\Gamma_{\max}^i| - b_{\max} \geq \epsilon > \alpha q_i|\Gamma_i'| - b_{\max}$). The user will win and be paid $b_{\max}$ by enlarging to $\Gamma_{\max}^i$ in the first iteration and we have $u(\Gamma_{\max}^i) = b_{\max} - c_i$. If she proposes Γ_i' instead of $\Gamma_{\max}^i$, she will be asked to decrease her bid or drop out in the first iteration. Eventually, she could lose or win with being paid $b_i' < b_{\max}$. Her utility could either be $u(\Gamma_i') = 0$ or $u(\Gamma_i') = b_i' - c_i$. We have $u(\Gamma_{\max}^i) > u(\Gamma_i')$.
- **Case 3** ($\epsilon > \alpha q_i|\Gamma_{\max}^i| - b_{\max} > \alpha q_i|\Gamma_i'| - b_{\max}$). Both $\Gamma_{\max}^i$ and Γ_i' will make the user face the choices of decreasing her bid or dropping out in the first iteration. If eventually she wins in both cases, then the number of iterations before she wins if she proposes $\Gamma_{\max}^i$ will be smaller than or equal to that of Γ_i'. The payments p_i and p_i' for the two cases satisfy $p_i \geq p_i'$ and we have $u(\Gamma_{\max}^i) \geq u(\Gamma_i')$. If she loses in both cases, then $u(\Gamma_{\max}^i) = u(\Gamma_i') = 0$. The last scenario is that she wins by proposing $\Gamma_{\max}^i$ and loses by proposing Γ_i' in the first iteration. Then, we have $u(\Gamma_{\max}^i) > 0 = u(\Gamma_i')$.

We have $u(\Gamma_{\max}^i) \geq u(\Gamma_i')$ with at least one scenario with strict inequality. Hence, user i enlarges bundle Γ_i to $\Gamma_{\max}^i$ in the first iteration. We arrive at the conclusion about any user's dominant strategy stated in Theorem 6. □

Theorem 7. *The QoI-MRC auction is individual rational.*

Proof. When a user is given the choices to decrease her bid or drops out of the auction, any user i will drop out if $\frac{b_i}{\beta} \leq c_i$. She becomes a loser and obtains $u_i = 0$. The user only chooses to divide b_i by β if $\frac{b_i}{\beta} > c_i$, which ensures that her payment $p_i > c_i$ if she wins. In this case, we have $u_i > 0$. Therefore, $u_i \geq 0$ and the QoI-MRC auction is individual rational. □

Then, we analyze the algorithmic properties of the QoI-MRC auction including its computational complexity and approximation ratio in Theorem 8 and 9.

Theorem 8. *The computational complexity of the QoI-MRC auction is $O(N)$.*

Proof. It is easily verifiable that the main loop of Algorithm 3 terminates after $O\big(\log_\beta \frac{b_{\max}}{c_{\min}}\big)$ number of iterations. The computational complexity inside the main loop is $O(N)$. Therefore, the computational complexity of the QoI-MRC auction is $O(N)$. □

In Theorem 9, we present our results about the approximation ratio of the QoI-MRC auction to the optimal social welfare. We use $\mathcal{S}_{\text{OPT}}$ to denote the winner set of the optimal solution of the MRC-WD problem, $q_{\max}$ to denote the maximum QoI in $\overrightarrow{q}$ and $\Gamma_{\max}$ to denote the maximum-cardinality bundle in $\{\Gamma_{\max}^1, \cdots, \Gamma_{\max}^N\}$.

Theorem 9. *The approximation ratio of the QoI-MRC auction to the optimal social welfare is $\frac{|\mathcal{S}|\epsilon}{|\mathcal{S}_{OPT}|(\alpha q_{\max}|\Gamma_{\max}| - c_{\min})}$.*

Proof. We use APP to denote the social welfare resulted by the QoI-MRC auction. From Theorem 6, every user $i \in \mathcal{N}$ enlarges her bundle to $\Gamma_{\max}^i$ in the first iteration. The winner set $\mathcal{S}$ output by Algorithm 3 consists of winners $\mathcal{S}_1$ that win in the first iteration and $\mathcal{S}_2$ that win in iteration $r_i > 1$ with bidding price $b_i^{r_i}$. We have

$$\begin{aligned}
\text{APP} &= \sum_{i\in\mathcal{S}} (\alpha q_i |\Gamma^i_{\max}| - c_i) \\
&\geq \sum_{i\in\mathcal{S}_1} (\alpha q_i |\Gamma^i_{\max}| - b_{\max}) + \sum_{i\in\mathcal{S}_2} (\alpha q_i |\Gamma^i_{\max}| - b_i^{r_i}) \\
&\geq |\mathcal{S}_1|\epsilon + |\mathcal{S}_2|\epsilon \\
&= |\mathcal{S}|\epsilon
\end{aligned}$$

Similarly, the optimal solution OPT is

$$\begin{aligned}
\text{OPT} &= \sum_{i\in\mathcal{S}_{\text{OPT}}} (\alpha q_i |\Gamma^i_{\max}| - c_i) \\
&\leq |\mathcal{S}_{\text{OPT}}|(\alpha q_{\max}|\Gamma_{\max}| - c_{\min}) \\
&= \frac{|\mathcal{S}_{\text{OPT}}|(\alpha q_{\max}|\Gamma_{\max}| - c_{\min})}{|\mathcal{S}|\epsilon} \cdot |\mathcal{S}|\epsilon \\
&\leq \frac{|\mathcal{S}_{\text{OPT}}|(\alpha q_{\max}|\Gamma_{\max}| - c_{\min})}{|\mathcal{S}|\epsilon} \cdot \text{APP}
\end{aligned}$$

Therefore, the approximation ratio of the QoI-MRC auction to the optimal social welfare is $\frac{|\mathcal{S}|\epsilon}{|\mathcal{S}_{\text{OPT}}|(\alpha q_{\max}|\Gamma_{\max}| - c_{\min})}$. □

6. PERFORMANCE EVALUATION

6.1 Baseline Method

The first baseline approach is a modified version of the traditional VCG auction [19, 20]. We integrate the concept of QoI and the QoI coverage constraint defined in Section 4 into the VCG winner determination (VCG-WD) problem. We call the modified VCG auction *quality of information aware VCG (QoI-VCG)* auction, in which the VCG-WD problem is solved optimally and the VCG pricing mechanism [19, 20] is utilized to derive winners' payments.

Another baseline method is the marginal social welfare greedy (MSW-Greedy) auction. Its winner determination algorithm firstly includes every user i with $w_i \geq 0$ into the winner set. Then, it selects the user with the largest marginal social welfare among the remaining users in every iteration until tasks' QoI requirements are fully satisfied. The pricing mechanism is similar to Algorithm 2 which essentially pays every winner her supremum bidding price to win given her current bidding bundle. It is easily verifiable that the MSW-Greedy auction is truthful and individual rational.

6.2 Simulation Settings

Setting	α	c_i	q_i	Q_j	$\lvert\overline{\Gamma}_i\rvert$	N	M
I	0.1	$[2, 4]$	$[1, 2]$	$[10, 13]$	$[20, 30]$	$[200, 500]$	100
II	0.1	$[4, 8]$	$[2, 4]$	$[10, 13]$	$[20, 30]$	300	$[300, 600]$

Table 5: Simulation settings for SRC auction

Setting	α	$b_{\max}$	c_i	q_i	$\lvert\overline{\Gamma}_i\rvert$	N	M
III	0.2	100	$[4, 6]$	$[1, 2]$	$[20, 30]$	$[200, 500]$	100
IV	0.2	100	$[6, 10]$	$[2, 4]$	$[20, 30]$	300	$[200, 400]$

Table 6: Simulation settings for MRC auction

For our simulation of the SRC auction, we consider the two settings described in Table 5. In setting I, we fix the number of tasks as $M = 100$ and vary the number of users from 200 to 500. In setting II, we fix the number of users as $N = 300$ and vary the number of tasks from 300 to 600. The parameter $\alpha = 0.1$ in both settings and the values of c_i, q_i, $|\overline{\Gamma}_i|$ for any user $i \in \mathcal{N}$ and Q_j for any task $\tau_j \in \mathcal{T}$ are generated uniformly at random from the ranges given in Table 5. User i's maximum executable task set $\overline{\Gamma}_i$ consists of $|\overline{\Gamma}_i|$ tasks selected uniformly at random from $\mathcal{T}$. Furthermore, the optimal solution to the VCG-WD problem of the QoI-VCG mechanism is calculated using the GUROBI optimization solver [43].

For our simulation of the MRC auction, we consider the two settings described in Table 6. In setting III, we fix the number of tasks as $M = 100$ and vary the number of users from 200 to 500. In setting II, we fix the number of users as $N = 300$ and vary the number of tasks from 200 to 400. The parameters $\alpha = 0.2$ and $b_{\max} = 0.2$ in both settings and the values of c_i, q_i, $|\overline{\Gamma}_i|$ for any user $i \in \mathcal{N}$ are generated uniformly at random from the ranges given in Table 6. User i's maximum executable task set $\overline{\Gamma}_i$ consists of $|\overline{\Gamma}_i|$ tasks selected uniformly at random from $\mathcal{T}$. User i's interested bundle set consists of randomly selected subsets of $\overline{\Gamma}_i$ whose union is $\overline{\Gamma}_i$.

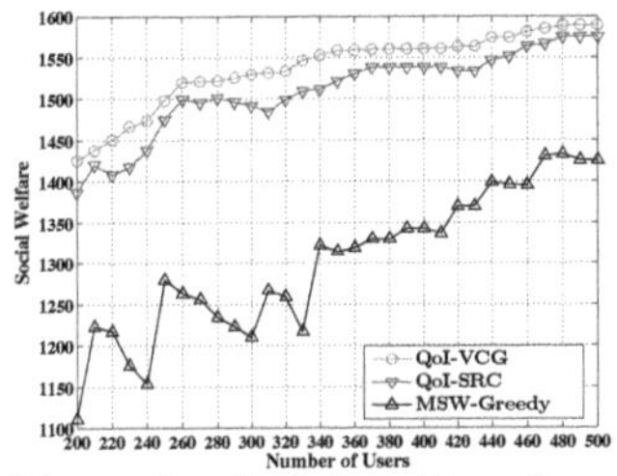

Figure 3: Social welfare for setting I

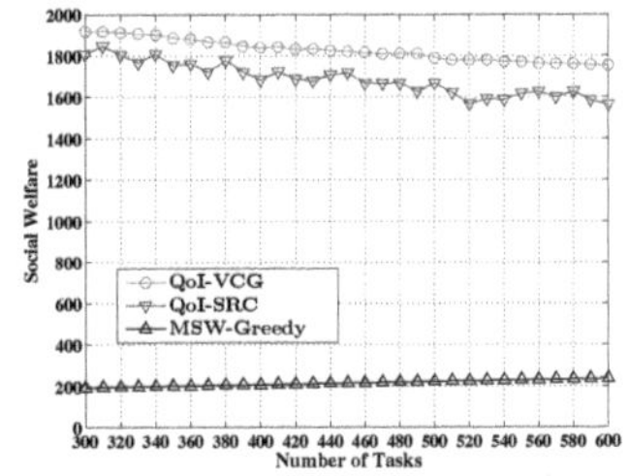

Figure 4: Social welfare for setting II

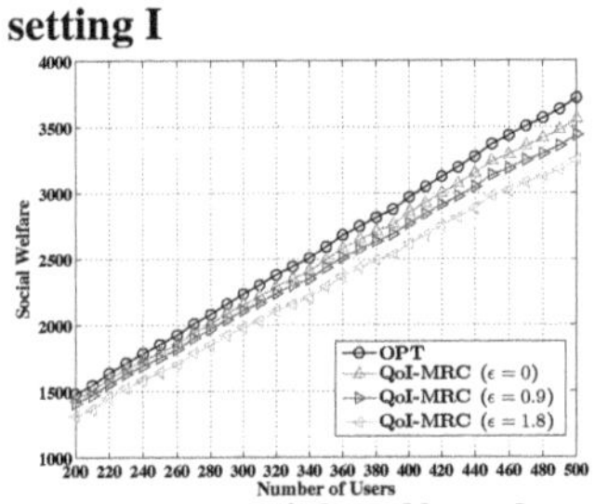

Figure 5: Social welfare for setting III (varying ϵ)

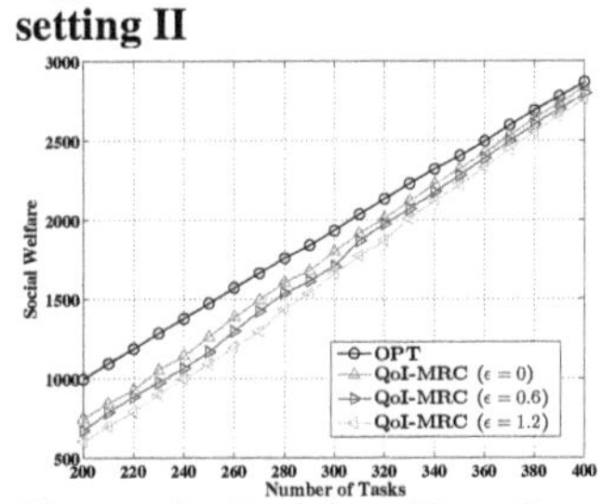

Figure 6: Social welfare for setting IV (varying ϵ)

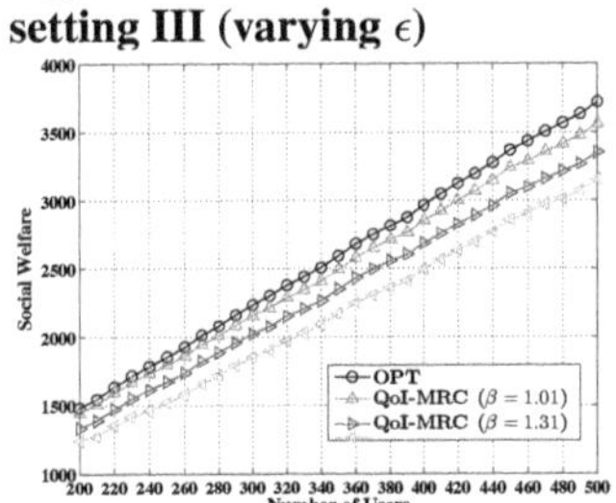

Figure 7: Social welfare for setting III (varying β)

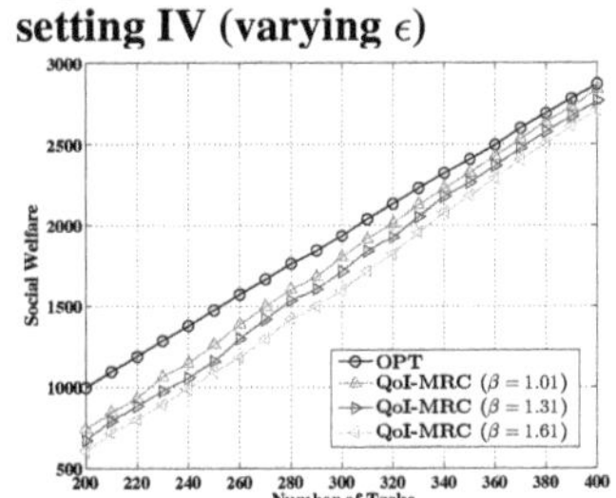

Figure 8: Social welfare for setting IV (varying β)

6.3 Simulation Results

In Figure 3 and 4, we compare the social welfare generated by the QoI-VCG auction, the QoI-SRC auction and the MSW-Greedy auction. The social welfare of the QoI-VCG auction equals to the optimal solution of the SRC-WD problem. From Figure 3 and 4, we arrive at the conclusion that the social welfare of the QoI-SRC auction is close to optimal and far better than that of the baseline MSW-Greedy auction.

In Table 7 and 8, we show the comparison of the execution time of the QoI-VCG and QoI-SRC auctions. It is obvious from these two tables that the QoI-SRC auction executes in significantly less time than the QoI-VCG auction. With the increasing of the number of users and tasks, the execution time of the QoI-VCG auction gradually becomes so long that makes it infeasible to be utilized in practice. In contrast, the QoI-SRC auction keeps low execution time regardless of the growth of the user and task numbers. The QoI-SRC auction is much more computationally efficient than the QoI-VCG auction.

In Figure 5 and 6, we compare the social welfare generated by the QoI-MRC auction with the optimal social welfare in both setting III and IV. We fix the parameter $\beta = 1.01$ and vary the choices of ϵ. From the two figures, we observe that the QoI-MRC auction obtains close-to-optimal social welfare and it becomes closer to the optimal social welfare when ϵ approaches 0.

N	200	220	240	260	280	300	320	340
QoI-VCG	10.19	16.06	11.22	11.71	58.64	63.14	79.37	10.51
QoI-SRC	0.019	0.014	0.015	0.015	0.020	0.022	0.018	0.019
N	360	380	400	420	440	460	480	500
QoI-VCG	43.52	93.44	94.25	273.6	52.54	72.26	860.9	2043
QoI-SRC	0.019	0.021	0.021	0.019	0.023	0.021	0.021	0.024

Table 7: Execution time (s) for setting I

M	300	320	340	360	380	400	420	440
QoI-VCG	18.70	1.337	2.715	15.47	21.42	43.38	88.57	224.3
QoI-SRC	0.066	0.076	0.075	0.076	0.073	0.090	0.075	0.077
M	460	480	500	520	540	560	580	600
QoI-VCG	67.85	50.68	183.5	229.3	474.8	751.1	1206	1269
QoI-SRC	0.079	0.117	0.099	0.130	0.111	0.122	0.123	0.147

Table 8: Execution time (s) for setting II

In Figure 7 and 8, we fix the parameter $\epsilon = 0.01$ and vary the choices of β. From these two figures, we also observe that the QoI-MRC auction obtains close-to-optimal social welfare and as β approaches 1, it becomes closer to the optimal social welfare.

7. CONCLUSION

In this paper, we design QoI aware incentive mechanisms for MCS systems based on RC auctions. For the SRC auction, we design a truthful, individual rational and computationally efficient mechanism that approximately maximizes the social welfare with a guaranteed approximation ratio. For the MRC auction, we design an iterative descending mechanism that achieves close-to-optimal social welfare with a guaranteed approximation ratio while satisfying individual rationality and computational efficiency. Moreover, our theoretical analysis is validated through extensive simulations.

References

[1] X. Sheng, J. Tang, X. Xiao, and G. Xue, "Sensing as a service: Challenges, solutions and future directions," *Sensors Journal, IEEE*, 2013.

[2] "Medwatcher app," http://www.fda.gov/MedicalDevices/Safety/ReportaProblem/ucm385880.htm.

[3] Y. Cheng, X. Li, Z. Li, S. Jiang, Y. Li, J. Jia, and X. Jiang, "Aircloud: A cloud-based air-quality monitoring system for everyone," in *SenSys*, 2014.

[4] D. Yang, G. Xue, X. Fang, and J. Tang, "Crowdsourcing to smartphones: Incentive mechanism design for mobile phone sensing," in *Mobicom*, 2012.

[5] L. Duan, T. Kubo, K. Sugiyama, J. Huang, T. Hasegawa, and J. Walrand, "Incentive mechanisms for smartphone collaboration in data acquisition and distributed computing," in *INFOCOM*, 2012.

[6] B. Faltings, J. Li, and R. Jurca, "Incentive mechanisms for community sensing," *Computers, IEEE Transactions on*, 2014.

[7] Z. Feng, Y. Zhu, Q. Zhang, L. Ni, and A. Vasilakos, "Trac: Truthful auction for location-aware collaborative sensing in mobile crowdsourcing," in *INFOCOM*, 2014.

[8] J.-S. Lee and B. Hoh, "Sell your experiences: a market mechanism based incentive for participatory sensing," in *PerCom*, 2010.

[9] Y. Zhang and M. van der Schaar, "Reputation-based incentive protocols in crowdsourcing applications," in *INFOCOM*, 2012.

[10] H. Xie and J. C. Lui, "Modeling crowdsourcing systems: Design and analysis of incentive mechanism and rating system," *SIGMETRICS Perform. Eval. Rev.*, 2014.

[11] H. Xie, J. C. Lui, J. W. Jiang, and W. Chen, "Incentive mechanism and protocol design for crowdsourcing systems," in *Allerton*, 2014.

[12] Z. Feng, Y. Zhu, Q. Zhang, H. Zhu, J. Yu, J. Cao, and L. Ni, "Towards truthful mechanisms for mobile crowdsourcing with dynamic smartphones," in *ICDCS*, 2014.

[13] X. Zhang, Z. Yang, Z. Zhou, H. Cai, L. Chen, and X. Li, "Free market of crowdsourcing: Incentive mechanism design for mobile sensing," *Parallel and Distributed Systems, IEEE Transactions on*, 2014.

[14] D. Zhao, X.-Y. Li, and H. Ma, "How to crowdsource tasks truthfully without sacrificing utility: Online incentive mechanisms with budget constraint," in *INFOCOM*, 2014.

[15] S. He, D.-H. Shin, J. Zhang, and J. Chen, "Toward optimal allocation of location dependent tasks in crowdsensing," in *INFOCOM*, 2014.

[16] I. Koutsopoulos, "Optimal incentive-driven design of participatory sensing systems," in *INFOCOM*, 2013.

[17] T. Luo, H.-P. Tan, and L. Xia, "Profit-maximizing incentive for participatory sensing," in *INFOCOM*, 2014.

[18] Z. Song, C. Liu, J. Wu, J. Ma, and W. Wang, "Qoi-aware multitask-oriented dynamic participant selection with budget constraints," *Vehicular Technology, IEEE Transactions on*, 2014.

[19] E. H. Clarke, "Multipart pricing of public goods," *Public Choice*, 1971.

[20] T. Groves, "Incentives in teams," *Econometrica: Journal of the Econometric Society*, 1973.

[21] J. Huang, R. A. Berry, and M. L. Honig, "Auction-based spectrum sharing," *Mob. Netw. Appl.*, 2006.

[22] X. Chen and J. Huang, "Spatial spectrum access game: Nash equilibria and distributed learning," in *MobiHoc*, 2012.

[23] J. Jia, Q. Zhang, Q. Zhang, and M. Liu, "Revenue generation for truthful spectrum auction in dynamic spectrum access," in *MobiHoc*, 2009.

[24] H. Jin, G. Sun, X. Wang, and Q. Zhang, "Spectrum trading with insurance in cognitive radio networks," in *INFOCOM*, 2012.

[25] M. Dong, G. Sun, X. Wang, and Q. Zhang, "Combinatorial auction with time-frequency flexibility in cognitive radio networks," in *INFOCOM*, 2012.

[26] D. Yang, X. Fang, and G. Xue, "Truthful auction for cooperative communications," in *MobiHoc*, 2011.

[27] X. Chen, B. Proulx, X. Gong, and J. Zhang, "Social trust and social reciprocity based cooperative d2d communications," in *MobiHoc*, 2013.

[28] Q. Yu, J. Chen, Y. Fan, X. Shen, and Y. Sun, "Multi-channel assignment in wireless sensor networks: A game theoretic approach," in *INFOCOM*, 2010.

[29] M. Dong, H. Jin, G. Sun, X. Wang, W. Liu, and X. Wang, "Non-cooperative game based social welfare maximizing bandwidth allocation in wsns," in *GLOBECOM*, 2011.

[30] Q. Zhang, Y. Wen, X. Tian, , X. Gan, and X. Wang, "Incentivize crowd labeling under budget constraint," in *INFOCOM*, 2015.

[31] Q. Li, Y. Li, J. Gao, B. Zhao, W. Fan, and J. Han, "Resolving conflicts in heterogeneous data by truth discovery and source reliability estimation," in *SIGMOD*, 2014.

[32] L. Su, Q. Li, S. Hu, S. Wang, J. Gao, H. Liu, T. Abdelzaher, J. Han, X. Liu, Y. Gao, and L. Kaplan, "Generalized decision aggregation in distributed sensing systems," in *RTSS*, 2014.

[33] Q. Li, Y. Li, J. Gao, L. Su, B. Zhao, M. Demirbas, W. Fan, and J. Han, "A confidence-aware approach for truth discovery on long-tail data," in *Proceedings of the VLDB Endowment*, 2014.

[34] S. Wang, D. Wang, L. Su, L. Kaplan, and T. F. Abdelzaher, "Towards cyber-physical systems in social spaces: The data reliability challenge," in *RTSS*, 2014.

[35] H. Li, B. Zhao, and A. Fuxman, "The wisdom of minority: Discovering and targeting the right group of workers for crowdsourcing," in *WWW*, 2014.

[36] L. Blumrosen and N. Nisan, "Combinatorial auctions," *Algorithmic Game Theory*, 2007.

[37] M. Babaioff, R. Lavi, and E. Pavlov, "Single-value combinatorial auctions and algorithmic implementation in undominated strategies," *J. ACM*, 2009.

[38] M. J. Osborne and A. Rubinstein, *A course in game theory*. Cambridge, USA: The MIT Press, 1994, electronic edition.

[39] M. Babaioff, R. Lavi, and E. Pavlov, "Mechanism design for single-value domains," in *AAAI*, 2005.

[40] Z. Zheng, F. Wu, S. Tang, and G. Chen, "Unknown combinatorial auction mechanisms for heterogeneous spectrum redistribution," in *MobiHoc*, 2014.

[41] R. B. Myerson, "Optimal auction design," *Mathematics of operations research*, 1981.

[42] S. Rajagopalan and V. Vazirani, "Primal-dual rnc approximation algorithms for (multi)-set (multi)-cover and covering integer programs," in *FOCS*, 1993.

[43] "Gurobi solver," http://www.gurobi.com/.

Pay as How Well You Do: A Quality Based Incentive Mechanism for Crowdsensing *

Dan Peng, Fan Wu†, and Guihai Chen
Shanghai Key Laboratory of Scalable Computing and Systems,
Department of Computer Science and Engineering, Shanghai Jiao Tong University, China
pd347@sjtu.edu.cn, {fwu, gchen}@cs.sjtu.edu.cn

ABSTRACT

In crowdsensing, appropriate rewards are always expected to compensate the participants for their consumptions of physical resources and involvements of manual efforts. While continuous low quality sensing data could do harm to the availability and preciseness of crowdsensing based services, few existing incentive mechanisms have ever addressed the issue of sensing data's quality. The design of quality based incentive mechanism is motivated by its potential to avoid inefficient sensing and unnecessary rewards. In this paper, we incorporate the consideration of data quality into the design of incentive mechanism for crowdsensing, and propose to pay the participants as how well they do, to motivate the rational participants to perform data sensing efficiently. This mechanism estimates the quality of sensing data, and offers each participant a reward based on her effective contribution. We also implement the mechanism and evaluate the improvements in terms of quality of service and profit of service provider. The evaluation results show that our mechanism achieves superior performance when compared to the uniform pricing scheme.

Categories and Subject Descriptors

C.2.1 [**Computer-Communication Networks**]: Network Architecture and Design

†F. Wu is the corresponding author.

*This work was supported in part by the State Key Development Program for Basic Research of China (973 project 2014CB340303), in part by China NSF grant 61422208, 61472252, 61272443, and 61133006, in part by CCF-Intel Young Faculty Researcher Program and CCF-Tencent Open Fund, in part by the Scientific Research Foundation for the Returned Overseas Chinese Scholars, and in part by Jiangsu Future Network Research Project No. BY2013095-1-10. The opinions, findings, conclusions, and recommendations expressed in this paper are those of the authors and do not necessarily reflect the views of the funding agencies or the government.

MobiHoc'15, June 22–25, 2015, Hangzhou, China.

http://dx.doi.org/10.1145/2746285.2746306.

Keywords

Crowdsensing; Incentive Mechanism; Quality Estimation; Maximum Likelihood Estimation; Information Theory

1. INTRODUCTION

Crowdsensing is a new paradigm of applications that enables the ubiquitous mobile devices with enhanced sensing capabilities to collect and to share local information towards a common goal [5, 12]. In recent years, a wide variety of applications have been developed to realize the potential of crowdsensing throughout everyday life, such as environmental quality monitoring [2, 3], noise pollution assessment [16, 24], road and traffic condition monitoring [19, 31], road-side parking statistics [18, 21], and indoor localization [23, 33]. However, the success of crowdsensing based services critically depends on sufficient and reliable data contributions from individual participants.

Sensing, processing, and transmitting data in crowdsensing applications requires manual efforts and physical resources. Therefore, appropriate rewards are always expected to compensate the owners of task-taking mobile devices. These owners, or say participants in the literature of crowdsensing, are commonly assumed to be rational, and would not make contributions unless there are sufficient incentives. Although researchers have proposed a number of incentive mechanisms for participation in crowdsensing [9, 11, 13, 15, 32, 36, 39, 40], they have not fully exploited the connection between quality of sensing data and rewards for contributions.

Sensing data of high quality, based on which the crowdsensing service provider aggregates and extracts information for accurate decision making and attentive service providing, is fundamentally important. In crowdsensing, quality of sensing data can be affected by the characteristics of mobile sensors, the clarity of task instructions, as well as the expertise and willingness of individual participants [14, 20, 25]. Particularly, participants with different spatial-temporal contexts and personal effort levels are likely to submit sensing data of diverse quality. Furthermore, rational participants tend to strategically minimize their efforts, while doing the sensing tasks, and thus may degrade the quality of sensing data. For example, careless or indifferent submissions are always found in crowdsensing based noise monitoring applications. When asked for environmental sound heard of neighborhood, a participant may perform the sensing tasks through a mobile device placed inside her pocket, rather than carefully taking out the device to sense accurately. Such a low quality submission would invalidate the estimation of noise pollution.

Continuous low quality sensing data undoubtedly do harm to the availability and preciseness of crowdsensing based services. However, to the best of our knowledge, few existing works have taken the observation of data quality into consideration, when designing incentive mechanisms for crowdsensing. It is very challenging to design quality based incentive mechanisms for crowdsensing.

Most of all, it is technically difficult to estimate the quality of sensing data without any prior knowledge of the sensing behavior of individual participants or the ground truth of targeted contexts. Subsequent quality verification would require significant investments in deploying particular infrastructures to do on-site sensing and ground truth collecting, like Model 831-NMS permanent noise monitoring system [4]. Lacking in flexibility and scalability, the deployment of traditional static sensing infrastructures, in turn, negates the necessity and benefits of crowdsensing.

Second, it is challenging to design incentive mechanisms that achieve both individual rationality and profit maximization. Here, individual rationality means that a participant should be rewarded no less than her sensing cost, and the profit of service provider is the difference between the value of crowdsensing based services and the total rewards to participants. Deliberate incentive mechanisms are required to motivate effective data contributions from rational participants, and to maintain a robust, profitable market for crowdsensing service provider.

Third, it is nontrivial to bridge the gap between quality of sensing data and rewards for contributions. Participants of crowdsensing, who perform the sensing tasks with heterogeneous physical resources and manual efforts, and therefore submit sensing data of diverse quality, may require appropriate rewards according to their contributions. While traditional uniform pricing scheme is unfair, the Pay-as-Bid pricing method used in most of the auction based incentive mechanisms is somehow troublesome for participants and indulgent of careless behavior. Both of these existing solutions ignore the quality issue, and thus are unlikely to encourage long-term, effective contributions.

In this paper, we incorporate the consideration of data quality into the design of incentive mechanism for crwodsensing, and propose to pay the rational participants as how well they do, to motivate efficient crowdsensing.

Our main contributions are listed as follows.

- To the best of our knowledge, we are the first to design a quality based incentive mechanism for crowdsensing that directly motivates individual participants to contribute high quality sensing data.
- Second, we extend the well-known Expectation Maximization algorithm that combines maximum likelihood estimation and Bayesian inference to estimate the quality of sensing data, and further apply the classical Information Theory to measure the effective contribution of sensing data. Based on the estimated quality and contribution, we can determine fair and proper rewards to the participants. The proposed incentive mechanism achieves individual rationality and profit maximization.
- Finally, we implement the incentive mechanism and extensively evaluate its performance. Our evaluation results show that it achieves superior performance in terms of quality assurance and profit management, when compared to the uniform pricing scheme.

The rest of the paper is organized as follows. We briefly review related work in Section 2 and present technical preliminaries in Section 3. The detailed design of our quality based incentive mechanism is presented in Section 4. In Section 5, we evaluate our incentive mechanism and show the results. Finally, we conclude this paper in Section 6.

2. RELATED WORK

The problem of data quality has been widely studied in organizational databases and information systems [7, 29], mainly focusing on quality category, attribute and contextual pattern from a perspective of data consumer. Sachidananda *et al.* [27] surveyed building blocks and existing approaches related to quality of information in wireless sensor networks.

For the paradigm of crowdsensing, Reddy *et al.* [26] developed a recruitment framework to identify and select well-suited participants to achieve high utility within a budget. Three stages are introduced, including qualifier, assessment, and progress review. Though reputation system based on performance has been built, this work focuses on the record of participation likelihood (whether the participant would take a sensing task when given a chance). In addition, it shows little consideration about incentives. On the other hand, although various empirical experiments [17, 20, 25, 35] demonstrate that financial and social incentives do have an impact on the performance of participants, such as engagement, compliance and quality, they fail to generalize an incentive model to adaptively guide the participants' behavior.

There are extensive researches targeting the incentive mechanism design for crowdsensing. Lee and Hoh [13] proposed a reverse auction based dynamic pricing scheme to motivate participants to sell their sensing data with claimed bids. Yang *et al.* [32] considered a platform-centric incentive model, where the reward is proportionally shared by participants in a Stackelberg game, and a user-centric incentive model, where participants in the auction bid for tasks and get paid no lower than the submitted bids. Koutsopoulos [11] designed an incentive mechanism to determine participation level and payment allocation to minimize platform's compensation cost with guaranteed service quality. Zhang *et al.* [37] and Zhao *et al.* [40] suggested online incentive mechanisms to flexibly recruit participants who appear opportunistically in the phenomena of interests. Luo *et al.* [15] studied an incentive mechanism based on all-pay auction with realistic constraints such as information asymmetry, population uncertainty, and risk aversion. Kawajiri *et al.* [10] deployed a crowdsensing based wireless indoor localization system, and steered participants to cover sufficient locations to improve the quality of service. There is no skill variance and device variance in their system. In general, these existing incentive mechanisms either have not considered the quality of sensing data or have addressed the incentive concerns and quality issues separately. Moreover, few of them have investigated the method to estimate the quality of sensing data.

In contrast, we systemically consider the participants' willingness to take a sufficient amount of efforts in crowdsensing, and bridge the gap between quality of sensing data and rewards for contributions, by providing a quality based incentive mechanism. The quality estimation method applied in this paper is originally introduced by Dawid and Skene [6], where the expectation maximization (EM) algorithm is used to obtain maximum likelihood estimates of observers' error

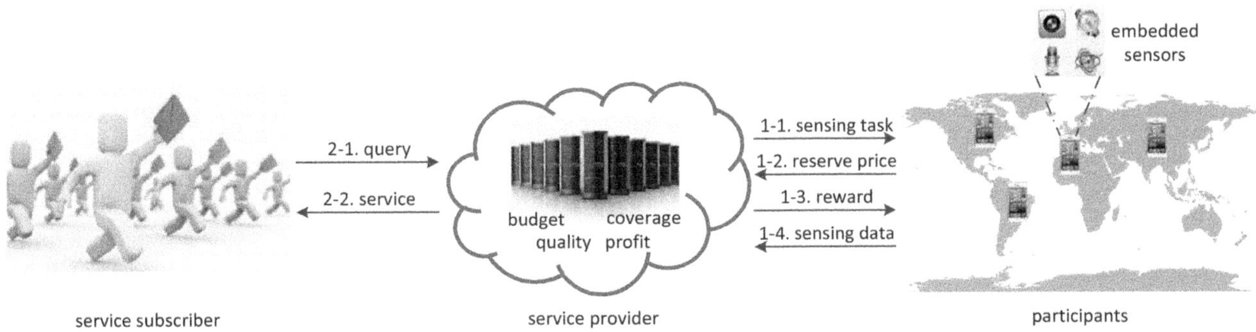

Figure 1: A general crowdsensing model.

rates and to infer the true response of patients. Wang and Ipeirotis [30] applied EM algorithm to estimate the quality of crowdsourced labeling workers. Zhang *et al.* [38] proposed to combine spectral methods and EM algorithm to address the problem of crowdsourced multi-class labeling with an optimal convergence rate up to a logarithmic factor. Beyond quality estimation, we also quantify the contribution of sensing data via information theory, and determine fair and proper rewards to participants.

3. PRELIMINARIES

In this section, we present the model of quality based crowdsensing, and key techniques for quality estimation.

3.1 Crowdsensing Model

As illustrated by Figure 1, there are three major components in the crowdsensing system, *i.e.*, service subscribers who request services, a service provider who conducts the crowdsensing campaign and provides services, and a crowd of participants who submit sensing data to support the services. The crowdsensing process (the right part) can be discribed as follows. First, the service provider releases a set $\mathbb{T}$ of sensing tasks (*e.g.*, noise sensing on campus at 10:00 am) with an incentive announcement and a quality requirement (*e.g.*, an error threshold). In the phenomena of interests, there is a set $\mathbb{A} = \{a_1, a_2, \ldots, a_n\}$ of participants, with sensors embedded in their mobile devices. Each participant $a_k \in \mathbb{A}$ bears a private reserve price/sensing cost c_k (*i.e.*, a monetary value for her consumptions of physical resources and involvements of manual efforts), and thus expects a reward for her contribution. Without sufficient rewards, the participants may not undertake the sensing tasks. The service provider estimates the quality q_k of sensing data from each participant a_k. By taking the profile of the participants' data quality and sensing costs into consideration, she selects a subset $W \subseteq \mathbb{A}$ of participants to perform each sensing task, and offers each $a_k \in W$ a certain amount of reward r_k according to her effective contribution. After collecting the sensing data for some tasks, the service provider updates quality estimation q_k for each $a_k \in W$ to guide the next round of recruitment (the right part), and extracts information to provide services (the left part).

We consider a general class of crowdsensing applications, in which the availability and preciseness of services significantly depends on the quality of sensing data, *e.g.*, urban noise pollution monitoring, which measures ambient noise pollution based on sensing data collected from mobile devices. For each piece of sensing data with an error below the specified threshold, the service provider gains a value V (*e.g.*, the subscription fee from service subscribers). For simplicity, we assume that V is fixed. The objective of the service provider is to maximize her own profit, by providing services with guaranteed quality, and recruiting participants with proper rewards. The profit is defined as

$$\text{Profit} \triangleq \sum_{a_k \in W} (V - r_k).$$

In this paper, we focus on the data quality that is specifically affected by participants' effort levels for sensing, and aim at designing incentive mechanisms for the service provider to stimulate high quality sensing and long-term, effective contributions.

3.2 Quality Estimation via EM

For crowdsensing, *e.g.*, urban noise sensing, it is reasonable to calibrate the sensing data, to tolerate the inherent uncertainty of mobile devices. Here, we divide the reading of sensing data into discrete intervals, and suggest the service provider to deliver a certain interval to the service subscribers, rather than an accurate reading, to mitigate the impact of device variance and device error. The discrete intervals are denoted as a set $\mathbb{D} = \{d_1, d_2, \ldots, d_m\}$, where each interval spans over a range of decibels, and the granularity of interval division can be determined by the tradeoff between accuracy and complexity.

Regarding the quality of sensing data as a result of the effort levels, we estimate "effort matrix" $\mathbf{e}^k$ for each participant a_k, and map this effort matrix into a scalar quality value through function $q_k = g(\mathbf{e}^k)$. Here, the effort matrix $\mathbf{e}^k$ is an $m \times m$ matrix, with element $e^k_{ij} \in [0, 1]$, $i = 1, \ldots, m$, $j = 1, \ldots, m$, indicating the probability that participant a_k submits a piece of sensing data in interval d_j while the true reading is in interval d_i. Particularly, $\{e^k_{ii} | i = 1, \ldots, m\}$ contains the probabilities that participant a_k obediently performs outside-pocket sensing for each of the m possible cases. Furthermore, the conditional probabilities satisfy $\sum_j e^k_{ij} = 1$.

We note that, the effort matrix can be measured when we have ground truth for all spatial-temporal contexts. However, for crowdsensing, the true reading, or even the interval, cannot be ascertained in most cases, making the direct verification of data quality and the discernment of effort matrix challenging. In this paper, we resort to the well-known expectation maximization (EM) algorithm [6] to estimate each participant's effort matrix.

The EM algorithm [6] is an iterative method for finding the Maximum Likelihood Estimation (MLE) of the parameters (*e.g.*, the effort matrix for each participant, and the true noise interval for each task), when there is missing data (*e.g.*, the indicators to tell right or wrong for sensing data) that precludes the straightforward estimation for the parameters. Here, MLE calculates the best estimation for parameters that maximizes the (log-)likelihood of the observations (*e.g.*, the submitted sensing data), and converges in probability to the true value of the unknown parameters when the number of observations is sufficiently large.

Given a set S of observed sensing data, a set P of missing true interval indicators, a set E of unknown effort matrices, and the density function f, the likelihood of unknown E is

$$L(E; P, S) = f(P, S|E).$$

To find the MLE of E, EM algorithm iteratively runs the following two steps until convergence (Supposing that $\widehat{E}^t$ is the current value of E after t iterations).

E-step calculates the expected value of likelihood function, with respect to the conditional distribution of P given observation S under the current estimation of E,

$$Q(E|\widehat{E}^t) = \mathbb{E}_{P|S,\widehat{E}^t}[L(E; P, S)].$$

M-step seeks the estimation $\widehat{E}$ that maximizes the expectation function,

$$\widehat{E}^{t+1} = \arg\max_{E} Q(E|\widehat{E}^t).$$

Inspired by [6], we extend the algorithm to estimate the true interval indicators and participants' effort matrices, by iterating the following two steps until convergence: 1) estimate the effort matrix and noise interval distribution via maximum likelihood estimation, based on the estimated true interval indicators; and 2) calculate new estimation of true interval indicators, according to the estimated effort matrices and noise interval distribution.

The converged estimation of participant's effort matrix indicates the quality of sensing data, while the noise interval distribution is suggestive of the noise pollution level.

4. QUALITY BASED INCENTIVE

In this section, we detail the design of our quality based incentive mechanism for crowdsensing. To pay each individual participant a_k as how well she does in sensing, we estimate her effort matrix $\mathbf{e}^k$, calculate her quality q_k of sensing data, quantify her effective contribution $c_m(q_k)$, and offer a proper reward r_k. Taking the quality of sensing data into consideration, our incentive mechanism can encourage long-term, effective contribution for crowdsensing based services.

4.1 A Simple Case

We first regard all of the submitted sensing data as qualified, and present a simple pricing scheme. We assume that the participants' sensing costs follow a probability distribution, with a probability distribution function $f(c_k)$, and a cumulative distribution function $F(c_k)$.

Table 1: Key notations

Notation	Definition
$\mathbb{T}$	Set of sensing tasks
$\mathbb{A}$	Set of participants
$\mathbb{D}$	Set of discrete noise intervals
$\mathbb{A}_t$	Set of participants who complete task $t \in \mathbb{T}$
$\mathbb{T}^k$	Set of tasks that $a_k \in \mathbb{A}$ performs
S	Set of observed sensing data
P	Set of missing true noise interval indicators
E	Set of unknown effort matrices
$L(E; P, S)$	Likelihood function of E
$\mathbf{e}^k$	Effort matrix of a_k
e_{ij}^k	Probability that a_k submits data in interval d_j while the true interval is d_i
Π	Noise interval distribution
$\mathbf{p}^t$	True noise interval indicator for task t
p_i^t	Probability of task t with true noise interval being d_i
d_t^k	Noise interval that a_k's sensing data for task t falls into
$I(d_t^k = d_j)$	Indicator function for the event $d_t^k = d_j$
q_k	Quality of a_k's sensing data
$c_m(q_k)$	Effective contribution of sensing data of quality q_k
c_k	Reserve price/sensing cost of a_k
r_k	Reward to a_k for her contribution
V	Value gained from qualified sensing data
r^*	Optimal quality based reward
r^u	Optimal uniform reward

A rational participant a_k will not do a given sensing task unless she gets a reward $r \geq c_k$. Therefore, the service provider's profit by providing services and recruiting participant a_k, which is defined as the difference between value V gained from the sensing data, and the reward r to participant a_k, where $V \geq r$, is formulated as

$$\text{Profit}(c_k, r) = \begin{cases} 0, & r < c_k, \\ V - r, & r \geq c_k. \end{cases}$$

While the distribution of c_k is independent of value V and reward r, the expected profit can be calculated as

$$\begin{aligned} \text{Profit}(r) &= \int_0^\infty \text{Profit}(c_k, r) f(c_k) dc_k \\ &= \int_0^r (V - r) f(c_k) dc_k = F(r)(V - r). \end{aligned}$$

Therefore, the service provider can maximize her profit by taking the first derivative of the function $\text{Profit}(r)$, solving the following equation, and getting the optimal reward,

$$r^* = V - \frac{F(r^*)}{f(r^*)}.$$

4.2 Quality Estimation

In practice, due to their various effort levels, different participants may submit sensing data of diverse quality. In this subsection, we extend the Estimation Maximization algorithm to estimate the effort matrix $\mathbf{e}^k$ for each participant a_k, and then estimate the quality of her sensing data as $q_k = g(\mathbf{e}^k)$.

Specifically, we denote the set of participants that submit sensing data to task t as $\mathbb{A}_t \subseteq \mathbb{A}$, and the set of tasks that participant a_k performs as $\mathbb{T}^k \subseteq \mathbb{T}$. For task $t \in \mathbb{T}^k$, the true noise interval is denoted as d_t^0, while the interval into which participant a_k's sensing data falls is denoted as d_t^k. An indicator function $I(d_t^k = d_j)$ (*i.e.*, $I(d_t^k = d_j) = 1$ when event $d_t^k = d_j$ is true; otherwise, $I(d_t^k = d_j) = 0$) is applied to describe the submission of sensing data.

We assume that the effort levels of participants are independent, and do not change for a period of time. So that we can periodically learn the effort matrix $\mathbf{e}^k$ for each participant a_k, and put this knowledge into practice. Without the true interval indicator, *i.e.*, $\mathbf{p}^t = \{p_i^t | i = 1, \ldots, m\}$ for each task t ($p_i^t = 1$ if $d_t^0 = d_i$ for sure) is unavailable, we resort to the EM algorithm that combines Maximum likelihood estimation and Bayesian inference to iteratively estimate the unknown effort matrix $\mathbf{e}^k$ and noise interval distribution $\Pi = \{\pi_i | i = 1, \ldots, m\}$.

The pseudo-code of this expectation maximization algorithm is shown in Algorithm 1, which runs as follows.

(1) Initialization: For each task t, the probability distribution of true noise interval indicator $\mathbf{p}^t$ is initialized as:

$$p_i^t = p(d_t^0 = d_i) = \frac{\sum_{a_i \in \mathbb{A}_t} I(d_t^k = d_i)}{|\mathbb{A}_t|}.$$

(2) Estimation of effort matrix and noise interval distribution: Given the likelihood function

$$L(E; P, S) = f(P, S|E),$$

and

$$L(E; S) = f(S|E) = \sum_P f(P, S|E),$$

where $E = \{\mathbf{e}^k | a_k \in \mathbb{A}\}$, $P = \{\mathbf{p}^t | t \in \mathbb{T}\}$, and $S = \{d_t^k | t \in \mathbb{T}, a_k \in \mathbb{A}_t\}$, the maximum likelihood estimate of E makes the observation S most likely to happen.

We note that the effort matrix $\mathbf{e}^k$ for each participant a_k follows the Multinomial Distribution. When participant a_k performs n_i^k independent tasks with true interval d_i, her sensing data for these tasks falls into interval d_j with probability e_{ij}^k, where $e_{ij}^k \geq 0$ and $\sum_j e_{ij}^k = 1$, $j = 1, \ldots, m$. Let $n_{i1}^k, \ldots, n_{im}^k$ be the number of submissions corresponding to interval $d_1, \ldots, d_m$, respectively. Then we have $\sum_j n_{ij}^k = n_i^k$, and the likelihood function of $\mathbf{e}_i^k$,

$$f(n_{i1}^k, \ldots, n_{im}^k | e_{i1}^k, \ldots, e_{im}^k) = \frac{n_i^k!}{\prod n_{ij}^k!} \prod (e_{ij}^k)^{n_{ij}^k}.$$

Taking the log-likelihood, Lagrange multipliers, and derivatives, we get the most natural estimates,

$$\widehat{e}_{ij}^k = \frac{n_{ij}^k}{n_i^k} = \frac{\sum_{t \in \mathbb{T}^k} p_i^t I(d_t^k = d_j)}{\sum_{t \in \mathbb{T}^k} p_i^t}, \quad j = 1, \ldots, m.$$

The noise interval distribution is estimated as

$$\widehat{\pi}_i = \frac{\sum_{t \in \mathbb{T}} p_i^t}{|\mathbb{T}|}, \quad i = 1, \ldots, m.$$

(3) Estimation of true noise interval indicator: Given the observed sensing data S, the effort matrices E, and the noise interval distribution Π, we apply the Bayesian inference to estimate the true noise interval indicators P. Considering the n independent observations $\{S^1, \ldots, S^n\}$ of sensing data from individual participants, where $S^i = \{d_t^i | t \in \mathbb{T}\}, i = 1, \ldots, m$, we have

$$p(P|S) = \frac{p(P)p(S|P)}{p(S)} = \frac{p(P)p(S^1|P) \ldots p(S^n|P)}{p(S)}.$$

When all terms not involving the true noise interval indicator are absorbed into the proportionality sign, we calculate the distribution of true noise interval indicator according to

$$p_i^t = \frac{\pi_i \prod_{a_k \in \mathbb{A}_t} \prod_j (e_{ij}^k)^{I(d_t^k = d_j)}}{\sum_q \pi_q \prod_{a_k \in \mathbb{A}_t} \prod_j (e_{qj}^k)^{I(d_t^k = d_j)}}, \quad i = 1, \ldots, m.$$

(4) Convergence: We iterate step $2-3$ until the two estimates converge, *i.e.*, $|\widehat{E}^{t+1} - \widehat{E}^t| < \varepsilon$, $|\widehat{P}^{t+1} - \widehat{P}^t| < \eta$, $\varepsilon > 0$, $\eta > 0$.

Algorithm 1: Effort Matrix Estimation

Input: A set $S = \{d_t^k | t \in \mathbb{T}, a_k \in \mathbb{A}_t\}$ of observations.
Output: Estimation of effort matrix E, marginal distribution of noise interval Π, and posterior estimation of true noise interval indicators P.

// Initialization of True Noise Interval Indicator
foreach $t \in \mathbb{T}$ **do**
  $cnt \leftarrow 0$; $\mathbf{cnt} \leftarrow \mathbf{0}$;
  foreach $a_k \in \mathbb{A}_t$ **do**
    $i \leftarrow d_t^k$; $cnt_i \leftarrow cnt_i + 1$; $cnt \leftarrow cnt + 1$;
  foreach $d_i \in \mathbb{D}$ **do**
    $p_i^t \leftarrow cnt_i / cnt$;
while *not converged* **do**
  // Estimation of Effort Matrix
  foreach $a_k \in \mathbb{A}$ **do**
    $\mathbf{cnt} \leftarrow \mathbf{0}$; $\mathbf{e}^k \leftarrow \mathbf{0}$;
    foreach $t \in \mathbb{T}^k$ **do**
      $j \leftarrow d_t^k$;
      foreach $d_i \in \mathbb{D}$ **do**
        $e_{ij}^k \leftarrow e_{ij}^k + p_i^t$;
        $cnt_i \leftarrow cnt_i + p_i^t$;
    foreach $d_i \in \mathbb{D}$ **do**
      foreach $d_j \in \mathbb{D}$ **do**
        $e_{ij}^k \leftarrow e_{ij}^k / cnt_i$;
  // Estimation of Noise Interval Distribution
  foreach $d_i \in \mathbb{D}$ **do**
    $\pi_i \leftarrow 0$;
    foreach $t \in \mathbb{T}$ **do**
      $\pi_i \leftarrow \pi_i + p_i^t$;
    $\pi_i \leftarrow \pi_i / |\mathbb{T}|$;
  // Estimation of True Noise Interval Indicator
  foreach $t \in \mathbb{T}$ **do**
    $smp \leftarrow 0$; $\mathbf{p}^t \leftarrow \mathbf{1}$;
    foreach $d_i \in \mathbb{D}$ **do**
      foreach $a_k \in \mathbb{A}_t$ **do**
        $j \leftarrow d_t^k$;
        $p_i^t \leftarrow p_i^t e_{ij}^k$;
      $smp \leftarrow smp + \pi_i p_i^t$;
    foreach $d_i \in \mathbb{D}$ **do**
      $p_i^t \leftarrow \pi_i p_i^t / smp$;
Return $E = \{\mathbf{e}^k | a_k \in \mathbb{A}\}, \Pi = \{\pi_i | i = 1, \ldots, m\}$, $P = \{\mathbf{p}^t | t \in \mathbb{T}\}$;

For each iteration (the while loop), the computation complexity is polynomial as $O(|\mathbb{A}||\mathbb{T}||\mathbb{D}|)$.

We claim that the EM algorithm increases the likelihood function in each iteration, and finally converges to a stable estimation. To circumvent the problem of getting trapped in a local optimum, we try different initializations for several executions of the algorithm. Although it is hard to provide theoretical guarantee for its performance, the EM algorithm has been widely used, and a provably optimal convergence rate up to a logarithmic factor has been shown in [38].

With the estimation for effort matrix $\mathbf{e}^k$, we can get the quality of a_k's sensing data through the mapping function. For simplicity, we focus on pure obedience, and set $q_k = g(\mathbf{e}^k) = \sum_i e^k_{ii}/m$. With the estimation for distribution of true noise interval indicator $\mathbf{p}^t = \{p^t_1, p^t_2, \ldots, p^t_m\}$ for task t, the interval d^*_i to be delivered is the one with maximum possibility, *i.e.*, $d^*_i = \arg\max_i p^t_i$.

4.3 Contribution Quantification

Various analyses and experiments have confirmed that expert work can be accomplished by the local crowd, even if they are lack of expert knowledge. However, the contribution of each individual participant remains unknown. Here, inspired by ideas in Information Theory and Shannon's Channel Coding Theorem [28, 34], we quantify the participants' contributions through information uncertainty reduction.

We regard the right part of crowdsensing system (Figure 1) as a signal transmission system (Figure 2), where the input signal X is the sensing data provided by the participants, and correspondingly, the output signal Y is the information that service provider receives on the sensing data. Transmitted through the channel, an input signal may be distorted in a random way depending on the channel condition, and thus the output signal may be different from the input signal. Here, the quality $q_k \in [0, 1]$ of the sensing data is expressed by a noise variable Z (independent of X) on the transmission channel, where $Pr(z = 0) = q_k$ indicates that the output signal is equal to the input signal with probability q_k, and $Pr(z = 1) = 1 - q_k$ indicates that an error occurs with probability $1 - q_k$.

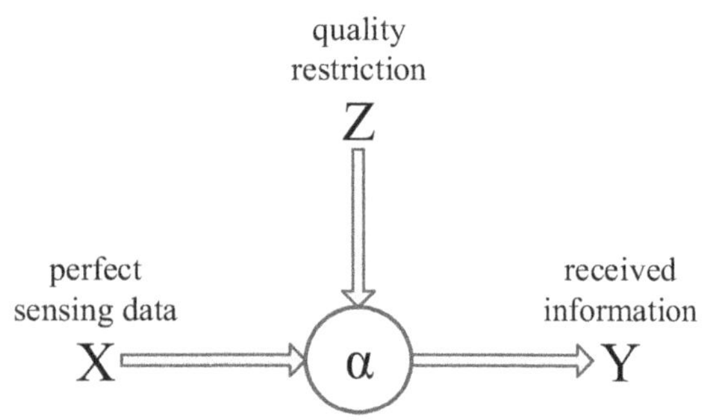

Figure 2: A discrete channel (α, Z), where $Y = \alpha(X, Z)$.

We assume that, in the signal transmission system, the input signal is perfect but interfered by the noisy channel with probability $1-q_k$. Thus, the output signal is equivalent to received information on sensing data of quality q_k. Similar to the capacity of a noisy channel [34], the contribution of the sensing data can be expressed as mutual information,

$$\begin{aligned} I(X;Y) &= H(Y) - H(Y|X) \\ &= H(Y) - \sum_x p(x) H(Y|X = x) \\ &= H(Y) - \sum_x p(x) h_b(q_k) \\ &= H(Y) - h_b(q_k), \end{aligned}$$

where $H(Y)$ is entropy of Y, $H(Y|X)$ is the conditional entropy of Y given X, and $h_b(q_k)$ is a binary entropy for the binary random noise Z with distribution $\{q_k, 1 - q_k\}$.

Intuitively, when no sensing data is submitted, all the m optional intervals are equally likely to be observed with probability $1/m$, making the uncertainty maximal at

$$H(Y) = -\sum_m (1/m)\log(1/m) = \log(m).$$

Given the sensing data, the information uncertainty is reduced to be

$$h_b(q_k) = -q\log(q_k) - (1 - q_k)\log(1 - q_k).$$

Generally, if Z is not a binary random variable, but distributed with q_k in the correct interval and equal probability $(1 - q_k)/(m - 1)$ for each of the $m - 1$ rest intervals, then the information uncertainty is calculated as

$$h_m(q_k) = -q_k\log(q_k) - \sum_{m-1}((1 - q_k)/(m - 1))\log((1 - q_k)/(m - 1)).$$

Therefore, the effective contribution of sensing data of quality q_k, can be formulated as

$$c_m(q_k) = \log(m) + q_k\log(q_k) + (1 - q_k)\log((1 - q_k)/(m - 1)).$$

With the convention $0\log 0 = 0$, sensing data of quality $q_k = 1$ will result in minimal uncertainty, $h_m(1) = 0$, and maximal contribution, $c_m(1) = \log(m)$. Though a binary channel which never makes errors and one always makes errors are equally good for communication, we only consider and reward sensing data of quality within the range $[0.5, 1]$.

Practically, with the same volume, sensing data of high quality carries larger amount of constructive information than that of low quality. Specifically, the high quality data contains intrinsic efficiency, while the low quality data needs extra information, functioning like error-correcting code (ECC), to detect and/or correct errors without resubmission. In crowdsensing, such kind of error correction, is more often conducted in the form of verification, such as recruiting another group of participants or sensing another kind of data (*i.e.*, light signal to determine if the device is out of pocket). Here, we elide the specific ECC and focus on its cost (*i.e.*, accounting for a part of the data volume), and quantify the effective contribution of sensing data as the information uncertainty reduction.

4.4 Reward Distribution

In this subsection, we take a step further and reward the participants proportionally to their quantified contributions, *i.e.*, $r(q_k) = rc_m(q_k)$, where r is a benchmark reward. Noting that we can learn the distribution $f(c_k, \mathbf{e}^k)$ asymptotically, we assume that the distribution is common knowledge.

We adjust parameters of the simple case. From participant a_k with an effort matrix $\mathbf{e}^k$, the profit that the service

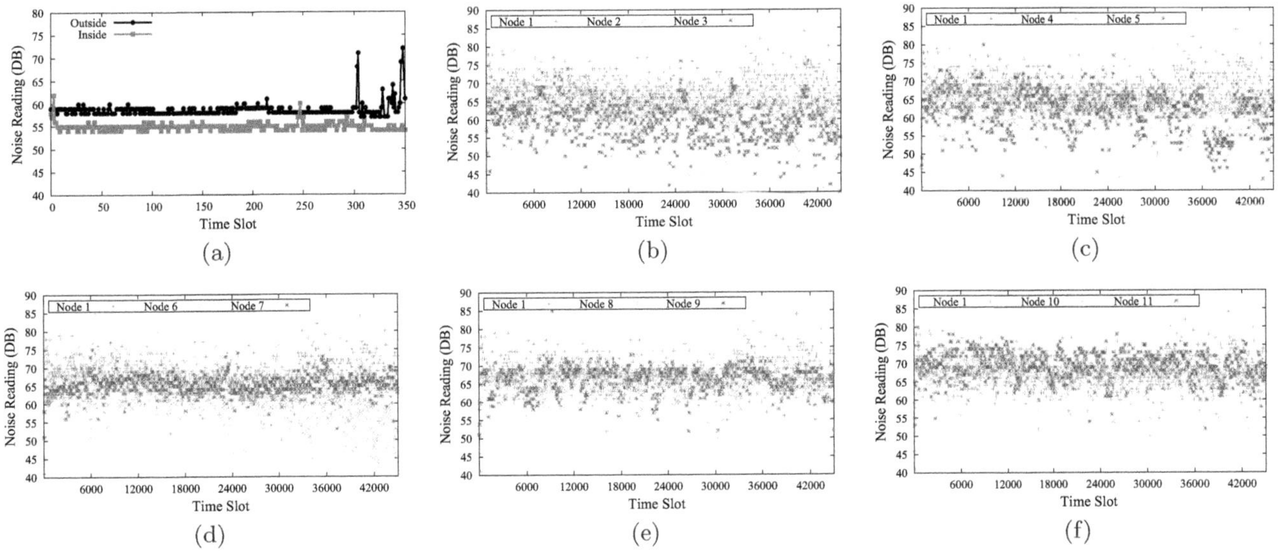

Figure 3: Accuracy of noise pollution monitoring with different effort levels of participants. (a)General noise reading differences between outside pocket sensing and inside pocket sensing; (b)-(f) Noise readings of ground truth (Node 1) and from the 10 participants (Node 2-11).

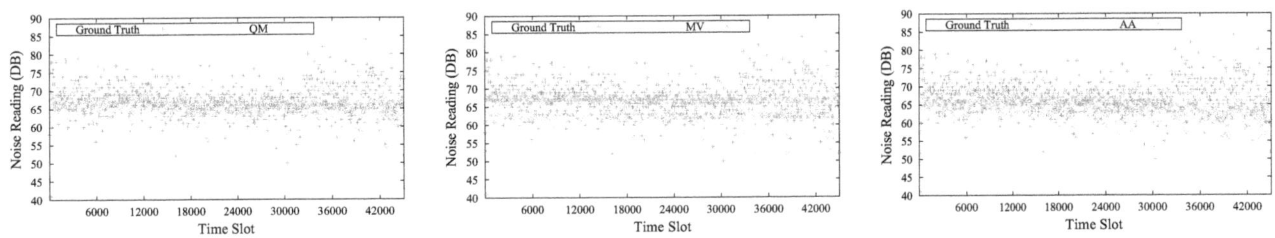

(a) Quality Measured Model (b) Majority Voting Model (c) All and Average Model

Figure 4: Comparison of monitoring accuracy of different models.

provider gains from the sensing data is

$$\text{Profit}(c_k, \mathbf{e}^k, r) = \begin{cases} 0, & rc_m(g(\mathbf{e}^k)) < c_k, \\ V - rc_m(g(\mathbf{e}^k)), & rc_m(g(\mathbf{e}^k)) \geq c_k. \end{cases}$$

Then, the optimal quality based reward is determined by

$$\begin{aligned} r^* &= \arg\max_r \text{Profit}(r) \\ &= \arg\max_r \int_{\mathbf{e}^k} \int_0^\infty \text{Profit}(c_k, \mathbf{e}^k, r) f(c_k, \mathbf{e}^k) dc_k d\mathbf{e}^k. \end{aligned}$$

For simple joint distribution $f(c_k, \mathbf{e}^k)$ of sensing cost and effort matrix, the optimal reward r^* can be calculated by solving the integral equation and taking the derivation of r. However, for complex cases, greedy algorithms can find the proper reward with approximate profit more efficiently.

5. EVALUATION RESULTS

In this section, we conduct simulations to evaluate performance of our quality based incentive mechanism. We first analyze the improvement in quality assurance. Then, we compare our quality based reward mechanism to the uniform pricing scheme, and illustrate the superior performance in profit management.

5.1 Quality Assurance

We install NoiseTube mobile app [1] on Google Nexus 7, and use the embedded acoustic sensor to measure noise in a meeting room. We recruit 10 participants to take part in the experiment, each of which carries a nexus and randomly puts it into his/her pocket or on the table. The participants are well told that accurate monitoring occurs when they put out the nexuses and keep them undisturbed.

The basic experiment is to test whether the participants' effort levels will effect the noise readings. As Figure 3(a) shows, the noise reading from a muffled microphone inside pocket is at least 5dBs lower than that of outside pocket sensing. The sensing data submitted by participants, as shown in Figure 3(b)-Figure 3(f), also presents such reading differences, based on which we can roughly tell the effort levels of participants, *i.e.*, node 10 is sensing with the highest effort level and submits almost perfect readings; node 7, node 8, node 9 and node 11 are 85% accurate with high effort levels at most of the time; node 2 and node 4 are helpful with 70% accuracy; node 6 is careless with high accuracy at first and then gradually slacks off; node 5 is indifferent with half accuracy and the other half deviation intermittently; and node 3 is sensing with the lowest effort level with all readings lower than ground truth.

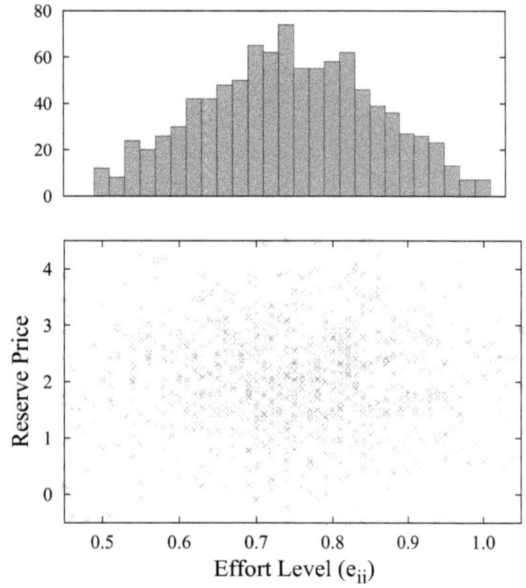

(a) No correlation, $\rho = 0.0$

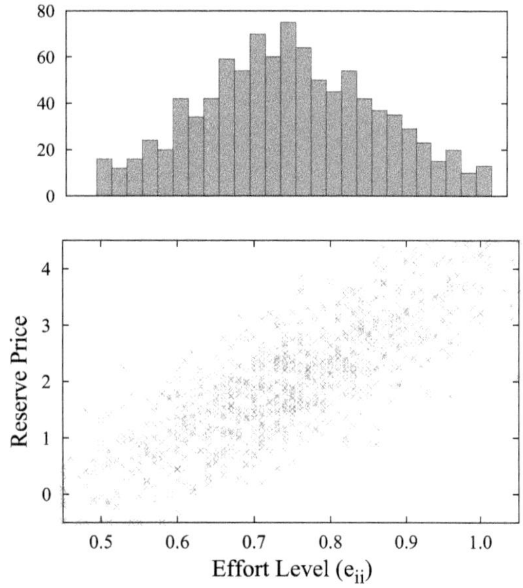

(b) Positive correlation, $\rho = 0.8$

Figure 5: Joint distribution of sensing cost and effort matrix.

Given the reading differences, we compare the quality assurance, *i.e.*, the overall monitoring accuracy, as a collective work from the crowd, in our quality measured model (QM), traditional majority voting model (MV), and all and average model (AA). The difference is: QM excludes sensing data with low quality (*i.e.*, with accuracy less than 50%) and assigns quality-estimated data with different weights; MV selects the most frequent noise interval at first, and then calculates the noise reading averagely; and AA takes in all submissions and figures out the average reading.

Results, as shown in Figure 4, indicate that QM outperforms the other two models, in monitoring the noise pollution more accurately (*i.e.*, the readings keep closely to the ground truth), and more robustly to the efforts fluctuation of participants, especially when careless and indifferent participants take up more than half of the whole population. Furthermore, the MV model may direct the monitoring into a fierce fluctuation when the noise interval is highly precise, which is 5dBs per interval in our setting. Despite a similar trend with QM, the AA model is more vulnerable to large amount of low quality submissions.

5.2 Profit Management

To test the performance of our quality based incentive mechanism in terms of profit management, we first generate the sensing costs and effort matrices for participants, and then compare the profit of our mechanism to that of the uniform pricing scheme.

We draw v_c and v_e from a bivariate normal distribution, $(c, e) \sim \mathcal{N}(\mu_1, \mu_2, \sigma_1^2, \sigma_2^2, \rho)$, where $\mu_1 = 2.0$, $\mu_2 = 0.75$, $\sigma_1 = 1.0$, $\sigma_2 = 0.125$, and $\rho = 0.0$ is set to indicate that there is no correlation between sensing cost and effort matrix (Figure 5(a)), or $\rho = 0.8$ for a strong positive correlation (Figure 5(b)). According to the $68 - 95 - 99.7$ rule/3σ rule [22], the 95.45% confidence interval is $\mu \pm 2\sigma$, which empirically states that about 95.45% data drawn from the normal distribution lies within $[0.0, 4.0] \times [0.5, 1.0]$ in our setting. Then, we transform v_c and v_e to c_k and $\mathbf{e}^k$ correspondingly by setting $c_k = \max(-0.5, \min(v_c, 4.5))$ and $e_{ii}^k = \max(0.45, \min(v_e, 1.05))$, $i = 1, \dots, m$. Therefore, the extreme data is excluded and the rest majority approximately follows the same normal distribution. Notably, other forms of distribution are also experimentally possible, and the exact joint distribution needs to be carefully estimated in practical crowdsensing markets [8].

After getting the joint distribution, we compare the profit of our quality based incentive mechanism and the uniform pricing scheme, where the profit is defined as the difference between the total value gained from the sensing data and the rewards for contributions. We note that, the quality based incentive mechanism gains a full value V from sensing data by providing an error-bounded service, and offers each participant a proper reward based on her effective contribution. In the uniform pricing scheme, the sensing data is regarded equally with the same quality, and the participants are offered the same reward,

$$r^u = \max_{a_k \in \mathbb{A}_t} c_k.$$

However, the gained value is restricted by the actual quality q_k of sensing data, *i.e.*, $v_k = y(V, q_k)$, which monotonously increases with quality q_k.

For simplicity, we consider that there are $|\mathbb{D}| = 2$ noise intervals, and omit the subscript of $\mathbf{e}$. Then, the effective contribution is calculated as

$$c_m(g(\mathbf{e})) = c_2(e) = 1 + e \log e + (1 - e) \log(1 - e).$$

Value function is set to be $v_k = V \sin(c_m(g(\mathbf{e})) \times \pi/2)$, which is concave with feasible $c_m \in [0, 1]$.

We select participants from sufficient crowd, in an increasing order of cost/contribution ratio, and calculate the optimal reward for the top proportion of them, ranging from 10% to 100%. The optimal reward, in our quality based incentive mechanism, is determined by

$$r^* = \arg\min_r r c_m(g(\mathbf{e}^k)) - c_k \geq 0, \forall a_k \in \mathbb{A}_t.$$

Each participant a_k will get a proper reward,

$$r_k = r^* c_m(g(\mathbf{e}^k)).$$

Results, as shown in Figure 6, indicate that our quality based incentive mechanism overwhelmingly outperforms the uniform pricing scheme, in both of the two distributions. The quality based incentive mechanism complies with the cost/contribution ratio to set the optimal reward in every stage, and thus can fully leverage the power of participants to complete the sensing tasks at a low cost, when compared to the uniform pricing scheme. Moreover, with the guaranteed value of service, the quality based incentive mechanism, with higher accuracy and less fluctuation in noise monitoring, is more appealing to the service provider.

The results also suggest the proper fraction of participants that the service provider should try to recruit, which is 80% for both schemes when sensing cost and effort matrix has no correlation, and 80% and 70%, for our quality based incentive mechanism and the uniform pricing scheme, respectively, when the factors are positively correlated. It is reasonable to see such a turning point in profit, from a smooth rise to a fall, since there are always some participants with sensing costs higher than what they deserve to be rewarded according to the their effective contributions, *i.e.*, with unreasonably high sensing costs for subpar contributions. The x-axis ends with 970 (Figure 6(a)) and 940 (Figure 6(b)), respectively, since we have excluded extreme data from the distribution.

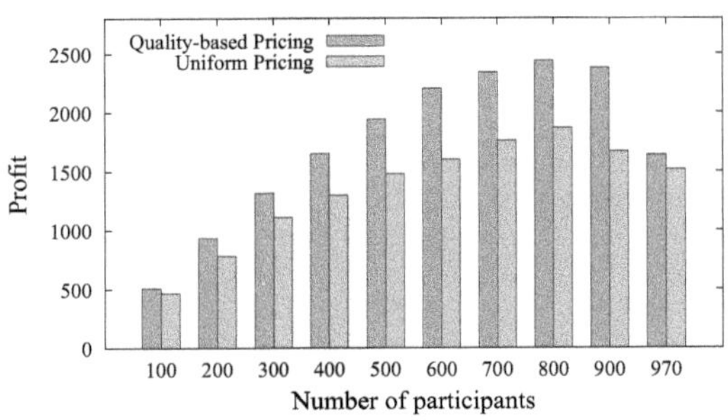

(a) No correlation, $\rho = 0.0$

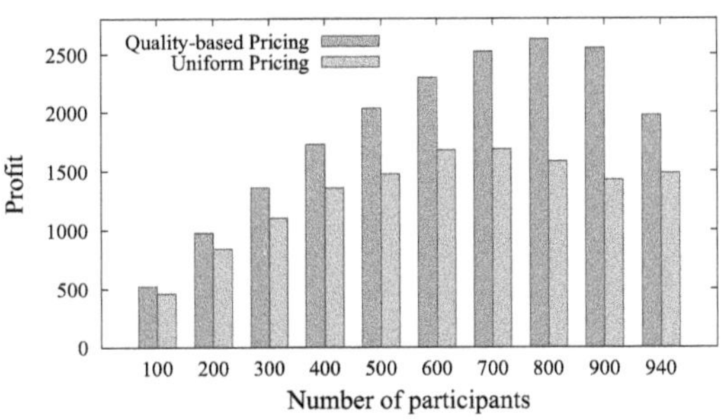

(b) Positive correlation, $\rho = 0.8$

Figure 6: Comparison on profit of different pricing schemes.

6. CONCLUSION

In this paper, we have incorporated the consideration of data quality into the design of incentive mechanism for crowdsensing. By applying the expectation maximization algorithm and information theory, we have bridged the gap between quality of sensing data and proper reward for contribution, and proposed the quality based incentive mechanism, which achieves both individual rationality and profit maximization. Our incentive mechanism estimates the effort matrix for each participant, calculates the quality of sensing data, and offers a reward in accordance with each effective contribution, aiming to motivate individual participants with different sensing costs to place sufficient manual efforts and submit high quality sensing data in crowdsensing. We have also implemented part of the mechanism with extensive experiments and simulations. Compared to the existing uniform pricing scheme, our mechanism achieves superior performance in profit management.

7. ACKNOWLEDGEMENTS

We appreciate the anonymous reviewers, whose comments led to an improvement of this paper. Our shepherd, Vishal Misra, gave us highly valuable comments to improve it.

8. REFERENCES

[1] Noisetube. http://www.noisetube.net/, 2008. [Online].

[2] Creek watch. http://creekwatch.researchlabs.ibm.com/, 2010. [Online].

[3] Opensense. http://www.opensense.ethz.ch/trac/, 2010. [Online].

[4] Noisemonitoring. http://www.larsondavis.com/, 2015. [Online].

[5] J. A. Burke, D. Estrin, M. Hansen, A. Parker, N. Ramanathan, S. Reddy, and M. B. Srivastava. Participatory sensing. *Center for Embedded Network Sensing*, 2006.

[6] A. P. Dawid and A. M. Skene. Maximum likelihood estimation of observer error-rates using the EM algorithm. *Applied Statistics*, pages 20–28, 1979.

[7] D. Hand. Principles of data mining. *Drug Safety*, 30(7):621–622, 2007.

[8] J. J. Horton and L. B. Chilton. The labor economics of paid crowdsourcing. In *Proceedings of the 11th ACM Conference on Electronic Commerce (EC)*, 2010.

[9] L. G. Jaimes, I. Vergara-Laurens, and M. A. Labrador. A location-based incentive mechanism for participatory sensing systems with budget constraints. In *Proceedings of the 2012 IEEE International Conference on Pervasive Computing and Communications (PerCom)*, 2012.

[10] R. Kawajiri, M. Shimosaka, and H. Kashima. Steered crowdsensing incentive design towards quality-oriented place-centric crowdsensing. In *Proceedings of the 16th ACM International Conference on Ubiquitous Computing (UbiComp)*, 2014.

[11] I. Koutsopoulos. Optimal incentive-driven design of participatory sensing systems. In *Proceedings of the 32nd Annual IEEE International Conference on Computer Communications (INFOCOM)*, 2013.

[12] N. D. Lane, E. Miluzzo, H. Lu, D. Peebles, T. Choudhury, and A. T. Campbell. A survey of mobile phone sensing. *IEEE Communications Magazine*, 48(9):140–150, 2010.

[13] J.-S. Lee and B. Hoh. Sell your experiences: a market mechanism based incentive for participatory sensing. In *Proceedings of the 2010 IEEE International Conference on Pervasive Computing and Communications (PerCom)*, 2010.

[14] H. Lu, W. Pan, N. D. Lane, T. Choudhury, and A. T. Campbell. Soundsense: Scalable sound sensing for people-centric applications on mobile phones. In *Proceeding of the 7th Annual International Conference on Mobile Systems, Applications, and Services (MobiSys)*, 2009.

[15] T. Luo, H.-P. Tan, and L. Xia. Profit-maximizing incentive for participatory sensing. In *Proceedings of the 33rd Annual*

IEEE International Conference on Computer Communications (INFOCOM), 2014.

[16] N. Maisonneuve, M. Stevens, M. Niessen, and L. Steels. Noisetube: Measuring and mapping noise pollution with mobile phones. In *Information Technologies in Environmental Engineering*. 2009.

[17] W. Mason and D. J. Watts. Financial incentives and the performance of crowds. *SIGKDD Explorations Newsletter*, 11(2):100–108, 2010.

[18] S. Mathur, T. Jin, N. Kasturirangan, J. Chandrasekaran, W. Xue, M. Gruteser, and W. Trappe. Parknet: Drive-by sensing of road-side parking statistics. In *Proceeding of the 8th Annual International Conference on Mobile Systems, Applications, and Services (MobiSys)*, 2010.

[19] P. Mohan, V. N. Padmanabhan, and R. Ramjee. Nericell: rich monitoring of road and traffic conditions using mobile smartphones. In *Proceedings of the 6th ACM Conference on Embedded Networked Sensor Systems (SenSys)*, 2008.

[20] M. Musthag, A. Raij, D. Ganesan, S. Kumar, and S. Shiffman. Exploring micro-incentive strategies for participant compensation in high-burden studies. In *Proceedings of the 13th ACM International Conference on Ubiquitous Computing (UbiComp)*, 2011.

[21] S. Nawaz, C. Efstratiou, and C. Mascolo. Parksense: a smartphone based sensing system for on-street parking. In *Proceeding of the 19th Annual International Conference on Mobile Computing and Networking (MobiCom)*, 2013.

[22] F. Pukelsheim. The three sigma rule. *American Statistician*, 44:88–91, 1994.

[23] A. Rai, K. K. Chintalapudi, V. N. Padmanabhan, and R. Sen. Zee: zero-effort crowdsourcing for indoor localization. In *Proceeding of the 18th Annual International Conference on Mobile Computing and Networking (MobiCom)*, 2012.

[24] R. K. Rana, C. T. Chou, S. S. Kanhere, N. Bulusu, and W. Hu. Ear-phone: An end-to-end participatory urban noise mapping system. In *Proceedings of the 9th ACM/IEEE International Conference on Information Processing in Sensor Networks (IPSN)*, 2010.

[25] S. Reddy, D. Estrin, M. Hansen, and M. Srivastava. Examining micro-payments for participatory sensing data collections. In *Proceedings of the 12th ACM International Conference on Ubiquitous Computing (UbiComp)*, 2010.

[26] S. Reddy, D. Estrin, and M. Srivastava. Recruitment framework for participatory sensing data collections. In *Proceedings of the 2010 IEEE International Conference on Pervasive Computing and Communications (PerCom)*, 2010.

[27] V. Sachidananda, A. Khelil, and N. Suri. Quality of information in wireless sensor networks: A survey. In *Proceeding of the 12th Annual International Conference on Information Quality (ICIQ)*, 2010.

[28] C. E. Shannon. A mathematical theory of communication. *The Bell System Technical Journal*, 27:379–423,623–656, 1948.

[29] D. M. Strong, Y. W. Lee, and R. Y. Wang. Data quality in context. *Communication of the ACM*, 40(5):103–110, 1997.

[30] J. Wang and P. G. Ipeirotis. Quality-based pricing for crowdsourced workers. In *Technical Report, New York University*, 2013.

[31] Y. Wang, X. Liu, H. Wei, G. Forman, C. Chen, and Y. Zhu. Crowdatlas: Self-updating maps for cloud and personal use. In *Proceeding of the 11th Annual International Conference on Mobile Systems, Applications, and Services (MobiSys)*, 2013.

[32] D. Yang, G. Xue, X. Fang, and J. Tang. Crowdsourcing to smartphones: incentive mechanism design for mobile phone sensing. In *Proceeding of the 18th Annual International Conference on Mobile Computing and Networking (MobiCom)*, 2012.

[33] Z. Yang, C. Wu, and Y. Liu. Locating in fingerprint space: wireless indoor localization with little human intervention. In *Proceeding of the 18th Annual International Conference on Mobile Computing and Networking (MobiCom)*, 2012.

[34] R. W. Yeung. *Information Theory and Network Coding*. Springer, 2008.

[35] L. Yu, P. André, A. Kittur, and R. Kraut. A comparison of social, learning, and financial strategies on crowd engagement and output quality. In *Proceedings of the 17th ACM Conference on Computer Supported Cooperative Work and Social Computing (CSCW)*, 2014.

[36] Q. Zhang, Y. Wen, X. Tian, X. Gan, and X. Wang. Incentivize crowd labeling under budget constraint. In *Proceedings of the 34th IEEE International Conference on Computer Communications (INFOCOM)*, 2015.

[37] X. Zhang, Z. Yang, Z. Zhou, H. Cai, L. Chen, and X. Li. Free market of crowdsourcing: Incentive mechanism design for mobile sensing. *IEEE Transactions on Parallel and Distributed Systems*, 25(12):3190–3200, 2014.

[38] Y. Zhang, X. Chen, D. Zhou, and M. I. Jordan. Spectral methods meet EM: A provably optimal algorithm for crowdsourcing. In *Proceedings of the 28th Annual Conference on Neural Information Processing Systems (NIPS)*, 2014.

[39] Y. Zhang and M. van der Schaar. Reputation-based incentive protocols in crowdsourcing applications. In *Proceedings of the 31st Annual IEEE International Conference on Computer Communications (INFOCOM)*, 2012.

[40] D. Zhao, X.-Y. Li, and H. Ma. How to crowdsource tasks truthfully without sacrificing utility: Online incentive mechanisms with budget constraint. In *Proceedings of the 33rd Annual IEEE International Conference on Computer Communications (INFOCOM)*, 2014.

An Online Approach to Dynamic Channel Access and Transmission Scheduling

Yang Liu, Mingyan Liu
Department of Electrical Engineering and Computer Science
University of Michigan, Ann Arbor
Email: {youngliu,mingyan}@eecs.umich.edu

ABSTRACT

Making judicious channel access and transmission scheduling decisions is essential for improving performance (delay, throughput, etc.) as well as energy and spectral efficiency in multichannel wireless systems. This problem has been a subject of extensive study in the past decade, and the resulting dynamic and opportunistic channel access schemes can bring potentially significant improvement over traditional schemes. However, a common and severe limitation of these dynamic schemes is that they almost always require some form of a priori knowledge of the channel statistics. A natural remedy is a learning framework, which has also been extensively studied in the same context, but a typical learning algorithm in this literature seeks only the best static policy (i.e., to stay in the best channel), with performance measured by *weak regret*, rather than learning a good dynamic channel access policy. There is thus a clear disconnect between what an optimal channel access policy can achieve with known channel statistics that actively exploits temporal, spatial and spectral diversity, and what a typical existing learning algorithm aims for, which is the static use of a single channel devoid of diversity gain. In this paper we bridge this gap by designing learning algorithms that track known optimal or suboptimal dynamic channel access and transmission scheduling policies, thereby yielding performance measured by a form of *strong regret*, the accumulated difference between the reward returned by an optimal solution when a priori information is available and that by our online algorithm. We do so in the context of two specific algorithms that appeared in [1] and [2], respectively, the former for a multiuser single-channel setting and the latter for a single-user multichannel setting. In both cases we show that our algorithms achieve sub-linear regret uniform in time and outperforms the standard weak-regret learning algorithms.

Categories and Subject Descriptors

F.1.2 [**Modes of Computation**]: Online Computation; C.2.1 [**Network Architecture and Design**]: Wireless Communication; G.3 [**Probability and Statistics**]: Distribution Functions

MobiHoc'15, June 22–25, 2015, Hangzhou, China.

http://dx.doi.org/10.1145/2746285.2746287.

General Terms

Algorithm, Design, Performance, Theory

Keywords

Dynamic and opportunistic spectrum access, stopping rule, multi-armed bandit, regret learning

1. INTRODUCTION

Making judicious channel access and transmission scheduling decisions is essential for improving performance (delay, throughput, etc.) as well as energy and spectral efficiency in wireless systems, especially those consisting of multiple users and multiple channels. Such decisions are often non-trivial because of the time-varying nature of the wireless channel condition, which further varies across different users and different spectrum bands. Such temporal, spatial and spectral diversity provide opportunities for a radio transceiver to exploit for performance gain and the past decade has seen many research advances in this area. For instance, a transmitter can seek the best channel through channel sensing before transmission, see e.g., [3–5] for such dynamic multi-channel MAC schemes that allow transmitters to opportunistically switch between channels in search of good instantaneous channel condition; if a transmitter consistently selects a channel with better instantaneous condition (e.g., higher instantaneous received SNR) from a set of channels, then over time it sees (potentially much) higher average rate [6–8]. Similarly, a transmitter can postpone transmission if the sensed instantaneous condition is poor in hopes of better condition later, see e.g., [1] for stopping rule based sequential channel sensing policies, in the single-user multichannel and single-channel multiuser scenarios, respectively. Variations on the same theme include [9] where a distributed opportunistic scheduling problem under delay constraints is investigated, and [2] where a generalized stopping rule is developed for the single-user multichannel setting.

These dynamic channel access schemes (both optimal and suboptimal) improve upon traditional schemes such as channel splitting [10, 11], multichannel CSMA [12], and multi-rate systems [13]. However, a common and severe limitation of these dynamic schemes is that they almost always require some form of a priori knowledge of the channel statistics. For instance, a typical assumption is that the channel conditions evolve as an IID process and that its distribution for each channel is known to the transmitter/user, see e.g., [1, 2, 5]. While in some limited setting such information may be acquired with accuracy and low latency, this assumption does not generally hold. Furthermore, the channel statistics may be time-varying, in which case such an assumption can only be justified if there exists a separate channel sampling process which keeps the assumed channel statistics information updated.

To relax such an assumption, it is therefore natural to cast the dynamic channel sensing and transmission scheduling problem in a learning context, where the user is not required to possess a priori channel statistics but will try to learn as actions are taken and observations are made. Within this context, the type of *online* learning or *regret* learning, also often referred to as the Multi-Armed Bandit (MAB) [14–16] framework, is particularly attractive, as it allows a user to optimize its performance throughout its learning process. For this reason, this learning framework has also been extensively studied within the context of multichannel dynamic spectrum access, see e.g., [17] for single-user and [18, 19] for multiuser settings. However, in most of this literature, the purpose of the learning algorithm is for a transmitter to find the best channel in terms of its average condition and then use this channel for transmission most of the time. It follows that the performance of such learning algorithms is measured by *weak regret*, the difference between a learning algorithm and the best single-action policy which in this context is to always use the channel with the best average condition. Accordingly, the key ingredient in these algorithms is to form accurate estimates on the average condition for each channel.

We therefore see a clear disconnect between what an optimal channel access policy can achieve with known channel statistics (e.g., by employing a stopping rule based algorithm) that actively exploits temporal, spatial and spectral diversity, and what a typical existing learning algorithm aims for, i.e., essentially the static use of a single channel, which unfortunately completely eliminates the utilization of diversity gain[1].

Our goal is to bridge this gap and seek to design learning algorithms that instead of trying to track the best average-condition channel, attempt to track a known optimal or sub-optimal channel access and transmission scheduling algorithm, thereby yielding performance measured by a form of *strong regret.* Our presentation and analysis strongly suggest that such learning algorithms may be constructed in a much broader context, i.e., they can be made to track any prescribed policy and not just those cited earlier or even limited to the dynamic spectrum access context. However, to make our discussion concrete, we shall present our results in the context of specific channel sensing and access algorithms.

Specifically, we present the general framework of such a learning algorithm, followed by the detailed instances designed to track the stopping rule policies given in [1] and [2], respectively. The choice of these two algorithms is not an arbitrary one. Our intention is to use two representatives to capture a fairly wide array of similar algorithms of this kind. The stopping rule algorithm in [1] is a relatively simple one, designed for multiple users competing for access to a single channel; it exploits temporal and spatial (multiuser) diversity, the idea being for a user to defer transmission if it perceives poor channel quality thereby giving the opportunity to another user with better conditions. The stopping rule algorithm in [2], on the other hand, is much more complex in construction; it is designed for a single user with access to multiple channels by exploiting spectral and temporal diversity, the idea being to find the channel with the best instantaneous condition. Both algorithms assume that channel qualities evolve in an IID fashion with known probability distributions, though different channels may have different statistics [2]; both are provably optimal (or near-optimal) under mild technical conditions. For other stopping-rule based policies see also [3–5]. We show that in both cases our algorithms achieve a sub-linear cumulative strong regret (against their respective reference algorithms from [1] and [2]), thus achieving zero-regret averaged over time.

[1]Some multiuser learning algorithms attempts to separate users into different channels, so do exploit to some degree the multiuser diversity gain, see e.g., [20].

The rest of the paper is organized as follows. Problem formulation is presented in Section 2, and the two reference optimal offline algorithms in Section 3. We present our online learning algorithms in Section 4 with performance analysis given in Section 5. Numerical results are given in Sections 6 and possible extensions to this work are discussed in Section 7. Section 8 concludes the paper.

2. PROBLEM FORMULATION

In this section we present two system models and their corresponding transmission scheduling problems. This lays the foundation for us to introduce the two offline optimal stopping-rule policies from [1] and [2], respectively in Section 3; these are the policies our learning algorithm presented in Section 4 aims to track.

2.1 Model I: multiuser, single-channel

Under the first model (studied in [1]), there is a finite number of users/transmitters, indexed by the set $\mathcal{M} = \{1, 2, ..., M\}$, $M \geq 1$, and a single channel. The system works in discrete time slots indexed by $n = 1, 2, \cdots$. Denote the channel quality by $X(n)$, $n = 1, 2, \cdots$. This quantity measures how good a channel is; for example, $X(n)$ could model the Signal-Noise-Ratio (SNR) for the channel at time n. At time n, if no one is transmitting on the channel, a user $i \in \mathcal{M}$ attempts to access with probability $0 \leq p_i \leq 1$ by sending a carrier sensing packet. A carrier sensing period takes a constant amount of time denoted by ζ (slots). The contention resolution is done by random access, i.e. an access attempt is successful with probability $p_s = \sum_{i \in \mathcal{M}} p_i \cdot \prod_{j \neq i}(1 - p_i)$, when there is only one user attempting access. Denote the random contention time between two successful accesses by η; it follows that $E[\eta] = \zeta / p_s$ (slots). We assume the process $\{X(n_k)\}_{k=1,2,...,}$ forms an IID process, where n_k is the time the k-th contention succeeds. That is we assume the samples collected at successful accesses are generated in an IID fashion (as assumed and argued in [1]). Upon a collision, the current slot will be abandoned and users re-compete in the next time slot. On the other hand, users keep silent if there is an active transmission on the channel. For simplicity it is assumed that $X(n)$ stays unchanged during each transmission, which may be justified if transmission times are kept on a smaller time scale than channel coherence times [21]. Once a user gains access right (and sees the channel quality $X(n)$), it has two options:

- access the channel right away for K time slots (*stop*); or
- give up the access opportunity, release the channel for all users to re-compete (*continue*).

This can be more formally stated as an optimal stopping rule (OSR) problem: users decide at which time to stop the decision process and use the channel. There are a number of variations of this problem with slightly different model, see e.g., [4]. The idea is when the channel quality is poor, a user would give up the transmission opportunity so that it is more likely that a user with better perceived channel quality will get to use it. Denote the stopping time by τ, then the objective is to design a stopping rule for all users so as to maximize the rate-of-return, which is the effective data rate for each successful access ([1])

$$J_I^* = \max_{\tau \in \Pi} J_I^\tau = \max_{\tau \in \Pi} E\left[\frac{X(\sum_{k=1}^{\tau} \eta_k) \cdot K}{K_\tau}\right] \underbrace{\longrightarrow}_{\text{Renewal theory}} \max_{\tau \in \Pi} \frac{E[X(\sum_{k=1}^{\tau} \eta_k) \cdot K]}{E[K_\tau]}, \quad (1)$$

where Π is the strategy space and η_k is the k-th contention time and $K_\tau = \sum_{k=1}^{\tau} \eta_k + K$ is the total amount of time spent for each successful transmission.

In this model, we regard the decision process between two consecutive successful transmissions (note that no successful transmission occurs if a user who wins access forgoes the transmission opportunity) as one *meta stage*. Suppose there are all together H meta stages (thus H successful transmissions). We define the following *strong regret* performance measure,

$$R_I(H) = \sup_{\tau \in \Pi^H} E^{\tau}\left[\sum_{l=1}^{H} \frac{X(\sum_{k=1}^{\tau_l} \eta_k) \cdot K}{K_{\tau_l}}\right] - E^{\alpha}\left[\sum_{l=1}^{H} \frac{X(\sum_{k=1}^{\alpha_l} \eta_k) \cdot K}{K_{\alpha_l}} | \mathcal{F}_{l-1}, ..., \mathcal{F}_0\right].$$

In the above formulation, since channel conditions are IID over time, for each meta stage we restart the clock, i.e., we always set the first time slot for each meta stage as $n = 1$. α_l is the stopping time for the l-th meta stage and $X(\sum_{k=1}^{\alpha_l} \eta_k)$ is the corresponding reward. Here we denote by the $\mathcal{F}_l := \cup_{j \in \mathcal{M}} \mathcal{F}_l^j$ the set of observations of channel qualities at meta stage l (with $\mathcal{F}_l^j$ for each user j).

2.2 Model II: single-user, multichannel

Under the second model (studied in [2]), there is a finite number of channels, denoted and indexed by $O = \{1, 2, ..., N\}$, each of which yields a non-negative reward when selected for transmission (e.g., throughput, delay etc). For any subset $S \subseteq O$ we will use $O - S$ to denote the set $\{j : j \in O \; \& \; j \notin S\}$. There is one decision maker (user/transmitter) within the system. The system again works in discrete time slots $n = 1, 2, ..., \tau \leq N$; these however are much smaller time units than those under Model I because they are used only for channel sensing and not transmission. The user sequentially chooses a set of channels to probe for their condition, stops at a stopping time τ using certain stopping rule, and selects a channel for transmission (over a period of time larger than a slot). The decision process thus consists of determining in which sequence to sense the channels, when to stop, and which channel to use for transmission when stopping.

For consistency we reuse the terminology *meta stage* to describe the above decision process between $n = 1$ and τ; this will be referred to as one *meta stage*. Each time a new meta stage starts the clock is reset to $n = 1$. The meta stages are indexed by $t = 1, 2, ..., T$. There is a period of transmission between two successive meta stages. It is assumed that the channel condition remains constant within a single meta stage and forms an IID process over successive meta stages. This is modeled by a reward X_i (to generate $\{X_i(t)\}_t$) for the i-th channel given by a pdf $f_{X_i}(\cdot)$ and cdf $F_{X_i}(\cdot)$, respectively. Channels are independent of each other, i.e., a specific channel i's realization $X_i(t; \omega)$ does not reveal any information for channels in $O - \{i\}$.

The transmitter is able to sense one channel (to observe X_i) at each decision step n with a finite and constant sensing cost $c_i \geq 0$ for each channel i. The system works in the following way at each n of meta stage t: The transmitter makes a decision between the following choices:

- continues sensing; if this is the case then furthermore decide which channel to probe next (*sense*);
- stops sensing and proceeds to transmit (*access*). Under this case there are two more options to choose from:
  - access the channel with the best observed instantaneous condition (*access with recall*);
  - access the best channel (with highest expected reward) from the un-probed set without sensing (*access with guess*).

For the offline problem, due to the IID assumption on the channel condition, the decision strategy at each meta stage t is the same. We thus suppress the time index t; the transmitter's objective is to choose the strategy that maximizes the collected reward minus the sum of probing costs:

$$J_{II}^* = \max_{\pi \in \Pi} J_{II}^{\pi} = \max_{\pi \in \Pi} E\left[X_{\pi(\tau)} - \sum_{n=1}^{\tau-1} c_{\pi(n)}\right], \quad (2)$$

where π denotes a probing strategy and τ the stopping time. From [2], it can be shown for time slots $n = 1, 2, ..., \tau$ at any meta stage t, a sufficient information state is given by the pair $(x(n), S_n)$ where S_n is the un-probed channel set and $x(n)$ is the highest observed reward among the set of probed channels $O - S_n$. Let $V(x, S)$ denote the value function, the maximum expected remaining reward given the system state is (x, S), the problem/decision process at the n-th decision step is equivalent to the following dynamic programming (DP) formulation

$$V(x(n), S_n) = \max\left\{\max_{j \in S_n}\{-c_j + E[V(\max\{x(n), X_j\}, S_n - j)]\}, x(n), \max_{j \in S_n} E[X_j]\right\}, \quad (3)$$

where the three terms on the RHS correspond to the decision options sense, access with recall and access with guess, respectively.

Our goal is to design an online algorithm $\alpha_t, t = 1, 2, ..., T$ based on past observed history $\mathcal{F}_{t-1}, ..., \mathcal{F}_1$, so as to minimize the following strong regret measure,

$$R_{II}(T) = \sup_{\pi \in \Pi^T} E^{\pi}\left[\sum_{t=1}^{T} (X_{\pi_t(\tau)}(t) - \sum_{n=1}^{\tau-1} c_{\pi_t(n)})\right] - E^{\alpha}\left[\sum_{t=1}^{T} (X_{\alpha_t(\tau)}(t) - \sum_{n=1}^{\tau-1} c_{\alpha_t(n)}) | \mathcal{F}_{t-1}, ..., \mathcal{F}_0\right], \quad (4)$$

where π_t is the optimal decision at meta stage t when the information on $\{X_i\}_{i \in O}$ is known and τ the stopping time; $\pi_t(n), n = 1, 2, ..., \tau$ are the channels selected at decision step n of each meta stage t. α_t is the decision actually made at t by the user based on past observations when channel statistics is unknown.

For both problems, if an algorithm can achieve regret $\frac{R_I(H)}{H}$ (respectively $\frac{R_{II}(T)}{T}$) $\rightarrow 0$ then it is called sub-linear in total regret and zero-regret in time average.

2.3 Weak regret

To contrast with strong regret, below we also illustrate the notion of weak regret, a more commonly used objective as mentioned earlier. It is the difference between an algorithm and the best single-action policy that always uses the option with the best average. For instance, under Model II the weak regret is given by

$$R^{\text{weak}}(T) = T \cdot \max_i E[X_i] - E[\sum_{t=1}^{T} X_{\alpha_t}]. \quad (5)$$

This can be similarity defined for Model I, where $\max_i E[X_i]$ corresponds to always letting the "best user" (with the highest average access rate) use the channel.

3. OFFLINE SOLUTIONS REVISITED

To be self-contained as well as to provide certain intuition for the design of the online algorithms, below we present the optimal offline solutions to the scheduling problems in Model I and Model II respectively.

3.1 Algorithm description: Model I

The solution for the scheduling problem in Model I is surprisingly clean and elegant, and can be easily described as follows. Within each meta stage l, the optimal stopping rule is given by a threshold policy [1]:

$$\tau^* = \min\{n \geq 1 : X(n) \geq x^*\}\ , \tag{6}$$

where x^* is given by the solution for u in the following equation:

$$E[X(n) - u]^+ = \frac{u \cdot \zeta}{p_s \cdot K}\ . \tag{7}$$

The corresponding algorithm is straightforward: at each n when a user needs to make a decision, if $X(n) \geq x^*$, a user will transmit and otherwise will release the channel. Intuitively this says that when the channel quality is sufficiently good (as compared to x^* which separates the decision regions for stop and continue), a user should transmit. This algorithm will be referred to as **Offline_MU** (MultiUser) in our subsequent discussion.

3.2 Algorithm description: Model II

The solution for Model II is much more involved; this is primarily due to it allowing *access with guess* as an option, which is very different from classical stopping time problems. In this sense this model presents a generalization. The optimal policy is shown to have three major steps in [2]: parameter calculation, sorting, and decision making, as detailed below.

STEP 1: Parameter calculation, $\forall j \in O$

$$a_j = \min\{u : u \geq E[X_j], c_j \geq E[\max(X_j - u, 0)]\}\ ,$$
$$b_j = \max\{u : u \leq E[X_j], c_j \geq E[\max(u - X_j, 0)]\}\ .$$

STEP 2: Channel sorting

1: Initialize $k = 1$, $S = O$.

2: First compute $\mathcal{R} := \left\{ j \in S, a_j = \max_{i \in S} a_i \right\}$, and then j^*:

$$j^* = \text{argmax}_{j \in \mathcal{R}} \left\{ I_{b_j = a_j} \cdot E[X_j] + I_{a_j > b_j} \cdot \left[E[X_j | X_j \geq a_j] - \frac{c_j}{P(X_j \geq a_j)} \right] \right\}.$$

3: Let $o_k = j^*$ (randomly select one if multiple j^* exists) and set $k := k+1$. $S = S - \{j^*\}$.

4: If $|S| \geq 1$, repeat **2**; o.w. return the sorted set $\{o_1, ..., o_N\}$.

5: Relabel the sorted set as $\{1, 2, ..., N\}$.

STEP 1 is based on a threshold property for the optimal policy proved in [2]. Intuitively speaking, a, b separate the decision region as follows. A state larger than a_j means further probing is not profitable whereas a state below b_j suggests gain from continued sensing. For **STEP 2** we refer to each of its sub-steps **m** as **STEP 2.m** (we will re-use this numbering style in later discussions). The sorting process is straightforward: we start with the full set O and at each step we first calculate $\mathcal{R}$, the set of channels with the highest a_j. Then within $\mathcal{R}$ we further order the channels based on the one-step reward of probing channel j when $x(n) = a_j$ and j being the only remaining channel. The ordering repeats until all channels are in order.

Given the current information state is $(x(n), S_n)$ at decision epoch n and denoting by d_s the solution to the following equation (solution is guaranteed to exist [2]):

$$V(0, S_n) = -c_1 + E[V(\max\{d_s, X_1\}, S_n - \{1\})]\ ,$$

STEP 3 : Decision Making

1: If $x(n) \geq \max_{i \in S_n} a_i$, stop and access the best sensed channel.

2: Otherwise if $x(n) > d_s$, probe the first channel in S_n.

3: If $x(n) \leq d_s$ consider the following sub-cases

(1) : If $b_1 \geq a_2$, then access/guess 1st channel (in S_n, w/o sensing).

(2) : If $b_2 \geq b_1$ or $g_1(0) \geq \max\{E[X_1], g_2(0)\}$, probe 1 in S_n.

(3) : There exists a unique b_0, where $b_1 > b_0 > b_2$ and $g_1(b_0) = \max\{E[X_1], g_2(0)\}$. If $x(n) \geq b_0$: probe 1st channel. $x(n) < b_0$: guess channel 1 if $E[X_1] \geq g_2(0)$; probe channel 2 o.w.

---

where $g_i(x) = -c_i + E[V(\max(X_i, x), -i+3)]$, $i = 1, 2$, and $g_1(x)$ is the expected reward of probing channel 1 facing information state $(x, \{1, 2\})$ while $g_2(x)$ is the reward for probing channel 2.

We denote the algorithm consisting of **(STEP 1, STEP 2, STEP 3)** as **Offline_MC** (MultiChannel) and it serves as the offline benchmark solution for the multichannel scheduling problem.

4. DESIGN OF ONLINE ALGORITHMS

We detail our online learning algorithm in this section. To generalize the discussion we shall refer to the users in Model I and the channels in Model II as *units*. Then for a unifying framework of the online learning process there are two main phases, *exploration* and *exploitation*, described as follows. (1) Exploration: sample the units with sampling times less than $D_1(t) = L \cdot t^z \cdot \log t$ up to meta stage t, with $L > 0$, $0 < z < 1$ being constant parameters. Here L is a sufficiently large (we shall specify its bounds later alongside the analysis) *exploration* parameter. When the unit represents a channel, the sampling process is to probe the channel quality; when such a unit represents a user, the process corresponds to letting the user gain access to the channel to gather samples. (2) Exploitation: execute the optimal scheduling policy using collected statistics as detailed in the offline solution, but with built-in tolerance for estimation errors as detailed below. The sensing results (possibly multiple) from exploitation phases will also be collected and utilized for training purpose.

The above steps are rather standard within the regret learning literature: when a unit has not been explored/sensed sufficiently (e.g., a user has not accessed a channel for a sufficient number of times in Model I or a channel has not been sampled sufficiently in Model II), the algorithm enters the exploration phase. Otherwise the algorithm mimics the procedures of calculating the optimal strategies as detailed in the offline solutions but with empirically estimated channel statistics. One notable difference here is that since the offline dynamic policies involve channel sensing as part of the decision process, effectively additional samples are collected during exploitation phases and used toward estimation. The general framework of this online approach is summarized as follows.

The exploitation phase is intended for the algorithm to compute and execute the optimal offline strategy using statistics collected during the exploration phase. However, due to the estimation error,

Online Solution : A unifying framework

1: *Initialization*: Initialize $L, z, t = 1$ and sample each unit at least once. Update the collection of sample as $\mathcal{F}_0$ and the number of samples for each unit j as $n_j(t)$.
2: *Exploration*: At stage t, if $\mathcal{E}(t) := \{j : n_j(t) < D_1(t)\} \neq \emptyset$, sense the set $\mathcal{E}(t)$ of units.
3: *Exploitation*: If $\mathcal{E}(t) = \emptyset$, calculate the optimal strategy according to steps in the corresponding offline algorithm (with relaxation) based on collected statistics $\{\mathcal{F}_{\hat{t}}\}_{\hat{t}=1}^{t-1}$.
4: *Update*: $t := t+1$; update sample set and for sampled unit j update $n_j(t) := n_j(t) + 1$.

Figure 1: A unifying framework

Online_MU : Algorithm details

1: *Initialization*: Initialize $L, z, l = 1$ and let each user access the channel once. Denote the collected sample for user j at stage l as $\mathcal{F}_l^j$. Update number of collected samples $n_j(0) = 1$ and $\mathcal{F}_0^j$.
2: *Exploration*: At stage l, let $\mathcal{E}(l) := \{j : n_j(l) < D_1(l)\}$. At any decision epoch, if $\mathcal{E}(l) \neq \emptyset$ and let user $j \in \mathcal{E}(l)$ transmit right away. If multiple such j exist, a user is selected randomly from $\mathcal{E}(l)$.
3: *Exploitation*: Otherwise if $\mathcal{E}(l) = \emptyset$, calculate the optimal threshold $\tilde{x}^*$ according to Eqn. (7) using collected statistics $\{\mathcal{F}_{\hat{l}}^j\}_{\hat{l}=0}^{l-1}$ for each user j and following the scheduling strategy detailed in **Offline_MU**.
4: *Update*: $l := l+1$; for user j who accessed the channel update $n_j(l) := n_j(l) + 1$ and its sample set $\{\mathcal{F}_{\hat{l}}^j\}_{\hat{l}=0}^{l}$.

Figure 2: Online_MU

Online_MC: Algorithm details

1: *Initialization*: Initialize $L, z, t = 1$ and sense each channel once. Update the number of channels being sensed and observed as $n_j(t) = 1$. Update the collection of sample for each channel j as $\{\tilde{X}_j(t_j(k))\}_{k=1}^{n_j(t)}$. ($\mathcal{F}_t = \cup_j \{\tilde{X}_j(t_j(k))\}_{k=1}^{n_j(t)}$)
2: *Exploration*: At meta stage t, if $\mathcal{E}(t) := \{j : n_j(t) < D_1(t)\} \neq \emptyset$, sense the set $\mathcal{E}(t)$ of channels sequentially and choose the one with best instantaneous condition.
3: *Exploitation*: If $\mathcal{E}(t) = \emptyset$ calculate the optimal strategy according to steps in **Offline_MC** (with relaxation) based on collected statistics $\{\mathcal{F}_{\hat{t}}\}_{\hat{t}=0}^{t-1}$ as follows:

Online.STEP 1: Calculate a_j, b_j according to the follows

$$\tilde{a}_j = \min\{u : u \geq E[\tilde{X}_j], c_j + \frac{1}{t^{z/2}} \geq E[\max(\tilde{X}_j - u, 0)]\} ,$$
$$\tilde{b}_j = \max\{u : u \leq E[\tilde{X}_j], c_j + \frac{1}{t^{z/2}} \geq E[\max(u - \tilde{X}_j, 0)]\} .$$

Online.STEP 2: Follow STEP 2 of **Offline_MC** but with the following relaxation

$$\tilde{\mathcal{R}} = \left\{ j \in S, |\tilde{a}_j - \max_{i \in S} \tilde{a}_i| < \frac{1}{t^{z/2}} \right\} .$$

Online.STEP 3: Follow STEP 3 of **Offline_MC** but with the following relaxation

$$\tilde{b}_1 \geq \tilde{a}_2 - \frac{1}{t^{z/2}} : (3.3.1);\ \tilde{b}_2 \geq \tilde{b}_1 - \frac{1}{t^{z/2}} : (3.3.2);$$
$$\tilde{g}_1(0) \geq \max\{E[\tilde{X}_1], \tilde{g}_2(0)\} - \frac{1}{t^{z/2}} : (3.3.2) .$$

4: *Update*: $t := t+1$; for sensed channel j update $n_j(t) := n_j(t) + 1$ and sample set $\mathcal{F}_t$.

Figure 3: Online_MC

the executed version has to be error tolerant, e.g., by relaxing the conditions for the steps involving strict equalities. We show how this relaxation is done for the problem in Model II below.

We now detail the online counterparts for **Offline_MU** and **Offline_MC** by filling the details in above general framework. As a notational convention, we will denote by $\tilde{y}$ the estimated version of y, $t_j(k)$ the meta stage when the k-th sample is collected for channel j and $E[\tilde{X}]$ the sample mean of X.

In **Online_MC**, besides the clear separation between exploration and exploitation phases, several relaxations are invoked and the relaxation term $\frac{1}{t^{z/2}}$ could be viewed as the tolerance/confidence region. This tolerance region decreases in time t and approaches 0 asymptotically as the estimation errors decrease as well. There is an inherent trade-off between exploration and the tolerance region. With more exploration steps (a larger z), a finer degree of tolerance region could be achieved. We shall further discuss the roles of z in the analysis.

5. REGRET ANALYSIS

In this section we analyze performance of the online algorithm. We present the main results for both **Online_MU** and **Online_MC**. Since **Online_MC** is a much more complex algorithm and its analysis can be easily adapted for **Online_MU**, as well as for brevity, we will only provide details for **Online_MC**.

Before formalizing the regret analysis for **Online_MC**, we outline the key steps. The regret consists of two parts: that incurred during exploration phases and that during exploitation phases. For exploration regret, we will try to bound the number of exploration steps that are needed. For the exploitation phase, the regret is determined by how accurate decisions are made using estimated values. Specifically, *Online.STEP 1* does not have a decision making step as it is simply a calculation, though we will show later in the proof the calculation of $\{a_j, b_j\}_{j \in O}$ does play an important role in the sorting and decision making process. In *Online.STEP 2* if the sorting is done incorrectly then this could lead to error in *Online.STEP 3.* as all decision making and sensing orders are based upon the ordering of the channels. *Online.STEP 3* has the following error: (1) error in the calculation of a_j, b_js, (2) error in calculating d_s, and (3) error in calculating a set of value functions for sub-step 3.3.

5.1 Assumptions

We state a few mild technical assumptions. We will assume non-trivial channels, i.e., $E[X_j] > 0, \forall j \in O$, so that they all have positive average rates. We will also assume all channel realizations are bounded, i.e., finite support over all channel condition, $0 \leq \sup_{j \in O, \omega} X_j(t; \omega) < \infty$, $\forall t$, ω being an arbitrary channel realization. This is not a restrictive assumption since in reality the transmission rate is almost always non-trivial and bounded.

Moreover denote

$$\Delta^* = \max_{t, i \neq j, \omega_i, \omega_j} |X_j(t; \omega_j) - X_i(t; \omega_i)| + \sum_{i \in O} c_i .$$

Δ^* can be viewed as an upper bound for a one step loss when a sub-optimal decision is made and $\Delta^* < +\infty$ (note c_is are finite). Finally, we assume the cdf of each channel i's condition satisfies the Lipschitz condition, i.e., there exists $\mathcal{L}$(note different from L), $\alpha >$

0 such that

$$|F_{X_i}(x+\delta) - F_{X_i}(x)| \leq \mathcal{L} \cdot |\delta|^{\alpha}, \forall i, x, \delta \, .$$

The Lipschitz condition has been observed to hold for various distributions, for example the exponential distribution and uniform distribution [22].

5.2 Main results for Online_MC

We first separate the regret for different phases. We have the following simple upper bound on the regret $R_{II}(T)$,

$$R_{II}(T) = R_e(T) + R_s(T) \leq R_e(T) + \Big(R_2(T) + R_3(T)\Big) \, .$$

The first term $R_e(T)$ is the regret from exploration phases. $R_s(T)$ is the regret from exploitation which could be further upper bounded by the two terms from *Online.STEP 2&3* of **Online_MC** respectively: $R_2(T)$ comes from the sorting procedure and $R_3(T)$ comes from the last step of decision making. Notice for *Online.STEP 1* there is no direct regret incurred by parameter calculation: the errors in the calculation are reflected in *Online.STEP 2&3* later. The idea of upper bounding the regret by a union bound will be repeatedly utilized in the following analysis. For example, we can show that the regret in each step above can again be upper bounded by the sum of regrets of each of its sub-steps. Therefore we will not restate the details of the bounding for the rest of the proof. Denote the sum $s_p(T) := \sum_{t=1}^{T} \frac{1}{t^p}$. We have our main result for the regret analysis summarized as follows.

THEOREM 1. *There exists a constant L such that the regret for **Online_MC** is bounded by*

$$R_{II}(T) \leq \Delta^* \Big\{ NLT^z \log T + C_1 \cdot s_{\alpha \cdot z/2}(T) + C_2 \cdot s_2(T) \Big\} \, ,$$

time uniformly, where $C_1, C_2 > 0$ *are constants.*

Here L is larger than a certain positive constant which we detail later. It is easy to notice since $T^z \log T$ and $s_{\alpha \cdot z/2}$ are both sub-linear terms ($s_{\alpha \cdot z/2}$ is on the order of $1 - \frac{\alpha \cdot z}{2}$ while $s_2(\cdot)$ is bounded by a constant since $s_p(T) < \infty, \forall p > 1, T$.), $R_{II}(T)$ is also sub-linear and asymptotically we achieve zero-regret on average ($\lim_{T \to \infty} R_{II}(T)/T = 0$). The first term $T^z \log T$ is due to the exploration while the term $s_{\alpha \cdot z/2}$ comes from exploitation. Clearly we see with a larger z (more exploration invoked), we will have a larger regret term from exploration phases; however the regret for exploitation will decrease. The balanced setting is achieved at $z = 1 - \frac{\alpha \cdot z}{2} \Rightarrow z = \frac{2}{2+\alpha}$.

5.3 Bounding the exploration regret

We start with bounding the exploration regret $R_e(T)$.

THEOREM 2. *The exploration regret* $R_e(T)$ *is bounded as*

$$R_e(T) \leq D_1(T) \cdot N\Delta^* \, . \qquad (8)$$

PROOF. Note since the exploration phase requires $D_1(T)$ samples for each channel up to time T, we know there are at most $N \cdot D_1(T)$ exploration phases being triggered. For each exploration phase, the regret is bounded by Δ^*, completing the proof. □

5.4 Bounding the exploitation regret

We next consider regret incurred during exploitation phases, that associated with the sorting (*Online.STEP 2*) and that associated with decision making (*Online.STEP 3*), respectively. Main steps and sketches of the proofs are given below, while the details can be found in the Appendix.

To bound the regret associated with sorting, we have the following result.

LEMMA 3. *Regret* $R_2(T)$ *is bounded as follows,*

$$R_2(T) \leq \Delta^* \cdot 2 \cdot N \sum_{t=1}^{T} \frac{2}{t^2} \, .$$

To bound the regret associated with decision making, we have the following result.

LEMMA 4. *Regret* $R_3(T)$ *is bounded as follows,*

$$R_3(T) \leq \Delta^* \cdot \Big(C_1 \cdot s_{\alpha \cdot z/2}(T) + C_2^* \cdot s_2(T) \Big) \, ,$$

where C_1, C_2^* *are positive constants.*

Combining $R_e(T), R_2(T), R_3(T)$ gives us the main result.

The general challenge in providing the above results lies in relating estimation errors to errors in decision making. For instance, in proving Lemma 3, we first show that the calculations of $E[X_j], a_j, b_j$ fall into certain confidence regions when the number of exploration steps is sufficiently large. This then allows us to bound the error in determining j^* which is characterized by two types. The first is in declaring whether $\tilde{a}_j = \tilde{b}_j$, and the second is in calculating the indices for determining j^* as detailed in STEP 2. Similarly, the proof of Lemma 4 is obtained by bounding the decision errors in each of the sub-steps *Online.STEP 3.1, 3.2, 3.3*.

5.5 Discussion on parameter L

In most of our proved results, we assumed L to be significantly large. We summarize the actual conditions on L below (please refer to the appendix for details):

$$\textbf{(Condition 1)}: L \geq \max\{4, 1/(\frac{\min_{a_{k_1} \neq a_{k_2}} |a_{k_1} - a_{k_2}|}{2 \max_j c_{1,j}})^2\} \, ,$$

$$\textbf{(Condition 2)}: L \geq 1/\varepsilon_o^2 \, ,$$

where $\{c_{1,j}\}_{j \in O}$ is a set of positive constants and ε_o is a solution of ε for $C \cdot (\varepsilon + \mathcal{L} \cdot (c_{1,j}+1)^{\alpha} \varepsilon^{\alpha}) \leq \frac{\min\{\varepsilon_3, \varepsilon_4\}}{2}$, where C is a positive constant and $\varepsilon_3 = \min_{j \neq k} |E[X_j] - E[X_k]|$, $\varepsilon_4 = \min_{j \neq k} |\frac{E[X_j]-c_j}{P(X \geq a_j)} - \frac{E[X_k]-c_k}{P(X \geq a_k)}|$ (we assume $\varepsilon_3, \varepsilon_4 > 0$).

From **(Condition 1)** we know when $\{a_i\}$s are closer to each other, L should be chosen to be larger. Also from **(Condition 2)** we know when channels' expected reward $E[X_j]$ and $\frac{E[X_j]-c_j}{P(X \geq a_j)}$ (can be viewed as potential term when sensed) are closer to each other, again L should be chosen to be larger. The intuition here is that in such cases a larger L can help achieve higher accuracy for the estimations to differentiate two channels that are similar.

The selection of L depends on a set of εs, which further depends on statistical information of X_js (though weaker as we only need to know a lower bound on them), but this is assumed unknown. Following a common technique [23], this assumption can be relaxed but with potentially larger regret. In particular one can show that at any time t with L being a positive constant the estimation error ε_t for any terms (e.g., a, b or $E[X_j]$) satisfy the following, $P(\varepsilon_t > \frac{1}{t^{\theta}}) \leq \frac{1}{t^{\nu}}$, with $\theta, \nu > 1$. Therefore with the error region ε_t being small enough, there would be no error associated with differentiating the channels of the algorithm. Thus there exists a constant T_0 such that, $\varepsilon_t < \min \varepsilon, \forall t > T_0$. Consider the the case

$\varepsilon_t \leq \frac{1}{t^\theta}$. Since when the error happens under this case, two estimated terms (the sub-optimal and optimal one) are separated by at most $2\varepsilon_t$. The probability of the corresponding term falls into this region is bounded as $|F_{X_i}(x+\varepsilon_t) - F_{X_i}(x-\varepsilon_t)| \leq \mathcal{L} \cdot 2^\alpha \cdot \frac{1}{t^{\alpha \cdot \theta}}$ by the Lipschitz condition. Therefore we have the extra error bounded by $\sum_{t=1}^{T_0} \mathcal{L} \cdot 2^\alpha \cdot \frac{1}{t^{\alpha \cdot \theta}}$, which is a constant growing sub-linearly up to time T_0.

5.6 Main results for Online_MU

For **Online_MU** we can similarly prove the following result

THEOREM 5. *There exists a constant L such that the regret for **Online_MU** is bounded by*

$$R_I(H) \leq \Delta^* \left\{ MLH^z \log H + \hat{C}_1 \cdot s_{\alpha \cdot z/2}(H) + \hat{C}_2 \cdot s_2(H) \right\},$$

time uniformly, where $\hat{C}_1, \hat{C}_2 > 0$ *are constants.*

Notice though $R_I(H)$ looks similar to $R_{II}(T)$, they may have very different parameters for each term, i.e, $\hat{C}_1, \hat{C}_2$ may be quite different from C_1, C_2, as well as different constraints for L due to the different statistical structure of the two problems. Again the first term is coming from exploration phases, the second term due to inaccurate calculations of x^* and last term bounds the event that $\tilde{x}^*$ is too different from x^*.

6. SIMULATION

In this section we show a few examples of the performance of the proposed online algorithm via simulation. We measure the average *regret* rate $R_I(l)/l(R_{II}(t)/t)$ and compare our performance to the optimal offline algorithm, a static best single channel policy, as well as that of a weak-regret algorithm.

For simplicity of demonstration we assume channel qualities follow *exponential distribution* but with different parameters [2]. The corresponding distributions' parameters are generated uniformly and randomly between $[0, 0.5]$. Users' attempt rate p_is are uniformly generated in the interval $[0, 0.5]$ (in Model I). The costs for sensing the channels (in Model II) are also randomly generated according to uniform distribution between $[0, 0.1]$. In the following simulation for Model I we have $M = 5$ users while for Model II we have $N = 5$ channels. Simulation cycle is set to be $H = T = 4{,}000$. In the set of results for performance comparison with offline solutions, we set the exploration parameters as $L = 10, z = 1/5$. Later on we show the performance comparison w.r.t. different selection of L and z.

6.1 Comparison with Offline Solution

We first take the difference between the oracle (**Offline_MU**) and **Online_MU** at each step t and divide it by t (i.e., we plot $R_I(t)/t$). This regret rate is plotted in Figure 4 and clearly we see a sub-linear convergence rate. We repeat the experiment for **Online_MC** and the regret convergence is shown in Figure 5, which validate our analytical results. To make the comparison more convincing, we compare the accumulated reward between **Online_MC**, **Offline_MC** and the best single-channel (action) policy, which always selects the best channel in terms of its average rate (channel statistics is assumed to be known a priori) in Figure 6. In particular we see the accumulated rewards of **Online_MC** (red square) is close to the performance of the oracle (blue circle) who has all channel statistical information and follows the optimal decision process as we previously depicted in **Offline_MC**. We observe the dynamic policies clearly outperform the best single channel policy.

[2] We have similar observations for other distributions. The details are omitted for brevity.

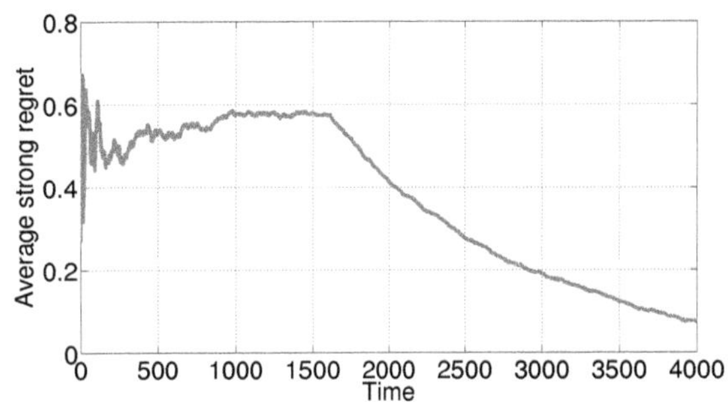

Figure 4: Convergence of average regret : Online_MU

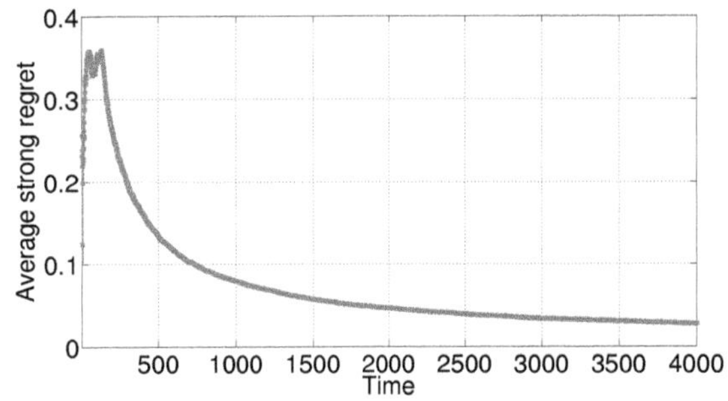

Figure 5: Convergence of average regret : Online_MC

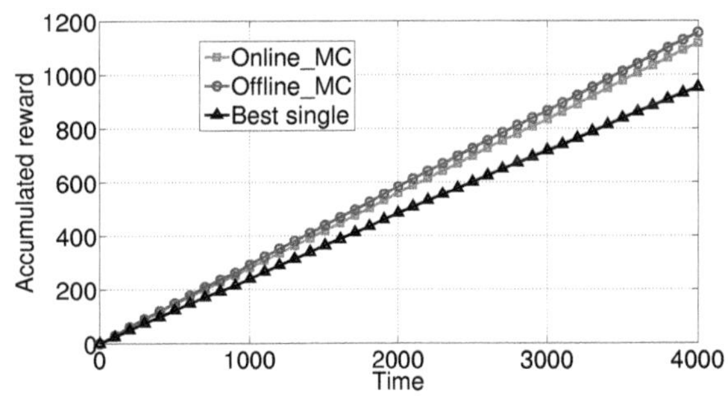

Figure 6: Online_MC v.s. Offline_MC v.s. Best single

6.2 Comparison with UCB1

We next demonstrate the advantages of our algorithm **Online_MC** by comparing it with UCB1, a classical online learning algorithm that achieves logarithmic weak regret for IID bandits [16]. The performance gain is quite clearly seen in Figure 7. It is worth pointing out that there also exists extensive literature in reinforcement learning (RL), which is generally targeted at a broader set of learning problems in Markov Decision Processes (MDPs) [24]. Bandit problems constitute a special class of MDPs, for which the regret learning framework (using index policies) is generally viewed as more effective both in terms of convergence and computational complexity.

6.3 Effects of parameter selection

We next take a closer look at the effects of parameter selection, primarily with L and z. We demonstrate with **Online_MC**. We repeat the above sets of experiment w/ different L, z combinations and tabulate the average reward per time step. From Table 1 we observe

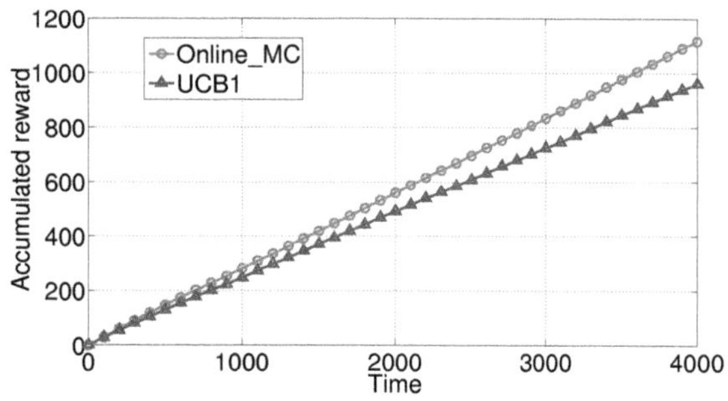

Figure 7: Online_MC v.s. UCB1

the selection of L is not monotonic: a smaller L incurs less exploration steps but more errors will be invoked at exploitation steps due to its less confidence in calculating the optimal strategy. On the other hand, a large L inevitably imposes higher burden on sampling and thus becomes less and less favorable with its increase. Similar observations hold for z since z controls the length of exploration phases jointly with L but with different scale. However it is indeed interesting to observe that when z grows large enough (e.g., $z=\frac{1}{2}$), the performance drops drastically: this is due to the fact in such a case more than enough efforts have been spent in sensing steps.

$L(z=1/5)$	5	10	20	30	40
Average reward	0.3391	**0.3522**	0.3353	0.3183	0.3166

Table 1: Diff. L (Avg. = 0.27 w/ random channel selection)

$z(L=10)$	1/6	1/5	1/4	1/3	1/2
Average reward	0.3411	0.3522	**0.3557**	0.3017	0.1949

Table 2: Diff. z (Avg. =0.27 w/ random channel selection)

7. DISCUSSION

In this section we discuss several possible extensions of the results presented in this paper, concerning the relaxation of assumptions on channel properties. Note that our basic idea and method of tracking an offline optimal (or near-optimal) algorithm by estimating key parameters remain unchanged regardless of the assumptions on the channel model. However, two factors will be at play with more challenging models: (1) Different channel models may lead to only sub-optimal offline solutions, or approximations which may or may not have a performance guarantee; tracking such algorithms would lead to a "weakened" strong regret measure. (2) If the computation of an offline algorithm is complex either in terms of computation or in the amount of information it requires, then this could also affect the effectiveness of our learning procedure.

For instance, throughout the paper we have assumed that the channel quality over time evolves as an IID process, though with unknown distributions. An immediate extension is to consider Markovian channel evolution, which leads to a restless bandit problem which does not have a known structured solution in general. In some special cases optimal solutions can be derived and may take on a simple form, see e.g., the greedy policy under the two-state channel model considered in [25,26], or the LP relaxation approximation developed in [27]. Tracking these algorithms requires the estimation of a set of two-state transition probability matrices, and conceptually can be done and likely will not change the order of the regret bound; however, none of these algorithms are generally optimal so in some cases we could be tracking a target with poor performance. On the other hand computing the optimal offline algorithm even with full channel statistics is computationally intensive (restless bandit problems are known to be PSPACE complete [28], so tracking it becomes non-trivial).

Similarly, throughout this study we have not considered interferences from multiple users; the channel quality perceived by a user is assumed to be entirely the result of factors like fading and shadowing but not interference. It would be an interesting extension to consider multiuser interference, and investigate the effectiveness our learning approach in tracking a certain offline multiuser algorithm. A natural way to design the learning procedure in this case is to combine stochastic bandit learning (for channels availability) with adversarial learning (for users interference). Possible candidates of target offline algorithms include e.g., [29] which studied a capacity maximization problem in distributed wireless network under SINR interference model and showed a constant factor approximation bound compared to the global optimum is achievable, by using an adversarial model to capture the effects of interference, and [30] that proposed a scheduling algorithms for a similar problem but under Reyleigh-fading interference models and showed a logarithmic order approximation.

Last but not least, the assumption that the channel statistics stay unchanged is needed only in deriving the bound under the current technique. It is however not needed for the learning algorithm to work as the exploration aspect of the algorithm is in principle designed to detect and adapt to changes in the underlying statistics. The challenge is in how to quantify the learning/adaptation performance when such changes are present. Some recent results may prove very helpful, see e.g., [31] on a sharp bound (sub-linear) for certain cases when such non-stationary statistical properties satisfy bounded variation [31].

8. CONCLUSION

In this paper we studied online channel sensing and transmission scheduling in wireless networks when channel statistics are unknown a priori. Without knowing such information we propose an online learning algorithm which helps collect samples of channel realization while making optimal scheduling decisions. We show our proposed learning algorithm (for both a multiuser and multichannel model) achieves sub-linear regret uniform in time, which further gives us a zero-regret algorithm on average.

Acknowledgment

This work is partially supported by the NSF under grant CNS 1217689.

9. REFERENCES

[1] D. Zheng, W. Ge, and J. Zhang. Distributed Opportunistic Scheduling for Ad hoc Networks with Random Access: an Optimal Stopping Approach. *IEEE Trans. Inf. Theor.*, 55(1):205–222, January 2009.

[2] N.B. Chang and M. Liu. Optimal Channel Probing and Transmission Scheduling for Opportunistic Spectrum Access. In *IEEE/ACM Transactions on Networking,vol. 17, no. 6*, pages 1805–1818, December 2009.

[3] V. Kanodia, A. Sabharwal, and E. Knightly. MOAR: A Multi-Channel Opportunistic Auto-Rate Media Access Protocol for Ad Hoc Networks. *Broadband Networks, International Conference on*, 0:600–610, 2004.

[4] T. Shu and M. Krunz. Throughput-efficient Sequential Channel Sensing and Probing in Cognitive Radio Networks under Sensing Errors. In *Proceedings of the 15th annual international conference on Mobile computing and networking*, MobiCom '09, pages 37–48, New York, NY, USA, 2009. ACM.

[5] A. Sabharwal, A. Khoshnevis, and E. Knightly. Opportunistic Spectral Usage: Bounds and a Multi-band CSMA/CA Protocol. *IEEE/ACM Transactions on Networking*, 2006:533545, 2006.

[6] Y. Liu and E. Knightly. Opportunistic Fair Scheduling over Multiple Wireless Channels. In *INFOCOM 2003. Twenty-Second Annual Joint Conference of the IEEE Computer and Communications. IEEE Societies*, volume 2, pages 1106 – 1115 vol.2, march-3 april 2003.

[7] M. Andrews, K. Kumaran, K. Ramanan, A. Stolyar, P. Whiting, and R. Vijayakumar. Providing Quality of Service over a Shared Wireless Link. *Communications Magazine, IEEE*, 39(2):150 –154, feb 2001.

[8] S. Borst and P. Whiting. Dynamic Rate Control Algorithms for HDR Throughput Optimization. In *INFOCOM 2001. Twentieth Annual Joint Conference of the IEEE Computer and Communications Societies. Proceedings. IEEE*, volume 2, pages 976 –985 vol.2, 2001.

[9] S.-S. Tan, D. Zheng, J. Zhang, and B Zeidler. *Distributed Opportunistic Scheduling for Ad-hoc Communications under Delay Constraints*. IEEE, 2010.

[10] A. Muqattash and M. Krunz. Power Controlled Dual Channel (PCDC) Medium Access Protocol for Wireless ad hoc Networks. In *INFOCOM 2003. Twenty-Second Annual Joint Conference of the IEEE Computer and Communications. IEEE Societies*, volume 1, pages 470 – 480 vol.1, march-3 april 2003.

[11] X. Yang and N.H. Vaidya. Explicit and Implicit Pipelining for Wireless Medium Access Control. In *Vehicular Technology Conference, 2003. VTC 2003-Fall. 2003 IEEE 58th*, volume 3, pages 1427 – 1431 Vol.3, oct. 2003.

[12] M.A. Marsan and F. Neri. A Simulation Study of Delay in Multichannel CSMA/CD Protocols. *Communications, IEEE Transactions on*, 39(11):1590 –1603, nov 1991.

[13] A. Kamerman and L. Monteban. WaveLAN-II: A High-Performance Wireless LAN for the Unlicensed Band. *Bell Labs Technical Journal*, 2(3):118–133, 1997.

[14] T. L. Lai and H. Robbins. Asymptotically Efficient Adaptive Allocation Rules. *Advances in Applied Mathematics*, 6:4–22, 1985.

[15] V. Anantharam, P. Varaiya, and J. Walrand. Asymptotically Efficient Allocation Rules for the Multiarmed Bandit Problem with Multiple Plays Part I: I.I.D. Rewards, Part II: Markovian Rewards. Technical Report UCB/ERL M86/62, EECS Department, University of California, Berkeley, 1986.

[16] P. Auer, N. Cesa-Bianchi, and P. Fischer. Finite-time Analysis of the Multiarmed Bandit Problem. *Mach. Learn.*, 47:235–256, May 2002.

[17] C. Tekin and M. Liu. Online learning in opportunistic spectrum access: A restless bandit approach. In *INFOCOM, 2011 Proceedings IEEE*, pages 2462–2470. IEEE, 2011.

[18] C. Tekin and M. Liu. Online learning in decentralized multi-user spectrum access with synchronized explorations. In *MILITARY COMMUNICATIONS CONFERENCE, 2012 - MILCOM 2012*, pages 1–6, Oct 2012.

[19] H. Liu, K. Liu, and Q. Zhao. Learning and sharing in a changing world: Non-bayesian restless bandit with multiple players. In *Information Theory and Applications Workshop (ITA), 2011*, pages 1–7. IEEE, 2011.

[20] C. Tekin and M. Liu. Performance and convergence of multi-user online learning. In *Game Theory for Networks*, pages 321–336. Springer, 2012.

[21] L. Zheng, D. Tse, and M. Médard. Channel Coherence in the Low-SNR Regime. *Information Theory, IEEE Transactions on*, 53(3):976–997, 2007.

[22] J. Heinonen. *Lectures on Lipschitz analysis*. 2005.

[23] R. Agrawal. The Continuum-Armed Bandit Problem. *SIAM journal on control and optimization*, 33(6):1926–1951, 1995.

[24] A. G Barto. *Reinforcement learning: An introduction*. MIT press, 1998.

[25] S.H.A. Ahmad, M. Liu, T. Javidi, Q. Zhao, and B. Krishnamachari. Optimality of myopic sensing in multichannel opportunistic access. *Information Theory, IEEE Transactions on*, 55(9):4040–4050, 2009.

[26] Y. Liu, M. Liu, and S.H.A. Ahmed. Sufficient conditions on the optimality of myopic sensing in opportunistic channel access: A unifying framework. *Information Theory, IEEE Transactions on*, 60(8):4922–4940, Aug 2014.

[27] JL Le Ny, M. Dahleh, and E. Feron. Multi-agent task assignment in the bandit framework. In *Decision and Control, 2006 45th IEEE Conference on*, pages 5281–5286. IEEE, 2006.

[28] D. Bertsimas and J. Niño-Mora. Restless bandits, linear programming relaxations, and a primal-dual index heuristic. *Operations Research*, 48(1):80–90, 2000.

[29] E. I. Asgeirsson and P. Mitra. On a game theoretic approach to capacity maximization in wireless networks. In *INFOCOM, 2011 Proceedings IEEE*, pages 3029–3037. IEEE, 2011.

[30] J. Dams, M. Hoefer, and T. Kesselheim. Scheduling in wireless networks with rayleigh-fading interference. *Mobile Computing, IEEE Transactions on*, PP(99):1–1, 2014.

[31] O. Besbes, Y. Gur, and A. Zeevi. Optimal exploration-exploitation in a multi-armed-bandit problem with non-stationary rewards. *Available at SSRN 2436629*, 2014.

[32] Y. Liu and M. Liu. An online approach to dynamic channel access and transmission schedulinge. Available: arXiv:1504.01050.

APPENDICES

Notations

We summarize the main notations in Table 3.

Outline of the proofs and main results

Due to space limitation we only sketch the main steps and results towards establishing the proved theorems. A more complete set of proofs can be found in [32].

Proof of regret for $R_2(T)$

LEMMA 6. *With sufficiently large* $L(\geq \frac{1}{\varepsilon^2})$, $\forall j$ *we have,*

$$P(|E[\tilde{X}_j] - E[X_j]| > \varepsilon) \leq \frac{2}{t^2},$$

Notations	Physical meaning
$M/\mathcal{M}$	number/set of users
N/O	number/set of channels
S	subset of channels
$X_i(X_i(t))$	channel i's reward (at time t)
c_i	cost for sensing channel i
p_i	access attempt rate of user i
$V(x,S)$	value function with state (x,S)
f_{X_i}, F_{X_i}	p.d.f./c.d.f. of channel i
π, α	access & sensing policies
t, n	system (meta) stage, decision step for each t
$R_{I(II)}(H(T))$	accumulated regret up to stage $H(T)$
$(x(n), S_n)$	information state at n-th epoch
L, z	exploration parameters
$\mathcal{L}, \alpha$	Lipschitz parameters

Table 3: Main Notations

and

$$P(|\tilde{a}_j - a_j| > c_{1,j}\cdot\varepsilon) \leq \frac{2}{t^2},\ P(|\tilde{b}_j - b_j| > c_{2,j}\cdot\varepsilon) \leq \frac{2}{t^2},$$

where $\varepsilon, c_{1,j}, c_{2,j}$ are positive constants.

Based on above results we could show

LEMMA 7. *At time t with sufficiently large L, and any iteration steps of the sorting procedure of Online.STEP 2 we have*

$$P(\mathcal{R} \neq \tilde{\mathcal{R}}) \leq N \cdot \frac{2}{t^2}.$$

Consider calculating j^* we have the following results,

LEMMA 8. *At time t with sufficiently large L, the error for sorting set S is bounded as,*

$$P(\tilde{S} \neq S) \leq N \cdot \frac{2}{t^2}.$$

Putting up all terms and multiple by Δ^* we have results claimed in Lemma 3.

Proof of regret for $R_3(T)$

We sketch the key steps towards getting the claim.

Online.STEP 3.1.

At first step of deciding whether $x(n) \geq a_1$ of *Online.STEP 3*, there will be no error when $x \leq \min\{\tilde{a}_1, a_1\}$ or $x \geq \max\{\tilde{a}_1, a_1\}$. Consider x falling in the middle. Make ε being small enough, $\varepsilon = \frac{1}{t^{z/2}}$. As we already proved $P(|\tilde{a}_1 - a_1| > c_{1,1}\cdot\varepsilon) < \frac{2}{t^2}$. Also due to the relaxation of $\mathcal{R}$, the difference between $\tilde{a}_1$ and the true a_1 is bounded away by at most $c_{1,1}\cdot\varepsilon + \varepsilon$. For $|\tilde{a}_1 - a_1| \leq (c_{1,1}+1)\cdot\varepsilon$, the probability that x falls within the middle is bounded as

$$\begin{aligned} &P(\exists i \text{ s.t. } X_i(t) \in [\min\{\tilde{a}_1, a_1\}, \max\{\tilde{a}_1, a_1\}]) \\ &\leq \sum_i P(X_i(t) \in [\min\{\tilde{a}_1, a_1\}, \max\{\tilde{a}_1, a_1\}]) \\ &\leq N \cdot |F_{X_i}(\tilde{a}_1) - F_{X_i}(a_1)| \leq \frac{N\mathcal{L}\cdot(c_{1,1}+1)^{\alpha}}{t^{\alpha\cdot z/2}}, \end{aligned}$$

by Lipschitz condition. Add up for all t we have a sub-linear term.

Online.STEP 3.2.

We first prove the following results.

LEMMA 9. *With sufficiently large L and information state (x,S), we have at time t $\forall\varepsilon > 0$*

$$P(|\tilde{V}(x,\tilde{S}) - V(x,S)| > |S|\cdot\varepsilon) \leq \frac{2}{t^2}.$$

Based on above results we prove that the estimation of d_s can be bounded by a confidence region, which we detail as follows.

LEMMA 10. *With sufficiently large L and channel set S*

$$P(|\tilde{d}_s - d_s| > \frac{2|S|+3}{C_{d_s}}\cdot\varepsilon) \leq \frac{4}{t^2},$$

at time step t, $\forall\varepsilon > 0$, where $C_{d_s} = P(X_1 \leq d_s)$.

(Sketch) The proof is primarily done via analyzing the estimation errors from both sides of the equation

$$V(0, S_n) = -c_1 + E[V(\max\{d_s, X_1\}, S_n - \{1\})],$$

which decides d_s. For bounding the value functions we repeatedly use Lemma 9. Taking $L \geq 4$ and $\varepsilon = \frac{1}{t^{z/2}}$ will lead to our bounds.

REMARK 11. *The above result invokes a constant $C_{d_s} = P(X_1 \leq d_s)$. If $P(X_1 \leq d_s) = 0$, i.e., $X_1(\omega) > d_s, \forall\omega$ our bound is not well defined. In fact under this case, what really matters is the overlapping between $[0, \tilde{d}_s]$ and $[\underline{X}_j, \overline{X}_j]$ (support of X_j). So long as the overlapping is bounded small enough, the decision error is again bounded.*

Online.STEP 3.3.

When $x(n) < d_s$, the optimal decision comes from one of three cases. For the first two cases, we have the following lemmas characterizing the regrets : for sub-steps *Online.STEP 3.3.1, 3.3.2* there are possibly three decisions to make and we have their error bounded as follows (detailed proofs omitted)

LEMMA 12. *With sufficiently large L, (1). if $b_1 \geq a_2$, $P(\tilde{b}_1 < \tilde{a}_2 - \frac{1}{t^{z/2}}) \leq \frac{2}{t^2}$. (2). If $b_2 \geq b_1$, $P(\tilde{b}_2 < \tilde{b}_1 - \frac{1}{t^{z/2}}) \leq \frac{2}{t^2}$. (3). If $g_1(0) \geq \max\{E[X_1], g_2(0)\}$, $P(\tilde{g}_1(0) < \max\{E[\tilde{X}_1], \tilde{g}_2(0)\} - \frac{2}{t^{z/2}}) \leq \frac{2}{t^2}$.*

(Sketch) For error in b_1 in *Online.STEP 3.3.2*, the analysis is the same as for a_1 as in *Online.STEP 3.1* since we already established its estimation error bounds.

For the last case in *Online.STEP 3.3.3*, first notice if $E[X_1] = g_2(0)$, there is no error associated with the last step since guess (access w/o sensing) the first channel and probe the second essentially return the same expected reward. Therefore we show the error analysis when $E[X_1] \neq g_2(0)$. We then bound the error of estimating b_0 (this is similar with proving the bound for d_s and we omit the details for proof) : with C_{b_0} being certain constant, $P(|\tilde{b}_0 - b_0| > \frac{2\varepsilon}{C_{b_0}}) \leq \frac{2}{t^2}$. Moreover we have the following results: (Details for proof omitted as it is quite similar to previous ones.) At time t $P(\mathbf{sign}(E[\tilde{X}_1] - \tilde{g}_2(0)) \neq \mathbf{sign}(E[X_1] - g_2(0))) \leq \frac{2}{t^2}$. These cover all parameters needed for the decision making queries. Putting up all terms we have results claimed in Lemma 4.

A High Reliability Asymptotic Approach for Packet Inter-Delivery Time Optimization in Cyber-Physical Systems

Xueying Guo*, Rahul Singh†, P. R. Kumar†, Zhisheng Niu*

*Tsinghua National Laboratory for Information Science and Technology, Tsinghua University, P. R. China
†Department of Electrical and Computer Engineering, Texas A&M University, USA
guo-xy11@mails.tsinghua.edu.cn, {rsingh1,prk}@tamu.edu, niuzhs@tsinghua.edu.cn

ABSTRACT

In cyber-physical systems such as automobiles, measurement data from sensor nodes should be delivered to other consumer nodes such as actuators in a regular fashion. But, in practical systems over unreliable media such as wireless, it is a significant challenge to guarantee small enough inter-delivery times for different clients with heterogeneous channel conditions and inter-delivery requirements. In this paper, we design scheduling policies aiming at satisfying the inter-delivery requirements of such clients. We formulate the problem as a risk-sensitive Markov Decision Process (MDP). Although the resulting problem involves an infinite state space, we first prove that there is an equivalent MDP involving only a finite number of states. Then we prove the existence of a stationary optimal policy and establish an algorithm to compute it in a finite number of steps.

However, the bane of this and many similar problems is the resulting complexity, and, in an attempt to make fundamental progress, we further propose a new *high reliability asymptotic* approach. In essence, this approach considers the scenario when the channel failure probabilities for different clients are of the same order, and asymptotically approach zero. We thus proceed to determine the asymptotically optimal policy: in a two-client scenario, we show that the asymptotically optimal policy is a "modified least time-to-go" policy, which is intuitively appealing and easily implementable; in the general multi-client scenario, we are led to an SN policy, and we develop an algorithm of low computational complexity to obtain it. Simulation results show that the resulting policies perform well even in the pre-asymptotic regime with moderate failure probabilities.

Categories and Subject Descriptors

C.2.1 [**Network Architecture and Design**]: Wireless Communication

MobiHoc'15, June 22–25, 2015, Hangzhou, China.

http://dx.doi.org/10.1145/2746285.2746305.

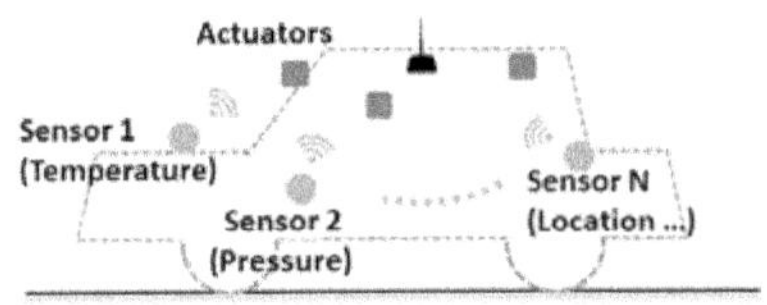

Figure 1: An in-vehicular network with an access point and several wirelessly connected sensors and actuators.

Keywords

Wireless Sensor Networks; Scheduling; Packet Inter-Delivery Time; High Reliability Asymptotic Approach

1. INTRODUCTION

Delay and throughput have long been regarded as important quality of service (QoS) metrics [9, 17, 25]. However, with the increasing deployment of real-time applications such as sensor networks, and surveillance applications over unreliable media such as wireless, guaranteeing small enough inter-delivery times between packets becomes important [14,15,19,20,22]. As an example, consider an in-vehicle wireless sensor network illustrated in Fig. 1. In-vehicle wireless sensor networks have been drawing increasing attention recently since they can significantly reduce the costs, reduce weight of the wiring harness and hence increase fuel efficiency, and are extensible and scalable, as compared to the wired in-vehicle networks [6, 24]. Such a cyber-physical system features several (about a hundred) wireless sensor nodes monitoring processes such as temperature and pressure, and continually transmitting their measurements to controllers which then choose appropriate actuation signals. In these systems, one is allowed to control the arrival process since outdated packets containing old sensor measurements can be replaced by newer packets. Since a large gap between updates can lead to system instability, inter-delivery times of these packets is an important QoS metric. Different clients may have different channel conditions and inter-delivery requirements, which further complicates the problem.

In this paper, our goal is to design scheduling policies that decide which client's packet to transmit in each time slot in such systems, so as to guarantee small enough inter-delivery times between packets.

To penalize severely the deviations in inter-delivery times that are larger than a certain threshold, we consider the exponential cost function,

$$\mathrm{E}\left[\exp\left(\theta \cdot \sum_{n=1}^{N}(D^{(n)} - \tau_n)^+\right)\right],$$

where $\theta > 0$ is a risk-aversion parameter. Here, $D^{(n)}$ is the inter-delivery time of client n, τ_n is a specified inter-delivery threshold for client n, and $(a)^+ := \max\{0, a\}$.

We formulate the optimization problem as a risk-sensitive Markov Decision Process (MDP) [4,5,7,11,12,16]. Though it is over an infinite state space, we show that there is an equivalent MDP that involves only a finite state space. For this equivalent MDP, we then prove the existence of a stationary optimal policy, and obtain an algorithm which determines the optimal policy in a finite number of steps.

The significant challenge of this and other modeling efforts is however the complexity of determining an optimal solution to the MDP, which is excessively large even for systems with a moderate number of states (e.g., a hundred nodes), as is of interest in many applications. To address this critical challenge, we further propose a new approach to channel modeling which we call the "high reliability asymptotic regime". In essence, this approach considers the scenario when the channel failure probabilities for different clients are of the same order, and asymptotically approach zero. We then proceed to determine the asymptotically optimal policy. Such a policy is expected to provide near optimal performance even when the channel failure probabilities are non-zero and range from small to moderate values. Philosophically, this approach can be regarded as similar to studying the high SNR asymptotics in network information theory [2].

In the case where there are two clients, the asymptotically policy has a very appealing structure, lending support to this approach. The asymptotically optimal policy is a structurally clean "modified-least-time-to-go" policy, which is both intuitively appealing and easily implementable.

Our interest, motivated by cyber-physical systems applications, is however in large systems with several sensors and actuators. For this general multi-client scenario, the asymptotic approach leads to an SN policy, and an algorithm of relatively low computational complexity to obtain it. The success of such an asymptotic approach however depends on its performance in the pre-asymptotic regime. We present simulation results showing that this is indeed the case.

The rest of the paper is organized as follows. We review the related works in Section 2. We present the system model in Section 3. We formulate the problem as a risk-sensitive MDP in Section 4, and reduce it to a finite state problem in Section 5. We prove the existence of a stationary optimal policy, and apply the classic risk-sensitive MDP approach in Section 6. We propose the high reliability asymptotic approach in Section 7. In Section 8, we design asymptotically optimal policies by analyzing the high reliability asymptote. Simulation results are presented in Section 9, followed by conclusions in Section 10.

2. RELATED WORK

Li, Eryilmaz and Li [15] and Li, Li and Eryilmaz [14] are apparently the first to consider inter-delivery time as a performance metric. These works analyzed this metric in the context of queueing systems, where the relevant trade-off is between stabilizing the queues and minimizing the sum of the inter-delivery times over all the clients. However, the situation is very different in wireless sensor networks where packets contain sensor measurements and one can simply replace older packets by newer packets, and thus resulting in no queues. Sadi and Ergen [21] have pointed out the periodic nature of sensor nodes in intra-vehicular wireless sensor networks. In another relevant work, Singh, Guo, and Kumar [22] have addressed the issue of trading off higher throughput for better performance with respect to variations in the inter-delivery times. However, this work does not allow tunable and heterogeneous inter-delivery requirements, and a buffer is maintained so as to mitigate the influence of variations in inter-delivery times. Guo, Singh, Kumar, and Niu [8] have further combined the inter-delivery time requirement with the system energy-efficiency. Singh and Stolyar [23] have shown that the service process under the Max Weight scheduling is asymptotically smooth.

The study of risk-sensitive MDPs dates back to Howard and Matheson [11]. There has been considerable work on proving the existence of stationary optimal policy in different conditions [4, 7, 16]. However, Chung and Sobel [5] have pointed out that, in contrast to the risk-neutral MDPs, even with a discounted cost, a stationary optimal policy need not exist for a general risk-sensitive MDP. This introduces an additional challenge to our study. In wireless communications, Altman et al [1] have applied risk-sensitive MDP techniques to design power control strategies aiming at minimizing the delivery failure probability in delay tolerant networks.

Avestimehr et al [2] have proposed a deterministic channel model to study the high SNR asymptotics in the field of network information theory, thus obtaining constant gap approximations to the capacity of wireless networks. This has led to near-optimal and easy-to-implement communication schemes for Gaussian relay networks. Kittipiyakul et al [13] and Zhang et al [26] have also employed such an asymptotic approach to analyze error performance in fading channels.

3. SYSTEM MODEL

Consider a system with N wireless sensors and one access point (AP). Time is discretized into slots. The AP broadcasts a control message at the beginning of each time-slot to announce which sensor can transmit in the slot. The assigned sensor then transmits a packet. The size of a time slot is the time required for the AP to send the control message plus the time for a client to prepare and transmit a packet. It is assumed that the wireless channel connecting sensor n and the AP has a *channel reliability* of $p_n \in (0, 1)$, which can be taken to be the probability that the control message from the AP and the transmission from client n are both successful. The system model can be generalized to take into account more general fading models.

The *QoS* requirement for client n is modeled through a specified value for the inter-delivery threshold τ_n. The cost incurred by the system in T time-steps is modeled as,

$$\mathrm{E}\left[\exp\left(\theta \sum_{n=1}^{N}\sum_{i=1}^{M_T^{(n)}}(D_i^{(n)} - \tau_n)^+ + (T - t_{D^{(n)}_{M_T^{(n)}}} - \tau_n)^+\right)\right], \quad (1)$$

where $D_i^{(n)}$ is the time between the $(i-1)$-th and i-th packet deliveries of client n, $M_T^{(n)}$ is the number of packets delivered for the n-th client by time T, $t_{D_i^{(n)}}$ is the time slot in which the i-th packet for client n is delivered, and $(a)^+ := \max\{a, 0\}$. The last term is included since, otherwise, the policy of never making any transmission at all will result in the least cost. The parameter $\theta > 0$ leads to a risk-aversion problem. The goal of the AP is to decide the client to transmit in each time slot, in order to minimize the above cost.

4. PROBLEM FORMULATION

We first describe the notations used: Vectors will be in bold font, e.g., $\boldsymbol{\tau} := (\tau_1, \ldots, \tau_N)$ and $\mathbf{x} := (x_1, \cdots, x_N)$. Define $a_n \wedge b_n := \min\{a_n, b_n\}$, and $\mathbf{a} \wedge \mathbf{b} := (a_1 \wedge b_1, \ldots, a_N \wedge b_N)$.

The system *state* at time t is denoted as

$$X(t) := (X_1(t), \ldots, X_N(t)),$$

where $X_n(t)$ is the time elapsed since the most recent packet delivered by client n. Thus, the *state space* is $\{0, 1, \cdots\}^N$, which is finite for the finite time horizon problem, but exponentially growing to infinity as the horizon increases. Let *control* $U(t)$ denote the client transmitting in time slot t. The system state evolves as,

$$X_n(t+1) = \begin{cases} 0 & \text{if a packet is delivered for client } n \text{ in slot } t, \\ X_n(t)+1 & \text{otherwise .} \end{cases}$$

As a consequence, the system forms a controlled Markov Chain, with transition probabilities,

$$\begin{aligned} &\mathrm{P}\left[X(t+1) = \mathbf{y} \middle| X(t) = \mathbf{x}, U(t) = u\right] \\ &= \begin{cases} p_u & \text{if } \mathbf{y} = (x_1{+}1, \cdots, x_{u-1}{+}1, 0, x_{u+1}{+}1, \cdots, x_N{+}1), \\ 1-p_u & \text{if } \mathbf{y} = \mathbf{x} + \mathbf{1}, \\ 0 & \text{otherwise,} \end{cases} \end{aligned}$$

where $\mathbf{1} := (1, \cdots, 1)$. The T-horizon optimal cost-to-go from initial state $\mathbf{x}$ is given by,

$$\begin{aligned} V_T(\mathbf{x}) := \min_{\pi} \mathrm{E}_\pi \Bigg[\exp \Bigg(\theta \sum_{t=0}^{T-1} \sum_{n=1}^{N} (X_n(t) + 1 - \tau_n)^+ \\ \cdot \mathbb{1}\{X_n(t+1) = 0\} \Bigg) \Bigg| X(0) = \mathbf{x} \Bigg], \end{aligned} \quad (2)$$

where $\mathbb{1}\{\cdot\}$ is the indicator function, and assuming $X(T) := \mathbf{0}$ so as to recover the last term in the cost (1). Here, the minimization is taken over all history-dependent scheduling policies π. Our goal is to design an optimal history-dependent policy that achieves the optimal cost-to-go $V_T(\mathbf{x})$ for any initial state $\mathbf{x}$.

Later in Section 6, equation (11), we will consider the infinite horizon cost $J(\pi, \mathbf{x})$ when $T \to \infty$.

5. REDUCTION TO FINITE STATE PROBLEM

We denote the problem in Section 4 as *MDP-1*. We now show that it is equivalent to another finite-state problem.

It directly follows from (2) that the DP recursive relationship of the optimal cost-to-go functions in MDP-1 is:

$$\begin{aligned} V_T(\mathbf{x}) = \min_n \{ p_n \exp\left(\theta \left(x_n + 1 - \tau_n\right)^+\right) V_{T-1}(\mathcal{S}_n(\mathbf{x})) \\ + (1{-}p_n) V_{T-1}(\mathbf{x} + \mathbf{1}) \}, \end{aligned} \quad (3)$$

where

$$\mathcal{S}_n(\mathbf{x}) := (x_1{+}1, \cdots, x_{n-1}{+}1, 0, x_{n+1}{+}1, \cdots, x_N{+}1), \quad (4)$$

i.e., the state that succeeds the state $\mathbf{x}$ in the event of a successful transmission for client n.

Lemma 1. For MDP-1, the following results hold:

1) For all $n \in \{1, \cdots, N\}$, and $\forall x_1, \cdots, x_N \geq 0$,

$$\begin{aligned} &V_T(x_1, \cdots, x_n + \tau_n, \cdots, x_N) \\ &= \exp(\theta x_n) \cdot V_T(x_1, \cdots, \tau_n, \cdots, x_N). \end{aligned} \quad (5)$$

Further, the optimal controls in the two states, $(x_1, \cdots, x_n{+}\tau_n, \cdots, x_N)$ and $(x_1, \cdots, \tau_n, \cdots, x_N)$, are the same.

2) The optimal cost function starting with any system state $\mathbf{x}$ such that $x_n \leq \tau_n, \forall n$ satisfies:

$$\begin{aligned} V_T(\mathbf{x}) = \exp\Big(\theta \sum_{n=1}^{N} \mathbb{1}\{x_n = \tau_n\}\Big) \min_u \Big\{ p_u V_{T-1}(\mathcal{S}_u(\mathbf{x}) \wedge \boldsymbol{\tau}) \\ + (1 - p_u) V_{T-1}((\mathbf{x} + \mathbf{1}) \wedge \boldsymbol{\tau}) \Big\}, \end{aligned} \quad (6)$$

where $\mathcal{S}_u(\mathbf{x})$ is as in (4);

3) $Y(t) := X(t) \wedge \boldsymbol{\tau}$ is a Markov Decision Process, i.e.,

$$\begin{aligned} &\mathrm{P}\big[Y(t+1) \big| Y(t), \cdots, Y(0), U(t), \cdots, U(0)\big] \\ &= \mathrm{P}\big[Y(t+1) \big| Y(t), U(t)\big]. \end{aligned}$$

Proof. The proof is omitted due to space constraints. □

Now, we construct a new *MDP-2*, and show in Theorem 1 that it is equivalent to MDP-1 in an appropriate sense. By slightly abusing notation, we still use the symbols $Y(t)$ and $U(t)$ for state and client-to-transmit.

Let us associate a state variable $Y_n(t)$ with each client n, with $Y_n(0) \in \{0, 1, \cdots, \tau_n\}$, which evolves as,

$$Y_n(t+1) = \begin{cases} 0 & \text{if a packet delivered for client } n \text{ in slot } t, \\ (Y_n(t)+1) \wedge \tau_n & \text{otherwise .} \end{cases}$$

Then the system *state space* is $\mathbb{Y} := \prod_{n=1}^{N} \{0, 1, \cdots, \tau_n\}$, which is finite, even for the infinite time horizon problem. The transition probabilities of the process $Y(t) := (Y_1(t), \cdots, Y_N(t))$ depend on the control $U(t)$ as,

$$\begin{aligned} &\mathrm{P}\big[Y(t+1) = \mathbf{y} \big| Y(t) = \mathbf{x}, U(t) = u\big] \\ &= \begin{cases} p_u & \text{if } \mathbf{y} = \mathcal{S}_u(\mathbf{x}) \wedge \boldsymbol{\tau}, \\ 1 - p_u & \text{if } \mathbf{y} = (\mathbf{x} + \mathbf{1}) \wedge \boldsymbol{\tau}, \\ 0 & \text{otherwise,} \end{cases} \end{aligned} \quad (7)$$

where $\mathcal{S}_u(\mathbf{x})$ is as in (4).

We associate the following cost to the system with starting state $\mathbf{x} \in \mathbb{Y}$, when policy π is applied:

$$V_T^\pi(\mathbf{x}) = \mathrm{E}_\pi\Big[\exp\Big(\theta \sum_{t=0}^{T-1} \sum_{n=1}^{N} \mathbb{1}\{Y_n(t) = \tau_n\}\Big) \Big| Y(0) = \mathbf{x}\Big]. \quad (8)$$

The optimal cost-to-go function is,

$$\tilde{V}_T(\mathbf{x}) := \min_\pi V_T^\pi(\mathbf{x}), \forall \mathbf{x} \in \mathbb{Y}. \quad (9)$$

Here, the superscript tilde is to distinguish it from the optimal cost for the MDP-1 in (2).

Theorem 1. The MDP-2 is equivalent to MDP-1 in the following senses:

1) The optimal cost-to-go functions of the two MDPs are equal in each time slot t for any starting state $\mathbf{x}$ such that $x_n \leq \tau_n, \forall n$, i.e.,

$$V_T(\mathbf{x}) = \tilde{V}_T(\mathbf{x}), \forall \mathbf{x} \in \mathbb{Y};$$

2) Any optimal control for MDP-1 in state $\mathbf{x}$ is also optimal for MDP-2 in state $\mathbf{x} \wedge \boldsymbol{\tau}$, and conversely.

Proof. The DP recursion for the optimal cost in MDP-2 is

$$\tilde{V}_T(\mathbf{x}) = \exp\Big(\theta \sum_{n=1}^{N} \mathbb{1}\{x_n = \tau_n\}\Big) \min_u \Big\{ \sum_{\mathbf{y}} P_u(\mathbf{x}, \mathbf{y}) \tilde{V}_{T-1}(\mathbf{y}) \Big\}, \quad (10)$$

where $P_u(\mathbf{x}, \mathbf{y}) := \mathrm{P}\big[Y(t+1) = \mathbf{y} \big| Y(t) = \mathbf{x}, U(t) = u\big]$. Recalling (7), we note that the r.h.s. of (6) and the r.h.s. of (10) evolve in exactly the same way. Thus, the optimal cost for MDP-1, i.e., $V_T(\mathbf{x})$, and the optimal cost for MDP-2, i.e., $\tilde{V}_T(\mathbf{x})$, have identical recursive relationships for $\mathbf{x} \in \mathbb{Y}$. Consequently, statement 1) follows.

In addition, due to the identical recursive relationships, the optimal controls at any state $\mathbf{x} \in \mathbb{Y}$ for the two systems are also identical. Combining this with the first statement of Lemma 1, we obtain statement 2). □

6. THE RISK-SENSITIVE APPROACH

The great advantage of the equivalent MDP-2 is that its state space is finite. Following Theorem 1, we focus exclusively on MDP-2 in the following.

To consider long-term operation, we define the *(risk-sensitive infinite horizon) average cost* under policy π starting at state $\mathbf{x}$,

$$J(\pi, \mathbf{x}) := \limsup_{T \to \infty} \frac{1}{\theta} \cdot \frac{1}{T} \ln V_T^{\pi}(\mathbf{x}), \forall \mathbf{x} \in \mathbb{Y}, \quad (11)$$

where $V_T^{\pi}(\mathbf{x})$ is as in (8).

A *stationary policy* is one that decides the current control (which client to transmit) by the current system state. Thus, it can be described by a map f from state space $\mathbb{Y}$ to control set $\{1, \cdots, N\}$, i.e., the control $U(t) = f(Y(t))$.

We now define the class of *Non-Exclusionary (NE)* policies as those stationary policies which do not serve a client n when the system state $\mathbf{x}$ is $(\tau_1, \cdots, \tau_{n-1}, 0, \tau_{n+1}, \cdots, \tau_N)$. It is shown in Appendix A that for any non-NE policy, either there is an NE policy out-performing it, or it is trivial to obtain the cost associated with it. Thus, we focus on NE policies.

In the following, we use the standard notations of transient/ non-transient states and communicating classes [18]. For a stationary policy f, let $\mathbf{P}^f$ denote its *transition probability matrix*,

$$(\mathbf{P}^f)_{\mathbf{x},\mathbf{y}} := \mathrm{P}\left[Y(t+1) = \mathbf{y} \middle| Y(t) = \mathbf{x}, U(t) = f(\mathbf{x})\right].$$

Further, let $\mathbf{L}^f$ denote the *dis-utility matrix* of f, such that,

$$(\mathbf{L}^f)_{\mathbf{x},\mathbf{y}} := \exp\Big(\theta \sum_{n=1}^{N} \mathbb{1}\{x_n = \tau_n\}\Big) \cdot (\mathbf{P}^f)_{\mathbf{x},\mathbf{y}}, \forall \mathbf{x}, \mathbf{y} \in \mathbb{Y}.$$

Let $\rho(\mathbf{L}^f)$ be its spectral radius.

Lemma 2. Consider any NE policy f,

1) There is exactly one non-transient communicating class, which includes the state $(\tau_1, \ldots, \tau_N)$.

2) For any transient state $\mathbf{y}$, we have, $(\mathbf{P}^f)_{\mathbf{y},\mathbf{y}} = 0$.

3) Assuming that there is only one communicating class (and thus non-transient) when f is applied, we have,

$$J(f, \mathbf{y}) = \rho(\mathbf{L}^f), \ \forall \mathbf{y}. \quad (12)$$

Proof. Since $p_n < 1$ for each client n, there is a positive probability that there will be no packet deliveries for $\tau_{\max} := \max_{n=1}^{N} \tau_n$ time slots, and so system state $(\tau_1, \cdots, \tau_N)$ is reachable from any state.

We now prove 2). From (7), we have, $(\mathbf{P}^f)_{\mathbf{y},\mathbf{y}} \neq 0$ implies either $\mathbf{y} = (\tau_1, \cdots, \tau_N)$, or $\exists n$ and $\mathbf{y}$ such that $f(\mathbf{y}) = n$ and $y_n = 0, y_l = \tau_l, \forall l \neq n$. However, the state $(\tau_1, \ldots, \tau_N)$ in the former case is non-transient, while the latter condition is ruled out because of the property of the NE policy.

Statement 3) is proved by matrix analysis techniques, and the proof is omitted here due to space constraints. □

In the following, we assume that for any NE policy, there is only one self-communicating class. This assumption is not restrictive considering the first statement in Lemma 2, since we at least can simply restrict the state space to the one non-transient communicating class. (In addition, by the second statement of Lemma 2, it follows that there is no one-state transient communicating class.) As a result, the average cost of any NE policy can be obtained by (12).

Next, let $p_{\max} := \max_{n=1}^{N} p_n$ and $\tau_{\max} := \max_{n=1}^{N} \tau_n$. We further denote $K := \lceil \tau_{\max}(1 - p_{\max})^{-\tau_{\max}} \rceil$.

Theorem 2. Let

$$\theta_{\text{th}} := \frac{\ln(K+1) - \ln(K)}{2N\,(K+1)}.$$

For the infinite-horizon MDP-2,

1) There exists a stationary optimal policy when $\theta < \theta_{\text{th}}$;

2) Further, this stationary optimal policy can be computed in a finite number of steps.

Proof. Denote by $T_{\text{Db}}(\mathbf{x})$ the first passage time from state $\mathbf{x}$ to $(\tau_1, \cdots, \tau_N)$, i.e.,

$$T_{\text{Db}}(\mathbf{x}) := \min\{t > 0 \big| Y(t) = (\tau_1, \cdots, \tau_N), Y(0) = \mathbf{x}\}.$$

We first prove the simultaneous Doeblin condition [4], i.e., that for any stationary policy f,

$$\mathrm{E}_f[T_{\text{Db}}(\mathbf{x})] \leq K, \ \forall \mathbf{x}. \quad (13)$$

Note that for any initial state $\mathbf{x}$, the state $\boldsymbol{\tau}$ will be hit if there are τ_{max} successive transmission failures. The probability of this event is $\geq (1 - p_{\max})^{\tau_{\max}}$. Consider the probability that the state τ is hit within $j\tau_{\max}$ time slots, then,

$$\mathrm{E}_f\left[T_{\text{Db}}(\mathbf{x})\right] \leq \sum_{j=1}^{+\infty} j\tau_{\max} \frac{(1-p_{\max})^{\tau_{\max}}}{[1-(1-p_{\max})^{\tau_{\max}}]^{-(j-1)}}$$

$$= \frac{\tau_{\max}}{(1-p_{\max})^{\tau_{\max}}}.$$

This proves (13). Consequently, statement 1) is proved by combining (13) with the Theorem 3.1 in [4].

In addition, since we can obtain the average cost of any stationary policy (the cost of NE policy by Lemma 2 and the cost of a non-NE policy by Appendix A), and since there are a finite number of possible stationary policies (resulting from finite state space and control set), statement 2) follows. □

7. THE HIGH RELIABILITY ASYMPTOTIC APPROACH

The risk-sensitive approach faces significant challenges on the issue of computational complexity: For MDP-2, denote the cardinality of the state space $\mathbb{Y}$ by $|\mathbb{Y}|$. Then, there are in total $|\mathbb{Y}|^N$ policies, each of which requires calculating the spectral radius of a $[0,1]^{|\mathbb{Y}|} \times [0,1]^{|\mathbb{Y}|}$ matrix to obtain the corresponding average cost (see Lemma 2). Further, the classic *policy iteration* technique [18] does not apply to this risk-sensitive problem, which has a non-irreducible structure, and has a communicating class changing for different policies, and thus one needs to compare the cost over all the policies in order to find the optimal policy. In addition, since $|\mathbb{Y}| = \prod_{n=1}^{N} (\tau_n + 1)$, the cardinality of the state-space is exponential in the number of clients, N.

However when the channel reliabilities are close to 1, i.e., the system of interest is in a high-reliability asymptotic regime, and we are able to show that a simple "modified-least-time-to-go" (MLG) policy, which is both structurally clean and easily implementable, is optimal. We note that the high-channel-reliability asymptotic is similar to the high SNR asymptotic in network information theory, see [2].

In this section, we derive some results useful for analyzing the MLG policy in the high-reliability regime. Later, in Section 8, we prove the optimality of the MLG policy in the case of two clients and propose a low-complexity policy for multi-clients which turns out to have good performance in the high-reliability regime.

For ease of exposition, we begin with the simple case of two clients sharing an AP.

7.1 Two-client Scenario and the MLG Policy

Consider two clients with channel reliabilities $p_1 = 1 - b_1\epsilon$, $p_2 = 1 - b_2\epsilon$, where $\epsilon > 0$ is a small quantity and $b_1, b_2 > 0$. Suppose, without loss of generality, that $\tau_1 = \tau$ and $\tau_2 = \tau + \Delta$, where $\Delta \geq 0$.

Define the *modified-least-time-to-go (MLG)* policy by,

$$f^{\mathrm{MLG}}(\mathbf{x}) = \begin{cases} 2 & \text{if } \mathbf{x} = (0, \Delta - 1), \\ \max_{n=1}^{N} \{\arg\min_{n=1}^{N} (\tau_n - x_n)\} & \text{otherwise.} \end{cases}$$

In words, the policy schedules the client with least $\tau_n - x_n$, i.e., "least time to go", in most of the states, and breaks the ties by selecting the client with larger threshold. There is only one exception: When $\mathbf{x} = (0, \Delta - 1)$, client 2 is scheduled, although $\tau_2 - x_2 = \tau_1 + 1 > \tau_1 - x_1 = \tau_1$.

We will show in Section 8 that this MLG policy is indeed optimal when $\epsilon \to 0$. We first explore its properties.

7.2 Regeneration Cycle

In the following, by the *cost incurred in time slots* $t_1, t_1 + 1, \ldots, t_2$, we mean the quantity,

$$\prod_{t=t_1}^{t_2} \exp\left(\theta \sum_{n=1}^{N} \mathbb{1}\{Y_n(t) = \tau_n\}\right). \tag{14}$$

The *regeneration point* of interest to us is defined as the time epoch when the system hits the state $(1,0)$, i.e., $Y(t) = (1,0)$.

A *regeneration cycle* is the time interval between two successive regeneration points. For any stationary policy f, let v_{cycle} be the *cost incurred in a regeneration cycle* (recall (14)), and let l_{cycle} be the *length of the regeneration cycle.* Since f is a stationary policy, v_{cycle} and l_{cycle} are random variables which are i.i.d. in different regeneration cycles. Thus, as in renewal theory, we have,

$$\begin{aligned} J(f, \mathbf{x}) &= \lim_{T\to\infty} \frac{1}{\theta} \cdot \frac{1}{T} \ln V_T^f(1,0) \\ &= \lim_{T\to\infty} \frac{1}{\theta}\frac{1}{T} \ln \mathrm{E}\left[\prod_{j=1}^{M_T^{(\mathrm{cycle})}} v_{\mathrm{cycle}}^{(j)}\right] \\ &= \lim_{T\to\infty} \frac{1}{\theta}\frac{M_T^{(\mathrm{cycle})}}{T} \ln \mathrm{E}\left[v_{\mathrm{cycle}}\right] \\ &= \frac{1}{\theta}\frac{\ln \mathrm{E}\left[v_{\mathrm{cycle}}\right]}{\mathrm{E}\left[l_{\mathrm{cycle}}\right]}, \forall \mathbf{x} \in \mathbb{Y}. \end{aligned} \tag{15}$$

where, the first equality follows from (11); since $v_{\mathrm{cycle}}^{(j)}$ denotes the cost incurred during the j-th regeneration cycle, the second equality follows from the definition of $V_T^{\pi}(\mathbf{x})$ in (8) with $M_T^{(\mathrm{cycle})}$ denoting the total number of regeneration cycles during T time slots, and the third equality holds since $v_{\mathrm{cycle}}^{(j)}, \forall j$ are i.i.d..

Result (15) reduces the analysis of the long-term average cost to the analysis of the expected cost and expected length of a regeneration cycle. Thus, it facilitates the following discussions.

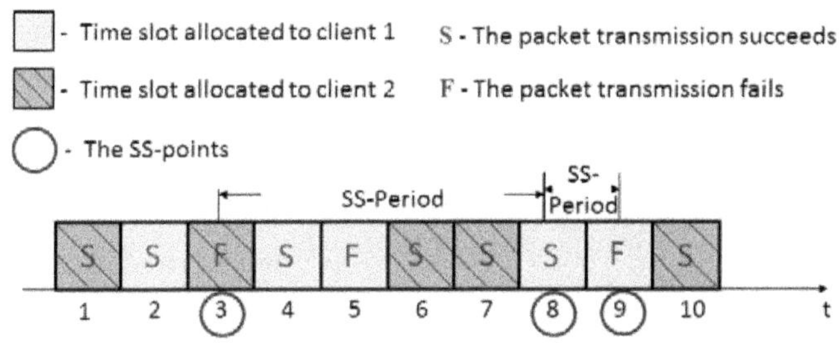

Figure 2: The SS-points and SS-periods are illustrated in a two-client scenario. (We arbitrarily allocate the time slots here just to give an example.)

7.3 SS-Point and SS-Period

Define the *SS-points* as the time slots such that the packet-transmissions in the two successive time slots preceding this time-slot are both successful. See the examples in Fig. 2. More formally,

$$\tau_j^{ss} := \begin{cases} \min\{t : t > 0 \text{ and slots } t-1, t-2 \text{ have} \\ \qquad \text{successful transmissions}\} \text{ for } j = 1 \\ \min\{t : t > \tau_{j-1}^{ss} \text{ and slots } t-1, t-2 \text{ have} \\ \qquad \text{successful transmissions}\} \text{ for } j = 2, 3, \ldots \end{cases} \tag{16}$$

Thus, τ_j^{ss} is the j-th SS-point.

Define the time interval between two successive SS-points as an *SS-period,* and let $v_{\mathrm{ss}}(\mathbf{x})$ be *the cost* (14) *incurred during an SS-period* when the system state at the beginning of the SS-period is $\mathbf{x}$. Under the application of a stationary policy the random variable $v_{\mathrm{ss}}(\mathbf{x})$ is i.i.d. across different SS-periods for each fixed $\mathbf{x}$.

It directly follows that, under an arbitrary NE policy (recall Appendix A),

$$\mathrm{P}\left(v_{\mathrm{ss}}(\mathbf{x}) > 1\right) = O(\epsilon), \tag{17}$$

which is obtained by noting that:

i) $v_{ss}(\mathbf{x}) > 1$ only if for some client n, we have $Y_n(t) = \tau_n$ for some time-slot t in this SS-period.

ii) However, $Y_n(t) = \tau_n$ for some time-slot t in this SS-period is possible only if the length of this SS-period is > 1 (which happens with probability $O(\epsilon)$).

The statement i) follows the definition of $v_{ss}(\mathbf{x})$, while the statement ii) holds because NE policies do not serve client 2 when the system state is $(\tau_1, 0)$, and do not serve client 1 when the state is $(0, \tau_2)$, and thus any possible starting state $\mathbf{x}$ of an SS-period satisfies $x_n < \tau_n, n = 1, 2$.

Further, if $P_{\mathbf{x}}^{(ss)}$ is the probability that in a regeneration cycle (i.e., time between two successive hits of the state $(1, 0)$, recall Section 7.2), there is at least one SS-period in which the starting state is $\mathbf{x}$, then,

$$\mathrm{E}\left[v_{\text{cycle}}\right] = 1 + \sum_{\mathbf{x}} P_{\mathbf{x}}^{(ss)} \left(\mathrm{E}\left[v_{ss}\left(\mathbf{x}\right)\right] - 1\right) + o(\epsilon^k), \quad (18)$$

where $k \geq 1$ is an integer such that $d_1\epsilon^k \leq \mathrm{E}\left[v_{\text{cycle}}\right] - 1 \leq d_2\epsilon^k$ for some $d_1, d_2 > 0$ when ϵ is sufficient small. This is obtained by noting that,

1) A regeneration cycle consists only of SS-periods.

2) For any regeneration cycle, $v_{\text{cycle}} > 1$ only if at least one of the SS-periods included in this cycle has $v_{ss}(\cdot) > 1$.

3) The probability that two or more SS-periods incur a cost $v_{ss}(\cdot) > 1$ is much less than the probability that only one of these SS-periods incurs a cost $v_{ss}(\cdot) > 1$, when ϵ is small enough. The probability of this event being small follows (17).

In the above, the proof of statements 1) and 2) is direct and omitted. It should be noted that the technique of ignoring events having relatively small probabilities, as employed in the proofs of statement 3) and (18), is frequently used in the remaining of this paper. These results facilitate our following analyses.

Now, we consider a *regeneration cycle consisting of only successful transmissions.* Denote $\mathbb{X}_{ss}$ as the set of all the system states hit during such a regeneration cycle.

Lemma 3. The following result holds:

1) For an arbitrary NE policy,

$$\mathrm{E}\left[v_{\text{cycle}}\right] \geq 1 + \sum_{\mathbf{x} \in \mathbb{X}_{ss}} \left(\mathrm{E}\left[v_{ss}\left(\mathbf{x}\right)\right] - 1\right) + o(\epsilon^k), \quad (19)$$

where k is an integer such that $d_1\epsilon^k \leq \mathrm{E}\left[v_{\text{cycle}}\right] - 1 \leq d_2\epsilon^k$ for some $d_1, d_2 > 0$ when ϵ is sufficient small.

2) When the MLG policy is applied,

$$\mathrm{E}\left[v_{\text{cycle}}\right] = 1 + \sum_{\mathbf{x} \in \mathbb{X}_{ss}} \left(\mathrm{E}\left[v_{ss}\left(\mathbf{x}\right)\right] - 1\right) + o(\epsilon^k), \quad (20)$$

where k is similarly defined as for (19).

3) Further, when the MLG policy is applied, and if $\Delta \geq 2$,

$$\mathbb{X}_{ss} = \{(1, 0), (0, x_2), \forall x_2 = 0, \cdots, \Delta - 1\} \quad (21)$$
$$\mathrm{E}[l_{\text{cycle}}] = \Delta + O(\epsilon); \quad (22)$$
$$\mathrm{E}[v_{ss}(1, 0)] = 1 + b_1^{\tau-1}\epsilon^{\tau-1}\left(\exp(\theta) - 1\right) + O(\epsilon^\tau), \quad (23)$$
$$\mathrm{E}[v_{ss}(0, x_2)] = 1 + O(\epsilon^\tau), \forall x_2 = 0, \cdots, \Delta - 1. \quad (24)$$

Similar results can be obtained for $\Delta = 0, 1$.

Proof. These results follow from (17), (18), and the definition of $\mathbb{X}_{ss}$. The proof is straightforward, and the details are omitted. □

8. ASYMPTOTICALLY OPTIMAL POLICIES

8.1 The Two-Client Scenario

Consider the case where there are two-clients sharing an AP, with channel reliabilities $p_1 = 1 - b_1\epsilon$, $p_2 = 1 - b_2\epsilon$, and thresholds $\tau_1 = \tau$, $\tau_2 = \tau + \Delta$. Without loss of generality assume $\Delta \geq 0$. Recall the definition of the MLG policy in Section 7.1, and note that $b_1, b_2, \epsilon > 0$. The following theorem establishes the optimality of the MLG policy.

Theorem 3. The following results hold:

1) The risk-sensitive cost under MLG policy is, $\forall \mathbf{x}$,

$$J(f^{\text{MLG}}, \mathbf{x}) = \begin{cases} A_0\epsilon^{\tau-1} + O(\epsilon^\tau) & \text{if } \Delta = 0 \\ \frac{e^\theta - 1}{2\theta}\epsilon^{\tau-1}\sum_{j=0}^{\tau-1} b_1^j b_2^{\tau-1-j} + O(\epsilon^\tau) & \text{if } \Delta = 1 \\ \frac{e^\theta - 1}{\theta\Delta} b_1^{\tau-1}\epsilon^{\tau-1} + O(\epsilon^\tau) & \text{if } \Delta \geq 2 \end{cases}$$

where

$$A_0 = \frac{e^\theta - 1}{\theta}\sum_{j=1}^{\tau-2} b_1^j b_2^{\tau-1-j} + \frac{b_1^{\tau-1} + b_2^{\tau-1}}{2\theta}\left(e^2 - 1\right).$$

2) The optimal cost $J^\star(\mathbf{x}) := \min_f J(f, \mathbf{x})$ has a lower bound,

$$J^\star(\mathbf{x}) \geq \begin{cases} A_0\epsilon^{\tau-1} + o(\epsilon^{\tau-1}) & \text{if } \Delta = 0 \\ \frac{e^\theta - 1}{2\theta} A_1\epsilon^{\tau-1} + o(\epsilon^{\tau-1}) & \text{if } \Delta = 1 \\ \frac{e^\theta - 1}{\theta} A_2\epsilon^{\tau-1} + o(\epsilon^{\tau-1}) & \text{if } \Delta \geq 2 \end{cases}$$

where

A_0 is as in the statement above

$$b_{\min} := \min\{b_1, b_2\}$$
$$A_1 := b_1^{\tau-1} + (\tau - 1)\, b_{\min}^{\tau-1}$$
$$A_2 := \min\left\{\frac{b_1^{\tau-1}}{\Delta}, \frac{b_1^{\tau-1} + (\tau_1 - 1)b_{\min}^{\tau-1}}{\Delta + 1}, \frac{b_1^{\tau-1} + (\tau_1 - 1)b_{\min}^{\tau-1} + \sum_{j=1}^{\tau-1} b_2^j b_1^{\tau-1-j}}{\Delta + 2}\right\}.$$

3) Thus, it follows from 1) and 2) above that the MLG policy is optimal in the high reliability asymptotic regime (i.e., small ϵ) if any of the following conditions is satisfied:

(i) $\Delta = 0$; (ii) $\Delta = 1$, and $b_1 \leq b_2$; (iii) $\Delta \geq 2$, and $b_1^{\tau-1} \leq \Delta(\tau - 1)b_2^{\tau-1}$.

Proof. We will only consider the case when $\Delta \geq 2$, since the analyses for the cases when $\Delta = 1$ or 0 follows similar arguments.

By Lemma 3, under the application of the MLG policy, we have,

$$\mathrm{E}[v_{\text{cycle}}] = 1 + b_1^{\tau-1}\epsilon^{\tau-1}\big(\exp(\theta) - 1\big) + O(\epsilon^\tau). \quad (25)$$

Thus, statement 1) follows by combining (15), (22) and (25).

To prove statement 2), we begin by deriving the lower bound of $\mathrm{E}[v_{ss}(\mathbf{x})]$ for any system state $\mathbf{x}$ of the form $(\cdot, 0)$ or $(0, \cdot)$. Note that, any possible starting state of an SS-period is of this form. In the following, we focus on the analysis of $\mathrm{E}[v_{\mathrm{ss}}(1,0)]$, since the analysis of the cost for the SS-period starting with any other state follows similar arguments.

Consider the evolution of system over an SS-period starting with state $(1,0)$ under the application of an arbitrary stationary policy. Then we have the following two possibilities,

(a) The policy serves client 2 before the earlier of these two events: *i*) a successful packet delivery for client 1, *ii*) the system hits the value $(\tau, \tau-1)$. Under such a policy, it can be shown that a cost $v_{\mathrm{ss}}(1,0) > 1$ is incurred with a probability $> d\epsilon^{\tau-2}$ for some $d > 0$.

(b) The policy does not serve client 2 before the earlier of the following two events: *i*) a successful packet delivery for client 1, *ii*) the system hits the value $(\tau, \tau-1)$. Then, if failures occur in all of the first $\tau-1$ time slots for the SS-period, the state $(\tau, \tau-1)$ will be hit. Thus, a cost $v_{\mathrm{ss}}(1,0) \geq \exp(\theta)$ is incurred with a probability $\geq b_1^{\tau-1}\epsilon^{\tau-1}$.

Consequently it follows from a) and b) above,

$$\mathrm{E}[v_{\mathrm{ss}}(1,0)] \geq 1 + b_1^{\tau-1}\epsilon^{\tau-1} + o(\epsilon^{\tau-1}).$$

Similar arguments lead us to conclude the following lower bounds on $\mathrm{E}[v_{\mathrm{ss}}(\mathbf{x})]$ under the application of an arbitrary stationary policy, (recall that $\mathbf{x}$ should be of the form $(0,\cdot)$ or $(\cdot,0)$ since it is a possible starting state of an SS-period)

i. $\forall \mathbf{x} \in \{(0,x_2)|x_2 \leq \Delta - 1\}$, $\mathrm{E}[v_{\mathrm{ss}}(\mathbf{x})] \geq 1$.

ii. $\forall \mathbf{x} \in \{(0,x_2)|x_2 \geq \Delta + 2\} \bigcup \{(x_1,0)|x_1 \geq 2\}$, $\mathrm{E}[v_{\mathrm{ss}}(\mathbf{x})] \geq 1 + d\epsilon^{\tau-2} + o(\epsilon^{\tau-2})$, with some $d > 0$.

iii. $\mathrm{E}[v_{\mathrm{ss}}(1,0)] \geq 1 + b_1^{\tau-1}\epsilon^{\tau-1}(\exp(\theta)-1) + o(\epsilon^{\tau-1})$.

iv. $\mathrm{E}[v_{\mathrm{ss}}(0,\Delta+1)] \geq 1 + \sum_{j=1}^{\tau-1} b_2^j b_1^{\tau-1-j}\epsilon^{\tau-1} + o(\epsilon^{\tau-1})$.

v. $\mathrm{E}[v_{\mathrm{ss}}(0,\Delta)] \geq 1 + (\tau-1)b_{\min}^{\tau-1}\epsilon^{\tau-1} + o(\epsilon^{\tau-1})$.

By combining these results with the inequality (19) and using equation (15), we obtain the second statement.

The third statement is a simple consequence of the first two statements. □

In Theorem 3, the first statement characterizes the risk-sensitive cost of the MLG policy, while the second provides a lower bound on the cost for any stationary policy. The third statement provides three sufficient conditions under which the MLG policy is asymptotically optimal. These conditions are related to the difference between the inter-delivery thresholds for different clients, and the difference in their relative failure probabilities.

8.2 The General Case: N Clients in the High-Reliability Regime

Now, we consider the general case where there are N clients sharing an AP, with the channel reliability of the n-th client being $p_n = 1 - b_n\epsilon$, where $\epsilon > 0$ is a small quantity and $b_n > 0$. The inter-delivery threshold of client n is τ_n. It is assumed that $N \leq \tau_1 \leq \tau_2 \leq \cdots \leq \tau_N$, with out loss of generality.

Since Theorem 2 implies that there exists a stationary policy that is optimal for the MDP-2, we focus exclusively on stationary policies. Now, we obtain characterization of the optimal policy.

We define a *regeneration point* as the time epoch when the system hits the state $(0,1,\cdots,N-1)$, i.e., time t is a regeneration point iff. $Y(t) = (0,1,\cdots,N-1)$. (Recall that for the case of 2 clients as discussed in Section 7.2, the regeneration point is the epoch when the state $(1,0)$ is hit.) The *regeneration cycle* is the time interval between two successive regeneration points. Now, consider a *regeneration cycle consisting of only successful transmissions*, and denote by $\mathbb{X}_{\mathrm{sN}}$ the sequence of system states hit during such a regeneration cycle. Note that $\mathbb{X}_{\mathrm{sN}}$ is a deterministic sequence with a given stationary policy. Let $|\mathbb{X}_{\mathrm{sN}}|$ be the length of this sequence, and $\mathbb{X}_{\mathrm{sN}}(j)$ be the j-th state in this sequence.

We also define an *SN-point* as the time slot when the packet transmissions in the N successive time slots preceding this time-slot are all successful. (This is similar to the definition of SS-point, in (16).) The *SN-period* is the time interval between two successive SN-points, and let $v_{\mathrm{sN}}(\mathbf{x})$ denote the cost (14) incurred during an SN-period when the system state at the beginning of the SN-period is $\mathbf{x}$, similar to the two-client case.

We further consider a time interval comprising of no less than N time-slots, which starts when the system state assumes the value $\mathbf{x}$ and ends when the nearest SN-point (such that the length of the period $\geq N$) is hit. Denote by $\tilde{v}_{\mathrm{sN}}(\mathbf{x})$ the cost (14) incurred during such a period. (Note that this is different from $v_{\mathrm{sN}}(\mathbf{x})$ because $v_{\mathrm{sN}}(\mathbf{x})$ is the cost incurred during an SN-period, and that an SN-period may have a length strictly less than N. An example of SN-period with length 1 is shown in Fig. 2 for the two-client scenario.)

Lemma 4. The optimal policy is a member of the set,

$$\{f : J(f,\mathbf{x}) = O(\epsilon), \forall \mathbf{x} \in \mathbb{Y}\}.$$

Further, for any policy f in this set, the following results hold:

1) The risk-sensitive cost is,

$$J(f,\mathbf{x}) = \frac{1}{|\mathbb{X}_{\mathrm{sN}}|}\sum_{j=1}^{|\mathbb{X}_{\mathrm{sN}}|}\left(\mathrm{E}\left[v_{\mathrm{sN}}(\mathbb{X}_{\mathrm{sN}}(j))\right]-1\right) + o(\epsilon^k), \tag{26}$$

for any system state $\mathbf{x}$, where $k \geq 1$ is an integer such that $d_1\epsilon^k \leq J(f,\mathbf{x}) \leq d_2\epsilon^k$ for some $d_1, d_2 > 0$ when ϵ is sufficient small.

2) For any possible starting state $\mathbf{x}$ of an SN-period, we have,

$$\mathrm{E}[\tilde{v}_{\mathrm{sN}}(\mathbf{x})] = 1 + \sum_{j=0}^{N-1}\left(\mathrm{E}\left[v_{\mathrm{sN}}(\mathcal{S}^j(\mathbf{x}))\right]-1\right) + o(\epsilon^k), \tag{27}$$

where $\mathcal{S}^1(\mathbf{x})$ is the state that succeeds state $\mathbf{x}$ in the event of a successful transmission when policy f is applied, i.e.,

$$\mathcal{S}^1(\mathbf{x}) := (x_1+1,\cdots,x_{f(\mathbf{x})-1}+1, 0, x_{f(\mathbf{x})+1}+1,\cdots,x_N+1)\wedge\tau;$$

$$\text{also } \mathcal{S}^{j+1}(\mathbf{x}) := \mathcal{S}\left(\mathcal{S}^j(\mathbf{x})\right), j = 1,2,\cdots; \mathcal{S}^0(\mathbf{x}) := \mathbf{x},$$

and k is an integer such that $d_1\epsilon^k \leq \mathrm{E}\left[\tilde{v}_{\mathrm{sN}}(\mathbf{x})\right] - 1 \leq d_2\epsilon^k$ for some $d_1, d_2 > 0$ when ϵ is sufficient small.

Proof. The results are obtained using arguments similar to the case of two-clients in the high reliability regime (See Section 7.2, 7.3, equations (15) (17) (18) (19)). □

One may note that the r.h.s. of (27) is closely related to the r.h.s. of (26), by noting that $\mathcal{S}^j(\mathbb{X}_{\text{sN}}(1)) = \mathbb{X}_{\text{sN}}(j+1), \forall j = 1, \cdots, |\mathbb{X}_{\text{sN}}|-1$, and that $|\mathbb{X}_{\text{sN}}| \geq N$ holds whatever policy is applied. Thus, the following assumption is not restrictive.

Assumption 1. A stationary policy that minimizes $\mathrm{E}[\tilde{v}_{\text{sN}}(\mathbf{x})]$ for each system state $\mathrm{x} \in \mathbb{Y}$, also minimizes $J(f, \mathrm{x})$.

Algorithm 1: SN Policy Algorithm

input : $N, \theta, \tau_1, \cdots, \tau_N, b_1, \cdots, b_N$.
output: Policy $g(\mathbf{x}), \forall \mathbf{x} \in \mathbb{Y}$.

1 $\mathbb{Y}_0 = \{\mathbf{x} : \exists A > 0, \min_\pi (\mathrm{E}[\tilde{v}_{\text{sN}}(\mathbf{x})]) = 1 + A + o(1)\}$;
2 **foreach** $\mathbf{x} \in \mathbb{Y}_0$ **do**
3 $\quad A(\mathbf{x})$ is as in Step 1;
4 $\quad g(\mathbf{x}) \leftarrow \arg\min_{n=1}^N A(\tilde{\mathcal{S}}_n(\mathbf{x}))$;
5 $\mathbb{Z} \leftarrow \emptyset$; $\mathbb{Y}_{\text{remain}} \leftarrow \emptyset$
6 **foreach** $k = 1$ *to* $(\min_{n=1}^N \tau_n)$ **do**
7 $\quad \mathbb{Z} \leftarrow \mathbb{Z} \cup \mathbb{Y}_{k-1}$;
8 $\quad \mathbb{Y}_k \leftarrow \{\mathbf{x} : \mathbf{x} + \mathbf{1} \in \mathbb{Y}_{k-1}$ and $\mathbf{x} \notin \mathbb{Z}\}$;
9 $\quad$ **repeat** $\mathbb{Y}_k \leftarrow \mathbb{Y}_k \cup \{\mathbf{x} : \tilde{\mathcal{S}}_n(\mathbf{x}) \in \mathbb{Z} \cup \mathbb{Y}_k, \forall n$ and $\mathbf{x} \notin \mathbb{Z} \cup \mathbb{Y}_k\}$ **until** Y_k *not extend;*
10 **foreach** $k = 1$ *to* $(\min_{n=1}^N \tau_n)$ **do**
11 $\quad \mathbb{Y}'_k \leftarrow \mathbb{Y}_k$;
12 $\quad$ **repeat**
13 $\quad\quad \mathbb{Y}''_k \leftarrow \mathbb{Y}'_k$; $\mathbb{Y}'_k \leftarrow \emptyset$;
14 $\quad\quad$ **foreach** $\mathbf{x} \in \mathbb{Y}''_k$ **do**
15 $\quad\quad\quad m \leftarrow \max\{j : \exists n, \tilde{\mathcal{S}}_n(\mathbf{x}) \in \mathbb{Y}_j\}$;
16 $\quad\quad\quad U_{\text{set}} \leftarrow \{n : \tilde{\mathcal{S}}_n(\mathbf{x}) \in \mathbb{Y}_m\}$;
17 $\quad\quad\quad$ **if** $m > k$ **then**
18 $\quad\quad\quad\quad [A(\mathbf{x}), g(\mathbf{x})] \leftarrow \min_{n \in U_{\text{set}}} b_n A((\mathbf{x}+\mathbf{1}) \wedge \boldsymbol{\tau})$;
19 $\quad\quad\quad$ **else if** $\exists n \in U_{set}$, $A(\tilde{\mathcal{S}}_n(\mathbf{X}))$ *not yet* **then**
20 $\quad\quad\quad\quad \mathbb{Y}'_k \leftarrow \mathbb{Y}'_k \cup \mathbf{x}$;
21 $\quad\quad\quad$ **else**
22 $\quad\quad\quad\quad [A(\mathbf{x}), g(\mathbf{x})] \leftarrow \min_{n \in U_{\text{set}}} A(\tilde{\mathcal{S}}_n(\mathbf{x})) + b_n A((\mathbf{x}+\mathbf{1}) \wedge \boldsymbol{\tau}) \mathbb{1}\{(\mathbf{x}+\mathbf{1}) \wedge \boldsymbol{\tau} \in \mathbb{Y}_{k-1}\}$;
23 $\quad$ **until** $\mathbb{Y}'_k = \emptyset$ *or* $\mathbb{Y}'_k = \mathbb{Y}''_k$;
24 $\quad$ **if** $\mathbb{Y}'_k \neq \emptyset$ **then**
25 $\quad\quad \mathbb{Y}_{\text{remain}} \leftarrow \mathbb{Y}_{\text{remain}} \cup \mathbb{Y}'_k$; $B(\mathbf{x}) \leftarrow 0, \forall \mathbf{x} \in \mathbb{Y}_k$;
26 $\quad\quad$ **foreach** $n = 1$ *to* $N - 1$ **do**
27 $\quad\quad\quad$ **foreach** $\mathbf{x} \in \mathbb{Y}_k$ **do**
28 $\quad\quad\quad\quad U'_{\text{set}} \leftarrow g(\mathbf{x})$ or U_{set};
29 $\quad\quad\quad\quad B(\mathbf{x}) \leftarrow \min_{n \in U'_{\text{set}}} B(\tilde{\mathcal{S}}_n(\mathbf{x})) + b_n A((\mathbf{x}+\mathbf{1}) \wedge \boldsymbol{\tau}) \mathbb{1}\{(\mathbf{x}+\mathbf{1}) \wedge \boldsymbol{\tau} \in \mathbb{Y}_{k-1}\}$
30 $\quad\quad$ **foreach** $\mathbf{x} \in \mathbb{Y}'_k$ **do**
31 $\quad\quad\quad [A(\mathbf{x}), g(\mathbf{x})] \leftarrow \min_{n \in U'_{\text{set}}} B(\tilde{\mathcal{S}}_n(\mathbf{x})) + b_n A((\mathbf{x}+\mathbf{1}) \wedge \boldsymbol{\tau}) \mathbb{1}\{(\mathbf{x}+\mathbf{1}) \wedge \boldsymbol{\tau} \in \mathbb{Y}_{k-1}\}$

Consequently, we design Algorithm 1 above to obtain a stationary policy, denoted *SN policy*, which tends to minimizes $\mathrm{E}[\tilde{v}_{\text{sN}}(\mathbf{x})]$ for any system state $\mathbf{x} \in \mathbb{Y}$. Here,

$$\tilde{\mathcal{S}}_n(\mathbf{x}) := (x_1+1, \cdots, x_{n-1}+1, 0, x_{n+1}+1, \cdots, x_N+1) \wedge \boldsymbol{\tau},$$

i.e., the state that succeeds the state $\mathbf{x}$ in the event of a successful transmission for client n in the MDP-2. This algorithm divides the state space into sets, $\mathbb{Y}_0, \mathbb{Y}_1, \cdots, \mathbb{Y}_{\min_{n=1}^N\{\tau_n\}}$, with,

$$\mathbb{Y}_k := \{\mathbf{x} : \exists A > 0, \min_\pi (\mathrm{E}[\tilde{v}_{\text{sN}}(\mathbf{x})]) = 1 + A\epsilon^k + o(\epsilon^k)\}, \quad (28)$$

for $k = 0, 1, \cdots, \min_{n=1}^N\{\tau_n\}$. Then it obtains or approximates the A in (28) for each system state $\mathbf{x}$ (denoted $A(\mathbf{x})$), and decides the optimal control based on $A(\mathbf{x})$.

Theorem 4. When Assumption 1 holds, and $\mathbb{Y}_{\text{remain}}$ in Algorithm 1 is empty, then the SN policy is optimal in the high reliability asymptotic regime.

Theorem 4 directly follows from Assumption 1 and the design of Algorithm 1.[1] The example in Fig. 5 illustrates the simulation for a multi-client system when these asymptotic conditions are satisfied.

9. SIMULATIONS

We now present the results of a simulation study comparing several wireless scheduling policies with respect to their risk-sensitive average costs. We present the results for the scenarios with clients requiring different inter-delivery thresholds and under heterogeneous channel reliabilities.

The wireless scheduling policies implemented include the optimal policy (OP) obtained from Theorem 2, the modified-least-time-to-go (MLG) policy (for two-client scenario) proposed in Section 8.1, and the SN policy proposed in Section 8.2. Also, two other heuristic policies are compared: the packet-level round-robin policy (PRR), and the largest-weighted-delivery-debt (WDD) policy, which serves the client with the largest weighted delivery debt, where:

$$\text{Delivery Debt}_n = \frac{t}{p_n \tau_n} - \frac{M_t^{(n)}}{p_n}.$$

(Recall $M_t^{(n)}$ is the number of packets delivered for the n-th client by time t, as in (1).) The WDD policy has been known to be "timely-throughput" optimal (see [10] for discussion).

Fig. 3 shows the costs incurred by these four wireless scheduling policies for different risk-sensitive parameters. It can be seen that the optimal policy always outperforms all the other policies.

Fig. 4 compares the scheduling policies under different channel reliabilities in the two-client scenario. It can be seen that even when the channel reliability probabilities are only moderate, e.g., $p_1 = 0.6$ and $p_2 = 0.8$, the MLG policy still achieves almost the optimal cost, and outperforms all other greedy policies.

Fig. 5 compares the scheduling policies in a multi-client scenario. It can be seen that even when the channel reliability probabilities are only moderate, e.g. 0.8, SN policy still approximates the optimal cost, and outperforms all other greedy policies. Here, we also employ the periodic scheduling (PS) policy [3], which is optimal when the failure probabilities are exactly zero. It can be seen that the PS policy performs extremely poorly even when the failure probability is very small, e.g., 0.01, since it gives rise to

[1]Note that the Algorithm 1 can be further improved by using $\tilde{S}(\tilde{S}(\mathbf{x}))$ in Step 19-22.

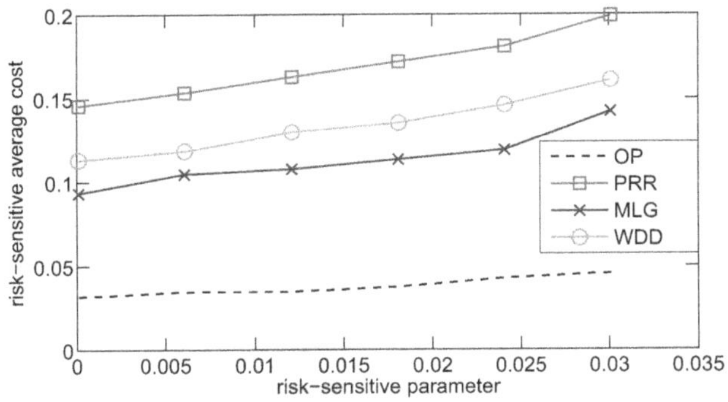

Figure 3: The risk-sensitive average cost vs. the risk-sensitive parameter θ for different wireless scheduling policies is shown. (The parameters are $N = 2$, $p_1 = 0.4$, $p_2 = 0.1$, $\tau_1 = 20$, $\tau_2 = 40$).

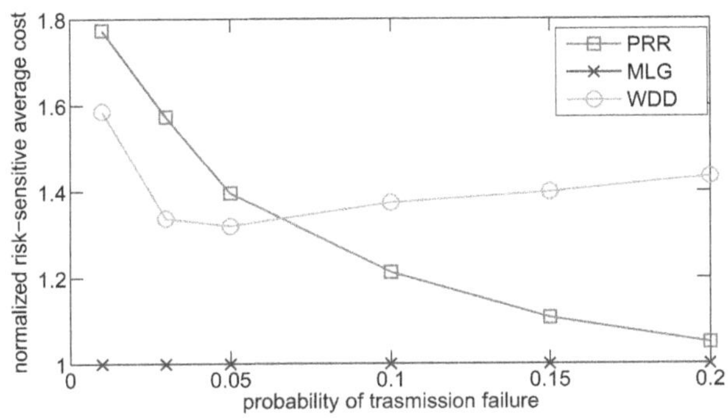

Figure 4: In two-client scenario, the normalized risk-sensitive average cost (normalized by the cost of the optimal policy) vs. the failure transmission parameter ϵ. ($p_1 = 1 - 2\epsilon$, $p_2 = 1 - \epsilon$, $\tau_1 = 3$, $\tau_2 = 5$, $\theta = 0.01$.)

open-loop policies. In contrast, the high-reliability asymptotic approach proposed for the scenario with sufficiently-small failure probability provides a well performing closed-loop scheduling policy. This confirms the value of the high-reliability asymptotic approach.

10. CONCLUSIONS

In this paper we have addressed the issue of designing scheduling policies in order to support inter-delivery requirements of wireless clients in cyber-physical systems. A novel risk-sensitive approach has been employed to penalize the "exceedance" over the allowable thresholds of inter-delivery times.

The resulting MDP that involves infinitely many states can be reduced to an equivalent MDP which involves only a finite number of states, thus showing that a stationary optimal policy exists when the risk-sensitive parameter θ is sufficient small. Based on this, we have designed a finite time algorithm to obtain the optimal policy.

To address the curse of dimensionality from MDP approach, we proposed a high-reliability asymptotic approach, and derived optimal policy for two-client scenario in the high-reliability regime. Further, we have designed an SN policy for a general number of clients based on our analysis result. The simulation results show that the proposed policies provide near-optimal performance even for moderately large values of the failure probabilities, justifying the approach.

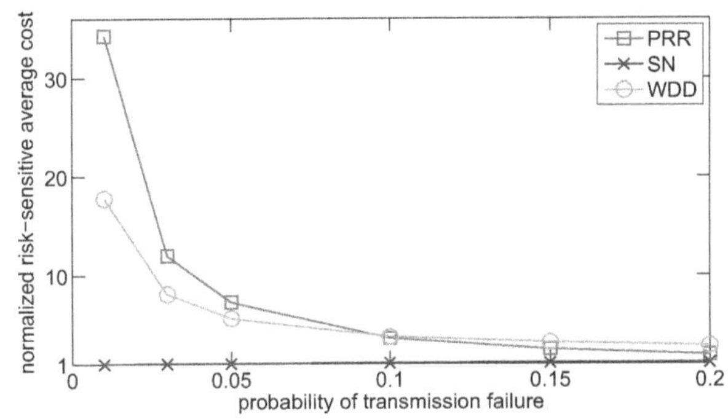

(a) Performance of the PRR, WDD, and SN policies

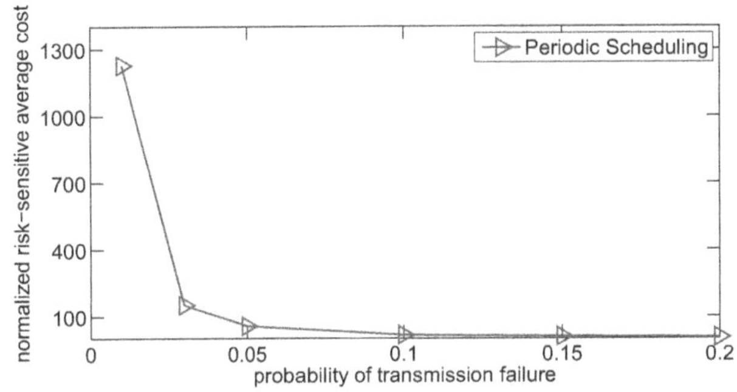

(b) Performance of Periodic Scheduling

Figure 5: In a multi-client scenario, the normalized risk-sensitive average cost (normalized by the cost of the optimal policy) vs. the failure transmission parameter ϵ is shown. (The parameters are $N = 3$, $p_1 = p_2 = p_3 = 1 - \epsilon$, $\tau_1 = 4$, $\tau_2 = 6$, $\tau_3 = 8$, $\theta = 0.05$.)

Acknowledgments

This work is sponsored in part by the National Basic Research Program of China (2012CB316001), the Nature Science Foundation of China (61201191, 61401250, 61321061, 61461136004), NSF under Contract Nos. CNS-1302182 and CCF-0939370, AFOSR under Contract No. FA-9550-13-1-0008, and Hitachi Ltd.

11. REFERENCES

[1] E. Altman, V. Kavitha, F. De Pellegrini, V. Kamble, and V. Borkar. Risk sensitive optimal control framework applied to delay tolerant networks. In *IEEE INFOCOM*, April 2011.

[2] A. S. Avestimehr, S. N. Diggavi, and D. N. Tse. Wireless network information flow: A deterministic approach. *IEEE Trans. on Info. Theory*, 2011.

[3] A. Bar-Noy, R. Bhatia, J. S. Naor, and B. Schieber. Minimizing service and operation costs of periodic scheduling. In *ACM Symposium on Discrete Algorithms*, 2002.

[4] R. Cavazos-Cadena and E. Fernandez-Gaucherand. Controlled Markov chains with risk-sensitive criteria:

Average cost, optimality equations, and optimal solutions. *Mathematical Methods of Operations Research*, 49(2), 1999.

[5] K.-J. Chung and M. J. Sobel. Discounted MDP's: Distribution functions and exponential utility maximization. *SIAM J. Control Optim.*, 25(1), 1987.

[6] T. ElBatt, C. Saraydar, M. Ames, and T. Talty. Potential for intra-vehicle wireless automotive sensor networks. In *IEEE Sarnoff Symposium*, March 2006.

[7] W. Fleming and D. Hernandez-Hernandez. Risk sensitive control of finite state machines on an infinite horizon. I. In *Decision and Control, IEEE Conference on*, Dec 1997.

[8] X. Guo, R. Singh, P. Kumar, and Z. Niu. Optimal energy-efficient regular delivery of packets in cyber-physical systems. In *IEEE ICC*, 2015.

[9] X. Guo, S. Zhou, Z. Niu, and P. Kumar. Optimal wake-up mechanism for single base station with sleep mode. In *IEEE International Teletraffic Congress*, Sept 2013.

[10] I.-H. Hou, V. Borkar, and P. Kumar. A theory of QoS for wireless. In *IEEE INFOCOM*, April 2009.

[11] R. A. Howard and J. E. Matheson. Risk-sensitive Markov decision processes. *Manage. Science*, 1972.

[12] S. C. Jaquette. A utility criterion for Markov decision processes. *Management Science*, 23(1), 1976.

[13] S. Kittipiyakul, P. Elia, and T. Javidi. High-snr analysis of outage-limited communications with bursty and delay-limited information. *Information Theory, IEEE Transactions on*, Feb 2009.

[14] B. Li, R. Li, and A. Eryilmaz. Heavy-traffic-optimal scheduling with regular service guarantees in wireless networks. In *MobiHoc*, 2013.

[15] R. Li, A. Eryilmaz, and B. Li. Throughput-optimal wireless scheduling with regulated inter-service times. In *IEEE INFOCOM*, April 2013.

[16] S. I. Marcus, E. Fernandez-Gaucherand, D. Hernandez-Hernandez, S. Coraluppi, and P. Fard. Risk sensitive Markov decision processes. In *Systems and control in the 21st century*, 1997.

[17] M. Neely, E. Modiano, and C. ping Li. Fairness and optimal stochastic control for heterogeneous networks. In *IEEE INFOCOM*, 2005.

[18] M. L. Puterman. *Markov Decision Processes: Discrete Stochastic Dynamic Programming*. John Wiley & Sons, Inc., 1st edition, 1994.

[19] Rahul Singh, I-Hong Hou and P.R. Kumar. Pathwise performance of debt based policies for wireless networks with hard delay constraints. In *IEEE 52nd Annual Conference on Decision and Control (CDC), 2013*, pages 7838–7843, Dec 2013.

[20] Rahul Singh, I-Hong Hou and P.R. Kumar. Fluctuation analysis of debt based policies for wireless networks with hard delay constraints. In *Proceedings of IEEE INFOCOM, 2014*, pages 2400–2408, April 2014.

[21] Y. Sadi and S. Ergen. Optimal power control, rate adaptation, and scheduling for uwb-based intravehicular wireless sensor networks. *IEEE Transactions on Vehicular Technology*, Jan 2013.

[22] R. Singh, X. Guo, and P. R. Kumar. Index policies for optimal mean-variance trade-off of inter-delivery times in real-time sensor networks. In *INFOCOM*, 2015.

[23] R. Singh and A. Stolyar. Maxweight scheduling: Asymptotic behavior of unscaled queue-differentials in heavy traffic. *In Proceedings of ACM SIGMETRICS*, June 2015.

[24] H.-M. Tsai, O. Tonguz, C. Saraydar, T. Talty, M. Ames, and A. MacDonald. Zigbee-based intra-car wireless sensor networks: a case study. *IEEE Wireless Communications*, December 2007.

[25] H. Xiong, R. Li, A. Eryilmaz, and E. Ekici. Delay-aware cross-layer design for network utility maximization in multi-hop networks. *Selected Areas in Communications, IEEE Journal on*, May 2011.

[26] Y. Zhang and C. Tepedelenlioglu. Applications of tauberian theorem for high-snr analysis of performance over fading channels. *Wireless Communications, IEEE Transactions on*, January 2012.

APPENDIX

A. NON-EXCLUSIONARY POLICIES ARE NOT RESTRICTIVE

We recall that Non-Exclusionary (NE) policies are those stationary policies which do not serve a client n when the system state $\mathbf{x}$ is $(\tau_1, \cdots, \tau_{n-1}, 0, \tau_{n+1}, \cdots, \tau_N)$. We next show that for a non-NE, either there is an NE policy out-performing it, or it is trivial to derive its cost function.

For a client n, denote $\mathbf{x}^{(na)}$ as the system state $(\tau_1, \cdots, \tau_{n-1}, a, \tau_{n+1}, \cdots, \tau_N)$ for integer $a \in [0, \tau_n]$. Similarly, for $n \neq l$, denote $\mathbf{x}^{(na_1, la_2)}$ as the state $\mathbf{x}$ such that $x_n = a_1$, $x_l = a_2$, and $x_j = \tau_j, \forall j \neq n, l$. In a T-horizon MDP-2 problem, denote by π the policy which transmits client n in the first time slot, and then follows the optimal policy. Similarly, $\tilde{\pi}$ as the policy which transmits client l in the first time slot and then follows the optimal policy. Then $V_T^{\pi}(\mathbf{x}), V_T^{\tilde{\pi}}(\mathbf{x})$ are the costs associated with these two policies with any initial state $\mathbf{x}$, respectively.

Lemma A.1. If there exists a client l such that $p_l > p_n$, then for each time slot T, we have $V_T^{\tilde{\pi}}(\mathbf{x}^{(n0)}) \leq V_T^{\pi}(\mathbf{x}^{(n0)})$. That is, if serving client n in state $\mathbf{x}^{(n0)}$ is optimal, serving client l is also optimal.

Lemma A.2. When $p_n = \min_l p_l$, if the optimal action in state $\mathbf{x}^{(n0)}$ with T time slots to go is to serve client n, then the optimal action in state $\mathbf{x}^{(na)}, \forall a \in \{1, \cdots, \tau_n\}$ with T time slots to go is also to serve client n.

The proofs for Lemma A.1 and Lemma A.2 are omitted due to space constraints.

Combining Lemma A.1 and Lemma A.2, for a non-NE stationary policy f which serves client n in state $\mathbf{x}^{(n0)}$, either there exists an NE policy which out-performs f (as in Lemma A.1), or f keeps serving client n (after hitting the state $\boldsymbol{\tau}$) following Lemma A.2 and therefore has a trivially computable cost.

QoE-Optimal Scheduling for On-Demand Video Streams over Unreliable Wireless Networks

I-Hong Hou
CESG and Department of ECE
Texas A&M University
College Station, TX 77843, USA
ihou@tamu.edu

Ping-Chun Hsieh
CESG and Department of ECE
Texas A&M University
College Station, TX 77843, USA
lleyfede@tamu.edu

ABSTRACT

Video streaming is anticipated to dominate wireless traffic in the near future. We study wireless systems where an access point delivers video streams to multiple clients over unreliable wireless channels. The performance of each client is measured by the amount of time that its video playback halts due to buffer underflow, which has been shown to have the most impact on client's perceived quality of experience (QoE).

We develop an analytical framework that jointly captures the video playback process and the unreliable and heterogeneous wireless channels. We derive the capacity region for QoE by establishing a lower bound of a weighted sum of video halt durations over all clients. We then propose a QoE-optimal policy that can achieve every point within the capacity region. Finally, we compare our policy against two commonly used policies. Both theoretical analysis and simulation results show that our policy greatly outperforms other policies.

Categories and Subject Descriptors

C.2.1 [**COMPUTER-COMMUNICATION NETWORKS**]: Network Architecture and Design—*Wireless communication*

Keywords

Wireless networks; scheduling; QoE; video streaming

1. INTRODUCTION

Many studies have predicted that on-demand video streaming will dominate wireless traffic in the near future. In on-demand video streaming, content providers, such as *Netflix* and *Youtube*, deliver packets to clients. Clients puts received packets in their buffers, and consume packets from the buffer during the video playback. When the buffer becomes empty, the video playback halts. It has been shown that video halts have the most significant impact on the quality of experience (QoE) of clients [16, 19].

In this paper, we aim to find the capacity of wireless networks for providing QoE, as well as scheduling policies that achieves the capacity. We propose an analytical model for wireless systems where an access point (AP) transmits video streams to a number of wireless clients over unreliable wireless channels. Different clients may have different channel qualities and consume packets at different rates. The performance of a client is then measured by the amount of time that it suffers from video halts.

We characterize the achievable duration of video halts for each client. Apparently, the duration of video halts is a random variable whose distribution is determined by the AP's scheduling policy. Using martingale theory, we first show that a weighted sum of the halt durations of all clients is stochastically lower-bounded by a random variable generated from a Brownian motion. This result provides a lower-bound of the capacity.

Next, we propose a simple on-line scheduling policy for providing the desirable QoE to each client. We prove that this policy is QoE-optimal in the sense that, given any vector of random variables whose weighted sum is larger than the lower-bound, the policy ensures that the halt durations of clients are no larger than the vector of random variables. In addition to being QoE-optimal, this policy also demonstrates that the lower-bound generated from the Brownian motion is indeed tight, and we are able to sharply characterize the capacity of QoE for wireless networks.

Further, we analytically study two widely-used scheduling policies, namely, the weighted random policy and the weighted round-robin policy. We derive the closed-form expression of the distribution of video halt duration of each client for both policies. We show that the performance of these policies can be much worse than our proposed policy. In particular, we show that when the total traffic load is fixed, the performance of the weighted random policy and the weighted round-robin policy deteriorates as the number of clients increases, while the performance of our policy remains the same for any number of clients.

Finally, we conduct simulations to verify our theoretical results. We implement our policy, the weighted random policy, and the weighted round-robin policy in ns-2. Simulation results suggest that our theoretical analysis is very accurate in characterizing the performance of each client. They also show that our proposed policy outperform other policies greatly under various scenarios. In particular, even when the weighted random policy and the weighted round-robin policy spend 5 times as much time to buffer incoming packets before playing videos, their video halt durations are still more than 5 times higher than the video halt duration of our policy.

MobiHoc'15, June 22–25, 2015, Hangzhou, China.

http://dx.doi.org/10.1145/2746285.2746288.

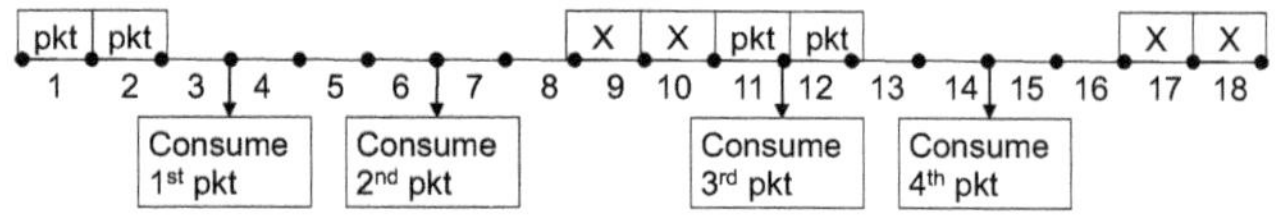

Figure 1: An example of video playback.

The rest of the paper is organized as follows. Section 2 describes our analytical model. Section 3 establishes some basic system properties, including a lower-bound for the achievable video halt durations. In Section 4, we propose a simple online scheduling policy and demonstrate that it is QoE-optimal. Section 5 shows that our analysis provides an accurate approximation for the actual system performance. In Section 6, we derive the closed-form expression of the performance under two popular policies. Section 7 demonstrates the simulation results. Section 8 summarizes some related work. Finally, Section 9 concludes the paper.

2. SYSTEM MODEL

Consider a wireless system where an access point (AP) serves a number of wireless clients, which are labeled as $n = 1, 2, \ldots, N$. We assume that time is slotted and numbered as $t = 1, 2, \ldots$. In each time slot, the AP can transmit to exactly one client.

Each wireless client is associated with an on-demand video stream. We assume that the bottleneck of a video stream is at the "last hop" between the AP and the client, which is a practical assumption for most scenarios and is used in many existing studies [14, 24]. Hence, the AP always has a packet ready for transmission to each client in each time slot. Each client has an infinite buffer so that it can buffer packets that are yet to be played. The playback process of a client is described as follows: Each client n *consumes* one packet in its buffer and plays its content every $\frac{1}{q_n}$ time slots. This also means that client n consumes packets at a rate of q_n packets per time slot. If a client is to consume a packet at time t, but its buffer is empty at that time, then we say that *outage* occurs at time t. Outage continues to occur in all subsequent time slots until the client receives a packet, at which time the client consumes the packet immediately. Outage corresponds to video halts, and the total number of slots that outage occurs is the total duration that the playback halts. We use $D_n(t)$ to denote the total number of slots that outage occurs for client n until time t.

Fig. 1 illustrates an example of the video playback process. In this example, we assume that $q_n = \frac{1}{3}$, and the client receives packets on time slots 1, 2, 11, and 12. As the client consumes one packet every three time slots, the first two packets that it receives are consumed at time 3 and 6, respectively. The client is to consume another packet at time 9. However, it does not have any packet in its buffer at that time, and hence outage occurs at time 9. Outage also occurs at time 10. At time 11, the client receives another packet, and it consumes the packet immediately and the video playback resumes. The client consumes another packet at time $14 = 11 + 3$, and is to consume one packet at time $17 = 14 + 3$. However, the client's buffer is empty at time 17, and hence outage occurs.

We now provide a more mathematical description on $D_n(t)$. Let $A_n^*(t)$ be the total number of packets that client n receives until time t, $C_n^*(t)$ be the total number of packets consumed by n until time t, and $B_n^*(t)$ be the number of packets in the buffer of n at time t. We set $A_n^*(0) = B_n^*(0) = C_n^*(0) = D_n(0) = 0$. We then have

$$C_n^*(t) = \lfloor q_n(t - D_n(t)) \rfloor, \tag{1}$$

because n consumes one packet every $1/q_n$ slots without outage. We also have

$$D_n(t) = \begin{cases} D_n(t-1)+1, & \text{if } \lfloor q_n(t - D_n(t-1)) \rfloor > A_n^*(t) \\ D_n(t-1), & \text{otherwise,} \end{cases} \tag{2}$$

since $\lfloor q_n(t - D_n(t-1)) \rfloor$ is the number of packets that n would consume if outage does not happen at slot t. Finally, we apparently have

$$B_n^*(t) = A_n^*(t) - C_n^*(t). \tag{3}$$

The definition of $C_n^*(\cdot)$ involves floor function and is difficult to operate with. We can simplify the expression of $D_n(t)$ by defining

$$A_n(t) := A_n^*(t) + (1 - q_n), \tag{4}$$

$$C_n(t) := q_n(t - D_n(t)), \tag{5}$$

$$B_n(t) := [A_n(t) - C_n(t)]^+. \tag{6}$$

We now have $D_n(t) = D_n(t-1) + 1$ if and only if

$$\lfloor q_n(t - D_n(t-1)) \rfloor = A_n^*(t) + 1 \tag{7}$$

$$\Leftrightarrow q_n(t - D_n(t-1) - 1) \geq A_n(t) \Leftrightarrow B_n(t) = 0, \tag{8}$$

where the last step of the derivation follows from $D_n(t) \leq D_n(t-1) + 1$. In other words, $D_n(t)$ increases when $B_n(t) = 0$.

The definitions of $A_n(t), C_n(t), B_n(t)$, and $D_n(t)$ can be viewed as a system where the client consumes q_n packets in each slot without outage and has an initial buffer size of $1 - q_n$. Let $X_n(t) := A_n(t) - q_n t$. Since client n is supposed to consume $q_n t$ packets by time t, $X_n(t)$ loosely reflects whether the number of packets delivered for n matches its consumption rate. We further note that the following relations hold:

$$B_n(t) = X_n(t) + q_n D_n(t) \geq 0, \tag{9}$$

$$X_n(t) = A_n(t) - q_n t, \tag{10}$$

$$[D_n(t) - D_n(t-1)] \in \{0, 1\}, \quad D_n(0) = 0, \tag{11}$$

$$B_n(t)[D_n(t) - D_n(t-1)] = 0. \tag{12}$$

We consider the unreliable wireless transmissions by assuming that the channel reliability of client n is p_n. When the AP transmits a packet to n, the transmission is successful with probability p_n. The AP has instant knowledge on whether the transmission is successful, and can retransmit the same packet if previous transmissions fail.

We further assume that clients choose their values of q_n so that it is feasible to provide a long-term average throughput of q_n packets per time slot to each client. In other words, there exists a scheduling policy under which $\liminf_{t\to\infty} \frac{A_n(t)}{t} \geq q_n$, or, equivalently, $\limsup_{t\to\infty} \frac{D_n(t)}{t} = 0$ for all n, almost surely.

Let $U_n(t)$ be the total number of times that the AP transmits to n until time t. Hou, Borkar, and Kumar [8] has shown that the long-term average throughput of n is at least q_n if and only if $\liminf_{t\to\infty} \frac{U_n(t)}{t} \geq \frac{q_n}{p_n}$. Since the AP transmits one packet in each time slot, we have:

LEMMA 1. *It is feasible to achieve* $\limsup_{t\to\infty} \frac{D_n(t)}{t} = 0$, *for all* n, *if and only if* $\sum_n \frac{q_n}{p_n} \leq 1$.

While the study of $\limsup_{t\to\infty} \frac{D_n(t)}{t} = 0$ reveals some important insights, it cannot precisely characterize $D_n(t)$ for videos with finite length. In this paper, we study the *diffusion limit* of $D_n(t)$, defined as

$$\hat{D}_n(t) := \lim_{k\to\infty} \frac{D_n(kt)}{\sqrt{k}}, 0 \le t \le 1. \tag{13}$$

We will mainly focus on the extreme case with $\sum_n \frac{q_n}{p_n} = 1$. In Section 4.1, we further demonstrate that some results for the extreme case also characterize the performance for the general case with $\sum_n \frac{q_n}{p_n} < 1$. In Section 7, we demonstrate that $\hat{D}_n(t)$ provides a very accurate approximation of $D_n(t)$ for videos that are at least a couple of seconds long.

$\hat{D}_n(t)$ is a random process whose distribution is determined by the scheduling policy. We compare the distributions of $\hat{D}_n(t)$ under different policies through stochastic ordering as defined as follows:

DEFINITION 1. *Let $\hat{D}_n^{\eta_1}(t)$ and $\hat{D}_n^{\eta_2}(t)$ be the process $\hat{D}_n(t)$ under policies η_1 and η_2, respectively. We say that $\hat{D}_n^{\eta_1}(t) \le_{st} \hat{D}_n^{\eta_2}(t)$ if*

$$Prob(\hat{D}_n^{\eta_1}(t) \ge x) \le Prob(\hat{D}_n^{\eta_2}(t) \ge x),$$

for all x and all $t \in [0,1]$. We say that η_1 minimizes $\hat{D}_n^{\eta_1}(t)$ if $\hat{D}_n^{\eta_1}(t) \le_{st} \hat{D}_n^{\eta}(t)$ for all η. □

We also define

$$\hat{X}_n(t) := \lim_{k\to\infty} \frac{X_n(kt)}{\sqrt{k}}, \tag{14}$$

$$\hat{B}_n(t) := \lim_{k\to\infty} \frac{B_n(kt)}{\sqrt{k}}. \tag{15}$$

The stochastic ordering of $\hat{X}_n(t)$ and $\hat{B}_n(t)$ under different policies are defined similarly.

In view of (9) - (12), we have

$$\hat{B}_n(t) = \hat{X}_n(t) + q_n\hat{D}_n(t) \ge 0, \tag{16}$$

$$\frac{d\hat{D}_n(t)}{dt} \ge 0, \quad \hat{D}_n(0) = 0, \tag{17}$$

$$\hat{B}_n(t)\frac{d\hat{D}_n(t)}{dt} = 0, \tag{18}$$

where we slightly abuse notation and define

$$\frac{d\hat{D}_n(t)}{dt} := \lim_{\delta\to 0^+} \frac{\hat{D}_n(t+\delta)}{\delta}.$$

We then have the following theorem:

THEOREM 1. *[5, Theorem 6.1] Given $\hat{X}_n(t)$, there exists a unique pair of $(\hat{B}_n(t), \hat{D}_n(t))$ that satisfies (16) - (18). Further, $\hat{D}_n(t) = \sup_{0\le\tau\le t}(\max\{0, -\frac{\hat{X}_n(\tau)}{q_n}\})$.*

3. FUNDAMENTAL SYSTEM PROPERTIES

Theorem 1 shows that $\hat{D}_n(t)$ can be characterized by $\hat{X}_n(t)$. Hence, we first study the behavior of $\hat{X}_n(t)$. Let $X(t) := \sum_n \frac{X_n(t)}{p_n} = \sum_n \frac{A_n(t)}{p_n} - t$, as $\sum_n \frac{q_n}{p_n} = 1$. Suppose the AP transmits to client n in time slot $t+1$, we have $X(t+1) = X(t) + \frac{1}{p_n} - 1$ with probability p_n, and $X(t+1) = X(t) - 1$ with probability $(1-p_n)$. Hence, no matter which client is scheduled at time $t+1$, we have $E[X(t+1)|\mathcal{H}_t] = X(t)$, where $\mathcal{H}_t$ is the system history up to time t. $X(t)$ is then said to be a martingale.

Suppose, given $\mathcal{H}_t$, the employed policy schedules client n at time slot $t+1$ with probability $r_n(t+1)$. Then, $\sigma_t^2 := E[(X(t+1) - X(t))^2|\mathcal{H}_t] = \sum_n r_n(t+1) \times (\frac{1}{p_n} - 1)$. If the employed policy achieves $\limsup_{t\to\infty} \frac{D_n(t)}{t} = 0$, then $\lim_{t\to\infty} \frac{U_n(t)}{t}$ exists and equals $\frac{q_n}{p_n}$, since $\sum_n \frac{q_n}{p_n} = 1$. Hence, we have $\lim_{t\to\infty} \frac{\sum_{\tau=1}^t r_n(\tau)}{t} = \frac{q_n}{p_n}$, and

$$\sigma^2 := \lim_{t\to\infty} \frac{\sum_{\tau=1}^t \sigma_\tau^2}{t} = \sum_n \lim_{t\to\infty} \frac{\sum_{\tau=1}^t r_n(\tau)}{t}(\frac{1}{p_n} - 1)$$
$$= \sum_n \frac{q_n}{p_n}(\frac{1}{p_n} - 1). \tag{19}$$

Further, for a fixed $t \in [0,1]$,

$$\lim_{n\to\infty} \sum_{\tau=1}^{\lfloor nt \rfloor} \sigma_\tau^2 / \sum_{\tau=1}^{n} \sigma_\tau^2 = t.$$

By the functional central limit theorem for martingale [3], we can establish that $\hat{X}(t) := \lim_{k\to\infty} \frac{X(kt)}{\sqrt{k}}$ is a driftless Brownian motion with variance σ^2. In particular, given $\hat{X}(\tau)$, for any $\tau, t \ge 0$ with $\tau + t \le 1$, $\hat{X}(\tau+t) - \hat{X}(\tau)$ is a Gaussian random variable with mean 0 and variance $\sigma^2 t$. Let $\Phi(x)$ be the cumulative distribution function (CDF) of a standard Gaussian random variable with mean 0 and unit variance. We then have

$$Prob(\hat{X}(\tau+t) - \hat{X}(\tau) \le b|\hat{X}(\tau)) = \Phi(b/\sqrt{\sigma^2 t}). \tag{20}$$

Let $\hat{D}(t) := \sup_{0\le\tau\le t}(\max\{0, -\hat{X}(\tau)\})$. Since $\hat{X}(t)$ is a Brownian motion for any policies that achieve $\lim_{t\to\infty} \frac{D_n(t)}{t} = 0$, the distribution of $\hat{D}(t)$ is the same for all such policies. We have the following two lemmas:

LEMMA 2. *The CDF of $\hat{D}(t)$ is given by*

$$Prob(\hat{D}(t) \le x) = \Phi(\frac{x}{\sqrt{\sigma^2 t}}) - \Phi(\frac{-x}{\sqrt{\sigma^2 t}}), \tag{21}$$

for all $x \ge 0, t \ge 0$. The probability density function of $\hat{D}(t)$ is $\sqrt{\frac{2}{\sigma^2 t\pi}} e^{-\frac{x^2}{2\sigma^2 t}}$.

PROOF. This is a direct result of Section 1.6 in [7]. □

LEMMA 3. *For any policy that achieves $\lim_{t\to\infty} \frac{D_n(t)}{t} = 0$, $\hat{D}(t) \le_{st} \sum_n \frac{q_n}{p_n}\hat{D}_n(t)$.*

PROOF. By definition, we have, for every sample path,

$$\hat{D}(t) = \sup_{0\le\tau\le t}(\max\{0, -\hat{X}(\tau)\})$$
$$= \sup_{0\le\tau\le t}(\max\{0, -\sum_n \frac{\hat{X}_n(\tau)}{p_n}\})$$
$$\le \sum_n \sup_{0\le\tau\le t}(\max\{0, -\frac{\hat{X}_n(\tau)}{p_n}\}) = \sum_n \frac{q_n}{p_n}\hat{D}_n(t).$$

□

We can also calculate the expected value of $\hat{D}(t)$ by

$$E[\hat{D}(t)] = \int_0^\infty x\sqrt{\frac{2}{\sigma^2 t\pi}} e^{-\frac{x^2}{2\sigma^2 t}} = \sqrt{\frac{2t}{\pi}\sum_n \frac{q_n}{p_n}(\frac{1}{p_n} - 1)}. \tag{22}$$

Motivated by Lemma 3, we define the *capacity region for QoE* of the system.

DEFINITION 2. *A vector* $\delta = [\delta_1, \delta_2, \dots, \delta_N]$ *is said to be* feasible *if there exists a scheduling policy so that* $\hat{D}_n(t) \leq_{st} \delta_n \hat{D}(t)/\frac{q_n}{p_n}$*, for all* n*. The* capacity region for QoE *is defined as the set of all feasible* δ. □

The following necessary condition for feasibility is then a direct result of Lemma 3.

THEOREM 2. *A feasible vector* δ *must have* $\delta_n \geq 0, \forall n$*, and* $\sum_n \delta_n \geq 1$. □

4. A QOE-OPTIMAL ONLINE POLICY

In this section, we introduce a simple online policy, namely, the *prioritized largest deficit policy*. We prove that the prioritized largest deficit policy is QoE-optimal in the sense that it can achieve every point in the capacity region for QoE.

The prioritized largest deficit policy divides clients into two groups, a *high-priority* group, denoted by S_1, and a *low-priority* group, denoted by S_2, with $S_2 \neq \phi$. In each time slot $t+1$, the AP calculates $\lfloor -X_n(t) \rfloor$ for all $n \in S_1$. The AP schedules an arbitrary client $n \in S_1$ with $\lfloor -X_n(t) \rfloor > 0$. If $\lfloor -X_n(t) \rfloor \leq 0$, for all $n \in S_1$, the AP schedules the client $m \in S_2$ with the largest value of $w_m(q_m t - A_m(t)) = w_m(-X_m(t))$, where w_m is a predetermined value with $w_m > 0$, for all $m \in S_2$.

In practice, the AP may choose the high-priority group and the weights of clients by its own pricing/service policy. For example, the AP may charge clients a premium to be put in the high-priority group, or to have larger w_n. We note that, in the special case where all clients are in the low-priority group, the prioritized largest deficit policy becomes similar to the max weight policy [21, 22] and the largest debt first policy [8], as it schedules the client with the largest value of $w_m(q_m t - A_m(t))$ in each time slot.

4.1 Performance of the High-Priority Group

We first study the performance of clients in the high-priority group. Define

$$Q(t) := \sum_{n \in S_1} \lfloor -X_n(t) \rfloor / p_n = Y(t) + Z(t),$$

where $Y(t)$ and $Z(t)$ are defined by

$$Y(t) := Q(t) + \sum_{n \in S_1} U_n(t) - t,$$

$$Z(t) := t - \sum_{n \in S_1} U_n(t).$$

Since $X_n(t+1) < X_n(t)$ unless n is scheduled in time slot $t+1$, and $|X_n(t+1) - X_n(t)| < 1$, for all t, the design of the prioritized largest deficit policy ensures that $(-X_n(t)) \geq 0$, for all $n \in S_1$ and all t. Hence, $Q(t) = Y(t) + Z(t) \geq 0$. Further, $Z(t)$ is non-decreasing and only increases when the AP schedules a client in S_1, which is equivalent to $Q(t) > 0$. Therefore, we have $Z(t) - Z(t-1) \geq 0$ and $Q(t)[Z(t) - Z(t-1)] = 0$. By a similar argument for Theorem 1, we can establish that

$$Z(t) = \sup_{0 \leq \tau \leq t} \max\{0, -Y(\tau)\}. \tag{23}$$

Next, we study the behavior of $Y(t)$. Let $\epsilon(t) := Q(t) + \sum_{n \in S_1} \frac{X_n(t)}{p_n}$. Then, $|\epsilon(t)| \leq \sum_{n \in S_1} \frac{1}{p_n}$. We can now rewrite $Y(t)$ as

$$Y(t) = \sum_{n \in S_1} (U_n(t) - \frac{A_n(t)}{p_n}) + (\sum_{n \in S_1} \frac{q_n}{p_n} - 1)t + \epsilon(t). \tag{24}$$

If a client n is scheduled at time slot $t+1$, we have,

$$U_n(t+1) - \frac{A_n(t+1)}{p_n} = \begin{cases} (U_n(t) - \frac{A_n(t)}{p_n}) + 1 - \frac{1}{p_n}, & \text{with probability } p_n, \\ (U_n(t) - \frac{A_n(t)}{p_n}) + 1, & \text{with probability } 1 - p_n. \end{cases}$$

On the other hand, if n is not scheduled at $t+1$, we have $(U_n(t+1) - \frac{A_n(t+1)}{p_n}) = (U_n(t) - \frac{A_n(t)}{p_n})$. In either case, $E[U_n(t+1) - \frac{A_n(t+1)}{p_n} | \mathcal{H}_t] = U_n(t) - \frac{A_n(t)}{p_n}$, for all n, and $\sum_{n \in S_1} (U_n(t) - \frac{A_n(t)}{p_n})$ is a martingale. By the martingale law of large numbers [6], $\lim_{t \to \infty} \frac{\sum_{n \in S_1} (U_n(t) - A_n(t)/p_n)}{t} = 0$, and hence $\lim_{t \to \infty} \frac{Y(t)}{t} = \sum_{n \in S_1} \frac{q_n}{p_n} - 1$. Since S_2 is not empty, $\sum_{n \in S_1} \frac{q_n}{p_n} < 1$. Hence, by (23), $\lim_{t \to \infty} \frac{Z(t)}{t} = 1 - \sum_{n \in S_1} \frac{q_n}{p_n}$, and $\lim_{t \to \infty} \frac{Q(t)}{t} = 0$. The latter further implies that $\lim_{t \to \infty} \frac{X_n(t)}{t} = 0$ and $\lim_{t \to \infty} \frac{U_n(t)}{t} = \frac{q_n}{p_n}$, for all $n \in S_1$.

Next, we study the diffusion limit of $Q(t)$, defined as

$$\hat{Q}(t) := \lim_{k \to \infty} \frac{Q(kt)}{\sqrt{k}}$$
$$= \lim_{k \to \infty} \frac{\sum_{n \in S_1} (U_n(kt) - A_n(kt)/p_n)}{\sqrt{k}} + \frac{(\sum_{n \in S_1} \frac{q_n}{p_n} - 1)kt + \epsilon(kt)}{\sqrt{k}} + \frac{Z(kt)}{\sqrt{k}}, 0 \leq t \leq 1.$$

Since $\lim_{t \to \infty} \frac{U_n(t)}{t} = \frac{q_n}{p_n}$, for all $n \in S_1$, by the functional central limit theorem for martingale,

$$\lim_{k \to \infty} \frac{\sum_{n \in S_1} (U_n(kt) - A_n(kt)/p_n)}{\sqrt{k}}$$

is a Brownian motion. Further, since $\sum_{n \in S_1} \frac{q_n}{p_n} < 1$,

$$\frac{(\sum_{n \in S_1} \frac{q_n}{p_n} - 1)kt + \epsilon(kt)}{\sqrt{k}} \to -\infty,$$

as $k \to \infty$. Therefore, the following lemma shows that $\hat{Q}(t) = 0$. Since $X_n(t) \geq 0$, for all $n \in S_1$ by the design of the prioritized largest deficit policy, we also have $\hat{X}_n(t) = 0$, for all $n \in S_1$.

LEMMA 4. *[5, Lemma 6.4] Let* $\{\theta_k\}$ *be a sequence of real numbers and* $\{x_k(t)\}$ *be a sequence of functions defined on* $t \in [0, 1]$ *with* $x_k(0) \geq 0$*. Let* $z_k(t) = x_k(t) + \theta_k + y_k(t)$*, and* $y_k(t) = \sup_{0 \leq \tau \leq t} \max\{0, -x_k(\tau) - \theta_k \tau\}$*. Suppose that as* $k \to \infty$*,* x_k *converges to a continuous function* x *and* $\theta_k \to -\infty$*. Then* $z_k(t) \to 0$. □

We summarize the performance of clients in the high-priority set in the following theorem:

THEOREM 3. *Under the prioritized largest deficit policy, for all* $n \in S_1$*,* $\lim_{t \to \infty} \frac{U_n(t)}{t} = \frac{q_n}{p_n}$*,* $\hat{X}_n(t) = 0$*, and* $\hat{D}_n(t) = 0$. □

We also note that the primary condition needed to establish Theorem 3 is $\sum_{n\in S_1}\frac{q_n}{p_n}<1$. Theorem 3 can therefore be used to establish the performance of systems with $\sum_n \frac{q_n}{p_n}<1$.

COROLLARY 1. *For any system with $\sum_{n=1}^{N}\frac{q_n}{p_n}<1$, it is feasible to achieve $\hat{D}_n(t)=0$, for all n.*

PROOF. For a system with $\sum_{n=1}^{N}\frac{q_n}{p_n}<1$, we can create a pseudo client $N+1$ and choose p_{N+1}, q_{N+1} so that $\sum_{n=1}^{N+1}\frac{q_n}{p_n}=1$. We then employ the prioritized largest deficit policy by choosing $S_1=\{1,2,\dots,N\}$ and $S_2=\{N+1\}$. By Theorem 3, we have $\hat{D}_n(t)=0$, for all $1\le n\le N$. □

4.2 Performance of the Low-Priority Group

Next, we study the performance of clients in the low-priority group S_2. We first demonstrate that $[\hat{X}_n(t)|n\in S_2]$ has the property of *state-space collapse* as described in the following:

THEOREM 4. *Under the prioritized largest deficit policy, for all $n,m\in S_2$, we have $w_n\hat{X}_n(t)=w_m\hat{X}_m(t)$, for all $t\in[0,1]$.*

PROOF. Let

$$p_n' := p_n(1-\sum_{m\in S_1}\frac{q_m}{p_m}), \tag{25}$$

$$V_n(t) := (-w_nX_n(t)) + (\sum_{m\in S_2}\frac{X_m(t)}{p_m'})/\sum_{m\in S_2}\frac{1}{w_mp_m'}. \tag{26}$$

The client with the smallest $w_nX_n(t)$ is then the one with the largest $V_n(t)$. We note that $(\sum_{m\in S_2}\frac{X_m(t)}{p_m'})/\sum_{m\in S_2}\frac{1}{w_mp_m'}$ is a weighted average of $w_nX_n(t)$. Therefore, $\max_{n\in S_2}V_n(t)\ge 0$, with equality holds if and only if $w_nX_n(t)=w_mX_m(t)$, for all $n,m\in S_2$.

We consider the fluid limit of the system and define $\bar{X}_n(t)=\lim_{k\to\infty}\frac{X_n(kt)}{k}=\lim_{k\to\infty}\frac{A_n(kt)}{k}-q_nt$, $\bar{V}_n(t)=\lim_{k\to\infty}\frac{V_n(kt)}{k}$. Without loss of generality, we assume that client 1 has the largest $\bar{V}_n(t)$ at time t in the fluid system. By Theorem 3, the fluid system spends a fraction $\sum_{m\in S_1}\frac{q_m}{p_m}$ of time serving clients in S_1, and therefore only spends a fraction $1-\sum_{m\in S_1}\frac{q_m}{p_m}$ of time serving client 1. We now have $\frac{d\bar{X}_1(t)}{dt}=p_1(1-\sum_{m\in S_1}\frac{q_m}{p_m})-q_1=p_1'-q_1$, and $\frac{d\bar{X}_n(t)}{dt}=-q_n, \forall n\neq 1, n\in S_2$. Therefore,

$$\begin{aligned}\frac{d\bar{V}_1(t)}{dt} &= -w_1p_1'+w_1q_1+\frac{\sum_{m\in S_2}\frac{q_m}{p_m'}-1}{\sum_{m\in S_2}1/w_mp_m'}\\ &= -w_1p_1'+w_1q_1,\\ \frac{d\bar{V}_n(t)}{dt} &= w_nq_n+\frac{\sum_{m\in S_2}\frac{q_m}{p_m'}-1}{\sum_{m\in S_2}1/w_mp_m'}\\ &= w_nq_n.\end{aligned}$$

Define a Lyapunov function $L(t)=\sum_{n\in S_2}\frac{1}{2w_np_n'}\bar{V}_n(t)^2$. The Lyapunov drift is then

$$\begin{aligned}\frac{dL(t)}{dt} &= \sum_{n\in S_2}\frac{1}{w_np_n'}\bar{V}_n(t)\frac{d\bar{V}_n(t)}{dt}\\ &= \sum_{n\in S_2}\frac{q_n}{p_n'}\bar{V}_n(t)-\bar{V}_1(t)\le 0,\end{aligned}$$

where the last inequality follows because $\sum_{n\in S_2}\frac{q_n}{p_n'}=1$, and $\bar{V}_1(t)\ge\bar{V}_n(t)$, for all $n\in S_2$.

Now, recall that $(\sum_{m\in S_2}\frac{X_m(t)}{p_m'})/\sum_{m\in S_2}\frac{1}{w_mp_m'}$ is a weighted average of $w_nX_n(t)$. Therefore, if $L(t)>0$, $w_1\bar{X}_1(t)<w_n\bar{X}_n(t)$, and $\bar{V}_1(t)>\bar{V}_n(t)$ for some $n\in S_2$. In this case, we have $\frac{dL(t)}{dt}<0$, and the fluid system is strongly stable. Therefore, the process $[V_n(t)]$ is positive recurrent, and we have $\lim_{k\to\infty}\frac{V_n(kt)}{\sqrt{k}}\to 0$. This establishes that $w_n\hat{X}_n(t)=(\sum_{m\in S_2}\frac{\hat{X}_m(t)}{p_m'})/\sum_{m\in S_2}\frac{1}{w_mp_m'}$, for all $n\in S_2$. □

Theorem 3 has already established that $\hat{X}(t)=\sum_n\frac{\hat{X}_n(t)}{p_n}=\sum_{n\in S_2}\frac{\hat{X}_n(t)}{p_n}$. By Theorem 4, we further have

$$\hat{X}_n(t)=\frac{1/w_n}{\sum_{m\in S_2}1/(p_mw_m)}\hat{X}(t).$$

Therefore,

$$\begin{aligned}\hat{D}_n(t) &= \sup_{0\le\tau\le t}\max\{0,-\frac{\hat{X}_n(\tau)}{q_n}\}\\ &= \frac{1/(p_nw_n)}{\sum_{m\in S_2}1/(p_mw_m)}\hat{D}(t)/\frac{q_n}{p_n}.\end{aligned} \tag{27}$$

The performance of the prioritized largest deficit policy can then be summarized as below:

THEOREM 5. *Under the prioritized largest deficit policy, $\hat{D}_n(t)=0$ for all $n\in S_1$, and $\hat{D}_n(t)$ is given by (27), for all $n\in S_2$.* □

By (22), we can derive the mean of $\hat{D}_n(t)$ as

$$E[\hat{D}_n(t)]=\sqrt{\frac{2t}{\pi}\sum_{m=1}^{N}\frac{q_m}{p_m}(\frac{1}{p_m}-1)}\frac{1/q_nw_n}{\sum_{m\in S_2}1/(p_mw_m)}, \tag{28}$$

for all $n\in S_2$.

4.3 Achieving Every Point in the Capacity Region

Based on Theorem 5, we can design an algorithm for the prioritized largest deficit policy to achieve every point in the capacity region for QoE. Assume that a vector $\delta=[\delta_n]$ with $\delta_n\ge 0$, for all n, and $\sum_n\delta_n\ge 1$ is given. We choose $S_1=\{n|\delta_n=0\}$, and $w_n=\frac{1}{p_n\delta_n}$ for all $n\notin S_1$. With this setting, we have $\hat{D}_n(t)=0=\delta_n\hat{D}(t)$, for all $n\in S_1$, and $\hat{D}_n(t)=\frac{\delta_n}{\sum_{m\in S_2}\delta_m}\hat{D}(t)/\frac{q_n}{p_n}\le_{st}\delta_n\hat{D}(t)/\frac{q_n}{p_n}$, for all $n\in S_2$. In addition, Theorem 5 and Theorem 2 provide a sharp description of the capacity region for QoE.

THEOREM 6. *The capacity region for QoE is the set of vectors δ with $\delta_n\ge 0$, for all n, and $\sum_n\delta_n\ge 1$.* □

5. STRONG APPROXIMATION OF THE DIFFUSION LIMIT

We focus on diffusion limit in this paper because it provides a much more precise characterization of $D_n(t)$ than the study of fluid limit, i.e., $\lim_{t\to\infty}\frac{D_n(t)}{t}$. Indeed, we can simply approximate $D_n(t)$ by $\hat{D}_n(t)$. In this section, we establish a strong approximation theorem for $\hat{D}(t)$. Our analysis is based on the following theorem:

THEOREM 7. *[20, Theorem 4.4] Let $W(t)$ be a martingale with $E[(W(t+1)-W(t))^2|\mathcal{H}_t]<\infty$ for all t. Define $G(t)=$*

$\sum_{i\le t} E[(W(i+1)-W(i))^2|\mathcal{H}_i]$. *If* $G(t)\to\infty$ *almost surely as* $t\to\infty$. *Also, there is a nondecreasing function* $f(t)$ *such that* $\frac{f(t)}{t}$ *is nonincreasing and*

$$\sum_{t\ge 0} f(G(t))^{-1}\int_{\mathcal{B}} x^2 dProb(W(t+1)-W(t)\le x|\mathcal{H}_t)<\infty, \tag{29}$$

where $\mathcal{B}=\{x: x^2>f(G(t))\}$, *then there exits a Brownian motion* $\hat{W}(t)$ *such that*

$$\sup_{i\le t}|W(i)-\hat{W}(i)| = o((tf(t))^{1/4}\log t), \tag{30}$$

almost surely. □

We now state and prove our strong approximation theorem for $\hat{D}(t)$:

THEOREM 8. *For any* $0<\varepsilon<\frac{1}{4}$, *there exists a random process* $D^*(t)$ *that has the same distribution as* $\hat{D}(t)$, *and*

$$|D(t)-D^*(t)| = o(t^{\frac{1}{4}+\varepsilon}), \tag{31}$$

almost surely.

PROOF. We first find a Brownian motion $X^*(t)$ such that $\sup_{i\le t}|X(i)-X^*(i)| = o(t^{\frac{1}{4}+\varepsilon})$. We choose

$$f(t) = [\frac{t^\varepsilon}{\log(\max\{t, e^{\frac{1}{\varepsilon}}\})}]^4,$$

which is a nondecreasing function, and $\frac{f(t)}{t}$ is nonincreasing. In Section 3 we already show that

$$\min_n \frac{1}{p_n}-1 \le E[(X(t+1)-X(t))^2|\mathcal{H}_t] \le \max_n \frac{1}{p_n}-1, \tag{32}$$

and $X(t+1)-X(t)\le \max_n\frac{1}{p_n}-1$, for all t and on all sample paths. Therefore, there exists a sufficiently large T such that $Prob(X(t+1)-X(t)\le x)=1$, for all x such that $x^2>f(G(t))$, for all $t>T$ and on every sample path. The condition (29) then holds. By Theorem 7, there exists a Brownian motion $X^*(t)$ such that $\sup_{i\le t}|X(i)-X^*(i)| = o(t^{\frac{1}{4}+\varepsilon})$, almost surely. Further, since $\hat{X}(t) := \lim_{k\to\infty}\frac{X(kt)}{\sqrt{t}}$ is also a Brownian motion, $X^*(t)$ must have the same distribution as $\hat{X}(t)$, and $D^*(t) := \sup_{0\le\tau\le t}(\max\{0,-X^*(\tau)\})$ has the same distribution as $\hat{D}(t)$.

Finally, we have

$$\begin{aligned}&|D(t)-D^*(t)|\\ =&|\sup_{0\le\tau\le t}(\max\{0,-X(\tau)\}) - \sup_{0\le\tau\le t}(\max\{0,-X^*(\tau)\})|\\ \le& \sup_{0\le\tau\le t}|X(\tau)-X^*(\tau)| = o(t^{\frac{1}{4}+\varepsilon}),\end{aligned}$$

almost surely. □

In Section 7, we will demonstrate that $\hat{D}_n(t)$ provides a very accurate estimate for videos that are at least a couple of seconds long through simulations.

6. PERFORMANCE OF POPULAR POLICIES

In this section, we discuss the performance of two popular policies, namely, the weighted random policy and the weighted round robin policy.

In the weighted random policy, the AP randomly picks a client and transmits a packet to it. The probability that a client n is chosen by the AP is $\frac{q_n}{p_n}$. Therefore, for a fixed client n, it receives a packet with probability q_n in each time slot. We have

$$X_n(t+1)-X_n(t) = \begin{cases} 1-q_n, & \text{with probability } q_n,\\ -q_n, & \text{with probability } 1-q_n.\end{cases}$$

$(X_n(t+1)-X_n(t))$ then has mean 0 and variance $q_n(1-q_n)$. By the functional central limit theorem, $\hat{X}_n(t)=\lim_{k\to\infty}\frac{X(kt)}{\sqrt{k}}$ is a driftless Brownian motion with variance $q_n(1-q_n)$. Since $\hat{D}_n(t)=\sup_{0\le\tau\le t}(\max\{0,\frac{-\hat{X}_n(\tau)}{q_n}\})$, we can derive the CDF of $\hat{D}_n(t)$ as follows:

THEOREM 9. *Under the weighted random policy, the CDF of* $\hat{D}_n(t)$ *is given by*

$$Prob(\hat{D}_n(t)\le x) = \Phi(\frac{xq_n}{\sqrt{q_n(1-q_n)t}}) - \Phi(\frac{-xq_n}{\sqrt{q_n(1-q_n)t}}), \tag{33}$$

for all $x\ge 0$, $t\ge 0$. *The expected value is*

$$E[\hat{D}_n(t)] = \sqrt{\frac{2t(1-q_n)}{\pi q_n}}. \tag{34}$$

□

Next, we study the weighted round robin policy. In the weighted round robin policy, the AP group time slots into *frames*, where each frame consists of the T time slots $\{jT+1, jT+2, \dots, (j+1)T\}$, for some positive integer j. The value of T is chosen as the least number such that $T\frac{q_n}{p_n}$ is an integer for each n. In each frame, the AP transmits to client n exactly $T\frac{q_n}{p_n}$ times.

Under the weighted round robin policy, the number of packets that client n receives in a frame is a binomial random variable. In particular, we have $X_n((j+1)T)-X_n(jT)=i-Tq_n$ with probability $\binom{Tq_n/p_n}{i}p_n^i(1-p_n)^{Tq_n/p_n-i}$. $X_n((j+1)T)-X_n(jT)$ then has mean 0 and variance $Tq_n(1-p_n)$. By the functional central limit theorem, for a fixed integers i and j, $lim_{k\to\infty}\frac{X_n(k(j+i)T)-X_n(kiT)}{\sqrt{k}}$ is a Gaussian random variable with mean zero and variance $Tq_n(1-p_n)j$. Further, for all $t\in[jT,(j+1)T]$, $|X_n(t)-X_n(jT)|\le T$. Therefore, $\hat{X}_n(t)$ is a Brownian motion with mean 0 and variance $q_n(1-p_n)$. We then have

THEOREM 10. *Under the weighted round robin policy, the CDF of* $\hat{D}_n(t)$ *is given by*

$$Prob(\hat{D}_n(t)\le x) = \Phi(\frac{xq_n}{\sqrt{q_n(1-p_n)t}}) - \Phi(\frac{-xq_n}{\sqrt{q_n(1-p_n)t}}), \tag{35}$$

for all $x\ge 0$, $t\ge 0$. *The expected value is*

$$E[\hat{D}_n(t)] = \sqrt{\frac{2t(1-p_n)}{\pi q_n}}. \tag{36}$$

□

In order to compare the performance of the weighted random policy and the weighted round robin policy against that of the prioritized largest deficit policy, we consider the symmetric case that all clients have the same channel reliability and they consume packets at the same rate. In particular, we

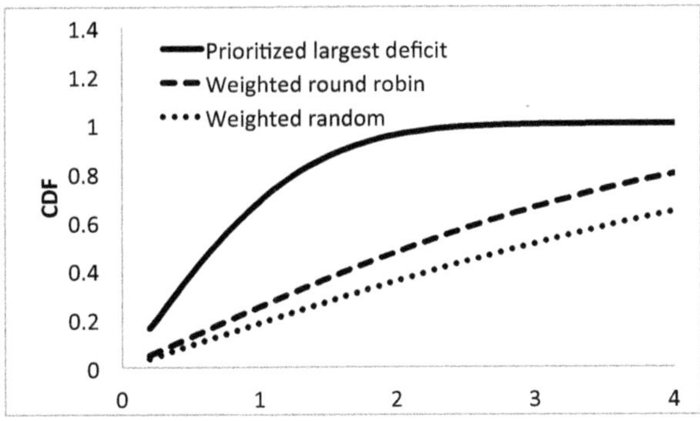

(a) $N = 10$

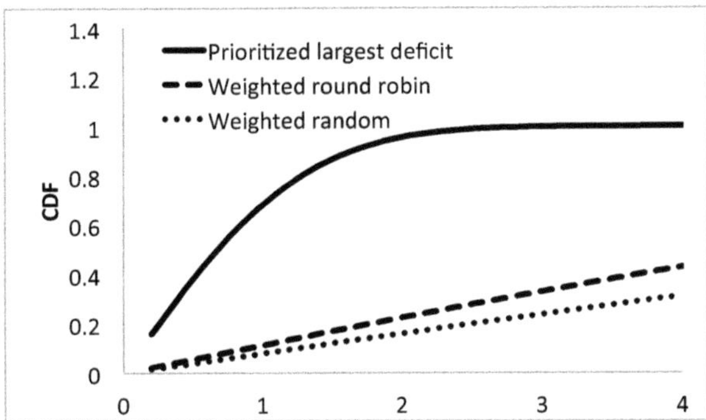

(b) $N = 50$

Figure 2: Comparisons of the three policies in a symmetric system.

set $p_n \equiv p$ and $q_n \equiv \frac{p}{N}$. We also set $S_1 = \phi$ and $\delta_n \equiv \frac{1}{N}$ for the prioritized largest deficit policy. By (19), (21), and (22), we have, under the prioritized largest deficit policy,

$$Prob(\hat{D}_n(t) \leq x) = \Phi(\frac{xp}{\sqrt{p(1-p)t}}) - \Phi(\frac{-xp}{\sqrt{p(1-p)t}}). \quad (37)$$

and

$$E[\hat{D}_n(t)] = \sqrt{\frac{2t(1-p)}{\pi p}}. \quad (38)$$

Since $q_n < p$, it is easy to see that

$$\hat{D}_n^{PLD}(t) \leq_{st} \hat{D}_n^{WRR}(t) \leq_{st} \hat{D}^{WR}(t),$$

where $\hat{D}_n^{PLD}(t), \hat{D}_n^{WRR}(t)$, and $\hat{D}^{WR}(t)$ denotes $\hat{D}_n(t)$ under the prioritized largest deficit policy, the weighted round robin policy, and the weighted random policy, respectively.

To illustrate the difference between the three policies, we plot the CDF of $\hat{D}_n(1)$ under the three policies for systems with 10 clients and 50 clients in Figure 2. We set $p = 0.5$ in both cases. Clearly, the prioritized largest deficit policy achieves much smaller $\hat{D}_n(1)$ than the other policies. In the system with 10 clients, $Prob(\hat{D}_n^{PLD}(1) \leq 2) = 0.95$, which is more than twice as large as $Prob(\hat{D}_n^{WRR}(1) \leq 2) = 0.47$ and $Prob(\hat{D}_n^{WR}(1) \leq 2) = 0.35$. The difference becomes larger as N increases. With 50 clients, $Prob(\hat{D}_n^{WRR}(1) \leq 2) = 0.22$, $Prob(\hat{D}_n^{WR}(1) \leq 2) = 0.16$, while the distribution of $\hat{D}_n^{PLD}(1)$ remains unchanged.

7. SIMULATION RESULTS

We have implemented our prioritized largest deficit policy, as well as the weighted round-robin and the weighted random policies in ns-2. In this section, we present our simulation results. In all simulations, we consider an IEEE 802.11a system where the AP transmits data at 54 Mbps. The time needed to transmit a packet and to receive an ACK is about 660 μs. All results presented in this section are the average of 50 simulation runs.

We first consider a system with 30 clients and $\sum_n \frac{q_n}{p_n} = 1$. We divide the clients into three groups: 10 clients are in the high-priority group, 10 clients are in the low-priority group with $w_n = 2$, and the other 10 clients are in the low-priority group with $w_n = 1$. Each group is further divided into two subgroups where clients in the first subgroup have $p_n = 0.75$ and $q_n = \frac{1}{40}$, while clients in the other subgroup have $p_n = 0.5$ and $q_n = \frac{1}{60}$. We simulate this system under different policies and compute the average outage of each client in each of the six subgroups.

Fig. 3 demonstrates the simulation results, where we use "PLD," "WRR," and "WR" to denote the prioritized largest deficit policy, the weighted round robin policy, and the weighted random policy, respectively. We also plot the estimate of $D_n(t)$ using $D_n(t) \approx \hat{D}_n(t)$, which is denoted by "predict." As can be seen in the figure, diffusion limit provides a very accurate estimate of $D_n(t)$ for each subgroup even for a small duration of time. This result suggests that $\hat{D}_n(t)$ is suitable for estimating the performance of on-demand video streams. In contrast, since $\lim_{t\to\infty} \frac{D_n(t)}{t} = 0$, for all n and for all simulated policies, it is clear that $\lim_{t\to\infty} \frac{D_n(t)}{t} = 0$ fails to capture important characteristics of videos with finite lengths. Further, we can also observe that the prioritized largest deficit policy outperforms the other two policies by large margins in all subgroups. Even for the low priority group with $w_n = 1$, which has the highest outage under our policy, the outage under our policy is still less than half of that under the other policies, as shown in Figs. 3(e) and 3(f).

Next, we consider a system that is slightly under-loaded, that is, $\sum_n \frac{q_n}{p_n} < 1$. The system setting is very similar to that in the previous paragraphs. The only difference is that we now set $p_n = 0.75$, and $q_n = \frac{1}{40}$ for half of the clients, and $p_n = 0.5$, $q_n = \frac{1}{65}$ for the other half. Under this setting, we now have $\sum_n \frac{q_n}{p_n} = \frac{25}{26}$.

Simulation results are shown in Fig. 4. Clearly, the prioritized largest deficit policy still outperforms the other two policies. Even for the two subgroups in the low priority group and have $w_n = 1$, their average amounts of outage within 20 seconds are only 25 and 23 time slots. Since wireless systems rarely operate on the boundary of the capacity regions, the simulation results show that our policy is still preferable for practical systems. We notice that the weighted round robin policy is in general better than the weighted random policy. This is consistent with the analysis in Section 6.

Finally, we evaluate the scenario where clients may buffer incoming packets and only start the playback when the number of packets in the buffer exceed a certain threshold. This is a popular approach to mitigate uncertainties of networks

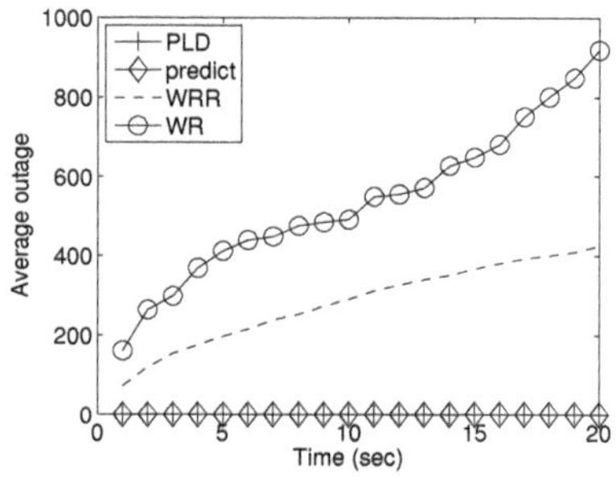

(a) High priority, $p_n = 0.75$, $q_n = 1/40$

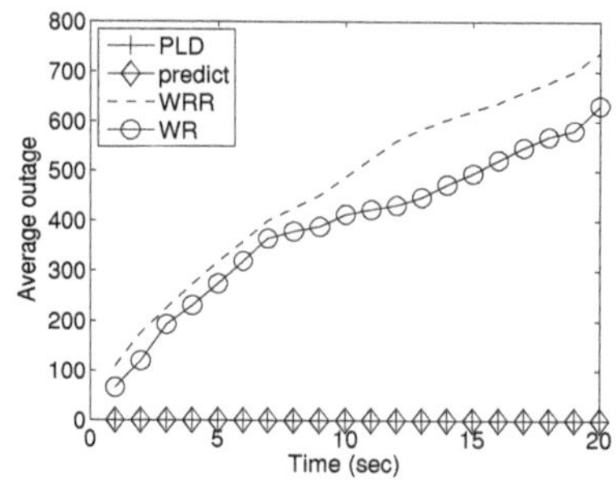

(b) High priority, $p_n = 0.5$, $q_n = 1/60$

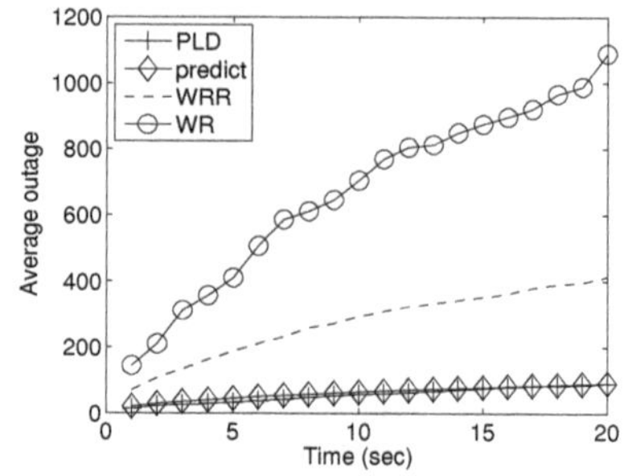

(c) Low priority, $p_n = 0.75$, $q_n = 1/40$, $w_n = 2$

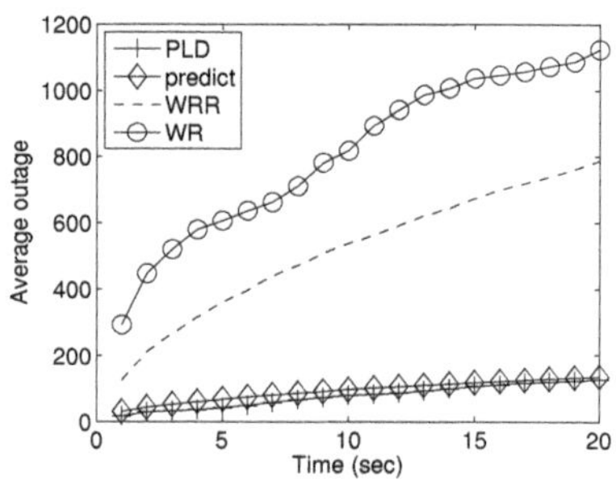

(d) Low priority, $p_n = 0.5$, $q_n = 1/60$, $w_n = 2$

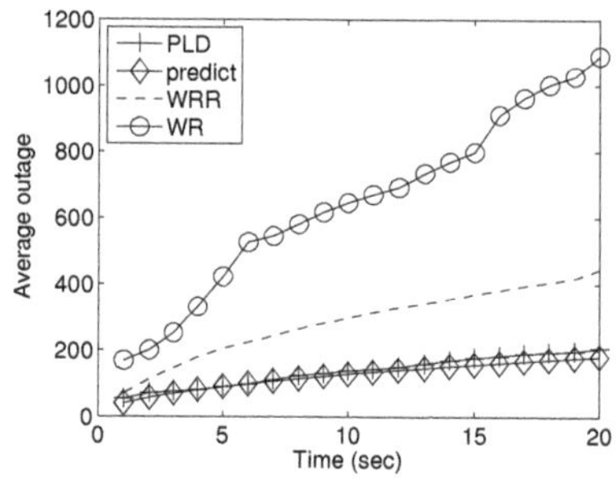

(e) Low priority, $p_n = 0.75$, $q_n = 1/40$, $w_n = 1$

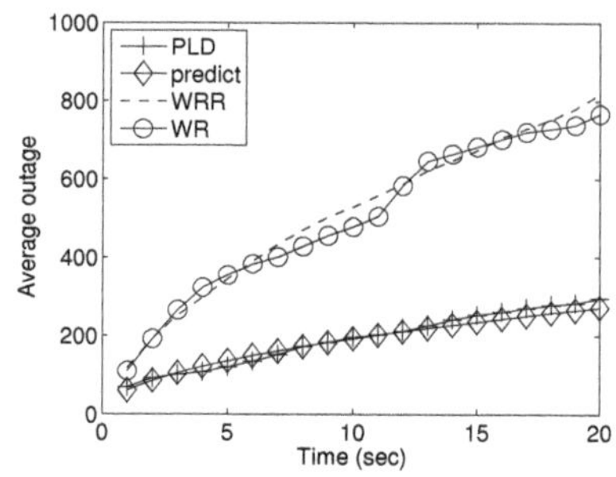

(f) Low priority, $p_n = 0.5$, $q_n = 1/60$, $w_n = 1$

Figure 3: Average outage for a system with $\sum_n \frac{q_n}{p_n} = 1$.

[15, 17, 23]. We consider the same system as that for Fig. 3. However, we assume that, when the system starts, each client has a certain number of packets in its buffer. We then simulate the per-client average outage in five minutes for different initial buffer sizes. To make the comparison fair, the prioritized largest deficit policy sets $S_1 = \phi$ and $\delta_n \equiv \frac{1}{N}$. In addition, we also compute the portion of clients that do not suffer from any outage in five minutes time.

Simulation results are shown in Fig 5. It is shown that our policy outperforms the other two greatly. With an initial buffer size as small as 25 packets, which corresponds to less than one second's video content, 96% of the clients do not encounter any outage through the playback under our policy. On the other hand, even when the weighted round-robin policy starts with an initial buffer size of 125 packets, its average video halt duration is still more than 5 times larger than that under our policy with an initial buffer size of 25 packets.

8. RELATED WORK

Many recent studies on video streaming have shifted emphasis from traditional quality of service (QoS) metrics, such as average delay and delay jitter, to QoE metrics that provide more direct measure on the perceived quality of end users. Video streaming needs to meet the strict deadline of each packet. Some studies model QoE by assuming that deadline misses cause packet losses and glitches in playback. Hou et al. [8], Jaramillo et al. [9], Li and Eryilmaz [13], Kim et al. [12] and Kang et al. [11] study the scheduling problem when each user has its requirements of per-packet deadline and deadline miss ratios. Li et al. [14] consider broadcasting an on-demand video stream where all packets are present at the beginning, but different packets have different deadlines. They then propose a network coding scheme to minimize the amount of packet losses.

In this paper, we focus on the scenario where deadline misses do not cause packet losses. Rather, they make video playback halt. Singh et al. [18] consider the radio resource management problem to reduce video halt. Chandur and Sivalingam [4] propose a scheduling heuristic to improve QoE. Bhatia et al. [2] propose a scheduling policy that exploits slow fading for on-demand video streaming. Joseph and de Veciana [10] propose a joint rate control and scheduling algorithm for optimizing QoE. These studies only focus on long-term average performance, and may be inadequate to capture important characteristics for videos with finite lengths.

Xu et al. [23] study the probability that video playback halts under a fixed scheduling discipline. ParandehGheibi et al. [17] study the tradeoff between rate, initial buffer size, and the probability of video halt. Anttonen and Mammelaa [1] derive an upper-bound of video halt probability for a G/G/1 queue. Yang et al. [25] uses large deviation theory to approximate video halt probability. These studies focus on the performance of a single user and does not consider the scheduling problem in a multi-user network.

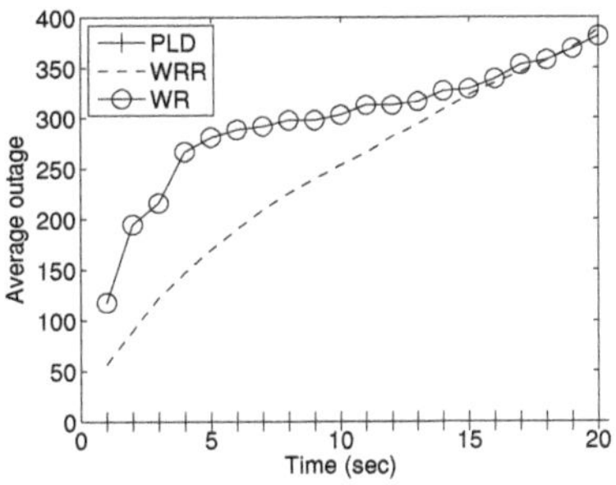

(a) High priority, $p_n = 0.75$, $q_n = 1/40$

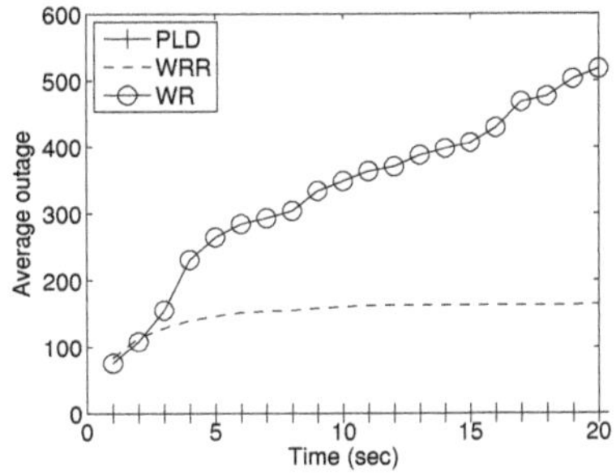

(b) High priority, $p_n = 0.5$, $q_n = 1/65$

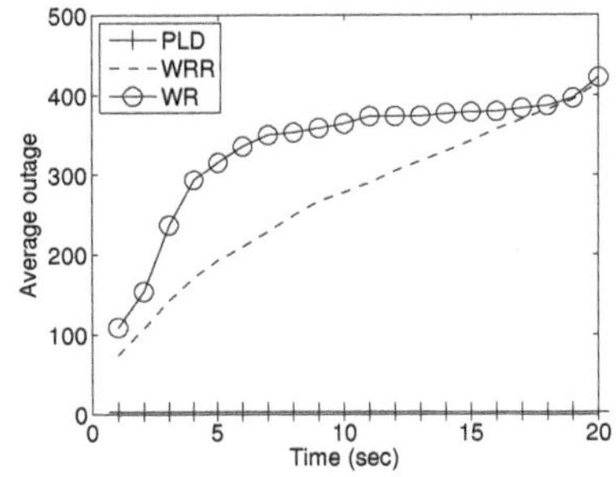

(c) Low priority, $p_n = 0.75$, $q_n = 1/40$, $w_n = 2$

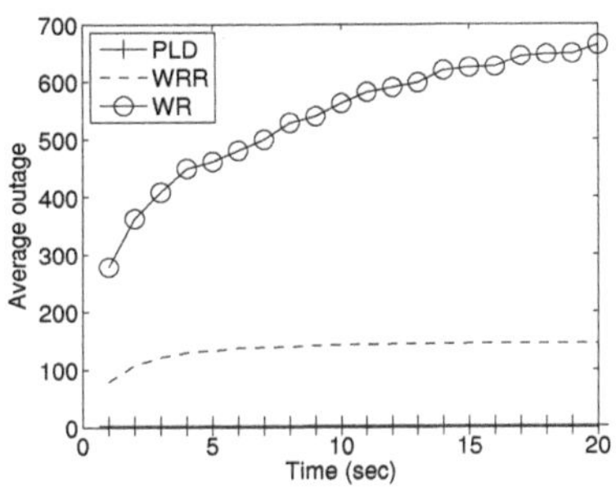

(d) Low priority, $p_n = 0.5$, $q_n = 1/65$, $w_n = 2$

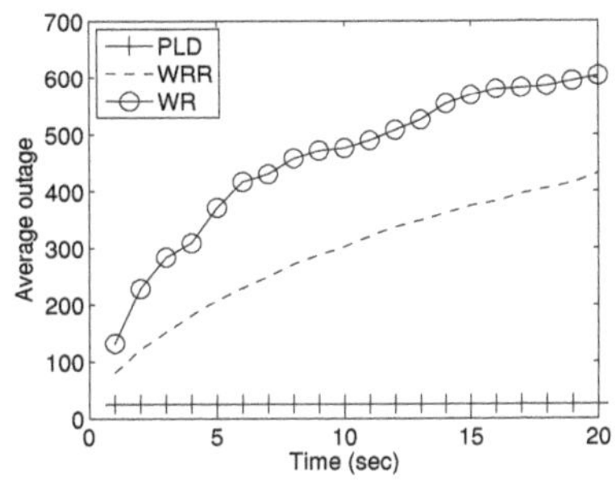

(e) Low priority, $p_n = 0.75$, $q_n = 1/40$, $w_n = 1$

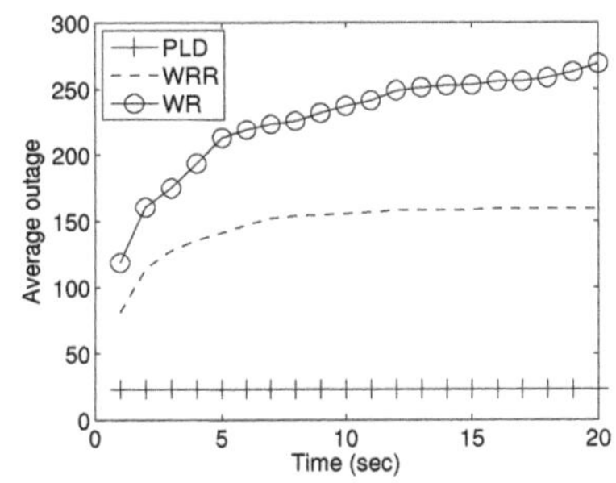

(f) Low priority, $p_n = 0.5$, $q_n = 1/65$, $w_n = 1$

Figure 4: Average outage for an under-loaded system.

9. CONCLUSIONS

In this paper, we study the capacity of wireless networks in providing quality of experience for on-demand video streams. We characterize the performance of a stream by the diffusion limit of its video halt duration. We derive a closed-form expression for the capacity region for QoE. We also propose a QoE-optimal scheduling policy that achieves every point in the capacity region. In addition, we study the performance of two other widely-used scheduling policies. Both theoretical analysis and simulation results demonstrate that our QoE-optimal policy outperforms other policies by large margins.

10. REFERENCES

[1] Anttonen, A., and Mammelaa, A. Interruption probability of wireless video streaming with limited video lengths. *Multimedia, IEEE Transactions on 16*, 4 (June 2014), 1176–1180.

[2] Bhatia, R., Lakshman, T., Netravali, A., and Sabnani, K. Improving mobile video streaming with link aware scheduling and client caches. In *INFOCOM, 2014 Proceedings IEEE* (2014), IEEE, pp. 100–108.

[3] Brown, B. M. Martingale central limit theorems. *The Annals of Mathematical Statistics 42*, 1 (1971), 59–66.

[4] Chandur, P., and Sivalingam, K. M. Quality of experience aware video scheduling in lte networks. In *Communications (NCC), 2014 Twentieth National Conference on* (2014), IEEE, pp. 1–6.

[5] Chen, H., and Yao, D. D. *Fundamentals of queueing networks: Performance, asymptotics, and optimization*, vol. 46. Springer, 2001.

[6] Csörgő, M. On the strong law of large numbers and the central limit theorem for martingales. *Transactions of the American Mathematical Society 131*, 1 (1968), 259–275.

[7] Harrison, J. M. *Brownian motion and stochastic flow systems*. Wiley New York, 1985.

[8] Hou, I.-H., Borkar, V., and Kumar, P. R. A theory of QoS for wireless. In *Proc. of INFOCOM* (2009).

[9] Jaramillo, J. J., Srikant, R., and Ying, L. Scheduling for optimal rate allocation in ad hoc networks with heterogeneous delay constraints. *Selected Areas in Communications, IEEE Journal on 29*, 5 (2011), 979–987.

[10] Joseph, V., and de Veciana, G. Nova: Qoe-driven optimization of dash-based video delivery in networks. In *INFOCOM, 2014 Proceedings IEEE* (April 2014), pp. 82–90.

[11] Kang, X., Wang, W., Jaramillo, J. J., and Ying, L. On the performance of largest-deficit-first for scheduling real-time traffic in wireless networks. In *Proceedings of the fourteenth ACM international symposium on Mobile ad hoc networking and computing* (2013), ACM, pp. 99–108.

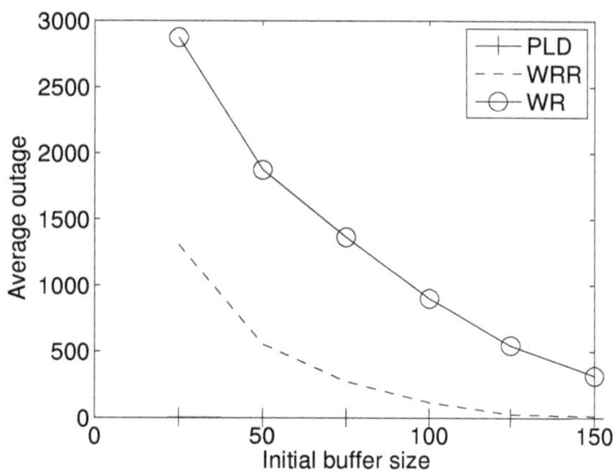

(a) Average outage

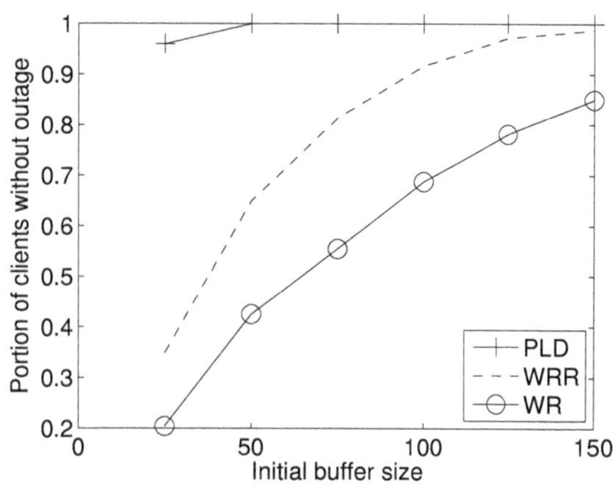

(b) Portion of clients without outage

Figure 5: Performance for different initial buffer sizes.

[12] Kim, K. S., Li, C.-P., and Modiano, E. Scheduling multicast traffic with deadlines in wireless networks. In *INFOCOM, 2014 Proceedings IEEE* (2014), IEEE, pp. 2193–2201.

[13] Li, R., and Eryilmaz, A. Scheduling for end-to-end deadline-constrained traffic with reliability requirements in multihop networks. *IEEE/ACM Transactions on Networking (TON) 20*, 5 (2012), 1649–1662.

[14] Li, X., Wang, C.-C., and Lin, X. On the capacity of immediately-decodable coding schemes for wireless stored-video broadcast with hard deadline constraints. *Selected Areas in Communications, IEEE Journal on 29*, 5 (May 2011), 1094–1105.

[15] Liang, G. Effect of delay and buffering on jitter-free streaming over random vbr channels. *Multimedia, IEEE Transactions on 10*, 6 (2008), 1128–1141.

[16] Mok, R., Chan, E., and Chang, R. Measuring the quality of experience of http video streaming. In *Integrated Network Management (IM), 2011 IFIP/IEEE International Symposium on* (May 2011), pp. 485–492.

[17] ParandehGheibi, A., Médard, M., Ozdaglar, A., and Shakkottai, S. Avoiding interruptions - a qoe reliability function for streaming media applications. *Selected Areas in Communications, IEEE Journal on 29*, 5 (2011), 1064–1074.

[18] Singh, S., Oyman, O., Papathanassiou, A., Chatterjee, D., and Andrews, J. G. Video capacity and qoe enhancements over lte. In *Communications (ICC), 2012 IEEE International Conference on* (2012), IEEE, pp. 7071–7076.

[19] Staelens, N., Moens, S., Van den Broeck, W., MarieÌLn, I., Vermeulen, B., Lambert, P., Van De Walle, R., and Demeester, P. Assessing quality of experience of iptv and video on demand services in real-life environments. *Broadcasting, IEEE Transactions on 56*, 4 (Dec 2010), 458–466.

[20] Strassen, V. Almost sure behavior of sums of independent random variables and martingales. In *Proceedings of the Fifth Berkeley Symposium on Mathematical Statistics and Probability, Volume 2: Contributions to Probability Theory, Part 1* (1967), University of California Press, pp. 315–343.

[21] Tassiulas, L., and Ephremides, A. Stability properties of constrained queueing systems and scheduling policies for maximum throughput in multihop radio networks. *Automatic Control, IEEE Transactions on 37*, 12 (1992), 1936–1948.

[22] Tassiulas, L., and Ephremides, A. Dynamic server allocation to parallel queues with randomly varying connectivity. *Information Theory, IEEE Transactions on 39*, 2 (1993), 466–478.

[23] Xu, Y., Altman, E., El-Azouzi, R., Haddad, M., Elayoubi, S., and Jimenez, T. Analysis of buffer starvation with application to objective qoe optimization of streaming services. *Multimedia, IEEE Transactions on 16*, 3 (April 2014), 813–827.

[24] Xu, Y., Elayoubi, S., Altman, E., and El-Azouzi, R. Impact of flow-level dynamics on qoe of video streaming in wireless networks. In *INFOCOM, 2013 Proceedings IEEE* (April 2013), pp. 2715–2723.

[25] Yang, J., Hu, H., Xi, H., and Hanzo, L. Online buffer fullness estimation aided adaptive media playout for video streaming. *Multimedia, IEEE Transactions on 13*, 5 (2011), 1141–1153.

On the Capacity Requirement of Largest-Deficit-First for Scheduling Real-Time Traffic in Wireless Networks

Xiaohan Kang
School of Electrical, Computer and Energy Engineering
Arizona State University
Tempe, AZ 85287
xiaohan.kang@asu.edu

I-Hong Hou
CESG and Department of ECE
Texas A&M University
College Station, TX 77843
ihou@tamu.edu

Lei Ying
School of Electrical, Computer and Energy Engineering
Arizona State University
Tempe, AZ 85287
lei.ying.2@asu.edu

ABSTRACT

We consider ad hoc wireless networks with real-time traffic, and study the capacity requirement of a low-complexity scheduling policy, called largest-deficit-first (LDF), for achieving the same quality of service (QoS) as the optimal policy in networks with unit capacity. We derive theoretical upper and lower bounds for general traffic. The bounds depend on the interference degree of the network and the max/min delay bound ratio. The performance of LDF is further evaluated using simulations and compared with two other algorithms. The simulation results show that LDF significantly outperforms the other two algorithms.

Categories and Subject Descriptors

C.2.1 [**Computer-Communication Networks**]: Network Architecture and Design—*wireless communication*

General Terms

Theory

Keywords

Capacity requirement; largest-deficit-first; real-time scheduling; quality of service; ad hoc networks

1. INTRODUCTION

With the rapid rise of various real-time applications such as video streaming, a large portion of the traffic in wireless networks is delay sensitive. For this kind of real-time traffic, there has been great interest in providing both high network throughput and minimum quality of service (QoS) guarantees for individual links. Following the analytical framework for scheduling traffic with hard deadlines proposed by Hou et al. [3], a lot of effort has been put in understanding the QoS performance of different scheduling policies with general network topology, heterogeneous traffic, channel fading etc. [4, 5, 6, 8] Other approaches have also been adopted to study QoS in multihop real-time traffic scenario. [13, 14] However, the problem of scheduling packets with hard deadlines in ad hoc wireless networks is largely unsolved except for some special cases as in Jaramillo et al. [9], where packet arrivals and deadline information are available before the packets arrive. Even with the required future information, the complexity of the algorithm in Jaramillo et al. [9] is prohibitively high. Because of that, Kang et al. [11] have studied the performance of a low-complexity algorithm, called the largest-deficit-first (LDF) scheduling, which maintains a deficit for each link and greedily selects links with the largest deficits,[1] and quantified the achievable delivery ratio of LDF compared to the optimal policy in the same network, which is called the *QoS efficiency ratio* in this paper. The QoS efficiency ratio quantifies the difference in delivery ratio between a greedy algorithm and the optimal algorithm. In particular, the QoS efficiency ratio is said to be γ if the number of successfully delivered packets under the greedy algorithm is at least γ faction of that under the optimal algorithm for any flow. This paper studies the performance of LDF from a different perspective and focuses on the amount of additional capacity required to *achieve the same delivery ratio as the optimal policy in networks with unit capacity*, which is named the *capacity efficiency ratio*.

We remark that these two concepts of efficiency ratios are very different because an increase in channel capacity does not necessarily result in the same amount of increase in delivery ratio. This can be easily seen from the following simple example. Consider a wireless channel with unit capacity and Poisson-distributed arrivals with rate λ. Assume the system is time-slotted; every packet is associated with a hard deadline of one time slot so a packet is either transmitted within the same time at which it arrives or discarded. In this simple example, the effective throughput of the system is

$$\mathbb{P}(A(t) \geq 1) = 1 - \frac{\lambda^0 e^{-\lambda}}{0!} = 1 - e^{-\lambda},$$

where $A(t)$ is the number of packet arrivals at the beginning of time slot t, and the delivery ratio is

$$(1 - e^{-\lambda})/\lambda.$$

Now if the channel capacity increases to two packets per time slot, then the effective throughput is

$$2\,\mathbb{P}(A(t) \geq 2) + \mathbb{P}(A(t) = 1) = 2 - (2 + \lambda)e^{-\lambda},$$

[1] A formal definition of LDF will be given in Section 2.3.

MobiHoc'15, June 22–25, 2015, Hangzhou, China.

ACM 978-1-4503-3489-1/15/06 ...$15.00.
http://dx.doi.org/10.1145/2746285.2746302.

and the delivery ratio becomes

$$(2 - (1 + 2\lambda)e^{-\lambda})/\lambda.$$

So when the bandwidth doubles, the increase in effective throughput or delivery ratio is less than 2-fold if $\lambda > 0.5$ (e.g., the increase is about $1.53 < 2$ when $\lambda = 2$). This is mainly because of the hard deadline constraint associated with each packet. If no deadline is imposed and $\lambda > 2$, then the effective throughput doubles when the channel capacity increases from one packet per time slot to two packets per time slot. We will later see in this paper that the bounds on the capacity efficiency ratio are completely different from the bounds on the QoS efficiency ratio.

We further comment that in Kang et al. [11], the authors proved that the QoS efficiency ratio of LDF is lower-bounded by $1/(1 + \beta)$, where β is the interference degree (see Chaporkar et al. [1]) of the network, i.e., the maximum number of links interfering with a single link that can be simultaneously activated in the network. In other words, the delivery ratio guaranteed by LDF is at least $1/(1+\beta)$ of the delivery ratio of the optimal policy. Since $\beta \geq 1$, the results in Kang et al. [11] can only be used to study the performance of LDF for those scenarios where the required delivery ratios are less than 0.5, and do not address the efficiency of LDF for applications which require higher delivery ratios. Therefore, to understand the performance of LDF for supporting high delivery ratios, we study the capacity efficiency ratio in this paper. In other words, the goal is to quantify the amount of additional capacity required for a greedy algorithm to achieve the same delivery ratios as the optimal policy for given traffic, where the delivery ratios can be close to one. The results in this paper are fundamentally different from the results in [11] as the results in [11] can only be applied to scenarios and applications where low delivery ratios are sufficient.

In this paper, we consider general network topology and traffic process, and derive theoretical bounds on the capacity efficiency ratio for LDF. Recall that the capacity efficiency ratio, denoted by K_{LDF}, is the minimum capacity required by LDF to guarantee at least the same QoS region achieved by the optimal policy with unit capacity.[2] We establish the following upper and lower bounds on K_{LDF}, where $\frac{\tau_{\max}}{\tau_{\min}}$ is the ratio of maximum packet delay bound to minimum packet delay bound, and β is the aforementioned interference degree of the network.

1. For i.i.d. traffic,
$$K_{\text{LDF}} \leq \left(2\frac{\tau_{\max}}{\tau_{\min}} + 2\log\frac{\tau_{\max}}{\tau_{\min}} + 3\right)\beta.$$
2. For i.i.d. traffic with unit delay bound ($\tau_{\min} = \tau_{\max} = 1$),
$$K_{\text{LDF}} \leq 2\beta.$$
3. There is non-i.i.d. probabilistic adversary such that
$$K_{\text{LDF}} \geq \frac{\tau_{\max}}{\tau_{\min}}.$$

We see from these bounds that to match the optimal but unknown policy with unit capacity, the required capacity for LDF depends on not only the topology characteristic but also the packet delay bound variation. While the upper and lower bounds are obtained under different assumptions, these bounds, along with the simulation results to be provided between LDF and other scheduling policies, provide basic understanding of the capacity requirements of LDF for supporting deadline-constrained traffic flows from various aspects of this problem.

The remaining of this paper is organized as follows. Section 2 introduces the model of the problem and defines the capacity efficiency ratio for capacity requirement characterization. We then present our main results regarding upper and lower bounds on the capacity efficiency ratio of LDF in Section 3. Simulation results are provided in Section 4. Section 5 concludes the paper.

2. MODEL

In this section we introduce the system model for the real-time scheduling problem. The wireless ad hoc network is modeled by a graph with potentially complex topology. The real-time data traffic is modeled to be (possibly infinitely many) packets with stochastic arrival times and hard deadlines. Then we describe the possible scheduling policies in a system with a certain capacity, and formally present the capacity efficiency ratio, which is the metric we use to characterize the performance of a scheduling policy.

We use $(x_i : i \in I)$ to denote the family (vector) of elements indexed by I. Curly braces with colons are reserved for set-builders. The size (cardinality) of a set A is denoted by $|A|$.

2.1 Network Model

We consider a time-slotted system with the set of links $\mathcal{N} = \{1, 2, \ldots, N\}$. The interference among the links is characterized by a conflict graph $G = (\mathcal{N}, \mathcal{E})$, where $\mathcal{N}$ is the set of vertices, each vertex corresponding to a link in the original network, and there is an edge (i_1, i_2) in $\mathcal{E}$ if link i_1 and link i_2 interfere with each other and thus cannot be scheduled simultaneously. Then $\mathcal{L} \subseteq \mathcal{N}$ is an independent set of the conflict graph if for any i_1, $i_2 \in \mathcal{L}$, we have $(i_1, i_2) \notin \mathcal{E}$. Let $\mathcal{I}$ be the set of all the independent sets of G. We then define the set of neighbors of link i to be those links that interfere with i, denoted by $\text{NB}(i) = \{i' \in \mathcal{N} : (i, i') \in \mathcal{E}\}$. Then the interference degree of G is given by

$$\beta = \max\{|\mathcal{L}| : i \in \mathcal{N}, \mathcal{L} \in \mathcal{I}, \mathcal{L} \subseteq \text{NB}(i)\}.$$

2.2 Traffic Model

At each time slot a number of packets with hard deadlines arrive on the links. The traffic of packets arriving in the system can be specified by a traffic sample path $J = ((n_i, b_i, e_i) : i \in \mathcal{N})$ with $b_i = (b_i(j) : 1 \leq j \leq n_i)$ and $e_i = (e_i(j) : 1 \leq j \leq n_i)$, where $n_i \leq \infty$ is the total number of packets arriving on link i in this traffic sample path, and $b_i(j)$ and $e_i(j)$ are the arriving time and the deadline of the jth packet on link i, respectively. Note that $n_i < \infty$ indicates that there are finitely many packets arriving on link i in the traffic sample path J, while $n_i = \infty$ indicates that there are infinitely many such packets in the traffic sample path J. Since the deadline is never before the arriving time, we have $b_i(j) \leq e_i(j)$ for all i and all j. The delay bound of the jth packet on link i, which is the maximum delay from

[2]The rigorous definition of the capacity efficiency ratio will be given in Section 2.4.

the arriving time to the time it is scheduled, is

$$\tau_i(j) = e_i(j) - b_i(j) + 1.$$

If the packet j on link i has not been scheduled by the end of time slot $e_i(j)$, it is considered useless and is discarded from the system. Let the number of arriving packets in J on link i at time slot t be $a_i(t) = |\{j : 1 \leq j \leq n_i, b_i(j) = t\}|$. By assuming the number of arriving packets on each link per time slot is at most $a_{\max}$ we have $a_i(t) \leq a_{\max}$ for any link i and any time t. Let $\mathcal{J}$ be the set of all traffic sample paths with delay bounds between $\tau_{\min}$ and $\tau_{\max}$ and maximum number of arriving packets $a_{\max}$.

2.3 Scheduling Policy

A scheduling policy determines a set of packets to be scheduled at each time slot. We assume reliable channels, so once scheduled a packet will be successfully delivered and leave the system. Let the set of available packets on link i at the beginning of time slot t be $\mathcal{A}_i(t) \subseteq \{1, 2, \ldots, n_i\}$. Then for any $j \in \mathcal{A}_i(t)$ we have $b_i(j) \leq t \leq e_i(j)$. Let the set of packets scheduled by a scheduling policy on link i at time slot t be $\mathcal{S}_i(t) \subseteq \mathcal{A}_i(t)$. For a system with unit capacity, at most one packet can be scheduled on a link each time slot (i.e., $|\mathcal{S}_i(t)| \leq 1$), and the set of links on which packets are scheduled must be an independent set of the conflict graph G due to the interference constraint (i.e., $\{i \in \mathcal{N} : |\mathcal{S}_i(t)| > 0\} \in \mathcal{I}$).

We now define the capacity of a system. We say a system has capacity k if each time slot is divided into k sub-slots, and the scheduling policy can choose a link activation set in each of the k sub-slots sequentially in a single time slot (this is the case for wireless networks where multiple orthogonal channels can be used for transmission).[3] Formally, given the packet$(\mathcal{A}_i(t) : i \in \mathcal{N})$ at time t, the set of scheduled packets on link i is

$$\mathcal{S}_i(t) = \bigcup_{k'=1}^{k} \mathcal{S}_i^{k'}(t),$$

where the sub-slot schedules $\left(\mathcal{S}_i^{k'}(t) : i \in \mathcal{N}, 1 \leq k' \leq k\right)$ satisfy the following constraints:

1. Only available packets can be scheduled; i.e.,

$$\mathcal{S}_i^{k'}(t) \subseteq \mathcal{A}_i(t) \quad \forall k' \leq k.$$

2. Each sub-slot of schedule has unit capacity; i.e.,

$$\left|\mathcal{S}_i^{k'}(t)\right| \leq 1 \quad \forall k' \leq k.$$

3. No packets can be (or need to be) scheduled twice since schedules in different sub-slots of a time slot are determined sequentially; i.e.,

$$\mathcal{S}_i^{k_1}(t) \cap \mathcal{S}_i^{k_2}(t) = \emptyset \quad \forall k_1, k_2 \leq k \text{ with } k_1 \neq k_2.$$

4. In each sub-slot the schedule satisfies the interference constraint; i.e.,

$$\left\{i \in \mathcal{N} : \left|\mathcal{S}_i^{k'}(t)\right| > 0\right\} \in \mathcal{I} \quad \forall k' \leq k.$$

[3]In this paper we consider uniform capacity over all the links in the network, which is the case when a particular wireless communication protocol is adopted in the ad hod network. E.g., IEEE 802.11a uses 52 subcarriers, which can be interpreted as a uniform capacity of 52 throughout the whole network.

The system, or the scheduling policy, is said to have unit capacity if it has capacity 1.

Naturally, we study maximal scheduling policies which do not idle when there is an available packet on a link that does not interfere with any other scheduled link. Note that some maximal policies are not feasible in practice since their decisions may depend on future traffic information.

We focus on a low-complexity greedy scheduling policy called the largest-deficit-first policy (LDF), which is the real-time variation of the extensively-studied longest-queue-first scheduling policy (see, e.g., Dimakis and Walrand [2] and Le et al. [12]). LDF maintains a nonnegative virtual queue $d_i(t)$, called the *deficit*, for each link i. The deficit evolves as follows.

1. The initial deficit is $d_i(0) = 0$ for all $i \in \mathcal{N}$.
2. Each time a packet arrives on link i, the deficit $d_i(t)$ increases by one with probability q_i, where q_i is the required delivery ratio for link i.[4]
3. Each time a packet on link i is scheduled, the deficit $d_i(t)$ decreases by one deterministically if $d_i(t) > 0$, and remain unchanged if $d_i(t) = 0$.

We can see that the deficit on a link is a nonnegative integer keeping track of the number of packets the scheduler owes to the link in order to meet the required delivery ratio, and when the deficit remains small, the required delivery ratio is achieved. In each sub-slot of the time slot t, LDF first sorts the links in $\mathcal{N}$ according to the current deficits $d_i(t)$, and obtains the index vector I such that $d_{I_1}(t) \geq d_{I_2}(t) \geq \cdots \geq d_{I_N}(t)$. LDF starts with the set of a single link that has the largest deficit, namely $\mathcal{B} = \{I_1\}$, and repeatedly considers link $i = 2, 3, \ldots, N$. The link I_i is included in the selection $\mathcal{B}$ if the following hold.

1. Link I_i does not interfere with any link in $\mathcal{B}$.
2. Link I_i has available packets on it for transmission.

After all links have been considered, the selection $\mathcal{B}$ is the scheduling decision given by LDF at this sub-slot of the time slot t.

2.4 Delivery Ratio Characterization

The goal of this paper is to provide individual quality-of-service (QoS) guarantee, which is usually more demanding than total throughput guarantee since some links may be over-served (getting more service than necessary) while others starved (getting insufficient service). In other words, the required delivery ratio for each link may not be achieved. That motivates us to study the relation between delivery ratio and capacity.

We model the stochastic traffic by the traffic process X, which is a $\mathcal{J}$-valued random element. We assume that LDF is associated with an arbitrary random tie-breaking process. We say the delivery ratio vector $q \in [0,1]^N$ is *achieved* by LDF$^{[k]}$ (LDF with capacity k) if for any $i \in \mathcal{N}$,

$$\mathbb{P}\left(\liminf_{T\to\infty} \frac{\mathrm{LDF}_i^{[k]}(X,T)}{\mathrm{CA}_i(X,T)} \geq q_i\right) = 1,$$

[4]We will elaborate on the meaning of the required delivery ratio q_i in Section 2.4.

where $\mathrm{LDF}_i^{[k]}(X,T)$ is the number of packets in X on link i scheduled by $\mathrm{LDF}^{[k]}$ in the first T time slots, and $\mathrm{CA}_i(X,T)$ is the cumulative number of arriving packets in traffic process X on link i before time T. Formally, for $X = ((n_i, b_i, e_i): i \in \mathcal{N})$,

$$\mathrm{CA}_i(X,T) = |\{j: 1 \le j \le n_i, b_i(j) \le T\}|.$$

Let the delivery ratio stability region of $\mathrm{LDF}^{[k]}$ for X be

$$\Lambda_{\mathrm{LDF}^{[k]}} = \left\{q \in [0,1]^N : q \text{ is achieved by } \mathrm{LDF}^{[k]}\right\}.$$

Define the delivery ratio stability region for traffic process X, denoted by Λ, to be the set of delivery ratios that can be achieved by some maximal policy with unit capacity. We then define the *capacity efficiency ratio* of LDF for traffic process X to be

$$K_{\mathrm{LDF}} = \min\{k: \ \mathrm{int}(\Lambda) \subseteq \Lambda_{\mathrm{LDF}^{[k]}}\},$$

where $\mathrm{int}(\cdot)$ is the interior. This definition is well-defined since sufficiently large capacity can guarantee that all packets will be delivered by any maximal scheduling policy when the number of arriving packets in each time slot is bounded.

3. MAIN RESULTS

We present upper and lower bounds on the capacity efficiency ratio of LDF in this section.

THEOREM 1. *For traffic process X that has i.i.d. arrival across time slots and i.i.d. delay bound across different packets on a link,*

$$K_{\mathrm{LDF}} \le \left(2\frac{\tau_{\max}}{\tau_{\min}} + 2\log\frac{\tau_{\max}}{\tau_{\min}} + 3\right)\beta.$$

We first state a lemma that gives an upper bound on the capacity efficiency ratio regardless of the stochastic nature of the traffic.

LEMMA 1. *For i.i.d. traffic process, the capacity efficiency ratio of LDF is upper-bounded by the minimum capacity that guarantees a maximal scheduling policy outperforms any unit-capacity policy in throughput over all traffic sample paths. Formally,*

$$K_{\mathrm{LDF}} \le \min\{k: \mu^{[k]}(J,T) \ge \nu^{[1]}(J,T) \quad \forall J \in \mathcal{J}, \forall T, \forall \mu^{[k]} \in \mathcal{P}(k), \forall \nu^{[1]} \in \mathcal{P}(1)\},$$

where $\mathcal{P}(k)$ and $\mathcal{P}(1)$ are the sets of all maximal scheduling policies with capacities k and 1, respectively, and $\mu^{[k]}(J,T)$ and $\nu^{[1]}(J,T)$ are the numbers of packets in traffic sample path J scheduled by $\mu^{[k]}$ and $\nu^{[1]}$ in the first T time slots.

Note that, by the definition of $\mathcal{P}(k)$ and $\mathcal{P}(1)$, $\mu^{[k]}$ and $\nu^{[1]}$ are two arbitrary maximal scheduling policies with capacities k and 1. So the right-hand-side of Lemma 1 is for the worst-case traffic sample paths and thus does not depend on the (probability) law of the traffic process. The proof of Lemma 1 can be found in Appendix A.

PROOF OF THEOREM 1. For any finite traffic sample path $J \in \mathcal{J}$ with $n_i < \infty$ for all $i \in \mathcal{N}$, let $\mathcal{L}^{\mathrm{P}}$ be the set of all packets on the links. For any $j \in \mathcal{L}^{\mathrm{P}}$, let $l(j)$ be the link of packet j, $b(j)$ the arriving time, $e(j)$ the deadline, and $\tau(j) =: e(j) - b(j) + 1$ the delay bound. We can then construct a conflict graph of the packets $G^{\mathrm{P}} = (\mathcal{L}^{\mathrm{P}}, \mathcal{E}^{\mathrm{P}})$, where there is an edge between $j \in \mathcal{L}^{\mathrm{P}}$ and $j' \in \mathcal{L}^{\mathrm{P}}$ if either $(l(j), l(j')) \in \mathcal{E}$ or $l(j) = l(j')$.

Let $\mathcal{O} \subseteq \mathcal{L}^{\mathrm{P}}$ be the set of packets scheduled by some policy ν with unit capacity, and let $\mathcal{M} \subseteq \mathcal{L}^{\mathrm{P}}$ be the set of packets scheduled by $\mathrm{MAX}^{[k]}$ (an arbitrary maximal scheduling policy with capacity k). By Lemma 1, to show the upper bound we only need to show that if $k = \left(2\frac{\tau_{\max}}{\tau_{\min}} + 2\log\frac{\tau_{\max}}{\tau_{\min}} + 3\right)\beta$ then $|\mathcal{M}| \ge |\mathcal{O}|$. Let t_j^{M} and t_j^{O} be the time slot that packet j is scheduled by $\mathrm{MAX}^{[k]}$ and ν respectively, and $t_j^{\mathrm{M}} = -1$ or $t_j^{\mathrm{O}} = -1$ if j is not scheduled by $\mathrm{MAX}^{[k]}$ or ν. For any $j \notin \mathcal{M}$, let

$$B_j := \left\{j' \in \mathcal{M}: b(j) \le t_{j'}^{\mathrm{M}} \le e(j), (j,j') \in \mathcal{E}^{\mathrm{P}}\right\}.$$

Then B_j can be understood as the potential set of blockers of j in $\mathcal{M}$, which are the packets that interfere with packet j and are are scheduled by $\mathrm{MAX}^{[k]}$ at a feasible scheduling time of j. Define the weights

$$w_j := \begin{cases} 1 & \text{if } j \in \mathcal{O} \cap \mathcal{M} \\ \frac{|B_j \backslash \mathcal{O}|}{(2+2\log(\tau_{\max}/\tau_{\min}))\beta\tau(j)} & \text{if } j \in \mathcal{O} \backslash \mathcal{M} \\ 0 & \text{if } j \notin \mathcal{O} \end{cases}.$$

To show $|\mathcal{M}| \ge |\mathcal{O}|$ we only need to show the following two inequalities:

$$\sum_{j \in \mathcal{L}^{\mathrm{P}}} w_j \le |\mathcal{M}|, \tag{1}$$

and

$$|\mathcal{O}| \le \sum_{j \in \mathcal{L}^{\mathrm{P}}} w_j. \tag{2}$$

To see (1) holds, we notice

$$\begin{aligned} &\sum_{j \in \mathcal{L}^{\mathrm{P}}} w_j - |\mathcal{M}| \\ &= \sum_{j \in \mathcal{O}} w_j - \sum_{j' \in \mathcal{M}} 1 \\ &= \sum_{j \in \mathcal{O} \backslash \mathcal{M}} \frac{|B_j \backslash \mathcal{O}|}{(2 + 2\log(\tau_{\max}/\tau_{\min}))\beta\tau(j)} - \sum_{j' \in \mathcal{M} \backslash \mathcal{O}} 1 \\ &= \sum_{j' \in \mathcal{M} \backslash \mathcal{O}} \left(\sum_{j \in \mathcal{O} \backslash \mathcal{M}} \frac{I_{B_j \backslash \mathcal{O}}(j')}{(2 + 2\log(\tau_{\max}/\tau_{\min}))\beta\tau(j)} - 1 \right), \end{aligned}$$

where

$$I_{B_j \backslash \mathcal{O}}(j') = \begin{cases} 1 & \text{if } j' \in B_j \backslash \mathcal{O} \\ 0 & \text{otherwise} \end{cases}.$$

Note in the above we rearranged the weights on $\mathcal{O} \backslash \mathcal{M}$ by the blockers in $\mathcal{M} \backslash \mathcal{O}$. By the definition of interference degree β, in each time slot there are at most β "neighbors" of $j' \in \mathcal{M}$ that are scheduled by ν. So for any τ with $\tau_{\min} \le \tau \le \tau_{\max}$,

$$\left|\{j \in \mathcal{O}: j' \in B_j, \tau(j) \le \tau\}\right| \le (2\tau - 1)\beta. \tag{3}$$

We can see this in Figure 1, where packet j' can block at most $(2\tau - 1)\beta$ packets in $\mathcal{O}$ with delay bounds less than or equal to τ. Hence,

$$\sum_{j \in \mathcal{O} \backslash \mathcal{M}} \frac{I_{B_j \backslash \mathcal{O}}(j')}{\tau(j)}$$

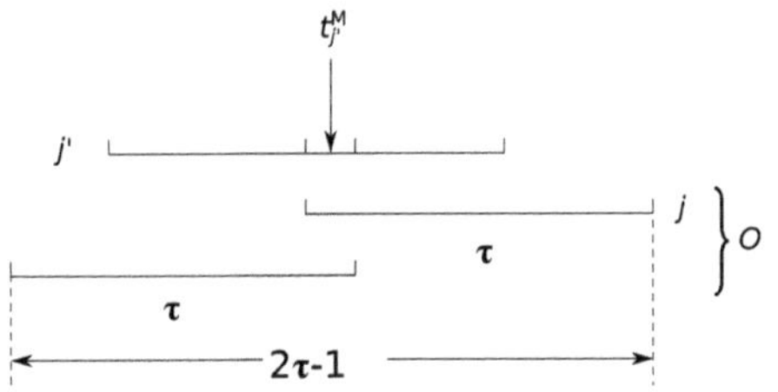

Figure 1: Demonstration of inequality (3).

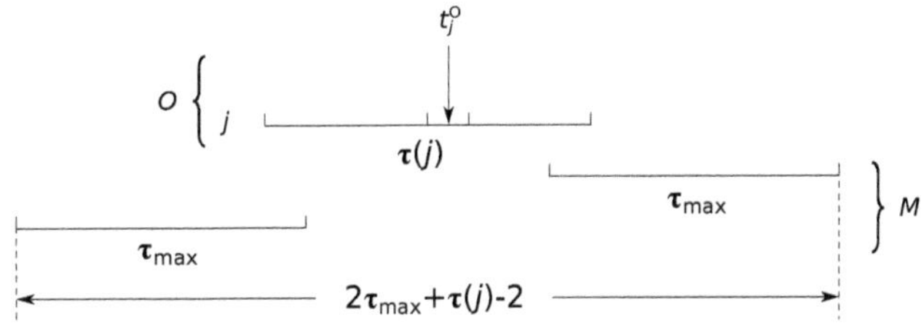

Figure 2: Demonstration of inequality (4).

$$
\begin{aligned}
&= \sum_{\tau=\tau_{\min}}^{\tau_{\max}} \sum_{\substack{j\in\mathcal{O}\setminus\mathcal{M}\\ \tau(j)=\tau}} \frac{I_{B_j\setminus\mathcal{O}}(j')}{\tau(j)} \\
&= \sum_{\tau=\tau_{\min}}^{\tau_{\max}} \frac{1}{\tau} \sum_{\substack{j\in\mathcal{O}\setminus\mathcal{M}\\ \tau(j)=\tau}} I_{B_j\setminus\mathcal{O}}(j') \\
&\le \sum_{\tau=\tau_{\min}}^{\tau_{\max}} \frac{1}{\tau} \left|\{j\in\mathcal{O}\colon j'\in B_j, \tau(j)=\tau\}\right| \\
&= \sum_{\tau=\tau_{\min}}^{\tau_{\max}} \frac{1}{\tau}(\left|\{j\in\mathcal{O}\colon j'\in B_j, \tau(j)\le\tau\}\right| \\
&\qquad - \left|\{j\in\mathcal{O}\colon j'\in B_j, \tau(j)\le\tau-1\}\right|) \\
&= \sum_{\tau=\tau_{\min}}^{\tau_{\max}-1} \left|\{j\in\mathcal{O}\colon j'\in B_j, \tau(j)\le\tau\}\right| \left(\frac{1}{\tau}-\frac{1}{\tau+1}\right) \\
&\quad + \left|\{j\in\mathcal{O}\colon j'\in B_j, \tau(j)\le\tau_{\max}\}\right| \frac{1}{\tau_{\max}} \\
&\le \sum_{\tau=\tau_{\min}}^{\tau_{\max}-1} (2\tau-1)\beta\left(\frac{1}{\tau}-\frac{1}{\tau+1}\right) + (2\tau_{\max}-1)\beta\frac{1}{\tau_{\max}} \\
&\le \left(\frac{2\tau_{\min}-1}{\tau_{\min}} + \frac{2}{\tau_{\min}+1} + \cdots + \frac{2}{\tau_{\max}}\right)\beta \\
&\le \left(2+2\log\frac{\tau_{\max}}{\tau_{\min}}\right)\beta.
\end{aligned}
$$

We then get

$$\sum_{j\in\mathcal{L}^{\mathrm{P}}} w_j - |\mathcal{M}| \le \sum_{j'\in\mathcal{M}\setminus\mathcal{O}} (1-1) = 0.$$

This completes the proof of (1).

Since $\mathrm{MAX}^{[k]}$ has capacity k, any $j\in\mathcal{O}\setminus\mathcal{M}$ must have been blocked by at least $k\tau(j)$ packets in $\mathcal{M}$. I.e.,

$$|B_j| \ge k\tau(j).$$

We call $B_j\cap\mathcal{O}$ the set of type I blockers of j, and $B_j\setminus\mathcal{O}$ the set of type II blockers of j. From Figure 2 we see that the type I blockers of j can be scheduled by ν in the $2\tau_{\max}+\tau(j)-2$ time slots except time slot t_j^{O}. By the interference degree, we must have

$$|B_j\cap\mathcal{O}| \le (2\tau_{\max}+\tau(j)-3)\beta. \tag{4}$$

Since j is blocked by some packet $j'\in\mathcal{M}\setminus\mathcal{O}$ every sub-slot within the delay bound of j, we have that the number of total blockers of packet j is at least the capacity k. So we can get a lower bound on the number of type II blockers of packet j as follow.

$$
\begin{aligned}
|B_j\setminus\mathcal{O}| &= |B_j| - |B_j\cap\mathcal{O}| \\
&\ge k\beta\tau(j) - (2\tau_{\max}+\tau(j)-3)\beta \\
&= \left(2\frac{\tau_{\max}}{\tau_{\min}} + 2\log\frac{\tau_{\max}}{\tau_{\min}} + 3\right)\beta\tau(j) \\
&\quad - (2\tau_{\max}+\tau(j)-3)\beta \\
&\ge \left(2+2\log\frac{\tau_{\max}}{\tau_{\min}}\right)\beta\tau(j).
\end{aligned}
$$

Finally,

$$
\begin{aligned}
\sum_{j\in\mathcal{L}^{\mathrm{P}}} w_j - |\mathcal{O}| &= \sum_{j\in\mathcal{O}} (w_j-1) \\
&= \sum_{j\in\mathcal{O}\setminus\mathcal{M}} \left(\frac{|B_j\setminus\mathcal{O}|}{\left(2+2\log\frac{\tau_{\max}}{\tau_{\min}}\right)\beta\tau(j)} - 1\right) \\
&\ge \sum_{j\in\mathcal{O}\setminus\mathcal{M}} (1-1) \\
&\ge 0.
\end{aligned}
$$

Thus (2) is proved. Combining (1), (2) and Lemma 1 we get Theorem 1. □

THEOREM 2. *For i.i.d. traffic process X with unit delay bound,*

$$K_{\mathrm{LDF}} \le 2\beta.$$

REMARK 1. *We note that Theorem 2 is stronger than Theorem 1 with i.i.d. traffic and $\tau_{\max}=\tau_{\min}=1$, which only gives an upper bound of 5β.*

PROOF. As in the proof of Theorem 1, we consider the packet conflict graph $G^{\mathrm{P}}=(\mathcal{L}^{\mathrm{P}},\mathcal{E}^{\mathrm{P}})$, where $\mathcal{L}^{\mathrm{P}}$ is the set of packets. Since the traffic has unit delay bound, we only need to consider one set of arriving packets $\mathcal{L}^{\mathrm{P}}$ with $b(j)=e(j)=1$ for all $j\in\mathcal{L}^{\mathrm{P}}$. Let

$$B_j := \left\{j'\in\mathcal{M}\colon (j,j')\in\mathcal{E}^{\mathrm{P}}\right\}.$$

We use the following weights:

$$w_j := \begin{cases} 1 & \text{if } j\in\mathcal{O}\cap\mathcal{M} \\ \frac{|B_j\setminus\mathcal{O}|}{\beta} & \text{if } j\in\mathcal{O}\setminus\mathcal{M} \\ 0 & \text{if } j\notin\mathcal{O} \end{cases}.$$

Similarly we can see that since the interference degree is β, we have

$$\sum_{j\in\mathcal{O}\setminus\mathcal{M}} I_{B_j\setminus\mathcal{O}}(j') \le \beta,$$

and then

$$\sum_{j\in\mathcal{L}^{\mathrm{P}}} w_j - |\mathcal{M}| = \sum_{j'\in\mathcal{M}\setminus\mathcal{O}} \left(\sum_{j\in\mathcal{O}\setminus\mathcal{M}} \frac{I_{B_j\setminus\mathcal{O}}(j')}{\beta} - 1\right) \le 0.$$

So (1) still holds. By choosing $k = 2\beta$ we have

$$|B_j \backslash \mathcal{O}| = |B_j| - |B_j \cap \mathcal{O}| \geq k - \beta = \beta.$$

So $\sum_{j \in \mathcal{L}^P} w_j \geq |\mathcal{O}|$. Thus $|\mathcal{M}| \geq |\mathcal{O}|$ and by Lemma 1 the proof is complete. □

We now give a lower bound on the capacity efficiency ratio of LDF by constructing a non-i.i.d. probabilistic adversary.

THEOREM 3. *Assume LDF is associated with the earliest-deadline-first (EDF) inter-link tie-breaking rule. There exists a probabilistic non-i.i.d. traffic process and deficit arrival process such that*

$$K_{\mathrm{LDF}} \geq \frac{\tau_{\max}}{\tau_{\min}}.$$

PROOF. For ease of presentation we only demonstrate a traffic process and a deficit arrival process with $\tau_{\max} = 3$ and $\tau_{\min} = 1$. General cases can be similarly constructed. Consider a network with three collocated links; i.e., the three links interfere with each other. We want to construct a traffic process such that LDF with capacity 2 cannot guarantee the full QoS region. Define the following traffic frames:

- J_1 with one packet per link. All packets arrive at the same time. The delay bounds for the three packets on links 1, 2 and 3 are 1, 2 and 3, respectively. The deficits increase at links 2 and 3;
- J_2 with one packet per link. All packets arrive at the same time. The delay bounds for the three packets on links 1, 2 and 3 are 2, 3 and 1, respectively. The deficits increase at links 1 and 2;
- J_3 with one packet per link. All packets arrive at the same time. The delay bounds for the three packets on links 1, 2 and 3 are 3, 1 and 2, respectively. The deficits increase at links 1 and 3;
- J_4 with one packet on link 1, two packets on link 2 and two packets on link 3. All packets arrive at the same time. The delay bounds are all 1. Each arriving packet increases the deficit by one.

Assume the initial deficits are all equal and in each frame we have arrival and deficit increases first, and then schedule according to current deficits. Let the adversarial traffic J be such that each big frame consists of (J_1, J_2, J_3) with probability $1 - \epsilon$, and (J_1, J_2, J_3, J_4) with probability ϵ, for some $\epsilon \in (0, 1)$. Then on average the deficit arrival is

$$\lambda = (1-\epsilon)\begin{pmatrix}2\\2\\2\end{pmatrix} + \epsilon\begin{pmatrix}3\\4\\4\end{pmatrix} = \begin{pmatrix}2+\epsilon\\2+2\epsilon\\2+2\epsilon\end{pmatrix}$$

per big frame, while on average LDF with EDF inter-link tie-breaking rule and capacity 2 schedules deficits

$$s_{\mathrm{LDF}} = (1-\epsilon)\begin{pmatrix}2\\2\\2\end{pmatrix} + \epsilon\begin{pmatrix}2\\3\\3\end{pmatrix} = \begin{pmatrix}2\\2+\epsilon\\2+\epsilon\end{pmatrix}$$

per big frame. So the deficits will increase linearly under LDF. We note that the optimal policy with unit capacity schedules

$$s_{\mathrm{OPT}} = \begin{pmatrix}3+\frac{1}{3}\epsilon\\3+\frac{1}{3}\epsilon\\3+\frac{1}{3}\epsilon\end{pmatrix}$$

per big frame. So for $\epsilon < 3/5$ we have

$$s_{\mathrm{LDF}} < \lambda < s_{\mathrm{OPT}}.$$

In other words, the capacity efficiency ratio for LDF with EDF tie-breaking rule under the given adversarial traffic process is at least $\tau_{\max}/\tau_{\min} = 3$. □

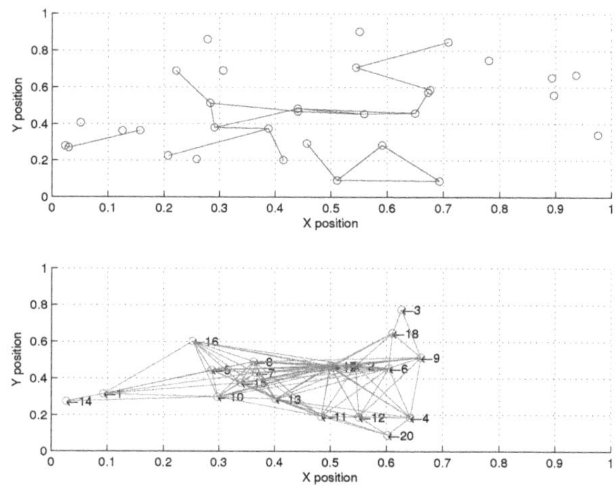

Figure 3: Network topology used in the simulations. The upper graph is the original graph and the lower graph is the conflict graph. The interference degree is 3.

4. SIMULATIONS

In this section we study the capacity efficiency ratio of different scheduling policies via simulations. We generated a randomly generated network shown in Fig. 3 with the unit-disk interference model.[5] In the original graph we place 32 nodes randomly in a unit square, and 20 links are randomly formed between pairs of nodes with distance less than the communication range $c = 0.25$. The interference is such that any two links interfere with each other if one transmitter or receiver is within the interference range $r = 0.21$ of the other transmitter or receiver. The number of packets arriving to each link at each time slot is $a_{\min} = 1$ with probability 0.5, and is $a_{\max} = 10$ otherwise. The delay bounds of the packets are $\tau_{\min} = 1$ for half random links, and $\tau_{\max} = 2$ for the other half. We varied some of the above default parameters in each specific simulation to show the impact they have on the system.

We compare LDF to two policies: the earliest-deadline-first policy with deficit-awareness (EDF-DA) and the shortest-delay-bound-first policy with deficit-awareness (SDBF-DA). The original versions of these two policies have been successfully used in real-time operating systems. EDF-DA is the QoS-guaranteeing version of the earliest-deadline-first scheduling algorithm, which is shown optimal on preemptive uniprocessors. It first gives priority to links with positive deficits, and then greedily choose packets with the earliest deadlines. SDBF-DA is the QoS-guaranteeing version of the rate-monotonic scheduling algorithm. It first gives priority

[5]The unit-disk model was first proposed to model ad hoc wireless networks by Huson and Sen [7], and later widely used in the analysis of scheduling problems in ad hod wireless networks (see, e.g., Joo et al. [10]).

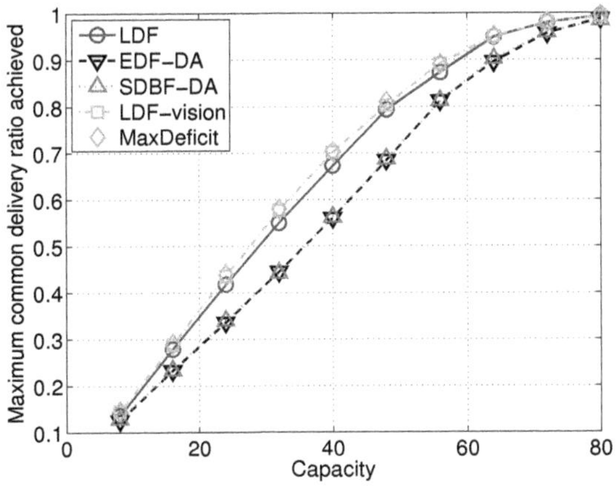

Figure 4: Maximum common delivery ratio achieved with different capacities for $\tau_{\max} = 1$.

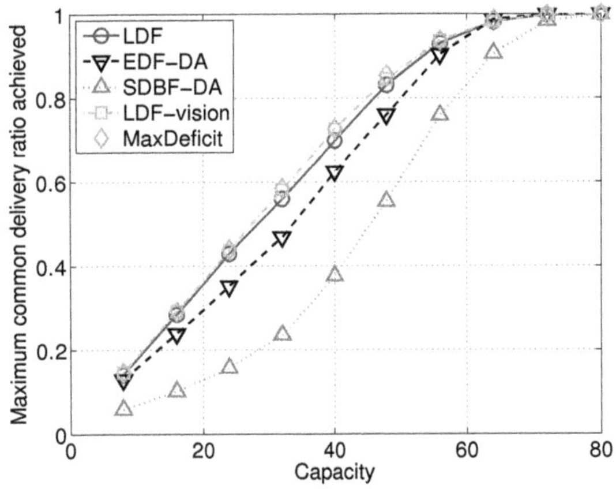

Figure 5: Maximum common delivery ratio achieved with different capacities for $\tau_{\max} = 2$.

to links with positive deficits, and then greedily choose packets with the shortest delay bound. Ties are broken uniformly at random.

We also consider two modified versions of LDF. The first one is LDF-vision, which starts with an empty selection, and in each repetition adds one or two feasible links to the selection in a greedy fashion such that the total deficit in the selection is maximized. We note that LDF-vision is a less greedy version of LDF, which greedily adds a single link to the selection. Intuitively LDF-vision has more global vision than LDF and may end up with a selection with larger total deficit. The other modified version of LDF is MaxDeficit, which gives the feasible schedule on the set of available links with the maximum total deficit. We can see that MaxDeficit is a max-weight scheduling with weight being the deficit. We note that MaxDeficit may incur much higher computational overhead than its greedy counterparts as the network size becomes large.

Once a link is chosen by the scheduler, SDBF-DA will schedule a packet with the shortest delay bound on that link, while all other policies will schedule a packet with the earliest deadline on that link.

REMARK 2. *Note that since the optimal policy for the delivery ratio is unknown, the capacity efficiency ratio cannot be calculated. So in the simulations, we plotted the delivery ratio versus the capacity for each low-complexity algorithm to study the performance improvement of each when additional capacity is added to the network.*

4.1 Homogeneous Delivery Ratios

We let the delivery ratios for all links be equal to a common delivery ratio $\bar{q}$ and study the maximum common delivery ratio value that each policy can achieve with various capacity. The results are shown in Figure 4 for homogeneous delay bounds, and Figure 5 for heterogeneous delay bounds. We see that the marginal delivery rate improvement brought by adding capacity decreases significantly as the capacity becomes large. For example in Figure 4 an additional amount of 8 units of capacity increases the maximum QoS of LDF from 0.45 to 0.59 at capacity 24, but only 0.95 to 0.98 at capacity 64. This phenomenon, known as *diminishing returns* in economics, demonstrate that it could be very demanding to achieve high delivery ratio of one by boosting capacity due to occasional bursty arrivals.

The comparison between different policies in both figures show that LDF has better delivery ratio performance than EDF-DA and SDBF-DA. While in the homogeneous delay bound case in Figure 4 EDF-DA and SDBF-DA are identical since all available packets have the same deadlines and delay bounds, in the heterogeneous delay bound case in Figure 5 EDF-DA outperforms SDBF-DA. We conjecture that LDF outperforms the two algorithms because it takes into account the full deficit information, as opposed to the other two policies which only use partial deficit information (whether the deficit is positive or not). We also note that SDBF-DA has a degraded performance for heterogeneous delay bounds since new packets with small delay bound may block packets with large delay bound that arrived in the previous time slots, leading to bad delivery ratio performance for links with large delay bounds.

Both LDF-vision and MaxDeficit have slightly better performance than LDF in the homogeneous scenario. This is intuitively because LDF-vision and MaxDeficit usually give scheduling decisions with larger total deficit. It should be noted that LDF-vision and MaxDeficit are much more computational expensive than LDF. Further comparison between LDF and its two modified versions on stability region will be provided in Section 4.2.

4.2 Heterogeneous Delivery Ratios

Now we randomly divide the links in the network into two groups: Group A and Group B. We let each group use a common delivery ratio, and plot the boundary delivery-ratio pairs where the deficits start to become unstable in Figure 6 and Figure 7. We first notice that LDF achieves the largest delivery ratio stability region among the three deficit-aware policies. We also note that the performance of the different policies change significantly when the heterogeneity of the delivery ratio increases. In particular the delivery ratio stability regions of EDF-DA and SDBF-DA are not convex. Comparing Figure 6 with Figure 7 we again see that heterogeneity in delay bounds benefits LDF and EDF-DA but harms SDBF-DA.

Comparing LDF and its two modified versions, namely LDF-vision and MaxDeficit, we see that the delivery ratio

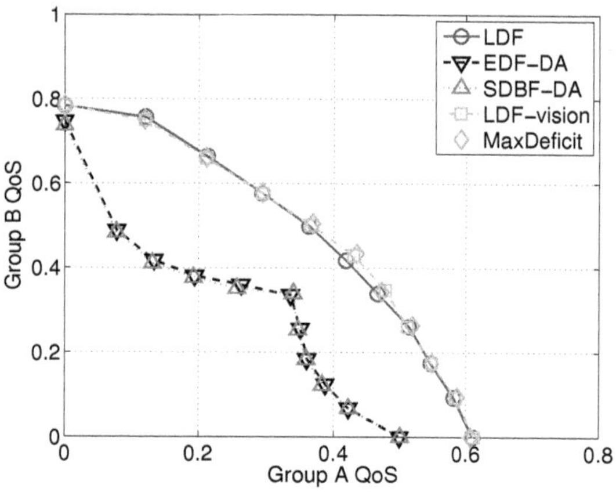

Figure 6: Delivery ratio stability region for $\tau_{\max} = 1$ with capacity 24.

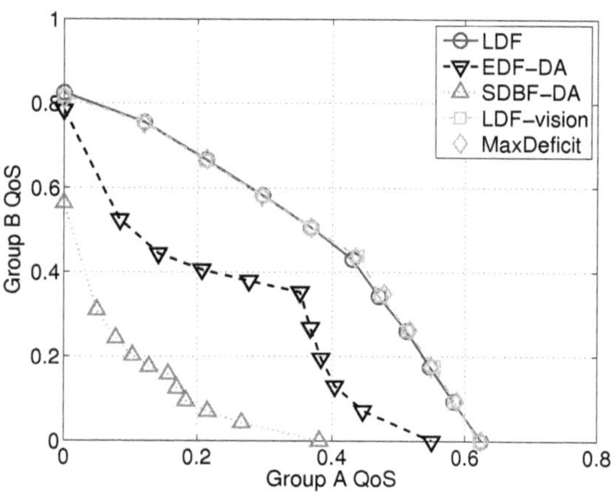

Figure 7: Delivery ratio stability region for $\tau_{\max} = 2$ with capacity 24.

stability regions for the three LDF-based policies are almost identical. The only noticeable difference between LDF and its modified versions is on the diagonal, i.e., the homogeneous case when the two groups have the same QoS. As a result, the computational advantage and the potential to be implemented distributedly makes LDF a good candidate for scheduling real-time traffic in ad hoc networks.

5. CONCLUSIONS

In this paper we studied the capacity requirements of ad hoc wireless networks with real-time traffic under the largest-deficit-first scheduling policy. We looked at the capacity efficiency ratio which is the amount of capacity needed for LDF to outperform the optimal policy with unit capacity. We derived upper and lower bounds on the capacity efficiency ratio of LDF in terms of max/min packet delay bound ratio and the interference degree of the conflict graph. We also used simulations to demonstrate the diminishing returns phenomenon of capacity.

6. ACKNOWLEDGMENTS

This work was supported in part by the National Science Foundation (NSF) under Grants CNS-1264012 and CNS-1262329, and the Defense Threat Reduction Agency (DTRA) under Grant HDTRA1-13-1-0030.

7. REFERENCES

[1] P. Chaporkar, K. Kar, X. Luo, and S. Sarkar. Throughput and fairness guarantees through maximal scheduling in wireless networks. *IEEE Trans. Inf. Theory*, 54(2):572–594, Feb. 2008.

[2] A. Dimakis and J. Walrand. Sufficient conditions for stability of longest queue first scheduling: Second-order properties using fluid limits. *Adv. Appl. Probab.*, 38(2):505–521, June 2006.

[3] I.-H. Hou, V. Borkar, and P. R. Kumar. A theory of QoS for wireless. In *Proc. IEEE Int. Conf. Computer Communications (INFOCOM)*, pages 486–494, Rio de Janeiro, Brazil, 2009.

[4] I.-H. Hou and P. R. Kumar. Admission control and scheduling for QoS guarantees for variable-bit-rate applications on wireless channels. In *Proc. ACM Int. Symp. Mobile Ad Hoc Networking and Computing (MobiHoc)*, pages 175–184, New Orleans, LA, 2009.

[5] I.-H. Hou and P. R. Kumar. Scheduling heterogeneous real-time traffic over fading wireless channels. In *Proc. IEEE Int. Conf. Computer Communications (INFOCOM)*, pages 1–9, San Diego, CA, 2010.

[6] I.-H. Hou and P. R. Kumar. Utility-optimal scheduling in time-varying wireless networks with delay constraints. In *Proc. ACM Int. Symp. Mobile Ad Hoc Networking and Computing (MobiHoc)*, pages 31–40, Chicago, IL, 2010.

[7] M. Huson and A. Sen. Broadcast scheduling algorithms for radio networks. In *Proc. IEEE Military Communications Conf. (MILCOM)*, volume 2, pages 647–651, San Diego, CA, Nov. 1995.

[8] J. J. Jaramillo and R. Srikant. Optimal scheduling for fair resource allocation in ad hoc networks with elastic and inelastic traffic. *IEEE/ACM Trans. Netw.*, 19(4):1125–1136, Aug. 2011.

[9] J. J. Jaramillo, R. Srikant, and L. Ying. Scheduling for optimal rate allocation in ad hoc networks with heterogeneous delay constraints. *IEEE J. Sel. Areas Commun.*, 29(5):979–987, May 2011.

[10] C. Joo, X. Lin, and N. B. Shroff. Understanding the capacity region of the greedy maximal scheduling algorithm in multihop wireless networks. *IEEE/ACM Trans. Netw.*, 17(4):1132–1145, Aug. 2009.

[11] X. Kang, W. Wang, J. J. Jaramillo, and L. Ying. On the performance of largest-deficit-first for scheduling real-time traffic in wireless networks. In *Proc. ACM Int. Symp. Mobile Ad Hoc Networking and Computing (MobiHoc)*, pages 99–108, Bangalore, India, July/Aug. 2013.

[12] L. B. Le, E. Modiano, C. Joo, and N. B. Shroff. Longest-queue-first scheduling under SINR interference model. In *Proc. ACM Int. Symp. Mobile Ad Hoc Networking and Computing (MobiHoc)*, pages 41–50, Chicago, IL, Sept. 2010.

[13] R. Li and A. Eryilmaz. Scheduling for end-to-end deadline-constrained traffic with reliability requirements in multi-hop networks. In *Proc. IEEE Int. Conf. Computer Communications (INFOCOM)*, pages 3065–3073, Shanghai, China, Apr. 2011.

[14] Z. Mao, C. E. Koksal, and N. B. Shroff. Online packet scheduling with hard deadlines in multihop communication networks. In *Proc. IEEE Int. Conf. Computer Communications (INFOCOM)*, pages 2463–2471, Turin, Italy, Apr. 2013.

APPENDIX

A. PROOF OF LEMMA 1

Let

$$C_{\text{MAX}} = \min\{k\colon \mu^{[k]}(J,T) \geq \nu^{[1]}(J,T)$$
$$\forall J \in \mathcal{J}, \forall T, \forall \mu^{[k]} \in \mathcal{P}(k), \forall \nu^{[1]} \in \mathcal{P}(1)\},$$

We only need to show that

$$\text{int}(\Lambda) \subseteq \Lambda_{\text{LDF}^{[k]}}$$

for $k = C_{\text{MAX}}$. Let $X(F)$ be the F-framed version of the traffic process X, which consists of all the packets j in X with $zF \leq b(j) \leq e(j) \leq (z+1)F$ for some integer z. Let the delivery ratio stability region with unit capacity for the F-framed traffic $X(F)$ be $\Lambda^{(F)}$. By definition of the stability region, for any $q \in \Lambda$ there exists a maximal scheduling policy with unit capacity, denoted by μ, that achieves q. Let $\mu^{(F)}$ be the F-framed version of μ, which only schedules packets in $X(F)$. Then

$$\mu_i^{(F)}(X,T) \geq \mu_i(X,T) - \frac{\tau_{\max} T}{F}.$$

Then with probability one,

$$\liminf_{T\to\infty} \frac{\mu_i^{(F)}(X,T)}{\text{CA}_i(X(F),T)} \geq \liminf_{T\to\infty} \frac{\mu_i(X,T) - \frac{\tau_{\max}T}{F}}{\text{CA}_i(X,T)}$$
$$\geq q_i - \frac{\tau_{\max}}{F\bar{a}_i},$$

where $\bar{a}_i$ is the arrival rate of traffic X on link i. Then we can see that the delivery ratio stability region for the F-framed traffic $X(F)$ approaches Λ as $F \to \infty$. So for any $q \in \text{int}(\Lambda)$ there exists F such that $q \in \Lambda^{(F)}$.

Let MW(F) be the scheduling policy that does a maximum weight schedule in each frame with size F. The weights are the deficits updated at the beginning of each frame. While this policy requires knowledge of the traffic in the whole frame at the beginning of each frame, it has been shown that this policy achieves the optimal delivery ratio region [9].

We now make use of a quadratic Lyapunov function and the above MaxWeight scheduling policy to show the stability of deficit process of LDF given a fixed $q \in \text{int}(\Lambda)$ and capacity $k = C_{\text{MAX}}$. Let $\Psi^{\text{LDF}}(t)$ be the queue state of the LDF policy at time t, which includes the number of packets and their delay bounds on each link. Let $D^{\text{LDF}}(t)$ be the deficit vector for LDF at time t. Note that $\left((D^{\text{LDF}}(t), \Psi^{\text{LDF}}(t))\colon t \geq 0\right)$ is a Markov chain. Let the Lyapunov function defined on deficit vector d and queue state ψ be

$$V(d,\psi) = \sum_i d_i^2.$$

Then

$$V\left(D^{\text{LDF}}(t+F), \Psi^{\text{LDF}}(t+F)\right)$$
$$- V\left(D^{\text{LDF}}(t), \Psi^{\text{LDF}}(t)\right)$$
$$= \sum_i \left(D_i^{\text{LDF}}(t+F)\right)^2 - \sum_i \left(D_i^{\text{LDF}}(t)\right)^2$$
$$= \sum_i \sum_{t'=t}^{t+F-1} \left(\left(D_i^{\text{LDF}}(t'+1)\right)^2 - \left(D_i^{\text{LDF}}(t')\right)^2\right)$$
$$= \sum_i \sum_{t'=t}^{t+F-1} \left(\left(\left(D_i^{\text{LDF}}(t') + A_i^{\text{D}}(t') - S_i^{\text{LDF}}(t')\right)^+\right)^2\right.$$
$$\left. - \left(D_i^{\text{LDF}}(t')\right)^2\right)$$
$$\leq \sum_i \sum_{t'=t}^{t+F-1} \left(2D_i^{\text{LDF}}(t')\left(A_i^{\text{D}}(t') - S_i^{\text{LDF}}(t')\right)\right.$$
$$\left. + \left(A_i^{\text{D}}(t') - S_i^{\text{LDF}}(t')\right)^2\right)$$
$$\leq \sum_i \sum_{t'=t}^{t+F-1} 2(D_i^{\text{LDF}}(t) + Fa_{\max})A_i^{\text{D}}(t')$$
$$- \sum_i \sum_{t'=t}^{t+F-1} 2(D_i^{\text{LDF}}(t) - Fk)S_i^{\text{LDF}}(t')$$
$$+ FN\left(a_{\max}^2 + k^2\right)$$
$$\leq \sum_i \sum_{t'=t}^{t+F-1} 2D_i^{\text{LDF}}(t)A_i^{\text{D}}(t')$$
$$- \sum_i \sum_{t'=t}^{t+F-1} 2D_i^{\text{LDF}}(t)S_i^{\text{LDF}}(t')$$
$$+ FN\left(a_{\max}^2 + k^2\right) + 2F^2N\left(a_{\max}^2 + k^2\right),$$

where $A_i^{\text{D}}(t)$ is the deficit arrival on link i in time slot t, and $S_i^{\text{LDF}}(t)$ is the deficit departure of LDF on link i in time slot t. For any deficit vector d and two subsets of the links $\mathcal{L}_1, \mathcal{L}_2 \subseteq \mathcal{N}$, we say $\mathcal{L}_1$ is *dominating in* $\mathcal{L}_2$ *under deficit* d if (1) $\mathcal{L}_1$ is nonempty, (2) $\mathcal{L}_1 \subseteq \mathcal{L}_2$, and (3) for any $i \in \mathcal{L}_1$ and any $j \in \mathcal{L}_2$,

$$d_i > d_j + F(k + a_{\max}).$$

By convention any nonempty subset of links $\mathcal{L} \subseteq \mathcal{N}$ is dominating in itself regardless of the deficit. We can then define the *smallest dominating set in subset* $\mathcal{L}$ *under deficit* d to be

$$\text{SDS}(\mathcal{L}, d) = \{\mathcal{L}_1 \subseteq \mathcal{L}\colon \mathcal{L}_1 \text{ is dominating in } \mathcal{L} \text{ under } d\}.$$

Then for $D^{\text{LDF}}(t)$ we let the first dominating group be

$$G_1(t) = \text{SDS}(\mathcal{N}, D^{\text{LDF}}(t)),$$

and define the first group deficit to be

$$\tilde{D}_{G_1}(t) = \max_i D_i^{\text{LDF}}(t).$$

If the jth dominating group $G_j(t) \neq \mathcal{N}$ for some $j \geq 1$ we can then define the $(j+1)$st dominating group to be

$$G_{j+1}(t) = G_j(t) \cup \text{SDS}(\mathcal{N}\backslash G_j(t), D^{\text{LDF}}(t)),$$

and define the $(j+1)$st group deficit to be

$$\tilde{D}_{G_{j+1}}(t) = \max_{i \in \mathcal{N}\backslash G_j(t)} D_i^{\text{LDF}}(t).$$

We note that $G_j(t) \subsetneq G_{j+1}(t)$. Since $\mathcal{N}$ is a finite set, there exists an integer $m \leq N$ such that $G_m(t) = \mathcal{N}$. Also by convention we let $G_0(t)=\emptyset$ and $\tilde{D}_{G_{m+1}}(t)=0$. Then we have

$$\emptyset = G_0(t) \subsetneq G_1(t) \subsetneq G_2(t) \subsetneq \cdots \subsetneq G_m(t) = \mathcal{N}.$$

By the definition of C_{MAX} we have for any deficit vector d, any queue initial state ψ, any traffic instance from t to $t+F-1$, and any subset of links $\mathcal{L}$ that have strictly larger deficits than any link in $\mathcal{N}\backslash\mathcal{L}$ throughout the whole frame $\{t, t+1, \dots, t+F-1\}$, if $D^{\text{LDF}}(t) = D^{\text{MW}(F)}(t) = d$, $\Psi^{\text{LDF}}(t) = \Psi^{\text{MW}(F)}(t) = \psi$, then

$$\sum_{i\in\mathcal{L}}\sum_{t'=t}^{t+F-1} S_i^{\text{LDF}}(t') \geq \sum_{i\in\mathcal{L}}\sum_{t'=t}^{t+F-1} S_i^{\text{MW}(F)}(t')$$

where $S_i^{\text{MW}(F)}(t)$ is the deficit departure of MW(F) on link i in time slot t. So,

$$\begin{aligned}
&\sum_i D_i^{\text{LDF}}(t) \sum_{t'=t}^{t+F-1} S_i^{\text{LDF}}(t') \\
&= \sum_{j=1}^{m} \sum_{i\in G_j(t)\backslash G_{j-1}(t)} D_i^{\text{LDF}}(t) \sum_{t'=t}^{t+F-1} S_i^{\text{LDF}}(t') \\
&\geq \sum_{j=1}^{m} \sum_{i\in G_j(t)\backslash G_{j-1}(t)} \Big(\big(\tilde{D}_{G_j}(t) - NF(k+a_{\max})\big) \\
&\quad \cdot \sum_{t'=t}^{t+F-1} S_i^{\text{LDF}}(t') \Big) \\
&\geq \sum_{j=1}^{m} \tilde{D}_{G_j}(t) \sum_{i\in G_j(t)\backslash G_{j-1}(t)} \sum_{t'=t}^{t+F-1} S_i^{\text{LDF}}(t') \\
&\quad - F^2N^2(a_{\max}+k)k \\
&= \sum_{j=1}^{m} \left(\tilde{D}_{G_j}(t) - \tilde{D}_{G_{j+1}}(t)\right) \sum_{i\in G_j(t)} \sum_{t'=t}^{t+F-1} S_i^{\text{LDF}}(t') \\
&\quad - F^2N^2(a_{\max}+k)k \\
&\geq \sum_{j=1}^{m} \left(\tilde{D}_{G_j}(t) - \tilde{D}_{G_{j+1}}(t)\right) \sum_{i\in G_j(t)} \sum_{t'=t}^{t+F-1} S_i^{\text{MW}(F)}(t') \\
&\quad - F^2N^2(a_{\max}+k)k \\
&= \sum_{j=1}^{m} \sum_{i\in G_j(t)\backslash G_{j-1}(t)} \tilde{D}_{G_j}(t) \sum_{t'=t}^{t+F-1} S_i^{\text{MW}(F)}(t') \\
&\quad - F^2N^2(a_{\max}+k)k \\
&\geq \sum_i D_i^{\text{MW}(F)}(t) \sum_{t'=t}^{t+F-1} S_i^{\text{MW}(F)}(t') \\
&\quad - F^2N^2(a_{\max}+k)k.
\end{aligned}$$

Then by Jaramillo et al. [9],

$$\begin{aligned}
&\mathbb{E}\Big[V\left(D^{\text{LDF}}(t+F), \Psi^{\text{LDF}}(t+F)\right) \\
&\quad - V\left(D^{\text{LDF}}(t), \Psi^{\text{LDF}}(t)\right) \\
&\quad \Big| D^{\text{LDF}}(t) = d, \Psi^{\text{LDF}}(t) = \psi\Big] \\
&\leq \mathbb{E}\left[\sum_i 2d_i \sum_{t'=t}^{t+F-1} A_i^{\text{D}}(t') \,\middle|\, D^{\text{MW}(F)}(t) = d, \right. \\
&\qquad\qquad \left. \Psi^{\text{MW}(F)}(t) = \psi \right] \\
&\quad - \mathbb{E}\left[\sum_i 2d_i \sum_{t'=t}^{t+F-1} S_i^{\text{MW}(F)}(t') \,\middle|\, D^{\text{MW}(F)}(t) = d, \right. \\
&\qquad\qquad \left. \Psi^{\text{MW}(F)}(t) = \psi \right] \\
&\quad + FN\left(a_{\max}^2 + k^2\right) + 2F^2N\left(a_{\max}^2 + k^2\right) \\
&\quad + F^2N^2(a_{\max}+k)k \\
&\leq B_1 - B_2 \sum_i d_i.
\end{aligned}$$

Then by the Foster–Lyapunov theorem the Markov chain $\left((D^{\text{LDF}}(t), \Psi^{\text{LDF}}(t)) \colon t \geq 0\right)$ is positive recurrent. So the delivery ratio vector q is achieved by LDF. Hence $K_{\text{LDF}} \leq C_{\text{MAX}}$.

Secure Communication through Jammers Jointly Optimized in Geography and Time

Yair Allouche
Dept. of Communication Systems Engineering
Ben-Gurion University
Beer-Sheva, Israel

Yuval Cassuto
Dept. Electrical Engineering
Technion – Israel Institute of Technology
Haifa 32000, Israel

Alon Efrat
Dept. of Computer Science
The University of Arizona
Tucson, AZ 85721, USA

Michael Segal
Dept. of Communication Systems Engineering
Ben-Gurion University
Beer-Sheva, Israel

Esther M. Arkin
Dept. Applied Mathematics and Statistics
Stony Brook University
Stony Brook, NY 11794, USA

Guy Grebla
Dept. Electrical Engineering
Columbia University
New York, NY 10027, USA

Joseph S. B. Mitchell
Dept. of Applied Mathematics and Statistics
Stony Brook University
Stony Brook, NY 11794, USA

Swaminathan Sankararaman
Akamai Technologies
Cambridge, MA 02142, USA

ABSTRACT

Security-sensitive applications, such as patient health monitoring and credit card transactions, are increasingly utilizing wireless communication systems, RFIDs, wireless sensor networks, and other wireless communication systems. The use of interference-emitting jammers to protect these sensitive communications has been recently explored in the literature, and has shown high potential. In this paper we consider optimization problems relating to the temporal distributions of jammers' activity, and the suitable coding regimes used for communication. Solving the joint problem optimally enables comprehensive security in space, at a low power consumption and low communication overhead. The joint optimization of jamming in space and time is driven by a new framework that uses the *bit-error probability* as a measure of communication quality. Under this framework, we show how to guarantee information-theoretic security within a geographic region, and with increased flexibility to tailor the coding regime to the problem's geometry. We present efficient algorithms for different settings, and provide simulations for various scenarios using the bit-error probability functions. These simulations demonstrate the efficiency of the scheme. We believe that our scheme can lead to practical, economical and scalable solutions for providing another layer of protection of sensitive data, in cases where encryption schemes are limited or impractical.

MobiHoc'15, June 22–25, 2015, Hangzhou, China.

DOI: http://dx.doi.org/10.1145/2746285.2746322.

1. INTRODUCTION

More and more, highly sensitive and private information is being transfered via wireless communication. Example systems include contactless smart cards [7], military sensor networks [1], emergency response systems employing wireless networks [12], and ambient living-assistance systems [15]; these systems use wireless communication to transmit banking/financial data, military intelligence, sensory patient health data, and other private information. The open nature of the wireless medium mandates that precautions be taken to protect the privacy of information, e.g., from potential eavesdropping. Unprotected communication, e.g. within sensor networks, also opens the door for various types of attacks on the network, such as sensor impersonation, sybil attacks and wormhole attacks.

Communication devices, such as RFID devices in smart cards, have limited computational capabilities, making cryptographic techniques impossible. Further limitations may come from application constraints, in which, e.g., emergency personnel are unable to enter passwords or use authentication methods to secure data transfer. To make the situation more complex, there may be multiple types of communication nodes, utilizing different frequencies, and the nodes may be changing over time, as nodes are removed or added or become mobile; thus, we are motivated to pursue security techniques that are impervious to variations in the structure of the system or the network.

Wireless jamming has been explored as a means of achieving security from eavesdroppers through the selective introduction of artificial noise [14,24]. In addition to making sure the eavesdropper's channel quality is degraded sufficiently, the quality of legitimate channels must not be compromised. This additional constraint marks a contrast between friendly jamming and traditional offensive jamming.

Sensitive communication may be on single or multiple frequencies and it is often imperative to secure all frequencies. In such scenarios, channel degradation at eavesdroppers may be achieved through several jamming techniques [18]. Some examples are *barrage jamming*, which transmits noise on all frequencies continuously, *narrowband jamming*, which is restricted to a single frequency, and *pulse jamming*, which sends periodic bursts of noise.

In many cases, legitimate communication is restricted to within a geographic region such as a warehouse, hospital or bank and must be protected from eavesdroppers outside this region. The communication inside the region may be highly dynamic, i.e., nodes may be mobile or may be added/removed and thus, jammers may only use minimal information about the communication taking place in order to intelligently configure themselves. In addition, the existence of only minimal information implies that jammers must be proactive rather than reactive, i.e., they cannot synchronize themselves with legitimate transmissions, nor with each other. Moreover, jammers do not need to have a (common) clock, and synchronization is not required. These assumptions render a collections of such jammers highly dynamic and easily adaptable to changes in the environment they protect. However, we do assume (and actually take advantage of) that jammers could produce noise for some portion of the time (affecting only a subset of the bits in a transmitted message), and burst distributions could be controlled by the user. These temporal jammers fall under the category of pulse jammers in [18].

We argue that temporal jamming has multiple advantages over continuous jamming in eavesdropping mitigation:

1. *Energy savings*: Guaranteed jamming can be achieved with low operation duty cycles.
2. *Simplicity*: Jammers can be fixed-power, and flexibly placed in space.
3. *Spatial separation:* A single-radio jammer can be active on different frequencies at different times, thus being able to secure multi-frequency communications.
4. *Robustness*: Temporal jamming is significantly more difficult to cancel at the eavesdropper's receiver, due to their bursty nature.
5. *Feasibility* There are examples where successful jamming that provides full privacy (in the formal meaning defined below) does not exist with a given set of continuous jammers, yet random temporal jamming is possible.

A central benefit of temporal jamming we explore in this paper is the possibility to employ advanced unconditionally secure coding techniques. Operating the jammers in the time domain allows us to reason about their effect on the most fundamental information unit: a single bit. Therefore, existing jamming optimization techniques can be complemented by coding performed on the transmitted information. When designed together, coding and geometric jammer layout can simultaneously provide reliable communication for legitimate nodes and unconditional privacy from eavesdropping.

Problem Statement. In this paper, we adopt the above approach and consider the combined problem: How should one select the fractions of time in which temporal jammers are active sending noise to secure the communication, and at which coding regime information needs to be communicated. The solution to this problem relies upon three important elements: a new framework for modeling temporal jamming using bit-error probabilities, a geometric optimization algorithm, and information theoretic definitions of reliable and secure communication. The geometric optimization problem aims at minimizing the total jamming power required to achieve reliability and secrecy constraints given the problem's geometry. It is important to note that the output of this optimization is some set of minimal activity fractions for all jammers, whose deployment does *not* require coordination between jammers on when to transmit.

Related Work. The wire-tap channel [31] has been considered within information theory [11, 14, 24, 29]: a single eavesdropper attempts to listen in on a legitimate communication between a pair of nodes. It is shown that perfect secrecy is possible when the eavesdropper's channel is worse than the legitimate channel. Prior work has considered the use of jammers to degrade the eavesdroppers' channel and has analyzed the channel capacity under various scenarios, such as cooperating or independent jammers, multiple eavesdroppers, etc. Within this same model of eavesdroppers, game-theoretic approaches for optimizing power consumption of jammers have been studied [6], as has the problem of designating regions where eavesdroppers cannot be located. Most of these prior works do not explore the geometry of the problem and are primarily of theoretical interest because of the simple scenarios considered.

Jamming has been considered as a possible security measure [8, 9, 16], designed to address the fact that RFID devices are extremely limited in power, making the use of cryptography difficult. Most works address the security of only a single RFID tag. Wireless sensor networks are another example of systems with low-capability devices; while, in many cases, cryptography is possible here [17], the focus has been on symmetric key cryptography due to the more resource-intensive nature of asymmetric key cryptography. Here, the primary problem occurs during the key distribution phase [23], where eavesdropping is still possible. It is, thus, viable to consider physical layer techniques in the context of sensor networks. On an interesting side note, [13] presents a method for securing against impersonation attacks in sensor networks by jamming nodes that are sent impersonated packets, in order to prevent receipt of the packets.

Only a few works consider the geography/geometry of the environment for security purposes. The model upon which this paper is based is presented in [19], where the authors present primarily theoretical results on power optimization and jammer placement. In addition, several other related works where the objective is to protect geographically restricted communication exist. Sheth *et al.* [22] present a method using directional antennas together with coding packets across multiple transmitters in order to define a secure region of coverage. Here, the region of coverage is restricted to the intersection of the ranges of the antennas. Tiwari holds a patent [26] for a method in which jammers are placed around a wireless network to secure it. However, security is achieved through active jamming and, thus, requires coordination between transmitters and jammers. In contrast, our methods do not require any coordination between jammers and legitimate nodes. Finally, using a model very similar to the one in this paper, Kim *et al.* [10] present an experimental study on how to create a secure zone around an access point using multiple friendly jammers. Tippenhauer *et al.* [25] show that the impact of friendly jamming can be eliminated using (carefully placed) multiple antennae; a potential advantage of our approach is to make such countermeasures less effective.

Gollakota *et al.* [4] have also used such a well-coordinated communication between source and jammers. These methods have significant advantages, but require reactive jammers (i.e., jammers synchronized with other jammers) and a flexible physical layer. None of these assumptions are required for our work.

Vilela and Barros [28] showed that without any assumptions on jammers and eavesdroppers' location, one could still use other nodes as friendly jammers, as long as they avoid co-transmitting with the legitimate transmitter and in the vicinity of a common destination. The authors show how to abstract this setting as a graph, and how to find an optimal subset of nodes using ILP. In [30] the authors study asymptotic behaviour in a stochastic setting in which jammers and eavesdroppers are at randomly distributed locations. In particular they study the concept of *Secure Throughput*, which is based on the probability that a message is successfully received only by the legitimate receivers.

Recently [21] suggested an elegant method for establishing friendly jamming where friendly nodes are able to communicate while enemy nodes are prevented from doing so. The idea is that a signal generated according to a secret key could appear as noise when key is not known. Gollakota *et al.* [4] have also used such a well-coordinated communication between source and jammers. These methods have significant advantages, but requires reactive jammers (that is, jammers synchronized with other jammers) and a flexible physical layer. None of theses assumptions are required for our work.

Finally, [2] studied schemes similar to our assumptions. They showed that allocating (optimally) equal-power jammers is an NP-hard problem and provided a PTAS for this problem. They have also provided an efficient scheme for pruning significant portions of the fence (see definitions below) so that various optimization problems can be addressed more efficiently.

Contributions. We measure the effect of jamming by modeling channel quality using the *bit-error probability* (BEP), which is a fundamental measure able to capture any specific scenario governing the physical layer. This new characterization of the jamming signals allows to improve the jamming quality via information-security codes tailored for the specific geometric setup. In particular, we present an algorithm that given a geometric and physical-layer setup finds the coding parameters that guarantee private reliable communication. To the best of our knowledge, this is the first time in jammer optimization where the optimal code parameters are found jointly with the assignment of the jammers' activity. The BEP framework is introduced in Section 2, and further developed in Section 3. In Section 4 we show that given the problem geometry it is possible to translate infeasible jamming specifications to a feasible specification by changing the coding parameters, without loss of security, reliability or communication rate. We then translate this possibility to efficient polynomial-time algorithms for computing optimal jammer parameters to meet the specifications, while minimizing energy requirements. The validity and efficiency of our scheme is shown through simulations in Section 5.

2. MODELS AND TOOLS

In this section we detail the settings within which the paper's results are obtained. We first introduce the models and tools pertaining to the *geometric* setup, then the *communications* model that drives the new temporal-jamming framework. The geometric model we use is essentially the same as considered in [19], with some adaptations. Using an established geometric model is a convenient choice, given that the key novelty of this paper lies in the tailoring of a wieldy communications model to practical geometric settings.

2.1 Geometric model and tools

Modeling communication in geographically restricted locations, we consider a *Storage/Fence* environment model, similar to the one in [19]. A depiction of this model is given in Fig. 1:

- We partition the region of interest into two (not necessarily connected) regions: the *controlled region*, $\mathcal{C}$, and its complement, the *uncontrolled region*, $\mathcal{U}$. Eavesdroppers may exist in $\mathcal{U}$ but not in $\mathcal{C}$. A polygonal fence $\mathcal{F}$ separates $\mathcal{U}$ from $\mathcal{C}$.
- Legitimate communication is enclosed within a polygonal region, or a set of polygonal regions, $\mathcal{S} \subset \mathcal{C}$, called the *storage*. The reader may wish to think of the storage as a warehouse containing items emitting sensitive information, e.g. RFID tags, sensors etc. Legitimate receivers and transmitters may be located at any point within $\mathcal{S}$. Note that $\mathcal{S}$ is in the controlled region.
- A set $\mathcal{J}$ of friendly jammers are placed in the region $\mathcal{A} = \mathcal{C} \setminus \mathcal{S}$, termed the *allowable region.* Note that jammers are not placed outside of the controlled area, since they could be destroyed physically, and they cannot be placed inside the storage $\mathcal{S}$, since they might interfere with legitimate communications.

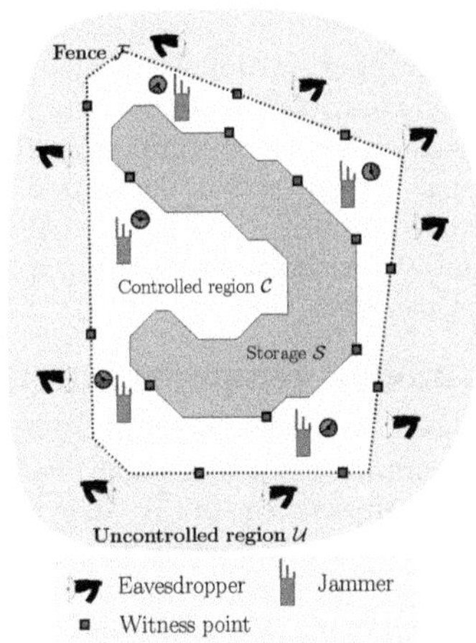

Figure 1. *An example scenario with a storage (dark gray) containing the communicating nodes, and surrounded by a fence (dotted). Jammers are placed within the controlled regions prevent eavesdroppers outside the fence from listening.*[1]

We believe that this model is applicable to multiple scenarios at which some geographic buffer zone separates the transmitting nodes from the potential eavesdroppers.

With a slight abuse of notation, we identify a node (receiver/jammer/eavesdropper) by its location p in $\mathbb{R}^2$. Consider a potential eavesdropper located at a point p in the uncontrolled region $\mathcal{U}$. Note that if any point $q \in \mathcal{S}$ may contain a transmitter, then for any communication model where reception quality is inversely proportional to distance, the highest risk of information leak heard by p is from the transmitter located at the nearest point to p from all storage point. Let us denote this point as $\mathsf{s}(p)$. That is, $\|p-\mathsf{s}(p)\| \leq \|p-q\|, \forall q \in \mathcal{S}$, where $\|a-b\|$ is the Euclidean distance between the two points a, b. Also assume that a set of jammers $\mathcal{J}$ is placed in $\mathcal{A}$.

Witness points. A major component in our toolbox is the *discretization* obtained by assigning only a polynomial relatively small number of *witness points* with the property that if required lower (resp. upper) bounds on jamming intensity are satisfied at these points, then the required conditions also hold for any point inside the storage (resp. outside the fence). It is clear that the number of these witness points we consider in lieu of the entire regions of interest affects the performance of the optimization algorithms dramatically. The operator can specify a tuning parameter $\varepsilon > 0$ trading accuracy vs. number of witness points and algorithmic efficiency. Given a parameter ε, we seek a set $\mathcal{W} = \{w_1 \ldots w_m\}$ of witness points in $\mathcal{U}$ such that for every point $p \in \mathcal{U}$, there is a witness point $w_i \in \mathcal{W}$ satisfying $\|p - \mathsf{s}(p)\| \leq (1+\varepsilon)\|w_i - \mathsf{s}(w_i)\|$. Moreover, $\|p-j\| \leq (1+\varepsilon)\|w_i - j\|$ for every jammer location $j \in \mathcal{J}$. In other words, for every potential eavesdropper $p \in \mathcal{U}$ (within the continuous domain), there is a witness point $w \in \mathcal{W}$ such that the distances from either p or w to the nearest legitimate transmitter are nearly equal. An analogous condition holds for a set of witness points within the storage, whose distances to the jammers are nearly equal to the distances between the legitimate receivers and the jammers. As shown in [19], such sets of witness points can be found with sizes equal to $\{(n+|\mathcal{J}|)\log(d)\}^2$ where d is the ration between $diam(\mathcal{F})$ and the minimum distance between storage and fence. Such polynomial-size sets of witness points imply the possibility to run jammer optimization algorithms on these sets with jamming guarantees on the true locations of receivers and eavesdroppers, for any jamming function that is "well behaved", e.g. inverse proportional to a polynomial of distance r) in small intervals $(r, r(1+\varepsilon))$. We note that all the jamming functions we consider in this paper indeed have this smoothness property.

2.2 Comm. model: temporal jamming

In this sub-section we introduce the *temporal jamming* model driving the jamming optimization results that follow. Temporal jamming refers to the ability of jammers to transmit the jamming signal intermittently, in fine time resolution of a single bit. This is in contrast with the more common *complete-duration* jammers, whose signals are set to be constant in time. We note from the outset that the benefits of temporal jamming shown later in the paper do *not* assume coordination between jammers, neither between jammers and transmitters. Rather, we only assume that each jammer is able to set its activity in time to a static value that is determined by the environment's geometry. To link the temporal-jamming model with the main thread of existing work, we first review the complete-duration jamming model.

Complete-Duration Jamming. When a jammer transmits a continuous signal at a certain power, it is convenient to formulate the jamming optimization in terms of *Signal to Interference Ratios* (*SIR*) at locations within the environment's geometry. Successful jamming is achieved if the *SIR* observed at all potential eavesdropper locations are below some specified threshold.

Formally, we express the signal decay due to path loss as follows: for an eavesdropper p_e listening to a transmitter $p_s \in \mathcal{S}$, the received power is $\tilde{P}\|p_s - p_e\|^{-\gamma}$, where $\tilde{P}$ is the transmitter's signal power and γ is the path-loss exponent. A similar formulation can be made for the received power at legitimate nodes, and for received jamming signal power. Recalling that for an eavesdropper p_e the nearest point on the storage is denoted $\mathsf{s}(p_e)$, we have

$$SIR(\mathcal{J}, p_e) = \frac{\tilde{P}\|\mathsf{s}(p_e) - p_e\|^{-\gamma}}{\max_{j\in\mathcal{J}} \hat{P}\|j - p_e\|^{-\gamma}},$$

where $\hat{P}$ is the jammer transmit power, and neglecting noise and the interference from the non-nearest jammers. An analogous (but slightly different) expression can be given for the *SIR* at legitimate-receiver locations.

The natural way to identify successful jamming is through an upper threshold, δ_1, on *SIR* for eavesdroppers, and a lower threshold, δ_2, on *SIR* for legitimate receivers. Thresholds on *SIR* are the widely accepted *"physical model"* described in [5]. Formally, any set of complete-duration jammers $\mathcal{J}$ needs to satisfy the following constraints

$$SIR(\mathcal{J}, p_e) \leq \delta_1, \forall p_e \in \mathcal{U} \text{ and} \quad (1)$$

$$SIR(\mathcal{J}, p_s) \geq \delta_2, \forall p_s \in \mathcal{S}. \quad (2)$$

Temporal Jamming. Moving from complete-duration to temporal jammers, it is clear that we can no longer use the *SIR* measure, as it carries no notion of temporal activity. To capture the temporal activity, we will work with the most fundamental communication unit: a *bit*, and its corresponding measure of equivocation: the *bit-error probability*[1]. Since jammers' activity is characterized as being on/off at a single-bit resolution, it is natural to measure the jamming quality by the bit-error probability induced upon an eavesdropper. Given a jammer active at some bit instant, the probability that it flips a bit at an eavsdropper location will be calculated based on a physical model considering signal and propagation characteristics. Later, this error probability will also include the randomness of whether a jammer is on or off at a given bit instant, assuming jammer activity epochs are drawn at random by each jammer independently. Formally, we denote by $\mathsf{BEP}(p)$ the bit-error probability at point p induced by a set of active jammers. We emphasize that the $\mathsf{BEP}(p)$ function captures the raw physical errors observed by the receivers, before any coding is considered, but after factoring in *all the assumptions* on the physical layer (modulation, antenna type, receiver sensitivity, etc). Clearly the function $\mathsf{BEP}(p)$ will depend on the number of active jammers and their position with respect to p. A detailed discussion of the functions $\mathsf{BEP}(p)$ is given in Section 3. When the bit-error probability considers random jammer activity in addition to the randomness of the communication medium, we denote it by $\mathsf{TBEP}(p)$. As an example, consider a single jammer that induces a bit-error probability of $\mathsf{BEP}(p)$ at point p when it is active. If this

[1]The same model extends readily from a bit to a higher-order symbol without fundamental changes.

jammer is active at bit instants i.i.d. with probability η, then the effective bit-error probability at point p will be $\mathsf{TBEP}(p) = \eta\mathsf{BEP}(p)$. In a similar way we can incorporate random partial-activity jamming into more involved scenarios with more than one jammer.

3. BIT-ERROR PROBABILITY

In the temporal jamming communications model that we described above, we wish to induce a high bit-error probability at eavesdropper locations, while keeping a low enough bit-error probability within the storage. To this end we defined the bit-error probability at point p using the abstract function $\mathsf{BEP}(p)$. In this section we further develop the model to discuss the properties of $\mathsf{BEP}(p)$ functions. The properties of a $\mathsf{BEP}(p)$ function will depend on whether p is in $\mathcal{S}$ or in $\mathcal{U}$, and on the number of jammers affecting the bit reception at p. Bit errors result from both the decay of the signal in space, and from the incidence of the jamming signal at the receiver. For points in $\mathcal{S}$ we assume below that signal decay is negligible, but this assumption is for convenience rather than necessity. For points in $\mathcal{U}$, which have larger distance from the transmitters in $\mathcal{S}$, the $\mathsf{BEP}(p)$ functions will incorporate both jamming and signal decay.

We now describe the $\mathsf{BEP}(p)$ functions from the simplest scenario of no jammers (only signal decay), followed by the single-jammer and multiple-jammers scenarios.

No Jammers. In the absence of jamming activity, bit errors are caused by the decay of communication signals in space. For legitimate receivers within $\mathcal{S}$, since we assume that the decay is negligible, the bit-error probability without jamming is identically zero. (We reemphasize that this assumption is only for ease of exposition, and not an essential one for the schemes to work.) For an eavesdropper at location $p_e \in \mathcal{U}$, a message is received with bit-error probability that depends on its distance to the transmitter. For the transmitter location we take the point in $\mathcal{S}$ closest to p_e, which is denoted $\mathsf{s}(p_e)$. Then we write the jamming-free bit-error probability at p_e as

$$\mathsf{BEP}_{\mathrm{free}}(p_e) = f_F(\|\mathsf{s}(p_e) - p_e\|), \quad (3)$$

where $f_F(\cdot)$ is a monotone non-decreasing function. $f_F(\cdot)$, as all the bit-error probability functions in the paper, admits values in $[0, 0.5]$. Bit-error probabilities above 0.5 are clearly not practically interesting.

A Single Jammer. At times when a jammer is active in location p_j, the noise it emits introduces bit-error events in addition to errors due to signal decay. The bit-error probability at location $p_e \in \mathcal{U}$ is in this case a function combining the two sources of bit errors

$$\mathsf{BEP}(p_e) = f(\|\mathsf{s}(p_e) - p_e\|; \|p_j - p_e\|), \quad (4)$$

where $f(\cdot;\cdot)$ is monotone non-decreasing in its left argument and monotone non-increasing in its right argument.
For legitimate receivers within $\mathcal{S}$ we assume negligible signal decay, so for these locations the bit-error probability is a function of jamming interference only

$$\mathsf{BEP}(p_s) = f_I(\|p_j - p_s\|), \quad (5)$$

where $f_I(d)$ can be regarded as a special case taking $f(0; d)$.

Multiple Jammers. For the case of multiple jammers *active at the same bit instant*, a bit-error event may be caused by any of the jammers, as well as by signal decay. To accommodate for multiple jammers, we extend the function $f(\cdot;\cdot)$ in (4) to have multiple right arguments

$$\mathsf{BEP}(p_e) = f(\|\mathsf{s}(p_e) - p_e\|; \|p_{j1} - p_e\|, \|p_{j2} - p_e\|, \ldots). \quad (6)$$

We mainly consider in this paper the case where f is symmetric in its right arguments, i.e., the bit-error probability depends on the jammers only through their distances to p_e (or p_s). This assumption is equivalent to equal-power jammers in the *SIR* model. At this point it is instructive to explain how the functions f_F, f_I, f are obtained in practice. There are different ways to do it, and the choice depends on the design stage at which the functions are needed. For the initial design of the system, one may use common communications models (power-decay with AWGN noise, fading etc.) to come up with estimates on these functions given some reasonable assumptions on the physical layer and communication medium. At a later stage when jammer activity assignments actually need to be decided, the exact system specifications are known, and so real measurements can yield f_F, f_I and f with good precision. In both cases we get an accurate characterization of the fundamental communication reliability that is better than known coarse characterizations such as SIRs. In Section 4.1 we give an example of natural parameterized functions for f_F, f_I, for which the modelling and measurement techniques mentioned above could be used to find the values of a small number of parameters per each system.

3.1 Decompositions and bounds for the BEP functions

For some optimization tasks, we would want to decompose the function f from (6) to separable functions in f's arguments. The main advantage of separability is in making f easier to measure and estimate in a deployed system. It is much easier to obtain the bit-error probability as a function of a single variable (e.g. distance to a single jammer) than as a complex function of multiple distances. When it is too complex to separate the effects of the multiple arguments, we use separable functions that give upper and lower bounds on f. The upper bounds allow to guarantee low enough error probabilities for legitimate receivers, and the lower bounds guarantee high enough error probabilities at eavesdropper locations.

When the bit-error probability is caused by a single active jammer, we use the interference-only function from (5)

$$\mathsf{BEP}_{\mathrm{jam}}(p_e) = f_I(\|p_j - p_e\|),$$

where we recall that $f_I(\cdot)$ is a monotone non-increasing function admitting values in $[0, 0.5]$. Now we wish to combine the single-jammer interference-only bit-error probability with that from signal decay given in (3). In order for a bit to be received in error, it needs to be flipped by either signal decay or by jamming interference, but not both. Assuming independence between the two error mechanisms, the resulting bit-error probability is

$$\mathsf{BEP}(p_e) = f_F(1 - f_I) + f_I(1 - f_F) = f_F + f_I - 2f_F f_I, \quad (7)$$

where f_F and f_I are short notations for $f_F(\|\mathsf{s}(p_e) - p_e\|)$ and $f_I(\|p_j - p_e\|)$, respectively. Since for any $f_F, f_I \leq 0.5$

we have $f_F + f_I - 2f_F f_I \geq \max[f_F, f_I]$, we get the following lower bound on the error probability

$$\mathsf{BEP}(p_e) \geq \max\left[f_F(\|\mathsf{s}(p_e) - p_e\|), f_I(\|p_j - p_e\|)\right]. \quad (8)$$

In addition to its simplicity, the max lower bound of (8) has the advantage that it is not specific to the independent bit flipping error model assumed in (7), but can rather be justified for other physical error sources.

Similarly, we can use the max function to combine the bit-error probabilities from multiple jammers, yielding the lower bound

$$\mathsf{BEP}_{\text{jam}}(p_e) \geq \max_{j \in J} f_I(\|p_j - p_e\|). \quad (9)$$

The multi-jammer error probability can again be combined with the decay error probability, obtaining the lower bound

$$\mathsf{BEP}(p_e) \geq \max\left[f_F(\|\mathsf{s}(p_e) - p_e\|), \max_{j \in J} f_I(\|p_j - p_e\|)\right]. \quad (10)$$

For eavesdropper locations we are interested in bounding the combined error probability from below, such that a jammer assignment guarantees no less than a certain amount of equivocation. Hence the right-hand side of (10) can replace the true bit-error probability requirement without loss of correctness. In contrast, for legitimate-receiver locations we look to bound the error probability from *above*, such that the actual error probability observed by legitimate clients is not worse than some guaranteed value. Consequently, for a legitimate-receiver location $p_s \in \mathcal{S}$ we may choose the sum combining, which is an obvious upper bound on the true combined error probability

$$\mathsf{BEP}(p_s) = \mathsf{BEP}_{\text{jam}}(p_s) \leq \sum_{j \in J} f_I(\|p_j - p_s\|). \quad (11)$$

Here the right-hand side of (11) can replace, without loss of correctness, the true bit-error probability requirement for legitimate receivers.

3.2 Partial-activity jammers

Now that we have set the basic formal infrastructure for calculating and bounding bit-error probabilities given a jammer setup, we move to treat partial-activity jammers, which are the key component of the temporal-jamming framework. A partial-activity jammer j transmits its jamming signal for an $\eta_j \in [0, 1]$ fraction of the time. In the remaining $1 - \eta_j$ fraction of time, the jammer is idle and does not contribute to the equivocation of the eavesdroppers and legitimate receivers. In the simplest case we assume that the jammer's activity on bit instants is drawn as i.i.d Bernoulli random variables with probability η_j. Consequently, a jammer is added as a right-argument to $f(\cdot;\cdot)$ at bit instants when it is drawn active, and excluded at other time instants. An example of activity instants of two jammers is given in the figure on the right, where Jammers 1 and 2 actively transmit for the duration of two bits at different times during the transmission of a message.

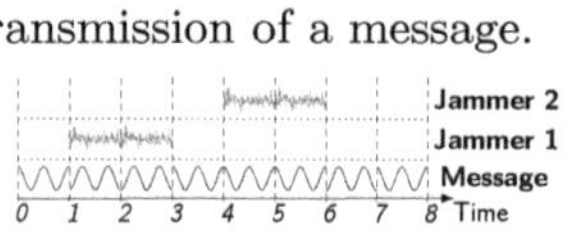

The design problem at hand is to set the activity fractions η_j of the deployed jammers to meet the privacy requirements induced by the system's geometry. Note that the random selection of activity instants simplifies the system operation, and in particular, no coordination is required between jammers.

The Two Nearest Jammer (2NJ) model. For solving various optimization problems addressed in this paper, we use either the NJ model (*nearest jammer*) or the 2NJ model (*two nearest jammers*). In 2NJ, the jamming impact of the third jammer and beyond on a point p could be neglected. This assumption is justified by the rapid decay of power with distance. Define $d_s(p) \triangleq \|\mathsf{s}(p) - p\|$, i.e., the distance from p to the nearest point on $\mathcal{S}$. The combined bit-error probability from two partial-activity jammers j_1, j_2 affecting p is calculated as

$$\begin{aligned}
\mathsf{TBEP}(p, j_1, j_2) = & \\
& (1 - \eta_{j_1})(1 - \eta_{j_2}) \cdot f_F(d_s(p)) && (12)\\
& + \eta_{j_1}(1 - \eta_{j_2}) \cdot f(d_s(p); \|p_{j_1} - p\|) && (13)\\
& + \eta_{j_2}(1 - \eta_{j_1}) \cdot f(d_s(p); \|p_{j_2} - p\|) && (14)\\
& + \eta_{j_1}\eta_{j_2} \cdot f(d_s(p); \|p_{j_1} - p\|, \|p_{j_2} - p\|). && (15)
\end{aligned}$$

Note that the expressions in (12)–(15) correspond to *disjoint* time instants within the transmission block. Hence combining with a sum is without loss of correctness. When $p = p_s$ is a location in the storage, we have $d_s(p_s) = 0$, and the left argument of each of the f functions in (13)–(15) is not applied while (12) is identically zero.

The motivation to stop at two nearest jammers, besides the decay of received power, is the decreasing probability $\eta_{j_1}\eta_{j_2}\eta_{j_3}\cdots$ to have a large number of simultaneous active jammers.

To achieve successful jamming, we need to satisfy the following constraints simultaneously

$$\mathsf{TBEP}(p_e, j1(p_e), j2(p_e)) \geq \tau_1, \; \forall p_e \in \mathcal{U}, \quad (16)$$

$$\mathsf{TBEP}(p_s, j1(p_s), j2(p_s)) \leq \tau_2, \; \forall p_s \in \mathcal{S}, \quad (17)$$

where $j1(p), j2(p)$ are the two nearest jammers to p, and τ_1 (resp. τ_2) is the lower (resp. upper) threshold of bit-error probability in $\mathcal{U}$ (resp. $\mathcal{S}$) locations. The solution should be given as an assignment to $\eta_1, \ldots, \eta_{|\mathcal{J}|}$ satisfying (16)–(17), with minimal total activity $\sum_{j=1}^{|\mathcal{J}|} \eta_j$.

4. ALGORITHMS FOR JAMMER ACTIVITY ASSIGNMENT

The purpose of this section is to provide constructive tools to find jammer activity assignments that satisfy the requirements of (16)–(17). The first such tool is called *threshold shifting*, which allows choosing "the best" pair of thresholds τ_1, τ_2 from all pairs that are equivalent in terms of the communication rate. The second tool are algorithms to solve the activity assignment problem for the NJ and the 2NJ models.

4.1 Threshold shifting through information-theoretic security

The principal benefit of working with the bit-error probability measure is its fundamental relations with *information theory*. These relations allow to cleverly employ information *coding* to aid the feasibility and efficiency of friendly jamming in a given geometric setup. In the sequel we show that geometric setups that do not admit a feasible assignment of η_j activity values to jammers, may be solved by shifting the lower and upper thresholds τ_1, τ_2 to values that are more favorable in terms of the geometric setup. Building on coding techniques, we are able to perform such a shift while allowing the same communication rate between legitimate nodes in the storage.

To see how coding fits in the solution, we examine the bit-error probability constraints in (16)–(17). While the left-hand side TBEP functions in the constraint inequalities are governed by the geometric setup of the problem, the right-hand side thresholds τ_1, τ_2 originate from informational – and not physical – features of reliable communication. In other words, the claim that τ_1 and τ_2 are sufficient thresholds must be backed by a code that provably guarantees that legitimate nodes can communicate reliably, while eavesdroppers gain no information from their received signals. As a corollary to that, it is possible to change the thresholds τ_1, τ_2 by changing the code used for communications. We call this operation threshold shifting. Suppose we have a code that gives the correct guarantees given a threshold pair τ_1, τ_2. Then we run an optimization algorithm to find η_j's that satisfy these thresholds. It may be the case that there is no feasible assignment to η_j's given τ_1, τ_2. Then we may look for an alternate pair τ_1', τ_2', for which a different code with the same rate exists, and solve a different optimization problem, with better success this time.

We briefly sketch the information-theoretic principles underlying threshold shifting and the associated code design problem. A detailed constructive treatment is deferred to future work. In information-theoretic terminology, communication between a transmitter and a legitimate receiver in location p_s in the storage is done over a *binary symmetric channel* (BSC) with parameter $\mathsf{TBEP}(p_s)$ given in (5). A BSC with parameter γ flips any bit i.i.d. with probability γ. Similarly, the communication between a transmitter and an eavesdropper in location p_e is done over a BSC with parameter $\mathsf{TBEP}(p_e)$ given in (6). The BSC is the most fundamental channel model, and a heavily studied one in information theory. For a BSC with parameter γ, it is known [20] that a communication rate of $1 - h(\gamma)$ is achievable using coding, and also optimal, where $h(\cdot)$ is the binary entropy function. This limiting rate $1 - h(\gamma)$ is called the *capacity* of the BSC. The scenario of a legitimate receiver communicating over one BSC with an eavesdropper communicating over another (worse) BSC is also a well studied problem in information theory called the *wire-tap channel* [31]. It is well known [27] that it is possible to communicate reliably with a legitimate receiver, while leaving the eavesdropper in complete equivocation, at a rate that is at most the difference

$$\Delta = \text{Capacity}(\mathsf{TBEP}(p_s)) - \text{Capacity}(\mathsf{TBEP}(p_e)). \quad (18)$$

In other words, we can change the bit-error probabilities of the legitimate receiver and the eavesdropper, and maintain the same communication rate so long as the difference between the respective channel capacities is maintained. Since both bit-error probabilities go in the same direction (either both upward or both downward), we refer to this operation as threshold shifting. To fit this into the jammer-activity optimization problem, we replace the individual TBEP values in (18) with the thresholds τ_1 (for p_e), and τ_2 (for p_s). The following example shows the potential of threshold shifting.

Example. Assume a simple configuration of a single legitimate node (denoted s), a single jammer (denoted j), and a single eavesdropper (denoted e) given in the Fig. 2. The distance between s and j is d_1, and the distance between j and e is d_2. Suppose the f functions governing the bit-error probabilities are given as follows. Bit error-probability due

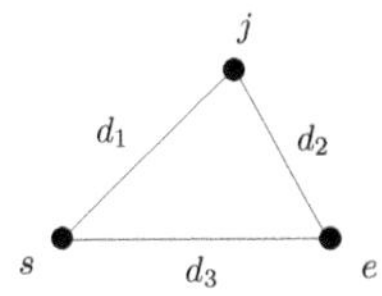

Figure 2. *The geometric layout of the legitimate node (s), the jammer (j), and the eavesdropper (e) in the example.*

to signal decay at distance x from the source is given by

$$f_F(x) = \frac{1}{2}\left[1 - e^{-\alpha_F x^{\gamma_F}}\right].$$

Bit error-probability due to interference at distance y from the jammer is given by $f_I(y) = \frac{1}{2}e^{-\alpha_I y^{\gamma_I}}$. The constants α_F, γ_F, α_I, γ_I allow fitting the functions to measured values in the particular system. For any choice of these parameters we have the desired properties that $f_F(0) = 0$, $f_I(0) = 0.5$, reflecting, respectively, no errors at the source and complete equivocation at the jammer. At the limit of distances going to infinity the behaviors are inverted, where f_F is tending to 0.5 and f_I is tending to 0. For the legitimate receiver s we assume to only have bit-error probability contribution from f_I (recall that s is located in a relatively small storage, hence very proximate to the transmitter). For the eavesdropper location e we have contributions from both functions, which we combine with the max function, as shown in (8). Altogether, assuming a jamming signal active at a η fraction of time, we have

$$\mathsf{TBEP}(s,j) = \eta f_I(d_1) = \frac{1}{2}\eta e^{-\alpha_I d_1^{\gamma_I}}$$

and

$$\begin{aligned}\mathsf{TBEP}(e,j) &= (1-\eta)f_F(d_3) + \eta \max\left[f_F(d_3), f_I(d_2)\right] \\ &= f_F(d_3) + \eta \max\left[f_I(d_2) - f_F(d_3), 0\right]\end{aligned}$$
$$= \frac{1}{2}\left[1 - e^{-\alpha_F d_3^{\gamma_F}} + \eta \max\left[e^{-\alpha_I d_2^{\gamma_I}} + e^{-\alpha_F d_3^{\gamma_F}} - 1, 0\right]\right].$$

Now with the closed-form expressions for $\mathsf{TBEP}(s,j)$ and $\mathsf{TBEP}(e,j)$ above, the jammer needs to set the activity factor η to guarantee that $\mathsf{TBEP}(e,j)$ is *above* some specified threshold τ_1 and $\mathsf{TBEP}(s,j)$ is *below* some specified threshold τ_2. The jammer's selection of η is best explained with a concrete numerical example. Suppose the measured parameters for propagation and jamming are found to be $\alpha_F = 0.1$, $\gamma_F = 2$, $\alpha_I = 3$, $\gamma_I = 2$. In addition, the distances of the problem are $d_1 = 0.8$, $d_2 = 0.6$, $d_3 = 0.9$. Then we can substitute these values into the f_I and f_F functions, and obtain in Fig. 3 the values of $\mathsf{TBEP}(s,j)$ (solid diagonal line) and $\mathsf{TBEP}(e,j)$ (dashed diagonal line) as a function of η. Given specified TBEP thresholds

$$\tau_1 = 0.1, \ \tau_2 = 0.03,$$

the solid vertical line in Fig. 3 marks the upper boundary of η values that satisfy $\mathsf{TBEP}(s,j) \le \tau_2$ (these values are marked by the shaded region on the bottom left). Similarly, the dashed vertical line marks the lower boundary of η values that satisfy $\mathsf{TBEP}(e,j) \ge \tau_1$ (these values are marked by the shaded region on the top right). It is clear from the figure that the intersection between the η values of the left and right regions is empty, hence there is no η that can satisfy both constraints, and jamming is impossible with these

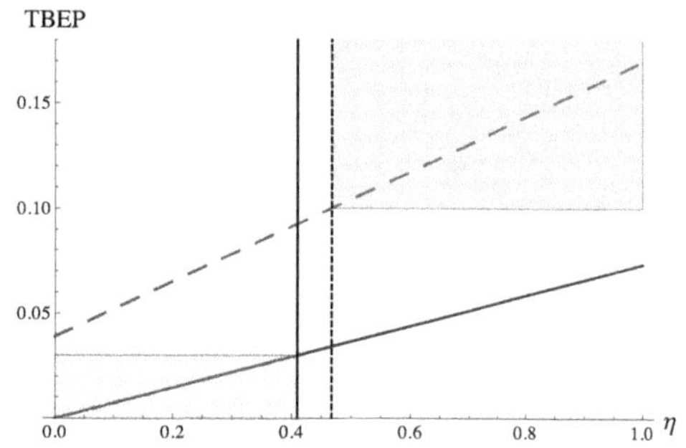

Figure 3. $\mathsf{TBEP}(s,j)$ *(solid) and* $\mathsf{TBEP}(e,j)$ *(dashed) as a function of* η*. Shaded regions represent* η *values that satisfy* $\mathsf{TBEP}(s,j) \leq \tau_2$ *(bottom-left) and* $\mathsf{TBEP}(e,j) \geq \tau_1$ *(top right). The intersection between allowed* η *values is empty.*

parameters. Now we show that using the threshold shifting technique, jamming will become possible *without any loss in information rate.* We choose the alternative thresholds $\tau_1' = 0.163$, $\tau_2' = 0.07$ which satisfy

$$\text{Capacity}(\tau_2') - \text{Capacity}(\tau_1') = h(\tau_1') - h(\tau_2') = 0.275.$$

This difference is identical to

$$\text{Capacity}(\tau_2) - \text{Capacity}(\tau_1) = h(\tau_1) - h(\tau_2) = 0.275.$$

Therefore, the same rate of communication (between legitimate nodes) can be maintained with the alternative thresholds, only changing the code used for communication. As a result, we repeat in Fig. 4 the same TBEP functions from Fig. 3, only this time marking the allowed regions specified by τ_1' and τ_2'. It can be observed in Fig. 4 that now the

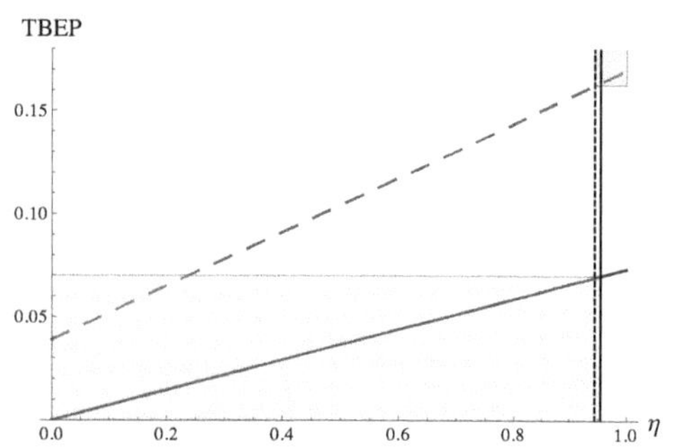

Figure 4. *The same* $\mathsf{TBEP}(s,j)$ *and* $\mathsf{TBEP}(e,j)$ *functions, now with shaded regions marking* η *values allowed by the shifted thresholds* τ_1' *and* τ_2'*. The intersection between allowed* η *values is non-empty.*

bottom-left and top-right shaded regions do intersect on η values between 0 and 1; hence, jamming is possible with these shifted thresholds.

This example can, of course, be generalized to much more complex jamming scenarios, as we see later in Section 5.

4.2 Computing $(\eta_1, \ldots, \eta_{|\mathcal{J}|})$ under the nearest-jammer model

Given a set of jammers $\mathcal{J}$ in specified locations, and a pair of threshold values τ_1, τ_2, we wish to set the activity fractions $\eta_1, \ldots, \eta_{|\mathcal{J}|}$ of the jammers to guarantee bit-error probability of at least τ_1 at eavesdropper locations, and at most τ_2 at locations in the storage. In addition to satisfying the bit-error probability thresholds, to save power we wish to achieve that with the lowest possible total activity sum $\sum_{j=1}^{|\mathcal{J}|} \eta_j$.

First we handle the nearest jammer model. That is, each point, on the storage or outside the fence, is influenced by the nearest jammer to the point, while more remote jammers' impact is neglected. The problem is, as above, to determine the values η_j for each jammer $j \in \mathcal{J}$.

1. Compute the set of witness points $\mathcal{W}$ as explained in Section 2.
2. Compute the Voronoi Diagram of $\mathcal{J}$, in $O|\mathcal{J}| \log |\mathcal{J}|)$ time (see [3]) .
3. Using the Voronoi Diagram, for each point in $\mathcal{W}$ find the nearest jammer in $\log |\mathcal{J}|$ time. Denote by $\mathcal{W}_j \subseteq \mathcal{W}$ the set of witness points whose nearest jammer is $j \in \mathcal{J}$.
4. For each $j \in \mathcal{J}$, compute L_j, the minimal η_j value that meets the $\mathsf{TBEP} \geq \tau_1$ threshold for all $p \in W_j \cap \mathcal{U}$.
5. For each $j \in \mathcal{J}$, compute U_j, the maximal η_j value that meets the $\mathsf{TBEP} \leq \tau_2$ threshold for all $p \in W_j \cap \mathcal{S}$.
6. If for every $j \in \mathcal{J}$, $L_j \leq U_j$ output $\eta_j = L_j$. If not, output "failure".

4.3 Computing $(\eta_1, \ldots, \eta_{|\mathcal{J}|})$ under the 2-nearest jammer model

Let $j1(p)$ (resp., $j2(p)$) be the first (resp., second) closest jammer to point p. Hence, $\{j1(p), j2(p)\} = 2NJ(p)$. Now we need to satisfy the constraints

$$\mathsf{TBEP}(p_e, j1(p_e), j2(p_e)) \geq \tau_1, \ \forall p_e \in \mathcal{W} \bigcap \mathcal{U}, \qquad (19)$$

$$\mathsf{TBEP}(p_s, j1(p_s), j2(p_s)) \leq \tau_2, \ \forall p_s \in \mathcal{W} \bigcap \mathcal{S}. \qquad (20)$$

We need to find an assignment to $\eta_1, \ldots, \eta_{|\mathcal{J}|}$ satisfying (19)–(20), with minimum total activity $\sum_{j=1}^{|\mathcal{J}|} \eta_j$. Note that this model is more involved than the single nearest jammer model, since the values η_j depend on each other. To overcome the computational difficulty, we use the geometric structure of the problem as follows. We assume the problem layout satisfies the *circular order assumption* (Figure 5): the jammers can be ordered $\mathcal{J} = (j_1, j_2, \ldots)$ such that each TBEP constraint involves either a single jammer j_i or a pair of jammers j_i, j_k, and furthermore, if a witness point $w \in \mathcal{W}$ is influenced by j_i (together with possibly another jammer), then no witness point w' is influenced by j_{i_1}, j_{i_2}, where $i_1 < i < i_2$. (Jammer indices wrap around, from $|\mathcal{J}|$ back to 1.) The implication is that once the values of η_i, η_k are fixed, then the values of $\eta_{i+1}, \ldots \eta_{k-1}$ (within the $[i, k]$ interval of indices) can be computed independently from the values of $\eta_{k+1}, \eta_{k+2} \ldots \eta_{i-1}$ (outside the $[i, k]$ interval of indices).

In the 2NJ model, the circular assumption amounts to some very natural topological assumptions on the shapes of the storage and warehouse, e.g. being simply connected. With this assumption, the region of influence of j_i on $\mathcal{S}$ and $\mathcal{U}$ may overlap with the regions of influence of j_{i-1} and j_{i+1}, but no other jammers.

Under the circular assumption, the solution can be simplified greatly with the following dynamic program. Let the η values be taken from a finite set D. For fixed value of η_i, η_j let $I_{i,j}(\eta', \eta'')$ be defined as *TRUE* if for $\eta_i = \eta', \eta_j = \eta''$ there is an assignment of $\eta_{i+1}, \eta_{i+2} \ldots \eta_{j-1}$ from D such that all inequalities that involve these indices are satisfied. (Recall that indices wrap from $|J|$ back to 1.) Note that

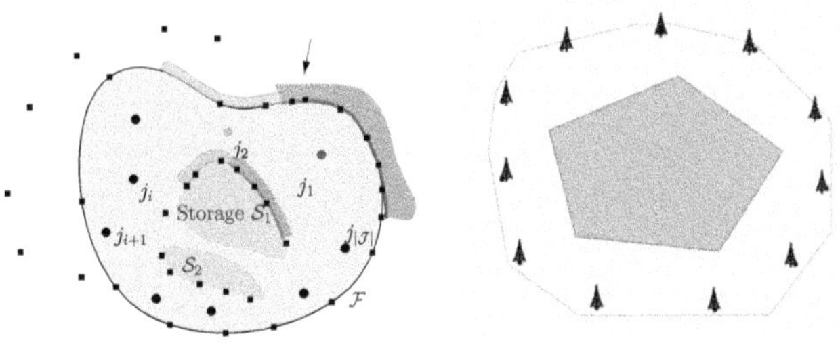

Figure 5. **Left** *An example of a setting in which the circular assumption holds. Squares indicate the witness points of $\mathcal{W}$. Jammers are indicated by disks. The portion of the fence and (boundary of) storage influenced by the orange jammer j_2 (resp., green jammer j_1) are highlighted in orange (resp., green). The arrow indicates a fence point influenced by both jammers.* **Right** *The Storage/Fence environment used in the simulations.*

$I_{ij}(\eta', \eta'') = TRUE$ and $I_{jk}(\eta'', \eta''') = TRUE$ imply that $I_{ik}(\eta', \eta''') = TRUE$.

The algorithm first computes $I_{i,i+1}(\eta', \eta'')$ for all $\eta', \eta'' \in D$ and $i = 1, 2, 3 \ldots$, then merges this data to compute $I_{i,i+2}(\eta', \eta'')$ for $i = 1, 3, 5 \ldots$ and so on. In each iteration the number of pairs considered is halved compared to the preceding iteration. Therefore, the time complexity is $O(|\mathcal{J}||D|^2 \log |\mathcal{J}|)$. Note that the storage $\mathcal{S}$ does not have to be connected, and could contain several components ($\mathcal{S}_1, \mathcal{S}_2$ in this example),

5. SIMULATION RESULTS

The goal of the following simulation study is to evaluate the new temporal-jamming framework in complex realistic jamming scenarios. The results build strongly on the tools developed in Section 4: they use the efficient algorithms for finding optimal jamming-activity assignments, and they reveal the benefits of the threshold-shifting technique. The Storage/Fence environment model used in the study is depicted in Figure 5. In this model, eleven friendly jammers are located along the fence (dotted) to protect the communications of nodes within the storage (gray). In the following, we use the 2NJ model with the f_F and f_I functions given in the example of Section 4.1. We fix three of the propagation and jamming parameters to $\gamma_F = \gamma_I = 2$ and $\alpha_I = 0.4$. The fourth parameter, α_F, is varied to model different scenarios. A small α_F implies slow decay of the information signals, and thus corresponds to poor separation between the storage and the fence, while a large α_F corresponds to better separation and an "easier" jamming problem. This can be seen in Fig. 6(a), where, given an upper threshold τ_2, a higher lower threshold τ_1 is achieved as α_F grows. Fig. 6(b) shows the delta capacity, which amounts to the achievable communication rate, as a function of the prescribed τ_2 value. This plot shows that for low α_F parameters, it is beneficial to raise (shift) τ_2 sufficiently in order to reach the maximum rate. Hence, it is seen that threshold shifting may be beneficial to overcome more challenging jamming scenarios. Fig. 6(c) and Fig. 6(d) provide information on the η values assigned by the optimal algorithm for each prescribed τ_2 value. Fig. 6(c) shows the maximum of the η_j values among the jammer set $\mathcal{J}$, and Fig. 6(d) shows the average over $\mathcal{J}$. These plots explain why Figs. 6(a,b) flatten out for large τ_2 values: due to saturation of jammer activity values, it becomes impossible to increase τ_1 further, regardless of the allowable τ_2.

6. CONCLUSION

In this paper, we considered the joint optimization problems arising out of the usage of friendly jammers for securing communication in a flexible manner, i.e., choosing jamming parameters optimally based on space as well as time. Our results are based on a new communication framework using the bit-error probability as a quality metric.

We first showed the benefits of temporal jamming where jammers' activity on individual bit instants are drawn as i.i.d Bernoulli random variables independent of other jammers. This scheme can be easily extended to the domain of multiple jamming frequencies. Next, we showed how to transform infeasible jamming specifications to feasible ones without any impact to security, reliability and communication rate by changing the coding parameters. Based on this, we presented two polynomial time approximation algorithms for computing jammers' activity parameters with a $(1+\varepsilon)$-approximation of the best achievable energy consumption. Our results demonstrate the benefits of choosing coding parameters in conjunction with assigning jammers' activity to efficiently manage secure reliable communication.

Acknowledgment A. Efrat was partially supported by the National Science Foundation (CNS-1017114). G. Grebla was partially supported by the Defense Threat Reduction Agency grant HDTRA 1-13-1-0021. E. Arkin and J. Mitchell were partially supported by the National Science Foundation (CCF-1018388) and by the US-Israel Binational Science Foundation (Grant 2010074).

7. REFERENCES

[1] D. S. Alberts, J. J. Garstka, and F. P. Stein. Network centric warfare: Developing and leveraging information superiority. Technical report, DTIC Document, 2000.

[2] E. Arkin, Y. Cassuto, A. Efrat, G. Grebla, J. S. B. Mitchell, S. Sankararaman, and M. Segal. Optimal placement of protective jammers for securing wireless transmissions in a geographic domain. In *ACM IPSN*, 2015.

[3] M. de Berg, M. Van Kreveld, M. Overmars, and O. C. Schwarzkopf. *Computational geometry*. Springer, 2000.

[4] S. Gollakota, H. Hassanieh, B. Ransford, D. Katabi, and K. Fu. They can hear your heartbeats: non-invasive security for implantable medical devices. *ACM SIGCOMM Computer Communication Review*, 41(4):2–13, 2011.

[5] P. Gupta and P. R. Kumar. The capacity of wireless networks. *IEEE Trans. Inf. Theory*, 46(2):388–404, 2000.

[6] Z. Han, N. Marina, M. Debbah, and A. H. rungnes. Physical layer security game: Interaction between source, eavesdropper, and friendly jammer. *EURASIP Journal on Wireless Communications and Networking*, 2009(1):452907, 2009.

[7] M. Hendry. *Multi-application Smart Cards: Technology and Applications*. Cambridge University Press, 2007.

[8] A. Juels and J. Brainard. Soft blocking: flexible blocker tags on the cheap. In *Proc. 2004 ACM Workshop on Privacy in the Electronic Society (WPES)*, pages 1–7, 2004.

[9] A. Juels, R. L. Rivest, and M. Szydlo. The blocker tag: selective blocking of RFID tags for consumer privacy. In *Proc. 8th ACM CCS*, pages 103–111, 2003.

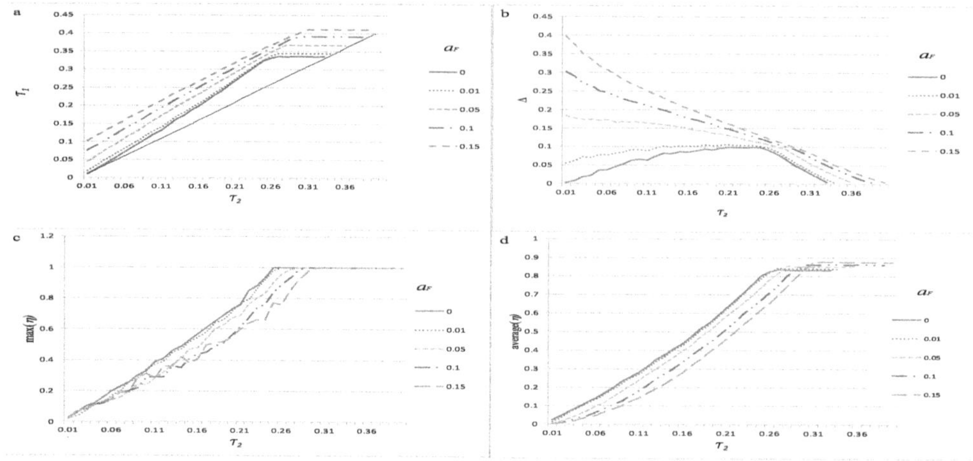

Figure 6. *Simulation results. For different α_F values, (a) presents the maximum achieved τ_1 threshold given τ_2. (b) presents the delta capacity, which is equivalent to the achievable communication rate. (c-d) present the maximum jammer activity and the average jammer activity versus τ_2, respectively.*

[10] Y. S. Kim, P. Tague, H. Lee, and H. Kim. Carving secure wi-fi zones with defensive jamming. In *ACM Symposium on Information, Computer and Communications Security*, ASIACCS '12, 2012.

[11] L. Lai and H. E. Gamal. The relay-eavesdropper channel: Cooperation for secrecy. *IEEE Trans. Inf. Theory*, 54(9):4005–4019, 2008.

[12] D. Malan, T. Fulford-Jones, M. Welsh, and S. Moulton. Codeblue: An ad hoc sensor network infrastructure for emergency medical care. In *Proc. 1st International Workshop on Wearable and Implantable Body Sensor Networks*, pages 55–58, 2004.

[13] I. Martinovic, P. Pichota, and J. B. Schmitt. Jamming for good: a fresh approach to authentic communication in wsns. In *Proc. ACM conference on Wireless network security*, WiSec, 2009.

[14] R. Negi and S. Goel. Secret communication using artificial noise. In *Proc. IEEE 62nd VTC*, pages 1906–1910, 2005.

[15] J. Nehmer, M. Becker, A. Karshmer, and R. Lamm. Living assistance systems: an ambient intelligence approach. In *Proc. 28th ICSE*, pages 43–50, 2006.

[16] P. Peris-Lopez, J. Hernandez-Castro, J. Estevez-Tapiador, and A. Ribagorda. RFID systems: A survey on security threats and proposed solutions. In *Personal Wireless Communications*, volume 4217 of *LNCS*, pages 159–170. Springer, 2006.

[17] A. Perrig, J. A. Stankovic, and D. Wagner. Security in wireless sensor networks. *Commun. ACM*, 47(6):53–57, 2004.

[18] R. A. Poisel. *Modern Communications Jamming Principles and Techniques.* Artech House, 2011.

[19] S. Sankararaman, K. Abu-Affash, A. Efrat, S. D. Eriksson-Bique, V. Polishchuk, S. Ramasubramanian, and M. Segal. Optimization schemes for protective jamming. In *Proc. 13th ACM MobiHoc*, pages 65–74, 2012.

[20] C. Shannon. A mathematical theory of communication. *Bell System Technical Journal*, 27(9):379–423, Oct. 1948.

[21] W. Shen, P. Ning, X. He, and H. Dai. Ally friendly jamming: How to jam your enemy and maintain your own wireless connectivity at the same time. In *IEEE Symp. on Security and Privacy*, 2013.

[22] A. Sheth, S. Seshan, and D. Wetherall. Geo-fencing: Confining wi-fi coverage to physical boundaries. In H. Tokuda, M. Beigl, A. Friday, A. Brush, and Y. Tobe, editors, *Pervasive Computing*, volume 5538 of *Lecture Notes in Computer Science*, pages 274–290. Springer Berlin Heidelberg, 2009.

[23] M. A. Simplício Jr., P. S. L. M. Barreto, C. B. Margi, and T. C. M. B. Carvalho. A survey on key management mechanisms for distributed wireless sensor networks. *Computer Networks*, 54(15):2591–2612, 2010.

[24] X. Tang, R. Liu, P. Spasojevic, and H. V. Poor. Interference assisted secret communication. *IEEE Trans. Inf. Theory*, 57(5):3153–3167, 2011.

[25] N. O. Tippenhauer, L. Malisa, A. Ranganathan, and S. Capkun. On limitations of friendly jamming for confidentiality. In *IEEE Security and Privacy (SP)*, pages 160–173, 2013.

[26] S. Tiwari. Wireless perimeter security device and network using same. US Patent 7917945, 2011.

[27] M. van Dijk. On a special class of broadcast channels with confidential messages. *IEEE Trans. Information Theory*, 43(2):712–714, 1997.

[28] J. P. Vilela and J. Barros. Collision-free jamming for enhanced wireless secrecy. In *IEEE (WoWMoM)*, pages 1–6, 2013.

[29] J. P. Vilela, M. Bloch, J. Barros, and S. W. McLaughlin. Wireless secrecy regions with friendly jamming. *IEEE Trans. Inf. Forensics Security*, 6(2):256–266, 2011.

[30] J. P. Vilela, P. C. Pinto, and J. Barros. Jammer selection policies for secure wireless networks. In *IEEE Communications (ICC)*, pages 1–6, 2011.

[31] A. D. Wyner. The Wire-tap Channel. *Bell Systems Technical Journal*, 54(8):1355–1387, 1975.

Mitigating Rate Attacks through Crypto-Coded Modulation

Triet D. Vo-Huu
vohuudtr@ccs.neu.edu

Guevara Noubir
noubir@ccs.neu.edu

College of Computer and Information Science
Northeastern University
Boston, MA 02115

ABSTRACT

Exposing the rate information of wireless transmissions enables highly efficient attacks that can severely degrade the performance of a network at very low cost. In this paper, we introduce an integrated solution to conceal the rate information of wireless transmissions while simultaneously boosting the resiliency against interference. The proposed solution is based on a generalization of Trellis Coded Modulation combined with Cryptographic Interleaving. We develop algorithms for discovering explicit codes for concealing any modulation in BPSK, QPSK, 8-PSK, 16-QAM, 64-QAM. We propose a 2-pass frequency correction and phase tracking mechanisms that enables the proposed schemes to reach their potential. We demonstrate that in most cases this rate hiding scheme has the side effect of boosting resiliency by up to 7dB (simulations) and 4dB (SDR experiments).

1. INTRODUCTION

Wireless communication is the key enabling technology of the Mobile Revolution that we are currently enjoying. Beyond enabling Mobile Phones, Wireless Sensor Networks, and the Internet of Things devices, it is also key to Cyber-Physical Systems such as SCADA Wireless Remote Terminal Units [46].

Achilles' Heel of Wireless. The broadcast nature of the wireless medium makes it vulnerable to two types of major attacks *denial of service*, and *information leakage*. Designing countermeasures to wireless DoS attacks before they become widespread is very important for both military and commercial applications. Due to a series of recent incidents, the FCC has stepped up its education and enforcement effort [12], rolled out a new jammer tip line (1-855-55NOJAM), and issued several fines [13]. At the same time jammers are becoming a commodity and are growing in sophistication and convenience of use and deployment. Beyond degrading a critical communication infrastructure, wireless DoS can also be the prelude to more sophisticated attacks where the adversary deploys rogue infrastructure [8]. Evidence of such attacks in the real world started emerging in the last few months [14, 42].

Weaknesses of Rate Adaptation Algorithms. We are interested in the impact of exposing the rate information, defined by the combination of Modulation and Coding Scheme (MCS), on enabling denial of service attacks. Recent work [33] showed that knowledge of the transmission rate enables selective jamming of packets resulting in very efficient attacks on all the Wi-Fi rate adaptation protocols investigated. Rate Adaptation Algorithms (RAA) adjust the physical layer transmission rate to the channel characteristics; ideally selecting a low rate MCS for a low SNR channel and a high rates for high SNR [5, 25, 26, 31, 34, 48, 50]. To illustrate the criticality of hiding the communication rate, we first provide some insights into rate adaptation attacks. The key idea in the highly efficient RAA-attack is to force a device to use a low rate (e.g., 1Mbps), by jamming all packets of higher rates. This allows: (1) a reflection attack where the victim is occupying the channel for very long time preventing other transmissions (i.e., 54 times channel occupancy for 802.11g to over 300 times for 802.11n), (2) a saturation of the network that induces a higher collision probability resulting in some RAA maintaining a network-wide low rate even when the adversary stops jamming. This self-sustained interference is called a congestion collapse. The RAA-attack is aggravated by the fact that jamming high rate packets is easier than jamming low rate packets and only requires interfering with few symbols. Furthermore, the comeback to higher rates is slow. Finally, the equiprobability of transmission among devices enables the adversary to focus on a single link to degrade the whole network [7]. Previous work [33, 36, 37] demonstrated both analytically and experimentally that smart RAA-aware jamming can lead to highly efficient attacks. The adversary only needs to jam a small carefully selected fraction (less than 5%) of the packets to achieve orders of magnitude more efficiency than blind jamming [33].

The fundamental reason why an adversary can selectively jam packets is because the rate information is either explicit (e.g., SIGNAL field of the IEEE 802.11 PLCP header) or implicit (analysis of I/Q constellation). Before describing our approach, we provide some context for our work in terms of related research.

Mitigating Jamming. Jamming at the physical layer has been extensively studied (cf. [39] for a recent monograph on this subject). Reliable communication in the presence of adversaries regained significant interest in the last decade, as new jamming attacks as well as the need for more complex applications and deployment environments have emerged (cf. [10, 38] and references therein). Specifically crafted attacks and counter-measures have been studied for packetized wireless data networks [20, 27, 28, 49], multiple access resolution [1, 2, 4], multi-hop networks [27, 44, 51], wireless sensor networks [52], spread-spectrum without shared secrets [23, 30, 43].

Related Work on RAA Attacks and Mitigations. Characterizing the vulnerabilities of RAA algorithms to jamming and developing countermeasures received increasing interest over the last

MobiHoc'15, June 22–25, 2015, Hangzhou, China.

http://dx.doi.org/10.1145/2746285.2746319.

few years from the first observations and mitigations through fixed rate communication during jamming [7, 37], to randomized mitigations [35, 36], to game theoretic randomization strategies [15–19]. However, previous work assumes that either the adversary is not able to selectively jam packets based on their rates [7, 35–37] (e.g., due to the slow reaction time of the jammer), or because the transmitter is able to effectively hide the rate [16, 18] (without proposing a concrete mechanism for rate-hiding). Unfortunately, over the last couple of years several recent work demonstrated that rate-selective reactive jammers are feasible on Ettus Software Defined Radio platforms, either on the host [33], or on the FPGA [32, 49]. RAA attacks are therefore fairly easy to implement on custom chips. As we will discuss in the next section, a key unresolved challenge in preventing RAA attacks is how to prevent an adversary from guessing the rate (Modulation, Coding information) during the transmission and therefore from selectively interfering with a packet.

A very recent work [41] proposed a modulation level encryption technique to hide the rate of communications. In essence, this technique always transmits with the highest order modulation, but the communicating nodes cryptographically agree on a subset of the constellation points to be used for each symbol. For example, BPSK modulation can be hidden in 16-QAM by only considering eight pairs of points. For every symbol to be transmitted a pair is cryptographically selected by the transmitter and is also known to the receiver through a shared key. The information bit of BPSK determines which element of the pair is sent. Since the eight pairs cover the whole constellation points, the adversary cannot distinguish between a BPSK communication embedded within 16-QAM or a true 16-QAM. While this scheme conceals the rate information, it does so at the cost of degrading the robustness of the communication. First, one can analytically show that 1-2dB are lost because of the constrained selection of the constellation pairs. Several additional dB are lost due to the poor performance of frequency offset correction, and phase tracking techniques.

Approach and contributions. One plausible approach to hide the implicit rate information, leaked by the constellation points, consists of always using the highest order modulation and combining it with a matching rate (e.g., uncoded BPSK can be hidden by using 16-QAM combined with a 1/4 rate coding scheme). As will be discussed and demonstrated in the next sections, such approach does not perform well, mainly because: (1) At low SNR several key components of the communication chain perform poorly, therefore degrading the performance of the system. These include the coding schemes, the frequency offset, and the phase tracking. This is one of the key reasons why most standards (both WLAN and Cellular) still rely on BPSK as a fallback solution for low SNR regimes. (2) Traditional codes maximize the Hamming distance between codewords and not the multi-dimensional Euclidean distance necessitated by the I/Q constellation of coded high order modulations. (3) An adversary can still guess the rate information by trying all possible modulation schemes. Traditional encryption schemes cannot prevent this attack since if they are applied post-coding/modulation they would render the error correction properties of the code useless (a single bit error would be amplified by the decryption process).

We introduce an integrated solution – Conceal and Boost Modulation (CBM) – to conceal the rate information of wireless transmissions while simultaneously boosting the communication resiliency against interference. The adversary sees all communications using the highest order modulation. The proposed solution is based on a Generalization of Trellis Coded Modulation (GTCM) with an integrated frequency offset and phase tracking technique combined with Cryptographic Interleaving. We developed novel algorithms for efficiently discovering and validating new trellis codes capable of upgrading any modulation constellation to any higher order constellation. While previous work on TCM was restricted to $\frac{k}{k+1}$ rate uniform trellis due to many reasons including complexity of searching over all possible trellis. We devise an efficient algorithm that finds the explicit codes for concealing any modulation in BPSK, QPSK, 8-PSK, 16-QAM, 64-QAM. In addition to the analytically proven properties of these codes, we show through simulations that in most cases this modulation hiding scheme has the side effect of boosting resiliency by up to 7dB over uncoded modulation and over 8dB in comparison with prior work [41]. However, in real experiments using a testbed of USRP N210 [11], we show that with a standard frequency offset correction and phase tracking, the performance of the proposed schemes is severely degraded. We develop a 2-pass frequency offset correction and phase tracking mechanisms that integrates within the GTCM decoder. This technique exploits the capability of today's baseband chips and SDR platforms to store a substantial number of samples therefore using information from the GTCM decoder to accurately track and correct the transient phase errors. Our final system achieves an experimentally measured performance boost of up to 4dB.

(a) 8-PSK (b) 16-QAM

Figure 1: Constellation guessing on USRP: Received symbols can be distinguished clearly after carrier synchronization and tracking.

2. RATE INFORMATION

2.1 Rate Information Leakage

Explicit rate information: In many communication protocols, the rate information of a transmission is unprotected. For instance in IEEE 802.11 networks, the rate is explicitly specified in the SIGNAL field of the physical layer's frames. An adversary can easily synchronize with the communication between two parties, analyze the data frames and extract the rate. This attack is very practical as demonstrated by [33]. Similarly, the rate information of a transmission in LTE cellular systems is exposed in the Modulation and Coding Scheme (MCS) field within the Downlink Control Information (DCI), which is itself encoded using a publicly known fixed rate $1/3$ convolutional code and QPSK modulation.

Modulation guessing: Even if the rate information is not explicitly provided within the packet header, the adversary can analyze the received signal in complex I/Q form. After performing the carrier synchronization, frequency and phase offset correction, the adversary can trace the received constellation pattern and determine the modulation in use. This method does not require the knowledge of the protocol's frame structure. We demonstrate the guessing attack by implementing a modulation detector on USRP, which can in real time identify the transmission's modulation (Figure 1). It can be easily extended to build a practical rate-aware jammer [33, 49] to selectively jam the high rate packets.

Code guessing: With more sophisticated techniques, an adversary could manage to identify not only the transmission's modulation, but also the codes in use. One such technique is to track the sequence of received symbols to guess the codes based on the fact that different codes produce different transitions from one coded symbol to another. Since most communication standards specify

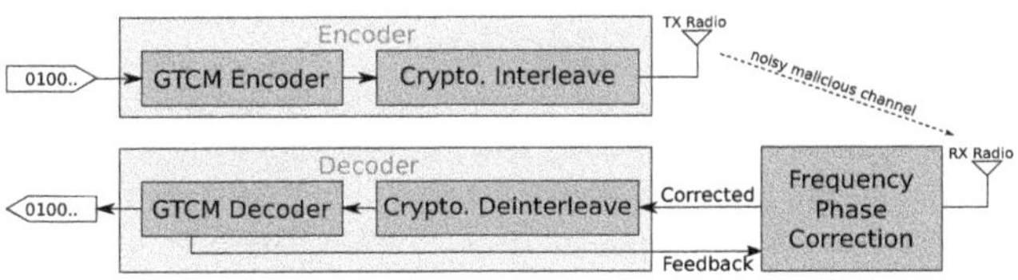

Figure 2: Overview of our CBM system.

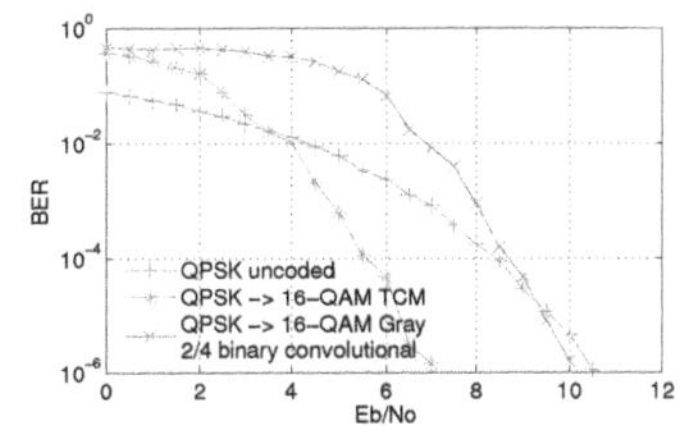

Figure 3: Performance comparison between (1) our TCM code with standard 16-QAM, and (2) best traditional binary code (from [9]) of rate $2/4$ with Gray coded 16-QAM.

a limited set of modulations and codes, guessing by matching and trial-and-error is efficient for the adversary.

2.2 Challenges to Rate Concealing

We now provide some insights why it is hard to hide the rate information.

Data Encryption: First, to hide the explicit rate information in the packet's protocol header, a straight-forward solution would be to encrypt the header. However, doing so does not prevent the modulation guessing attack, as a transmission still exposes the modulation to the complex I/Q analyzing adversary, who does not even need to decrypt the header to learn the rate.

Using Single Modulation: Alternatively, in order to avoid modulation guessing, a naive solution could be always using only one modulation for communications. This, however, lacks the flexibility and adaptivity to the environment, such as preventing the user from benefiting from high data rates at high SNR.

Modulation Level Encryption: Recently, the modulation level encryption technique developed by Rahbari and Krunz [41] can hide the rate from modulation guessing by a random mapping into a higher-order modulation based on a shared secret between two parties. However, their solution sacrifices the resiliency by 1-2dB in simulation, and several dB in real world due to imperfect frequency offset correction.

Coding: To improve the system robustness, one can propose using binary error correction codes combined with the highest order modulation. However without a careful design of the codes, the transmission performance is not guaranteed even with the best binary codes (as we show later in Section 4). Moreover, simply applying coding with modulation level encryption still leaks the rate information to code guessing attacks.

3. APPROACH

Our scheme – Conceal and Boost Modulation (CBM) – is depicted in Figure 2. The General Trellis Coded Modulation (GTCM) module's functionalities are two-fold. First, it makes the constellation pattern indistinguishable to the adversary, therewith countering the modulation guessing attacks. Second, it boosts the system resiliency against interference. The Cryptographic Interleaving (CI) module conceals the rate information from explicit rate exposing and implicit code guessing attacks.

Our idea for hiding the constellation is to always use a *single unifying* modulation (the highest order) to transmit data in order to create the same constellation observed by the adversary. To preserve the bit rate and robustness supported by the original modulation, the GTCM module encodes the data by a suitable code of rate matching the bit rate ratio between the original modulation and the target modulation. To be precise, let's consider a system that supports a set of different modulations ordered by the number of bits per symbol (bps) $b_1 \leq \ldots \leq b_{\mathcal{N}}$, where $\mathcal{N}$ denotes the highest-order modulation of bit rate $n = b_{\mathcal{N}}$. Assume that the on-going transmission is desired to be carried at a bit rate $k = b_{\mathcal{K}}$ bps for some modulation $\mathcal{K}$. In order to conceal the constellation, we encode the data using an adequate code of rate k/n and transmit the encoded data using the target modulation $\mathcal{N}$. Since the adversary will always observe the same constellation $\mathcal{N}$, the actual rate is concealed from modulation guessing attacks.

To counter the code guessing attacks, we develop a cryptographic module, which interleaves the modulated symbols before transmission. We emphasize that the interleaving process is performed at the baseband samples level, i.e., complex symbols produced by the GTCM module are interleaved per block of transmitted symbols. We note that straightforward encryption of data *before* modulating does not conceal the rate information, as the adversary can clearly observe the constellation of encrypted data. We derive a specific method to efficiently generate cryptographic interleaving functions used for permuting the output symbols from the GTCM module in such a way that the transmit stream does not leak the rate information. For the receiver to be able to decode the data, the rate information is embedded into the packet in an encrypted form such that only the receiver, who shares the secret key with the transmitter, can decrypt the information.

It is important to understand the implications of rate hiding. On one hand, the highest-order modulation creates redundancy by the constellation expansion. On the other hand, the constellation points' pair-wise distances are closer than in the original constellation. Without good design specifically targeting to the upgraded modulation's constellation, the system can become less resilient against interference. For example, the modulation unification technique [41] results in loss of 1-2dB of robustness compared to regular rate-exposing systems. This is because no coding is used in their system. However, even using good traditional binary codes cannot guarantee the robustness of the system because they maximize the Hamming distance between codewords and are not designed for coded modulation. An illustration is shown in Figure 3. We take the best code $\begin{pmatrix} 17 & 13 & 05 & 02 \\ 10 & 03 & 17 & 15 \end{pmatrix}$ of rate $2/4$ from Table VII in [9], and use it with Gray coded 16-QAM modulation. Comparing it with our derived TCM code $\begin{pmatrix} 01 & 12 & 16 & 11 \\ 01 & 13 & 16 & 11 \end{pmatrix}$ of the same rate and constraint, we see a gain of about 4dB is achieved with our code (Figure 3), while the binary code almost gives no advantage over uncoded QPSK at BER $= 10^{-6}$. Therefore, with good codes designed for the target modulation, we can gain instead of losing.

Searching for good codes for the rate-hiding systems must take into account the constellation description defined by the highest-order modulation. This idea is rooted in the Trellis Coded Modulation (TCM) technique introduced by Ungerboeck [45], who focused on devising modulation codes of rate $k/(k+1)$. In the literature, finding good TCM codes is a challenging problem, for which only heuristic solutions have been studied such as the set partitioning rules established in [45]. Unfortunately, there is no polynomial time algorithm for constructing the optimal general TCM codes. In this work, we introduce a new heuristic approach for upgrading

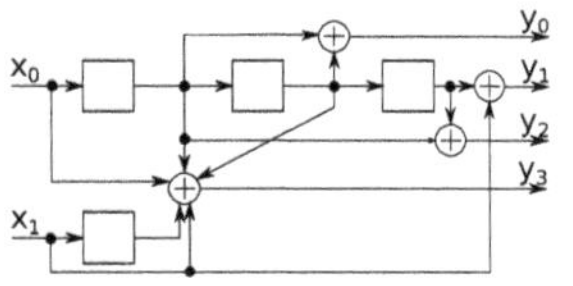

Figure 4: Our best TCM code of rate $2/4$ (QPSK $\rightarrow$ 16-QAM) and constraint length 4. Its boosting gain over uncoded QPSK is 3.8dB.

arbitrary modulations. Our heuristic solution is not based on the conventional set partitioning technique. Instead, we generate the code by randomizing the mapping between the inputs, shift registers, and the outputs of the general code structure. Our results show that this approach can find codes at least as good as the ones found in [45]. In practice only applying codes to an existing system is not sufficient due to imperfections caused by frequency and phase offset. We address these issues by devising a two-pass synchronization mechanism, which will be discussed in Section 6.

4. GENERAL TCM

In this section, we describe the fast search procedure for TCM codes of arbitrary rate k/n, which are used to encode data originally modulated by a modulation $\mathcal{K}$ of order 2^k (bit rate k) to the highest-order modulation $\mathcal{N}$ of order 2^n (bit rate n), without any uniformity restriction. For convenience, we give a brief overview of TCM codes. A TCM code is a convolutional code (k, n) defined by a set of k shift registers storing the code's k input bits, and a generator matrix which specifies the input-output relation (e.g., Figure 4). Deeper shift registers have higher potential gain and decoding complexity. Thus, we classify the codes by their constraint length v defined as $v = \sum_{i=1}^{k} v_i$, where v_i is the length of the i-th shift register. In our search procedure, we only consider the feed-forward construction of convolutional codes, because any construction with feedback can be transformed into a feedback-free construction that produces equivalent codewords [29]. To represent a code, we use the conventional generator polynomial form $G(D) = \{g_{ij}(D), i = 1 \ldots k, j = 1 \ldots n\}$, where $g_{ij}(D) = \sum_{l=0}^{v_i} a_l D^l$ is a univariate polynomial, and the indeterminate D represents the delay of the input bit in the corresponding shift register. If $a_l = 1$, the i-th input's current value (for $l = 0$) and past values (for $l > 0$) are $GF(2)$ added (exclusive-or) to the j-th output. For example, the convolutional code $(2, 4)$ in Figure 4 has the generator matrix/polynomials $G = \begin{bmatrix} D + D^2 & D^3 & D + D^3 & 1 + D + D^2 \\ 0 & 1 & 0 & 1 + D \end{bmatrix}$.

Unlike binary convolutional codes whose performance depends on the Hamming distance of the binary output symbols, TCM codes' performance is determined by the free *Euclidean* distance d^∞, which is the minimum Euclidean distance of any two distinct complex-symbol sequences produced by the code and modulation $\mathcal{N}$. Since binary codes are not designed for coded modulation, they do not take into account the constellation mapping. The best binary code with regards to Hamming distance can have a significantly small Euclidean distance between transmitted complex symbols and result in poor performance when combined with a specific modulation. For example, Figure 3 shows that our TCM code (QPSK$\rightarrow$16-QAM) outperforms the best binary $2/4$ convolutional code in [9] applied to a Gray-coded 16-QAM modulation, by 3dB at BER=10^{-6}. In the search for good TCM codes, we use as comparison metrics the asymptotic coding gain ratio measured by $\beta = d^\infty_{\mathcal{N}} / \Delta_{\mathcal{K}}$, where $\Delta_{\mathcal{K}}$ is the minimum Euclidean distance between constellation points in the original modulation $\mathcal{K}$. Good TCM codes must have high β ratio.

4.1 Code search algorithm

We introduce a new heuristic approach for searching for good TCM codes. For a given code specification $(k, n, \{v_i\})$, the coefficients of the generator polynomials g_{ij} are randomly selected. Since each combination of coefficients corresponds to a unique code construction, we check the generated code for its free Euclidean distance and if it satisfies additional critical properties such as structure information leakage. The search is performed for a fixed number of trials independent of the code specification, thus it is substantially faster than a full search which evaluates all possible codes. Yet, as shown in Section 4.3, our randomization approach can achieve the same results as a full search. The search procedure is illustrated in the RANDOMCODESEARCH algorithm below.

Our random search is characterized by the number of trials T performed by the algorithm. A randomly generated code, might be (1) *catastrophic*, i.e., there exists a non-zero input sequence that can produce all-zero output sequence; or (2) *non-equiprobable*, i.e., the output values are not uniformly distributed, which can help the adversary deploy statistical attacks to distinguish the mapping we aim to conceal. Therefore, the generated code is first validated against above properties, then its free distance d^∞ is computed.

```
RANDOMCODESEARCH(k, n, {v_i}, M, T)
d∞ = 0                // free distance of current best code
for i = 1 to T
    C = generateCode(k, n, {v_i})
    if valid(C)  // non-catastrophic and equiprobable check
        d = COMPUTEDISTANCE(C, M, d∞)
        if d > d∞
            d∞ = d        // update free distance
            C* = C        // store new best code
return (C*, d∞)
```

4.2 Free distance computation algorithm

The computational bottleneck of the code search lies in the computation of the Euclidean free distance, since it is performed for every generated code. In the conventional TCM code construction method based on set partitioning rules [45], computing the free distance only involves finding the minimum distance to the all-zero sequence. However, our GTCM approach does not restrict the search by the set partitioning rule, as we consider a higher-dimension space so that better codes can be found (including non-uniform ones). As a result, computing the free Euclidean distance involves all pairs of output sequences. Nevertheless, we devise an efficient algorithm – COMPUTEDISTANCE – whose running time is on average less than 2ms, on a 3GHz CPU desktop computer, for the modulations and depths we consider. COMPUTEDISTANCE's algorithm consists of traversing the trellis of the code and appropriately updating the *state-distances*, which is defined below.

First, we introduce some convenient notations. Let $I = \{0, \ldots, 2^k - 1\}$ be the set of inputs, $O = \{0, \ldots, 2^n - 1\}$ the set of output symbols, and $\Lambda = \{0, \ldots, 2^v - 1\}$ the set of possible states corresponding to a code C. A path P of length L is defined as a sequence of 3-tuples $P = \{(S_i, x_i, y_i), i = 0 \ldots L - 1\}$, where $S_i \in \Lambda, x_i \in I$ are respectively the state and input of the code at time i, and $y_i \in O$ is the output symbol due to input x_i at state S_i. The encoding can start from any initial state S_0. Since the output symbol is mapped to a specific constellation $\mathcal{M}$, the Euclidean distance between two paths P and $\tilde{P}$ of length L is dependent on $\mathcal{M}$ and computed by $d_{\mathcal{M}}(P, \tilde{P}) = \sum_{i=0}^{L-1} d_{\mathcal{M}}(y, \tilde{y})$, where $d_{\mathcal{M}}(y, \tilde{y})$ gives the Euclidean distance between two points y and $\tilde{y}$ on the target coded modulation $\mathcal{M}$'s constellation. Now, we define the state-distance $D[S, \tilde{S}] \triangleq \min\{d(P, \tilde{P})\}$ of two states S and $\tilde{S}$ as the minimum Euclidean distance between all possible paths of the same length ending at state S and $\tilde{S}$, respectively.

The key idea of our algorithm is that we update $D[S, \tilde{S}]$ gradually when traversing the trellis with increasing L. When two paths P and $\tilde{P}$ merge at the same state $S = \tilde{S}$, the free distance d^∞ is checked and updated with $D[S, \tilde{S}]$.

ComputeDistance($C, \mathcal{M}, d^\infty_{best}$)

1 $D[S, \tilde{S}] = \infty$ for all $(S, \tilde{S}) \in V^2$ // state-distances
2 $d^\infty = \infty$ // C's free distance
3 **for each** $S \in \Lambda$, $(x, \tilde{x}) \in I^2, x \neq \tilde{x}$
4 UpdateDistance($S, x, S, \tilde{x}$)
5 **repeat**
6 **for each** $(S, \tilde{S}) \in \Lambda^2, S \neq \tilde{S}, D[S, \tilde{S}] < d^\infty$
7 **for each** $(x, \tilde{x}) \in I^2$
8 UpdateDistance($S, x, \tilde{S}, \tilde{x}$)
9 **if** $d^\infty \leq d^\infty_{best}$
10 **return** d^∞ // not the best, return now
11 **until** $(S, \tilde{S})$ not found in line 6
12 **return** d^∞ // we found a better code

The algorithm ComputeDistance starts by initializing the state-distances to the distance between any path P and $\tilde{P}$ starting from any *same* state S (line 1–4). We make the paths diverge from the same state (line 3), then compute the distance between them (line 4). In the main loop (line 5–11), the state-distances are repeatedly updated for each new segment added (line 7) to the paths until there exist no more state pairs $(S, \tilde{S})$ whose state-distance $D[S, \tilde{S}]$ is less than d^∞ (line 11). The maintenance and update of state-distances in both the initialization and the main loop are performed by UpdateDistance, which keeps records of $D[S, \tilde{S}]$ for all $S, \tilde{S}$. Whenever two paths P and $\tilde{P}$ merge at a state S, the corresponding state-distance $D[S, S]$ is checked to update d^∞.

UpdateDistance($S, x, \tilde{S}, \tilde{x}$)

1 $T = C.nextState(S, x)$; $y = C.output(S, x)$
2 $\tilde{T} = C.nextState(\tilde{S}, \tilde{x})$; $\tilde{y} = C.output(\tilde{S}, \tilde{x})$
3 **if** $S = \tilde{S}$
4 $d = d_{\mathcal{M}}(y, \tilde{y})$ // update at initialization
5 **else**
6 $d = d_{\mathcal{M}}(y, \tilde{y}) + D[S, \tilde{S}]$ // update loop
7
8 **if** $d < D[T, \tilde{T}]$
9 $D[T, \tilde{T}] = d$
10 **if** $d < d^\infty$ **and** $T = \tilde{T}$ // two paths merge
11 $d^\infty = d$

Furthermore in RandomCodeSearch, where each generated code is computed for the free distance, we speed up the search by storing the best free distance d^∞_{best} associated to the best code C^* discovered so far in order to quickly eliminate codes of free distance shorter than d^∞_{best} (line 9 in ComputeDistance).

Correctness. To prove the correctness of the algorithm, we show that the state-distances $D[S, \tilde{S}]$ keep records of the distances of all possible "close" paths. The proof is based on the following lemma.

Lemma 1. *At any time i on the code trellis, for any pair of paths P and $\tilde{P}$, if there exists another pair of paths Q and $\tilde{Q}$ such that $S_i^{(P)} = S_i^{(Q)}$, $S_i^{(\tilde{P})} = S_i^{(\tilde{Q})}$, and $D[Q, \tilde{Q}] < D[P, \tilde{P}]$, then P and $\tilde{P}$ can be eliminated.*

Proof (sketch). By the lemma's assumption, P merges with Q and $\tilde{P}$ merges with $\tilde{Q}$ at time i. It is followed that at time $i + 1$, any new pair evolved from P and $\tilde{P}$ will find a similar new pair evolved from Q and $\tilde{Q}$. Therefore, the pair $(P, \tilde{P})$ cannot have shorter distance and can be eliminated from searching. □

Proof of correctness. At initialization of ComputeDistance, $D[S, \tilde{S}]$ are set to non-infinity values only for pairs of paths starting from the same state (line 3). This means that $D[S, \tilde{S}]$ properly reflect the distances of paths at initial states. In the main loop, the algorithm traverses every transition of the trellis and updates the state-distances. By Lemma 1, the macro UpdateDistance will discard paths corresponding to greater distance $D[S, \tilde{S}]$ and keep the ones corresponding to the shortest distance so far (line 9). Therefore, no closest pairs are eliminated by the algorithm.

To see that the algorithm terminates, we show that there exists a time such that $D[S, \tilde{S}] \geq d^\infty$ for all state pairs. It is enough to show that $D[S, \tilde{S}]$ are increasing while d^∞ is decreasing. The former is correct because evolving paths always contain transitions that results in positive increment in distance. The latter is due to the update in UpdateDistance. This concludes the proof.

Computational Complexity. The time complexity $g(t)$ of ComputeDistance depends on the length L of paths where the free distance is found. We estimate $g(t)$ in the worst case as follows. First, since UpdateDistance requires a constant number of operations, we judge the time complexity in terms of number of calls to UpdateDistance. The initialization of $D[S, \tilde{S}]$ requires 2^{v+2k} updates (line 3–4). At each iteration of time i in the main loop (line 5–11), the number of updates is at most 2^{2v+2k}. Therefore, the worst-case complexity of ComputeDistance is $g(t) = 2^{v+2k} + 2^{2v+2k}L = O(2^{2(v+k)}L)$. In our experimental search results, we observe that the value of L can be bounded by $L \leq 3v$ for any code. The running time of the algorithm on a 3GHz CPU desktop computer is less than 2ms, which is significantly faster than the naive approach that compares all pairs of paths.

4.3 Search results

In this section, we list the GTCM codes found by our randomization approach (Tables 1 to 3), and discuss their performance in comparison with traditional uniform TCM codes, as well as with a full search approach. The lists are compiled for codes of constraint length up to $v = 10$ and for each pair of original modulation $\mathcal{K}$ and target coded modulation $\mathcal{N}$ in {BPSK, QPSK, 8-PSK, 16-QAM, 64-QAM}. We note that previous work [45] discovered codes for only 1 bit constellation expansion. The asymptotic coding gain β is measured in dB, and the generator matrix G is presented in the standard octal form adopted from [9, 29]. Our symbol mapping of m-PSK constellations is $p(s) = e^{j2\pi s/m}$, where $s = 0 \dots m-1$ is the transmitted symbol, $j = \sqrt{-1}$. For square m-QAM constellations, our mapping is $p(s) = (x_0 + s_L\Delta_m) + j(y_0 + s_H\Delta_m)$, where Δ_m is the minimum separation in m-QAM, (x_0, y_0) are coordinates of the zero symbol ($s = 0$) located at the bottom-left corner of the constellation, and $s_L = s \bmod (\sqrt{m})$, $s_H = (s - s_L)/\sqrt{m}$ correspond to low-order and high-order bits of s. We note that (1) for some cases of short constraint length, there are no good codes with positive boosting gain; (2) our code search algorithm is independent of symbol mapping, thus can be used to find good generalized TCM codes for any constellation required by the application.

Comparison with uniform codes search. As an example shown in Table 2 for QPSK → 8-PSK, we achieve better codes than the ones in [45] for constraint lengths $v = 6, 8, 10$, which confirms the intuition that better codes can be discovered if the uniform mapping property of the set partitioning rules is relaxed.

Comparison with full search. To verify that the codes discovered using our randomization techniques are actually the best for each category, we also perform a full search for some "small" tuples[1] $(\mathcal{K}, \mathcal{N}, v)$ and compare the results with codes found by Random-

[1]Larger values of $\mathcal{K}, \mathcal{N}$ or v make the *full* search intractable.

BPSK → QPSK			BPSK → 8-PSK			BPSK → 16-QAM			BPSK → 64-QAM		
v	β	G	v	β	G	v	β	G	v	β	G
1	1.76	(3 1)	2	3.72	(5 2 4)	3	3.42	(17 4 5 10)	5	3.94	(63 10 40 47 4 2)
2	3.98	(7 2)	3	4.77	(10 2 17)	4	4.15	(33 10 27 2)	6	4.63	(117 10 40 55 104 100)
3	4.77	(13 4)	4	5.36	(31 4 2)	4	4.15	(33 10 27 2)	6	4.63	(117 10 40 55 104 100)
4	5.44	(35 4)	5	6.02	(10 2 71)	5	5.05	(67 10 55 4)	7	4.91	(227 4 60 371 44 210)
5	6.02	(64 33)	6	6.53	(107 20 12)	6	5.31	(31 100 167 2)	8	5.17	(573 12 52 745 100 362)
6	6.99	(135 56)	7	6.99	(251 102 4)	7	5.8	(212 20 327 40)	9	5.35	(1747 16 344 1277 60 10)
7	6.99	(374 147)	8	7.24	(661 102 30)	8	6.13	(725 14 757 200)	10	5.61	(2473 12 3436 3341 62 6)
8	7.40	(457 142)	9	7.63	(1715 336 400)	9	6.33	(1453 346 1137 30)			
9	7.78	(1312 665)	10	7.78	(3575 1400 14)	10	6.63	(2653 16 3103 774)			
10	8.45	(2175 1256)									

Table 1: BPSK → QPSK/8-PSK/16-QAM/64-QAM TCM codes.

QPSK → 8-PSK			QPSK → 16-QAM			QPSK → 64-QAM		
v	β	G	v	β	G	v	β	G
1	1.12	(3 2 1) (1 0 0)	2	2.55	(3 0 1 1) (1 2 2 1)	4	3.01	(1 0 2 3 0 1) (12 4 6 1 6 6)
2	3.01	(1 5 2) (1 0 0)	3	3.42	(5 2 0 6) (1 0 3 0)	5	3.41	(5 0 2 1 0 4) (12 4 4 15 2 10)
3	3.6	(1 4 2) (2 1 0)	4	3.8	(7 2 2 7) (2 0 5 0)	6	3.68	(1 0 2 3 0 0) (75 30 76 72 2 40)
4	4.13	(13 10 6) (3 1 0)	5	4.15	(1 2 3 0) (37 14 10 2)	7	3.94	(5 0 0 3 1 0) (66 44 20 71 26 6)
5	4.59	(1 4 0) (13 17 4)	6	4.47	(7 16 13 1) (11 16 12 1)	8	4.1	(61 54 34 46 32 34) (15 7 6 3 4 0)
6	5.01	(20 1 12) (3 4 0)	7	5.05	(17 0 4 0) (2 5 25 12)	9	4.26	(12 2 4 7 0 4) (73 62 6 110 16 24)
7	5.01	(7 2 0) (30 75 10)	8	5.05	(10 24 35 12) (25 12 3 15)	10	4.63	(220 46 140 231 102 330) (17 0 4 7 2 12)
8	5.75	(1 6 0) (134 165 42)	9	5.56	(10 24 35 12) (25 12 3 15)			
9	5.75	(311 250 122) (6 1 0)	10	5.56	(116 10 27 70) (23 30 31 5)			
10	6.02	(763 227 376) (7 6 0)						

Table 2: QPSK → 8-PSK/16-QAM/64-QAM TCM codes.

$\mathcal{K}$	$\mathcal{N}$	$T_{\text{full}}(s)$	$T_{\text{random}}(s)$
BPSK	QPSK	1	≈ 0
BPSK	8-PSK	4	≈ 0
BPSK	16-QAM	263	15
QPSK	8-PSK	57	44
QPSK	16-QAM	7101	54

Table 4: Running time comparison for searching codes of constraint length $v = 5$: random search is significantly faster than full search.

CODESEARCH. As we conjectured, the full search does not find any code better than RANDOMCODESEARCH. Yet, RANDOMCODESEARCH is extremely fast (cf. Table 4). The search results indicates that good codes are distributed randomly in the search space, thus randomized searching is a viable approach, and especially useful for large constraint length and high-order modulations.
Asymptotic coding gain. The search results show that with a large enough constraint length there are codes such that in addition to modulation hiding, the resiliency of the system can be boosted up. For example, concealing BPSK in QPSK is about 8.5dB more robust than uncoded BPSK systems.

5. CRYPTOGRAPHIC INTERLEAVING

While encoding the data with the highest-order constellation can hide the modulation, information about the trellis codes still leaks. A powerful adversary can attempt to decode the received stream of samples with all possible codes (which are publicly known) in parallel. The attacker can then infer the rate from the code that has the highest likelihood (i.e., lowest errors). It is necessary to prevent the adversary from being able to try the decoding. Our key idea is to randomize the transitions between the coded symbols. However, we note that naive randomization does not work. For instance, simply applying conventional encryption algorithms on the coded symbols (post-GTCM) will significantly reduce the system performance, as an error occurring during the transmission can spread out to many errors after decryption (by definition of a good encryption algorithm), which would exceed the code's error correcting capability. We therefore propose "Cryptographic Interleaving" as a solution for the code concealing problem. While cryptographic interleaving has been proposed to alleviate the impact of malicious jamming [28], its use for concealing code information, as far as we are aware of, is first identified in this work. Based on cryptographic functions, we design an efficient mechanism to permute the order of GTCM-coded baseband symbols without changing their values.

Crypto-Interleaving Process: In order to prevent an adversary from distinguishing between sequences encoded by different codes, we require: (1) the transmitted symbols should be indistinguishable from a sequence produced by a random code, (2) symbols belonging to different packets are permuted differently, and (3) the user identity is not revealed. We assume a shared key between the transmitter and receiver, which will be used as the seed to generate a secret random interleaving function. For convenience, we assume that the coded symbols produced by the GTCM Encoder can be divided into multiple blocks, each has m symbols, and each frame contains b blocks. A block is identified by the tuple (K, s, i), where K is the shared secret belonging to the communication session, s is the frame number, and i denotes the block index within the frame.

Let's consider a pool of N generated interleaving functions $\mathcal{P} = \{f_0 \dots, f_{N-1}\}$, where N is the security parameter, and each interleaving function $f_n : I \to I, I = \{0, \dots, m-1\}, n \in \{0, \dots N-1\}$ is an invertible index-mapping of symbols within a block. The permutation of symbols in a block (K, s, i) is performed in two steps. First, an interleaving function $f = f_n$ is selected from the pool $\mathcal{P}$ by $n = h_K(s|i) \bmod N$, where h is a key-hashed pseudo-random function (e.g., truncated HMAC-SHA3). Then, the symbol sequence $(y_0, \dots, y_{m-1})$ is permuted to $(y_{f^{-1}(0)}, \dots, y_{f^{-1}(m-1)})$.

Generating Crypto-Interleaving Functions: The efficiency of the crypto-interleaving process depends on the computation of the permutation. While a naive solution can precompute the pool of index-mapping, it does not scale with the block size. Moreover, significant memory is required for the precomputation. In our CBM system, we propose an efficient method for generating the interleaving functions. Our technique assumes that the number of symbols per block, m, is a prime. We note that while this constraint can be easily overcome to support various frame size, e.g., by padding, it has the side effect of preventing length-based attacks, which exploit the observations of different frame size to infer the code information. We define the following linear interleaving functions: $f_{A,B}(x) = Ax + B \bmod m$, where $A \in \{1 \, . . \, m-1\}, B \in \{0 \, . . \, m-1\}$. It is easy to see that any pair (A, B) corresponds to a bijective function $I_{A,B}(x)$ with respect to x; therefore, $f_{A,B}(x)$ is a proper interleaving function (i.e., invertible). The interleaving process is carried out by first generating the coefficients A, B based on the block identifier (K, s, i) by

$$A = (h_K(|s|i|0) \bmod (m-1)) + 1, \quad B = h_K(s|i|1) \bmod m.$$

8-PSK → 16-QAM			8-PSK → 64-QAM			16-QAM → 64-QAM		
v	β	G	v	β	G	v	β	G
1	3.11	(1 3 0 1) (0 0 1 0) (1 0 1 0)	3	4.15	(5 1 7 5 3 2) (2 3 3 1 2 0) (1 0 0 0 0 0)	2	3.31	(0 0 1 2 3 0) (1 3 1 1 3 2) (1 0 0 1 0 0) (1 0 0 0 0 0)
2	4.36	(3 3 2 3) (1 0 3 1) (1 0 0 0)	4	4.66	(0 14 1 0 15 4) (2 0 0 1 1 0) (1 0 0 1 0 0)	3	3.31	(1 2 1 1 3 2) (0 3 0 1 0 2) (2 0 1 2 3 2) (0 0 0 1 0 0)
3	5.33	(3 5 1 7) (0 1 3 1) (1 0 1 0)	5	5.12	(37 21 13 24 35 4) (3 1 0 1 0 0) (1 0 0 1 0 0)	4	4.18	(0 5 6 11 10 1) (1 2 0 0 3 0) (1 0 0 1 0 0) (0 0 0 1 0 0)
4	6.12	(5 6 6 4) (4 1 2 3) (1 0 1 0)	6	5.53	(71 75 36 70 53 12) (2 2 0 1 2 0) (1 0 0 1 0 0)	5	4.56	(10 3 4 17 24 14) (1 2 1 2 3 0) (0 0 0 1 0 0) (1 0 0 1 0 0)
5	6.12	(5 4 2 2) (0 3 7 3) (2 0 1 0)	7	5.73	(6 47 4 10 27 12) (3 2 0 1 2 0) (2 2 0 3 2 0)	6	4.91	(63 57 30 12 14 32) (0 2 1 1 3 0) (0 0 0 1 0 0) (1 0 0 0 0 0)
6	6.79	(16 3 6 7) (16 17 13 13) (1 0 1 0)	8	5.91	(124 157 6 270 254 172) (3 0 0 0 0 2) (1 0 0 1 0 1)	7	5.23	(10 3 4 17 24 14) (11 16 5 12 17 14) (0 0 0 1 0 0) (1 0 0 1 0 0)
7	7.37	(23 17 11 17) (2 16 15 10) (1 0 1 0)	9	6.26	(26 21 300 303 272 1) (5 3 0 1 2 0) (1 0 0 1 0 0)	8	5.53	(24 0 15 26 23 0) (31 37 15 5 27 26) (1 0 0 1 0 0) (1 0 0 0 0 0)
8	7.37	(21 20 15 16) (15 5 17 3) (1 0 2 0)	10	6.42	(471 475 236 670 653 12) (6 6 0 1 2 0) (1 0 0 1 0 0)	9	5.81	(73 177 42 123 25 55) (10 7 4 2 12 1) (1 0 0 1 0 0) (1 0 0 0 0 0)
9	7.37	(77 336 10 332) (2 1 5 1) (1 0 1 0)				10	5.81	(36 737 302 641 151 317) (4 7 2 6 6 1) (1 0 0 1 0 0) (1 0 0 0 0 0)
10	7.37	(15 35 33 5) (13 16 10 15) (16 10 0 15)						

Table 3: 8-PSK → 16-QAM/64-QAM TCM codes.

The interleaving function f is selected as $f = f_{A,B}$. The symbol sequence $\{y_0, \dots, y_{m-1}\}$ is accordingly permuted to $\{y_{f^{-1}(0)}, \dots, y_{f^{-1}(m-1)}\}$.

Header Format and Encoding: Since the interleaving processing on the coded symbols of the user data involves using not only the secret key K, but also the packet number s and block index i, the transmitter needs to embed this information along with the rate information into the transmitted frame.

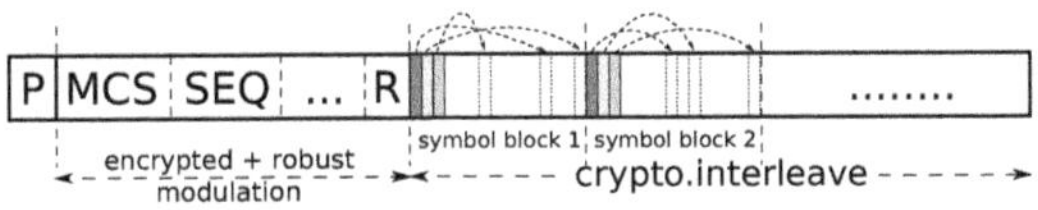

At the packet beginning, the preamble P assists with the frame detection and synchronization at the receiver. The MCS field identifies the modulation and coding scheme for the payload. The packet number required for cryptographic interleaving is specified by SEQ. The R field stores a random number generated per packet by the transmitter. The frame header is encrypted by $E_K(MCS|SEQ|\dots|R)$ using AES encryption E with the shared secret key K. The header is encoded by a public robust coding scheme and along with the preamble is modulated by a public robust modulation.

Security: Since the interleaving functions are generated using a key-hashed pseudorandom function h with secret key K applied on the packet number s and block index i, the coefficients A and B are indistinguishable [3], thus the interleaved symbol sequences are also indistinguishable.The header is also semantically secure due to the use of random R with AES encryption.

6. SYNCHRONIZATION MECHANISMS

As we will show in Section 7, the simulation results exhibit a significant gain in system robustness while the rate information is concealed from the adversary. However, when evaluating our CBM scheme over a real radio system with a standard set of synchronization mechanisms, we experience a substantial performance loss. Chief among the mechanisms impacted by the imperfections of the radio front end are the frequency and phase correction. At low SNR, such imperfections impact high order modulation much more severely than low order modulation. As in many other communication systems, synchronization with transmitter is required at the receiver in order to decode the data. Traditional synchronization techniques for symbol timing, frequency and phase recovery are realized by means of phase locked loop (PLL) circuits [22, 40]. However, in the context of our work, where the channel SNR can be very low due to adversarial interference, conventional methods perform poorly, making synchronization mechanisms bottleneck of the system. To make our CBM system robust, we developed a set of new efficient digital signal processing algorithms for coarse and fine frequency and phase offset correction relying on an integrated process of estimations based on preambles and iterative soft decoding. Our algorithms also exploit the fact that today's radio receivers can have ample memory to store a whole packet, and many standards already require multi-pass iterative soft-decoding, e.g., LDPC decoding in DVB-S2, IEEE 802.11n/ac. In Section 7, we show that our techniques achieve significantly better performance than traditional solutions. It is also worth mentioning that the impact of asynchronization attacks, which focus jamming energy on the beginning of each frame to destroy the synchronization information, is also alleviated in our system by using a long preamble with good correlation properties (cf., Section 6.2).

6.1 Overview of Transmitter and Receiver

We designed and implemented our transmitter and receiver on the USRP N210 SDR [11] using GNU Radio [6]. The transmit and receive chains of our CBM system are depicted in Figure 5.

Transmitter: The key components of the transmitter are the GTCM Encoder and Cryptographic Interleaving blocks. On transmission of a packet, the binary payload is encoded with an appropriate trellis code and target modulation (Tables 1 to 3) by the GTCM Encoder to produce coded complex symbols. The sequence of symbols is then permuted using the Cryptographic Interleaving block according to the shared key between the two parties. The packet modulating process is completed by prepending the payload with the header and preamble. Finally, it is resampled by the root-raised cosine TX filter before transmission by the RF front end.

Receiver: As in many communication systems, our receiver first obtains the sequence of symbols from the RF front end after they are preprocessed with the Automatic Gain Control (AGC) and symbol timing synchronizer to stabilize the attenuated input signal and lock to the receiver sampling clock.

The key to improving the robustness of our CBM system to overcome the RF front end imperfections consists of improving the accuracy of frequency offset and phase correction. Our mechanisms start with the Frame Synchronizer. First, we estimate the coarse frequency offset based on the preamble of each received packet. The header and payload symbols are then corrected with the estimates. To improve the estimation accuracy, we employ a phase locked loop (PLL) combined with a soft pre-decoding of the packet. This integration results into a 2-pass decoding process. The feedback from the soft pre-decoding re-encoding loop is applied to the PLL to improve the correction. Finally, the corrected sequence passes through the Cryptographic Deinterleaver and GTCM Decoder to recover the original data. In the following subsections, we discuss in details our efficient algorithms of those mechanisms.

6.2 Frame Synchronization

The Frame Synchronizer uses the preamble for both frame detection and frequency offset estimation. The principle of our synchronization mechanisms is to analyze the phase-difference sequence of the received symbols. While our technique for frequency offset estimation partly shares similarity with previous work [24], we improve the estimation by averaging over multiple packets. More importantly, we can identify the frame and estimate the phase offset at the same time, and fine-tune the estimation with feedback from the soft decoding process. We consider the received symbol

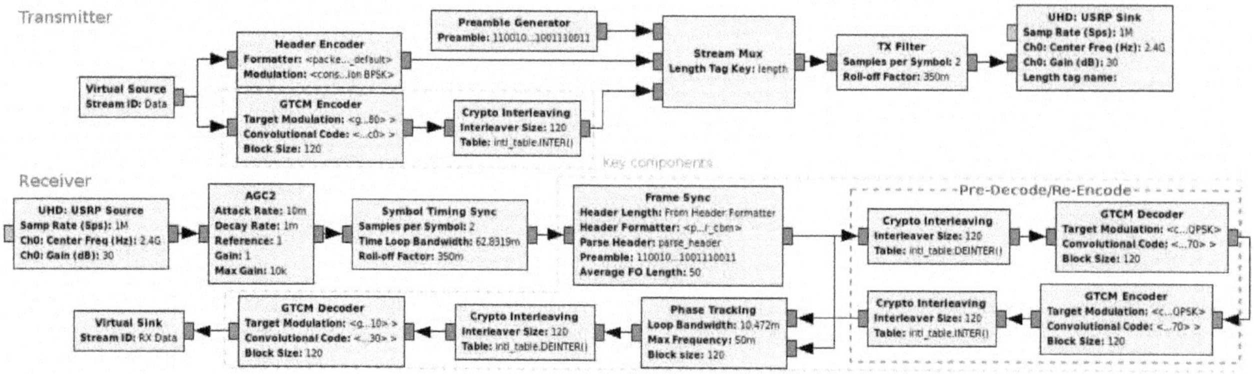

Figure 5: Transmitter and Receiver block diagram

$y_i = x_i e^{j(\theta i+\phi)} + w_i$ at discrete sampling time i, after the signal has been normalized by the AGC, and the symbol sampling period has been synchronized with the receiver clock. The transmitted symbol x_i is distorted by the unknown frequency offset θ, phase offset ϕ due to the mismatched clock between the transmitter and receiver, and interference w_i. The unknown parameters θ and ϕ are considered as constants during a short period of preamble, and zero-mean variables during the packet transmission period.

Frame Detection: Let $\{p_1, \ldots, p_L\}$ denote the complex valued preamble, and $\Delta p_i = p_{i+1}p_i^*$ be the phase-difference indicator between two adjacent preamble symbols. The transmitted stream consists of multiple frames: $\{x_i\} = \{p_1, \ldots, p_L, d_{1,1}, \ldots, d_{1,m}, \ldots, p_1, \ldots, p_L, d_{s,1}, \ldots, d_{s,m}, \ldots\}$, where $d_{s,j}$ denotes the s-th frame's j-th data symbol. To detect the start of each transmitted frame in the received signal, we first compute the phase-difference sequence of received symbols $\Delta y_i = y_{i+1}y_i^* = x_{i+1}x_i^* e^{j\theta} + z_i$, where z_i represents the phase-difference with interference. We then match $\{\Delta y_i\}$ with $\{\Delta p_i\}$, i.e., computing the cross-correlation

$$C = \sum_{i=1}^{L-1} \Delta y_i \Delta p_i^* = \sum_{i=1}^{L-1} x_{i+1}x_i^* \Delta p_i^* e^{j\theta} + \sum_{i=1}^{L-1} z_i \Delta p_i^*.$$

We select the preamble as a maximum length sequence such that $\sum p_i x_i^* = L$ only if $\forall i, x_i = p_i$. When the preamble is present in the received signal, i.e., $x_i = p_i$, we obtain $C \approx (\sum_i^{L-1} |\Delta p_i|^2) e^{j\theta}$. When it is not present, C becomes small due to uncorrelation between $\{p_i\}$ and $\{y_i\}$. Our experimental evaluation suggests that the frame be best detected, if $|C| \geq \alpha \sum_{i=1}^{L-1} |\Delta p_i|^2$ with $\alpha = 0.8$.

Frequency Offset Estimation: Once the frame is detected, the frequency offset is immediately estimated from the cross-correlation: $\tilde{\theta} = \angle C \approx \theta$. Under low SNR conditions, $\tilde{\theta}$ may not closely approximate the actual θ. Instead, we compute the average $\hat{\theta} = E[\tilde{\theta}]$ over multiple packets, and use $\hat{\theta}$ for succeeding processing.

Phase Offset Estimation: Knowing the frequency offset $\hat{\theta}$, we estimate the phase offset by correcting the received preamble y_i with $\hat{\theta}$: $\hat{y}_i = y_i e^{-j\hat{\theta} i}$, and computing the cross-correlation with the expected preamble p_i as: $A = \sum_{i=1}^{L} \hat{y}_i p_i^* \approx \sum_{i=1}^{L} p_i e^{j(\theta - \hat{\theta})i + \phi} p_i^* \approx \sum_{i=1}^{L} |p_i|^2 e^{j\phi}$. The phase offset $\hat{\phi}$ is estimated as $\hat{\phi} = \angle A \approx \phi$.

6.3 Phase Tracking

While preamble based frequency and phase offset estimation can provide accurate estimates at the frame beginning, the environment variations make these initial estimates deviated from the actual values over time, especially when reaching the end of the frame. To over come this issue, standard phase tracking mechanisms usually deploy decision-aided methods, which rely on the distance between the received symbols and the reference constellation points. BPSK modulation has less symbol errors and therefore the phase tracking works quite well. For higher order modulations, the density of the constellation makes the estimation of the phase errors harder at low SNR, as incorrect constellation points are guessed more frequently. These errors accumulate and end up exceeding the error correction capability of the GTCM code. This partially explains for low SNR scenarios why many current standards still rely on low order modulations instead of coded high order modulations. In pilot-aided synchronization systems such as OFDM, low SNR can result in loss of orthogonality of the carriers, preventing the receiver to recover the signal's phase and amplitude.

To improve the resiliency of our system, we first add a PLL logic in the Frame Synchronizer to keep track of minor changes of the frequency and phase. The loop bandwidth of the PLL is set to a reasonably small value in order to be sufficient to track the small variations, but not to be disturbed by interference.

The key technique to improve the estimation accuracy, consists of a pre-decoding and re-encoding mechanism, in which we first decode the phase-corrected symbols (by running them one first time through the Cryptographic Deinterleaver and GTCM Decoder), then re-encode the resulted binary data back to complex symbols. Now by comparing the re-encoded symbols (which have few symbol errors) and the previously received signal, we can rerun the phase tracking mechanism overcoming synchronization mistakes of the first pass. During the second-pass phase tracking, we carefully skip all the symbols for which there is a discrepancy between what was received and what was decoded. We observe that this significantly reduced the phase tracking errors. This frequency/phase corrected sequence of symbols is then sent to the Cryptographic Deinterleaver and GTCM Decoder for the final decoding.

7. EVALUATION

We report on the evaluation of our CBM system with both simulation results in MatLab and experimental results in our USRP N210 SDR testbed. We use the bit error rate (BER) and normalized signal-to-noise ratio E_b/N_0 as metrics for the system robustness.

7.1 Simulation Results

First, we assess the robustness of our codes found in Section 4 by simulation in MatLab to avoid impact of imperfect RF front ends such as frequency offset or phase noise. We simulate the transmission of packets encoded by the best TCM codes (constraint length

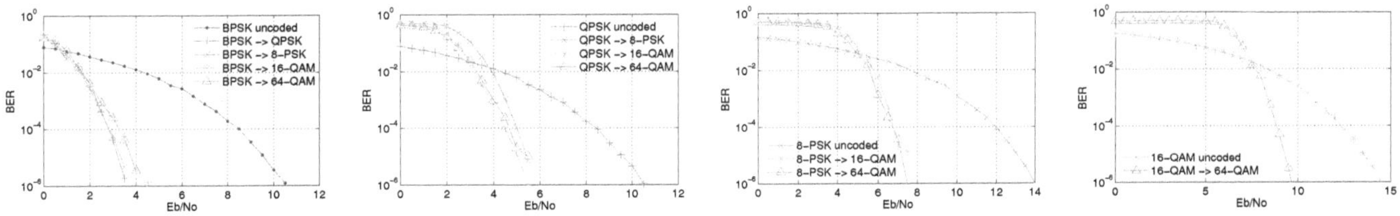

(a) Conceal & Boost BPSK (b) Conceal & Boost QPSK (c) Conceal & Boost 8-PSK (d) Conceal & Boost 16-QAM

Figure 6: Simulation results: Resiliency Boost of Coded over Uncoded Modulations

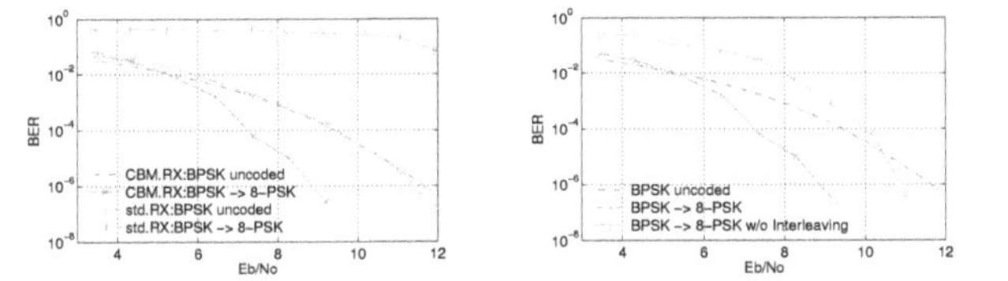

(a) Synchronization: CBM Receiver vs. Standard Receiver. (b) Robustness with and without Cryptographic Interleaving.

Figure 7: Performance of CBM's Synchronization and Cryptographic Interleaving mechanisms.

$v = 10$) for each pair of original modulation $\mathcal{K}$ and target modulation $\mathcal{N}$. The simulated noise is additive white Gaussian.

At BER $= 10^{-6}$, Figure 6a shows that, in addition to hiding the rate, our codes provide up to 7dB gain over uncoded BPSK modulation when concealing it into any higher-order modulation. Compared to the modulation level encryption technique proposed in recent related work [41] whose performance degrades by about 1.2dB for hiding BPSK modulation in 64-QAM modulation, we gain up to 8.2dB. In Figures 6b to 6d, we also achieve significant improvements when concealing QPSK, 8-PSK, and 16-QAM to higher-order modulations. It can be observed that when 64-QAM modulation is used for rate concealing, we obtain at least 5dB resiliency over any original uncoded modulation.

7.2 Experimental Results

As noted by previous work [45], the frequency offset and phase noise, due to channel variations and imperfect RF front ends, can severely reduce the decodability of TCM codes. To assess our system in realistic conditions, we implemented our solution in our USRP N210 SDR testbed to evaluate our system performance. The setup consists of one transmitter, one receiver, and one jammer. The experiments were both carried through an RF cable and a combiner adding the TX signal to the jammer signal (for a precise control of the SNR), and over the air as a second check.

Impact of Synchronization Mechanisms: As discussed in Section 6, the low SNR conditions prevent traditional synchronization techniques from performing well. Figure 7a shows the performance comparison between two systems: (1) one uses the standard synchronization techniques with band-edge filter combined with phase locked loop circuits [21, 22], (2) CBM receiver with our synchronization mechanisms. We observe that the coded modulation with standard synchronization techniques performs worse than the uncoded modulation due to low SNR. With our 2-pass synchronization, the accuracy of frequency and phase offset correction is much improved, resulting in the resiliency boost of the system.

Effect of Interleaving: While the main goal of Cryptographic Interleaving is to conceal the underlying modulations and codes from the adversary, it has a side effect of increasing the system robustness by scattering the burst errors over the whole block. To show the contributions of Cryptographic Interleaving in terms of resiliency boost, we compare the performance of our CBM system with and without interleaving. Figure 7b shows that interleaving increases the performance gain by roughly 2dB. We note that without our synchronization mechanism, the interleaving does not help.

CBM vs. Uncoded: Now we evaluate our CBM system in comparison with the uncoded system. We conduct the experiments for concealing any modulation $\mathcal{K}$ under any higher-order modulation $\mathcal{N}$ from the set of 5 different supported modulations. The results are shown in Figures 8a to 8d. First, we observe that in the real world environments, our system resiliency drops roughly $4-6$dB due to the unpleasant frequency and phase offset. Yet, comparing to the uncoded system, we obtain up to 4dB gain in resiliency while simultaneously concealing the rate information.

8. CONCLUSION AND DISCUSSION

We proposed a solution to the problem of hiding the rate of a communication while simultaneously increasing its robustness to interference. To the best of our knowledge, this is the first system that can achieve this goal. Our approach relies on algorithms for discovering new General TCM codes, and a cryptographic interleaving scheme. These algorithms include new efficient techniques to determine the free distance of non-uniform TCM codes. We explicitly derived 85 codes for upgrading any modulation in {BPSK, QPSK, 8-PSK, 16-QAM, 64-QAM} into any higher order modulation. These are the best codes among uniform and non-uniform TCM codes specifically designed for coded modulation and that conceal the underlying rate information. The GTCM codes and Crypto-Interleaving are complemented by new frequency correction and phase tracking techniques. We demonstrate analytically, and through simulations and experimentation, that beyond achieving rate-hiding, an order of magnitude improvement of energy efficiency is achieved in comparison with recent related work. The proposed solution is easily deployable in software defined radios. Our implementation source code is available at [47]. An interesting avenue of future research is to explore generalizations of turbo and LDPC codes to higher order modulations with an integrated frequency and phase correction mechanism.

Acknowledgement. This material is based upon work supported by the National Science Foundation under Grant CNS-1409453.

References

[1] B. Awerbuch, A. W. Richa, and C. Scheideler. A jamming-resistant MAC protocol for single-hop wireless networks. PODC'08, 2008.

[2] E. Bayraktaroglu, C. King, X. Liu, G. Noubir, R. Rajaraman, and B. Thapa. On the performance of IEEE 802.11 under jamming. In *IEEE INFOCOM*, 2008.

[3] M. Bellare. New Proofs for NMAC and HMAC: Security Without Collision-Resistance. In C. Dwork, editor, *Advances in Cryptology -*

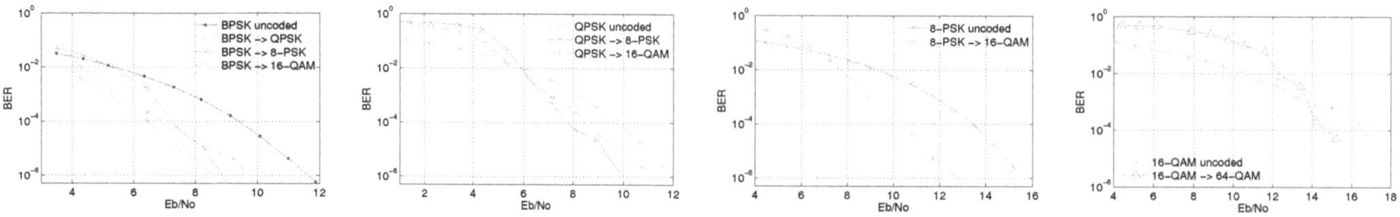

(a) Conceal & Boost BPSK (b) Conceal & Boost QPSK (c) Conceal & Boost 8-PSK (d) Conceal & Boost 16-QAM

Figure 8: Experimental results: Resiliency Boost of Coded over Uncoded Modulations

CRYPTO 2006, volume 4117 of *Lecture Notes in Computer Science*. Springer Berlin Heidelberg, 2006.

[4] M. A. Bender, M. Farach-Colton, S. He, B. C. Kuszmaul, and C. E. Leiserson. Adversarial contention resolution for simple channels. SPAA '05, pages 325–332, New York, NY, USA, 2005. ACM.

[5] J. C. Bicket. Bit-rate selection in wireless networks. Master's thesis, Massachusetts Intitute of Technology, 2005.

[6] E. Blossom. GNU Radio: Tools for Exploring the Radio Frequency Spectrum. *Linux J.*, 2004(122), June 2004.

[7] I. Broustis, K. Pelechrinis, D. Syrivelis, S. V. Krishnamurthy, and L. Tassiulas. Fiji: Fighting implicit jamming in 802.11 wlans. In *Security and Privacy in Communication Networks*. 2009.

[8] A. Cassola, W. Robertson, E. Kirda, and G. Noubir. A practical, targeted, and stealthy attack against wpa enterprise authentication. NDSS, 2013.

[9] J.-J. Chang, D.-J. Hwang, and M.-C. Lin. Some extended results on the search for good convolutional codes. *Information Theory, IEEE Transactions on*, 43, 1997.

[10] Y. Chen, W. Xu, W. Trappe, and Y. Zhang. *Securing Emerging Wireless Systems: Lower-layer Approaches*. Springer, 2009.

[11] Ettus Research. Universal Software Radio Peripheral.

[12] FCC. FCC enforcement bureau steps up education and enforcement efforts against cellphone and gps jamming, 2013.

[13] FCC. FCC fines jammers, 2013.

[14] FCC. Marriott hotels fined $600,000 by FCC for jamming Wi-Fi hotspots, October 2014.

[15] K. Firouzbakht, G. Noubir, and M. Salehi. Superposition coding in an adversarial environment. CISS, March 2011.

[16] K. Firouzbakht, G. Noubir, and M. Salehi. On the capacity of rate-adaptive packetized wireless communication links under jamming. WISEC '12. ACM, 2012.

[17] K. Firouzbakht, G. Noubir, and M. Salehi. On the performance of multi-layer superposition coding scheme under constrained jamming. CISS, March 2013.

[18] K. Firouzbakht, G. Noubir, and M. Salehi. On the performance of adaptive packetized wireless communication links under jamming. *Wireless Communications, IEEE Transactions on*, 2014.

[19] K. Firouzbakht, G. Noubir, and M. Salehi. Packetized wireless communication under jamming, a constrained bimatrix game. GLOBECOM, Dec 2014.

[20] S. Gilbert, R. Guerraoui, and C. Newport. Of malicious motes and suspicious sensors: On the efficiency of malicious interference in wireless networks. In *OPODIS*, 2006.

[21] F. Harris. Let's assume the system is synchronized. In *Globalization of Mobile and Wireless Communications*. Springer, 2011.

[22] F. J. Harris. *Multirate Signal Processing for Communication Systems*. Prentice Hall PTR, Upper Saddle River, NJ, USA, 2004.

[23] T. Jin, G. Noubir, and B. Thapa. Zero pre-shared secret key establishment in the presence of jammers. MobiHoc, 2009.

[24] S. Kay. A fast and accurate single frequency estimator. *Acoustics, Speech and Signal Processing, IEEE Transactions on*, Dec 1989.

[25] J. Kim, S. Kim, S. Choi, and D. Qiao. CARA: Collision-aware rate adaptation for IEEE 802.11 WLANs. In *INFOCOM*, 2006.

[26] M. Lacage, M. H. Manshaei, and T. Turletti. IEEE 802.11 rate adaptation: a practical approach. In *Proceedings of ACM MSWiM*, 2004.

[27] M. Li, I. Koutsopoulos, and R. Poovendran. Optimal jamming attacks and network defense policies in wireless sensor networks. In *INFOCOM*, 2007.

[28] G. Lin and G. Noubir. On link layer denial of service in data wireless lans. *Wiley Journal on Wireless Communications and Mobile Computing*, May 2005.

[29] S. Lin and D. J. Costello. *Error Control Coding*. 2 edition, 2004.

[30] A. Liu, P. Ning, H. Dai, Y. Liu, and C. Wang. Defending DSSS-based broadcast communication against insider jammers via delayed seed-disclosure. ACSAC'10.

[31] MadWifi-Project. Bit-rate selection algorithms, 2012.

[32] D. Nguyen, C. Sahin, B. Shishkin, N. Kandasamy, and K. R. Dandekar. A real-time and protocol-aware reactive jamming framework built on software-defined radios. SRIF '14, pages 15–22, New York, NY, USA, 2014. ACM.

[33] G. Noubir, R. Rajaraman, B. Sheng, and B. Thapa. On the robustness of IEEE 802.11 rate adaptation algorithms against smart jamming. ACM WiSec '11, pages 97–108, 2011.

[34] Onoe. MadWifi rate control, 2011.

[35] C. Orakcal and D. Starobinski. Jamming-resistant rate control in Wi-Fi networks. In *IEEE GLOBECOM*, 2012.

[36] C. Orakcal and D. Starobinski. Jamming-resistant rate adaptation in wi-fi networks. *Performance Evaluation*, 75-76(0):50–68, 2014.

[37] K. Pelechrinis, I. Broustis, S. V. Krishnamurthy, and C. Gkantsidis. Ares: an anti-jamming reinforcement system for 802.11 networks. In *Proceedings of ACM CoNEXT*, 2009.

[38] K. Pelechrinis, M. Iliofotou, and S. V. Krishnamurthy. Denial of service attacks in wireless networks: The case of jammers. *Communications Surveys & Tutorials, IEEE*, 2011.

[39] R. Poisel. *Modern communications jamming principles and techniques*. Artech House Publishers, 2011.

[40] J. G. Proakis and M. Salehi. *Digital Communications*. 5 edition, 2007.

[41] H. Rahbari and M. Krunz. Friendly CryptoJam: A Mechanism for Securing Physical-layer Attributes. WiSec '14, 2014.

[42] B. Schneier. Fake cell phone towers across the US, Sep. 2014.

[43] M. Strasser, C. Popper, S. Capkun, and M. Cagalj. Jamming-resistant key establishment using uncoordinated frequency hopping. In *IEEE SP*, 2008.

[44] P. Tague, D. Slater, G. Noubir, and R. Poovendran. Linear programming models for jamming attacks on network traffic flows. In *WiOpt*, 2008.

[45] G. Ungerboeck. Channel coding with multilevel/phase signals. *Information Theory, IEEE Transactions on*, 28(1):55–67, Jan 1982.

[46] vMonitor and ICL. SCADA wireless systems, 2011.

[47] T. D. Vo-Huu and G. Noubir. CBM source code. http://www.ccs.neu.edu/home/noubir/projects/cbm.

[48] M. Vutukuru, H. Balakrishnan, and K. Jamieson. Cross-layer wireless bit rate adaptation. In *Proceedings of ACM SIGCOMM*, 2009.

[49] M. Wilhelm, I. Martinovic, J. B. Schmitt, and V. Lenders. Short paper: reactive jamming in wireless networks: how realistic is the threat? In *Proceedings of ACM WiSec*, 2011.

[50] S. Wong, H. Yang, S. Lu, and V. Bharghavan. Robust rate adaptation for 802.11 wireless networks. In *ACM MobiCom*, 2006.

[51] W. Xu, K. Ma, W. Trappe, and Y. Zhang. Jamming sensor networks: attack and defense strategies. *IEEE Network*, 20(3):41–47, 2006.

[52] W. Xu, W. Trappe, and Y. Zhang. Defending wireless sensor networks from radio interference through channel adaptation. *ACM Transactions on Sensor Networks*, 4, September 2008.

Temporally or Spatially Dispersed Joint RFID Estimation Using Snapshots of Variable Lengths

Qingjun Xiao
Key Lab of Computer Network and Information Integration (Southeast University)
Ministry of Education, China
csqjxiao@seu.edu.cn

Min Chen   Shigang Chen   Yian Zhou
Department of Computer and Information Science and Engineering
University of Florida, Gainesville, FL, USA
{min, sgchen, yian}@cise.ufl.edu

ABSTRACT

Radio-frequency identification (RFID) technology has been widely used in applications such as inventory control, object tracking, supply chain management. An important research is to estimate the number of tags in a certain area covered by readers. This paper extends the research in both temporal and spatial dimensions to provide much richer information for monitoring the dynamics of distributed RFID systems. More specifically, we are interested in estimating the joint properties of any two snapshots taken at arbitrary locations and arbitrary times in a system. With many practical applications, there is however little prior work on this problem. We propose a joint RFID estimation protocol based on a simple yet versatile snapshot construction. Given the snapshots of any two tag sets, although their sizes may be very different, we design a way to combine their information and more importantly derive formulas to extract the joint properties of the two tag sets from the combined information, with an accuracy that can be arbitrarily set. Through formal analysis, we determine the optimal system parameters that minimize the execution time of taking snapshots, under the constraints of a given accuracy requirement. Our simulation results show that the proposed protocol can reduce the execution time by multifold when comparing with the best alternative approach in the literature.

Categories and Subject Descriptors

C.2.4 [**Computer-Communication Networks**]: [Distributed Systems]; C.4 [**Performance of Systems**]: [Measurement techniques]; H.4 [**Information Systems Applications**]: Miscellaneous

General Terms

Performance, Algorithm

Keywords

RFID; Cardinality Estimation; Random Hashing

MobiHoc'15, June 22–25, 2015, Hangzhou, China.

http://dx.doi.org/10.1145/2746285.2746289.

1. INTRODUCTION

Radio-frequency identification (RFID) technology has been widely used in various commercial applications, including inventory control, object tracking, supply chain management, auto-payment, etc [13, 7, 3, 9, 10]. RFID tags (each carrying a unique identifier) are attached to merchandise at retail stores, equipments at hospitals, or goods at warehouses, allowing an RFID reader to quickly identify products, access properties of each individual item, or collect statistical information about a group of items.

An important system function is called *RFID estimation* [5, 4, 12, 8, 22, 15, 16, 21, 2], which is to estimate the number of tags in a certain area covered by readers. This basic function can be used to monitor the inventory level in a warehouse, the sales in a retail store, and even the popularity of attractions in tourism [2]. It can also serve as a pre-processing step to make other functions (such as tag identification [18, 11, 6]) more efficient. RFID estimation takes much less time to perform than a full system scan that collects all tag IDs. This makes it valuable since RFID systems operate at low wireless rates and the execution time has been the key performance metric in system design. Moreover, it does not identify any tags, which avoids the privacy issue, particularly in scenarios where the party performing the operation (such as warehouse or port authority) does not own the tagged items.

Motivation: This paper extends RFID estimation in both temporal and spatial dimensions to provide much richer information about the dynamics of a distributed RFID system. We use two applications to explain the problems of temporally dispersed RFID estimation and spatially dispersed estimation, respectively. Consider the application of monitoring the inventory dynamics of a warehouse over time. We are interested in the amount of goods moving in (i.e., the number of new tags) and the amount moving out (i.e., the number of departure tags) between *any two* reference time points, without identifying the tag IDs, where the reference time points may be evenly spaced by time intervals of a certain length. The problem cannot be easily solved simply by estimating the number of tags in the warehouse after each time interval by traditional approaches [5, 4, 12, 8, 22, 15, 16, 21, 2]. For instance, if the number of tags at time 1 is estimated to be 1000 and so does the number at time 2, we will not be able to know whether no new tag has moved in or 1000 new tags have moved in while all old tags have moved out. To handle this problem, we need to take *snapshots* with more detailed information about existing tags, such that from any two snapshots taken at different times, we will be able to estimate the joint properties of the corresponding two tag sets, such as their union, intersection and difference, which provide information for stocking dynamics about product inflow and outflow.

In the second application, consider the supply chain management in a large logistics network. As tagged products are shipped from location (component factory, assembly line, warehouse, port, or other storage/retail facility) to location, if each location takes periodic snapshots of its tag set and keeps a series of such snapshots over time, we will be able to make queries for joint estimation between *any two* snapshots, which may be taken from different locations or from the same location at different times. Such joint estimation, when performed over time across the network, gives a picture about how goods flow through the logistics network. For one application, this information can help diagnose erratic shipments by identifying unexpected volumes that move over supply chains with significant deviation from a pre-established business plan — it has been reported that, due to such logistic errors, more than 65% of the inventory records did not match the physical inventory [14]. Without any automatic tools, we will have to resort to manual inventory check to discover the errors, which is laborious, expensive and slow, especially when such inventory task needs to be performed at daily basis.

Moreover, comparing with traditional RFID estimation [5, 4, 12, 8, 22, 15, 16, 21, 2] (which were designed to operate at a single time and a single place), the ability to jointly consider any two temporally or spatially dispersed snapshots will enable us to expand the applications mentioned earlier, for example, by providing more detailed information about changes in inventory and sales, by monitoring the flows of tourists moving from place to place in a theme park, or by serving as a pre-processing step to make some sophisticated functions such as continuous tag monitoring [17] more efficient.

Problem, Challenge and Prior Art: From the above applications, we abstract the problem of *joint RFID estimation*, which is to estimate the joint properties of two arbitrary sets of tags at different times or different locations in a large distributed RFID system. The joint properties include the cardinalities of the union, intersection and difference of the two sets.

The key challenge is that when a snapshot is taken for one tag set, we do not know which other set (at different time/location) the joint estimation will be made with. In fact, the snapshot can be paired with any other snapshot taken in the past or future in the system.

There is little prior work on this practically interesting problem. Directly related is the differential estimation method (DiffEstm) [20], which focuses on the difference between two sets and adopts a different problem model. It uniformly sets the sizes of all snapshots based on the worst-case situation so that any two can be paired. This is very inefficient because the tag sets in a system can have very diverse sizes. For example, in the previous logistics network application, a warehouse may sometimes be almost empty, while carrying tens of thousands of items at other times. Suppose the largest set the system can handle is 50,000. Even if a tag set at a certain time is down to hundreds, the size of its snapshot will still have to be set according to 50,000 in [20].

Our Contributions: First, we propose a new solution for the generalized joint RFID estimation problem based on a simple yet versatile snapshot construction. It takes only one pass of communication between a reader and tags to construct the snapshot of a given tag set. The size of the snapshot is roughly proportional to the size of the tag set, instead of being fixed to a large worst-case value. Given the snapshots of any two tag sets, although their sizes may be very different, we propose a way to combine their information and more importantly derive formulas to extract the joint properties of the two sets from the combined information.

Second, we formally analyze the means and variances of the estimated properties computed from the formulas. We show that the formulas produce asymptotically unbiased results and they estimate the joint properties with an absolute (probabilistic) error bound that can be set arbitrarily. We also derive the formulas for determining the optimal system parameters that minimize the execution time of taking snapshots, under the constraints of a given accuracy requirement for joint estimation.

Third, we perform extensive simulations to complement the theoretical analysis. The results show that by allowing the snapshots to have variable sizes, the new solution significantly outperforms the existing method. For example, under the same accuracy requirement, the new solution achieves about 240% improvement in execution time when comparing with DiffEstm.

2. PROBLEM DEFINITION

Consider a large distributed RFID system such as a supply-chain network, consisting of multiple locations, where tagged objects are shipped from location to location. At any time and any location, there is a set of tags. Consider two arbitrary sets of tags, N and N', at different locations or at the same location but different times. We study the joint properties of the two sets, including their intersection, union and difference.

Let $n = |N|$, $n' = |N'|$, $u = |N \cup N'|$, $m = |N \cap N'|$, $d = |N - N'|$, and $d' = |N' - N|$. With loss of generality, we assume N is a larger set than N', and hence $n \geq n'$. The *joint RFID estimation problem* is to provide estimations $\hat{u}$, $\hat{m}$, $\hat{d}$, and $\hat{d'}$ for u, m, d and d' respectively, such that the following pre-defined accuracy requirements are met:

$$Prob\{\hat{u} - k \leq u \leq \hat{u} + k\} \geq \alpha \tag{1}$$

$$Prob\{\hat{d} - k \leq d \leq \hat{d} + k\} \geq \alpha \tag{2}$$

$$Prob\{\hat{m} - k \leq m \leq \hat{m} + k\} \geq \alpha \tag{3}$$

$$Prob\{\hat{d'} - k \leq d' \leq \hat{d'} + k\} \geq \alpha, \tag{4}$$

where α is a probability value, and k is a probabilistic error bound. For example, if $\alpha = 95\%$ and $k = 100$, it requires that the absolute error of each estimation should be within k for a probability of no less than 95%.

An alternative way of specifying the estimation accuracy is based on a relative error $\epsilon \in (0, 1)$.

$$Prob\{\hat{u}(1 - \epsilon) \leq u \leq \hat{u}(1 + \epsilon)\} \geq \alpha \tag{5}$$

$$Prob\{\hat{d}(1 - \epsilon) \leq d \leq \hat{d}(1 + \epsilon)\} \geq \alpha \tag{6}$$

$$Prob\{\hat{m}(1 - \epsilon) \leq m \leq \hat{m}(1 + \epsilon)\} \geq \alpha \tag{7}$$

$$Prob\{\hat{d'}(1 - \epsilon) \leq d' \leq \hat{d'}(1 + \epsilon)\} \geq \alpha, \tag{8}$$

where the relative errors $\frac{\hat{u}-u}{\hat{u}}$, $\frac{\hat{d}-d}{\hat{d}}$, $\frac{\hat{m}-m}{\hat{m}}$ and $\frac{\hat{d'}-d'}{\hat{d'}}$ are bounded by $\pm\epsilon$ at a probability of at least α.

We do not adopt this model because it is very expensive or even impossible to achieve as the values of m, d and d' can be very small (down to zero). Consider $m = 0$. In this case, we will have to make sure that $\hat{m} = m = 0$ in order for (7) to be met, which means *precise measurement* of the empty intersection, i.e., $Var(\hat{m}) = 0$. Because $\hat{m}$ is derived from the two snapshots, these snapshots cannot carry any positive variance in their information based on which $\hat{m}$ is computed; note that the snapshots are independent due to $N \cup N' = \emptyset$. Recording precise information (such as IDs of all tags) is very expensive; all existing RFID estimation methods collect imprecise information from tags with non-zero variance to save time for information collection.

One critical problem is that at the time when the snapshot is taken for any tag set, we do not know which other snapshot it will be paired with for joint estimation. Because it is possible to pair with another snapshot with no common tag, we will have to make the snapshot precise (thus expensive) due to the requirement (7).

Finally, it arguably makes more sense to specify absolute error bound in some practical scenarios. Consider the logistics network application. Suppose we want to monitor the volume of products flowing from a number of factories to a number of assembly plants. Further suppose the volume from a particular factory to a particular plant may range from zero to ten of thousands in each pair of snapshots. To get a rough idea about the volume, we may specify the accuracy requirement as an absolute error bound of ± 50 items with 95% confidence. If the actual volume is 10, even though the relative error will be large, it does not change the fact that the estimated volume remains very small, giving correct assessment. On the contrary, if we specify a relative error of 1% and the actual volume is 10, it will require the estimation to have an absolute error of ± 0.1 item, which is not only expensive to achieve but also unnecessary. Note that in this example we estimate small intersection from snapshots of two large sets, not estimating the cardinality of one tag set from its snapshot (e.g, bitmap) as the traditional RFID estimation does.

3. PRIOR WORK

3.1 Differential Estimation

DiffEstm [20] gives a relative error model similar to (6)-(8) but does not prove that its estimation results meet those requirements. In fact, DiffEstm cannot always meet the relative error bound because it has positive variance in its snapshots, whereas the relative error model requires snapshots to carry precise information as we have argued previously.

We give a simplified description of DiffEstm's snapshot construction: A reader makes a request $(f, p, ...)$ to tags in its coverage area. After a tag receives the request, with a probability p, it will transmit in a slot randomly selected from an ALOHA frame of size f. The reader will turn the time frame into a bitmap snapshot of length f, with each busy slot being 1 and each idle slot being 0. In the original paper, the request carries a frame size F and a parameter f. Each tag transmits in a randomly chosen slot, and the reader only listens to the first f slots. This approach is equivalent to a frame size of f with a sampling probability $p = \frac{f}{F}$.

Figure 1 illustrates how DiffEstm works. After two bitmap snapshots (on the top of the figure) are taken for two tag sets, they are bitwise-ORed to produce a combined bitmap (at the bottom). The difference and intersection of the two

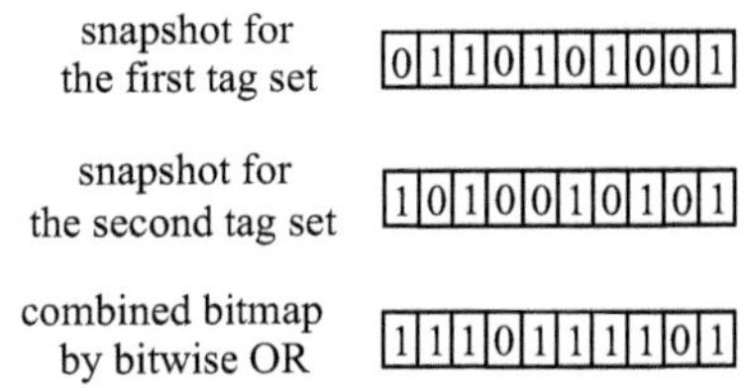

Figure 1: DiffEstm estimates the difference and intersection between two tag sets by combining their bitmap snapshots, which must have the same length and the same sampling probability.

sets will then be derived from the information in the three bitmaps, which must all contain a sufficient number of zeros to ensure estimation accuracy [20].

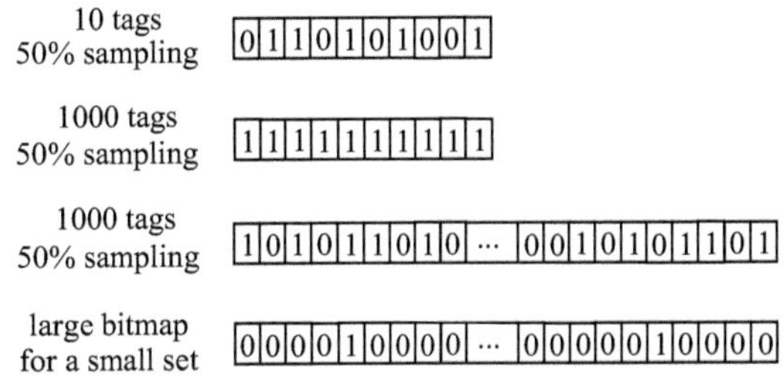

Figure 2: Large snapshots for small tag sets.

In order to support bitwise-OR, DiffEstm requires that all snapshots must have the same size and use a common sampling probability. For any small tag set, if the common sampling probability is very small, too few or even no tag will be sampled for the snapshot construction. Hence, the sampling probability will have to be reasonably large, as illustrated by the top bitmap in Figure 2, where 10 tags are recorded with 50% sampling probability. However, for a large set, a significant sampling probability will cause all bits to be set as ones (the second bitmap in the figure), unless the bitmap size is sufficiently large (the third bitmap in the figure). Now because the same large size has to be applied to all snapshots, it becomes a great waste for small tag sets (the fourth bitmap). Since each bit takes one time slot to get, a large bitmap size means a long time for taking a snapshot, even for a very small tag set.

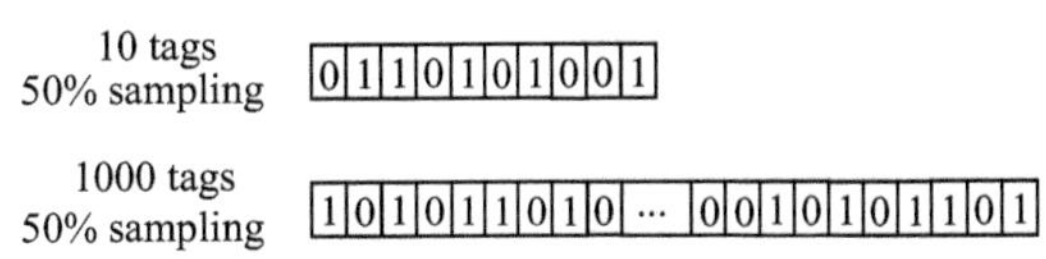

Figure 3: Snapshots of variable sizes.

Naturally, it is desirable to let each snapshot have a different size, depending on the size of the tag set it records, as illustrated in Figure 3. This will require us to develop new methods of combining two snapshots (or two bitmaps) with variable sizes. The real difficulty is not at how to combine two bitmaps per se; there are simple ways to combine them. The real difficulty comes after the combination — how to perform analysis on the information combined from non-uniform snapshots, how to use that information for joint estimation, and most importantly how to ensure the accuracy requirements in (1)-(4). These are the tasks that have not been investigated in the literature.

3.2 RFID Estimation and Union Estimation

There is a rich set of literature that estimate the cardinality n of a single tag set [5, 12, 4, 8, 22, 15, 16, 21, 2], typically giving an estimate $\hat{n}$ with a relative error model of

$$Prob\{\hat{n}(1-\epsilon) \leq n \leq \hat{n}(1+\epsilon)\} \geq \alpha, \quad (9)$$

which is different from the model of joint estimation where intersection and difference between two sets are estimated. The execution time is a function of the relative error bound ϵ. For example, the time of LOF is $\mathcal{O}(\frac{1}{\epsilon^2}\log n)$ [12], that of PET is $\mathcal{O}(\frac{1}{\epsilon^2}\log\log n)$ [22], and that of ZOE is $\mathcal{O}(\frac{1}{\epsilon^2} + \log\log n)$ [21]. The recent work of two-phase simple RFID counting (SRC) [2] has the best performance to date.

When the tag set cannot be covered by a single reader, multiple readers will be needed, each covering a subset. Many of the RFID estimation solutions can be easily extended for estimating the union size of the subsets. Among them, SRC_M [2] performs the best, achieving a reduction in execution time by up to 300%, when comparing with others. SRC_M also uses bitmaps. For each subset, it create multiple bitmaps, each under a different sampling probability. It then identifies the best sampling probability and combines the bitmaps of that probability from different subsets by bitwise OR. The combined bitmap records all tags in the union and can thus be used to estimate the union cardinality with the method from [5].

What makes SRC_M efficient is that as it scans one subset after another, it leverages the information learned from the previous subsets to reduce the number of bitmaps (different sampling probabilities) it needs for each subsequent subset. However, this method cannot be extrapolated to temporally/spatiall dispersed joint estimation where we do not know which tag sets will be jointly estimated beforehand and thus cannot leverage one set's information to help reduce the overhead for the other.

If we nevertheless want to apply SRC_M to joint estimation, we may use a common sampling probability that is optimized for the worst-case scenario such that an error bound for the union estimation will always be met. In this case, SRC_M will become DiffEstm except that the former considers only union while the latter also addresses difference and intersection (which are more difficult to estimate and analyze).

4. JOINT RFID ESTIMATION PROTOCOL

This section presents our joint RFID estimation protocol (JREP). Our protocol consists of two components: an online encoding component for measuring the information of each tag set and storing it in a bitmap called *snapshot*, and an offline data analysis component for estimating the joint properties of two arbitrary sets such as intersection/union/difference cardinalities, using their snapshots. We use an asymmetric design to push most complexity to the offline component, while keeping the online component as efficient as possible.

4.1 Online Encoding

Consider a snapshot taken at an arbitrary location and an arbitrary time in a large RFID system of multiple locations. Let N be the set of tags existing at the location and the time when the snapshot is taken, and n be the number of tags in N. The reader that performs the snapshot will first get a rough estimation for the value of n by using an existing cardinality estimation protocol [8, 12, 22]. It determines a frame size f for the snapshot as follows:

$$f = \min_{p\in(0,1]}\{2^{\lceil\log_2(\frac{np}{\omega})\rceil}\}, \quad (10)$$

where p is a sampling probability and

$$\omega = -\frac{3}{4} + \frac{\sqrt{3}}{4}\sqrt{4p\Big(\frac{k^2}{n_{\max}{Z_\alpha}^2} + 2\Big) - 5}.$$

We use Z_α to denote the $\frac{1+\alpha}{2}$ percentile for the unit normal distribution. For example, when $\alpha = 95\%$, $Z_\alpha = 1.96$. Later we will formally derive the above formulas that minimize the time overhead of online encoding and the storage overhead of the snapshot in the worst case, under the constraints of (1)-(4). Let p^* be the sampling probability that minimizes (10). The value of p^* only depends on $n_{\max}$, k, and α. Hence, it is pre-determined for a system once these parameters are set.

The encoding process is described as follows: The reader broadcasts an encoding request with parameters f and p^*. Upon receipt of the request, each tag decides with probability p^* whether it will participate in the encoding. If it does, it selects a slot uniformly at random and transmit a pulse during that slot. The reader monitors the status of each slot — with the detection of a pulse, it records the slot as a bit '1'; otherwise, it records a bit '0'. After the frame, the reader has a bitmap of ones and zeros, which will be stored and used later for joint estimation. We call this bitmap as a snapshot of the tag set N.

The implementation of sampling may be done as follows: Let M be a large integer. The reader broadcasts an integer $\lfloor p^*M\rfloor$ instead of a floating number p^*. A tag computes a pseudo-random value $R(ID)$, where ID is the tag's identifier and R is a pseudo-random function (required by the C1G2 standard). The tag is sampled if $R(ID) \bmod M < \lfloor p^*M\rfloor$. The slot selection also leverages the random function R. The tag computes $R(ID\,|\,r) \bmod f$, where r is a randomly-chosen constant pre-configured with all tags, to make the values of $R(ID\,|\,r)$ and $R(ID)$ independent of each other. With these implementations, we have the following property established.

PROPERTY 1. *Consider an arbitrary common tag in any two sets N and N', whose frame sizes are f and f' respectively, with $f \geq f'$. A tag is either sampled for encoding in both frames or neither. $\forall j \in [0, f)$, if the tag is sampled and does not select the $(j \bmod f')$th slot in the frame of f', then it will not select the jth slot in the frame of f.*

PROOF. It is easy to see that the tag will be either sampled for both frames or neither, because the same pseudo-random value $R(ID)$ is used for sampling.

Suppose the tag does not select the $(j \bmod f')$th slot in the frame of f'. That is, $R(ID\,|\,r) \neq j \bmod f'$. Because both f and f' are the powers of two and $f \geq f'$, f' must be able to divide f. Hence, $R(ID\,|\,r) \neq j \bmod f$, which means the jth slot in frame of f is not selected. □

4.2 Offline Joint RFID Estimation

Given two arbitrary snapshots, B and B', which may be taken at the same location but different times or at different locations, we give the formulas for estimating their difference, intersection and union.

4.2.1 Expanded OR

Let f and f' be the sizes of B and B', respectively. Without losing generality, suppose $f \geq f'$. According to (10), we know that both f and f' are the powers of two. The reason for them to be powers of two is to support the following operation that combines the information from the snapshots of two arbitrary tag sets for joint estimation.

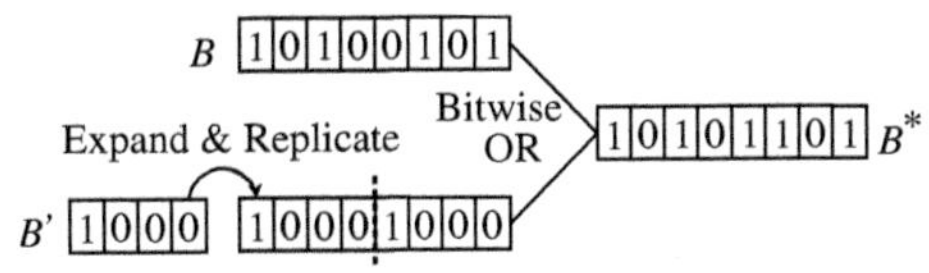

Figure 4: Expanded OR of two bitmaps B and B'.

We introduce an auxiliary bitmap, which is called the *expanded OR* between B and B', and is denoted as B^*. The expanded OR, which has been illustrated in Fig. 4, is defined as follows: We know that f is a multiple of f'. If $f \neq f'$, we will replicate B' for $\frac{f}{f'}$ times, such that it is expanded to the same length of B. We then perform bitwise OR between the two bitmaps, and the resulting B^* is f bits long.

The operation of expanded OR may appear to be trivial, but the implication of replicating the information of one bitmap when combining with another bitmap is not obvious at all. It requires rigorous analysis for its impact on estimation accuracy as the technique was never used in RFID estimation before.

Let N be the original tag set that is encoded by bitmap B. The size of N is denoted as n. Let X_j, $0 \leq j < f$, be the event that the jth bit in B remains zero after the n tags are randomly sampled and encoded into this bitmap.

$$Prob\{X_j\} = (1 - \frac{p}{f})^n \tag{11}$$

Let V be a random variable for the fraction of bits in B that are zeros (We can also measure an instance value of V from the snapshot B. This instance value will be used in the estimator derived later). We have

$$V = \frac{1}{f}\sum_{i=0}^{f-1} 1_{X_j},$$

where 1_{X_j} be the indicator variable of X_j, whose value is 1 when the event X_j occurs and 0 otherwise. Clearly, $E(1_{X_j}) = Prob\{X_j\}$. Hence,

$$E(V) = \frac{1}{f}\sum_{i=0}^{f-1} E(1_{X_j}) = \frac{1}{f}\sum_{i=0}^{f-1} Prob\{X_j\} = (1-\frac{p}{f})^n. \tag{12}$$

Let N' be the tag set encoded by B', n' be the set size, and Y_j, $0 \leq j < f'$, be the event that the jth bit in B' is zero.

$$Prob\{Y_j\} = (1 - \frac{p}{f'})^{n'} \tag{13}$$

The above equation is also true for any bit in the expanded B' (for producing B^*). Let Z_j, $0 \leq j < f$, be the event that the jth bit in B^* is zero. Since this bit is OR of the jth bit in B and the (j mod f')th bit in B', the event Z_j happens when both events X_j and $Y_{j \bmod f'}$ happens. Hence, we have

$$\begin{aligned} Prob\{Z_j\} &= Prob\{X_j \wedge Y_{j \bmod f'}\} \\ &= Prob\{X_j \,|\, Y_{j \bmod f'}\} \cdot Prob\{Y_{j \bmod f'}\} \\ &= (1-\frac{p}{f})^d(1-\frac{p}{f'})^{n'}, \end{aligned} \tag{14}$$

where $Prob\{Y_{j \bmod f'}\} = (1-\frac{p}{f'})^{n'}$ is from Eq. (13), and we have $Prob\{X_j \,|\, Y_{j \bmod f'}\} = (1-\frac{p}{f})^d$, because the condition $Y_{j \bmod f'}$, according to Property 1, suggests that all common tags of N and N' won't select the jth slot in the frame of f, and consequently only the d tags in $N - N'$ may select this slot.

Following a similar process of deriving (12), we have

$$E(V') = (1 - \frac{p}{f'})^{n'} \tag{15}$$

$$E(V^*) = (1 - \frac{p}{f})^d(1 - \frac{p}{f'})^{n'}, \tag{16}$$

where $V' = \frac{1}{f'}\sum 1_{Y_j}$ and $V^* = \frac{1}{f}\sum 1_{Z_j}$.

In the following, we give the estimators for the joint properties of N and N', including d, d', m, and u.

4.2.2 Estimator of Set Difference $d = |N - N'|$

Replacing the first term $(1-\frac{p}{f'})^{n'}$ in (16) by $E(V')$, we have

$$E(V^*) = E(V')(1 - \frac{p}{f})^d,$$

$$d = \frac{\ln E(V^*) - \ln E(V')}{\ln(1 - \frac{p}{f})}. \tag{17}$$

Replacing $E(V^*)$ and $E(V')$ by their instance values V^* and V' measured from B^* and B', we obtain the estimator $\hat{d}$.

$$\hat{d} = \frac{\ln V^* - \ln V'}{\ln(1 - \frac{p}{f})} \tag{18}$$

Such replacement with instance values produces asymptotically unbiased results, which originates from the central limit theorem and the multivariate δ-method [1], as explained below. Since V' (or V^*) is the arithmetic mean of a large number of independent random variables $V' = \frac{1}{f'}\sum 1_{Y_j}$ (or $V^* = \frac{1}{f}\sum 1_{Z_j}$), according to the central limit theorem, it approximates a Gaussian distribution, and its variance is inversely proportional to the number of random variables f' (or f). Further consider that $\hat{d}$ in (18) is a function of V' and V^* with continuous first partial derivatives. We can apply the multivariate δ-method, and conclude that the estimation $\hat{d}$ approximates a Gaussian distribution, whose expected value is $E(\hat{d}) \approx \frac{\ln E(V^*) - \ln E(V')}{\ln(1-\frac{p}{f})}$. Combined with (17), we have $E(\hat{d})$ equal to d asymptotically, when f and f' are large enough. Later, we will derive the mean of $\hat{d}$ with better accuracy.

Below we use a similar approach to derive the estimators of d', m and u.

4.2.3 Estimator of Set Difference $d' = |N' - N|$

Based on the definitions of d and d', we know that $d = n + d' - n'$, where $n + d'$ is the number of tags in $|N \cup N'|$. Applying it to (16), we have

$$\begin{aligned} E(V^*) &= (1 - \frac{p}{f})^{n+d'-n'}(1 - \frac{p}{f'})^{n'} \\ &= E(V)(1 - \frac{p}{f})^{d'} E(V') \,/\, (1 - \frac{p}{f})^{n'} \\ &= E(V)(1 - \frac{p}{f})^{d'} E(V') \,/\, E(V')^{\ln(1-\frac{p}{f})/\ln(1-\frac{p}{f'})}. \end{aligned}$$

Solving the above equation for d', we have

$$d' = \frac{\ln E(V^*) - \ln E(V) - \ln E(V')}{\ln(1 - \frac{p}{f})} + \frac{\ln E(V')}{\ln(1 - \frac{p}{f'})}.$$

Similar to the previous estimator, we can substitute the expected values $E(V)$, $E(V')$ and $E(V^*)$ by their instance values V, V' and V^* measured from B, B' and B^*, and have an asymptotically unbiased estimator $\hat{d}'$ of approximately Gaussian distribution for the intersection cardinality d'.

$$\hat{d}' = \frac{\ln V^* - \ln V - \ln V'}{\ln(1-\frac{p}{f})} + \frac{\ln V'}{\ln(1-\frac{p}{f'})} \tag{19}$$

4.2.4 Estimator of Set Intersection $m = |N \cap N'|$

We rewrite the expected value of V^* in (16) as

$$E(V^*) = (1-\frac{p}{f'})^{n'}(1-\frac{p}{f})^{n-m} = E(V')E(V)(1-\frac{p}{f})^{-m}$$

$$m = \frac{\ln E(V) + \ln E(V') - \ln E(V^*)}{\ln(1-\frac{p}{f})}.$$

Substitute the expected values $E(V)$, $E(V')$ and $E(V^*)$ by their instance values V, V' and V^*, we have an asymptotically unbiased estimator $\hat{m}$ of approximately Gaussian distribution for the intersection cardinality m.

$$\hat{m} = \frac{\ln V + \ln V' - \ln V^*}{\ln(1-\frac{p}{f})} \tag{20}$$

4.2.5 Estimator of Set Union $u = |N \cup N'|$

Multiplying both sides of Eq. (16) with $(1-\frac{p}{f})^{n'}$, we have

$$E(V^*)(1-\frac{p}{f})^{n'} = (1-\frac{p}{f})^{d+n'}E(V')$$

$$E(V^*)E(V')^{\ln(1-\frac{p}{f})/\ln(1-\frac{p}{f'})} = (1-\frac{p}{f})^{u}E(V')$$

$$u = \frac{\ln E(V^*) - \ln E(V')}{\ln(1-\frac{p}{f})} + \frac{\ln E(V')}{\ln(1-\frac{p}{f'})}.$$

Substitute the expected values $E(V')$ and $E(V^*)$ by their instance values V' and V^*, we have an estimator $\hat{u}$ of approximately Gaussian distribution for the union cardinality.

$$\hat{u} = \frac{\ln V^* - \ln V'}{\ln(1-\frac{p}{f})} + \frac{\ln V'}{\ln(1-\frac{p}{f'})} \tag{21}$$

4.2.6 Traditional Estimator of $n = |N|$ and $n' = |N'|$

We estimate n and n' based on the classical work in [19]:

$$\hat{n} = \frac{\ln V}{\ln(1-\frac{p}{f})} \qquad \hat{n'} = \frac{\ln V'}{\ln(1-\frac{p}{f'})}, \tag{22}$$

where $\hat{n}$ and $\hat{n'}$ denote the estimated values.

4.2.7 Reduction to DiffEstm [20] and PZE [5]

It is interesting to see that when we set $f = f'$, the estimators (18), (19) and (20) are reduced to the estimators of DiffEstm. If we further set the sets identical, i.e., $N = N'$, the union estimator (21) becomes the PZE estimator in [5], similar to those in (22) for a single set. Hence, DiffEstm and PZE are special cases of our estimators. Note that PZE repeats a small frame with a small sampling probability many times to reduce estimation variance. Here we use a larger bitmap (with a larger sampling probability) to reduce variance. The two approaches are equivalent [2].

The most fundamental difference in (18), (19), (20) and (21) from the prior art is the generalized semantics of $V*$, which is the fraction of bits that are zeros in the bitmap B^* combined from two bitmaps of variable sizes, f and f', where each bit in the smaller bitmap has to be used multiple times in order to enable bitwise OR. However, it is not intuitive why this multiple use of the same bits will work in estimation until we formally analyze the estimation accuracy under such a maneuver of combining information from non-uniform bitmaps.

5. ANALYSIS

In this section, we analyze the accuracy of the joint estimations $\hat{d}$, $\hat{d'}$, $\hat{m}$ and $\hat{u}$. To derive them, we will need the mean and variance of $\hat{n}$ ($\hat{n'}$), which can be found in [19]:

$$E(\hat{n}) \approx n + \frac{1}{2p}(e^{\omega} - \omega p - 1) \tag{23}$$

$$Var(\hat{n}) \approx \frac{f}{p^2}(e^{\omega} - \omega p - 1), \tag{24}$$

where $\omega = \frac{pn}{f}$ is called the *load factor* of bitmap B;

$$E(\hat{n'}) \approx n' + \frac{1}{2p}(e^{\omega'} - \omega' p - 1) \tag{25}$$

$$Var(\hat{n'}) \approx \frac{f'}{p^2}(e^{\omega'} - \omega' p - 1), \tag{26}$$

where $\omega' = \frac{pn'}{f'}$ is the load factor of bitmap B'.

5.1 Mean and Variance of $\hat{d}$

We first derive $E(\hat{d})$ and $Var(\hat{d})$. From (18) and (22), we rewrite the formula for $\hat{d}$ as

$$\hat{d} = \frac{\ln V^*}{\ln(1-\frac{p}{f})} - \hat{n'} \cdot \frac{\ln(1-\frac{p}{f'})}{\ln(1-\frac{p}{f})}. \tag{27}$$

The statistical properties of $\hat{n'}$ are known. The values of p, f, f' are also known. The first term is denoted as $\hat{n^*}$:

$$\hat{n^*} = \frac{\ln V^*}{\ln(1-\frac{p}{f})}. \tag{28}$$

We have derived the mean and variance of $\hat{n^*}$. Due to space limitation, we omit the process, which will be reported in a longer journal version.

$$E(\hat{n^*}) \approx n^* + \frac{1}{2p}(e^{\omega^*} - \omega^* p - 1)$$

$$Var(\hat{n^*}) \approx \frac{f}{p^2}(e^{\omega^*} - \omega^* p - 1),$$

where

$$n^* = d + n'\frac{f}{f'}, \qquad \omega^* = \frac{pd}{f} + \frac{pn'}{f'}, \tag{29}$$

and ω^* is the load factor of B^*. When $f = f'$, we see that (28) and (21) are equivalent. In this case, $\hat{n^*} = \hat{u}$, and B^* can be regarded as an encoding of the union of the two sets.

Based on (27) and (29), using the fact that $\ln(1-x) \approx -x$ when x is sufficiently small, the expected value of $\hat{d}$ is

$$E(\hat{d}) = E\Big(\hat{n^*} - \hat{n'} \cdot \frac{\ln(1-\frac{p}{f'})}{\ln(1-\frac{p}{f})}\Big) \approx E(\hat{n^*} - \frac{f}{f'}\hat{n'})$$

$$= d + \frac{1}{2p}(e^{\omega^*} - \omega^* p - 1) - \frac{f}{f'}\frac{1}{2p}(e^{\omega'} - \omega' p - 1).$$

Recall from the previous section that all proposed estimators are asymptotically unbiased.

The variance of $\hat{d}$ is derived as follows.

$$Var(\hat{d}) \approx Var(\hat{n^*} - \tfrac{f}{f'}\hat{n'})$$
$$= Var(\hat{n^*}) + \tfrac{f^2}{f'^2}Var(\hat{n'}) - 2\tfrac{f}{f'}Cov(\hat{n^*}, \hat{n'})$$

We have derived that $Cov(\hat{n^*}, \hat{n'}) \approx \frac{f}{f'} Var(n')$; the process is omitted due to space limitation. Hence,

$$Var(\hat{d}) \approx Var(\hat{n^*}) - \frac{f^2}{f'^2} Var(\hat{n'}). \quad (30)$$

The above equation implies that $Var(\hat{d})$ is smaller than $Var(\hat{n^*})$. Intuitively, because $\hat{d}$ is calculated from $\hat{n^*}$ and $\hat{n'}$, the estimation $\hat{d}$ should contain the estimation error of both $\hat{n^*}$ and $\hat{n'}$. However, our analysis shows that the two estimates $\hat{n^*}$ and $\hat{n'}$ positively correlate with each other, i.e., $Cov(\hat{n^*}, \hat{n'}) > 0$, which causes the variance of $\hat{d}$ smaller.

5.2 Mean and Variance of $\hat{u}$

From (21), (22), and (28), by the fact that $\ln(1-x) \approx -x$ when x is sufficiently small, we have $\hat{u} \approx \hat{n^*} - \frac{f-f'}{f'}\hat{n'}$. Hence,

$$\begin{aligned}
E(\hat{u}) &\approx E(\hat{n^*}) - \frac{f-f'}{f'} E(\hat{n'}) \\
&= u + \frac{1}{2p}(e^{\omega^*} - \omega^* p - 1) - \frac{f-f'}{f'}\frac{1}{2p}(e^{\omega'} - \omega' p - 1) \\
Var(\hat{u}) &\approx Var(\hat{n^*}) + \frac{(f-f')^2}{f'^2} Var(\hat{n'}) - 2\frac{f-f'}{f'} Cov(\hat{n^*}, \hat{n'}).
\end{aligned}$$

Since $Cov(\hat{n^*}, \hat{n'}) \approx \frac{f}{f'} Var(n')$, we have

$$Var(\hat{u}) \approx Var(\hat{n^*}) - \frac{f^2 - f'^2}{f'^2} Var(\hat{n'}). \quad (31)$$

5.3 Mean and Variance of $\hat{m}$

From (20), (22), (28), we have $\hat{m} \approx \hat{n} + \frac{f}{f'}\hat{n'} - \hat{n^*}$. Hence,

$$\begin{aligned}
E(\hat{m}) \approx& E(\hat{n}) + \frac{f}{f'} E(\hat{n'}) - E(\hat{n^*}) \approx m + \frac{1}{2p}(e^{\omega} - \omega p - 1) \\
&+ \frac{f}{f'}\frac{1}{2p}(e^{\omega'} - \omega' p - 1) - \frac{1}{2p}(e^{\omega^*} - \omega^* p - 1) \\
Var(\hat{m}) \approx& Var(\hat{n}) + \frac{f^2}{f'^2} Var(\hat{n'}) + Var(\hat{n^*}) \\
&+ 2\frac{f}{f'} Cov(\hat{n}, \hat{n'}) - 2Cov(\hat{n^*}, \hat{n}) - 2\frac{f}{f'} Cov(\hat{n^*}, \hat{n'}).
\end{aligned}$$

We have derived that $Cov(\hat{n}, \hat{n'}) = \frac{f}{p^2}(e^{\frac{mp}{f}} - \frac{m}{f}p^2 - 1)$ and that we have derived that $Cov(\hat{n^*}, \hat{n}) \approx Var(\hat{n}) + (\frac{f}{f'} - 1)\frac{f}{p^2}(e^{\frac{mp}{f}} - \frac{m}{f}p^2 - 1)$. Also using $Cov(\hat{n^*}, \hat{n'}) \approx \frac{f}{f'} Var(n')$, we have

$$\begin{aligned}
Var(\hat{m}) \approx& Var(\hat{n}) + \frac{f^2}{f'^2} Var(\hat{n'}) + Var(\hat{n^*}) \\
&+ 2\frac{f}{p^2}(e^{\frac{mp}{f}} - \frac{m}{f}p^2 - 1) - 2Var(\hat{n}) - 2\frac{f^2}{f'^2} Var(\hat{n'}) \\
=& Var(\hat{n^*}) - Var(\hat{n}) - \frac{f^2}{f'^2} Var(\hat{n'}) + 2\frac{f}{p^2}(e^{\frac{mp}{f}} - \frac{m}{f}p^2 - 1).
\end{aligned} \quad (32)$$

5.4 Mean and Variance of $\hat{d'}$

From (20), (22), (28), we have $\hat{d'} \approx \hat{n^*} - \hat{n} - \frac{f-f'}{f'}\hat{n'}$. Hence, we can calculate

$$\begin{aligned}
E(\hat{d'}) \approx& E(\hat{n^*}) - E(\hat{n}) - \frac{f-f'}{f'} E(\hat{n'}) \\
\approx& d' + \frac{1}{2p}(e^{\omega^*} - \omega^* p - 1) - \frac{1}{2p}(e^{\omega} - \omega p - 1) \\
&- \frac{f-f'}{f'}\frac{1}{2p}(e^{\omega'} - \omega' p - 1) \\
Var(\hat{d'}) \approx& Var(\hat{n^*}) + Var(\hat{n}) + (\frac{f-f'}{f'})^2 Var(\hat{n'}) \\
&+ 2\frac{f-f'}{f'} Cov(\hat{n}, \hat{n'}) - 2Cov(\hat{n^*}, \hat{n}) - 2\frac{f-f'}{f'} Cov(\hat{n^*}, \hat{n'}).
\end{aligned}$$

The three covariances are known when we previously derive the variance of $\hat{m}$. Therefore,

$$\begin{aligned}
Var(\hat{d'}) =& Var(\hat{n^*}) + Var(\hat{n}) + (\frac{f-f'}{f'})^2 Var(\hat{n'}) \\
&- 2Var(\hat{n}) - 2\frac{f-f'}{f'}\frac{f}{f'} Var(\hat{n'}) \\
=& Var(\hat{n^*}) - Var(\hat{n}) - \frac{f^2 - f'^2}{f'^2} Var(\hat{n'}).
\end{aligned} \quad (33)$$

Because the estimators approximate Gaussian distributions, the accuracy requirements of (1)-(4) can be turned into a set of constraints on bounded $Var(\hat{d})$, $Var(\hat{d'})$, $Var(\hat{m})$, and $Var(\hat{u})$. The following property shows that these constraints can be turned into a single one on $Var(\hat{n^*})$, which will be used to determine the optimal system parameters. The proof of the property is omitted due to space limitation.

PROPERTY 2. *$Var(\hat{n^*})$ is an approximately tight upper bound of $Var(\hat{d})$, $Var(\hat{d'})$, $Var(\hat{m})$, and $Var(\hat{u})$.*

6. SYSTEM PARAMETERS

We have already known that the distributions of joint estimations, $\hat{d}$, $\hat{d'}$, $\hat{m}$, and $\hat{u}$, approximate Gaussian distributions. Our requirement is to bound the estimation error of each joint property by a constant k with high probability, as stated in (1)-(4). In this section, we try to set the optimal system parameters f and p to minimize the protocol execution time, subject to the accuracy requirement.

6.1 Load Factor

Consider the requirement (1) on the union cardinality estimation $\hat{u}$, which specifies a confidence interval of width $2k$ at a confidence level of α. For a Gaussian distribution with $E(\hat{u}) \approx u$, the requirement on $\hat{u}$ is translated to:

$$Z_\alpha \sqrt{Var(\hat{u})} \le k \qquad Var(\hat{u}) \le \frac{k^2}{{Z_\alpha}^2}, \quad (34)$$

where Z_α denotes the $\frac{1+\alpha}{2}$ percentile for the unit Gaussian distribution. Similar, the requirement (3)-(4) can be translated to

$$Var(\hat{m}) \le \frac{k^2}{{Z_\alpha}^2}, \quad Var(\hat{d}) \le \frac{k^2}{{Z_\alpha}^2}, \quad Var(\hat{d'}) \le \frac{k^2}{{Z_\alpha}^2}. \quad (35)$$

In order to cover all possible cases, due to Property 2, all these constraints (1)-(4) can be replaced by $Var(\hat{n^*}) \le \frac{k^2}{{Z_\alpha}^2}$.

$$\begin{aligned}
&\frac{f}{p^2}(e^{\omega^*} - \omega^* p - 1) \le \frac{k^2}{{Z_\alpha}^2} \\
&\frac{n}{p\omega}\left((1-p)\omega^* + \frac{1}{2}\omega^{*2} + \frac{1}{6}\omega^{*3}\right) \le \frac{k^2}{{Z_\alpha}^2} \quad \text{Taylor Expansion}
\end{aligned} \quad (36)$$

From (29), we have $\omega^* = \frac{pd}{f} + \frac{pn'}{f'} = \frac{pn}{f} - \frac{pm}{f} + \frac{pn'}{f'} = \omega + \omega' - \frac{pm}{f}$. If $m = 0$, then $\omega^* = \omega + \omega'$, which maximizes the left side of (36). We consider this worst-case constraint in terms of m. Hence,

$$\frac{n}{p\omega}\Big((1-p)(\omega+\omega') + \frac{1}{2}(\omega+\omega')^2 + \frac{1}{6}(\omega+\omega')^3\Big) \le \frac{k^2}{Z_\alpha{}^2}$$
$$\frac{1}{\omega}\Big((1-p)(\omega+\omega') + \frac{1}{2}(\omega+\omega')^2 + \frac{1}{6}(\omega+\omega')^3\Big) \le \frac{k^2 p}{Z_\alpha{}^2 n}.$$

To satisfy the above constraint in the worst case in terms of n (which is bounded by $n_{\max}$), we have

$$\frac{1}{\omega}\Big((1-p)(\omega+\omega') + \frac{1}{2}(\omega+\omega')^2 + \frac{1}{6}(\omega+\omega')^3\Big) \le \frac{k^2 p}{Z_\alpha{}^2 n_{\max}}. \quad (37)$$

In our system design, we shall set both w and w' for a system-wide optimal load factor. With $\omega' = \omega$, we have

$$\frac{1}{\omega}\Big((1-p)2\omega + \frac{1}{2}(2\omega)^2 + \frac{1}{6}(2\omega)^3\Big) \le \frac{k^2 p}{Z_\alpha{}^2 n_{\max}}$$

$$\omega \le -\frac{3}{4} + \frac{\sqrt{3}}{4}\sqrt{4p\Big(\frac{k^2}{n_{\max} Z_\alpha{}^2} + 2\Big) - 5}. \quad (38)$$

Because $w = \frac{np}{f}$, it is inversely proportional to the frame size f, which measures the protocol execution time when encoding the tags in B. Hence, we should set our target load factor as

$$\omega = -\frac{3}{4} + \frac{\sqrt{3}}{4}\sqrt{4p\Big(\frac{k^2}{n_{\max} Z_\alpha{}^2} + 2\Big) - 5}. \quad (39)$$

We justify our choice of setting $\omega = \omega'$ above. The left side of (37) is an increasing function in both ω and ω'. If we allow $\omega' \neq \omega$ and still set their values to be as small as possible, then one of them will be greater than the right side of (39) and the other will be smaller. Because N and N' are arbitrary tag sets under consideration, it means that some tag sets will be encoded with their load factors greater than the right side of (39) and some others will have smaller load factors. Let N_1 and N_2 be two sets with load factors greater than (39). We should be able to perform joint estimation on any two encoded sets without violating the accuracy requirement. However, if we perform joint estimation on N_1 and N_2, because their load factors are larger than (39), the constraint of (37) will not hold.

6.2 Frame Size and Sampling Probability

From (38) and $w = \frac{np}{f}$, we have

$$f \ge \frac{np}{-\frac{3}{4} + \frac{\sqrt{3}}{4}\sqrt{4p(\frac{k^2}{n_{\max} Z_\alpha{}^2} + 2) - 5}}. \quad (40)$$

Recall that the value of f is set to be a power of two in order to support expanded OR between the snapshots of any two tag sets. We want to choose the optimal sampling probability that minimizes the protocol execution time by keeping the frame size f as small as possible. Hence, we have the formula for the frame size as quoted in Section 4.1:

$$f = \min_{p \in (0,1]} \{2^{\lceil \log_2(\frac{np}{\omega}) \rceil}\}, \quad (41)$$

where p is a sampling probability and the load factor ω is determined by Eq. (39). It requires a prior knowledge of n, the number of tags in N, which can be estimated through an existing protocol such as GMLE [8], LOF [12] and PET [22].

The optimal sampling probability p^* that minimizes f depends on the pre-determined parameters $n_{\max}$, k and α. Hence, it can be pre-computed.

7. SIMULATION RESULTS

7.1 Simulation Setting

We evaluate the performance of the proposed JREP protocol and compare it to DiffEstm [20] for joint estimation. For the union estimation, we also want to compare with SRC_M, the best protocol among those that were originally designed to estimate the cardinality of a tag set covered by multiple readers. Assuming that the optimal sampling probability is known, SRC_M becomes equivalent to DiffEstm in union estimation. See Section 3.2.

We consider two performance metrics. First, when the two protocols are subject to the same average execution time, we compare *their probabilities of meeting a given error bound*. The probability is measured as the number of joint estimations that meet the error bound divided by the total number of joint estimations performed in the simulation. In favor to DiffEstm and SRC_M, we assume that they know the optimal sampling probability that maximizes their worst-case probabilities of meeting the error bound. The original paper [20] does not give a formula for this optimal sampling probability. We obtain it through exhaustive search by simulations. Second, given an accuracy requirement as defined in (1)-(4), we compare the *execution times* of the two protocols. The execution time is measured as the number of time slots it takes the reader to encode a tag set in a snapshot bitmap, including the frame size f and other slots needed to give an initial rough estimation of n (Section 6). For JREP, we invoke GMLE [8] to generate a raw estimation of n with a 95% confidence interval of ±10% error.

The system model is a distributed RFID system of multiple locations, where each reader periodically takes a snapshot of its local set of tags, whose number ranges from 0 to 50,000, with $n_{max} = 50,000$. The average number of tags in a set is chosen to be 10,000, which reflects that the normal business flow of tagged objects is smaller than the worst-case number that the system is designed to handle. The size of each tag set will be taken from a truncated normal distribution $Norm(10000, 2000^2)$ in the range of $[0, n_{max}]$. For the accuracy requirement, we set $\alpha = 95\%$ and $k = 500$ by default. We will also perform simulation with other values of k and α.

7.2 Estimation Accuracy under Same Execution Time

We first set the parameters for JREP so that it satisfies the accuracy requirement of $\alpha = 95\%$ and $k = 500$, i.e., the difference between the estimated values ($\hat{d}$, $\hat{d}'$, $\hat{u}$, $\hat{m}$) and the true values (d, d', u, m) is bounded by 500 with 95% probability. We can compute the value of ω from (39) and then the values of f and p from (41). However, since the value of f is rounded up to the power of two to support the operation of expanded OR, these two parameters are in fact set conservatively. Alternatively, we can set their values empirically through simulations (similar to [2]). We first compute the initial value of ω from (39) and then perform bi-section search to reduce it as small as possible such that the resulting values of f and p from (41) will still satisfy the accuracy requirement. As a result, the load factor ω is 0.735.

Table 1: Probability for intersection cardinality estimation (m) by JREP ($\omega = 0.735$) to meet the bound $k = 500$

$n(\times 10^3)$ \ $n'(\times 10^3)$	[0, 5)	[5, 10)	[10, 15)	[15, 20)	[20, 25)	[25, 30)	[30, 35)	[35,40)	[40, 45)	[45, 50)
[0, 5)	1.00	—	—	—	—	—	—	—	—	—
[5, 10)	1.00	1.00	—	—	—	—	—	—	—	—
[10, 15)	1.00	1.00	1.00	—	—	—	—	—	—	—
[15, 20)	1.00	1.00	1.00	1.00	—	—	—	—	—	—
[20, 25)	1.00	1.00	1.00	1.00	1.00	—	—	—	—	—
[25, 30)	1.00	1.00	1.00	1.00	1.00	1.00	—	—	—	—
[30, 35)	1.00	1.00	1.00	1.00	1.00	1.00	1.00	—	—	—
[35, 40)	0.99	1.00	1.00	1.00	1.00	1.00	1.00	1.00	—	—
[40, 45)	0.99	0.99	0.99	1.00	0.99	1.00	1.00	1.00	1.00	—
[45, 50)	**0.98**	0.99	0.99	1.00	0.99	1.00	1.00	1.00	0.99	0.99

Table 2: Probability for union cardinality estimation (u) by JREP ($\omega = 0.735$) to meet the error bound $k = 500$

$n(\times 10^3)$ \ $n'(\times 10^3)$	[0, 5)	[5, 10)	[10, 15)	[15, 20)	[20, 25)	[25, 30)	[30, 35)	[35,40)	[40, 45)	[45, 50)
[0, 5)	1.00	—	—	—	—	—	—	—	—	—
[5, 10)	1.00	1.00	—	—	—	—	—	—	—	—
[10, 15)	1.00	1.00	1.00	—	—	—	—	—	—	—
[15, 20)	1.00	1.00	1.00	1.00	—	—	—	—	—	—
[20, 25)	0.99	1.00	1.00	1.00	0.99	—	—	—	—	—
[25, 30)	1.00	1.00	1.00	1.00	0.99	1.00	—	—	—	—
[30, 35)	0.99	0.99	0.99	0.99	0.99	1.00	1.00	—	—	—
[35, 40)	0.98	0.98	0.99	0.99	0.97	1.00	0.99	0.99	—	—
[40, 45)	0.97	0.97	0.97	0.97	0.96	0.99	0.99	0.98	0.97	—
[45, 50)	**0.95**	0.96	0.97	0.98	0.96	0.99	0.97	0.98	0.97	0.96

Table 3: Probability for intersection cardinality estimation (m) by DiffEstm ($f = 18405$) to meet $k = 500$

$n(\times 10^3)$ \ $n'(\times 10^3)$	[0, 5)	[5, 10)	[10, 15)	[15, 20)	[20, 25)	[25, 30)	[30, 35)	[35,40)	[40, 45)	[45, 50)
[0, 5)	1.00	—	—	—	—	—	—	—	—	—
[5, 10)	1.00	1.00	—	—	—	—	—	—	—	—
[10, 15)	1.00	1.00	1.00	—	—	—	—	—	—	—
[15, 20)	1.00	1.00	1.00	1.00	—	—	—	—	—	—
[20, 25)	1.00	1.00	1.00	1.00	0.98	—	—	—	—	—
[25, 30)	1.00	1.00	0.99	0.98	0.97	0.94	—	—	—	—
[30, 35)	1.00	1.00	0.98	0.97	0.94	0.89	0.85	—	—	—
[35, 40)	1.00	1.00	0.96	0.96	0.91	0.89	0.82	0.76	—	—
[40, 45)	1.00	0.99	0.94	0.89	0.86	0.79	0.72	0.73	0.67	—
[45, 50)	1.00	0.96	0.92	0.88	0.82	0.77	0.74	0.68	0.61	**0.51**

Table 4: Probability for union cardinality estimation (u) by DiffEstm/SRC$_{\mathrm{M}}$ ($f = 18405$) to meet $k = 500$

$n(\times 10^3)$ \ $n'(\times 10^3)$	[0, 5)	[5, 10)	[10, 15)	[15, 20)	[20, 25)	[25, 30)	[30, 35)	[35,40)	[40, 45)	[45, 50)
[0, 5)	1.00	—	—	—	—	—	—	—	—	—
[5, 10)	1.00	1.00	—	—	—	—	—	—	—	—
[10, 15)	1.00	1.00	1.00	—	—	—	—	—	—	—
[15, 20)	1.00	1.00	1.00	0.99	—	—	—	—	—	—
[20, 25)	1.00	0.99	0.99	0.98	0.94	—	—	—	—	—
[25, 30)	0.99	0.97	0.95	0.93	0.91	0.87	—	—	—	—
[30, 35)	0.96	0.94	0.90	0.88	0.85	0.81	0.75	—	—	—
[35, 40)	0.91	0.89	0.84	0.84	0.78	0.76	0.71	0.67	—	—
[40, 45)	0.86	0.82	0.77	0.73	0.70	0.66	0.62	0.61	0.56	—
[45, 50)	0.78	0.72	0.69	0.67	0.64	0.60	0.59	0.56	0.51	**0.42**

Table 1 shows the probability for the intersection estimation $\hat{m}$ by JREP to meet the error bound 500. We simulate two tag sets of sizes n and n', with $n \geq n'$. The first column shows the range from which n is chosen uniformly at random. For example, the first range is $[0, 5000)$ and the last range is $[45000, 50000)$. Be ware that the numbers of in the first column have a unit of 1000. The first row shows the range from which n' is chosen. Similarly its first range is $[0, 5000)$ and the last range is $[45000, 50000)$. Because we require $n \geq n'$, the combinations of n and n' above the diagonal are invalid. Each cell in the table shows the probability of meeting the error bound when n and n' are chosen from specified ranges. For example, consider the left bottom cell inside the table, where n is chosen from $[45000, 50000)$ and n' from $[0, 5000)$. The probability of meeting the error bound is 98%, which is measured from 1,000 simulation runs, each with two tag sets N and N' arbitrarily generated and the number m of common tags randomly chosen from the range $[0, n']$.

Table 2 shows the probability for the union estimation $\hat{u}$ by JREP to meet the error bound 500. All probabilities in both tables are greater than 95%, which confirms our

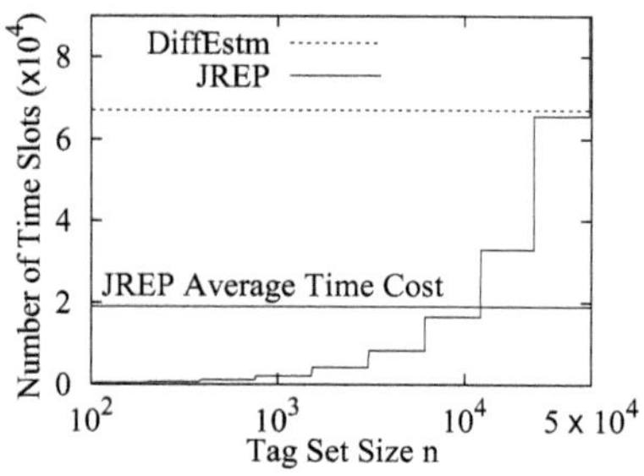

Figure 5: Time comparison with $k = 500$ and $\alpha = 95\%$

analytical results that the proposed estimators satisfy the accuracy requirements (1) and (3). The same is true for difference estimations $\hat{d}$ and $\hat{d}'$, which are not shown due to space limitation.

For JREP, the frame size depends on the size of tag set to be encoded. With an average size of 10,000 tags and $\omega = 0.735$, the average execution time of JREP is 18,405 slots in our simulation. We use the same number of slots for DiffEstm (or SRC_M), and the simulation results are shown in Tables 3 and 4, where the probability for m to meet the error bound 500 can be as low as 51% when both n and n' are large, and the probability for u to meet the error bound can be as low as 42%, which is much worse than what JREP can achieve at the same time cost.

7.3 Execution Time to Achieve Same Accuracy

Next, we fix the accuracy requirements with $\alpha = 95\%$ and $k = 500$, and compare the execution times of JREP and DiffEstm for taking a bitmap snapshot of a tag set. Because DiffEstm is not designed for absolute error bound, there is no formula to compute its frame size. With $n_{max} = 50,000$, we use exhaustive search by simulation to find its minimum frame size that can meet the error bound. The results are shown in Fig. 5, where the horizontal axis is the size of a tag set, which varies from 100 to 50000, and the vertical axis is the number of time slots needed to take a bitmap snapshot of the set. Due to the nature of its design, DiffEstm uses a constant frame size of 67,000 slots. The frame size of JREP is variable. It is small when the tag set is small. For example, for a set of 5000 tags, the number of time slots needed by JREP is 8,192, only 12% of what's needed by DiffEstm. The average time cost of JREP is shown by the solid horizontal line. Similar results are observed from simulations with different accuracy requirements (whose results cannot be included due to limited space).

8. CONCLUSION

This paper studies the problem of joint cardinality estimation: Given any two tag sets in a large RFID system, estimating their union cardinality, intersection cardinality, and difference cardinalities. We propose a solution called JREP that adapts its snapshot based on the size of the tag set that it records. Variable-sized snapshots are combined through expanded OR to support joint estimation. We derive a full set of estimators, analyze their accuracies, and provide formulas for setting the optimal system parameters. We demonstrate that the new solution is much more efficient than the prior art.

9. ACKNOWLEDGMENTS

This work was supported in part by the National Natural Science Foundation of China under Grant 61300024, Jiangsu Provincial Natural Science Foundation of China under Grant BK20130634, China Specialized Research Fund for the Doctoral Program of Higher Education under Grant 20130092120036, and National Science Foundation of United States under grants CNS-1409797 and CNS-1115548.

10. REFERENCES

[1] G. Casella and R. L. Berger. *Statistical Inference.* 2nd Edition, Duxbury Press, 2002.

[2] B. Chen, Z. Zhou, and H. Yu. Understanding RFID counting protocols. *Proc. of ACM MOBICOM*, 2013.

[3] M. Chen, W. Luo, Z. Mo, S. Chen, and Y. Fang. An efficient tag search protocol in large-scale RFID systems. *Proc. of IEEE INFOCOM*, April 2013.

[4] H. Han, B. Sheng, C. Tan, Q. Li, W. Mao, and S. Lu. Counting RFID tags efficiently and anonymously. *Proc. of IEEE INFOCOM*, 2010.

[5] M. Kodialam and T. Nandagopal. Fast and reliable estimation schemes in RFID systems. *Proc. of ACM MOBICOM*, 2006.

[6] S.-R. Lee, S.-D. Joo, and C.-W. Lee. An enhanced dynamic framed slotted aloha algorithm for RFID tag identification. *Proc. of IEEE MOBIQUITOUS*, pages 166–174, 2005.

[7] T. Li, S. Chen, and Y. Ling. Efficient protocols for identifying the missing tags in a large RFID system. *IEEE/ACM Transactions on Networking*, 21(6), 2013.

[8] T. Li, S. Wu, S. Chen, and M. Yang. Energy efficient algorithms for the RFID estimation problem. *Proc. of INFOCOM*, 2010.

[9] W. Luo, Y. Qiao, and S. Chen. An efficient protocol for RFID multigroup threshold-based classification. *Proc. of IEEE INFOCOM*, April 2014.

[10] W. Luo, Y. Qiao, S. Chen, and T. Li. Missing-tag detection and energy-time tradeoff in large-scale RFID systems with unreliable channels. *IEEE/ACM Transactions on Networking*, 22(4):1079 – 1091, August 2014.

[11] J. Myung and W. Lee. Adaptive splitting protocols for RFID tag collision arbitration. *Proc. of ACM MOBIHOC*, 2006.

[12] C. Qian, H. Ngan, and Y. Liu. Cardinality estimation for large-scale RFID systems. *Proc. of IEEE PERCOM*, 2008.

[13] Y. Qiao, S. Chen, T. Li, and S. Chen. Energy-efficient polling protocols in RFID systems. *Proc. of ACM Mobihoc*, May 2011.

[14] Y. Rekik. Inventory inaccuracies in supply chains: How can RFID improve the performance? *Wiley Encyclopedia of Operations Research and Management Science*, 2010.

[15] V. Shah-Mansouri and V. Wong. Cardinality estimation in RFID systems with multiple readers. *IEEE Transactions on Wireless Communications*, 10(5):1458–1469, May 2011.

[16] M. Shahzad and A. X. Liu. Every bit counts: Fast and scalable RFID estimation. *Proc. of ACM MOBICOM*, 2012.

[17] B. Sheng, Q. Li, and W. Mao. Efficient continuous scanning in RFID systems. *Proc. of IEEE INFOCOM*, 2010.

[18] H. Vogt. Efficient object identification with passive RFID tags. *Proc. of IEEE PERCOM*, 2002.

[19] K.-Y. Whang, B. T. Vander-Zanden, and H. M. Taylor. A linear-time probabilistic counting algorithm for database applications. *ACM Transactions on Database Systems*, 15(2):208–229, June 1990.

[20] Q. Xiao, B. Xiao, and S. Chen. Differential estimation in dynamic RFID systems. *Proc. of IEEE INFOCOM*, 2013.

[21] Y. Zheng and M. Li. Zoe: Fast cardinality estimation for large-scale RFID systems. *Proc. of IEEE INFOCOM*, pages 908–916, 2013.

[22] Y. Zheng, M. Li, and C. Qian. Pet: Probabilistic estimating tree for large-scale RFID estimation. *Proc. of IEEE ICDCS*, June 2011.

Performance and Energy Consumption Analysis of a Delay-Tolerant Network for Censorship-Resistant Communication

Yue Liu† David R. Bild† David Adrian† Gulshan Singh†
Robert P. Dick† Dan S. Wallach‡ Z. Morley Mao†

†University of Michigan
Ann Arbor, MI, USA
{liuyue,drbild,davadria,gulshan}@umich.edu
{dickrp,zmao}@eecs.umich.edu

‡Rice University
Houston, TX, USA
dwallach@cs.rice.edu

ABSTRACT

Delay Tolerant Networks (DTNs) composed of commodity mobile devices have the potential to support communication applications resistant to blocking and censorship, as well as certain types of surveillance. We analyze the performance and energy consumption of such a network, and consider the impact of random and targeted denial-of-service and censorship attacks. To gather wireless connectivity traces for a DTN composed of human-carried commodity smartphones, we implemented and deployed a prototype DTN-based microblogging application, called 1am, in a college town. We analyzed the system during a time period with 111 users. Although the study provided detailed enough connectivity traces to enable analysis, message posting was too infrequent to draw strong conclusions based on user-initiated messages, alone. We therefore simulated more frequent message initiations and used measured connectivity traces to analyze message propagation. Using a flooding protocol, we found that with an adoption rate of 0.2% of a college town's student and faculty population, the median one-week delivery rate is 85% and the median delivery delay is 13 hours. We also found that the network delivery rate and delay are robust to denial-of-service and censorship attacks eliminating more than half of the participants. Using a measurement-based energy model, we also found that the DTN system would use less than 10.0% of a typical smartphone's battery energy per day in a network of 2,500 users.

Categories and Subject Descriptors

C.2.1 [**Computer-Communication Networks**]: Network Architecture and Design—*Distributed networks, Store and forward networks*; C.4 [**Performance of Systems**]: Performance attributes, Reliability, availability, and serviceability

MobiHoc'15, June 22–25, 2015, Hangzhou, China.

http://dx.doi.org/10.1145/2746285.2746320.

Keywords

Delay Tolerant Networks, Opportunistic networks, Microblogging, Censorship resistance, Energy overhead

1. INTRODUCTION

Delay Tolerant Networks (DTNs) composed of human carried devices have the potential to support blocking-, censorship-, and surveillance-resistant communication applications. Unlike the Internet, the non-hierarchical, device-to-device structure of DTNs makes it difficult to block, modify, or monitor a large portion of network traffic via attacks on a few devices.

The demand for the functionality offered by infrastructureless communication systems is suggested by the response to intentional widespread service disruption for users of social media applications such as Twitter and Facebook during the Arab Spring [1], ongoing political censorship in Iran and China, and growing awareness of global surveillance of individuals without reasonable cause to believe they have committed crimes. Recently in Hong Kong, in response to the threat of potential denial of service attacks on the Internet-based Instagram, there were 200,000 downloads of a local mesh networking chat program called FireChat between 28 and 30 September 2014 [2]. This application supports text messaging and photo transfer mediated by device-to-device Bluetooth connections [2]. Popular social networking/microblogging services are now commonly censored throughout much of the world. For example, Twitter is coerced to censor its users on a country-by-country basis by the threat of punishment by various governments [3]. In response to this trend, we have evaluated the feasibility, performance, and energy consumption of a DTN system composed of commodity smartphones and tablets when subjected to random and targeted denial-of-service and censorship attacks.

DTNs composed of commodity smartphones and tablets are influenced by constraints on battery energy, computation speed, and network throughput. We evaluate the potential of DTNs to support microblogging using a flooding protocol variant that avoids redundant transmissions. Message delivery rates and latencies, as well as battery energy overheads, are evaluated using contact traces gathered via a deployment study. We developed a prototype microblogging application on Android, named *1am* [4], and made it available to volunteers in a university town for installation on their personally owned smartphones.

Over a period of seven months in 2013, 1am had 291 users, with 111 users during a month of high activity on which our analysis focuses. Although users employed the app for microblogging, the limited number of postings made it difficult to draw strong conclusions based on app usage patterns. However, these volunteers' device-to-device wireless connectivity traces enabled findings on feasibility, performance, energy consumption, and resistance to denial-of-service and censorship attacks. The 1am traces are publicly available (see Section 8 for the URL).

- Feasibility and performance: Our analysis indicates that in a college town in which 0.2% of the population install the app, the system has a median delivery rate of 0.85 and a median delivery delay of 13 hours. We pay special attention to the system's performance variations and study their causes. We find that the delivery delays of DTN flooding protocols follow a power law distribution that varies from hours to days (Figure 8), which may be of interest to application designers.
- Robustness to denial-of-service and censorship attacks: We found that attacks that randomly remove half of the network participants only reduce delivery rates to the remaining participants by 3%. Targeted attacks, which remove nodes that appear most frequently on the most rapid message delivery paths, were more harmful, causing the delivery rate to decrease precipitously when half of the participants were removed. However, even when subjected to targeted attacks, the network only suffered a 13% decrease in delivery rate when a third of its participants were removed.
- Energy consumption: We analyzed the impact of participating in the proposed infrastructureless microblogging network on smartphone battery lifespan and found negligible impact on battery energy for participants in our 111-user study. Based on a measurement-based wireless communication aware smartphone power consumption model, our analysis shows that participants in a network of 2,500 active users will each expend 10% of their battery energy during a single day of use.

2. RELATED WORK

The idea of using infrastructureless networks to support censorship-resistant communication is shared by various existing work [5, 6, 7]. Al-Akkad et al. use mobile ad hoc networks (MANETs) to enable continuous tweet dissemination when network infrastructure is disrupted [5], which has fewer applications than DTN-based systems because MANETs require instantaneous end-to-end connections. Hossmann et al. describe a DTN-based Twitter application for disaster communication. They do not provide evaluation results due to the lack of contact traces specific to disaster scenarios [6]. Our goal is providing daily microblogging services in local communities. We therefore use daily human contact traces to study achievable message delivery performance and energy consumption in such systems.

Due to the difficulty of collecting large-scale human contact traces, most existing work on DTNs [8, 9] uses a few existing traces [10, 11] for evaluation. The Dartmouth traces record the association histories of all participants on Dartmouth College's campus WiFi network [10]. Most of the recorded devices are laptops, whose mobility and contact patterns may differ from smartphones. The UCSD traces were collected from participants who used experimental PDAs during the deployment [11]. Their traces show a trend of declining user engagements [11] that is uncommon for normal smartphone users. To gather traces representative of the mobility and contact patterns of modern smartphone users, we installed data collection software on participants' personally owned smartphones.

We are unaware of existing models for the energy consumptions of common DTN routing protocols or applications. Socievole et al. evaluated the energy consumption of five DTN routing protocols via simulation [12]. They modeled Bluetooth communication, while we modeled 802.11 ad hoc communication. In addition, their analysis considered networks with a maximum size of 200 nodes, while we considered networks with 50,000 nodes.

Various existing work on improving the energy overhead of DTN flooding protocols assumes a simple linear relationship between the network's energy consumption and the average number of copies per message [13, 14]. However, our energy model shows that the cost of learning each node's received and not-yet-received messages to avoid redundant transmissions is the leading energy contributor in large networks, as this cost scales quadratically with network size. This result suggests the simple linear model is inadequate, and possibly misleading.

3. 1AM: MICROBLOGGING ON DTNS

This section describes the design of *1am*, an infrastructureless DTN-based microblogging service. This information is provided to give background and context to the subsequent analysis sections of the paper.

3.1 Overview

1am is designed to functionality similar to Twitter. Posts are public text messages containing up to 514 characters. Users can post new messages, make comments, and retransmit (analogous to retweet) messages and comments from others. Its main user interface (UI) displays a timeline of incoming messages.

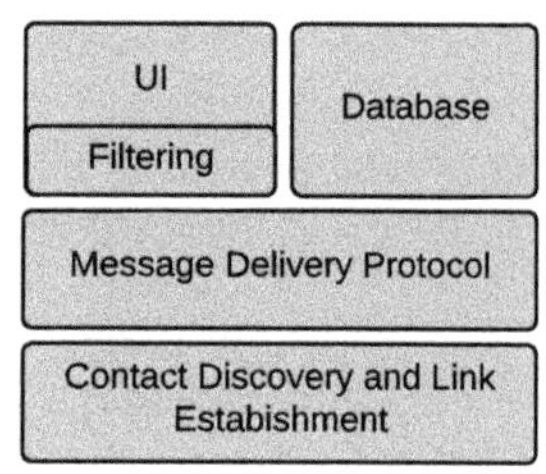

Figure 1: 1am architecture.

We now describe some of 1am's characteristics and features.

Identity Management: 1am has no central registry that might be used to enable blocking, censorship, or surveillance attacks; it uses a fully distributed design. Users are uniquely identified by self-generated public keys, created locally during application installation. In other words, the public key is the identity, eliminating any need of certification authorities for certifying identity-key associations. We allow 1am users to have human readable user names, which may collide. We resolve user name collisions by comparing public keys that are extremely unlikely to collide. The UI is designed to make the implications clear to users when the same user name is associated with different keys.

Message Authenticity: Like all public communication systems, 1am is subject to rumors and misinformation. Conventional solutions relying on centralized filtering or censorship cannot be used, due to 1am's decentralized architecture. To increase the cost of disinformation campaigns, we protect the authenticity of 1am posts with digital signatures, which are individually verified by each receiver. The intention is for credible 1am users to gradually build up positive reputations. In addition, it would be possible to use distributed spam or propaganda detection techniques [15]. There is no requirement for users to associate their actual identities with their 1am identities.

Multimedia Support: Bandwidth is a scarce resource in device-to-device networks: 1am cannot support content of arbitrary size. Our study shows that it is feasible to support images. However, without re-designs of the message delivery protocol or major improvements on wireless transceiver energy efficiency, video sharing cannot be supported in our system (see Section 7).

Figure 1 illustrates the architecture of 1am. From the bottom up, the first layer is in charge of **contact discovery and link establishment**. It detects contact opportunities, establishes an 802.11 ad hoc channel with discovered peers, and informs higher level protocols. Note that this layer is not 1am-specific and should be shared by all DTN applications. The second layer is the **message delivery protocol** that routes 1am messages to intended receivers. Finally, when a 1am message arrives, the **UI** is informed and the message is stored in a **database** for future use, e.g., re-transmission. The UI's displays messages according to given filtering rules, e.g., those from immediate wireless communication neighbors or "followed" identities.

We choose 802.11 ad hoc technology over Bluetooth for device-to-device communication, because the former has longer transmission range. We avoided WiFi Direct due to the inconvenience of its pairing process, which requires human involvement, as well as its lack of broadcast support.

Although modern smartphone hardware and operating systems support 802.11 ad hoc communications, at the time of the study an API was not provided by Android. During our 1am deployment study, to avoid requiring users to "root" their phones, we used an ad hoc network emulation layer to identify direct wireless connectivity, deliver messages, and gather data[1] (See Section 4.1 for more details).

3.2 Message Delivery Protocol

We use a flooding protocol for message delivery for two reasons. First, flooding protocols can be used to support arbitrary filtering rules. At this stage we are not sure which rules are most appropriate for DTN-based microblogging services and therefore avoid any premature optimization tying the system design to specific rules. Second, in non-congested situations, e.g., for applications with small traffic volume, flooding protocols have the best message delivery performance and worst energy consumption among all routing protocols. Therefore, they serve as good reference points for understanding the limitations of the underlying network and provide guidance for further optimization.

To avoid redundant message transmissions, we exchange Bloom filters during each contact to learn about each node's received and not-yet-received messages. Bloom filters are compact data structures for storing elements and testing set membership [16]. They are widely used in DTN routing protocols for their space- and bandwidth-efficiency. Specifically, each node stores all its received messages in a Bloom filter that is exchanged at each contact. The other party could then test which of its own messages have not been received by the node. Classic Bloom filters use 14.4 bits per key for a 10^{-3} set membership test error rate [16]. This is much smaller than the original message it documents.

[1]We subsequently developed an application-level method that supports direct device-to-device WiFi communication on Android platforms.

4. USER TRACE COLLECTION

We developed a prototype of 1am and provided it to volunteers in a college town with a student and faculty population of 50,000. The application was instrumented (with knowledge of the study participants) to gather mobility and wireless connectivity data. This section describes the data collection platform and provides some statistics on the gathered traces. It gives an overview of participants' motion and contact patterns, and provides background for understanding the performance numbers in Section 5.

4.1 Deployment Platform

Commodity Android devices do not support appropriate 802.11 ad hoc communication [17]. Enabling it would require rooting participants' phones, which we consider an unacceptable barrier to study participation. Instead, we applied a widely used technique in the DTN research community to estimate 802.11 contact opportunities. To simplify, two devices with simultaneous visibility of common WiFi access points are considered to be capable of direct communication [9, 18].

We use a data collection platform we designed for assisting DTN protocol deployments, called MANES [19]. It gathers time-varying location and wireless environment measurements. It also estimates contact opportunities based on WiFi scan results and provides applications with an emulated 802.11 ad hoc communication interface. MANES replaces the "contact discovery and link establishment" layer in Figure 1.

MANES has two components, an Android client that gathers GPS and WiFi scan measurements, and a backend server that aggregates and stores user traces. Location data are uploaded as soon as they become available to support up-to-date topology estimation, as the server uses the estimated topology to relay packets between 802.11 neighbors.

To save energy for the client, automated sampling frequency adjustment is used when taking both WiFi and GPS measurements. If there are no significant changes since the last measurement, further WiFi scans are postponed for 120 seconds and further GPS scans are postponed for five minutes. Otherwise, the WiFi sampling frequency is 30 seconds and the GPS sampling frequency is one minute. Because humans are usually stationary, the average WiFi measurement period in the collected traces is 114.5 seconds.

4.2 Participant Recruitment

1am traces are collected from fully informed users with their consent. We released 1am to the university community and advertised via posters, gifts of promotional water bottle, and word of mouth. We had 291 users, each of whom used the application at least three days from March to October in 2013. Most were university students. The median trace duration per user is 24 days. We use the first 31 days of traces, the month with the maximum number of participants, for the analysis in the rest of this paper. We refer to this period as the *study period*. During the study period, we had

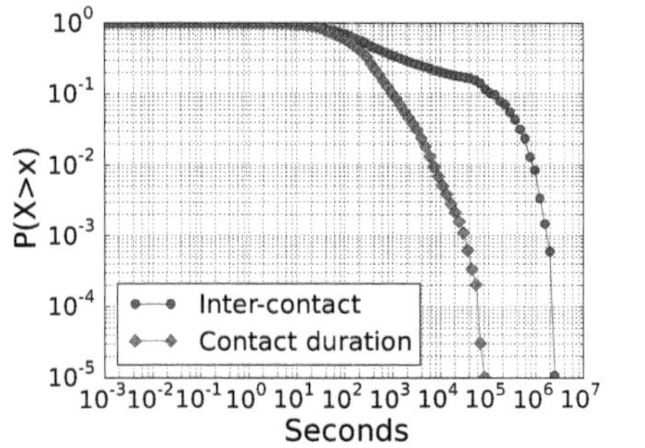

Figure 2: Contact duration and inter-contact time distributions, each following (truncated) power law distributions.

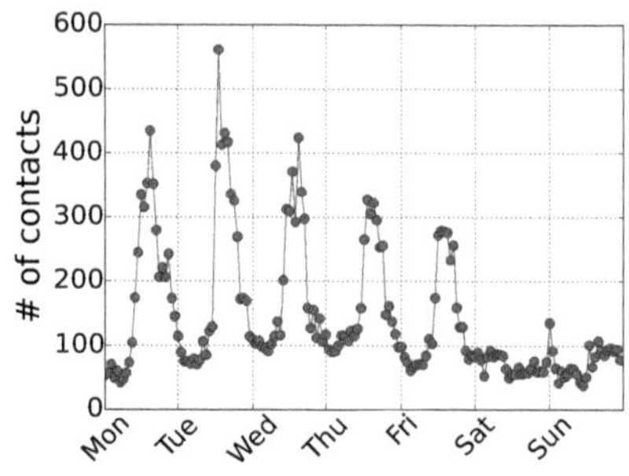

Figure 3: Average # of contacts by weekday, showing a strong weekday/weekend pattern.

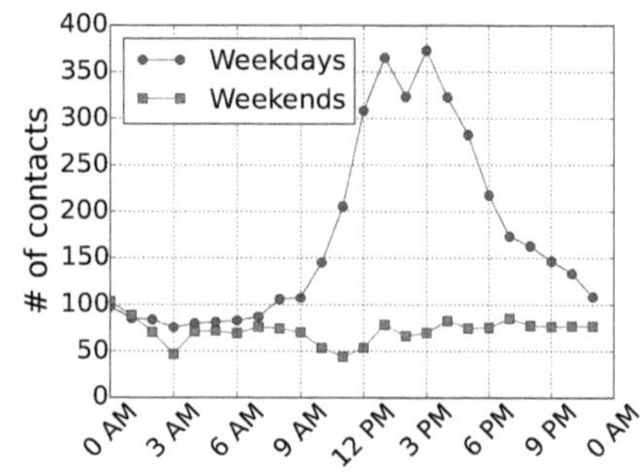

Figure 4: Average # of contacts by hours, showing a strong diurnal pattern with its peak in the early afternoon.

Table 1: Comparison of Contact Traces

	UCSD	Dartmouth	1am
Year	2002	2003/2004	2013
Device	PDA	Laptop/PDA	Smartphone
Duration (days)	77	114	31
Granularity (seconds)	120	300	114.5
Devices participating	273	6,648	111
Number of contacts	195,364	4,058,284	98,072
# contacts/pair/hour	0.0028	0.000067	0.033

111 active study participants, with an average of 85 active participants each day.

4.3 Contact Statistics

During the study period, 98,072 inter-participant wireless communication contacts were made, with an average of 20 contacts, six of which were unique, per user, per day. 10% of users made no contacts. The average contact rate is 0.0329 contacts per pair per hour, which is much higher than the rate of other WiFi-based contact traces widely used in the DTN community (see the last row in Table 1). We suspect there have been changes in normal smartphone users' behaviors since those traces were gathered. In our study, users were carrying their own modern, compact, highly functional smartphones and in the UCSD [11] and Dartmouth traces [10], they were carrying either limited-functionality PDAs or laptops; these devices were carried less frequently than modern smartphones, resulting in decreased contact frequency. It is also possible that 1am users tend to recruit friends and acquaintances with whom they have frequent contact. Previous research shows correlation between physical proximity and social relationships [20].

Figure 2 shows the distributions of contact duration and inter-contact time. The contact duration has a median of 149 seconds. The inter-contact time has a (truncated) power law distribution in the 30 s–1 day range, with a coefficient of 0.3. This is consistent with prior research findings [18].

4.4 Diurnal Patterns

Figure 3 and Figure 4 illustrate a weekly and diurnal pattern of contact numbers, which is expected for a population that is working or studying during weekdays. Note that a pair can meet and have contacts multiple times in a day. On an average weekday (Figure 4, "Weekdays"), the contact number starts to rapidly increase at 9 a.m. and is at its highest from 1 p.m. to 3 p.m. It then gradually decreases, reaching a minimum at around 3 a.m. On an average weekend (Figure 4, "Weekends") the contact number stays almost constant at the minimum level of the average weekday. This difference would be expected for a population in which most contacts result from co-location during weekday work or study.

4.5 Geographic Patterns

To better understand the study population, we examined the geographic locations of contacts. Not all contacts are associated with GPS readings (only 27.6% are), but all are associated with WiFi scan results. This is expected, as humans typically spend most of their time indoors and GPS readings are often not available indoors. We used the following algorithm to estimate GPS locations based on WiFi scan results. We first estimate the GPS locations of WiFi access points using location samples containing both GPS readings and WiFi scan results; the location of one access point is the average of the GPS locations for all measurements with WiFi scans containing that access point. We then estimate the location of each contact event associated with only WiFi scans as the estimated location of the access point with the highest signal strength in these scans. This algorithm allows us to estimate the locations of 99.4% of the contact events.

To simplify explanation and analysis, we divide the entire area into 100 m×100 m discrete locations that we associate contact events with. There are 239 discrete locations with at least one contact, each. Contacts are distributed unevenly. If the locations are ordered by frequency of contacts, we find that 90% of the contacts occur in the first 25% of locations. Figure 5 shows the map of the first 100 locations, with the shade indicating number of contacts. These locations are visually clustered into two components, clearly outlining the two campuses of the university that where the study was done. The Northeast Campus, where the study was most heavily promoted, has more contacts.

To further understand the context of the contacts on each campus, we consider their temporal patterns. Figure 6 shows the average number of contacts in the two campuses by weekday. The Northeast Campus curve ("Location1") has clear weekly and diurnal patterns, while the Southwest Campus curve ("Location2") does not. This suggests that most 1am users work in the Northeast Campus (in fact in a few very concentrated areas of that campus, i.e., the darkest few grid elements), instead of the Southwest Campus.

4.6 Discussion

The above statistics show that 1am users in these traces are a community of people whose contacts are generally a result of work- or study-related co-location. Most of their

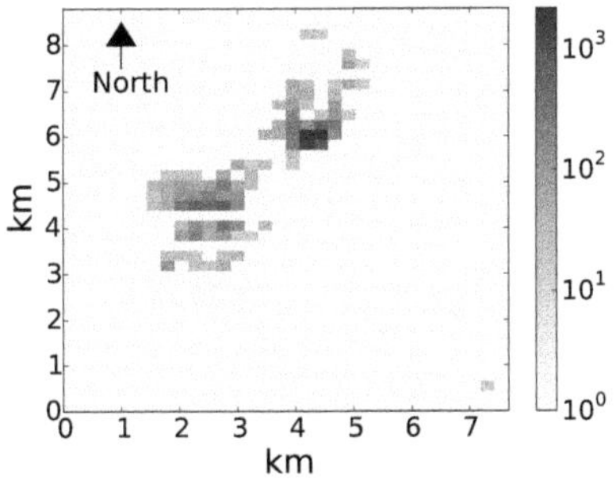

Figure 5: Geographic distribution of the contacts, illustrating the two university campuses. The majority of contacts occured in the Northeast Campus.

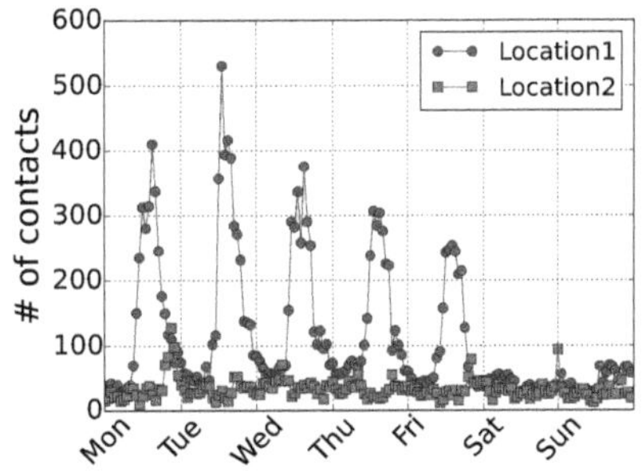

Figure 6: Total # of contacts in the two campuses in an average week. "Location1" (the Northeast Campus) shows weekly and diurnal patterns. "Location2" (the Southwest Campus) does not have obvious patterns.

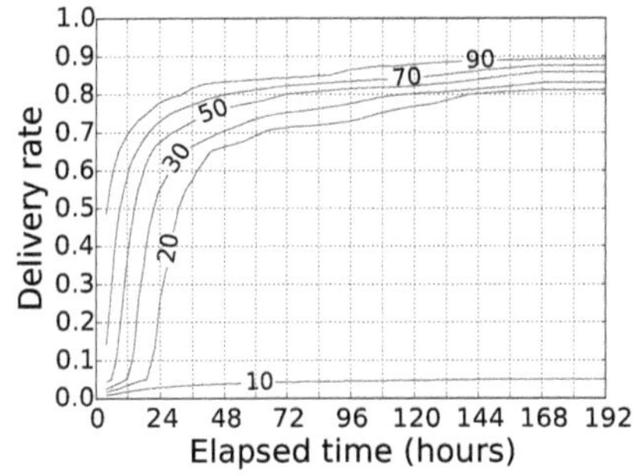

Figure 7: 1am's message delivery rate over time, showing two stages with significantly different propagation speeds. A point on the X-percentile line represents the X-percentile delivery rate at the considered time of the flooding processes.

contacts occur within a few work/study areas. Their motion patterns are less concentrated and correlated during nights and weekends. They continue to have contacts at these times, but with lower frequency. Our conclusions in the rest of the paper will be most relevant to similar deployment scenarios.

5. MESSAGE DELIVERY PERFORMANCE

In this section we evaluate 1am's message delivery performance using two metrics, **message delivery rate**, the percentage of intended receivers that have successfully received a message, and **message delivery delay**, the elapsed time from message initiation to its successful delivery. We also discuss the robustness of the system when subjected to a variety of potential attacks.

5.1 Methodology

Because 1am users initiated too few posts during the study period (on average, around one post per user per month), we cannot draw strong conclusions based on user-initiated messages. We instead simulated more frequent message initiations. In order to fully explore the dynamics of the underlying network, we cause every device in the trace to initiate a message every six minutes. We do not initiate messages from a particular smartphone when it is inactive, i.e., in sleep mode or powered off.

Since 1am uses a flooding protocol to distribute messages, we use timed shortest path analysis to obtain message delivery rates and delays. While this method overlooks performance degradation in congested situations when some messages are forced to follow circuitous routes, it produces an upper bound on message delivery performance that is fairly tight for applications with small traffic volume.

We calculate the shortest-path message distribution tree for each initiated message. The following analysis is based on the aggregated shortest-path trees associated with all message initiations.

5.2 Overall Performance

Figure 7 illustrates the progress of the simulated flooding processes over time. The X-axis shows the elapsed time in hours since message initiation. The Y-axis shows the delivery rate: the ratio of active nodes that have received the message. If a message has not reached a participant within a week of initiation, we consider the delivery failed. As there are too many flooding processes to illustrate individually, we use percentile lines to show the distributions of their delivery rates. For example, at 24 h, the 50th percentile line has a delivery rate of 0.68, meaning 24 h after message initiation the median delivery rate of all the flooding processes is 0.68.

The 50th percentile line shows that it takes a median of 14 hours to reach 60% of participants, 24 hours to reach 70%, and a week to reach 85%. The fastest-spreading 10% of messages (the 90th percentile line) take 6 hours to reach 60% of participants, 12 hours to reach 70%, and a week to reach 90%. The slowest 10% of messages (the 10th percentile line) reached almost no other participants, because 10% of participants had no contacts during the study period.

The message propagation speed (the slope of the percentile lines) has two stages. To reach the first 60% of participants it takes 3 hours for every 10% of progress, but it becomes increasingly difficult to reach the rest of the participants. For example, the median case (the 50th percentile line) takes only 18 hours to progress from 0% to 60%, but 50 hours to progress from 60% to 80%. The power-law distribution of delivery delays in Figure 8 also illustrates this phenomenon.

To explain this change in propagation speed and understand why it takes so long to reach the last 40% of participants, we examine the difference in contact numbers for receivers reached in different stages of the flooding processes. Different flooding processes have different propagation speeds. Therefore, we did not use absolute elapsed time to quantify a receiver's stage. For example, 9 h is late in a flooding process that finishes in 10 hours, but is early in another one that finishes in 100 hours. To define a metric independent of propagation speed, we order the receivers in each flooding process by their reception times and set the stage of a receiver based on its comparative order, i.e., the delivery rate upon that receiver's message reception. We aggregate same-stage receivers of all the flooding processes and show their contact number distributions in Figure 9. The X-axis shows the stages of receivers using delivery rates. The Y-axis is a node's total number of contacts during the study period. As there are multiple nodes at the same stage, we use percentile lines to show their contact number distributions.

There is a clear change in trend at the stage associated with 60% delivery rate. Below that, the contact number distributions are almost constant. Above that, the number of contacts per node decreases dramatically. This is consistent

Figure 8: Message delivery delay distribution, which follows a (truncated) power law.

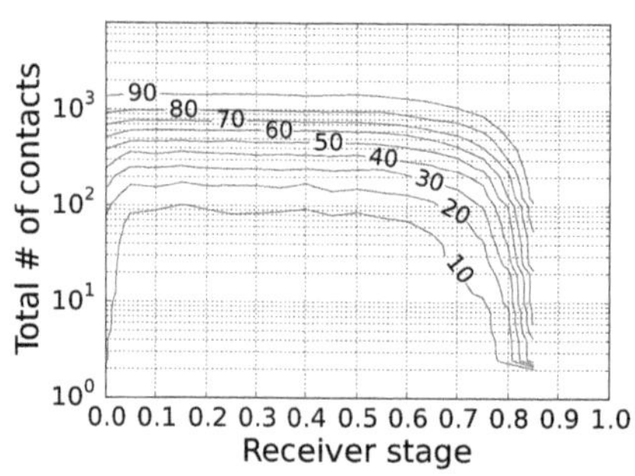

Figure 9: Contact number distributions of different-stage receivers, showing a transition at 0.6 delivery rate. A point on the X-percentile line represents the X-percentile contact number of receivers reached at the considered stage.

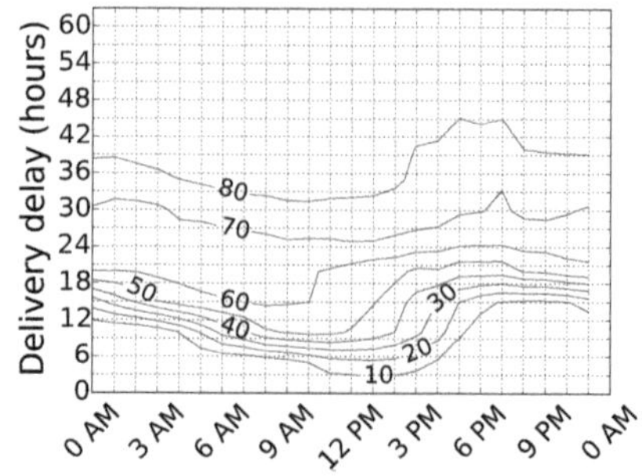

Figure 10: Delivery delays (to reach 60% of the network) of messages with different initiation hours, showing significant variations. A point on the X-percentile line represents the X-percentile delivery delay of the considered initiation hour.

with Figure 7, which shows a constant propagation speed before reaching 60% delivery rate, and a decreasing speed after that. This result suggests that diminishing contact opportunities prolong delivery delays for the last 40% nodes.

In summary, due to the participants' differences in contact opportunities, the 1am communication system has two stages in its delivery performance. It has a constant propagation speed (3 hours per 10% progress) for the first 60% of the participants, who are well connected with each other. It is increasingly difficult to reach the remaining nodes, which have fewer and fewer contacts. Overall, with a message lifetime of one week, the system has a median delivery rate of 0.85 and a median delivery delay of 13 hours.

5.3 Initiation Time

We also look into the influence of message initiation time on delivery performance. There is a significant difference between weekday and weekend initiations. Weekday initiations have a significantly faster delivery; it takes a median of 12 hours to reach 60% of the network on weekdays, compared to 30 hours on weekends. This is consistent with Figure 4 showing that there are significantly more contacts on weekdays than weekends.

There are also significant performance variations by hour-of-day, as illustrated in Figure 10. The X-axis shows the initiation hour. The Y-axis shows the delivery delay to reach 60% of the network. For example, in the median case (the 50th percentile line), a message sent at 11 a.m. only takes 10 hours to reach 60% of the network, while another sent at 8 p.m. takes 21 hours.

In general, the closer before noon a message is initiated, the shorter its delay. The later after noon a message is initiated, the longer the delay. The shortest delay occurs at around 12 p.m., and the longest delay occurs at around 7 p.m. This trend is consistent with 1am's daily contact dynamics. The majority of the contacts occur between 10 a.m. and 6 p.m. (Figure 4). Messages initiated before this period have the advantage of using all these contact opportunities. Those initiated after the start of this period have fewer contact opportunities and longer delays.

6. ROBUSTNESS

As a natural consequence of their distributed, non-hierarchical structures, DTNs are robust to blocking and censorship accomplished by removing or controlling network resources. Evaluating a network's robustness to resource removal can be used to determine its robustness to both attacks. The relationship between resource removal and blocking (denial-of-service) attacks is straightforward; an attacker might eliminate smartphones, perhaps via malware or by jamming their wireless signals at specific locations. The relationship with censorship is slightly more complex; censorship can be seen as a selective form of resource removal. Because censorship requires control over network devices, or their communication channels, a network structure robust to resource removal is also robust to censorship.

Resistance to attacks in which many network participants simultaneously and rapidly inject messages requires additional consideration. Non-hierarchical networks remain vulnerable to such denial-of-service attacks. However, resisting them is possible. Recall that 1am messages are signed using the private keys of the sending identities. It is practical for receiving mobile devices to detect when particular identities are sending messages at an undesirable rate and then cease forwarding them. An attacker might conceivably adopt a new identity and use it to launch an attack. That strategy can be defeated by assigning higher priorities to messages from nodes that have previously sent messages of interest.

Increasing the cost of surveillance is a secondary goal. 1am messages are public by design. However, there remains value in increasing the cost of reprisal-oriented network surveillance, e.g., associating messages with senders or receivers, or associating identities with individuals. The use of a non-hierarchical device-to-device network has the potential to increase the cost of reprisal-oriented surveillance because it requires a physical presence throughout a large portion of the network to observe enough traffic to associate senders and receivers. Associating identities with messages is also expensive because attackers would require a widespread physical presence, perhaps capable of wireless signal triangulation, to determine the location of the mobile device originating a particular message.

6.1 Attacks

We now explain the evaluation of 1am when subjected to two classes of resource removal attacks: the removal of participating devices and the removal of communication channels. Device removal attacks prevent specific network nodes from transmitting or relaying specific (censorship) or

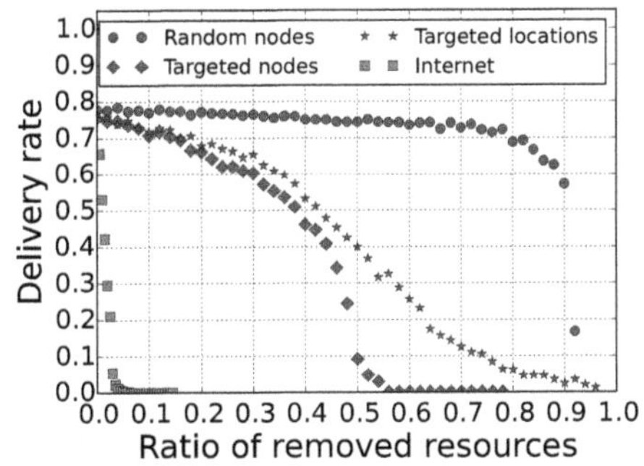

Figure 11: Degradation of message delivery rates under resource removal attacks. "Random node removal" has almost no effect while "targeted node removal" is the most effective. Under "targeted node removal", the Internet is fragmented much faster than the 1am network.

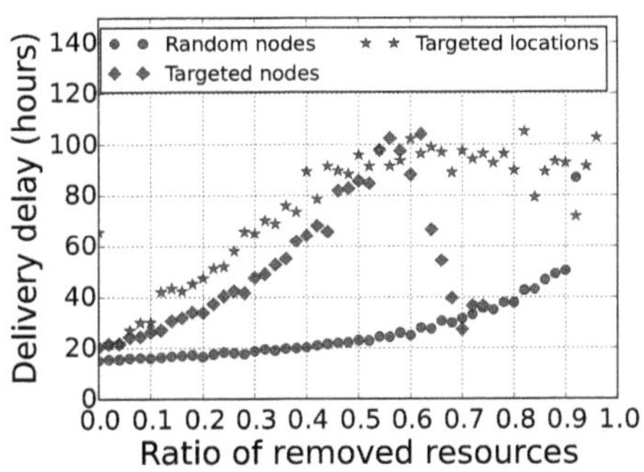

Figure 12: Degradation of message delivery delay under resource removal attacks. Again, "Random node removal" has almost no effect. Both targeted removal attacks are more effective, with "targeted location removal" resulting in faster delay increase.

all (blocking) messages, e.g., through malware deployment, physical attacks, or wireless signal jamming. Two specific strategies are considered. "Random device removal" disables devices at random, and "targeted device removal" disables devices in order of their importance. More *important devices* occur more frequently on the shortest message delivery paths.

The other class of attack disrupts physically local communications, e.g., via radio jamming on 802.11 frequencies [21]. We call this "location removal attacks" because it disables all communication within a local area, or location. We defined a *location* to be a 100 m×100 m grid element, i.e., a region with an area similar to that covered by an 802.11b transmitter. Only "targeted location removal" is discussed because "random location removal" is less effective and we believe intelligent attackers would be capable of identifying *important locations*, i.e., ones with most contact occurrences.

We simulated the effects of both classes of attacks by recalculating the message delivery performance when subject to them. In the case of device removal attacks, all contacts involving the affected devices are removed. In the case of location removal attacks, all contacts occurring within the affected locations are removed.

6.2 Attack Performance

Figures 11 and 12 illustrate how attacks affect message delivery rates and delays. The X-axis shows the ratio of removed (controlled) resources. The Y-axis in Figure 11 is the median delivery rate after a week, and Y-axis in Figure 12 is the median delivery delay.

Figure 11 shows that random device removal has almost no effect on delivery rates until more than 80% of devices are removed. Targeted removal attacks more quickly impact delivery rates. Targeted device removal and targeted location removal have similar impact with the first being slightly more effective. Targeted device removal causes delivery rate to deteriorate rapidly after 30%–40% of the most important devices are removed and the network collapses when 50% are removed. Targeted location removal does not have the same cutoff effect at the 50% removal ratio.

Figure 12 shows that random device removal has almost no effect on delivery latency until more than 60% of nodes are removed. On the other hand, both targeted removal attacks have immediate influence on delay. For example, the targeted location removal incurs around 20 hours increase in delay per 10% of removed devices. It is interesting that contrary to its impact on delivery rate, targeted location removal has a larger impact on message delivery latency than does targeted device removal. The following explanation is consistent with our observations. When a location is removed, it is likely that devices will meet in other locations to complete the delivery process with higher delay. In contrast, when a node is removed, this can terminate further distribution of messages, resulting in reduced in delivery rates, without reducing the delivery delays of the remaining messages.

6.3 Comparison to the Internet

We are interested in comparing the performance degradation of the 1am network and the Internet when subject to resource removal attacks. Albert, Jeong, and Barabasi studied the fragmentation of the Internet when its most critical routers are removed [22]. They quantity network fragmentation using the relative size of the largest cluster, which is an upper bound of the network's average delivery rate. We therefore plotted Internet fragmentation as a function of the percent of removed routers from their paper, in direct comparison with 1am's delivery rate curve in Figure 11. Figure 11 shows that when the same ratio of resources are removed, the Internet becomes much more fragmented than the 1am network. This is due to its hierarchical structure; its normal function relies on a few backbone servers. We do not claim that the 1am network is more robust than the Internet under attacks of the same scale, because it may be more difficult to eliminate or compromise 5% of resources on the Internet than on the 1am network.

6.4 Conclusion and Discussion

Our analysis shows that it is ineffective to block or censor 1am communications by randomly removing network resources, unless the majority (more than 80%) of the resources are removed. It is more effective to target the most important resources, i.e., devices with numerous contacts and locations where many contacts occur. Even using this strategy, it is necessary to eliminate a large percentage of the 1am network, relative to a hierarchical network. The Internet is fragmented when less than 5% of its most critical routers are removed, while the 1am network does not degrade rapidly until more than 30% of its devices or locations are removed. Eliminating 30% of network devices, or radio jamming 30%

Table 2: Power Model Parameters

	Meaning	Value
N	Network size	Deployment dependent
E_f	Energy cost of send+receive one 802.11b frame	26.4 mJ
f_m	Message initiation frequency	Message type dependent (see Table 5)
F_m	# of 802.11b frames per message	Message type dependent (see Table 5)
B_{frame}	# of data bits per frame	4095/2
$R_{contact}$	Avg. # of contacts per pair per hour	0.0329 (1am trace)

Table 3: Operation/State Dependent WiFi Power

P_{idle} (idle state)	210 mW
P_{high} (send/receive state)	341 mW
E_{sw} (one power state switch from low-high-low)	242 mJ
E_{ping} (send+receive one 802.11b frame (ping))	2.16 mJ
E_{send} (send one 802.11b frame (UDP))	19.6 mJ
E_{recv} (receive one 802.11b frame (UDP))	6.8 mJ

of the public areas in a town or campus is likely to be an expensive undertaking for an attacker.

7. ENERGY MODEL

This section describes an energy model for 1am running on commodity smartphones and describes the relationship between battery depletion and network scale. We first develop an energy model for the WiFi component in 802.11 ad hoc mode based on measurements, then elaborate on the three contributors to energy consumption for 1am: contact discovery, communication, and computation. For the convenience of the readers, Table 2 lists a few parameters frequently used throughout this section.

We use a Monsoon power monitor [23] to measure power consumption. The devices used for power modeling are rooted Samsung Galaxy Nexus smartphones running CyanogenMod 10.2.1-toro (Android 4.3.1). The wireless chip of these devices is Broadcom BCM4330. The CPU is a Dual-Core 1.2 GHz ARM Cortex-A9.

7.1 WiFi Component in 802.11 Ad hoc Mode

We measure the smartphone's power consumption for different packet transmission frequencies. The experimental setup follows. Two devices are put into 802.11b ad hoc mode and a 2 Mbps communication channel is established. One device uses the "ping" program to send periodic ICMP packets, which are padded into maximum 802.11b frames. We measure the power consumption of the other device, which is placed in sleep mode with only the WiFi component awake. The ping frequency (f_{ping}) is varied from 0.1 Hz to 100 Hz.

We observe clear changes in wireless interface power management states as f_{ping} changes. When $f_{ping} < 0.5$ Hz, the WiFi component switches on and off for each frame and consumes significant energy, as the energy cost for one power state switch is much larger than that for one send/receive operation. When $f_{ping} > 1$ Hz, the WiFi component stays in the high power state. From 0.5 Hz to 1 Hz, the frequency of power state switches gradually decreases, and we see a decreasing power consumption despite the increase in ping frequency. Based on this result, we use a conservative two-stage model for the WiFi component. Send/receive operations separated by more than one second cause power state switches. In other words, the device stays in the high power state until there is a gap between operations longer than one second.

Table 3 summarizes the measured energy numbers for different power states/operations. Note that we also measured the energy cost of sending/receiving one (maximum) 802.11b frame through an application program operating UDP sockets (E_{send} and E_{recv}), as these numbers are more relevant for application energy modeling.

7.2 Ongoing Contact Discovery

In order to avoid relying on centralized control and scheduling, we used Zheng's and Hou's asynchronous activation algorithm [24] to check for contact opportunities periodically. The activation pattern within each period is deliberately designed so that two unsynchronized devices have overlapping activation times. The authors showed that it is possible to achieve a 9/73 duty cycle [24]. Therefore, the hourly energy cost for contact discovery is $E_{base} = P_{idle} \cdot 3,600\,\text{seconds} \cdot \frac{9}{73}$, where P_{idle} is the idle power consumption for staying awake in 802.11 ad hoc mode, the minimal power state in which devices could discover each other.

7.3 Communication

Communication happens upon each contact, causing the following sequence of operations. The two devices first switch into the high power state, then exchange Bloom filters to learn about each other's received and not-yet-received messages, then deliver the not-yet-received messages, and finally switch back into the low-power state. The communication energy consumption is therefore the sum of the Bloom filter exchange (we also call it metadata exchange) and message delivery energy consumptions.

7.3.1 Message Delivery Cost

All messages are flooded to the whole network, so the number of messages received per node per hour is the total number of messages generated by the network per hour, Nf_mF_m. f_m is the message initiation frequency (in 1/hour) and N is the number of nodes in the network. F_m is the number of 802.11b frames each message consumes (see Table 5 for typical message sizes). Therefore, the hourly energy cost for message delivery is $E_{msg} = E_f(Nf_mF_m)$. E_f is the energy cost of sending and receiving one maximum size 802.11b frame, $E_f = E_{send} + E_{recv}$.

7.3.2 Metadata Exchange Cost

The metadata of each node's received messages within the preceeding seven days are recorded in Bloom filters—recall that 1am's message lifetime is one week. We now derive the size of each node's Bloom filter. Each node receives in total $Nf_m \cdot 12\,\text{hours} \cdot 7\,\text{days} \cdot F_m$ messages per week, as we assume 12 hours of active time per day for initiating messages. Each message requires 14.4 bits in the Bloom filter (recall Section 3.2), so the size of each node's Bloom filter (measured in 802.11b frames) is $\frac{14.4\,\text{b}\cdot(Nf_m\cdot 12\,\text{h}\cdot 7\,\text{d}\cdot F_m)}{B_{frame}}$, where B_{frame} is the maximum number of data bits carried by one 802.11b frame.

As each node's Bloom filter is exchanged upon each contact, the energy cost per contact is $E_f\frac{14.4\,\text{b}\cdot(Nf_m\cdot 84\,h\cdot F_m)}{B_{frame}} + E_{sw}$. The extra term E_{sw} is the energy cost of switching on and off the WiFi component to enable communication (see Table 3). On the other hand, each node's average contacts per hour is $NR_{contact}$, as $R_{contact}$ is the average number of contacts per pair per hour. Therefore, each node's hourly cost for

Table 4: Energy Cost of 1am Computations

	Execution time for 5,000 runs (ms)	Energy cost per run (mJ)
Signature (OpenSSL)	741.9 [25]	0.1
Verification (OpenSSL)	3819.7 [25]	0.6
Verification (SpongeCastle)	1,572,347	239
Others	65,776	10.0

metadata exchange is

$$E_{md} = N R_{contact} \left(E_f \frac{14.4\,\mathrm{b} \cdot (N f_m \cdot 84\,\mathrm{h} \cdot F_m)}{B_{frame}} + E_{sw} \right).$$

Overall, the hourly communication energy cost per node is $E_{comm} = E_{msg} + E_{md}$, which scales with N^2 as E_{md} scales with N^2 and E_{msg} scales with N.

7.4 Computation

Each node's hourly energy cost for computation is $E_{comp} = N f_m E_{mcomp}$, where $N f_m$ is the number of 1am messages received per node per hour, and E_{mcomp} is the energy cost of processing one message, which includes the cost of signing, verification, and all other operations, e.g., serialization/deserialization and database queries and insertions[2].

Table 4 lists the computation time and energy cost for various message handling operations[3]. For digital signature and verification, 1am uses ECDSA with nistp256 for their space-friendly public keys [26]. Unfortunately Android's default cryptography library, SpongeCastle [27], is much less energy efficient (2,000× less) than an unsupported native library, OpenSSL [28] (see Table 4). Because it is non-trivial to port OpenSSL to Android and measure its performance, we used a previous paper's reported computation time for the considered algorithm parameters, CPU model, and OS [25]. In summary, $E_{mcomp} = 0.1\,\mathrm{mJ} + 0.6\,\mathrm{mJ} + F_m \cdot 10.0\,\mathrm{mJ}$, for signing, verification, and other operations, respectively. The cost for all operations except signing and verification is proportional to the message size, as reflected in the last term of E_{mcomp}.

Summing the cost of contact discovery, communication, and computation yields 1am's total hourly energy cost

$$E = E_{base} + E_{comm} + E_{comp}, \quad (1)$$

which scales in $\mathcal{O}(N^2)$, as E_{base} is constant, E_{comp} is $\mathcal{O}(N)$, and E_{comm} is $\mathcal{O}(N^2)$. Note that this model assumes an uniform pairwise contact rate ($R_{contact}$) independent of the network size (N). In reality, $R_{contact}$ may decrease as N increases, offsetting the $\mathcal{O}(N^2)$ trend, because an increasing number of nodes may never meet as the network becomes larger and more geographically distributed. Nevertheless, this model produces an upper bound on energy consumption that is fairly tight for small local communities with sufficient mixing, e.g., a university campus.

7.5 Energy Cost for Multimedia Support

Using the energy model in Equation 1, we study 1am's energy overhead for various network sizes (N) and message types (text, image, and video). N is varied from 100 to 50,000, which correspond to 0.2%–100% adoption rates among students and faculty on a university campus. Table 5 shows the sizes (measured in 802.11b frames) and message initiation frequencies (f_m) of different multimedia messages. Each 1am text message contains at most 514 characters, so one frame per message is sufficient. The text initiation frequency is based on Twitter's average rate, around 2 per user per day [29]. We consider images of sizes typical for microblogging applications, 100 KB. The image initiation frequency is based on Facebook users' photo posting statistics [30]. We consider 352×288 video encoded at 1 Mbps, i.e., high-quality MPEG, of 4 minutes duration, the average video length on the Internet [31]. The video initiation frequency is based on YouTube's statistics [32].

[2]In fact signing is only conducted once by the message initiator while every receiver verifies. We simplified the model by assuming that signing and verification occur the same number of times, leading to an upper bound cost estimation.

[3]The energy cost is the product of the computation time and P_{CPU}, the smartphone's power level with CPU being awake, which is 760 mW according to our measurement.

Table 5: Message Sizes (F_m) and Initiation Frequencies (f_m)

Type	Message size	F_m (frames/msg.)	f_m (msg./hour)
Text	514 characters	1	0.16667
Image	100 KB	44	0.02536
Video clip	1 Mbps × 240 seconds	12000	0.00054

Table 6: Hourly Energy Consumptions for Different Network Sizes and Message Types

N (network size)	Text		Image		Video	
	J	%	J	%	J	%
100	95	0.41	99	0.42	122	0.52
400	101	0.43	124	0.53	257	1.10
700	108	0.46	162	0.70	467	2.00
1,500	138	0.59	327	1.40	1K	5.96
2,000	164	0.70	476	2.04	2K	9.59
5,000	430	1.84	2K	9.08	12K	50.0
50,000	27K	117.6	181K	775.2	1048K	4491.6

Energy percentages are for a 6.48 watt-hour battery.

Table 6 shows the hourly energy consumption of different scenarios. We report both in Joules and the percent of energy in a 6.48 Wh battery, a commodity lithium-ion battery widely used in smartphones. We consider the maximum acceptable daily energy consumption to be 25% of the battery, i.e., ~2.1% per hour assuming 12 hours of active time per day. The shaded cells in Table 6 shows the cases we believe would impose unacceptable battery charging burdens on users.

Table 6 shows that it is practical to flood text and image messages in networks with up to 5,000 and 2,000 nodes, respectively. However, video messages can only be supported in networks with fewer than 700 nodes, despite a much smaller initiation frequency. In an extreme case when video messages are initiated as frequently as text messages, the battery will be depleted in less than 3 hours even in a 100-node network. If both text and image messages are supported, it is practical to have networks with 1,500 nodes. If all three types are supported, the network is limited to 400 nodes.

Metadata exchange ($E_{md} \propto N^2$) is the main cause of energy consumption in large networks. This result suggests that simple energy models that ignore metadata exchange and only consider data transmission [13, 14] are inaccurate and possibly misleading. We note that the key to designing more energy-efficient DTN message distribution protocols is to offset the $\mathcal{O}(N^2)$ trend in energy consumption without greatly degrading performance.

8. CONCLUSIONS

Thanks to their structure, DTNs composed of commodity smartphones have the potential to resist blocking and censorship, and make surveillance expensive. Such networks are capable of supporting text microblogging applications without much reducing participant smartphones' battery lifespan for towns with populations of 50,000 and adoption rates below 5%. Supporting frequent image or video distribution without new dissemation ideas is impractical at similar network scales. The network was able to deliver messages to most participants within a day with only a 0.2% adoption rate in a college town with a population of 50,000. It degrades more gracefully than a hierarchical infrastructure network when subjected to attacks that eliminate participants or geographic locations, suggesting robustness to blocking and censorship. The 1am traces are publicly available at http://ziyang.eecs.umich.edu/projects/whisper/traces.html.

There is evidence of substantial demand for communication applications that are robust to blocking, censorship, and surveillance but developing such applications requires an understanding of how design decisions influence performance, security, and energy consumption properties. This work takes a first step toward this understanding.

9. ACKNOWLEDGMENTS

The authors would like to thank Rongrong Tao and Junzhe Zhang for helping implementing prototypes and performing experiments, and Paul Myers for proofreading the paper. This work was supported in part by the US National Science Foundation (NSF) under Award TC-0964545 and in part by the University of Michigan.

10. REFERENCES

[1] P. N. Howard, A. Duffy, D. Freelon, M. Hussain, W. Mari, and M. Mazaid, "Opening closed regimes: What was the role of social media during the Arab Spring," Project on Information Technology & Political Islam, Jan. 2011.

[2] J. Cook, "Hong Kong protesters are communicating via a mobile app that doesn't actually use the Internet," *businessinsider.com*, Sept. 2014.

[3] B. Ries, "Twitter blocks pro-Ukrainian political account for Russian users," *Mashable.com*, May 2014.

[4] "1am: Censorship-resistant microblogging," 2013, http://1am-networks.org.

[5] A. Al-Akkad, C. Raffelsberger, A. Boden, L. Ramirez, and A. Zimmermann, "Tweeting when online is off? Opportunistically creating mobile ad-hoc networks in response to disrupted infrastructure," in *Proc. Int. Conf. Information Systems for Crisis Response and Management*, May 2014, pp. 662–671.

[6] T. Hossmann, F. Legendre, P. Carta, P. Gunningberg, and C. Rohner, "Twitter in disaster mode: Opportunistic communication and distribution of sensor data in emergencies," in *Proc. Extreme Conf. on Communication: The Amazon Expedition*, Sept. 2011, pp. 1:1–1:6.

[7] G. Fanti, Y. Ben David, S. Benthall, E. Brewer, and S. Shenker, "Rangzen: Circumventing government-imposed communication blackouts," University of California, Berkeley, Tech. Rep. UCB/EECS-2013-128, July 2013.

[8] P. Hui, J. Crowcroft, and E. Yoneki, "BUBBLE rap: Social-based forwarding in delay tolerant networks," *IEEE Trans. Mobile Computing*, vol. 10, no. 11, pp. 1576–1589, Nov. 2011.

[9] L. Song and D. Kotz, "Evaluating opportunistic routing protocols with large realistic contact traces," in *Proc. Wkshp. Challenged Networks*, Sept. 2007, pp. 35–42.

[10] T. Henderson, D. Kotz, and I. Abyzov, "The changing usage of a mature campus-wide wireless network," *Computer Networks*, vol. 52, no. 14, pp. 2690–2712, 2008.

[11] M. McNett and G. M. Voelker, "Access and mobility of wireless PDA users," *ACM SIGMOBILE Mobile Computing and Communications Review*, vol. 9, no. 2, pp. 40–55, 2005.

[12] A. Socievole and S. Marano, "Evaluating the impact of energy consumption on routing performance in delay tolerant networks," in *Proc. Int. Conf. Wireless Communications and Mobile Computing*, Aug. 2012, pp. 481–486.

[13] Y. Li, Y. Jiang, D. Jin, L. Su, L. Zeng, and D. O. Wu, "Energy-efficient optimal opportunistic forwarding for delay-tolerant networks," *IEEE Trans. Vehicular Technology*, vol. 59, no. 9, pp. 4500–4512, 2010.

[14] X. Lu and P. Hui, "An energy-efficient n-epidemic routing protocol for delay tolerant networks," in *Proc. Int. Conf. Networking, Architecture and Storage*, July 2010, pp. 341–347.

[15] D. R. Bild, Y. Liu, R. P. Dick, Z. M. Mao, and D. S. Wallach, "Aggregate characterization of user behavior in Twitter and analysis of the retweet graph," *ACM Trans. Internet Technologies*, accepted, in press.

[16] F. Putze, P. Sanders, and J. Singler, "Cache-, hash-, and space-efficient Bloom filters," *J. of Experimental Algorithms*, no. 4, pp. 108–121, 2007.

[17] S. Trifunovic, B. Distl, D. Schatzmann, and F. Legendre, "WiFi-Opp: ad-hoc-less opportunistic networking," in *Proc. Wkshp. Challenged Networks*, Sept. 2011, pp. 37–42.

[18] A. Chaintreau, P. Hui, J. Crowcroft, C. Diot, R. Gass, and J. Scott, "Impact of human mobility on opportunistic forwarding algorithms," *IEEE Trans. Mobile Computing*, vol. 6, no. 6, pp. 606–620, 2007.

[19] "Manes: a mobile ad hoc network emulation system," 2013, http://ziyang.eecs.umich.edu/projects/whisper/manes/.

[20] D. Wang, D. Pedreschi, C. Song, F. Giannotti, and A.-L. Barabasi, "Human mobility, social ties, and link prediction," in *Proc. Int. Conf. Knowledge Discovery and Data Mining*, Aug. 2011, pp. 1100–1108.

[21] E. Bayraktaroglu, C. King, X. Liu, G. Noubir, R. Rajaraman, and B. Thapa, "Performance of IEEE 802.11 under jamming," *Mobile Networks and Applications*, vol. 18, no. 5, pp. 678–696, 2013.

[22] R. Albert, H. Jeong, and A.-L. Barabási, "Error and attack tolerance of complex networks," *Nature*, vol. 406, no. 6794, pp. 378–382, 2000.

[23] Monsoon, "Monsoon power monitor," 2008, http://www.msoon.com/LabEquipment/PowerMonitor/.

[24] R. Zheng, J. C. Hou, and L. Sha, "Asynchronous wakeup for ad hoc networks," in *Proc. Int. Symp. Mobile Ad Hoc Networking and Computing*, June 2003, pp. 35–45.

[25] A. M. Braga and E. N. Nascimento, "Portability evaluation of cryptographic libraries on Android smartphones," in *Proc. Int. Symp. Cyberspace Safety and Security*, Dec. 2012, pp. 459–469.

[26] J. Lopéz and R. Dahab, "An overview of elliptic curve cryptography," Institute of Computing, State University of Campinas, Tech. Rep. IC–00-10, 2000.

[27] "Sponge Castle," 2014, http://rtyley.github.io/spongycastle/.

[28] "OpenSSL," 2014, https://www.openssl.org/.

[29] "Twitter usage," 2015, https://about.twitter.com/company.

[30] "A focus on efficiency, a whitepaper from Facebook, Ericsson and Qualcomm," internet.org, Sept. 2013.

[31] ComScore, "ComScore releases December 2013 U.S. online video rankings," *conscore.com*, Jan. 2014.

[32] "YouTube statistics," 2014, https://www.youtube.com/yt/press/statistics.html.

Tracking Vital Signs During Sleep Leveraging Off-the-shelf WiFi

Jian Liu†, Yan Wang†, Yingying Chen†, Jie Yang*, Xu Chen†, Jerry Cheng§
†Stevens Institute of Technology, Hoboken, NJ 07030, USA
*Florida State University, Tallahassee, FL 32306, USA
§Rutgers University, North Brunswick, NJ 08902, USA
†{jliu28, ywang48, yingying.chen}@stevens.edu, *jyang5@fsu.edu, †xchen30@stevens.edu,
§jcheng1@rwjms.rutgers.edu

ABSTRACT

Tracking human vital signs of breathing and heart rates during sleep is important as it can help to assess the general physical health of a person and provide useful clues for diagnosing possible diseases. Traditional approaches (e.g., Polysomnography (PSG)) are limited to clinic usage. Recent radio frequency (RF) based approaches require specialized devices or dedicated wireless sensors and are only able to track breathing rate. In this work, we propose to track the vital signs of both breathing rate and heart rate during sleep by using off-the-shelf WiFi without any wearable or dedicated devices. Our system re-uses existing WiFi network and exploits the fine-grained channel information to capture the minute movements caused by breathing and heart beats. Our system thus has the potential to be widely deployed and perform continuous long-term monitoring. The developed algorithm makes use of the channel information in both time and frequency domain to estimate breathing and heart rates, and it works well when either individual or two persons are in bed. Our extensive experiments demonstrate that our system can accurately capture vital signs during sleep under realistic settings, and achieve comparable or even better performance comparing to traditional and existing approaches, which is a strong indication of providing non-invasive, continuous fine-grained vital signs monitoring without any additional cost.

Categories and Subject Descriptors

H.4 [**Information Systems Applications**]: Miscellaneous

Keywords

Vital Signs; Channel State Information (CSI); WiFi; Sleep Monitoring

1. INTRODUCTION

Vital signs, such as breathing rate and heart rate, indicate the state of a person's essential body functions. They are the essential components to assess the general physical health of a person and identify various disease problems. Correlating the vital signs with our sleep quality can further enable sleep apnea diagnosis and treatment [1], treatment for asthma [2] and sleep stage detection [3]. However, the traditional way to monitor vital signs during sleep requires a patient to perform hospital visits and wear dedicated sensors [4], which are intrusive and costly. The obtained results may be biased because of the unfamiliar sleeping environments in the hospital. Moreover, it is difficult, if not possible, to run long-term sleep monitoring in clinical settings. Thus, a solution that can provide non-invasive, low-cost and long-term vital signs monitoring without requiring hospital visits is highly desirable.

Recently, Radio Frequency (RF) based monitoring solutions [5, 6, 7, 8] have drawn considerable attention as they provide non-invasive breathing rate monitoring. For example, F. Adib et al. utilize Universal Software Radio Peripheral (USRP) and Frequency Modulated Continuous Wave (FMCW) radar to monitor a person's breathing rate by detecting the chest fluctuations caused by breathing [7, 8]. Doppler radar [5] and ultra-band radar [6] are utilized to catch a person's breathing respectively. These systems involve specialized devices with high complexity, which prevent them from large-scale and long-term deployment. Furthermore, N. Patwari et al. [9, 10] use coarse-grained channel information (i.e., received signal strength (RSS)) extracted from wireless sensor nodes to detect breathing rate. Their approach requires additional wireless network infrastructure (i.e., dedicated sensor nodes), and the coarse-grained channel information is not able to capture the vital signs of heart rate. Another new direction is using wearable sensors (such as Fitbit [11] and Jawbone [12]) to track people's fitness at any time. But they only have the capability of performing coarse-grained sleep monitoring without capturing the breathing rate, which is critical to many sleep problem diagnosis including sleep apnea. Additionally, users are required to wear these fitness sensors even during their sleep, which could be a challenge for elder people.

To address these issues, our work aims to perform continuous long-term vital signs monitoring with low cost and without the requirement of wearing any sensor. We show that it is possible to track breathing rate and heart rate during sleep by using off-the-shelf WiFi. This will largely increase the opportunity for wide deployment and in-home use. Indeed, our system re-uses existing WiFi network for tracking vital signs without dedicated/wearable sensors or additional wireless infrastructure. Furthermore, by exploiting fine-grained channel information, Channel State Information (CSI), provided by off-the-shelf WiFi device, our system captures not

MobiHoc'15, June 22–25, 2015, Hangzhou, China.

http://dx.doi.org/10.1145/2746285.2746303.

only the breathing rate but also heart rate. Specifically, our system utilizes the readily available channel information to detect the minute movements caused by breathing and heart beats (i.e., inhaling, exhaling, diastole and systole).

Using channel state information has significant implication on how fine-grained minute movements can be captured for vital signs monitoring. Comparing to the traditional RSS, which only provides a single measurement of the power over the whole channel bandwidth, the fine-grained CSI provides both amplitude and phase information for multiple OFD-M subcarriers. For instance, the mainstream WiFi systems such as 802.11 a/g/n are based on OFDM where the relatively wideband $20MHz$ channel is partitioned into 52 subcarriers. Due to the frequency diversity of these narrowband subcarriers, the multipath effect and shadow fading at different subcarriers may result in significant difference in the observed amplitudes. This means that a small movement in physical environment may lead to the change of CSI at some subcarriers, whereas such change maybe smoothed out if we examine the signal strength over the whole channel bandwidth. Our system thus takes advantage of the fine-grained CSI provided by off-the-shelf WiFi device to capture the minute movements for vital signs monitoring.

Our system uses only a single pair of WiFi device and wireless AP for detecting the breathing rate and heart rate during sleep. The breathing rate detection algorithm first obtains time series of CSI from off-the-shelf WiFi device (e.g., desktop, laptop, tablet, and smartphone) and then analyzes the information in time domain and frequency domain. It achieves high accuracy for both single and two-person in bed scenarios. To detect heart rate, our algorithm first applies a bandpass filter to eliminate irrelevant frequency components, and then estimates the heart rate in the frequency domain by locating the frequency peak in the normal heart rate range. Extensive experiments are conducted in lab environment and two apartments with difference sizes. The results show that our system provides accurate breathing rate and heart rate estimation not only under typical settings but also covering challenging scenarios including long distance between the WiFi device and AP, none-line-of-sight (NLOS) situation and different sleep postures. This demonstrates that our approach can provide device-free, continuous fine-grained vital signs monitoring without any additional cost. It has the capability to support large-scale deployment and long-term vital signs monitoring in non-clinical settings.

The main contributions of our work are summarized as follows:

- We show that the existing WiFi network can be re-used to capture vital signs of breathing rate and heart rate through using only one AP and a single WiFi device. Such an approach can also be extended to non-sleep scenarios when the user is stationary.
- Our proposed system extracts fine-grained channel state information (CSI) from off-the-shelf WiFi device to detect the minute movements and provide accurate breathing and heart rates estimation concurrently.
- We develop algorithms that have the capability to track breathing rates of a single person as well as two-person in bed cases, which cover typical in-home scenarios.
- Extensive experiments in both lab and two apartments over a three-month period show that our system can achieve comparable or even better performance as compared to existing dedicated sensor based approaches.

2. RELATED WORK

Breathing rate, heart rate and statistics of sleep events are important indicators for evaluating one's sleep quality, stress level and various health conditions. In general, the methods used to track such information during sleep can be categorized into four groups: dedicated sensor based, smartphone and wearable sensor based, touch-free sensor based and RF signal based.

Traditional approaches use dedicated sensors to measure vital signs during sleep. For example, Polysomnography (PSG) [4] measures body functions including breathing rate, eye movements (EOG), heart rhythm (ECG) and muscle activity by attaching multiple sensors to a patient. Such systems incur high cost and are usually limited to clinical usage. Recent advances of smartphones and wearable sensors have enabled in-home sleep monitoring by utilizing the built-in accelerometer and microphone [13, 14, 11, 12]. These methods mainly provide coarse-grained monitoring including the detection of body movements, snoring, or regular sleep events, and are not able to monitor breathing rate, which is a critical indication of sleep irregularity such as sleep apnea. They also require users to place smartphones close-by and wear sensors during sleep. Touch-free sensor based solutions either use the sensors attached to the mattress [15] or install a camera to capture the chest movement for breathing rate estimation [16]. These systems however require professional installations and cannot estimate heart rate.

Most related to our work is the RF signal based monitoring mechanisms, such as the use of Doppler radar [5], ultra-wideband [6], Frequency Modulated Continuous Wave (FMCW) radar [8, 7] or Received Signal Strength (RSS) [9, 10] for monitoring the vital signs of breathing rate. In particular, these mechanisms [5, 6, 7, 8] rely on specialized hardware including Universal Software Radio Peripheral (USRP), FMCW radar and Doppler radar. These systems incur high cost and high complexity, making them impractical for large scale deployment. N. Patwari et al. [9, 10] use received signal strength (RSS) measurements (e.g., using 16 frequency channels in IEEE 802.15.4) extracted from wireless sensor nodes to detect the breathing rate. Their approaches require additional wireless network infrastructure and high-density placement of sensor nodes. And the coarse-grained channel information of RSS is not able to capture the heart rate.

Different from the previous work, our system re-uses existing WiFi network for tracking vital signs of breathing and heart rates concurrently without dedicated/wearable sensors or additional wireless infrastructure. By exploiting fine-grained channel state information provided by off-the-shelf WiFi devices, our system captures both the breathing rate as well as heart rate. Our system thus performs device-free, continuous fine-grained vital signs monitoring without any additional cost. It has the potential to be widely deployed in home and many other non-clinical environments.

3. SYSTEM DESIGN

In this section, we discuss the preliminaries, design challenges and overview of our system design.

3.1 Preliminaries

While proliferating WiFi networks are usually used for wireless Internet access and connecting local area networks, such as an in-home WiFi network involving both mobile and stationary devices (e.g., laptop, smartphone, tablet, desktop, smartTV), they have great potential to sense the environment changes and capture the minute movements caused by

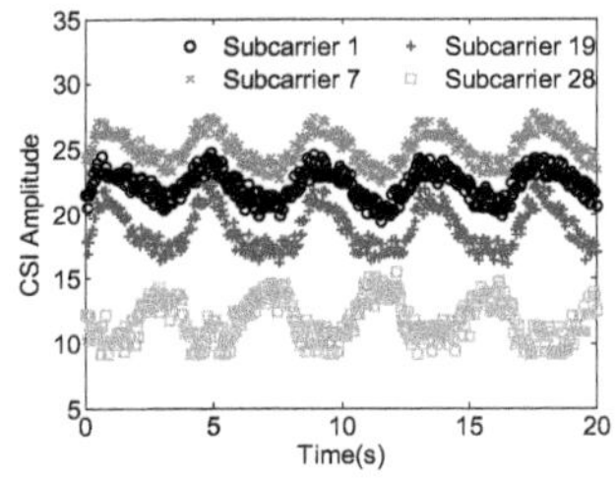

Figure 1: CSI amplitude of four subcarriers over time when a person is asleep.

human body [17]. Indeed, WiFi signals are affected by human body movements at various scales during sleep, such as large scale movements involving going to bed and turn over, minute movements including inhaling/exhaling for breathing and diastole/systole for heart beats. By extracting and analyzing the unique characteristics of WiFi signals, we could capture and derive the semantic meanings of such movements including both breathing rate and heart beats during sleep. We are thus motivated to re-use existing WiFi network to monitor the fine-grained vital signs during sleep as it doesn't require any dedicated/wearable sensors or additional infrastructure setup.

To monitor the minute movements of breathing and heart beats, we exploit the Channel State Information (CSI) provided by off-the-shelf WiFi devices as opposed to the commonly used Received Signal Strength (RSS). While the coarse-grained channel information of RSS provides the averaged power in a received radio signal over the whole channel bandwidth, the fine-grained CSI of WiFi signal (based on OFDM) describes at each subcarrier how a signal propagates from the transmitter to the receiver and represents the combined effect of, for example, scattering, fading, and power decay with distance. For example, in 802.11 a/g/n, a relatively wideband $20MHz$ OFDM channel (or carrier) is partitioned into 52 subcarriers. And we could examine the amplitude and phase at each subcarrier, which could be thought of as a narrowband channel, for extracting the minute movements. Due to the relative narrowband channel, the scattering and reflecting effects caused by minute movements could result in totally different amplitudes and phases at each subcarrier. Such difference however is usually smoothed out if we look at the averaged power over the whole channel bandwidth (i.e., RSS). Analyzing the CSI at each subcarrier thus provides great opportunity to capture the minute movements from not only breathing but also heart beats.

Figure 1 shows the CSI amplitude of four subcarriers (i.e., subcarrier 1, 7, 19 and 28) extracted from a laptop in a 802.11n network over time when a person is asleep. His bed is in between an AP and the laptop with 3 meters apart. The person does not carry any sensor in his body. We observe that the CSI amplitude of these four subcarriers exhibits an obvious periodic up-and-down trend. Such a pattern could be caused by the person's breathing during sleep. This observation strongly suggest that we may achieve device-free fine-grained vital signs monitoring by leveraging the CSI from off-the-shelf WiFi devices.

3.2 Challenges

Our goal is to track human vital signs of breathing and heart rates simultaneously using CSI measurements from a single pair of WiFi devices. To build such system under realistic settings as a typical in-home scenario, a number of challenges need to be addressed.

Robustness to Real Environments. The placement of WiFi devices in real environments could change over time, and different persons present different sleeping postures. Our system should be able to provide accurate vital sign monitoring under such challenging conditions including various distances between the AP and WiFi devices, presence of walls between WiFi devices (creating none-line-of-sight (NLOS) scenarios), and different sleeping postures. In addition, our system should be able to identify regular sleep related events (such as turnover or getting out of bed) to facilitate vital signs monitoring.

Tracking Breathing & Heartbeat Simultaneously. Both breathing and heart beat only involve small body movements, presenting significant challenges when tracking such vital signs simultaneously under realistic settings. Even if the repeatable CSI changing pattern caused by breathing could be detected as shown in Figure 1, it is difficult to capture heartbeat movements using WiFi links at the same time. Because the noisy environments will also affect CSI measurements, making it much harder to distinguish the minute movements caused by breathing (i.e., inhaling and exhaling) and heart beats (i.e., diastole and systole).

Sensing with Single Pair of AP and WiFi Device. Our approach should work with existing WiFi infrastructure, which may have only a single wireless link (between the AP and the device) across the human body. This presents additional challenges when two people are in-bed together. Our system should be able to distinguish and measure breathing rates coming from two people. Furthermore, the system should use WiFi traffic as little as possible, such as only utilizing existing beaconing traffic.

3.3 System Overview

The basic idea of our system is to track vital signs during sleep through capturing the unique patterns embedded in WiFi signals. As illustrated in Figure 2, the system takes as input time-series CSI amplitude measurements, which can be collected at an off-the-shelf WiFi device by utilizing existing WiFi traffic or system-generated periodic traffic (if network traffic is insufficient) during people's sleep. The data is then processed to filter out the CSI measurements that contain sleep events (e..g, going to bed and turn over) or large environmental changes such as people walking by via *Coarse Sleep Event Detection and Filtering*. The measurements belonging to the regular sleep events can be further classified to detailed events such as going to bed, getting off bed and turnovers. Moreover, our work is based on the fact that breathing and heart rates of resting people have different frequency ranges (e.g., breathing rate ranges from 10 to 37 bpm [18, 19], and heart rate ranges from 60 to 80 bpm [20]). This useful information leads us to work on different frequency bands of the CSI measurements for accurate vital signs estimation.

The core components of our system are *Breathing Rate Estimation* and *Heart Rate Estimation*. After coarse sleep event detection and data filtering, based on the different frequency information embedded inside the CSI measurements, the input is fed into *Breathing Rate Estimation* and *Heart Rate Estimation* respectively. In particular, the lower-frequency information of the CSI measurements is processed by the *Breathing Rate Estimation* component. Our system first performs *Data Calibration* and *Subcarrier Selection* to preprocess the data and select only the subcarriers sensitive to minute human body movements (i.e., subcarriers with

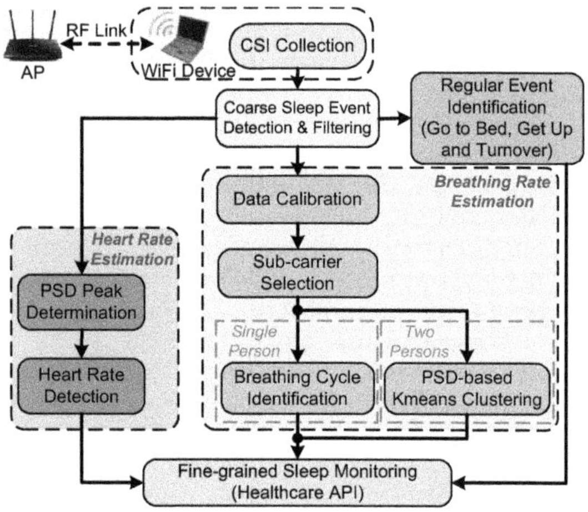

Figure 2: Overview of system flow.

large variances). We then develop two methods, *Breathing Cycle* and *PSD-based K-means Clustering*, to estimate the breathing rate for single and two-person in-bed scenarios respectively. *PSD* denotes power spectral density. Following the similar principle, *PSD-based K-means Clustering* can be easily extended to handle the case of estimating breathing rates for multiple people simultaneously given the number of people under study is known. The higher-frequency information of the CSI measurements is fed into the *Heart Rate Estimation* component. The heart rate is then derived in the frequency domain by examining the peaks in power spectral density (PSD) of CSI measurements. We leave the detailed presentation of *Breathing Rate Estimation* and *Heart Rate Estimation* to Section 4 and Section 5, respectively.

4. BREATHING RATE ESTIMATION

We first describe *Data Calibration* and *Subcarrier Selection*, and then present *Breathing Cycle Identification* for estimating an individual's breathing rate. We finally show how to estimate breathing rates for two persons in-bed case.

4.1 Data Calibration

Data calibration is used to improve the reliability of the CSI by mitigating the noise presented in the collected CSI samples in real environments. The noise sources could come from environment-related changes, radio signal interference, etc. Our data calibration first utilizes the Hampel filter [21] to filter out the outliers which have significant different values from other neighboring CSI measurements. Specifically, we apply the Hampel filter with a sliding window at each subcarrier to remove such outliers. After that, we further apply a moving average filter, which further removes high-frequency noise that is unlikely to be caused by breathing or heart beats as the corresponding minute movements usually present in a fixed frequency range. Figure 3 illustrates the effectiveness of our data calibration by comparing the CSI amplitude before and after data calibration under a none-line-of-sight case with severe signal outliers: the CSI amplitude shown in the figure is from a single subcarrier collected from a WiFi device, which trasmits/receives packets from an AP with a wall between them. As we can see from the figure, after data calibration, the sinusoidal waves in CSI amplitude can clearly reflect the periodic up-and-down chest and belly movements caused by breathing.

4.2 Subcarrier Selection Strategy

We observe that the amplitudes of different subcarriers have different sensitivity to inhaling and exhaling caused by

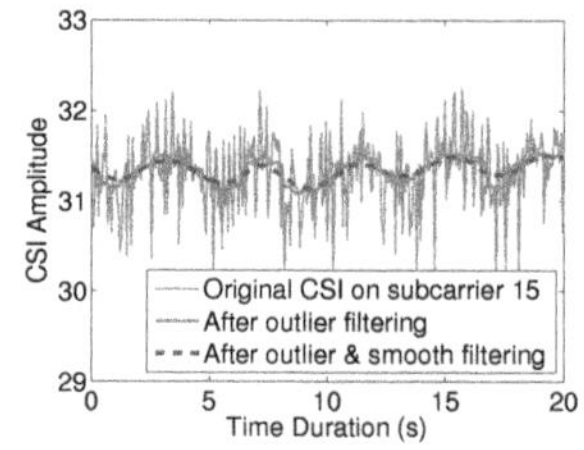

Figure 3: Illustration of data calibration of a single subcarrier.

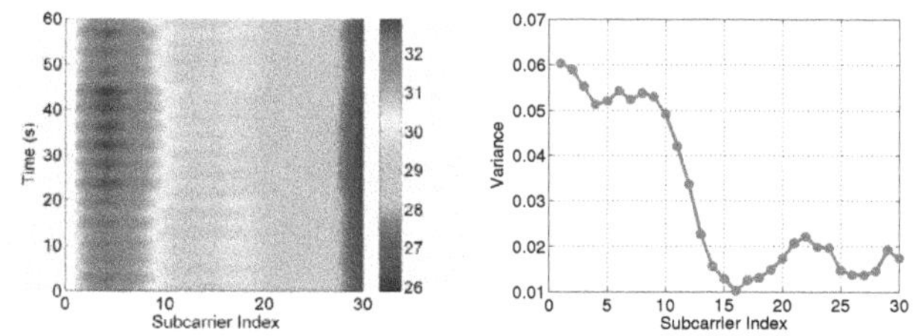

(a) CSI time series patterns after data calibration. (b) Variance of each subcarrier.

Figure 4: Example of CSI amplitude pattern at 30 subcarriers and the corresponding variance.

breathing due to frequency diversity. Figure 4(a) presents an example of CSI amplitude over time on 30 subcarriers extracted from a laptop in WiFi network when a person is asleep. We find that the CSI from the smaller subcarrier indices is significantly affected by the minute movements caused by breathing, while CSI from the higher subcarrier indices (i.e., from 15 to 30) is less sensitive. This is because different subcarriers have different central frequencies, which have different wavelengthes. Combining the effect of multipath/shadowing with different frequencies, CSI measurements at different subcarriers thus have different amplitudes. Those subcarriers not sensitive to the breathing activity should be filtered out. We utilize the variance of CSI amplitude in a moving time window to quantify the subcarrier's sensitivity to minute movements. Figure 4(b) shows the variance of 30 subcarriers. We can see that subcarriers with higher variance are more sensitive to minute movements. We thus use a threshold based method to select subcarriers having large variance of CSI amplitude in a time window for breathing rate estimation.

4.3 Breathing Cycle Identification

As breathing involves periodic minute movements of inhaling and exhaling, our breathing cycle identification aims to capture the periodic changes in CSI measurements caused by breathing. From Figure 1, we observe the CSI amplitude on the selected subcarrier indeed presents a sinusoidal-like periodic changing pattern over the time due to breathing. This observation suggests that we can identify breathing cycles by measuring the peak-to-peak time interval of sinusoidal CSI amplitudes. We thus first identify peaks of sinusoidal CSI amplitude patterns to calculate peak-to-peak intervals. We then combine the peak-to-peak intervals from multiple subcarriers to improve the robustness and the accuracy of breathing cycle identification.

Local Peak Identification. A typical peak finding algorithm determines a data sample as a peak if its value is larger than its two neighboring samples. However, such simple method produces many *fake peaks* (i.e., the identified peaks that are not at the location of real peaks of the sinusoidal CSI amplitude pattern) as illustrated in Figure 5. The

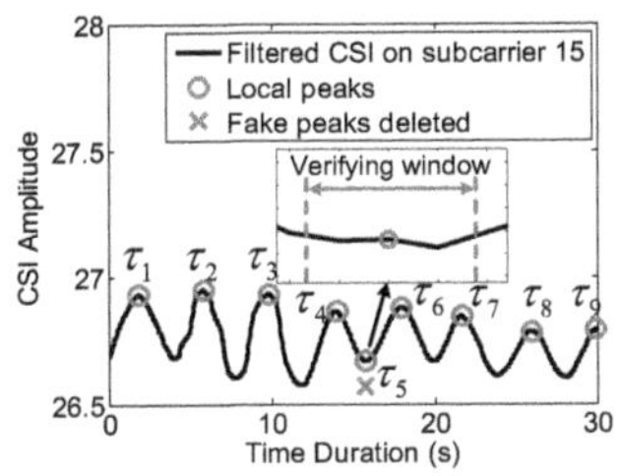

Figure 5: Illustration of fake peak removal.

peak τ_5 has larger value than its two neighboring samples, yet, it is a fake peak among these nine identified peaks. In order to filter out the fake peaks, we apply a threshold to the minimum distance between two neighboring peaks based on human's maximum possible breathing rate. In addition, we develop a *Fake Peak Removal* algorithm to further reduce the number of fake peaks.

Specifically, adults usually breathe at 10-14 breathes per minute (bpm) [19], while new born babies breathe at around 37 bpm [18]. We therefore set the range of breathing rates being considered in our work to 10-37 bpm which covers a broad range including fast and slow breathing rates. We further adopt a minimum acceptable interval σ_{mpd} that corresponds to the maximum possible breathing rate as a threshold to remove the peaks that are too close to each other. If a peak has its backward interval (i.e., the interval between previous peak and current peak) less than the minimum acceptable interval length, it will be identified as a fake peak. In particular, we set the minimum acceptable interval $\sigma_{mpd} = 60 \cdot f/37$ samples, which corresponds to the maximum possible breathing rate for infants. The parameter f is the sampling rate of CSI measurements that corresponds to WiFi packet transmission rate.

In addition, we confirm the identified peaks by comparing its value to multiple data samples within a verification window centered at the peak. The system only keeps the identified peak when its value is greater than all the data samples in the verification window. The algorithm of fake peak removal is provided in Algorithm 1. In our experiments, we observe that a short verification window of one second is good enough to remove fake peaks.

Breathing Cycles Combination. Once we capture all the local peaks from the selected subcarriers, a more clear pattern can be obtained as shown in Figure 6. The referenced signal is derived from the NEULOG Respiration Monitor Logger Sensor [22], which is connected to a monitor belt attached to the user's ribcage while asleep. Next, our system estimates the breathing rate by combining peak-to-peak intervals obtained crossing all selected subcarriers. We denote a set of peak-to-peak intervals obtained from P selected subcarriers as $L = [l_1, ..., l_i, ..., l_P]'$, where $l_i = \{l_i(1), ..., l_i(N_i - 1)\}$ is a vector of N_i peak-to-peak intervals obtained from the ith subcarrier. Then the estimated breathing cycle E_i from the ith subcarrier can be obtained by using the following equation:

$$\arg\min_{E_i} \sum_{n=1}^{N_i-1} |E_i - l_i(n)|^2. \quad (1)$$

Considering the subcarriers with larger variance are more sensitive to the minute movements, we utilize a weighted mean of estimated breathing cycles crossing all selected subcarriers to obtain a more accurate estimation of breathing

Algorithm 1 Fake Peak Removal.

Require:
CSI time series on subcarrier i: $c_i = \{c_i(1), ..., c_i(M)\}$;
Local peak set: $MaxSet = \{\tau_k, 1 \leqslant k \leqslant K\}$;
Length of the verifying window: N;
Ensure:
$MaxSet$ after removing fake maximums;
for k=1: K **do**
  $locs$:= location(τ_k);
  amp := amplitude(τ_k);
  for m := $locs$-$\lfloor \frac{N-1}{2} \rfloor$: $locs$+$\lfloor \frac{N-1}{2} \rfloor$ **do**
    if $m < 0 \,\|\, m > M$ **then**
      continue;
    end if
    if $amp < c_i(m)$ **then**
      delete τ_k from $MaxSet$;
      break;
    end if
  end for
end for
return $MaxSet$;

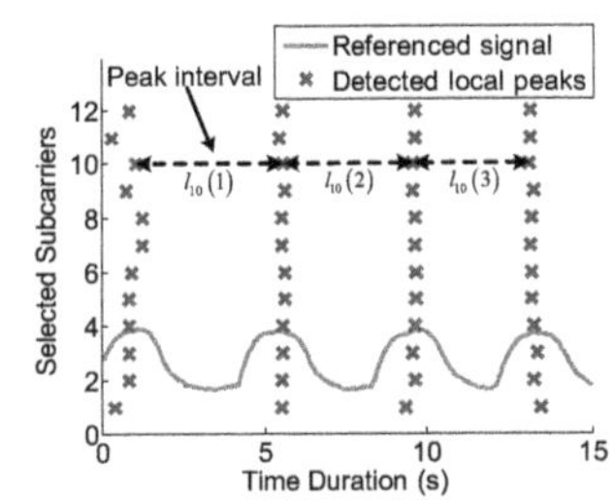

Figure 6: Local peaks of all selected subcarriers.

cycle E, which is defined as follows:

$$E = \sum_{i=1}^{P} \frac{\text{var}(c_i) \cdot E_i}{\sum_{i=1}^{P} \text{var}(c_i)}, \quad (2)$$

where P is the number of validated subcarriers, c_i is the CSI amplitude measurements on the ith subcarrier. The breathing rate finally can be identified as $60/E$ bpm.

4.4 Breathing Rate Estimation of Two Persons Scenario

Estimating breathing rate becomes challenging when there are two persons in bed as the CSI measurements would be affected by two independent movements simultaneously due to breathing. It is hard to observe a clear sinusoidal pattern in the time series of CSI amplitude. Nevertheless, the frequency of the breathing coming from two persons is still preserved if we transfer the time series of CSI to the frequency domain. We therefore develop a mechanism to determine two people's breathing rates simultaneously by examining the frequency components in CSI measurements.

In particular, our system analyzes the time series of CSI amplitude in frequency domain by using the power spectral density (PSD). The PSD transforms the time series of CSI measurements on each subcarrier to its power distribution in the frequency domain. It is used to identify the frequencies having strong signal power. A strong sinusoidal signal generates a peak at the frequency corresponding to the period of the sinusoidal signal in PSD. Therefore, the CSI amplitude measurements collected when two persons in bed should present two strong peaks at the frequency corresponding to

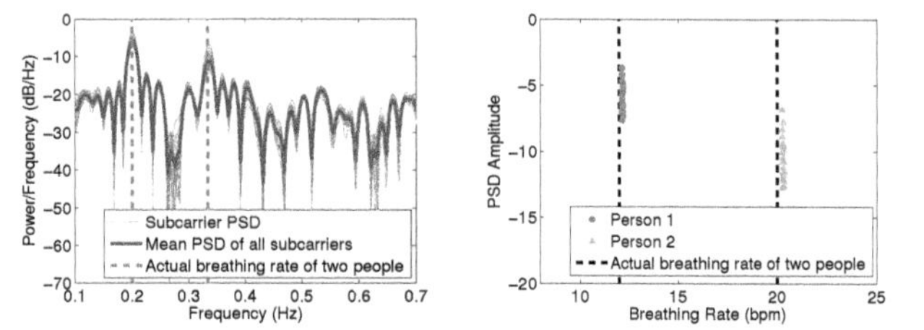

(a) PSD of CSI measurements. (b) K-means clustering of subcarriers' peaks.

Figure 7: Illustration of two people breathing at different frequencies (12*bpm* and 20*bpm*).

the breathing rate of two persons, respectively. The PSD on the ith subcarrier with N CSI amplitude measurements can be calculated with following equation:

$$PSD_i = 10\log_{10}\frac{(abs(FFT(c_i)))^2}{N}, \quad (3)$$

where c_i is the vector of CSI measurements on subcarrier i.

For each selected subcarrier, we utilize a threshold based approach to identifying the candidate peaks within its PSD. We then use a K-means clustering method to classify the candidate peaks into two clusters based on two dimensional feature including PSD amplitude and corresponding frequency. The number of targeted people (i.e., K in K-means) can be either estimated using existing work (e.g., [23]) or entered manually from the users. The average values of the frequencies in two clusters are identified as the breathing rates of these two people. Figure 7 shows an example of estimating two persons' breathing rate using PSD based method. The ground truths of two persons' breathing rates are 12*bpm* and 20*bpm* (i.e., $0.2Hz$ and $0.33Hz$ respectively). Figure 7(a) depicts that there are two strong peaks in the PSD of selected subcarriers near these two frequencies, respectively. Figure 7(b) shows that our PSD based K-means clustering method can effectively estimate the breathing rates of two persons in bed simultaneously. We note that the proposed approach still works even when two people have the same breathing rates. Under such scenario, our approach returns two close-by PSD peaks on each selected subcarrier in the frequency domain after K-means clustering. In addition, the person's chest or belly that is closer to the wireless link has bigger impact on the CSI changes, which creates more obvious periodic changes of CSI. This leads to the stronger peak corresponds to that person's breathing or heart beat rate. We thus can map the detected breathing or heart rates to each individual based on the strength of the peak and the proximity of the individual to the wireless link.

5. HEART RATE ESTIMATION

Heart rate is a very important indicator of the persons' sleep status, quality and overall health condition. While the breathing patterns can be observed in the CSI measurement, the heart rates don't produce observable periodic CSI change patterns in the time series CSI measurements. This is because the vibration of blood vessels caused by heart beat (i.e., diastole and systole) are smaller minute movements than that of breathing. Thus, the effect of minute movement of heartbeat is overlapped with and covered by the chest and belly movements of breathing. On the other hand, the heartbeat has much higher frequency than breathing. We thus can filter out the interference of breathing in order to facilitate the heart rate estimation.

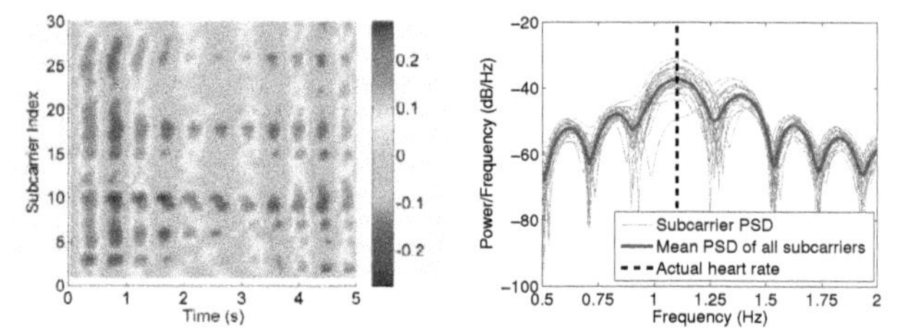

(a) CSI time series patterns. (b) PSD of CSI measurements on all subcarriers.

Figure 8: Recovered heart beats by applying pass band filtering and PSD of CSI measurements.

In particular, after Coarse Sleep Event Detection and Filtering, the CSI measurements with the frequency range related to normal heart rate range of resting people (i.e., 60*bpm* to 80*bpm* which corresponds to $1Hz$ to $1.33Hz$) will be separated and served as input to our Heart Rate Estimation. The patterns of CSI measurements of all subcarriers after such band-pass filtering are illustrated in Figure 8(a), from which we can observe the CSI changing that accompany the heart beats. With the aid of the band-pass filter, the mean PSD curve for all subcarriers displays a noticeable peak in the PSD graph at the frequency of $1.095Hz$, namely 65.7*bpm*, in Figure 8(b). In the same figure, there is a black dashed line representing the ground truth of 66*bpm* measured by a commercial fingertip pulse sensor during such time period. We then analyze the CSI amplitude on each subcarrier in frequency domain and generate the power spectral density (PSD) (refer to Equation 3) to identify the frequencies having strong signal power. We can thus determine the heart rate by locating the maximum power in the average PSD of all subcarriers in the normal heart rate range. For two person's heart rates monitoring, we can identify two heart rates simultaneously by using the similar approach to the breathing rate estimation of two persons illustrated in Section 4.4.

6. SYSTEM IMPLEMENTATION

6.1 Coarse Sleep Event Detection & Environmental Change Filtering

Coarse sleep event detection and filtering is used to detect and filter out the sleep events or environmental changes that interfere with the minute movements of breathing and heart beat during sleep. These sleep events, such as turnovers (i.e., changing sleeping postures) and getting up, and occasional changes of environments, such as people walking by, involve large scale body movements which significantly affect the CSI measurements and are irrelevant to vital signs monitoring. Our system thus performs coarse determination of CSI segments containing such inference factors and filters them out to facilitate accurate vital signs monitoring during sleep.

In particular, we employ a threshold-based approach to determine whether a segment of CSI measurements contains sleep events/environmental changes or not by examining the short-time energy of the moving variance of the CSI measurements. The rationale behind this is that the sleep events or environmental changes involving large body movements (e.g., going to bed and turn over) result in much larger changes of CSI measurement than that of minute movements of breathing and heart beat. The large movements thus can be detected once the variance energy of the corresponding CSI measurements exceeds a particular threshold.

We denote the CSI samples of P subcarriers as $C = [C_1, \ldots, C_p, \ldots, C_P]'$, where $C_p = \{c_p(1), \ldots, c_p(T)\}$ represents T

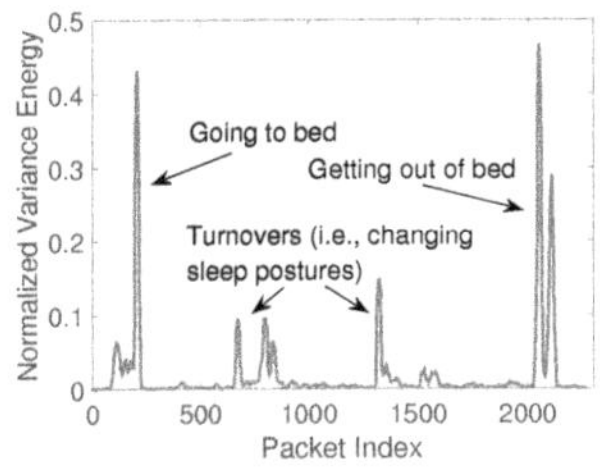

Figure 9: Short time energy of the variance of difference sleep events.

CSI amplitudes on the pth subcarrier. We further denote the moving variances of the P subcarriers as $V = [V_1, \ldots, V_p, \ldots, V_P]'$, where $V_p = \{v_p(1), \ldots, v_p(T)\}$ are the moving variances derived from C_p. Our system can then calculate the cumulative moving variance energy of CSI samples accessing P subcarriers as:

$$E = \frac{1}{NP} \sum_{p=1}^{P} \sum_{n=1}^{N} |v_p(n)|^2, \quad (4)$$

where N denotes the window length of short time energy.

We empirically determine the variance energy to be 0.02 as the threshold in this work. Figure 9 illustrates the normalized moving variance energy of CSI measurements that are collected when the participant involves different sleep events during sleep. We observe that all sleep events generate significantly large variance energy comparing to that of the minute movements of only breathing and heart beats.

6.2 Regular Sleep Event Identification

Given the detected sleep events, we further classify them into detailed events such as going to bed, getting off bed and turnovers. Generating statistic of such detailed events can help quantify the sleep quality. For example, frequent getting up or turning overs may suggest that the person has difficulty falling asleep. This information contributes to many healthcare applications such as elderly care and medical diagnosis. As shown in Figure 9, sleep events involving relative larger-scale movements (i.e., going to bed and getting out of bed) result in much larger variance energy than those involving relative smaller-scale movements (i.e., turn overs). We thus can distinguish sleep events with larger-scale movements from those with smaller-scale movements by comparing the variance energy from Equation (4). To further distinguish larger-scale movements, we can exploit the changes of the number of persons in bed to infer these two events. The number of persons in bed can be obtained by using a profile based approach as studied in existing work (e.g., [23]).

7. PERFORMANCE EVALUATION

In this section, we evaluate our system of tracking vital signs during sleep in both lab and two apartments.

7.1 Device and Network

We conduct experiments in an 802.11n WiFi network with a single off-the-shelf WiFi device (i.e., Lenovo T500 Laptop) connected to a commercial wireless Access Point (AP) (i.e., TP-Link TL-WDR4300). The laptop runs Ubuntu 10.04 LTS with the 2.6.36 kernel and is equipped with an Intel WiFi Link 5300 card for measuring CSI [24]. Unless mentioned otherwise, the packet transmission rate is set to $20pkts/s$. How the packet rate affects the performance will be discussed in Section 7.5.4. For each packet, we extract CSI for 30 subcarrier groups, which are evenly distributed in the 56 subcarriers of a $20MHz$ channel [24].

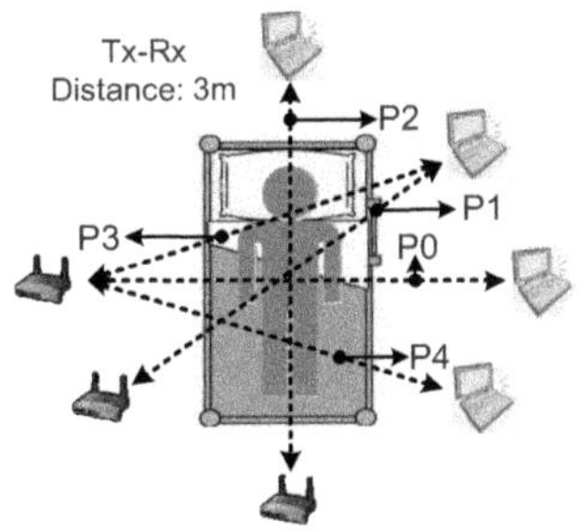

(a) Setup of WiFi device-AP pair with different relative positions.

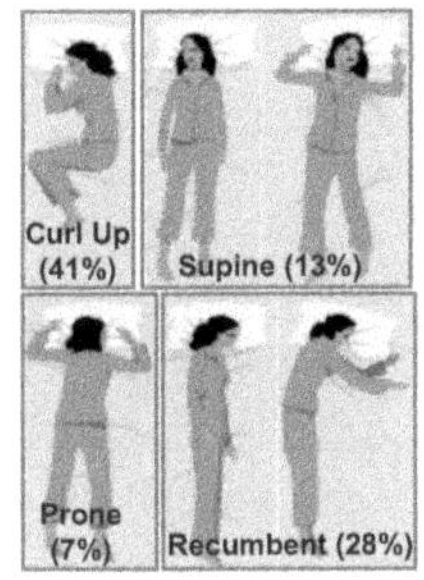

(b) Different sleep postures in bed [25].

Figure 10: Setup of relative position of WiFi device and AP and sleeping postures.

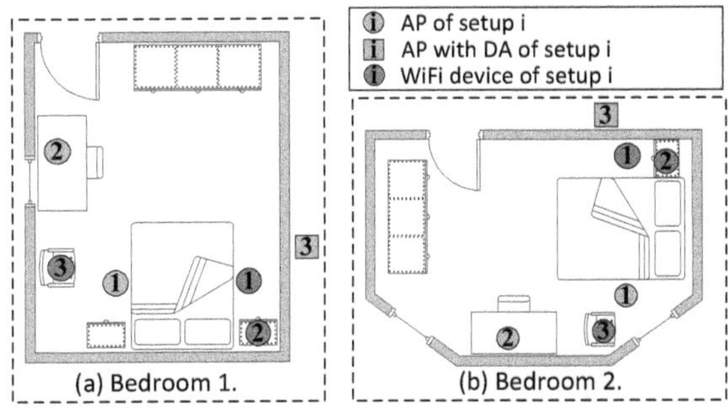

Figure 11: Two apartment setup.

7.2 Experimental Methodology

The experiments are conducted in both lab and two apartments with 6 participants over a three-months time period. The lab environment is a large room with office cubic around. It is used to study the impact of various factors such as obstacles, the various distances between the AP and the WiFi device, and sleep postures. The participants lie on a bed and control their breathing rate to follow various steady beats from a metronome, which is set to a rhythm ranging from $12bpm$ to $18bpm$.

We also conduct experiments in two apartments with different bedroom sizes. Figure 11 illustrates the environmental setup in two bedrooms, in which both beds are queen size. The smaller one (i.e., bedroom 1) has the size of about $12ft \times 9ft$, whereas the larger one (i.e., bedroom 2) is about $15ft \times 12ft$. As shown in Figure 11, we have three setups in both apartments: setup 1 is the ideal scenario where the AP and WiFi device are placed at two sides of the bed. This setup is useful for persons who want to optimize the performance of the vital signs monitoring during sleep. Setup 2 represents a typical scenario where there is a AP inside the room and a WiFi device, such as smartphone, laptop or tablet, is put on the bed table. Setup 2 has larger distance between the AP and the WiFi device than setup 1. Setup 3 is a challenging scenario where the AP and the WiFi device are placed in different rooms with a concrete wall between them. The distance between the AP and the WiFi device is the largest among three setups. In this setup, we utilize directional antennas (i.e., TL-ANT2406A) to enhance the reception of WiFi signals. The ground truths of breathing and heart rates are monitored by the NEULOG Respiration

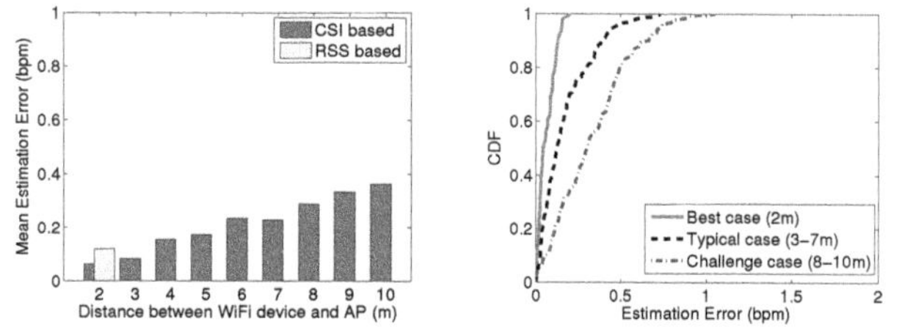

(a) Mean estimation error. (b) CDF of estimation error.

Figure 12: Performance under different distances between WiFi device and AP.

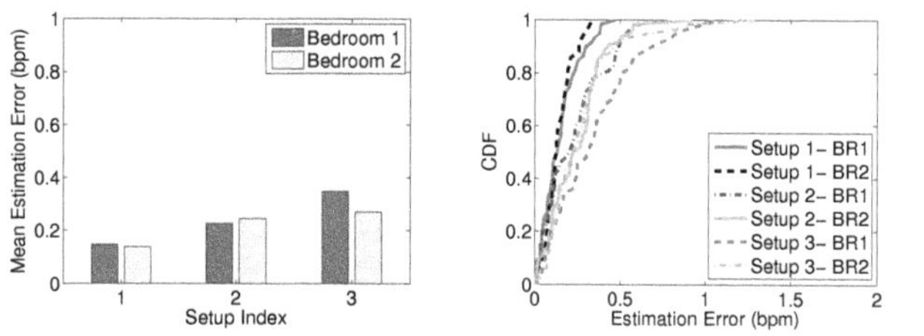

(a) Mean estimation error. (b) CDF of estimation error.

Figure 13: Performance in two real apartments.

Monitor Logger Sensor [22] and a fingertip pulse oximeter, respectively.

7.3 Evaluation of Breathing Rate Estimation

We evaluate the overall performance of breathing rate estimation under different scenarios including different distances between the AP and WiFi, evaluation in two real apartments and two persons in bed case.

7.3.1 Effect of Device Distance

As typical bedroom has limited space, we choose a large lab environment to study the performance of breathing rate estimation under various distances. The AP and the WiFi devices are placed at two sides of the bed (i.e., *P0* setup in Figure 10(a)) with distances from 2 to 10 meters. Figure 12(a) presents the mean error in terms of beat per minute (bpm) of breathing rate estimation under different distances when there is a single person in bed. Overall, we observe that the mean estimation error of our breathing rate estimation is lower than $0.4bpm$, which demonstrates that our system is very accurate across different distances including very large distances such as 5 to 10 meters. In addition, shorter distance between the AP and the WiFi device results in better performance. For example, the mean error is within $0.2bpm$ when the distance is under 5 meters. This is because the received WiFi signals are stronger with shorter communication distances, providing more reliable measurements to capture the minute movements of breathing. Comparing to the result of existing work using RSS [10] which only tested with the distance of $2m$, as shown in yellow bar in Figure 12(a), our system provides significantly better performance (i.e., the error is reduced by about 67%). Figure 12(b) depicts the Cumulative Density Function (CDF) of the breathing rate estimation error for three categories of distances between the AP and WiFi device: *best case* (i.e., $2m$), *typical case* (i.e., $3m$-$7m$ covering mid-sized bedrooms), and *challenging case* (i.e., $8m$-$10m$ covering huge-sized bedrooms). As we can see that for both *best case* and *typical case*, over 90% estimation errors are less than $0.4bpm$. Even for the *challenging case*, over 80% of estimation errors are smaller than $0.5bpm$. This suggests that our system can achieve highly accurate breathing rate estimation by using a single pair of AP and WiFi device. And it supports large distance between them.

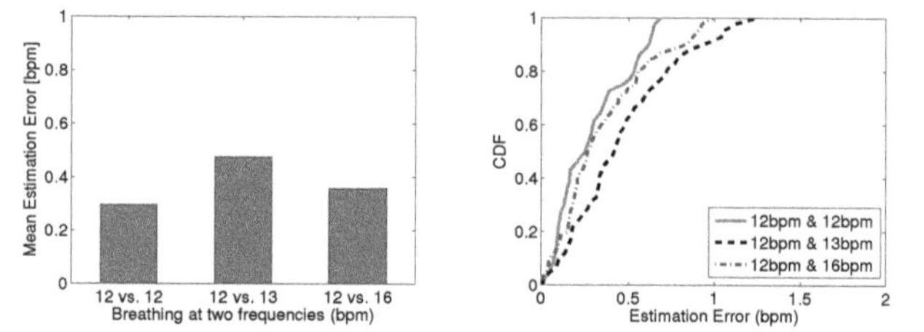

(a) Mean estimation error. (b) CDF of estimation error.

Figure 14: Breathing rate estimation of two persons in bed.

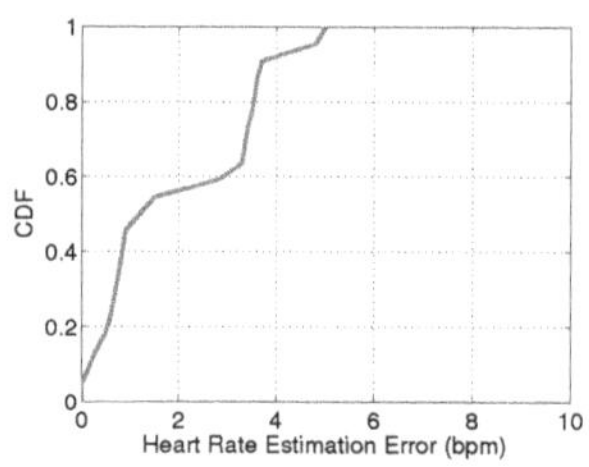

Figure 15: Performance of heart rate estimation.

7.3.2 Evaluation in Real Apartments

We next evaluate the breathing rate estimation in two different-size apartment bedrooms with different deployments of the AP and WiFi device, as shown in Figure 11. Figure 13(a) presents the mean estimation error for each setup in two bedrooms. We find that the setup 1 achieves the lowest estimation error of about $0.15bpm$ in both bedrooms due to the shortest distance between the AP and WiFi device. The estimation error of setup 2 increases as the distance between two devices increases. Still, setup 2 has the estimation error as low as $0.22bpm$ and $0.24bpm$ in bedroom 1 and bedroom 2, respectively. In addition, we observe that although setup 3 involves the obstacle (i.e., a 6-inch wall) that blocks the line-of-sight signal transmission and longer distance between the AP and WiFi device, we can still achieve less than $0.3bpm$ mean estimation error with a single pair of AP and WiFi device. Moreover, Figure 13(b) shows that more than 80% estimation errors are less than $0.5bpm$ for all of those three setups in two real bedrooms, indicating that our system is accurate and robust in real apartment environments. The above results show that our system provides effective breathing rate monitoring under various distances of WiFi device and AP and is robust across different environments.

7.3.3 Two Persons in Bed Case

We further test our system with two persons in bed using bedroom 1 setup. The AP and WiFi device are placed at two sides of the bed with the distance of $3m$. Two participants are breathing with different rates as: $\{12bpm, 12bpm\}$, $\{12bpm, 13bpm\}$ and $\{12bpm, 16bpm\}$). Figure 14 depicts the mean estimation error and the CDF of the breathing estimation error. We observe that the mean error is within $0.5bpm$ for all combination of different breathing rates. In addition, we find that over 90% of estimation errors are less than $1bpm$, which is comparable to that of commercial physical contact devices (e.g., zephyr[26]). Given that we only use a single pair of AP and WiFi device, such accuracy of breathing rate monitoring is very encouraging.

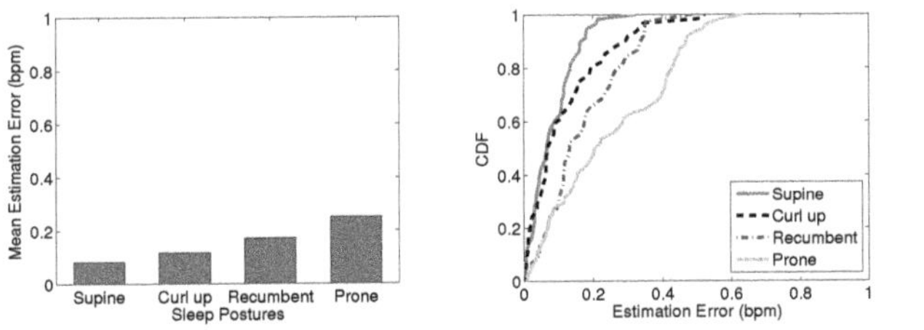

(a) Mean estimation error. (b) CDF of estimation error.

Figure 16: Effect of sleep postures.

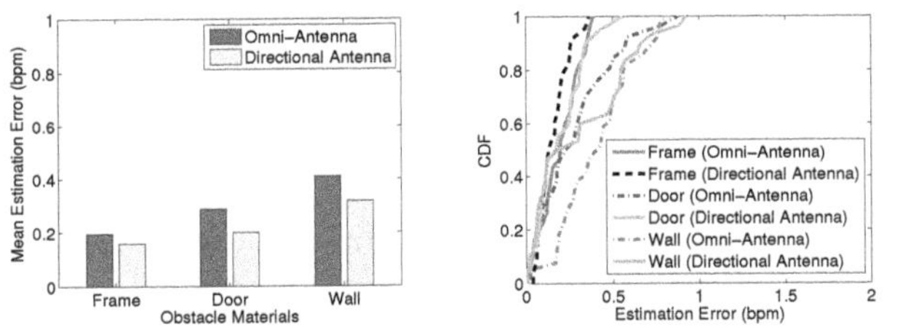

(a) Mean estimation error. (b) CDF of estimation error.

Figure 17: Effect of obstacle between WiFi device and AP.

7.4 Performance of Heart Rate Estimation

Figure 15 illustrates the CDF of heart rate estimation error when one person is in bed using setup 1 in bedroom 1 with the AP equipped with directional antennas. We observe that about 57% of estimation errors are less than $2bpm$ and over 90% of estimation errors are less than $4bpm$. The results are very encouraging as our system achieves comparable accuracy to that of commercial sensors, e.g., Zephyr [26] and SleepIQ [15]. Comparing with these commercial products, our system re-uses existing WiFi network without dedicated/wearable sensors or additional cost. Our system thus is able to support large-scale deployment and long-term vital signs monitoring in non-clinical settings. To the best of our knowledge, our work is the first to achieve device-free heart rate estimation leveraging off-the-shelf WiFi.

7.5 Impact of Various Factors

In this subsection, we perform detailed study of breathing rate estimation under various factors.

7.5.1 *Sleep Postures*

We experiment with different sleep postures as shown in Figure 10(b). The AP and laptop are placed at two sides of the bed with the distance of $3m$. Figure 16(a) compares the mean error of breathing rate estimation resulted from different sleep postures. Overall, our system achieves less than $0.3bpm$ mean error for all sleep postures, which demonstrates the effectiveness and robustness of our system. In particular, the mean estimation errors of supine, curl up, and recumbent positions are about $0.07bpm$, $0.1bpm$ and $0.158pm$, respectively. Figure 16(b) shows the CDF curves of estimation error for all postures. We find that our system can obtain less than $0.2bpm$ error for more than 80% of typical sleep postures. The prone posture has the largest mean estimation error of about $0.25bpm$ for the reason that the body movements, which are caused by breathing, are mainly in the chest and belly and would be absorbed and blocked by the soft mattress. Still, our system achieves 93% of estimation errors less than $0.5bpm$ for prone posture.

7.5.2 *Obstacles/Walls*

We evaluate our system with obstacles of different materials in between of AP and WiFi device with $P0$ deployment in

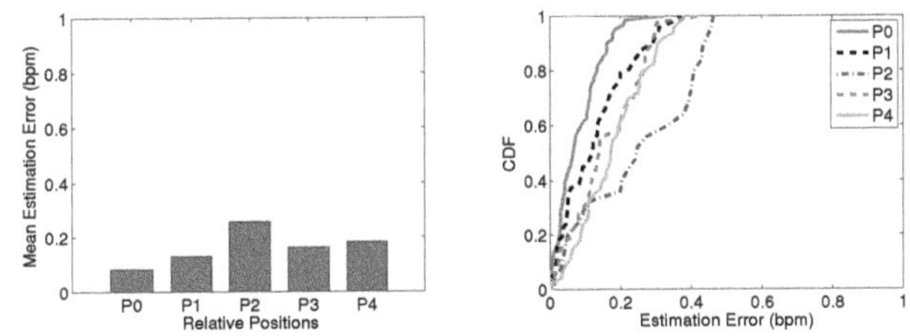

(a) Mean estimation error. (b) CDF of estimation error.

Figure 18: Effect of relative position of WiFi device and AP.

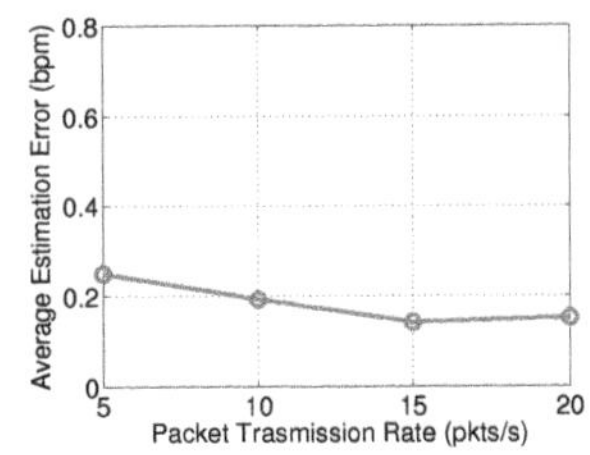

Figure 19: Effect of packet transmission rate.

Figure 10(a). These obstacles are commonly used materials in home environments including a plastic frame of $1inch$, a solid wood door of $2inches$, and a concrete wall of $6inches$. As more and more people use directional antenna to boost the wireless signal reception in home WiFi network, we use both directional and omnidirectional antennas in the experiments. From Figure 17(a), we observe that the mean error is less than $0.4bpm$ for all materials. Obviously, with the concrete wall, the performance is slightly worse than that of door and plastic frame. In addition, by using the directional antenna, the mean error decreases about $0.1bpm$, indicating the directional antenna can enhance the performance of breathing rate estimation due to stronger received signals. Figure 17(b) shows the CDFs of estimation error. We observe that the error is always within $0.5bpm$ and $1bmp$ for the plastic frame and wall respectively. The results show that our system can work under different obstacles and the directional antenna could improve the performance. A more comprehensive study of the system performance in various environments with more obstacles and walls will be presented in our future work.

7.5.3 *Relative Position of WiFi device and AP*

Figure 18(a) shows the mean error of breathing rate estimation under different relative positions of Tx-Rx pair (i.e., the AP and WiFi device), as shown in Figure 10(a). We find that the deployment $P2$ has the largest mean error at about $0.26bpm$ among all deployments (i.e., $P0, P1, P2, P3, P4$) since the WiFi signals are partially blocked by the human body (i.e., head and feet). In addition, Figure 18(b) depicts the CDFs of breathing rate estimation errors. We observe that the estimation errors are all within than $0.5bpm$ even for the worst case deployment $P2$. Above results show that our system is effective under different relative positions of WiFi device-AP pair.

7.5.4 *Packet Transmission Rate*

As higher packet transmission rate results in more CSI measurements for vital signs monitoring, we are interested in how the packet rate affects the performance of our system. Furthermore, we study whether our system can work with existing WiFi beaconing packets. Figure 19 presents the mean breathing rate estimation error versus packet transmission rate when varying the transmission rate from $5pkt/s$ to $20pkt/s$ using the dataset from apartment experiment (i.e., Bedroom 1, setup 1). We observe that high packet transmission rate slightly improves the performance. Overall, our system is not very sensitive to packet transmission rate, given the range from $5pkt/s$ to $20pkt/s$. Specifically, when the packet transmission rate is as low as $5pkts/s$ or $10pkts/s$, our system has about $0.24bpm$ and $0.2bpm$ mean estimation error, respectively. As the commercial access points have the beaconing of $10pkts/s$ to broadcast their SSID, our system is able to use such beacons for accurate breathing rate estimation. These results show that our system can not only work with existing AP beaconing packets but also provide accurate breathing rate monitoring with even less packet rate, such as $5pkts/s$.

8. CONCLUSION

In this paper, we show that the WiFi network could be exploited to track vital signs during sleep including breathing and heart rates using only one AP and a single WiFi device. In particular, our system exploits fine-grained channel state information from off-the-shelf WiFi devices to detect the minute movements associated with breathing and heartbeat activities. Our algorithms grounded on CSI information in both time and frequency domain have the capability to estimate the breathing rate of a single person as well as two-person in bed cases. Extensive experiments in both lab and two apartments over a three-month time period confirm that our proposed approach using the existing WiFi network can achieve comparable or even better accuracies as compared to existing dedicated sensor based approaches. This WiFi-based approach opens up a new direction in performing device-free and low-cost vital sign monitoring during sleep in non-clinical settings.

9. ACKNOWLEDGEMENT

We thank our shepherd, Dr. Lili Qiu, and the anonymous reviewers for their insightful feedbacks. This work was partially supported by the National Science Foundation Grants CNS-1217387, SES-1450091, CNS-1464092 and CNS-1318748.

10. REFERENCES

[1] "Sleep apnea: What is sleep apnea?" *NHLBI: Health Information for the Public. U.S. Department of Health and Human Services*, 2010.

[2] P. X. Braun, C. F. Gmachl, and R. A. Dweik, "Bridging the collaborative gap: Realizing the clinical potential of breath analysis for disease diagnosis and monitoring–tutorial," *IEEE Sensors Journal*, vol. 12, no. 11, pp. 3258–3270, 2012.

[3] G. S. Chung, B. H. Choi, K. K. Kim, Y. G. Lim, J. W. Choi, D.-U. Jeong, and K. S. Park, "Rem sleep classification with respiration rates," in *6th International Special Topic Conference on Information Technology Applications in Biomedicine (ITAB)*. IEEE, 2007, pp. 194–197.

[4] C. A. Kushida, M. R. Littner, T. Morgenthaler, C. A. Alessi, D. Bailey, J. Coleman Jr, L. Friedman, M. Hirshkowitz, S. Kapen, M. Kramer *et al.*, "Practice parameters for the indications for polysomnography and related procedures: an update for 2005," *Sleep*, vol. 28, no. 4, pp. 499–521, 2005.

[5] Y. Chen, D. Misra, H. Wang, H.-R. Chuang, and E. Postow, "An x-band microwave life-detection system," *IEEE Transactions on Biomedical Engineering*, vol. 33, no. 7, pp. 697–701, 1986.

[6] J. Salmi and A. F. Molisch, "Propagation parameter estimation, modeling and measurements for ultrawideband mimo radar," *IEEE Transactions on Antennas and Propagation*, vol. 59, no. 11, pp. 4257–4267, 2011.

[7] F. Adib, Z. Kabelac, H. Mao, D. Katabi, and R. C. Miller, "Demo: Real-time breath monitoring using wireless signals," in *MobiCom*, 2014.

[8] F. Adib, Z. Kabelac, and D. Katabi, "Multi-person motion tracking via rf body reflections," *MIT technical report*, 2014.

[9] N. Patwari, L. Brewer, Q. Tate, O. Kaltiokallio, and M. Bocca, "Breathfinding: A wireless network that monitors andlocates breathing in a home," *IEEE Journal of Selected Topics in Signal Processing*, vol. 8, no. 1, pp. 30–42, 2014.

[10] O. J. Kaltiokallio, H. Yigitler, R. Jäntti, and N. Patwari, "Non-invasive respiration rate monitoring using a single cots tx-rx pair," in *IPSN*, 2014, pp. 59–70.

[11] Fitbit, http://www.fitbit.com/.

[12] Jawbone Up, https://jawbone.com/up.

[13] Sleep as Android, https://sites.google.com/site/sleepasandroid/.

[14] T. Hao, G. Xing, and G. Zhou, "isleep: unobtrusive sleep quality monitoring using smartphones," in *Sensys*, 2013.

[15] SleepIQ, http://bamlabs.com/.

[16] J. Penne, C. Schaller, J. Hornegger, and T. Kuwert, "Robust real-time 3d respiratory motion detection using time-of-flight cameras," *International Journal of Computer Assisted Radiology and Surgery*, vol. 3, no. 5, pp. 427–431, 2008.

[17] Y. Wang, J. Liu, Y. Chen, M. Gruteser, J. Yang, and H. Liu, "E-eyes: device-free location-oriented activity identification using fine-grained wifi signatures," in *MobiCom*, 2014, pp. 617–628.

[18] J. F. Murray, *The normal lung: the basis for diagnosis and treatment of pulmonary disease*. Saunders, 1986.

[19] P. Sebel, M. Stoddart, R. Waldhorn, C. Waldman, and P. Whitfield, *Respiration, the breath of life*. Torstar Books New York, 1985.

[20] "Target heart rates - aha," *Target Heart Rates. American Heart Association*, 2014.

[21] L. Davies and U. Gather, "The identification of multiple outliers," *Journal of the American Statistical Association*, vol. 88, no. 423, pp. 782–792, 1993.

[22] "NEULOG Respiration Monitor Logger Sensor," http://www.neulog.com/.

[23] W. Xi, J. Zhao, X. Li, K. Zhao, S. Tang, X. Liu, and Z. J., "Electronic frog eye: Counting crowd using wifi," in *INFOCOM*, 2014.

[24] D. Halperin, W. Hu, A. Sheth, and D. Wetherall, "Tool release: gathering 802.11 n traces with channel state information," *ACM SIGCOMM Computer Communication Review*, vol. 41, no. 1, pp. 53–53, 2011.

[25] "Sleep position gives personality clue," 2003, http://news.bbc.co.uk/2/hi/health/3112170.stm.

[26] Zephyr Technology, http://zephyranywhere.com/.

UbiBreathe: A Ubiquitous non-Invasive WiFi-based Breathing Estimator

Heba Abdelnasser
Computer and Sys. Eng. Dep.
Alexandria University
heba.abdelnasser@alexu.edu.eg

Khaled A. Harras
Computer Science Dep.
Carnegie Mellon University
kharras@cs.cmu.edu

Moustafa Youssef
Wireless Research Center
E-JUST
moustafa.youssef@ejust.edu.eg

ABSTRACT

Monitoring breathing rates and patterns helps in the diagnosis and potential avoidance of various health problems. Current solutions for respiratory monitoring, however, are usually invasive and/or limited to medical facilities. In this paper, we propose a novel respiratory monitoring system, *UbiBreathe*, based on ubiquitous off-the-shelf WiFi-enabled devices. Our experiments show that the received signal strength (RSS) at a WiFi-enabled device held on a person's chest is affected by the breathing process. This effect extends to scenarios when the person is situated on the line-of-sight (LOS) between the access point and the device, even without holding it. *UbiBreathe* leverages these changes in the WiFi RSS patterns to enable ubiquitous non-invasive respiratory rate estimation, as well as apnea detection.

We propose the full architecture and design for *UbiBreathe*, incorporating various modules that help reliably extract the hidden breathing signal from a noisy WiFi RSS. The system handles various challenges such as noise elimination, interfering humans, sudden user movements, as well as detecting abnormal breathing situations. Our implementation of *UbiBreathe* using off-the-shelf devices in a wide range of environmental conditions shows that it can estimate different breathing rates with less than 1 breaths per minute (bpm) error. In addition, *UbiBreathe* can detect apnea with more than 96% accuracy in both the device-on-chest and hands-free scenarios. This highlights its suitability for a new class of anywhere respiratory monitoring.

Categories and Subject Descriptors

J.3 [**Computer Applications**]: Life and Medical Sciences

Keywords

Non-invasive breathing monitoring; WiFi-based breathing estimation; apnea detection; device-free activity recognition

1. INTRODUCTION

Monitoring breathing rates is an important predictor of a number of serious problems such as cardiac arrests, strokes, or chronic obstructive pulmonary diseases [7,28]. Existing breathing monitors used in hospitals typically require special devices attached to the human body (e.g. a mask or a nasal cannula). These special devices are usually annoying for patients, limit their movement, and more importantly are not appropriate for remote patient monitoring. The camera on a mobile phone has also been used to measure the respiration rate of a user by analyzing the user's chest motion [31]. This approach, however, requires a certain amount of light to work properly, and therefore, cannot for instance be used to monitor a sleeping infant's breathing rate in a dark room. In addition, in other scenarios, the mobile phone camera usage would quickly consume the battery power, and raise privacy concerns. Recently, a number of RF-based techniques, e.g. [5, 6, 9, 21, 29] have been proposed for contact-free breathing monitoring. Nevertheless, such systems have a limited range, high cost, and/or high deployment overhead.

In this paper, we present *UbiBreathe*: A system that provides affordable, pervasive, non-intrusive and easy to use/deploy respiration monitoring. *UbiBreathe* is a software-only solution that can work with any WiFi-enabled device without the need of any special hardware, can monitor multiple persons in parallel, detect breathing anomalies, and display the full breathing signal in realtime. The basic idea *UbiBreathe* leverages is that the chest/lungs are large organs, and the inhaling and exhaling motion of a breathing person causes a dominant periodic component in the received WiFi signal at a receiver positioned on the user's chest. This "modulated" WiFi signal due to the breathing process can be analyzed to extract different useful information about the person's breathing pattern. Moreover, this effect extends to the scenario when the person is on the line-of-sight (LOS) between the AP and WiFi-enabled device, without carrying any device. This is particularly useful in appli-

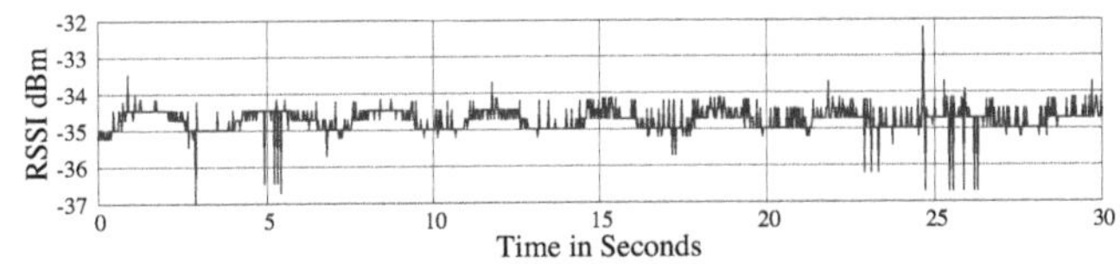

(a) Raw measured WiFi signal strength.

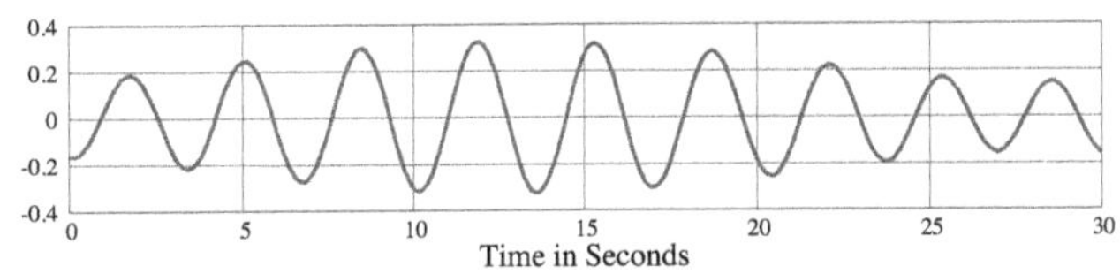

(b) The breathing waveform after processing by *UbiBreathe*.

Figure 1: *UbiBreathe* can extract the embedded breathing signal from the noisy signal strength. The ground truth breathing rate is 18 bpm.

MobiHoc'15, June 22–25, 2015, Hangzhou, China.

DOI: http://dx.doi.org/10.1145/2746285.2755969 .

cations such as in-home sleep apnea diagnostic systems for the elderly, or monitoring a baby's respiration while sleeping to avoid Sudden Infant Death Syndrome (SIDS), which is the leading cause of death among infants one month to one year old [23].

We present the *UbiBreathe* system architecture along with the details of how it can extract the breathing signal and different respiratory information from the noisy WiFi received signal strength (RSS), while handling different practical challenges. An example of a typical RSS input and resulting output from our *UbiBreathe* system is shown in Figure 1. To obtain such output, *UbiBreathe* employs a number of processing modules to reduce the effect of interfering humans, handle sudden user movement, and detect outliers. Moreover, *UbiBreathe* analyzes the extracted breathing signal in realtime and raises alarms about the loss of the breathing signal, indicating the presence of apnea.

We implement *UbiBreathe* using standard WiFi APs, laptops, and cell phones, and evaluate its performance in two different environments including a typical apartment, and one floor in our engineering building, under varying environmental parameters. Overall, our results show that *UbiBreathe* can achieve a high breathing rate detection accuracy of less than 1 breaths per minute (bpm) error for different breathing rates. In addition, it can detect apnea with more than 92% accuracy and less than 10% false positive and false negative rates based on the readings of a single AP. This accuracy further increases to 96% and less than 4% false positive and false negative rates based on the RSS of five overheard APs.

In summary, our contributions are three-fold:

- We present the design and architecture of a non-intrusive system for estimating breathing rates and detecting apnea using off-the-shelf WiFi-enabled devices. The system works in both device-on-chest and hands-free scenarios.

- We present the details of different signal processing modules to handle a number of practical scenarios covering noise reduction, human interference, sudden user movement, and signal outliers.

- We implement the system on different Android devices and thoroughly evaluate it in two different testbeds under different environmental conditions, interfering users, and operational scenarios.

The remainder of this paper is organized as follows. Section 2 provides an overview on related work. Section 3 presents the architecture and overview of *UbiBreathe* followed by a detailed description of various system components in Section 4. The evaluation setup and system assessment in real environments are detailed in Section 5. Finally, we conclude and discuss future work in Section 6.

2. RELATED WORK

We break down prior work related to our system into recent breathing monitoring systems and the state-of-the-art WiFi-based event detection systems.

2.1 Respiration Monitoring Systems

Respiration monitoring systems often used in hospitals typically require special *contact-based* devices attached to the human body. Capnometers [24], for example, are widely used in practice and require patients to have a mask or nasal cannula constantly attached to them. Photoplethysmography (PPG) [41], an optical technique used to detect blood volume changes in the microvascular tissues by illuminating the skin and measuring light absorbtion changes, is also used by hospitals in ICUs via sensors attached to a patient's finger (e.g. pulse oximeters) to monitor breathing and heart rates. These solutions, however, use special hardware, may be annoying to the user, limit her movement, and may not be suitable for remote patient monitoring at home.

Along the same line, recent studies have demonstrated the feasibility of measuring heart rates by placing the index finger over a cellphone camera with its flash turned on or through special heart rate sensors (e.g. as in the Samsung Galaxy S5 phone). The camera or sensor records the light absorbed by the finger tissue, and from that video, each frame is processed by splitting each pixel into RGB components whose values can be used to acquire a PPG signal [14, 30, 38]. Mobile phones have also been shown to measure the respiration rate of a user by analyzing the chest motion [31]. These camera-based or sensor-based solutions share the drawbacks of consuming a lot of the scarce phone energy, requiring a certain amount of light to work properly (therefore not suitable for monitoring a person sleeping in a dark room), requiring special sensors, requiring direct contact with the user skin, and/or raising privacy concerns.

Due to skin sensitivity and other issues that inhibit attaching sensors to the body, *contact-free* RF respiration monitoring devices were proposed including microwave doppler radars [5, 9], ultra-wideband (UWB) radars [6, 21], and ISM-based systems [15, 29]. These systems can provide high accuracy in respiration rate detection due to the special frequency band used and/or dense device deployment. However, their main drawbacks are the limited range of high frequency devices used, as well as their high cost. In addition, [15] uses special ZigBee devices with high gain directional antennas.

UbiBreathe, on the other hand, provides a ***software-only solution*** that uses off-the-shelf WiFi devices installed on a ubiquitous scale and available in various user devices. It can provide accurate estimation with only one AP-device pair. However, it has to deal with the challenges associated with the WiFi signal characteristics and low device density.

2.2 WiFi-based Event Detection Systems

With the ubiquity of WiFi-enabled devices and infrastructure, various WiFi-based event detection systems have been proposed. For example, device-free activity recognition relying on RSSI fluctuations, or the more detailed channel state information (CSI) in standard WiFi networks, have emerged as ubiquitous solutions for presence detection [1, 4, 10–12, 18, 20, 34, 36, 40, 44], tracking individuals [19, 33, 35, 39], recognition of different human activities [3, 8, 16, 42], and gesture recognition systems [2, 32].

UbiBreathe extends these systems to a new domain: ubiquitous health-care. It monitors breathing signal information of multiple users simultaneously (each user needs to carry her own device), and provides apnea detection capabilities.

3. SYSTEM OVERVIEW

The goal of *UbiBreathe* is to monitor the breathing of a person by exploiting resulting fluctuations in standard WiFi signals using off-the-shelf mobile devices. The basic idea *UbiBreathe* leverages is that a dominant periodic component is introduced in the received WiFi signal as a result of the volume change in the chest/lungs when a person is inhaling and exhaling. Therefore, the WiFi RSS can be analyzed to extract different useful information about the person's breathing pattern. For simplicity of illustration, we present the current and following sections assuming that the mobile device is held on the person's chest. However, the same principles apply to the hands-free mode of operation, where the person is away from

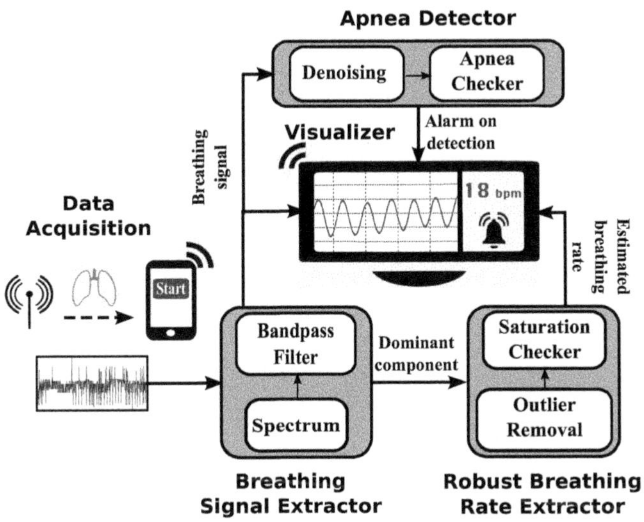

Figure 2: *UbiBreathe* architecture. *UbiBreathe* has four components: Breathing Signal Extractor, Robust Breathing Rate Extractor, Apnea Detector, and Realtime Visualizer modules.

the mobile device but in the line-of-sight between a transmitter and a receiver (e.g. an AP or any other WiFi-enabled device). We quantify the system accuracy for both configurations in Section 5.

The architecture of our system, depicted in Figure 2, includes four major modules: the Breathing Signal Extractor, the Robust Breathing Rate Extractor, the Apnea Detector, and the Realtime Visualizer. All modules can be run on the user device, offloaded to the cloud, or to a local user device (e.g. a nearby laptop) [25, 26]. The process starts when the user activates the breathing estimation process through the system GUI on her phone. This trigger-based activation helps in reducing the system's energy consumption, as it is not running all the time; this activation also partially reduces the effect of interference. The data acquisition module on the user's mobile device then begins collecting the WiFi received signal strength (RSS) in realtime.

Overall, the system modules operate as follows. The RSS is first processed by the *Breathing Signal Extractor* module that filters the noise from the input signal and extracts the breathing signal from sliding windows over the input RSS stream as well as the instantaneous breathing rate in realtime. The extracted breathing signal is then passed to the *Robust Breathing Rate Extractor* module that filters outliers and provides a more stable signal reading (e.g. for the patient's chart) by fusing the different estimates over successive windows. The *Apnea Detector* module applies further denoising techniques to the breathing signal and accordingly checks for the absence of the breathing pattern. Finally, the *Realtime Visualizer* module combines the output of the different modules in a user friendly visual output and raises alarms when an apnea is detected.

We note that different information can be dispatched to different user devices. For example, the full information (full breathing signal, instantaneous rate, and apnea alarm) can be displayed on the user's nearby laptop or sent over the Internet for remote monitoring by a health-care facility or a close family member. Alternatively, a single time reading can be displayed on the user's cell phone after a stable reading is obtained (indicated by an audible beep); or an apnea alarm can be sent to the cell phone of the parent of a monitored sleeping child.

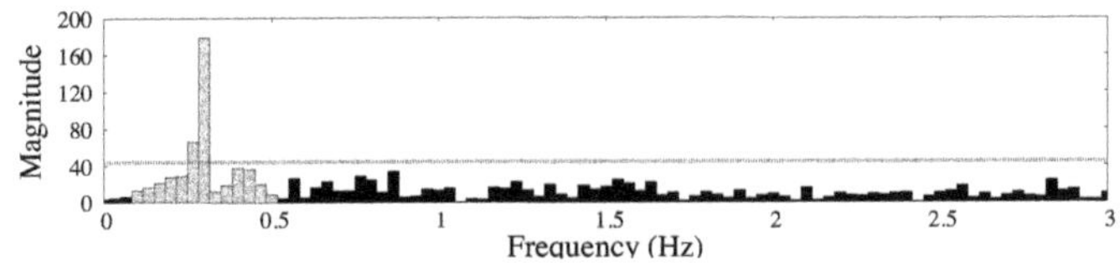

Figure 3: The FFT of the raw WiFi signal in Figure 1. A band pass filter (red frequencies) is applied to the signal spectrum to limit it to the human breathing range (6 to 30 bpm) and remove the DC component. Another filtering stage based on magnitude/energy thresholds is further applied to the band-limited spectrum (horizontal line).

4. THE UBIBREATHE SYSTEM

In this section, we discuss the details of the four modules of the *UbiBreathe* system shown in Figure 2.

4.1 Breathing Signal Extractor

The goal of this module is to extract the full breathing signal from the received noisy WiFi RSS values. We first describe the base operational case with a single steady user and then discuss how *UbiBreathe* handles interfering humans in the environment and sudden actions from these users. The output from this module is fed to all other modules simultaneously for different purposes as described in Section 3.

4.1.1 Basic Operation

Figure 3 shows the Fast Fourier Transform (FFT) for the WiFi signal in Figure 1. The person's breathing rate is 18 breaths per minute (bpm) (i.e. 0.3 Hz). The figure shows that the frequency spectrum of the WiFi signal influenced by the breathing person has a strong component close to the actual breathing rate. This behavior is consistent over different experiments, as we show later in the evaluation section.

UbiBreathe leverages this observation to estimate the breathing rate. In particular, we begin by obtaining the frequency spectrum by applying the FFT to a sliding window of the WiFi raw signal of length n samples taken over W seconds[1]. A band pass filter is then applied to limit the frequencies to those within the range of the normal human breathing rates [22] (red frequencies in Figure 3). The band pass cut-off frequencies are therefore set from 0.1 to 0.5Hz, which correspond to breathing rates between 6 and 30bpm. The breathing rate ($\hat{r}$) is finally estimated as the frequency with the maximum magnitude in the human breathing rate range. More formally:

The breathing rate ($\hat{r}$) is finally estimated as the frequency with the maximum magnitude in the human breathing rate range. More formally:

$$\hat{r} = \underset{r_{min} \le r \le r_{max}}{\arg\max} \; |\text{FFT}(x_{1\ldots n})| \tag{1}$$

where r_{min} is the minimum human respiration rate, r_{max} is the maximum human respiration rate, and $x_{1\ldots n}$ are the RSS values in the current sliding window.

This ***instantaneous*** estimated rate is passed to the next system modules for further processing. To reconstruct the breathing signal, noting that the dominant frequency components in a signal have high energy, we first apply another noise reduction step by trimming all frequencies with low energy, i.e. whose amplitude falls below 25% of the amplitude of the dominant breathing frequency (green line in Figure 3). Finally, an inverse FFT operation is

[1]The effect of these parameters on system performance is analyzed in Section 5.

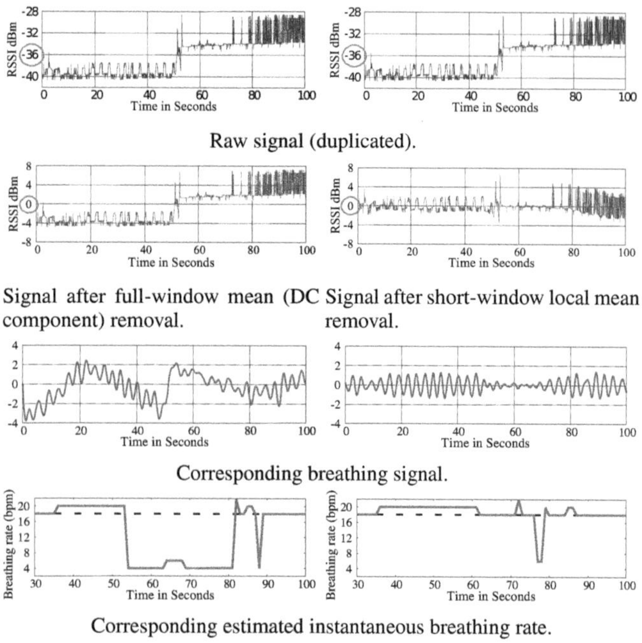

(a) Simple mean removal. (b) **Proposed** sub-window local mean removal.

Figure 4: Different mean removal techniques for handling sudden changes from the user or other interfering humans. Ground truth breathing rate is shown as a horizontal dotted black line. A simple full-window mean (i.e. DC component) removal does not remove the effect of the sudden change at time $t = 52$ sec which affects the estimated breathing rate for an extended period. The proposed sub-window local mean removal technique balances the raw input signal and reduces the sudden change effect.

performed to obtain the time domain breathing signal (Figure 1b), which is passed to the visualization module.

4.1.2 Handling Sudden Changes

Sometimes the user may make a sudden action/move or other users may interfere within the line of sight. These actions can lead to large sudden changes in the RSS, and hence the breathing signal as shown in Figure 4. A simple mean removal (i.e. DC component removal) does not solve this issue as shown in Figure 4a, making the impact of such actions span a long duration as it appears in multiple overlapping FFT windows. To reduce this effect, we apply a ***within-window local*** mean removal technique. Specifically, we subtract from each raw RSS value in the FFT window the mean of a shorter window centered around this value (currently set to 5 seconds in our implementation). This ***local*** mean removal balances the signal and leads to reducing the sudden change effect as shown in Figure 4b.

We note that using multiple RSS streams from ***different heard APs*** further reduces the effect of an external user cutting the LOS with a specific AP. This is not discussed in this paper due to space constraints. In addition, the outlier detection sub-module of the *Robust Breathing Rate Extractor* module described in the next section further diminishes the impact of sudden changes.

4.2 Robust Breathing Rate Extractor

Once both the breathing signal and the *instantaneous* breathing rate are estimated, this module aims to increase the robustness of the breathing rate estimation based on fusing different overlapping

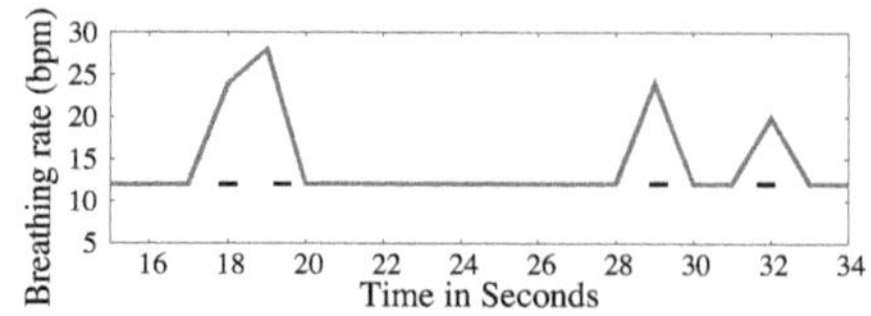

(a) Instantaneous breathing rate ($\hat{r}$), the output of the *Breathing Signal Extractor* module.

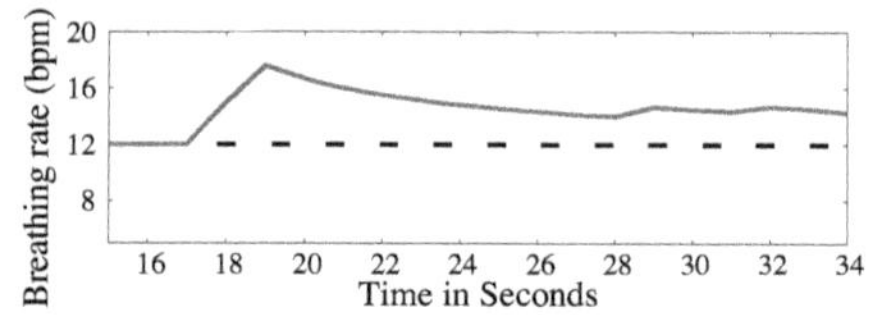

(b) Output after applying a standard moving average filter.

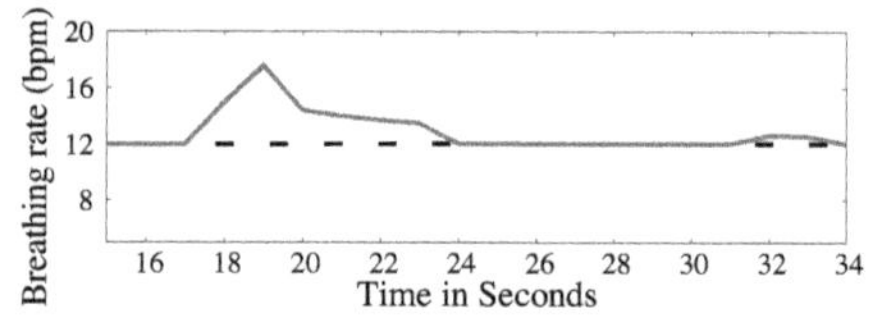

(c) Output after applying a moving α-trimmed mean filter ($\alpha = 0.25$).

Figure 5: Using the α-trimmed mean filter effect for outliers detection. The black dashed line is the ground truth (12bpm). The α-trimmed mean filter converges faster and more accurately to the true value.

consecutive windows. This is particulary useful in scenarios where a single stable reading is needed, e.g. to be logged in the patient's chart. The module contains two sub-modules: the *Outlier Detector* module and *Robustness Enhancement* module.

4.2.1 Outlier Detector

To further reduce the impact of outliers (e.g. the sudden change at time $t = 52$ sec in Figure 4), *UbiBreathe* uses an α-trimmed mean filter [43] over a sliding window of previous instantaneous estimations. An α-trimmed mean filter sorts the values within the input window and then trims the highest and lowest α values. The remaining values are then averaged to obtain the smoothed filter value corresponding to the input window. More formally, given a window of q sorted instantaneous breathing rate estimates ($\hat{r}_i$'s), such that $\hat{r}_1 \leq \hat{r}_2 \leq \cdots \leq \hat{r}_q$, the output of the filter r is given by:

$$r = \frac{1}{q - 2\lceil \alpha q \rceil} \sum_{i=\lceil \alpha q \rceil + 1}^{q - \lceil \alpha q \rceil} \hat{r}_i \qquad (2)$$

where $0 \leq \alpha < 0.5$.

We note that for $\alpha = 0$, the filter is reduced to a standard moving average filter, while for $\alpha = 0.5$, the filter is reduced to a standard median filter. An α-trimmed mean filter has the advantage of handling both impulse and gaussian noise, as compared to median and mean filters that can handle only one of them. Therefore, we set α to 0.25. Figure 5 shows the effect of applying both a standard moving average filter and the α-trimmed mean filter to the output of the *Breathing Signal Extractor* module. The figure shows that the α-trimmed mean filter can successfully reduce the effect of the outliers as well as converge faster and more accurately to the ground truth breathing rate compared to a standard moving average filter.

4.2.2 Robustness Enhancer

Since the breathing signal is continuously changing, *UbiBreathe* can provide a more robust breathing rate estimate compared to the

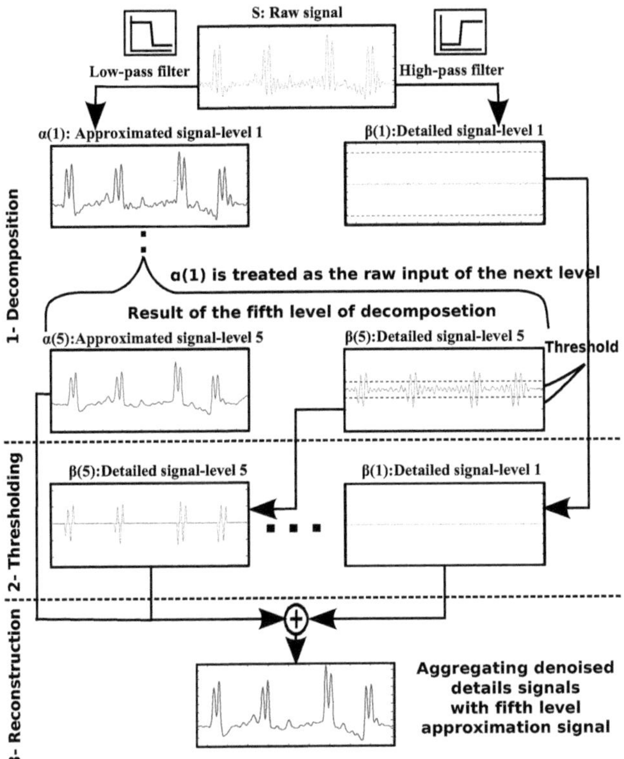

Figure 6: Wavelet Denoising stages: the input signal is first decomposed using high- and low-pass filters. Then the details are thresholded using soft thresholding, such that the wavelet coefficients smaller than a given threshold (the doted blue lines) are set to zero and the coefficients above the threshold reduced by the value of the threshold. Finally, the thresholded coefficients are added to the last level approximation signal to get the reconstructed denoised signal.

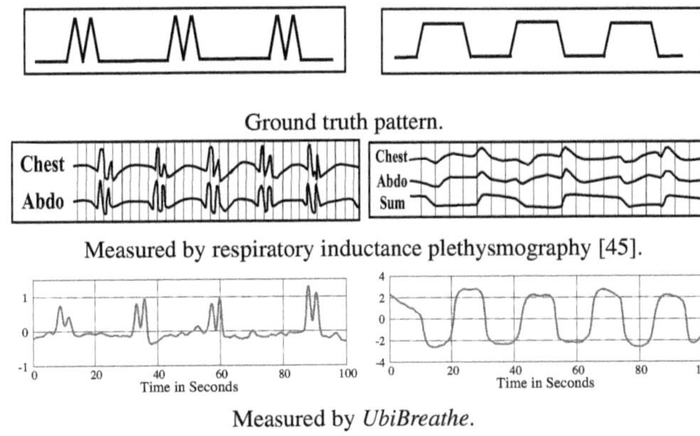

(a) Biot's Respiration: a respiratory pattern characterized by periods or "clusters" of rapid respirations of near equal depth followed by regular periods of apnea.

(b) Apneustic Respiration: has a prolonged inspiratory phase followed by a prolonged expiratory phase commonly believed to be apneic phases [45].

Figure 7: The figures compare between the visualization of respiratory inductance plethysmography that typically uses invasive techniques and the visualization of *UbiBreathe*.

instantaneous output of the α-trimmed mean filter. The idea is to make sure that the breathing rate estimation has saturated. This is achieved by checking whether all breathing rate estimates within the last 10 seconds are consistent within a small error margin (taken as 0.75 bpm in our experiments) or not. For example, the breathing signal starts saturating after 24 seconds in Figure 5c. Note that the system needs to wait for the signal to saturate, introducing a slight delay for the initial robust reading. This initial delay is quantified in the evaluation section and *does not affect the latency of the other modules* that operate in realtime.

4.3 Apnea Detector

This module aims at detecting apnea, which is the cessation of the oro-nasal airflow (i.e. the absence of breathing) for at least 10 seconds in duration [13]. Apnea is the main characteristic that marks almost all abnormal breathing patterns [45]. During apnea, there is no movement of the inhalation muscles and the volume of the lungs remains unchanged. This fact should map to a non-changing RSS signal in *UbiBreathe*, modulo small changes caused by environmental noise. The Apnea Detector module works in two phases: denoising and apnea detection.

4.3.1 *Denoising*

To detect apnea, *UbiBreathe* further removes the noise from the breathing signal using wavelet denoising [37], which is based on the Discrete Wavelet Transform (DWT). In DWT, the generic step splits the signal into two parts: an approximation coefficient vector and a detail coefficient vector. This splitting is applied recursively in a number of steps (i.e. levels), J, to the approximation coefficient vector only to obtain finer details from the signal. At the end, DWT produces a coarse approximation projection (scaling) coefficients $\alpha^{(J)}$, together with a sequence of finer detail projection (wavelet) coefficients $\beta^{(1)}, \beta^{(2)}, ..., \beta^{(J)}$. The DWT coefficients in each level can be computed using the following equations:

$$\alpha_k^{(J)} = \langle x_n, g_{n-2^J k}^{(J)} \rangle_n = \sum_{n \in \mathbb{Z}} x_n \, g_{n-2^J k}^{(J)}, \quad J \in \mathbb{Z} \qquad (3)$$

$$\beta_k^{(\ell)} = \langle x_n, h_{n-2^\ell k}^{(\ell)} \rangle_n = \sum_{n \in \mathbb{Z}} x_n \, h_{n-2^\ell k}^{(\ell)}, \quad \ell \in \{1, 2, ..., J\} \qquad (4)$$

where x_n is the nth input point, $\langle . \rangle$ is the dot product operation, and g's and h's are two sets of discrete orthogonal functions called the wavelet basis (we used the Haar basis functions in our system). The inverse DWT is given by

$$x_n = \sum_{k \in \mathbb{Z}} \alpha_k^{(J)} \, g_{n-2^J k}^{(J)} + \sum_{\ell=1}^{J} \sum_{k \in \mathbb{Z}} \beta_k^{(\ell)} \, h_{n-2^\ell k}^{(\ell)} \qquad (5)$$

Wavelet denoising builds on the DWT as shown in Figure 6 by running through three phases. In the beginning, the raw input signal is subjected to a decomposition phase using DWT to break the signal down into an approximation signal, and a wavelet detail coefficient. This process is conducted recursively to each resulting approximation signal up to five levels. Afterwards, dynamic thresholding is applied to the wavelet detail coefficients resulting from each level to remove their noisy components. Finally, inverse wavelet transform is performed on all the resulting coefficients, in addition to the approximated signal from the last level, to reconstruct a final denoised signal. Compared to other techniques, wavelet denoising runs efficiently in linear time with respect to the size of the input signal. In addition, it does not make any assumptions about the nature of the signal and permits discontinuities in the input signal [27] (similar to those caused by apnea).

4.3.2 Apnea detection

Some of the typical apnea patterns, involving repeated prolonged loss of breath, are shown in Figure 7. To detect the loss of the breathing signal for more than 10 seconds, a sliding moving window of samples covering 10 seconds is used over the denoised input signal. The difference between the maximum and minimum signal values within this window is compared to a threshold (θ). If this difference is below the threshold, then there is no breathing signal and an apnea alarm is raised. More formally, for a given window of denoised samples $y[1..m]$, an alarm is raised if:

$$\max(y[1..m]) - \min(y[1..m]) \underset{\text{No Apnea}}{\overset{\text{Apnea Det.}}{\lessgtr}} \theta \qquad (6)$$

where θ is the detection threshold.

To make apnea detection adapt to dynamic environments, we use a dynamic threshold rather than a fixed one. The threshold (θ) is taken as a percentage (τ) of the range of the last detected breathing signal. We quantify the effect of τ on performance in the evaluation section. Overall, Figure 7 compares the results of *UbiBreathe* when applied to a person emulating the ground truth patterns shown at the top of the figure, with the plethysmography measurements of those with the same apnea pattern.

Finally, *UbiBreathe* leverages multiple RSS streams received from the different APs naturally deployed in an environment to increase the system accuracy and resilience to noise. In this case, a simple majority vote on the detected state (apnea/ normal breathing) from each stream is used to fuse the detection of the different APs for enhanced accuracy.

4.4 Realtime Visualization Module

The goal of the *Realtime Visualization* module is to combine the output of the different system modules in a user friendly manner. In particular, the output from these modules is collected and streamed to a pre-defined user device, e.g. a laptop to show the breathing signal, the breathing rate, as well as raise an audible and visual alarm if apnea is detected.

Among these outputs, the breathing signal is of specific importance. Since abnormal respiratory rates and changes in them are broad indicators of major physiological instability [17], displaying the breathing waveform can help medical practitioners detect different breathing anomalies. In particular, normal ventilation is an automatic, seemingly effortless inspiratory expansion and expiratory contraction of the chest cage. This act of normal breathing has a relatively constant rate and inspiratory volume that together constitute the normal respiratory rhythm (inspiration = expiration). Abnormality may occur in the rate, rhythm, and in the effort of breathing. These properties are clear in the RSS waveform after being processed by *UbiBreathe* as shown in Figure 7. Note that, due to space constraints, we only provide the details for detecting apnea and leave detecting its specific type to future work.

4.5 Discussion

UbiBreathe applies a number of techniques to handle the noisy wireless environment and interfering nearby users. Specifically, using a band pass filter within the normal human breathing rates helps in removing other sources of interference in the frequency spectrum. Moreover, *UbiBreathe* explicitly handles sudden changes in the received WiFi signal using the local mean removal technique. In addition, using the α-trimmed mean filter helps in removing outliers and speeds the convergence time.

The system can leverage multiple APs to increase the accuracy of both the breathing rate estimation and apnea detection as well as reduce the effect of interfering humans that usually interfere with the stream from only one AP.

The design of the user interface that initiates the estimation process based on user request makes the system more resilient to outliers and helps in reducing its computational requirements. In addition, since the measurements are done at the user's device, multiple users can estimate their own breathing rate in ***parallel***, with no cross-interference on each other leveraging the broadcast nature of the wireless channel.

Since human breathing rate is a low frequency signal, the normal beacon transmission rate of WiFi (IEEE 802.11 standard) is well above the Nyquist frequency. This makes *UbiBreathe*'s energy consumption within the normal range required for WiFi operation.

5. EVALUATION

In this section, we analyze the performance of *UbiBreathe* in two typical environments as depicted in Figure 8: (a) An apartment covering a 10×12 m^2 area and consisting of a living room connected to the dining area, three bedrooms, kitchen, and a bathroom. (b) The

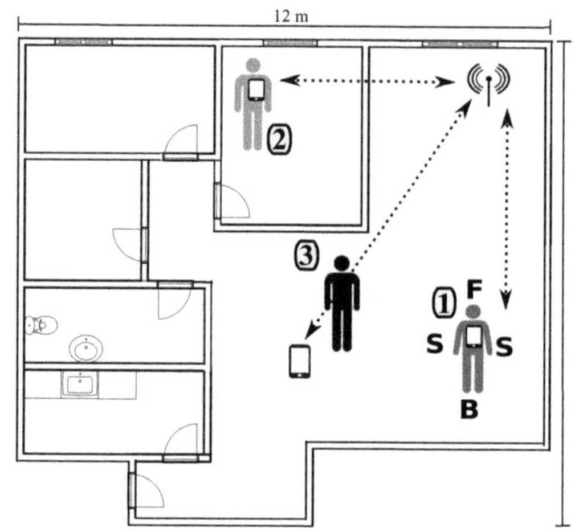

(a) First test environment (apartment).

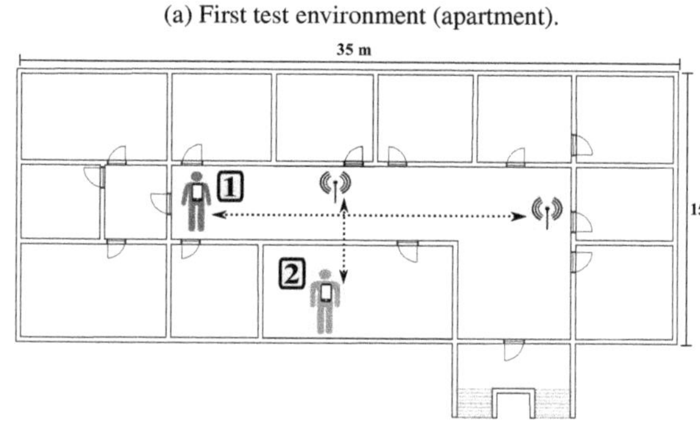

(b) Second test environment (one floor of the engineering building where our lab is located).

Figure 8: Floorplans of the two test environments used for evaluating *UbiBreathe*. The labeled persons denote different *UbiBreathe* scenarios, 1) Holding-the-device: The user is holding the mobile device on her chest. 2) Holding-the-device through-the-wall: The user and AP are in two rooms while the user is holding the mobile device on her chest. 3) Hands-free On LOS: The user is standing between the AP and the device. The orientation characters in holding-the-device scenarios indicate the possible user orientations relative to the AP.

Parameter	Range	Default value
FFT window size (w)	$10-60$ sec	30sec
Sampling rate (Fs)	$1-10$ Hz	10 Hz
Breathing rate ground truth	$12, 18, 24$ bpm	18bpm
Distance between the AP and mobile device	$1-14$ m	8 m
Apnea detection threshold (τ)	33 - 67%	50% , 67%
Number of Streams	1-5	1
Orientation	Front, side, back	Front
Testbeds	Apt., Eng. building	Both

Table 1: Parameter ranges and default values.

second floor of our engineering building which contains 12 rooms connected by a large corridor with a total area of 35×15 m^2.

In both environments, a Samsung Galaxy S4 Mini mobile and a Samsung Galaxy Note II devices as well as an HP EliteBook laptop are used as receivers with the typical WiFi sampling rate of 10Hz. The used APs are Cisco Linksys X2000. We run the experiments with three different users at different times of the day over a period of two weeks. A custom-made breathing metronome application that instructs the users about their breathing rate/time is used to regulate the breathing rate of these users and acts as the ground truth. In all experiments, there were a varying number of interfering users in their normal daily activities, reaching up to three users in the same room, in addition to other unknown persons in the other rooms and offices.

We extensively evaluate *UbiBreathe* in three different scenarios shown in Figure 8: **1) Holding-the-device**: The user is holding the mobile device on her chest, **2) Holding-the-device, through-the-wall**: The user and AP are in two different rooms while the user is holding the mobile device on her chest, and **3) Hands-free On-LOS**: The user is standing between the AP and the device. We evaluate the system accuracy in these three scenarios and then evaluate it for multiple users breathing with different rates. Table 1 shows the default values of the system parameters utilized in our experiments. All accuracy numbers are based on the output of the *Robust Breathing Rate Extractor* module.

5.1 Holding the Device Scenario

In this section, we study the system performance in the holding-the-device scenario under different sampling rates, distances from the AP, and user orientations. Both the LOS and through-the-wall scenarios are evaluated.

5.1.1 Impact of sampling parameters

Figure 9 shows the system performance for different sampling rates (Fs) and different FFT window sizes (parameter w). ***Other parameters are set to their default values as in Table 1.*** The figure shows that, in general, the accuracy of breathing estimation increases with the increase in the FFT window size. However, this accuracy comes at the cost of increasing the ***initial*** latency of the *Robustness Enhancer* module. Using the typical WiFi beaconing rate of 10 Hz, we can obtain a low estimation error of 0.2 bpm using a window size of 30 sec. We use these values for the remainder of our evaluation section.

5.1.2 Impact of distance separating the device and AP

Figure 10 shows the effect of changing the distance between the device and the AP on the system's accuracy. We observe that the

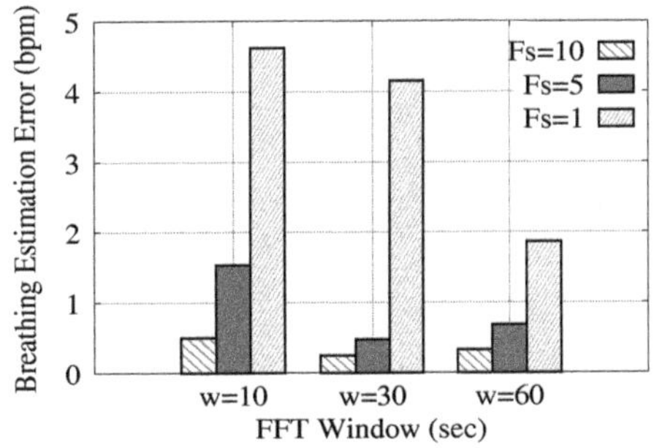

(a) Estimation error.

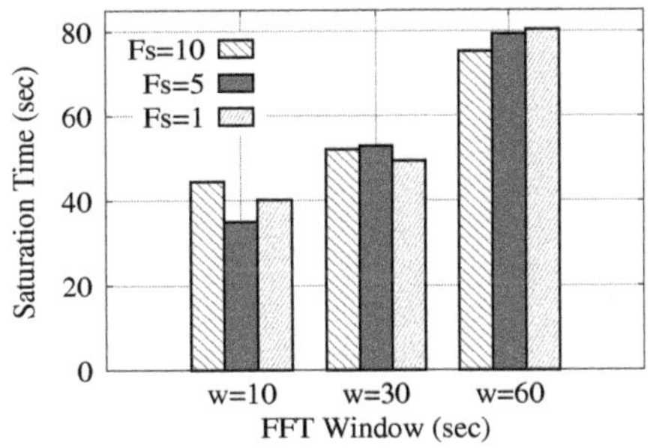

(b) Required **initial** time to saturate (latency of the *Robustness Enhancer* module). Other modules work in ***realtime***.

Figure 9: Effect of sampling parameters on system performance for the device-on-chest scenario. The ground truth breathing rate is 18 bpm. Other parameters are set to their default values in Table 1.

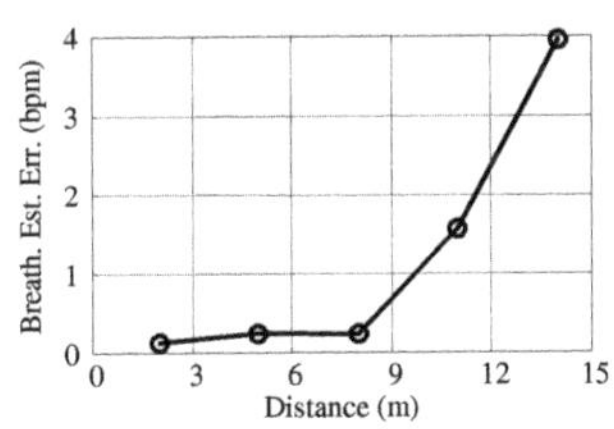

(a) No-wall.

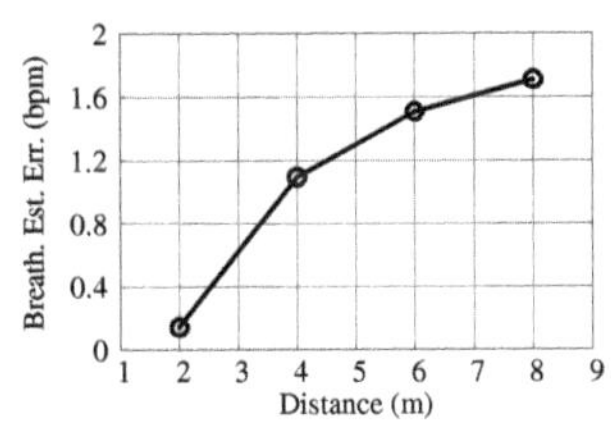

(b) Through-the-wall.

Figure 10: Effect of the distance between the AP and user device on system performance for the device-on-chest scenario.

breathing rate estimation accuracy decreases when increasing the separation distance. This is because a stronger RSS leads to a higher signal-to-noise ratio (SNR) and hence better accuracy. In other words, a weaker signal leads to lower changes in the signal strength in response to the chest movement, leading to less sensitivity. *UbiBreathe*, however, can still be within 1.6bpm from the ground truth for distances up to 11m in the no-wall scenario and 1.7bpm for distances up to 8m in through-the-wall scenario.

5.1.3 Impact of user orientation relative to the AP

Figure 11 shows the effect of different user orientations relative to the AP (front, back, and side) on the accuracy of *UbiBreathe*. We observe that the system achieves the highest performance (estimation error of 0.24bpm) in the front orientation. This result occurs when the user's body is essentially not blocking the LOS, and hence, the received signal is relatively stronger compared to the other orientations. For the other two orientations (side and back), *UbiBreathe* still maintains a high estimation accuracy of less than 2.5bpm error.

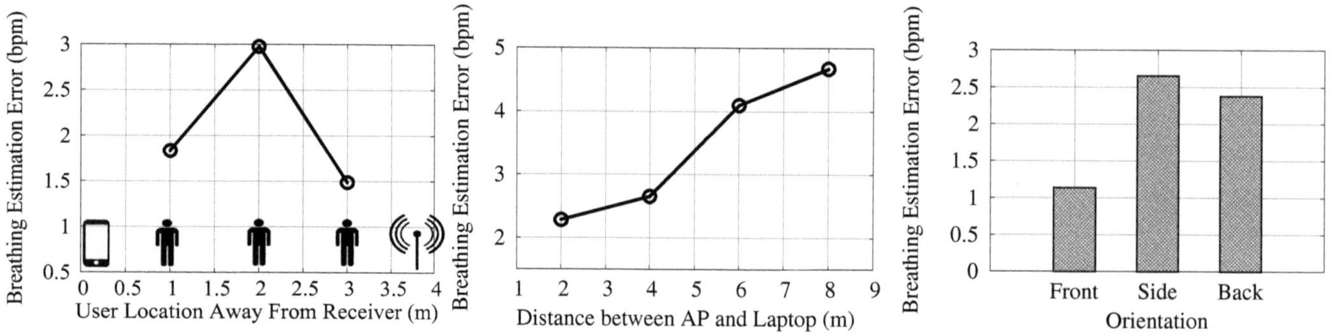

(a) The user at different positions between the AP and mobile device.

(b) Varying the distance between the AP and device with user fixed.

(c) The impact of user orientation relative to the AP.

Figure 12: This figure shows the performance of *UbiBreathe* in terms of breathing estimation error under different hands-free scenarios including: (a) varying the position of the user between the AP and device, (b) varying the distance between the AP and device while keeping the user fixed $1m$ away from the mobile device, and (c) examining the performance with different user orientations.

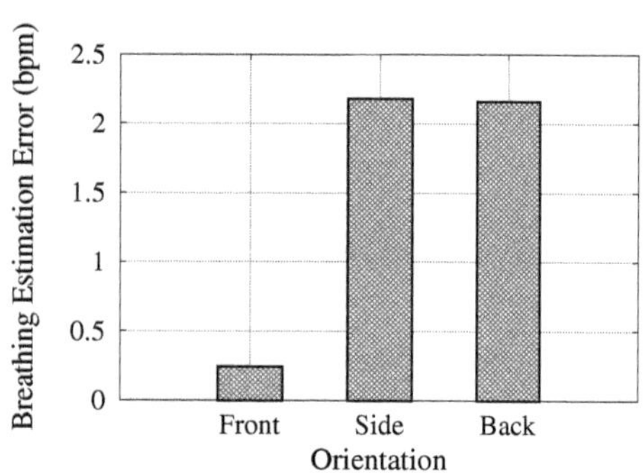

Figure 11: Effect of the user orientation relative to the AP on performance for the device-on-chest scenario.

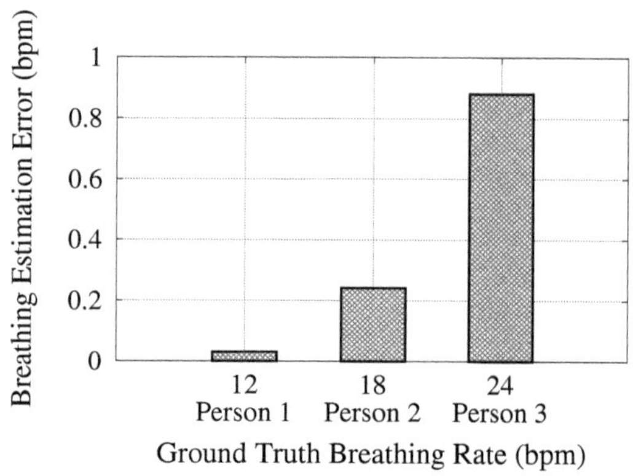

Figure 13: Performance for three concurrent measurements from different persons with different breathing rates.

5.2 Hands-free in LOS Scenario

We now move to the in-LOS scenario (i.e. hands-free scenario) shown in Figure 8 where the user is not carrying the device but rather standing between the AP and device. This scenario is suitable for many applications that require some form of constant monitoring during long periods of time, such as infant or elderly breathing monitoring during their sleep.

5.2.1 Impact of the user distance relative to the device and AP

In this experiment, the distance between the AP and the device is set to 4m, and the error rate is recorded for users situated at different points within this range. Figure 12a shows the results. We can observe that the system's performance is improved when the user is standing near the AP or the mobile device than when she is standing in the middle. This result is due to the fact that when the user is closer to either the transmitter or receiver, she blocks the majority of signal paths between them. Given the application scenarios mentioned earlier, it is highly likely to have users closer to one of the devices (e.g. when a person has a mobile device next to her during sleep).

5.2.2 Impact of distance between the device and AP

In this experiment, we evaluate the system performance for different distances between the AP and device in the hands-free scenario. The purpose of this experiment is to obtain an idea of when the system starts becoming less accurate relative to typical room sizes where such monitoring would take place. The user is stationary at a distance of 1 meter away from the mobile device. Figure 12b shows that, similar to the mobile on chest case, the system performance decreases when the distance between the AP and the mobile device increases due to the noisier signal.

5.2.3 Impact of orientation

Figure 12c shows the effect of different user orientations relative to the AP. The figure shows that, similar to the device on chest case, the system achieves the highest performance in the front orientation, with a worst case accuracy among all orientations of 2.6 bpm error.

5.3 Multiple Persons Case Study

We evaluate the system in the apartment environment using one AP and three users ***concurrently*** holding their devices while breathing with different rates 12, 18, and 24 bpm (as in Figure 8a). The results in Figure 13 show that, since *UbiBreathe* leverages the standard broadcast nature of WiFi networks, different users do not interfere with each other. Higher breathing rates are slightly more challenging to capture due to their corresponding required higher sampling rate. However, within the normal human breathing rate, *UbiBreathe* can achieve a high accuracy of 0.9 bpm error.

5.4 Apnea Detection

In this section, we investigate the system's performance in detecting apnea, i.e. absence of the breathing signal. The distance

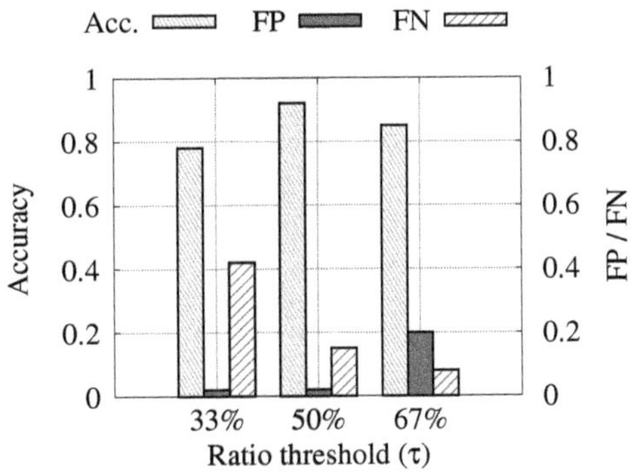

(a) Holding device.

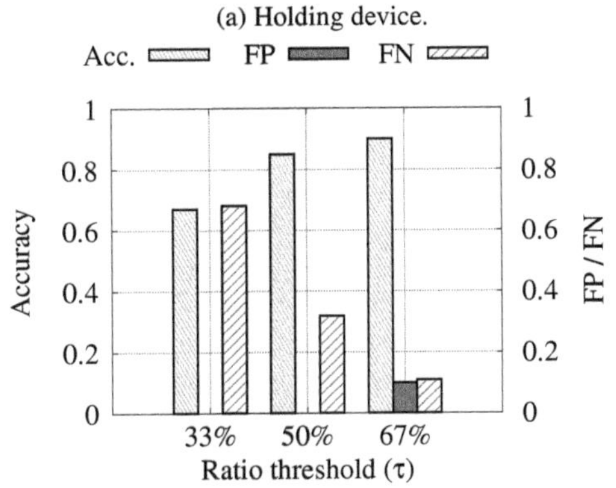

(b) Hands-free.

Figure 14: Apnea detection accuracy for the two modes of operation using a single stream.

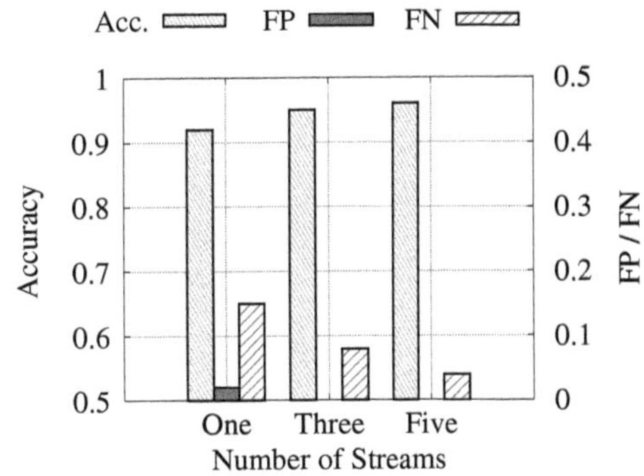

(a) Holding device.

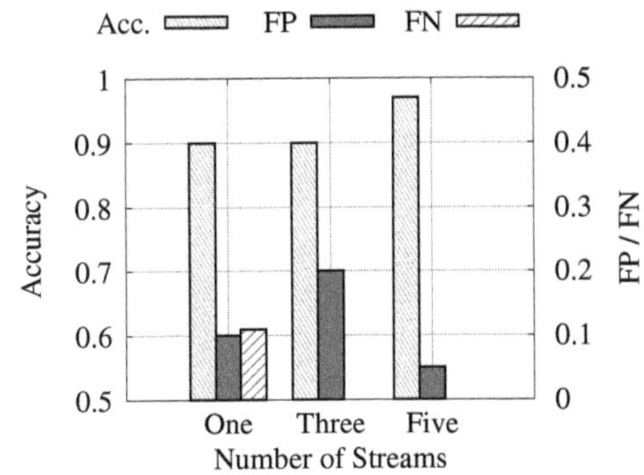

(b) Hands-free.

Figure 15: Apnea detection accuracy for the two modes of operation using multiple streams.

between the device and the AP is set to 2m in this experiment. The users are requested to simulate the breathing pattern in Figure 7b, following the ground truth pattern with the help of our custom-made breathing metronome application.

5.4.1 Impact of detection threshold ratio (τ)

Figure 14 shows the effect of the detection threshold ratio (τ) on accuracy (True positives+True negatives/Total samples), false positive rate, and false negative rate. We observe that, as expected, increasing the detection threshold ratio (τ) reduces the false negative rate while increasing the false positive rate. A value of τ between 50% to 67% leads to the best accuracy of 92% for both the device-on-chest and hands-free scenarios.

5.4.2 Impact of multiple APs

Figure 15 shows the effect of using more than one stream on apnea detection accuracy in the two modes of operation. A majority vote between all streams is used to select the correct state (apnea/normal breathing). The figure shows that increasing the number of streams generally increases the apnea detection performance under all metrics. Using five streams, *UbiBreathe* can achieve at least 96% accuracy and 5% false-negative and false positive rates.

5.5 Summary

The results in this section show that *UbiBreathe*, through its different modules, can achieve a high accuracy of breathing rate extraction with an error less than 1 bpm in different scenarios with interfering humans performing their normal daily activities. This performance accuracy is robust to distances between the AP and device up to 8 m in through-the-wall scenario and 11 m for the no-wall scenario. The front user orientation provides the best accuracy due to the higher SNR. Other orientations still give a decent accuracy, with less than 2.6 bpm error

UbiBreathe can achieve a robust single time reading from its *Robustness Enhancer* sub-module within 50 sec in all scenarios using the default parameters. This initial latency is useful for some applications, e.g. logging in the patient's chart, and does not affect the latency of the other system modules that *all run in realtime*.

The false-negative rate is critical for apnea detection. Our results show that using the WiFi RSS streams from multiple overheard APs decrease the apnea detection false-negative rate to only 4% in the on-chest scenario and zero in the hands-free scenario.

6. CONCLUSION AND FUTURE WORK

We presented *UbiBreathe*: a system for ubiquitous non-intrusive breathing rate monitoring based on the standard WiFi equipment. *UbiBreathe* combines a number of modules to extract the breathing signal from the noisy wireless channel as well as handle abrupt user actions and interfering humans. Implementation of *UbiBreathe* on different off-the-shelf WiFi devices showed that it can achieve a high accuracy of less than 1 bpm error under different realistic deployments in the device-on-chest and hands-free scenarios. Moreover, it can provide a robust reading for the patient's records in less than 50 seconds. *UbiBreathe*, in addition, can detect apnea with more than 96% accuracy with less than 5% false positive and negative rates. This allows it to be used in diverse scenario including remote patient monitoring, automatic early health-issues detection, fitness monitoring, infants sleeping monitoring, among others.

Currently, we are expanding *UbiBreathe* in different directions including detecting the exact apnea types, and performing clinical trials with real patients.

7. REFERENCES

[1] H. Abdel-Nasser et al. MonoPHY: Mono-stream-based device-free WLAN localization via physical layer information. In *IEEE WCNC*, 2013.

[2] H. Abdelnasser et al. WiGest: A ubiquitous WiFi-based gesture recognition system. In *IEEE INFOCOM*, 2015.

[3] A. Al-Husseiny and M. Youssef. RF-Based traffic detection and identification. In *IEEE VTC Fall*, 2012.

[4] H. Aly et al. New insights into WiFi-based device-free localization. In *ACM UbiComp*, 2013.

[5] T. Ballal et al. Breathing rate estimation from a non-contact biosensor using an adaptive IIR notch filter. In *IEEE BioWireleSS*, 2012.

[6] Y. Chen and P. Rapajic. Human respiration rate estimation using ultra-wideband distributed cognitive radar system. *International Journal of Automation and Computing*, 2008.

[7] D. De Backer et al. Influence of respiratory rate on stroke volume variation in mechanically ventilated patients. *Anesthesiology*, 2009.

[8] Y. Ding et al. RFTraffic: passive traffic awareness based on emitted RF noise from the vehicles. In *IEEE ITST*, 2011.

[9] A. D. Droitcour et al. Signal-to-noise ratio in doppler radar system for heart and respiratory rate measurements. *IEEE Microwave Theory and Techniques*, 2009.

[10] K. El-Kafrawy et al. Propagation modeling for accurate indoor WLAN RSS-based localization. In *IEEE VTC*, 2010-Fall.

[11] K. El-Kafrawy et al. Impact of the human motion on the variance of the received signal strength of wireless links. In *PIMRC*, 2011.

[12] A. Eleryan et al. Synthetic generation of radio maps for device-free passive localization. In *IEEE GLOBECOM*, 2011.

[13] A. S. Fauci et al. *Harrison's principles of internal medicine*. McGraw-Hill Medical New York, 2008.

[14] E. Jonathan and M. Leahy. Investigating a smartphone imaging unit for photoplethysmography. *Physiological measurement*, 2010.

[15] O. J. Kaltiokallio et al. Non-invasive respiration rate monitoring using a single COTS TX-RX pair. In *IEEE IPSN*, 2014.

[16] N. Kassem et al. RF-based vehicle detection and speed estimation. In *IEEE VTC Spring*, 2012.

[17] W. A. Knaus et al. APACHE II: a severity of disease classification system. *Critical care medicine*, 1985.

[18] A. Kosba et al. Robust WLAN device-free passive motion detection. In *IEEE WCNC*, 2012.

[19] A. E. Kosba et al. Analysis of a device-free passive tracking system in typical wireless environments. In *IEEE NTMS*, 2009.

[20] A. E. Kosba et al. RASID: A robust WLAN device-free passive motion detection system. In *IEEE PerCom*, 2012.

[21] A. Lazaro et al. Analysis of vital signs monitoring using an IR-UWB radar. *Progress In Electromagnetics Research*, 2010.

[22] W. Lindh et al. *Delmar's comprehensive medical assisting: administrative and clinical competencies*. Cengage Learning, 2013.

[23] J. J. McKenna et al. Why babies should never sleep alone: a review of the co-sleeping controversy in relation to SIDS, bedsharing and breast feeding. *Paediatric respiratory reviews*, 2005.

[24] M. L. R. Mogue and B. Rantala. Capnometers. *Journal of clinical monitoring*, 1988.

[25] A. Mtibaa et al. Towards computational offloading in mobile device clouds. In *IEEE CloudCom*, 2013.

[26] A. Mtibaa et al. Towards resource sharing in mobile device clouds: Power balancing across mobile devices. In *ACM SIGCOMM MCC Workshop*. ACM, 2013.

[27] S. Nibhanupudi. *Signal denoising using wavelets*. PhD thesis, University of Cincinnati, 2003.

[28] R. Parkes. Rate of respiration: the forgotten vital sign: Racheal parkes explains why emergency department nurses should document the respiratory rates of all patients, irrespective of their presenting complaints. *Emergency Nurse*, 2011.

[29] N. Patwari et al. Breathfinding: A Wireless Network That Monitors and Locates Breathing in a Home. *IEEE J-STSP*, 2014.

[30] P. Pelegris et al. A novel method to detect heart beat rate using a mobile phone. In *IEEE EMBC*, 2010.

[31] M.-Z. Poh et al. Non-contact, Automated Cardiac Pulse Measurements Using Video Imaging and Blind Source Separation. *Optics Express*, 2010.

[32] Q. Pu et al. Whole-home gesture recognition using wireless signals. In *ACM MobiCom*, 2013.

[33] I. Sabek et al. ACE: An accurate and efficient multi-entity device-free WLAN localization system. *IEEE Transactions on Mobile Computing*, 2014.

[34] I. Sabek and M. Youssef. Multi-entity device-free WLAN localization. In *IEEE GLOBECOM*, 2012.

[35] I. Sabek and M. Youssef. Spot: An accurate and efficient multi-entity device-free WLAN localization system. *CoRR*, 2012.

[36] A. Saeed et al. Ichnaea: A low-overhead robust WLAN device-free passive localization system. *IEEE J-STSP*, 2014.

[37] S. Sardy et al. Robust wavelet denoising. *IEEE Signal Processing*, 2001.

[38] C. Scully and other. Physiological parameter monitoring from optical recordings with a mobile phone. *IEEE Biomedical Engineering*, 2012.

[39] M. Seifeldin et al. Nuzzer: A large-scale device-free passive localization system for wireless environments. *IEEE Transactions on Mobile Computing*, 2013.

[40] M. Seifeldin and M. Youssef. A deterministic large-scale device-free passive localization system for wireless environments. In *ACM PETRA*, 2010.

[41] N. H. Shariati and E. Zahedi. Comparison of selected parametric models for analysis of the photoplethysmographic signal. In *IEEE CCSP*, 2005.

[42] S. Sigg et al. RF-based device-free recognition of simultaneously conducted activities. In *ACM UbiComp*, 2013.

[43] J. Yang, Y. Ge, et al. Performing joint learning for passive intrusion detection in pervasive wireless environments. In *IEEE INFOCOM*, 2010.

[44] M. Youssef et al. Challenges: device-free passive localization for wireless environments. In *ACM MobiCom*. ACM, 2007.

[45] G. Yuan et al. Respiratory rate and breathing pattern. *The McMaster University Medical Journal*, 2013.

Taming Wireless Fluctuations by Predictive Queuing Using a Sparse-Coding Link-State Model

Stephen J. Tarsa
Harvard University
Cambridge, MA

Marcus Comiter
Harvard University
Cambridge, MA

Michael B. Crouse
Harvard University
Cambridge, MA

Bradley McDanel
Harvard University
Cambridge, MA

H. T. Kung
Harvard University
Cambridge, MA

ABSTRACT

We introduce State-Informed Link-Layer Queuing (SILQ), a system that models, predicts, and avoids packet delivery failures caused by temporary wireless outages in everyday scenarios. By stabilizing connections in adverse link conditions, SILQ boosts throughput and reduces performance variation for network applications, for example by preventing unnecessary TCP timeouts due to dead zones, elevators, and subway tunnels. SILQ makes predictions in real-time by actively probing links, matching measurements to an overcomplete dictionary of patterns learned offline, and classifying the resulting sparse feature vectors to identify those that precede outages. We use a clustering method called *sparse coding* to build our data-driven link model, and show that it produces more variation-tolerant predictions than traditional loss-rate, location-based, or Markov chain techniques.

We present extensive data collection and field-validation of SILQ in airborne, indoor, and urban scenarios of practical interest. We show how offline unsupervised learning discovers link-state patterns that are stable across diverse networks and signal-propagation environments. Using these canonical primitives, we train outage predictors for 802.11 (Wi-Fi) and 3G cellular networks to demonstrate TCP throughput gains of 4x with off-the-shelf mobile devices. SILQ addresses delivery failures solely at the link layer, requires no new hardware, and upholds the end-to-end design principle to enable easy integration across applications, devices, and networks.

Categories and Subject Descriptors

C.2.1 [**Network Architecture and Design**]: Wireless networking, 802.11 (Wi-Fi), cellular data networks, TCP, sparse coding, data-driven model learning

1. INTRODUCTION

Wireless networks struggle to cope with link fluctuations in everyday scenarios. Any user who has accessed in-flight Wi-Fi, checked a smart phone on an elevator, or browsed the web on a train can attest to frustrating pockets of dismal throughput. Such disruptions result from the drastic changes in signal propagation that occur as users travel through complex environments with varying sources of multipath reflection, distances to base stations, line-of-sight occlusions, and interference. Generous provisioning of network infrastructure is the de-facto solution in practice, but more flexible and scalable strategies are needed [1].

Addressing delivery failure at the link layer is attractive because it shields higher layers of the network stack from transient link variations without changing radio hardware [2, 3]. When packet delivery is stable, applications and protocols like TCP realize higher throughput with lower variation, simplifying design and improving user experience [4]. However, predicting wireless link state at the scale of individual packets is difficult in real-world scenarios where steady-state assumptions like stable loss rates or location-dependence have limited efficacy. For example, we see in indoor experiments that the relationship between physical location and packet loss can change without warning if a coworker politely holds open a metal door, extending a link's range. These effects are common, especially in environments where construction predates pervasive wireless communication.

In response, we present State-Informed Link-Layer Queuing (SILQ), a system that uses data-driven learning to mitigate the destabilizing effects of wireless link loss. SILQ predicts link state at the 100ms time-scale to anticipate tempo-

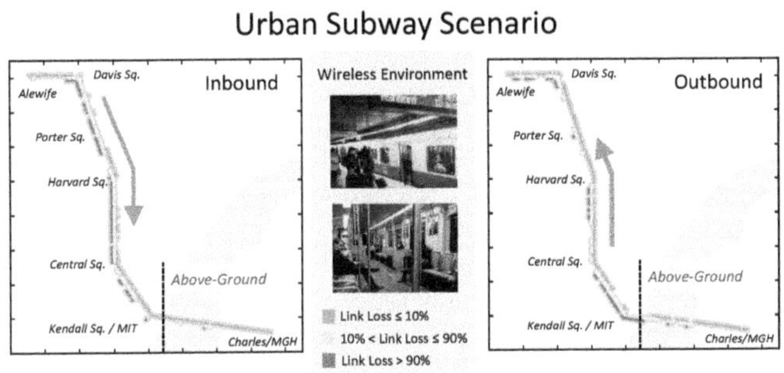

Figure 1: Packet loss rates over a 3G cellular network are shown on the subway in Boston, MA. Temporary dead zones in tunnels cause connection timeouts that leave links under-utilized, even when the train comes above-ground.

MobiHoc'15, June 22–25, 2015, Hangzhou, China.

http://dx.doi.org/10.1145/2746285.2746318.

rary outages and buffer packets accordingly. Real-time predictions are made by actively probing links, matching the resulting measurement sequences to an overcomplete dictionary of prominent patterns learned offline, and then classifying these *sparse feature vectors* to determine if they precede an outage. By preempting transmissions that are unlikely to succeed, SILQ reduces performance degradation caused when higher layers of the network stack react adversely to missing packets, for instance when TCP times out in a subway tunnel. Unlike prior cross-layer approaches to this problem, SILQ does not break connections in the middle of the network or modify transport protocols [4, 5, 6].

SILQ's prediction model improves upon past data-driven link models by expressing state as a linear combination of a few canonical packet-loss patterns, called features. This *sparse linear model* cuts away noise and restores missing data to improve statistical accuracy in the face of real-world data variations [7]. More-stable feature vectors can then be classified with a linear Support Vector Machine (SVM) to identify outages [8]. This method produces stable predictions looking further ahead in time than standard techniques like regression [9]. We demonstrate that this noise-, variation-, and deletion-tolerant model is computationally simple enough for real-time operation on mobile devices, and also supports the design flexibility to trade prediction accuracy for bandwidth and power improvements.

We build our predictive link model by first learning a dictionary of link-state features offline. Training data consists of UDP packet receptions recorded in three scenarios:

- An Unmanned Aerial Vehicle (UAV) flying over rural farmland
- Users walking throughout an active office building and riding an elevator
- Users traveling through a city on the subway

We show that features captured by sparse coding, a form of unsupervised clustering [10], reflect the effects of line-of-sight occlusions, radio range limitations, and interference. Furthermore, we show that features are often universal across rural, urban, indoor, outdoor, high mobility, and low mobility links. In contrast, we find that our supervised SVM outage-predictors are specific to an environment, though predictions remain accurate over days, weeks, and months.

This paper presents a full implementation of SILQ on off-the-shelf Linux and Android devices, and validates it in the field over 802.11b/g and 3G cellular networks. We compare our sparse-coding link model to traditional modeling approaches based on loss-rate and heuristics in terms of both statistical accuracy and network throughput under predictive queuing. Ultimately, we show that SILQ boosts throughput in an indoor office by 2x when used with Linux TCP, while achieving 4x lower variation. SILQ further improves throughput by 4x on the Boston subway where 3G coverage is spotty. Finally, we show that the power overhead of our approach can be reduced to only 4-5% above a baseline data connection by updating predictions less frequently when the link is in a steady state.

2. TEST SCENARIOS

We begin by describing our UAV, indoor office, and urban subway scenarios. In each environment, we collect initial link measurements by transmitting 66-byte (66B) UDP probe packets every 1ms from a mobile node to a nearby base station that logs sequence numbers. We detect lost probes from non-sequential receptions and construct contiguous streams of probe deliveries, called "traces." These high-granularity traces are used to build a link model in Section 4, though we introduce an adaptive probing mechanism in Section 5.1 to reduce SILQ's runtime probing overheads.

Figure 2: Our UAV's flight path over fields and farmland in upstate New York is shown. Ground receivers are placed in three locations to capture the link characteristics of an open field, dense forest, and parking lot with surrounding ground structures.

In our experiments, transmitters and receivers are all off-the-shelf mobile devices. For 802.11 measurements in the UAV and indoor office scenarios, we use an array of laptops, Mobile Internet Devices (MIDs), and BeagleBone Blacks depending on weight, power, and portability restrictions. Each accesses the wireless medium using a T-Link TL-WN727 USB dongle, and we disable hardware retransmissions by sending packets in broadcast mode. For subway experiments, we access the 3G cellular network with an Android smartphone or by tethering nodes to an Apple iPhone 6. In this case, we cannot disable ARQ with cell towers, though the effect is constant throughout data.

Given the speed and range of our UAV links, we transmit at 1Mbps modulation for best symbol resilience. In order to compare results across environments, we rate-limit links in the office and subway to 1Mbps. In practice, SILQ has been scaled to 20Mbps and deployed on commercial 802.11, 3G, and LTE cellular networks.

2.1 UAV Air-to-Ground Communication

Our UAV scenario consists of a fixed-wing SIG Rascal 110 flying a dumbell shaped pattern over an airfield in upstate New York on precipitation-free days, as shown in Figure 2. Autopilot maintains a consistent flight path to within 15m across laps, while keeping altitude steady at 100m and velocity at 20m/s. The property spans forest and farmland, contains fewer than 50 ground structures or cars at any time, and is free of 802.11 interference. Data collection is conducted over 802.11b with a single broadcast transmitter attached face-down to the UAV's wing.

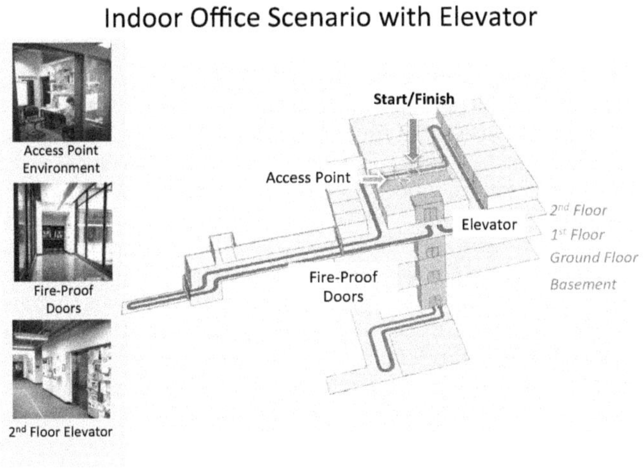

Figure 3: Our walking tour throughout an active office is shown in blue. Links are attenuated by concrete and brick, and obstructed by fire-proof doors and an elevator car.

Ground receivers are placed in identical orientations in three groups throughout the property to capture different signal-propagation characteristics:

1. *Field* nodes at the end of the runway have clean line-of-sight to the UAV during most of the flight. For them, packet loss is driven primarily by radio range.

2. *Ground structure* nodes are placed in a parking lot partially surrounded by several 5m-tall metal buildings. Between 4 and 6 cars are parked within 10m of nodes, and vehicle positions change across flights. These structures create line-of-sight occlusions and multipath reflections that affect packet delivery depending on geometry and UAV position.

3. *Forest* nodes are placed in a grove of fir trees at the end of the runway. They capture similar link conditions to field nodes, though uneven ground, trees, branches, and leaves affect line-of-sight transmission.

This UAV scenario is of both experimental and operational interest. First, the simple interference-free environment is ideal for conducting controlled wireless experiments to serve as building blocks for more complicated scenarios. Second, UAV wireless communication has commercial applications in bridge and crop inspection, rural Internet relay, package delivery, and a myriad of military scenarios.

2.2 Indoor Office

Our indoor office scenario is shown in Figure 3. A user carries a laptop throughout an office building while transmitting data to an 802.11 access point in a second-floor office. For each experiment, the user repeats a walking tour that crosses a footbridge to a nearby building and then returns for an elevator ride down three floors to the basement.

All experiments are conducted during high-traffic daytime hours when the building is used by several hundred students and faculty. We observe strong fluctuations in link quality due to signal attenuation through brick and concrete, as well as blockages from fire-proof doors and the elevator car. We also observe that signals are powerful enough to reach several floors to the basement, but that links can be blocked at ranges as short as 15m should fire doors occlude transmission. For this scenario, our data includes cross-channel interference from the building's 802.11 network.

2.3 Subway

Our subway scenario is shown in Figure 1. A user travels between Cambridge and Boston, MA in a train car that passes both below and above ground. Train speed varies depending on track conditions, and precise positioning is unknown within tunnels. The user transmits data from a mobile device to a server accessed via a first-hop 3G cellular connection and subsequent hops over wired Internet. We observe that round trip delays average 150ms and fluctuate within a manageable distribution. Queuing delays cause UDP probe packets to arrive in bursts of roughly consistent length and spacing.

As illustrated in Figure 1, we observe many regions of poor reception, but also extended regions of excellent reception when 3G repeaters are nearby or the subway crosses an above-ground bridge. This scenario is completely uncontrolled and is used to validate SILQ's methodology in an everyday situation of particular aggravation to the authors.

3. PREDICTIVE LINK-STATE MODELING

In order to implement predictive queueing, we first build a model of wireless packet delivery for our three scenarios. In the literature, link models typically reflect two approaches: physical models that use signal propagation to explain packet loss, and data-driven models that mathematically capture those effects with statistics like correlation between packet receptions. The former group includes distance-based attenuation, two-ray interference, and geometric occlusion models [11, 12, 13], while the latter includes loss-rate and Markov-chain models that reproduce distributions of consecutive receptions [14, 15, 16]. Though physics-driven methods are intuitive, they require detailed environment-specific information as inputs. On the other hand, generic data-driven models can require training datasets that grow exponentially with temporal scale.

These two extremes are sometimes blended by location-based statistical models [17, 18]. However, we find that location information is generally a poor predictor of individual packet losses. For example, we observe in our UAV experiments that slight changes to antenna orientation drive major swings in link loss. We also see that the location of a single car close to ground-structure nodes causes drastic changes in packet loss behavior due to multipath reflection. Indoors, we see that loss characteristics change when doors are closed or metal objects are moved within offices. And in the subway, location information is not even available once the train descends underground. For these reasons, we *purposefully* eschew location information in pursuit of a more accurate, general packet loss model.

Our data-driven link model combines unsupervised sparse coding, a form of clustering, with supervised Support Vector Machine (SVM) classification. This approach is closely related to state-of-the-art learning systems for vision and speech recognition that capture complicated features while tolerating non-Gaussian data variations [19]. Though ours is the first sparse-feature model for wireless packet transmission to our knowledge, other learning techniques are gaining traction in networking scenarios. At the transport layer, game-theoretic simulations can discover TCP protocols tailored to network conditions [20]. At the physical layer, learning has been used to adapt forward-error-correction (FEC) to congestion in simulation [21]. Our approach stands out both by our use of sparse feature representation to cope with real-world measurement artifacts, as well our emphasis on live, online operation aboard mobile devices.

3.1 A Sparse Coding Link Model

Sparse coding is an unsupervised clustering method that solves for an overcomplete matrix of recurring patterns in training data. We call that matrix a *dictionary* and its column vectors *features* [10, 22]. Under this framework, a data vector can be approximated as a linear combination of features. By constraining the number of features used, approximations are represented by *sparse* coefficient vectors with only a few non-zero entries. For data with noise or non-Gaussian variations like deletions, sparse approximations latch measurements to exemplar patterns, truncating weakly expressed information and restoring missing values. This process improves variation-tolerance in subsequent statistical analysis.

3.1.1 Offline Dictionary Training

We learn dictionaries offline from a large set of link traces, effectively exploiting past data to improve statistical accuracy for future data. Several formulations for dictionary training exist [23]; we use an optimization method based on the Least Absolute Shrinkage and Selection Operator (LASSO) that relaxes sparse coding's constraint on the number of non-zero feature coefficients by instead penalizing the sum of coefficient magnitudes [24]:

$$\min_{\alpha,D} \ \frac{1}{2}||x - D\alpha||_2^2 + \lambda||\alpha||_1 \qquad (1)$$

where D is a $w \times m$ dictionary containing m features of length w, x a normalized binary measurement vector representing the outcomes of w back-to-back probe transmissions, α its sparse feature representation, and λ a tunable positive value. To implement dictionary training, we segment field traces into T windows of w measurements x_t for $t = 1...T$. This objective produces qualitatively similar results to sparse coding but is convex, yielding stable, accurate solutions for D.

3.1.2 Online Measurement Encoding

While LASSO is effective for offline dictionary learning, it is too computationally intensive to compute sparse codes in real-time on mobile devices. Therefore, we use a D found by LASSO and solve for α online according to:

$$\min_{\alpha,D} \ ||x - D\alpha||_2^2 \text{ s.t. } ||\alpha||_0 \le k \qquad (2)$$

with k a hard sparsity threshold. This alternative formulation can be greedily solved by Matching Pursuit (MP) [25] using a series of inner-product tests that iteratively select k features to reduce a residual. MP has $O(mw)$ complexity and we show in Section 6.4 that feature encoding is a negligible part of SILQ's running time.

Our sparse-feature-based link model is related to state models like Markov chains in the literature [14, 16]. The process of learning a dictionary by clustering can be thought of as a data-driven method for reducing the space of possible states in the model. For example, if we train a dictionary with many features and a small penalty parameter (e.g. $m \approx 200$ and $\lambda \approx 0.1$), then D captures *templates* of frequently occurring link states. New link measurements are then matched to the closest template by setting $k = 1$. However, if the number of dictionary features is chosen to be small and lambda is chosen to be large (e.g. $m \approx 20$ and $\lambda \approx 4$), then training will extract a small number of the most prominent patterns in each training example. This produces a set of more-general features that can be combined to enumerate observed link states, for example by encoding with $k = 8$. We call these features *primitives.* In Section 4, we will show that these latter linear-combinational models generalize well across networks and environments, addressing a key limitation of traditional wireless link models.

3.2 Outage Prediction With SVMs

Using learned link primitives, we can build a predictive statistical model for all sorts of link-layer events that affect network performance. In this work, we use bulk data transport via TCP as an application vehicle to demonstrate SILQ's gains and define the prediction target to be *any upcoming sequence of 192 probe measurements containing a single delivery failure.* This represents back-to-back transmission failures of 1500B MTU data packets sent at 1Mbps with the Linux default 7 ARQ retries, assuming a round-trip time less than 100ms. Since most TCP implementations can recover quickly from a single packet drop using fast-retransmit, we instead try to detect these two-packet outages. We note that video streaming and transaction processing are other candidate applications for SILQ with potentially different prediction targets.

To implement binary event prediction, we use a linear SVM classifier, which finds a separating plane between training data belonging to two classes, designated by class *labels*; later, new data vectors are compared to the separating plane using an inner-product and threshold test to predict their class membership. Since SVM training data in our application requires both sparse feature vectors and corresponding labels, it is considered a supervised technique. To derive labels y_t for our data, we annotate a subset of traces from each environment, setting $y_t = 1$ when an outage followed the measurement vector in the trace and $y_t = 0$ otherwise. In Section 4.2, we show how to optimize over SVM configuration parameters.

4. TRAINING MODELS

4.1 Learned Link Primitives

We first train dictionaries on field-collected traces using LASSO and examine the link primitives discovered in each of our scenarios. We learn separate dictionaries of size $m = 20$ with $\lambda = 4$ from each type of receiver: UAV field nodes, UAV forest nodes, UAV ground-structure nodes, indoor office nodes, and subway nodes. Figure 4 shows several features found often in each trace, with dips reflecting patterns of delivery failure and peaks capturing delivery successes.

We see that primitives learned across UAV ground receiver types are similar. Taken together, they capture examples of abrupt changes to the link, gradual transitions, intermittent packet drops, and temporary outages lasting 10's of milliseconds. When we examine the distributions of nonzero coefficients in each trace's sparse representations, we find that field and forest nodes more often map to long runs of delivery successes or smooth gradual changes in link quality. This aligns with our experiment configuration, in which these nodes have the best connectivity, are far from any structures that can suddenly occlude line-of-sight transmission, and are affected mostly by radio range limitations. In contrast, the coefficients computed for ground-structure nodes more-often map to abrupt transitions as buildings block line-of-sight until the UAV is immediately overhead.

Primitives learned in the office environment bear a striking resemblance to those learned from UAV receivers. We see a mixture of temporary outages affecting strong links, as well as abrupt on-to-off and off-to-on transitions. These links exhibit a greater degree of noisy variation than UAV nodes, possibly due to 802.11 cross-channel interference from the building's wireless network.

Subway atoms reflect the same general shapes, but prominently exhibit regular 10ms-long oscillations in delivery. According to log files, average probe inter-arrival times over the 3G network display 10ms bursts of back-to-back deliveries, likely due to queueing delays. This means that unsupervised learning captures primitives reflecting both wireless-link and network effects.

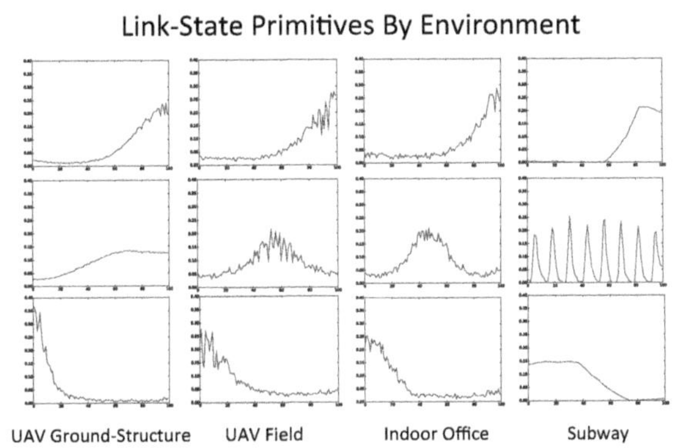

Figure 4: Common link primitives learned from different environments using LASSO with $m = 20$ and $\lambda = 4$ are shown. They capture fast and slow link transitions as well as bursts of delivery successes.

4.1.1 Separating Network Effects

As discussed in Section 3.1, sparse feature models can be configured either to match link states to a single template, or to express them as linear combinations of primitives. The practical result of this choice can be seen by comparing the primitives in Figure 4 to the template in Figure 5 learned from subway data using $m = 200$ and $\lambda = 0.1$. We see that templates simultaneously represent the concurrent effects of wireless link loss *and* network queuing delays. This contrasts with models based on linear combinations of primitives that automatically separate these effects.

This observation highlights the power of applying sparse coding to link modeling: our approach naturally expresses complicated network measurements in a simple, well-separated vector of high-level information – statistics can then be computed relative to this meta-information. In addition to supporting stable, intuitive statistical models, our method uses data-driven learning to identify link states that generalize

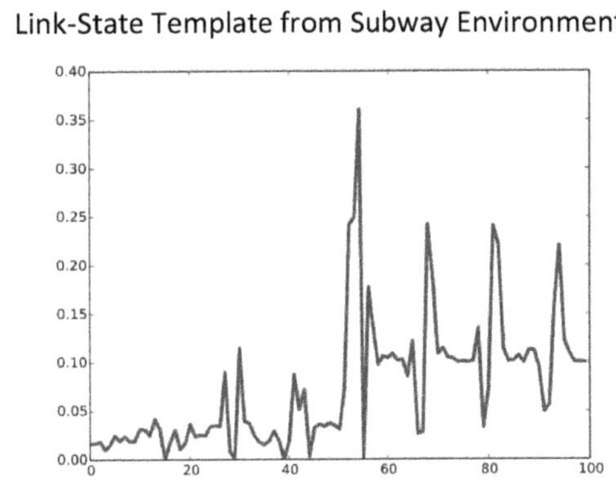

Figure 5: A link-state template learned from subway data is shown. The effects of link loss and bursts due to network delays are captured together, contrasting with Figure 4 where they are separated into different primitives.

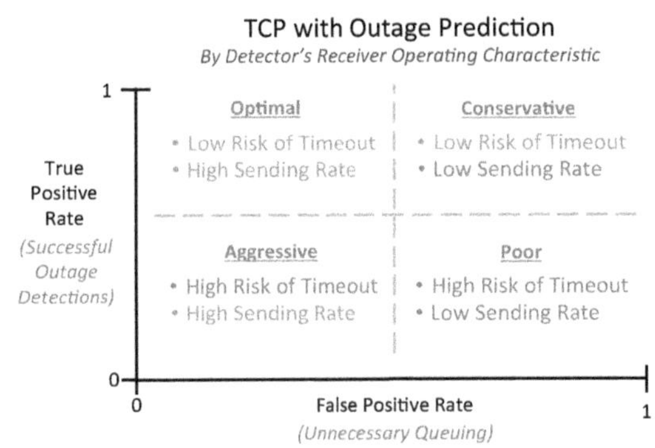

Figure 6: The effect of outage-detection sensitivity on TCP is illustrated. Detectors that forward data aggressively run a high risk of timeout. Those that forward conservatively rarely time out, but often under-utilize the link.

beyond just their training data, reducing the need for extensive data collection in new scenarios.

4.2 Tuning an SVM Predictor for Temporary Link Outages

We next show how to tune a linear SVM to predict outages from sparse-coded link measurements. Fundamentally, SVMs separate classes of data by solving for a max-margin separator between training examples of each class. When used for detection, this allows us to obtain a tradeoff between true positive and false positive rates by shifting the SVM separator toward one class or another.

Within SILQ, a predictor's sensitivity ultimately affects realized network performance. Figure 6 illustrates this relationship in the context of an outage predictor and TCP throughput. Predictors tuned to forward packets aggressively raise few alarms, achieving low false positives but also low true positives. The result is a fast sending rate but a high risk of TCP timeout when outages are not well-predicted. At the other end of the spectrum are predictors tuned to forward data conservatively by raising many alarms, leading to

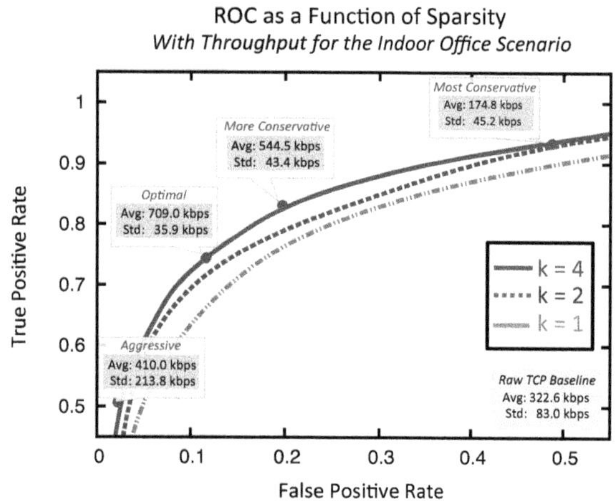

Figure 7: Throughput is shown at various points on our outage detector's ROC profile, empirically demonstrating the relationship described in Figure 6 in our indoor office scenario. We also see that training parameters such as encoding sparsity k affect the ROC profile of our outage detector.

a high true positive rate but also many false positives. These detectors rarely let timeouts happen, but severely underutilize links in good conditions.

In Figure 7, we show the empirical effect that prediction sensitivity has on throughput, measured in our indoor office scenario with the methodology of Section 6.2. We see that aggressive models achieve poor average throughput with a high standard deviation – while they opportunistically grab all available sending opportunities, they also often time out and cause throughput to drop to zero for a long period of time. However, overly conservative models end up realizing *lower* throughput since they fail to send often enough when the link is usable.

We also see in Figure 7 that optimizing over sparse coding parameters like m, λ, and k changes the resulting SVM predictor's ROC profile. For example, if we set $m = 20$, but $k = 2$, then the detector is strictly *worse* than setting $k = 4$.

Guided by these results, we reason that the best link model in terms of TCP throughput should maximize correct outage predictions while ensuring plenty of sending opportunities. We implement this by choosing the model that maximizes outage recall, provided non-outage (i.e. sending opportunity) recall is above a threshold of 0.75. Varying m, λ, k, and the SVM's test threshold, we train dictionaries and SVMs while holding out a subset of traces for evaluation to obtain $m = 20$, $\lambda = 4$, and $k = 4$ as our best configuration. Examining our optimized link model, we notice that the SVM heavily weights three particular dictionary primitives, suggesting that TCP throughput is highly sensitive to a small number of link states.

4.3 Transferring Features

While some link-state primitives may be unique to a particular environment, Section 4.1 showed that similar features are found among scenarios. Intuitively, these should represent common drivers of link loss like range effects in large open environments or abrupt transitions due to occlusions. We next empirically verify that learning captures canonical link characteristics that are common across diverse environments.

For Figure 8, we learn primitives from a single scenario and use them to compute sparse feature representations and train outage predictors in a different scenario. We not only see that primitives generalize well across environments, but that some amount of data diversity actually improves outage recall, possibly serving as a defense against overfitting. We note that this trend does *not* hold when we use a template model – for example, we find that templates from the office scenario do not accurately characterize the queuing effects of the subway, hurting recall.

We also found that SVM separators do not port as well as dictionaries across scenarios, since the precise relationships between link states over time are environment-dependent. For example, a fast subway train may produce shorter temporal correlation between a degrading link and an upcoming outage than in the office scenario. However, we saw that SVMs trained on months-old data still provided good performance in the field, suggesting that such relationships are fundamentally stable. Since SVM training is less computationally intensive and requires less data than dictionary training, SILQ implements this function on-device to allow fast adaptation to new environments.

Outage-Prediction Recall when Transferring Primitives

		SVM Training & Test Environments		
		UAV	Indoor Office	Urban Subway
Dict. Training Environment	UAV	0.81	0.82	0.74
	Indoor Office	0.83	0.79	0.79
	Urban Subway	0.81	0.81	0.73

Figure 8: Outage-prediction recall is reported when dictionary primitives are learned in one scenario and applied in another. This establishes that learned link primitives are often universal across environments and networks.

5. SILQ ARCHITECTURE

To demonstrate throughput gains from the predictions of our sparse-coding link model, we implement SILQ for Linux and Android devices. At runtime, SILQ nodes each measure their outgoing links by transmitting UDP probes at a regular interval. Reception reports are then bounced back to senders, piggybacked on probes traveling in the opposite direction. After a regular measurement interval (100ms for all results in this paper), each SILQ node computes a link prediction using the prior w measurements. If an outage is predicted, SILQ holds all data packets at the link layer until a new prediction indicates otherwise.

5.1 Measurement Protocol

SILQ's measurement protocol is shown in Figure 9. Nodes maintain a bitmap $\texttt{Link}_{in}$ marking the last w incoming probes relative to the most recent, denoted $\texttt{Seq}_{\texttt{in}}$. An arriving probe's sequence number is compared against $\texttt{Seq}_{\texttt{in}}$ to detect delivery failures before updating $\texttt{Link}_{in}$ and $\texttt{Seq}_{\texttt{in}}$. Our UDP probes use 69B to carry a reception report consisting of $\texttt{Link}_{in}$ as a 3B bitmap and $\texttt{Seq}_{\texttt{in}}$ as a 2B **`unsigned short`**.

Nodes also maintain a round-trip-time estimate d_{RTT} to detect lost reception reports. For example, if $\texttt{Seq}_{\texttt{out}} = 20$

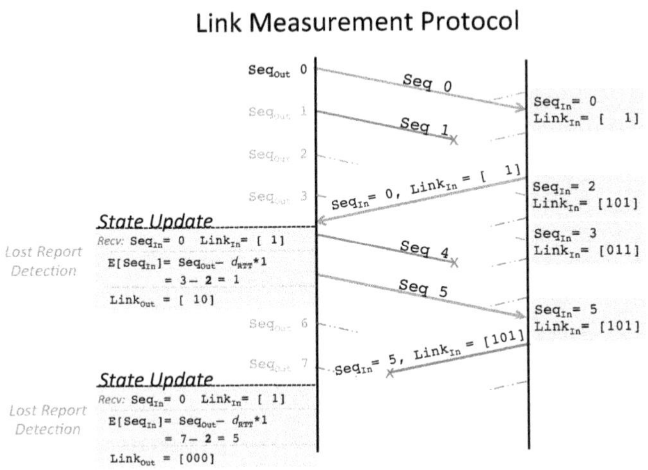

Figure 9: SILQ's measurement protocol piggybacks reception reports containing a bitmap of incoming probe receptions on outgoing probes. Senders use estimated round-trip-time d_{RTT} to detect lost reception reports.

probes are sent and only the first report successfully bounces back, the sender must compute how many reports *should* have arrived: $\texttt{Seq}_{\text{out}} - d_{\text{RTT}} \frac{w}{100\text{ms}} = 19$. This means that bi-directional probing captures asymmetric link effects, except when many reception reports are lost at the end of an interval. In this case, we make the conservative assumption that the link is off in both directions. In practice, we find that disruptions due to d_{RTT} fluctuation resolve after one or two missed $100ms$ windows, even on a crowded carrier network.

5.1.1 Managing Probing Overheads

Probing consumes both power and network bandwidth, resources that must be balanced against measurement fidelity. For example, in Section 6, Figures 12 and 14 show us that sending 20 probes per 100ms consumes 22% of bandwidth for a 1Mbps link and 9% additional battery for a laptop with a power-hungry USB radio.

Beyond simply reducing probe rate, we introduce a strategy for managing overhead by updating predictions less-frequently when the link is in a stable steady-state. This *steady-state sleep* mode detects sustained strong-connectivity or sustained outage by 3 consecutive all-1 or all-0/missing link reports, respectively. In this mode, SILQ updates predictions every t_{Sleep}ms using a single round of probing. We set t_{Sleep} so that regular prediction will resume in two cases:

Case 1: Good-to-Bad Transition When a good link degrades, outgoing data will be vulnerable to loss due to a stale state prediction. We therefore compute the portion of SILQ's sending queue at risk and set t_{Sleep} to ensure tolerable loss:

$$t_{\text{Sleep}} = d_{\text{TX}} * (Q_{\text{SILQ}} - P_{\text{Min}}) - d_{\text{RTT}} \quad (3)$$

where P_{Min} is the minimum number of packets that must be delivered to maintain the connection, Q_{SILQ} is the current send-queue size, d_{TX} is the transmission time of an MTU data packet, and d_{RTT} is the time needed for a full link report to bounce back. For example, TCP uses a triple-duplicate-ACK to trigger fast recovery, so we set $P_{\text{Min}} = 3$. With $d_{\text{RTT}} = 110$ms, $d_{\text{TX}} = 12$ms, and a sending queue of $Q_{\text{SILQ}} = 50$ packets, we can set $t_{\text{sleep}} = 454$ms.

Case 2: Bad-to-Good Transition When the link is unavailable, we can save power by turning the wireless radio off and waking periodically to check link status. In this case, a large t_{sleep} risks underutilizing the link by slowing SILQ's reaction time. We tune this quantity empirically – for example we see an average 3s delay between restored connectivity and SILQ's first predicted sending opportunity in our office scenario and conservatively set $t_{\text{Sleep}} = 900$ms to ensure that the link is checked every 1s.

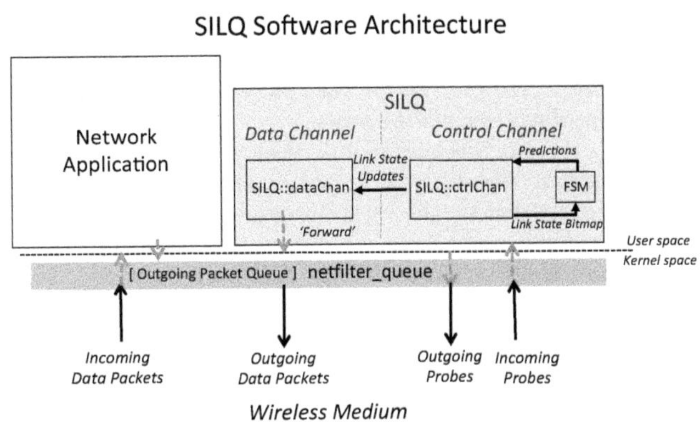

Figure 10: The SILQ architecture consists of logically separated data and control channels that isolate link measurement protocols from data forwarding protocols. In our testbed, both access the same wireless medium using the same interface.

5.2 Software Architecture & Implementation

SILQ's software architecture is shown in Figure 10. It is implemented in user space for Linux and Android devices using **`netfilter_queue`** to administer packets within the kernel. Each node runs both *data channel* and *control channel* controllers – the data channel controller holds or forwards packets based on the current predicted link state, while the control channel controller is responsible for probing and providing measurements to a *finite-state machine (FSM)* link-model module. The logical separation between channels simplifies probing and data-delivery protocols, however both access the same wireless medium using the same wireless interface for all results in this paper.

SILQ's FSMs are modular, allowing us to compare sparse coding to traditional modeling approaches in the field. We implement `NO_OP` (i.e. always-forward), *Loss Rate Threshold*, *Heuristic Hold*, and *Sparse Coding* FSMs. For all but the `NO_OP` FSM, trivial all-0 measurement vectors always predict outage, and trivial all-1 measurement vectors predict no-outage. For *Loss Rate Threshold* and *Heuristic Hold*, we use a "conservative" parameter to require back-to-back no-outage predictions before turning a bad link back on. This stabilization procedure is needed for loss-rate and heuristic predictors to achieve any throughput gains in the field. In contrast, we optimize the sparse coding FSM for stable prediction using the statistical methods of Section 4.2.

6. SYSTEM EVALUATION

We evaluate SILQ in the UAV, office, and subway scenarios by measuring TCP throughput, power consumption, and CPU utilization. For these experiments, we train dictionaries and SVMs as in Section 4 and then transfer a large file from a mobile device to a remote server via TCP. We compare raw TCP to SILQ using predictions from sparse coding, loss-rate threshold, and heuristic models. Our heuristic holds data packets if all probes in a previous window are lost, representing the simplest method of coping with the long out-of-range regions in our UAV and subway tests. We empirically tune a loss-rate threshold and "conservative" parameters for comparison methods to maximize throughput.

Our baseline TCP protocol is the Linux default TCP Cubic. We enable SACK-enhanced F-RTO for resilience over wireless links, use 9 keep alive probes, and allow 15 back-to-back timeouts before terminating a connection. Our wireless adapters use 7 ARQ retries for data packets, while we disable ARQ for probes over 802.11 links.

To control for differences in link quality, we compare *overall* throughput for different experiments using total data transferred divided by the total number of transmission opportunities for data packets. To illustrate the effect of small changes in experiment parameters like walking speed, Figures 11(a) and 11(b) plot loss rate for two runs in our office scenario using faint green, yellow, and red bars. We see that the durations of both outages and regions with strong connectivity differ, biasing total throughput by affording more transmission opportunities during the run shown in Figure 11(a) independent of network protocol. Our comparison metric corrects for this effect in post-processing by counting only stable regions with back-to-back probe deliveries in our throughput denominator.

6.1 UAV Throughput in Emulation

Due to logistical barriers related to personnel, budget, and weather, we validate throughput in the UAV scenario using a lightweight link emulator. During emulated flights, SILQ runs on our UAV payload and ground nodes, while probe and data packets are sent over wired interfaces to a central controller that replays field traces. The emulation controller forwards packets to their destination only if a packet reception was recorded in the field trace. We emulate a 1Mbps link and compare 1500B MTU data packets against 12 back-to-back 1ms probes to reflect a 12ms transmission time. An error in any probe causes the data packet to be dropped. The controller simulates both ARQ and CSMA. Emulated traces are held out of the training datasets used for dictionary and SVM training.

We find that SILQ boosts throughput by 22% over a raw TCP connection for links to ground-structure nodes. This improvement from 529 kbps to 644kbps is attributed to the high-quality predictions of our sparse coding link model, as heuristic and loss-rate predictions hurt throughput by 5% and 10%, respectively. For field and forest nodes, SILQ produces little benefit to average throughput, but yields an extremely low throughput deviation of 19kbps across flights.

Examining UAV links by type, we find that SILQ's sparse-coding predictions help most when link conditions vary often. Our learning approach successfully captures measurement sequences with strong predictive power caused by the complex geometry of nearby buildings and cars. In contrast, when loss is intermittent at radio range extremes, ARQ is enough to fix isolated losses. In all cases, we found that loss-rate and heuristic predictors underperform sparse coding – our heuristic only captures coarse outages lasting hundreds of milliseconds, while loss-rate predictions map both outages and intermittent losses to a single metric.

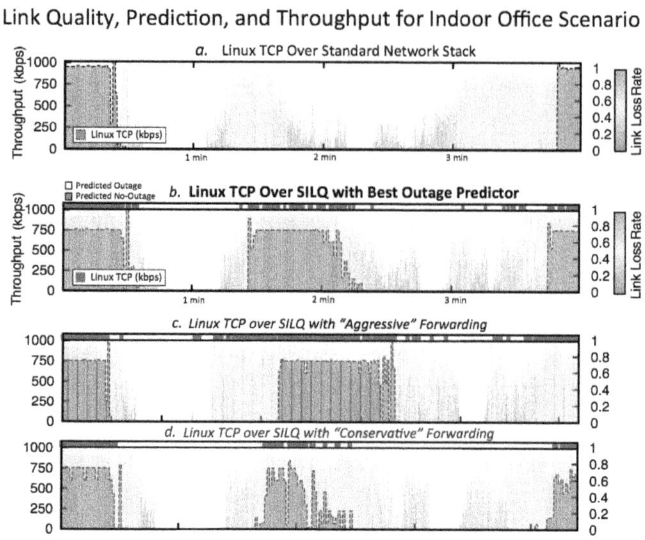

Figure 11: TCP throughput is plotted against the left axis in our indoor office scenario. For reference, link loss is plotted against the right axis using faint green, yellow, and red bars. Link-state predictions are represented by pink and white markers at the top of each plot. SILQ's optimal, aggressive, and conservative forwarders behave as anticipated, and TCP connections wake up quickly with SILQ.

6.2 Indoor Elevator/Office Environment

Next, we deploy SILQ in our indoor office environment. For these experiments, wireless links are stable when users are close to an access point, but exhibit both abrupt outages due to fire doors and gradual degradation caused by an elevator car.

Averaging five runs, SILQ improves throughput by 2x over a raw TCP connection, while reducing throughput variation by 4x. Predictions from our sparse coding model produce 15% higher throughput than the heuristic and 50% higher throughput than loss-rate predictions. We found it difficult to tune either comparison prediction-method to perform well over the entire walking tour – unlike sparse-coding, neither could cope with both abrupt link transitions *and* gradual link degradation using a single configuration. Figure 12 shows that sparse-coding predictions are also more resilient to lower probe rates than heuristic or loss-rate models. In Section 6.4, we show that this allows us to better match SILQ's power consumption to available resources.

Figure 11 shows a closer look at SILQ's performance over example runs in the indoor office. For reference, we plot link loss against the right axis using faint green and red bars. When appropriate, SILQ's link state predictions are shown at the top of a plot, with a pink marker indicating that the link is predicted to be on, and whitespace showing a predicted outage. TCP throughput is plotted against the left axis using black and blue shaded curves.

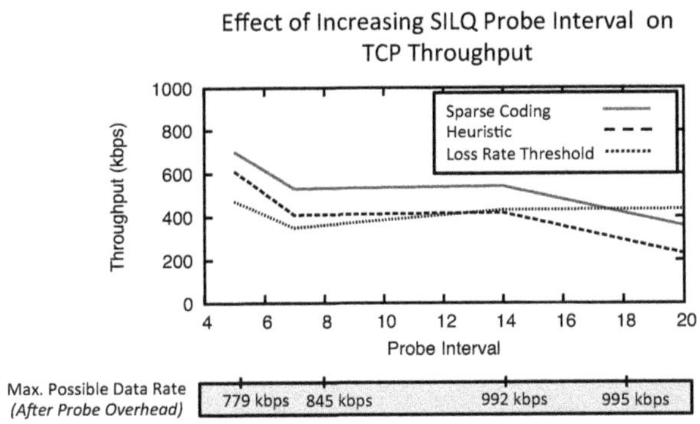

Figure 12: Average throughput in our indoor office scenario is shown as we reduce probe rate. Predictions from a sparse coding model are more resilient to low probe rates than heuristic or loss rate models.

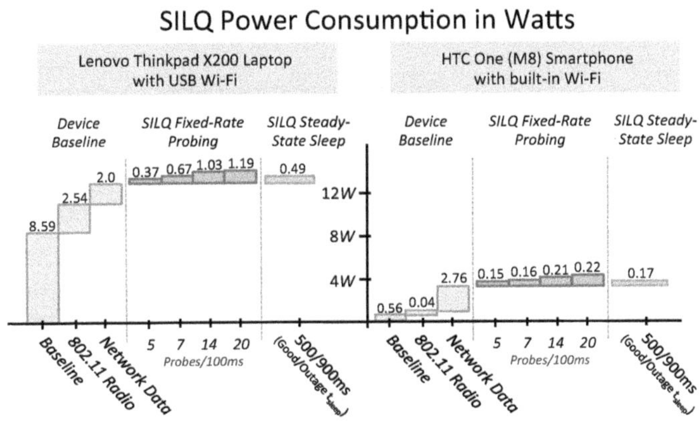

Figure 14: In our office environment, our steady-state sleep mode reduces power consumption to 4% and 5% above an active data connection, depending on device. This method forgoes predictions when the link is in a steady-state.

In Figure 11(a), we see that TCP times out as soon as link conditions degrade and does not wake up until several minutes later. This causes the mobile device to miss sending opportunities during nearly 40% of the tour. In contrast, Figure 11(b) shows SILQ running with our best-tuned sparse-coding model, which predicts impending outages well and causes TCP to wake up rapidly. We also show SILQ's performance when our SVM outage predictor is tuned according to the True Positive/False Positive tradeoffs discussed in Section 4. We see how the more aggressive forwarder in Figure 11(c) sends often, but times out due to its optimism about link state. In contrast, the conservative forwarder in Figure 11(d) misses large portions of sending opportunities in an effort to avoid timeouts.

6.3 Real-World Subway Environment

Our subway scenario validates SILQ "in the wild". This scenario exhibits a great deal of uncontrolled complexity – mobile nodes experience fast changes in velocity, sudden occlusions from tunnels, spotty connectivity to 3G repeaters, and competing wireless traffic. This scenario serves to demonstrate the strength of SILQ's end-to-end design since no code alterations or network configuration changes were needed for the system to function.

Figure 13 compares raw TCP to SILQ with a sparse coding predictor over subway rides between the Harvard Square and Charles-MGH stops. Note that Figure 13(a) represents an inbound trip from Harvard to Charles-MGH, and Figure 13(b) represents an outbound trip between the two stops in the opposite order. While a raw TCP connection times out for minutes at a time, SILQ utilizes nearly every available sending window and improves throughput by 4x over a six minute train ride.

6.4 Profiling CPU & Battery Overheads

Finally, we profile SILQ's performance on two of our experimental devices: a Lenovo X200 laptop running a 1.86GHz Intel Core 2 Duo processor with a T-Link TL-WN722N USB wireless radio, and an HTC One (M8) smartphone running a 2.36GHz Qualcomm Snapdragon 801 ARM processor with onboard Wi-Fi. We run SILQ on each device with only baseline background-process activity. Throughout, screens are kept at their default brightness. On the laptop, we create network data traffic by transferring a large file via TCP to a remote server. On the phone, we have a user request popular web pages at a rate of roughly one site per 4 seconds. For both devices, we measure CPU utilization and battery consumption by averaging over 30 seconds.

We observe that SILQ uses only 2% CPU on the Intel chip, and 4% on the smartphone. Less than 1% of SILQ's runtime is spent computing predictions, with most time spent servicing packets. Using a dictionary of 30 atoms for $w = 20$ probes per interval, SILQ's memory footprint is 972KB.

Figure 14 shows SILQ's power consumption for each device. We see that lower probe rates reduce SILQ's power overhead significantly – for example, by 14% on the laptop and 6% on the phone when we drop from 20 to 14 probes per 100ms. We also report savings from our steady-state sleep mode in the indoor office environment. Since our devices prevent us from easily powering radios on and off without re-associating with access points, this savings is calculated in post-processing from SILQ's logs, based on recorded steady-state regions. When we compare SILQ's battery consumption overhead using the steady-state sleep mode to the power consumed by an active data connection, we see that our method only costs an additional 4% and 5% per device, utltimately for a 2-4x boost in throughput.

7. CONCLUSION

This paper presented SILQ, a link layer queuing system that uses machine learning to predict link outages so that packet loss can be avoided. Using sparse coding, we demonstrated that a link model based on combinations of simple primitives makes better use of training data and leads to higher quality predictions than models requiring steady-state assumptions about link quality. SILQ can be easily deployed on Linux and Android devices, and has been demonstrated to achieve up to 4x throughput gains in scenarios of practical interest.

Acknowledgements

This research was supported in part by gifts from the Intel Corporation. Stephen Tarsa is supported by a fellowship from the Siebel Foundation.

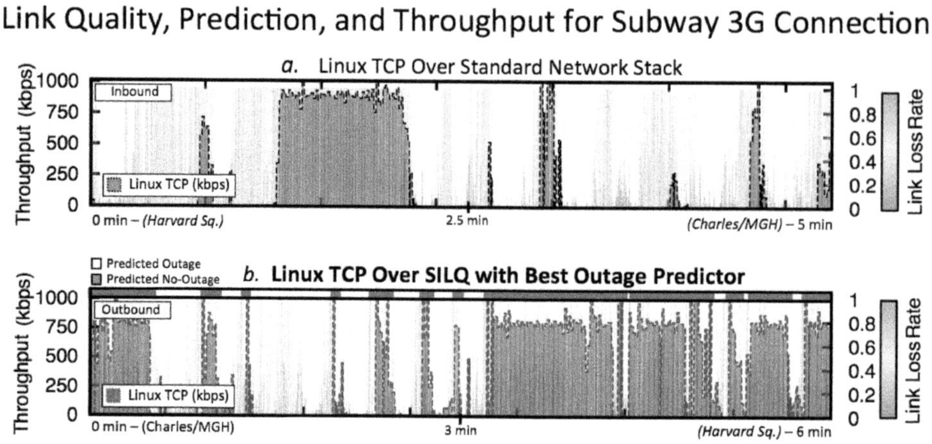

Figure 13: We compare a raw TCP connection to TCP atop SILQ using predictions from a sparse-coding link model during inbound and outbound subway rides. Over a 3G cellular network, raw TCP times out quickly and misses many sending opportunities. With SILQ, timeout is avoided and throughput increases by 4x.

8. REFERENCES

[1] J. Andrews, H. Claussen, M. Dohler, *et al.*, "Femtocells: Past, Present, and Future," *2012 IEEE Selected Areas in Communications.*

[2] H. Balakrishnan, V. N. Padmanabhan, S. Seshan, and R. Katz, "A Comparison of Mechanisms for Improving TCP Performance over Wireless Links," *1997 IEEE/ACM Trans. on Networking.*

[3] C. Parsa and J. Garcia-Luna-Aceves, "TULIP: A Link-Level Protocol for Improving TCP over Wireless Links," in *1999 IEEE Wireless Comms. and Networking Conf.*

[4] H. Balakrishnan, S. Seshan, and R. Katz, "Improving Reliable Transport and Handoff Performance in Cellular Wireless Networks," *1995 Wireless Networks.*

[5] A. Bakre and B. Badrinath, "I-TCP: Indirect TCP for Mobile Hosts," in *1995 IEEE Distr. Computing Sys.*

[6] T. Goff, J. Moronski, D. Phatak, *et al.*, "Freeze-TCP: A True End-to-End TCP Enhancement Mechanism for Mobile Environments," in *2000 IEEE INFOCOM.*

[7] S. Tarsa and H.-T. Kung, "Hierarchical Sparse Coding for Wireless Link Prediction in an Airborne Scenario," in *2013 IEEE MILCOM.*

[8] C. Burges, "A Tutorial on Support Vector Machines for Pattern Recognition," *1998 Springer Data Mining and Knowledge Discovery.*

[9] S. Tarsa, A. Kumar, and H.-T. Kung, "Workload Prediction for Adaptive Power Scaling Using Deep Learning," in *2014 IEEE Int. Conf. on IC Design & Tech.*

[10] B. Olshausen, D. Field, *et al.*, "Sparse Coding With An Overcomplete Basis Set: A Strategy Employed By VI?," *1997 Vision Research, Pergamon Press.*

[11] R. Valenzuela, "A Ray Tracing Approach to Predicting Indoor Wireless Transmission," in *2003 IEEE Vehicular Technology Conference.*

[12] J. Andersen *et al.*, "Propagation Measurements and Models for Wireless Communications Channels," *IEEE Comms. Magazine, 1995.*

[13] M. Ylianttila, J. Mäkelä, and K. Pahlavan, "Analysis of Handoff in a Location-Aware Vertical Multi-Access Network," *2005 Computer Networks.*

[14] E. Gilbert *et al.*, "Capacity of a Burst-Noise Channel," *1960 Bell Syst. Tech. J.*

[15] K. Farkas, T. Hossmann, F. Legendre, B. Plattner, and S. Das, "Link Quality Prediction in Mesh Networks," *2008 Computer Communications.*

[16] A. Konrad, B. Zhao, A. Joseph, and R. Ludwig, "A Markov-Based Channel Model Algorithm for Wireless Networks," *2003 Wireless Networks.*

[17] H.-T. Kung, C.-K. Lin, T.-H. Lin, S. Tarsa, and D. Vlah, "A Location-Dependent Runs-and-Gaps Model for Predicting TCP Performance over a UAV Wireless Channel," in *2010 IEEE MILCOM.*

[18] B. Ferris, D. Fox, and N. Lawrence, "WiFi-SLAM Using Gaussian Process Latent Variable Models.," in *2007 IEEE IJCAI.*

[19] T.-H. Lin and H.-T. Kung, "Stable and Efficient Representation Learning with Non-Negativity Constraints," in *2014 Intl. Conf. on Machine Learning.*

[20] K. Winstein and H. Balakrishnan, "TCP Ex-Machina: Computer-Generated Congestion Control," in *2013 ACM SIGCOMM Computer Communication Review.*

[21] H. Seferoglu, A. Markopoulou, U. Kozat, M. Civanlar, and J. Kempf, "Dynamic FEC algorithms for TFRC flows," *2010 IEEE Trans on Multimedia.*

[22] J. Mairal, F. Bach, J. Ponce, and G. Sapiro, "Online Learning for Matrix Factorization and Sparse Coding," *2010 Journal of Machine Learning Research.*

[23] F. Bach, R. Jenatton, J. Mairal, and G. Obozinski, "Optimization with Sparsity-Inducing Penalties," *2012 Foundations and Trends in Machine Learning.*

[24] R. Tibshirani, "Regression Shrinkage and Selection via the LASSO," *1996 Journal of the Royal Stats. Society.*

[25] S. Mallat and Z. Zhang, "Matching Pursuits with Time-Frequency Dictionaries," *1993 IEEE Transactions on Signal Processing.*

TRINITY: A Practical Transmitter Cooperation Framework to Handle Heterogeneous User Profiles in Wireless Networks

Shailendra Singh*
University of California, Riverside
singhs@cs.ucr.edu

Karthikeyan Sundaresan
NEC Labs America, Inc.
karthiks@nec-labs.com

Srikanth V. Krishnamurthy
University of California, Riverside
krish@cs.ucr.edu

Xinyu Zhang
University of Wisconsin-Madison
xyzhang@ece.wisc.edu

Amir Khojastepour
NEC Labs America, Inc.
amir@nec-labs.com

Sampath Rangarajan
NEC Labs America, Inc.
sampath@nec-labs.com

ABSTRACT

To handle increased capacity demands, sophisticated MIMO-based transmission strategies, based on transmitter cooperation, have emerged. However, different types of users' channels (e.g., static vs mobile, stable vs dynamic channels) that make up today's enterprises, require different MIMO transmission strategies. With the wrong strategy, a user could even see a degradation in performance. Our overarching goal is to design and implement a framework, TRINITY, that can simultaneously cater to a heterogeneous mix of users, by intelligently combining a plurality of MIMO transmission strategies wherein the transmitters at different nodes can cooperate to deliver significant performance gains. Three key challenges that we address in building TRINITY are: (i) how to categorize users into channel profiles such that a single transmission strategy caters to the users of a profile, (ii) how to combine strategies to communicate with users of different profiles simultaneously, and (iii) what is the granularity of transmitter cooperation needed to balance efficiency with complexity. We implement and evaluate TRINITY on our WARP radio testbed. Our extensive experiments show that TRINITY's intelligent combining of transmission strategies improves the total network rate by 50%-150%, satisfies the QoS requirements of thrice as many users, and improves PSNR for video traffic by 10 dB compared to individual transmission strategies.

Categories and Subject Descriptors

C.2.1 [**Network Architecture and Design**]: Wireless communication

*Shailendra Singh interned in the Mobile Communications and Networking department at NEC Laboratories America Inc., Princeton during this work.

MobiHoc'15, June 22–25, 2015, Hangzhou, China.

http://dx.doi.org/10.1145/2746285.2746321.

General Terms

Algorithms, Experimentation, Measurement, Performance

Keywords

Network MIMO, Distributed Antenna System (DAS), Transmitter Cooperation, Heterogeneous user profiles

1. INTRODUCTION

Enterprises previously dominated by wireless static users with devices like laptops are increasingly seeing mobile users, thanks to smartphones and Bring-Your-Own-Device (BYOD) initiatives. At the same time, wireless transmission strategies have evolved to cope with increased capacity demands. Specifically, the past decade has seen the emergence of sophisticated MIMO-based strategies.

While standards have emerged for both single user (802.11n) and multi-user (802.11ac) MIMO, they still only dictate transmissions within a cell. Recent research has led to networked MIMO systems, wherein the APs of different cells can cooperate and transmit simultaneously. With *network multiplexing*, such cooperation can control interference to deliver a scalable, network-wide multiplexing gain (scales with the number of transmitters [16]). With *network diversity*, the cooperation could lead to higher robustness to fading and mobility due to a diversity gain. Transmission cooperation could lead to significant throughput gains over conventional systems that simply reuse the spectrum (e.g., using CSMA).

Different types of users need different strategies: However, harnessing the potential gains from transmission cooperation in a heterogeneous setting is not easy. While network multiplexing (e.g., using netMIMO [16]; Fig. 1c) supports concurrent data flows from transmitters in close proximity (e.g., APs of neighboring cells) and could thus, maximize throughput, it can only apply to static users. This is because, such multiplexing can only be realized if the entire process (eg. for netMIMO) of estimating channel state information (CSI) at a receiver, feeding back the CSI to the transmitter and subsequently, transmitting the data are completed within the coherence time (the time after which the CSI can be expected to change) of a channel. Applying netMIMO for mobile users or for users with short coherence times, can even hurt performance by as much as 70% for a 3-user network as shown later. For mobile users, one can conceivably apply network diversity, where there is no need for CSI feedback; here, multiple versions of the same data stream are sent from the different transmitters (e.g., distributed antenna system or DAS technology or space-time codes; Fig. 1b). The diversity gain increases the reliability of the transmission as the channel state changes rapidly. It also provides a much larger transmission footprint (at the expense of spatial reuse) that allows mobile users to receive data reliably as they move around without handoffs. Note here that static clients would obtain much lower throughputs with network diversity, than that with netMIMO.

With both network multiplexing and network diversity we veer from traditional WiFi access (e.g., CSMA) by having the base stations (each possibly with multiple antennas) in close proximity coordinate their transmissions. However, there could be static clients that experience low coherence times due to the dynamics of the environment they are in (e.g., human motion, closing/opening of doors). For such clients, using network diversity that limits spatial reuse is an overkill since they do not move from the footprint of one transmitter to that of another. On the other hand, one cannot apply network multiplexing since the CSI changes rapidly. For such clients, the use of traditional CSMA type spectrum reuse policies seems to be the best way to go as shown via experiments in Section 2.2.

Classification of users and strategies: To cater to a mix of users with diverse channel and mobility characteristics (referred to as user/channel *profiles*), our thesis is that one must tailor transmission strategies to user profiles towards maximizing performance and improving user quality of experience. The users in an enterprise network can be categorized as follows based on the above discussion. First, they can be categorized into those with large and small channel coherence times. Further, among those with small coherence times, they can be classified based on the contributing factor - user mobility or environment dynamics. Similarly, the gamut of wireless transmission strategies can be grouped into three distinct categories based on transmitter cooperation and CSI availability. At the top level, we have those that allow transmitter cooperation and those that do not. We refer to the latter as simply Reuse strategies (eg. CSMA). Schemes that enable transmitter cooperation can be further classified into (a) *network multiplexing* requiring CSI feedback (e.g., netMIMO, MU-MIMO), and (b) *network diversity* without requiring CSI feedback (e.g., space-time block codes, DAS etc.). Note that this classification subsumes conventional diversity-multiplexing strategies (e.g., 802.11n) in single transmitter settings (the multiple antennas are treated as separate transmitters). With real-world experiments, we show that applying the right strategy for each user profile is important not just for improving performance but more importantly to prevent any performance degradation (from applying the wrong strategy).

Challenges: Many challenges arise in ensuring that the right strategy is applied to each user profile in practice: (i) What is the overhead in obtaining timely CSI ? (ii) Can CSI by itself suffice in categorizing users into the different profiles or are other forms of feedback needed ? (iii) Given the high CSI overhead of netMIMO, how can one scale transmission cooperation to a large network ? (iv) How can a transmitter simultaneously apply the different transmission strategies in the presence of a heterogeneous mix of users ?

Contributions: In this paper, we design and implement a practical framework, TRINITY, that can (i) accurately categorize users into the various profiles, (ii) combine multiple strategies at transmitters to effectively cater to users of various profiles simultaneously, and (iii) determine the appropriate granularity of transmitter cooperation to balance performance against overhead and complexity. Briefly, TRINITY is deployed at a central controller (managing enterprise networks) and incorporates three key design elements.

1. It enables simultaneous operation of all strategies by intelligently combining them in either frequency or time. We focus on the frequency domain since it allows for power pooling [9] benefits not available with time domain operations. Moreover, most of today's networks (802.11n, WiMAX, LTE) are based on OFDM; the available OFDM spectrum units (called *sub-carriers*) are split between different strategies. However, note that the design can be trivially modified to combine the strategies in the time domain.

2. The resources (e.g., # sub-carriers) allocated to a strategy depends on the traffic load of the corresponding user profile and is integrated with a user categorization process. A measurement (CSI and SNR) driven approach coupled with sensor hints (e.g., accelerometer [17]), is used to accurately categorize users into profiles.

3. To optimize network performance, we propose a novel scheme for clustering transmitters that addresses the performance-complexity trade off with network multiplexing and the coverage-capacity trade off with network diversity, in large networks.

We implement and evaluate TRINITY via extensive experiments on our 13 node WARP [4] testbed and with large-scale simulations. We see that TRINITY categorizes users with 90-95% accuracy. Tailoring transmission strategies to heterogeneous user profiles at finer time-scales compared to application layer dynamics, TRINITY can benefit both throughput and delay sensitive applications. It improves network rate by 50%-150%, satisfies QoS requirements for *thrice* as many users, and improves PSNR for video traffic by 10 dB, compared to individual transmission strategies.

2. APPLYING THE RIGHT STRATEGY

We first provide a primer on transmission cooperation strategies. Later, we determine what strategy to use for each user profile.

2.1 Classification of Strategies

Network Multiplexing: With network multiplexing, multiple independent data streams are transmitted concurrently from multiple cooperating APs to different users by converting interference into a multiplexing gain; an example of this is network (distributed) MIMO [16]. The data streams for different users are shared at all APs, which are tightly synchronized (at the carrier signal level). From the PHY layer perspective, this can be realized using a data encoding (called precoding) scheme called zero-forcing beamforming (ZFBF) [23]; this applies a precoding matrix (computed from inverse of the channel matrix between APs and the clients) to send a linear combination of the data streams through each AP, such that unwanted streams (interference) cancel out at each client, leaving only the desired stream. A simple scenario is shown in Fig. 1c. Network MIMO (netMIMO) allows the capacity to scale *linearly* with the number of cooperating APs. However, this comes at the cost of tight phase synchronization across APs and overhead caused by clients' channel state information (CSI) feedback to the APs. We refer to variants of closed-loop (requiring CSI) precoding schemes (e.g., netMIMO, adaptive beamforming, MU-MIMO) both across and within APs collectively, as *network multiplexing* schemes.

Network Diversity: These schemes send multiple, coherent versions of a data stream via multiple transmitters to provide transmit diversity. An example is the use of distributed Alamouti space-time (ST) codes [23]; when APs 1 and 2 employ the 2×1 Alamouti code to jointly transmit to client 1, the resulting diversity gain scales the SNR at the client by the factor $|h_{11}|^2 + |h_{21}|^2$, where h_{ij} is the complex channel gain between AP i and user j. A simpler form of transmit diversity is to transmit the same data (symbols) from multiple transmitters as shown in Fig. 1b, wherein client 1 receives a combination of the streams transmitted from all APs over a composite channel $\tilde{h} = h_{11} + h_{21} + h_{31} + h_{41}$. The power pooled from the multiple transmitters contributes to a combining (SNR) gain on average. This form of network diversity is similar in principle to

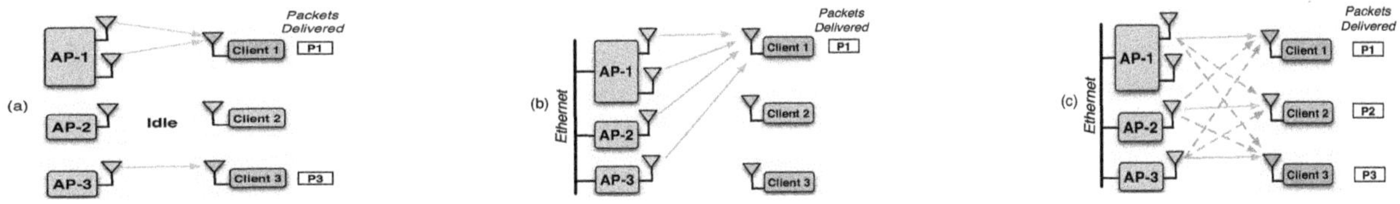

Figure 1 (a) Reuse: Two slot schedule: AP1, AP3 active simultaneously in slot 1, AP2 in slot 2. (b) DAS: 3 slot schedule - 3 APs sending same data to one client in each slot. (c) netMIMO: 3 APs sending 3 data streams to 3 clients in each slot.

broadcast and is referred to as a distributed antenna system (DAS). Unlike ST diversity, DAS does not require a receiver to *estimate* the state with respect to the individual channels from the different transmitters (no associated pilot overhead). This has made it highly popular for deployments in both WiFi and cellular frameworks [1].

These schemes not only improve coverage and robustness - factors critical for handling mobility, but also provide a diversity (SNR) gain that translates to a *logarithmic* increase in capacity. Further, they do not need timely CSI feedback (from the clients to the APs). We refer to such schemes broadly as *network diversity* schemes.

Spectrum reuse: In addition to network multiplexing and diversity, it is also important to consider *non-cooperating* transmitters. This includes conventional time-divisioned access (e.g., CSMA) wherein, APs defer transmissions in the presence of interference (a busy channel) while spatial reuse is automatically leveraged otherwise. In the example in Fig. 1a , APs 1 and 3 can transmit in tandem on the same channel, while AP 2 time shares the medium with 1 and 3. Such schemes (e.g., distributed CSMA or centralized scheduling [19]) will collectively be referred to as *Reuse* schemes.

2.2 Guidelines for Strategy Selection

Users in enterprise networks can be categorized into one of the following three categories based on their mobility and channel coherence characteristics: **(i)** *Mobile users with Short Coherence Times (Mobile)*: Coherence time (Tc) varies based on the speed of a client which can range from walking speeds of 3-4 Kmph (Tc = 10 ms) to vehicular speeds of 75 Kmph[1] (Tc = 1.1 ms). **(ii)** *Static Users with Short Coherence Time (Short-Tc)*: Static users can also experience short Tc (10-20 ms or less) due to dynamic settings where objects or other users move. **(iii)** *Static Users with Long Coherence Time (Static)*: Clients in static settings in the absence of mobility, experience a more stable channel (longer Tc, 100 ms or more).

Experimental Study Next, we perform experiments to determine the appropriate transmission strategy for each user category; our studies here form the basis for TRINITY's design. We will use CSMA (a Reuse strategy), DAS and netMIMO as the representative transmission strategies. Our experimental set-up (more details in Section 5) shown in Figures 1a, 1b and 1c is deployed in an indoor lab with three transmitters and three clients using a WARP testbed. For all mobile experiments, we placed the WARP radios on a cart and moved it on the same path at the same walking speed. Aggregate network rate (throughput normalized to unit bandwidth, bits/s/Hz) is used as the metric and depends on both client SNR received as well as the schedules indicated in Figs. 1a, 1b and 1c. The reported results are averaged over multiple runs.

Static Clients: From Fig. 2a, we see that *when all the clients are static, netMIMO is the most appropriate strategy*, outperforming Reuse and DAS by up to 69.8%. It achieves high network rate by multiplexing three data streams to three clients at the same time. Since the channel coherence time in our static environment is large, all clients can decode their data with high reliability. Further, *since the benefit of spatial reuse (absent in DAS) outweighs the diversity gain in static environments, Reuse performs better than DAS.*

[1]Vehicular speeds are considered as our schemes are also applicable to outdoor small cell (eg. LTE) mobile networks.

Mobile Clients: However, as we vary the number of mobile clients in the network, the performance of both netMIMO and Reuse start to degrade; the degradation for netMIMO is especially severe. On the other hand, *owing to coverage and combining gain in SNR from three transmitters without reliance on any CSI, DAS is unaffected by client mobility.* Thus, DAS outperforms netMIMO and Reuse by up to 96.7% depending on the number of mobile clients.

To better understand the behavior of these transmission schemes, we also recorded the received SNR of the symbols from each transmitter. Fig. 2b shows the average SNR of the mobile clients under Reuse, DAS and netMIMO over multiple runs. For DAS and netMIMO, we only report the SNR values of a single client; other clients also exhibit a similar trend. In the Reuse scheme, client-1(C1) is associated with AP-1, client-2(C2) with AP-2, client-3(C3) with AP-3. During experiments, client-1 is moved from left to right while client-3 is moved from right to left. Client-2 is moved in both directions. It can be inferred from Fig. 2b that each client in Reuse, experiences a high SNR only when they are near their respective APs. In DAS, a mobile client experiences a high SNR throughout the experiment due to the coverage and the signal combining effect from the three transmitters, with about 5-6 dB of SNR gain over the highest SNR possible with Reuse (with ideal handoffs).

Why not Reuse or netMIMO for Mobile Clients? *In addition to link degradation, mobility also impacts the benefits of spatial reuse in Reuse.* Even for centralized schemes [19] to leverage reuse, interference conflicts have to be determined (from transmitters to various clients) to establish appropriate reuse schedules - a process that is executed only once every several packets to reduce overhead/complexity. In the presence of client mobility, tracking interference conflicts of mobile clients accurately is not practical; this in turn affects the Reuse performance with respect to such clients.

In netMIMO, the SNR drops if the client becomes mobile. We see in Fig. 2c that unlike for a static client, there is a large variation in channel phase (20°-40°) and magnitude (1-2 dB) for a walking client even with a CSI feedback rate of once every 10 ms. Since precoding depends on CSI to remove interference between concurrent streams, *stale CSI from such variations from mobility has a bigger impact on netMIMO performance*. Further, if there are N clients/AP, M APs and S sub-carriers in a OFDM transmission, to apply netMIMO, one needs to measure channel qualities from each of the M APs (sequentially, M transmissions) to all the $M \cdot N$ clients on all the S sub-carriers ($S \cdot M \cdot N$ channels). This has to be then fed back from each of the clients ($M \cdot N$ transmissions) to construct the channel matrix required by the precoding algorithm. Further, a few measurements per client are typically needed for stable channel estimates. Thus, it is hard to accomplish this entire process within the channel coherence times of even walking clients.

The expanded coverage along with combining gain in SNR, without reliance on any CSI, makes DAS the strategy that is least impacted by (and thus, best suited for dealing with) client mobility.

Short-Tc Clients: A static client can also experience fluctuating channel conditions due to environment dynamics etc. This can result in small channel coherence times (≈ 10 ms) even if the client is static as seen in Fig. 2c, where a static client is in a busy indoor cafe. Fig. 2d shows the aggregate network rate achieved by each scheme with an increasing number of such static clients.

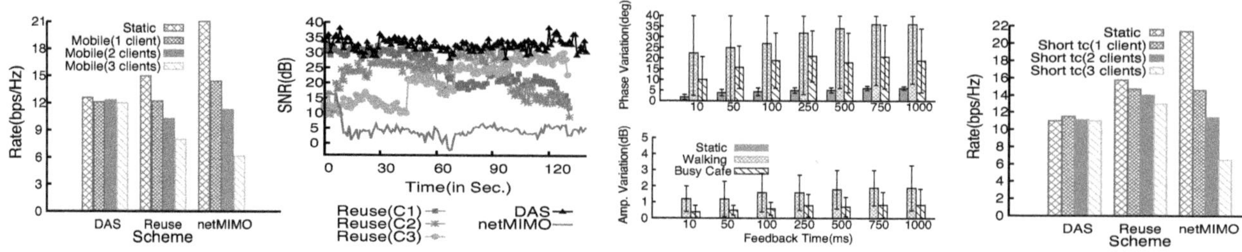

(a) (b) (c) (d)

Figure 2 : (a) Static vs. Mobile. (b) Impact of Mobility. (c) Channel variations. (d) Static with Short Tc.

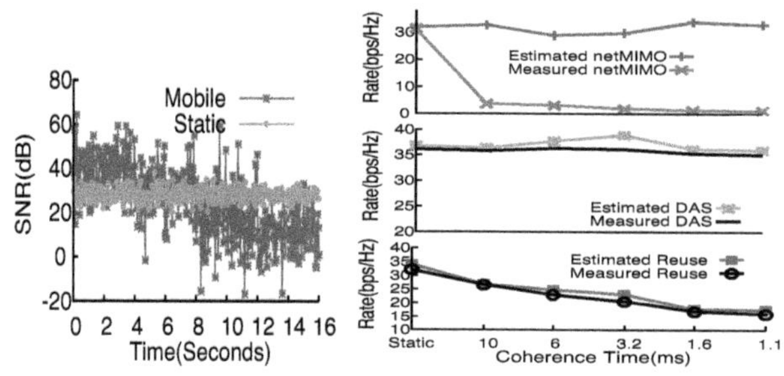

(a) (b)

Figure 3 : (a) SNR: Mobile Vs. Static. (b) Estimated vs. Measured.

With phase variations as high as 20°, even with a CSI feedback period of 10 ms, netMIMO is highly susceptible to stale CSI and the achieved rate degrades in a manner similar to that in the mobile scenario. However the degradation in Reuse is now less pronounced. While link quality is impacted, since the topology (interference pattern) does not change, spatial reuse is not impacted and thus, Reuse outperforms DAS (reuse gains will increase with topology size). Hence, interestingly, *a simple Reuse scheme is the best for static clients that experience small coherence times.*

Our work in perspective: Our strategy classification is based on core features related to transmitter cooperation and CSI availability and is generic enough to accommodate most open-loop and closed-loop transmission schemes. A few important remarks are in order. **(A)** Our classification of multiplexing, diversity and reuse, is from the *network* perspective, accounting for transmitter cooperation; it subsumes conventional multiplexing-diversity schemes applied at a single transmitter. When transmitters and clients have multiple antennas themselves, each transmitter in our network-level open-loop (no CSI) schemes (Reuse and network diversity) can in addition apply 802.11n's (MIMO) open loop multiplexing/diversity. **(B)** The focus of our work is to exploit transmission cooperation to maximize the performance of the network as a whole, and not of specific individual clients; however, the latter also improves as a by-product. For example, for a static client with poor links to the multiple spatially dispersed transmitters, DAS may yield its highest individual throughput; however, DAS prevents the transmitters from multiplexing other clients and thus hurts aggregate network performance. **(C)** Network multiplexing only refers to the ability to multiplex multiple streams across different transmitters and does not preclude diversity. Indeed, by inherently accounting for client link qualities (based on CSI) [8], it determines the appropriate number of streams that can be sent to each client. If clients with poor but stable channels are chosen for the multiplexing session, then more antennas would automatically be used to generate fewer streams (i.e. providing diversity) to these clients, such that it maximizes the aggregate throughput performance of the session.

3. DESIGN OF TRINITY

In applying the right strategy to each user profile based on the aforementioned inferences, two key challenges arise in practice: (i) How to categorize users into various profiles? and (ii) How to intelligently combine various strategies to cater to a heterogeneous set of users simultaneously and manage resources effectively between strategies? We now present the key elements in TRINITY designed to address these challenges. TRINITY is implemented at a central controller that manages a set of distributed transmitters.

3.1 Categorization

While device-based categorization (smartphone ⇒ mobile, laptop ⇒ static) is simple, it does not capture a user's true channel state (e.g., laptop in a busy cafe). However, measuring the channel coherence time of a user directly is hard. Hence, TRINITY uses indirect indicators such as mobility cues (sensor/SNR hints) along with rate degradation (from CSI estimates) *jointly* for categorizing users.

3.1.1 Mobility Triggers

Sensor hints: Most mobile devices (smartphones/tablets) have GPS and accelerometers. While GPS provides a good estimate of user speeds outdoors (especially for vehicular users), accelerometer readings have been successfully used (e.g., [17]) to decipher user mobility indoors with high accuracy. When accelerometer data is available, TRINITY employs the approach in [17]. Briefly, for each new accelerometer sample, the standard deviation of the sample's magnitude is computed over a sliding window (w) of samples. If this standard deviation exceeds a threshold (a), movement is detected. If it is within the threshold for n successive windows, the device is deemed stationary. We use the values $w = 5$, $a = 0.15$ m/s^2, and $n = 10$; in [17] it was experimentally shown that with these values, device movement can be detected with an accuracy over 95%.

SNR hints: While sensor hints provide high accuracy, they may not be always available. In such cases, TRINITY uses SNR hints to decipher user mobility using an approach similar to that in [11]. Specifically, the variation in the average SNR of a client is used for this purpose. Consider a simple experiment where a mobile client is moving away from the AP at walking speed; we record the SNR variation that it experiences with time. We perform 20 such trials and the SNR trace from one such trial is compared against that of a static client in Fig. 3a. As expected, the SNR variation for a mobile client is high due to the dynamic environment. We find that this variation is consistently more than 10 dB in all 20 trials. Similar experimental results are also reported in [11]. Using this value as a threshold, we consider a user to be mobile (mobility hint) as follows: we compute the standard deviation (σ) over a moving window (2 seconds) of 10 measured samples of average SNR over a 200 ms (t_o) interval. If $\sigma > 10$ dB, the user is considered mobile.

Compared to sensor hints, SNR hints only provide an accuracy of just over 80%. Hence, TRINITY employs sensor hints for detecting user mobility whenever available and resorts to SNR hints only when the former is not present.

3.1.2 *Sensitivity of netMIMO*

Finally, netMIMO's sensitivity to fluctuating channels can also be effectively used for categorization. When channel states are measured from the transmitters to users for netMIMO, one can estimate the SINR and thus, the rate *expected* at users when netMIMO is applied (calculated using standard techniques [22]). When netMIMO is executed, the resulting SINR or rate can be *measured* and then compared against the estimated value. A significant drop in measured rate compared to the expected rate will result if netMIMO can no longer be supported by the user's channel. To understand the validity of our claim, we simulate a scenario with different channel coherence times to create mobility. Instead of transmitting the symbols over the air we pass them through a flat AWGN channel, so as to keep it constant over the coherence time (channel feedback rate is 20ms), after which it changes independently to a new realization. We find that (Fig. 3b) netMIMO rate drastically degrades for a client when it changes its state from being static to mobile even at walking speed. Unlike DAS or Reuse, the deviation between the estimated and measured rates is very large for netMIMO (more than 50% consistently) due to its strong reliance on CSI.

CSI alone is insufficient: Instead of using sensor/SNR hints, one might wonder if CSI estimates alone are sufficient for user categorization. Such an approach has two major shortcomings. First, it requires CSI estimation/feedback overhead for all users, regardless of whether or not they can support netMIMO; this will be prohibitive in terms of overhead. Second, CSI is limited to characterizing coherence times, but cannot attribute reasons to why coherence times are short; this is important to distinguish between DAS and Reuse.

3.1.3 *Proposed Algorithm*

TRINITY leverages the above two indicators *jointly* to categorize users with high accuracy as follows.

Initial Step 1: When a user joins the network, with sensor and/or SNR hints, it first determines if the user is mobile and if so categorizes it to be a DAS user. Otherwise, it aggressively assumes the user to be a netMIMO user.

Initial Step 2: During netMIMO operation, if there is a significant gap between the estimated (from CSI feedback) and measured netMIMO rates (by more than 50%) for the user, then the user is removed from the netMIMO category. If the user cannot support netMIMO and if its sensor and/or SNR hints do not indicate it to be a DAS user, only then the user is classified as a Reuse user.

Recurring Step: Since a user's profile can change temporally, categorization cannot be a one-time process. If the user is a netMIMO or Reuse user and if its profile degrades to a lower multiplexing (rate) category (netMIMO→reuse→DAS), then this would automatically be reflected in its rate (for netMIMO) and sensor/SNR hints (for Reuse). Using these triggers, the user can then be appropriately assigned to DAS or Reuse. To account for temporal changes, categorization is implicitly integrated within TRINITY.

3.2 Joint Application of Strategies

In reality, users of different profiles are inter-twined in various regions of the network. Hence, it is inevitable that we combine different strategies (at each transmitter) either in the time or frequency domain to serve such a mix of users.

TRINITY combines the strategies in the frequency domain. Thus, it can leverage *power pooling* benefits at the transmitters [9]. The sub-carriers in an OFDM system (say N in total) are split orthogonally (e.g., N_m to netMIMO, N_d to DAS, $N - N_m - N_d$ to Reuse; see Fig. 6) between the various strategies. Each transmitter then transmits with the appropriate subset of sub-carriers carrying data for users of the corresponding profile. On the downlink (AP→users), when an AP (with fixed transmit power) has users that do not span *all* profiles, the power on the sub-carrriers assigned to the unused strategie(s) will be pooled to the sub-carriers assigned to the remaining strategies in operation. This results in a higher SNR on the sub-carriers in operation, a gain termed as *power pooling gain*. Note that when strategies are combined in the time-domain (which TRINITY can do), all sub-carriers are used for a given strategy at a time and thus there is no room for power pooling.

3.3 Resource Management

Once users are categorized, an estimate of the traffic loads from each category are collected by the central controller (from the APs). The different user profiles (i) are then weighted (v_i) based on the traffic load, and the allocation of number of sub-carriers to each of the strategies across the entire network is made proportional to their weights (e.g., $N_i = \frac{v_i N}{\sum_i v_i}$). Note that other weight choices based on priority/QoS can also be employed. Once the v_i's are determined, the sub-carrier allocation is done by the central controller, and is updated periodically at coarse time-scales to track traffic load variations. Among the sub-carriers allocated to a strategy, users in the respective profile are then scheduled based on a desired fairness model (proportional fairness in our case, details are in [7]). Since resource management is tightly coupled with user categorization, it continuously adapts to dynamics in user profiles. Once resources have been allocated to different strategies (user profiles), the next step is to determine how the transmitters serving users in different categories access these resources.

4. MEDIUM ACCESS IN TRINITY

While the Reuse strategy can be realized in a completely distributed manner, cooperation strategies like netMIMO and DAS require a central controller to manage synchronization, processing, etc. Thus, in TRINITY downlink transmissions are *scheduled* by its central controller. However, media access in TRINITY can also be easily realized in a quasi-distributed manner as discussed later in Section 4.2. Further, since the resources allocated to the strategies are orthogonalized in the frequency domain, it is sufficient to consider scheduling within each strategy in isolation. We later discuss (Section 4.4) how the various strategies are integrated at a transmitter.

4.1 Clustering for netMIMO and DAS

Need for Clustering: For netMIMO, the ideal operation would be to execute one large netMIMO between all the transmitters in the network and the users in the netMIMO category. While this would provide the maximum number of concurrent streams (scaling with the # of transmitters), this would also incur the overhead of synchronizing all the transmitters, measuring (and feeding back) CSI from all transmitters to all netMIMO users and sharing of all netMIMO users' data streams across all transmitters. Clearly this is not scalable beyond a few transmitters (as in [12, 16]).

Similarly with DAS, grouping all transmitters in one big DAS set-up eliminates the need to identify appropriate transmitters for various clients. However, the cost incurred is that the data on each sub-carrier is broadcast by all the transmitters, thereby significantly limiting reuse in the network. Given that users' mobility may be restricted to regions of the network for a given period of time, this could cause a gross under-utilization of the spectrum.

Approach: To address these issues, TRINITY groups the transmitters into smaller, contiguous clusters (e.g., Fig. 5), and netMIMO and DAS are applied only within each cluster. Interference between clusters is avoided either in the time or frequency domain. Applying cooperation strategies at cluster granularity ensures feasibility and scalability for netMIMO, and allows for spectrum reuse across clusters in DAS. The maximum cluster size (Q,

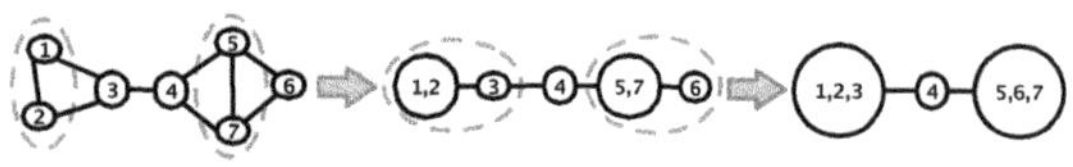

Figure 4 : Graph coarsening with $Q = 3$

decided based on practical considerations), and the clusters themselves can be different for netMIMO and DAS.

Clustering Algorithm: To establish clusters, we design a novel, topology-aware clustering algorithm for TRINITY. The underlying principle is that transmitters within each cluster should have strong mutual interference, in order to maximize the cooperation or combining gain. Moreover, transmitters across different clusters should be weakly coupled, so as to maximize frequency reuse opportunities. TRINITY adopts a graph coarsening approach to clustering (executed by the central controller), whereby neighboring vertices are consolidated (merged) recursively based on a desired metric.
Step 1: For each strategy, the entire network can be represented by a conflict graph $G(V, E)$, where transmitters constitute the vertices V and an edge $(u, v) \in E$ indicates interference (to clients) between transmitters u and v operating under the given strategy.
Step 2: For each randomly selected vertex v, the algorithm finds the neighbor u that with v, suspends the locally maximum *clique* (members interfere with each other). Then, it merges u, v and their edge into a single vertex u', which is added to the conflict graph.
Step 3: This process is applied recursively on the new conflict graph, until no more vertices can be merged or the cluster size constraint Q is reached. Each vertex in the resultant conflict graph contains multiple transmitters in the original network, which then form the desired clusters (Fig. 4).

TRINITY employs *maximum clique* as its coarsening metric as it creates clusters with good cooperation gain, while also reducing the interference across clusters. Note that the above conflict graph is determined at coarse time scales as it depends only on the AP layouts (which do not change) and aggregate client distributions around each AP (which only change gradually).

4.2 Interference Avoidance across Clusters

An inevitable feature of clustering in netMIMO and DAS is that transmitters on the edge of the clusters will receive interference from neighboring clusters, albeit only from transmitters using the same strategy. To eliminate such inter-cluster interference, TRINITY takes the following approach through resource allocation.
Step 1: It considers a conflict graph with clusters themselves as vertices (an edge exists between adjoining clusters) and performs a simple, (degree-based) greedy multi-coloring on the set of sub-carriers allocated to the strategy.
Step 2: The orthogonal sets of sub-carriers assigned to the clusters are then used by their cluster-edge (interfering) transmitters *only* to remove inter-cluster interference. *All* sub-carriers allocated to the strategy are used by the cluster-interior (non-interfering) transmitters, thereby allowing for efficient reuse of resources across all the clusters. In the example in Fig. 5, APs 3 and 4 are cluster-edge, interfering transmitters and hence operate on orthogonal sub-carriers (first 24 sub-carriers), while the other APs operate on all sub-carriers (see Fig. 6) for their netMIMO clients.

Note that with *Reuse*, there is no clustering (the cluster size is one with every transmitter being an edge transmitter).

Random access approach: While TRINITY adopts a scheduled approach, it can also use a distributed random access MAC to handle interference between clusters. Such a quasi-distributed approach would retain coordination only within the clusters (for applying cooperative strategies), while decoupling operations across clusters.

4.3 Framing Transmissions

TRINITY combines multiple strategies in the frequency domain at a transmitter, which amounts to transmitting to multiple clients in a single frame. This is the essence of OFDMA, which is popular in cellular networks (LTE, WiMAX). Like a conventional OFDMA frame, TRINITY's transmission frames are two-dimensional in time and frequency (time symbols and sub-carriers), and consists of a preamble followed by a control region. The control region contains information on which sub-carriers carry data for which user, and the MCS (modulation and coding rate) to be used for decoding the data. The controller ensures that data for users on a specific strategy are scheduled only on sub-carriers assigned to that strategy. Training or reference signals/pilots are embedded in the frame (similar to WiMAX/LTE, 802.11n/ac) to enable frequency synchronization, channel measurement and CSI reporting for netMIMO.

4.4 TRINITY: Summary of Operations

We summarize the operations in TRINITY with the simple example in Fig. 5; there are 6 APs and 9 clients, six of which (1,2,3,5,6,7) are static, two (4,8) are short-Tc and one (9) is mobile.
1. With sensor and/or SNR hints, an uncategorized user is first checked to see if it is a DAS user (client 9). Otherwise, it is assumed to be a netMIMO user. Channels are estimated for that user and netMIMO is then applied. Based on the estimated and observed rates for netMIMO operation, and coupled with sensor/SNR hints, the user is appropriately categorized as either netMIMO or a Reuse user (clients 1,2,3,5,6,7 are netMIMO; 4,8 are Reuse users).
2. Sub-carriers in the frequency domain are partitioned between strategies based on traffic loads of users in the associated categories, priority and fairness. (Assuming identical traffic load for all clients, netMIMO, Reuse and DAS strategies receive 24, 8 and 4 sub-carriers respectively out of a total of 36 sub-carriers.)
3. For a given cluster size constraint ($Q_{netMIMO} = 3$, $Q_{DAS} = 6$), transmitters are clustered for netMIMO and DAS, using the heavy clique graph coarsening approach (two clusters for netMIMO and one for DAS). Transmitters in the cluster interior (APs 1,2,5,6 for netMIMO; all APs for DAS) use all sub-carriers assigned to the strategy; those at the cluster edge operate on a subset determined by multi-coloring to avoid interference (for netMIMO, APs 3 and 4 operate on orthogonal sets of 12 sub-carriers out of the allocated 24). For Reuse, transmitters use multi-coloring to determine their frequency resources (APs 2 and 5 do not interfere and use all 8 sub-carriers assigned for Reuse). Clients are then scheduled at each transmitter for each strategy on the appropriate set of sub-carriers.
4. Data for multiple clients belonging to different profiles are combined in the frequency domain and transmitted simultaneously from each AP (frame transmissions at each AP are shown in Fig. 6).
5. While netMIMO users are re-categorized automatically when their channel state changes to one with low multiplexing gain, Reuse and DAS users are explicitly moved to netMIMO periodically to see if they have moved to a state with a higher multiplexing gain.

5. IMPLEMENTATION AND TEST-BED

5.1 Implementation

We prototype TRINITY on the WARP (FPGA-based) SDR platform using the WARPLab framework. Multiple WARP boards can be connected to a host PC via an Ethernet switch. The host PC performs the (de-) construction and processing of baseband waveforms transmitted (received) to (from) the FPGA board with the RF front-end. TRINITY and all its components are executed on the Host PC, which also serves as the central controller. Single antenna WARP boards are used for both the AP and clients.

Transmission Strategies: Our PHY layer implementation for Reuse is a centralized version of 802.11g with standard (de-) modulation techniques with 64 sub-carriers per OFDM symbol. When

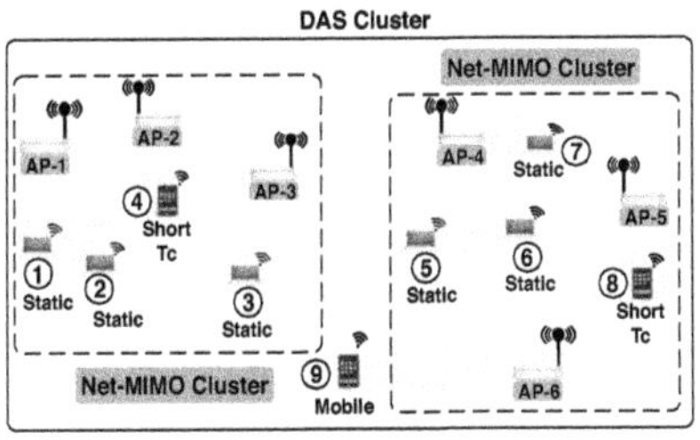

Figure 5 : Sample network topology

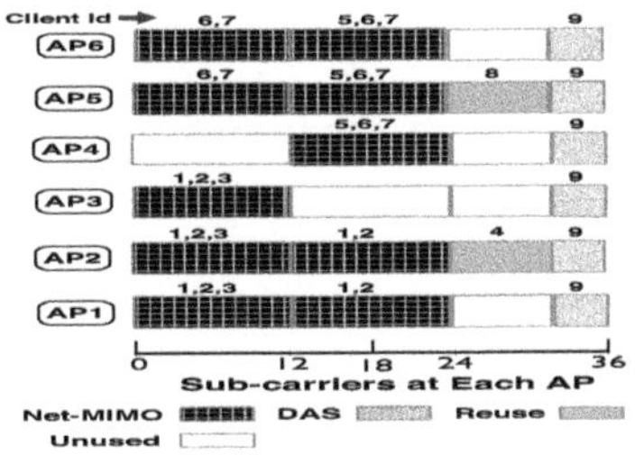

Figure 6 : Execution of Trinity

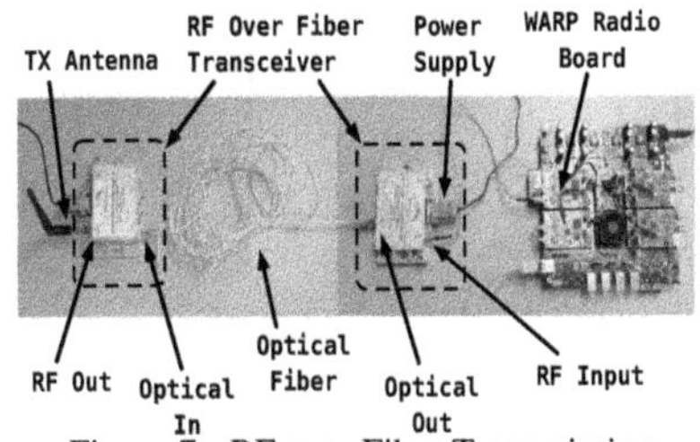

Figure 7 : RF over Fiber Transmission

Frequency	2.48GHz	Bandwidth	10MHz
Feedback Rate	50ms	Symbols/Pkt	1024
Symbol Time	$20\mu s$	Modulation	BPSK

Table 1 : Physical layer parameters

transmitters apply netMIMO, the central controller performs a linear combination of the BPSK symbols (zero-forcing beamforming precoding [23]) to be sent by the different transmitters so as to pre-cancel their mutual interference. The channel matrix, whose inverse provides the precoding matrix, is obtained before netMIMO operation from the CSI piggy-backed (by clients) on the most recently received ACK packets. Each receiver estimate its CSI based on pilots from the last few OFDM symbols received in the previous frame. Due to the nature of WARPLab framework, the minimum feedback delay for CSI is 50 ms; this is still sufficient for enabling netMIMO for static clients. The DAS mode is an extension to the Reuse PHY. The same data symbols are modulated and sent over the air by different transmitters simultaneously without precoding.

Categorization: The central controller collects and keeps track of rate information (for netMIMO clients), and sensor and SNR hints needed for categorization. SNR hints are realized from measurements from the sent and received data bits. However, WARP devices do not provide sensor hints unlike modern mobile devices. Several WARP-based PHY layer designs [4] have employed WARP's User I/O push buttons for events such as switching antenna mode, changing modulation and coding etc. Similarly, in TRINITY we program one of the push buttons to generate the sensor hint to the central controller that the client is mobile once it starts walking.

5.2 Deployment and Synchronization

In our implementation, we make the transmitters lightweight (serve as just RF boards that transmit signals). All the baseband processing is pushed to the central controller. This allows for an efficient and practical realization of netMIMO, especially for synchronizing, estimating channels and sharing of data streams across APs over a large geographic area. With each WARP mother board serving 4 daughter RF boards, we move the mother boards to the central controller, while the daughter boards serve as the RF transmitters. The RF signals processed at the mother boards are carried to the RF daughter boards through optical fibers (as shown in Fig. 7) that have very low latency (≈ 5 μs/Km), thereby preserving the symbol-level synchronization needed for netMIMO. The RF signal is modulated to optical through an off-the-shelf commercial RoF (radio over fiber) transceiver, carried over the fiber and then converted back to RF signal at the other end. Co-locating multiple WARP mother boards also enables easier clock and phase synchronization between them (using approaches recently proposed in [18]) - a feature imperative for the functioning of netMIMO. Note that the above distributed, *thin* AP deployment model has recently become a very cost-effective and popular option for cellular and WiFi coverage in convention centers, hospitals, etc. [5].

5.3 Experimental Set-up

Our WARP testbed, consisting of 6 transmitters and 7 clients, is deployed in an indoor office setting as shown in Fig. 8. Different scenarios are created by moving the transmitters and clients to different locations. For mobility, WARP clients placed on a cart are moved at (timed and repeatable) fixed walking speeds on the same path across all experiments. Since a controlled environment is not possible for short-Tc clients (e.g., busy cafe), for repeatability, we emulate their channel variations by moving only their antennas in the proximity of their original location. Fig. 9 shows that such emulation produces channel variations very similar to a busy cafe, while allowing for repeatability.

To avoid external interference, we use channel 14 (unused by other devices) in the 2.4 Ghz band. Back to back packets are sent for 6 minutes using appropriate strategies in each experiment and the results are averages over multiple runs unless otherwise stated.

Metrics: The main metrics of evaluation are aggregate network rate (bits/s/Hz or bits/s as appropriate) and utility. A client's rate is obtained from its achievable Shannon rate ($log(1+\rho)$) and depends on the average received SINR (ρ, per sub-carrier) per transmitted OFDM symbol, and the number of sub-carriers allocated to the client. For netMIMO, transmission rates are implicitly determined as part of the pre-coding phase once CSI is known. For Reuse and DAS, where CSI is not employed, any of the conventional SNR based rate adaptation schemes can be used. However, due to the inherent feedback latency in WARP, rate adaptation is currently not supported for Reuse and DAS in our test-bed. In a way, measuring the rate directly from SINR of received symbols assumes ideal rate adaptation and hence prevents the vagaries of rate adaptation algorithms from influencing the inferences on strategies. Utility is used to characterize fairness among clients in the same category. The utility of a user is the logarithm of its rate ($\log(R_i)$) [3]. We seek to maximize the sum of the utilities of all users (network wide utility); this results in proportional fairness [3].

To evaluate QoS, we consider video delivery. Specifically, we consider typical video file [6] (encoding rate = 1Mbps, frames per second = 30) downloads and estimate the achieved Peak-Signal-to-Noise-Ratios (PSNR) for quantifying the delivered QoS. PSNR is defined as a function of the mean squared error (MSE) between the pixels of the decoded video and that of the original version. It is computed as follows: $PSNR = 10\log_{10}\frac{2^L-1}{MSE}\ [dB]$, where L is the number of bits used to encode pixel luminance (8 bits).

6. EVALUATION

6.1 Categorization

We use a sample network topology containing 3 APs and 6 clients as shown in Figure 10. Two scenarios are considered: (1) categorizing a single client (client 4) in isolation, and (2) categorizing two clients (2 and 4) simultaneously. To emulate a realistic scenario, where newly joined clients in the network need to be categorized, we assume that the pre-existing clients in the network are already

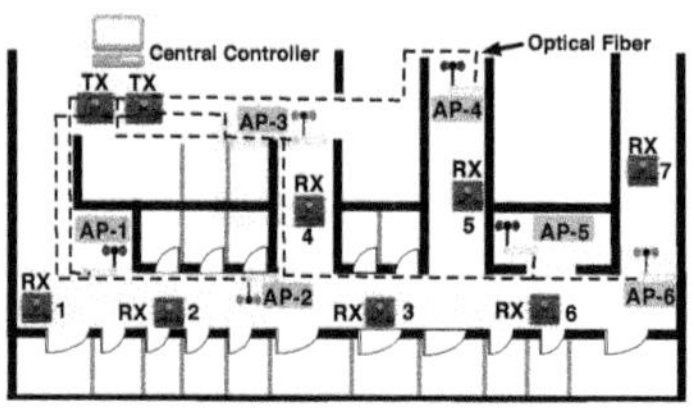

Figure 8 : Testbed deployment

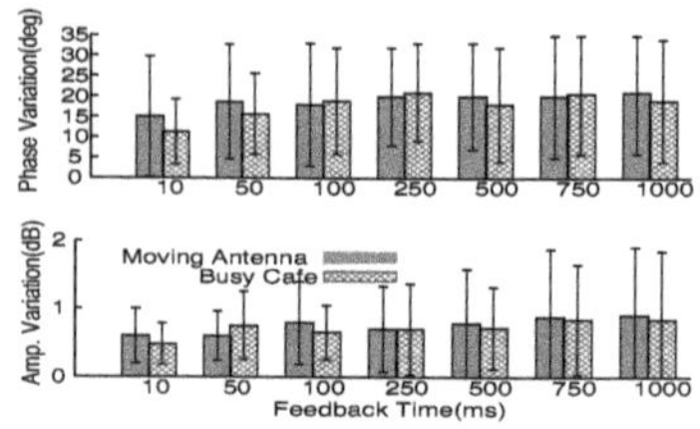

Figure 9 : Channel Variation

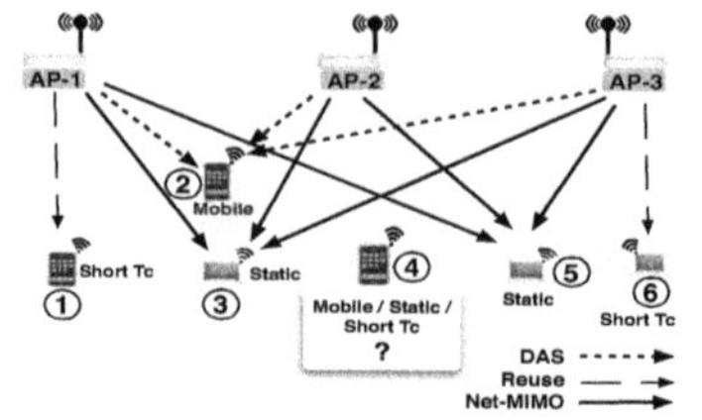

Figure 10 : Sample categorization topology

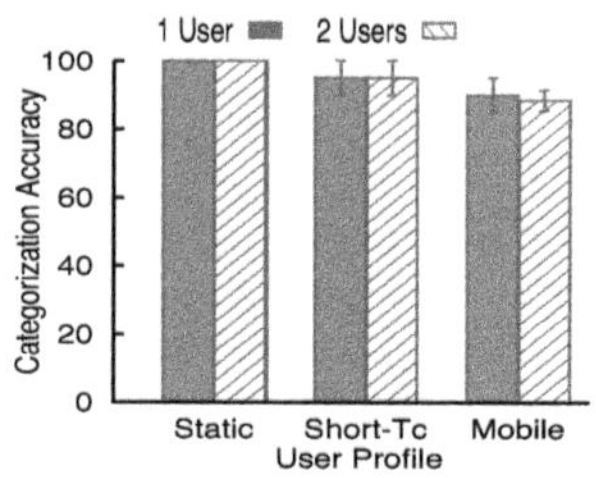

Figure 11 : Categorization Accuracy

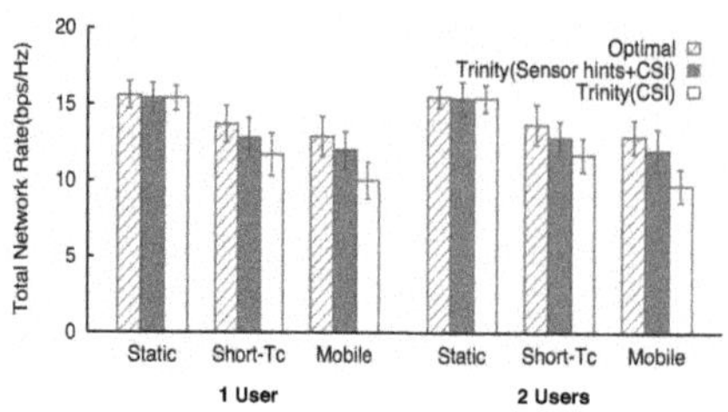

Figure 12 : Impact on Network Rate

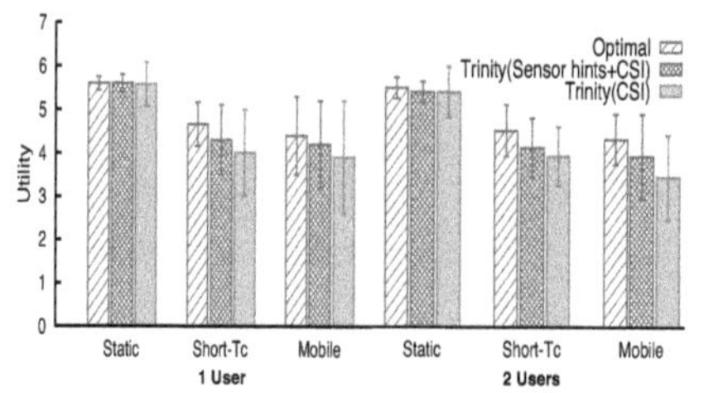

Figure 13 : Impact on Network Utility

categorized accurately. Given that all devices may not provide sensor hints, we also consider two variants - one with sensor hints and one without sensor hints (only SNR hints and CSI).

Accuracy with and without sensor hints: Client 4's channel state is set to be in one of 3 states: static, mobile or short-Tc. 20 trials are performed with each state. In the case of two clients (4 and 2), we experiment over all possible combinations of their profiles. Categorization accuracy is evaluated by comparing the profile categorized by TRINITY against *ground truth*, which is the profile that yields the highest aggregate network rate. To determine a client's optimal profile, we perform an exhaustive search over all possible combinations of strategies (DAS, Reuse and netMIMO) for each client, to find the combination which maximizes the overall network rate.

As seen in Fig. 11, TRINITY achieves a high accuracy of 95% for netMIMO users, 90-95% for Reuse users and 80-85% for DAS users. The accuracy is highest for netMIMO, where rate discrepancies provide a clear indicator, while channel dynamics for DAS users cause some classification errors. The accuracy with sensor hints is about 11% higher on average, than without it, indicating that SNR hints may be sufficient in providing an accurate classification of DAS and Reuse users, although at the expense of network performance. Further, introducing multiple clients for simultaneous categorization does not impact the accuracy of categorization. This is expected as categorization is specific to individual clients.

Impact on network rate and utility: Next, we examine the implication of the accuracy on on the aggregate network rate. Here, after categorization, the apt transmission schemes are used to transfer data to clients and the aggregate network rate is measured. The results in Fig. 12 clearly indicate that the impact of making local categorization decisions for users, although sub-optimal compared to the exhaustive global approach (e.g., some slow moving users may be under Reuse), does not incur appreciable loss (compared to optimal), while providing a large reduction in complexity. Given the high accuracy of categorizing netMIMO users, their loss in network rate is negligible. For Reuse and DAS users, the loss is small with sensor hints; in its absence it can get to 10% and 15%, respectively, but still remains within reasonable limits. Similar results are seen when utility is used to capture the fairness in Fig. 13.

The above experiments demonstrate *TRINITY's ability to categorize users appropriately with high accuracy using a combination of standard CSI/SNR and sensor hints, thereby yielding close-to optimal network performance.*

6.2 Combining Strategies in Frequency

For all the strategy-combining experiments, a topology where 2 APs jointly apply netMIMO to 2 netMIMO clients and DAS to a single DAS client, is used. In addition, one of the APs serves a single Reuse client. Since different number of sub-carriers may be employed for each strategy when combining them in a frame, we use rate in bit/s (accounting for # sub-carriers) as our metric. In the interest of space, we defer results on feasibility of frequency-domain combining, power pooling and flexible resource allocation policies in TRINITY to [7].

To understand the implication of power pooling gains with frequency domain combining (FDC), we consider its impact on network rate compared to time domain combining (TDC). In our experimental topology, when the Reuse client is associated with AP1, the sub-carriers allocated for Reuse at AP2 are un-used and their power is redirected to those that serve netMIMO and DAS users. Considering an equal split of sub-carriers between strategies, this results in about a 10% gain in the aggregate network rate compared to TDC (Fig. 14a). When the DAS user is removed, its sub-carriers are re-allocated between netMIMO and Reuse users. This results in additional un-used sub-carriers (and their power) from the Reuse strategy at AP2, which are used to serve the netMIMO users. This further increases the rate gain to $\approx$ 15%.

Increasing the number of APs, increases the possibility of more sub-carriers being left un-used at APs, since all APs may not be serving users from all profiles. To see if this contributes to increased network rate, we increase the number of APs within the interference range of the current two APs in our topology. Indeed, Fig. 14b shows that increasing the number of APs can harness additional power pooling gains from FDC and contribute to $\approx$ 20% increase in network rate compared to TDC. Note that, while in practice the amount of power that can be pooled is limited by FCC regulations [2], it can still deliver appreciable gains [9].

6.2.1 Case study in a dynamic network

We consider a sample case study to highlight TRINITY's adaptation to network dynamics (more cases in [7]). The experiment consists of 6 APs and 6 clients as shown in Figure 14c. APs 1 and 6 do not interfere with other APs, whereas APs 2, 3, 4 and 5 are in a cluster, where they interfere with each other and can invoke either netMIMO or DAS. There are 3 static and 3 short-Tc clients at the start of the experiment. We depict TRINITY's operations and reactions on a time line in Fig. 15. We see that at the start of the ex-

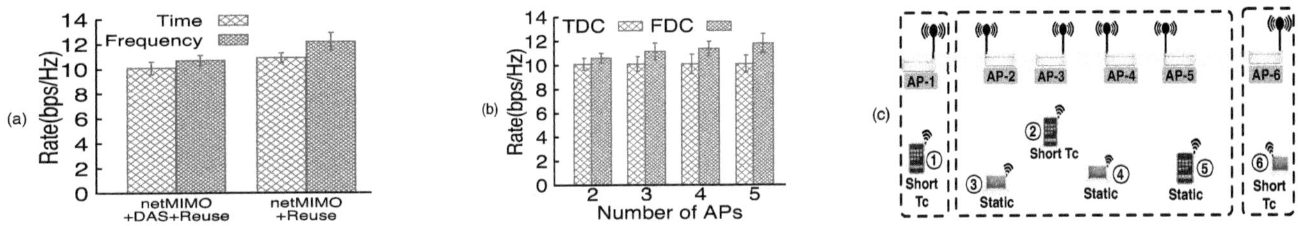

Figure 14 :(a) TDC Vs. FDC. (b) Impact of # APs on FDC. (c) Sample network topology for case study.

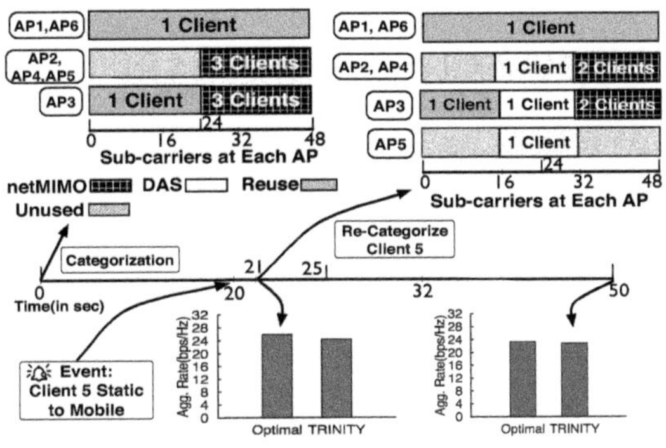

Figure 15 : Execution of TRINITY on sample topology.

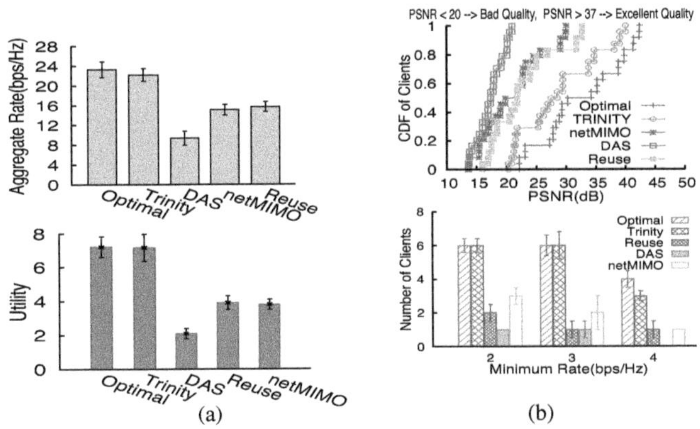

Figure 16 : (a) Performance of TRINITY (b) QoS

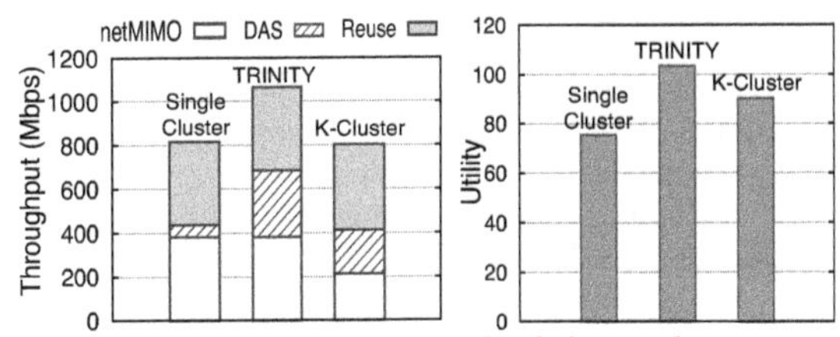

Figure 17 : Trace-driven simulation results.

periment, TRINITY categorizes the clients accurately into different profiles - static clients are assigned to netMIMO, whereas short-Tc clients are assigned to Reuse. TRINITY then runs its strategy combining algorithm to apply these strategies on orthogonal frequencies (see Fig. 15) and begins transmissions. APs 2, 3, 4 and 5 split their sub-carriers between netMIMO (served by APs 2,3,4,5) and reuse (served by AP 3) in the cluster. Hence, APs 2, 4 and 5 benefit from the power pooled from their un-used Reuse sub-carriers.

At the 20th second, we change client 5's state from static to mobile; we move it at walking speed in the vicinity of APs 2, 3, 4 and 5 until the experiment ends. The change in profile to a lower multiplexing one (from netMIMO) is identified automatically.

TRINITY re-categorizes client 5 within a second, into the DAS profile and obtains the new sub-carrier mapping for the APs as shown in Fig. 15. To understand the impact on network rate during network dynamics, we compare TRINITY's rate against that of the optimal (exhaustive search) solution which is also executed immediately after re-categorization as well as after 50s. It can be seen that the loss in network performance during the re-categorization process (latency to find the new profile) is small and gets further amortized when measured over a longer time window. Note that the time line experiment is part of a longer 6 min. experiment but only the first 50 seconds are shown here.

6.3 Integrating TRINITY Components

Impact on Network Rate/Utility: To understand TRINITY's performance (network-level), we compare it with four other schemes: optimal (exhaustive search), netMIMO-only, DAS-only and Reuse-only. The latter three are baseline strategies that apply only one strategy to all users irrespective of their profile and is hence representative of state of the art schemes that do not differentiate between user profiles. Our evaluations include various network topologies with 6 APs and 6 clients in our testbed, similar to those in Figs. 5 & 14c but with a more comprehensive set of clustering patterns for the APs, namely topologies with (i) linear placement of APs (only neighboring APs interfere with each other's clients), (ii) two clusters of 3 APs each, (iii) three clusters of 2 APs each, (iv) clusters of size 1, 2 and 3 APs, and (v) a single cluster of 6 APs. In each topology, clients' locations and profiles are randomly configured, and the APs transmit back-to-back data for 180 seconds.

Fig. 16a shows the average of the aggregate network rate and utility respectively, achieved over all scenarios for each scheme. We see that *TRINITY's performance is very close to that of optimal and outperforms other schemes by almost 50-150% in network rate and by two folds in utility.* This exemplifies the merit of catering transmission strategies to user profiles with TRINITY.

6.3.1 Impact on User Quality of Experience

Since we consider clients of various profiles, a given rate or throughput may not be valued the same by clients with different profiles. Hence, we also evaluate TRINITY in terms of client QoS satisfaction (using same set of topologies as previous experiment). To this end, we first consider a simple metric, wherein each client requires a minimum rate for its application for satisfactory experience and the goal is to see how many clients' requirements can be satisfied. Fig. 16b (bottom) shows the number of clients satisfied by a given scheme as a function of their increasing minimum rate requirement. We see that TRINITY is capable of satisfying as many clients as the optimal scheme in most of the cases. Further, *it can cater to thrice as many clients as the other individual strategies.* Next, we consider a standard encoded video of rate 1 Mbps with 30 frames per second for each client to understand the direct impact on application performance in Fig. 16b (top). Here, we see that *TRINITY is able to improve clients' video quality significantly by providing a large (median) gain of 10 dB in PSNR.*

6.3.2 *Large-scale Trace-driven Simulations*

Since it is hard to scale a testbed running netMIMO on WARP to larger topologies, we now evaluate the *complete* TRINITY solution using trace-driven simulations. To create traces for a realistic network topology, we move the WARP nodes to various locations of an office building, and collect the per-subcarrier CSI (both magnitude and phase distortion) between nearby transceiver pairs. These WARP nodes together form a network of 20 APs and 30 clients. Each AP has 2 to 6 neighboring APs within its sensing range, and serves 1 to 3 clients within its communication range. Among the clients, there are 8 Reuse, 10 netMIMO and 12 DAS users. The CSI and interference relations between neighboring nodes are then fed into a simulator executing TRINITY. We evaluate TRINITY against its variants, where its clustering component is replaced by one of the following schemes: (i) Single Cluster, which aggregates all netMIMO or DAS APs into a single cluster; (ii) K-Cluster, which greedily clusters nearby K transmitters (K is fixed to 4 in our experiments). In TRINITY, the maximum cluster size is 4.

Fig. 17(a) shows that Single Cluster achieves the highest throughput for netMIMO users owing to its global synchronization and data sharing across all netMIMO APs. However, TRINITY suffers only a small loss in performance due to splitting the APs into small clusters of practical size. This is because not all APs interfere with each other in a large network, and TRINITY can leverage spatial reuse between remote APs in different clusters. The K-cluster scheme does not account for the topology factor in its clustering process, *i.e.*, weak/strong interference between nearby APs, and thus it loses 26.1% throughput compared to TRINITY.

For DAS users, Single Cluster achieves the lowest performance, as it completely sacrifices spatial reuse for diversity, causing substantial throughput loss when there are multiple DAS users spread over a large area. TRINITY and K-cluster strike a good balance between diversity (needed for mobility) and spatial reuse. For Reuse clients, all the schemes achieve a comparable level of performance (Similar inferences can be made for utility results in Fig. 17(b)).

7. RELATED WORK

Experimental software radio platforms have allowed network practitioners to take sophisticated PHY layer multiplexing schemes like beamforming (e.g., [13]), multi-user MIMO (e.g.,[10]), interference alignment [12, 13], network MIMO (e.g., [16]),from theory to practice. Similar efforts exist with respect to Reuse [19] and diversity [15] strategies as well. While these works have made great strides in highlighting the potential and practical limitations of such schemes, their focus has understandably been on static clients with stable channels (for reliable CSI estimation) as a first step. On the theory front, works [14] are now exploring how to effectively leverage outdated CSI. However, their use in netMIMO is still in its early stages and is hence not considered here.

Given the heterogeneity of user profiles in both enterprises and outdoor cellular (e.g., LTE/WiMAX small cells) networks, it is important to understand which *strategies* are apt for which user profiles and how to combine them. While [20] articulated the need for using different strategies for different user profiles, no system was designed or implemented towards realizing this vision.

8. DISCUSSIONS AND CONCLUSIONS

We design, implement and evaluate a practical framework TRINITY, that identifies and optimizes transmission (cooperation) strategies to cater to a heterogeneous mix of users effectively, thereby improving their quality of experience in wireless networks.

Complexity and Overhead: TRINITY requires only as much overhead as any closed-loop transmission scheme like beamforming or netMIMO. By identifying the right set of netMIMO clients, it saves on the complexity and feedback overhead incurred in applying netMIMO generically to all clients. Further, by restricting netMIMO to clusters, its complexity and overhead are further reduced.

Uplink: Realizing OFDMA on the uplink requires sub-carrier level synchronization between clients being multiplexed, which is challenging although doable [21]. Thus, TRINITY is currently limited to FDC on the downlink, while using TDC on the uplink.

9. REFERENCES

[1] DAS in Action : Atlanta. `http://bit.ly/ACRt4V`.

[2] Fcc rules for unlicensed wireless equipment operating in the ism bands. `http://www.afar.net/tutorials/fcc-rules/`.

[3] Network utility maximization. `http://bit.ly/1el4QAb`.

[4] Rice University WARP project. `http://warp.rice.edu`.

[5] Wired is the new wireless. `http://bit.ly/UaD2AC`.

[6] Xiph.org video media. http://media.xiph.org/video/derf/.

[7] Tailoring wireless transmission strategies to user profiles in wireless networks: Tech. report. `http://bit.ly/1suD5xO`, 2013.

[8] A.H., M., AND A., N. Diversity of MIMO linear precoding. In *IEEE Trans. on Info. Theory* (2014).

[9] ARSLAN, M. Y., SUNDARESAN, K., KRISHNAMURTHY, S. V., AND RANGARAJAN, S. Design and implementation of an integrated beamformer and uplink scheduler for ofdma femtocells. In *ACM MobiHoc* (2012).

[10] ARYAFAR, E., AN, N., SALONIDIS, T., AND KNIGHTLY, E. W. Design and Experimental Evaluation of Multi-user Beamforming in Wireless LANs. In *ACM MobiCom* (2010).

[11] FARKAS, K., HOSSMANN, T., LEGENDRE, F., PLATTNER, B., AND DAS, S. K. Link quality prediction in mesh networks. *Elsevier Comput. Commun.* (2008).

[12] GOLLAKOTA, S., PERLI, S. D., AND KATABI, D. Interference alignment and cancellation. In *ACM SIGCOMM* (2009).

[13] KUMAR, S., CIFUENTES, D., GOLLAKOTA, S., AND KATABI, D. Bringing cross-layer mimo to today's wireless lans. In *ACM SIGCOMM* (2013).

[14] MADDAH-ALI, M. A., AND TSE, D. Completely stale transmitter channel state information is still very useful. In *Allerton* (2010).

[15] RAHUL, H., HASSANIEH, H., AND KATABI, D. Sourcesync: a distributed wireless architecture for exploiting sender diversity. In *ACM SIGCOMM* (2010).

[16] RAHUL, H. S., KUMAR, S., AND KATABI, D. JMB: Scaling Wireless Capacity with User Demand. In *ACM SIGCOMM* (2012).

[17] RAVINDRANATH, L., NEWPORT, C., BALAKRISHNAN, H., AND MADDEN, S. Improving Wireless Network Performance Using Sensor Hints. In *USENIX NSDI* (2011).

[18] SHEPARD, C., YU, H., ANAND, N., LI, E., MARZETTA, T., YANG, R., AND ZHONG, L. Argos: practical many-antenna base stations. In *ACM Mobicom* (2012).

[19] SHRIVASTAVA, V., AHMED, N., RAYANCHU, S., BANERJEE, S., KESHAV, S., PAPAGIANNAKI, K., AND MISHRA, A. Centaur: realizing the full potential of centralized wlans through a hybrid data path. In *ACM Mobicom* (2009).

[20] SINGH, S., SUNDARESAN, K., KHOJASTEPOUR, A., RANGARAJAN, S., AND KRISHNAMURTHY, S. V. One strategy does not serve all: Tailoring wireless transmission strategies to user profiles. In *ACM HotNets* (2012).

[21] TAN, K., FANG, J., ZHANG, Y., CHEN, S., SHI, L., ZHANG, J., AND ZHANG, Y. Fine-grained channel access in wireless lan. In *ACM SIGCOMM* (2010).

[22] TARIGHAT, A., SADEK, M., AND SAYED, A. A multi user beamforming scheme for downlink mimo channels based on maximizing signal-to-leakage ratios. In *IEEE ICASSP* (2005).

[23] TSE, D., AND VISWANATH, P. Fundamentals of wireless communication. Cambridge University Press, 2005.

Device-to-Device Communication Overlaying Two-Hop Multi-Channel Uplink Cellular Networks

Jiajia Liu
School of Computer Science and Technology
Xidian University
Xi'an, China
liujiajia@xidian.edu.cn

Nei Kato
Graduate School of Information Sciences
Tohoku University
Sendai, Japan
kato@it.ecei.tohoku.ac.jp

ABSTRACT

Different from previous works, in this paper, we adopt D2D communication as a routing extension to traditional cellular uplinks thus enabling a two-hop route between a user and the serving BS via a D2D relay. Specifically, a BS establishes a cellular link with a mobile user only if the pilot signal strength received from the user is above a specified threshold; otherwise, the user may establish a D2D link with a neighboring user and connect to a nearby BS in a two-hop manner. We present a stochastic geometry based framework to analyze the coverage probability and average rate in such a two-hop multi-channel uplink cellular network where mobile users adopt the fractional channel inversion power control with maximum transmit power limit. As validated by extensive numerical results, the developed framework enables network designers to efficiently determine the optimal control parameters so as to achieve the optimum system performance. Our results show that employing D2D link based two-hop connection can significantly improve both the network coverage and average rate for uplink traffic.

Categories and Subject Descriptors

C.2.1 [**Computer-Communication Networks**]: Network Architecture and Design—*Wireless Communication*

General Terms

Performance

Keywords

Device-to-device communication, uplink, fractional power control, multi-channel cellular network, stochastic geometry

1. INTRODUCTION

Among all the Long Term Evolution (LTE)-Advanced communication techniques, device-to-device (D2D) communication, defined to directly route data traffic between spatially closely located mobile users, has been regarded as one of the most promising techniques to improve energy and spectrum efficiency, especially for Proximity-based Services (ProSe) [1, 3] and Group Communication System Enablers for LTE (GCSE_LTE) [2]. Besides the intensive research activities and meetings organized by 3GPP TSG RAN WG1, recently, there has been a surging interest from academia and industry in D2D communication. Depending to the implementation details, a D2D pair may communicate in the same cellular band (as an underlay) or in reserved frequency resources (as an overlay) [5, 6]. A detailed survey can be found in [5].

So far, D2D communication has been mostly studied for direct downlink traffic offloading between two mobile users within proximity, such as interference management, resource allocation, performance evaluation, etc. That is, for a cellular user, the requested data is delivered from the buffer of a neighboring user via D2D communication, without traversing through the serving BS or the core network. It is noticed that there has been some pioneer works exploring D2D communication in uplink transmission [9, 12, 13]. In [9], the authors proposed a distributed power control algorithm to minimize the overall per user power consumption. In [12, 13], the D2D pair reuse the uplink frequency and the focus is to manage the interference from cellular users to the D2D receiver. A common feature of these works is that the authors studied the issues of interference control and resource allocation among cellular users and D2D users by focusing on a D2D pair in only one or two cells. Consequently, it cannot be applied to the general deployment scenario with a large number of BSs and mobile users, where the network-wide accumulated interference as well as the spatial distributions of BSs and users play an important role in determining the achievable network performance.

To the best of the authors' knowledge, the work most close to this work is [11]. In [11], the authors considered both the underlay mode and the overlay mode for allocating spectrum resources to D2D communications, where the BSs are regularly placed at the center of hexagonal cells. Note that for each D2D transmitter in [11], it is assumed that there is a specific D2D receiver just located within the transmission range of the D2D transmitter. Therefore, each D2D transmitter is always able to establish a D2D link and transmit its data to a D2D receiver, leaving the problem how the D2D receiver further uploads the received data to the core network unexplored. In practical scenarios, however, even the success probability of establishing such one-hop D2D links is

MobiHoc'15, June 22–25, 2015, Hangzhou, China.

http://dx.doi.org/10.1145/2746285.2746311.

severely limited by the spatial distributions of mobile users and the hit rate of interested content [6].

Based on the above observation, in this paper, we adopt D2D communication as a routing extension to traditional cellular uplinks thus enabling a two-hop route between a user and the serving BS via a D2D relay. Specifically, a BS establishes a cellular link with a mobile user only if the pilot signal strength received from the user is above a specified threshold; otherwise, the user may establish a D2D link with a neighboring user and connect to a nearby BS in a two-hop manner. We present a stochastic geometry based framework to analyze the coverage probability and average rate in such a two-hop multi-channel uplink cellular network where mobile users adopt the fractional channel inversion power control with maximum transmit power limit. As validated by extensive numerical results, the developed framework enables network designers to efficiently determine the optimal control parameters so as to achieve the optimum system performance. Our results show that employing D2D link based two-hop connection can significantly improve both the network coverage and average rate for uplink traffic.

The remainder of this paper is outlined as follows. Section 2 introduces system models and deriving methodology. We provide stochastic geometric analysis of SINR statistics in cellular links and D2D links, per user coverage probability as well as average rate in Section 3. In Section 4, we present numerical results to illustrate the performance gains brought by employing D2D communications in upstream transmission, and finally conclude the whole paper in Section 5.

2. SYSTEM MODELS AND METHODOLOGY

2.1 Network Models

We consider a multi-channel cellular network consisting of BSs and users. The spatial distributions of BSs and users are mutually independent. Specifically, the BSs follow an independent homogeneous Poisson point process (PPP) Φ_b of density λ_b. The users are spatially distributed in the network region according to another independent PPP Φ_u of density λ_u. Since the user density will significantly affect the performances of the D2D communication based two-hop uplink cellular network, we present in this work a stochastic geometric model together with comprehensive analysis to address the relationship between the SINR distributions and λ_b, λ_u, as well as the number of available channel resources at each BS. Note that the considered network scenario is more general than that in [4, 7, 8] where the density of users λ_u is assumed to be large enough such that all channel resources will be assigned to users at each BS, which corresponds to some partial or special cases, such as the peak time during a day.

We focus on the uplink communications where each user always has data to upload to the BS. The data uploading from each user to a nearby BS is limited to at most two hops. That is, each user either directly transmits to the BS, or first transmits the data to a nearby user (relay) which then forwards the data to the BS. The former case is via a one-hop cellular link, while the latter is via a two-hop route consisting of a D2D link and a cellular link, as illustrated in Fig. 1. Note that in the latter case, as the BS receiving the uplink data may not be the one that is nearest to the requesting user, it is able to provide more flexibility and wider coverage for cell-edge users.

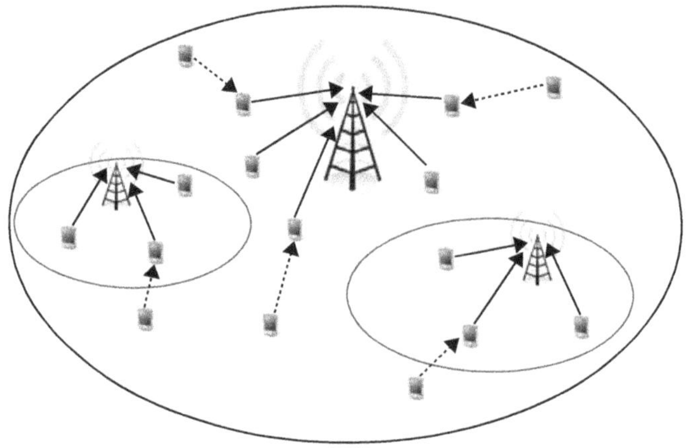

Figure 1: Illustration of D2D communication based two-hop uplink cellular network, where a user can upload its data via a one-hop cellular link or via a two-hop route consisting of a D2D link and a cellular link.

2.2 Uplink Association and D2D Link Establishment

For the considered two-hop uplink cellular network, users decide their uplink association and establish D2D links as follows. First, each user registers to its nearest BS. As the BSs will result in a Poisson-Voronoi (PV) cell tessellation in the network region, each user indeed registers to the BS located within the same PV-cell. Note that since we consider the uplink transmission and each user selects its associated BS according to their spatial distance, the generated PV-cell tessellation is actually non-weighted. Second, each user transmits a pilot signal to its associated BS to test the channel quality. If the pilot signal strength received at the BS is above a specified threshold β, the user establishes a cellular link with the BS and uploads its data directly to the BS; otherwise, the user operates in D2D mode and tries to establish a D2D link with adjacent one-hop cellular users. For the case that multiple users request to form a D2D link with a one-hop cellular user, it selects the nearest one out of them as the D2D transmitter. The maximum transmission range for establishing D2D links is d_m.

The threshold β may be interpreted as a control parameter which corresponds to the antenna design and signal processing capability at the BSs. It can also be interpreted as a basic requirement for accessing the uplink cellular frequency resources. Here we adopt it to optimize the spectrum efficiency and other network performances. The event whether a received pilot signal strength falls below β or not, is totally random and actually depends on a lot of factors, such as the spatial distance between the user and the BS, the channel quality, etc. Statistically speaking, if the value of β is too big, the number of users establishing cellular links and D2D links will become very limited and thus a lot of users remain unconnected; on the other hand, if β is too small, the spectrum resources assigned for cellular links suf-

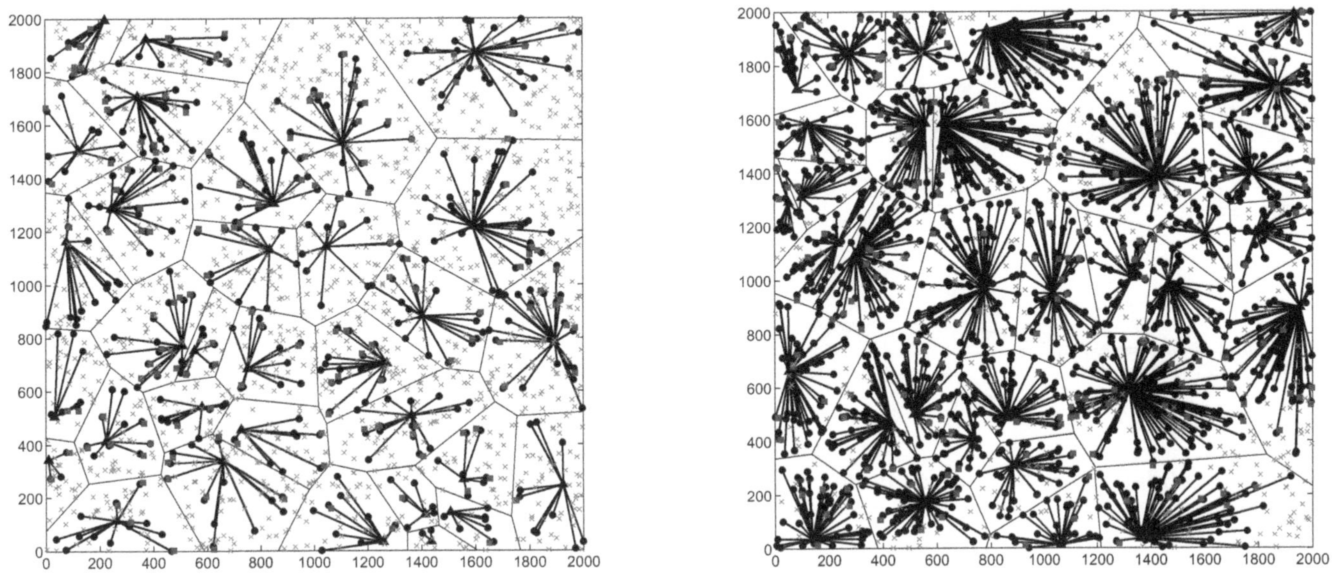

(a) $\beta = -68$ dBm

(b) $\beta = -75$ dBm

Figure 2: Illustration of uplink associations and D2D link establishment under different settings of β, where the cellular links between BSs (black triangles) and one-hop cellular users (black points) are denoted by black lines, D2D links are denoted by blue lines, users operating in D2D modes are denoted by blue squares, and the users remaining unconnected are denoted by red crosses. We set $\lambda_b = 10/\text{km}^2$, $\lambda_u = 500/\text{km}^2$, $d_m = 20\text{m}$.

fer from severe congestion while the advantages of D2D communications are underutilized. An illustrating example can be found in Fig. 2, where $\beta = -68$ dBm and $\beta = -75$ dBm are selected to represent the above two cases, respectively.

2.3 Frequency Allocation and Channel Models

To facilitate the data forwarding at the intermediate relay of a two-hop route, we assume that each user is equipped with two independent air interfaces and is able to transmit and receive in different frequency bands simultaneously. All BSs share the same frequency resources, and specifically, we evenly divide the frequency resources into $|N|+|M|$ orthogonal channels, denoted as $\{n_1, n_2, \dots, n_{|N|}, m_1, m_2, \dots, m_{|M|}\}$. The first $|N|$ channels, i.e., channels $n_1, n_2, \dots, n_{|N|}$, are allocated for direct cellular link transmissions; while the channels $m_1, m_2, \dots, m_{|M|}$ are reserved for D2D link transmissions, which corresponds to the inband overlay case in practical scenario. Therefore, for the uplink data reception at a BS in channel n_i, $1 \le i \le |N|$, it will be interfered only by the surrounding users which transmit directly to their BSs in the same channel n_i. Regarding the channel assignment of cellular links, each BS randomly selects a channel from the set $\{n_1, n_2, \dots, n_{|N|}\}$ and assigns it to a cellular link until all $|N|$ channels are used up. Note that depending on the number of users choosing to establish cellular links in each PV cell, there may be users in some cells suffering "channel outage" due to the lack of channel resources; while in some other cells there may be unassigned idle channels. For D2D communications, each D2D transmitter randomly selects a channel from $\{m_1, m_2, \dots, m_{|M|}\}$ for data transmission.

The general power-law propagation model is adopted to characterize the path-loss effect of all cellular link transmissions and D2D link transmissions. The channel noise power is assumed to be additive and of constant value σ^2. The channel gain h between a transmitter-receiver pair is assumed to be exponentially distributed. Therefore, the signal power received at a distance r from the transmitter (of unit transmit power), can be denoted as $h \cdot r^{-\alpha}$, where $\alpha > 2$ is the path-loss exponent. Considering the fact that a D2D link of short transmission range may usually have a better channel quality than a cellular link, we denote by h_b and h_u the fading coefficients of cellular links and D2D links, respectively, and let $h_b \sim \exp(\mu_b)$, $h_u \sim \exp(\mu_u)$. We assume all the fading coefficients are independent of each other, and all cellular links and D2D links share the same path-loss exponent α.

2.4 Power Control

Similar to [11, 15], we adopt the fractional channel inversion power control for uplink transmissions of all cellular links, where users utilize distance-proportional fractional power control to adapt their transmit power. In particular, given the per user maximum transmit power P_m and the communication distance r between a user-BS pair, the user adopts a transmit power p_t

$$p_t = \begin{cases} \epsilon \cdot r^{\alpha \cdot \eta} & \text{if } \epsilon \cdot r^{\alpha \cdot \eta} < P_m, \\ P_m & \text{otherwise.} \end{cases} \quad (1)$$

where α is the path-loss exponent, $\alpha > 2$, ϵ is the coefficient of proportionality, $0 < \epsilon \ll 1$, and η is the power control factor, $0 \le \eta \le 1$. One can see that such power control enables

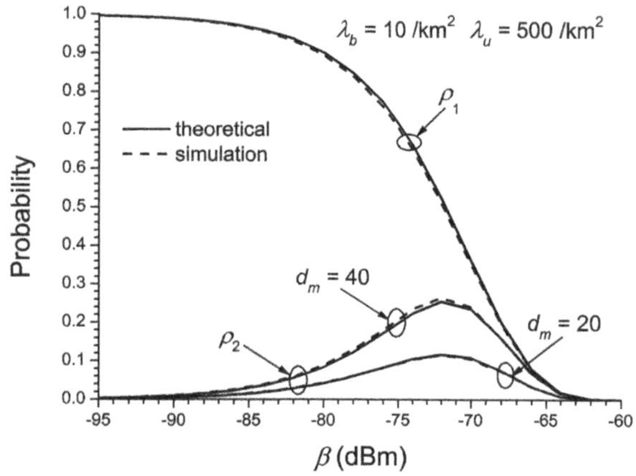

Figure 3: Validation for ρ_1 and ρ_2 under different settings of d_m, where $\epsilon = -100$ dB, $\mu_b = 1$, $\eta = 1$.

a user closer to the BS to transmit with a smaller transmit power under the maximum transmit power constraint, which improves the power-efficiency of mobile users while mitigating the interference. The special setting of $\eta = 0$ corresponds to the case of performing no channel inversion; while the setting of $\eta = 1$ corresponds to the case of complete channel inversion. Regarding the D2D communication in all D2D links, the transmitters perform no power control and transmit with the maximum transmit power P_m.

2.5 Deriving Methodology

For the considered two-hop multi-channel uplink cellular network, the performance metrics of interest are the coverage probability and average rate. Our target is to explore the performance gains brought by utilizing D2D communication for two-hop uplink transmissions, and how to properly tune the controlling parameters such as β and ϵ for network performance optimization.

Our deriving methodology is as follows. First, we calculate the spatial density of users transmitting directly to BSs with cellular links and the density of users able to establish D2D links. Second, we derive the probability density function (pdf) and moments for the transmit power of an active cellular transmitter (i.e., the user winning a channel for uplink cellular transmission). Third, we further obtain the Laplace transform of the accumulated interference received at a typical BS in a given channel, and utilize the stochastic geometry theory to derive the complementary cumulative distribution function (ccdf) of the SINR. Finally, after deriving the ccdf for the SINR of a D2D link, we are able to obtain the coverage probability and average rate for a generic cellular link and D2D link, respectively.

3. MODELING AND ANALYSIS OF TWO-HOP UPLINK TRANSMISSIONS

3.1 Densities of Users Establishing Cellular Links and D2D Links

LEMMA 1. *For the considered two-hop multi-channel uplink cellular network, if we denote by ρ_1 the probability that a generic user deciding to establish a cellular link with the nearest BS, and denote by ρ_2 the probability that a generic user being able to establish a D2D link, then we can determine ρ_1 as*

$$\rho_1 = \pi\lambda_b \int_0^{(\frac{P_m}{\epsilon})^{\frac{2}{\alpha\cdot\eta}}} e^{-\frac{\mu_b\beta}{\epsilon}t^{\frac{\alpha(1-\eta)}{2}}-\pi\lambda_b t}dt + \pi\lambda_b \int_{(\frac{P_m}{\epsilon})^{\frac{2}{\alpha\cdot\eta}}}^{\infty} e^{-\frac{\mu_b\cdot\beta}{P_m}t^{\frac{\alpha}{2}}-\pi\lambda_b t}dt \quad (2)$$

Furthermore, ρ_2 can be approximated by

$$\rho_2 = \rho_1 \cdot \left(1 - e^{-\frac{1-\rho_1}{\rho_1}\left(1-e^{-\pi d_m^2 \rho_1 \lambda_u}\right)}\right) \quad (3)$$

PROOF. We first derive ρ_1. Recall that each user first registers to the nearest BS, then transmits a pilot signal to the BS to check the channel status. The user chooses to establish a cellular link with the BS if and only if the pilot signal strength received at the BS is above a specified threshold β. If we denote by r_b the distance between a user and its nearest BS, then we have

$$\Pr(r_b > x) = e^{-\lambda_b \pi x^2}$$

and thus the pdf of r_b

$$f_{r_b}(x) = 2\pi\lambda_b x e^{-\pi\lambda_b x^2} \quad (4)$$

Consider a generic user-BS pair. Note that whether the received pilot signal strength is above β or not is a random event, which depends on the transmission distance, channel fading, etc. Then, we have

$$\begin{aligned}
\rho_1 &= \Pr(p_t \cdot h_b \cdot r_b^{-\alpha} > \beta) \\
&\overset{(i)}{=} \int_0^{(\frac{P_m}{\epsilon})^{\frac{1}{\alpha\cdot\eta}}} e^{-\frac{\mu_b\beta}{\epsilon}x^{\alpha(1-\eta)}} \cdot f_{r_b}(x)dx + \int_{(\frac{P_m}{\epsilon})^{\frac{1}{\alpha\cdot\eta}}}^{\infty} e^{-\frac{\mu_b\cdot\beta}{P_m}x^{\alpha}} \cdot f_{r_b}(x)dx \\
&\overset{(ii)}{=} \pi\lambda_b \int_0^{(\frac{P_m}{\epsilon})^{\frac{2}{\alpha\cdot\eta}}} e^{-\frac{\mu_b\beta}{\epsilon}t^{\frac{\alpha(1-\eta)}{2}}-\pi\lambda_b t}dt + \pi\lambda_b \int_{(\frac{P_m}{\epsilon})^{\frac{2}{\alpha\cdot\eta}}}^{\infty} e^{-\frac{\mu_b\cdot\beta}{P_m}t^{\frac{\alpha}{2}}-\pi\lambda_b t}dt
\end{aligned}$$

where (i) follows after applying the definition of p_t in (1), and (ii) follows after substituting (4) and replacing the variable $t = x^2$.

From (2), one can see that a generic user chooses to establish a D2D link with surrounding users with probability $1-\rho_1$. Note that it can only choose the nearest one-hop cellular users (i.e., the users establishing cellular links) to form a D2D link. If we treat the one-hop cellular users as potential D2D receivers, the spatial density of potential D2D receivers can be determined as $\rho_1\lambda_u$. Accordingly, the spatial density of potential D2D transmitters can be determined as $(1-\rho_1)\lambda_u$. Therefore, the density of successful D2D links can be approximated as the density of active D2D transmitters or active D2D receivers, and then (3) can be obtained (Theorem 2 in [14]). □

Remark 1. There will be users of density $(1-\rho_1-\rho_2)\lambda_u$ remaining in outage, due to failure in establishing one-hop cellular links or D2D link based two-hop routes. Fig. 3 presents a validation for ρ_1 and ρ_2 derived in Lemma 1, where the simulation results were collected by a Matlab based simulator. One can observe from Fig. 3 that, as β increases, ρ_1 monotonically decreases; while the behavior of ρ_2 is totally different, for which there exists an optimum setting of β to achieve the maximum value. Furthermore, a careful observation of Fig. 3 shows that a bigger range d_m for allowing D2D communication, can effectively improve the value of ρ_2 (i.e., the success probability of establishing D2D links); while ρ_1 is independent of d_m, as indicated in (2).

3.2 SINRs in Cellular Links and D2D Links

From Fig. 2, one can see that the one-hop cellular users form clusters around their BSs. Due to the variations among the number of one-hop cellular users within different PV-cells, the sizes of formed clusters also vary significantly from BS to BS. Furthermore, the remaining potential D2D transmitters follow a Poisson hole process [10], which is analytically intractable due to the unknown probability generating functional. As each BS assigns channels to its one-hop cellular users randomly, for analytical tractability, we neglect the weak dependence among the distances between users and their BSs [15], and treat the spatial distribution of one-hop cellular users transmitting in the same channel as an independent PPP [8]. Similarly, we assume the D2D transmitters using the same channel follow another independent PPP.

We first derive the pdf and moment for the transmit power in cellular uplinks. According to the transmit power p_t of a generic one-hop cellular user defined in (1), we have $p_t = \epsilon \cdot r^{\alpha\cdot\eta}$, when the distance r between the user and its nearest BS satisfies $0 < r < (\frac{P_m}{\epsilon})^{\frac{1}{\alpha\cdot\eta}}$. Therefore, we can determine the pdf of p_t as

$$f_{p_t}(x) = \frac{2\pi\lambda_b}{\alpha\eta\epsilon} \frac{(\frac{x}{\epsilon})^{\frac{2}{\alpha\eta}-1} e^{-\pi\lambda_b(\frac{x}{\epsilon})^{\frac{2}{\alpha\eta}}}}{1 - e^{-\pi\lambda_b(\frac{P_m}{\epsilon})^{\frac{2}{\alpha\eta}}}} \tag{5}$$

when $0 < x < P_m$, $0 < \eta \leq 1$.

Therefore, the moment of p_t can be derived as

$$\begin{aligned} &\mathbf{E}[(p_t)^k] \\ &= \int_0^{(\frac{P_m}{\epsilon})^{\frac{1}{\alpha\eta}}} (\epsilon \cdot x^{\alpha\eta})^k f_{r_b}(x)dx + \int_{(\frac{P_m}{\epsilon})^{\frac{1}{\alpha\eta}}}^{\infty} (P_m)^k \cdot f_{r_b}(x)dx \\ &= \frac{\epsilon^k}{(\pi\lambda_b)^{\frac{\alpha\eta k}{2}}} \cdot \gamma\Big(\frac{\alpha\eta k}{2} + 1, \pi\lambda_b\Big(\frac{P_m}{\epsilon}\Big)^{\frac{2}{\alpha\eta}}\Big) \\ &\qquad + (P_m)^k e^{-\pi\lambda_b\left(\frac{P_m}{\epsilon}\right)^{\frac{2}{\alpha\eta}}} \end{aligned} \tag{6}$$

where $\gamma(s,x) = \int_0^x t^{s-1}e^{-t}dt$ is the lower incomplete Gamma function.

Recall that the transmitter in each D2D link randomly selects a channel from the set $\{m_1, m_2, \ldots, m_{|M|}\}$ for data transmission, while one-hop cellular users transmit in channels $\{n_1, n_2, \ldots, n_{|N|}\}$. Therefore, there is no cross-tier interference between cellular links and D2D links. For a typical cellular link, the interference received at the BS is from the surrounding one-hop cellular users which transmit in the same channel.

Lemma 2. *For the considered two-hop multi-channel uplink cellular network, if the distribution of one-hop cellular users transmitting in a given channel follows a homogeneous PPP $\hat{\Phi}$ of density $\hat{\lambda}$, then the ccdf for the SINR received at the BS of a typical cellular link $F_c(\hat{\lambda}, \hat{\theta}) = \Pr(SINR_c > \hat{\theta})$, can be determined as*

$$\begin{aligned} F_c(\hat{\lambda},\hat{\theta}) &= \pi\lambda_b \int_0^{(\frac{P_m}{\epsilon})^{\frac{2}{\alpha\eta}}} \exp\Big\{ - \pi\lambda_b x - \frac{\mu_b\hat{\theta}\sigma^2}{\epsilon} x^{\frac{\alpha}{2}(1-\eta)} \\ &\quad - \pi\hat{\lambda}(\frac{\hat{\theta}}{\epsilon})^{\frac{2}{\alpha}} x^{1-\eta}\mathbf{E}[(p_t)^{\frac{2}{\alpha}}] \int_0^\infty \frac{dy}{1+y^{\frac{\alpha}{2}}} \Big\} dx \\ &\quad + \pi\lambda_b \int_{(\frac{P_m}{\epsilon})^{\frac{2}{\alpha\eta}}}^{\infty} \exp\Big\{ - \pi\lambda_b x - \frac{\mu_b\hat{\theta}\sigma^2}{P_m} x^{\frac{\alpha}{2}} \\ &\quad - \pi\hat{\lambda}(\frac{\hat{\theta}}{P_m})^{\frac{2}{\alpha}} x\mathbf{E}[(p_t)^{\frac{2}{\alpha}}] \int_0^\infty \frac{dy}{1+y^{\frac{\alpha}{2}}} \Big\} dx \end{aligned} \tag{7}$$

where $\mathbf{E}[(p_t)^{\frac{2}{\alpha}}]$ is as calculated in (6).

Proof. This lemma follows after evaluating the Laplace transform of the accumulated interference measured at a BS. See Appendix A for details. □

Lemma 3. *For the considered two-hop multi-channel uplink cellular network, suppose the D2D transmitters transmitting in a given channel are distributed according to a PPP $\hat{\Phi}$ of density $\hat{\lambda}$. The ccdf for the SINR received at the receiver of a typical D2D link $F_d(\hat{\lambda}, \hat{\theta}) = \Pr(SINR_d > \hat{\theta})$, can be determined as*

$$\begin{aligned} F_d(\hat{\lambda},\hat{\theta}) = \frac{\pi\rho_1\lambda_u}{1-e^{-\pi\rho_1\lambda_u d_m^2}} \int_0^{d_m^2} \exp\Big\{ - \pi\rho_1\lambda_u x \\ - \frac{\mu_u\hat{\theta}\sigma^2}{P_m} x^{\frac{\alpha}{2}} - \pi\hat{\lambda}\hat{\theta}^{\frac{2}{\alpha}} x \int_{\hat{\theta}^{-\frac{2}{\alpha}}}^{\infty} \frac{dt}{1+t^{\frac{\alpha}{2}}} \Big\} dx \end{aligned} \tag{8}$$

Proof. See Appendix B for details. □

Note that although (8) in Lemma 3 is obtained for the case of D2D transmitters performing no power control, it can be readily extended to the case of utilizing distance-proportional fractional power control, after following derivations similar to that of Lemma 2.

3.3 Coverage Probability

Before deriving the coverage probability of a generic user in the uplink transmission, we first present some basic results regarding the probability mass function (pmf) of the number of one-hop cellular users in a general PV cell, the pdf of a channel n_i, $i \in [1, |N|]$, being assigned for cellular transmission in a PV cell, as well as the probability of a generic one-hop cellular user being allocated channel n_i by the serving BS.

Note that the area of a generic PV cell cannot be precisely calculated. In this paper, we adopt the following approximation for the pdf of PV cell area ([16])

$$f_{PV}(x) \approx \frac{\lambda_b^c c^c}{\Gamma(c)} x^{c-1} e^{-c\lambda_b x} \tag{9}$$

where λ_b is the density of Poisson distributed BSs, $\Gamma(x) = \int_0^\infty t^{x-1}e^{-t}dt$ is the Gamma function, and c is a constant $c = 3.575$.

If we denote by $q(k)$ the probability that there are k one-hop cellular users in a general PV cell, then we have

$$\begin{aligned} q(k) &= \int_0^\infty \frac{(\rho_1\lambda_u x)^k}{k!} e^{-\rho_1\lambda_u x} \cdot f_{PV}(x)dx \\ &= \frac{(\rho_1\lambda_u)^k (c\lambda_b)^c}{(\rho_1\lambda_u + c\lambda_b)^{k+c}} \cdot \frac{\Gamma(k+c)}{\Gamma(c)\Gamma(k+1)} \end{aligned} \quad (10)$$

where (10) follows after substituting (9).

Recall that within each PV cell, the BS randomly assigns channels $n_1, n_2, \ldots, n_{|N|}$ to one-hop cellular users until all channels are used up. Therefore, there is no difference between utilization probabilities among the $|N|$ channels. Without loss of generality, we denote by $\mathcal{S}_{|N|}$ the probability of a channel n_i being assigned for uplink transmission in a PV cell. Then, we have

$$\begin{aligned} \mathcal{S}_{|N|} &= \sum_{k=0}^{|N|} q(k) \cdot \frac{k}{|N|} + \sum_{k=|N|+1}^{\infty} q(k) \cdot 1 \\ &= 1 - \sum_{k=0}^{|N|} \frac{q(k)(|N| - k)}{|N|} \end{aligned} \quad (11)$$

Consider a PV cell which has at least a one-hop cellular user inside. We denote by $\mathcal{G}_{|N|}$ the probability that a generic one-hop cellular user being assigned channel n_i for uplink transmission, $i \in [1, |N|]$. Then, we have

$$\begin{aligned} \mathcal{G}_{|N|} &= \frac{\sum_{k=1}^{|N|} q(k) \cdot 1 \cdot \frac{1}{|N|} + \sum_{k=|N|+1}^{\infty} q(k) \cdot \frac{|N|}{k} \cdot \frac{1}{|N|}}{1 - q(0)} \\ &= \frac{1}{1 - q(0)} \Big(\sum_{k=1}^{|N|} \frac{q(k)}{|N|} + \sum_{k=|N|+1}^{\infty} \frac{q(k)}{k} \Big) \end{aligned} \quad (12)$$

Now we are ready to derive the coverage probability for a generic user. Given the SINR threshold θ defined for signal outage, then the coverage probability $P_c(\beta, \epsilon, \theta)$ can be given by the following theorem.

THEOREM 1. *For the considered two-hop multi-channel uplink cellular network, given the SINR threshold θ defined for outage, the coverage probability $P_c(\beta, \epsilon, \theta)$ can be determined as*

$$P_c(\beta, \epsilon, \theta) = |N| \cdot \mathcal{G}_{|N|} \cdot F_c(\mathcal{S}_{|N|} \cdot \lambda_b, \theta) \Big(\rho_1 + \rho_2 F_d(\frac{\rho_2\lambda_u}{|M|}, \theta) \Big) \quad (13)$$

where $F_c(x, \theta)$, $F_d(x, \theta)$, $\mathcal{S}_{|N|}$, and $\mathcal{G}_{|N|}$ are as defined in (7), (8), (11), and (12), respectively.

PROOF. We denote by $P_c^1(\beta, \epsilon, \theta)$ and $P_c^2(\beta, \epsilon, \theta)$, respectively, the coverage probability of a generic user in one-hop cellular link and that in a D2D based two-hop route. Then, we can determine the coverage probability as

$$P_c(\beta, \epsilon, \theta) = \rho_1 P_c^1(\beta, \epsilon, \theta) + \rho_2 P_c^2(\beta, \epsilon, \theta) \quad (14)$$

Consider a generic one-hop cellular user. From (12), one can see that it may be assigned channel n_i, $i \in [1, |N|]$ for uplink transmission with probability $\mathcal{G}_{|N|}$. As the density of one-hop cellular users transmitting in the same channel n_i can be given by $\mathcal{S}_{|N|}\lambda_b$, combining with Lemma 2, we have

$$P_c^1(\beta, \epsilon, \theta) = \sum_{i=1}^{|N|} \mathcal{G}_{|N|} \cdot F_c(\mathcal{S}_{|N|} \cdot \lambda_b, \theta) = |N| \cdot \mathcal{G}_{|N|} F_c(\mathcal{S}_{|N|} \cdot \lambda_b, \theta) \quad (15)$$

Considering the independence between the D2D link transmission and the cellular link transmission in a two-hop route, the coverage probability of a two-hop route can be given by

$$P_c^2(\beta, \epsilon, \theta) = P_c^1(\beta, \epsilon, \theta) \cdot \Pr(\text{SINR}_d > \theta) \quad (16)$$

According to Lemma 1, the spatial density of D2D transmitters is $\rho_2\lambda_u$. Since each D2D transmitter randomly selects a channel from $\{m_1, m_2, \ldots, m_{|M|}\}$ for data transmission, the density of D2D transmitters using the same channel, say m_i, is $\frac{\rho_2\lambda_u}{|M|}$. Based on Lemma 3, therefore,

$$\Pr(\text{SINR}_d > \theta) = F_d(\frac{\rho_2\lambda_u}{|M|}, \theta) \quad (17)$$

Substituting (17) into (16), we get

$$P_c^2(\beta, \epsilon, \theta) = P_c^1(\beta, \epsilon, \theta) \cdot F_d(\frac{\rho_2\lambda_u}{|M|}, \theta) \quad (18)$$

Combining (15), (18), and (14), we finish the proof for Theorem 1. □

3.4 Average Rate

THEOREM 2. *For the considered two-hop multi-channel uplink cellular network, if we denote by $R_c(\beta, \epsilon)$ the average rate (nats/s/Hz) in a general cellular link, and denote by $R_d(\beta, \epsilon)$ the average rate in a D2D link, then the average rate of a generic mobile user can be determined as*

$$R(\beta, \epsilon) = \rho_1 \cdot R_c(\beta, \epsilon) + \rho_2 \cdot \min\big(R_c(\beta, \epsilon), R_d(\beta, \epsilon)\big) \quad (19)$$

where

$$R_c(\beta, \epsilon) = \frac{|N| \cdot \mathcal{G}_{|N|}}{|M| + |N|} \cdot \int_0^\infty F_c(\mathcal{S}_{|N|} \cdot \lambda_b, e^t - 1)dt \quad (20)$$

and

$$R_d(\beta, \epsilon) = \frac{1}{|M| + |N|} \cdot \int_0^\infty F_d(\frac{\rho_2\lambda_u}{|M|}, e^t - 1)dt \quad (21)$$

PROOF. We can directly obtain (19) according to Lemma 1. As the frequency resources are evenly divided into $|N| + |M|$ channels, the frequency bandwidth of a single channel is $\frac{1}{|M|+|N|}$. Regarding $R_c(\beta, \epsilon)$, we have

$$\begin{aligned} R_c(\beta, \epsilon) &= \frac{|N| \cdot \mathcal{G}_{|N|}}{|M| + |N|} \cdot \mathbf{E}\Big[\ln\left(1 + \text{SINR}_c\right)\Big] \\ &= \frac{|N| \cdot \mathcal{G}_{|N|}}{|M| + |N|} \cdot \int_0^\infty \Pr\left(\text{SINR}_c > e^t - 1\right)dt \\ &= \frac{|N| \cdot \mathcal{G}_{|N|}}{|M| + |N|} \cdot \int_0^\infty F_c(\mathcal{S}_{|N|} \cdot \lambda_b, e^t - 1)dt \end{aligned}$$

Following similar derivations, (21) can be obtained. Then we finish the proof for Theorem 2. □

Remark 2. Note that in previous works [4, 7, 8], to facilitate the analysis of coverage probability and average rate for a user occupying a given channel, it assumed a large enough user density such that the channel will always be occupied in all cells, while neglecting the fact that it actually becomes more difficult for a user to obtain a channel as the user density increases. That is, the users may suffer from "channel outage" due to the limited frequency resources (channels) in a cell. Different from previous models, the results obtained in Theorems 1 and 2 enables a full range study on the actual coverage probability and average rate as the network

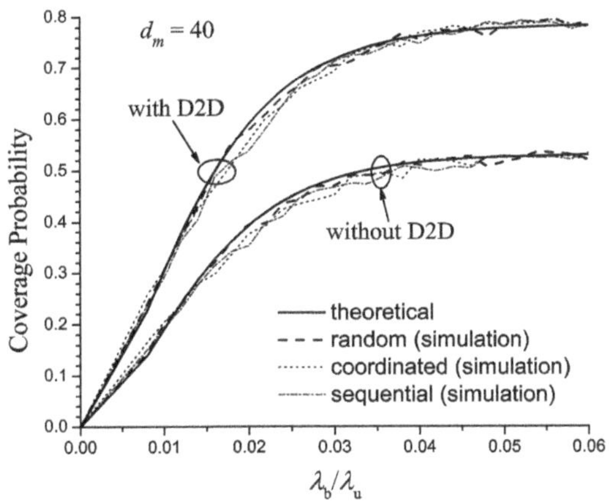

Figure 4: Comparison between theoretical results and simulation results obtained under the schemes of random channel assignment, sequential channel assignment, and coordinated channel assignment.

varies from sparsely distributed to densely distributed, by carefully addressing the dynamic impact of user density, BS density, and available channels on these fundamental performance metrics. One can observe from (13) and (20) that as $\lambda_u \to \infty$ we have $\mathcal{S}_{|N|} \to 1$, i.e., any given channel will be surely assigned for uplink transmission in all cells.

4. NUMERICAL RESULTS

4.1 Parameter Settings

In this section, we present extensive numerical results to illustrate the performance gains that can be achieved by the developed framework. Unless otherwise specified, we consider hereafter an interference-limited multi-channel uplink cellular network, i.e., the noise power $\sigma^2 = 0$, and set the number of channels for cellular transmission and for D2D communications as $|N| = 25$, $|M| = 5$. According to the maximum output from a UMTS/3G mobile phone, the transmit power limit of mobile users is set as $P_m = 27$ dBm. We fix the power control factor as $\eta = 1$, and select the coefficient of proportionality as $\epsilon = -100$ dB. The spatial densities of BSs and mobile users are chosen as $\lambda_b = 10$ BS/km^2 and $\lambda_u = 500$ user/km^2, respectively. Regarding the path-loss exponent and fading coefficients of cellular links and D2D links, we set $\alpha = 4$ and the mean coefficient as $\mu_b = 1$, $\mu_u = 1$. Finally, we set the signal strength threshold for establishing one-hop cellular link as $\beta = -72$ dBm, the SINR threshold for outage as $\theta = -50$ dB, and the maximum D2D transmission range as $d_m = 60$ m.

4.2 Model Validation

We summarize in Fig. 4 a comparison between the theoretical results from Theorem 1 and the simulation results by a Matlab based simulator. Besides the random channel assignment considered in Section 2, we also conducted extensive simulations under another two commonly adopted OFDMA channel assignment schemes, i.e., sequential channel assignment, and coordinated channel assignment. In the former assignment scheme, each BS assigns channels according to the sequential order of channel index. In the latter scheme, all BSs are first divided into two sets; BSs in one set assign channels in a top-down logic while BSs in the other set assign channels in a bottom-up logic. One can easily observe from Fig. 4 that, although our analytical model was developed for the case of random channel assignment, it is able to provide an effective reference for studying the behaviors of coverage probability under the other two untractable channel assignment schemes.

4.3 Coverage Probability

Fig. 5 shows how the coverage probability of a generic user varies with control parameters β, ϵ, λ_b/λ_u, and $|N|$, where the curves of with and without D2D communications correspond to $P_c(\beta, \epsilon, \theta)$ and $\rho_1 P_c^1(\beta, \epsilon, \theta)$, respectively. One can easily observe from (a), (b), (c), and (d) that, employing D2D communication based two-hop route can significantly improve the coverage probability of a generic user in various network scenarios.

As shown in Figs. 5(a) and 5(b), there exist optimum settings of β and ϵ at which the coverage probability can be maximized. What's more, a relatively stable coverage probability can be achieved when β decreases to a small value, while the coverage probability quickly diminishes to zero as β increases up. Actually, such behavior can be interpreted as follows: when β is very small, a certain ratio of users (which depends on the power control parameters ϵ and P_m) can establish direct one-hop cellular links and thus a number of D2D links can be successfully established; while for a large β, only a very limited number of users (i.e., the users that are very close to the BSs) can establish cellular links and D2D links. It is also noticed from Fig. 5(b) that no user can be covered when ϵ is too small. This is because that the signal power received at the BS becomes very weak (much less than θ) due to the fractional channel inversion power control which necessarily results in a vanishing coverage probability.

It is interesting to observe from Fig. 5(c) that, as λ_b/λ_u increases up, the curves of coverage probability under all settings of d_m converge to constant values, i.e., the performance gains over the curve of without D2D communication remain stable. That is, for a fixed density of users, the coverage probability cannot be infinitely improved by simply deploying more BSs, which further corroborates the conclusions obtained for the multi-tier cellular networks [7]. Furthermore, one can observe from Fig. 5(d) that for the considered multi-channel two-hop uplink cellular network, when the total number of frequency resources is fixed, the performance gain of coverage probability achieved by D2D communication actually increases with $|N|$, i.e., the number of channels allocated for cellular communications.

4.4 Average Rate

We summarize in Fig. 6 the relationship between average rates $R(\beta, \epsilon)$, $\rho_1 R_c(\beta, \epsilon)$ and the network parameters, where the performance gains over the case of without D2D communication can be clearly observed. In Fig. 6(a), there exist optimal settings of β to achieve the optimum $R(\beta, \epsilon)$ for all the three settings of ϵ there, similar to that in Fig. 5(a).

A careful comparison of Fig. 6 with Fig. 5 shows that, the behaviors of average rate with ϵ, λ_b/λ_u, and $|N|$ in Fig. 6 are totally different from that of coverage probability in Fig. 5. Specifically, in Fig. 6(b), both the average rates of with and without D2D communications monotonically increase with ϵ

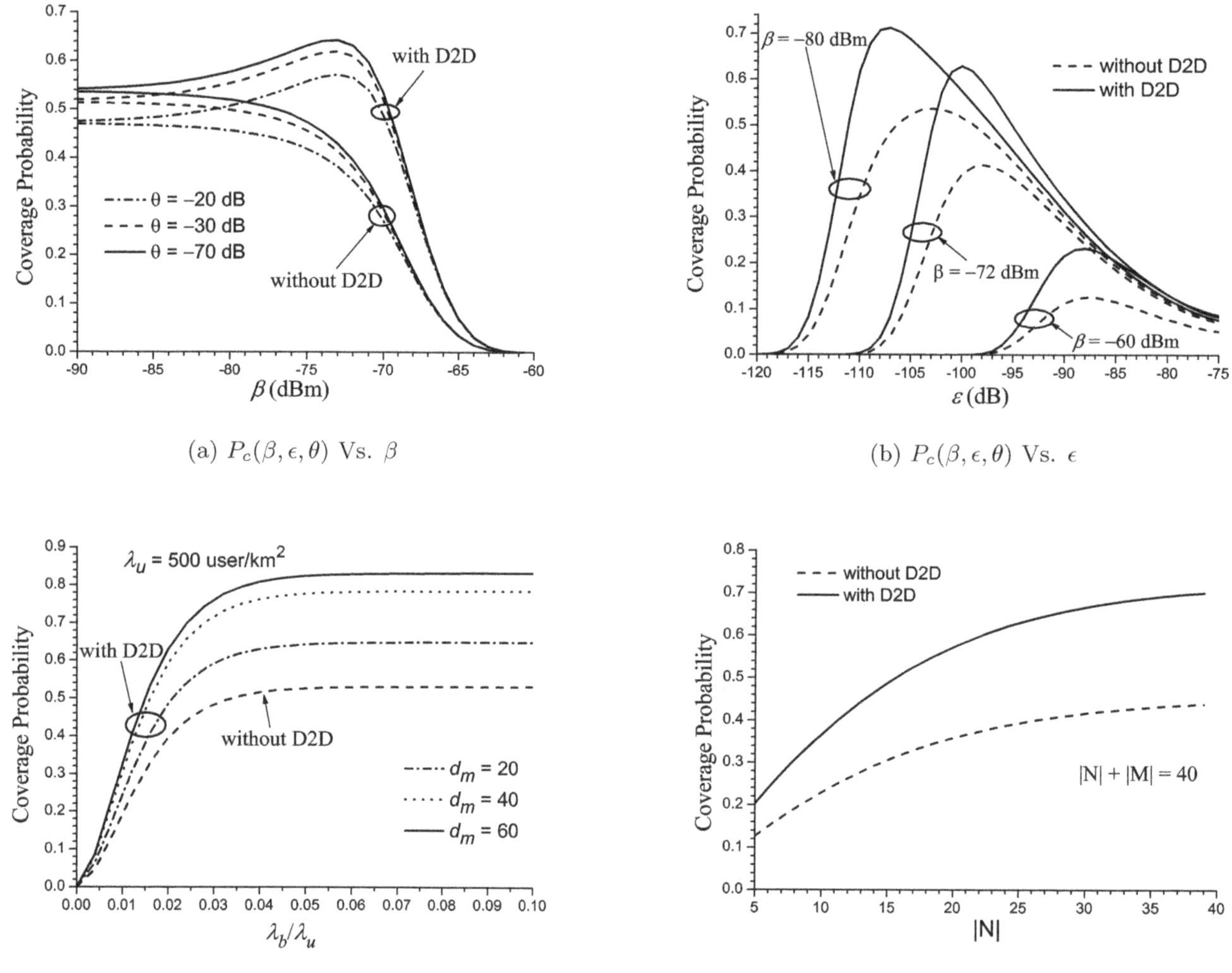

(a) $P_c(\beta, \epsilon, \theta)$ Vs. β

(b) $P_c(\beta, \epsilon, \theta)$ Vs. ϵ

(c) $P_c(\beta, \epsilon, \theta)$ Vs. λ_b/λ_u

(d) $P_c(\beta, \epsilon, \theta)$ Vs. $|N|$

Figure 5: Illustration of coverage probability $P_c(\beta, \epsilon, \theta)$ for a generic user.

and saturate to constant values as ϵ is large enough. This is because the number of one-hop cellular users transmitting with the maximum transmit power increases with ϵ, and the limiting case is that all users employ the same transmit power P_m.

It is noticed from Fig. 6(c) that, when the user density λ_u is fixed, the average rates of both with and without D2D communications monotonically increase with λ_b/λ_u. That is, a higher average rate can be achieved by deploying more BSs, although not able to improve the coverage probability (as illustrated in Fig. 5(c)). Regarding Fig. 6(d), one can see that there exist optimal values of $|N|$ to maximize the average rate for both the cases of with and without D2D communications. Actually, given the value of $|M|$, the effects of increasing $|N|$ are two folds: on one hand, it is able to increase the coverage probability since more channels can be allocated for establishing cellular links; on the other hand, it decreases the frequency bandwidth of a single channel as the unit frequency band is evenly divided into $|N| + |M|$ orthogonal channels.

5. CONCLUSIONS

In this paper, we have investigated the potential gains of D2D communication in extending network coverage and enhancing spectral efficiency of uplink cellular networks. A stochastic geometry based model was presented to characterize the complicated effects of operation mode selection (related to β), transmit power control (related to ϵ and η), channel allocation (related to $|N|$ and $|M|$), as well as relative deployment density (related to λ_u/λ_b). Our results indicate that these parameters may affect the per user coverage probability and average rate in quite different ways and most importantly, the performance gains of employing D2D communication can be maximized after properly tuning the parameters.

6. ACKNOWLEDGMENTS

This work was partially supported by the National Natural Science Foundation of China under grants 61372073, 61373043, 61202394, 61472367, and 61432015, and by the

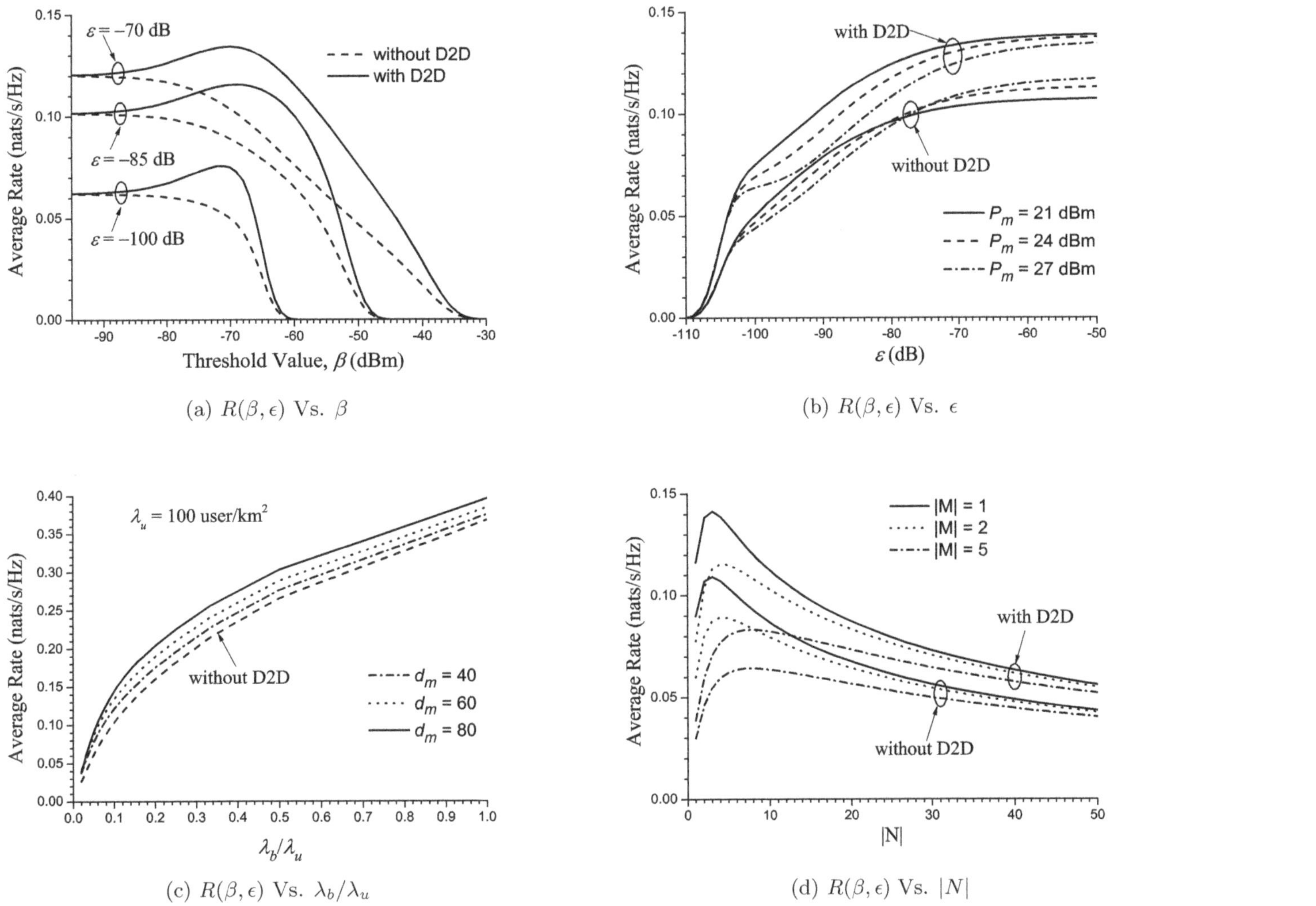

(a) $R(\beta, \epsilon)$ Vs. β

(b) $R(\beta, \epsilon)$ Vs. ϵ

(c) $R(\beta, \epsilon)$ Vs. λ_b/λ_u

(d) $R(\beta, \epsilon)$ Vs. $|N|$

Figure 6: Illustration of average rate $R(\beta, \epsilon)$ for a generic user, where the default parameters are set as $\lambda_b = 10$ BS/km^2, $\lambda_u = 100$ user/km^2, $\beta = -70$ dBm, $d_m = 60$ m, $P_m = 21$ dBm, $|M| = 1$, $|N| = 5$.

Key Program of and NSFC-Guangdong Union Foundation U1135002.

7. REFERENCES

[1] 3GPP. 3rd generation partnership project; technical specification group SA; feasibility study for proximity services (ProSe) (Release 12). TR 22.803 V12.2.0, June 2013.

[2] 3GPP. 3rd Generation Partnership Project; Technical Specification Group Services and System Aspects; Group Communication System Enablers for LTE (GCSE_LTE) (Release 12). TS 22.468 V12.0.0, June 2013.

[3] 3GPP. 3rd generation partnership project; technical specification group SA; study on architecture enhancements to support proximity services (ProSe) (Release 12). TR 23.703 V2.0.0, March 2014.

[4] J. G. Andrews, F. Baccelli, and R. K. Ganti. A tractable approach to coverage and rate in cellular networks. *IEEE Transactions on Communications*, 59(11):3122–3134, November 2011.

[5] A. Asadi, Q. Wang, and V. Mancuso. A survey on device-to-device communication in cellular networks. *IEEE Communications Surveys & Tutorials*, 16(4):1801–1819, 2014.

[6] X. Bao, Y. Lin, U. Lee, I. Rimac, and R. R. Choudhury. DataSpotting: Exploiting Naturally Clustered Mobile Devices to Offload Cellular Traffic. In *INFOCOM*, 2013.

[7] H. S. Dhillon, R. K. Ganti, F. Baccelli, and J. G. Andrews. Modeling and analysis of k-tier downlink heterogeneous cellular networks. *IEEE Journal on Selected Areas in Communications*, 30(3):550–560, April 2012.

[8] H. ElSawy and E. Hossain. On stochastic geometry modeling of cellular uplink transmission with truncated channel inversion power control. *IEEE*

Transactions on Wireless Communications, 13(8):4454–4469, August 2014.

[9] G. Fodor and N. Reider. A distributed power control scheme for cellular network assisted D2D communications. In *GLOBECOM*, 2011.

[10] C. han Lee and M. Haenggi. Interference and outage in poisson cognitive networks. *IEEE Transactions on Wireless Communications*, 11(4):1392–1401, April 2012.

[11] X. Lin, J. G. Andrews, and A. Ghosh. Spectrum sharing for device-to-device communication in cellular networks. *IEEE Transactions on Wireless Communications*, 13(12):6727–6740, September 2014.

[12] H. Min, J. Lee, S. Park, and D. Hong. Capacity enhancement using an interference limited area for device-to-device uplink underlaying cellular networks. *IEEE Transactions on Wireless Communications*, 10(12):3995–4000, December 2011.

[13] H. Min, W. Seo, J. Lee, S. Park, and D. Hong. Reliability improvement using receive mode selection in the device-to-device uplink period underlaying cellular networks. *IEEE Transactions on Wireless Communications*, 10(2):413–418, February 2011.

[14] P. H. J. Nardelli, P. Cardieri, and M. Latva-aho. Efficiency of wireless networks under different hopping strategies. *IEEE Transactions on Wireless Communications*, 11(1):15–20, January 2012.

[15] T. D. Novlan, H. S. Dhillon, and J. G. Andrews. Analytical modeling of uplink cellular networks. *IEEE Transactions on Wireless Communications*, 12(6):2669–2679, June 2013.

[16] A. Okabe, B. Boots, and K. Sugihara. *Spatial Tessellations: Concepts and Applications of Voronoi Diagrams*. John Wiley and Sons, New York, 1992.

APPENDIX

A. PROOF OF LEMMA 2

Starting from the definition of $F_c(\hat{\lambda},\hat{\theta})$, we have

$$\begin{aligned} F_c(\hat{\lambda},\hat{\theta}) &= \int_0^\infty \Pr\left(\frac{p_t h_b x^{-\alpha}}{I_c+\sigma^2} > \hat{\theta}\right)\cdot f_r(x)dx \\ &= \int_0^{\left(\frac{P_m}{\epsilon}\right)^{\frac{1}{\alpha\eta}}} \Pr\left(h_b > \frac{\hat{\theta}(I_c+\sigma^2)}{\epsilon\cdot x^{\alpha(\eta-1)}}\right)\cdot 2\pi\lambda_b x e^{-\pi\lambda_b x^2}dx \\ &+ \int_{\left(\frac{P_m}{\epsilon}\right)^{\frac{1}{\alpha\eta}}}^\infty \Pr\left(h_b > \frac{x^\alpha\hat{\theta}(I_c+\sigma^2)}{P_m}\right)\cdot 2\pi\lambda_b x e^{-\pi\lambda_b x^2}dx \end{aligned} \tag{22}$$

For the first part of (22),

$$\begin{aligned} &\int_0^{\left(\frac{P_m}{\epsilon}\right)^{\frac{1}{\alpha\eta}}} \Pr\left(h_b > \frac{\hat{\theta}(I_c+\sigma^2)}{\epsilon\cdot x^{\alpha(\eta-1)}}\right)\cdot 2\pi\lambda_b x e^{-\pi\lambda_b x^2}dx \\ &= 2\pi\lambda_b \int_0^{\left(\frac{P_m}{\epsilon}\right)^{\frac{1}{\alpha\eta}}} e^{-\pi\lambda_b x^2 - \frac{\mu_b\hat{\theta}\sigma^2}{\epsilon\cdot x^{\alpha(\eta-1)}}}\cdot \mathbf{E}_{I_c}\left[e^{-\frac{\mu_b\hat{\theta}I_c}{\epsilon\cdot x^{\alpha(\eta-1)}}}\right]xdx \\ &= 2\pi\lambda_b \int_0^{\left(\frac{P_m}{\epsilon}\right)^{\frac{1}{\alpha\eta}}} e^{-\pi\lambda_b x^2 - \frac{\mu_b\hat{\theta}\sigma^2}{\epsilon\cdot x^{\alpha(\eta-1)}}}\cdot \mathcal{L}_{I_c}\left(\frac{\mu_b\hat{\theta}x^{\alpha(1-\eta)}}{\epsilon}\right)xdx \end{aligned} \tag{23}$$

where $\mathcal{L}_{I_c}(s)$ is the Laplace transform of the accumulated interference I_c received at the BS of a typical cellular link

$$\begin{aligned} \mathcal{L}_{I_c}(s) &= \mathbf{E}[e^{-I_c\cdot s}] \\ &= \mathbf{E}_{\hat{\Phi},p_t,R,h_b}\Big[\prod e^{-p_t R^{-\alpha}h_b s}\Big] \\ &= \mathbf{E}_{\hat{\Phi},p_t,R}\Big[\prod \mathbf{E}_{h_b}\Big\{e^{-p_t R^{-\alpha}h_b s}\Big\}\Big] \\ &= \mathbf{E}_{\hat{\Phi},p_t,R}\Big[\prod \frac{\mu_b}{\mu_b+p_t R^{-\alpha}s}\Big] \\ &\overset{(i)}{=} \exp\left\{-2\pi\hat{\lambda}\int_0^\infty \mathbf{E}_{p_t}\left[1-\frac{\mu_b}{\mu_b+p_t s x^{-\alpha}}\right]xdx\right\} \\ &\overset{(ii)}{=} \exp\left\{-2\pi\hat{\lambda}\Big(\frac{s}{\mu_b}\Big)^{\frac{2}{\alpha}}\mathbf{E}_{p_t}\Big[(p_t)^{\frac{2}{\alpha}}\Big]\int_0^\infty \frac{y^{1-\alpha}}{1+y^{-\alpha}}dy\right\} \end{aligned} \tag{24}$$

where (i) follows after applying the probability generating functional of PPP and (ii) follows after substituting $y = x(\frac{p_t s}{\mu_b})^{-\frac{1}{\alpha}}$. Similarly, for the second part of (22),

$$\begin{aligned} &\int_{\left(\frac{P_m}{\epsilon}\right)^{\frac{1}{\alpha\eta}}}^\infty \Pr\left(h_b > \frac{x^\alpha\hat{\theta}(I_c+\sigma^2)}{P_m}\right)\cdot 2\pi\lambda_b x e^{-\pi\lambda_b x^2}dx \\ &= 2\pi\lambda_b \int_{\left(\frac{P_m}{\epsilon}\right)^{\frac{1}{\alpha\eta}}}^\infty e^{-\pi\lambda_b x^2 - \frac{\mu_b\hat{\theta}\sigma^2}{P_m}x^\alpha}\cdot \mathcal{L}_{I_c}\Big(\frac{\mu_b\hat{\theta}x^\alpha}{P_m}\Big)xdx \end{aligned} \tag{25}$$

After plugging (24) into (23) and (25) and setting $s = \frac{\mu_b\hat{\theta}x^{\alpha(1-\eta)}}{\epsilon}$ and $s = \frac{\mu_b\hat{\theta}x^\alpha}{P_m}$, respectively, we finish the proof for Lemma 2.

B. PROOF OF LEMMA 3

From Lemma 1, we know that the spatial density of potential D2D receivers is $\rho_1\lambda_u$. Since each D2D transmitter selects the nearest potential D2D receiver to establish a D2D link, the pdf of the distance r_d between a D2D transmitter and its receiver can be determined as

$$f_{r_d}(x) = \frac{2\pi\rho_1\lambda_u x e^{-\pi\rho_1\lambda_u x^2}}{1-e^{-\pi\rho_1\lambda_u d_m^2}} \tag{26}$$

Following the definition of $F_d(\hat{\lambda},\hat{\theta})$, we have

$$\begin{aligned} F_d(\hat{\lambda},\hat{\theta}) &= \Pr\Big(\frac{P_m h_u r_d^{-\alpha}}{I_d+\sigma^2} > \hat{\theta}\Big) \\ &= \int_0^{d_m} \Pr\left(h_u > \frac{\hat{\theta}x^\alpha(I_d+\sigma^2)}{P_m}\right)\cdot f_{r_d}(x)dx \\ &\overset{(i)}{=} \frac{2\pi\rho_1\lambda_u\int_0^{d_m} e^{-\pi\rho_1\lambda_u x^2 - \frac{\mu_u\hat{\theta}\sigma^2}{P_m}x^\alpha}\cdot \mathcal{L}_{I_d}\big(\frac{\mu_u\hat{\theta}x^\alpha}{P_m}\big)xdx}{1-e^{-\pi\rho_1\lambda_u d_m^2}} \end{aligned}$$

where (i) follows after substituting (26), and $\mathcal{L}_{I_d}(s)$ is the Laplace transform of the interference I_d measured at the typical D2D receiver. Given the distance x between the receiver and the transmitter in the typical D2D link, following similar derivations, we can derive $\mathcal{L}_{I_d}(s)$ as

$$\mathcal{L}_{I_d}(s) = \exp\left\{-\pi\hat{\lambda}\Big(\frac{P_m s}{\mu_u}\Big)^{\frac{2}{\alpha}}\int_{(\frac{\mu_u}{P_m s})^{\frac{2}{\alpha}}x^2}^\infty \frac{dt}{1+t^{\frac{\alpha}{2}}}\right\} \tag{27}$$

Then (8) can be obtained after substituting (27) in $F_d(\hat{\lambda},\hat{\theta})$ and setting $s = \frac{\mu_u\hat{\theta}x^\alpha}{P_m}$.

On the Decomposition of Cell Phone Activity Patterns and their Connection with Urban Ecology

Blerim Cici[†◇⋆], Minas Gjoka[◇⋆], Athina Markopoulou[†‡◇⋆], Carter T. Butts[‡◇⋆]
Networked Systems[†], CalIT2[⋆], CPCC[◇], EECS Dept.[‡]
Sociology Dept.[○] & Statistics Dept.[○]
UC Irvine, Irvine, USA
{bcici, mgjoka, athina, buttsc}@uci.edu

ABSTRACT

The goal of this paper is to infer features of urban ecology (i.e., social and economic activities, and social interaction) from spatio-temporal cell phone activity data. We present a novel approach that consists of (i) time series decomposition of the aggregate cell phone activity per unit area using spectral methods, (ii) clustering of areal units with similar activity patterns, and (ii) external validation using a ground truth data set we collected from municipal and online sources. The key to our approach is the spectral decomposition of the original cell phone activity series into seasonal communication series (SCS) and residual communication series (RCS). The former captures regular patterns of socio-economic activity within an area and can be used to segment a city into distinct clusters. RCS across areas enables the detection of regions that are subject to mutual social influence and of regions that are in direct communication contact. The RCS and SCS thus provide distinct probes into the structure and dynamics of the urban environment, both of which can be obtained from the same underlying data. We illustrate the effectiveness of our methodology by applying it to aggregate Call Description Records (CDRs) from the city of Milan.

Categories and Subject Descriptors

H.2.8 [**Database Management**]: Database Application— *data mining, spatial databases*; J.4 [**Social and Behavioral Sciences**]: Sociology—*Smart Cities, Urban Planning*

Keywords

Mobile networks; Call-Description Records (CDRs); Time Series Decomposition; Urban Ecology.

1. INTRODUCTION

The modern urban environment is a complex ecosystem, characterized by distinct geographical regions sharing common patterns of socio-economic activity, infrastructure, social cohesion, etc. [5, 24]; further, some of these regions are strongly interacting (via mobility, communication, etc.), while others are relatively isolated from one another [16, 18]. We refer to this intra-urban structure as "urban ecology." Historically, the detection of urban ecology has been difficult as it usually requires extensive local knowledge of the area in question and investigation using time-consuming and expensive techniques (e.g., informant interviews, ethnographic observation, etc.). This poses challenges for urban governance—e.g., urban planning, infrastructure management, administration, and law enforcement—particularly in an era of increasingly rapid urban growth and change (e.g., due to shifting patterns of immigration and economic activity). Likewise for the private sector, effective siting of businesses requires extensive knowledge of the urban landscape; in a global economy, obtaining such knowledge via years of experience "on the ground" in a given location may be expensive or impractical.

It is estimated that within the next forty years, two-thirds of the world's population will be living in expanding urban centers, and the level of urbanization is expected to increase in all major areas of the developing world [2]. Given this, there is clearly a need for methods that will cheaply yield up-to-date information on urban environments, without extensive on-the-ground investigation. A promising tool in that regard is the use of aggregate geo-located data on communication activity, a resource that is increasingly available given the near-universal penetration of mobile devices within urban populations. Because communication behavior is a fundamental aspect of virtually all social and economic interaction, even aggregated communication data can provide rich information on the types and volumes of activities occurring within a given geographical area, and on the degree of interaction (or lack thereof) between occupants of different areas. Such data is inexpensive, can be collected and distributed in a privacy-preserving

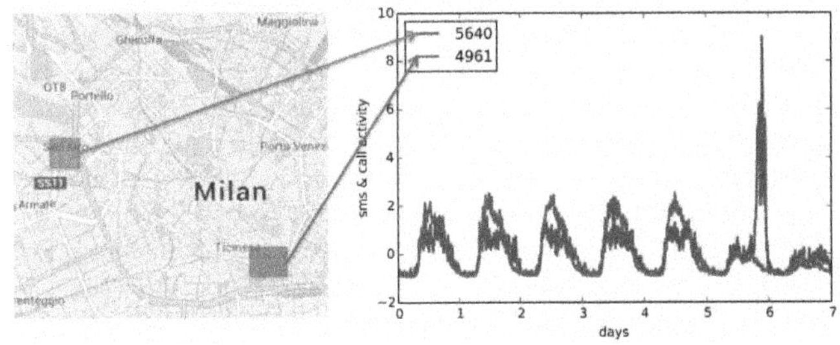

Figure 1: Cell phone activity series (normalized) for two grid squares of Milan, for the week of 11/4/2013–11/10/2013. Square 5640 is located close to the San Siro stadium, while square 4961 is located in a university region. Differences in seasonal patterns (weekday/weekend) reflect stable differences between the university and stadium environments.

This work has been supported by AFOSR MURI award FA9550-09-0643, and NSF CDI award 1028394. This work is based on data made available by Telecom Italia for the *Big Data Challenge* [3].

MobiHoc'15, June 22–25, 2015, Hangzhou, China.
Copyright 2015 ACM 978-1-4503-3489-1/15/06 ...$15.00.
http://dx.doi.org/10.1145/2746285.2746292.

manner (e.g., in the case of aggregate activity), and can be monitored to track developments within the urban landscape.

The question, then, is how aggregate mobile communication data can be used to provide information on urban ecology. In this paper, we provide an approach to this problem that draws on the notion of seasonal decomposition from the field of classical time series analysis. By decomposing communication data across time, frequency, and space, we create distinct time series that provide (respectively) information on routine activities and on deviations from those routines. Subsequent analysis of the resulting multivariate time series allows for the identification of socio-economically distinct regions within the urban environment, identification of socially interacting regions, and other goals of interest to the analyst. As we show, these analyses can be performed efficiently and in an unsupervised or semi-supervised manner, facilitating their use in settings for which the analyst has only limited resources for additional data collection.

Key idea: As is well known, a time series can be decomposed into three components (the *classical decomposition* [6]): a *trend*, representing systematic, non-periodic change over the time scale of observation; a *seasonal* component, representing systematic periodic variation in the phenomenon of interest (possibly with multiple characteristic frequencies); and a *residual* component, representing variation due to idiosyncratic factors and exogenous shocks. The value of the decomposition approach arises from the fact that many social processes either generate gradual, systematic change (e.g., population growth) or are strongly periodic (e.g., on hourly, daily, weekly, or annual time scales); the trend and seasonal components of the time series "selects out" such processes, allowing them to be either measured or removed from analysis (as desired). By turns, many other social processes are characterized by short-term responses to exogenous perturbations, and (when integrated over all perturbations) have little or no systematic component. Information on these processes is contained in the residual series, which can thus be used to study them without contamination from their systematic counterparts.

Data: The data that we use in this study consists of time series of aggregate cell phone traffic sent or received by persons within small areal units in the city of Milan (see Fig. 1), for approximately one-month period. In particular, we use aggregate call-description-records (CDRs) and aggregate SMS activity per area unit, made available for the *Big Data Challenge* [3] competition. In addition, we collected ground truth data from the municipality of Milan and online sources, containing elements such as universities, residential areas, sport centers, parks, etc. This latter data is used here for external evaluation of our methodology and is made publicly available at [4].

Methodology and Results Overview: We apply our approach to the cell phone activity series, using the decomposed series to characterize distinct aspects of urban ecology. We proceed as follows:

First, we begin by decomposing the original cell phone activity series for each areal unit into seasonal and residual components. The decomposition is done using FFT, with the seasonal component corresponding to high-amplitude frequencies and the residual component corresponding to the deseasonalized series in the time domain. The seasonal communication series (SCS) are due to typical patterns of socio-economic activity within an area; e.g. a university generates higher traffic during weekdays and lower traffic during weekends and holidays than a residential neighborhood. The residual communication series (RCS), on the other hand, can represent irregular traffic (e.g. an area may have higher traffic than usual due to a protest or sporting event, or lower traffic than usual due to a strike) and/or due to the influence of one area on another (e.g., due to mobility and/or social interaction).

Second, we perform hierarchical clustering of different areas based on the different time series and we validate the results using the ground truth data. We show that our SCS clustering scheme successfully segments areas dominated by distinct types of socio-economic activity, and allows for discovery of regions whose activity patterns differ markedly from the rest of the city. The results compare favorably with state-of-the-art approaches such as [26], since SCS can incorporate regular patterns occurring on any time scale; by contrast, state-of-the-art methods estimate regular patterns using average weekday and weekend days (evaluated using binned averages), and cannot therefore exploit patterns of change that occur across multiple days. In addition to using the SCS to identify regular patterns, we show that its counterpart, the RCS, enables the detection of regions that are subject to mutual social influence or in direct communication contact; this was not previously possible using mere activity data. More specifically, we show that the structure of lagged spatial correlations in RCS across areas allows for the detection of regions that are subject to mutual social influence (i.e., disruptions in one area propagate to the other), and of regions that are in direct communicative contact. We validate the latter by showing that RCS correlations between areas are significantly related to the volume of inter-area cell phone traffic, and that this relationship is substantially stronger than for SCS.

In summary, the RCS and SCS provide distinct probes into the structure and dynamics of the urban environment, both of which can be obtained from the same underlying communication data.

The structure of the rest of the paper is as follows. Section 2 reviews related work. Section 3 presents our data sets, and the ground truth we collected. Section 4 presents the decomposition of the original series into SCS and RCS, and some key insights from basic properties of these series. Section 5 presents the clustering methodology. Section 6 presents the results of applying clustering to SCS and its comparison to ground truth, as well as the findings of the RCS analysis. Section 7 concludes the paper.

2. RELATED WORK

This section summarizes the most relevant related work in the intersection between urban dynamics and human activity data. Data generated by human activity can be divided into two broad categories: (1) self-reported data and (2) behavioral traces. In self-reported data, users decide to report their semantically annotated location via check-ins e.g. in Foursquare a user selects a venue from a list of venues that are detected nearby his location. In behavioral traces, users are passively monitored and do not actively select the information that is being revealed. Cell phone activity patterns are an example of behavioral traces, in which some aspects of the users' behavior are *fully* revealed, but without any *semantic information* i.e. the user location is not annotated to indicate venue or category type. This work uses cell phone activity patterns.

Behavioral traces. Cell phone activity patterns, also commonly known as Call Description Records (CDR), capture important aspects of human activity in a city [23], and they have been used to study human mobility, social networks, and urban ecology. Since the focus of this paper is on the latter, we mainly review related work in that area, and we only briefly mention other work in the broad area of cell phone activity analysis.

Toole et al. [27] used aggregated CDRs in order to infer land usage in Boston. They used a supervised learning technique: they built various features from activity series and used them to classify areas of the city into five different categories (residential, commercial, industrial, parks, and other). Their ground truth was a data set of zoning regulations from the municipality of Boston. However, the classifier's accuracy was worse than classifying every area to belong in the dominant category, due to the high percentage of residential areas. In contrast, we use clustering, a form of unsupervised learning, our ground truth data set contains the facilities in each area, and we study the city of Milan.

Soto et al. [26] also followed an unsupervised learning approach to characterize areas in the city of Madrid. They clustered areas of the city based on their activity signature, *i.e.* the activity pattern for a typical weekday and a typical weekend, where "typical" is defined as average activity in a period of 3 months. They produce five different clusters: industrial and offices, business and commercial, nightlife, leisure and touristic, and residential. We follow a different clustering approach that facilitates selecting solutions for specific purposes (e.g., segmentation versus anomaly detection), and employ a more general time series decomposition that can be used in settings with regular patterns that do not fit into the typical weekday/typical weekend day typology. In Section 6 we compare our spectral approach to that of [26] and show that our approach allows us to detect additional information that is lost under averaging. Additionally, our work differs from [26] in that we make use of residual fluctuations in the time series, which can be used to detect interactions between areas. We note that our clustering and residual analysis techniques could be applied to the averaging scheme used by [26], and many aspects of our approach are hence complementary to this work.

Similar decompositions of activity series have been applied in other settings as well. Calabrese et al. [9] applied eigendecomposition to extract features from Wi-Fi time-series, and then used those features, produced from the top 4 eigenvectors, to cluster access points with similar traffic. We apply time series decomposition on a different type of series and we also take advantage of the residual communication to highlight important aspects of the data.

Finally, CDRs have been used for human mobility analysis, [17], [15], [8] as well as for studying social interactions [14]. These studies have answered various questions, including: what is the potential of ride-sharing for reducing traffic in a city [12]; which are the poorest areas of a city [25], etc.

Self-reported data. Work on urban dynamics and self-reported locations is primarily focused on Foursquare check-ins [13, 20, 21]. The authors of [21] use the categories of Foursquare check-ins in order to cluster similar areas of the city, i.e. two areas are similar if their normalized check-ins are also similar (e.g. both have 70% restaurant and 30% work check-ins). More specifically, each area is represented by a vector of category check-ins aggregated over a time period. Spectral clustering with a cosine similarity measure is used to create clusters of similar areas. However, the paper provides no external validation of the clustering results. In contrast, our evaluation results make use of a separately obtained ground truth data from the official city records and our method does not require semantically annotated location information.

The authors of [13] use the same clustering approach as [21], with some modifications in the distance function, and they validate they results through interviews with city residents. However, the distance function in [13] requires per-user and per-venue check-in information whereas our method is suitable with spatially aggregated data over all users in the same area.

[28] considers that the function of an area is a combination of two aspects: places of interest (POI) categories and human mobility data (e.g. number of people arriving or leaving) in a region. They cluster similar areas using a topic model-based method that combines both aspects. They evaluate their method by using well-known locations, and interviews with residents of the city. However [28] aggregates the human mobility data in typical weekday/weekend fashion, an approach that we show looses information. Additionally, their method requires as input POI categories which, unlike ours, assumes existing knowledge about the city.

3. DATA SETS

Table 1 summarizes the data sets used in our analysis.

Name	Period	Source
Milan Activity	Nov.4-Dec.1 2013	Telecom Italia [3]
Milan Square-to-Square	Nov.4-Dec.1 2013	Telecom Italia [3]
Universities, Businesses, Parks, Population per area, Sport Centers, Bus stops	Jan.1-Dec.31 2013	City of Milan [1]

Table 1: Data Sets

3.1 Cell phone data

The first two data sets were provided by Telecom Italia Mobile as a part of the *Big Data Challenge* [3] competition. They consist of telecommunications activity records in the city of Milan. In this paper, we focused on a 4-week period of November 2013. The decisions about spatial and temporal granularity in the dataset, were already made by the dataset provider (Telecom Italia) when they made the data sets available for the *Big Data Challenge*, and were out of our control. In particular, the city of Milan, an area of 550 km^2, was divided into a 100×100 square grid. Each grid square has the same dimensions: a side length of 0.235 km and an area of 0.055 km^2. This is the areal unit we use throughout the paper, and we refer to it as a "square". The temporal unit is the 10-minute interval.

In the Milan Activity dataset, the activity is aggregated within each grid square for each 10-minute interval. Each activity record consists of the following entries: square ID, time-stamp of 10-minute time slot, country code, incoming SMS activity, outgoing SMS activity, incoming call activity, and outgoing call activity. According to the data set release information [3], each activity value corresponds to the level of interaction of all the users in the square with the mobile phone network, *e.g.* the higher the number of outgoing calls made by the users, the higher the outgoing Calls activity. Values of incoming/outgoing Call and SMS activity are normalized and have the same scale. Therefore, we sum up the latter four values,[1] over all country codes in order to come up with a single value which describes the total activity volume in a square during each 10-minute time slot; this is the *original time series*, used in Section 4. Fig. 1 shows an example of the original time series for two grid-squares over a one week-period.

The Milan Square-to-Square dataset contains information regarding the "directional interaction strength" (as per terminology in [3]) between two squares, based on the calls exchanged between users in them. Each activity record consists of the following fields: ID of square i where call was initiated from, ID of unit j where the call was made to, time slot, and value of directional strength from i to j. We can obtain the total directional strength from square i to square j, by summing up over all time slots in the 4-week period.

3.2 Ground Truth

We collect additional data sets at the Municipality of Milan's Open Data website [1], in order to use them as ground truth, for external validation of clustering, in Section 6. For each square defined in the main data sets, we gathered the following *category* information: population, %green area, #sport centers, #of universities, #businesses, and #bus stops. The blue shaded area in Fig. 2 marks

[1] This aggregation helps avoid data sparsity.

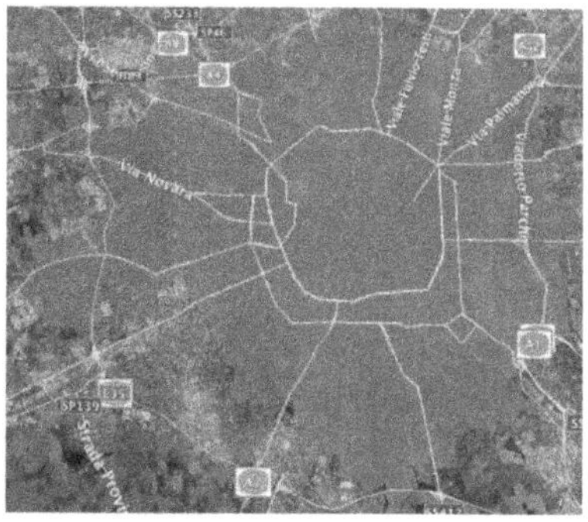

Figure 2: Local identity units of Milan. The blue shaded area shows the part of the city for which we have ground truth information. Ground truth information consist of information regarding facilities in each area, as well as census data.

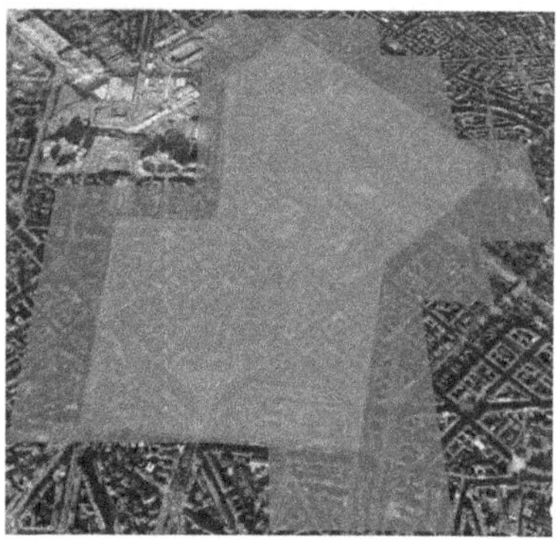

Figure 3: Squares inside the local identity unit of Pagano. Some squares have full overlap, while others have only partial overlap. The Population of Pagano will be spread uniformly to the overlapping grid-squares proportionally to the overlapping area (between a square and Pagano). Also, the population of a square may be reduced even further if the square contains green areas. A square can receive population from multiple local identity units.

the neighborhoods (or "local identity units") in the city of Milan, for which category information is available.

Gathering the category data and putting them in a ready-to-use format was non-trivial. First, we performed basic data cleaning and post-processing of the collected data. This involved removing duplicate entries in each category, transformation of coordinates from the Italian Gauss-Boaga projection to standard latitude-longitude, and mapping of addresses to latitude-longitude using Google Maps API. Second, we assigned every ground truth element in each category to the corresponding square. Information that appeared as a single latitude-longitude coordinate was easy to assign to a single square; those included businesses, universities, bus stops and sport centers. However, assigning categories such as green areas (which appear as geometric shapes with multiple points) and demographic information (which is reported on top of the local identity units) to the grid squares was more challenging. In the case of the green areas, we calculate the overlapping area between a specific square and a given green area as a percentage of the square.[2] Fig. 3 shows

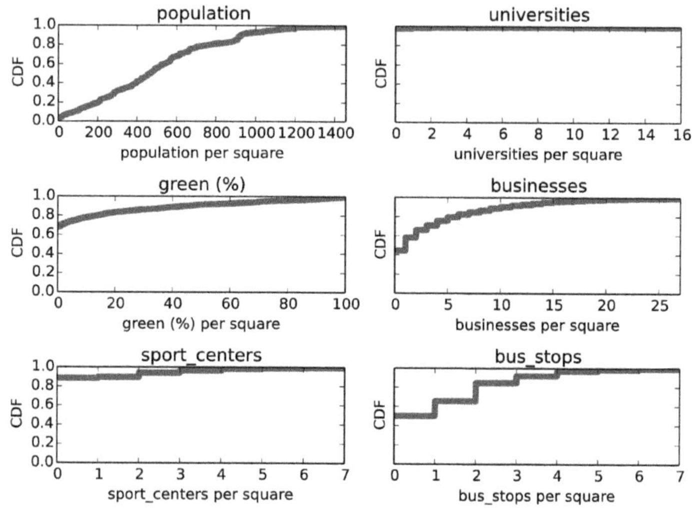

Figure 4: Number of ground truth elements in each square. The above figures indicate how uniformly each ground truth element is distributed in the city. For example we observe that the vast majority of the squares have zero universities, and universities are distributed to only a handful of squares.

the overlap between squares and local identity areas. Fig. 4 shows how ground truth elements are distributed over the grid. Finally, we make the processed ground truth dataset publicly available at [4].

Limitations: Using ground truth to evaluate urban dynamics has some inherent limitations and, in fact, leads to – conservatively – underestimating the success of our method. For example, we were constrained to use only the portion of the data (30% of the squares) for which we were able to obtain ground truth. Furthermore, a category as defined in the ground truth (e.g. "universities") may not capture subtle differences (e.g. universities in the periphery vs. universities in the center), which the time-series approach may be able to correctly capture. These challenges in evaluating clustering based on urban dynamics using ground truth data, have also been observed by previous papers [27]; while other papers choose to use interviews with city residents [26, 28] .

4. ACTIVITY IN TIME AND FREQUENCY DOMAINS

Let $S = [1, n]$ be the set of all grid squares, where $n = 10^4$. Also, let $T = \{t_1, t_2, ..., t_m\}$ be the set of all time units (10-minute time slots as defined by the data provider) in our 4-week period, where $m = 4032$. Finally, for each square $i \in S$, we denote the original activity series as $O_i(T) = \{o_i(t_1), o_i(t_2), ..., o_i(t_m)\}$.

The original time series is expected to have strong periodicity, since it depends on human activity. Therefore, we first map our time series into the frequency domain to identify the dominant seasonal components. We apply the fast Fourier transform (FFT) to convert $O_i(T)$, for all $i \in S$, from the time domain to the frequency domain. FFT is suitable for our purpose because it is a non-parametric method that extracts periodicity, it is useful for series with no obvious trend and provides a spectrogram that is easily interpretable [11]. Fig. 5 shows the power spectrum of all series in the frequency domain. We observe several frequencies with high power (e.g., weekly, daily, and 12-hour cycles). These high-power frequencies dominate the seasonal component of the com-

[2]For example, if the park was large and the whole square was inside it then the square was considered to be 100% green space. For demographic data, we calculate the overlapping area between a square and a local identity unit, we subtract the green-space area, and we assign part of the population of the local identity unit to the square, proportionally to the size of the remaining overlapping area as a percentage of the local identity unit.

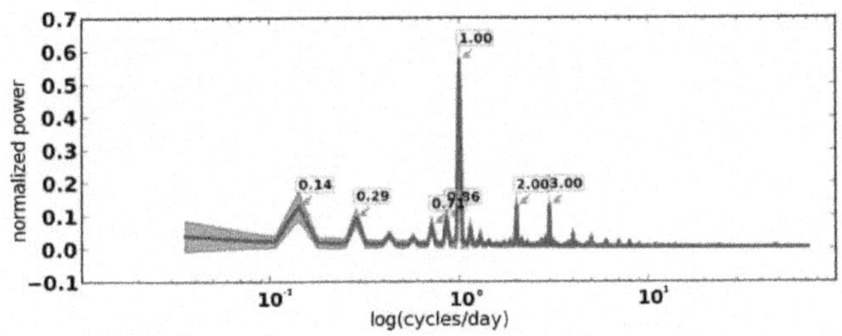

Figure 5: Power spectrum of activity aggregated over all grid squares (blue line indicates mean, shaded area ±1 std dev); marks indicate high-amplitude frequencies, e.g. daily (1 $cycles/day$) and weekly (0.14 $cycles/day$.

munication series, and indicate endemic social processes taking place within the city.

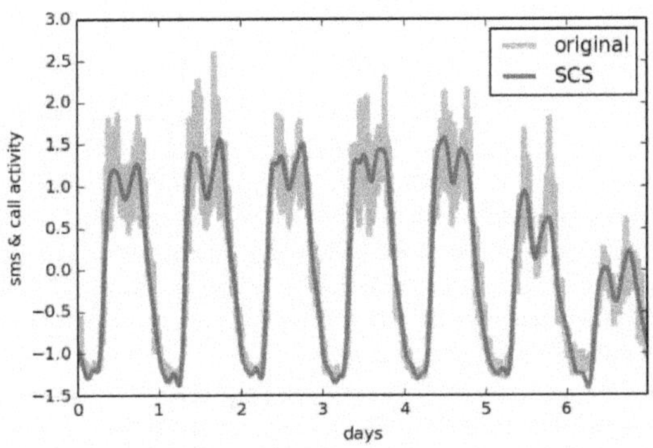

(a) Original series and derived SCS; SCS contains only systematic information, and is hence smoother.

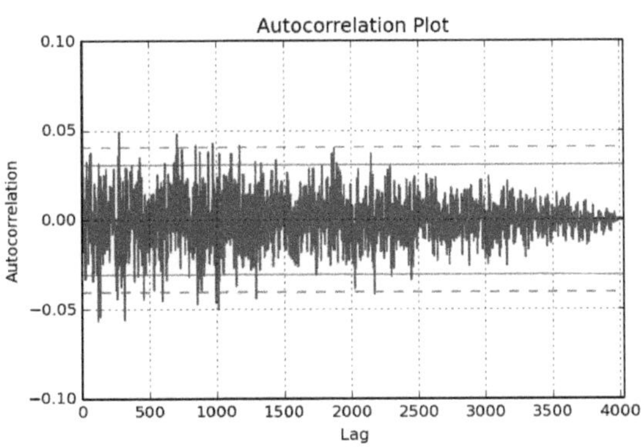

(b) RCS autocorrelation. Low autocorrelation values verify that systematic components have been removed. Note that the y-axis is zoomed in the interval (-0.1, 0.1).

Figure 6: Decomposition of original activity series for grid square 5071.

For each grid square $i \in S$, we decompose the original time-series $O_i(T)$, into *seasonal* and *residual* components through the following steps.

1. We select its k highest-power frequencies.
2. We regenerate the seasonal communication series $SCS_i(T)$ using only the top k frequencies of the grid-square, where $SCS_i(T) = \{scs_i(t_1), ..., scs_i(t_m)\}$.
3. We obtain the residual communication series $RCS_i(T)$ by subtracting the basic series from the original series: $RCS_i(T) = \{o_i(t_1) - scs_i(t_1), ..., o_i(t_m) - scs_i(t_m)\}$.

The data analysis in the remainder of the paper uses $k = 30$; this was selected by finding the smallest k such that the RCS autocorrelation function does not differ significantly from that of a white noise sequence, as shown in Fig 6(b). Please note that SCS captures regular activity (which we use in Section 6.1 for clustering of areas in the city), while RCS carries information about similarity of residual activity between two squares (which we use in Sec. 6.2.1 to study cross-square interactions.)

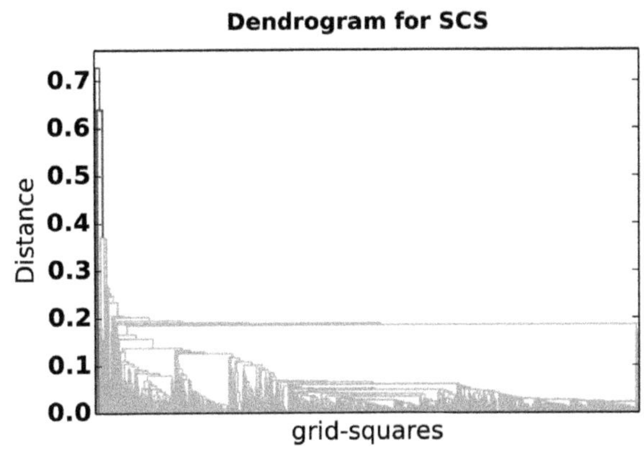

(a) Dendrogram

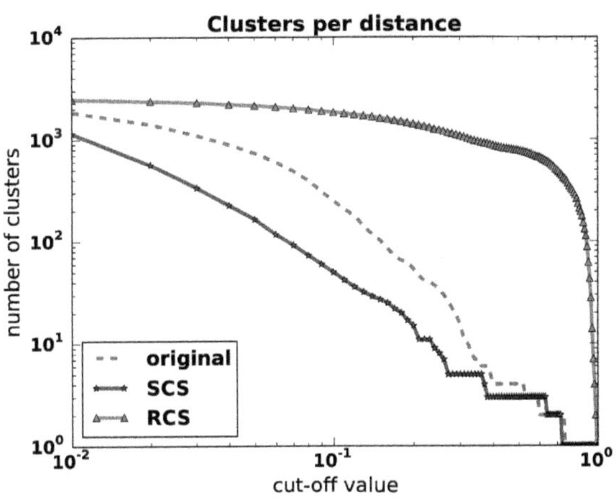

(b) Number of clusters per cut-off distance.

Figure 7: Cut-off distances and clusters. (a) shows the dendrogram for clustering the SCS. At distance 0.74 all squares have been merged into one cluster. By looking at the dendrogram we see that most squares in Milan have quite similar traffic, *i.e.* highly correlated activity series, with a few special squares that are different from the rest. Also, we summarize clustering with SCS, original, and RCS in (b), which shows the number of clusters per cut-off distance.

Insights from decomposition and neighborhoods: Here we discuss observations on the correlation of a square and its neighbors w.r.t. the different time series, namely, original, SCS and RCS. These are important to guide the clustering based on these time series, discussed in the next section.

Fig 8(a) evaluates the correlation between neighboring and non-neighboring squares for the original, SCS, and RCS series. In RCS,

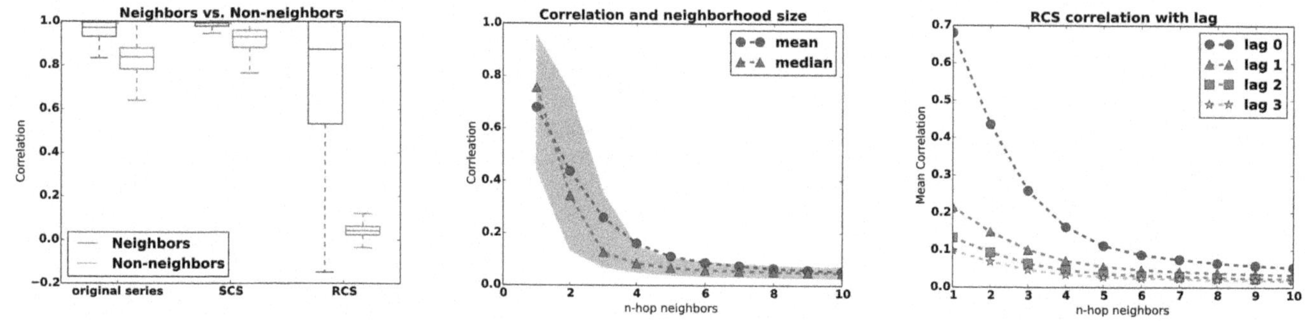

(a) Correlation between neighbors vs. non-neighbors for original, SCS, and RCS. (b) Correlation for n-hop neighbors for RCS. (c) Correlation and lag.

Figure 8: Correlation and neighborhood. In (a) we observe that in all three cases, the correlation between neighbors is stronger than non-neighbors. However, the difference in the correlation between neighbors and non-neighbors varies. In (b) we observe that as the size of the neighborhood increases the mean correlation decreases – the filled area of the graph represent the region between 25th-percentile and the 75th-percentile. And, in (c) we observe that even when we look at lagged correlation for the RCS, we observe higher correlation, on average, between neighboring squares and a decline in the mean correlation as distance increases. Correlation also decreases when time lag increases.

the correlation between neighbors is much stronger than the correlation between non-neighbors; this is a clear indication that when something occurs in a square, it often spreads to its neighbors. On the other hand, the correlation between non-neighbors is close to zero, which indicates that perturbations of activity are spatially restricted; this is even more clear when we look at Fig. 8(b) that shows how the correlation among neighbors decreases as the size of the neighborhood increases. Also, in Fig. 8(c), we see that what happens in a square at time slot t_0 will affect its neighbors at a later time slot, with the effect dampening over time. This is compatible with an underlying diffusion process.

Fig 8(a) also shows that in SCS the correlation between both neighbors and non-neighbors increased when compared to the original series. Moreover, the difference of the correlation between neighbors and non-neighbors decreased. This shows that SCS is dominated by the day-to-day activity patterns, and is stripped from perturbations that are spatially constrained.

5. CLUSTERING

Our goal is to use the result of the decomposition to segment the city into distinct areas, where the members of same area would have similar activity patterns. We hypothesize that if two squares have similar communication patterns then they have similar local ecologies, whereas if their communications patterns differ then they have different local socio-economic activities; *e.g.* one would expect a university and a stadium to have different activity patterns, since people visit them during different hours.

To achieve our goal, we cluster squares via agglomerative hierarchical clustering. We employ hierarchical clustering because of its generality (requiring no particular assumptions regarding the underlying distance measure) and because it yields a family of solutions (generally expressed as a dendrogram) that contains more information than a single clustering solution. As we show, this information can be exploited to perform both segmentation and anomaly/outlier detection from a single dendrogram. The distance function used in the rest of the paper is based on the Pearson correlation between activity series. More specifically, for two grid-squares $i, j \in S$, their distance in a given activity series A is:

$$dist(A_i, A_j) = 1 - correlation(A_i, A_j)$$

This distance function takes values in the range [0,2]; when two grid-squares are fully correlated they will have a distance of 0, when they are completely uncorrelated a distance of 1, and when they are inversely correlated a distance of 2. Also, we used the average linkage criterion to build the dendrogram since it had the highest cophenetic coefficient in comparison with other linkage types – the cophenetic coefficient is a measure of how faithfully a dendrogram preserves the pairwise distances.

Fig. 7 shows the high-level clustering results. Fig. 7(a) shows the dendrogram for the clustering via SCS; by looking at it we see that for small cut-offs, *e.g.* values between 0.02 and 0.08, we get a segmentation of the city into multiple areas, while for large cut-offs, *e.g.* values higher than 0.28, we get a very large cluster and a few small ones – hence, high cut-offs can be used for segmentation and low cut-offs can be used to detect areas with anomalous activity, without requiring additional computation.

Fig. 7(b) evaluates the number of clusters generated in the original, SCS, and RCS series for the full range of cut-off distances from 0-1. We observe that the results of clustering with RCS differ significantly from that with SCS and original. More specifically, clustering with RCS yields a large number of clusters (1000s) until cut-off distance ~ 0.90. On the other hand, clustering with SCS yields a low number of clusters for cut-off distance as small as 0.10. We speculate that the reason for this result is due to the degree of correlation between neighbors and non-neighbors (also see figures 8(a) and 8(b)). Intuitively, SCS provides information on routine activities in the city. Thus, where the analyst's goal is to cluster urban areas based on regular patterns of activity, the SCS should be employed.

6. RESULTS

The results presented in this section are limited to the grid squares that overlap with the ground truth; this corresponds to the approximately 3K squares represented in the colored area of Fig. 2.

6.1 Clustering based on the SCS

SCS hierarchical clustering requires a choice of where to cut the dendrogram. Examination of the number of clusters by distance, Fig. 7(b), shows that this alone does not produce a natural cutting point for the SCS; thus, we also factor in skewness of cluster sizes,

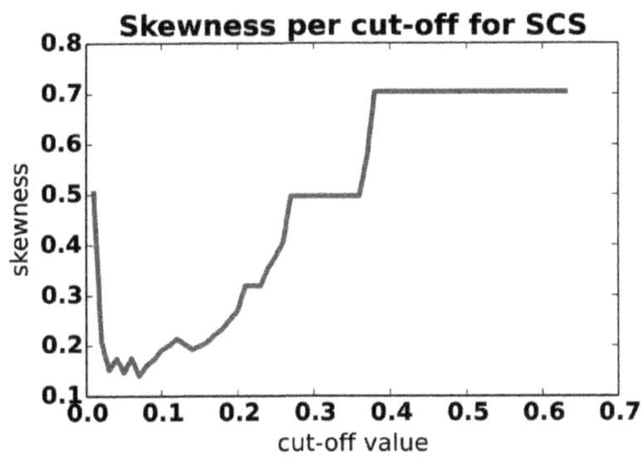

Figure 9: Skewness plot for SCS clustering. We use Pearson's second skewness coefficient: (mean-median)/(standard deviation). The minimum skewness is at cut-off = 0.07.

defined as (mean-median)/(standard deviation). Fig. 9 shows the calculated skewness for the full range of cut-off values in the SCS clustering. The rationale for employing skewness to guide distance selection is as follows. One expects that a segmentation of the urban environment into distinct functional areas, *e.g.* university areas, residential areas, *etc.*, will produce clusters of relatively comparable size, with correspondingly low skewness. On the other hand, if the distribution is very skewed, then there is a small number of large clusters which contain the vast majority of squares, and various small clusters with unique activity patterns that are quite different from the rest of the city, *e.g.* stadiums. By choosing low versus high-skewness cut-points, one can then choose to break the city into a few large areas of similar activities, or (respectively) detect small, anomalous areas in the city against an "average" background pattern. Both options provide distinct information, and it is not necessary to employ only one; here, we show both cases.

Low-skewness segmentation: In this case we seek to divide the city into comparably sized clusters, and hence choose a cut-point that yields a size distribution with low skewness. Per Fig. 9, we obtain this via a distance threshold of 0.07, which is the minimum skewness value in the SCS clustering. As Fig. 11 shows, the clusters of Fig. 10(a) successfully segment the city by features of the urban environment. For instance, clusters c1 and c5 have a high density of universities, while cluster c3 has a high density of green space; density is the ratio of the number of ground truth elements over cluster size. Thus, we conclude that the clusters indeed reflect regions with distinct socio-economic and environmental characteristics as reflected by their differences in SCS.

High-skewness anomaly detection: In this case we seek to identify one large cluster reflecting the range of "typical" activity patterns and several small areas of anomalous activity; we thus select a cutoff leading to a skewed distribution e.g. Fig. 10(b) with cutoff 0.30 which contains five clusters. In Fig. 12 we see the normal activity in the city in cluster c0, while the other clusters represent strongly anomalous traffic. For instance, cluster c1 corresponds to the San Siro stadium, while cluster c3 contains the Otomercato, a wholesale market for fruit and vegetable.

SCS vs. original series: In Fig. 13 we show a comparison between the clustering with SCS, and the clustering with the original in regard to coverage for the full range of cut-off distances $0 - 1$. We confirm that clustering with SCS yields better results. This verifies our expectation that removing idiosyncratic variation from the signal clarifies the regular activity within a grid square.

SCS vs. Typical Weekday/Weekend : Prior work [26] handles clustering of time series by aggregating cell phone activity in a typical weekday/weekend over all users in an area. Our method fits data better and requires less assumptions compared to that approach. We compare the performance of our method with that of a typical weekday/weekend using the Entropy of the density distribution for a given category, which is a common external clustering evaluation measure [29]. Table 2 shows the obtained values of Entropy for our method and the clustering via K-means and typical weekday/weekend from [26]. We observe that our method performs better for all ground truth categories. The intuition behind that is that our way of summarizing the cell phone activity is superior in the sense that the seasonal component of FFT (our SCS) holds more information than the typical weekday/weekend approach, as shown in Fig. 14. To quantitatively illustrate that point, we calculate the normalized sum of squared errors for each grid-square i, for both methods as follows:

$$e_i = \frac{\sum_{t=1}^{t=T} (O_i(t) - B_i(t))^2}{T}$$

Category	Entropy for hierarchical SCS	Entropy for [26]
Universities	0.96	0.97
Businesses	0.82	1.33
Green (%)	0.94	1.27
Population	0.97	1.34

Table 2: Segmentation performance via Entropy (lower value is better). Hierarchical SCS clustering produces more functionally distinct clusters for all categories.

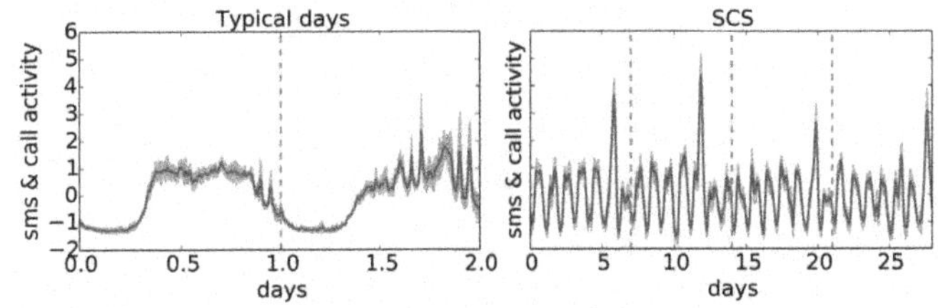

Figure 14: The left figure shows how the typical weekday/weekend approach summarizes the cell phone activity series for the San Siro area. Notice that the high peaks are lost when traffic is aggregated. The right figure shows the SCS traffic in the San Siro area for one month (our method).

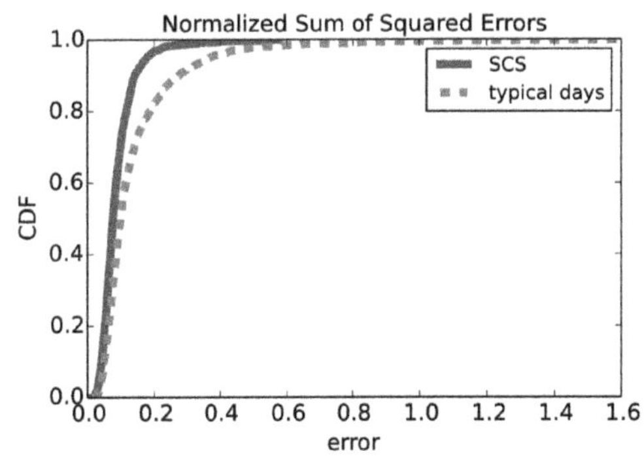

Figure 15: The figure shows how much information is lost from the original series, when we use SCS and when we use typical days. Despite the fact that SCS is created using the top-30 frequencies, while the typical days series is created using a vector of 288 values – 144 values for weekdays, and 144 for weekends – the SCS can reconstruct the original series much better.

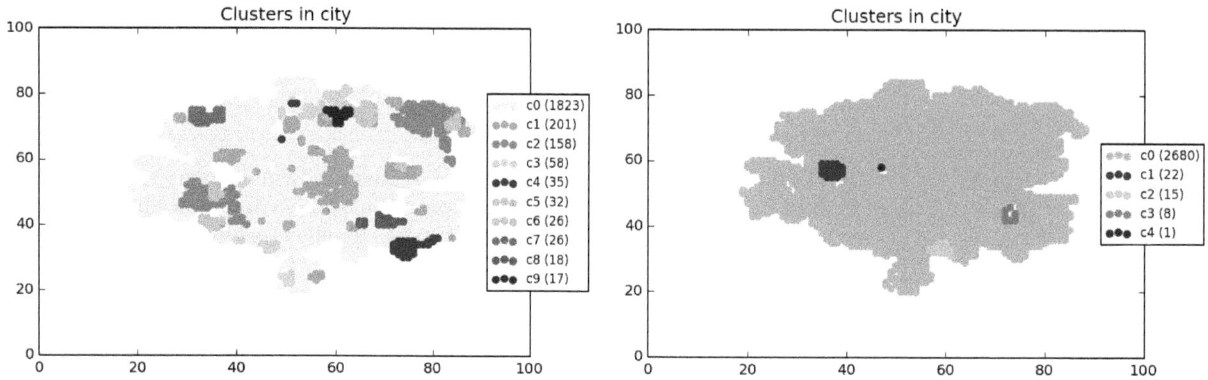

(a) Segmenting Milan (cut-off 0.07)

(b) Detecting anomalous areas (cut-off 0.30)

Figure 10: Clusters generated by low skewness (left) and high skewness (right) segmentation. When the number of clusters exceeds 10, we show only the top 10 largest clusters.

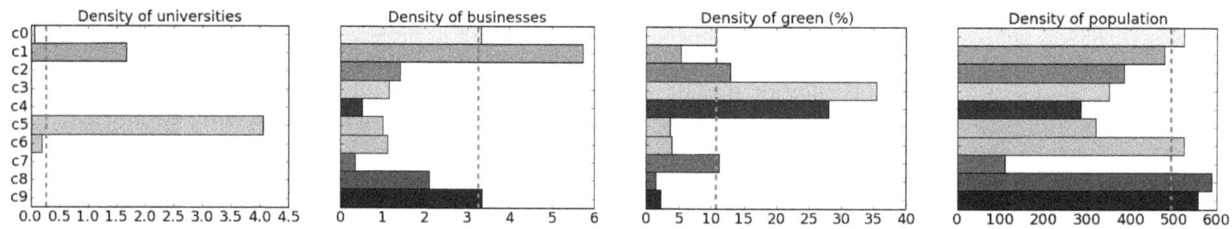

Figure 11: Densities per category for top 10 clusters of Fig. 10(a); red dashed line indicates the Milan average. SCS clustering separates regions with distinct urban environments (e.g., commercial vs. green space).

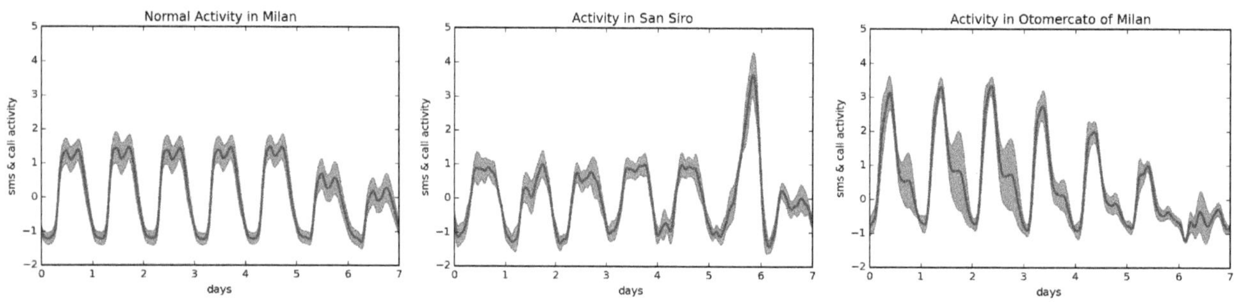

(a) Normal area (c0)

(b) San Siro (c1)

(c) Otomercato (c4)

Figure 12: Average activity series for the clusters of Fig. 10(b); different clusters have very distinct seasonal patterns.

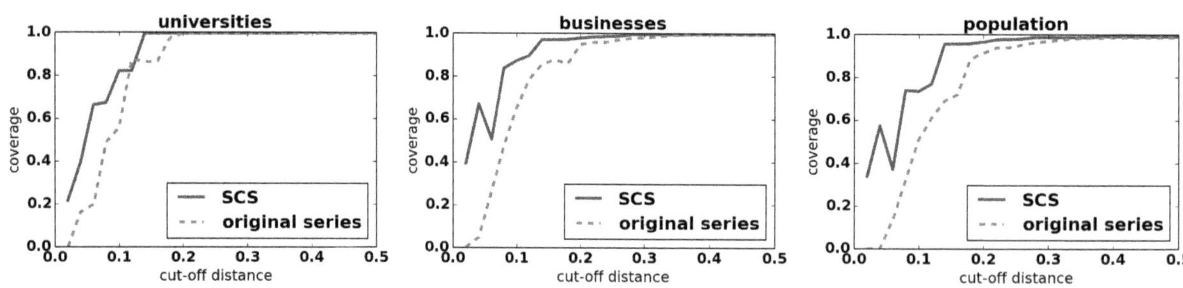

(a) Universities

(b) Businesses

(c) Population

Figure 13: Coverage for SCS clusters vs. original series clustering. Coverage is defined as the percentage of the ground-truth elements "covered" by the clusters with higher than mean concentration of the element type. SCS clustering shows stronger segmentation (higher coverage) for all cut-off values.

In our method $B_i(t) = SCS_i(t)$, whereas in the method of [26] $B_i(t)$ is obtained by using the typical weekday five times and the typical weekend twice to create a typical week, and repeating the typical week four times to create a time series of length T, which corresponds to a month. Fig. 15 shows the cumulative distribution of the errors over all grid-squares. SCS has smaller errors which indicates that it holds more information.

Our method requires less assumptions regarding the nature of the data. It works well in a different culture, e.g. some countries, such as Egypt, designate Friday as a weekend day, while others have Thursday-Friday weekends. To apply the typical weekday and weekend division requires knowledge of the culture, while our approach does not require that. Additionally, the typical weekday approach does not capture mid-week variations that might appear in certain areas.

6.2 What we learn from RCS

RCS reflects the response to perturbations rather than regular behavior. Therefore, we treat them differently: we use cross-correlation between the RCS time series of grid squares, and we investigate how the RCS of one square affects its neighbors and how it correlates with square-to-square communications.

6.2.1 *Using RCS to study cross-square interactions*

A more powerful use of the RCS is to examine interactions between grid squares. Specifically, examination of lagged cross-correlations in the RCS for two squares shows how squares affect each other: i.e., for two cross-correlated squares, a perturbation in one square at time t will be associated with a change in the other square at a later point in time. We denote the cross-correlation "distance" for squares B_i, B_j at a given lag by:

$$dist'(Bi, Bj, lag) = 1 - correlation(Bi, Bj, lag)$$

Note that, unlike a true distance, $dist'$ is not symmetric, i.e. $dist'(Bi, Bj, lag) \neq dist'(Bj, Bi, lag)$. We thus build a directed graph where the nodes are the grid squares and square i is adjacent to square j at a given lag iff

$$dist'(Bi, Bj, lag) < thresh$$

where $thresh$ is an analyst-selected threshold that filters out weak time-lagged correlations. We set $lag = 1$ which corresponds to a 10-minute difference between two squares; it is the most fine-grained unit we can get from our data. We found experimentally that a threshold 5 standard deviations away from the mean yields good results. Given the cross-correlation digraph, we may examine the strongly connected components of the graph to find areas that are subject to mutual social influence (e.g., there are paths by which events in any square can affect communication activity in any other square at a later time).

What we learn from the strong connected components of the graph: In Fig. 16(b) we show the top 10 strongest connected components of the graph, as described in the previous paragraph. We observe a different, but interesting, segmentation of the city from that obtained by SCS, with a clear structure becoming apparent. The center of the city is a connected component (green color), completely separate from the rest. This means that perturbations occurring inside a grid-square on the center, will most likely propagate to other grid-squares in the center. Another example is the dark blue connected component on the center-right side which corresponds to the Milan Linate airport. More generally, the large clusters identified in Fig. 16(b) reflect *socially connected regions* of the city, with events in any given square tending to reverberate within its regional cluster (but not to propagate beyond).

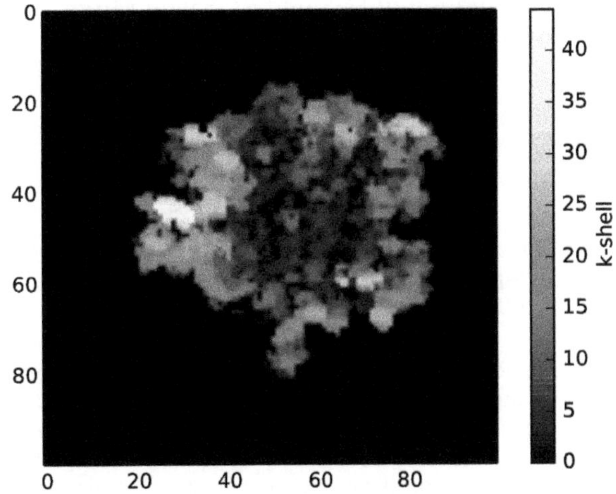

(a) Heat-map showing the k-shell score of each grid square. We observe that squares in the center of the city have lower k-shell scores in comparison with the periphery. This shows that, for this particular directed graph, squares in the periphery are more socially well-connected than squares in the center.

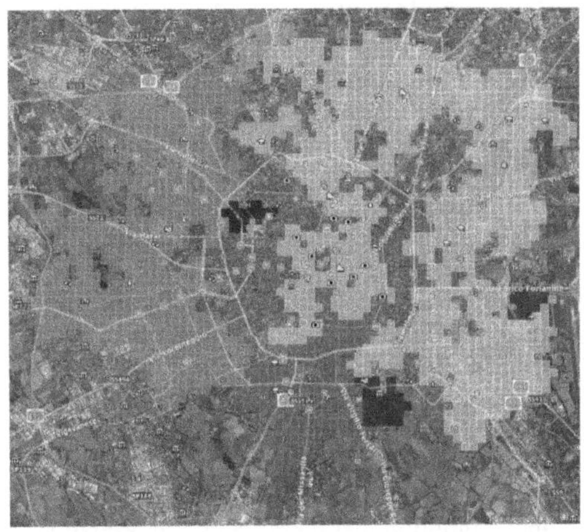

(b) Largest Strongest Connected Components

Figure 16: k-shell heat-map, and 10 largest strongly connected components for the directed graph of RCS cross-correlations with $lag = 1$.

What we learn from the k-shell decomposition: k-shell decomposition is a well-known technique in graph theory for identifying regions of high local cohesion [22] and has been used as a visualization tool for studying networks such as the Internet [10]. It involves identifying maximal sets of nodes with at least k neighbors who are also in the set (k-cores) and then identifying the highest-number to which each core belongs. In this article, we apply the k-shell decomposition on the RCS-based digraph, identifying the squares that are more/less cohesively connected to their neighbors; spatial regions with high values of k are strongly interactive (in the sense that perturbations in one location can propagate to other locations in the region through multiple, redundant correlation paths). In Fig. 16 we observe that squares in the center of the city have lower k-shell scores in comparison with the periphery. This shows that, within Milan, there are several spatially peripheral regions with high local connectivity, while squares near the city and along major arterials tend to be either isolated (with respect to propagation of shocks) or connected via locally tree-like structures.

6.2.2 Correlation of SCS and RCS with Milan Square-to-Square Communication

QAP test results	SCS	RCS
Correlation	**0.05**	**0.27**
Min random	-0.018	-0.005
Mean random	0	0
Max random	0.011	0.004

Table 3: Correlation of SCS and RCS inter-square correlations with Milan Square-to-Square data set, with QAP test replications ($n = 100$). Correlations are significant at p <0.01.

Finally, we compared the Milan Square-to-Square call volume data set with the SCS and RCS square-to-square cross-correlations, assessing the resulting relationship using the Quadratic Assignment Procedure (QAP) [19, 7]. QAP is a technique for testing an observed bimatrix statistic (here, matrix correlation) against a null hypothesis of no association, while controlling for the underlying structure of the matrices being compared; the technique is a form of matrix permutation test, in which the distribution of bimatrix statistics obtained under row-column permutation of the input matrices is used to form a null distribution.

We transformed the Milan Square-to-Square data set into a NxN matrix, where N is the number of grid squares, and we denote it as MM. An entry $MM_{i,j}$ corresponds to the symmetrized communication strength between squares i, j in the Square-to-Square data set. Similarly, we created two additional NxN matrices: 1) matrix RM, with $RM_{i,j} = RCS\_Correlation(i, j)$, corresponding to the residual correlation for squares i, j, and 2) matrix BM, with $BM_{i,j} = SCS\_Correlation(i, j)$, corresponding to the SCS correlation for squares i, j.

As we can see from Table 3, there is a significant correlation between the Square-to-Square data set both for SCS and RCS (p <0.01 in both cases), but for the residual series it is almost six times stronger. Thus, we see that the cross-correlations between squares are associated with direct contact between persons in the respective areas, and this is a substantially stronger effect than the baseline similarity in calling pattern within each square. This further validates our above intuition that the RCS cross-correlations provide information on social interaction across areas within the city.

7. CONCLUSION

In this paper, we studied the decomposition of cell phone activity series, via FFT, into two series: 1) the seasonal communication series (SCS) produced from high-amplitude frequencies, and 2) the residual communication series (RCS) produced after subtracting SCS from the original series. As shown, the SCS can be used to characterize typical patterns of socio-economic activity within an area, while the RCS can be used to capture both irregularities due to novel events and the influence of one area on another. For the first part, we perform an external evaluation of the produced clusters using a ground truth data set that we gathered from the municipality of Milan. Our SCS clustering, produces clusters of areas with similar characteristics as shown in ground truth data. RCS allows to identify regions such that disruptions in one area propagate to the other, and regions that are in direct communicative contact. The RCS and SCS thus provide distinct probes into the structure and dynamics of the urban environment, both of which can be obtained from the same underlying data.

Our techniques are applicable to other geo-social activity data sets,e.g. Twitter and Foursquare, and can be used to reveal patterns of how areas related to each other; in future work we plan to apply our techniques to cell phone activity data from other cities, as well as other type of geo-social activity data. These findings will provide the network operator with information that can improve planning, operations and anomaly detection. In future work, we plan to exploit our findings in order to do cell phone activity prediction.

8. REFERENCES

[1] Milan's public data. `http://dati.comune.milano.it/`, '14.

[2] World urbanization prospects: The 2011 revision. United Nations Department of Economic and Social Affairs/Population Division.

[3] Big data challenge. `http://www.telecomitalia.com/tit/en/bigdatachallenge.html`, 2014.

[4] Source code and data release. `odysseas.calit2.uci.edu/cellphoneactivity`, 2014.

[5] A. S. Berger. *The City: Urban Communities and their Problems, '78.*

[6] P. J. Brockwell and R. A. Davis. *Time Series: Theory and Methods.* Springer-Verlag, New York, second edition, 1991.

[7] C. T. Butts. Perform quadratic assignment procedure (qap) hypothesis tests for graph-level statistics., 2014.

[8] F. Calabrese, M. Colonna, P. Lovisolo, D. Parata, and C. Ratti. Real-time urban monitoring using cell phones: A case study in rome. *IEEE Transactions on Intelligent Transportation Systems*, 2011.

[9] F. Calabrese, J. Reades, and C. Ratti. Eigenplaces: Segmenting space through digital signatures. *IEEE Pervasive Computing*, 2010.

[10] S. Carmi, S. Havlin, S. Kirkpatrick, Y. Shavitt, and E. Shir. A model of internet topology using k-shell decomposition. *PNAS*, 2007.

[11] C. Chatfield. *The Analysis of Time Series: An Introduction.* 1995.

[12] B. Cici, A. Markopoulou, E. Frias-Martinez, and N. Laoutaris. Assessing the potential of ride-sharing using mobile and social data: A tale of four cities. In *Proc. of Ubicomp*, 2014.

[13] J. Cranshaw, R. Schwartz, J. Hong, and N. Sadeh. The Livehoods Project: Utilizing Social Media to Understand the Dynamics of a City. In *Proc. of ICWSM*, 2012.

[14] N. Eagle, A. Pentland, and D. Lazer. Inferring friendship network structure by using mobile phone data. *PNAS*, 2009.

[15] M. Ficek and L. Kencl. Inter-Call Mobility Model: A Spatio-temporal Refinement of Call Data Records Using a Gaussian Mixture Model. In *Proc. of Infocom*, 2012.

[16] C. S. Fischer. Toward a subculture theory of urbanism. *AJS*, 1975.

[17] V. Frias-Martinez, C. Soguero, and E. Frias-Martinez. Estimation of urban commuting patterns using cellphone network data. In *Proc. UrbComp*, 2012.

[18] R. Grannis. The importance of trivial streets: Residential streets and residential segregation. *American Journal of Sociology*, 1998.

[19] D. Krackhardt. QAP Partialling as a Test of Spuriousness. *Social Networks*, 9:171–186, 1987.

[20] A. Noulas, C. Mascolo, and E. Frias-Martinez. Exploiting foursquare and cellular data to infer user activity in urban environments. In *Proc. of MDM*, 2013.

[21] A. Noulas, S. Scellato, C. Mascolo, and M. Pontil. Exploiting semantic annotations for clustering geographic areas and users in location-based social networks. In *Proc. of SMW*, 2011.

[22] B. Pittel, J. Spencer, and N. Wormald. Sudden emergence of a giant k-core in a random graph. *Journal of Combinatorial Theory*, 1996.

[23] C. Ratti, S. Williams, D. Frenchman, and R. Pulselli. Mobile landscapes: using location data from cell phones for urban analysis. *Environment and Planning b Planning and Design*, 33(5):727, 2006.

[24] R. J. Sampson, S. W. Raudenbush, and F. Earls. Neighborhoods and violent crime: A multilevel study of collective efficacy. *Science 1997.*

[25] C. Smith-Clarke, A. Mashhadi, and L. Capra. Poverty on the cheap: Estimating poverty maps using aggregated mobile communication networks. In *Proc. of CHI*, 2014.

[26] V. Soto and E. Frias-Martinez. Automated Land Use Identification using Cell-Phone Records. In *Proc. of HotPlanet*, 2011.

[27] J. L. Toole, M. Ulm, M. C. González, and D. Bauer. Inferring land use from mobile phone activity. In *Proc. of UrbComp*, 2012.

[28] J. Yuan, Y. Zheng, and X. Xie. Discovering regions of different functions in a city using human mobility and pois. In *KDD*, 2012.

[29] Y. Zhao and G. Karypis. Criterion functions for document clustering: Experiments and analysis. Technical report, 2001.

Signpost: Scalable MU-MIMO Signaling with Zero CSI Feedback

Anfu Zhou*†, Teng Wei†, Xinyu Zhang†, Min Liu* and Zhongcheng Li*
*Institute of Computing Technology, Chinese Academy of Sciences, †University of Wisconsin - Madison
{zhouanfu, liumin, zcli}@ict.ac.cn, twei7@wisc.edu, xyzhang@ece.wisc.edu

ABSTRACT

Poor scalability is a long standing problem in multi-user MIMO (MU-MIMO) networks: in order to select concurrent uplink users with strong channel orthogonality and thus high total capacity, channel state information (CSI) feedback from users is required. However, when the user population is large, the overhead from CSI feedback can easily overwhelm the actual channel time spent on data transmission. Moreover, due to spontaneous uplink traffic, uplink user selection cannot rely on the access point's central assignment and needs a distributed realization instead, which makes the problem even more challenging.

In this paper, we propose a fully scalable and distributed uplink MU-MIMO protocol called *Signpost*. Firstly, Signpost is scalable, i.e., it achieves *zero CSI overhead* by exploiting a novel orthogonality evaluation mechanism that enables each user to speculate its orthogonality to other users, using its own CSI only. Secondly, Signpost realizes distributed user selection through a two-dimensional prioritized contention mechanism, which can single out the best users efficiently by utilizing both the time and frequency domain resources. The contention mechanism includes a unique collision recovery scheme, which enables Signpost to achieve a collision probability as low as one-tenth compared with traditional 802.11-like mechanism. Software-radio based implementation and testbed experimentation show that Signpost significantly outperforms state-of-the-art user selection methods under various traffic patterns and node mobility.

Categories and Subject Descriptors

C.2.1 [**Computer-Communication Networks**]: Network Architecture and Design—*Wireless Communications*

General Terms

Algorithms, Design, Theory, Performance

Keywords

Multi-user MIMO; MU-MIMO; 802.11ac; User selection

1. INTRODUCTION

MU-MIMO is an emerging wireless technology that allows multiple users to transmit concurrently towards the same multi-antenna access point (AP), or vice versa. It holds the potential to substantially improve network throughput. To fully realize this potential, only the best user group should be served in each MU-MIMO transmission, because users are coupled and their achievable rates depend on the orthogonality of their instantaneous channel states [1, 13]. However, selecting the best user group usually requires a signaling stage, wherein all users feed back their CSI to the AP. When the user population is large, channel time spent on CSI feedback can easily overwhelm the actual channel time spent on data transmission. Therefore, a user selection mechanism must be *scalable* – given a growing user population, it should limit the CSI overhead while maximizing the link capacity, in order to optimize the overall throughput.

Besides, particularly for uplink (UL) MU-MIMO, the user selection mechanism must be fully *distributed* and executed by the users themselves instead of the AP. The users may be mobile, have bursty traffic demands, or join/leave the MU-MIMO cell dynamically. Thus, they should coordinate with each other spontaneously to form the best user group for each UL MU-MIMO transmission.

Recent MU-MIMO protocols have addressed the scalability of *downlink* (DL) MU-MIMO user selection [15, 18]. One state-of-the-art approach is OPUS [18] which bounds CSI overhead via the AP's iterative probing. Suppose M is the number of antennas on the AP and N is the number of client users in the network. OPUS requires only M rounds of CSI feedback from the client users to the AP, instead of N rounds in previous studies.

One may handle the UL scenario in a similar manner as DL (i.e., the AP is in charge of choosing an optimal set of concurrent users, and then the selected users transmit following the AP's commands [17]). However, such an approach falls short of scalability and goes against the distributed nature of UL MU-MIMO. First of all, M rounds of CSI feedback still entail a non-trivial overhead. For example, when $M = 2$, the time spent on CSI feedback is usually more than half of the time spent on data transmission (More details are in Sec. 6). Second, in UL scenarios, a client needs to compete for transmission opportunities upon traffic demand [16, 17]. When the user population grows, collisions happen frequently and network performance degrades severely, which in turn leads to poor MU-MIMO scalability. Due to these challenges, recent wireless standards like 802.11ac, LTE and WiMax only permit MU-MIMO DL, whereas efficient UL MU-MIMO remains an open problem.

In this paper, we propose Signpost – a scalable and distributed user selection protocol for UL MU-MIMO. *Firstly*, Signpost can decide on a high-throughput concurrent user set without requiring any CSI feedback, which means *zero CSI overhead* under any user population. To achieve this, our key observation is that *the orthogonality between users could be speculated through an indirect way instead of directly collecting CSI from users*. Specifically, suppose we want to choose 2 users for concurrent uplink transmission towards a 2-antenna AP. Our basic idea is to predefine two orthogonal channel vectors (called *Signpost directions*). Before each uplink transmission, each user can compute the angle between its own CSI and each signpost direction. Suppose that among all users, user i is best aligned with one Signpost direction, and another user j is best aligned to the other Signpost direction. Then we can conjecture that the two users have strong

MobiHoc'15, June 22–25, 2015, Hangzhou, China.

http://dx.doi.org/10.1145/2746285.2746286.

orthogonality, since they are aligned to two orthogonal Signpost directions[1].

One may question whether this indirect method can group orthogonal users as reliably as one that directly collects CSI. We provide a positive answer through both theoretical analysis and a test-bed measurement study in Sec.3. We also find that this desirable benefit is unique to UL scenarios, and does not hold true in the opposite DL scenarios.

Secondly, to facilitate a distributed realization, we design an efficient two-dimensional (2-D) prioritized contention protocol to single out users with strong orthogonality. Instead of equal-chance random access as in 802.11, here the MAC layer contention priority of a user is derived from its PHY layer information of alignment metrics (i.e., how well the user's CSI is aligned to Signpost directions). In this way, we can guarantee that a preferred set of concurrent users will be selected.

In addition, unlike conventional channel contention, here multiple users are contending for multiple Signpost directions simultaneously. Thus, collision rate can easily become overwhelming. To achieve contention efficiency, we utilize different OFDM subcarriers to separate the contention from different Signpost directions. Combining this with the time-domain random backoff, we design a unique collision recovery mechanism that allows users to detect a collision and recover from the collision in a distributed and cooperative way. In a network consisting of 30 users with saturated traffic, the resulting collision probability is only about 2$\sim$3%, whereas that in state-of-the-art work is more than tenfold higher. Signpost's contention mechanism preserves the distributed nature of UL scenarios, and hence works well under various traffic patterns and node mobility.

We have built a prototype of Signpost on the WARP [30] software radio platform, and have conducted extensive experiments under different scenarios to compare its performance with three state-of-the-art user selections works including SAM [16], MIMOMate [17] and OPUS [18]. The main results are as follows:

(i) In terms of PHY-layer throughput, Signpost achieves a gain of 1.16$\times$ to 1.70$\times$ under saturated-traffic scenarios, 1.13$\times$ to 1.56$\times$ under non-saturated scenarios, and 1.04$\times$ to 1.56$\times$ under mobile scenarios, in a typical 802.11 MU-MIMO WLAN with a 2-antenna AP and 14 users.

(ii) After taking the MAC overhead into account, Signpost achieves remarkably higher MAC-layer throughput gain. In particular, it is 1.44$\times$ to 2.96$\times$, 1.55$\times$ to 1.93$\times$, and 1.70$\times$ to 2.57$\times$ under the three scenarios.

(iii) Signpost scales well in medium to large sized networks. For a 3-antenna AP, we vary the number of users from 6 to 46, and for each setting half of the users are statically located and the other half mobile, and traffic on each user is random. The resulting gain is 1.72$\times$, 1.56$\times$ and 1.49$\times$ compared with SAM, MIMOMate and OPUS respectively, averaged over all network sizes.

The rest of this paper is organized as follows. We discuss more related works in Sec. 2, and then present Signpost's indirect user orthogonality evaluation in Sec. 3 and 2-D prioritized contention in Sec. 4, and the complete Signpost protocol operations in Sec. 5. We evaluate Signpost's performance in Sec. 6 and conclude the paper in Sec. 7.

2. RELATED WORK

The potential of MU-MIMO and the impact of user selection have long been recognized in communication theory [1]. Early works [2–8] assumed that perfect CSI is available and focused on designing low-complexity algorithms to approximate the maximum capacity. However, in practice, obtaining CSI incurs huge overhead, which renders these theoretical approaches infeasible [18, 19].

Recently, many experimental studies [9–18] have explored MU-MIMO in practical scenarios. For the DL case [15, 18], MU-MIMO transmission is more straightforward since user selection could be achieved in a centralized manner at the AP side. However, how to realize scalable and distributed MU-MIMO transmission is a far more challenging problem. Existing UL MU-MIMO protocols [13, 16] still adopt the traditional 802.11 random contention mechanism to select concurrent users, which not only fails to select concurrent transmitters according to their channel characteristic, but also wastes much channel time due to high collision probability.

A recent protocol called MIMOMate [17] optimizes UL user selection through a centralized approach, where the AP is in charge of selecting concurrent users. The AP learns the CSI passively, and then matches users into groups according to their CSI. Then for each round of UL transmission, only group leaders are involved in contention, thus saving channel contention time. However, such a centralized approach is not applicable when users are mobile or have non-saturated traffic, since the passively learned CSI usually becomes outdated and leads to an inappropriate selected users set. Moreover, it also adds protocol complexity. To our knowledge, Signpost represents the first distributed UL MU-MIMO mechanism with zero CSI overhead. Therefore, it can maximally deliver the gain of MU-MIMO, as will be verified in Sec. 6.

Signpost's zero-feedback principle shares similar spirit with random beamforming (RBF) [8] which is used for *downlink* MU-MIMO. An RBF AP randomly beamforms to multiple directions, requires users to feed back their alignment with each direction, and then beamforms to users with best alignment. To our knowledge, RBF has only been discussed in theory and lacks a MAC protocol that supports its operations in practice. More importantly, although RBF is asymptotically optimal (i.e, its information-theory capacity grows at the same order as that obtained with known CSI, as the number of users N and the number of antennas M approach infinity [8]), we show that under practical networks with a reasonable number of N and M, RBF has poor performance. This fact indicates that having exact CSI is critical for DL MU-MIMO beamforming in practice. In contrast, we demonstrate that CSI feedback is not necessarily required to achieve high performance in UL scenarios. We contrast Signpost and RBF in more details in Sec. 3.4.

In terms of Signpost MAC, the 2-D prioritized contention mechanism is inspired by the frequency domain contention mechanism Back2F [20], but it differs in several aspects. *First*, Signpost jointly utilizes the resource from both frequency domain and time domain for efficient contention. *Second*, the Signpost MAC supports MU-MIMO through concurrent multi-directional contention, while Back2F is designed for traditional single-transmission scenarios. Finally, Back2F requires at least two antennas to enable concurrent transmission and carrier sensing, which is not needed in Signpost.

3. INDIRECT ORTHOGONALITY EVALUATION

In this section, we first introduce the relevant background, including the impact of users' CSI orthogonality and traditional direct orthogonality evaluation mechanisms. Then we describe Signpost's indirect approach followed by both analytical and experimental validation.

3.1 Background

In MU-MIMO networks, the throughput of a user depends not only on the user's own channel state, but also on the channel state

[1]Since these predefined orthogonal vectors could be used to indicate client users' direction, we can image them as the signposts along a sidewalk. We thus name our approach "Signpost".

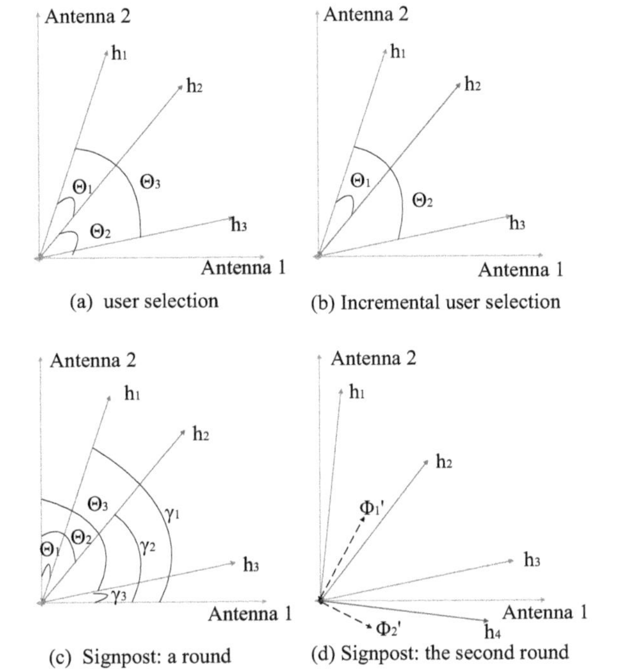

(a) user selection (b) Incremental user selection

(c) Signpost: a round (d) Signpost: the second round

Figure 1: User selection in MU-MIMO.

of other concurrent users [1, 13]. We briefly review this point as follows. Consider a typical MU-MIMO WLAN with a 2-antenna AP, when a single user u_1 transmits a symbol x_1 alone, the received symbol $\boldsymbol{y}$ on the AP is as follows:

$$\begin{cases} y_1 = h_{11}x_1 + n_1 \\ y_2 = h_{21}x_1 + n_2 \end{cases} \tag{1}$$

where $\boldsymbol{h_1} = (h_{11}, h_{21})$ is the channel coefficients between the AP and u_1, and n_i represents zero-mean Gaussian noise with variance N_0. Through Maximal Radio Combining (MRC) [1], we can recover the symbol and the resulting SNR of the symbol, denoted by SNR_{alone}, is:

$$SNR_{alone} = E[\|\boldsymbol{h_1}x_1\|^2]/N_0 \tag{2}$$

Next, suppose another user u_2 transmits a symbol x_2 concurrently with u_1, then the received symbol $\boldsymbol{y}$ can be represented as:

$$\begin{cases} y_1 = h_{11}x_1 + h_{12}x_2 + n_1 \\ y_2 = h_{21}x_1 + h_{22}x_2 + n_2 \end{cases} \tag{3}$$

To recover each symbol, say x_1, the AP migrates the interference from the other symbol using a *zero-forcing* (ZF) technique as in [13]. Specifically, ZF projects $\boldsymbol{y}$ on a direction orthogonal to $\boldsymbol{h_2}$ so as to null out x_2, and gets an estimate of x_1 (denoted by $\hat{x}_1$) as follows:

$$\hat{x}_1 = x_1 + \frac{h_{22}n_1 - h_{12}n_2}{h_{22}h_{11} - h_{21}h_{12}} \tag{4}$$

From (4), we can compute the resulting SNR of x_1, denoted by SNR_{con}:

$$SNR_{con} = SNR_{alone}(1 - \cos^2(\theta)) \tag{5}$$

where θ is the angle between $\boldsymbol{h_1}$ and $\boldsymbol{h_2}$, that is,

$$\cos^2(\theta) = \frac{\|\boldsymbol{h_1 h_2}\|^2}{\|\boldsymbol{h_1}\|^2\|\boldsymbol{h_2}\|^2} \tag{6}$$

From (5), we can observe that the channel quality of u_1, SNR_{con}, depends on the angle between the two users' channel coefficients. When the two users are nearly orthogonal (i.e., θ is close to $\frac{\pi}{2}$), the channel quality will be as good as that when u_1 transmits alone. But when θ is small, the channel quality will degrade significantly, which in consequence leads to poor performance. For example, when $\theta = 45°$, SNR_{con} is only half of SNR_{alone}. Therefore, *it is critical to select and group users with strong channel orthogonality.*

A straightforward approach for selecting an optimal user set is to allow the AP to collect all users' CSI first, evaluate the orthogonality of each possible user set, and then choose the one with the best orthogonality. We illustrate this by an example shown in Fig. 1(a), where we assume a 2-antenna AP, and three users u_1, u_2 and u_3 with CSI $\boldsymbol{h_1}$, $\boldsymbol{h_2}$ and $\boldsymbol{h_3}$, respectively. When CSI of all three users is available on the AP, the AP can compute their pairwise angles, and select the two users (in fact, u_1 and u_3) with the most orthogonal angle[2].

However, this approach has many drawbacks in practice. First, obtaining full CSI of all users usually incurs large overhead, which grows linearly with the number of users and can easily overwhelm the actual channel time spent on data transmission [18, 19]. Moreover, even if we can get the full CSI, the computational complexity may become formidable as it increases exponentially with the user population.

To cope with the computational cost, many suboptimal incremental user selection algorithms [4–7] have been proposed, which choose the first user according to a performance metric, and then select additional users one by one that provides the best potential performance when grouped with those previously selected ones. The procedure repeats until M users are selected (M is the number of antennas on the AP). For example, in Fig. 1(b), suppose we choose u_1 as the first user, then by computing the angle θ_1 between u_1 and u_2, and the angle θ_2 between u_1 and u_3, we will find that u_3 should be the next selected user. Although some incremental user selection methods (e.g., SUS [4]) have been shown to well approximate the optimal capacity at low computational complexity [7], they still incur large overhead, since in each round of user selection, identifying the next best user still requires full CSI from all unselected users. To reduce such CSI overhead, a recent work, OPUS [18], proposed a novel incremental user selection method, which requires CSI of M users in each round, instead of full CSI of all users. However, as we will show in Sec. 6, the overhead of OPUS is still high due to its contention and feedback overhead.

In retrospect, these existing approaches could be categorized into a class of **direct** approach for user selection, as the orthogonality is derived by directly computing the angle between the users' CSI. In consequence, CSI is necessary and hence the overhead is unavoidable.

3.2 UL User Selection with Zero CSI Feedback

Now we introduce the principle of indirect user selection in Signpost. The key idea is to allow each user to speculate its orthogonality with others by using its local CSI only.

Suppose we want to determine the orthogonality between two users u_i and u_j with channel gain $\boldsymbol{h_i}$ and $\boldsymbol{h_j}$, respectively. We predefine some vectors (say, $\boldsymbol{\phi_1}$, $\boldsymbol{\phi_2}$, and called Signpost directions) with orthogonal directions. Each user then computes the angles between its channel gain and the Signpost directions. If user i has good *alignment* with $\boldsymbol{\phi_1}$ and j also has good *alignment* with $\boldsymbol{\phi_2}$, we can conjecture that the angle between $\boldsymbol{h_i}$ and $\boldsymbol{h_j}$ is close to orthogonal since $\boldsymbol{\phi_1}$ and $\boldsymbol{\phi_2}$ are orthogonal.

For example, in Fig. 1(c), we can set the directions along two axes of coordinates as the Signpost directions, i.e., $\boldsymbol{\phi_1} = (1, 0)$ and $\boldsymbol{\phi_2} = (0, 1)$. Suppose these Signpost directions are known to all three users, then each user can evaluate its alignment to each Signpost direction, by computing the angle between its CSI and that

[2]Besides angles, some works also take the SNR of each user into account. Here we just use angle for simplicity, but the principle is the same.

Signpost direction. For direction ϕ_1, the angles are θ_1, θ_2 and θ_3 for the three users respectively. Then u_1 with the smallest angle θ_1 will be selected. Similarly, on the second Signpost direction ϕ_2, u_3 (with the smallest angle γ_3) will be selected.

Note that if we use a fixed set of Signpost directions, there will be unfairness problem since the same set of users will always be selected. To solve this problem, we predefine multiple sets of Signpost vectors, and use them alternately across different rounds of user selection. For example, in Fig. 1(d), in the second round, we use a different set of Signpost directions (i.e, $\phi_1^{'}$ and $\phi_2^{'}$) than the first round. Consequently, a different set of users (u_2 and u_4) is likely to be selected along the new directions.

We now extend the above basic idea to the general case. For a MU-MIMO network with an M-antenna AP and N users, each client user i computes $g_{i,j}$ ($j = 1, \cdots, M$), the *alignment metric* between its channel state $\boldsymbol{h_i}$ and the jth Signpost vector $\boldsymbol{\phi_j}$ as follows:

$$g_{i,j} = \frac{||\boldsymbol{h_i \phi_j}||^2}{||\boldsymbol{h_i}||^2} \quad (7)$$

From a centralized perspective, Signpost user selection operates in an iterative manner. *First*, we pick the maximum value among all $g_{i,j}$ ($i \in [1, N]$ and $j \in [1, M]$), and denote it as $g_{i_{max}, j_{max}}$. We then put the corresponding user i_{max} into the set of selected users, and remove the j_{max} Signpost direction out of consideration. *Second*, we find the next maximum alignment metric among the remaining Signpost directions and remaining users, that is, among all $g_{i,j}$ ($i \in [1, i_{max} - 1] \cup [i_{max} + 1, N]$) and $j \in [1, j_{max} - 1] \cup [j_{max} + 1, M]$. Then we can select the second user and remove it and the its corresponding Signpost direction. The process iterates until we select M users (or N if the user population $N < M$). Before describing a decentralized realization of the iterative procedure (Sec. 4), we first justify this design through both analysis and testbed measurement.

3.3 Analytical Verification

One may question whether Signpost's indirect approach can select appropriate user sets that result in large overall throughput. After all, it is an indirect approach, and each user only uses its local CSI without knowing other users' CSI. The following analysis provides a positive answer.

We first analyze the advantage of Signpost by comparing it with a baseline random user selection. We first show, for any Signpost direction, how well the selected users can be aligned. We define the alignment metric (denoted by $\hat{g}$) between the selected user on the jth Signpost direction as:

$$\hat{g} \triangleq \max_{i \in [1,N]} g_{i,j} \quad (8)$$

For a simple case of $M = 2$, we compute a closed-form expression of $E\{\hat{g}\}$ as follows. From the definition of $\hat{g}$, it is clear that for any $cos^2(\theta) \in [0, 1]$, $\hat{g} \leq cos^2(\theta)$ requires that all $g_{i,j}$ ($i \in [1, N]$) should be no larger than $cos^2(\theta)$. Then, we know the probability that $\hat{g} \leq cos^2(\theta)$ is

$$F(\hat{g} \leq cos^2(\theta)) = \prod_{i=1}^{N} F(g_{i,j} \leq cos^2(\theta)) \quad (9)$$

We assume the CSI of any user is a random vector in the M dimension space, then the cosine of the angle between the user and a Signpost direction follows a distribution as that of the minimum of (M-1) i.i.d. uniform random variables in [0,1] (from Lemma 3.2 in [26]). For our specific case of $M = 2$, this means that the angle follows a uniform distribution in [0, $\frac{\pi}{2}$]. So

$$F(g_{i,j} \leq cos^2(\theta)) = 1 - \frac{2\theta}{\pi} \qquad \forall i \in [1, N] \quad (10)$$

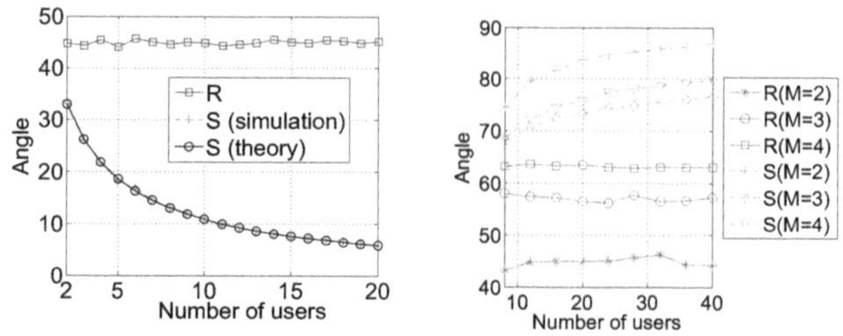

Figure 2: Mean angle (a) between users and signpost directions (b) between selected users.'R' means Random method, and 'S' means Signpost.

Putting (10) into (9), we have

$$F(\hat{g} \leq cos^2(\theta)) = (1 - \frac{2\theta}{\pi})^N \quad (11)$$

Then the expectation of $\hat{g}$ becomes

$$E(\hat{g}) = \int_{\theta=0}^{\frac{\pi}{2}} \left[cos^2(\theta) N (1 - \frac{2\theta}{\pi})^{(N-1)} (-\frac{2}{\pi}) d\theta \right] \quad (12)$$

Solving the integration above, we can have a closed-form equation as follows,

$$E\{\hat{g}\} = \frac{1}{2}\Big[1 + \sum_{i=0}^{N-1} \frac{(\frac{1+(-1)^i}{2})(-1)^{\frac{i}{2}-1} \prod_{j=0}^{i-1}(N-j)}{\pi^i} + \frac{(1+(-1)^N)(-1)^{\frac{N}{2}-1} \prod_{j=0}^{N-1}(N-j)}{\pi^N}\Big] \quad (13)$$

From (13), we obtain the average angle (denoted by $\hat{\theta}$) between the selected user and the corresponding Signpost direction as:

$$\hat{\theta} = \arccos(\sqrt{E\{\hat{g}\}}) \quad (14)$$

Fig. 2(a) (the 'theory' Line) plots $\hat{\theta}$ as the number of users N grows from 2 to 20. We also verify the analysis with simulation: for each N, we generate N users with random CSI, and select two users using Signpost and Random method, respectively. We repeat 1000 rounds of simulation for each N setting. The results show that the simulation perfectly match with theory. The angle between a user and its corresponding Signpost direction $\hat{\theta}$ decreases rapidly with N. When $N \geq 12$, $\hat{\theta}$ is smaller than $10°$. In contrast, under random user selection, a selected user always has an average angle of $45°$ to any Signpost direction, regardless of N.

Therefore, our user selection scheme can ensure the selected users are well aligned with the corresponding Signpost directions. Since the Signpost directions are orthogonal, we expect that the selected users will be near-orthogonal. The simulation results in Fig. 2(b) confirm this point. Under $M = 2$, if $N \geq 12$, the angle between two users selected by Signpost is larger than $77°$, and approaches $90°$ as N further increases. We also find that Signpost keeps much advantage over the random user selection as M increases.

3.4 Measurement Validation

Now we show that strong orthogonality achieved by Signpost leads to much higher network performance, using a test-bed based measurement. We set up the test-bed in Fig.12 using WARP [30] on a 20-MHz channel, where we use a 3-antenna AP, and collect CSI of 30 distinct locations by varying the location of the two clients (more details of the implementation are in Sec. 6). Then we feed the CSI into different channel orthogonality evaluation and user selection methods, and compare the resulting per-user SINR from Signpost, Random User Selection (RUS) and the Optimal upbound derived by an exhaustive search among all possible user combinations. The results are given in Fig. 3(a). We can observe that Signpost is much

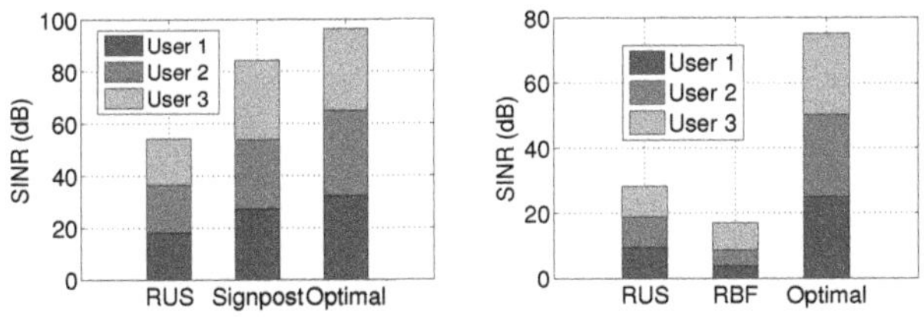

Figure 3: (a) UL SINR (b) DL SINR.

closer to the optimal bound, and the ratio is 87.3%, while that of RUS is only 56.1%.

More importantly, we find that this desirable benefit is unique to UL scenarios, and it does not hold true in the opposite DL scenarios. We plot the result for the DL scenario in Fig. 3(b). Here we compare RUS, the Optimal bound and Random Beamforming (RBF) [8]. RBF could be considered as the DL version of Signpost. Similar to Signpost, RBF also applies indirect orthogonality evaluation without CSI feedback. A RBF AP randomly beamforms to multiple directions, asks the users to feed back their alignment along each direction, and then beamforms to users with best alignment. It is proved in [8] that when both the number of antennas on the AP M and the user population N go to infinity, the information-theory capacity of RBF is at the same order with that of the Optimal. However, as we can observe from Fig. 3(b), RBF exhibits poor performance, even much worse than RUS in practice with reasonable M and N.

We find the reason as follows. After user selection, the AP needs to know the exact CSI to perform precoding before beamforming to users. However, RBF only precodes with the randomly selected directions without CSI feedback, which causes much capacity loss. In contrast, for the UL case, the AP will finally get all CSI after it receives upcoming transmissions, which can be used to decode all of them. In this way, the AP exploits full potential of selected users with strong orthogonality. To sum up, this fact indicates that having exact CSI is critical for downlink beamforming in practice, while Signpost demonstrates that CSI feedback is not necessarily required in uplink scenarios.

4. 2-D PRIORITIZED CONTENTION

Now we present the contention mechanism that realizes the Signpost user selection in a distributed way. Compared with traditional SISO scenarios, it is far more challenging when designing an efficient contention mechanism for MU-MIMO. In traditional SISO networks, the aim is to single out *one random user* while minimizing collisions. For MU-MIMO, the objective is to single out *a preferred set of users with strong orthogonality* while minimizing the contention and collision overhead.

To meet the objective, we propose a cross-layer approach, which connects the alignment metrics computed from PHY layer CSI with the MAC layer contention aggressiveness of users. The larger the metrics, the smaller the contention aggressiveness is. On one hand, this makes users with strong orthogonality more likely to win the contention. On the other hand, this prioritized contention causes an extra difficulty in avoiding collisions. In particular, when different users have similar alignment metrics, they will end up in collision since they have similar contention time. One straightforward method for avoiding collisions is to increase the contention window. For 802.11 contention, this will work since users pick a random contention time in the contention window. The larger the window, the more likely they will choose different contention time so as to avoid collisions. However, this will not work for prioritized contention, since the contention time is not randomly picked but pre-defined by the alignment metrics. One may increase the contention window to a

Algorithm 1 2-D prioritized contention algorithm.

Input: h: the user's CSI; Φ: the Signpost directions; W: the contention window;
Output: *sel*: the selected status of the user;

Initialize: *sel* = 0; the selected Signpost direction $sel\_dir = 0$; contention status *cont* = 1; *slot* = 1;
Compute the alignment metrics using (7)
Create M backoff timers using (15), (16), (17) and (18);
while slot $\leq W$ **do**
  if *cont* == 1 $\&$ a timer on any direction m expires **then**
    cont = 0
    sel = 1;
    $sel\_dir = m$;
  end if
  if hear a CA on any direction m **then**
    if *cont* == 1 **then**
      Quit contention on direction m;
      Disable the corresponding timer ;
    end if
    if *cont* == 0 $\&$ $sel\_dir == m$ **then**
      sel = 0; ▷ Detect own collision, cancel the selection
    end if
  end if
  if hear multiple CAs on any direction m **then**
    if *cont* == 1 **then**
      Detect other users' collision, keep contention;
    end if
    if *cont* == 0 $\&$ $sel\_dir == m$ **then**
      sel = 0; ▷ Detect own collision, cancel the selection
    end if
  end if
  slot++;
end while

very large value so that close alignment metrics can still be mapped into different contention slots. But clearly, this will waste too much channel time.

To overcome this problem, we design a two-dimensional (2-D) contention method. Besides the time domain backoff used in 802.11, we also utilize frequency domain by using different OFDM subcarriers to separate the contention from different Signpost directions. In this way, we alleviate contention intensity and reduce collision probability. Moreover, by leveraging both time and frequency domain knowledge, we design a unique collision recovery mechanism that allows users to detect collisions, and recover from the collisions in a cooperative and distributed way. Combining these two techniques, Signpost achieves distributed user selection efficiently. Next, we present an overview of the 2-D prioritized contention mechanism, followed by more details for each component.

4.1 Overview

For a network with N users and a M-antenna AP, the contention mechanism works as follows. Recall each user i can locally compute M alignment metrics, one metric per Singpost direction. Thereafter, the user employs a *mapping mechanism* to project each metric to a 2-D coordinate: along frequency (subcarrier index) and time (backoff timer), respectively. Then, a 2-D CSMA-based contention procedure begins. Specifically, each user picks the Signpost direction with smallest backoff timer and starts counting down. After the timer expires, it contends with others by transmitting a contention announcement (CA, the design is in Sec. 5) on the specified subcarrier. If a user hears a CA on this Signpost direction before its timer

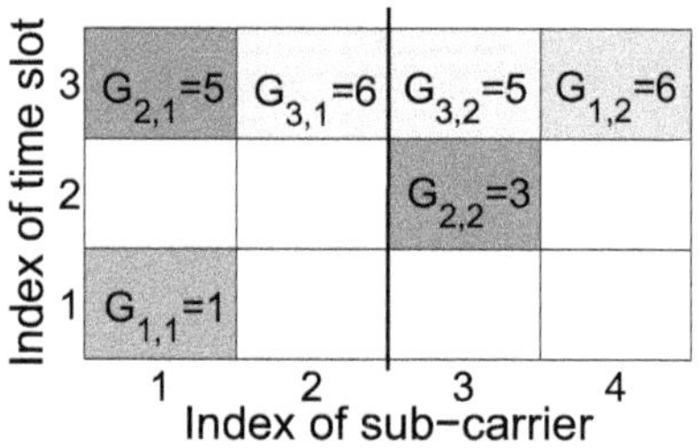

Figure 4: An example of Signpost contention.

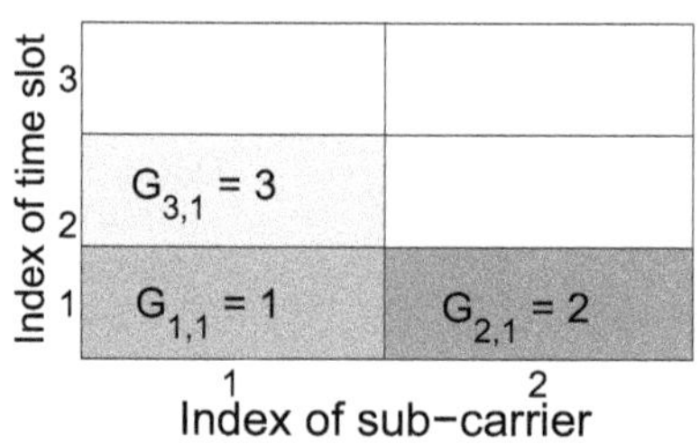

Figure 5: An example of collision recovery

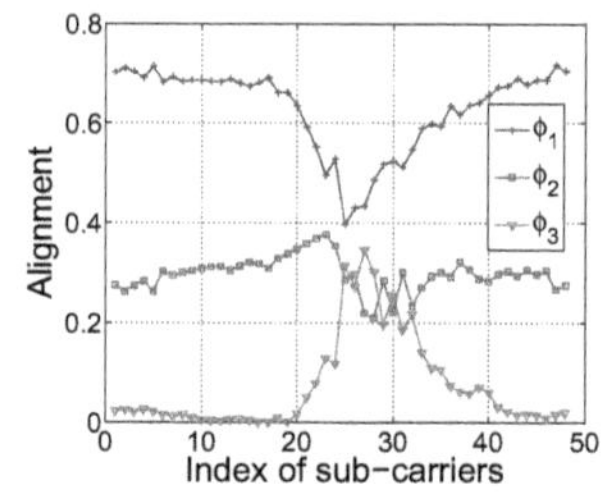

Figure 6: Alignment consistency

expiration, it will infer that someone else has better alignment and then it quits contention on this Signpost direction. Then it contends for next Signpost direction with the second smallest backoff time. However, if a user hears more than one CAs on the same Signpost direction at the same time, it will infer that a collision happens and then it keeps contending to recover from the collision. Once it wins a contention on any direction, it stops contention. The contention procedure running on each user is given in Algorithm 1. Next we explain each component of the algorithm.

4.2 Mapping

An alignment metric is mapped to a specified subcarrier index and a specified backoff timer in two steps. First, we separate contention from different Signpost directions by assigning a different segment of consecutive subcarriers to each Signpost direction. Given S subcarriers in total, we first divide them into M segments, each containing $L \triangleq \lfloor \frac{S}{M} \rfloor$ subcarriers. Then alignment metrics belonging to the j_{th} Signpost direction will be mapped to the j_{th} subcarrier segments. In the second step, we decide the exact subcarrier and backoff timer for each alignment metric. Suppose we use a contention window with length of W time slots. Then an alignment metric $g_{i,j}$ (i.e., the alignment of user i on direction j, $0 \le g_{i,j} \le 1$) is first quantized to $G_{i,j}$ as follows:

$$G_{i,j} = \lfloor (1 - g_{i,j})LW \rfloor \tag{15}$$

Then, the backoff timer $t_{i,j}$ is specified as:

$$t_{i,j} = \left\lceil \frac{G_{i,j}}{L} \right\rceil \tag{16}$$

and the subcarrier index $s_{i,j}$ is specified as follows. First we compute

$$\hat{s}_{i,j} = mod(G_{i,j}, L) \tag{17}$$

then we shift this subcarrier into the jth subcarrier segment as:

$$s_{i,j} = (j-1)L + \hat{s}_{i,j} \tag{18}$$

We illustrate the mapping mechanism using an example in Fig. 4, where we assume $M = 2$, $N = 3$, contention window $W = 3$, and number of subcarriers $S = 4$. The alignment metrics for these three users are $\{G_{1,1} = 1, G_{1,2} = 6\}$, $\{G_{1,2} = 5, G_{2,2} = 3\}$, and $\{G_{3,1} = 6, G_{3,2} = 5\}$, respectively. Following the above mapping mechanism, we compute the corresponding subcarrier index and backoff timer for each alignment metric, which is given in Fig. 4. We can see that user 1 will win the contention on the first direction, while user 2 will win on the second direction.

4.3 Collision Recovery

Collision happens when multiple users have the same or very close alignment metric on the same Signpost direction. An example is shown in Fig. 5, with a similar setting as in Fig. 4 but with focus on the contention from the first Signpost direction. The contention on other Signpost directions is similar but independent since we use different subcarrier segments to separate them.

We assume three users with $G_{1,1} = 1$, $G_{2,1} = 2$ and $G_{3,1} = 3$. User 1 and user 2 will transmit a CA each at the same time slot, on subcarrier 1 and subcarrier 2. Note that user 2 has a larger backoff timer and hence a lower contention priority, and ideally it should know that user 1 has won the contention. But in practice, it has no such knowledge. When it transmits a CA on subcarrier 2, it is unable to hear the CA on subcarrier 1 from user 1 since 802.11 radios are half-duplex, which finally leads to a collision.

We design a collision recovery scheme to tackle such challenges. The basic idea is to let other users keep contending on this direction (and will transmit a CA once the nearest timer expires), if they detect multiple CAs in the same slot but on more than one subcarriers. Then, the previous users involved in the collision, after hearing that there are still active contenders, will learn that they have been involved in a collision. In consequence, they will give up the transmissions, and finally avoid the collision. Continuing on the above example, user 3 will hear two CAs on two different subcarriers, thus aware of a collision. Then, instead of quitting the contention, user 3 will still transmit a CA at its backoff timer expiration point, i.e., the second time slot. Meanwhile, user 1 and 2 upon hearing the new CA, will know that they collide and give up the transmissions. Finally, user 3 wins the contention without collision. In this way, the collision is resolved.

Note that the collision recovery mechanism may fail under two cases. The first case is that there are no later users to help collision recovery. In the previous example, if there are only 2 users, the collision cannot be recovered. The second case is that more than one users have exactly the same quantized alignment metric, and hence transmit on the same subcarrier at the same backoff time. For this case, later users cannot detect that more than one users' CAs collide on the same subcarrier, and therefore will not start collision recovery. However, these two kinds of collisions could be limited to a minimum using a reasonable contention window. In Sec. 6, we will show that in a network of 30 users with saturated traffic, the collision probability of Signpost is only about 2~3%, while that of random contention based methods is more than tenfold.

In the description above, we focus on the single collision domain where all contending users can hear each other, but Signpost can naturally handle multiple collision domains. For example, suppose three contending users A, B and C, where A and B can carrier sense each other, B and C can sense each other, but A and C cannot sense each other. Suppose A wins the contention by first sending out a CA. After hearing this CA, user B in the same domain with user A will quit the contention by not sending out any CA. In consequence, user C can still have a transmission opportunity even when it has a lower contention priority than user B. In this way, Signpost users in different collision domains can transmit in parallel and thus reuse the spatial diversity.

We have assumed that each client only has one antenna for ease of exposition. However, Signpost can be applicable to multi-antenna clients by a straightforward adaptation. The basic idea is to treat each separate antenna as a "virtual" user. All virtual users contend the transmission opportunities following the same 2-D prioritized contention mechanism. In this way, Signpost can still choose an

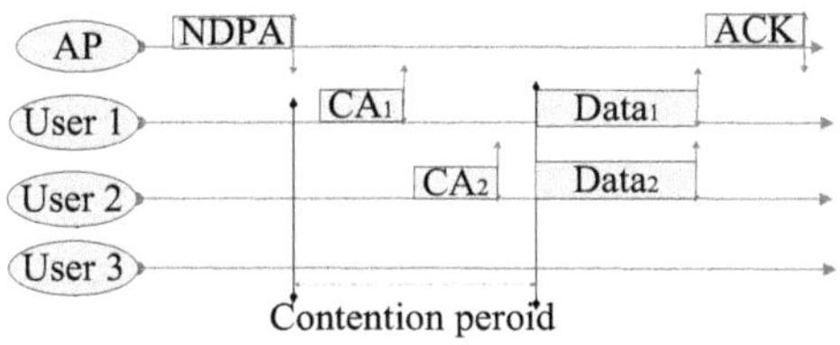

Figure 7: Signpost operations

optimal concurrent user set while simultaneously taking into account the fairness among users with different number of antennas.

5. PROTOCOL OPERATIONS

Now we put the indirect orthogonality evaluation and 2-D prioritized contention mechanisms together to design a complete Signpost uplink MU-MIMO protocol. Fig. 7 illustrates a typical flow of operations in Signpost. Signpost operates in a similar way as the basic operations in 802.11ac, but it works for uplink MU-MIMO and avoids CSI probing. We re-engineer the 802.11ac NDPA packet to indicate the Signpost directions, and add a new packet type called contention announcement (*CA*) to indicate that some users have won contention. At a high level, Signpost works as follows:

(i): First, the AP broadcasts a NDPA packet to start a new *round* of uplink transmission. The NDPA contains a training sequence that allows each user to estimate its own CSI to the AP (assuming calibrated reciprocal channel as in 802.11 beamforming [31, Ch. 20.3.12.1]). In addition, it contains a Signpost index number that indicates to users the corresponding Signpost vectors in this round.

(ii): Each user evaluates its alignment metrics. Specifically, each user i computes the alignment between its channel state vector $\boldsymbol{h_i}$ and each of the M Signpost vectors (directions). Thus, it obtains M orthogonality metrics, one for each direction (Sec. 3.2).

(iii): Then, the users contend for medium access following the proposed 2-D prioritized contention scheme. This scheme ensures that for each Signpost direction, the user that best aligns to it will win with high probability. The winner then declares itself by transmitting a *CA*. Upon hearing the *CA*, others quit contention on this direction, but can still contend on other directions (Sec. 4.3).

(iv): The contention can end up with one winner along each Signpost direction. All the M winners then start uplink transmission concurrently, and the AP acknowledges the reception through a block ACK.

Steps *(i)-(iv)* are repeated for each round of uplink transmission. Note that for a new round, a new set of Signpost vectors should be used for fairness among users. We realize this by embedding a new index number in the NDPA. Note that multiple data packets can follow one user-selection procedure, provided that they span much shorter duration than the channel coherence time.

5.1 Design of Signpost Vectors

For a M-antenna AP, the CSI of each user is a M dimension vector. Thus, there can be up to M orthogonal Signpost directions, each being a M dimension vector. These M Signpost vectors constitute a Signpost matrix Φ, which is a unit orthogonal matrix.

To generate a Signpost matrix Φ, we first generate a random unit vector $\boldsymbol{\phi_1}$, and use it as the first Signpost direction. Then we generate other $M-1$ Signpost directions (i.e, $\boldsymbol{\phi_2}, \boldsymbol{\phi_3}, \cdots, \boldsymbol{\phi_M}$) by computing the $\boldsymbol{\phi_1}$'s orthogonal basis: $null(\boldsymbol{\phi_1})$.

We repeat the above to generate P different Signpost matrices, and assign index numbers to them as Φ^1, Φ^2,..Φ^P. Since these Signpost matrices are generated randomly, they have very diverse Signpost directions. In each round of uplink transmission, we use a different Signpost matrix so that different set of users can be selected for fairness. To do so, we should have two preparations. *First*, users should have a consistent knowledge of the collection of Signpost matrices and corresponding index numbers. This is easy to achieve, since the Signpost matrices could be generated off-line and standardized among users. *Second*, we embed an index number in each NDPA, which indicates the Signpost matrix to be used. By hearing the NDPA, all users are synchronized to use the same Signpost matrix in each round.

Note that a very small storage space is required for storing these Signpost matrices in each AP or user device. We use a complex number to represent an element in a Signpost matrix, requiring 64 bit. For a 4-antenna AP and 100 Signpost matrices in total, 12.5KB of storage space suffices.

5.2 Design of Contention Announcement

The contention announcement (CA) is produced by sending a symbol on the mapped subcarrier (using similar technique as in [20]). The length of a symbol is 3.6 μs. Taking into account the propagation delay and hardware circuit delay, we set the duration of CA to be an 802.11 slot length of 9 μs.

5.3 Handling OFDM Systems

Modern wireless systems such as WiFi and LTE widely use OFDM, which decomposes a user's channel into multiple subcarriers. Due to frequency diversity, the subcarriers may have different channel gains, which makes the user selection problem more sophisticated. In particular, for each user, one subcarrier s_1 may be better aligned with a Signpost direction, whereas another subcarrier s_2 may be better aligned to a different direction. In this case, it is hard to tell which Signpost direction the whole channel is close to.

However, we find that in practical OFDM channels, different subcarriers usually have consistency of alignment with Signpost directions, despite minor fluctuation. We presents an experimental example in Fig. 6, which plots the alignment of each subcarrier of an OFDM channel with three Signpost directions $\boldsymbol{\phi_1}$, $\boldsymbol{\phi_2}$ and $\boldsymbol{\phi_3}$. The per-subcarrier CSI is collected from a WARP testbed (Sec. 6) deployed in an office environment with rich multipath reflections (and hence frequency diversity). We can see that although there exist some bumps on some subcarriers, on average the alignment of the entire OFDM channel with three Signpost directions could be clearly separated out in descending order as: $\boldsymbol{\phi_1}$, $\boldsymbol{\phi_2}$ and $\boldsymbol{\phi_3}$.

Based on the above observation, we can define the alignment metric of an OFDM channel with a Signpost direction by averaging the alignment metrics among all subcarriers. Then the user selection process remains the same as introduced before. Our actual experiments of Signpost always focus on OFDM systems. Note that instead of using the averaging approach, one may further improve Signpost performance by incorporating a more advanced multi-subcarrier alignment metric like the effective SNR metric in [27], but this is beyond the scope of our work. Also note that one could select users on a per-subcarrier basis, but this will significantly increase the overhead (e.g., by almost 48× in 802.11 which has 48 data subcarriers). Therefore, we insist on the simple averaging based metric in Signpost.

6. PERFORMANCE EVALUATION

In this section, we evaluate the performance of Signpost in comparison with existing methods. After introducing the implementation and experimental setup, we first examine the network capacity improvement from Signpost's indirect user selection approach. Then we take MAC overhead into account, and examine the MAC-layer throughput. Finally, we run a system test under various traffic patterns and node mobility.

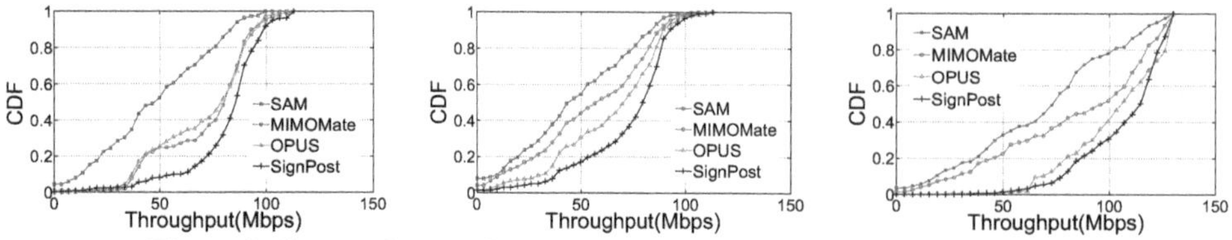

Figure 8: Comparison under (a) saturation, (b) non-saturation (c) mobile.

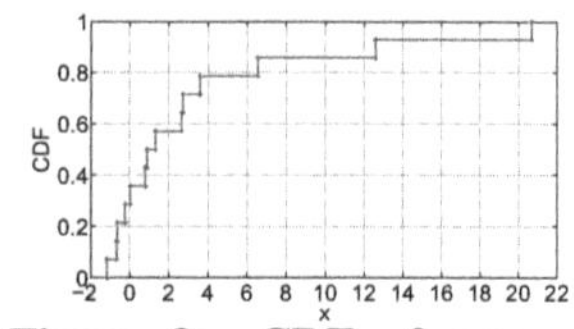

Figure 9: CDF of per-user throughput gap

6.1 Implementation and Experimental Setup

We have prototyped Signpost on top of an 802.11ac-compatible MU-MIMO OFDM library that we built on WARP [30]. The library's PHY-module implements OFDM modulation, packet detection and synchronization, channel estimation and symbol demodulation, and MMSE based MU-MIMO decoding [19]. To realize Signpost, we implement the computation and quantization of the alignment metric, and the 2-D prioritized contention mechanism in the prototype. Due to the interface latency of WARP, we cannot directly implement a real-time version of the Signpost MAC. However, since all WARP radios in our testbed are connected to a PC controller, we emulate the contention on the PC, which then commands the winning contender to start the data transmission over the air. Similarly, we also emulate an optimal bit-rate adaptation on the PC for all comparing user selection methods, so we can separately study the effect of user selection. In practice, rateless coding mechanisms [28, 29] can be used to adapt a user's bit-rate to its channel quality without any channel state feedback.

For performance comparison, we have also implemented three state-of-the-art user selection schemes:

(i): SAM [16]. SAM is the fist experimental work to validate the performance gain of uplink MU-MIMO through implementation on a software radio platform. SAM inherits the traditional 802.11 CSMA contention mechanism and uses a *random* backoff mechanism to select each concurrent user with equal probability, so it does not require CSI feedback.

(ii): MIMOMate [17]. MIMOMate optimizes SAM's user selection by introducing a leader-contention-based contention mechanism. It first matches clients into groups according to their CSI. Then for each round of uplink transmission, it elects a leader through SAM-like random contention, and then the followers matched to the leader transmit one by one without contention. For computing the optimal matching sets, CSI of all users is required, which causes substantial overhead. Therefore, MIMOMate abandons the CSI feedback, and allows the AP to learn CSI passively from normal uplink frames. One problem with the leader-based contention is that a follower may not always have traffic to transmit (i.e., bursty traffic pattern, which is often true in practice). To handle this problem, we combine MIMOMate with a random contention to let other users (i.e., users with traffic but not in the leader's matching set) fill these transmission opportunities [3].

(iii): OPUS [18]. OPUS is a scalable incremental user selection approach for downlink MU-MIMO, but can be readily applied to uplink. OPUS handles the user selection in M rounds. In each round, the AP broadcasts a probing direction. Each remaining user can evaluate its orthogonality metric against the existing selected users by comparing its CSI to the probing direction, and the one with the largest metric will be selected. Unlike Signpost, the probing direction is computed from the CSI of the existing selected user, so in each round, the selected user should feed back its CSI to the AP.

Table 1: Average PHY layer throughput (Mbps)

	SAM	MIMOMate	OPUS	Signpost
Saturated	47.7	72.2	70.3	81.2
Non-saturated	46.2	54.7	63.6	72.0
Mobile	68.4	83.51	102.5	106.5

Our experiments are conducted on a testbed located in an office environment. All MU-MIMO transmissions run on a 2.4GHz channel unused and non-overlapping with ambient wireless devices. Other PHY parameters follow the 802.11ac default (e.g., 20MHz bandwidth and 64 subcarriers). Packet size is 1.5KB unless noted otherwise. Due to limited hardware, for experiments involving more than 4 clients simultaneously, we move the testbed nodes to different locations, collect the per-subcarrier uplink channel matrices, and feed the CSI traces to our implementation in place of WARP's over-the-air channel.

6.2 PHY Layer Throughput

We first check whether Signpost can select better user sets and result in larger network capacity, so here we ignore MAC overhead and examine users' time-averaged bit-rates. We run a 2-antenna AP and 14 users, with the topology and user positions shown in Fig. 12.

6.2.1 Saturated Traffic

In this experiment, we set all 14 users static with saturated traffic, and run 400 rounds of uplink transmissions. We compute the sum bitrates of all selected users in each round, and plot the CDF of sum bitrates in Fig. 8(a), and also give the average of sum bitrates in Table I. From the results, we see that SAM has much lower throughput than the other three methods, since it selects users randomly without considering their channel characteristics. Moreover, Signpost achieves the highest throughput among all schemes. Its gain is 1.70×, 1.12×, and 1.16× compared with SAM, MIMOMate and OPUS, respectively. The gain comes from the fact that Signpost selects more orthogonal concurrent users.

The experiment results show that an indirect user selection approach can indeed have better performance than direct approaches. We analyze the reason as follows. Essentially speaking, MIMOMate, OPUS and Signpost all use greedy approximation to an exhaustive search, and there is no guarantee that they can find the optimal user set. However, the difference is that both MIMOMate and OPUS are incrementally greedy, that is, they first select a user, and then they find next user best matched to the selected user, and so on. In this case, the decision is made based on more local information. In contrast, Signpost simultaneously considers multiple orthogonal directions, and the decision is made from much more global information.

6.2.2 Non-saturated Traffic

We now evaluate Signpost when users have non-saturated traffic. To emulate bursty traffic patterns, we generate packets following a Poisson distribution with rate 0.55 packet/round. Fig. 8(b) plots

[3]Besides the random contention mechanism, one may use angle-based [17] or SINR-based [18] contention mechanisms to select users to fill the transmission opportunities. However, these mechanisms require CSI exchange among all client users [17], which incurs large overhead. Therefore, in this paper we suppose no CSI exchange between client users and use the random contention when MIMOMate is facing this situation.

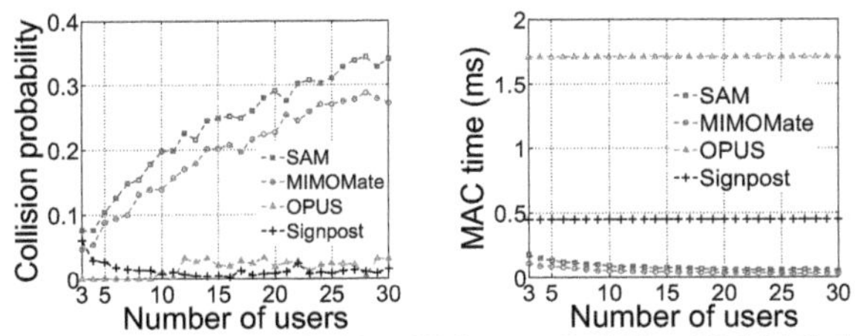

Figure 10: Overhead: (a) collision probability (b) MAC time

the CDF and Table I gives the average per-round throughput. The average gain of Signpost is 1.56×, 1.32× and 1.13× over the other three methods, respectively. The throughput of all four methods drops when compared with the saturated case because there are fewer users to select from. A closer inspection shows that non-saturated traffic affects MIMOMate the most. The throughput of MIMOMate drops by about 24% while that of OPUS and Signpost drops by about 10% and SAM barely changes. This fits our expectation because MIMOMate AP pre-defines each set of selected users. Additional users are selected randomly to fill transmission opportunities when some selected users have no packets to send. As a result, the users that finally transmit concurrently may not form an originally pre-defined set and hence the performance degrades significantly. On the other hand, OPUS and Signpost can still select better concurrent user sets from the users that have traffic.

6.2.3 Mobile Scenario

In this experiment, we set up a mobility environment by letting the client users move at a walking speed. The results (Fig. 8(c) and Table I) show that MIMOMate is affected by the mobility, with throughput about 78% of that of Signpost, in comparison with 89% in static scenario. The reason lies in MIMOMate's passive CSI learning scheme. The passively learned CSI easily becomes outdated under mobile scenarios and hence leads to suboptimal user matching. On average, the gain of Signpost is 1.56×, 1.28× and 1.04× over the other three methods, respectively.

6.2.4 Fairness

We examine Signpost's fairness issue by using SAM as a baseline, since SAM gives equal transmitting probability to all users. Here we present results under the saturated scenario, but the conclusion holds true under other scenarios. For each user, we compute the throughput gap (denoted with x) by subtracting SAM's throughput from Signpost's throughput. We plot the CDF of x in Fig.9 and make two observations *(i)*: Signpost increases throughput for more than 70% users. *(ii)* For users whose throughput drops, the decrease is less than 2Mbps. On the other hand, the increase for other users is much larger and is up to 20Mbps. Overall, we can conclude that Signpost improves throughput by selecting users with strong orthogonality, *not* by unfairly starving a fraction of the users.

6.3 MAC Overhead

In this section, we use our MAC emulator to examine Signpost's MAC overhead, including collision probability and channel time spent on contention. We still use a 2-antenna AP, and vary the number of users from 3 to 30. SAM and MIMOMate inherit the backoff mechanism of 802.11 For MAC parameters. We set the initial contention window to 32 and the contention window doubles if collision happens and up to a maximum of $32 * (2^7) = 4096$. OPUS uses a fixed contention time of 8 contention slots each lasting 27 μs [18]. Signpost use a fixed contention time of $W = 50$ 802.11 slots of 9 μs each (A smaller W leads to less contention time but a larger collision probability, and vice versa. Our experiments show that $W = 50$ achieves the best tradeoff in medium to large sized networks). We run saturated traffic as it incurs the worst-case overhead for Signpost.

6.3.1 Collision Probability

Fig. 10(a) plots the collision probability as the number of users increases. We observe that: *(i)* Random contention based methods, SAM and MIMOMate, have much larger collision probability, which is consistent with previous studies on 802.11 MAC [21–25]. Between them, MIMOMate is better because MIMOMate only needs contention to select the leading user. *(ii)* Prioritized contention methods, OPUS and Signpost, have many fewer collisions. Interestingly, Signpost's collision probability is slightly higher when the number of users N is small. The reason lies in its collision recovery mechanism: with fewer users, there rarely exist any other users for collision recovery (Sec. 4.3), which leads to higher collision probability.

6.3.2 Time Spent on MAC

Fig. 10(b) shows the mean channel time spent on MAC-level signaling before each transmission. OPUS has the largest expense, since it requires two rounds of CSI feedback. Other methods only need to waste time for contention. Also, Signpost and OPUS's MAC time is fixed regardless of the user population, since they use a fixed contention time. Whereas, the MAC time of SAM and MIMOMate decreases as the user population increases, since the contention is fiercer and hence users will be selected faster.

6.4 MAC Layer Throughput

Now we take into account the MAC overhead and check the MAC-layer throughput. The network setting is the same as in Sec. 6.2. Modern high speed wireless standards like 802.11n and 802.11ac widely adopt frame aggregation to amortize MAC protocol overhead across frames. In 802.11ac, a frame can be aggregated up to 5.5ms. In our following experiment, we aggregate 5 frame together, and the final frame duration will be about 2.3ms under an intermediate data rate of 18Mbps.

Fig. 11 presents the average throughput under 3 scenarios. Compared with the PHY throughput in Table I, the advantage of Signpost magnifies significantly under all scenarios. In particular, the throughput of Signpost is 1.93× to 2.96× over SAM, 1.44× to 1.72× over MIMOMate and 1.64× to 1.83× over OPUS. The extra gain over SAM and MIMOMate comes from Signpost's low collision probability, while the extra gain over OPUS comes from Signpost's low MAC time.

6.5 A Comprehensive Test

Finally, we examine the scalability of Signpost in a more complex mixed scenario consisting of a 3-antenna AP and users varying from 6 to 46. For each user population, we set half of the users statically located and the other half mobile. Meanwhile, we set traffic intensity for each user randomly within a range of [0, 1]. As shown in Fig.13, the experiment result has similar trend as in Fig.11: the throughput of MIMOMate and OPUS is not far from SAM, due to the impact of mobility, non-saturation and MAC overhead. Signpost significantly outperforms other schemes, especially as the user population grows. Its throughput is 1.72×, 1.56× and 1.49× compared with SAM, MIMOMate and OPUS, averaged over all network sizes.

7. CONCLUSION

In this paper, we have presented Signpost, a scalable and distributed signaling and user selection protocol for uplink MU-MIMO. Signpost enables a user to speculate its orthogonality with other users by computing the angle between its local CSI and some pre-defined orthogonal directions, without requiring other users' CSI.

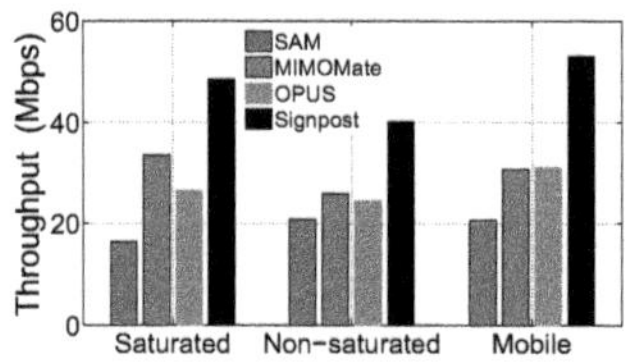

Figure 11: MAC throughput

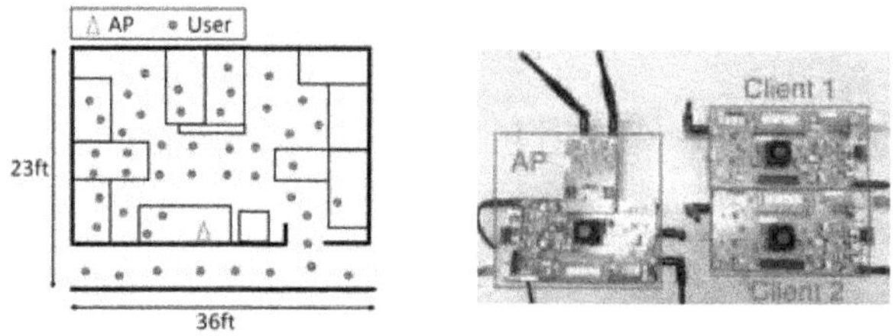

Figure 12: Testbed floor map and software-radio nodes.

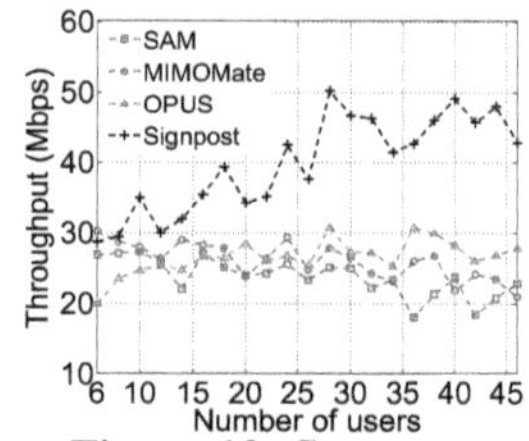

Figure 13: System test.

This lightweight orthogonality evaluation method is integrated with a 2-D prioritized contention mechanism that singles out the best M users for an M-antenna AP. The contention mechanism enables the users to detect and avoid collisions cooperatively in a distributed way so as to achieve an efficient contention with low overhead and low collision probability. Our software-radio based prototype implementation and experiments show that the gain of Signpost is usually more than 1.5× compared with three state-of-the-art MU-MIMO user selection methods, under various network scenarios with static or mobile users, saturated or non-saturated traffic.

Acknowledgements

The work reported in this paper was supported in part by the National Natural Science Foundation of China (61202410, 61132001, 61120106008, 61272475, 61272474, 61472404, 61472044 and 61472402), and the US NSF under Grant CNS-1318292, CNS-1343363, CNS-1350039 and CNS-1404613.

8. REFERENCES

[1] D. Tse and P. Vishwanath, *Fundamentals of Wireless Communications.* Cambridge University Press, 2005.

[2] Y. Zhang, C. Ji, Y. Liu, W. Malik, D. O'Brien, and D. Edwards, "A Low Complexity User Scheduling Algorithm for Uplink Multiuser MIMO Systems," *IEEE Trans. on Wireless Communications*, vol.7, no.7, 2008.

[3] X. Chen, H. Hu, H. Wang, H.-H. Chen, and M. Guizani, "Double Proportional Fair User Pairing Algorithm for Uplink Virtual MIMO Systems," *IEEE Trans. on Wireless Communications*, vol.7, no.7, 2008.

[4] Z. Shen, R. Chen, and etc., "Low Complexity User Selection Algorithms for Multiuser MIMO Systems with Block Diagonalization," *IEEE Trans. on Signal Processing*, vol.54, no.9, 2006.

[5] T. Yoo, N. Jindal, and A. Goldsmith, "Multi-Antenna Downlink Channels with Limited Feedback and User Selection," *IEEE JSAC*, vol.25, no.7, 2007.

[6] T. Ji, and etc., "Low Complex User Selection Strategies for Multi-User MIMO Downlink Scenario," in *Proc. of IEEE WCNC*, 2007.

[7] D. Gesbert, M. Kountouris, R. W. Heath, C.-B. Chae, and T. Salzer, "Shifting the MIMO Paradigm," *IEEE Signal Processing Magazine*, vol. 24, no. 5, 2007.

[8] M. Sharif and B. Hassibi, "On the Capacity of MIMO Broadcast Channels with Partial Side Information," *IEEE Trans. on Information Theory*, vol.51, no.2, 2005.

[9] E. Aryafar, N. Anand, T. Salonidis, and E. W. Knightly, "Design and Experimental Evaluation of Multi-user Beamforming in Wireless LANs," in *Proc. of ACM MobiCom*, 2010.

[10] H. Yu, L. Zhong, A. Sabharwal, and D. Kao,"Beamforming on Mobile Devices: a First Study," in *Proc. ACM MobiCom*, 2011.

[11] S. Gollakota, S. D. Perli, and D. Katabi, "Interference Alignment and Cancellation," in *Proc. ACM Sigcommm*, 2009.

[12] K. C.-J. Lin, S. Gollakota, and D. Katabi, "Random Access Heterogeneous MIMO Networks," in *ACM SIGCOMM*, 2011.

[13] W. Shen, Y. Tung, K. Lee, K. Lin, "Rate Adaptation for 802.11 Multiuser MIMO Networks," in *Proc. ACM Mobicom*, 2012.

[14] C. Shepard, H. Yu, N. Anand, L. Li, T. Marzetta, Y. Yang, and L. Zhong, "Argos: Practical Base Stations with Many Antennas," in *Proc. ACM MobiCom*, 2012.

[15] X. Zhang, K. Sundaresan, M. A. A. Khojastepour, S. Rangarajan, and K. G. Shin, "NEMOx: Scalable Network MIMO for Wireless Networks," in *Proc. ACM MobiCom*, 2013.

[16] K. Tan, H. Liu, J. Fang, W. Wang, J. Zhang, M. Chen, and G. M. Voelker, "SAM: Enabling Practical Spatial Multiple Access in Wireless LAN," in *Proc. ACM MobiCom*, 2009.

[17] T. Kuo, K. Lee, K. Lin and M. Tsai, "Leader Contention Based User Matching for 802.11 Multiuser MIMO Networks," *IEEE Trans. on Wireless Communications*, 2014

[18] X. Xie, X. Zhang, "Scalable User Selection for MU-MIMO Networks," in *Proc. IEEE INFOCOM* 2014.

[19] X. Xie, X. Zhang, K. Sundaresan, "Adaptive Feedback Compression for MIMO Networks," in *ACM Mobicom*, 2013.

[20] S. Sen, R. Choudhury and S. Nelakuditi, "No Time to Countdown: Migrating Backoff to the Frequency Domain," in *Proc. ACM Mobicom*, 2011.

[21] G. Bianchi, "Performance Analysis of the IEEE 802.11 Distributed Coordination Function," *IEEE Journal on Selected Areas in Communications*, vol.18, no.3, 2000.

[22] M. Heusse, F. Rousseau, R. Guillier, A. Duda,"Idle Sense: An Optimal Access Method for High Throughput and Fairness in Rate Diverse Wireless LANs," in *Proc. ACM Sigcomm*, 2005

[23] V. Ramaiyan, A. Kuma, E. Altman, "Fixed Point Analysis of Single Cell IEEE 802.11e WLANs: Uniqueness, Multistability and Throughput Differentiation," in *ACM Sigmetrics*, 2005

[24] H. Ma, Y. Liu,"On Coverage Problems of Directional Sensor Networks," *Mobile Ad-hoc and Sensor Networks, Lecture Notes in Computer Science*, vol. 3794, 2005

[25] J. Wu, B. Cheng, C. Yuen, Y. Shang, J. Chen, "Distortion-Aware Concurrent Multipath Transfer for Mobile Video Streaming in Heterogeneous Wireless Networks," *IEEE Transactions on Mobile Computing*, vol. 14, no. 4, 2015.

[26] K. Jagannathan, S. Borst, P. Whiting and Eytan Modiano, "Efficient Scheduling of Multi-User Multi-Antenna Systems," in *Proc. WiOpt*, 2006

[27] D. Halperin, W. Hu, A. Sheth and D. Wetherall, "Predictable 802.11 Packet Delivery from Wireless Channel Measurements," in *Proc. ACM Sigcommm*, 2010

[28] J. Perry, P. Iannucci, K. Fleming, H. Balakrishnan, and D. Shah, "Spinal Codes," in *Proc. ACM Sigcomm*,2012

[29] A. Gudipati and S. Katti, "Strider: Automatic Rate Adaptation and Collision Handling," in *Proc. ACM Sigcomm*,2011

[30] Rice University, "Wireless Open-Access Research Platform," http://warp.rice.edu/trac/wiki, Jul. 2014.

[31] "Wireless LAN Medium Access Control (MAC) and Physical Layer (PHY) Specifications", in *IEEE Std. 802.11n*, 2009.

Cross-Cell DoF Distribution: Combating Channel Hardening Effect in Multi-Cell MU-MIMO Networks

Xiufeng Xie and Xinyu Zhang
University of Wisconsin-Madison
{xiufeng, xyzhang} @ece.wisc.edu

Eugene Chai
NEC Labs America
eugene@nec-labs.com

ABSTRACT

Equipped with the multi-user MIMO (MU-MIMO) technology, a WiFi access point (AP) with M antennas can achieve M degrees-of-freedom (DoF) in theory. Existing MU-MIMO protocols strive to maximize DoF usage by serving M users simultaneously. In this paper, through a MU-MIMO testbed measurement, we found that the correlation between users' channels can severely compromise network throughput under a DoF-maximizing strategy. To combat this problem, we propose Kardia that judiciously distributes the DoF to least-correlated users within an AP's cell, and coordinates neighboring APs such that each can serve the best set of users while nulling mutual interference. The key challenge in Kardia lies in efficiently determining which set of users to serve without knowing the channel state from all of them. We propose a lightweight mechanism that enables APs to collaboratively infer the correlation between users through precoded probing packets. Our analysis shows that Kardia's DoF distribution framework has a provable performance guarantee. Our testbed implementation further reveals that Kardia can significantly boost the performance of multi-cell MU-MIMO networks, in contrast to legacy protocols like 802.11ac.

Categories and Subject Descriptors

C.2.1 [**Computer-Communication Networks**]: Network Architecture and Design—*Wireless Communications*

General Terms

Algorithms, Design, Theory, Performance

Keywords

Multi-user MIMO; MU-MIMO; 802.11ac; Channel Hardening

1. INTRODUCTION

Multi-user MIMO (MU-MIMO) is a hallmark of the recent WLAN standard 802.11ac, with which an M_{tx}-antenna AP can simultaneously transmit up to M_{tx} data streams to different users, thus achieving a maximum *degree-of-freedom* (DoF) of M_{tx}. However, exploiting MU-MIMO's full potential is a non-trivial issue in practice. The M_{tx}-fold capacity gain is attainable only if channels of all M_{tx} users are *orthogonal* [1] to each other, *i.e.*, the pairwise angles between their *channel vectors*[1] all equal 90°. Consider the example in Figure 1(a), to suppress the mutual interference, the AP precodes U1's data along a direction $\boldsymbol{w}_1$ orthogonal to U2's channel $\boldsymbol{h}_2$. Consequently, U1 receives the signal $\boldsymbol{h}_1\boldsymbol{w}_1$, *i.e.*, a projection of $\boldsymbol{w}_1$ along $\boldsymbol{h}_1$ as shown in Figure 1(b), and thus the received signal strength is $|\boldsymbol{h}_1||\boldsymbol{w}_1|\sin\theta$. Ideally, when U1 and U2 are fully orthogonal, U1's received signal strength is $|\boldsymbol{h}_1||\boldsymbol{w}_1|$. However, the actual signal strength can be much lower — measurement of real MIMO networks revealed that users' channels are often *correlated*, with pairwise angle θ concentrated between 20° and 70° [2].

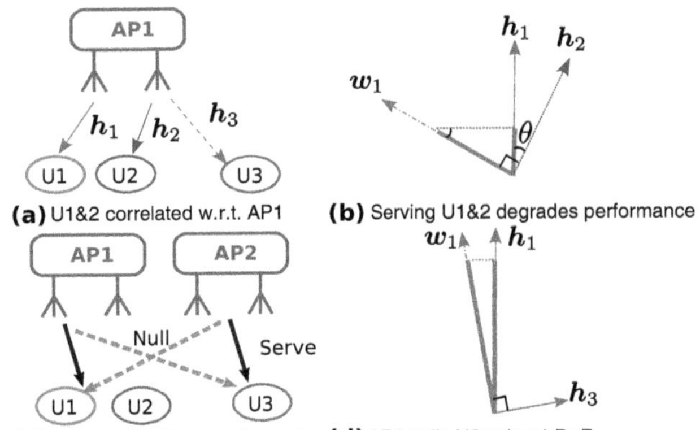

(**a**) U1&2 correlated w.r.t. AP1 (**b**) Serving U1&2 degrades performance (**c**) Migrate 1 DoF to another cell (**d**) AP1 nulls U3 using 1 DoF

Figure 1: Impact of user orthogonality in MU-MIMO (a)(b), and how Kardia addresses this problem (c)(d).

Channel hardening bounds throughput. For a given AP, as we add more concurrent downlink users, we increase the probability of serving a pair of users with a small channel angle θ. Thus, MU-MIMO throughput does not scale linearly as more users are added. This so-called *channel hardening* effect has been predicted in theoretical models [3] and also observed in our measurement of indoor MU-MIMO networks (§2). If an AP simply leverages all its spatial DoFs, then the network capacity may be compromised by those strongly correlated users. Hence, the optimal number of DoF used for transmission (*i.e.*, the *usable* DoF) is not always equal to the maximum DoF number supported by the AP. To maximize network throughput, an AP must select a subset of users with optimal mutual channel orthogonality. However, finding such an optimal user set in a large network is an intractable combinatorial problem even for an oracle that knows all users' channels [4].

Kardia. We propose a MAC/PHY cross-layer framework, called Kardia[2] to combat the aforementioned channel hardening effect in MU-MIMO networks. The basic principle of Kardia is *cross-cell DoF distribution*. Specifically, we allow an AP to only serve $S \leq M_{tx}$ users that are "most orthogonal" to each other. Its remaining $(M_{tx} - S)$ DoFs are exploited to enable neighboring cells to transmit in parallel. While serving its own users, each AP nullifies its interference to users in other cells (Figure 1(c)(d)). Such a DoF distribution mechanism begs two new questions: *(i) how do we determine the number of usable DoFs, and (ii) how do we distribute these usable DoFs within and across WLAN cells?*

[1]The channel of a single-antenna user can be described as an M_{tx}-element *channel vector*, comprised of its channel gain *w.r.t.* each of the AP's transmit antennas.

[2]"Kardia" is a Greek word meaning "Heart", the core organ that distributes blood flows.

MobiHoc'15, June 22–25, 2015, Hangzhou, China.

http://dx.doi.org/10.1145/2746285.2746290.

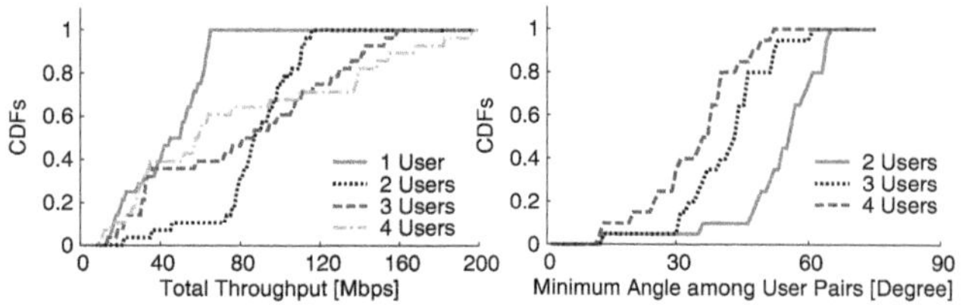

(a)Distribution of total throughput (b)Distribution of minimum channel angles

Figure 2: Network throughput and channel angle when a 4-antenna AP serving from 1 to 4 single-antenna users.

Ideally, given the channel vectors or channel state information (CSI) of *all users*, an AP can search for the user combination with maximum downlink capacity [4–6]. However, in practice, CSI needs to be obtained from users' feedback. Even if the feedback overhead can be reduced based on channel reciprocity [7] or CSI compression [8], the overhead to obtain global CSI still grows linearly with the total number of users, which can easily overwhelm the actual data transmission time [8]. In addition, selecting the APs that yield the highest cooperation gain is equally challenging. The APs' downlink capacity becomes correlated, and searching through all AP combinations in a large multi-cell network is computationally intractable, even for an oracle that knows global CSI. To meet the above challenges, Kardia employs cross-cell DoF distribution, with three key features:

(a) Iterative DoF distribution. Kardia employs a lightweight and scalable MAC protocol, which iteratively groups users and APs before each downlink transmission. The protocol ensures that, within each cell, selected users are most orthogonal to each other, and between cells, every selected AP can effectively nullify its own interference to other cells. This protocol proved to achieve at least 50% of the network capacity of an oracle scheduler.

(b) Multi-cell orthogonality probing (MOP). Kardia employs a lightweight MOP mechanism to provide channel orthogonality information and facilitate user/AP selection. It is accomplished without extensive user feedback or global CSI. The AP *learns users' orthogonality with partial CSI knowledge no more than that required for MU-MIMO precoding*, thus bounding feedback overhead.

(c) Orthogonality-aware subcarrier selection (OAS) allows an AP to turn frequency selectivity into an advantage. It concentrates transmit power on subcarriers that tend to have strong CSI orthogonality when used by selected users.

We prototype Kardia based on the WARP platform. Our testbed first realizes a MU-MIMO OFDM physical layer following the 802.11ac specification. Then, we build the Kardia components on top of the PHY module. Our testbed experiments demonstrate that:

(i) Kardia's DoF distribution mechanism effectively picks capacity maximizing users/APs combinations, and can achieve near-optimal performance in practical network topologies.

(ii) Kardia has a low overhead. It only collects CSI from selected users rather than all users in the network. As a result, Kardia bears comparable signaling overhead as vanilla 802.11ac, and its overhead is bounded even for a large network with up to 100 users.

(iii) In large-scale testbed experiments, Kardia achieves around 2.07× and 1.56× throughput gain over vanilla 802.11ac and state-of-the-art MU-MIMO user selection scheme [9], respectively.

2. MOTIVATION

In this section, we motivate Kardia's design components through micro-benchmark measurements on a MU-MIMO testbed.

Using All DoFs is Ineffective. Real-world MU-MIMO transmissions are subject to the aforementioned *channel hardening* effect. As a result, the sum-rate of a transmitter does not increase linearly with the number of downstream users. We study the prevalence of this channel hardening effect through a MU-MIMO testbed with a 4-antenna AP and single-antenna users (§6 details our testbed). We conduct the experiments over 20 different topologies. In each topology, we record the total throughput when the AP serves from 1 to 4 users, respectively. Figure 2(a) shows the resulting throughput distribution for different user numbers. We observe that the median throughput doubles from 40 to 80Mbps when we increase the user number from 1 to 2. However, it *decreases* as we further increase the user number to 4 — *For almost half of the cases, serving 2 users renders a higher sum-rate than serving 4 users.*

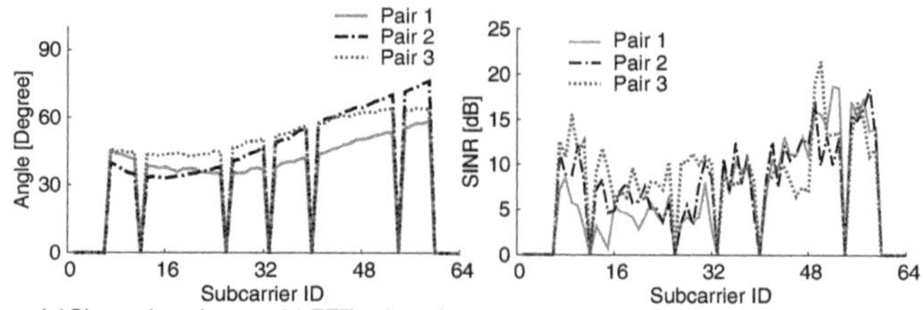

(a)Channel angle over 64 FFT subcarriers (b)SINR over 64 FFT subcarriers

Figure 3: SINR and channel angle over 64 subcarriers. 0-notches correspond to omitted pilot subcarriers.

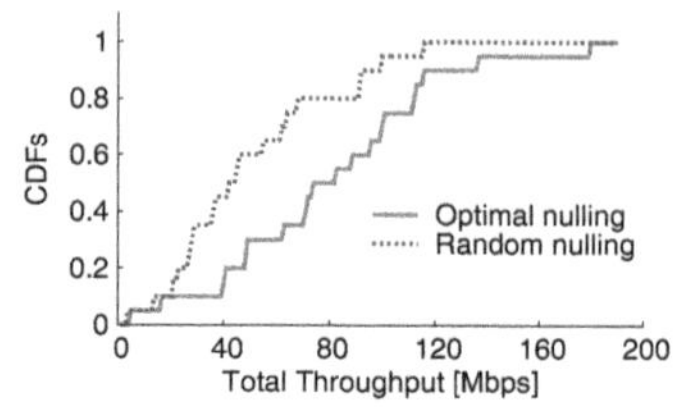

Figure 4: Randomly choosing users for concurrent transmission does not lead to optimal throughput.

Such channel hardening effect roots in the spatial correlation between user's channels, which bottlenecks MU-MIMO capacity [3]. Under the above setting, Figure 2(b) shows the distribution of minimum pairwise angles between users (*i.e.*, the indicator for spatial channel correlation, as discussed in §1). Note that if we blindly select 4 users for a MU-MIMO transmission, the minimum pairwise angle is below 35° for 50% of the cases, thus crippling the achievable throughput and explaining the results in Figure 2(a).

Using All Subcarriers is Ineffective. In a frequency-selective channel, the CSI varies across subcarriers. Hence, the degree of channel orthogonality between a pair of users will also vary across subcarriers. Figure 3(a) shows the angle between three distinct user pairs over 64 subcarriers in a 20MHz band. Observe that for a given pair of users, the channel angle between them can vary significantly across subcarriers. Consequently, the SINR and associated throughput over the subcarriers can vary substantially, as seen in Figure 3(b). Since the sum power of subcarriers is always bounded by the transmitter's total power budget, it will be beneficial to transmit only over subcarriers with high user orthogonality.

Blind Interference Nulling is Ineffective. When an AP serves its own users while nulling its interference to other-cells' active users, interestingly, the AP's choice of other-cell-users to be nulled also affects the throughput of its own users. Figure 4 compares the total throughput achieved with optimal and random nulling. In each scenario, a 4-antenna AP selects either 2 or 3 MU-MIMO users and uses the remaining DoF for nulling additional users. For optimal nulling, we select the additional users that are most orthogonal to the users to be served, while for random nulling, nulled user(s) are selected at random. We observe that optimal nulling almost doubles the median throughput among the MU-MIMO users. Hence, we must carefully choose the optimal nulling candidates when performing DoF distribution in Kardia.

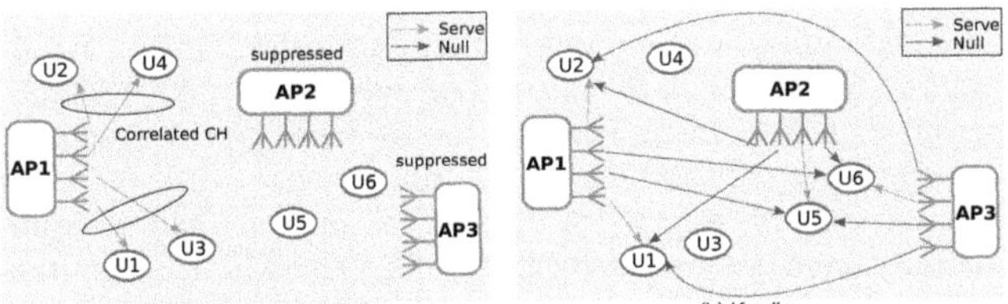

(a) Conventional MU-MIMO (b) Kardia

Figure 5: Final schedule in an example topology.

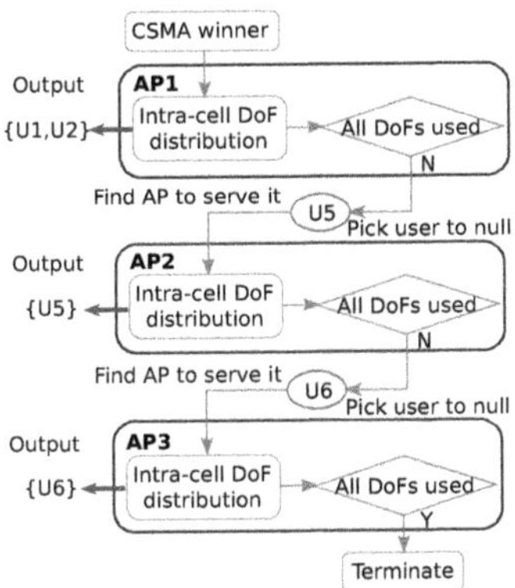

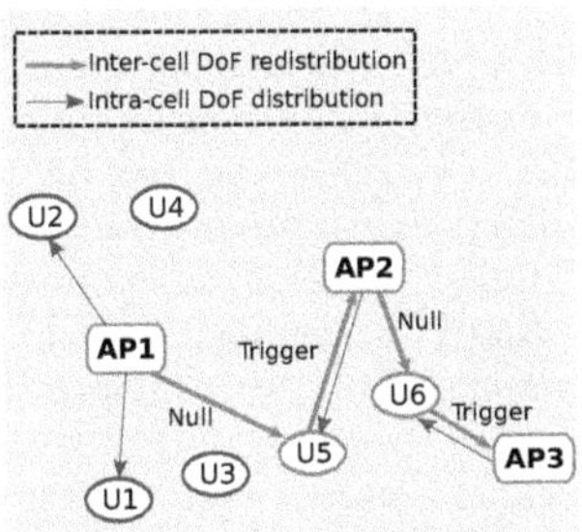

Figure 6: Kardia operation flow for the example in Fig. 5. **Figure 7: Iterative search path in user/AP selection.**

3. Kardia: A CASE STUDY

To understand how Kardia works, let us first focus on an example network shown in Figure 5, where each AP has $M_{tx} = 4$ antennas and serves *single-antenna* users. We assume a single contention domain, *i.e.*, all users can be reached by all APs in this network. We further assume that the channels of U1 and U3 *w.r.t.* AP1 are correlated (*i.e.*, the channel angle between AP1→U1 and AP1→U3 is close to 0°). Similarly, U2 and U4 are correlated as well. U5 is uncorrelated with all other users, but has the lowest channel gain since it is furthest away from AP1.

Suppose AP1 wins channel contention, vanilla 802.11ac will allow AP1 to exhaust the DoFs and serve *all* 4 downlink users, causing low performance. In contrast, Kardia allows AP1 to identify the usable DoFs and serve the best un-correlated *subset* of users (say {U1,U2} in this example). AP1 then uses its remaining 2 DoFs to nullify its interference to users that may be served by other APs, thus enabling concurrent transmissions of multiple APs (Fig. 5(b)).

To maximize the capacity of concurrent downlink transmission, Kardia optimizes the AP/user selection as follows (Fig. 6 and 7).

Intra-cell DoF distribution. Kardia is initiated by AP1 immediately after it gains channel access. AP1 first instantiates *intra-cell DoF distribution* (§4.1.2) to *iteratively* add users into its MU-MIMO transmission group to maximize intra-cell downlink capacity. The first user (U1 in this example) to add is randomly picked with a probability ensuring proportional fairness (§4.5). Then U2 is added since its channel is the most orthogonal to U1's.

At this stage, combining any more user along with U1 and U2 will result in an increased channel condition number [1] and thus degrades downlink capacity. AP1 thus stops adding downlink users with 2 unallocated DoFs "blocked" by the channel hardening effect.

Inter-cell DoF distribution. To leverage the unallocated DoFs, after AP1 terminates its intra-cell DoF distribution, Kardia selects a *bridge client* for AP1 to nullify. It employs multi-cell orthogonality probing (MOP, §4.2) to ensure that the bridge client can be simultaneously served by a neighboring AP, and that the resulting inter-cell interference can be nulled by AP1.

In this example, AP1 selects U5 as the *bridge client*. Although U5 is uncorrelated to U1 and U2, AP1 does not directly serve them together as this will degrade downlink capacity[3], however, steering the downlink beams away from U5 will only cause trivial signal power loss on U1 and U2 since they are uncorrelated, hence AP1 can nullify its interference to U5 without affecting the performance of U1 and U2. U5 then triggers a new AP (AP2 in this case) to serve it as shown in Figure 7.

The newly activated AP2 then continues to run its own intra-cell DoF distribution. Note that each AP needs to nullify its interference to other APs' selected users. Since U3 and U4 are correlated to AP1's selected users (U1 and U2), they may reduce total network capacity when selected by AP2. Therefore, AP2 excludes U3 and U4, and instead selects a bridge client (U6) uncorrelated to all currently selected users *w.r.t.* all current APs. The bridge client U6 then triggers a new AP (AP3) to serve it.

Termination of Kardia. Such iterative user-AP selection process continues until one of the APs has no DoF left. In the final schedule shown in Figure 5(b), this happens after U6 is paired with AP3 and consequently each AP has 4 users to serve/null in total. Thereafter, each AP activates its MU-MIMO PHY-layer transmission module to serve its own users while nulling other APs' users.

It is worth noting that although we introduce Kardia's work flow here based on single-antenna users, our design can be easily extended to multi-antenna users. In effect, we can treat each antenna on a multi-antenna user as a separated "single-antenna user".

Algorithm 1 Kardia's outline.

1. The *lead AP* wins CSMA channel contention
2. Add the *lead AP* in the set of selected APs $\mathcal{A}$
3. The *lead AP* picks its first user and gets CSI feedback
4. **While** the minimum Tx DoF among all APs > 0
5. /*Set current scheduling AP j to be the newly added AP*/
6. AP j performs *intra-cell DoF distribution* (Algorithm 2)
7. AP j determines its set of users $\mathcal{U}_j$ to serve
8. Any other selected AP k updates its set of users to null $\mathcal{N}_k$
9. **If** remaining DoF $D_j > 0$
10. AP j performs *inter-cell DoF distribution* (Algorithm 3)
11. Add the newly selected AP j' to the set $\mathcal{A}$
12. **Output**: the set of all selected APs $\mathcal{A}$
    the users to be served by each AP $\{\mathcal{U}_1, \mathcal{U}_2, ..., \mathcal{U}_{|\mathcal{A}|}\}$
    the users to be nulled by each AP $\{\mathcal{N}_1, \mathcal{N}_2, ..., \mathcal{N}_{|\mathcal{A}|}\}$

4. Kardia DESIGN

4.1 Iterative DoF Distribution

4.1.1 An outline of operations

We now generalize the above example and detail Kardia's iterative DoF distribution protocol. The protocol outputs a near-optimal set of APs/users that maximizes the sum capacity of concurrent downlink transmissions, while minimizing costly CSI feedback. Algorithm 1 summarizes the major steps. Here we assume homogeneous APs, each with M_{tx} transmit antennas[4].

The DoF distribution protocol is activated whenever an AP gains channel access following CSMA. This AP is referred to as the *lead AP*. The lead AP then announces its intention for MU-MIMO trans-

[3]In MU-MIMO, the user with a much worse channel gain than others will take most of the transmit power after precoding, nulling this user avoids the problem since no power is allocated to that user.

[4]It is straightforward to extend our algorithm to heterogeneous AP cases, where the total number of DoFs is bounded by the antenna number on the AP that wins the CSMA contention first. This is because Kardia basically transfers the DoFs of this first AP to other cells when the DoFs are "blocked" by the channel hardening effect.

Algorithm 2 Intra-cell DoF distribution.

Input: current AP j, CSI of its first user $\boldsymbol{H}_0 = \boldsymbol{h}_{1j}$, its remaining DoF $D_j = M_{tx} - 1$
While $D_j > 0$
  AP j precodes and sends the probing frame
  If Any unselected user has orthogonality metric $> \tau_o$
    Unselected users perform distributed ranking (§4.2).
    The winner user k feeds back CSI to AP j
    AP j adds user k to the selected group $\mathcal{U}_j$
    AP j reduces the remaining DoF $D_j = D_j - 1$
Else AP j times out if no reply. Break.
Output: selected user group $\mathcal{U}_j$, remaining DoF D_j

mission through an 802.11ac signaling packet called *NDP*. The first user to be served is picked based on proportional fairness (§4.5) and also announced in NDP. The first user U_i then feeds back its CSI, *i.e.*, its channel vector $\boldsymbol{h}_{ij}$ *w.r.t.* the *lead AP j*. Thereafter, AP j instantiates *intra-cell DoF distribution* (§4.1.2) to iteratively add users to serve, which ensures that each newly selected user has the highest potential to boost capacity. If an AP terminates its *intra-cell DoF distribution* early and leaves surplus DoFs, Kardia proceeds with *inter-cell DoF distribution* (§4.1.3), allowing the AP to use its surplus DoFs to null additional users so that they can be served by other APs. The intra- and inter-cell DoF distribution iterates until all available APs terminate or all M_{tx} DoFs are distributed.

4.1.2 Intra-cell DoF distribution

Algorithm 2 summarizes the *intra-cell DoF distribution* in Kardia, which is designed to achieve the following property:

Property 1. *Whenever a new user is added, among all unselected users, it has maximum orthogonality to any existing selected users w.r.t. any existing selected APs.*

Below we introduce the intra-cell DoF distribution design.

Multi-cell Orthogonality Probing (MOP). At the start of *intra-cell DoF distribution*, AP j already has its first user to serve. It instantiates Kardia's core component, *i.e.*, multi-cell orthogonality probing, to iteratively add more users. To single out the user mostly orthogonal to currently selected ones, a naive approach is to collect CSI feedback from all unselected users. Yet this causes formidable overhead. Instead, the Kardia AP beamforms a customized *probing frame* toward directions orthogonal to the CSI of any currently selected user. The probing frame enables unselected users to estimate their channel quality and orthogonality to currently selected ones *w.r.t.* AP j based on the received SNR. After hearing the *probing frame*, the unselected users initiate a *distributed ranking*, where the one with the highest orthogonality metric wins and feeds back its CSI to AP j. The AP keeps adding users successively by repeating the above steps. We defer the detailed design of probing frame, orthogonality estimation, and distributed ranking to Section 4.2.

Termination when adding more users is harmful. To guarantee the channel orthogonality within the selected user set $\mathcal{U}_j$, only users with orthogonality metric higher than a threshold τ_o are allowed to participate in the distributed ranking after AP j's probing frame. If in a certain iteration, the AP hears no CSI feedback, then all unselected users must have orthogonality metric $< \tau_o$. In this case, AP will time out and terminate intra-cell DoF distribution early, even if it has unallocated DoFs. Otherwise the algorithm iterates until the AP's DoF is exhausted.

Algorithm 3 Inter-cell DoF distribution.

Input: current AP j, set of its downlink users to serve $\mathcal{U}_j$
AP j broadcasts a notification to pick nulling target
Unselected users perform distributed ranking
If Any unselected user has orthogonality metric $> \tau_n$
  User l most orthogonal to $\mathcal{U}_j$ wins and feeds back its CSI
  Every selected AP $\in \mathcal{A}$ adds user l in its nulling set N
  CSI feedback from user l triggers additional AP selection
  Unselected AP evaluates orthogonality if it joins $\mathcal{A}$
AP j' who ensures the best user orthogonality joins $\mathcal{A}$
Output: U_l to be nulled by AP j, the new AP j' to serve U_l

4.1.3 Inter-cell DoF distribution

Algorithm 3 summarizes the *inter-cell DoF distribution* in Kardia, which is geared toward the following goal:

Property 2. *Whenever a new AP is added, among all unselected APs, it maximizes the channel orthogonality of all existing selected users (which it needs to null).*

Below we detail the inter-cell DoF distribution design.

Step1: Selecting a user to null. Suppose an AP j terminates intra-cell DoF distribution early and leaves surplus DoFs due to channel hardening, it then starts the *inter-cell DoF distribution* by picking a user to null, *i.e.*, the *bridge user*. The choice here is as important as selecting a user to serve, since nulling an improper user may ruin the performance of existing selected users (§2).

To pick the optimal user to null, AP j broadcasts a short frame to notify other users/APs that it has already terminated intra-cell DoF distribution with DoFs left. All unselected users overhearing this notification then conduct a special distributed ranking based on an orthogonality metric estimated from AP j's last probe (detailed in §4.2). Specifically, to ensure nulling the bridge user will not significantly affect the downlink capacity of AP j, among the unselected users, only those with orthogonality metric greater than a threshold τ_n can join this distributed ranking. The user U_l most orthogonal to AP j's existing users wins and feeds back its CSI.

Step2: Selecting new AP. The bridge user U_l then elects a new AP j' to serve it. This AP should have the highest potential capacity when serving the users nulled by previous AP(s) and nulling users served by previous AP(s). To gauge its potential, each AP who overheard the CSI feedback from U_l evaluates the *condition number* of the channel matrix containing all CSI feedbacks it has overheard up to now. A smaller condition number implies a smaller correlation between channels and thus higher potential capacity [1]. These candidate APs report their evaluated condition number to a central coordinator via a wireline control channel as in [10]. The AP with the smallest condition number is then selected.

Step3: User selection for the new AP. The newly added AP then continues to run its own intra-cell DoF distribution procedure. Note that all previous AP(s) need to nullify interference to the new AP's selected users. Essentially, each AP schedules a set of users to serve/null, and each user can join multiple AP's scheduled sets (served in one set, nulled in all other sets). The challenge here is to let each user ensure the channel orthogonality in every scheduled set it takes part in. Kardia adopts a simple but effective solution: if a user has found itself correlated to any selected user in an AP's intra-cell DoF distribution iteration, it will simply ignore future probes from new APs and hence will not be selected by any of them for this downlink MU-MIMO transmission.

Step4: Termination of DoF distribution. Such joint user-AP selection iterates until the network's DoF is exhausted, *i.e.*, the total number of users to serve reaches M_{tx}. The final output is a downlink transmission schedule including a set of APs, each to serve its own set of users and null those belonging to other APs. Afterwards, each AP further examines the user coupling across its bandwidth via an *orthogonality-aware subcarrier selection* (OAS) scheme (§4.3). Finally, each AP runs Zero-Forcing Beamforming (ZFBF), a standard MU-MIMO precoding algorithm [1], to serve

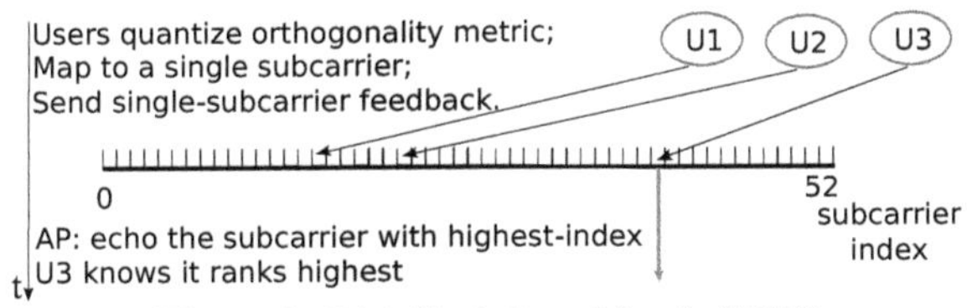

Figure 8: Distributed ranking in MOP.

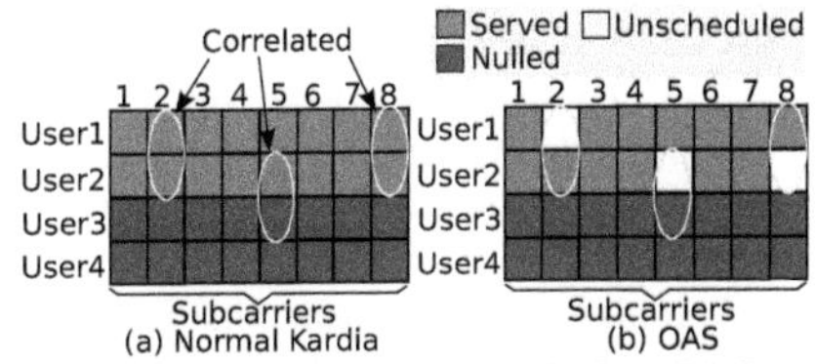

Figure 9: Simple example for OAS.

its users while nulling other APs' users. Note that the CSI used in ZFBF is exactly that collected during Kardia's AP/user selection. No extra CSI feedback is required. Therefore, we have:

Property 3. *Kardia does not require global CSI knowledge. The number of users who feed back their CSI equals the number of users served in the subsequent MU-MIMO transmission, which is typically much smaller than the total user population in the network.*

4.2 Multi-cell Orthogonality Probing (MOP)

We now detail the basic primitives in multi-cell orthogonality probing (MOP), the key PHY-layer operation to enable the DoF distribution protocol discussed above.

Probing frame. Before adding a user to serve/null, the AP sends a probing frame to help unselected users assess their orthogonality with already selected ones. The basic idea is to probe channel directions that are orthogonal (in the channel vector space) to channels of already selected users. Each channel direction carries a training sequence embedded inside the frame's preamble. The probing frame design follows existing single-cell MU-MIMO signaling schemes [9]. We thus omit more details here.

Orthogonality metric. A user's orthogonality metric in MOP reflects its potential contribution to downlink capacity when grouped with selected users, and served/nulled by existing APs. More specifically, it should reflect the user's: *(i)* channel quality *w.r.t.* the probing AP, and *(ii)* channel orthogonality to already selected users *w.r.t.* the probing AP. Since the probing directions are orthogonal to channels of selected users, the *maximum SNR among all probing directions* exactly meets the two requirements above. A user can evaluate its SNR values along each probing direction by decoding the corresponding known training sequence. The training sequence with highest SNR corresponds to the most orthogonal direction. We screen users with orthogonality metric lower than τ_o (§4.1.2), a threshold set to 6 dB (SNR threshold for the lowest modulation level). We validate this orthogonality metric design in §7.1.

Note that for the *bridge client,* MOP should only gauge its channel *orthogonality* to already selected users, and isolate the effect of channel quality (reflected by link SNR). We thus subtract the bridge client's link SNR from the orthogonality metric (only when selecting the bridge client). The link SNR is estimated directly from the probing AP's preamble following [8]. Correspondingly, the threshold τ_n (§4.1.3) equals τ_o subtracting the link SNR.

Distributed Ranking. MOP's distributed ranking mechanism is inspired by recent work in frequency-domain contention in CSMA [11, 12]. Instead of random access, however, it is used to single out the user with highest orthogonality metric. Specifically, after receiving a probing frame, each unselected user k computes and quantizes its orthogonality metric g_k into integers within $[0, G_m]$. The quantized value $\hat{g}_k$ is then mapped to index of OFDM subcarriers ranging from 0 to G_m. Then, the user sends an OFDM symbol with only the $\hat{g}_k$-th subcarrier carrying a non-zero data symbol $(1+j)$, as illustrated in Figure. 8. After receiving the feedback, the AP employs energy detection over frequency domain to identify the active subcarrier with highest index. It considers a subcarrier to be active if the energy level is τ dB above the noise floor (estimated by the average energy of unpopulated guardband subcarriers). An empirical value of $\tau = 3$ dB is found to achieve high detection accuracy in practice. Afterwards, the AP echoes back an OFDM symbol by activating the highest-index subcarrier, so that the corresponding user knows it is selected.

A notable feature of our distributed ranking design is its constant overhead irrespective of the user population. But when the users have similar quantized orthogonality metric, a collision may occur. MOP employs several counter-measures: *(i)* Only users with orthogonality metric above a lower limit τ_o can participate in the distributed ranking, hence the spectrum becomes less congested. *(ii)* Kardia also employs an upper limit corresponding to the maximum SINR that AP observes among all users it can serve. These two limits bound the range of orthogonality metric to quantize, resulting in a high resolution after quantization. We choose [7, 30] dB as the default range. With 52 subcarriers (excluding guardband) in 802.11, the resolution becomes 23/52 = 0.44dB. In practice, this resolution ensures that users in a medium sized network can seldom share the same highest quantized orthogonality metric (§7.1). A larger number of subcarriers can lead to even higher resolution. *(iii)* In the rare event when collision occurs, the AP may receive CSI feedbacks from multiple users and cannot resolve them. It will terminate the probing and instruct all already selected users/APs to start MU-MIMO transmission, so as not to waste the channel time.

4.3 Orthogonality-Aware Subcarrier Selection

To bound the signaling overhead, Kardia selects users based on an orthogonality metric that averages the heterogeneous channels of different subcarriers and thus may not properly capture the frequency diversity. We resolve this issue through Orthogonality-Aware Subcarrier Selection (OAS), a post-schedule refinement to Kardia's output. As illustrated in Figure 9, OAS excludes a user on a certain subcarrier if it bears weak orthogonality to other users there. This brings two benefits: *(i)* It focus more signal power on subcarriers with good channel orthogonality, thus improving SNR. *(ii)* Even if such additional power boost is small, eliminating some selected users on the "bad orthogonality" subcarriers is still critical since they will otherwise induce high bit error rates to other users who could have much better performance without them.

To execute OAS, for each subcarrier, an AP computes the Hermitian angle between each pair of users that it needs to serve/null. Since the users already fed back their CSI, the AP has enough CSI knowledge to perform this operation. If the angle of a pair is less than a threshold θ_a, one of the users will be excluded on this subcarrier. The user with bad channel orthogonality to more users will be excluded with higher priority. We empirically set $\theta_a = \pi/6$, a relative angle where two users only achieve half of the effective transmit power compared with the fully orthogonal case (§1).

4.4 SINR estimation for MU-MIMO downlink

Finally, before MU-MIMO transmission, each AP needs to determine the modulation level for each user. The key challenge here lies in the link quality estimation. Each MU-MIMO transmission may involve a different set of user combinations, whose SINR depend their orthogonality, and therefore, history based adaptation no longer works. Ideally, the AP can model the SINR following the well-known MU-MIMO capacity equation [1]. However, it is non-trivial to obtain the noise level in practice. Simply measuring the "idle" energy level fails to take into account the channel noise (*e.g.*, caused by imperfect channel estimation) which may vary among different APs. It is possible to directly measure and feedback SINR by individual test transmission, but this incurs enormous overhead.

Kardia employs a lightweight method to obtain SINR. In a user U_i's CSI feedback, it piggybacks its orthogonality metric, expressed as a 16-bit float point number in dB scale. The orthogonality metric can be modeled as: $SINR_i^p = S_i^p/(I_i^p + N_i)$, where $S_i^p = \boldsymbol{h}_i\boldsymbol{p}$ is the received power of U_i along probing direction $\boldsymbol{p}$ (the direction where it experiences the highest SINR) and N_i is the noise level. I_i^p is the leakage interference from other directions to direction p. Note that leakage interference exists because the probing packet is not directly beamformed to U_i. Meanwhile, the AP computes the signal to leakage-interference ratio: $SLR_i^p = S_i^p/I_i^p$, based on the fact that $I_i^p = \sum_{q \neq p} \boldsymbol{h}_i\boldsymbol{q}$.

Since both $SINR_i^p$ and SLR_i^p are ratio between power levels, we can circumvent the unknown scalars introduced by the transceivers' power amplifiers and other analog components. After receiving the feedback, the AP can obtain the noise level: $N_i = (SINR_i^p)^{-1} - (SLR_i^p)^{-1}$. Then, the expected SINR of U_i if served by AP j can be modeled as $SINR_i = \gamma_j \boldsymbol{h}_i\boldsymbol{w}_i/N_i$. Note that ZFBF dictates that $I_i = 0$. γ_j is the power scalar that respects the AP's power budget. When OAS is enforced, γ_j is scaled by the ratio between total number of subcarriers and actual number that carriers data.

4.5 Other Practical Issues

Fairness control. Kardia employs a randomized algorithm to arbitrate proportional throughput fairness among users. Specifically, in the beginning of MOP, the lead AP selects the first user with a probability weighted by users' historical throughput record, which the AP learns from ACKs. The probability that user k is selected as the first user is $p_k = (1/\overline{\phi_k})/\sum_{j\in\mathcal{K}}(1/\overline{\phi_j})$, where $\overline{\phi_k}$ is its average throughput and $\mathcal{K}$ is the set of all users. Such a scheduling mechanism has proven to achieve proportional fairness [1].

Overhead of Kardia. Owing to its light-weight MOP, Kardia only adds marginal overhead over vanilla 802.11ac. In particular, *its number of probing/feedback rounds is bounded by M_{tx}, irrespective of the network size.* In each round, *(i)* The probing frame contains the 802.11ac STF, LTF and VHT-LTF preambles, $20\mu s$ in total. *(ii)* The implicit CSI feedback contains STF and LTF, $16\mu s$ in total). *(iii)* The distributed ranking consists of two OFDM symbols ($8\mu s$) plus a TX/RX switching time ($9\mu s$ in 802.11), costing $17\mu s$ in total. When $M_{tx} = 4$, MOP's overhead is approximately $(20+16)+(20+16+17)\times(M_{tx}-1) = 195\mu s$ (note that the first round does not entail distributed ranking). Compared with vanilla 802.11ac, the outstanding overhead of Kardia lies in the frequency-domain distributed ranking, which is only $17(M_{tx} - 1)\mu s$. In practice, frame aggregation is commonly enforced on MU-MIMO transmissions to amortize the overhead, which is evaluated in §7.1.

Multiple contention domains. Our previous description of Kardia has been restricted to a single contention domain where APs/-users can sense each other. In a large network, the current Kardia design arbitrarily partition it into multiple clusters, each being one contention domain. Only APs/users inside each cluster coordinate and run Kardia. Those in different clusters either follow the contend-and-reserve protocol in 802.11ac, or relies on a TDMA scheduler running by a central coordinator. It is possible to further optimize the clustering as in [13], but this is left as our future work.

Synchronization. Kardia's PHY layer leverages two mature communications technologies, including intra-cell MU-MIMO precoding and inter-cell interference nulling. Neither require sophisticated carrier frequency or phase synchronization among distributed APs or clients. The latter does require coarse time synchronization to within an OFDM cyclic prefix length [10], which is 0.8 μs in 802.11ac. Existing system prototype has verified the feasibility of interference nulling under such synchronization requirement using commodity WiFi cards [10]. We remark that distributed ranking design in Kardia also requires similar level of coarse synchronization among clients and AP within an OFDM cyclic prefix length.

Channel coherence time. It should be noted that multiple rounds of downlink transmissions can follow one DoF distribution, provided that they span much shorter time than the channel coherence time and thus CSI remains stable. Existing experiments [13] observed that for indoor environment with low-mobility and short-distance links (*i.e.*, the targeted scenario of Kardia), MU-MIMO capacity is unaffected as long as CSI is refreshed every 15 ms. In our evaluation, MOP is performed based on a conservative update threshold of 5.5 ms[5], *i.e.*, it is initiated before a MU-MIMO transmission, if more than 5.5 ms has elapsed since the last MOP. This conservative approach tends to amplify the overhead of Kardia.

Natural regression to 802.11ac mode. When the APs are sparsely deployed, *i.e.*, we have independent cells without interference to each other, the 802.11ac can simply work in each cell. In this case, Kardia naturally regresses to the vanilla 802.11ac. In the example in Sec. 3, if AP2 does not interfere with the users of AP1, then the CSI feedback of AP1's users will never reach AP2 due to channel reciprocity. Hence AP2 still has its full M_{tx} DoFs to serve its own users. Such graceful regression guarantees Kardia can achieve a throughput no less than vanilla 802.11ac in any scenario.

5. Kardia: PERFORMANCE GUARANTEE

Kardia's iterative DoF distribution algorithm tries to maximize user orthogonality in each iteration, without incurring the formidable computational and feedback overhead in an exhaustive search. But how far can it deviate from a global exhaustive search? We now answer this question by lower-bounding Kardia's performance in the basic multi-cell MU-MIMO and interference nulling setup (§4.1).

(a) DoF distribution as an optimization problem. We introduce an indicator variable $x_{uj} \in 0, 1$, denoting whether AP j serves user u. We assume the network is dense, such that for each user, there are a sufficient number of users (belonging to any APs) that can form an orthogonal group with it. Even under this assumption, it is non-trivial to solve the problem of DoF distribution that maximizes total network capacity, which can be formulated as a non-linear integer program, as follows:

$$\max_{\boldsymbol{x}} \quad g(\boldsymbol{x}) \tag{1}$$

$$\text{s.t.} \quad \textstyle\sum_{j\in\mathcal{A}} x_{uj} \leq 1, \forall u \in \mathcal{U} \tag{2}$$

$$\textstyle\sum_{j\in\mathcal{A}}\sum_{u\in\mathcal{U}} x_{uj} \leq M_{tx} \tag{3}$$

where $\mathcal{A}$ and $\mathcal{U}$ denote set of APs and users to choose from. Eq. (2) says that a user is served by at most one AP, whereas Eq. (3) captaures the DoF constraint, *i.e.*, total users to be served should be no larger than M_{tx}, the number of antennas on each AP.

Our objective is to maximize $g(\boldsymbol{x})$, the total network capacity for a given user-grouping and AP selection strategy $\boldsymbol{x}$. Suppose each AP has a power budget of P, then under ZFBF precoding, the AP j projects equal power γ_j towards each user it serves. Thus, for each AP j, we have:

$$\sum_{u\in\mathcal{U}} \frac{\gamma_j x_{uj}}{||\vec{h}_{uj}||^2} = P, \text{and } \gamma_j = \Big(\sum_{u\in\mathcal{U}} ||\vec{h}_{uj}||^{-2} x_{uj}\Big)^{-1} P \tag{4}$$

Then, the total network capacity can be written as:

$$g(\boldsymbol{x}) = \sum_{j\in\mathcal{A}}\sum_{u\in\mathcal{U}} x_{uj} \log(1 + \frac{\gamma_j}{N_0}) \approx \sum_{j\in\mathcal{A}}\sum_{u\in\mathcal{U}} x_{uj} \log \frac{\gamma_j}{N_0} \tag{5}$$

[5] 5.5 ms is the maximum allowable frame duration in 802.11ac.

(b) Submodularity of objective function.

Definition 1: Submodular function. If Ω is a set and 2^{Ω} its power set, then a set function f is submodular *w.r.t.* Ω if: For every $X, Y \subseteq \Omega$ with $X \subseteq Y$ and every $e \in \Omega \backslash Y$, we have $f(X \cup e) - f(X) \geq f(Y \cup e) - f(Y)$.

Submodularity is a diminishing returns property, stating that adding an element to a smaller set helps more than adding it to a larger set. In our problem, intuitively, as the user set becomes larger, orthogonality is more likely to become worse when a new user is added (§2). Thus, the objective function is likely to be submodular. We formalize this intuition as follows.

Lemma 1. *The function $g(\boldsymbol{x})$ is submodular.*

Proof sketch: Define $\Omega = \{(u, j) : u \in \mathcal{U}, j \in \mathcal{A}\}$, then $\boldsymbol{x}$ is its power set. For a given set $U^0 = \{(u, j) \in \Omega : x_{uj} = 1\}$, suppose one more element $(u', j') \notin U^0$ is added to U^0. Then, for the same element (u', j') added to V^0, a subset created by removing one element from U^0, we can easily prove that $[g(U^0 \cup (u', j')) - g(U^0)] - [g(V^0 \cup (u', j')) - g(V^0)]$ is non-negative. By induction, we can prove $g(\boldsymbol{x})$ satisfies the submodularity definition. We ommit the details due to space constraint. □

(c) Worst-case performance bound. Problem (1) resembles the classical problem of maximizing a submodular set function, particularly the maximum general assignment problem [14, Ch. 3]. Approximation ratio of assignment problems with exclusive constraint like (2) is well known (see a survey in [14] and recent works, *e.g.*, [15, 16]). However, the DoF constraint (3), which limits the cardinality of set $\boldsymbol{x}$, is unique in our setting. To our knowledge, performance bound of iterative solutions to such a problem has not been analyzed in prior work.

Theorem 1. *The performance of Kardia's iterative user/AP selection mechanism is at least $\frac{1}{2}$ of the global optimum.*

Proof: Our performance analysis extends the lower-bounding techniques used in optimizing submodular functions defined over a *partition matroid* [17]. We partition the ground set Ω into $|\mathcal{U}|$ sets, with the u-th set being: $\mathcal{S}_u = \{(u, j) : j \in \mathcal{A}\}$, *i.e.*, collection of links with the same user u. Then the set of sets $\mathcal{F} = \{\cup_{u=1}^{|\mathcal{U}|} | \mathcal{F}_u$, where $\mathcal{F}_u \subseteq \mathcal{S}_u$ and $|\mathcal{F}_u| \leq 1, \forall u = 1, 2, \cdots, |\mathcal{U}|\}$ becomes a partition matroid. Note that the constraint of $|\mathcal{F}_u| \leq 1$ is equivalent to Eq. (2).

We now show that the cardinality constraint (3) reduces Kardia's iterative algorithm to an early-termination version of the classical greedy solution to optimizing a partition matroid [17], but the approximation ratio of $\frac{1}{2}$ still holds.

Denote L^* as the set of user-AP pairs in the optimal solution to (1), and L as Kardia's algorithm. Let $\rho_e(A)$ be the increment to the objective function when a new element e is added to the solution set, *i.e.*, $\rho_e(A) = g(A \cup e) - g(A)$. Following a well known property of submodular set functions [17], we have:

$$g(L^*) \leq g(L) + \textstyle\sum_{l \in L^* \backslash L} \rho_l(L) \tag{6}$$

Let e be the element in L that has the minimum increment when it is added. L_e denotes the solution set right before e is added. The submodularity of $g(\cdot)$, along with the selection step of Kardia, implies that:

$$\textstyle\sum_{l \in L^* \backslash L} \rho_l(L) \leq \sum_{l \in L^* \backslash L} \rho_l(L_e) \leq \sum_{l \in L^* \backslash L} \rho_e(L_e) \tag{7}$$

Further, $\sum_{l \in L^* \backslash L} \rho_e(L_e) = |L^* \backslash L| \rho_e(L_e)$ (8)

$$\leq M_{tx} \rho_e(L_e) \leq \textstyle\sum_{l \in L} \rho_l(L_l) \tag{9}$$

$$= g(L) \tag{10}$$

Inequality (9) follows the definition of e. Combining Eq. (10) with (6), we have $g(L) \geq \frac{1}{2} g(L^*)$, which completes the proof. □

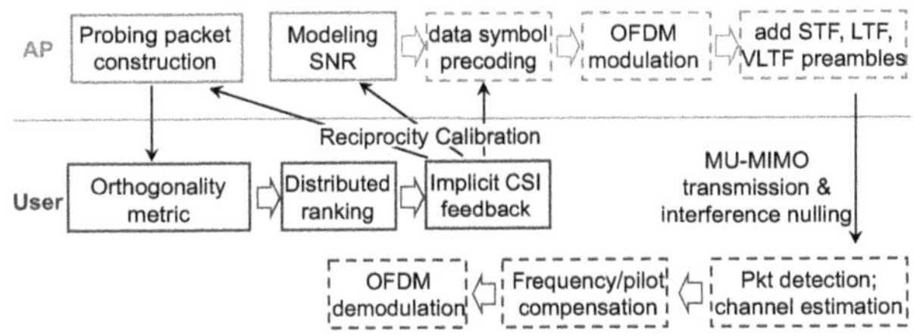

Figure 10: Implemented modules in Kardia. Boxes with broken lines represent 802.11-compliant PHY modules.

6. IMPLEMENTATION

We build a prototype of Kardia using the WARP software radio platform. Figure 10 shows the basic modules and work flow of our implementation. The AP's probing packet is first constructed using the precoding mechanism described in §4.2. Upon receiving the probing packet, each user computes its orthogonality metric, and then starts distributed ranking. The winner feeds back its implicit CSI, which is implemented using the channel reciprocity calibration mechanism in 802.11 [18, Ch. 20.3.12.1]. The performance of MU-MIMO beamforming based on implicit CSI feedback has been validated in [7]. The winner's CSI is in turn leveraged to construct the next probing packet. After each AP selects its users to serve/null, the AP models per-user SNR (§4.4) and selects the corresponding modulation rate. MU-MIMO transmission and interference nulling start immediately afterwards.

The MU-MIMO transmission module of Kardia builds on top of 802.11 OFDM PHY. By default, it has a 20 MHz channel divided into 64 subcarriers, including 48 data subcarriers, 4 pilots, 1 DC and 11 guardband subcarriers. Modulated symbols (*e.g.*, using BPSK) on each data subcarrier are first precoded using ZFBF, mapped to different transmit antennas, and then modulated by OFDM. Standard 802.11 preambles, including STF (for synchronization), LTF (per-antenna channel estimation) and VHT-LTF (estimating the channel of precoded symbols), are prepended to the OFDM-modulated symbols. At the receiver side, correlation-based algorithms are used to detect incoming packets, estimate the CSI, and compensate for frequency offset. The resulting OFDM symbols in the packet are then demodulated and mapped into data bits. Note that the OFDM-symbol-level synchronization requirement of interference nulling is natively satisfied by the WARP platform.

Due to the processing latency and interface delay between the WARP radio and its PC host, we cannot directly reproduce MAC/PHY level mechanisms that require instantaneous feedback/response or in-hardware computation. In particular, precoding/decoding a packet costs several hundred milliseconds in WARPLab, which is orders of magnitude longer than that in real WiFi hardware. To circumvent this problem, we build a backend module on top of WARPLab, which uses a virtual clock for time-critical operations. Kardia's key MAC components including MOP, OAS, beamforming rate adaptation, and PHY layer MU-MIMO transmission and interference nulling, are first run over the air. Then, the virtual clock replaces the WARP-induced inter-frame latency with the response time of real WiFi hardware (the 9 μs SIFS for inter-frame time). This ensures the achievable throughput of each transmission is faithfully reproduced. The resulting network performance is thus consistent with that when Kardia is running in actual WiFi radios.

7. EVALUATION

In this section, we first evaluate each module of Kardia through micro-benchmark experiments based on the testbed implementation detailed in §6. We then conduct a system-level test to benchmark Kardia against the state-of-the-art MU-MIMO schemes.

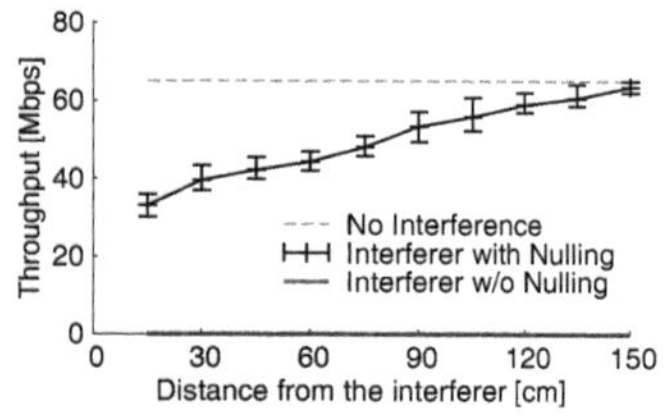

Figure 11: The effectiveness of interference nulling. Error bars indicate max/min across 10 experiment runs.

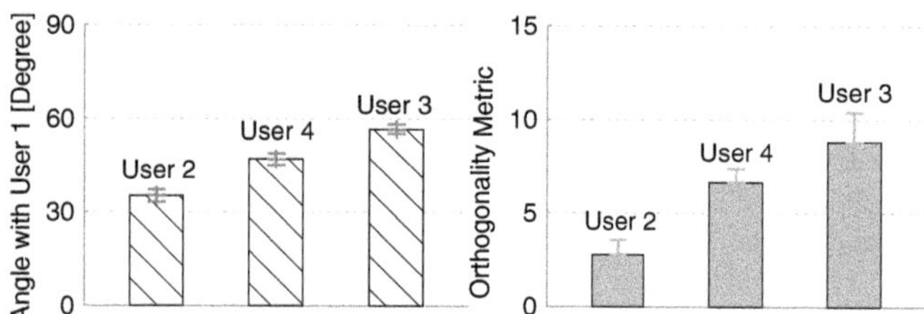

(a) Angle with selected User 1 (b) Orthogonality metric in probing

Figure 12: MOP's probing result faithfully reflects the orthogonality between users.

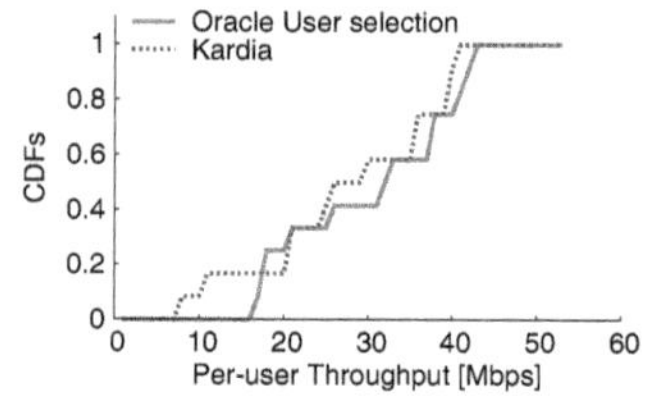

Figure 13: MOP's user selection in contrast to an oracle.

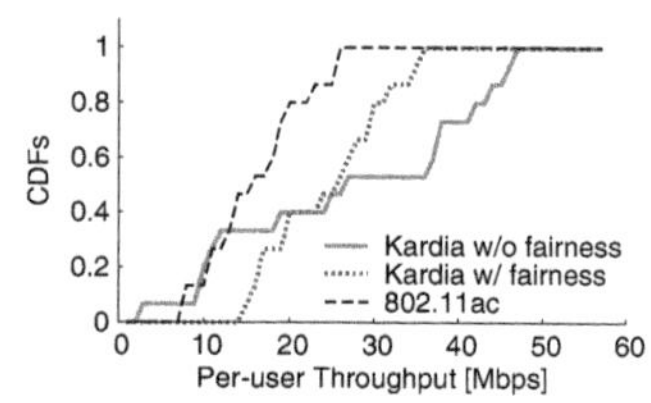

Figure 14: Per-user throughput and fairness of Kardia.

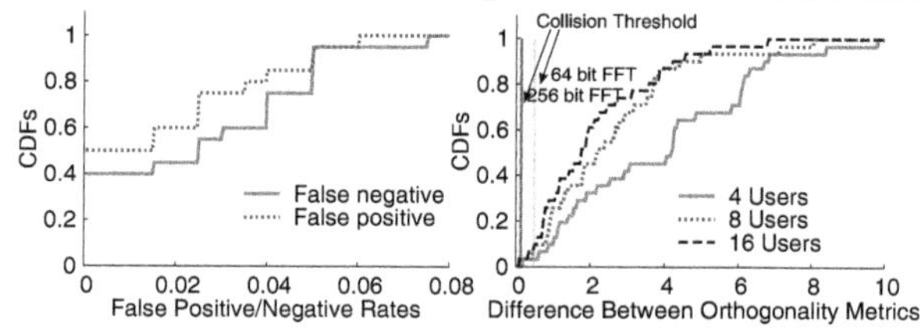

(a) Feedback detection (b) Feedback collision

Figure 15: Performance of distributed ranking.

7.1 Micro-benchmark evaluation

Validation of interference nulling. To verify the efficacy of inter-cell interference nulling in our Kardia implementation, we measure the throughput of a SISO link (link distance 3 m) in the presence of an interfering transmission. The interferer nulls its transmission at the SISO receiver through zero-forcing precoding. Figure 11 shows the throughput achieved at the SISO receiver when it is separated by varying distances from the interferer. Without interference nulling, no frame can be correctly received. If interference nulling is enabled, the receiver can almost achieve its interference-free throughput when the distance separation is beyond 120 cm. Below that separation, leakage interference still exists and may halve the throughput in extreme cases. In practice, the typical distance between a user and interfering AP is larger than that separation, interference nulling should be even more effective.

Validation of orthogonality probing in MOP. We verify MOP's orthogonality metric design using a 4-antenna AP, which first selects a user (user1), and then probes all 3 remaining directions that are orthogonal to user1's channel. Figure 12 shows that the unselected users' performance metrics are closely correlated with their channel angles *w.r.t.* user1. The "more orthogonal" (closer to $\frac{\pi}{2}$) it is, the higher the orthogonality metric. Therefore, this metric can effectively single out users most orthogonal to existing ones.

Optimality of DoF distribution. In theory, Kardia's DoF distribution can achieve at least 50% of the optimal throughput (§5). We now experimentally compare Kardia with a an *oracle* that obtains a globally optimal user selection solution via an exhaustive search based on global CSI knowledge. Both Kardia and the oracle run in our testbed topology with one 4-antenna AP and 10 randomly located users. Figure 13 shows CDF of per-user throughput. We observe that Kardia's performance closely approximates that of the oracle solution, with a median loss of only 8%. Due to exponential complexity of the exhaustive search, we were unable to compute the oracle result for multi-AP case. We will evaluate this case shortly using 802.11ac as benchmark (§7.2).

Proportional fairness control. Recall Kardia uses a weighted 'first-user selection' scheme to approximate proportional throughput fairness (Sec 4.5). To validate its effectiveness, we compare the throughput performance of Kardia with and without such fairness control. Figure 14 plots the per-user throughput distribution of Kardia with and without proportionally fair user selection, in contrast to 802.11ac. The results are obtained from 3 testbed topologies, each with the same number of AP/users as above. Observe the median throughput levels of Kardia with and without proportionally fair user selection are similar. But, the throughput variance of Kardia is smaller with fairness control enabled. It delivers substantial throughput gain over 802.11ac, for all users in the network.

Distributed ranking. Next we verify Kardia's frequency-domain distributed ranking. Figure 15(a) shows the CDF of false positive/negative rates in a 10-user topology running Kardia, where false positive is defined as a user wins the distributed ranking that it did not join. Recall that not all users will join each ranking due to the pruning of low orthogonality-metric users. Thus, both false positive and negative rates are very low. Consequently, the AP can accurately single out the user with highest metric.

Collisions happen when the difference of users' orthogonality metrics fall lower than the resolution of quantization mechanism (§4.2). However, Figure 15(b) shows that the probability of such collisions under various topologies is below 5% when 64-subcarriers are used. With 256 subcarriers, the resolution of orthogonality metric quantization improves and the collision in distributed ranking becomes negligible. Note that collisions on lower-index subcarriers will not affect the performance of Kardia. It only matters when both of the colliding users have the same highest orthogonality metric, and thus choose the same set of upper subcarriers.

Accuracy of rate adaptation. We next investigate the accuracy of the SNR estimation method (§4.4) using two 4-antenna APs. Each AP transmits to 2 users and nulls the another 2 users served by the other AP. Figure 16 shows the difference between our estimation and ground truth (measured through post-processing of received packets), distributed across 30 different real-world topologies. Observe that our SNR estimation method bears a maximum error of 1.88dB and average 0.65dB, which suffices for bit-rate adaptation with a reasonable accuracy.

Effectiveness of OAS. We now verify the OAS (§4.3) in a random topology with a 2-antenna AP and 10 users. Figure 17 shows that Kardia's simple subcarrier selection can improve the mean data rate of all users from about 55Mbps to 75Mbps — a 36% increase. Note that this increase comes despite the fact that not all OFDM subcarriers are utilized. Therefore, the OAS can accurately avoid poorly performing subcarriers to improvement overall throughput.

Kardia's overhead. The overhead in Kardia includes *(i)* the orthogonality probing frame, *(ii)* the distributed ranking and *(iii)* the implicit CSI feedback. Because the WARPLab platform cannot meet 802.11ac timing demands, we evaluate the overhead using a

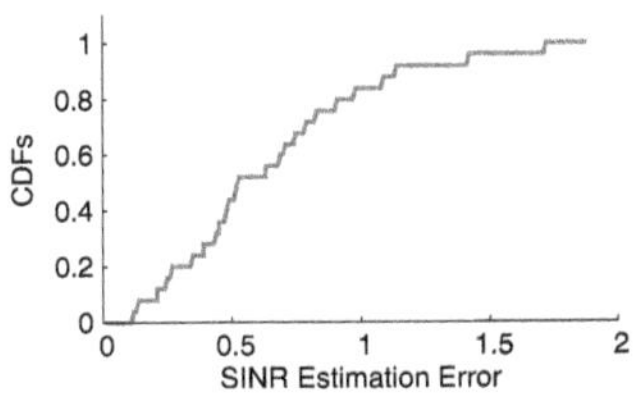

Figure 16: Accuracy of Kardia SNR estimation.

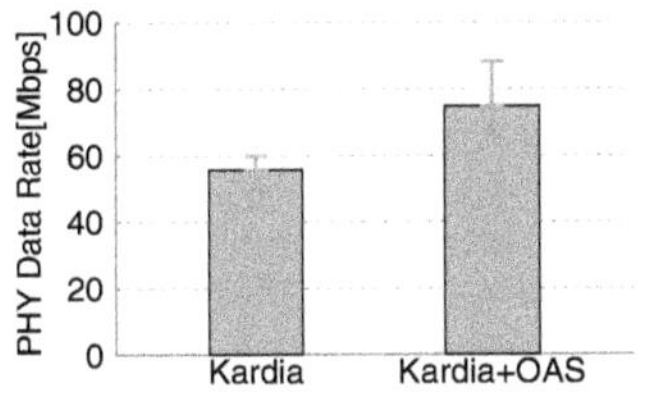

Figure 17: Average (and std.) rate over 10 users using OAS.

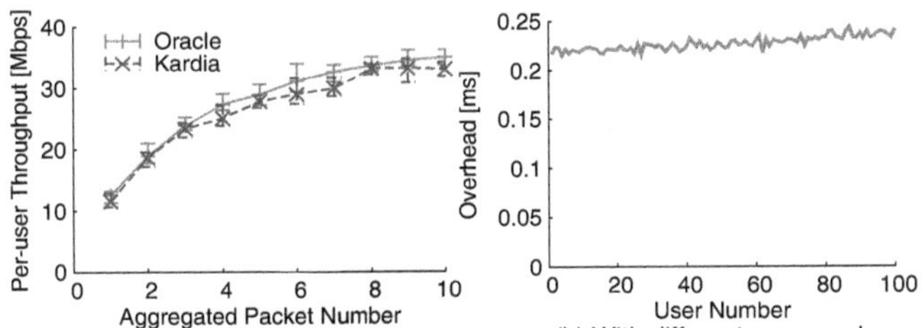

(a) With different packet aggregation size (b) With different user number

Figure 18: Overhead analysis for Kardia.

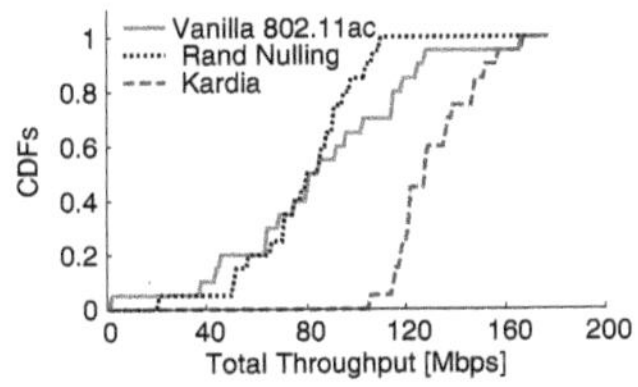

Figure 19: Throughput in small scale network.

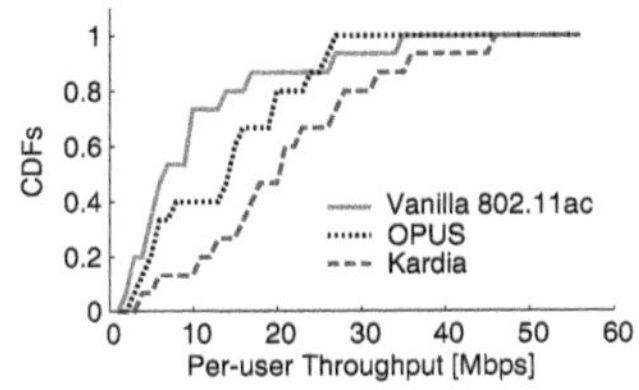

Figure 20: Throughput in large scale network.

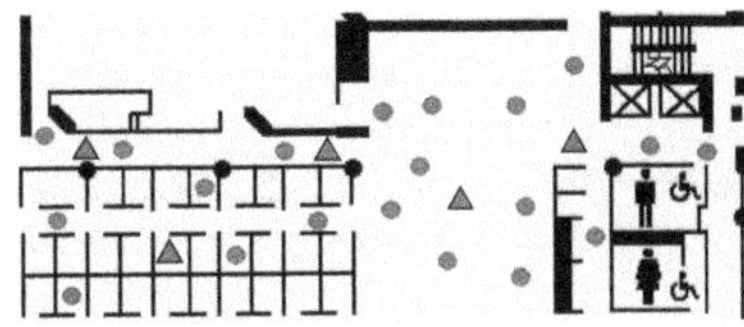

Figure 21: The testbed topology. Blue and red markers denote the user and AP locations, respectively.

simulated network (§6) of 10 4-antenna APs and 100 users. We compare the overhead of Kardia with that of an oracle which has no overhead for user/AP selection, but still incurs the implicit CSI feedback overhead needed for MU-MIMO transmission.

Figure 18(a) shows that Kardia has similar performance to the oracle scheme under a variety of frame aggregation levels (with 1.5 KB per-frame). This is because *(i)* orthogonality probing only incurs short preambles, and *(ii)* each distributed ranking only occupies a short period of 17 μs (§4.2). Note that the throughput of both Kardia and oracle scheme degrade significantly with low frame aggregation level. This is attributed to the unavoidable probing/feedback overhead in all closed-loop MU-MIMO networks.

Figure 18(b) further reveals Kardia's scalability as its overhead is almost independent of user population. We can observe that the overhead only increases slightly under much larger user number. This increase is caused by collisions in the distributed ranking. Since the collision probability remains very low under large user number, the amount of such increase is trivial.

7.2 System level evaluation

In this section, we integrate all Kardia components for performance evaluation in practical topologies.

Small scale experiments. We first test Kardia in a small scale prototype implementation of 2 APs and 6 users. Kardia is compared with (a) random nulling, where the 2 APs randomly select users to serve and null, and (b) vanilla 802.11ac, which only allows single cell transmission. We vary the location of APs and users and repeat the experiment for 30 different topologies. Figure 19 shows the CDF of total network throughput among all topologies. On average, Kardia improves the total network throughput by 54% over vanilla 802.11ac and 67% over random nulling. The performance gain here comes from both orthogonality-based user scheduling within each cell and the DoF distribution over the two cells.

Performance in large scale networks. The DoF distribution capability of Kardia reaps even greater throughput gains in larger and denser networks. Here, we evaluate Kardia over a larger network of 5 APs and 20 users, partitioned into 2 contention domains following §4.5. Due to a limited number of available WARP boards, we adopt a trace-based emulation approach similar to [8]. We collect channel matrices between all APs and clients in the testbed locations (Figure 21). We then emulate Kardia by replacing the WARP hardware with per-frame channel distortion following the traces.

Figure 20 compares the per-user throughput of different protocols, in which we also include OPUS [9], an orthogonality-aware user selection scheme that essentially limits itself to intra-cell DoF distribution. Experimental results reveal that *(i)* vanilla 802.11ac has the worst performance, with a total network throughput of only 152Mbps. *(ii)* OPUS outperforms vanilla 802.11ac, but its intra-cell user selection alone does not explore the full network capacity. *(iii)* Kardia achieves the highest performance, with a total throughput of 314 Mbps. The capability of DoF distribution amongst different cells allows Kardia to achieve 2.07× and 1.56× of average throughput gain over vanilla 802.11ac and OPUS, respectively.

8. RELATED WORK

Multi-cell coordinated beamforming. Coordinated beamforming has been well explored in infrastructure networks [19, 20]. A common theme lies in joint optimization of precoding matrix among APs to maximize capacity. Such optimization is solvable only for a given set of APs and users with known CSI. A recent algorithm [21] allows a MIMO node to transmit through a direction orthogonal to existing transmissions, but it requires lengthy learning phase. ProBeam [22] exploits switched-beamforming to optimize spatial reuse in WiMax. Owing to a discrete set of beam directions, the problem can be cast into a matching between the transmitters' beams and receiver set, which is further mapped to the generalized assignment problem [23]. In contrast, Kardia runs ZFBF beamforming that derives a unique set of beams for each user combination, rendering the user/AP selection problem much harder.

Recently, multi-cell coordinated beamforming in WLAN has become a research hotspot. However, existing works [24, 25] mainly focus on *multi-antenna* clients. Their design principle is to make the most of the multiple DoFs at the *client* side. In contrast, Kardia focus on the optimal utilization of the DoFs at the *AP* by employing multi-cell transmission to combat the channel hardening effect. Kardia works even for *single-antenna* clients.

User grouping in single-cell MU-MIMO. Current wireless standards, including 802.11ac, WiMax and LTE, can run MU-MIMO only for a given set of users irrespective of their orthogonality. Substantial theoretical work has devised iterative algorithms to combat user coupling [4–6] for single-cell MU-MIMO. These algorithms aim to compute an optimal user combination, but assuming global CSI is known to the AP. Alternative algorithms [26] use the statistical instead of full CSI. But practical wireless channels are hard to be characterized by a stationary model due to multi-path fading. Kardia is partly inspired by OPUS [9], where an AP incrementally selects users based on their orthogonality to existing ones in its own cell. Kardia addresses a more comprehensive problem of multi-cell joint selection of users and APs, and derives an algorithm with provably good performance. Our experiments verified that it is superior over a stand-alone counterpart where each AP selects users separately (Figure 20).

Cross-layer MU-MIMO protocols. State-of-the-art MU-MIMO systems [2, 24, 27, 28] commonly adopt random access protocols, *i.e.*, random user selection. They are employed only to maximize the number of concurrent users, rather than the sum capacity. Such systems can be further enhanced by Kardia to combat channel hardening and thus better harness the downlink DoFs.

Network MIMO [13, 29, 30] and interference alignment [31] can increase DoF linearly with the *total* number of transmit antennas in the network (assuming channel hardening is circumvented). However, both approaches rely on *coherent* signal combination/alignment between distributed transmitters, which in turn requires carrier phase and sampling clock synchronization [31]. In contrast, although Kardia advocates multi-cell cooperation, it only requires APs to synchronize their packet transmission time, and can tolerate jitters within a CP duration ($0.8\mu s$). This has proven feasible for COTS APs with a wireline backhaul [10].

Combining MU-MIMO and DAS (Distributed Antenna System) [32] can improve spatial reuse and alleviate hidden terminals. However, this design allows multiple widely-distributed transmit antennas to access the channel independently, which severely suppresses legacy 802.11ac transmissions nearby. In contrast, Kardia will naturally regress to legacy 802.11ac mode if all APs nearby ignore the extra transmission opportunities offered by the Kardia AP.

9. CONCLUSION

In a distributed MU-MIMO network, channel orthogonality among users has a significant impact upon the network throughput. Improper grouping of MU-MIMO downlink users, particularly those with poor orthogonality, is detrimental to the overall network throughput. We have designed and evaluated Kardia, a novel framework that can efficiently identify the throughput-maximizing users/APs combinations within a WLAN cell and across cells. System evaluations show that Kardia improves the throughput in a large-scale network by 107% over 802.11ac. Kardia has potential to enhance a broad class of MU-MIMO protocols that group users randomly.

Acknowledgement

This research was supported in part by the NSF under Grant CNS-1318292, CNS-1343363, CNS-1350039 and CNS-1404613.

10. REFERENCES

[1] D. Tse and P. Viswanath, *Fundamentals of Wireless Communication*. Cambridge University Press, 2005.

[2] W.-L. Shen, Y.-C. Tung, K.-C. Lee, K. C.-J. Lin, S. Gollakota, D. Katabi, and M.-S. Chen, "Rate Adaptation for 802.11 Multiuser MIMO Networks," in *Proc. of ACM MobiCom*, 2012.

[3] B. Hochwald and S. Vishwanath, "Space-time multiple access: Linear growth in the sum rate," in *in Proc. 40th Annual Allerton Conf. Communications, Control and Computing*, 2002.

[4] T. Yoo, N. Jindal, and A. Goldsmith, "Multi-Antenna Downlink Channels with Limited Feedback and User Selection," *IEEE JSAC*, vol. 25, no. 7, 2007.

[5] T. Ji, C. Zhou, S. Zhou, and Y. Yao, "Low Complex User Selection Strategies for Multi-User MIMO Downlink Scenario," in *IEEE WCNC*, 2007.

[6] M. Trivellato, F. Boccardi, and F. Tosato, "User Selection Schemes for MIMO Broadcast Channels with Limited Feedback," in *Proc. of IEEE Vehicular Technology Conference*, 2007.

[7] C. Shepard, H. Yu, N. Anand, E. Li, T. Marzetta, R. Yang, and L. Zhong, "Argos: Practical Many-Antenna Base Stations," in *Proc. of ACM MobiCom*, 2012.

[8] X. Xie, X. Zhang, and K. Sundaresan, "Adaptive Feedback Compression for MIMO Networks," in *ACM MobiCom*, 2013.

[9] X. Xie and X. Zhang, "Scalable User Selection for MU-MIMO Networks," in *Proc. of IEEE INFOCOM*, 2014.

[10] S. Kumar, D. Cifuentes, S. Gollakota, and D. Katabi, "Bringing Cross-Layer MIMO to Today's Wireless LANs," in *Proc. of ACM SIGCOMM*, 2013.

[11] K. Tan, J. Fang, Y. Zhang, S. Chen, L. Shi, J. Zhang, and Y. Zhang, "Fine-Grained Channel Access in Wireless LAN," in *Proc. of ACM SIGCOMM*, 2010.

[12] S. Sen, R. Roy Choudhury, and S. Nelakuditi, "No time to countdown: Migrating backoff to the frequency domain," in *Proc. of ACM MobiCom*, 2011.

[13] X. Zhang, K. Sundaresan, M. A. Khojastepour, S. Rangarajan, and K. G. Shin, "NEMOx: Scalable Network MIMO for Wireless Networks," in *Proc. of ACM MobiCom*, 2013.

[14] L. Bordeaux, Y. Hamadi, and P. Kohli, *Tractability: Practical Approaches to Hard Problems*. Cambridge University Press, 2014.

[15] G. Calinescu, C. Chekuri, M. Pál, and J. Vondrák, "Maximizing a Submodular Set Function Subject to a Matroid Constraint," in *IPCO*, 2007.

[16] J. Lee, V. S. Mirrokni, V. Nagarajan, and M. Sviridenko, "Maximizing Nonmonotone Submodular Functions Under Matroid or Knapsack Constraints," *SIAM J. Discret. Math.*, vol. 23, no. 4, 2010.

[17] M. Fisher, G. Nemhauser, and L. Wolsey, "An Analysis of Approximations for Maximizing Submodular Set Functions – II," *Mathematical Programming Studies*, 1978.

[18] "Wireless LAN Medium Access Control (MAC) and Physical Layer (PHY) Specifications," *IEEE Std. 802.11n*, 2009.

[19] H. Dahrouj and W. Yu, "Coordinated Beamforming for the Multicell Multi-Antenna Wireless System," *IEEE TWC*, vol. 9, no. 5, 2010.

[20] C.-B. Chae, I. Hwang, R. Heath, and V. Tarokh, "Interference Aware Coordinated Beamforming in a Multi-Cell System," *IEEE TWC*, vol. 11, no. 10, 2012.

[21] Y. Noam and A. Goldsmith, "Exploiting Spatial Degrees of Freedom in MIMO Cognitive Radio Systems," in *Proc. of IEEE ICC*, 2012.

[22] J. Yoon, K. Sundaresan, M. A. Khojastepour, S. Rangarajan, and S. Banerjee, "ProBeam: A Practical Multicell Beamforming System for OFDMA Small-Cell Networks," in *Proc. of ACM MobiHoc*, 2013.

[23] L. Fleischer, M. X. Goemans, V. S. Mirrokni, and M. Sviridenko, "Tight Approximation Algorithms for Maximum General Assignment Problems," in *Proc. of ACM-SIAM SODA*, 2006.

[24] K. C.-J. Lin, S. Gollakota, and D. Katabi, "Random Access Heterogeneous MIMO Networks," in *ACM SIGCOMM*, 2011.

[25] H. Yu, O. Bejarano, and L. Zhong, "Combating Inter-cell Interference in 802.11ac-based Multi-user MIMO Networks," in *Proc. of ACM MobiCom*, 2014.

[26] D. Gesbert, M. Kountouris, R. W. Heath, C.-B. Chae, and T. Salzer, "Shifting the MIMO Paradigm," *IEEE Signal Processing Magazine*, vol. 24, no. 5, 2007.

[27] K. Tan, H. Liu, J. Fang, W. Wang, J. Zhang, M. Chen, and G. M. Voelker, "SAM: Enabling Practical Spatial Multiple Access in Wireless LAN," in *Proc. of ACM MobiCom*, 2009.

[28] S. Gollakota, S. D. Perli, and D. Katabi, "Interference Alignment and Cancellation," in *Proc. of ACM SIGCOMM*, 2009.

[29] H. S. Rahul, S. Kumar, and D. Katabi, "JMB: Scaling Wireless Capacity With User Demands," in *Proc. of ACM SIGCOMM*, 2012.

[30] H. V. Balan, R. Rogalin, A. Michaloliakos, K. Psounis, and G. Caire, "Achieving High Data Rates in a Distributed MIMO System," in *Proc. of ACM MobiCom*, 2012.

[31] O. El Ayach, S. Peters, and J. Heath, R.W., "The Practical Challenges of Interference Alignment," *IEEE Wireless Communications*, vol. 20, no. 1, 2013.

[32] J. Xiong, K. Sundaresan, K. Jamieson, M. A. Khojastepour, and S. Rangarajan, "MIDAS: Empowering 802.11ac Networks with Multiple-Input Distributed Antenna Systems," in *CoNEXT*, 2014.

A Distributed Algorithm to Construct Multicast Trees in WSNs: An Approximate Steiner Tree Approach

Hongyu Gong
Dept. of Electronic Engineering
Shanghai Jiao Tong University
ann@sjtu.edu.cn

Lutian Zhao
Dept. of Mathematics
Shanghai Jiao Tong University
golbez@sjtu.edu.cn

Kainan Wang
Dept. of Computer Science
Shanghai Jiao Tong University
sunnywkn@sjtu.edu.cn

Weijie Wu
School of Information Security Engineering
Shanghai Jiao Tong University
weijiewu@sjtu.edu.cn

Xinbing Wang
Dept. of Electronic Engineering
Shanghai Jiao Tong University
xwang8@sjtu.edu.cn

ABSTRACT

Multicast tree is a key structure for data dissemination from one source to multiple receivers in wireless networks. Minimum length multicast tree can be modeled as the Steiner Tree Problem, and is proven to be NP-hard. In this paper, we explore how to efficiently generate minimum length multicast trees in wireless sensor networks (WSNs), where only limited knowledge of network topology is available at each node. We design and analyze a simple and distributed algorithm, which we call Toward Source Tree (TST), to build multicast trees in WSNs. We show three metrics of TST algorithm, i.e., running time, tree length and energy efficiency. We prove that its running time is $O(\sqrt{n \log n})$, the best among all existing solutions to our best knowledge. We prove that TST tree length is in the same order as Steiner tree, give a theoretical upper bound and use simulations to show the ratio between them is only 1.114 when nodes are uniformly distributed. We evaluate energy efficiency in terms of the number of forwarding nodes in multicast trees, and prove that it is order-optimal. We give an efficient way to construct multicast tree in support of transmission of voluminous data.

Categories and Subject Descriptors

C.2.1 [**Computer-Communication Networks**]: Network Architecture and Design—*Wireless Communication*

Keywords

Multicast Tree; Steiner Tree; Wireless Sensor Networks

MobiHoc'15, June 22–25, 2015, Hangzhou, China.

http://dx.doi.org/10.1145/2746285.2746296.

1. INTRODUCTION

Wireless Sensor Network (WSN) is a network of wireless sensor nodes into which sensing, computation and communication functions are integrated. Sensors are self-organizing and deployed over a geographical region [1]. Multicasting, i.e., one-to-many message transmission, is one of the most common data transmission patterns in WSNs. Tree is the topology for non-redundant data transmission. To enable efficient multicast, multicast tree has been proposed and widely used. It has not only been applied to multicast capacity analysis in wireless networks [2–4], but has also been used to support a wide range of applications like distance education, military command and intelligent systems [5].

Many researchers have been working on constructing efficient multicast trees [6–8]. They have proposed a number of algorithms so as to minimize the routing complexity as well as achieve the time and energy efficiency (for details, please refer to the next section), but most of them did not focus on an important performance measure: the tree length. This is a critical metric since larger tree length clearly results in longer delay. To enable the messages to be forwarded farther, sensors have to increase their transmission power, causing more energy consumption as well as more serious interference to neighboring nodes. Besides, as the transmission distance increases, the messages suffer from higher probability of transmission failure.

Recently, GEographic Multicast (GEM), inspired by Euclidean Steiner Tree, was proposed for routing in dense wireless networks [9]. Formally, given a network $G = (V, E)$, the weight of each edges, and a set of terminals $S \subseteq V$, the Steiner Tree Problem is to find a tree in G that spans S with the minimum total weight [10]. This problem has been proven to be NP-hard [11], and has not been visited for a long time. Former forms of its approximate implementation were not appropriate for constructing multicast trees in WSNs for various reasons (details will be discussed in the following section.) In GEM, the authors took the first step to utilize the Steiner tree for constructing multicast trees in WSNs, achieving routing scalability and efficiency. This approach can potentially reduce the tree length, but this very simple form of utilization only considers the hop count in an unweighted graph, but not the total length of the multicast tree in a weighted graph. Furthermore, as for the performance analysis, the statistical properties were all under the assumption that all nodes are uniformly distributed, making it difficult to tell its efficiency under a realistic network environment.

In this paper, inspired by taking the advantage of the Steiner tree property, we design a novel distributed algorithm to construct an approximate minimum-length multicast tree for wireless sensor networks, aiming at achieving energy efficiency, ease of implementation and low computational complexity, at an affordable cost on the sub-optimality of tree length. In what follows, we call our design Toward Source Tree Algorithm, or TST for short. We quantitatively evaluate TST algorithm performance under general node distribution, and show that TST has the following satisfactory metrics:

- Its running time is $O(\sqrt{n \log n})$, the best among all existing solutions for large multicast groups.
- Its tree length is in the same order as Steiner tree, and simulation shows the constant ratio between them is only 1.114 with uniformly distributed nodes.
- The number of nodes that participate in forwarding is order-optimal, yielding high energy efficiency during transmission for sensor networks.

The rest of paper is organized as follows. Section 2 states related work. In Section 3, we introduce our network model. In Section 4, we present our Toward Source Tree Algorithm to construct a multicast tree. In Section 5, 6 and 7, we evaluate the performance of our algorithm mainly from three aspects: multicast tree length, running time and energy efficiency separately. In Section 8, we use extensive simulations to further evaluate the performance. Section 9 concludes this paper.

2. RELATED WORK

We review related works in two categories: the multicast tree construction and the approximate Steiner tree.

Multicase tree construction. Many studies focus on multicast routing in wireless networks, and useful techniques for routing have been proposed in WSN. Sanchez *et al.* proposed Geographic Multicast Routing (GMR), a heuristic neighborhood selection algorithm based on local geographic information [6]. Later Park *et al.* [15] combined distributed geographic multicasting with beaconless routing. In Localized Energy-Efficient Multicast Algorithm (LEMA), forwarding elements apply the MST algorithm locally for routing [7]. Dijkstra-based Localized Energy-Efficient Multicast Algorithm (DLEMA) finds energy shortest paths leading through nodes with maximal geographical advance towards desired destinations [8]. However, few works have considered minimizing the distance of multicast routing or providing comprehensive quantitative analysis theoretically on the performance of routing policies.

Approximate Steiner Tree. Shortest Path Heuristic (SPH) and Kruskal Shortest Path Heuristic (KSPH) add new nodes to existing subtrees through the shortest paths [12]. Average Distance Heuristic (ADH) joins subtrees that contain receivers by a path passing non-receivers with minimal average distance to existing subtrees [13]. Santos *et al.* push forward distributed dual ascent (DA) algorithm, achieving good performance in practice [14]. The comparison of these algorithms with our TST algorithm is shown in Table 1. These algorithms were proposed for point-to-point networks. In this paper, we consider the Steiner Tree Problem in wireless sensor networks that are broadcast in nature. In addition, each node has limited computation and storage capability. Devices are usually battery-powered, and therefore energy-efficiency is of great importance. Due to these specific features and requirements, existing algorithms for P2P are not suitable for WSN.

To sum up, there have been extensive existing works focusing on multicast tree construction or the approximate Steiner tree problems, but we have not found a perfect adoption of Steiner tree into constructing multicast trees.

3. NETWORK MODEL

Let us first use a mathematical model to capture a wireless sensor network. We assume the network consists of n nodes in total (or we call the *network size* is n), distributed independently and identically in a unit square. Each node is assigned with a unique identifier to be distinguished from others. Each time when a source needs to transmit messages, it chooses m receivers randomly. In other words, m is the number of nodes that participate in a multicast group, or we call it the *multicast group size*. For our statistical analysis, we focus on the dense network and large multicast group where m and n are both very large, and $m \leq n$. This is particularly suitable to describe a wireless sensor network.

The geographical distribution of nodes is described by a density function $f(\mathbf{x})$ where $\mathbf{x}$ is the position vector. Here we allow $\mathbf{x}$ to be of any dimension; in the rest of this paper we let it be a two-dimensional vector for ease of presentation, but it does not hurt any generality. We assume $f(\mathbf{x})$ is independent of n and m. We also assume that $0 < \epsilon_1 \leq f(\mathbf{x}) \leq \epsilon_2$ where ϵ_1 and ϵ_2 are both constants, i.e., a node has a positive probability to be located at any point of this area.

To ensure the connectivity of the whole network, we set the transmission range $r = \Theta\left(\sqrt{\frac{\log n}{n}}\right)$ [16]. For all nodes, r is the same and fixed. We assume that two nodes u and v can communicate with each other directly if and only if the Euclidean distance between them, d_{uv}, is no larger than r. Every node can obtain its own geographical location, e.g., via the Global Position System (GPS). However, nodes do not know the exact location of other nodes until they receive messages containing that piece of information.

Table 2: System Parameter

n	number of all nodes in the network
m	number of multicast group members
r	transmission range
r_c	search coverage range
L_V	length of a temporary tree
L_M	length of a multicast tree

4. ALGORITHM

In this section, we describe our Toward Source Tree algorithm in detail. This algorithm consists of three phases.

Table 1: Comparison of Distributed Algorithm for Approximate Steiner Construction

Algorithm	Expected tree length	Expected time	Assumptions
SPH [12]	2-approximation Steiner tree, $O(\sqrt{m})$	$O(m\sqrt{\frac{n}{\log n}})$	Shortest paths need to be known; Applied in Point-to-point network.
KSPG [12]		$O(m\sqrt{\frac{n}{\log n}})$	
ADH [13]		$O(m\sqrt{\frac{n}{\log n}})$	
DA [14]	$O(\sqrt{m})$	$O(n^2)$	No shortest path information required; Applied in Point-to-point network.
TST	$O(\sqrt{m})$	$O(\sqrt{n}\log n)$	No shortest path information required; Applied in Wireless network.

In the first phase, the source broadcasts a message and wakes up all receivers it chooses. In the second phase, every receiver chooses the closest neighboring receiver that has shorter Euclidean distances to the source node than the receiver node itself, and then a temporary tree can be established among all receivers. However, till the end of this stage cycles might exist. Hence we eliminate these cycles in the third phase. In what follows we describe the process in detail, and we will use an example to illustrate how to generate such a tree at the end of this section.

4.1 Phase 1: Identifying Receivers

Each node has a label indicating its role in the multicast tree: "S" stands for the source and "R" for receivers. In this phase, a message containing all receivers' identifiers is sent from the source so that all nodes in the network can be aware whether they are receivers. Upon receiving this message, receivers then wake up, label themselves with "R" and be ready to participate in the multicast routing.The source will also specify its own location in this message.

This step is necessary for multicast routing since no one except the source knows which nodes the messages are destinated for. In this phase, the broadcast information will notify the nodes who are selected into the multicast group, and all receivers will be awakened.

4.2 Phase 2: Connecting All Receivers

In this phase, we first build a "temporary tree" consisting of only the multicast group members, and then find the minimum-hop shortest path between each pair of members that are directly connected in the "temporary tree". All multicast group members will be connected with the newly added relays.

Step 1: Searching Receivers in the Neighorhood

In this step, each multicast member chooses an appropriate neighbor to connect to. The neighboring member selection criteria is: each member chooses the closest one from the set of members that have shorter Euclidean distances to the source node than this node itself. If no such neighboring member can be found, then this multicast member directly connects to the source.

When a member tries to contact its neighbor members, it is regarded as the sender that sends *request message*. Its form is: <*sender id, sender location, location of previous hop, coverage range r_c, node sequence, total hop H, path length p*>. *Sender id* is used to identify the multicast members sending the *request message*, and *path length* can be updated with the location of previous hop and current hop. The coverage range r_c sets the range within which the multicast member searches for its neighboring members. The Euclidean distance between the sender and current node can be calculated with sender location, and messages will be discarded if the distance is larger than r_c. *Node sequence* records in order the nodes through which this message has passed, which acts as a guide for response from neighboring receivers so that the response can be routed via the available path. The hop count H is the number of hops the message has passed through, and p is the path length the message have been through when it reaches the current node.

Algorithm 1 Neighbor Request from Multicast Members

for all receiver R in a multicast group **do**
  the number of request session: $k \leftarrow 0$
  coverage range: $r_c \leftarrow r$
  time out interval: $T_0 \leftarrow \Theta\left(2^k \log n\right)$
  set the node sequence as $\{R\}$
  total hop: $H \leftarrow 0$
  path length: $p \leftarrow 0$
  forward the *request message* to its neighborhood
  while no response is received when time is out for the kth request session **do**
    $k \leftarrow k+1$
    $r_c \leftarrow 2^k r$
    $T_{k+1} \leftarrow 2T_k$
    set the node sequence as $\{R\}$
    $H \leftarrow 0$
    $p \leftarrow 0$
    forward the *request message* to its neighborhood
  end while
end for

In each search session, the member broadcasts the *request message* within search coverage range. The sender sets an appropriate timeout interval. Once the sender receives replies from neighboring nodes, the search session terminates. Then it enters step 2. However, if time runs out and no reply is obtained, it means that no appropriate neighboring members are found. The sender then doubles its search range and initiates another search. In Algorithm

1, we show how a multicast group member connects to their neighboring members or the source.

A node may receive more than one *request message* from the same sender. If it is within *coverage range*, it will choose the one with the fewest hops among all the messages. If the numbers of hops are the same, it picks out the message with the shortest path length. Then it modifies this message. It adds itself to the *node sequence*, increases the *hop count* by 1 and calculate new *path length* given the location of the previous hop. With these information updated, it forwards the message. Algorithm 2 describes how nodes deal with *request messages* in detail.

Algorithm 2 Request Forwarding

for all node u receiving *request message* **do**
  dist = || location of u - sender location ||
  if dist $< r_c$ **then**
    add u to node sequence
    $H \leftarrow H + 1$
    newDist = ||location of u - location of previous hop||
    $p \leftarrow p +$ newDist
    forward the *request message* to its neighborhood
    if u is in the multicast group **then**
      nodeSourceDist = || location of u - source location ||
      senderSourceDist = || sender location - source location ||
      if nodeSourceDist < senderSourceDist **then**
        send *respond message* back to the sender
      end if
    end if
  end if
end for

When a multicast member finds it closer to the source than the sender of the *request message*, it might be chosen as the neighbor by the sender. Therefore, this member will choose a path to the sender and respond with the *respond message*. The form of the *respond message* is: *<sender id, respondent id, node sequence, total hop H, path length p>*. The *respond message* can be routed with the path information provided by the node sequence.

Step 2: Connecting to the Nearest Neighbor

With *respond messages*, every member selects the closest neighbor. Once a neighbor is chosen, the *connect message* is forwarded via the minimum-hop shortest path. The *connect message* is used to establish a connection between nodes in the multicast group. At the same time, all relay nodes on the minimum-hop shortest path record this pair of members, previous hop and the next hop on the path. When all receivers send the *connect message*, a "temporary tree" among all mutlicast group members including the source is constructed.

4.3 Phase 3: Eliminating Cycles

In Phase 2, we construct a "temporary tree" made up of multicast group members. However, when other nodes are added to it as relays, cycles might be formed. In particular, when paths connecting different pairs of multicast members share the same relay nodes, such node may receive redundant information, which indicates that cycles come into being. Therefore, we check the existence of cycles in this phase and eliminate them if any.

Suppose a node u acts as a relay for k ($k > 1$) pairs of nodes in the multicast group, which are directly connected in the temporary tree, denoted as (R_{11}, R_{12}), (R_{21}, R_{22}),..., (R_{k1}, R_{k2}). Let us assume that in each pair, R_{i1} is closer to source than R_{i2} ($1 \le i \le k$). A relay stores its previous and the next hop of the path from R_{i1} to R_{i2}, and they are denoted as PH_i and NH_i respectively. Then it chooses one pair randomly, say, (R_{j1}, R_{j2}) and keeps the information: $(R_{j1}, R_{j2}, PH_j, NH_j)$. For other pairs (R_{i1}, R_{i2}) where $R_{i1} \neq R_{j1}$, the relay modifies their information as $(R_{j1}, R_{i2}, PH_j, NH_i)$. Define a set Q, where $Q = \{q \mid q =< R_{i1}, R_{i2}, PH_i >, \forall\ R_{i1} \neq R_{j1}\}$. Last, it sends "*Eliminate* message Q" and its previous hops delete unnecessary edges accordingly. In Algorithm 3, we show how to wipe out the cycles.

Algorithm 3 Cycle Elimination

for all node u engaged in paths between k pairs of members **do**
  choose an integer j such that $1 \le j \le k$
  for all i such that $1 \le i \le k$ and $i \neq j$ **do**
    forward *Eliminate* message $Q_i =< R_{i1}, R_{i2}, PH_i >$
  end for
end for
for all node w receiving "*Eliminate* message Q_i" **do**
  if w is exactly PH_i **then**
    if w is not in the multicast group **then**
      $PH_i \leftarrow$ previous hop of w on path (R_{i1}, R_{i2})
      forward the modified Q_i to the previous hop
      eliminate information: $(R_{i1}, R_{i2}, PH_i, NH_i)$
    end if
  end if
end for

4.4 Proof of Tree Topology

The previous subsections describe how we can connect mutlicast group members using our TST algorithm. Now let us prove that the topology constructed by TST algorithm is exactly a tree. We first show that temporary tree formed in the second phase has a tree topology in Lemma 4.1. But relays are added into the temporary tree to connect receivers, which might result in the existence of cycles. In Theorem 4.1 we show that cycle elimination can in fact guarantee the tree topology.

Lemma 4.1. *The temporary tree connecting m receivers has a tree topology.*

PROOF. We prove it by contradiction. Suppose that a cycle exists and k nodes are contained in this cycle, denoted by $n_1, n_2, ..., n_k$. All of them are multicast members. Without loss of generality, we assume n_i selects n_{i+1} as its neighboring member, $i = 1, \cdots, k-1$, and that n_k chooses n_1 as its neighbor. According to the criteria of neighbor selection, we know that n_{i+1} is closer to source than n_i for $i = 1, \cdots, k-1$. Therefore, n_k must be closer to source than n_1. Due to the fact that n_k's selection is n_1, we conclude that n_1 must be closer to source than n_k, which is a contradiction. This concludes the proof. □

Based on Lemma 4.1, we have the following theorem:

Theorem 4.1. *The topology connecting nodes generated by TST algorithm is a tree that spans all multicast group members.*

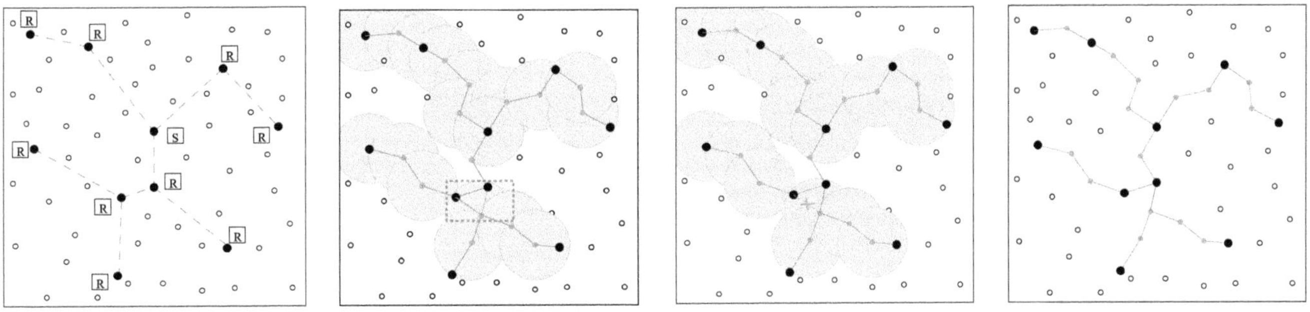

(a) Building a temporary tree spanning multicast group members

(b) Adding relay nodes

(c) Eliminating redundant edges and maintaining the topology of tree

(d) Constructing the multicast tree with relays added

Figure 1: Steps of the TST algorithm

PROOF. The existence of cycles means that some nodes in the multicast tree may receive redundant messages, i.e., some nodes have more than one previous hop. For these nodes, they send "Eliminate messages" and ensure that they have only one previous hop. When all nodes in the multicast tree have only one previous hop, no cycle exists.

Multiple previous hops also indicate that multiple paths may exist between two nodes. Once some previous hops are unnecessary, the paths involving these hops can also be eliminated. Thus Algorithm 3 can eliminate these unnecessary paths, and this completes our proof. □

4.5 Illustration

We use an example to illustrate our TST algorithm. Nodes are distributed in the unit square as shown in Figure 1(a). Solid nodes represent source nodes labeled by "S", or multicast members labeled by "R". The hollow nodes can be chosen as relays. The first step is to build a temporary tree spanning all multicast members. The dashed lines denote virtual connections between two members. Then nodes on the minimal-hop shortest path are engaged as relays between two neighboring members. They form the topology as shown in Figure 1(b). Note that there exists a cycle marked with dotted rectangular box. The last step is to eliminate unnecessary edges as is done in Figure 1(c). Finally we obtain the multicast tree as is shown in Figure 1(d).

5. ANALYSIS ON TREE LENGTH

The previous section describes our Toward Source Tree algorithm. In this and the following three sections, we will discuss its performance in terms of tree length, time complexity, and energy efficiency. In this section, we discuss the length of TST. We first obtain the length of temporary tree, assuming uniform distribution of nodes and then extending to a general setting. Next we explore the length of minimal-hop shortest path that connects two receivers. Combining the length of temporary tree and the path, we can derive the upper bound for the multicast tree length.

5.1 Temporary Tree in Uniform Distribution

Assuming that all nodes are uniformly distributed, we start by discussing the tree length of the temporary tree.

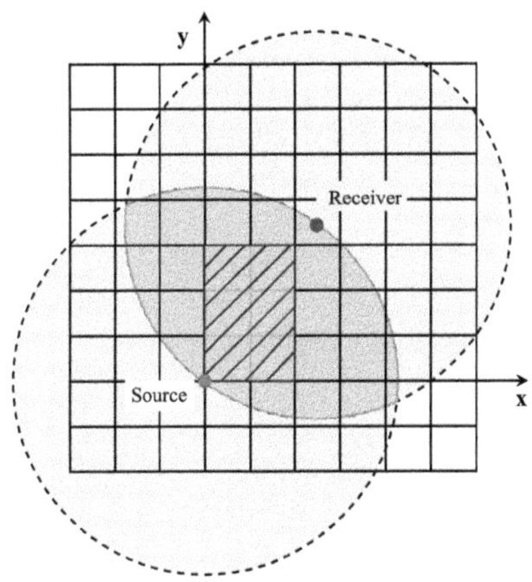

Figure 2: Two-dimensional coordinate system, actual and approximate neighbor regions

Lemma 5.1. *Assume nodes are uniformly distributed in a unit square. The expected length of the temporary tree is upper bounded by* $c\sqrt{m}$*, where* $c = 5.622$.

PROOF. We establish a two-dimensional coordinate system shown in Figure 2. Let the source be the origin, and X-axis as well as Y-axis parallel to the square edge. The whole network is divided into m square cells, and the edge length of each cell is $\frac{1}{\sqrt{m}}$. In the coordinate system, the edge length is normalized to be 1, so intersections in Figure 2 have integer coordinates. In Figure 2, the red node is the source node S and the blue node is the receiver R whose coordinate is (x, y). Without loss of generality, suppose that x and y are both positive. Set the radius to be the Euclidean distance between S and R, and draw two circles with the center in S and in R respectively. The intersected region of the unit square and two circles' overlapping area is the shaded region. According to criteria for neighbor receiver selection, the shaded region is where the possible neighbor receivers of R are located. If no receiver lies in this shaded area, R connects to S directly.

We shrink the possible neighbor region and consider an approximate region marked with parallel lines in Figure 2.

The shrinking region is denoted by N'_R, where

$$N'_R = \{(a,b) | 0 \le a \le \lfloor x \rfloor, 0 \le b \le \lfloor y \rfloor\}. \quad (1)$$

We also rearrange the nodes in each cell. Suppose that the coordinate of a node is (a, b), then we move it to the point with coordinate $(\lfloor a \rfloor, \lfloor b \rfloor)$. All nodes are now further from receiver R after the rearrangement. By shrinking the possible neighbor region and rearranging the nodes, we can derive the upper bound of the temporary tree length.

Let M_R denote the set of all receivers. We use the coordinate of the point farthest from origin in a cell as the coordinate of this cell, and let $p_{i,j}$ be the probability that the node in the cell (i,j) is chosen by the receiver R as a neighbor to connect to. Let p_S be the probability that the receiver directly connects to the source. Assume that the nodes in cell (i,j) is chosen if all cells (i',j') are empty, where $i \le i' \le \lfloor x \rfloor$ and $j \le j' \le \lfloor y \rfloor$. This assumption makes the edge length estimation larger than the actual edge length. We have

$$p_{i,j} \le \left(1 - \frac{(\lfloor x \rfloor + 1 - i)(\lfloor y \rfloor + 1 - j) - 1}{m}\right)^{m-1} - \left(1 - \frac{(\lfloor x \rfloor + 1 - i)(\lfloor y \rfloor + 1 - j)}{m}\right)^{m-1}, \quad (2)$$

$$p_S \le (1 - \frac{\lfloor x \rfloor \lfloor y \rfloor}{m})^{m-1}. \quad (3)$$

The expected length of temporary tree is:

$$E(L_V) \le \frac{1}{\sqrt{m}} \sum_{R \in M_R} E(\sum_{i=1}^{\lfloor x \rfloor} \sum_{j=1}^{\lfloor y \rfloor} p_{i,j} \sqrt{(x-i+1)^2 + (y-j+1)^2} + p_S \sqrt{x^2+y^2}). \quad (4)$$

Combining (2), (3) and (4), we can derive the upper bound of tree length with some integration and summation methods, and finally obtain $E(L_V) \le 5.622\sqrt{m}$. □

5.2 Temporary Tree in General Distribution

We further study the case that nodes are non-uniformly distributed. We partition the unit square into k small squares, where $m = k^{1+\gamma}$ and $0 < \gamma < 1$. Lemma 5.2 can be applied to estimate the intra-square connection, and we study the inter-square connection in Lemma 5.3. With both inter- and intra- square edge estimation, we derive upper bound for temporary tree length in general distribution.

Lemma 5.2. *Let m nodes be independently distributed in a unit square with a density function $f(\mathbf{x})$. The source S is located outside the square. Let each node connect to the closest neighbor that has shorter Euclidean distance to S than the node itself. If no such receiver exists, it does not connect to other nodes. A tree can be constructed among m nodes, and the expected length of such a tree is upper bounded by $c\sqrt{m}$, where $c = 5.622$.*

PROOF. We denote the tree generated in the way described in this lemma as T. There is a difference of this lemma from Lemma 5.1, since the source S is located outside the square as is shown in Figure 3(a). Point S' is the closest point to S among all nodes in the network. With S' as the source, a temporary tree as mentioned in TST algorithm can be established spanning all nodes in the network. We denote the temporary tree as T'. In the following,

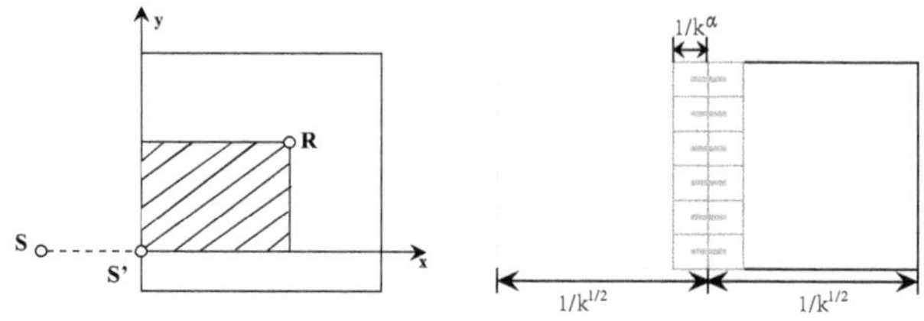

(a) Approximate neighbor region when the source is located outside the square

(b) Inter-square edges between nodes in adjacent square cells

Figure 3: Intra- and inter-square edges

we demonstrate that the tree length of T' can be used to estimate the upper bound of tree length of T.

For a node R, we use N_R to denote the regions where nodes might be selected by R as a its neighbor. We use a rectangular region as approximate neighbor region N'_R, and $N'_R \subseteq N_R$. The approximate neighbor region is the region marked with parallel lines in Figure 3(a). We use the method adopted in the proof of Lemma 5.1 to obtain the length of the temporary tree T'.

We can observe that the approximate neighbor regions are the same in both cases that we take S as the source and that we take S' as the source. There are some details that need to be clarified. Firstly, when we only consider the nodes in approximate neighbor region, the estimated tree length is larger than actual length, because we ignore the nodes that are closer to node R in accurate neighbor region. Secondly, if neighbors exist in the approximate region, the estimations of edge length are the same for both T and T'. Thirdly, if no neighbor is found in approximate region for a node, we assume that it doesn't connect to others in T but it connects to the source in T' in our calculation. From the analysis above, we can conclude that length of T is upper bounded by the length of T'.

Also recall that in our proof of Lemma 5.1, and $5.622\sqrt{m}$ is the upper bound for the length of temporary tree wherever S' is. In summary, we can directly use estimated tree length in Lemma 5.1 as the upper bound of the tree length of T. This completes our proof. □

Lemma 5.3. *Let m nodes be independently distributed in a unit square with density function $f(\mathbf{x})$. The unit square $[0,1] \times [0,1]$ can be partitioned into k square cells with edge length of $\frac{1}{\sqrt{k}}$, where $m = k^{1+\gamma}$ and $0 < \gamma < 1$. The expected minimal distance between two nodes in adjacent cells is in the order of $o\left(\frac{1}{\sqrt{k}}\right)$.*

PROOF. We partition the cells with edge length of $\frac{1}{\sqrt{k}}$ into smaller grids with edge length of $\frac{1}{k^\alpha}$, where $\alpha > \frac{1}{2}$. Then we look for a pair of nodes located in adjacent grids of the adjacent cells, as is shown by green lines in Figure 3(b). Denote P as the probability that one pair of such nodes exists, and we have

$$P = 1 - \left(1 - \left(1 - \left(1 - \frac{1}{k^{2\alpha-1}}\right)^{\frac{me_1}{k}}\right)^2\right)^{k^{\alpha-1/2}}. \quad (5)$$

when $\alpha < \gamma + \frac{1}{2}$, we have

$$P \sim 1 - \exp(-2\epsilon_1 k^{1/2-\alpha+\gamma} - \frac{\epsilon_1}{\log 2} k^{1/2-\alpha}). \quad (6)$$

Furthermore, we can show that

$$P^k \to 1. \quad (7)$$

Hence the probability that k pairs of nodes exist at the same time in adjacent grids of k adjacent cells converges to 1. We conclude that the expectation of minimal distance between two nodes in adjacent cells is in an order of $o\left(\frac{1}{\sqrt{k}}\right)$. The minimal total length of inter-square edges connecting k cells is $o(\sqrt{k})$, and is therefore $o(\sqrt{m})$. □

With both inter- and intra-square edges, we derive upper bound for the length of temporary tree in general distributions in the following lemma.

Lemma 5.4. *Let m nodes be independently distributed with a density function $f(\mathbf{x})$. The expectation for the total length of temporary tree is $E[L_V] \leq c\sqrt{m} \int_{\mathbf{x}\in[0,1]^2} \sqrt{f(\mathbf{x})}d\mathbf{x}$, where $c \approx 5.622$.*

PROOF. We partition the unit square into k small squares with edge length of $\frac{1}{\sqrt{k}}$. We estimate the temporary tree length in the case of non-uniform distribution by considering two types of edges between nodes. One is intra-square edge, i.e., a node chooses to connect to another node located in the same square. The other is inter-square edge, i.e., a node connects to another one located in a different square.

We first consider the intra-square edges. We use a modified neighbor selection criteria to build a tree among nodes in the same small squares: a node connects to the nearest one that is closer to source and in the same square. Considering that the source is located outside the square, Lemma 5.2 can be used to derive the upper bound of the length of intra-square edges: $\frac{c}{\sqrt{k}}\sqrt{m\int_{Sq_i} f(x)dx}$, where Sq_i is a small square region in the set of k regions $\{Sq_1, \cdots, Sq_k\}$.

When modified neighbor selection criteria is applied, more constraints are added to neighbor selection. Therefore, the distance between a node and its selected neighbor may increase. Temporary tree length should be no larger than the sum of intra-square edge length and inter-square edge length. The length of intra-square edges within k squares is

$$\sum_{i=1}^{k} c\frac{1}{\sqrt{k}}\sqrt{m\int_{Sq_i} f(\mathbf{x})d\mathbf{x}}. \quad (8)$$

By Riemann-Stiejies integration, we have

$$\sum_{i=1}^{k} c\frac{1}{\sqrt{k}}\sqrt{m\int_{Sq_i} f(\mathbf{x})d\mathbf{x}} \leq c\sqrt{m}\int_{\mathbf{x}\in[0,1]^2}\sqrt{f(\mathbf{x})}d\mathbf{x}. \quad (9)$$

The length of inter-square edges is $o(\sqrt{m})$ according to Lemma 5.3, and it can be ignored compared with intra-square edge length. Therefore, the temporary tree length is upper bounded by $c\sqrt{m}\int_{\mathbf{x}\in[0,1]^2}\sqrt{f(\mathbf{x})}d\mathbf{x}$. □

5.3 Path with Minimal Hops

Members are connected by the minimal-hop shortest path. In this part, we study the relationship between the path length and the Euclidean distance between two nodes.

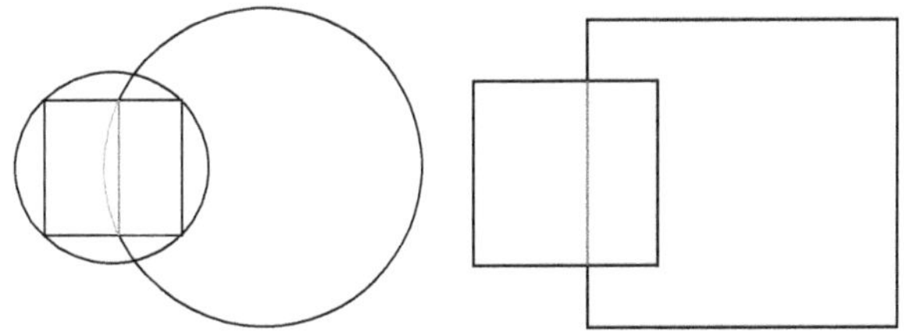

(a) 2-norm (b) infinite-norm

Figure 4: We estimate the probability of points on the red segment instead of green arc

Lemma 5.5. *Let n nodes be independently and identically distributed over $[0,1] \times [0,1]$ with a distribution function $f(\mathbf{x})$. Suppose that the Euclidean distance between two nodes u and v is x. The following properties hold:*

1. *The expected number of fewest relays that are needed to connect u and v converges to $\frac{x}{r}$ as n approaches ∞;*
2. *The expected length of the path connecting uv and involving the fewest relays converges to x.*

PROOF. We set the transmission range as $r = \sqrt{\frac{2}{\epsilon_1}}\sqrt{\frac{\log n}{n}}$. The left circle in Figure 4(a) shows the transmission range of u. The circumscribed square is embedded properly in this left circle. The right circle with center in v has a radius of x. The intersection of the square and the right circle is marked as the green arc. For simplicity, we consider the red segment rather than the green arc in the following analysis to estimate number of relays, and this will overestimate the hop count. Then we can use ∞-norm in Figure 4(b) for estimation instead of the 2−norm.

Let A be the event that the next relay exists with distance s from u, and let B be the event that there is a node within its transmission region. We have

$$P(A|B) = \frac{e^{-2n\epsilon_1 r^2}}{1 - e^{-2n\epsilon_1 r^2}}(e^{2n\epsilon_1 sr} - 1). \quad (10)$$

Denote $E_r(x)$ as the expected number of relay nodes on the path with the minimal hops between u and v. Here we consider that the square with side length r in the ∞-norm is contained in a circle with diameter $\sqrt{2}r$ in the 2−norm. We have the following functional equation when plugging in $r = \epsilon_1^{-1/2}\sqrt{\frac{\log n}{n}}$:

$$\begin{aligned} E_r(x) &= \int_0^r (1 + E_r(x-s))\frac{2n\epsilon_1 r e^{-2n\epsilon_1 r^2}}{1 - e^{-2n\epsilon_1 r^2}} e^{2n\epsilon_1 sr} ds \\ &= 1 + \frac{2\log n}{n^2 - 1}\int_0^1 E_r(x - \alpha r)n^{2\alpha}d\alpha. \end{aligned} \quad (11)$$

Clearly, the lower bound of $E_r(x)$ is x/r. As for the upper bound of hop count, we can prove that for a fixed $d > 1$, $E_r(x) \leq d(x/r)+1$ by induction. $E_r(x) = 1$ when $x \in (0, r)$. Suppose that $E_r(x - \alpha r) \leq d\frac{x-\alpha r}{r} + 1$, then we can prove

$$\begin{aligned} E_r(x) &\leq 2 + \frac{2\log n}{n^2 - 1}\int_0^1 d\frac{x - \alpha r}{r} n^{2\alpha} d\alpha \\ &= 2 + d\frac{x}{r} - d\frac{n^2}{n^2 - 1} + \frac{d}{2\log n} \leq d(x/r) + 1. \end{aligned} \quad (12)$$

The last inequality in (12) holds for

$$d \geq \frac{2\log n(n^2-1)}{n^2(2\log n - 1)+1}. \tag{13}$$

From (12) and (13), $E_r(x)$ converges to x/r as n approaches ∞, so the first property holds. Since the transmission range is r, path length approaches x. Hence the second property also holds. □

5.4 Length of Multicast Tree

Based on the lengths of temporary tree and minimum-hop shortest path, now we derive the length of multicast tree constructed by TST algorithm in the following theorem.

Theorem 5.1. *Let n nodes be independently and identically distributed in a unit square with density function $f(\mathbf{x})$. The expected length of Toward Source Tree spanning m receivers randomly chosen from n nodes is upper bounded by $c\sqrt{m}\int_{\mathbf{x}\in[0,1]^2}\sqrt{f(\mathbf{x})}d\mathbf{x}$, where $c = 5.622$.*

PROOF. Denote $e_{i,j}$ as the edge connecting receivers i and j in the temporary tree T_V, and denote $l_{i,j}$ as the length of the minimal-hop shortest path between these two receivers. Since redundant links are eliminated, it holds that

$$E(L_M) \leq \sum_{e_{i,j}\in T_V} E(l_{i,j}). \tag{14}$$

The path length converges to the Euclidean distance as network size approaches ∞ according to Lemma 5.5. Therefore we have:

$$E(L_M) \leq c\sqrt{m}\int_{\mathbf{x}\in[0,1]^2}\sqrt{f(\mathbf{x})}d\mathbf{x}. \tag{15}$$

This completes our proof. □

Remark: We derive an upper bound for the Toward Source Tree, but it is not a tight bound. In Section 8, we will show that TST algorithm has even better empirical performance than our theoretical bound. Let l_{MST} and l_{ST} denote the lengths of the minimum spanning tree and the Steiner tree connecting m receivers respectively. Steele proved that when m nodes are independently distributed in a unit square with density function $f(\mathbf{x})$, then $l_{MST} = c_1\sqrt{m}\int_{[0,1]^2}\sqrt{f(\mathbf{x})}d\mathbf{x}$ where c_1 is a constant [17]. Roberts estimates that $c_1 = 0.656$ [18]. Du *et al.* proved that $l_{ST} \geq \frac{\sqrt{3}}{2}l_{MST}$ [19]. Therefore the lower bound of Steiner tree length is

$$L_{ST} \geq \frac{\sqrt{3}}{2}c_1\int_{[0,1]^2}\sqrt{f(\mathbf{x})}d\mathbf{x}. \tag{16}$$

The length of Toward Source Tree with m receivers is in the same order as that of Steiner tree, and thus the difference between them is only a constant ratio less than 10.

6. ANALYSIS ON TIME COMPLEXITY

Wireless sensor networks have dynamic topology since some sensors run out of energy while new ones are added to the network. To enable information to arrive at destinations in a short time, we expect the algorithm for multicast tree construction to be at small time costs. In this section, we derive the time complexity of TST.

Theorem 6.1. *Let n nodes be independently and identically distributed in a unit square. The running time of TST algorithm has an upper bound of $O(\sqrt{n\log n})$ and a lower bound of $O\left(\sqrt{\frac{n}{\log n}}\right)$.*

PROOF. There are three serial phases in TST algorithm, so we discuss the time cost of each phase one by one. In Phase 1, the messages containing location information of the source are broadcast in the network. The furthest distance between the source and another node is $O(1)$, so $O\left(\frac{1}{r}\right)$ relays are needed for a message to reach one node. In expectation, there are $\pi r^2\epsilon_2 n = O\left(nr^2\right)$ nodes within transmission range of a node and hence a node has to wait for $O\left(nr^2\right)$ time slots to transmit a message at most. The time cost in Phase 1 is

$$O\left(\frac{1}{r}\right) \leq E(t_1) \leq O(nr). \tag{17}$$

In Phase 2, the dominant time cost comes from searching for neighboring receivers. In the kth search session, the coverage range is $2^k r$. We need $O\left(2^k\right)$ relays to forward *request messages* from one receiver to any other nodes within its search coverage range. Since the coverage range does not exceed $\sqrt{2}$, the number of search sessions cannot be more than $\left\lceil\log_2\frac{\sqrt{2}}{r}\right\rceil$.

$$E(t_2) \leq O\left(\sum_{k=0}^{\left\lceil\log_2\frac{\sqrt{2}}{r}\right\rceil} 2^k nr^2\right) \leq O(nr). \tag{18}$$

In Phase 3, the worst case is that relays on the path whose length is $O(1)$ form cycles. Time for cycle elimination is

$$E(t_3) = O\left(\frac{1}{r}nr^2\right) = O(nr). \tag{19}$$

Given that $E(t) = \sum_{i=1}^{i=3} E(t_i)$ and $r = O\left(\sqrt{\frac{\log n}{n}}\right)$, the total running time is

$$O\left(\sqrt{\frac{n}{\log n}}\right) \leq E(t) \leq O(\sqrt{n\log n}). \tag{20}$$

This completes our proof. □

Remark: For any algorithm to construct a multicast tree among a group of nodes, broadcast in Phase 1 is necessary. Since no node has a knowledge of the multicast group except the source, such information has to be forwarded to every node in the network so that they can know whether they should participate in multicasting. The lower bound of time for multicast tree construction is $O\left(\sqrt{\frac{n}{\log n}}\right)$. Since TST achieves the time complexity upper bounded by $O(\sqrt{n\log n})$, the minimal time cost to construct a multicast tree is also upper bounded by $O(\sqrt{n\log n})$. Hence the time complexity of TST algorithm shares the same upper and lower bounds as the minimal time cost, and the ratio between these two bounds is only $O(\log n)$.

The length of multicast trees have a great influence on communication quality in terms of transmission delay and wireless interference. Construction of minimum-length trees is an NP-hard problem, and takes exponential time. Approximate algorithms achieve larger tree length with lower time complexity. Now we explore the relationship between tree length and time complexity in Figure 5. Since the lower bound of time needed for multicast tree construction

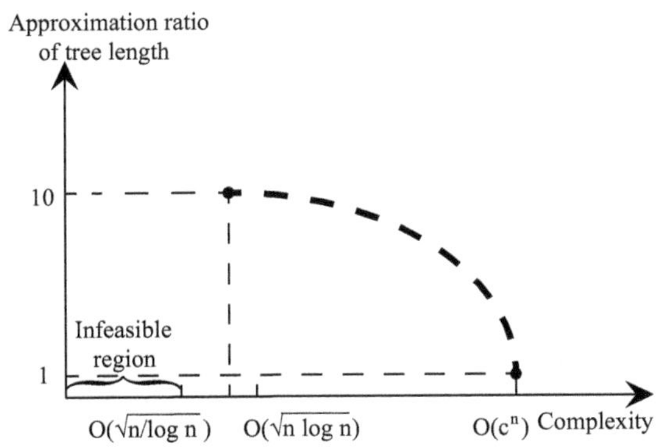

Figure 5: Relationship between tree length and time complexity

is $O\left(\sqrt{\frac{n}{\log n}}\right)$, the region with time complexity smaller than $O\left(\sqrt{\frac{n}{\log n}}\right)$ is infeasible. Accurate solution to Steiner tree problem achieves the approximation ratio of 1 at the cost of exponential time, and our algorithm achieves the ratio of 10. The approximation ratio of other algorithms like those in Table 1 approaches 1 but they have larger time costs.

7. ANALYSIS ON ENERGY EFFICIENCY

Energy is a primary consideration in wireless sensor networks, since sensors are battery-powered and their energy is limited. There are two main types of energy consumption: 1) the energy consumed to construct such multicast trees; and 2) the energy needed to send messages along the tree constructed by this algorithm. When a large amount of information is transmitted, the latter type is the dominant part in energy consumption. Therefore in this section, we focus on the energy consumed in message forwarding along the constructed tree.

Since the transmission range is fixed, the number of forwarding nodes in the tree determines the energy consumption for information propagation. We evaluate the number of forwarding nodes in Theorem 7.1.

Theorem 7.1. *Let n nodes be independently and identically distributed in the unit square. The number of forwarding nodes in the multicast tree is*

$$N_{TST} = \begin{cases} \Theta\left(\sqrt{\frac{mn}{\log n}}\right), & m = O\left(\frac{n}{\log n}\right); \\ \Theta(m), & m = \omega\left(\frac{n}{\log n}\right). \end{cases} \tag{21}$$

When $m = O(n/\log n)$, the number of forwarding nodes in TST algorithm is order-optimal.

Proof. Let T_V be the temporary tree, and $e_{i,j}$ be an edge in the temporary tree connecting two receivers i and j, and $d_{i,j}$ be the Euclidean distance between them. When m is small, relay nodes are the dominant part of the forwarding nodes in our multicast tree. The total number of transmitting nodes is $N_{TST} = \Theta\left(\sum_{e_{i,j}\in T_V} \frac{d_{ij}}{r}\right) = \Theta\left(\frac{\sqrt{m}}{r}\right)$. As m grows larger, receivers are closer to each other and thus fewer relay nodes are added. Therefore, receivers are the dominant part of all nodes in the multicast tree, so $N_{TST} = \Theta(m)$. The critical value of m to distinguish the two cases satisfies $\Theta\left(\frac{\sqrt{m_c}}{r}\right) = \Theta(m_c)$, so $m_c = \Theta\left(\frac{n}{\log n}\right)$.

Denote N_{min} as the minimal number of nodes that are engaged in message propagation. The upper bound of N_{min} is given assuming that nodes are uniformly distributed [2]. We use its technique and obtain N_{min} in general distribution,

$$N_{min} = \begin{cases} \Theta\left(\sqrt{\frac{mn}{\log n}}\right), & m = O\left(\frac{n}{\log n}\right); \\ \Omega\left(\frac{n}{\log n}\right), & m = \omega\left(\frac{n}{\log n}\right). \end{cases} \tag{22}$$

As we can see, when $m = O\left(\frac{n}{\log n}\right)$, the number of forwarding nodes in TST algorithm is optimal in the order sense. □

Remark: When $m = \omega\left(\frac{n}{\log n}\right)$, energy consumption of TST algorithm may not be order-optimal. However, to achieve the minimal energy consumption, we have to find the minimum connected dominating set of a given graph, which is proven to be NP-complete [20] and requires global information of network topology. Therefore, we regard it as an acceptable cost of energy to achieve the feasibility and time-efficiency in practice.

8. PERFORMANCE EVALUATION

We perform extensive simulations to evaluate the empirical performance of Toward Source Tree algorithm in terms of the multicast tree length and energy consumption. We consider two common distribution patterns in this part: uniform distribution and normal distribution.

8.1 Uniform Distribution

We first consider nodes are uniformly distributed in a unit square and transmission range is set to be $r = \sqrt{\frac{\log n}{n}}$. We explore the effect of multicast group size m on the tree length. Assuming that the network size is fixed as 1000, we obtain the lengths of the Stenier tree and TST when the value of m varies. The length of the Steiner tree can be obtained via NewBossa in [21]. Two curves in Figure 6(a) describe the relationship between multicast group size and the lengths of the Toward Source Tree as well as the Steiner Tree. It is shown that the length of TST is larger than that of the Steiner Tree but quite close to it. We change the network size in the range [200, 2200] and change the multicast group size accordingly, and run extensive simulations. According to the statistics, the ratio of the tree length achieved by the two algorithms is 1.114 on average. When nodes are uniformly distributed, Toward Source Tree is a good approximation of the Steiner Tree.

Next we evaluate energy consumption by considering the number of forwarding nodes engaged in multicasting. To derive the statistical properties of TST, we set the network size as 100,000. In Figure 6(c), when the multicast group is small, the first part of the curve indicates that the number of forwarding nodes is $O(\sqrt{m})$. As there are more multicast group members, the number of forwarding nodes grows linearly with the group size.

8.2 Non-uniform Distribution

For the case of non-uniform distribution, we first choose the source location $\mathbf{x_s}$ randomly in the unit square. Then we consider that other nodes satisfy the normal distribution:

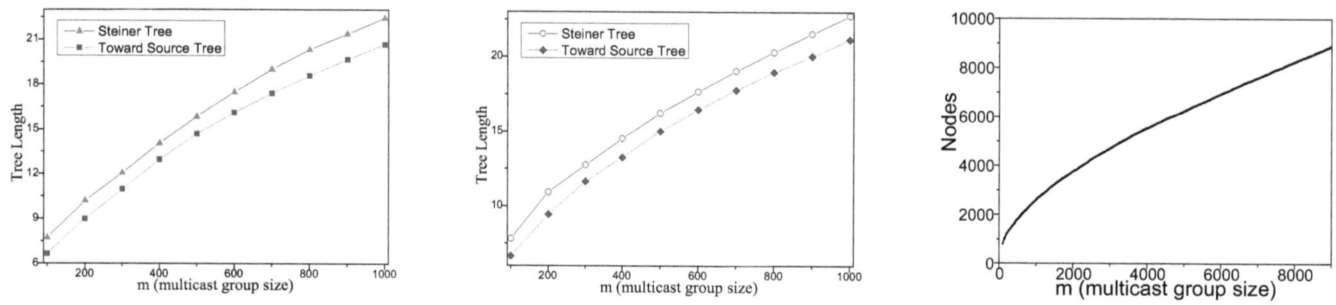

(a) Tree length in uniform distribution (b) Tree length in normal distribution (c) Number of forwarding nodes

Figure 6: Algorithm evaluation when nodes are uniformly distributed

$f(\mathbf{x}) = \frac{1}{\sqrt{2\pi}} e^{-\frac{\|\mathbf{x}-\mathbf{x_s}\|^2}{2}}$, where $\|\mathbf{x} - \mathbf{x_s}\|$ is the Euclidean distance between the node and the source.

In normal distribution, the length of Toward Source Tree is only a little larger than the optimal length as is shown in Figure 6(b), when the network size is 1000. When the network size and multicast group size change, a large amount of statistics show that the ratio between them is 1.110 on average. Similar to the case of uniform distribution, the number of forwarding nodes in the multicast tree is also linear with $\sqrt{m}$, and becomes linear with m as m increases and the network size keeps unchanged.

9. CONCLUSION

In this paper, we propose a novel algorithm, which we call Toward Source Tree, to generate approximate Steiner Trees in wireless sensor networks. The TST algorithm is a simple and distributed scheme for constructing low-cost and energy-efficient multicast trees in the wireless sensor network setting. We prove its performance measures in terms of tree length, time complexity and energy efficiency. We show that the tree length is in the same order as, and is in practice very close to, the Steiner tree. We prove its running time is the shortest among all existing solutions. We prove that the number of nodes that participate in forwarding is order-optimal, yielding high energy efficiency for applications.

10. ACKNOWLEDGEMENT

This work is supported by NSF China (No.61325012, 61271219, 61221001, 61428205); China Ministry of Education Doctor Program(No.20130073110025); Shanghai Basic Research Key Project (12JC1405200, 11JC1405100); Shanghai International Cooperation Project (No.13510711300).

11. REFERENCES

[1] M Segal J row ro t and evin m roved tru ture or data olle tion in wirele en or network n *Proc. of IEEE INFOCOM* age 1375–1383 2014

[2] H R Sadjad our Z Wang and J J Gar ia una A eve A uni ing er e tive on the a a it o wirele ad ho network n *Proc. of IEEE INFOCOM* 2008

[3] X Y i Multi a t a a it o wirele ad ho network *IEEE/ACM Trans. Netw.* 17(3): 50– 61 200

[4] X iu S Shakkottai and R Srikant The multi a t a a it o large multiho wirele network *IEEE/ACM Trans. Netw.* 18(6):16 1–1770 2010

[5] U ar hne Multi a t over wirele network *Communications of ACM* 45(12):31–37 2002

[6] P M Ruiz J A San hez and Stojmenovi Gmr: Geogra hi multi a t routing or wirele en or network n *Proc. of IEEE SECON* age 20–2 2006

[7] J A San hez and P M Ruiz ema: o alized energ effi ient multi a t algorithm a ed on geogra hi routing n *Proc. of 31st IEEE Conference on Local Computer Networks* age 3–12 2006

[8] M Barto z B Mu zni ki and P Zwierz kow ki Dijk tra a ed lo alized multi a t routing in wirele en or network n *Proc. of IEEE CSNDSP* age 1–6 2012

[ ] G Mora ito Gallu io and S Palazzo Geogra hi multi a t (gem) or den e wirele network : roto ol de ign and er orman e anal i *IEEE/ACM Trans. Netw.* 21(4):1332–1346 2013

[10] T Rothvo J B rka F Grandoni and Sanità Steiner tree a roximation via iterative randomized rounding *Journal of the ACM* 60(1):6 2013

[11] R M Kar *Reducibility among Combinatorial Problems* S ringer 1 72

[12] F Bauer and A arma Di tri uted algorithm or multi a t ath etu in data network *IEEE/ACM Trans. Netw.* 4(2):181–1 1 1 6

[13] G o Re Gatani and S Gaglio An effi ient di tri uted algorithm or generating multi a t di tri ution tree n *Proc. of IEEE ICPP Workshops* age 477–484 2005

[14] M A Drummond M Santo and E U hoa Di tri uted dual a ent algorithm or teiner ro lem in network n *Anais do Simpósio Brasileiro de Redes de Computadores* age 381–3 6 2007

[15] et al H Park J ee Di tri uted multi a t roto ol a ed on ea onle routing or wirele en or network n *Proc. of IEEE ICCE* age 522–523 2013

[16] M D Penro e A trong law or the longe t edge o the minimal anning tree *The Annals of Probability* 27(1):246–26 1

[17] J M Steele Growth rate o eu lidean minimal anning tree with ower weighted edge *The Annals of Probability* 16(4):1767–1787 1 88

[18] F D K Ro ert Random minimal tree *Biometrika* 55(1):255–258 1 68

[1] F Hwang D Du A roo o the gil ert ollak onje ture on the teiner ratio *Algorithmica* 7(1):121–135 1 2

[20] R G Mi hael and S J David *Computers and Intractability: A Guide to the Theory of NP-completeness* W H Freeman 1 78

[21] De t o S at Prin eton Bo a `http://www.cs.princeton.edu/~rwerneck/bossa/` Jul 2014

Virtually Moving Base Stations for Energy Efficiency in Wireless Sensor Networks

Runwei Zhang
I&C, EPFL
Lausanne, Switzerland
runwei.zhang@epfl.ch

Patrick Thiran
I&C, EPFL
Lausanne, Switzerland
patrick.thiran@epfl.ch

Martin Vetterli
I&C, EPFL
Lausanne, Switzerland
martin.vetterli@epfl.ch

ABSTRACT

Energy efficiency of wireless sensor networks (WSNs) can be improved by moving base stations (BSs), as this scheme evenly distributes the communication load in the network. However, physically moving the BSs is complicated and costly. In this paper, we propose a new scheme: *virtually moving the BSs*. We deploy an excessive number of BSs and adaptively re-select a subset of active BSs so as to emulate the physical movement. Beyond achieving high energy-efficiency, this scheme obviates the difficulties associated with physically moving the BSs.

The challenges are (i) that the energy efficiency of BSs should be considered as well, in addition to that of the sensor nodes and (ii) that the number of candidate subset of active BSs is exponential with the number of BSs. We show that scheduling the virtual movement of BSs is NP-hard. Then, we propose a polynomial-time algorithm that is guaranteed under mild conditions to achieve a lifetime longer than 62% of the optimal one. In practice, as verified through extensive numerical simulations, the lifetime achieved by the proposed algorithm is always very close to the optimum.

Categories and Subject Descriptors

C.2.1 [**Network Architecture and Design**]: Wireless communication, Distributed networks; C.2.2 [**Network Protocols**]: Routing protocols

General Terms

Theory

Keywords

Wireless sensor networks, moving base stations, energy efficiency, load balancing

1. INTRODUCTION

Energy efficiency is a key issue in wireless sensor networks (WSNs), because the batteries of sensor nodes have limited capacity. Specifically-designed routing protocols [21, 7, 1] can, to some extent, improve the energy efficiency of the WSN. Yet, they can do little for the *energy-hole* problem: sensor nodes close to the base stations (BSs)[1] forward much more data and drain their batteries much faster than other sensor nodes. The uneven distribution of the energy consumption is a culprit for the poor energy efficiency.

Moving BSs [13, 18, 9, 3, 14] addresses the energy-hole problem, as it increases the degree of freedom for evenly distributing the energy consumption in the WSN. Properly scheduled movements of BSs can greatly improve the energy efficiency of the WSN. However, all existing approaches exploiting BS mobility have a major drawback: they make BSs physically move, which requires BSs to have additional implements for mobility. As a result, practical implementations of these approaches are complicated and costly.

Can we reap the benefits of moving BSs, while avoiding the hassles of the physical movement? We give an affirmative answer by proposing a new scheme: *virtually moving the BSs*. To emulate the physical movement, we deploy an excessive number of BSs in the sensing field and continue re-selecting a subset of active BSs. Active BSs turn on long-range communication and forward data to the remote server; and passive BSs turn off the long-range communication and perform like sensor nodes. Simply by switching on and off the long-range communication, we balance the energy-consumption load of all sensor nodes and all BSs. In this scheme, BSs are also deployed in the sensing field and are supplied with limited available energy. Therefore, keeping all deployed BSs always active is not energy efficient and we have to optimize both the energy efficiency of BSs and that of sensor nodes. We term this joint optimization problem a *virtually-moving BSs problem*. This problem is much more complicated than the traditional maximum lifetime routing problem (e.g., [7]), because active BSs consume a large and fixed amount of energy for using long-range communications. Based on our measurement through a digital oscilloscope, a typical GSM/GPRS module on BSs has to be activated for around 35 seconds just to start and close each long-range communication connection. In the meantime, depending on the sensor sampling rate of the WSN, it only takes a few seconds for actually transmitting the sensing samples. Therefore, BSs can consume energy an order of magnitude more on the fixed energy-consumption than on actually transmitting the sensing samples. This fixed energy-consumption

[1]BSs are the devices that forward data from all sensor nodes across the WSN to a remote server through long-range communication, *e.g.*, GSM/GPRS, EDGE, 3GPP or LTE.

MobiHoc'15, June 22–25, 2015, Hangzhou, China.
Copyright © 2015 ACM 978-1-4503-3489-1/15/06 ...$15.00.
http://dx.doi.org/10.1145/2746285.2746291.

of BSs makes the virtually-moving problem NP-hard, as we will present a reduction from the 3-SAT [6].

The virtually-moving BSs problem cannot be solved using the traditional Garg-Konemann typed algorithms [10], as these algorithms only deal with linear packing problems. We propose a novel scheme that transform the problem into a sequence of *uncapacitated facility-location* (UFL) problems [12] by using the constrained gradient method [8]. Under very mild conditions, the obtained UFL problems have approximate solutions with an approximation ratio of 1.61 [12]. By adaptively solving the sequence of UFL problems, our proposed algorithm yields a lifetime at least 62% of the optimum. The proposed algorithm is adaptive, has low computational complexity and requires easily available information as input. It is therefore a perfect fit for the WSN paradigm.

Through extensive simulations, we show that virtually moving multiple BSs is more energy efficient compared to other existing schemes for organizing WSNs. We also show that the achieved lifetime of the proposed scheduling algorithm is always close to the optimum.

The main contributions of this paper are as follows:

1. We propose a new scheme for organizing WSNs which virtually moves the BSs. This scheme not only achieves high energy-efficiency, but it also circumvents the challenges of physically moving BSs. The idea of load balancing by virtually moving devices can be used in other networked systems, including super-node selection in peer-to-peer networks and cooperative beamforming in cellular networks.

2. We show that the scheduling problem of virtually moving BSs is NP-hard, and we propose an adaptive algorithm to solve it. The proposed algorithm is computationally light, only requires easily available information as input and guarantees, under mild conditions, to yield a lifetime that is at least 62% of the optimal one. Due to the general formulation, the proposed scheduling algorithm has merits beyond the WSNs.

The outline of this paper is as follows. First, we review the related works in Section 2. Then, we show the system model in Section 3 and formally formulate the scheduling problem of virtually moving BSs in Section 4. Next, we analyze the complexity of the scheduling problem in Section 5 and propose the adaptive algorithm in Section 6. Finally, we show simulation results in Section 7 and conclude in Section 8.

2. RELATED WORK

Energy efficiency is a key issue in the design of WSNs. Since the emergence of WSNs, researchers have proposed many schemes to enhance the energy efficiency of WSNs.

A traditional WSN has a single BS and a number of sensor nodes deployed around the BS. At the very beginning, researchers have proposed to optimize the multi-hop routing of the short-range communication of sensor nodes [21, 7, 1]. These schemes, to some extent, improve the energy efficiency of the WSN. Yet, they can do little for the energy-hole problem: sensor nodes near the single BS deplete their batteries much faster than other sensor nodes. The uneven distribution of the energy consumption greatly undermines the energy efficiency of the network.

To mitigate the energy-hole problem, researchers propose to deploy multiple BSs [5, 11, 17]: Instead of using one single BS, they set up multiple BSs and let sensor nodes around all BSs share the high communication load. By optimizing the positions of the multiple BSs, the energy-consumption load is more evenly balanced, resulting in a higher energy efficiency.

To completely solve the energy-hole problem, researchers propose to physically move BSs [13, 4, 15, 9, 16, 2, 14]. These schemes have high energy-efficiency because they increase the degree of freedom for evenly distributing the communication load. However, optimizing the continuous moving trace of BSs is hard. Even in WSNs with one BS, the optimal trace of the BS can only be found when the sensing field has specific geometric shapes, such as, circles [13]. Then, researchers propose to discretize the continuous moving traces of BSs by restricting the positions of BSs to a set of candidate positions. Shi *et al.* [15] show that such a discretization incurs an arbitrarily small loss of precision by constructively selecting the candidate positions. Then, Wang *et al.* [2] discusses the scheduling problem for moving a single BS on a finite set of candidate positions. The recent work of Luo *et al.* [14] discuss the problem of moving a given number of BSs on a finite set of candidate positions. They show that this problem is NP-hard and present an approximation algorithm for scheduling the movements.

Because physically moving the BSs is complicated and costly, we propose a new scheme that virtualizes this movement. It offers two additional differences with physical motion of the BSs (*e.g.*, [2, 14]): (i) In the virtual-movement scheme, the number of active BSs selected at different times can be changed, contrary to the physical-movement scheme, and (ii) in the virtual-movement scheme, BSs are considered to have a finite energy supply like sensor nodes because BSs are also installed in the sensing field; whereas in the physical-movement scheme, BSs are, to the best of our knowledge, always assumed to have an infinite energy supply. In our recent work [19], we discussed virtually moving one active BS and implemented this scheme in a real WSN. In this paper, we consider the more general scheme where multiple BSs are virtually moving.

3. SYSTEM MODEL

We model the WSN as a directed graph whose vertices are a set of BSs V_b, a set of sensor nodes V_r and a remote server S. The edges in the directed graph consist of (i) short-range communication links among all BSs and sensor nodes $V_b \cup V_r$, and (ii) long-range communication links from BSs V_b to the remote server S. We now introduce the definitions for data communication and energy consumption in the considered WSN. The notations are summarized in Table 1.

3.1 Data Communication

Each sensor node $i \in V_r$ generates data with a constant rate $r \in \mathbb{R}^+$, whereas BSs do not generate data. All data has to be transmitted to active BSs by short-range multi-hop communications. Active BSs forward the collected data to the remote server S via long-range communication. Although active BSs are adaptively changed, sensor nodes are always actively sensing and uploading data to the remote server via active BSs. Let $x_{ij} \in \mathbb{R}_0^+$ be the data rate sent on the short-range communication link from i to j ($i, j \in V_b \cup V_r$). Let $y_i \in \mathbb{R}_0^+$ be the data rate sent on the long-range communication link from BS $i \in V_b$ to the remote server S. Because the rate of data inflow and outflow should

Table 1: Notations

r	data generating rate of each sensor node
x_{ij}	data rate on short-range communication link from i to j
$\boldsymbol{x}$ ($\boldsymbol{x}^{(n)}$)	data rates on all short-range communication links (at time slot n)
y_i	data rate on long-range communication link of BS j
$\boldsymbol{y}$ ($\boldsymbol{y}^{(n)}$)	data rates on long-range communication link of all BSs (at time slot n)
z_i	indicator activity state of BS i
$\boldsymbol{z}$ ($\boldsymbol{z}^{(n)}$)	vector of indicators showing the active states of all BSs (at time slot n)
c_i	energy consumption rate of node i
$\boldsymbol{c}$ ($\boldsymbol{c}^{(n)}$)	energy consumption rates of all sensor nodes and BSs (at time slot n)
$c_{\rm c}$, $c_{\rm st}$, $c_{\rm sr}$, $c_{\rm lc}$, $c_{\rm lt}$	constant parameters for modelling the energy consumption rates
e_i	initially availaible energy of node i
$\boldsymbol{e}$ ($\boldsymbol{e}^{(n)}$)	initially availaible energy of all sensor nodes or BSs (at time slot n)
$\mathcal{L}$	the set of all candidate configurations
$\mathcal{L}^{[k]}$	the set of candidate configurations given that $\boldsymbol{z} = \boldsymbol{z}^{[k]}$, $1 \le k \le 2^{\|V_b\|} - 1$
θ_i	average energy decrease rate of node i
$\boldsymbol{\theta}$ ($\boldsymbol{\theta}^{(n)}$)	average energy decrease rate of all sensor nodes or BSs (at time slot n)
T^*	the optimal lifetime of the virtually-moving BSs problem (5)
τ	length of a time slot
N^*	number of time slots that the WSN can sustain when using Algorithm 1

be balanced both on sensor nodes and on BSs, we have

$$\begin{cases} \sum_{j\in V_b\cup V_r} x_{ij} = \sum_{j\in V_b\cup V_r} x_{ji} + r, \forall i \in V_r, \\ \sum_{j\in V_b\cup V_r} x_{ij} + y_i = \sum_{j\in V_b\cup V_r} x_{ji}, \forall i \in V_b, \\ x_{ij} \ge 0,\ i,j \in V_b \cup V_r, \\ y_i \ge 0,\ i \in V_b. \end{cases} \quad (1)$$

Let z_i ($i \in V_b$) be a binary variable indicating the state of BS i : if BS i is active, $z_i = 1$, and otherwise $z_i = 0$. When BS i is passive, its data rate of long-range communication y_i should be 0. Therefore,

$$y_i \le |V_r| r z_i, \quad (2)$$

where $|V_r|r$ is the total data rate transmitted in the whole WSN. If BS i is active, (2) imposes no constraint on y_i.

3.2 Energy Consumption

We denote the energy consumption rate of either a sensor node or a BS $i \in V_b \cup V_r$ by c_i ($c_i \in \mathbb{R}^+$). (i) On the one hand, for a sensor node,

$$c_i = c_{\rm c} + c_{\rm st} \sum_{j\in V_b\cup V_r} x_{ij} + c_{\rm sr} \sum_{j\in V_b\cup V_r} x_{ji}, \forall i \in V_r, \quad (3)$$

where $c_{\rm c}$ denotes the constant energy consumption rate for sensing and initiating the short-range communication, and $c_{\rm st}$, $c_{\rm sr}$ denote the energy consumption rates for transmitting and receiving unit data via short-range communication, respectively. (ii) On the other hand, for a BS,

$$c_i = c_{\rm c} + c_{\rm st} \sum_{j\in V_b\cup V_r} x_{ij} + c_{\rm sr} \sum_{j\in V_b\cup V_r} x_{ji} + c_{\rm lc} z_i + c_{\rm lt} y_i, \forall i \in V_b, \quad (4)$$

where $c_{\rm lc}$ denotes the fixed energy-consumption rate for initiating and closing long-range communication and $c_{\rm lt}$ denotes the energy consumption rate for actually transmitting unit data via long-range communication.

Let the initially availaible energy of each sensor node or BS i ($i \in V_b \cup V_r$) be denoted by e_i.

For simplicity of discussion, we group $\{x_{ij}\}_{i,j\in V_b\cup V_r}$ into a vector $\boldsymbol{x}$, group $\{y_i\}_{i\in V_b}$ into a vector $\boldsymbol{y}$, group $\{z_i\}_{i\in V_b}$ into a vector $\boldsymbol{z}$, group $\{c_i\}_{i\in V_b\cup V_r}$ into a vector $\boldsymbol{c}$ and group $\{e_i\}_{i\in V_b\cup V_r}$ into a vector $\boldsymbol{e}$.

Notice that the state of a WSN is characterized by the data rates of short-range communication $\boldsymbol{x}$, the data rates of long-range communication $\boldsymbol{y}$, the selection of active BSs $\boldsymbol{z}$ and the energy consumption rates $\boldsymbol{c}$. We call the four-tuple $(\boldsymbol{x}, \boldsymbol{y}, \boldsymbol{z}, \boldsymbol{c})$ a *configuration* of the network.

4. PROBLEM FORMULATIONS

Scheduling the virtual movement of BSs is equivalent to finding a set of configurations and finding the time durations. In this section, we first describe the optimization space for selecting the configurations. Then, we will formally formulate the scheduling problem, namely, the *virtually-moving BSs problem*. At the end of this section, we will show why our proposed scheme is more energy efficient than the previously proposed schemes [5, 11, 17, 2, 19].

4.1 The Optimization Space

We denote the set of all candidate configurations by

$$\mathcal{L} = \{(\boldsymbol{x}, \boldsymbol{y}, \boldsymbol{z}, \boldsymbol{c}) | (1), (2), (3) \text{ and } (4) \text{ hold}\}.$$

Because $\boldsymbol{z}$ is a binary vector taking $2^{|V_b|} - 1$ possible values (there should be at least one active BS, therefore we cannot have $\boldsymbol{z} = \boldsymbol{0}$), we can separate $\mathcal{L}$ into $2^{|V_b|} - 1$ subsets based on different values of $\boldsymbol{z}$. We denote the possible values of $\boldsymbol{z}$ by $\boldsymbol{z}^{[1]}, \boldsymbol{z}^{[2]}, \cdots, \boldsymbol{z}^{[2^{|V_b|}-1]}$ with a non-decreasing order of the number of active BSs. In particular, the first $|V_b|$ elements, $\boldsymbol{z}^{[1]}, \boldsymbol{z}^{[2]}, \cdots \boldsymbol{z}^{[|V_b|]}$ denote the BSs selections where only one BS is active. For any $1 \le k \le 2^{|V_b|} - 1$, we denote by $\mathcal{L}^{[k]}$ the subset of $\mathcal{L}$ satisfying $\boldsymbol{z} = \boldsymbol{z}^{[k]}$:

$$\mathcal{L}^{[k]} = \{(\boldsymbol{x}, \boldsymbol{y}, \boldsymbol{z}^{[k]}, \boldsymbol{c}) | (1), (2), (3), (4) \text{ hold}\},$$

which is a simplex because constraints (1), (2), (3), (4) are linear after fixing $\boldsymbol{z} = \boldsymbol{z}^{[k]}$. Decomposing $\mathcal{L} = \bigcup_{k=1}^{2^{|V_b|}-1} \mathcal{L}^{[k]}$ enables us to simplify the optimization problem, as will be explained in the following.

4.2 The Virtually-moving BSs Problem

Because $\mathcal{L}^{[k]}$ is a simplex for all $1 \le k \le 2^{|V_b|} - 1$, the convex combination of any two configurations in $\mathcal{L}^{[k]}$ is still in $\mathcal{L}^{[k]}$. Let $(\boldsymbol{x}^{[1]}, \boldsymbol{y}^{[1]}, \boldsymbol{z}^{[k]}, \boldsymbol{c}^{[1]}) \in \mathcal{L}^{[k]}$ and $(\boldsymbol{x}^{[2]}, \boldsymbol{y}^{[2]}, \boldsymbol{z}^{[k]}, \boldsymbol{c}^{[2]}) \in \mathcal{L}^{[k]}$ be used for time durations $t^{[1]}$ and $t^{[2]}$. Using these two configurations is equivalent to using their convex combination

$$\left(\frac{t^{[1]}\boldsymbol{x}^{[1]} + t^{[2]}\boldsymbol{x}^{[2]}}{t^{[1]} + t^{[2]}}, \frac{t^{[1]}\boldsymbol{y}^{[1]} + t^{[2]}\boldsymbol{y}^{[2]}}{t^{[1]} + t^{[2]}}, \boldsymbol{z}^{[k]}, \frac{t^{[1]}\boldsymbol{c}^{[1]} + t^{[2]}\boldsymbol{c}^{[2]}}{t^{[1]} + t^{[2]}}\right),$$

which is still in $\mathcal{L}^{[k]}$, for a time duration $t^{[1]} + t^{[2]}$. This further implies that any number of configurations in the same set $\mathcal{L}^{[k]}$ can be substituted by only one configuration—their convex combination.

Therefore, in the virtually-moving BSs problem, we seek at most $2^{|V_b|} - 1$ configurations: for each $1 \le k \le 2^{|V_b|} - 1$, we select a configuration $(\boldsymbol{x}^{[k]}, \boldsymbol{y}^{[k]}, \boldsymbol{z}^{[k]}, \boldsymbol{c}^{[k]}) \in \mathcal{L}^{[k]}$ and a time duration $t^{[k]}$, such that the total lifetime[2] $\sum_{k=1}^{2^{|V_b|}-1} t^{[k]}$ is maximized given the initially availaible energy $\boldsymbol{e}$:

$$\begin{aligned} \max_{\{\boldsymbol{x}^{[k]},\boldsymbol{y}^{[k]},\boldsymbol{z}^{[k]},\boldsymbol{c}^{[k]},t^{[k]}\}_{k=1}^{2^{|V_b|}-1}} \quad & \sum_{k=1}^{2^{|V_b|}-1} t^{[k]} \\ \text{s.t.} \quad & \sum_{k=1}^{2^{|V_b|}-1} t^{[k]}\boldsymbol{c}^{[k]} \le \boldsymbol{e}, \\ & \left(\boldsymbol{x}^{[k]}, \boldsymbol{y}^{[k]}, \boldsymbol{z}^{[k]}, \boldsymbol{c}^{[k]}\right) \in \mathcal{L}^{[k]}, \forall 1 \le k \le 2^{|V_b|} - 1, \\ & t^{[k]} \ge 0, \forall 1 \le k \le 2^{|V_b|} - 1. \end{aligned} \tag{5}$$

We denote the optimal lifetime of (5) by T^*. To differentiate with other schemes that will be mentioned below, we call this scheme *MultiMove*, which schedules the virtual movement of multiple BSs by solving problem (5).

4.3 Comparisons to Other Schemes

In the following, we compare MultiMove with some other existing schemes.

MultiFixed [5, 11, 17]: This scheme selects a subset of BSs to be always active and selects the routes of short-range communications. This boils down to selecting only one configuration $(\boldsymbol{x}, \boldsymbol{y}, \boldsymbol{z}, \boldsymbol{c}) \in \mathcal{L}$, so that the lifetime of the WSN is maximized:

$$\begin{aligned} \max_{\boldsymbol{x},\boldsymbol{y},\boldsymbol{z},\boldsymbol{c},t} \quad & t \\ \text{s.t.} \quad & (\boldsymbol{x}, \boldsymbol{y}, \boldsymbol{z}, \boldsymbol{c}) \in \mathcal{L}, \\ & t\boldsymbol{c} \le \boldsymbol{e}, \end{aligned} \tag{6}$$

where t denotes the lifetime of the network, and $t\boldsymbol{c}$ denotes the total energy consumption that should be no larger than the initially availaible energy $\boldsymbol{e}$.

OneMove [2, 19]: In this scheme, we schedule the virtual movement of one BS on a finite set of candidate locations for maximizing lifetime. This is equivalent to selecting at most $|V_b|$ configurations: for each $1 \le k \le |V_b|$ (in contrast to $1 \le k \le 2^{|V_b|} - 1$ as in the MultiMove scheme), we select one configuration $(\boldsymbol{x}^{[k]}, \boldsymbol{y}^{[k]}, \boldsymbol{z}^{[k]}, \boldsymbol{c}^{[k]}) \in \mathcal{L}^{[k]}$ in each set $\mathcal{L}^{[k]}$ with the time duration $t^{[k]}$, such that the total lifetime $\sum_{k=1}^{|V_b|} t^{[k]}$ is maximized:

$$\begin{aligned} \max_{\{\boldsymbol{x}^{[k]},\boldsymbol{y}^{[k]},\boldsymbol{z}^{[k]},\boldsymbol{c}^{[k]},t^{[k]}\}_{k=1}^{|V_b|}} \quad & \sum_{k=1}^{|V_b|} t^{[k]} \\ \text{s.t.} \quad & \sum_{k=1}^{|V_b|} t^{[k]}\boldsymbol{c}^{[k]} \le \boldsymbol{e}, \\ & \left(\boldsymbol{x}^{[k]}, \boldsymbol{y}^{[k]}, \boldsymbol{z}^{[k]}, \boldsymbol{c}^{[k]}\right) \in \mathcal{L}^{[k]}, \forall 1 \le k \le |V_b|, \\ & t^{[k]} \ge 0, \forall 1 \le k \le |V_b|. \end{aligned} \tag{7}$$

[2]There are many possible ways of defining the lifetime. Throughout this paper, we use the time that the first node drains out of energy as the lifetime of the WSN.

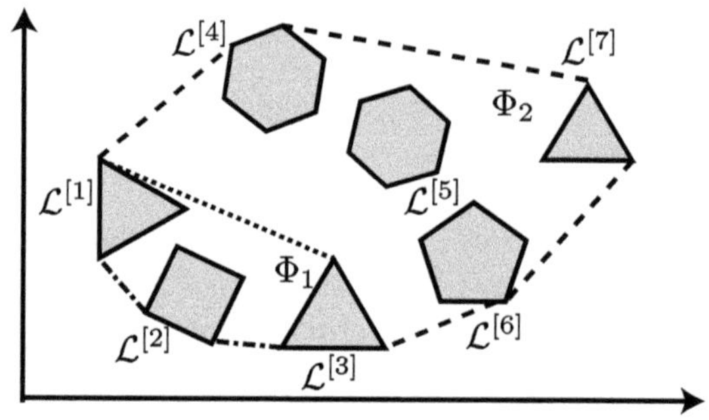

Figure 1: Optimization spaces of different schemes when the WSN has three BSs. The whole space for candidate configurations $\mathcal{L}$ is the union of simplexes $\mathcal{L}^{[1]}, \mathcal{L}^{[2]}, \cdots, \mathcal{L}^{[7]}$ which are denoted by the grey polygons. The optimization spaces of MultiFixed is $\mathcal{L}$. The optimization space of OneMove is illustrated by the space $\Phi_1 = \text{conv}(\bigcup_{k=1}^{3} \mathcal{L}^{[k]})$, whose edges are denoted by the dotted lines. The optimization space of MultiMove is illustrated by the space $\Phi_2 = \text{conv}(\mathcal{L})$, whose edges are denoted by the dashed lines. The common edges of Φ_1 and Φ_2 are denoted by dash-dot lines. We see that MultiMove has an optimization space larger than both MultiFixed and OneMove.

MultiMove is more energy efficient than the other schemes mentioned above. In the MultiFixed scheme, we select one configuration in the optimization space $\mathcal{L}$. In the MultiMove scheme, we select one configuration $(\boldsymbol{x}^{[k]}, \boldsymbol{y}^{[k]}, \boldsymbol{z}^{[k]}, \boldsymbol{c}^{[k]}) \in \mathcal{L}^{[k]}$ and a time duration $t^{[k]}$ for any $1 \le k \le 2^{|V_b|} - 1$. This virtually creates a new configuration whose average energy consumption rates are $\sum_{k=1}^{2^{|V_b|}-1} \boldsymbol{c}^{[k]} t^{[k]} / \sum_{k=1}^{2^{|V_b|}-1} t^{[k]}$, a convex combination of $\boldsymbol{c}^{[1]}, \boldsymbol{c}^{[2]}, \cdots, \boldsymbol{c}^{[2^{|V_b|}-1]}$. Therefore, the optimization space of MultiMove for selecting configurations is virtually expanded from $\mathcal{L}$ to its convex hull $\text{conv}(\mathcal{L})$. Similarly, in the OneMove scheme, the optimization space is virtually expanded from $\bigcup_{k=1}^{|V_b|} \mathcal{L}^{[k]}$ (the subset of configurations where only one BS is active) to $\text{conv}(\bigcup_{k=1}^{|V_b|} \mathcal{L}^{[k]})$. We illustrate the optimization spaces of different schemes in Figure 1 with an example of a WSN with three BSs.

5. COMPLEXITY ANALYSIS

In this section, we will analyze the complexity of the virtually-moving BSs problem.

The problem is unsurprisingly "very hard" because (i) there is an exponential number of candidate subsets of active BSs, and (ii) active BSs have the fixed energy-consumption rate c_{lc} for using long-range communication, which makes the problem non-convex. To formally evaluate the hardness of the problem, we define the **decision version of**

the virtually-moving BSs problem as follows: Given the topology of the WSN, the constant parameters c_c, c_{st}, c_{sr}, c_{lc}, c_{lt}, the data generating rate r, the initially availible energy $\boldsymbol{e}$, the sets of possible configurations $\{\mathcal{L}^{[k]}\}_{k=1}^{2^{|V_b|}-1}$ defined by (1), (2), (3) and (4), and a number T, does there exist a configuration in each simplex $(\boldsymbol{x}^{[k]}, \boldsymbol{y}^{[k]}, \boldsymbol{z}^{[k]}, \boldsymbol{c}^{[k]}) \in \mathcal{L}^{[k]}$ and a time duration $t^{[k]}$ for each $1 \leq k \leq 2^{|V_b|} - 1$, such that the lifetime of the network $\sum_{k=1}^{2^{|V_b|}-1} t^{[k]} \geq T$ under the energy constraint $\sum_{k=1}^{2^{|V_b|}-1} t^{[k]}\boldsymbol{c}^{[k]} \leq \boldsymbol{e}$?

THEOREM 1. *The virtually-moving BSs problem is NP-complete.*

PROOF. First of all, the decision version of the problem is NP because we can verify a valid instance in polynomial time. Now we show that the problem is NP-hard. We reduce the 3-SAT problem [6] to the virtually-moving BSs problem. Consider a 3-SAT instance with l variables a_1, a_2, $\cdots$, a_l and m clauses b_1, b_2, $\ldots$, b_m (Notice that each clause is a 3-element subset of $\{a_i, \bar{a}_i\}_{1\leq i\leq l}$). We define an $2l+1$-th variable w other than $\{a_i, \bar{a}_i\}_{1\leq i\leq l}$ and define a few sets:

- $P_i = \{a_i, \bar{a}_i\} \cup \{b_j | b_j \text{ contains } a_i\}$, $\forall 1 \leq i \leq l$,
- $Q_i = \{a_i, \bar{a}_i\} \cup \{b_j | b_j \text{ contains } \bar{a}_i\}$, $\forall 1 \leq i \leq l$,
- $W_1 = \{w\} \cup \{a_1, a_2, \cdots a_l\} \cup \{b_1, b_2, \cdots b_m\}$,
- $W_2 = \{w\} \cup \{\bar{a}_1, \bar{a}_2, \cdots \bar{a}_l\}$.

We construct an instance of the virtually-moving BSs problem as follows. Let P_1, P_2, $\cdots$, P_l, Q_1, Q_2, $\cdots$, Q_l, W_1, W_2 be associated with a BS each, and let a_1, a_2, $\cdots$, a_l, b_1, b_2, $\ldots$, b_m, w be associated with a sensor node each. Let each BS have a long-range communication link to the remote server S. Excluding the remote server S, the graph of the WSN is bipartite where every edge connects a BS to a sensor node, and this edge only exists when the set associated with the BS contains the variable associated with the sensor node. Let the initially availible energy of each BS be 1 and let that of each sensor node be 2. Let the constants for energy consumption be $c_c = 0$, $c_{st} = 1$, $c_{sr} = 0$, $c_{lc} = 1$, $c_{lt} = 0$, and let the data generating rate $r = 1$. Then, we set the tentative lifetime $T = 2$.

Because the data generating rate $r = 1$, $c_{st} = 1$ and because of (3), the energy consumption rate of any sensor node is at least 1. Remember that the initially availible energy of any sensor node is 2, the lifetime of the considered virtually-moving BSs problem is at most $T = 2$. In the following, we will show that if the constructed virtually-moving BSs problem achieves the lifetime $T = 2$, the original 3-SAT problem is satisfiable. We start with four deductions, given that the lifetime $T = 2$ is achievable:

(i) To be active, BSs W_1 and W_2 alternate, and each for a time duration 1. First, because of (4) and because $c_{lt} = 1$, the energy consumption rate of any BS is at least 1, therefore any BS has an active time duration at most 1 given the initially availible energy 1. Then, because BSs W_1 and W_2 are the only neighbours of sensor node w and because they have to serve w for a whole lifetime 2, both BSs W_1 and W_2 have to be active for a time duration 1 and they cannot be simultaneously active.

(ii) The energy consumption rate of every sensor node is 1 at any time. On the one hand, it is at least 1, as shown above. On the other hand, it cannot exceed 1, because every sensor node has to sustain a lifetime 2 with an initially availible energy 2.

(iii) Passive BSs do not forward data for other sensor nodes at any time, otherwise, at least one sensor node would receive data from passive BSs. Using (3), we see that this would result in an energy consumption rate exceeding 1, which would contradict (ii).

(iv) In the configuration where BS W_2 is active (BS W_1 is passive because of (i)), one and only one BS between BS P_i and BS Q_i is active for any $1 \leq i \leq l$. First, at least one of them has to be active in order to forward data from sensor node a_i because they are the only neighbours of a_i. Then, they cannot be simultaneously active, because they have to forward data for sensor node a_i for a lifetime 2 with the total available energy 2 and because $c_{lt} = 1$.

Because of deduction (i), we have a configuration in which BS W_2 is active and BS W_1 is passive. We will use this configuration to construct a valid assignment for the original 3-SAT problem. Because of deduction (iv), one and only one BS between BSs P_i and Q_i is active for any $1 \leq i \leq l$ in that configuration. This enables us to construct an assignment for the 3-SAT problem by setting the variable $a_i = 1$ if BS P_i is active and setting $a_i = 0$ if BS Q_i is active. Then, because of deduction (iii), each sensor node in $b_1, b_2, \cdots b_m$ connects to at least one active BS because passive BSs do not forward data from sensor nodes. Therefore, every clause b_j $(1 \leq j \leq m)$ in the 3-SAT problem is satisfied: If sensor node b_j connects to the active BS P_i, clause b_j is satisfied because it contains variable a_i and $a_i = 1$; if sensor node b_j connects to the active BS Q_i, clause b_j is also satisfied because it contains variable $\bar{a}_i$ and $a_i = 0$. In summary, if we can solve the constructed virtually-moving BSs problem, we can also solve the original 3-SAT problem. Therefore, the virtually-moving BSs problem is NP-hard as 3-SAT is known to be NP-hard. □

6. SCHEDULING ALGORITHM

In this section, we will propose a scheme for adaptively scheduling the virtual movement of multiple BSs. The proposed algorithm is computationally light, only requires easily available information as input, and guarantees, under mild conditions, a network lifetime at least 62% of the optimal one.

The adaptive scheduling scheme works as follows. Time is discretized into slots of length τ, during which we use only one configuration. Before the start of each time slot, the remote server collects the information about the current available energy of all BSs and all sensor nodes. Using only this information as input, the remote server selects the configuration to be used in the next time slot and notifies all BSs. As τ is usually much larger than the sampling interval of sensor nodes, this scheme has negligible overhead for collecting the required information and distributing the configuration determined by the server.

We denote the available energy of all sensor nodes and BSs at time n $(n \in \mathbb{N})$ by $\boldsymbol{e}^{(n)}$. In particular, the initially availible energy $\boldsymbol{e}^{(0)} = \boldsymbol{e}$. Denote the configuration selected for time slot n by $(\boldsymbol{x}^{(n)}, \boldsymbol{y}^{(n)}, \boldsymbol{z}^{(n)}, \boldsymbol{c}^{(n)}) \in \mathcal{L}$. The available energy evolves according to

$$\boldsymbol{e}^{(n)} = \boldsymbol{e}^{(n-1)} - \tau\boldsymbol{c}^{(n)}. \quad (8)$$

If we sum up the iterative equation (8) from time 0 to time n and use $\boldsymbol{e}^{(0)} = \boldsymbol{e}$, we have

$$\boldsymbol{e}^{(n)} = \boldsymbol{e} - \tau \sum_{t=1}^{n} \boldsymbol{c}^{(t)}. \quad (9)$$

Denote by N^* the maximum number of time slots before the first sensor node depletes its energy,

$$N^* = \max\{n | \boldsymbol{e}^{(n)} \geq \boldsymbol{0}\}, \quad (10)$$

and the lifetime of the WSN is τN^*.

In the following, to find the optimal configurations, we first propose to use the constrained gradient method [8] and to transform the virtually-moving BSs problem into adaptively solving a sequence of subproblem called the *min-weight configuration problems*. Then, we will discuss how to solve the min-weight configuration problems.

6.1 The Constrained Gradient Method

First of all, we define auxiliary variables

$$p^{[k]} = t^{[k]} \Big/ \sum_{k=1}^{2^{|V_b|}-1} t^{[k]}, \quad (11)$$

$$\boldsymbol{\theta} = \sum_{k=1}^{2^{|V_b|}-1} p^{[k]} \boldsymbol{c}^{[k]}. \quad (12)$$

Here $p^{[k]}$ denotes the fraction of time for using configuration $(\boldsymbol{x}^{[k]}, \boldsymbol{y}^{[k]}, \boldsymbol{z}^{[k]}, \boldsymbol{c}^{[k]})$ for all $1 \leq k \leq 2^{|V_b|} - 1$ and $\boldsymbol{\theta}$ denotes the average energy decrease rates for all sensor nodes and BSs. Next, we recast problem (5) as the auxiliary problem

$$\begin{aligned} \min_{\{\boldsymbol{x}^{[k]}, \boldsymbol{y}^{[k]}, \boldsymbol{z}^{[k]}, \boldsymbol{c}^{[k]}, p^{[k]}\}_{k=1}^{2^{|V_b|}-1}, \boldsymbol{\theta}} \quad & F(\boldsymbol{\theta}) = \max_{i \in V_b \cup V_r} \theta_i / e_i \\ \text{s.t.} \quad & \boldsymbol{\theta} = \sum_{k=1}^{2^{|V_b|}-1} p^{[k]} \boldsymbol{c}^{[k]}, \\ & \left(\boldsymbol{x}^{[k]}, \boldsymbol{y}^{[k]}, \boldsymbol{z}^{[k]}, \boldsymbol{c}^{[k]}\right) \in \mathcal{L}^{[k]}, \forall 1 \leq k \leq 2^{|V_b|} - 1, \\ & \sum_{k=1}^{2^{|V_b|}-1} p^{[k]} = 1, \\ & p^{[k]} \geq 0, \forall 1 \leq k \leq 2^{|V_b|} - 1, \end{aligned} \quad (13)$$

where θ_i is the i-th element of $\boldsymbol{\theta}$. Note that the objective value of (13) is the inverse of the objective value in (5).

We relax the objective function $F(\boldsymbol{\theta})$ in problem (13) into a differentiable function

$$f(\boldsymbol{\theta}) = \frac{1}{\alpha} \log \left(\sum_{i \in V_b \cup V_r} \exp\left(\frac{\alpha \theta_i}{e_i}\right) \right) \quad (14)$$

by introducing a real parameter $\alpha > 0$. We can check that

$$f(\boldsymbol{\theta}) - \frac{1}{\alpha} \log |V_b \cup V_r| \leq F(\boldsymbol{\theta}) \leq f(\boldsymbol{\theta}). \quad (15)$$

Therefore, using $f(\boldsymbol{\theta})$ as an approximation of $F(\boldsymbol{\theta})$ incurs an arbitrarily small loss of precision when α is large.

We define $\boldsymbol{\theta}^{(n)}$ as the average energy decrease rates during the first n time slots

$$\boldsymbol{\theta}^{(n)} = \frac{1}{n} \sum_{t=1}^{n} \boldsymbol{c}^{(t)} = \frac{\boldsymbol{e} - \boldsymbol{e}^{(n)}}{n\tau}, \quad (16)$$

Algorithm 1: The constrained gradient method for selecting configurations

Input: The parameters $c_c, c_{st}, c_{sr}, c_{lc}, c_{lt}, r$, the initially availaible energy $\boldsymbol{e}$, and a β-approximate algorithm for solving the min-weight configuration problem (18).

Output: N^*, $\{(\boldsymbol{x}^{(n)}, \boldsymbol{y}^{(n)}, \boldsymbol{z}^{(n)}, \boldsymbol{c}^{(n)})\}_{1 \leq n \leq N^*}$.

Initialize $\boldsymbol{\theta}^{(0)} \longleftarrow \boldsymbol{0}$, $\boldsymbol{e}^{(0)} \longleftarrow \boldsymbol{e}$, $n \longleftarrow 1$.
while $\boldsymbol{e}^{(n-1)} \geq \boldsymbol{0}$ **do**
  Calculate $\boldsymbol{\theta}^{(n-1)}$ from $\boldsymbol{e}^{(n-1)}$ and (16).
  Calculate the gradient $\boldsymbol{\nabla}^\top f(\boldsymbol{\theta}^{(n-1)})$ using (17).
  Select configuration $(\boldsymbol{x}^{(n)}, \boldsymbol{y}^{(n)}, \boldsymbol{z}^{(n)}, \boldsymbol{c}^{(n)})$ by using a β-approximate algorithm to solve the min-weight configuration problem (18) where $\boldsymbol{\lambda} = \boldsymbol{\nabla}^\top f(\boldsymbol{\theta}^{(n-1)})$.
  Update $\boldsymbol{e}^{(n)} \longleftarrow \boldsymbol{e}^{(n-1)} - \boldsymbol{c}^{(n)}$.
  Update $n \longleftarrow n + 1$.
Set $N^* = n - 1$.

where the second equality follows from (9). The purpose is to adaptively select the configurations of the WSN such that the sequence $\{\boldsymbol{\theta}^{(n)}\}_{n \in \mathbb{N}^+}$ gradually approaches the desired $\boldsymbol{\theta}$ in (13). Note that $\boldsymbol{\theta}^{(n-1)}$ is known at time slot n because $\boldsymbol{e}^{(n-1)}$ is already known and because of (16).

As shown in Algorithm 1, we iteratively do the following in each time slot $n \in \mathbb{N}^+$ as long as $\boldsymbol{e}^{(n-1)} \geq \boldsymbol{0}$:

(i) First, we calculate the energy decrease rates in the first $n-1$ time slots $\boldsymbol{\theta}^{(n-1)}$ using $\boldsymbol{e}^{(n-1)}$ and using (16), and we calculate the gradient of the relaxed objective function $\boldsymbol{\nabla}^\top f(\boldsymbol{\theta}^{(n-1)})$ whose i-th element ($i \in V_b \cup V_r$) is

$$\nabla_i^\top f\left(\boldsymbol{\theta}^{(n-1)}\right) = \frac{\exp\left(\alpha \theta_i^{(n-1)} / e_i\right)}{e_i \sum_{i \in V_b \cup V_r} \exp\left(\alpha \theta_i^{(n-1)} / e_i\right)}. \quad (17)$$

Here, e_i in (17) is the initially availaible energy of node i.

(ii) Then, we define a weight vector $\boldsymbol{\lambda} = \boldsymbol{\nabla}^\top f(\boldsymbol{\theta}^{(n-1)})$ and select a configuration $(\boldsymbol{x}^{(n)}, \boldsymbol{y}^{(n)}, \boldsymbol{z}^{(n)}, \boldsymbol{c}^{(n)})$ by solving

$$\begin{aligned} \min_{\boldsymbol{x}, \boldsymbol{y}, \boldsymbol{z}, \boldsymbol{c}} \quad & \boldsymbol{\lambda}^\top \boldsymbol{c} \\ \text{s.t.} \quad & (\boldsymbol{x}, \boldsymbol{y}, \boldsymbol{z}, \boldsymbol{c}) \in \mathcal{L}, \end{aligned} \quad (18)$$

which is termed as the *min-weight configuration problem*.

When the algorithm terminates, the lifetime of the network is τN^*, as defined in (10). Because N^* is dependent on τ and α, we will use $N^*(\tau, \alpha)$ for N^* to show explicitly the dependencies in the following.

The min-weight configuration problem is still combinatorial because there could be an exponential number of candidate configurations in $\mathcal{L}$. Nontheless, we will show in Theorem 2 that if the min-weight configuration problem has a β-approximate algorithm (β can be either a constant or a big-O function of $|V_b \cup V_r|$), the virtually-moving BSs problem also has a β-approximate algorithm.

THEOREM 2. *Using Algorithm 1 for selecting the configurations $\{(\boldsymbol{x}^{(n)}, \boldsymbol{y}^{(n)}, \boldsymbol{z}^{(n)}, \boldsymbol{c}^{(n)})\}_{n \in \mathbb{N}^+}$ with a β-approximation algorithm for solving the min-weight configuration problem (18), the achieved lifetime $\tau N^*(\tau, \alpha)$ satisfies*

$$\frac{\tau N^*(\tau, \alpha) + \tau}{T^*} > \frac{1}{\beta + \gamma_1(\alpha) + \gamma_2(\tau, \alpha)},$$

Table 2: Mapping from the min-weight configuration problem into an UFL problem

Facility set $\mathcal{F}$	BSs V_b
Open facility set $\mathcal{F}_o$	Active BSs $\{u \in V_b \mid z_u = 1\}$
Customer set $\mathcal{C}$	Sensor nodes V_r
Facility cost h_u ($u \in \mathcal{F}$)	$\lambda_u c_{\text{lc}}$, $u \in V_b$
Service cost g_{uv} ($u \in \mathcal{F}, v \in \mathcal{C}$)	$L_{uv} + \lambda_v c_{\text{c}}$, where L_{uv} is the length of the shortest-path from sensor node $v \in V_r$ to S via BS $u \in V_b$ with the distance assignment (22).

where

$$\gamma_1(\alpha) = \frac{\beta T^* \ln |V_b \cup V_r|}{\alpha},$$

$$\gamma_2(\tau, \alpha) = \frac{\alpha \tau |V_b \cup V_r|^2 c_{\max}^3 T^* (\ln \frac{e_{\min}}{\tau c_{\max}} + 1)}{2 e_{\min}^3},$$

with $e_{\min}$ denoting the minimum element of $\mathbf{e}$ and $c_{\max}$ denoting an upper-bound on the energy consumption rate of any BS or any sensor node

$$c_{\max} = c_{\text{c}} + c_{\text{lc}} + (c_{\text{st}} + c_{\text{sr}} + c_{\text{lt}})|V_b \cup V_r| r.$$

If we set $\tau \to 0$ and then set $\alpha \to \infty$, we have

$$\lim_{\alpha \to \infty} \lim_{\tau \to 0} \frac{\tau N^*(\tau, \alpha)}{T^*} \geq \frac{1}{\beta}.$$

Details of the proof can be found in the technical report [20].

6.2 The Min-weight Configuration Problem

We propose an algorithm for solving the min-weight problem with a guaranteed approximation ratio $\beta = 1.61$ by using previous results in the uncapacitated facility-location (UFL) problems [12].

The UFL problem can be stated as follows. Let $\mathcal{F}$ be a set of facilities and let $\mathcal{C}$ be a set of customers. Let $h_u > 0$ be the fixed cost for opening the facility $u \in \mathcal{F}$ and let $g_{uv} > 0$ be the service cost for each $u \in \mathcal{F}$ and $v \in \mathcal{C}$. We seek a subset of open facilities $\mathcal{F}_o \subseteq \mathcal{F}$, such that all customers are served and the sum of facility costs and service costs

$$\sum_{u \in \mathcal{F}_o} h_u + \sum_{v \in \mathcal{C}} \min_{u \in \mathcal{F}_o} g_{uv} \tag{19}$$

is minimized. A special type of UFL problems is called *metric uncapacitated facility-location* (metric-UFL) problems where the service costs are metric, that is,

$$g_{uv} + g_{u'v} + g_{u'v'} \geq g_{uv'}, \forall u, u' \in \mathcal{F}, \text{ and } v, v' \in \mathcal{C}. \tag{20}$$

In [12], Metric-UFL problems are solved by using an approximation algorithm with an approximation ratio 1.61.

We will convert the min-weight configuration problem (18) into an UFL problem with the mappings shown in Table 2:

(i) We set $\mathcal{F} = V_b$ and $\mathcal{C} = V_r$. The open facility set we are looking for is the set of active BSs

$$\mathcal{F}_o = \{u : z_u = 1, u \in V_b\}. \tag{21}$$

(ii) We assign a length d_{ij} for each edge of the WSN,

$$d_{ij} = \begin{cases} \lambda_i c_{\text{st}} r + \lambda_j c_{\text{sr}} r, & i, j \in V_b \cup V_r, \\ \lambda_i c_{\text{lt}} r, & i \in V_b, j = R, \\ \infty, & \text{othewise}, \end{cases} \tag{22}$$

where λ_i is the i-th element of the weight vector $\boldsymbol{\lambda}$.

(iii) For each sensor node $v \in V_r$ and each BS $u \in V_b$, we calculate the shortest path from sensor node v to the remote server S via BS u, which we denote by L_{uv}. We let the service cost g_{uv} for BS u forward the data packets from sensor node $v \in V_r$ be

$$g_{uv} = L_{uv} + \lambda_v c_{\text{c}}, \tag{23}$$

and we let the facility cost h_u for activating BS $u \in V_b$ be

$$h_u = \lambda_u c_{\text{lc}}. \tag{24}$$

The UFL problem constructed from the mappings in Table 2 is not metric in general, because the length of a path under the distance assignment (22) is not symmetric: the length of the shortest path from sensor node v to BS u is not equal to the reverse path from BS u to sensor node v. In the following theorem, we show the conditions that ensure the UFL to be metric.

THEOREM 3. *Given the parameters c_{c}, c_{st}, c_{sr}, c_{lc}, c_{lt}, r, and a weight vector $\boldsymbol{\lambda}$, we construct an instance of the UFL problem from the min-configuration problem (18) by using the mappings shown in Table 2. The constructed UFL problem*

- *has the same optimal objective value as that of the min-weight configuration problem (18), and*
- *is metric (20) under the condition that $c_{\text{sr}} \leq c_{\text{st}} \leq 2c_{\text{lt}} + c_{\text{sr}}$.*

Details of the proof can be found in the technical report [20].

We then use the 1.61-approximation algorithm proposed in [12] to solve the constructed UFL problem. For simplicity of discussion, we define the set of unconnected customers as $\mathcal{C}_u$. Let the two-tuple $(i, \mathcal{C})$ denote a star that is composed of a facility $i \in \mathcal{F}$ and a set of customers $\mathcal{D} \subseteq \mathcal{C}$ connected to facility i. The cost of the star $(i, \mathcal{D})$ is defined as the total cost divided by the number of unconnected customers in $\mathcal{D}$:

$$\text{cost}(i, \mathcal{D}) = \begin{cases} \dfrac{h_i + \sum_{j \in \mathcal{D}} q_{ij}}{|\mathcal{C}_u \cap \mathcal{D}|}, & i \notin \mathcal{F}_o, \\ \dfrac{\sum_{j \in \mathcal{D}} q_{ij}}{|\mathcal{C}_u \cap \mathcal{D}|}, & i \in \mathcal{F}_o, \end{cases} \tag{25}$$

where

$$q_{ij} = \begin{cases} g_{ij}, & j \in \mathcal{C}_u, \\ \min(0, g_{ij} - \min_{k \in \mathcal{F}_o} g_{kj}), & j \notin \mathcal{C}_u. \end{cases}$$

The procedure of the algorithm is as follows:

(i) At the beginning, we set $\mathcal{F}_o = \emptyset$ and $\mathcal{C}_u = \mathcal{C}$.

(ii) As long as the set of unconnected customers $\mathcal{C}_u \neq \emptyset$, find the most cost-efficient star $(i, \mathcal{D})$ for all $i \in \mathcal{F}$ and $\mathcal{D} \subseteq \mathcal{C}$. Connect all customers in $\mathcal{D}$ to i and set $\mathcal{C}_u = \mathcal{C}_u \backslash \mathcal{D}$. If BS $i \notin \mathcal{F}_o$, activate BS i and $\mathcal{F}_o = \mathcal{F}_o \cup \{i\}$.

We note that in step (ii), although the number of stars is exponential with the number of customers, it is easy to find

Algorithm 2: Approximation algorithm for solving the min-weight configuration problem

Input: The parameters $c_c, c_{st}, c_{sr}, c_{lc}, c_{lt}, r$, and a weight vector $\boldsymbol{\lambda}$.

Output: A configuration $(\boldsymbol{x}, \boldsymbol{y}, \boldsymbol{z}, \boldsymbol{c}) \in \mathcal{L}$.

Assign the lengths of edges in the WSN as shown in (22).
Set $\mathcal{F} \longleftarrow V_b$ and set $\mathcal{C} \longleftarrow V_r$.
Calculate the shortest path L_{uv} from each sensor node $v \in \mathcal{C}$ to the remote server S via each BS $u \in \mathcal{F}$.
Assign the service costs g_{uv} $(u \in \mathcal{F}, v \in \mathcal{C})$ and the facility costs h_u $(u \in \mathcal{F})$ as shown in (23) and (24), respectively.
Set $\mathcal{F}_o \longleftarrow \emptyset$ and set $\mathcal{C}_u \longleftarrow \mathcal{C}$.
while $\mathcal{C}_u \neq \emptyset$ **do**
  Find the most cost-effective star $(i, \mathcal{D})$ where $i \in \mathcal{F}$ and $\mathcal{D} \subseteq \mathcal{C}$ with the cost of the stars defined in (25).
  Connect all sensor nodes in $\mathcal{D}$ to BS i along the shortest paths with edge lengths defined in (22). Set $\mathcal{C}_u \longleftarrow \mathcal{C}_u \backslash \mathcal{D}$.
  Enable BS i to be active and set $\mathcal{F}_o \longleftarrow \mathcal{F}_o \cup \{i\}$.

the most cost-effective one star. It is sufficient to consider stars $(i, \mathcal{D}_k^i)$ for $i \in \mathcal{F}$ and $k \in \{1, \cdots, |\mathcal{C}_u|\}$, where $\mathcal{D}_k^i$ denotes the set containing all connected customers $j \in \mathcal{C} \backslash \mathcal{C}_u$ whose $q_{ij} < 0$ and containing k unconnected customers $j \in \mathcal{C}_u$ with the smallest positive q_{ij}. Clearly, other stars cannot be more cost-effective (More details can be found in [12]).

We summarize the whole procedure for finding the approximate min-weight configuration as in Algorithm 2.

THEOREM 4. *Algorithm 2 guarantees to find a configuration* $(\boldsymbol{x}, \boldsymbol{y}, \boldsymbol{z}, \boldsymbol{c}) \in \mathcal{L}$, *such that the weight* $\boldsymbol{\lambda}^\top \boldsymbol{c}$ *is at most* $\beta = 1.61$ *times the optimal objective value of the min-weight configuration problem (18) under the condition that* $c_{sr} \leq c_{st} \leq 2c_{lt} + c_{sr}$.

In summary, the results in both Theorems 2 and 4 yield that our proposed algorithm achieves, under mild conditions, a lifetime at least 62% of the optimal one.

7. SIMULATIONS

In this section, we will show how we evaluate the proposed scheme by running extensive simulations.

We consider a 150 m × 150 m sensing field where we randomly generate a connected WSN with $|V_r| = 40$ and $|V_b| = 5$ (The default network size is small so that problem (5) can be solved exactly). All sensor nodes generate data with a rate of $r = 1$ and BSs do not generate data. Data generated by sensor nodes are transmitted to active BSs using short-range communication whose per-hop transmitting range is 40 m. Time is partitioned into slots with the length of a time slot $\tau = 1$. Let the constants of energy consumption rates be $c_{sc} = 1$, $c_{st} = 1$, $c_{sr} = 1$, $c_{lc} = 10$ and $c_{lt} = 1$ (We select these parameters to reflect the real energy consumptions of BSs and sensor nodes. More details can be found in our recent paper [19]). Let the initially availaible energy of all BSs be $e_i = 5000, \forall i \in V_b$ and let that of all sensor nodes be $e_i = 3000, \forall i \in V_r$. Let the parameter $\alpha = 10000$ in (14).

Here, we simulate five schemes: (i) *OneFixed*, the traditional scheme that uses one always-active BS, (ii) *MultiFixed* that uses multiple always-active BSs, where the locations of active BSs are optimized through (6), (iii) *OneMove* that schedules the virtual movement of one BS through (7), (iv) *MultiMove* that schedules the virtual movement of multiple BSs by solving (5) without approximation (considered as the optimum in the following), and (v) *MultiMove-A* that schedules the virtual movement of multiple BSs by using our proposed Algorithm 1 and Algorithm 2 to approximately solve (5). The details of MultiFixed, OneMove, MultiMove are discussed in Section 4.3. Without the fixed energy-consumption of long-range communication, both MultiFixed and MultiMove are optimal, they will always activate all BSs and use the maximum lifetime routing [7]. Because problem (5) is computationally hard, MultiMove is only applicable when the network is small.

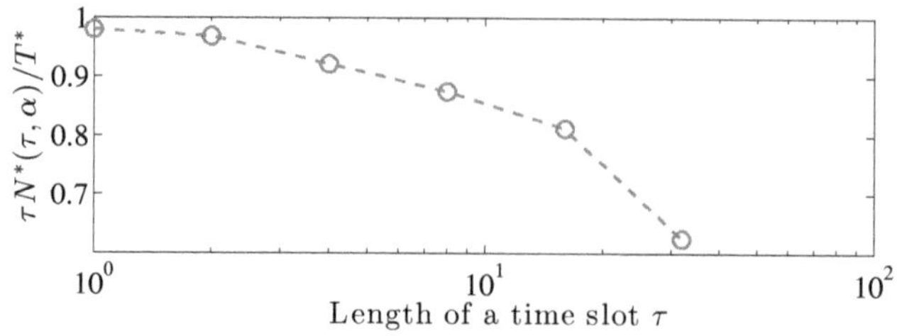

Figure 2: The ratio between the lifetime of MultiMove-A and that of MultiMove $\tau N^*(\tau, \alpha)/T^*$ versus the length of time slot τ. We see that the ratio decreases as τ increases. If τ is set small ($\tau < 10$), MultiMove-A yields a lifetime very close to the optimum achieved by MultiMove.

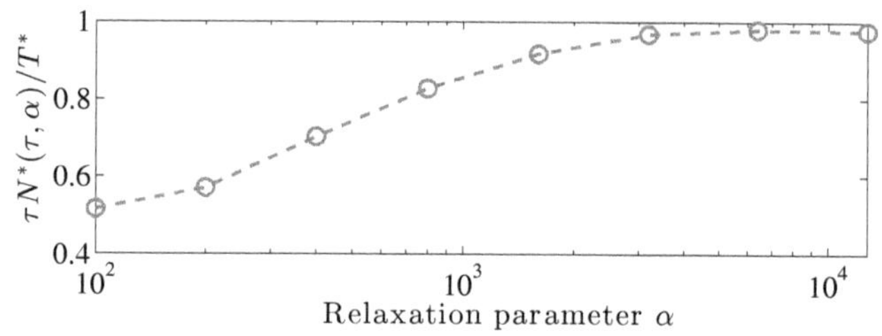

Figure 3: The ratio between the lifetime of MultiMove-A and that of MultiMove $\tau N^*(\tau, \alpha)/T^*$ versus the relaxation parameter α. We see that when α is sufficiently large ($\alpha > 1000$) , MultiMove yields a lifetime very close to the optimum.

7.1 Parameter Selection

As shown in Theorem 2, the performance of MultiMove-A depends on the parameters including the length of a time slot τ and the relaxation parameter α. We show how these parameters influence the ratio between the lifetime achieved by MultiMove-A and that by MultiMove $\tau N^*(\tau, \alpha)/T^*$.

In Figure 2, we show the ratio $\tau N^*(\tau, \alpha)/T^*$ versus the length of a time slot τ. When τ is small, MultiMove-A yields a lifetime very close to the optimum achieved by MultiMove, as the algorithm exploits the fine granularity of the time slot.

In Figure 3, we show the ratio $\tau N^*(\tau, \alpha)/T^*$ versus the relaxation parameter α in (14). When α is large, the relaxation of the objective function is precise, and MultiMove-A yields a lifetime very close to the optimum.

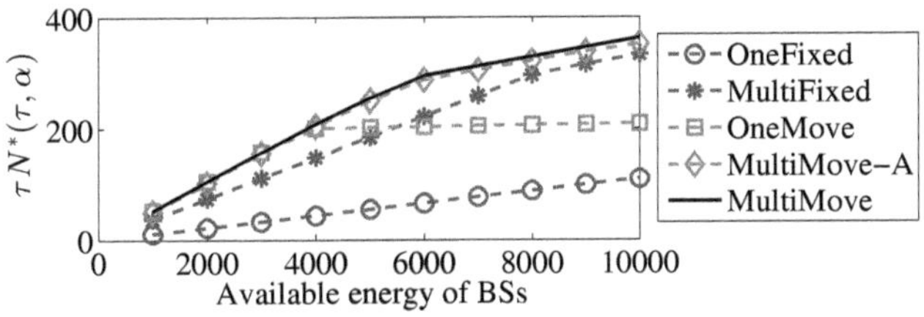

Figure 4: The network lifetime $\tau N^*(\tau, \alpha)$ versus the initially availaible energy of BSs when running different schemes..

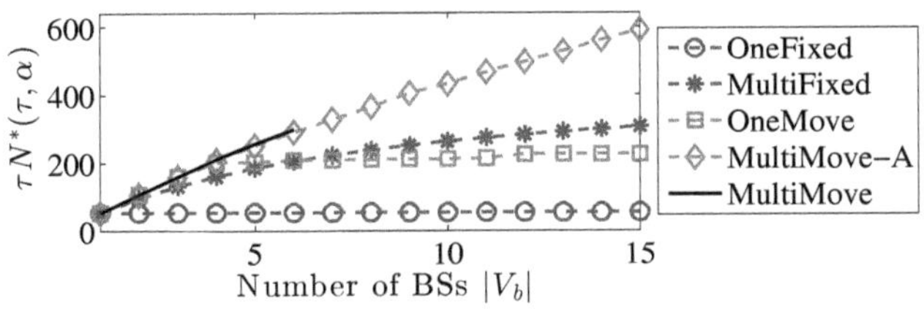

Figure 5: The network lifetime $\tau N^*(\tau, \alpha)$ versus the number of BSs $|V_b|$ when running different schemes..

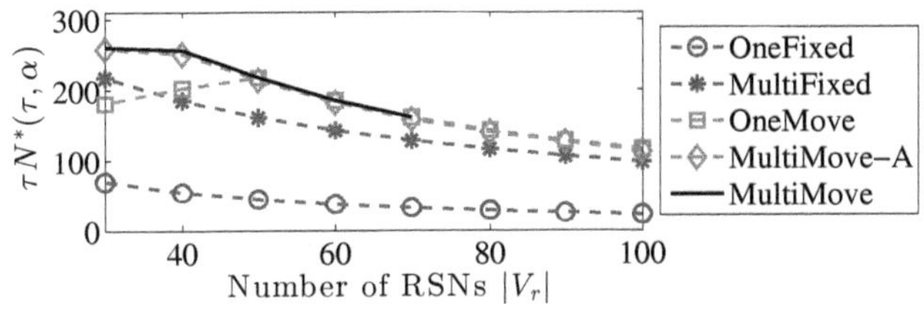

Figure 6: The network lifetime $\tau N^*(\tau, \alpha)$ versus the number of sensor nodes $|V_r|$ when running different schemes.

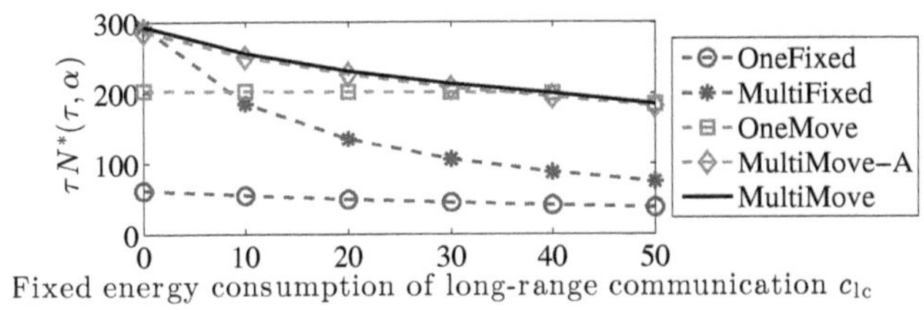

Figure 7: The network lifetime $\tau N^*(\tau, \alpha)$ versus the fixed energy-consumption of long-range communication c_{lc} when running different schemes.

7.2 Performance Comparison

To simulate different scenarios, we vary five parameters of the network: (i) the initially availaible energy of BSs, (ii) the number of BSs $|V_b|$, (iii) the number of sensor nodes $|V_r|$, (iv) the fixed energy-consumption rate of using long-range communication c_{lc}, and (v) the data rate of sensor nodes r.

We summarize the simulation results as follows: (i) In some scenarios, BSs are bottlenecks of the network lifetime, *e.g.*, when the initially availaible energy of BSs is low, when $|V_b|$ is small, when $|V_r|$ is large, when c_{lc} is large and when r is small. In these scenarios, OneMove outperforms MultiFixed, because OneMove improves the energy efficiency of BSs by rotating one active BS among multiple BSs. (ii) In other scenarios, sensor nodes are bottlenecks of the network lifetime, for example, when the initially availaible energy of BSs is high, when $|V_b|$ is large, when $|V_r|$ is small, when c_{lc} is small and when r is large. In these scenarios, MultiFixed outperforms OneMove, because MultiFixed reduces the energy consumption of sensor nodes by reducing the hop-distance from sensor nodes to BSs. (iii) In all scenarios, the lifetime achieved by MultiMove-A is always very close to the optimum achieved by MultiMove and is always longer than those achieved by both OneMove and MultiFixed.

Lifetime versus the initially availaible energy of BSs: In Figure 4, we show the lifetime of the WSN $\tau N^*(\tau, \alpha)$ versus the initially availaible energy of BSs. We fix the initially availaible energy of sensor nodes $e_i = 3000, \forall i \in V_r$, and we vary the initially availaible energy of BSs (all BSs have the same amount though). When the initially availaible energy of BSs is small, OneMove is very close to the optimum achieved by MultiMove and MultiMove-A. Therefore, in this scenario, virtually moving multiple BSs degrades into the scheme of virtually moving one BS as in [19]. When the initially availaible energy of BSs increases, the increase of lifetime of OneMove diminishes and Multi-Fixed outperforms OneMove, because the bottleneck of the network lifetime is shifted from BSs to sensor nodes.

Lifetime versus the number of BSs: In Figure 5, we show the lifetime of the WSN $\tau N^*(\tau, \alpha)$ versus the number of BSs $|V_b|$. We see similar results as that in Figure 4. When $|V_b|$ is small, OneMove outperforms MultiFixed and performs close to the optimum as MultiMove-A does. This is because when BSs are bottlenecks of the network lifetime, rotating one active BS is the optimal solution. When $|V_b|$ is large, sensor nodes become bottlenecks of the lifetime of the WSN, and MultiFixed outperforms OneMove.

Lifetime versus number of sensor nodes: In Figure 6, we show the lifetime of the WSN $\tau N^*(\tau, \alpha)$ versus the number of sensor nodes $|V_r|$. There is a clear trend that when $|V_r|$ increases, the lifetime of the network decreases. When $|V_r|$ is small, sensor nodes limit the lifetime of the WSN, and therefore OneMove performs poorly. When $|V_r|$ is large, BSs cause bottlenecks of the network lifetime, and OneMove performs close to the optimum achieved by MultiMove and MultiMove-A.

Lifetime versus the fixed energy-consumption of long-range communication: In Figure 7, we show the lifetime of the WSN $\tau N^*(\tau, \alpha)$ versus the fixed energy consumption rate of long-range communication c_{lc}. There is a trend that when c_{lc} increases, the lifetime of the network decreases. Still, MultiMove-A and MultiMove only decrease mildly because they can evenly distribute the high energy-consumption load among the whole WSN. Meanwhile, we see that the lifetime curve of OneMove is flat when c_{lc} is small, because the bottleneck of lifetime is due to the sensor nodes rather than BSs in these scenarios.

Lifetime versus the data rate of sensor nodes: In Figure 8, we show the achieved lifetime $\tau N^*(\tau, \alpha)$ versus the data rate r using different schemes. For better illustration, we set $e_i = 5000, \forall i \in V_b$ and $e_i = 1000, \forall i \in V_r$. We see similar results as that in Figure 7. When r is low, BSs are bottlenecks in the lifetime, and OneMove outperforms MultiFixed. When r becomes high, sensor nodes cause the bottleneck of the network lifetime, and the lifetime achieved by MultiFixed is very close to the optimum.

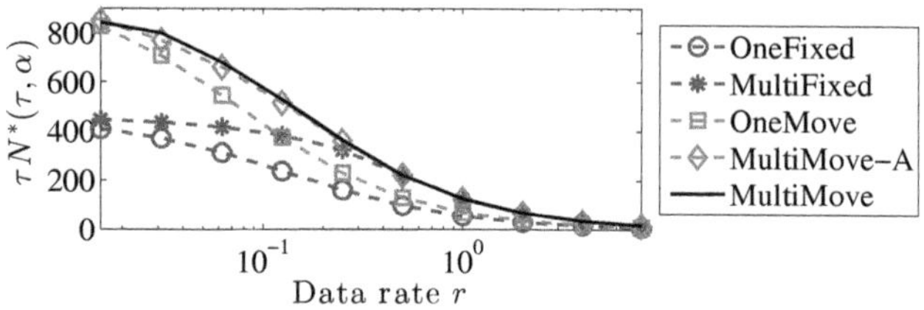

Figure 8: The network lifetime $\tau N^*(\tau, \alpha)$ versus the data rate of sensor nodes r when running different schemes.

8. CONCLUSION

In this paper, we have presented and evaluated the scheme of virtually moving the BSs in WSNs, where we adaptively re-elect an active subset of BSs. This scheme not only achieves a high energy-efficiency but also avoids the difficulty of physically moving the BSs. We have shown that the problem of virtually moving BSs is in fact NP-hard. We have proposed an adaptive algorithm for scheduling the virtual movement by using the constrained gradient method and using previous results in uncapacitated facility-location problems. Under mild conditions, this algorithm guarantees to yield a lifetime at least 62% of the optimum. The idea of load balancing by virtually moving devices can be used in other networked systems, including super-node selection in peer-to-peer networks and cooperative beamforming in cellular networks. As a consequence, the proposed scheduling algorithm has merits beyond the WSNs.

9. ACKNOWLEDGEMENTS

The work presented in this paper was supported (in part) by the Swiss National Science Foundation under grant number 200021-146423.

10. REFERENCES

[1] G. Barrenetxea, B. Berefull-Lozano, and M. Vetterli. Lattice networks: capacity limits, optimal routing, and queueing behavior. *Networking, IEEE/ACM Transactions on*, 14(3):492–505, June 2006.

[2] S. Basagni, A. Carosi, E. Melachrinoudis, C. Petrioli, and Z. M. Wang. Controlled sink mobility for prolonging wireless sensor networks lifetime. *Wirel. Netw.*, 14(6):831–858, Dec. 2008.

[3] L. Ben Saad and B. Tourancheau. Multiple mobile sinks positioning in wireless sensor networks for buildings. In *Sensor Technologies and Applications, 2009. SENSORCOMM.*, June 2009.

[4] Y. Bi, L. Sun, J. Ma, N. Li, I. Khan, and C. Chen. Hums: An autonomous moving strategy for mobile sinks in data-gathering sensor networks. *Eurasip Journal on Wireless Communications and Networking*, 2007.

[5] A. Bogdanov, E. Maneva, and S. Riesenfeld. Power-aware base station positioning for sensor networks. In *INFOCOM 2004. Twenty-third Annual Joint Conference of the IEEE Computer and Communications Societies*, 2004.

[6] A. Z. Broder, A. M. Frieze, and E. Upfal. On the satisfiability and maximum satisfiability of random 3-cnf formulas. *Proceedings of the Fourth Annual ACM-SIAM Symposium on Discrete Algorithms*, pages 322–330, 1993.

[7] J.-H. Chang and L. Tassiulas. Maximum lifetime routing in wireless sensor networks. *Networking, IEEE/ACM Transactions on*, 12(4):609–619, Aug 2004.

[8] M. Frank and P. Wolfe. An algorithm for quadratic programming. *Naval Research Logistics Quarterly*, 3(1-2):95–110, 1956.

[9] S. Gandham, M. Dawande, R. Prakash, and S. Venkatesan. Energy efficient schemes for wireless sensor networks with multiple mobile base stations. In *IEEE Global Telecommunications Conference 2003.*

[10] N. Garg and J. Könemann. Faster and simpler algorithms for multicommodity flow and other fractional packing problems. *SIAM J. Comput.*, 37(2):630–652, May 2007.

[11] P. Gonzalez-Brevis, J. Gondzio, Y. Fan, H. Poor, J. Thompson, I. Krikidis, and P.-J. Chung. Base station location optimization for minimal energy consumption in wireless networks. *IEEE Vehicular Technology Conference*, 2011.

[12] K. Jain, M. Mahdian, E. Markakis, A. Saberi, and V. V. Vazirani. Greedy facility location algorithms analyzed using dual fitting with factor-revealing lp. *J. ACM*, 50(6):795–824, Nov. 2003.

[13] J. Luo and J. Hubaux. Joint mobility and routing for lifetime elongation in wireless sensor networks. *2005. 24th Annual Joint Conference of the INFOCOM*, 2005.

[14] J. Luo and J.-P. Hubaux. Joint sink mobility and routing to maximize the lifetime of wireless sensor networks: The case of constrained mobility. *IEEE/ACM Trans. Netw.*, 18(3):871–884, June 2010.

[15] Y. Shi and Y. Hou. Some fundamental results on base station movement problem for wireless sensor networks. *IEEE/ACM Trans. Netw.*, 2011.

[16] Y. Tanaka, S. Imahori, M. Sasaki, and M. Yagiura. An lp-based heuristic algorithm for the node capacitated in-tree packing problem. *Computers and Operations Research*, 39(3):637–646, 2012.

[17] Z. Vincze, R. Vida, and A. Vidacs. Deploying multiple sinks in multi-hop wireless sensor networks. In *Pervasive Services, IEEE International Conference on*, pages 55 –63, july 2007.

[18] Y. Yun and Y. Xia. Maximizing the lifetime of wireless sensor networks with mobile sink in delay-tolerant applications. *Mobile Computing, IEEE Transactions on*, 9(9):1308–1318, Sept 2010.

[19] R. Zhang, F. Ingelrest, G. Barrenetxea, P. Thiran, and M. Vetterli. The beauty of the commons: Optimal load sharing by base station hopping in wireless sensor networks. *Selected Areas in Communications, IEEE Journal on*, PP(99):1–1, 2015.

[20] R. Zhang, P. Thiran, and M. Vetterli. Virtually Moving Base Stations for Energy Efficiency in Wireless Sensor Networks. *Technical report, http://infoscience.epfl.ch/record/206994.*

[21] G. Zussman and A. Segall. Energy efficient routing in ad hoc disaster recovery networks. In *INFOCOM 2003. Twenty-Second Annual Joint Conference of the IEEE Computer and Communications. IEEE Societies*, volume 1, pages 682–691 vol.1, March 2003.

An Operator Calculus Approach for Multi-constrained Routing in Wireless Sensor Networks

Bilel Nefzi
LORIA-University of Lorraine
bilel.nefzi@live.com

René Schott
LORIA-University of Lorraine
schott@loria.fr

Ye Qiong Song
LORIA-University of Lorraine
song@loria.fr

G. Stacey Staples
Southern Illinois University Edwardsville
sstaple@siue.edu

Evangelia Tsiontsiou
LORIA-University of Lorraine
evangelia.tsiontsiou@loria.fr

ABSTRACT

Wireless sensor networks (WSN) are inherently multi - constrained. They need to preserve energy while offering reliable and timely data reporting for a non-negligible number of scenarios. This is particularly true when a node should decide which forwarder has to be chosen for routing a packet. Nevertheless, solving multi-constrained routing problems is NP-complete. Most approaches involve transforming the problem into a single constrained problem using a cost function, although this may lead to suboptimal solutions. Some other solutions are based on heuristics. However, their high implementation complexity prevents their online use. Hence, they are not suitable for highly dynamic WSNs. In this paper we make use of Operator Calculus (OC) methods on graphs to solve path selection in the presence of multiple constraints. OC has lower resolution time complexity compared to other techniques. Based on OC, we develop a distributed algorithm for path selection in a graph. We develop a new routing protocol which makes use of this algorithm: the Operator Calculus based Routing Protocol (OCRP). In OCRP, a node selects the set of eligible next hops based on the given constraints and the distance to the destination. It then sends the packet to all eligible next hops. The protocol is implemented in Contiki OS and emulated for TelosB motes using Cooja. We compare its performance against tree and directional flooding routing and show the advantages of our technique.

Categories and Subject Descriptors

C.2.2 [**Computer-Communication Networks**]: Network Protocols-Routing protocols

General Terms

Algorithms, Design, Performance, Reliability

MobiHoc'15, June 22–25, 2015, Hangzhou, China.
Copyright 2015 ACM 978-1-4503-3489-1/15/06 ...$15.00
http://dx.doi.org/10.1145/2746285.2746301 .

Keywords

Multi-constrained Routing, WSNs, Routing protocols, QoS

1. INTRODUCTION

Routing in wireless sensor networks is fundamentally a multi-constrained problem. On the one hand, nodes in these networks need to handle energy and memory constraints. On the other hand, an increasing number of applications require additional guarantees, like minimal delay and reliability, for the packets they generate. Therefore, a good routing protocol needs to select best paths through several existing ones to balance energy and memory consumption and guarantee the application's constraints. Those QoS metrics could have different nature. They could be additive like delay, multiplicative like reliability or more generally obey any function.

IETF has already standarized a routing protocol for Low Power and Lossy networks (RPL) [16]. RPL is a simple distance vector routing protocol that builds a Destination Oriented Directed Acyclic Graph (DODAG) rooted at a sink node. Each node can have multiple parents directed to the sink, but only one parent is chosen according to an Objective Function (OF). IETF has introduced several metrics for the OF like node state, energy, hop count, throughput, latency, link quality and ETX. Different DODAGs can be built according to different optimization metrics over the same physical topology, that can be identified by the *instance-id.* However, if more than one metric has to be considered, there is no indication about the way that this can be achieved, solving the multi-constrained problem.

In this paper we make use of the Operator Calculus (OC) theory [8] to solve path selection in the presence of multiple constraints. OC is a dynamic programming algorithm which constructs the "nilpotent adjacency matrix" related to a finite graph and solves the shortest path problem by the powers of that matrix, removing the cycles of the paths. OC makes use of constraints algebra that automatically removes from consideration any path whose weight fails to simultaneously satisfy the constraints. A concrete example of how OC works is given in Section IV. Many existing algorithms can not deal with min\max metrics, so they use techniques like omitting the links which do not satisfy the respective constraints in an initialization phase and then apply the algorithm on the modified graph [11]. OC is able to deal with metrics that are not necessarily additive during the algorithm execution.

Although the implementation of OC may look like “brute force” if one only thinks in terms of trying all paths and making comparisons before removing infeasible paths, however, the ideal implementation of OC requires no such development and comparisons. In fact, an implementation in an "algebraic architecture" would require none of that. The properties of the algebra automatically kill the cycles and the infeasible paths. Moreover, the approach is flexible – the OC formulations of all problems look alike. We simply change the set of weights and adjust the binary operation. Nevertheless, in this paper, as an use case example, we are mainly interested in finding, among all feasible paths, only the hop-minimal because its practical interest in a WSN. Of course, in case that one wants to optimize other metrics, e.g., the energy consumption, it is possible to collect a number of feasible paths and then apply another choice function that allows selecting the preferred path.

Based on OC, we derive a distributed algorithm for path selection in a graph and develop a new routing protocol that makes use of this algorithm: the Operator Calculus based Routing Protocol (OCRP). To the best of our knowledge, OC is the only algorithm which is able to simultaneously consider those different kind of metrics.

The rest of this paper is organized as follows. In the next section we present the related work in routing algorithms. In Section III we review the OC theory. In Section 4, we illustrate through an example the path selection algorithm using OC and derive a distributive version of it. Section 5 details the implementation of OCRP in Contiki OS. Section 6 provides a performance analysis of OCRP. We conclude the paper in Section 7.

2. RELATED WORK

Several routing protocols have been developed for WSNs, trying to provide the demanding QoS. Most approaches handle this problem through the use of cost functions which regroup multiple constraints into a single function, *e.g.* Speed [1] family, RPAR [2] and MQoSR [14]. This has the advantage of transforming the problem into a single-constrained problem which is easier to solve. Nevertheless, this approach is not possible when the metrics have different natures. Moreover, if constraints are taken individually, using cost functions may lead to paths which violate some constraints. Huang and Fang [15] propose a multi-constrained QoS multi-path routing protocol where the end-to-end delay is formulated as an optimization problem and then an algorithm based on linear integer programming is applied to solve the problem. However, the information is always routed over a min-hop path which leads to more energy consumption.

Multi-constrained path selection algorithms offer the possibility of selecting a different function for each constraint. For example, we could use the sum function for delay, the product function for reliability, the *min* function for link quality and energy, etc. Nevertheless, multi-constrained routing is NP-complete [10]. However, Van Mieghem and Kuipers [11] suggest that multi-constrained routing in realistic networks may not be NP-complete. More specifically, they suggest that multi-constrained routing problems confinded to a particular class of networks (topology and link weight structure) may not be NP-complete.

Other heuristic and approximation algorithms have been developed to identify paths given particular QoS requests. For example, in [12] and [13], the writers study the NP-hard multi-constrained routing problem of seeking a path from a source to a destination in the presence of multiple additive end-to-end QoS constraints.

A novel multi-constrained algorithm is proposed in this paper which avoids the use of heuristics or construction of trees to prevent combinatorial explosion. As referred before, OC can simultaneously deal with different kind of metrics.

3. OPERATOR CALCULUS ON GRAPHS

Operator calculus (OC) methods on graphs have been developed in a number of earlier works by Schott and Staples, summarized in the recent book *Operator Calculus on Graphs* [8]. The principle idea underlying the approach is the association of graphs with algebraic structures whose properties reveal information about the associated graphs. For example, an element a of a ring or algebra is said to be *nilpotent* if $a^n = 0$ for some positive integer n. By constructing the “nilpotent adjacency matrix” associated with a finite graph, information about self-avoiding structures (paths, cycles, trails, etc.) in the graph are revealed by computing powers of the matrix. Cycles are removed from consideration automatically by the algebra itself.

The operator calculus approach is further extended through the introduction of the *constraints algebra* that automatically removes from consideration any path whose weight fails to simultaneously satisfy multiple constraints [8]. The resulting constrained path algebra is then used to devise algorithms for computing multi-constrained paths in weighted graphs.

Consider a directed graph $G = (V, E)$ on n vertices such that associated with each edge $(v_i, v_j) \in E$ is a vector weight $\mathbf{w}_{ij} = (w_{ij1}, \ldots, w_{ijm}) \in \mathbb{R}^m$. For the case $m = 1$, Dijkstra's algorithm finds all single source minimum paths in a directed graph on n vertices with nonnegative edge weights in $\mathcal{O}(n^2)$ time [6]. The Bellman-Ford algorithm finds single source minimal paths in digraphs with nonnegative cycles and arbitrary edge weights and runs in $\mathcal{O}(n\,|E|)$ time [3, 7].

In the more general case $m \geq 1$, Corley and Moon [4] presented an algorithm for finding all Pareto non-negative cycles and paths with computational complexity $\mathcal{O}(mn^{2n-3} + mn^n)$.

Given an initial vertex v_0 and terminal vertex v_∞ in a weighted graph, the collection of *feasible paths* from v_0 to v_∞ refers to all paths whose associated total costs satisfy some predefined constraints. OC approach aims to find all hop-minimal feasible paths satisfying multiple constraints involving weights that are not necessarily additive.

Described herein is a new routing protocol based on the approach developed in [8] to find this set of feasible paths. Essential details of the approach are summarized below.

Definition 1. Multi-Constrained Path Problem (or MCP problem): Given a finite graph $G(N, E)$, where V is the set of nodes and E is the set of links, each edge $(v_i, v_j) \in E$ is weighted with a vector of m non-negative integers $w_{ij} = (w_{ij1}, \ldots, w_{ijm})$ and a constraint vector $\mathfrak{C} = (c_1, \ldots, c_m)$. The multi-constrained path problem is to find paths $\mathbf{p}$ from source vertex v_0 to target vertex v_∞ in the graph G such that

$$\mathrm{wt}(\mathbf{p}) \preceq (c_1, \ldots, c_m) = \mathfrak{C}, \qquad (1)$$

where $\text{wt}(\mathbf{p})$ is the weight vector of each path $\mathbf{p}$. In other worlds, MCP problem finds the collection of feasible paths from source to destination whose associated total costs satisfy some predefined constraints.

Definition 2. The *constraints algebra*, denoted $\mathcal{A}_{\mathfrak{C}}$, is the real associative unital algebra generated by $\{\xi^{\mathbf{x}} : \mathbf{x} \in \mathbb{R}^m\}$ with (formal) unit $\xi^{\mathbf{0}}$ having multiplication defined according to

$$\xi^{\mathbf{x}}\,\xi^{\mathbf{y}} := \begin{cases} \xi^{\mathbf{x}*\mathbf{y}} & \text{if } \mathbf{x}*\mathbf{y} \preceq \mathfrak{C}, \\ 0 & \text{otherwise.} \end{cases} \tag{2}$$

EXAMPLE 1. *Consider $m = 3$: end-to-end delay, reliability and node residual energy. The requirements are the following:*

- *The total end-to-end delay must be less or equal to $d_{\max}$.*
- *The link quality of total path must be greater or equal to $lq_{\min}$.*
- *The remaining energy of each node in the path must be greater or equal to $re_{\min}$.*

In this case, $* = (+, \cdot, \min)$, $\mathfrak{R} = (\leq, \geq, \geq)$, *and* $\mathfrak{C} = (d_{\max}, lq_{\min}, re_{\min})$. *If we consider* $\mathfrak{C} = (10, 0.6, 50)$, *we have the following computations:*

$$\xi^{(1,0.7,60)}\,\xi^{(9,0.9,80)} = \xi^{(1+9,0.7\cdot 0.9,\min\{60,80\})} = \xi^{(10,0.63,60)}.$$

On the other hand,

$$\xi^{(1,0.7,30)}\,\xi^{(12,0.9,35)} = 0$$

because $1 + 12 = 13 > 10$ *and also because* $\min\{30, 35\} = 30 < 50$.

In this example, the multiplicative identity (unit) of $\mathcal{A}_{(10,0.6,50)}$ is formally defined as $\xi^{\mathbf{0}} := \xi^{(0,1,\infty)}$.

Given a constraint vector $\mathfrak{C} = (c_1, \ldots, c_m) \in \mathbb{R}^m$, properties of the constraints algebra $\mathcal{A}_{\mathfrak{C}}$ can be used to sieve out the feasible paths from the collection of all paths. The feasible paths can then be ranked and an optimal path can be chosen.

For fixed positive integer n, consider the alphabet $\Sigma_n := \{\omega_i : 1 \leq i \leq n\}$. For convenience, we adopt the following *ordered multi-index* notation. In particular, letting $\mathbf{u} = (u_1, \ldots, u_k)$ for some k, the notation $\omega_{\mathbf{u}}$ will be used to denote a *sequence* (or *word*) of distinct symbols of the form

$$\omega_{\mathbf{u}} := \omega_{u_1}\omega_{u_2}\cdots\omega_{u_k}. \tag{3}$$

Appending 0 to the set Σ_n, multiplication is defined on the words constructed from elements of Σ_n by

$$\omega_{\mathbf{u}}\omega_{\mathbf{v}} = \begin{cases} \omega_{\mathbf{u}.\mathbf{v}} & \text{if } \mathbf{u} \cap \mathbf{v} = \emptyset, \\ 0 & \text{otherwise,} \end{cases} \tag{4}$$

where $\mathbf{u}.\mathbf{v}$ denotes sequence concatenation.

One thereby obtains the noncommutative semigroup Ω_n, whose elements are the symbol 0 along with all *finite words* on distinct generators (i.e., finite sequences of distinct symbols from the alphabet Σ_n). Defining (vector) addition and real scalar multiplication on the semigroup yields the semigroup algebra $\mathbb{R}\Omega_n$. This semigroup algebra will be referred to as a *path algebra*.

THEOREM 1. *Given a multi-weighted graph G on n vertices and a constraint vector $\mathfrak{C} = (c_1, \ldots, c_m)$, let v_0 and v_∞ denote distinct source and target vertices, respectively. If Ψ is the $\mathfrak{C}$-constrained path-identifying nilpotent adjacency matrix associated with G, then the collection of feasible paths $v_0 \to v_\infty$ in G is given by*

$$\xi^{\mathbf{0}}\omega_0 \sum_{\ell=1}^{n} \langle v_0 | \Psi^\ell | v_\infty \rangle = \sum_{\substack{\text{paths } \mathbf{p}: v_0 \to v_\infty \\ \text{wt}(\mathbf{p}) < \mathbf{c}}} \xi^{\text{wt}(\mathbf{p})}\omega_{\mathbf{p}}. \tag{5}$$

More specifically, feasible paths exist if and only if $\xi^{\mathbf{0}}\omega_0 \sum_{\ell=1}^{n} \langle v_0 | \Psi^\ell | v_\infty \rangle$ is nonzero. For the case $v_0 = v_\infty$, one has

$$\langle v_0 | \Psi^\ell | v_0 \rangle = \sum_{\substack{\text{cycles } \mathbf{p}: v_0 \to v_0 \\ \text{wt}(\mathbf{p}) < \mathbf{c}}} \xi^{\text{wt}(\mathbf{p})}\omega_{\mathbf{p}}. \tag{6}$$

4. PATH SELECTION ALGORITHMS

In this section, two path selection algorithms are illustrated. In the first one, we suppose that there is a central entity (a server for example) which has a global view of the network and therefore can construct the Ψ matrix of the whole graph. We refer to this version as the centralized path selection algorithm. In the centralized algorithm, the graph is assumed to be static. The second algorithm presented, referred to as the online path selection algorithm, is a distributed version of the first one. In the online algorithm, each node in the graph is assumed to have a partial view of the whole graph (one-hop, two-hop, etc.) and is capable of constructing the Ψ matrix of this sub-graph. We note that OCRP uses the online version where the sub-graph of every node consists of its one-hop neighbors.

The graph example presented in Figure 1 is used to illustrate both path selection algorithms. Similar to Example II.4, the delay, link quality and node's residual energy are used as constraints with a constraint vector $\mathfrak{C} = \{9, 30, 70\}$ with the difference that the link quality in that case is expressed by *min* constraint in each hop, since it is equavalent to a multiplicative constraint in a whole path. The same product functions as the example are also used. In order to conserve space, parentheses have been omitted from exponents and multi indices.

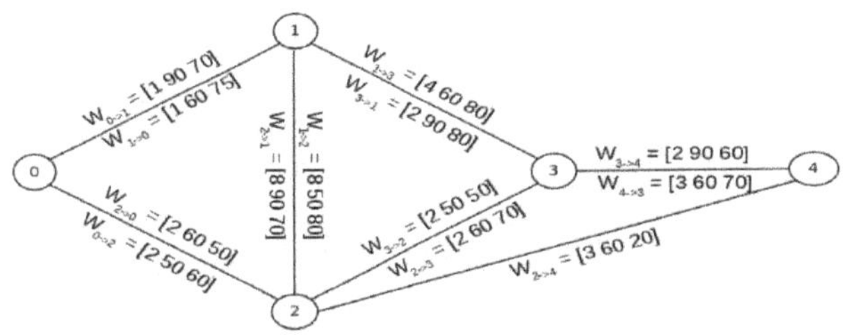

Figure 1: A graph example with links having a vector of weights. We observe that links may be unidirectional ($2 \to 4$) and links $i \to j$ and $j \to i$ have different weights.

The associated path-identifying nilpotent adjacency matrix Ψ of the above example is represented below.

4.1 Centralized path selection algorithm

The first centralized algorithm considered here is applied to a fixed graph, i.e., the static case. The topology of the

$$\begin{bmatrix} 0 & \overset{1,90,70}{\xi}\ \omega_{01} & \overset{2,50,60}{\xi}\ \omega_{02} & 0 & 0 \\ \overset{1,60,75}{\xi}\ \omega_{10} & 0 & \overset{8,50,80}{\xi}\ \omega_{12} & \overset{4,60,80}{\xi}\ \omega_{13} & 0 \\ \overset{2,60,50}{\xi}\ \omega_{20} & \overset{8,90,70}{\xi}\ \omega_{21} & 0 & \overset{2,60,70}{\xi}\ \omega_{23} & \overset{3,60,20}{\xi}\ \omega_{24} \\ 0 & \overset{2,90,80}{\xi}\ \omega_{31} & \overset{2,50,50}{\xi}\ \omega_{32} & 0 & \overset{2,90,60}{\xi}\ \omega_{34} \\ 0 & 0 & 0 & \overset{3,60,70}{\xi}\ \omega_{43} & 0 \end{bmatrix}$$

entire network is known at all times. Using the result of Theorem 1, Algorithm 1 enumerates all feasible hop-minimal paths from initial vertex v_0 to terminal vertex v_∞. Applying a choice function then allows the user to select a preferred path for the routing.

It is worth noting that OC eliminates at early stage any encountered infeasible path, leading thus to drastically decrease the search space, so largely reduce the total complexity. However, the number of solutions depends on how tight the constraints are. Tighter the constraints, fewer the solutions. Looser constraints give more solutions and require longer runtimes.

Algorithm 1 expresses the centralized algorithm in pseudocode.

input : Source node v_0, target node v_∞, and constrained path-identifying nilpotent adjacency matrix Ψ.
output: Component of row vector $\mathbf{u}$ representing all multi-weighted paths of minimal length from v_0 to v_∞ satisfying the constraint vector.

$\mathbf{u} := \mathbf{v}_0\Psi$
while $[(\mathbf{u} \neq \mathbf{0}\ \mathbf{and}\ \mathbf{u}_{v_\infty} \neq 0)]$ **do**
$\mathbf{u} := \mathbf{u}\Psi$
end
return $\mathbf{u}_{v_\infty}$

Algorithm 1: StaticCentralizedPaths (pseudocode)

At each iteration of the loop, a partial path is evolved one step. The algorithm terminates in two cases:

1. The partial paths all ultimately revisit vertices or violate the constraints. In this case the algorithm returns 0.
2. Any feasible path $v_0 \to v_\infty$ is found. At this point, the algorithm returns all existing feasible hop-minimal paths within the frame sequence considered.

Note that replacing the final line of Algorithm 1 by

$$\textbf{return}\ \gimel(\mathbf{u}_{v_\infty})$$

allows one to compute the *preferred* hop-minimal path from v_0 to v_∞.

Given initial vertex v_0, target vertex v_∞, and constrained path-identifying nilpotent adjacency matrix Ψ, the centralized algorithm proceeds as follows.

1. Compute the action of the matrix Ψ on the initial vertex v_0 and prepend the initial vertex to create a row vector, $\mathbf{u}$, containing partial paths of length 1. Simply stated, this is the v_0th row of Ψ with each entry left-multiplied by the element ω_{v_0}. In the pseudocode, this is denoted by $\mathbf{v}_0\Psi$.
2. If target has not been reached (v_∞-component of $\mathbf{u}$ is zero), apply the matrix Ψ to $\mathbf{u}$, thereby appending one step to each partial path.
3. Repeat step 2 until either the target has been reached or all partial paths have self-intersected, in which case $\mathbf{u} = 0$.
4. Return all existing hop-minimal paths to target (zero if no path exists). This information is found in the v_∞ component of $\mathbf{u}$.

Note that as a matrix, Ψ acts on row vectors by right-multiplication.

Applying the algorithm to the graph of Fig III.I, the task is to compute all feasible hop-minimal paths from 0 to 4, satisfying the constraint vector $\mathfrak{C}$. Setting $\mathbf{v}_0 := (\overset{0,\infty,\infty}{\xi}\ \omega_0)$, one-hop feasible paths with initial vertex 0 are recovered by computing the row vector

$$\mathbf{u} = \mathbf{v}_0\Psi = \begin{bmatrix} 0 & \overset{1,90,70}{\xi}\ \omega_{01} & \overset{2,50,60}{\xi}\ \omega_{02} & 0 & 0 \end{bmatrix}.$$

All two-hop feasible paths with initial vertex 0 can be found by computing $\mathbf{u} * \Psi = \mathbf{v}_0\Psi^2 =$

$$\begin{bmatrix} 0 & 0 & \overset{9,50,70}{\xi}\ \omega_{012} & \overset{5,60,70}{\xi}\ \omega_{013} + \overset{4,50,60}{\xi}\ \omega_{023} & 0 \end{bmatrix}.$$

The reader can verify that the second and fifth component of this vector is zero because the paths $\{021\}$ *and* $\{024\}$ are infeasible and are removed by the algebra, i.e., $\overset{2,50,60}{\xi}\ \overset{3,60,20}{\xi} = 0$ in the constraints algebra.

Respectively, the three-hop paths can be found by $\mathbf{v}_0\Psi^3 =$

$$\begin{bmatrix} 0 & \overset{6,50,60}{\xi}\ \omega_{0231} & 0 & 0 & \overset{6,50,60}{\xi}\ \omega_{0234} + \overset{7,60,60}{\xi}\ \omega_{0134} \end{bmatrix}.$$

In that point, the destination has been reached by the paths $\{0234\}$ and $\{0134\}$ and the algorithm terminates returning the two hop-minimal feasible paths.

The complexity of enumerating all feasible k-paths from v_0 to v_∞ with the operator calculus approach is

$$\mathcal{O}(n \cdot \sharp\{\mathbf{p} \in \mathcal{F}_{v_0} : |\mathbf{p}| \leq k-1\}),$$

where $\mathcal{F}_{v_0}$ denotes the collection of all feasible paths having initial vertex v_0, and $|\mathbf{p}|$ denotes the length (i.e., number of hops) of the path $\mathbf{p}$ [8].

4.2 Complexity evaluation of OC algorithm and comparison with SAMCRA

Since the complexity of OC approach depends on the number of feasible paths are found, we would like to give a numerical insight of the efficiency of the proposed algorthim. For that reason we evaluate OC experimentally and we compared it with SAMCRA, identifying their complexity under the same topology and same demands. SAMCRA is a well-known centralized, multi-constrained algorithm [11]. It terminates as soon as it finds one feasible path between two nodes. Comparing both algorithms in a fair way, OC stops the multiplication process whenever it finds one feasible path.

SAMCRA returns the path which has the minimum non-linear length l that satisfies all the constraints. If we consider a path P with k links: $P = \{e_1, e_2, \ldots, e_k\}$, the length of P is [11]:

$$l(P) = max_{1 \leq i \leq m}(\frac{\sum_{j=1}^{k} W_i^{e_j}}{L_i})$$

where m is the number of weights and L the constraint vector.

SAMCRA is based on two more principles: the $k-$shortest path approach and the non-dominance. The k-shortest path approach is used when more than one possible paths between a source and a destination is needed to be found. In SAMCRA, this approach is applied only to the intermediate nodes, where we store not only one but multiple sub-paths from the source to each intermediate node, only when these paths are non-dominated. In each step, SAMCRA chooses the sub-path with the minimum path length and stops whenever the first feasible path is found.

For comparing SAMCRA with OC, we limit ourselves to additive metrics since SAMCRA considers only this type of constraint. Both algorithms are compared under the randomly generated 128-node graph of Fig. 2. A weight vector of 3 additive metrics is associated to each link. 5 different constraint vectors are used that are depicted in Table 1 and each of them has three additive constraints, A, B and C. The weight of a path p corresponding to each metric is equal to the sum of weights of its links for this metric and has to be less or equal to the respective constraint. The constraint vector C_i represents stricter constraints than the constraint vector C_{i+1}.

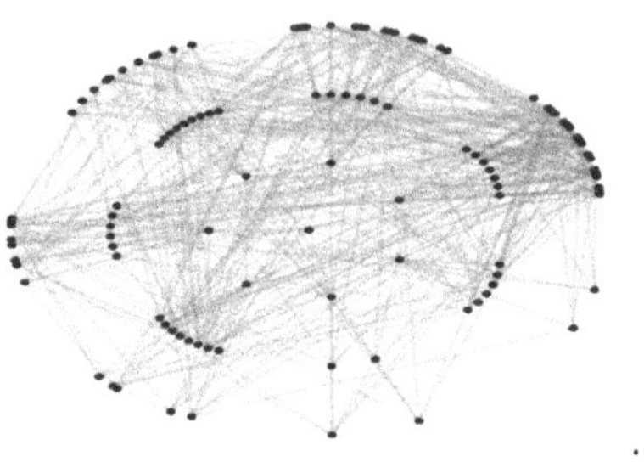

Figure 2: Randomly generated 128-node graph.

Constraints	A	B	C
$\mathfrak{C}_1$	1.61604	2.41987	68.1328
$\mathfrak{C}_2$	2.83083	4.75579	185.967
$\mathfrak{C}_3$	3.91719	6.85752	330.864
$\mathfrak{C}_4$	4.75373	10.1413	428.139
$\mathfrak{C}_5$	5.07585	14.1619	643.696

Table 1: Table of constraints

	C_1	C_2	C_3	C_4	C_5
SAMCRA	5262.9	5262.4	5398.3	5449.5	5438.0
OC	278.9	177.6	51.6	44.9	44.6

Table 2: Execution time in msec of 100 (centralized) random requests over a 128-node graph

Table 2 depicts the total computation time of 100 random requests of SAMCRA and OC on the graph of Fig. 2, using the 5 constraint vectors of Table 1. As we can observe, SAMRA needs more execution time than OC for computing all 100 requests.

Both SAMCRA and OC are exact, so they are able to find a solution, if a solution exists. SAMCRA is Dijkstra-based and this is the main reason that it is not enough efficient in terms of complexity when it is applied in big graphs. It's complexity depends on the number of nodes and the density of the graph. SAMCRA has to explore each unique link of the graph to find the optimal one. On the other hand, OC, using the nilpotent adjacency matrix needs less time for the graph search process.

Moreover, we can see in Table 2 that the execution time of SAMCRA is slightly increased as the constraints are relaxed. Relaxed constraints means that there is more space to explore or more sub-paths can be feasible. However, this is not the case for OC approach. The matrix multiplication process requires almost stable execution time, so more relaxed constraints enables OC to find more quickly a feasible solution. It seems that matrix multiplication is more efficient approach than the exhaustive graph search applied in SAMCRA.

SAMCRA can only work with positive and additive weights. The advantage of OC is its flexibility of the fact that it can work with both positive and negative weights and it can also deal with additive, concave and multiplicative metrics. Moreover, if we take into consideration the numerical results in terms of complexity, OC seems to be a very interesting approach for applications that demand high number of nodes.

Both algorithms have been implemented in Java 1.6.0.27 and computed in Ubuntu 12.04.3 with 2x3 Intel Core 2 Duo processor and 8 GB DDR2.

4.3 Distributed path selection algorithm

The distributed routing algorithm is implemented at individual nodes. Each node receiving a packet is able to choose a route for passing the packet along, based on some partial information the node has about the current network topology. The distributed algorithm described here makes use of the following assumption:

While the topology of the graph is not known at any time, each node "knows" its own best-case minimal distance from every other node in the underlying graph. This is the minimum number of hops between a node and every other node in the underlying graph assuming all links are valid. Writing $\mathcal{P}_{ij}$ for the set of all paths $\mathbf{p} : v_i \to v_j$ in the underlying graph G, let $d : V \times V \to \mathbb{N}_0 \cup \{\infty\}$ be the function defined by

$$d(v_i, v_j) := \begin{cases} \min_{\mathbf{p} \in \mathcal{P}_{ij}} \{|\mathbf{p}|\} & \text{if } \mathcal{P}_{ij} \neq \emptyset, \\ \infty & \text{otherwise.} \end{cases} \quad (7)$$

In other words, $d(v_i, v_j)$ is the minimum number of hops required to reach v_j from v_i among all existing paths in the underlying graph. If no such path exists, $d(v_i, v_j) = \infty$.

In order to determine whether an evolving path is getting closer to the destination, a "distance oracle" function is employed. We define the *distance oracle* $\Delta : (\mathcal{A}_{\mathfrak{C}} \otimes \Omega_n) \times (\mathcal{A}_{\mathfrak{C}} \otimes$

$\Omega_n) \to \mathbb{N}_0$ by

$$\Delta\left(\sum_{\mathbf{p}\in\mathcal{P}_1\subseteq\mathcal{P}} \xi^{\mathrm{wt}(\mathbf{p})}\omega_{\mathbf{p}}, \sum_{\mathbf{q}\in\mathcal{P}_2\subseteq\mathcal{P}} \xi^{\mathrm{wt}(\mathbf{q})}\omega_{\mathbf{q}}\right) := \min_{\substack{\mathbf{p}\in\mathcal{P}_1\\ \mathbf{q}\in\mathcal{P}_2}} d(\mathbf{p}_{|\mathbf{p}|}, \mathbf{q}_{|\mathbf{q}|}). \quad (8)$$

REMARK 1. *The distance oracle reveals the minimum number of hops required to reach the terminal vertex of a path in $\mathcal{P}_2$ from the terminal vertex of a path in $\mathcal{P}_1$.*

Given a finite path $\mathbf{b}$, denote by $\Psi_{(\mathbf{b},t_k)}$ the $\mathbf{b}$-*neighborhood adjacency matrix* at time t_k. This matrix represents the adjacency of the *neighborhood* $\mathcal{N}(\mathbf{b}_{|\mathbf{b}|})$ in the graph at time t_k.

Algorithm 2 is implemented at each node of the underlying graph. It is worthwhile to note that computations are being performed in a sequence of algebras.

For convenience, define the canonical *path projection* $\pi_\Omega : \mathcal{A}_{\mathfrak{C}} \otimes \Omega_n \to \mathcal{P}$ by linear extension of

$$\pi_\Omega(\xi^{\mathrm{wt}(\mathbf{b})}\omega_{\mathbf{b}}) := \mathbf{b}. \quad (9)$$

Algorithm 2 simulates the nodewise implementation to choose a preferred multi constrained path $v_0 \to v_\infty$ in the graph process $(G_{t_k} : k \in \mathbb{N}_0)$. It will be assumed that the time is discretized and the graph sequence is adapted such that topology changes cannot occur during a hop.

Algorithm 2 proceeds by developing multiple paths in parallel with source vertex v_0. At each time step, the partial paths are augmented by one step such that the constraints are still satisfied and the absolute distance (number of hops) from the target is not increased. The algorithm terminates when the time exceeds a final allowable time or when a feasible path $v_0 \to v_\infty$ is found.

Let us consider our graph example. In this example, we assume that each node can see only the one hop neighbors. The neighborhood adjacency matrix of node 0 is equal to:

$$\Psi_{(0,t)} = \begin{bmatrix} 0 & \overset{1,90,70}{\xi}\omega_{01} & \overset{2,50,60}{\xi}\omega_{02} \\ \overset{1,60,75}{\xi}\omega_{10} & 0 & 0 \\ \overset{2,60,50}{\xi}\omega_{20} & 0 & 0 \end{bmatrix}$$

The minimum number of hops required to reach the destination is $\delta = 2$ by the path $\{0, 2, 4\}$. The constraint vector of the online algorithm includes δ, so $\mathfrak{C} = \{2, 9, 30, 60\}$ and $\mathbf{v}_0 := (\overset{0,\infty,\infty}{\xi}\omega_0)$. Applying OC in node 0, leads to the following row vector, which represents the extention of the partial path by one step.

$$\mathbf{u} = \mathbf{v}_0\Psi_{(0,t)} = \begin{bmatrix} 0 & \overset{1,90,70}{\xi}\omega_{01} & \overset{2,50,60}{\xi}\omega_{02} \end{bmatrix}$$

Node 0 knows that 1 and 2 are closer to the destination. Therefore, algorithm 3 selects both nodes as next-hops.

The neighbourhood adjacency operator matrix of node 1 and 2 is given below:

input : Source vertex v_0, target node v_∞, initial time t_0, final allowable time t_∞, and neighborhood adjacency matrix $\Psi_{(v_0,t_k)}$ valid at time step t_0.
output: Algebraic element ψ representing a feasible path $v_0 \to v_\infty$ if one is found, zero otherwise.

Initialize frame counter (k), best case distance (in hops) from source to target (δ), constraints, and preferred first step from v_0.
$k := 0$
$\delta := \Delta(\xi^{\mathbf{0}}\omega_{v_0}, \xi^{\mathbf{0}}\omega_{v_\infty})$
$\mathfrak{C} := (\delta, c_1, \ldots, c_m)$
$\psi := \daleth\left(\langle \xi^{\mathbf{0}}\omega_{v_0} | \Psi_{(v_0,t_0)} | \mathbf{1}\rangle\right)$
Repeat until maximum frames considered or until remaining distance to target is zero.
while $\left[(t_k \le t_\infty)\ \mathbf{and}\ [\Delta(\psi, \xi^{0}\omega_{v_\infty}) \neq 0\right]$ **do**
  Advance frame counter.
  $k := k + 1$
  Extend partial path by one step.
  $\psi :=$
  MultiplePathEvolve$[\xi^{\mathbf{0}}\omega_{v_0}, v_\infty, t_k, \Psi_{(\pi_\Omega(\psi),t_k)}]$
end
Return preferred feasible path if one found. Otherwise, return zero.
return ψ

Algorithm 2: DistributedChoosePath

$$\Psi_{(1,2t)} = \begin{bmatrix} 0 & \overset{1,90,70}{\xi}\omega_{01} & 0 & 0 \\ \overset{1,60,75}{\xi}\omega_{10} & 0 & \overset{8,50,80}{\xi}\omega_{12} & \overset{4,60,80}{\xi}\omega_{13} \\ 0 & \overset{8,90,70}{\xi}\omega_{21} & 0 & 0 \\ 0 & \overset{2,90,80}{\xi}\omega_{31} & 0 & 0 \end{bmatrix}$$

$$\Psi_{(2,2t)} = \begin{bmatrix} 0 & 0 & \overset{2,50,60}{\xi}\omega_{02} & 0 & 0 \\ 0 & 0 & \overset{8,50,80}{\xi}\omega_{12} & 0 & 0 \\ \overset{2,60,50}{\xi}\omega_{20} & \overset{8,90,70}{\xi}\omega_{21} & 0 & \overset{2,60,70}{\xi}\omega_{23} & \overset{3,60,20}{\xi}\omega_{24} \\ 0 & 0 & \overset{2,50,50}{\xi}\omega_{32} & 0 & 0 \\ 0 & 0 & 0 & 0 & 0 \end{bmatrix}$$

In the next time step, both node 1 and 2 run OC and choose next valid hops and so on. The final row vector of node 3 is:

$$\mathbf{u} = \begin{bmatrix} 0 & 0 & 0 & \overset{6,50,60}{\xi}\omega_{0234} + \overset{7,60,60}{\xi}\omega_{0134} \end{bmatrix}$$

We need to remark that in the distributed version of OC the number of paths may be limited compared to the centralized version because of the parameter δ. In our example, the path $\{0231\}$ is not found by the distributed OC because node 3 cannot send the packet to node 2, since both nodes have same δ. Sender-nodes can forward a packet to nodes which have a strictly lesser δ.

input : Algebraic monomial $\xi^{\mathrm{wt}(\mathbf{b})}\omega_{\mathbf{b}} \in \mathcal{A}_{\mathfrak{C}} \otimes \Omega_n$, target node v_∞, and discrete time t_k. The element $\xi^{\mathrm{wt}(\mathbf{b})}\omega_{\mathbf{b}}$ represents a multi-weighted partial path (of length $|\mathbf{b}|$) from fixed initial vertex v_0 to vertex $v_{\mathbf{b}_{|\mathbf{b}|}}$. The constraint vector is $\mathfrak{C} = (\delta, c_1, \ldots, c_m)$.

Data: Neighborhood adjacency matrix $\Psi_{(\mathbf{b},t_k)}$ valid at time step t_k is assumed to be available, as this is implemented at each node.

output: Algebraic element ψ representing all feasible multi-weighted paths of length $|\mathbf{b}|+1$ emanating from v_0, satisfying the fixed constraint vector, and whose last steps do not increase the minimal distance to v_∞ over the previous partial path.

Get best-case remaining distance from target.
$\delta' := \Delta(\xi^{\mathbf{b}}\omega_{\mathbf{b}}, \xi^{\mathbf{0}}\omega_{v_\infty})$

Reset constraints so remaining distance cannot increase during path evolution.
$\mathfrak{C} := (\delta, c_1, \ldots, c_m)$

Extend partial path by one step, and return feasible paths.
return $\langle \xi^{\mathrm{wt}(\mathbf{b})}\omega_{\mathbf{b}} | \Psi_{(\mathbf{b},t_k)}$

Algorithm 3: MultiplePathEvolve

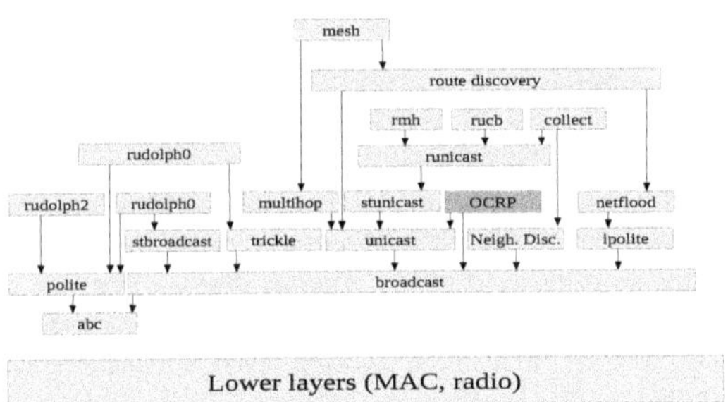

Figure 3: Rime stack

5. IMPLEMENTATION OF OCRP

OCRP is a multi-constrained routing protocol that applies OC methods to find the set of feasible paths from a source node to a destination. The OC method is implemented in a distributive manner on every node of the network and is applied for every generated and received data packet. OCRP is implemented in Contiki OS [20].

Each path must satisfy three constraints: end-to-end delay, link quality, and nodes' residual energy. The total end-to-end delay must be less than d_{max}, the link quality of each hop must be greater than lq_{min}, and the remaining energy of each node in the path must be greater than re_{min}. Other constraints can be easily added.

The OCRP implementation is based on the RIME stack as described in the next section.

5.1 General description of OCRP

OCRP is implemented on top of the broadcast module and unicast module as illustrated in Figure 3. It is independent of the MAC protocol. OCRP implements three different modules, described next.

Neighbor discovery and maintenance.

This module is responsible for maintaining an up-to-date neighbor table. It is an important feature since all other modules rely on the neighbor table for its functionality. Every node uses either hello messages or data messages to broadcast its internal state to neighbors. A node generates a hello message and broadcasts it if no data is generated or forwarded during the last period of time. A broadcast process is responsible for setting the period's length and handling its expiration within each node. The hello or data packets include the remaining energy of the node. A neighbor node that receives a hello packet computes the link quality using the LQI and RSSI values of the packet.

Delay Estimator.

This module measures the round trip time (RTT) for every neighbor node. It is called every random amount of time selected within a given interval. This interval is chosen such that the RTT for all neighbors are computed within a reasonable amount of time and for all situations compared to data generation, while limiting its effect on traffic. During each call, a node selects the next neighbor in the neighbor table and sends a unicast PING message to it. On reception of the PING message, the neighbor sends back a PONG message. The PING originating node then calculates the last RTT and updates its weighted moving average according to equation 10. We note here that we could not implement delay estimation using data messages since data may be forwarded to multiple receivers in a single broadcast; therefore no acknowledgements are used.

$$\overline{RTT}_{n+1} = \alpha \overline{RTT_n} + (1-\alpha) RTT_{n+1} \tag{10}$$

Data broadcast protocol.

This module is responsible for the generation and routing of data packets. It is detailed in the next section.

In addition to the processes described, OCRP uses an implicit time synchronization protocol, called timesynch. "The time synchronization is implicit in that no explicit time synchronization messages are sent: the module relies on the underlying network device driver to timestamp all radio messages, both outgoing and incoming. The code currently only works on the Tmote Sky platform (TelosB0) [22] and the cc2420 driver [21].

Time synchronization eases the calculation of the remaining time before the end-to-end delay deadline expires. A data message is time stamped before being queued by the transmitting node. The receiving node uses this information to calculate the message transfer time and subsequently update the remaining time before deadline expiration.

5.2 Data broadcast protocol

The data broadcast protocol (DBP) is responsible for the generation and the routing of data packets to the destination. Hereafter we describe how it works from the generation to the final reception.

After the generation or the reception of a data packet, a node executes the following steps:

1. It executes the OC method to select the set of valid next-hops.
2. It includes the set of valid next-hops in the data packet header.
3. It transmits the packet.

When a packet is received from the MAC layer, a node determines whether it is the destination. If the answer is yes, the data are extracted from the packet and no further actions are taken. Otherwise, it determines whether its address is included in the set of valid next-hops. If the answer is no, the packet is deleted and no further actions are taken. Otherwise, it tests whether the packet is processed for the first time or not. If the answer is no, then the packet is deleted and no further actions are taken. If the node is included in the list of next-hops and the packet is processed for the first time, then it executes stages 1, 2, and 3 as described above.

A node stores the sequence numbers and the source addresses of the last received packets. Therefore, it can verify if a packet has already been received.

The following paragraph details how a valid next hop is selected.

Computing a valid next-hop. The neighbor discovery and maintenance module and the delay estimator module ensure that every node in the network knows its list of neighbors, their remaining energy, and the link quality and estimated delay to reach each neighbor.

In addition, each node knows its distance as well as its neighbors' relative distances to a given sink node. In the actual implementation, this information is embedded in hello and data messages. Initially, a sink node advertises a rank equal to zero to itself and other nodes advertise an infinite rank to any sink. Whenever a node receives a rank value strictly lesser than its actual rank for a given sink, it updates its new rank as the received rank plus one and advertises it in its hello and data packets.

For any given packet to transmit, a neighbor is valid if the following two conditions are met. First, the distance of the neighbor to the destination is strictly less than the distance of the actual node to the destination. Second, the progression of a packet to this neighbor does not violate the constraints imposed on this packet.

The OC algorithm is then implemented as follows. First, the node computes the set of nodes that respect the first condition. The node has now a partial view of the network graph (limited to its neighbors) for which it builds its 'nilpotent adjacency matrix', Ψ. The path selection algorithm is finally applied to Ψ and the list of valid next-hops is derived.

5.3 Other implementation details

The broadcast and unicast procedures implement a retry counter. Each packet is transmitted up to $MaxRetriesCount$ times until the packet is successfully forwarded to the next-hop. In each attempt, the underlying protocol sends an indication to OCRP to indicate whether or not the message has been successfully transmitted. Note that a successful transmission does not imply that the next-hop has effectively received the packet. This depends on the MAC protocol in use.

OCRP uses one transmission queue for broadcast and unicast packets. Therefore, the RTT calculations take the queueing delay into account. This is an important feature since the queueing delay largely affects the per hop packet transfer delay.

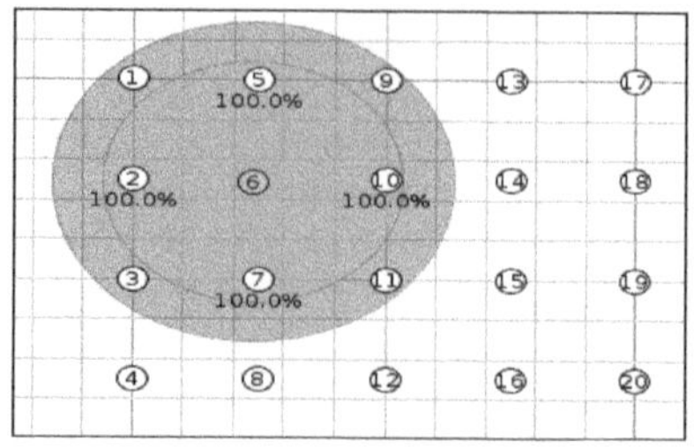

Figure 4: Simulated scenario. Nodes are organized in grid. Chequered green circle delimits the transmission radio. Grey circle delimits the interference zone

6. PERFORMANCE ANALYSIS

6.1 Simulation setup

We consider two multi-hop networks composed of 20 and 40 nodes organized in a grid and distributed in a surface of $100 \times 100m^2$. An example of the 20-node graph is illustrated in Figure 4. Node (1), located in the upper left of the network, is the sink node and the remaining nodes are senders. The transmission range is fixed to $20m$ with an interference radius equal to $30m$. Cooja simulator tool was used to compare the performance of OCRP with tree and directional flooding routing. The TelosB sky motes were emulated to obtain higher fidelity results. The radio model is the UDGM radio loss [1].

A node generates periodically a data packet each 0.25, 0.5, 1, 2 and 10 msecs. This means that each node generates 4, 2, 1, 0.5 and 0.1 packets per second respectively. All the packets are sent to node (1). The nodes' radios are always on. We opted for this choice to measure the intrinsic performance of routing protocols. Nodes have a unique queue for transmitting data, hello messages and unicast PING messages. Its length is fixed to 10 in the simulations. We note that increasing queue length penalizes static tree routing and flooding protocols since OCRP selects the nodes which have the lowest RTT. In fact, RTT calculation captures the queueing delay.

The delay (in ms), link quality (percentage) and nodes' residual energy (percentage) were used as constraints, $\mathfrak{C} = (d_{\max}, lq_{\min}, re_{\min})$. $* = (+, \min, \min)$, $\mathfrak{R} = (<, >, >)$. In the simulations, $\mathfrak{C} = (100, 30, 30)$ for the 20-node graph and $\mathfrak{C} = (200, 30, 30)$ for the 40-node graph.

We measured the *end-to-end delay*, the *rate of packet delivery within deadline* and the *energy consumption*. The *end-to-end delay* is defined as the average end-to-end delay of all received packets, considering only the first reception of the same packet. The *rate of packet delivery within deadline* is defined as the number of received packets which respected the deadline divided by the total number of generated packets. The *energy consumption* is defined as the average units of energy consumed per second. Here we assume that a broadcast packet and a unicast packet consume 1 unit and 0.5 units of energy, respectively. We simply assume that the

[1] Unit Disk Graph Model.

energy cost to transmit a broadcast packet is twice the cost of transmitting a unicast packet. This is particularly true for some duty-cycled MAC protocols like B-MAC, X-MAC, and Contiki-MAC [17, 18, 19]. In fact, the broadcast is repeatedly transmitted during a whole duty-cycle period to ensure that the packet is received by all neighbor nodes.

We compared the performance of OCRP, tree routing and directional flooding routing. We recall that each node in OCRP selects multiple valid next-hops according to $\mathfrak{C}$. Directional flooding selects all the next-hops that are closer to the destination (lower rank) and tree routing works by sending the packet to the static parent of the node.

6.2 Simulation results

Figures 5 and 8 show the ratio of packet delivery within deadline (PDD). According to the results, tree routing and OCRP have similar performance in case of 20-node graph but OCRP is slightly better in case of 40-node network. Directional flooding obtains the worst results. Overall results degrade when the traffic increases.

OCRP removes in advance all the partial paths that do not satisfy the constraints, while the other protocols forward the packets without any limit. This means that the PDD of OCRP totally depends on the deadline. Nevertheless, we can observe that the performance of both OCRP and tree routing is close in terms of PDD. Tree routing loose many packets because it is static. It uses predifined paths and high traffic deteriorates its performance due to the fact that the parents, particularly the ones located in the destination neighborhood, get congested. They are busy forwarding packets, and their queues have higher utilization. Hence, the number of received packets, as well as the number of received packets within deadline, decrease. This behavior results also in higher end-to-end delays as shown in Figure 7 and 10. OCRP dynamically selects next-hops according to neighbor's state. It thereby dynamically balances load among all its neighbors, which leads to better PDD and end-to-end delay results.

In directional flooding, since every packet is forwarded to all neighbors that are closer to the destination, multiple copies of the same packet are transmitted for each newly generated one. This has the effect of overloading the nodes– especially the immediate neighbors of the destination. Another impact is the high number of collisions between the nodes which try to transmit. As a consequence, this high load impacts not only the number of received packets within deadline, but also the energy consumption and the end-to-end delay as shown in all other figures.

Since reliability is one of the most important issues in WSNs, recovery processes are needed in case of failures in the network. OCRP and even directional flooding are more reliable in that case, since they use the multi-path approach and each new generated packet may follow different paths. On the other hand, tree routing keeps predefined static paths and this does not define it as a fault tolerant routing protocol. For instance, if a sensor node is out of battery, all the packets that traverse from this node will be dropped.

The proposed delay estimation, link quality and delay measurements implementation may be further improved. Nevertheless, these encouraging results show that OCRP algorithm could be effectively implemented in wireless sensor networks. This is a proof of concept for a new multi-constrained routing strategy that will be improved in future work. We note that the code has been successfully uploaded and tested using five TelosB nodes. However, a bigger network has to be deployed to get meaningful results.

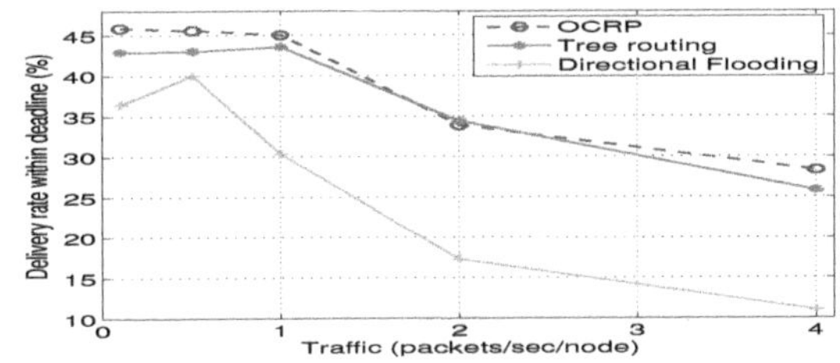

Figure 5: Ratio of delivery within deadline for 20-node graph.

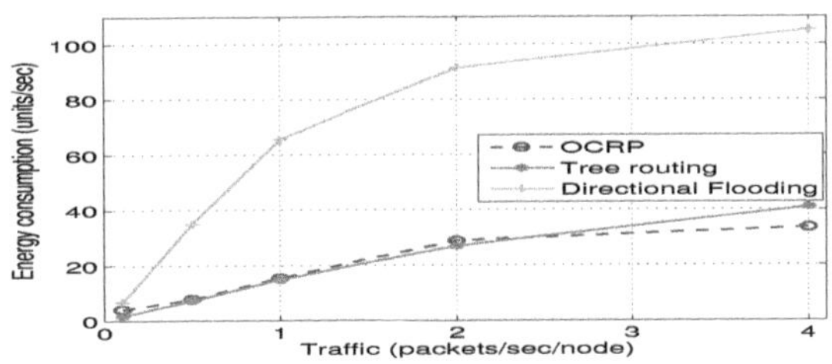

Figure 6: Energy consumption for 20-node graph.

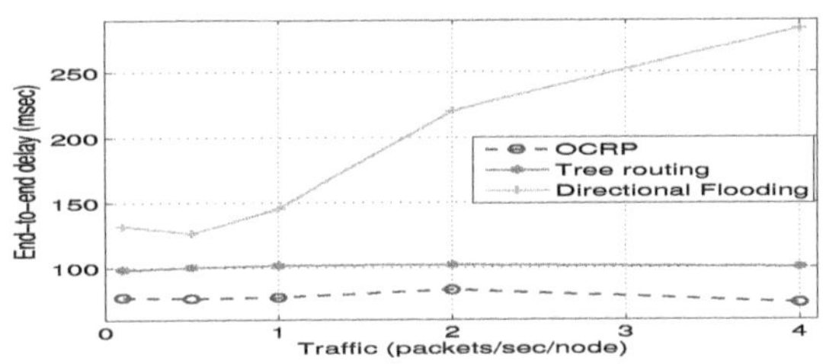

Figure 7: End-to-end delay for 20-node graph.

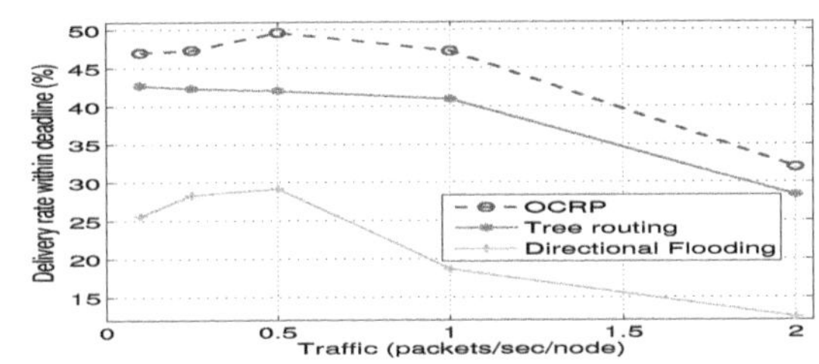

Figure 8: Ratio of delivery within deadline for 40-node graph.

7. CONCLUSIONS

Operator calculus method on graphs is a new and innovative approach for solving multi-constrained routing problems. Based on this approach, we developed a new algorithm for solving multi-constrained path selection in graphs. We presented centralized offline and distributed online versions of this algorithm. The offline version is implemented within a node and assumes a global knowledge of the graph structure. The online version is implemented within every node

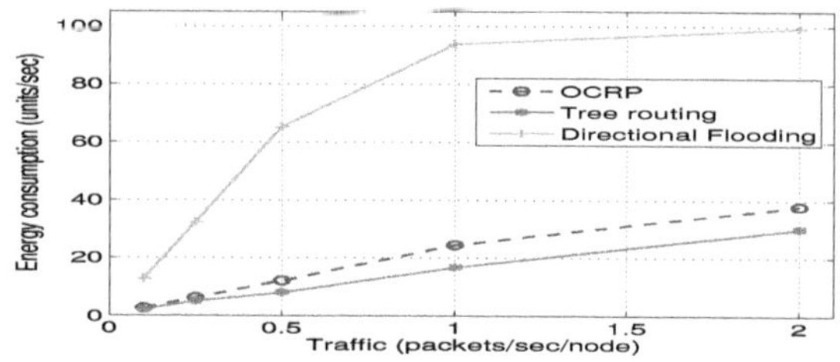

Figure 9: Energy consumption for 40-node graph.

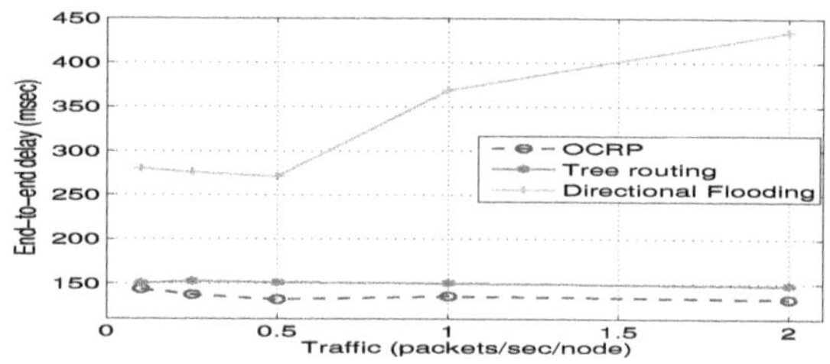

Figure 10: End-to-end delay for 40-node graph.

and assumes that each node has a partial view of the network. We did an experimental evaluation of OC, we compared it with SAMCRA and we show that OC is more efficient than SAMCRA in terms of execution time.

We presented a new dynamic routing protocol, called OCRP, which successfully implements the distributed algorithm within ContikiOS. In addition to the multi-constrained path selection, the RTT estimation, link quality and delay measurement protocols ensure that OCRP adapts its behavior according to the network's state. We showed through emulation using Cooja and uploading to real nodes that our distributed multi-constrained path selection algorithm is well supported by resource-constrained wireless sensor nodes.

In future work, we will improve OCRP using more reliable RTT and link quality estimation. We also plan to move from RIME to uIP stack and compare OCRP with RPL routing protocol. Finally, we plan to use IoT-LAB for more large-scale implementations.

8. ACKNOWLEDGMENTS

This work was supported in part by Quasimodo project (ANR 2010 INTB 0206 01) and Lorraine AME Satelor project.

9. REFERENCES

[1] T. He, J. Stankovic, C. Lu, and T. Abdelzaher, "SPEED: A Stateless Protocol for Real-Time Communication in Sensor Networks", *Proceedings of IEEE International Conference on Distributed Computing Systems*, pp. 46-55, 2005.

[2] Chipara, O.; He, Z.; Guoling Xing; Qin Chen; Xiaorui Wang; Chenyang Lu; Stankovic, J.; Abdelzaher, T., "Real-time Power-Aware Routing in Sensor Networks", *14th IEEE International Workshop on Quality of Service (IWQoS 2006)* , pp.83-92, June 2006.

[3] R. Bellman, "On a routing problem", *Quarterly of Applied Mathematics*, **16** (1958),87-90.

[4] H.W. Corley, I.D. Moon, "Shortest paths in networks with vector weights", *Journal of Optimization Theory and Applications*, **46** (1985), 79-86.

[5] H. Cruz-Sánchez, G.S. Staples, R. Schott, Y-Q. Song, "Operator calculus approach to minimal paths: Precomputed routing in a store-and-forward satellite constellation", *Proceedings of IEEE Globecom 2012*, Anaheim, USA, December 3-7. pp. 3438-3443.

[6] E.W. Dijkstra, "A note on two problems in connexion with graphs", *Numerische Mathematik*, **1** (1959), 269271.

[7] L.R. Ford Jr., D.R. Fulkerson, *Flows in Networks*, Princeton University Press, 1962.

[8] R. Schott, G.S. Staples. *Operator Calculus on Graphs (Theory and Applications in Computer Science)*, Imperial College Press, London, 2012.

[9] R. Schott, G.S. Staples, "Operator calculus on generalized zeon algebras: theory and application to multi-constrained path problems", *Prépublications de l'Institut Elie Cartan*, 2011/18, (2011). Online at `http://hal.archives-ouvertes.fr/hal-00603748/PDF/staceyQoSjune11.pdf`.

[10] Z. Wang, J. Crowcroft, "QoS routing for supporting resource reservation", *IEEE Journal on Selected Areas in Communications*, **14** (1996), 1228–1234.

[11] P. Van Mieghem, F. A. Kuipers, "On the complexity of QoS routing", *Computer Communications*, **26** (2003), 376–387.

[12] G. Xue, W. Zhang, J. Tang, K. Thulasiraman, "Polynomial time approximation algorithms for multi-constrained QoS routing", *IEEE/ACM Transactions on Networking*, **16** (2008), 656–669.

[13] G.Liu and K. G. Ramakrushnam, "A* Prune: an algorithm for finding K shortest paths subject to multiple constraints" IEEE INFOCOM 2001 2(April 2001) 743-749.

[14] H. Alwan and A. Agarwal,"MQoSR: A Multiobjective QoS Routing Protocol for Wireless Sensor Networks,âĂİ ISRN Sensor Networks, vol. 2013, Article ID 495803, 12 pages, 2013.

[15] X. Huang, Y. Fang, Multiconstrained QoS multipath routing in wireless sensor networks, Journal of Wireless Networks 465-478

[16] RPL: IPv6 Routing Protocol for Low power and Lossy Networks - http://tools.ietf.org/html/draft-ietf-roll-rpl-19

[17] J. Polastre, J. Hill, and D. Culler. "Versatile low power media access for wireless sensor networks", *International Conference on Embedded Networked Sensor Systems (ACM SenSys)*, Baltimore, MD, USA, 2004.

[18] M. Buettner, G. V. Yee, E. Anderson, and R. Han, "X-MAC: a short preamble MAC protocol for duty-cycled wireless sensor networks", *International Conference on Embedded Networked Sensor Systems (ACM SenSys)* , Boulder, Colorado, USA, 2006.

[19] A. Dunkels, *The ContikiMAC Radio Duty Cycling Protocol* , SICS Technical Report T2011:13, ISSN 1100-3154, December 2011.

[20] Contiki OS. `http://www.contiki-os.org/`

[21] Timesynch module. `http://contiki.sourceforge.net/docs/2.6/a01741.html`

[22] TelosB data sheet. `http://www.willow.co.uk/TelosB_Datasheet.pdf`.

Poster: An Adaptive Copy Spraying Scheme for Data Forwarding in Mobile Opportunistic Networks

Peiyan Yuan
School of Computer and Information Engineering
Henan Normal University
Xinxiang, China
peiyan@htu.cn

Wei Wang
School of Computer and Information Engineering
Henan Normal University
Xinxiang, China
wangwei6800@gmail.com

Chenyang Wang
School of Computer and Information Engineering
Henan Normal University
Xinxiang, China
mkingsun@foxmail.com

ABSTRACT

Mobile opportunistic network (MON) is a new paradigm which exploits node contacts to forward data, enabling numerous and impressive applications. The data copy spraying scheme is a challenging problem in MON, due to the mobility of nodes and lack of global knowledge, it hence captures great interests from research communities. Traditional algorithms allocate data copies with node's statistical information and neglect the temporal contact feature, resulting in a poor delivery performance. We propose AS, an adaptive data copy spraying scheme in MON. AS adjusts the number of copies dynamically based on the temporal contact feature among nodes. Theoretical analysis verifies that AS achieves a lower mean delivery delay than SprayWait, one of the state-of-the-art works. Simulation results show that AS improves the packet delivery ratio simultaneously.

Categories and Subject Descriptors

C.2.1 [**Computer-Communication Networks**]: Network Architecture and Design—*Store and forward networks*

General Terms

Algorithms, Design, Analysis

Keywords

data forwarding; copy spraying; mobile opportunistic networks

1. INTRODUCTION

With recent advancements in wireless communication and mobile sensing technologies, current smart devices have powerful sensing abilities and communication functions, which triggers research in leveraging them to collect data from physical world or share interests among communities. Such sensing/communicaton paradigm is generally called mobile opportunistic networks (MON) [4]. Compared to the traditional wireless sensor networks and ad hoc networks, one of the most characteristics of MON is that they do not require a fully connected end-to-end path between node pairs. This new feature makes them very suitable for scenarios with temporal topology, and enables numerous applications ranging from wild monitoring to crowd sensing [1], from rural communications to metropolitan awareness of issues [6], etc.

Delivering packets is challenging due to the intermittent links in the above scenarios. To improve data transmission efficiency, many quota based routing protocols have been proposed, which mainly include SprayWait [2], Hug [5] and HS [3]. These algorithms achieve a better tradeoff between the packet delivery ratio and mean delivery delay by limiting the number of copies. Hoverver, all of them allocate copies of packets with node's statistical information and neglect the temporal contact feature, making them less efficient. Considering this issue, we propose AS, an adaptive copy spraying scheme in MON. AS sprays data copies among nodes based on their temporal contact ratios. We outline the details of AS in subsequent sections.

2. ADAPTIVE COPY SPRAYING

We observe that node's contact ratio is temporal even in a homogenous scenario (i.e., all nodes follow the same mobility model). We would like to exploit the temporal contact feature to improve delivery performance by doing adaptive spraying. Each node carries a counter to record the number of contacts between itself and other nodes in the past time window W, where the parameter W can be set one hour, one day or one week based on the granularity of data sets. When two nodes I and J encounter, they make the following decision.

2.1 Decision making

For any node I receiving a packet with l copies, if it has a contact with another node J without copies, it forwards $\left\lfloor {}^{l\beta_j}/_{(\beta_i+\beta_j)} \right\rfloor$ copies to node J and keeps $\left\lceil {}^{l\beta_i}/_{(\beta_i+\beta_j)} \right\rceil$ for itself, where β_i and β_j denote the contact ratio of nodes I and J at moment t, respectively. The difference among AS, HS and SprayWait is illustrated in Fig.1, where the subscripts denote the number of copies nodes carry.

Suppose the node I carry 8 copies. Fig.1(a) shows the copy spraying process of SprayWait, it takes a binary way to allocate copies, so each node eventually carries 4 copies. In Fig.1(b), node I will deliver all copies to node J if the latter is a homing node. If data copies are sprayed by the AS

MobiHoc'15, June 22–25, 2015, Hangzhou, China.
ACM 978-1-4503-3489-1/15/06.
http://dx.doi.org/10.1145/2746285.2764862.

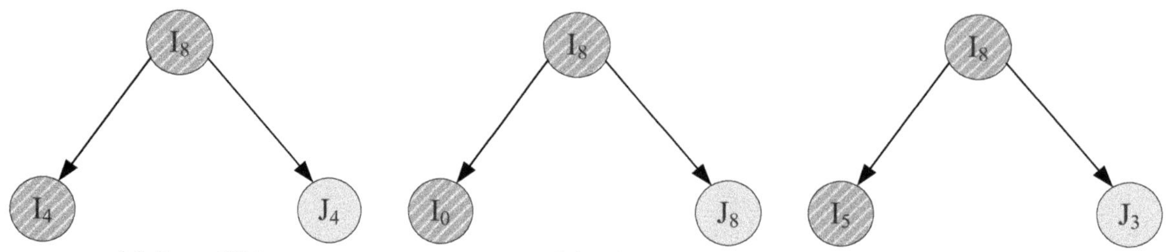

(a) SprayWait (b) HS (c) AS

Figure 1: The copy spraying process between two nodes under the three algorithms.

algorithm as shown in Fig.1(c), node I will allocate 3 copies to node J and leave 5 copies to itself (suppose $\beta_i = 0.5$ and $\beta_j = 0.3$).

From the aforementioned, we know that AS is equivalent to SprayWait if $\beta_i \equiv \beta_j$, and if $\beta_i << \beta_j$ it turns into HS. That is, AS generalizes both SprayWait and HS by dynamically adjusting the number of copies. We next prove AS achieves the optimal delivery performance.

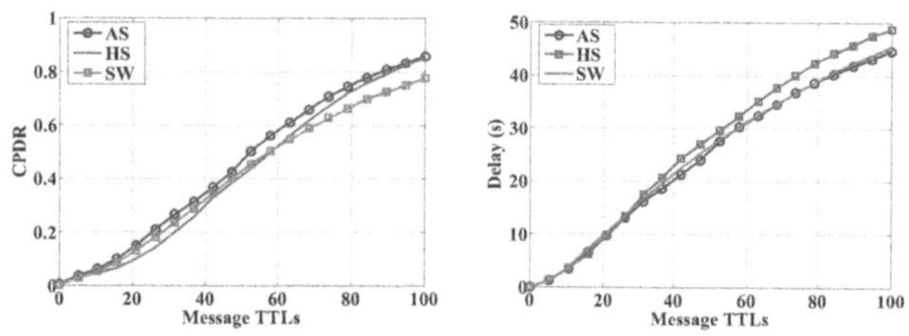

(a) CPDR (b) MDD

Figure 2: The CPDR and MDD under different message TTLs, where the number of nodes is 100 and the community mobility model is implemented.

2.2 Performance analysis

THEOREM 1. *AS achieves the optimal delivery performance.*

PROOF. Suppose there exits another scheme called OS and $\beta_i > \beta_j$, in which node I leaves $\lceil l\alpha/(\beta_i + \beta_j) \rceil$ for itself $(0 \leq \alpha \leq \beta_i + \beta_j)$ and the left for node J.

When $\alpha \geq \beta_i$, it indicates node I carries more copies in OS than in AS, so node I needs to spend more time to allocate copies in OS. Now we suppose $\alpha < \beta_i$, that is, node J carries more copies in OS than in AS, considering the fact that $\beta_i > \beta_j$, we conclude that node I sprays more faster than that of node J given the same number of copies they carry.

When $\beta_i \leq \beta_j$, we get the same conclusion by analyzing node J. □

2.3 Performance evaluation

Fig.2 shows the cumulative packet delivery ratio (CPDR) and mean delivery delay (MDD), where the term "SW" denotes SprayWait. It's obvious to see that AS achieves the highest CPDR and the shortest MDD compared to HS and SprayWait. It improves CPDR about by 8% and MDD by 10%, respectively. Both the two results demonstrate that the AS achieves a better performance since it can adaptively adjust the number of copies among nodes.

3. CONCLUSION AND FUTURE WORK

In this paper, we present a novel routing metric, called AS, to improve the performance of mobile opportunistic networks. We exploit the temporal contact feature to design utility function. We prove and show the performance gain from both the theoretical analysis and experimental evaluation. In the future, the use of time window to compute node's contact ratio will be investigated. Neglecting to do this will result in divergent contact ratios, impacting the AS performance. Extensive simulations under various scenarios will be run to evaluate the protocol, and to explore the influence of different parameter settings and forwarding metrics.

4. ACKNOWLEDGMENTS

This work was supported by the National Natural Science Foundation of China under Grant No. U1404602, the Science and Technology Foundation of Henan Educational Committee under Grant No.14A520031 and the Dr. Start-up Project of Henan Normal University under Grant No. qd14136.

5. REFERENCES

[1] H. Ma, D. Zhao, and P. Yuan. Opportunities in mobile crowd sensing. *Communications Magazine, IEEE*, 52(8):29–35, August 2014.

[2] T. Spyropoulos, K. Psounis, and C. S. Raghavendra. Efficient routing in intermittently connected mobile networks: the multiple-copy case. *Networking, IEEE/ACM Transactions on*, 16(1):77–90, February 2008.

[3] J. Wu, M. Xiao, and L. Huang. Homing spread: Community home-based multi-copy routing in mobile social networks. In *INFOCOM, 2013 Proceedings IEEE*, pages 2319–2327. IEEE, 2013.

[4] P. Yuan and P. Liu. Data fusion prolongs the lifetime of mobile sensing networks. *Journal of Network and Computer Applications*, 49:51–59, March 2015.

[5] P. Yuan and H. Ma. Hug: Human gathering point based routing for opportunistic networks. In *Wireless Communications and Networking Conference (WCNC), 2012 IEEE*, pages 3024–3029. IEEE, 2012.

[6] P. Yuan, H. Ma, and H. Fu. Hotspot-entropy based data forwarding in opportunistic social networks. *Pervasive and Mobile Computing*, 16:136–154, January 2015.

Poster: Compressed Sensing Inspired Approaches for Path Reconstruction in Wireless Sensor Networks

Rui Liu Yao Liang Xiaoyang Zhong
Department of Computer and Information Science
Indiana University – Purdue University Indianapolis, Indiana, USA
{liurui, yliang, xiaozhon}@cs.iupui.edu

ABSTRACT
In this work, we investigate routing dynamics in mobile ad hoc wireless sensor networks (WSNs), which is of great importance for network performance analysis, operation optimization, system maintenance, and network diagnosis. We study packet path recovery for data collection in multi-hop dynamic WSNs at the sink based on compressed sensing approach. We extend our previous outing topology recovery (RTR) approach and evaluate its performance in comparison with the recent CSPR. Our work provides insights into the understanding of the profound impacts of different compressed sensing inspired approaches on their respective path reconstruction performance, and the resource requirement on sensor nodes. The evaluation results show that RTR can significantly outperform CSPR in various WSN setups.

Categories and Subject Descriptors
C.2.1 [**Computer-Communication Networks**]: Network Architecture and Design – *Wireless communication.*

Keywords
Wireless sensor networks; routing topology; compressed sensing; path reconstruction.

1. INTRODUCTION
It is increasingly important to understand packet routing dynamics in multi-hop and large-scale WSNs for network analysis, operation optimization, system maintenance, and network diagnosis. While a simple way is to directly record individual forwarding node's ID along the route in each packet, it is not scalable and also not resource-efficient. To address this challenge, several novel approaches for path-reconstruction in WSNs have been proposed recently, including Multi-hop Network Tomography (MNT) [1], PathZip [2], Routing Topology Recovery (RTR) [3], Pathfinder [4], and Compressive Sensing based Path Reconstruction (CSPR) [5]. MNT and Pathfinder rely on anchor packets to take advantage of the inter-packet correlation to infer packet path. PathZip compresses the path information into a hash value carried by each packet, in which the computation complexity grows exponentially with the size of WSN and thus may suffer from its scalability issue. RTR and CSPR are inspired by compressed sensing (CS). Recently, authors of CSPR [5] showed that CSPR performed better than MNT and Pathfinder.

This work focuses on the CS inspired approaches for path reconstruction in WSNs. Compressed sensing is a breakthrough technique in information theory and signal processing, which enables to recover a sparse signal from a small number of measurements. We note that the formulations of the RTR [3] and the recent CSPR [5] are very different. In view of this, we intend to understand if the two different CS-based formulations would have any profound impacts on their respective performances, as well as their resource requirements on each sensor node. In our RTR approach, the concept of base topology is introduced for WSN routing for data gathering, defined as the superset of all possible routing topologies of the WSN. Given a WSN of size n, the total number of directed wireless links (due to asymmetry wireless channel property) in the link space associated to the WSN base topology should be $N=n(n-1)-(n-1)=(n-1)^2$, modeled as a directed acyclic graph G(V, E) without those wireless links outgoing from the sink. Our RTR approach is based on the observation that a WSN routing path, in principle, can be represented as a sparse ***link*** vector, each element in which corresponds to a link in the WSN link space of dimension $N=(n-1)^2$. In contrast, a path in CSPR is represented as a sparse ***node*** vector whose element corresponds to a node in the WSN. Therefore, in CSPR, the path representation space has its dimension $N=n$ for a given WSN of size n.

We extend our original RTR approach by devising new decoding algorithms for both reliable and lossy WSNs. We then evaluate the extended RTR versus the CSPR via careful network simulations. We present not only the evaluation results, but also our insights and analysis.

2. RTR
RTR formulates the path recovery as a novel CS-inspired problem. Let matrix $\Phi = \{\varphi_{i,j}\}$ ($1 \le i \le n-1$, $1 \le j \le (n-1)^2$) represent a routing matrix in a WSN of size n (including the sink), whose elements $\varphi_{i,j}$ are defined as

$$\varphi_{i,j} = \begin{cases} 1, & \text{the ith path traverses over the jth link;} \\ 0, & \text{otherwise.} \end{cases}$$

Given a path measurement vector Y at the WSN sink for a collection cycle, reconstruct the link vector X and matrix Φ, so that

$$\hat{X} = arg\,min||X||_0 \text{ subject to } Y = \hat{\Phi}X,$$

where l_0-norm $||X||_0$ is the number of nonzero elements in X.

The original RTR algorithms [3] assume very little information available for path reconstruction, and thus require that packets are received at the sink in sequence, which may not be always true in practice. We extend the original RTR by devising new decoding algorithms to overcome this limitation. We assume that source node ID, hop count, and source node's parent ID are available in

MobiHoc'15, June 22–25, 2015, Hangzhou, China.
ACM 978-1-4503-3489-1/15/06.
http://dx.doi.org/10.1145/2746285.2764863

each packet. However, as hop count and source node's parent node ID are already available in WSN routing protocols such as Collection Tree Protocol (CTP), the enhanced RTR will make use of this available information without adding new overhead to WSN packet.

Each packet carries an aggregated path measurement, which initially is set to zero. The measurement encodes the path information along its route towards the sink, updated at each intermediate forwarding node. With a small and fixed overhead, RTR in-network encoding operations are the modular sum and XOR of the carried measurement in the packet and the value of currently traversed link in the route. RTR computes the unique label value $l_{u,v}$ of each individual link *e(u, v)* online using the simple labeling function given in [3], based on unique IDs of the two endpoint nodes *u* and *v*. If a node's ID has 16 bits, a link value then is 32 bits. Thus, a path measurement will have 32 bits for each modular sum and XOR result, resulting in total eight bytes overhead per packet. Once a packet arrives at the sink, its routing path will be decoded by our devised algorithms using its aggregated path measurement.

3. EVALUATIONS

We conducted detailed lossy WSN simulations using TOSSIM, the standard network simulator in TinyOS. Two important WSN topologies, the line topology and the grid topology are considered. For line topology, the sink node sits at one end of the line; for grid topology, the sink node sits at a corner. The sink collects WSN sensor readings from all nodes every five minutes. Table I gives a summary of the statistics of the simulations.

We evaluate the performance of RTR versus CSPR on per-packet path reconstruction as well as on path group reconstruction. CSPR adopts a CS solver CoSaMP to recover a path vector with *M* measurements, and requires that $k<N/2$ and $M \geq 3k$, with *k* non-zero items in the path vector of dimension *N*; otherwise, it outputs "Fail". Fig. 1 shows the performance comparison of RTR versus CSPR approaches for line and grid topologies. In both topologies, RTR performs significantly better than CSPR in per-packet path recovery. For path group reconstruction, RTR outperforms CSPR even more drastically. The insights are as follows. In WSN line topology with n nodes, for example, the sparsity requirement of CSPR (due to CoSaMP) will not be satisfied if the number of hops is equal or larger than $(n-2)/2$. Hence, in the simulation with 15 nodes, all the path groups with hop counts equal or larger than 6 are unrecoverable by the CSPR because their node vectors are not sparse. It is found that only 16.58% of the path groups in line topology meet the sparsity property (hop count ≤ 6), among which 76.29% cannot collect sufficient packets for path reconstruction. In summary, 96.07% and 98.07% of the path groups cannot be recovered by the CSPR for the line and grid WSN topology, respectively.

4. CONCLUSIONS

We devise new RTR path decoding algorithms, and compare the two CS-inspired WSN path reconstruction approaches RTR versus CSPR. The evaluation results profoundly reveal that due to the different problem formulations, the RTR and CSPR exhibit dramatic difference between their respective performances. In particular for path group reconstruction, the CSPR was only able to recover 3.93% and 1.93% of the total path groups for simulated line and grid WSNs respectively. In contrast, the RTR was able to recover 94.36% and 81.48% of the total path groups for line and grid topology WSNs respectively. We show that the undesirable performance of CSPR is mainly caused by two critical drawbacks in its formulation: (1) the path node vector would largely violate the sparsity requirement of CS solvers for linear WSNs and other similar WSN topologies; and (2) most of the highly dynamic paths may not occur so frequently that the CSPR could not collect the sufficient number of packets in those path groups to recover them even after a long collection time (e.g., more than 2100 data collection cycles).

Table 1. Simulation statistics

WSN Topology (size)	Line (15)	Grid (225)
Packet reception rate	98.60%	87.10%
Total received packets	29962	44855
Total collection cycles	2173	230
Total path groups	585	19380
Longest path (hops)	14	27

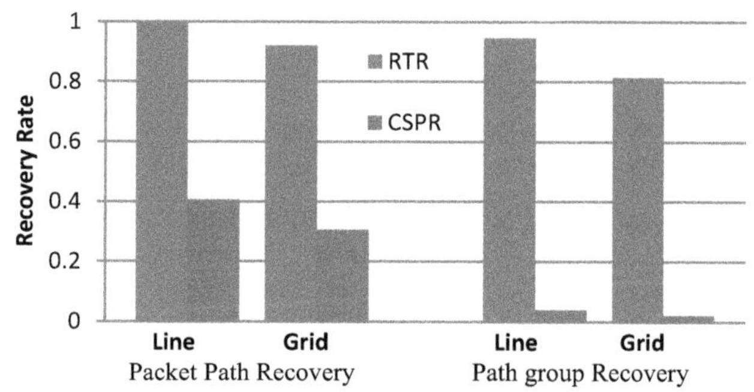

Figure 1. Performance evaluation of RTR vs. CSPR.

In addition, RTR uses much less resource for path encoding than CSPR. While both RTR and CSPR have the same packet overhead of eight bytes, CSPR requires 200 bytes in each node for storing its dictionary, whereas RTR needs none.

5. ACKNOWLEDGMENTS

This work was supported in part by NSF under CNS-1320132.

6. REFERENCES

[1] M. Keller, J. Beutel, and L. Thiele. How was your journey? Uncovering routing dynamics in deployed sensor networks with multi-hop network tomography. *Proc. of SenSys*, Nov. 2012.

[2] X. Lu, D. Dong, Y. Liu, X. Liao, and L. Shanshan. Pathzip: Packet path tracing in wireless sensor networks. *Proc. of MASS*, Oct. 2012.

[3] Y. Liang, and R. Liu. Routing Topology Inference for Wireless Sensor Networks. *Computer Communication Review*, Vol. 43, No. 2, pp. 22-27, April 2013.

[4] Y. Gao, W. Dong, C. Chen, J. Bu, G. Guan, X. Zhang, and X. Liu. Pathfinder: Robust path reconstruction in large scale sensor networks with lossy links. *Proc. of ICNP*, Oct. 2013.

[5] Z. Liu, Z. Li, M. Li, W. Xing, and D. Lu. Path reconstruction in dynamic wireless sensor networks using compressive sensing. *Proc. of MobiHoc*, Aug. 2014.

Poster: Full-duplex WiFi: Achieving Simultaneous Sensing and Transmission for Future Wireless Networks

Yun Liao, Kaigui Bian, Lingyang Song
State Key Laboratory of Advanced Optical Communication Systems and Networks, School of Electrical Engineering and Computer Science, Peking University
Beijing, China
{yun.liao, bkg, lingyang.song}@pku.edu.cn

Zhu Han
Electrical and Computer Engineering Department, University of Houston
Houston, TX, USA
zhan2@uh.edu

ABSTRACT

With the booming exploitation of WiFi networks based on the conventional CSMA/CA access scheme, the frequent long collision period becomes unbearable. To better utilize the WiFi spectrum, in this poster, we propose a novel WiFi protocol with the assistance of full-duplex (FD) technique that allows users to sense the spectrum while transmitting, and stop transmission once collision is detected. Analytical and simulated results show that the average collision length is sharply reduced and the normalized throughput can be significantly improved by the proposed FD-WiFi protocol compared with the conventional CSMA/CA.

Categories and Subject Descriptors

C.2.1 [**Network Architecture and Design**]: Wireless communication

Keywords

Full-duplex, WiFi protocol design

1. INTRODUCTION AND MOTIVATION

Conventionally, the WiFi networks are deployed based on the CSMA/CA scheme in which users sense the carrier before accessing to it [1]. However, once collision happens, all collided users cannot be aware of collision before finishing their transmissions. This becomes a severe problem under crowded conditions where collision may happen frequently.

In this poster, we introduce full-duplex (FD) [2] technique which enables simultaneous transmitting and receiving into WiFi networks. This leads to the possibility of a new WiFi protocol design in which users are not assumed "blind" when transmitting. Analytical saturation throughput of the FD-WiFi protocol is derived with the consideration of imperfect sensing brought by residual self-interference (RSI) in the PHY layer[3]. Both analytical and simulation results indicate that the normalized saturation throughput of the proposed FD-WiFi protocol can significantly outperforms the conventional CSMA/CA under various network conditions.

MobiHoc '15, June 22-25, 2015, Hangzhou, China
ACM 978-1-4503-3489-1/15/06.
http://dx.doi.org/10.1145/2746285.2764864.

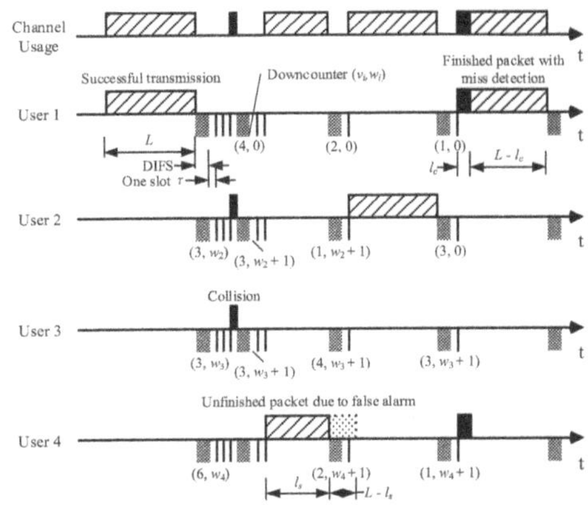

Figure 1: FD-WiFi Protocol, in which (v_i, w_i) denotes the residual backoff time and the backoff stage of user i.

2. FD-WIFI PROTOCOL

2.1 System Model

We consider a system with M FD-enabled contending users operating under the saturated condition, i.e., each user always has a packet to transmit. With the existence of the RSI, the sensing of transmitting FD users can never be perfect. For simplicity and comparison fairness, we omit the noise term as is commonly assumed in the analysis of CSMA, and only consider the impact of RSI in sensing[3]. Furthermore, we assume perfect sensing when more than two users collide, since the received signal from other users overwhelms the RSI. Thus, the effects of imperfect sensing are considered only in the following two cases: (1) one single user occupies the channel and falsely detects collision with probability P_f; and (2) one user collides with another without awareness with probability P_m.

2.2 Protocol Design

Fig. 1 illustrates the procedure of channel access in the proposed protocol consisting of the following several parts.

FD sensing: All users keep sensing continuously regardless of their own activity, and make decisions of the channel usage at the end of each slot with duration τ, which is the required time to reliably detect others' transmissions.

Backoff mechanism: Once the channel is judged idle without interruption for a certain period of time as long as a distributed interference space (DIFS), users check their own backoff timers. If their timers have counted down to zero, a random backoff time for additional deferral is generated as

$$\text{Backoff Time} = v \times \tau = \text{Random}(W) \times \tau, \tag{1}$$

where $W = 2^w W_0$ represents the contention window length, v is a random integer drawn from the uniform distribution over $[0, W)$, and $w \in [0, w_x]$ is the backoff stage depending on the number of unsuccessful transmissions for a packet. The countdown starts right after the DIFS, and suspends when the channel is detected as occupied by others.

Channel access and transmission suspension: A user accesses the channel when its timer reaches zero, and stops transmission and swifts to the backoff procedure once a collision is detected by FD transceivers. If the packet is finished, the user resets the the backoff state $w = 0$. Otherwise, it sets $w = \min\{w + 1, w_x\}$.

3. PERFORMANCE ANALYSIS

In this section, the saturation throughput of the FD-WiFi is derived and compared with the CSMA/CA.

3.1 Transmission Probability

We follow the assumption in [1] that each packet gets collided with a same probability independent of the value of W_i. Then the probability p that one user starts transmission in the next slot can be derived from the probability of successfully finishing a packet p_s as

$$p = \frac{2(2p_s - 1)}{(2p_s - 1)(W_0 + 1) + (1 - p_s) W_0 (1 - (2 - 2p_s)^{w_x})}. \quad (2)$$

Then, consider the probability of finishing a packet after a user starts transmission, which requires at least one user transmits the entire packet without awareness of collision. For simplicity, we assume fixed packet length L, and we have

$$\begin{aligned} p_s &= \sum_{l=0}^{L} \left[P\left(\text{collide for } l\right) \cdot P\left(\text{finish the residual } L - l\right) \right] \\ &= (1-p)^{M-1}(1-P_f)^L \\ &+ (M-1)p(1-p)^{M-2} P_m \cdot \frac{(1-P_f)^L - P_m^{2L}}{1 - P_f - P_m^2}. \end{aligned} \quad (3)$$

Combining (2) and (3), the values of p and p_s can be solved numerically.

3.2 Throughput

We use the time fraction that the channel is occupied for successful transmission as the normalized throughput, i.e., the throughput is defined as,

$$\begin{aligned} C &= \frac{\mathbb{E}\left[\text{Successful transmission length}\right]}{\mathbb{E}\left[\text{Consumed time for a successful transmission}\right]} \\ &= P_s L_s / \left[P_e + P_s\left(L_s + \text{DIFS}\right) + P_c\left(L_c + \text{DIFS}\right)\right], \end{aligned} \quad (4)$$

where $P_s = Mp(1-p)^{M-1}$ denotes the probability that a successful transmission occurs, $P_e = (1-p)^M$ is the probability that the channel is empty, $P_c = 1 - P_e - P_s$ represents the collision probability, and L_s, L_e, and L_c denote the average length of successful transmission, empty state, and collision, respectively. The average length of successful transmission and collision can be calculated as, respectively,

$$L_s = \frac{1 - (1-P_f)^{L-1}}{P_f} + (1-P_f)^{L-1}, \quad (5)$$

$$L_c = 1 + C_M^2 p^2 (1-p)^{M-2} \frac{P_m^2 \left(1 - P_m^{2L-2}\right)}{P_c \left(1 - P_m^2\right)}. \quad (6)$$

Then the throughput is readily obtained from (4).

It can be seen in (6) that the average collision length L_c is slightly more than one slot, which is sharply reduced compared with the length of a packet in CSMA/CA.

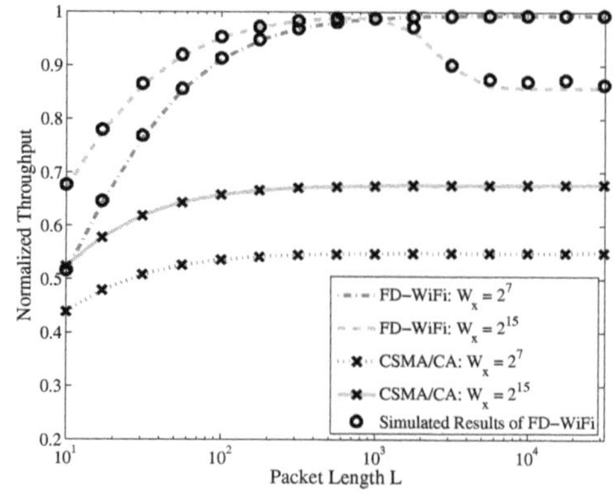

Figure 2: Saturated throughput vs. packet length L, where $W_0 = 2^4$ slots, and $w_x = \{3, 11\}$.

4. SIMULATION RESULTS

In the simulation, we set the number of users $M = 100$, DIFS length as 2 slots, minimum contention window $W_0 = 2^4$ slots, sensing error probabilities $P_m = 10^{-2}$ and $P_f = 10^{-3}$. 10^6 transmission attempts are simulated to evaluate the system performance. It is shown in Fig. 2 that FD-WiFi can achieve much higher throughput in most cases. In the CSMA/CA, the system throughput monotonously approaches the asymptotic performance with the increase of packet length, which, according to [1], is the probability that a transmission is successful. On the other hand, in the proposed FD-WiFi, when the packet is sufficiently long, a collision-free transmission is likely to stop in the middle due to false alarm and the user backoffs and prolongs W. When the system goes stable, it is likely that all users adopt the largest W even if they rarely collide. Thus, when the packet length exceeds the average successful transmission length L_s, which is approximately $1/P_f = 10^3$ slots when L is large according to (5), the throughput may decrease, as shown in the dashed line.

5. CONCLUSIONS

In this poster, we employed FD technique to WiFi and proposed a new protocol for the future FD-WiFi, in which users can keep sensing and monitoring the channel usage state when they are transmitting. In the new protocol, the average collision length is largely reduced due to the continuous detection of channel usage, and the higher channel utilization ratio can be achieved compared to the CSMA/CA scheme.

6. ACKNOWLEDGEMENTS

This work was supported by the National 973 Project under Grant 2013CB336700, by the National Natural Science Foundation of China under Grants 61222104, U1301255, and 61428101.

7. REFERENCES

[1] G. Bianchi. Performance analysis of the ieee 802.11 distributed coordination function. *IEEE Trans. on Selected Areas in Comm.*, 18(3):535–547, March 2000.

[2] M. Jain, J. I. Choi, T. M. Kim, D. Bharadia, S. Seth, K. Srinivasan, P. Levis, S. Katti, and P. Sinha. Practical, real-time, full duplex wireless. In *Proc. of the 17th MobiCom*, pages 301–312. ACM, September 2011.

[3] Y. Liao, T. Wang, L. Song, and Z. Han. Listen-and-talk: Full-duplex cognitive radio. In *Proc. of Globecom'14*. IEEE, December 2014.

Poster: Avoiding Rollback Traffic during the Switch of Snapshot Routing in Cyclic Mobile Networks

Zhu Tang, Wanrong Yu, Zhenqian Feng, Wei Han, Baokang Zhao, Chunqing Wu
College of Computer, National University of Defense Technology, Changsha, Hunan, China
{tangzhu, wlyu, bkzhao, wuchunqing}@nudt.edu.cn, z_q_feng@163.com, hanwei_phd@126.com

ABSTRACT
In this paper, we propose a rollback traffic avoidance method for the snapshot routing in cyclic mobile networks. Since the snapshot routing tables are switched simultaneously, part of the traffic may be sent back on some links if the new routing path contains the same links but with reversed forwarding direction against the old one. Since the selection of routing paths to avoid the rollback traffic is NP-hard, we propose an approximate algorithm called Inter-Snapshot Rollback Traffic Avoidance (ISRTA), to pursuit the approximate optimal solutions. Evaluation is performed based on the typical cyclic mobile network – Iridium satellite system, and the simulation results show that our method can efficiently eliminate the rollback paths and traffic in the Iridium system.

Keywords
Rollback Traffic Avoidance, Snapshot Routing, Cyclic Mobile Networks

1. INTRODUCTION
Cyclic mobile network is a kind of networks whose node moving trajectories are periodical and predictable (e.g. vehicular ad hoc networks, mobile social networks and non-geostationary earth orbit (NGEO) satellite networks [1]). Therefore, the routing paths based on the prediction information can be pre-calculated offline and stored in each mobile nodes. The snapshot routing algorithm [2][3] is firstly proposed for the satellite networks, which divides the orbit period into many small time intervals (i.e. *snapshots*) according to the link on/off change or equal duration. Each snapshot is designed to contain a relative stable network topology. Based on the predictability of node movements, the snapshot routing tables in all nodes are switched simultaneously to predefined new ones at a predefined time. New routing tables would be quite fit for the new mobile network topology and other quality of service requirements. Snapshot routing algorithm can efficiently reduce the impact of dynamic network topology to the routing performance in mobile networks. Consequently, it is applied in the practical operational satellite network - Iridium system [4], which is a typical cyclic mobile network.

Since the instantaneous switch of routing tables updates the routing paths in the whole network, the forwarding paths of packets might be changed after the switch. If the new routing path contains same links but with reversed forwarding direction from the old path, the packets sent through these links just now will be sent back, finally resulting in the transient loop traffic. Unfortunately, these loops can cause more disordered packets, extra end to end delay and larger packet drop rate.

MobiHoc'15, June 22-25, 2015, Hangzhou, China
ACM 978-1-4503-3489-1/15/06.
http://dx.doi.org/10.1145/2746285.2764865

For example in Figure 1, the source node is $S_{i,j}$ and the destination node is $S_{i+1,j+1}$. In snapshot n, the link ($S_{i,j+1}$, $S_{i+1,j+1}$) is shorter than link ($S_{i,j}$, $S_{i+1,j}$), so the routing path from $S_{i,j}$ to $S_{i+1,j+1}$ prefers $S_{i,j}$→$S_{i,j+1}$→$S_{i+1,j+1}$. Thus, packets 1~6 are sending along this path to the destination node $S_{i+1,j+1}$ (Figure 1(a)). At the end of snapshot n, the link ($S_{i,j+1}$, $S_{i+1,j+1}$) breaks down predictably (Figure 1(b)). Then the routing tables switch to snapshot n+1 in each satellite, and the routing path from $S_{i,j}$ to $S_{i+1,j+1}$ changes to $S_{i,j}$→$S_{i+1,j}$→ $S_{i+1,j+1}$, while the routing path from $S_{i,j+1}$ to $S_{i+1,j+1}$ changes to $S_{i,j+1}$→$S_{i,j}$→$S_{i+1,j}$→ $S_{i+1,j+1}$. Now, the packets 4, 5, 6 arrived at $S_{i,j+1}$ need to be sent back to $S_{i,j}$, and then be forwarded to the destination (Figure 1(c)). Consequently, the traffic on link ($S_{i,j}$, $S_{i,j+1}$) is reversed. In this paper, these reversed forwarding packets are called *rollback traffic*, the paths such as $S_{i,j}$→$S_{i,j+1}$→ $S_{i+1,j+1}$ and $S_{i,j+1}$→$S_{i,j}$→$S_{i+1,j}$→$S_{i+1,j+1}$ are called *rollback paths*, and the links containing the rollback traffic such as (S_i, S_j) are called *rollback links*.

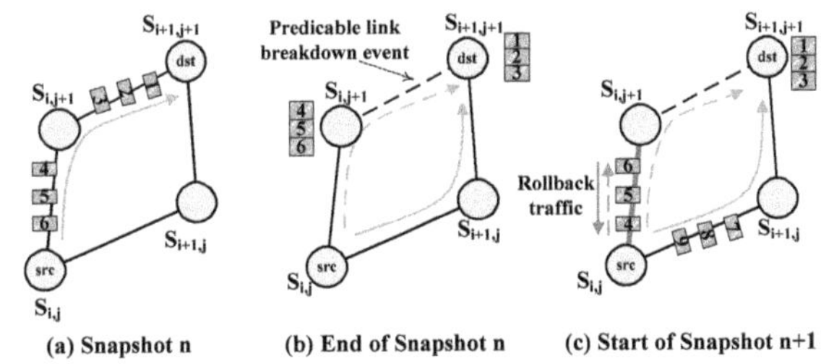

Figure 1: Rollback traffic in snapshot routing algorithm.

Although the duration of these routing loops is short, the extra end to end delay, packet disorder and link congestion caused by the rollback traffic could not be ignored. Since the selection of routing paths to avoid the rollback traffic is a mixed integer linear programming problem and is NP-hard, we propose a simple approximate algorithm - Inter-Snapshot Rollback Traffic Avoidance (ISRTA) to pursuit the approximate optimal solutions.

2. INTER-SNAPSHOT ROLLBACK TRAFFIC AVOIDANCE ALGORITHM

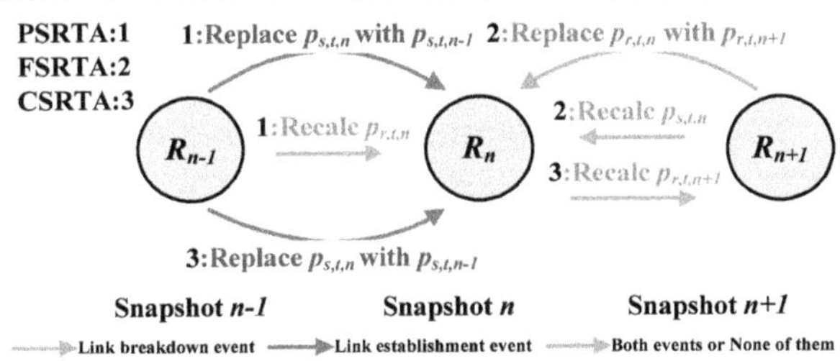

Figure 2: Three avoidance operations of ISRTA for R_n.

The ISRTA algorithm is circularly performed on each snapshot until the rollback paths are eliminated or the iteration count reaches the upper bound. The ISRTA algorithm performs three avoidance operations on each snapshot routing path set (R_n), such as previous-snapshot rollback traffic avoidance (PSRTA), following-snapshot rollback traffic avoidance (FSRTA) and cross-

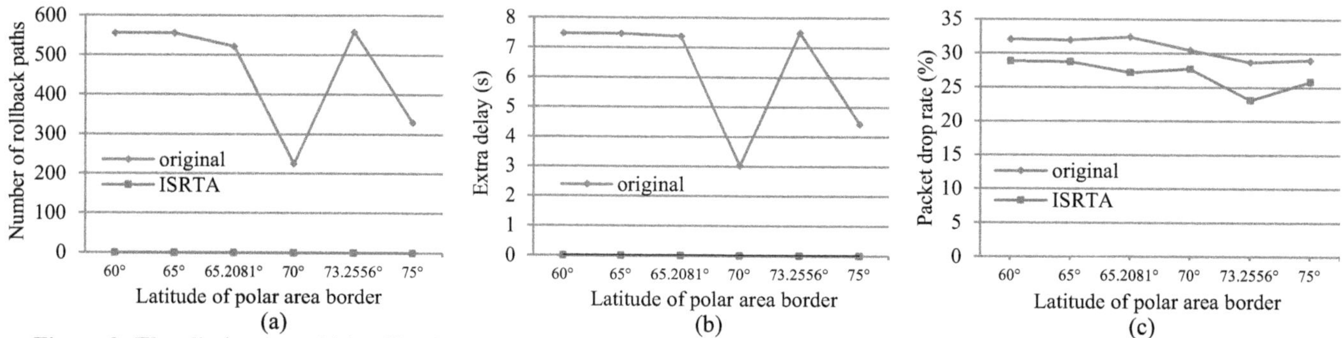

Figure 3: The elimination of (a) rollback paths, (b) extra delay and reduction of (c) packet drop rate with ISRTA algorithm.

snapshot rollback traffic avoidance (CSRTA). The PSRTA and FSRTA are designed to solve the rollback paths of R_n with previous R_{n-1} and following R_{n+1}, while CSRTA is used to recheck and solve the rollback paths between R_{n-1} and R_{n+1} after the PSRTA and FSRTA are performed on R_n. The three avoidance operations of ISRTA algorithm illustrated in Figure 2 contain different replacement strategies described in the next paragraph.

The rollback traffic can be characterized by three factors $p_{s,t,n-1}$, $p_{r,t,n}$ and $E_n = p_{s,t,n-1} \cap_{link} p_{r,t,n}$, where $p_{s,t,n-1}$ denotes the path from s to t before the snapshot switch, $p_{r,t,n}$ denotes the path from r to t after snapshot switch and E_n denotes the reversed links carrying the rollback traffic between $p_{s,t,n-1}$ and $p_{r,t,n}$. Since the rollback traffic is caused by the routing path changes between snapshots, the rollback paths are replaced depending on the trigger event for routing path changes. For each snapshot routing path set R_n, we propose to replace $p_{s,t,n}$ with $p_{s,t,n-1}$ of R_{n-1} if the path change is triggered by the link establishment event (red lines in Figure 2), and replace $p_{r,t,n}$ with $p_{r,t,n+1}$ of R_{n+1} if the path change is triggered by the link breakdown event (blue lines in Figure 2). In this way, the rollback paths are avoided and the modified paths are also applicable for the current snapshot n. If the routing path changes are triggered by both link breakdown and link establishment event, or triggered by none of them but the link cost reduction or link cost increase event, new paths excluding current rollback links are recalculated to avoid the rollback traffic (orange lines in Figure 2).

3. PERFORMANCE EVALUATION

The performance evaluation of the ISRTA algorithm is carried out in NS2. The network scenario is mainly based on the typical cyclic mobile networks – Iridium satellite system. The Iridium system contains 66 satellites uniformly distributed in 6 orbit planes, each satellite maintains two constant intra-plane ISLs (inter-satellite links) and one/two variable inter-plane ISLs. The connectivity of inter-plane ISLs changes periodically when the latitude of polar area border (L_{pa}) is specified.

3.1 Network Performance Improvement

As we can see in Figure 3(a)~(b), the values of rollback paths, extra delay caused by the reversed forwarding under different latitude of polar borders are reduced to 0. This is mainly because the Iridium system is a typical Manhattan Street Network, and there always exist alternative paths for multipath routing. Therefore, we can replace the rollback paths with appropriate alternative paths by ISRTA algorithm. Since the rollback traffic is avoided here, the local link congestion is weakened, and the packet drop rate is reduced as a result (see Figure 3(c)).

3.2 Increase of Average Network Delay

However, the end to end path delay might be prolonged if the new paths could not select the shortest delay paths. The increase of global average network delay for each snapshot is illustrated in Figure 4. Since alternative equal cost multi-paths always exist in the Iridium system, the end to end delay is not prolonged sharply after ISRTA is applied. After all, compared to the reduction of extra delay which is illustrated in Figure 3(b), the slight increment of global network delay caused by ISRTA is acceptable.

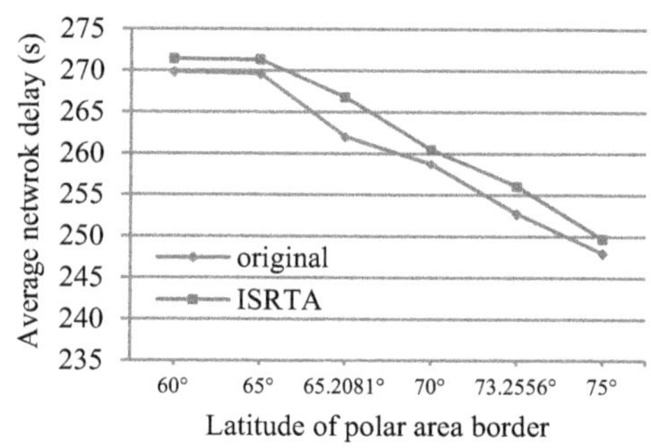

Figure 4: The increase of global average network delay.

4. CONCLUSIONS

In this paper, the rollback traffic avoid problem for snapshot routing algorithm in cyclic mobile networks is analyzed. We then propose the inter-snapshot rollback traffic avoidance (ISRTA) algorithm to pursuit the approximate optimal solutions. Simulation results show that our method can efficiently eliminate the rollback traffic in the Iridium system with little increment of global average network delay. In future work, we will continue to evaluate and improve our algorithm in terrestrial cyclic mobile networks, such as the vehicular ad hoc networks and mobile social networks.

5. ACKNOWLEDGMENTS

This work was partially supported by the project of National Natural Science Foundation of China under grant No.61103182, 61202488, 61272482 and 61379147.

6. REFERENCES

[1] Yue, C. and Zhili, S. Routing in Delay/Disruption Tolerant Networks: A Taxonomy, Survey and Challenges. *Commun. Surveys & Tutorials, IEEE*, 15(2): 654-677, 2013.

[2] Werner, M. A dynamic routing concept for ATM-based satellite personal communication networks. *Selected Areas in Communications, IEEE Journal on*, 15(8): 1636-1648, 1997.

[3] Fischer, D., Basin, D., Eckstein, K. and Engel, T. Predictable Mobile Routing for Spacecraft Networks. *Mobile Computing, IEEE Transactions on*, 12(6): 1174-1187, 2013.

[4] Evans, J. V. Satellite systems for personal communications. *Proceedings of the IEEE*, 86(7): 1325-1341, 1998.

Poster: Design and Implementation of IoT-enable Mobile E-Learning Platform for Medical Education

Chia-Wei Chang†, Phone Lin†, Chi-Wei Tseng† and Yi-Kai Kong†
†Department of Computer Science and Information Engineering, National Taiwan University, Taipei, Taiwan
r02922103@ntu.edu.tw, plin@csie.ntu.edu.tw, d95922034@ntu.edu.tw, b99902124@ntu.edu.tw
Wan-Ching Lien‡, Meng-Che Wu§, and Cheng-Yi Wu‡
‡Department of Emergency Medicine, National Taiwan University Hospital, Hsin-Chu branch, Taiwan
§Department of Emergency Medicine, National Taiwan University Hospital, Taipei, Taiwan
wanchinglien@ntu.edu.tw, mengcher111@gmail.com, pluswu@gmail.com *

Keywords

Internet of Things (IoT); Medical Training; Mobile E-learning

ABSTRACT

This poster proposes an IoT-enabled mobile e-learning platform to enhance the performance of a learning process (i.e., assembling of fragmented learning time for a trainee) and the efficiency of learning material management. The informatics framework and implementation methodology for the proposed platform are described in the poster. The proposed platform has been used in the emergency department of National Taiwan University Hospital (NTUH) for training junior ultrasound physicians.

Categories and Subject Descriptors

H.4 [**Information Systems Applications**]: Miscellaneous

1. INTRODUCTION

With the rapid growth and development of the information and communication technologies, e-learning has evolved quickly over the past decade. For example, mobile e-learning enables learning at anywhere and anytime. Summarized from [1], most of e-learning solutions come with the disadvantages, such as the static learning materials and the fragmented learning time, which decreases the performance of a learning process significantly. In this poster, we propose an IoT-enabled mobile e-learning platform to resolve the above issues. We use the ultrasound education in the emergency department in the hospital as a use case to show the informatics and implementation methodology for the proposed platform. The ultrasound education is based on formal curricula teaching speech and bedside hand-on individual practice. There are usually limited number of case studies in the traditional ultrasound education, which makes the education incomprehensive. We implement the concept of the IoT perception layer to collect real data (i.e., medical record) from IoT smart sensors (e.g., X-Ray, MRI machine or ultrasound machine) to the platform, and generate learning materials from raw data to meaningful learning materials. Furthermore, it usually takes time for the learners (i.e., junior emergency physicians) to have good diagnostic accuracy. Since the learners do not have a continuous long time period to sit in front of a computer to use the e-learning platform, our platform implements the "memorizing" functionality for mobile learners to record the learning stage and assemble the fragmented time.

*P. Lin's work was supported in part by MOST of Taiwan under Grants 103-2627-E-002-008, 103-2221-E-002-249-MY3, 103-2221-E-002-152-MY3, 104-2923-E-002-005-MY3, 103-2622-E-009-012, 103-2218-E-002-032, by Chunghwa Telecom, by ICL/ITRI, by MoE ATU Plan.

MobiHoc'15, June 22–25, 2015, Hangzhou, China.
ACM 978-1-4503-3489-1/15/06.
http://dx.doi.org/10.1145/2746285.2764866.

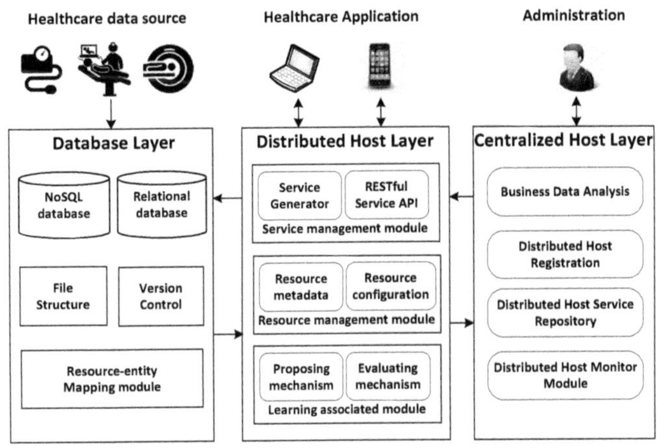

Figure 1: The framework of the IoT-enabled mobile e-learning platform

2. FRAMEWORK

Fig. 1 illustrates the framework for the platform, which consists of three layers elaborated as follows: There are three main modules in the **Database** layer, including File Structure, NoSQL Database, and Relational Database. We follow the study [2] to define NoSQL Database and Relational Database, where NoSQL Database manages the data collected from IoT sensors (e.g., scanning data and log data), and Relational Database manages the data by pre-defined schema, e.g., user profile, usage status, accounting. File Structure stores other files of big size (e.g., the images and videos) that are not stored in the two databases. We adopt the distributed file structure for the huge amount of data. The **Distributed Intelligence Host** layer is implemented in one or more distributed hosts. Each host is responsible for providing services to a dedicated training course such that the latency of data access could be shorten. This layer consists of the Service Management, Resource Management, and Learning Associated modules. Service Management provides APIs to the learning applications, which follows the RESTful protocol [3]. Resource Management configures the metadata for the learning materials and serves as the bridge **Distributed Intelligence Host** and **Database**. Learning Associated recommends learning materials to learners and evaluate the learning status of learners. The **Centralized Host** layer is responsible for evaluating the learning performance of learners and monitoring the operation status of the **Distributed Intelligence Host** layer. Comparing to **Distributed Intelligence Host** that receives frequent requests from the learning applications, the **Centralized Host** layer handles less requests. Therefore **Distributed Intelligence Host** is implemented in a centralized node. In **Centralized Host**, the Business Data Analysis module is used to collect long-term statistic data (monthly or yearly) from distributed intelligence hosts. The Distributed Host Registration module manages the registration history for the distributed hosts. The Host Service Repository module provides mapping between the learning applications and the URL of the distributed hosts.

3. CASE STUDY

We install the proposed platform in NTUH for the ultrasound education. Fig. 2 shows a snapshot of the platform. We evaluate the learning performance for the learners using the platform as follows. Our study was conducted from Aug., 2014 to Feb., 2015. The junior emergency physicians in the NTUH were enrolled in this training. We choose four topics in this program: focused assessment with sonography in trauma (FAST), abdominal aortic aneurysm, acute cholecystitis, and hydronephrosis. We compare the difference of accuracy of image interpretation before and after the use of the platform. Data analysis was performed using the SPSS statistical software, version 18.0. Paired t-test was used. A p-value <0.05 was considered statistically significant. The preliminary data regarding test results of the platform. There were only 10 participants until now joining the testing and attending the training program. All of them were senior emergency physicians. For example in the topic of abdominal aorta, all of them had experience more than 10 scans of abdominal aorta. In the second stage of imaging education, the participants had an average accuracy of 85% (shown in Fig. 3a). The average time to interpret one image was 15.12 ± 16.38 seconds (shown in Fig. 3b). In the third stage of learning evaluation, they got an accuracy of 100%.

4. CONCLUSION

In this poster, we proposed an IoT-enabled mobile e-learning platform. We presented the framework for the proposed platform. We used the ultrasound education as a case study and ran the platform in NTUH to study the performance of the platform for learning process. Our study showed that the proposed platform helps the physicians do the learning process more efficiently. More learning performance result will be shown when the system collect more case studied (i.e., more learners use the platform) in the future. According our literature survey, our study is the first one to apply mobile e-learning for emergency ultrasound training.

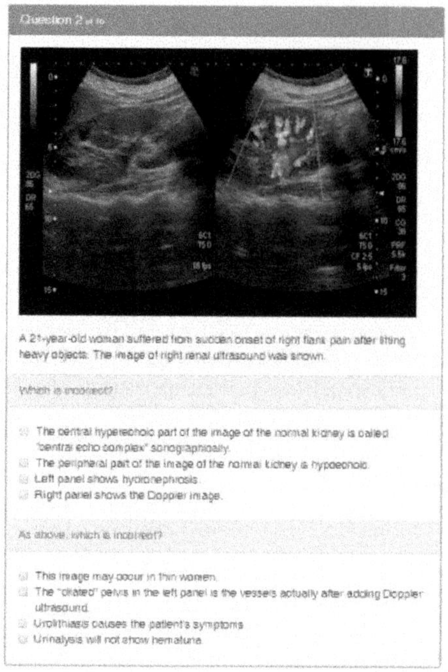

Figure 2: A Snapshot of mobile e-learning platform for medical education

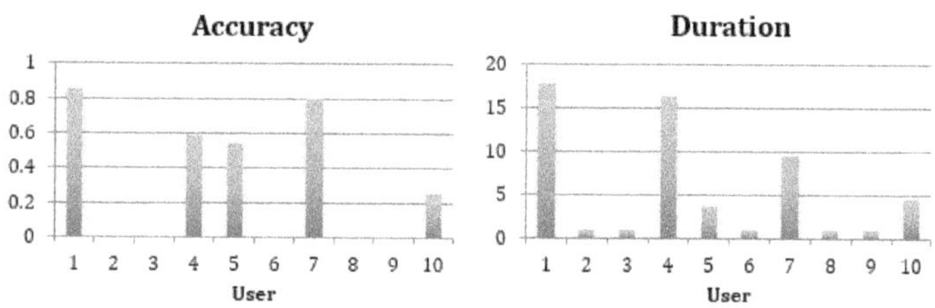

a Accuracy of test results   b Duration of test results

Figure 3: Statistic result for the learning performance

5. REFERENCES

[1] Jorge G. MD Ruiz, Michael J. MD Mintzer, and PhD Leipzig, Rosanne M. MD. The impact of e-learning in medical education. *IT in Medical Education*, 81(3):207–212, March. 2006.

[2] MongoDB. Top 5 considerations when evaluating nosql databases. [Online]. Avaliable: `http://info.mongodb.com/rs/mongodb/images/10gen_Top_5_NoSQL_Considerations.pdf`, 2014.

[3] F. Belqasmi, R. Glitho, and Chunyan Fu. Restful web services for service provisioning in next-generation networks: a survey. *Communications Magazine, IEEE*, 49(12):66–73, December 2011.

Poster: Roadside Unit Caching Mechanism for Multi-Service Providers

Zhiwen Hu, Zijie Zheng, Tao Wang, and Lingyang Song
School of Electronics Engineering and Computer Science
Peking University, Haidian District, Beijing, China
{zhiwen.hu, zijie.zheng, wangtao, lingyang.song}@pku.edu.cn

ABSTRACT

Roadside units (RSUs) with caching abilities are becoming an important part for the future transportation system, enabling both Internet accesses and local caching services for vehicular users. In this paper, we address the caching problem which involves the coexistence of multiple service providers who intend to cache their own contents into the RSUs by competitions to improve the data disseminations. And we propose a mechanism based on multi-object auctions, which can achieve a sub-optimal outcome. Simulation results also show the effectiveness of our solution.

Categories and Subject Descriptors

C.2.1 [**Computer-Communication Networks**]: Network Architecture and Design—*wireless communication*

Keywords

Vehicular network, road-side caching, multi-object auction

1. INTRODUCTION

With the application of the high-end facilities on vehicles and the deployment of roadside units (RSUs), vehicular users can resort to resource-intensive online services, which may drain the limited wireless resources due to large amount of data requests. One way to relief the burden of the system is to equip the RSUs with caching abilities. Therefore popular contents of service providers (SPs) that requested by vehicular users can be obtained without the crowded backhaul links from RSUs to the Internet [1].

However, the diversity of the vehicular traffic and the overlapping of adjacent RSUs make it quite complicated to optimize the caching scheme. Moreover, the competitions caused by the coexistence of multiple service providers are challenging the feasibility of applying caching schemes in practical scenes. In this paper, we propose a novel mechanism based on multi-object auctions to solve the problem with the consideration of both difficulties above. Simulation results have testified the effectiveness of our solution, where the average download percentage of vehicular users has elevated remarkably with the proposed auction mechanism.

MobiHoc'15, June 22–25, 2015, Hangzhou, China.
ACM 978-1-4503-3489-1/15/06.
http://dx.doi.org/10.1145/2746285.2764867.

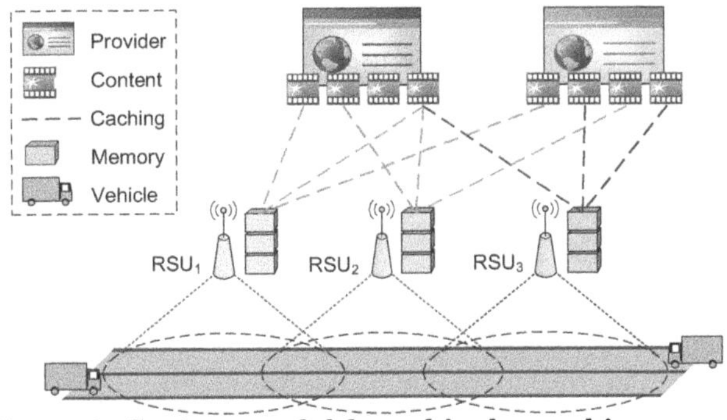

Figure 1: System model for vehicular caching among multiple content providers.

2. SYSTEM MODEL

We consider a two-way street where RSUs with caching abilities are equidistantly distributed. Vehicular users that move in both directions can get accesses to nearby RSUs and therefore download contents from the Internet. We assume that each vehicular user starts to download one of the contents once he drives into the street. During the whole journey, users can always continue downloading if there are RSUs nearby, but experience higher download speed if the desired contents are cached in nearby RSUs. The downloading process may not complete by the end of the street, so we aim to maximize the average download percentage for vehicular users. Our model is demonstrated in Fig. 1.

Contents: We denote the content providers by $\mathcal{P} = \{P_l | 1 \leq l \leq L\}$ and all of their contents by $\mathcal{C} = \{C_n | 1 \leq n \leq N\}$. These contents are assumed to have the same size S, and only differ in their popularity. The popularity of C_n is denoted by ϕ_n, representing the probability of C_n being requested by each vehicular user. And to normalize the probability, we also have $\sum_{n=1}^{N} \phi_n = 1$.

RSUs: We denote RSUs by $\{RSU_m\}$, where $1 \leq m \leq M$. The caching ability of each RSU is U, representing that each RSU can cache no more than U contents at the same time. The coverage length of a RSU in the street is denoted by l, and the total length of the street is L_s.

Vehicular traffic: We suppose that the traffic condition on each side of the road is uniform in a period of time, and the vehicular speed v and the vehicular density d can also be predicted. The traffic flow $f = v \cdot d$ represents the average number of vehicles that travel through the street per second from a given direction. On one side of the street, we denote these three parameters by v_1, d_1 and f_1 respectively, while on the other side of the street, by v_2, d_2 and f_2 respectively.

Wireless traffic: We assume that the backhaul-link between any RSU to the Internet has a constant transmission rate r_{back} for each user, while the down-link between an RSU and one of its nearby vehicles has a variant transmission rate r_{down} which depends on the vehicular density. We suppose that $r_{down} = \min\{\frac{r_{max}}{l(d_1+d_2)}, r_{max}\}$, where r_{max} is the maximum download rate and $l(d_1 + d_2)$ is the number of vehicles that are under the RSU's cover. The final transmission rate to vehicular users is (1) r_{down} for cached contents and (2) $\min\{r_{down}, r_{back}\}$ for uncached contents, and we denote them by r_c and r_u respectively for simplicity.

Effective coverage length: We first use the boolean matrix Λ to represent the caching scheme, whose element $\lambda_{m,n} = 1$ if RSU_m caches C_n, and $\lambda_{m,n} = 0$ if not. Based on this, we use $L(\Lambda, n)$ to denote the length of the street which is under the cover of RSUs that cache C_n, where $L(\Lambda, n)$ shows the effective coverage length of C_n.

Download percentage: Once the vehicular user determines to download C_n when entering the street, the final download percentage for him is given by

$$\begin{cases} D_{1,n} = min\{1, \left[r_c\frac{L(\Lambda,n)}{v_1} + r_u\frac{L_s-L(\Lambda,n)}{v_1}\right]/S\}, \\ D_{2,n} = min\{1, \left[r_c\frac{L(\Lambda,n)}{v_2} + r_u\frac{L_s-L(\Lambda,n)}{v_2}\right]/S\}, \end{cases} \quad (1)$$

where $D_{1,n}$ is for the users who request C_n from the left entrance, and $D_{2,n}$ is for the right. To take into account the popularity of different contents, we can calculate the average download percentage from both entrances given by

$$\begin{cases} D_1 = \sum_{n=1}^{N} \phi_n D_{1,n}, \\ D_2 = \sum_{n=1}^{N} \phi_n D_{2,n}. \end{cases} \quad (2)$$

Objective function and constraint: We aim to maximize the average download percentage on both sides of the street. The weight of each side depends on f_1 and f_2, so we give the final objective function and its constraint as

$$\begin{cases} \arg\max\{D_1 \cdot \eta_1 + D_2 \cdot \eta_2\}, \\ s.t.\ \sum_{n=1}^{N} \gamma_{m,n} \le U, \quad \forall m, \end{cases} \quad (3)$$

where $\eta_1 = f_1/(f_1 + f_2)$, $\eta_2 = f_2/(f_1 + f_2)$, and the constraint shows the limited storages of RSUs.

3. AUCTION BASED SOLUTION

3.1 The proposed mechanism

In our system, $U \cdot M$ memory blocks of RSUs are used to cache contents. The complexity brought by overlapping among RSUs makes the optimization problem intractable. So we propose a multi-step multi-object auction mechanism to give a sub-optimal solution. Our proposal is to auction for U times, in which way the uth memory blocks of all the M RSUs are auctioned off in the uth auction.

In the uth auction, there are N contents playing the role of bidders and M memory blocks from different RSUs playing the role of objects, which can be denoted as $\{B_n\}$ and $\{O_m\}$ respectively. The valuation that B_n estimates O_m is denoted by $v_{n,m}$, which can be calculated as:

$$v_{n,m} = \phi_n\left[(D_{1,n}^{t'} - D_{1,n}^{t})\eta_1 + (D_{2,n}^{t'} - D_{2,n}^{t})\eta_2\right], \quad (4)$$

where $D_{1,n}^{t}$ and $D_{2,n}^{t}$ are based on the current allocation, while $D_{1,n}^{t'}$ and $D_{2,n}^{t'}$ are based on the hypothesis that content C_n is allocated to RSU_m.

3.2 The core algorithm

Our algorithm of multi-object auction is originated from [2], which uses bipartite graph to get a perfect matching among bidders and objects. This algorithm guarantees the maximum social welfare, and is proved to satisfy the VCG principle, where bidders' best strategy is to bid truthfully.

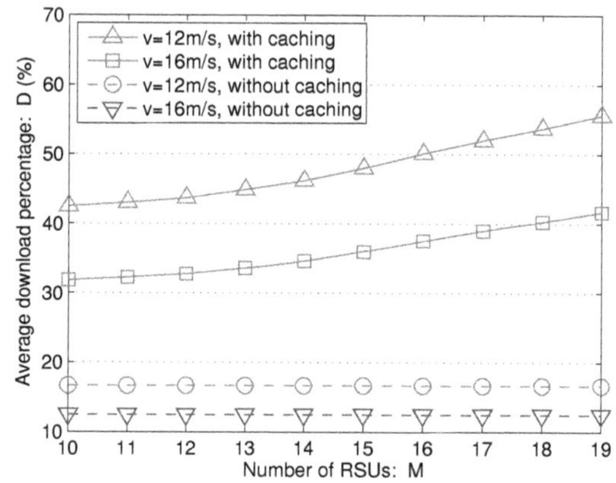

Figure 2: Average download percentage with different vehicular speed v and numbers of RSUs M.

The first step is to add $N - M$ virtual objects with zero valuations therefore the numbers of bidders and objects are equal, and also, the initial prices of objects are all set as zero. Given the valuation matrix and the prices of objects, a preferred-object graph can be established, which is essentially a bipartite graph where each bidder node is only connected to the object nodes which bring most profit. By continually applying breadth-first-search (BFS) in this graph, the matching is enlarged until no more augmenting path exists. If we get a perfect matching, then the auction is completed, otherwise a set of constricted object nodes can be found during BFS. We raise the price of this set of objects until at least one of the bidders changes his most preferred objects, leading to a new structure of the preferred-object graph. And we repeat these steps until the graph contains a perfect matching which represents the auction result.

4. SIMULATION RESULTS

Without the loss of generality, we only simulate one situation where $v_1 = v_2 = v$ and $d_1 = d_2 = d$. We set $N = 100$, $U = 15$, $d = 0.1m^{-1}$, $r_{back} = 1Mbps$, $r_{max} = 100Mbps$, $S = 500Mbits$, and we let ϕ_n obey Zipf-like distribution. The simulation result is shown in Fig. 2, where the impact of vehicular speed v and numbers of RSUs M is illustrated.

By comparing the differences between the strategies that with and without caching, we can see the effectiveness of our algorithm in elevating average download percentage. With a fixed number of RSUs, a lower vehicular speed results in a higher download percentage due to the longer download time. And with a fixed vehicular speed, more RSUs being deployed can also benefit the outcome of our solution.

5. ACKNOWLEDGEMENTS

This work was supported by the National 973 Project under Grant 2013CB336700, by the National Natural Science Foundation of China under Grants 61222104 and U1301255, and 61428101.

6. REFERENCES

[1] R. Ding, T. Wang, L. Song, Z. Han, and J. Wu. Roadside-Unit Caching in Vehicular Ad Hoc Networks for Efficient Popular Content Delivery. In *proc. IEEE Wireless Comunication and Networking Conference (WCNC)*, New Oleans, US, April 2015.

[2] G. Demange, D. Gale, and M. Sotomayor. Multi-item auctions. *Journal of Political Economy*, 94(4):863–872, August 1986.

Poster: Disseminating Content in Interest-centric Opportunistic Social Networks

Chenguang Kong
Department of Computer Science
Georgia State University
Atlanta, Georgia
ckong3@student.gsu.edu

Xiaojun Cao
Department of Computer Science
Georgia State University
Atlanta, Georgia
cao@cs.gsu.edu

1. INTRODUCTION

In the Mobile social network, users can leverage the short range communication technologies to disseminate free or self-generated content during the opportunistic contacts[1][3]. Merchants or organizations are also willing to disseminate their commercial or advertisement content, such as coupons, advertisements and event invitations, to the interested customers through opportunistic communication. Those commercial or advertisement content can bring some benefit or reward to the content provider(CP) when the content is adopted by a user. For instance, a user (or customer) redeems the coupon and purchases goods which can increase the income of the merchant. Different users can bring different amount of reward to the content provider. The reward is highly related to how much the users are interested in the content. Thus, it is the goal of the content provider to disseminate a limited number of content to the interested users to maximize the total reward.

Since there is cost associated with content generation, we assume that only the CP can generate a limited number of content copies, and disseminates those copies to users during the opportunistic contact. A user cannot copy or generate content copies and will retain one copy for self usage after receiving some content copies. The users are motivated to help disseminate the rest copies to others during future opportunistic contact because of the incentive mechanism provided by the CP. The dissemination process terminates if all users in the network hold at most one copy of the content.

The intermittent network connectivity and contact uncertainty in mobile social networks make the content dissemination process unpredictable and difficult. In this paper, we define a content dissemination problem in the Interest-centric Opportunistic Social Network (IOSN). In the IOSN, users move around for the activities or locations they are interested in. For instance, conference attendees move among several sections they are interested. The users with similar interests may have similar trajectories in IOSNs. Based on this observation, we propose the Social Connection Pattern (SCP) to model the interest distributions of users' social connections. We then develop the Social Connection Pattern based Dissemination (SCPD) algorithm to identify a proper content dissemination strategy when two users contact, such that the overall expected reward is maximized.

MobiHoc'15, June 22–25, 2015, Hangzhou, China.
ACM 978-1-4503-3489-1/15/06.
http://dx.doi.org/10.1145/2746285.2764868.

2. SOCIAL CONNECTION PATTERN

We employ the Social Connection Pattern (SCP) to model the interest distribution of users' contactors and connectors. User u's **contactors** are the users who have directly contacted with user u while u's **connectors** are the users who have not directly contacted with user u but there have been a connection path from those users to u

The SCP of a users u_i consists of two elements: a social connection pattern matrix P_{it} and a counting vector C_{it}. The matrix P_{it} records the interest distribution of the users who have directly contacted or connected through intermediate users with user i till time t. The jth row in P_{it} is used to record the interest distribution of the j-hop connectors of user i at time t as shown in Eq. (1), where N is the largest hop number.

We use **weight** as the measurement of user's interest in the content, which is corresponding to the reward generated by the user. We assume that W is the largest possible weight. In P_{it}, a vector $x_{ijt} = [p_{ij1t}, ..., p_{ijwt}, ..., p_{ijWt}]$ is used to describe the interest distribution of j-hop connectors of user i at time t. p_{ijwt} is the probability that a j-hop connector of user i at time t has a weight of w.

$$P_{it} = [x_{i1t}, x_{i2t}, ..., x_{iNt}]^T = \begin{bmatrix} p_{i11t} & p_{i12t} & \cdots & p_{i1Wt} \\ p_{i21t} & p_{i22t} & \cdots & p_{i2Wt} \\ \vdots & \vdots & \vdots & \vdots \\ p_{iN1t} & p_{iN2t} & \cdots & p_{iNWt} \end{bmatrix} \tag{1}$$

The counting vector C_{it} in SCP counts the number of connectors of user i at time t, which describes the ability that user i connect with others as shown in Eq. (2):

$$C_{it} = [c_{i1t}, c_{i2t}, ..., c_{ijt}, ..., c_{iNt}] \tag{2}$$

where c_{ijt} is the number of j-hop connectors and obtained by exchanging information with user i's contactors.

3. SCP BASED CONTENT DISSEMINATION ALGORITHM

In this section, we introduce the SCP based content Dissemination(SCPD) algorithm to efficiently disseminate content in IOSNs. Assume there are total M content copies generated by content provider. The objective is to disseminate those M copies to M users in IOSNs so that the total reward from the users who receive the content copies is maximized.

Suppose user u receives $s+1$ ($M > s \geq 1$) copies of the content and needs to disseminate s content copies. The s content copies are expected to return some reward, denoted as $g_u(s)$. When user u encounters another user v at time t, user u calculates how many content copies should be delivered to v. If user u delivers m content copies to user v, we define $f_v(m)$ as the expected reward generated by the m content copies. The basic idea of our SCPD algorithm is to find out the optimal m, denoted by m^*, such that the increase of total expected reward is maximized as Eq. (3).

$$m^* = argmax_m\{(g_u(s-m)+f_v(m)) - g_u(s)\} \quad \text{s.t.} 0 \le m \le s \tag{3}$$

In Eq. (3), the expected reward of the m content copies disseminated to user v (i.e., $f_v(m)$) is calculated based on the SCP of user v as shown in Eq. (4).

$$f_v(m) = \max_{m_j} w_v + \sum_{j=1}^{N}\sum_{w=1}^{W} p_{vjwt} \times m_j \tag{4}$$

$$\text{s.t.} \sum_{j=1}^{N} m_j \le m-1 \tag{5}$$

$$\frac{m_j}{m_{j-1}} \le \frac{c_{vjt}}{c_{v(j-1)t}}, \text{ for all } 1 < j \le N \tag{6}$$

$$\forall m_j \in \mathbb{Z} \tag{7}$$

Similarly, if user u holds s content copies, the expected reward $g_u(s)$ is calculated as in Eq. (8).

$$g_u(s) = \max_{s_j} w_u \sum_{j=1}^{N}\sum_{w=1}^{W} p_{ujwt} \times s_j$$
$$\text{s.t.} \sum_{j=1}^{N} s_j \le s \tag{8}$$
$$\frac{s_j}{s_{j-1}} \le \frac{c_{ujt}}{c_{u(j-1)t}}, \text{ for all } 1 < j \le N$$
$$\forall s_j \in \mathbb{Z}$$

To efficiently resolve this maximization problems, we propose the SCP based Dissemination(SCPD) algorithm, which is based on the Branch and Bound algorithm [2]. Take $f_v(m)$ as the example, the sketch of our algorithm is described as follows:

(*I*) **Initialization**: We set $i = 1$ and the value of m_i as 1 to $m-1$ to generate m *possible solutions*. The $f_v(m)$ of each possible solution is calculated by ignoring the constraint in Eq. (6).

(*II*) **Bound**: We check if any possible solution satisfies the constraint in Eq. (6) as well. If yes, select the possible solution with the largest $f_v(m)$ as the *available solution*, and remove any other possible solutions with smaller $f_v(m)$. If the available solution is the only possible solution left, the algorithm terminates; otherwise, go to Step (*III*).

(*III*) **Branch**: We set the value of m_{i+1} as 1 to $m - |s| - 1$ to generate new possible solutions. The $f_v(m)$ of each new possible solution is calculated by ignoring the constraint in Eq. (6). Update $i = i + 1$ and go to Step (*II*) to continue.

With the above algorithm calculating $f_v(m)$ and $g_u(s)$, users u can identify the optimal m^* in Eq. (3) by traversing all m in the range of $0 \le m \le s$.

4. SIMULATION AND EVALUATION

In our simulation, the opportunistic social network dataset Infocom2006 is used. In our simulation, the reward received by the content provider is represented by the weight sum of the content receivers. The weights of users are normalized within the range $[0, 100]$.

To evaluate the efficiency of our algorithm, we compare it with the Flooding algorithm. In the Flooding algorithm, when a user B meets a new contactor C who does not obtain the content before, B will deliver half of B's content copies to C.

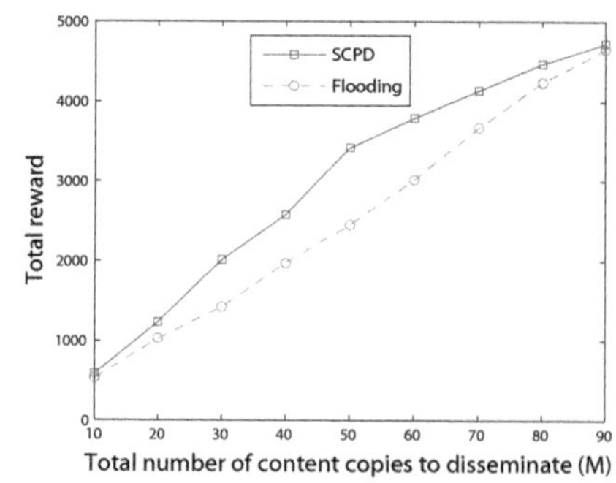

Figure 1: Dissemination results of Infocom dataset

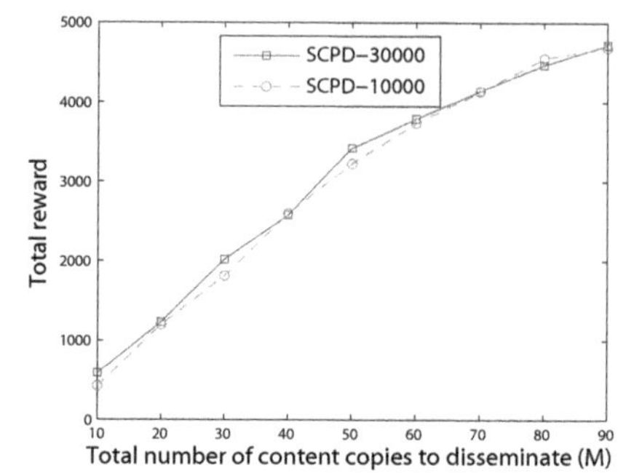

Figure 2: Dissemination results of Infocom dataset on training length

As shown in the x-axis of Fig. 1, we randomly select a user as the content provider, who intends to disseminate $M(10 \le M \le 90)$ content copies to users in the network. The y-axis records the total reward obtained from the content receivers who hold one content copy when the dissemination process terminates. The results show that the total reward obtained by the SCPD algorithm is significantly higher than the total reward obtained by the Flooding algorithm.

We use two training length (i.e., 30000 and 10000) to learn the SCP, and the results are shown in Fig. 2. One can see that the total reward of the content receivers with different training length is close to each other. It demonstrates that the proposed SCPD is stable and reliable to predict the future connections.

5. CONCLUSION

In Interest-centric Opportunistic Social networks (IOSNs), users move around the interested locations and have a user interest related probability to meet with other users. In this paper, we have formulated the problem of content dissemination in IOSNs. We have derived the Social Connection Pattern (SCP) to statistically describe the interest distribution of contactors and connectors. We have also proposed the Social Connection Pattern based Dissemination (SCPD) algorithm to maximize the reward generated by all content receivers.

6. REFERENCES

[1] R. Ciobanu and et al, Onside: Socially-aware and interest based dissemination in opportunistic networks, in *Proc. of NOMS*, 2014.

[2] A. Land and et al, An automatic method of solving discrete programming problems, *Econometrica*, 28(3):497–520, 1960.

[3] K. Lin and et al, Preference-aware content dissemination in opportunistic mobile social networks, in *Proc. of INFOCOM*, 2012.

Poster: A Time-Saving Scheme for Ambulance Transportation with Support of Software-Defined Networking

Depeng Li
Department of Information and Computer Sciences
University of Hawaii at Manoa
1680 East West Road, Honolulu, HI, USA
1+(808) 956-3973
depengli@hawaii.edu

ABSTRACT
If Software-Defined Networking (SDN) is deployed on the ambulance, the doctor / care giver could remotely diagnose / take care of the patient after the patients are onboard. The patient get more chance to survive. After analyzing how to present patients earlier care, this paper's goals are to (1) enable an ambulance to transport the patient to hospitals as early as possible (2) ensure the paramedic provide care earlier via SDN. A set of graphic algorithms have been proposed and the experimental results demonstrate the feasibility of our solution.

Categories and Subject Descriptors
C.2.0 [**Computer-Communication Network**]: General – *Data communications*; G.2.2 [**Graph Theory**]: Graph Theory – *Graph algorithms, Network problems*; K.6.0 [**Management of Computing and Information System**]: General – *Economics.*

Keywords
Ambulance; Emergency Medical System; Mobile Ad hoc Networks; Software Defined Networking.

1. INTRODUCTION
An ambulance offers transportation services to pick up patients from scene of an incident and also driving them to hospitals. If an ambulance could transport a patient to the hospital a few minutes earlier, there is a higher possibility to save the patient's life [6]. Since 1970's, a rich amount of research has studied Location and Relocation model for ambulance: in order to maximize the expected covered demands, a dynamic relocation model is used under an assumption that the number of ambulances is limited in a region [2].

In this paper, we intend to carefully re-think the whole picture of the Emergency Medical System (EMR) which, so far, highly emphasizes on how to reduce response time [2]. Nevertheless, we believe that the essence of EMR is to give the earliest possible medical service to patients, locally or remotely. Driving patients to the hospital is the most reliable solution but not the only one: recent network communication advances in Software Defined Networking (SDN) technologies [5] makes a paradigm shift. It enables the possibility for doctors/nurses to remotely monitor the victim through SDN service on Ambulance. Though the quality of the service cannot achieve the same level as that in the hospital, patients could get the least medical service after they are positioned at the ambulance. Thus, this could significantly minimize the responding time and may further result in a potential life-saving. Furthermore, since the topic that how to dispatch ambulances in responding to an incident has already been well-studied, this paper basically endeavors to learn how to reduce the time to transport patients from the scene to the hospitals with SDN service.

The *objective* of this paper is to analyze the time-saving scheme which decreases the patients' waiting time for care givers. Our contributions are, with the deployment of SDN for ambulances, (1) adapt the metric of Mobile Ad hoc Networks (MANET) which is constructed to accommodate EMR system, (2) propose a set of graphic algorithms to calculate the nearest available hospital, and (3) execute preliminary experiment, whose results demonstrate the feasibility of our solution.

MobiHoc'15, June 22–25, 2015, Hangzhou, China.
ACM 978-1-4503-3489-1/15/06
http://dx.doi.org/10.1145/2746285.2764869

2. BACKGROUND
2.1 Ambulance
A *Patient Transport Ambulance* (PTA) is used for transportation of a sick or injured person from or between a scene and a hospital [1]. This paper studies the PTA which is equipped with two-way radio, mobile data terminal and SDN. In general, crew members include an ambulance driver, care assistant, paramedic, and emergency medical technician who could perform a wide range of emergency care skills, e.g. defibrillation, spinal immobilization, bleeding control, splinting of suspected fractures, assisting the patient with certain medications, and oxygen therapy [1].

2.2 Maximum Matching Algorithm
A matching on a graph is a set of edges, no two of which share a vertex. A maximum matching contains the greatest number of edges possible. M is a maximum matching if no matching on the graph contains more edges than M. The self-stabilizing Synchronous Maximal Matching (SMM) algorithm is proposed for ad hoc networks [3]. It will be deployed as one of our two solutions. The other solution, the maximum matching algorithm based on the depth-first spanning tree, is also proposed.

2.3 Software Defined Networking
Decoupling the control plane from the data plane, Software-Defined Networking (SDN) is a new programmable network framework which could offer users a set of flexible tools to design

and control the network. Leveraging SDN, we could design and develop some innovations e.g. ambulance communication systems to gain critical features such as fixed network bandwidth and quality of services. In addition, control management can be dynamically changed by users through a set of software [5].

3. OUR SOLUTIONS

Our solution is comprised of three components: (1) network model, (2) new metrics of edges' weight in network model, and (3) scheduling algorithms to calculate the best-serving path along which the patients could be delivered from the scene to available hospitals by using maximum matching algorithms if two or more than two ambulances are demanding hospitals simultaneously.

3.1 MANET of EMR

The MANET of EMR is denoted as $M = (\{m_1; \cdots; m_{|M|}\}; L)$ where m_i is an ambulance/hospital node and L is the set of paths established by two nodes. M is modeled as a connected, directed graph $G = (\{n_1; \cdots; n_{|M|}\},\ E, W(e))$ where vertex n_i corresponds to node m_i in M, E denotes the set of edges in L and W is the set of weights for all edges. There is an edge in E starting from vertices n_i and ending at n_j if nodes m_i and m_j in M enable successful path in such a way that the ambulance can drive from m_i to m_j directly.

3.2 Metrics of Edges' Weight

Each edge $e_{i,j} =< n_i, n_j >$ is associated with a weight number, ŵ, which is calculated by formula (1) below:

$$\hat{w} = \lambda \cdot t + (1 - \lambda)q \qquad (1)$$

where t is the estimated time for an ambulance to drive from m_i to m_j , q is quality of the SDN service (e.g. which is closely related with the network quality of $e_{i,j}$) when driving from m_i to m_j , and $0 \le \lambda \le 1$ is an coefficient. We can deduce formula (2).

$$\hat{w} = \begin{cases} t & when\ \lambda = 1 \\ q & when\ \lambda = 0 \\ \lambda \cdot t + (1-\lambda)q & \text{otherwise} \end{cases} \qquad (2)$$

Here, we can infer three points: (1) if $\lambda = 1$, then $\hat{w} = t$. It is corresponding to the case that our EMR system solely focus on the time to transport patients from scenes to hospitals. This scenario happens when the service of SDN is not provided or is not counted in. We call this *time-oriented.* (2) if $\lambda = 0$, then $\hat{w} = q$. It means that our EMR system takes account of nothing but the quality of SDN. This case most probably infers that the care can be provided via the other remote end of SDN and how long the patient can be delivered to hospitals is not important anymore. We call it *SDN-oriented.* (3) if $0 \le \lambda \le 1$, it is called *hybrid.* Both time and the quality of SDN are counted in. This is a more common scenario. If $0 \le \lambda < 0.5$, q is more important than t and vice versa.

3.3 Scheduling Algorithms

If there is only one ambulance requesting to transport the patients from the scene back to the hospitals, the shortest path algorithm (e.g. Dijkstra's algorithm) is invoked where formula (1) is called to calculate the weight of each edge in G and its output will be preferred hospital. This algorithm also applies to scenarios in which a hospital can accommodate more than one ambulance.

However, sometimes, a hospital may only have one device, d, but more than one ambulances request d for their patients. In such case, the hospital cannot accommodate more than one such kind of ambulance and the rest ambulances have to find other hospital equipped with d. To handle this case, this paper proposes two Maximum Matching Algorithm, (1) SMM [3] and (2) Maximum Matching Depth-first Spanning Tree (MM-DST) [4]. Since the former is described in [3], we mainly explain the latter.

Algorithm 1: Maximum Matching Depth-first Spanning Tree algorithm
/ $n_i \in G$ is a node. */*

Step 1: All nodes in G start up minimum Depth-first Spanning Tree algorithm (DST). The roots will be the nodes with the smallest ID comparing with their neighbors. A collection of independent spanning trees is generated.

Step 2: DST is executed to get a full spanning forest E which connects all spanning trees.

Step 3: The post-order walking algorithm over spanning forest E is executed by the source node. Then, a sequence $S = \{n_1, \ldots, n_i\}$ is constructed.

Step 4: Delete all repeated n_i in S. If corresponding to neither an available hospital nor an ambulance which is required to deliver a patient back to hospital, n_i should be deleted, too. A new sequence $S' = \{n'_1, \ldots, n'_k\}$ is obtained.

Step 5: n'_{2j-1} and n'_{2j} are matched where $n'_{2j-1} \in S'$ and $n'_{2j} \in S'$ and $1 \le j \le \frac{k}{2}$ if one of n'_{2j-1} and n'_{2j} is hospital and the other ambulance. If not, right shift pointer, j, till find the one satisfying the requirement.

4. EXPERIMENTAL RESULTS

The network simulation-2 (ns-2) is a widely used simulation tool. In this paper, to achieve a routing function, AODV, a routing protocol, is deployed to connect wireless nodes and forward packets from one node to another. A multicast AODV (MAODV) module is extended at ns-2 to multicast packets for this project. Specifically, this simulation utilized the test scenario components listed below: *Network: Mobile Ad Hoc Network (MANET); Routing Protocol: AODV; Area: 1500 x 300 meters; Number of nodes: 50; Number of repetitions: 10.* The test results are illuminated in Fig. 1. We conclude that our solution is feasible since its communication overhead is affordable.

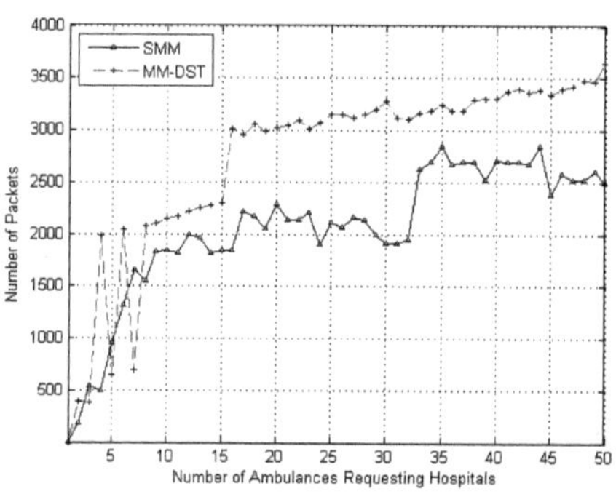

Figure 1. Maximum Matching Algorithms over EMR.

5. REFERENCES

[1] http://en.wikipedia.org/wiki/Ambulance, 2015

[2] L. Brotcorne, G. Laporte and F. Semet. "Ambulance location and relocation models." *European journal of operational research* vol. 147, no. 3 (2003): pp. 451-463.

[3] W. Goddard, S. T. Hedetniemi, D. P. Jacobs, and P. K. Srimani, "Self-stabilizing protocols for maximal matching and maximal independent sets for ad hoc networks", *Parallel and Distributed Processing Symposium*, pp.87-96, 2003.

[4] D. Li and S. Sampalli. "An efficient group key establishment in location-aided mobile ad hoc networks." 2nd ACM PE-WASUN 05.

[5] N. McKeown. "Software-defined networking." *INFOCOM* keynote talk 17, no. 2 (2009): 30-32.

[6] S. Saisubramanian, P. Varakantham, and H. C. Lau. "Risk based optimization for improving emergency medical systems." *AAAI'*15.

Poster: Toward a Theoretical Privacy Framework for Electronic Locks in Context of Home Security Monitoring System for Clouds of Things

Depeng Li
Department of Information and Computer Sciences
University of Hawaii at Manoa
1680 East West Road, Honolulu, HI, USA
depengli@hawaii.edu

ABSTRACT

Current popular schemes e.g. homomorphic cryptography are extensively deployed to preserve privacy in a limited level but without a formal privacy model, we can neither offer privacy guarantee nor quantify the privacy loss. In this paper, we raise a few privacy-related questions, one after another, with the e-Lock state changes in a smart home as an example. In a novel privacy framework we proposed, the questions are partially addressed with the utilization of a set of theoretical models e.g. hidden markov model, differential privacy and information flow with belief. Since our paper is still at its start phase, we plan to accomplish the framework and wish can inspire colleagues' interests in this area.

Categories and Subject Descriptors

K.4.1 [**Computer and Society**]: Public Policy Issues – *Privacy*;

Keywords

Electronic Lock; Formal Privacy Model; Privacy Preservation.

1. INTRODUCTION

In smart homes, proliferation of sensors and actuators equipped with communication capability enable occupants to remotely access or control an array of automated home electronic devices by entering a single command or a PIN number [1]. A current trend is that smart home, with occupancies' consent, could cooperate with third parties such as a home security monitoring company to get 24/7 security protection service. However, the participatory sensing application could potentially reveal the true data of occupants - it is highly possible that they are misused without well-designed privacy preservation.

The privacy violation for smart home [2] - even for some simple appliance such as electronic locks (e-Lock) [3], - is a pressing challenge today and increasingly affects all occupancies given the fact that captured true data can be misused to infer personal activities. The insight is based on the observation that some intermittent activities such as e-Lock switched on/off could possibly infer personal absence/presence at the smart home.

A power replay attack [3] is explored against most popular and commercially endorsed electronic lock. However, privacy preservation and privacy analyses (e.g. [4]) for e-Lock in context of smart home security monitoring system has not been presented. More importantly, it lacks a formal model of privacy analysis – privacy guarantee and quantitative evaluation are desirable. The pertinent privacy related questions should be addressed regarding time-series e-Lock state data: (1) How much privacy is lost and to what extend if all e-Lock states in smart home are open for access? (2) If perturbation methods which introduce uncertain noise to true personal data is deployed, could aggregator still queries leak privacy? (3) If the aggregator (e.g. server or the cloud of the security company) is not trusted, could we protect the privacy by access control scheme based on information flow?

Our contributions: we supply a theoretical privacy framework to analyze the privacy leakage through accommodating fundamental functionality e.g. sharing / hiding, perturbation and access control for aggregated time-series e-Lock state dataset for smart home system stored in cloud of things. We not only carefully study potential privacy inference but also try to address corresponding concerns about privacy loss in case of true dataset, of distorted dataset and of dataset under information flow protection:

(1) When the switching on/off operations of e-Locks are open to access, they are treated as the input and, in turn, could be modeled as real-valued correlated Gaussian random variable. Based on that, hidden Markov Chain model is provided to measure the occupancies' absence in correlation with the e-Lock's switching on/off operations

(2) To offer privacy protection, perturbing noisy into real data is assumed. We then invoke differential privacy method to analyze significant distinguish for specific occupancies' absence of the smart home.

(3) Turning on/off operations of e-Locks are transmitted to the security companies' server or even their cloud. They may be borrowed by third party for investigation in future. It is possible that aggregator is untrusted. An attempt to utilize hyberproperty information flow is taken to shield privacy.

2. ARCHITECTURE OF E-LOCK IN SMART HOME

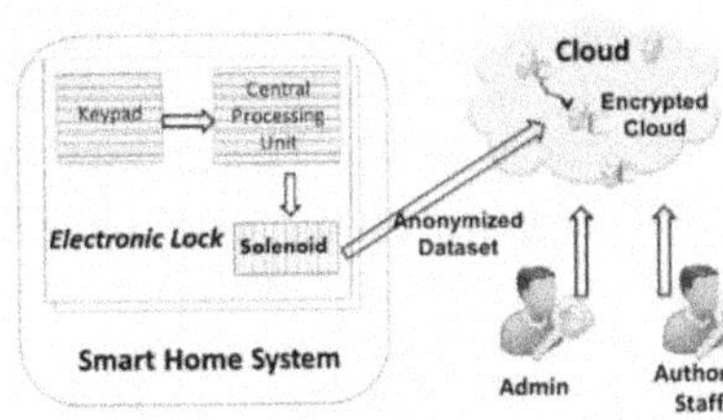

Figure 1 – Overview of e-Lock [3] in Smart Home of Cloud Things

MobiHoc'15, June 22–25, 2015, Hangzhou, China.
ACM 978-1-4503-3489-1/15/06.
http://dx.doi.org/10.1145/2746285.2764870

Figure 1 demonstrates the overview of the e-Lock in context of smart home with the cloud-things services. E-Locks in a smart home includes three components – keypad, central processing unit and solenoid (actuator). If the credential inputted at keypad is valid, a signal is sent to solenoid to changes the e-Lock's state from off to on. The application generates time-series categorical data which is aggregated to the server/cloud of the security company through secure communication channel. The admin or even authority staffs (e.g. policeman) may be able to query or even access the anonymized dataset from now on.

3. PRIVACY LOSS AND THREAT MODEL

3.1 Privacy Loss Scenario

Privacy for residence occupancy: An e-Lock state change C_i can let an adversary infer that the resident is presence or absence with the support of a temporal correlation of participatory sensing data.

Example I: Alice is the only one at home and then e-Lock's state is changed. Eve can probably infer that Alice may open the door and leave or Alice has accompany. If it is the former, Eve can take the risk to break in.

Untrusted third party aggregator that peek privacy: An adversary queries the collected data-set to steal the privacy by taking advantage of the strong correlation among successive values in the series.

Example II: Eve observe that Alice left the community. Eve can query the number of e-Lock state changes in the community at two successive time slots to guess which house Alice left.

Untrusted third party: the collected dataset could be borrowed by third party to accomplish research duties such as optimization or investigation tasks such as criminal inquiry. Unveiling time-series true/raw data may violate householder's privacy.

3.2 Threat Models

Like other researches [5] in areas of privacy preservations, we assume that smart devices (e.g. e-Lock, etc.) in smart home and the cloud/server obey network communication schemes. However, both users and the aggregators could be untruthful since they can lie and they also have the intension to combine the information if possible. However we need at least a fraction of them (e.g. a majority) are honest.

4. PROPOSED PRIVACY FRAMEWORK

4.1 Markov Chain

We assume that the state of an e-Lock L_i, (where $L_i \in L = \{L_1, L_2, ..., L_n\}$, n is the number of e-Locks in households) is sampled when there is an unlock/lock action. $L_i \in \{0,1\}$ where 0 denotes unlocked and 1 locked. Let array L_t^n denote the state of all e-Lock at time t. There are 2^n possible state of all e-Locks.

Assume there are m family memebers. The presence of each person in the household is also monitored as $P_i \in \{0,1\}$ where 0 denotes absence and 1 presence. At the time instant t, the presence of all members $\{P_1, P_2, ..., P_m\}$ is denoted as an array P_t^m. There are 2^m possible state of the presence of all m family members.

Thus, we model the joint probability distribution of the e-Lock states and the presence state over x time instants:

$$P(L_t^n, P_t^m) = \prod_{t=1}^{x} P(L_t^n | L_{t-1}^n) P(P_t^m | L_t^n) \qquad (1)$$

Based on (1), we can deduce a hidden Markov model for presence of persons, which can be characterized by three parameters: (a) the initial presence, (b) a state distribution and (c) a conditional distributions. After defining the 3 inputs with concrete details, our hidden Markov model should assess the interrelated association between the pair (L, P) in which, array P with all elements being 0 is what both the burglar and the security company are interested in.

4.2 Differential Privacy

Let I_i denote all e-Lock state change data related with one smart home or even a community. Denote $I = \sum_i^n I_i$ which is the collected dataset related with n persons $\{I_1, I_2, ..., I_n\}$. We demand the following holds

$$\Pr[A(I) = x] \le e^{\epsilon} \Pr[A(I') = x] \qquad (2)$$

where Pr is a probability distribution over randomness of algorithm $A(I)$ where I is the input, I' is the addition or removing of one single user, and x is an any value output.

Let $\boldsymbol{Q} = \{Q_1, Q_2, ... Q_n\}$be any query sequence, we demand the following holds:

$$|Q(I) - Q(I')|_p \le \Delta_p(Q) \qquad (3)$$

where $p \in \{1,2\}$, $Q(I)$ and $Q(I')$ are each vectors, $\Delta_1(Q)$ measures Manhattan distance $\sum_i |Q_i(I) - Q_i(I')|$ and $\Delta_2(Q)$ Euclidean distance ($\sqrt{\sum_i (Q_i(I) - Q_i(I'))^2}$).

4.3 Hyberproperty

The malicious third-party may query the true data and revise its belief from the keep going interaction thereafter [6]. An experiment $£ =< S, b_H, \sigma_H, \sigma_L >$ is processed where S is the query system, b_H denotes prebelief about high state, σ_H denotes high state and σ_L denotes low state. The third-party / agent predicts the output distribution p'_A and S produces a state $\sigma' \in p' = [\![S]\!](\dot{\sigma_L} \oplus \dot{b_H})$. The agent can infer a postbelief: $b'_H = (p'_A | o) \upharpoonright H$ where o is the low projection of the output state. With £, we, instantiating Bayes' rule on these probabilities, get Bayesian inference:

$$BI(£, o) = \frac{b_H(\sigma_H) \bullet ([\![S]\!]\dot{\sigma_L} \oplus \dot{\sigma_H} \upharpoonright H))(o)}{(\sum \sigma'_H : b_H(\sigma'_H) \bullet ([\![S]\!]\dot{\sigma_L} \oplus \dot{\sigma_H} \upharpoonright H))(o))} \qquad (4)$$

5. DISCUSSION AND FUTURE WORKS

Our future works will centrally focus on privacy preservation via perturbing distributed noisy information to time-series e-Lock state change data to minimize the privacy loss with lower utility-privacy tradeoff. In addition, how to extend hidden Markov Chain method to precisely quantify privacy loss and corresponding countermeasures via differentially private protection will be studied.

6. REFERENCES

[1] D. J. Cook, "How smart is your home?" *Science,* vol. 335, no. 6076, pp. 1579-1581, 2012.

[2] T. Kim, L. Bauer, J. Newsome, A. Perrig, and J. Walker. "Access right assignment mechanisms for secure home networks." *Journal of Communications and Networks*, vol. 13, no. 2, pp. 175-186, April 2011.

[3] S. Oh, J. Yang, A. Bianchi, and H. Kim, "Poster: power replay attack in electronic door locks", extended abstract, IEEE Sym. Security and Privacy, pp. 1-2, 2014, San Jose, CA.

[4] C. Dwork, "Differential privacy: A survey of results." *In Theory and Applications of Models of Computation*, pp. 1-19, 2008.

[5] V. Rastogi and S. Nath, "Differentially private aggregation of distributed time-series with transformation and encryption." In *2010 ACM SIGMOD* pp. 735-746. ACM, 2010.

[6] M. Clarkson, A. Myers, and F. Schneider. "Quantifying information flow with beliefs." *Journal of Computer Security* vol. 17, no. 5: pp. 655-701,2009.

Poster: Unified Resource Allocation for Small Cell Networks Using Matching Theory

Shuhang Zhang
School of Electronics Engineering and Computer Science, Peking University, Beijing, China
zhangshuhang@pku.edu.cn

Boya Di
School of Electronics Engineering and Computer Science, Peking University, Beijing, China
diboya@pku.edu.cn

Lingyang Song
School of Electronics Engineering and Computer Science, Peking University, Beijing, China
lingyang.song@pku.edu.cn

ABSTRACT

In this paper, we study the resource allocation problem in a small cell Orthogonal Frequency Division Multiple Access (OFDMA) network consisting of multiple access points (APs) and subscribed users. We formulate the subchannel allocation and the user assignment as a joint optimization problem, and solve it utilizing a novel three-sided matching algorithm. In the proposed algorithm, a unified cooperative framework is constructed in which we discuss both the non-overlapping and the overlapping coalitions formed by the APs, as well as the traditional non-cooperative case.

Categories and Subject Descriptors

C.2.1 [**Computer-Communication Networks**]: Network Architecture and Design - Wireless Communication

Keywords

Small Cell, Resource Allocation, Matching Theory

1. INTRODUCTION

Small cell networks are considered as one of the most promising solutions for future access technologies. There exist several challenges such as the interference management and the user assignment of the access points (APs). Typically, an OFDMA small cell network consists of one macro AP (MAP), multiple femtocell APs (FAPs), non-overlapping sub-channels(SCs) and multiple user equipments (UEs). To achieve a satisfying sum-rate of the network, the UEs need to be associated to the APs, and the APs then allocate the SCs to the UEs for communication. Given the potential interference caused by different UEs over the same SCs subscribed to various FAPs, the conflicting FAPs can choose to cooperate with each other to share the spectrum resources or allocate the SCs separately. Note that one FAP can cooperate with multiple FAPs to avoid the conflicts on different SCs, and together they form overlapping coalitions to allocate these SCs. Most existing works are focusing on whether to form the cooperation between the FAPs or not, and a unified resource allocation solution for the small cell work should be considered in which both the cooperative and the non-cooperative behaviours of the FAPs are depicted.

In this work, we formulate the resource allocation problem as a joint optimization problem, and then model it as a three-sided matching problem utilizing the *matching theory* [1], [2]. We then propose a novel matching algorithm to effectively solve it in which we regard the sets of UEs, APs, and SCs as selfish and rational players who try to maximize their own interests. We extend the traditional matching algorithm by introducing the coalition formation games so as to unify the non-cooperative scheme and the cooperative scheme including the formation of both the non-overlapping and the overlapping coalitions.

2. SYSTEM MODEL

We consider an OFDMA small cell downlink network, as depicted in Fig.1, with one MAP, N FAPs and E UEs. Let $\mathcal{N} = \{1, 2, \cdots N\}$ denote the set of FAPs and $\mathcal{E} = \{1, 2, \cdots E\}$ denote the set of UEs. Each FAP has access to multiple SCs, denoted by $\mathcal{K}_{SC} = \{1, 2, \cdots K\}$. The MAP transmits its signals on another set of orthogonal sub-channels, denoted by $\mathcal{L} = \{1, 2, \cdots L\}$, which satisfies $L \cap K = \varnothing$. Each UE can only be served by one FAP or the MAP, and then the AP allocates multiple SCs or MAP-SCs to it. Since the FAPs are resource-constrained, each FAP_j can serve a maximum of q_j^{FAP} UEs, while the MAP can serve a maximum of q^{MAP} UEs, satisfying $q^{MAP} \gg q_j^{FAP}$. Considering user fairness, we assume that each UE can only be assigned with a maximum number of X_{max} SCs or MAP-SCs.

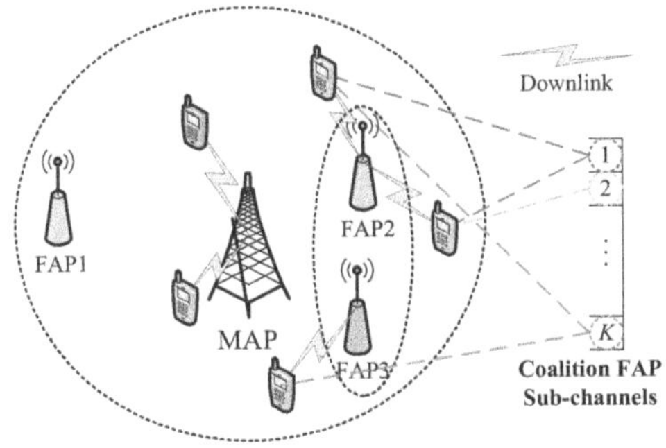

Figure 1: System model of the OFDMA smallcell downlink network.

Since the spectrum band of the FAPs is different from the MAP, there is no FAP-MAP interference. Note that the inter-FAP interference occurs when two FAPs use the same SC to serve different UEs. We denote P_i^k as the power that UE_i receives over SC_k, and $h_{i,j,k}$ as the channel coefficient,

MobiHoc'15, June 22–25, 2015, Hangzhou, China.
ACM 978-1-4503-3489-1/15/06.
http://dx.doi.org/10.1145/2746285.2764871.

respectively. The signal to interference noise ratio (SINR) of UE_i that is connected to FAP_j over SC_k is given by

$$R_{i,j}^{FAP}(k) = \frac{P_i^k |h_{i,j,k}|^2 / d^\alpha}{{\sigma_n}^2 + \sum\limits_{j' \in \mathcal{D}_\mathcal{J}} P_i^k |h_{i,j',k}|^2 / d^\alpha}, \tag{1}$$

where ${\sigma_n}^2$ is the noise variance, d^α is the path loss function, and $\mathcal{D}_\mathcal{J}$ is the set of FAPs adjacent to FAP_j. Therefore, the SINR of UE_i that is connected to the MAP at MAP-SC_k is given by

$$R_i^{MAP}(k) = \frac{P_i^{MAP}(k)|h_{i,k}|^2 / d^\alpha}{{\sigma_n}^2}, \tag{2}$$

where $P_i^{MAP}(k)$ is the transmission power that UE_i receives over MAP-SC_k.

To better describe the user association and sub-channel pairing, we define a $E \times N$ UE-FAP pairing matrix $\mathbf{\Phi}$, in which the binary variable $\phi_{i,j}$ denotes whether UE_i and FAP_j are paired with each other. We also define a $E \times K$ UE-SC paring matrix $\mathbf{\Psi}$, in which $\psi_{i,k} = 1$ if UE_i and SC_k are paired and $\psi_{i,k} = 0$ otherwise. Respectively, we use a binary indicator θ_i to describe whether or not UE_i is connected to the MAP, and a $E \times L$ UE-MAPSC paring matrix $\mathbf{\Omega}$, in which the binary variable $\omega_{i,l}$ denotes whether UE_i and $MAPSC_l$ are paired with each other. Our objective is to maximize the total sum-rate by jointly determining the variables $\{\phi_{i,j}, \psi_{i,k}, \theta_i, \omega_{i,l}\}$, which can be formulated as:

$$\begin{aligned} \max_{\{\mathbf{\Phi},\mathbf{\Psi},\mathbf{\Theta},\mathbf{\Omega}\}} & \sum_{i=1}^{E}\sum_{j=1}^{N}\sum_{k=1}^{K} \log_2 \left[1 + R_{i,j}^{FAP}(k)\phi_{i,j}\psi_{i,k}\right] \\ & + \sum_{i=1}^{E}\sum_{g=1}^{L} \log_2 \left[1 + R_i^{MAP}(l)\theta_i\omega_{i,l}\right] \\ \boldsymbol{s.t.} \quad & \text{constraints}, \end{aligned} \tag{3}$$

where the constraints include:1) each FAP has a quota number for its UE q_j^{FAP}; 2) the MAP has a quota number for its UE q^{MAP}; 3) each UE cannot pair with more than X_{max} SCs and MAP-SCs.

3. MATCHING ALGORITHMS

We assume that the power is equally allocated over each SC by each AP, and then perform a three-sided matching algorithm in which we consider the APs, the UEs, and the SCs as three disjoint sets of players who aim at maximizing their own interests when matching with the members in the other two parties. Considering the existence of the inter-FAP interference in the matching process, we introduce the cooperation between the FAPs, i.e., the conflicting FAPs can choose to cooperate with each other on whether to share the SC together. When two FAPs agree that they avoid allocating the same SC to two different users, we say they cooperate with each other and form a coalition, otherwise, they behave non-cooperatively to allocate this SC. If one FAP cooperate with multiple FAPs over different SCs, it forms overlapping coalitions with other FAPs.

The detailed matching algorithm is described as bellow. Each UE lists its possible SC-AP choices and obtains the preference lists over all the SC-AP pairs according to the data rates it can get. In each round, each UE that is possible to make a profitable deviation proposes to its favourite AP-SCs pairs that haven't rejected it in the former rounds. The APs that have received more than one offers then decide whether to accept the proposing UEs. For a proposed FAP, it negotiates with other FAPs which cause potential inter-FAP interference on whether to form a coalition, and then it determines how to allocate the SCs to the proposed UEs. The matching will stop until no UE is willing to make new offers, i.e., the matching converges to a stable matching.

4. SIMULATION RESULT

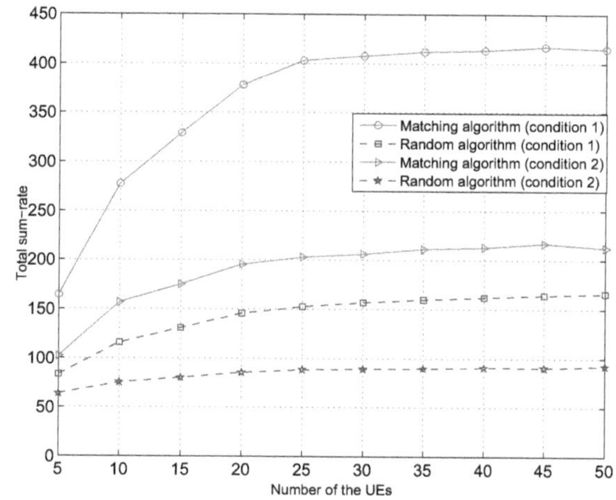

Figure 2: Total sum-rate vs. Total UE number.

For the simulation, we set P_i^{MAP} to 46 dBm, P_i^{FAP} to 43 dBm, q_j^{FAP} to 5, q^{MAP} to 8, X_{max} to 3 and the the path loss exponent α to 2. We also set the location of the APs and UEs and the condition of each SC randomly. To evaluate the performance of our proposed matching algorithm, we utilized a random matching algorithm. We then compared our results with the results of a random matching algorithm in two different conditions, as shown in Figure 2. In condition 1, there are 10 FAPs, 15 SCs and 5 MAPSCs in the network and in condition 2, there are 4 FAPs, 8 SCs and 2 MAPSCs in the network. Figure 2 illustrates the relation between the UE number and the total sum-rate. The total sum-rate raises rapidly when when there's few UE, and it goes saturated when the UE number increases. It's obvious to see that our proposed algorithm outperforms the random algorithm, and the sum-rates in condition 1 always outperform those in condition 2, because of a ampler resource.

5. CONCLUSION

In this paper, we studied the resource allocation problem in an OFDMA small cell network. We proposed a novel three-sided matching algorithm to jointly match the UEs, SCs and the APs as well as present the cooperation between the FAPs. Simulation results show that our proposed algorithm performs better than the random matching algorithm.

6. ACKNOWLEDGEMENT

This work was supported by the National 973 Project under Grant 2013CB336700, by the National Natural Science Foundation of China under Grants 61222104 and U1301255, and 61428101.

7. REFERENCES

[1] A. Roth and M. Sotomayor, *Two-Sided Matching: A Study in Game-Theoretic Modeling and Analysis*, Cambridge University Press, 1992.

[2] S. Bayat, R. Louie, Z. Han, B. Vucetic and Y. Li, "Distributed User Association and Femtocell Allocation in Heterogeneous Wireless Networks," in *IEEE Transactions on Communications*, pp. 3027-3043, vol. 62, no. 8, Aug. 2014.

Demo: Proximity-based Information Propagation

Soranut Midtrapanon, Takkachai Rittirat,
Sornrakitch Thanumaiweerakun
Faculty of ICT
Mahidol University, Thailand
[soranut.mid,takkachai.rit,
sornrakitch.tan]@student.mahidol.ac.th

Wantanee Viriyasitavat
Faculty of ICT
Mahidol University, Thailand
wantanee.vir@mahidol.ac.th

ABSTRACT

In this paper, we propose and implement a proximity-based information propagation framework based on Android devices. With the ubiquity of the smartphones and a drastic increase in demands of cellular traffic, the information propagation mechanism proposed and implemented in this paper entirely relies on the mobile-to-mobile (i.e., ad-hoc) communications. In contrast to the WiFi Direct technology (i.e., single-hop ad hoc communications), the pure ad-hoc communications enabled in our proposed framework allows multi-hop message propagation. In addition, a mitigation technique is also implemented to prevent the broadcast storm problems caused by redundant rebroadcasts. The implementation of the pure ad-hoc and multi-hop communications have been tested in several Android phone models and in a few tests scenarios which were conducted to determine the feasibility as well as the limitation of using mobile devices for the proximity-based information propagation.

Categories and Subject Descriptors

C.2.1 [**Computer Communication Networks**]: Network Architecture and Design

Keywords

Mobile-to-mobile communications, Wireless ad-hoc networks

1. INTRODUCTION

Smartphones have become an important part in our daily life as they are ubiquitous and they have transformed how people communicate and interact. As a result, cellular networks have been the main communications means for smartphones and their communication throughputs have been improved drastically over the past years (i.e., 4G/LTE/5G). While the cellular networks have been proven to be able to support current traffic demands, it is envisioned that in the era of the Internet of Things, the cellular networks may not be sufficient to support traffic from billions of devices. In addition, the cellular network infrastructure may not be available in some remote regions and/or are destroyed in disastrous situations. As a result, relying solely on the cellular networks might not be adequate and a communication alternative might become useful in such the situations. In this paper, we therefore propose the proximity-based information propagation based solely on the ad-hoc (i.e., infrastructureless) communications between mobile devices (i.e., Android devices). Besides being robust (i.e., it is able to function in all scenarios), the proposed framework enables the proximity-based communications without prior information about the nearby devices. The device or user is able to specify if the information is location-specific and should be relayed only within the certain region (i.e., without uploading it onto the Internet).

The contribution of this demo paper can be summarized as follows: i) the implementation of a new ad-hoc communications based on IEEE 802.11 standard; rather than the Wi-Fi Direct technology that does not operate in a pure ad-hoc manner (i.e., one of the devices has to take the role of a virtual access point); ii) the proof-of-concept prototype that has been comprehensively tested and evaluated in a number of Android mobile platforms; and iii) the example Android application that allows messages to be broadcasted efficiently and effectively in a multi-hop manner.

MobiHoc'15, June 22–25, 2015, Hangzhou, China.
ACM 978-1-4503-3489-1/15/06.
http://dx.doi.org/10.1145/2746285.2764927.

2. IMPLEMENTATION

In our implementation, the newest APIs and tools provided from Netlink via *nl80211* were used to enable the ad-hoc mode in the Android mobile devices. Despite the latest APIs, the ad-hoc implementation described in this paper is backward compatible with some of the older APIs. The *iw* tool is used to set up the device's wireless interface to work in IBSS mode[1] and in order to support the new security layer introduced in Android 5.0 (API 21), we precompiled the tool[2] with Android NDK for both PIE (Position-Independent Executable) and non-PIE supported Android version. In addition, the devices must have i) able to gain the root access, ii) have a cfg80211/mac80211 wireless device, and iii) the kernels must support IBSS mode. The above implementation was successfully implemented and tested in 5 various Android devices: Samsung Nexus S, Samsung Galaxy Nexus, HTC Desire, HTC One, and LG Nexus 5.

While the above implementation enables pure ad-hoc communications between Android devices, it does not allow the

[1]https://wireless.wiki.kernel.org/en/developers/documentation/cfg80211
[2]http://git.kernel.org/cgit/linux/kernel/git/jberg/iw.git

message to be relayed in a multi-hop manner. This one-hop communication could significantly and negatively affect the information propagation coverage especially when the mobile phone is run in a power-limited mode. As a result, a multi-hop message rebroadcast is implemented whereby a broadcast storm mitigation technique is applied in order to avoid the excessive and redundant rebroadcasts of the messages (i.e., known as the broadcast storm problem) [1]. In this technique, each mobile device, upon receiving a message, waits for a certain amount of time computed in 1 before rebroadcast the message. If the wait time expires and the device has not received any message, the device rebroadcasts; otherwise, the device cancel its scheduled message rebroadcast.

$$t(d) = \begin{cases} 0, & \text{if } d > D_{max} \\ \left(1 - \frac{d}{D_{max}}\right) \cdot 500ms, & \text{if otherwise} \end{cases} \quad (1)$$

where d is the distance between its current location and the sender of the message and D_{max} is the maximum communication range. Observe that the wait time is inversely proportional to the distance between the sender and the current location; i.e., the further the phone is from the sender, the smaller the wait time. This mechanism favors the further devices to do the rebroadcast so that the information can be propagated in a faster and more efficient manner.

3. EXPERIMENTS

In addition to the device implementation, we have conducted a few test scenarios to determine the feasibility and limitation of using the low-power Android devices for mobile-to-mobile communications. The first test scenario was conducted to determine the maximum communication range between two Android devices. In this scenario, both devices are associated with the same SSID with pre-assigned unique IP addresses. Both phones have been calibrated to use the fixed maximum power allowed by the chipset. Packet Delivery Ratio (PDR) results are collected for different distances (with a 20-meter increment) and for different orientations. In this test scenario, the receiver phone shown in the left figure of Figure 1 always faces its backside toward to the sender while the sender changes in one of the four orientations as shown in Figure 2. Back in Figure 2 indicates that with the phone is put perpendicular to the ground; the sender faces its backside toward to the receiver. Based on the results shown in Figure 2, the communication range of an Android phone could be up to 480m and the orientation of the sender and the receiver could significantly affect the packet reception. Note that this result serves as a preliminary evaluation to determine the maximum communication range; this range may differ significantly depending on the environment and specific Android phones.

Furthermore, in order to put the proposed proximity-based information propagation into a perspective, we developed an Android application, namely RoadCast. This application is envisioned to be used for broadcasting information about traffic incident to drivers or passengers in the surrounding areas. This information may include the traffic incident type, estimated duration, severity as well as the GPS location of the accident. Three phones are used in this experiment (e.g., two Nexus 5 and one HTC One).

The experiment shown in Figure 3 was conducted to verify the functionality and effectiveness of the broadcast storm mitigation technique implemented in the proposed framework. In this experiment, all three devices are put next to one another (hence, each can establish direct communication with the other two). However, the locations of all the three phones are simulated to the locations shown in the left figure of Figure 3. In this experiment, device A (shown in red color) broadcasts a message to the other two devices (shown in green color). Upon receiving the message from the sender, both devices compute the wait time to rebroadcast the message received. The experiment shows that in this scenario, while both devices receive the message, the device located further from the sender is the only one that rebroadcasts. This is expected since the further device has a smaller wait time and thus rebroadcasts time; while the closer device receives the redundant rebroadcasts, it cancels its scheduled rebroadcast. reducing the number of devices that perform the broadcast.

Figure 1: A test scenario to determine the maximum communication range of Android phone. Both phones used in this scenario are the Nexus 5 models.

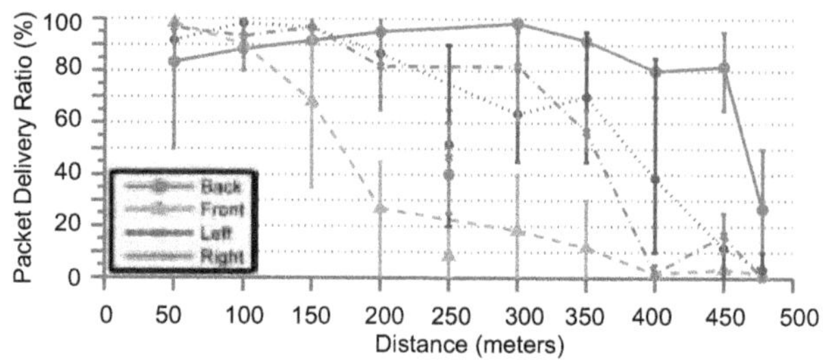

Figure 2: The packet delivery ratio results for the scenario shown in Figure 1.

Figure 3: A scenario conducted to determine the effectiveness of the broadcast mitigation technique.

4. REFERENCES

[1] Wisitpongphan, N. and et al. Broadcast storm mitigation techniques in vehicular ad hoc networks. IEEE Wireless Communications Magazine, 2007.

Demo: LIVES: Learning through Interactive Video and Emotion-aware System

Min Chen
EPIC Lab
Huazhong Univ. of Science and Technology
Wuhan, China
minchen@ieee.org

Yixue Hao
EPIC Lab
Huazhong Univ. of Science and Technology
Wuhan, China
yixue.epic@gmail.com

Yong Li
Department of Electronic Engineering
Tsinghua University
Beijing, China
liyong07@tsinghua.edu.cn

Di Wu
School of Info. Sci. & Tech.
Sun Yat-Sen University
Guangzhou, China
wudi27@mail.sysu.edu.cn

Dijiang Huang
Department of CSE
Arizona State University
Arizona, USA
Dijiang.Huang@asu.edu

ABSTRACT

In order to improve the accuracy and efficiency of emotion recognition, we design a novel system called Learning through Interactive Video and Emotion-aware System (LIVES). LIVES includes data collection, emotion recognition, and result validation, as well as emotion feedback. We adopt transfer learning to label and validate moods in LIVES, while the emotion can be classified into six types of mood in a reasonable accuracy. Through transfer learning, the time-consuming and labor-intensive processing cost on data collection and labeling can also be greatly reduced. In our prototype system, LIVES is used to enhance an emotion-aware robot's intelligence provided by cloud. LIVES-based emotion recognition is executed in the remote cloud while corresponding result is sent to the robot for emotion feedback. The experimental results demonstrate LIVES significantly improves the accuracy and effectiveness of emotion classification.

Keywords

Affective interaction, transfer learning, sentiment anlysis

1. INTRODUCTION

Nowadays, there are lots of works on emotion recognition. Previous work on emotion recognition can be categorized as follows: (1) body signal-based recognition [4]; (2) audio-visual data based recognition, including method through face video processing [5], and (3) recognition based on the usage pattern of smartphone [7]. However, it is challenging to fuse large-scale heterogeneous emotion data in multi-dimensional spaces for analyzing user's emotion while proactively activating surrounding hardware resources to perform personalized actions to comfort user's emotion. LIVES based solution is the first to tackle above challenges through multi-space emotion data collection, emotion recognition, validation and feedback. Especially, LIVES explores transfer learning on top of robotics and cloud-terminal integration technologies.

MobiHoc'15, June 22–25, 2015, Hangzhou, China.
ACM 978-1-4503-3489-1/15/06.
http://dx.doi.org/10.1145/2746285.2764928 .

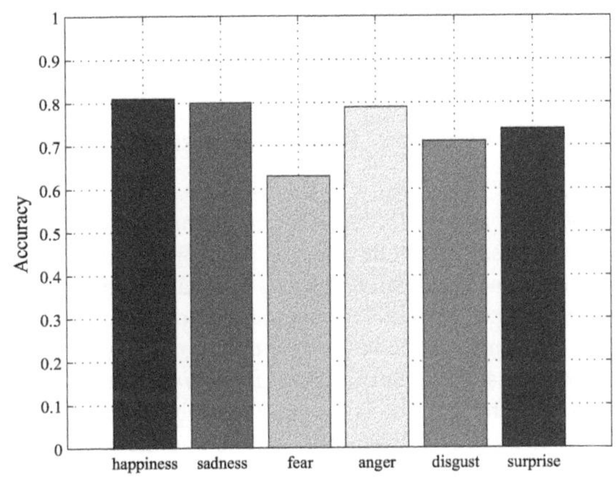

Figure 1: Accuracy of mood recognition

2. LIVES FRAMEWORK

2.1 LIVES Description

In LIVES, user's physical, cyber and social domain's data are first collected by wearable device, mobile devices and network devices. Physical data include physiological data, activity level, location, environmental and face/interactive video. Cyber data consist of call, SMS, email, application usage, WiFi and network control. Social network data include SNS content or image post, repost and comment. Then, the data are preprocessed. After preprocessing, we extract the data feature. For the emotion space, the data are labeled and validated by transfer learning based on previously labeled results. Now we introduce the label and validate phase. In the label phase, the source domain data x_s input come from ten users' personal information in terms of physical data, cyber and social network data and moods. The target domain data x_t input data come from other personal information. Our goal is to estimate the mood c probability $p(c|x_t)$, since the x_s and x_t may be in a different feature space, So we first need to find a translator to link the two feature spaces [3]. since the f_s and f_t are features and are conditionally independent x_s, where $x_s \in \chi_s$, so we can calculate $p(f_s, f_t)$ as

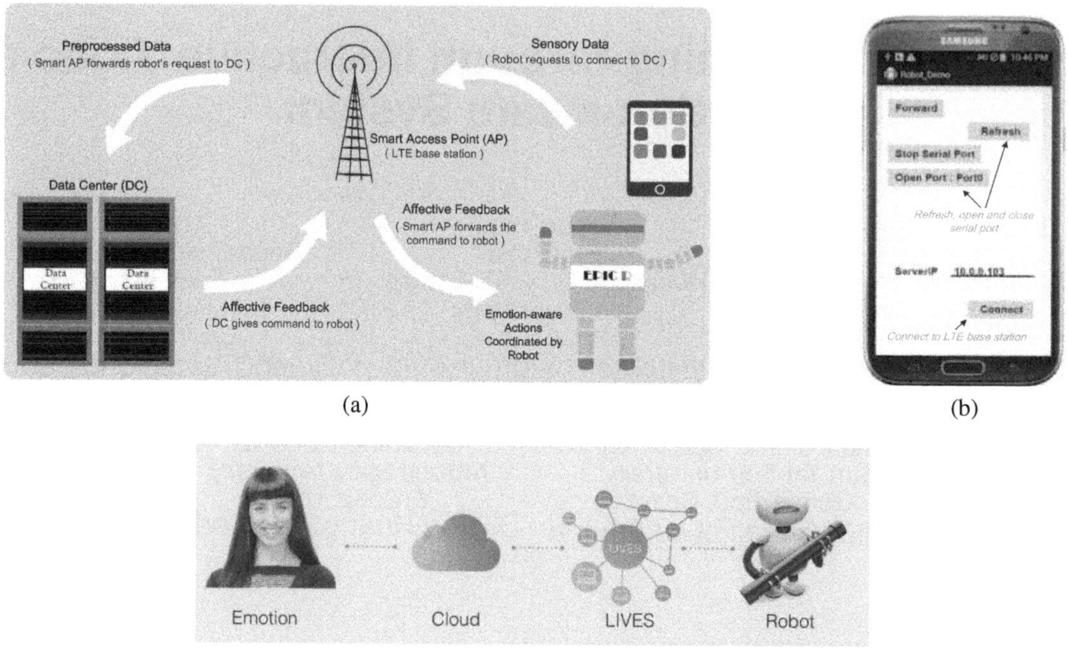

Figure 2: LIVES based Testbed: (a) System architecture; (b) Control messages shown in LTE cell phone; (c) Test scenario.

follows: $p(f_t, f_s) = \int_{\mathcal{X}_s} p(f_t, x_s)p(f_s|x_s)dx_s$, Now we link the unlabel feature f_t and x_s through Jensen-Shannon divergence. In the validation phase, We overhear users' input of their own emotion when they use some applications such as Moodagent. But one principal problem is that, the mood we overhear is not the same as mood label space C. Thus, we need to compare the similarity of the label space C and the user's input mood as $M = \{m_1, \ldots, m_n\}$ which is collected in each time slot as ground-truth label. Using a framework similar to transfer learning [6], we can find the similarity between mood c and m as follows: $\text{sim}(c, m) = \text{MMD}^2[D_c, D_m]$, The $\text{MMD}^2[D_c, D_m]$ is the maximum mean discrepancy [1], we validate the label which the most similar in C, Through transfer learning the time-consuming and labor-intensive processing cost can be reduced extensively. After a certain time of labeling and validation through transfer learning, the training sets are established. By the utilization of Hidden Markov model, the emotion data are classified into six mood. These mood classification results are forwarded to EPIC robot which is developed in Embedded and Pervasive Computing (EPIC) lab. During emotion feedback stage, EPIC robot system carries out hardware resource cognition then performs a series of actions to comfort user's emotion using Markov decision process. For example, a personalized video will be shown in an available screen such as a projector. If the user is not satisfied with the emotion feedback actions, video contents and display method can be fine tuned through continuous learning until user's emotions are cared more accurately and efficiently. This is called feedback data through the interaction between user and system. In order to improve the accuracy of emotion recognition, we use physical data, cyber data, social network data and feedback data in next time.

2.2 Demonstration

As shown in Fig. 2(a), we implement LIVES in AIWAC testbed [2], which consists of robot, smart access point (AP), and data center (DC). The testbed provides a version of software available to run in Linux in the DC, which generates command queue according the analyzed mood and these commands are transmitted from DC to the robot via TCP protocol. Fig. 2(b) illustrates control messages shown in LTE cell phone. In Fig. 2(c), we use LIVES to predicate the user's mood compared with the mood given by users, we can obtain the accuracy as shown in Fig. 1, where the recognition of user's moods is achieved with acceptable accuracy which is higher than Moodscope [7]. When we find people in a unpleasant mood, we use robot to do some interactive actions to care user's mood.

Acknowledgment

Many thanks to Yujun Ma, Yin Zhang, Hang Ruan, Wenye Wang, Shan Zhao, Chuanbei Wu for making tremendous system-building efforts on the testbed, where LIVES experiments are run.

3. REFERENCES

[1] K. Borgwardt, A. Gretton, and et al. Integrating stuctured biological data by kernel maximum mean discrepancy. In *Proc. of ISMB'06*, 2006.

[2] M. Chen, Y. Zhang, Y. Li, and et al. Aiwac: affective interaction through wearable computing and cloud technology. *IEEE Wireless Communications*, 22(1):20–27, Feb. 2015.

[3] W. Dai, Y. Chen, G.-R. Xue, Q. Yang, and Y. Yu. Translated learning: Transfer learning across different feature spaces. In *Proc. of ACM NIPS*. ACM, 2008.

[4] A. Gluhak, M. Presser, L. Zhu, and et al. Towards mood based mobile services and applications. In *Proc. of ACM EuroSSC*, pages 159–174. ACM, 2007.

[5] J. Hernandez, M. Hoque, W. Drevo, and R. Picard. Mood meter: Counting smiles in the wild. In *Proc. of Int'l Conf. on Ubiquitous Computing (UbiComp)*, pages 301–310. ACM, Sept. 2012.

[6] D. H. Hu, V. W. Zheng, and Q. Yang. Cross-domain activity recognition via transfer learning. *Pervasive and Mobile Computing*, 7(3):344–358, 2011.

[7] R. LiKamWa, Y. Liu, N. D. Lane, and L. Zhong. Moodscope: Building a mood sensor from smartphone usage patterns. In *Proc. of ACM MobiSys'13*, pages 84–89. ACM, June 2013.

Demo: Software-Defined Device to Device Communication in Multiple Cells

Huanyu Zhang
School of Electronics Engineering and Computer Science, Peking University, Beijing 100871, China
zhy99@pku.edu.cn

Mingxin Zhou
School of Electronics Engineering and Computer Science, Peking University, Beijing 100871, China
mingxin.zhou@pku.edu.cn

Lingyang Song
School of Electronics Engineering and Computer Science, Peking University, Beijing 100871, China
lingyang.song@pku.edu.cn

Shengli Zhang
Department of Communication Engineering, Shenzhen University, 518060, China
zsl@szu.edu.cn

ABSTRACT

This work aims to design a novel multi-hop device-to-device (D2D) communication system across multiple cells, by applying the spirit of software-defined networking, where the controllers regulate the data flows between the device-level switches in a centralized way. We utilize a hierarchical control plane, where the global controller handles the cross-cell D2D transmission, and the local controller determines the intra-cell D2D routing and scheduling. Specifically, by collecting the network information periodically, the controllers can generate the topology of D2D network and provide it to the applications. Through the use of USRP hardware, we demonstrate the feasibility of our proposed system.

Categories and Subject Descriptors

C.2.1 [**Computer-Communication Networks**]: Network Architecture and Design—*Wireless Communications*

Keywords

Multi-hop cross-cell D2D communications, software-defined networking

1. INTRODUCTION

Device-to-device (D2D) communication is envisioned as a promising technique to supplement the cellular network, which can enhance the spectral efficiency, extend the coverage, and create new services. However,the current D2D communication only supports one-hop communication within one cell. In order to achieve the potentials of D2D, multi-hop transmission must be supported, since the communication distance of D2D is too short to connect relatively far nodes. To support a multi-hop D2D communication (even intra-cell), the routing and scheduling algorithms must be carefully designed.

In addition, the cross-cell D2D communication also needs to be supported. D2D communication tends to be utilized at the edge of the cell to extend the coverage and reuse the resources allocated to the center cellular users. In this case, the D2D communication at the edge of multiple cells may affect with each other. To alleviate the interference, negotiation between base stations (BSs) of multiple adjacent cells increases the signal overheading significantly. Besides, cross-cell transmission seems impossible without a centralized entity to manage the data routing involving multiple cells.

To this end, we attempt to design a novel system to support multi-hop cross-cell D2D transmission, based on the concept of software-defined networking (SDN), where the distributed data flows are regulated by the centralized controllers. SDN is a revolutionary paradigm which decouples the control plane from data plane. The controllers in the control plane define the rules that the switching devices follow in the data plane.

As illustrated in Fig. 1, the wireless nodes are classified as potential-switching nodes (PSN) that can forward packets for others due to the broadcast nature and cellular nodes (CN) that can only communicate with the BS. Generally speaking, the wireless nodes static or at low speed and with relatively long residual battery life can act as a PSN. Besides, to facilitate routing management, we regard BS as a PSN with larger power that can relay data packets for mobile devices. We propose to employ a global controller (GC) and several local controllers (LC) to manage cross-cell routing and scheduling, and several local controllers (LC) to perform intra-cell routing and scheduling.

2. SYSTEM DESIGN

This system adopts the TDMA MAC protocol, consisting of the control phase and data phase. We utilize the standard graph-based network and interference model to capture the characteristics of the wireless environment and represent the topology. To support cross-cell multi-hop D2D transmission, in the control phase, the controllers collect network information, abstract the D2D networks as connectivity graphs and

MobiHoc'15, June 22–25, 2015, Hangzhou, China.
ACM 978-1-4503-3489-1/15/06.
http://dx.doi.org/10.1145/2746285.2764929.

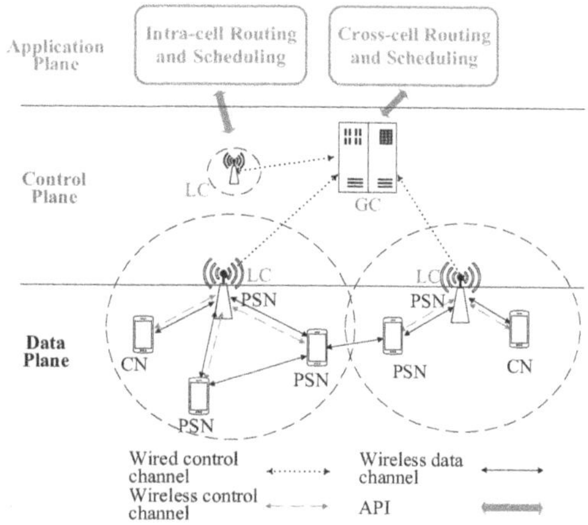

Figure 1: Abstraction of the proposed system

contention graphs, and provide abstraction for the higher level application programs through an open interface. After the applications solve the problems, the controllers then translate the program output into standard rules that can be parsed by the mobile devices. In the data phase, the data packets are disseminated based on the rules received in the control phase. In this demo, the application is to manage joint routing and scheduling in the D2D network.

The network information that should be updated consists of topology information and flow information. In this demo, the topology information contains the location, velocity and residual battery life of each node, and the flow information includes the previous, current and forthcoming flow information. The previous flow information refers to the statistics which is kept track of in the flow table of each node, which is used for automatic calibration of the topology. The current flow information needs to be updated if a current flow needs more bandwidth or is about to end. The forthcoming flow information contains the requested source, its corresponding destination, and the QoS requirement.

After collecting the topology information, the LC partitions the mobile devices in its cell into 3 sets: the center mobile devices, the edge PSNs, and the edge CNs. The LC abstracts the D2D network within its coverage as a connectivity graph and a contention graph with the corresponding distance constraints of connectivity and interference. The program on top of the LC solves the joint routing and scheduling problem of the inner network[1], every time when the topology of the network or the source/destination changes. The joint routing and scheduling is a classic multi-commodity problem and can be solved using linear programming [2].

Then, the mobile devices in the inner network of a LC and itself can be aggregated as a "big" PSN, and GC can tackle the routing and scheduling problem of several big PSNs and edge PSNs, with the knowledge of the time slots already been occupied by the inner network. The GC then notifies the LCs of the time slots for the cross cell transmission. At this stage, if there are still time slot resources left, the LCs allocate them to the edge CNs. We argue that the resource for an edge CN should be allocated at last, because the channel condition tends to be worse than the center mobile devices, and due to its high mobility, it may become a center mobile device in the next period.

[1]Inner network is defined as the network only contains center mobile devices.

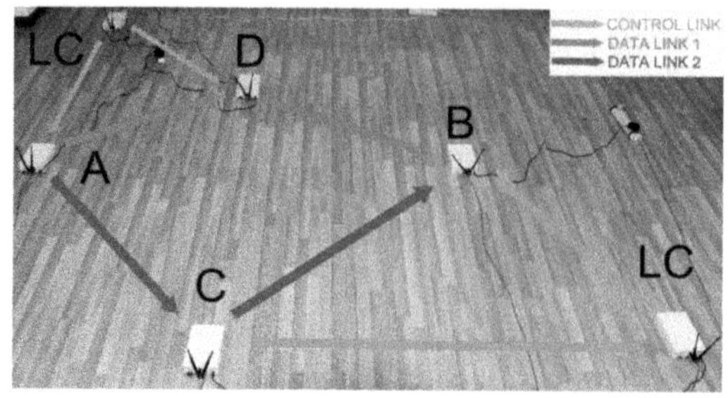

Figure 2: The overview of the experiment

We then briefly describe the calibration mechanism. The aforementioned topology is based on the location and velocity of the mobile devices. We assume a fixed positive link capacity if the two corresponding nodes satisfy the connectivity constraint. Sometimes, due to some non-location-based effects such as fading and a blockage, the topology obtained in this way may be inaccurate. Thus, we employ the statistics of the previous flow information to calibrate the topology. Specifically, for the last n period, if the data delivery ratio of a link is less than a threshold γ_d, the link is treated blocked. Note that n period should be at the scale of seconds to avoid too frequent modification of the topology and reduce computation complexity.

3. DEMONSTRATION

The demonstration employs the USRP hardware and the GNU Radio software to evaluate the feasibility of our proposed system. We adopt the physical layer of a single user point-to-point IEEE 802.11 a/g/p transceiver [1], and add the TDMA-based MAC layer and network layer to support multi-hop cross-cell D2D transmission. We use a commodity PC to serve as the global controller which connects with the local controllers. In addition, we also perform an experiment to demonstrate the automatic calibration property of our system. As shown in Fig. 2, the system consists of 1 GC, 2 LCs, and 4 edge PSNs, i.e., nodes A, B, C, and D. There are two main parts of this experiment. Initially, based on the topology and flow information, the controllers abstract the network and inform the application with the connectivity graph and contention graph to regulate the data flows. The routing is defined as from A to B to D. Then, we put a metal plate to block the signal from A to B. Through the automatic calibration, the controllers re-direct the data flows, i.e., from A to C to D.

4. ACKNOWLEDGEMENT

This work was supported by the National 973 Project under Grant 2013CB336700, by the National Natural Science Foundation of China under Grants 61222104 and U1301255, and 61428101.

5. REFERENCES

[1] B. Bloessl. An ieee 802.11 a/g/p transceiver for gnu radio. https://github.com/bastibl/gr-ieee802-11.

[2] K. Jain, J. Padhye, V. N. Padmanabhan, and L. Qiu. Impact of interference on multi-hop wireless network performance. In *Proceedings of the 9th Annual International Conference on Mobile Computing and Networking*, pages 66–80. ACM, 2003.

Demo: RecDroid— An Android Resource Access Permission Recommendation System

Bahman Rashidi, Carol Fung, Gerrit Bond, Steven Jackson, Marcus Pare
Dept. of Computer Science, Virginia Commonwealth University
Richmond, Virginia, USA
{rashidib,cfung,bondg,jacksonst4,pareme}@vcu.edu

Tam Vu
Dept. of Computer Science and Engineering, University of Colorado Denver
Denver, Colorado, USA
tam.vu@ucdenver.edu

ABSTRACT

Nowadays, it is prohibitive for apps market places, such as Google App Store, to thoroughly verify an app's resource permission requests to be legitimate or malicious. As a result, mobile users are left to decide for themselves whether an app is safe to use or not. To assist users to make correct decisions as for whether to accept a permission request or not, we propose RecDroid. RecDroid is a crowdsourcing recommendation framework that collects apps' permission requests and users' responses to those requests, from which an experts ranking algorithm is used to seek expert users in the system and a recommendation algorithm is used to suggest appropriate responses to permission requests (accept or reject) based on experts' responses. In this demo, we demonstrate a user case to show how the RecDroid system assists users in permission control. We also explain the major principles and processes behind that support the RecDroid recommendation system.

Keywords

Permission; Android; Recommendation; Policy-based; Smartphone

1. INTRODUCTION

In current Android architecture, users are the key to resource control to applications. Users need to grant all resource access requests before installing and using an app. This type of permission control mechanism, however, has been proven ineffective to protect users privacy and resource from malicious apps. Study shows that more than 70% of smart phone apps request to collect data irrelevant to the main function of the app. When installing a new app, only a small portion (3%) of users pay attention and make correct answers to permission granting questions, since they tend to rush through prompted permission request screens to get to use the application. In addition, the current Android permission warnings do not help most users make correct security decisions.

Realizing these shortcomings in the current Android architecture, much efforts have been put towards to address the problems.

MobiHoc'15, June 22–25, 2015, Hangzhou, China.
ACM 978-1-4503-3494-5/15/05.
http://dx.doi.org/10.1145/2746285.2764930.

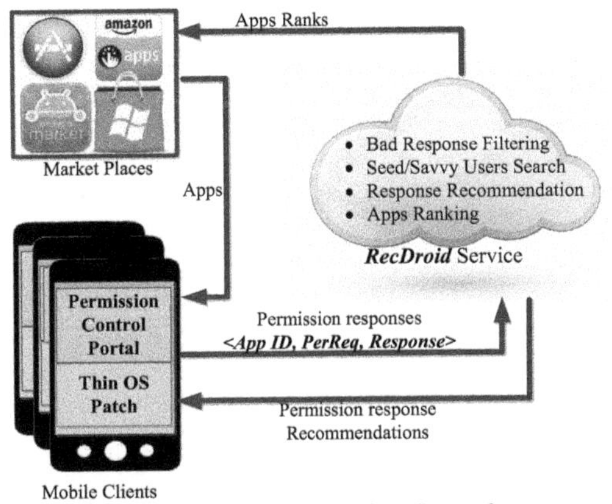

Figure 1: RecDroid Service Overview

In particular, we provide a framework, called *RecDroid*, to assist mobile users to control their resource and privacy. First, the framework allows users to use apps without giving all permissions and receive help from expert users when permission requests appear. RecDroid allows users to install untrusted apps under a *"probation"* mode, while the trusted ones are installed in normal *"trusted"* mode. In probation mode, users make real-time resource granting decisions when apps are running. Second, the framework also facilitates a user-help-user environment, where expert users' decisions are recommended to inexperienced users. The framework provides the following functionalities [1, 2]:

- Two app installation modes for apps: *trusted mode* and *probation mode*. In the probation mode, an app requests permissions from users at run time to access sensitive resources (e.g. GPS traces) when the resource is needed. In the trusted mode, the app is fully trusted and all permissions are granted.
- An architecture to intercept and collect apps' permission requests and responses, from which recommendations are made on whether a permission should be granted or not.
- A recommendation system to guide users with permission granting decisions, by serving users with recommendations from expert users on the same apps.
- A user-based ranking algorithm to rank security risks of mobile apps.

2. SYSTEM DESIGN AND IMPLEMENTAION

We designed and implemented RecDroid with four major functional components. In particular, RecDroid (1) captures resource

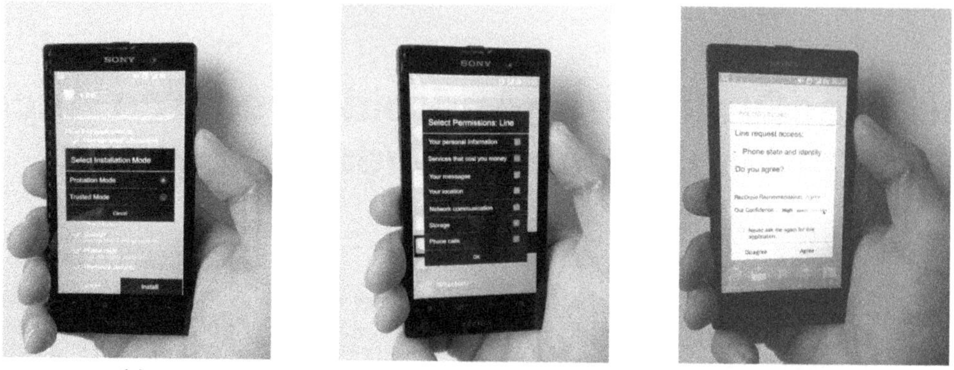

(a) (b) (c)

Figure 2: An example of RecDroid on Line app: (a) probation and trusted installation modes; (b) Users pick which critical resources to be monitored; (c) Pop-up for permission granting with suggestion from RecDroid and its confidence

access request on the phone and pops up dialogs to interact with users when such events happen, (2) recommends users with low-risk responses to permission requests based on expert users' responses, (3) collects users' permission-request responses and reports them to the server, and (4) allows users to configure monitored resources through a management portal. The architecture overview of RecDroid system is shown in Figure 1. The system consists of of a *thin OS patch* and a *RecDroid server*. The *thin OS patch* enables RecDroid to capture local permission requests and interact with users regarding permission control. It also communicates with the server to report user responses to those permission request and receive recommended responses from the server.

We implemented the request capturing function of RecDroid by modifing the permission management component of the Android OS. We set up a RecDroid server on a desktop to handle data storage and recommendation algorithm. We also created an Android app named *Permission Control Portal* for users to monitor and manage resource access permissions at fine-grain level.

3. DEMONSTRATION

3.1 User Interaction

The RecDroid supports users with fine-grained permission control and guided permission decision making with RecDroid recommendation system. We use the app "Line" as an example. The first screenshot (Figure 2(a)) shows two options on app installation, *probation mode* or *trusted mode*. If a user selects the probation mode, the application will be added to the list of RecDroid monitored apps. Otherwise, if the user selects the trusted mode, the application will be installed with all requested permissions granted.

For the installed apps, users can use the RecDroid's *Permission Control Portal* app to view a list of apps which have been installed under the probation mode. If a user selects an app in the list, a list of its requested permissions (Figure 2(b)) will be shown and the user can select some of them to be monitored resources. By default all sensitive resources are monitored.

If an app is installed under the probation mode, whenever the app attempts to access a monitored resource, RecDroid will detect it and the user will be notified through a pop-up dialog (Figure 2(c)). The RecDroid system provides a recommendation with a confidence level to assist users to make decisions regarding whether or not to grant the resource access. If the user select agree, the requested resource will be served; otherwise the access is blocked.

3.2 Experiment Scenario

In our demo, we will show the performance and usability of the RecDroid system through an interactive process. We will show that how the RecDroid system discovers expert users and makes low-risk recommendations to permission requests. In the demo, we will show the interception design of RecDroid and explain the background processes that support the functions of RecDroid. We will show the entire process of RecDroid from installing an app to permission decision making assisted by RecDroid recommendation.

To prepare for the demo, we build a customized Android ROM (Android 4.3, Jelly Bean) equipped with RecDroid system and install it on 5 LG Nexus 4 devices. We also install 20 apps including known Malicious and non Malicious apps. In addition to installed apps, we have developed some apps with different required permissions and users can install them by themselves under probation or trusted mode. After setting up the phones, users will work with the devices. Whenever an installed app requests to get access to a resource, users will be informed through a pop-up dialog to decide whether to accept or reject the request.

RecDroid records all responses from users and store them on an online server hosted by the Computing Center of Virginia Commonwealth University. We use the collected responses to identify the expertise levels of users through our expert seeking algorithm. After ranking the users, we aggregate the responses to a permission request from different users using a weighted voting technique to generate a recommendation on whether to grant the resource access request. We will demonstrate that the RecDroid recommending system can generate high quality recommendations to assist users to protect their security and privacy.

In this demonstration we are planning to show the following aspects of the RecDroid system:

Interaction. In this part of the demo, we show the usability of the system by demonstrating the entire process of the interaction between RecDroid and users. We also demonstrate how users can use RecDroid app to configure the system.

Recommendation System. In this part of the demo, we will show how RecDroid identifies expert users and how it utilizes expert users to make recommendations.

3.3 Equipmet and Settings

We will bring 1 laptops, 4 mobile phones (Nexus 4) and some brochure to demonstrate RecDroid. In addition, we ask for a demonstration table, a poster board, and an electronic screen (around 31.5inch and above) for the video demonstration. We also need the WiFi access for our Mobile phones to communicate with the server.

4. REFERENCES

[1] B. Rashidi, C. Fung, and T. Vu. Recdroid: A resource access permission control portal and recommendation service for smartphone users. In *Proceedings of the ACM MobiCom Workshop on Security and Privacy in Mobile Environments*, SPME '14, pages 13–18, New York, NY, USA, 2014. ACM.

[2] B. Rashidi, C. Fung, and T. Vu. Dude, ask the experts!: Android resource access permission recommendation with recdroid. In *14th IFIP/IEEE International Symposium on Integrated Network Management (IM 2015)*. IEEE, Ottawa, Canada, 2015.

Demo: WiFi Multihop - Implementing Device-to-Device Local Area Networks by Android Smartphones

Chao Yao
State Key Laboratory of Advanced Optical Communication Systems and Networks, Peking University, Beijing, China
chao.yao@pku.edu.cn

Hongliang Zhang
State Key Laboratory of Advanced Optical Communication Systems and Networks, Peking University, Beijing, China
hongliang.zhang@pku.edu.cn

Lingyang Song
State Key Laboratory of Advanced Optical Communication Systems and Networks, Peking University, Beijing, China
lingyang.song@pku.edu.cn

ABSTRACT

WiFi Direct is a new technology proposed by WiFi Alliance to enable direct device to device communications using the same spectrum as WiFi. In some scenarios, communication distance between two devices cannot be covered by one hop, and thus, multihop Device to Device (D2D) communication is required to solve this problem. However, existing WiFi Direct protocol doesn't provide multihop message routing. In this paper, we propose a multihop D2D communication protocol based on WiFi Direct, and implement it on Android smartphone. Devices will form a group in consideration of power and topology condition, delay-tolerant routing between two groups is supported by the protocol.

Categories and Subject Descriptors

C.2.2 [**Computer-Communication Networks**]: Network Protocols—*Routing protocols*

Keywords

Device-to-Device Communications, Multihop Networks, Wifi Direct

1. INTRODUCTION

In many scenarios, wireless communication is set up using base station or Access Point. However, infrastructure nodes may fail to provide service in some hostile scenario. In such a scenario, D2D communication is a promising technique adopted to solve the communication disability. The original IEEE 802.11 standard has enabled D2D communication by means of the ad hoc mode. Unlike the previous technology, WiFi Direct builds upon the successful IEEE 802.11 infrastructure mode and lets devices negotiate who will take over the AP-like functionalities [2]. The virtual AP will take control of the clients, and once the virtual AP can access to the infrastructure node, the clients can also communicate with the infrastructure node as well.

MobiHoc'15, June 22–25, 2015, Hangzhou, China.
ACM 978-1-4503-3489-1/15/06
http://dx.doi.org/10.1145/2746285.2764931.

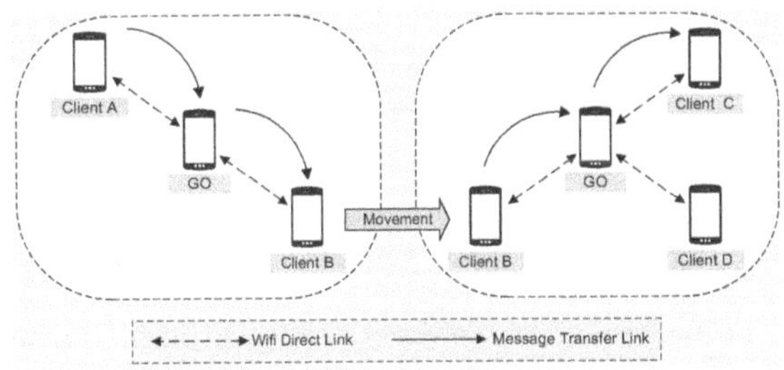

Figure 1: A simple illustration of multihop D2D communication model.

However, the limitation of WiFi Direct is that it only defines D2D communications in its coverage, but long-haul communications are not supported. For this reason, multihop D2D communication is adopted to support the long-haul communications. However, multihop D2D communications based on WiFi Direct still face many technical challenges. In WiFi Direct standard, the source only knows the next receiver, the routing is one challenge for a network without centralized control. Secondly, a device with low battery cannot work as the relay node to forward messages, power control is another challenge. To address this issue, we propose a WiFi Direct based protocol to support multihop D2D communications by the means of delay-tolerant routing, which considers both topology and power.

2. PROTOCOL DESIGN

The most significant feature in our design is that a device can transmit message to another device via multihop WiFi Direct communications without the assist of infrastructure nodes. In our proposed protocol, the mobility of the devices is utilized, and by the means of multihop D2D communication, the message can be forwarded to the destination. Detailed protocol process is presented in Fig. 2.

2.1 Group Formation

Initially, devices scan the devices in its neighbor as the operation mode defined in WiFi Direct standard [1]. After P2P discovery, it supports group formation by the means of selecting a group owner (GO) which has the highest intent value among all clients to take control of the group. The intent values of the devices depend on the number of neighbors and the Received Signal Strength Indicator (RSSI) from the neighbor devices. From the topology perspective, a device

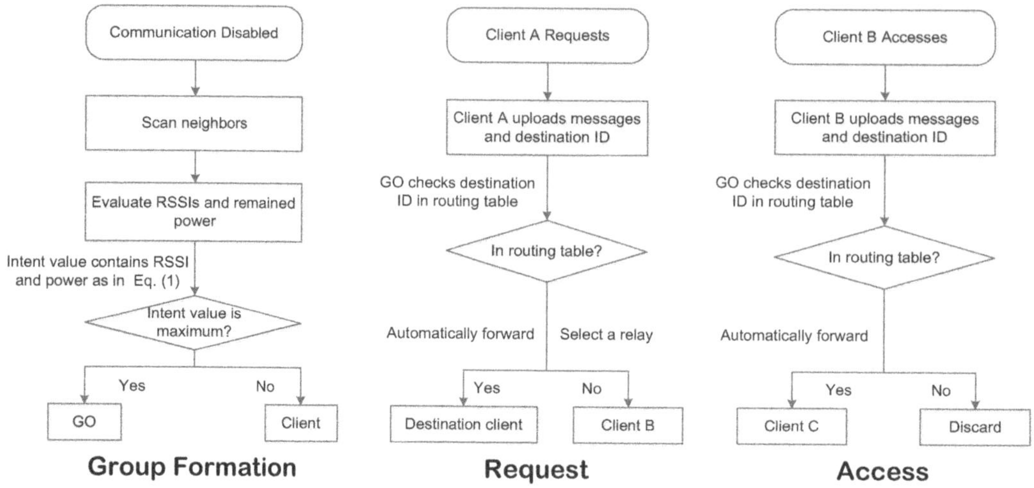

Figure 2: The detailed process of multihop D2D communication protocol in Fig. 1.

has a sufficient large number of neighbors, which indicates that the device is in a more centralized position. Therefore, it should have more probability to become a GO.

At the beginning of the discovery, each device initializes the P2P negotiation. Each device evaluates the values of RSSIs for all the neighbors and the power remained in the device. According to the received RSSIs and the remained power, the intent value can be caculated as follow:

$$IV = \left[\frac{\alpha}{N} \sum_{i=1}^{N} R_i + \beta P \right], \tag{1}$$

where N denotes the number of neighbors, R_i denotes the RSSI from the neighbor i, and P denotes the current power. The RSSI and power are evaluated as integers varying from 1 to 15. The parameters α and β denote the significance level of power and centrality, in our demo, $\alpha = 0.7$ and $\beta = 0.3$. After comparing the intent values, the GO is selected and all the other devices are worked as clients connected to GO.

2.2 Data Forwarding

During the data transmission process, the unique ID to specify device is its telephone number. Therefore, after group formation, the GO device will set up a routing table which contains the numbers of all the devices in this group. Once a device wants to transmit message to other device, the device should upload the message and destination ID to the GO. If GO finds the destination ID in the routing table, the GO will forward the message to the destination device automatically. Otherwise, the GO will find a client to relay the message. When the GO detects that the RSSI from one client becomes lower in a fixed length frame window, the client will be decided the tendency to leave the group. In this way, the GO will deliver the forwarding message to the client which has moving potential.

A moving device once detects a group, the device will join the group as a client. Then, the client will upload the copies of message to the GO, then GO will check its routing table whether the destination device is in this group. If the GO finds the destination device is not in its group, it will discard the copy of message and then return a response. Otherwise, the GO finds the destination device is in its routing table, the GO will forward the message to the target device automatically, and return an acknowledgement information.

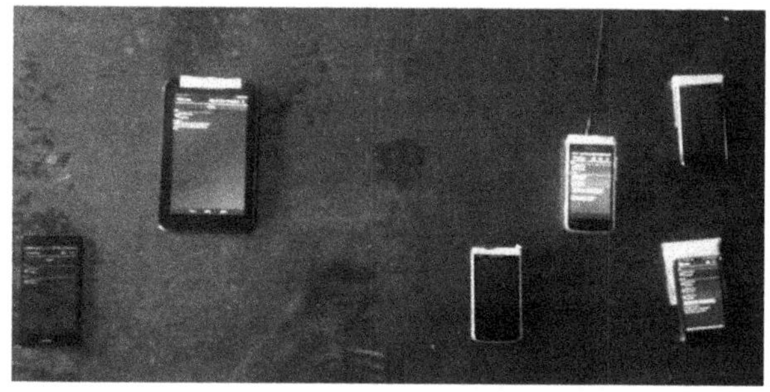

Figure 3: Overview of the experiment settings.

3. DEMONSTRATION DESCRIPTION

In this demo, we demonstrate and explain the detailed experiment settings and the WiFi Direct based multihop D2D communication protocol, the experiment settings in demo are shown in Fig. 3. In the demo, we highlight the core idea of our design, including the group formation and data forwarding, by visualizing the evaluation process of the intent values of each device and the selection process of GO. In addition, the process of message forwarding across different groups is presented in the demo.

4. ACKNOWLEDGEMENT

This work was supported by the National 973 Project under Grant 2013CB336700, by the National Natural Science Foundation of China under Grants 61222104 and U1301255, and 61428101.

5. REFERENCES

[1] Wi-fi peer-to-peer (p2p) technical specification v1.2. Technical report, P2P Technical Group, WiFi Alliance, December 2012.

[2] D. Camps-Mur, A. Garcia-Saavera, and P. Serrano. Device-to-device communications with wi-fi direct: overview and experimentation. *IEEE Wireless Communications*, 20(3):96–104, June 2013.

Demo: Concurrent Spectrum Sensing and Transmission for Cognitive Radio using Self-Interference Cancellation

Andrew Austin
andrew.austin@epfl.ch

Orion Afisiadis
orion.afisiadis@epfl.ch

Alexios Balatsoukas-Stimming
alexios.balatsoukas@epfl.ch

Andreas Burg
andreas.burg@epfl.ch

Telecommunications Circuits Laboratory, École Polytechnique Fédérale de Lausanne, Switzerland

ABSTRACT

A demonstration of a cognitive radio network that supports concurrent spectrum sensing and transmission is presented. To detect primary users while transmitting, the secondary user node must suppress the self-interference signals. The system is implemented on a National Instruments Universal Software Radio Peripheral (USRP) platform. The demonstration will show that continuous spectrum sensing avoids the overhead for dedicated sensing periods and can detect the primary user within at most 10 ms from the start of transmission.

1. INTRODUCTION

Cognitive radio has been proposed to improve spectral efficiency by introducing opportunistic reuse of temporarily under- or un-used frequency spectrum [6]. Fig. 1(a) shows a simplified cognitive radio system, where a secondary user communicates with the receiver nodes when the primary user is not active. Primary users may have priority access rights to some frequency bands (e.g., licensed spectrum). Therefore, secondary users with cognitive radio capability must be able to rapidly detect the presence of these primary users and switch to other unoccupied frequency bands.

Many spectrum sensing algorithms and techniques have been proposed and implemented (for an overview, refer to [6]). Typically, sensing is not performed concurrently with transmission, as the antennas connected to transmit and spectrum-sensing circuits are usually physically close and significant levels of self-interference would 'swamp' the sensing procedure. Accordingly, most approaches rely on periodically stopping secondary user transmissions to sense the channel [6], i.e., to 'listen' for the primary users, as illustrated in Fig. 1(b). There is a trade-off in establishing appropriate sensing periods and duration: shorter intervals between sensing or longer listening periods reduces the efficiency of the secondary users; however, increasing the interval or re-

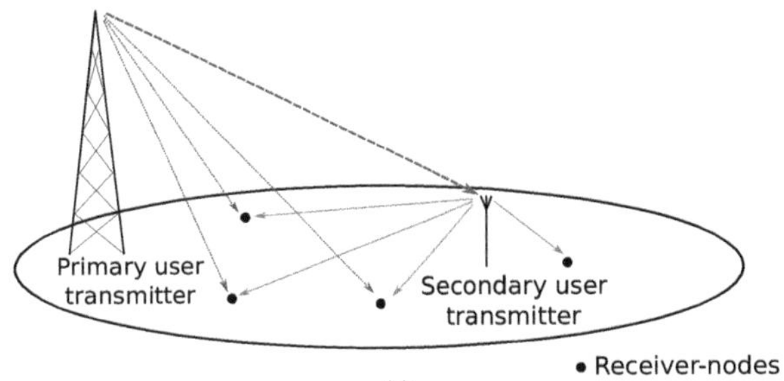

(a)

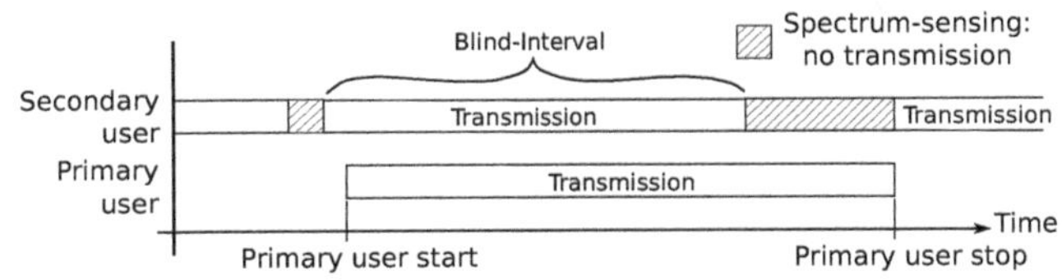

(b)

Figure 1: (a) Overview of a cognitive radio system. (b) Primary and secondary user transmissions over time.

ducing the duration potentially increases interference to the primary users. In addition, the 'blind-interval' between sensing periods can increase the latency between the start of primary user transmissions and the stop of the secondary user, which is a concern for 5G systems where low latency is required.

In this demonstration we present the first hardware implementation of a concurrent transmission and spectrum-sensing cognitive radio system. We avoid overloading and 'swamping' the spectrum-sensing circuit by actively suppressing the (known) self-interference transmitted signal using an appropriately generated RF cancellation signal. It has been shown that concurrent spectrum-sensing can improve secondary user throughput [4] and lowers the risk of interference to a primary user [2]. However, these and other similar studies are largely theoretical and neither hardware implementations nor demonstrations have been previously reported.

An important contribution of this demonstration is the evaluation of spectrum-sensing algorithms under realistic conditions, i.e., in the presence of residual self-interference. For example, [4] and [2] use energy-detection algorithms to identify primary user transmissions by assuming near-

MobiHoc'15, June 22–25, 2015, Hangzhou, China.
ACM 978-1-4503-3489-1/15/06.
http://dx.doi.org/10.1145/2746285.2764932.

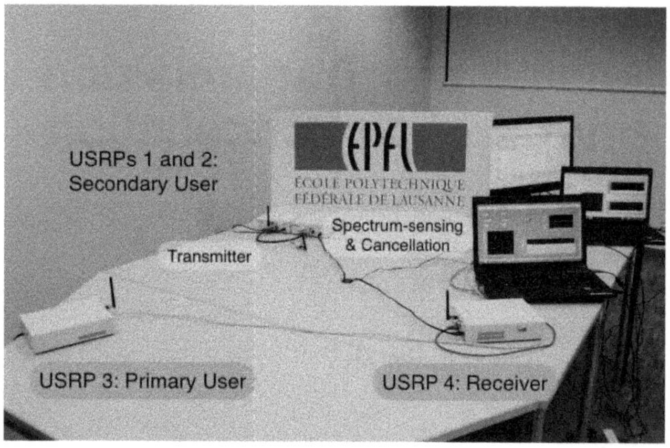

Figure 2: Annotated photograph of the cognitive radio network proposed for demonstration.

perfect cancellation of the self-interference (i.e., suppression below the thermal noise-floor). In practise, perfect suppression is usually not attained, due to phase-noise, other hardware impairments, and uncertainty in the channel estimates [5]. For typical operating conditions, the residual self-interference is above the noise-floor, and this can make it difficult to demodulate weak external signals. However, for cognitive-radio, the goal is only to *detect* the presence of a primary user, and not necessarily to correctly decode the transmissions. In this case, reliable spectrum-sensing performance may be achieved at a lower signal-to-noise ratio, again often involving a trade-off with detection latency.

2. OVERVIEW OF DEMONSTRATION

The demonstration is implemented on four National Instruments (NI) 2920 USRP transceivers [1]. The NI USRP-2920 operates at carrier frequencies of 50 MHz to 2.2 GHz and provides output power ranging from −11 dBm to 20 dBm. The nominal operating frequency of the demonstration system is 2.2 GHz (with 200 kHz bandwidth), although this can be adjusted to other available frequency bands. The USRPs are programmed over Ethernet from a laptop computer, running the LABVIEW software platform, which also performs data processing. If the spectrum-sensing algorithms detect transmission from a primary user, the cognitive radio will quickly switch the transmitter to an unoccupied channel (or off). In the demonstration, the remote receiver will then receive from the primary user. In order to quickly distinguish the received signals in the demonstration, the primary user will transmit BPSK, while the secondary user will transmit QPSK (other combinations are also possible).

2.1 Self-Interference Cancellation

Two of the USRP transceivers (USRPs 3 and 4 in Fig. 2) are assigned the roles of primary user transmitter and remote-user receiver respectively. The two remaining USRPs are used to form the secondary user full-duplex transmit node, as shown in Fig. 2. In the demonstration, the nodes will be separated by approximately 2 meters. USRP 1 acts as the transmitter, modulating and sending data into the channel, while spectrum-sensing is performed by the receiver in USRP 2. USRP 2 also sounds and estimates the self-interference channel, and generates an appropriate RF cancellation signal. The cancellation signal is then 'subtracted' from the incoming signal via an external combiner, reducing the power of the self-interference so that transmissions from the primary user may be detected. The self-interference signal is also attenuated when propagating between the transmitting and spectrum-sensing antennas and further suppression is performed in the digital domain [5].

A 10 MHz reference clock is shared between transmit and cancellation USRPs. The carrier is regenerated within each USRP from this reference signal. In this configuration, each local oscillator has independent phase-noise, which tends to limit the self-interference cancellation that can be achieved [3]. Therefore, primary-user detection algorithms that perform well in the presence of noise and interference are required. In this demonstration we use energy- and waveform-based detection algorithms to sense the channel under realistic noise and self-interference conditions. Our cognitive radio system implementation can detect the presence of the primary user (and responds appropriately by turning off the secondary user) within 10 ms from the start of transmission. It should be noted that a significant component of this latency is due to the need to avoid underflow in the USRPs transmit buffers. The decision latency of the secondary user is much less and depends on the sampling rate and sensing algorithms; for an implementation of energy-detection, with 200 kHz sampling frequency, this is approximately 2.5 ms.

2.2 Requirements

To successfully demonstrate our concurrent cognitive radio system at MOBIHOC'15 we will require:

- A 2 × 2 m table to position the USPRs and laptops;
- Power and internet connections; and
- Space and a supporting board to hang a poster showing some further details and statistical results.

The required set up time is approximately 30 minutes. All other required equipment will be brought by the authors.

3. REFERENCES

[1] NI USRP-292x/293x Datasheet. http://www.ni.com/datasheet/pdf/en/ds-355.

[2] W. Afifi and M. Krunz. Adaptive transmission-reception-sensing strategy for cognitive radios with full-duplex capabilities. In *Proc. IEEE Intl. Symp. Dynamic Spectrum Access Networks (DYSPAN)*, pages 149–160, 2014.

[3] A. Balatsoukas-Stimming, P. Belanovic, K. Alexandris, and A. Burg. On self-interference suppression methods for low-complexity full-duplex MIMO. In *Proc. Asilomar Conference on Signals, Systems and Computers*, pages 992–997, 2013.

[4] T. Riihonen and R. Wichman. Energy detection in full-duplex cognitive radios under residual self-interference. In *Proc. Cognitive Radio Oriented Wireless Networks and Communications (CROWNCOM)*, pages 57–60, 2014.

[5] A. Sabharwal, P. Schniter, D. Guo, D. Bliss, S. Rangarajan, and R. Wichman. In-band full-duplex wireless: Challenges and opportunities. *IEEE J. Sel. Areas Commun.*, 32(9):1637–1652, 2014.

[6] T. Yücek and H. Arslan. A survey of spectrum sensing algorithms for cognitive radio applications. *IEEE Commun. Surveys Tuts.*, 11(1):116–130, 2009.

Demo: An Efficient and Reliable Wireless Link for Mobile Video Surveillance Systems

Li'an Li
Department of Automation
Shanghai Jiao Tong University
li_li_an@sjtu.edu.cn

Cailian Chen
Department of Automation
Shanghai Jiao Tong University
cailianchen@sjtu.edu.cn

Wenbin Yu
Department of Automation
Shanghai Jiao Tong University
yuwb980214@qq.com

Yiyin Wang
Department of Automation
Shanghai Jiao Tong University
yiyinwang@sjtu.edu.cn

Xinping Guan
Department of Automation
Shanghai Jiao Tong University
xpguan@sjtu.edu.cn

ABSTRACT

In this demo, an efficient and reliable wireless link is designed for mobile video surveillance systems. In the link, the idea of cognitive radio is utilized and an adaptive channel switching mechanism is employed to avoid unpredictable interferences. Packets pipelining and accumulative acknowledgement (ACK) is proposed based on the stop-and-wait ARQ protocol to improve the communication efficiency of the link. Moreover, an integration design of the ACK packet is used to piggyback different kinds of control messages. With the efficient and reliable wireless link, a cognitive radio prototype is developed for video transmission between the telerobot and teleoperator. The video information from the telerobot can be transmitted back to the teleoperator quickly and reliably even under channel interferences. The telerobot can also be controlled timely and accurately. A video demo shows the whole story and performance.

Keywords

ARQ; cognitive radio; throughput; SDR

1. INTRODUCTION

Co-channel or adjacent-channel interference becomes more and more serious in the ISM band because of the proliferation of wireless devices and standardized protocols in this licensed free band. The conventional static wireless protocols may not guarantee the quality of service (QoS) requirements for some specific applications under the complex and dynamic spectrum environment. With the recent advances in software-defined radio (SDR) technology and hardware, the design and implementation of wireless protocols with adaptive and dynamic adjustment ability is a trend. In this demo, we design an efficient and reliable wireless link for mobile video surveillance systems to embrace this trend. These systems can be used for industrial surveillance, customs and border protection and disaster environment exploration. As shown in Fig. 1, a telerobot can be sent into some surveillance environments to obtain the video information, which needs to be transmitted back to a teleoperator timely and reliably. Then the teleoperator can have a understanding of the detected environment and operate the telerobot precisely and efficiently. However, the crowded spectrum environment with unknown interferences set up a barrier for the real-time requirement. Facing the dynamic interferences, the standardized protocols such as 802.15.4, 802.11 may not perform well without adaptive capacity. Hence, an efficient and reliable wireless link is designed and implemented on the SDR platforms as shown in Fig. 1. The USRP node on the telerobot and the PXI platform as the teleoperator are SDR transceivers with frequency-agile ability. The newly designed wireless link is based on the popular stop-and-wait automatic repeat-request (ARQ) protocol.

MobiHoc'15, June 22–25, 2015, Hangzhou, China.
ACM 978-1-4503-3489-1/15/06.
http://dx.doi.org/10.1145/2746285.2764934.

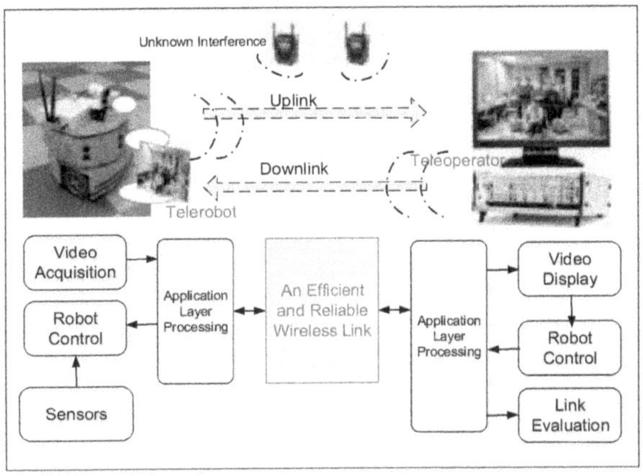

Figure 1: Setup of demonstration and system architecture.

2. WIRELESS LINK DESIGN

In the wireless link, two different strategies are proposed to improve the communication efficiency and reliability. Moreover, integrated design of the ACK packet reduces the ACK overhead and improves the throughput further.

2.1 Packets Pipelining and Accumulative ACK

Since the wireless link is unreliable, ACK and retransmission are necessary to guarantee the quality of video trans-

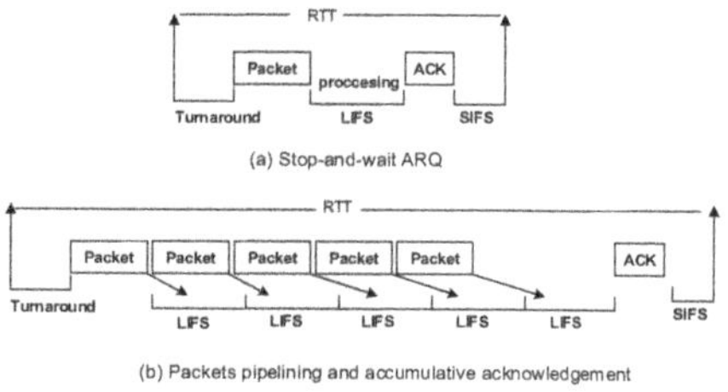

Figure 2: Time cost of a round-trip communication.

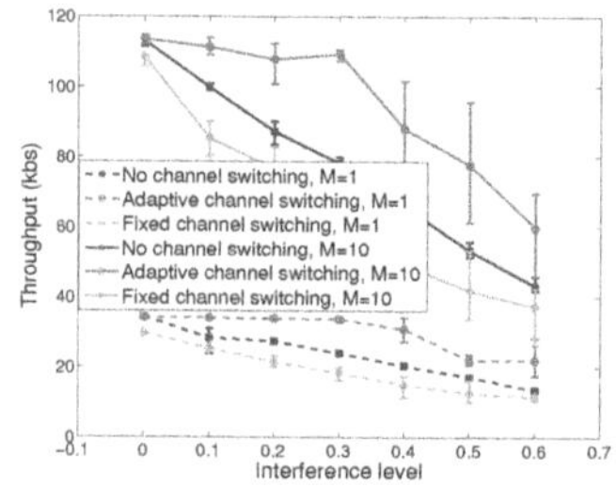

Figure 3: Throughput vs. interference level.

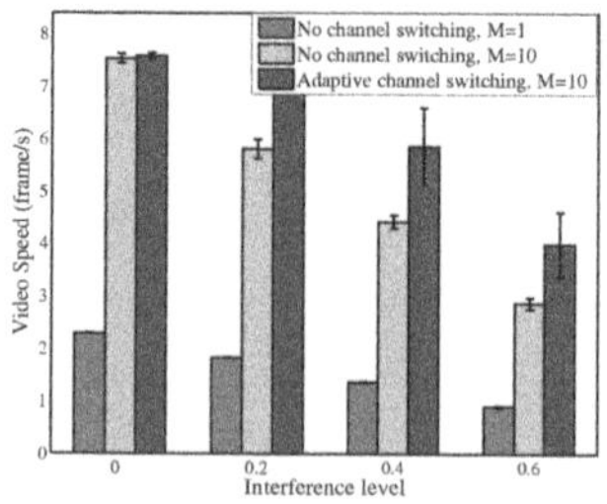

Figure 4: Video speed vs. interference level.

mission. For the stop-and-wait ARQ protocol, the time costs for each round communication are shown as Fig. 2 (a). The turnaround time (T_{td}) is the switching delay from receiving to transmitting state. The packet and the ACK time (T_{packet}, T_{ack}) are the transmission time of a packet and an ACK given a specified data rate respectively. The LIFS time (T_{LIFS}) is the processing delay of each packet and the SIFS time (T_{SIFS}) is the processing delay of the ACK. Because of the signal processing delay [2], T_{LIFS} and T_{SIFS} are larger than the packet and ACK transmission time. Hence, the traditional stop-and-wait ARQ is inefficient because of waiting cost and frequently ACK overhead.

To improve the communication efficiency of the wireless link, we modify the traditional stop-and-wait ARQ protocol and propose packets pipelining and accumulative ACK strategy as shown in Fig. 2 (b). The transmitter continues to send a number of packets specified by a window size M in a pipelined way. The receiver captures and processes the packets in a concurrent way to improve efficiency. After processing all packets in the round, then the receiver acknowledges the transmitter with an accumulative ACK to reduce overhead. The round-trip time (RTT) for the both strategies is given by $RTT = T_{td} + T_{packet} + M * T_{LIFS} + T_{ack} + T_{SIFS}$. The communication efficiency [1] is defined as $\eta = M * T_{packet}/RTT$. Obviously, the communication efficiency increase with M. When $M = 1$, it is the traditional stop-and-wait ARQ protocol. However, M cannot be set too large because large M leads to a longer retransmission delay of the false packet.

2.2 Adaptive channel switching

To combat the dynamic and unpredictable channel interferences at the crowded ISM band. An adaptive channel switching mechanism is employed for the wireless link. After decoding all packets in each round communication, the receiver analysis the link quality based on packets lost probability P_e in each round. The receiver senses another available channel if P_e is larger than a threshold δ. The channel switching information is integrated into the ACK packet and is shared with the transmitter by downlink transmission from the receiver. Both devices adjust the communication channel according to channel switching information. The link failure is inevitable because of ACK lost or deliberately jamming. Hence, we introduce a SYN (Synchronization) state that devices enter into when they detect a link failure. The transmitter will enter into the SYN state if it does not receive any ACK after retransmitting the packets R rounds. If the receiver does not receive any data for a time period T_s, it will also transfer to the SYN state. In the SYN state, devices communicate on a dedicated narrow-band channel to exchange the channel switching information.

3. IMPLEMENTATION AND EVALUATION

We fully implement the efficient and reliable link on National Instruments (NI) SDR platforms including NI-USRP nodes and NI-PXI platform as shown in Fig. 1. The performance is evaluated between the traditional stop-and-wait ARQ protocol and the proposed packets pipelining and accumulative ACK strategy with window size $M = 10$. Moreover, the throughput is also compared between adaptive channel switching mechanism, fixed channel switching mechanism and no channel switching mechanism. There are three channels for the transmitter and receiver. Three interference nodes are set to interfere a dedicated channel respectively. The interference level is a ratio between the time duration that interference nodes transmit on the channel and the total time consumption of each experiment.

In Fig. 3, the throughput increases almost 4 times for our proposed strategy ($M = 10$) compared with the traditional ARQ protocol ($M = 1$). Moreover, adaptive channel switching strategy always perform the best when dealing with channel interference. Especially when the interference level at each channel is relatively low (less than 0.3), the effective throughput nearly keeps the same level as no channel interference existing. The adaptive channel switching mechanism not only avoids channel interference smartly, but also saves unnecessary channel switching cost when no interference appears. Hence, the wireless link throughput can be improved greatly when we combined the two strategies together in the communications.

A mobile video surveillance system based on the wireless link is implemented, the performance is as Fig. 4, and the demonstration can be seen from a video [1] [2].

4. ACKNOWLEDGMENTS

The work was partially supported by NSF of China under U1405251, 61273181, 61221003, 61290322 and 61174127.

5. REFERENCES

[1] M. Heusse, F. Rousseau, G. Berger-Sabbatel, and A. Duda. Performance anomaly of 802.11 b. In *INFOCOM 2003*, pages 836–843, USA, Mar. 2003.

[2] T. Schmid, O. Sekkat, and M. B. Srivastava. An experimental study of network performance impact of increased latency in software defined radios. In *WiNTECH 2007*, pages 59–66, Canada, Sept. 2007.

[1] `https://youtu.be/-YhhA3qslNU`

[2] `http://v.youku.com/v_show/id_XOTMOMDkyNzk2.html`

Demo : A Low-cost, Highly Customizable Robotic Platform for Testing Mobile Sensor Networks

Eduardo Castello
Graduate School of Engineering Science
Osaka University, Japan
eduardo.Castello@irl.sys.es.osaka-u.ac.jp

Sinan Y. Hanay
Center for Information and Neural Networks
NICT, Japan
hanay@nict.go.jp

ABSTRACT

Developing a mobile platform which can be useful for sensor network scientists is a challenging task. In this paper, we propose a low-cost, highly customizable robotic mobile platform in order to test mobile sensor network algorithms within lab environments. Using 3D printing technology and user friendly electronics, we provide a useful tool for mobile networking community. This way, the community will have the opportunity to test their algorithms before the deployment in real sensor nodes. A brief market study about the mobile platforms field is given in the paper which reveals that current platforms are either more expensive or simply do not meet the requirements for our target scenario.

Categories and Subject Descriptors

C.2.4 [**Computer-Communication Networks**]: Distributed Systems

General Terms

Design, Experimentation

Keywords

Mobile Sensor Network, Implementation

1. INTRODUCTION

Mobile sensor networks have many applications area. They can be used to monitor environments, by gathering ecological, climatic or seismic data. Researchers believe that these networks would not only be an important tool for environmental surveillance, but also for providing reliable information to robots in pervasive environments.

Many research groups are actively conducting research on the algorithms that distribute the tasks and govern the behavior of a group of mobile sensor nodes. However, it is difficult to transfer these simulation based algorithms into real systems which can resemble the environmental conditions real nodes will face.

Fortunately, 3D printing technology is gathering an increasing amount of attention in research labs where customized hardware and cheap prototypes are needed. Robotics have already benefited from 3D printing technology in a wide variety of projects. However, the problem of creating a mobile robotic platform using this technology has not been address yet. One of the long-term aims is to show that 3D printing technology is a feasible solution in order to create groups of robots that can be useful for important topics such as the mobile sensor network field.

In this paper, we propose a low-cost, highly customizable "do-it-yourself (DIY)" mobile platform named "Epimeteo". This platform is an easy assemble solution in order to test mobile sensor network algorithms within lab environments. We intend to provide a useful tool for researchers in the field in order to test their algorithms before they are deployed in real sensor nodes.

Platform	Price (€)	Disadvantage	Diameter (cm)
Khepera III [1]	2000	Expensive	13
Turtle Bot [2]	750	Expensive	42
Epuck [4]	600	Expensive	7
iRobotsense [3]	230	Large Size	34
Epimeteo	300	DIY	12

Table 1: Comparison of Several Robotic Platforms

2. EXISTING PLATFORMS

A wide range of robot platforms have been used for mobile sensor research. In this section we intend to briefly survey a few of them remarking its relevant capabilities. Table 1 summarizes platforms available to the community.

Even though, previous platforms provided a good initial step towards developing adaptive robotic nodes for sensor networks they couldn't provide an easily reproducible solution to the scientific community.

None of the platforms outlined in section 2 fulfills these requirements. In one hand, the majority of robots have big proportions and therefore need larger environments than a lab setting in order to operate correctly. On the other hand, robots with small dimensions are either expensive or have limited functionalities. Finally, a very small number of these platforms provides free access to their programming code. This motivated us to create the Epimeteo mobile robot.

MobiHoc'15, June 22–25, 2015, Hangzhou, China.
ACM1-4503-3489-1/15/06.
http://dx.doi.org/10.1145/2746285.2764935.

3. EPIMETEO DESIGN

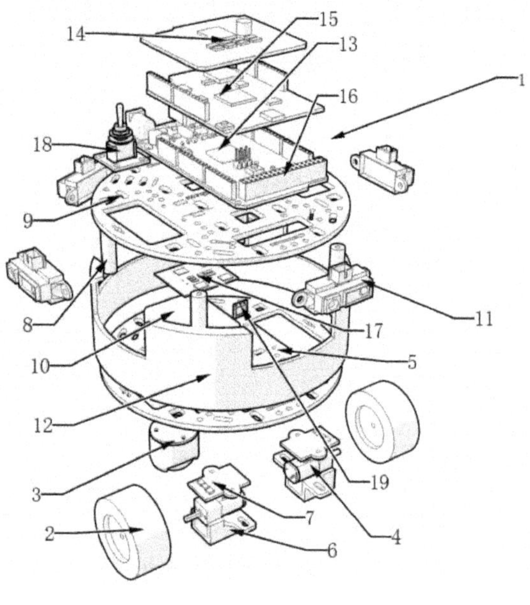

Figure 1: 3D Images of Epimeteo : The mobile robotic base for sensor networks

A detailed description of Epimeteo's components is depicted in Figure 1. The Epimeteo mobile base (1) is a differential drive device in which two wheels (2) – and a ball caster (3) – are used in order to move the whole robot. Both wheels are propelled by two brushed DC metal-gear motors (4) which are attached to the lower chassis (5) by two brackets (6). Two encoders (7) were added in order to calculate the exact distance wheels have travelled.

Four pillars (8) separate the lower and the upper chassis (9) layers, leaving some space in between. Within this space a Lithium ion battery (10) is placed in order to provide enough energy to the whole system. A re-charger circuit is also provided (17).

Epimeteo uses 5 of the popular Sharp GP2Y0A21 IR sensors (11) which are able to sense objects up to 80 cm distance with an angle of 31 degrees. These sensors enable Epimeteo to avoid big obstacles, such as outer walls or other robots. A red "skirt" (12) is included in order to avoid noisy reading from other IR sensors.

Epimeteo uses an Arduino Mega 2560 (13) as main processing unit. This board is based in the popular ATmega 2560 microprocessor, which is very common among roboticists. Besides providing the possibility of connecting a wide variety of sensors, the Arduino board is able to connect with several "Shields". These "Shields" are circuit boards specifically designed to provide extra functionality to the Arduino platform.

The first "Shield" used in this research is called Ardumotor (14) and provides current as well as instructions to both motors. Finally, a WiFi shield (15) is used in order to provide high-bandwidth connectivity.

We believe that the combination of 3D printed pieces such as the two chassis layers, motor brackets, ball caster and Arduino make this kind of devices an ideal candidate for indoor mobile network research, due to its high-customizability and its ease of replication. Figure 2 shows one of the first prototypes ready to be deployed.

One disadvantage of Epimeteo is that, after all pieces are printed it needs to be assembled by hand. However, this assembly process does not require any special skill, and a single robot can be assembled in a short time.

Figure 2: One of the first prototypes

4. SUMMARY

We propose a low-cost, highly customizable robotic platform suitable for mobile sensor networks research. Thanks to the benefits of 3D printing technology, and user friendly electronics we provide a useful solution in order to test sensor networks algorithms. A brief market survey reveals that current platforms are either more expensive or simply do not meet the requirements for lab scenarios.

Currently, we are at the stage of building a medium-size team (10-15 units) of Epimeteo robots in order to test the feasibility of our platform in collective groups. We will test and analyze different types of algorithms for mobile sensor network nodes. Finally, we will provide all needed information (i.e.the 3D model file and the library) to reproduce our prototype through a website.

5. REFERENCES

[1] Khepera iii. `http://www.k-team.com`. Accessed: 2015-04-15.

[2] W. Garage. Turtlebot. `http://turtlebot.com`. Accessed: 2015-04-15.

[3] S. Janansefat, I. Senturk, K. Akkaya, and M. Gloff. A mobile sensor network testbed using irobots. In *37th Annual IEEE Conference on Local Computer Networks (LCN)*, 2012.

[4] F. Mondada, M. Bonani, X. Raemy, J. Pugh, C. Cianci, A. Klaptocz, S. Magnenat, J.-C. Zufferey, D. Floreano, and A. Martinoli. The e-puck, a robot designed for education in engineering. In *Proceedings of the 9th conference on autonomous robot systems and competitions*, volume 1, pages 59–65, 2009.

Demo: Real LTE Experimentation in a Controlled Environment

Vasilis Maglogiannis[1], Dries Naudts[1], Ingrid Moerman[1]
Nikos Makris[2], Thanasis Korakis[2]
[1]Ghent University - iMinds, Department of Information Technology (INTEC), Ghent, Belgium
[2]University of Thessaly - Department of Electrical and Computer Engineering, Volos, Greece
{vasilis.maglogiannis, dries.naudts, ingrid.moerman}@intec.ugent.be, {nimakris, korakis}@uth.gr

ABSTRACT
LTE, commonly known as 4G, stands for Long-Term Evolution and is a wireless communication technology standardized by 3GPP. LTE adoption has increased drastically over the last years, and today is integrated widely in a vast number of wireless devices. However, significant restrictions, such as the increased equipment cost and the acquisition of licensed spectrum, renders experimentation with real LTE equipment very difficult. Recently, iMinds w-iLab.t testbed has been extended with commercial LTE equipment and an EPC (Evolved Packet Core) software platform, offering the opportunity to orchestrate and execute real LTE experiments, hereby providing full access to the most relevant configurable LTE parameters of the network. In this paper, we describe an LTE demonstration scenario that showcases various use cases and the respective experimental settings that can be conducted on the LTE testbed.

Keywords
LTE; wireless; experimentation; testbed; replicability; controlled mobility

1. INTRODUCTION
LTE is a wireless technology, which due to its innovative architecture provides enhanced spectrum management, increased capacity (approaching the Shannon limit [1]), high user data rates and low latency. These characteristics render LTE a very appealing wireless technology currently being deployed worldwide at an increasing rate. LTE is designed to operate in licensed spectrum and as such only mobile operators owning frequency licenses have the right to deploy it. As a consequence end-to-end experimental networks using real LTE equipment are very scarce. Additionally, experimentation in a commercial operated LTE network is not recommended, because of non-replicable experimental conditions. The iMinds w-iLab.t testbed [2] has obtained a test license for LTE frequencies assigned by the BIPT[1] and has been recently extended with both LTE hardware and EPC software. Since early 2015, iMinds offers open access to a fully operational LTE test network for designing and performing end-to-end LTE experiments in a well-controlled environment. The controlled conditions of the LTE testbed offer the immense advantage of performing replicable and reliable experiments. The experimenter can modify various LTE parameters that are normally not accessible to users.
Furthermore, an experimenter can exploit other technologies supported in the w-iLab.t testbed such as Wi-Fi and Bluetooth, in order to perform multi-RAT (Radio Access Technology) experiments. Adequate monitoring tools, e.g. a spectrum analyzer, and cognitive radio platforms, such as WARPs and USRPs, the latter also available with LTE compatible front ends, can assist the monitoring and the validation of the experiments.
Various types of experiments can be performed in the testbed, for instance designing and studying interference scenarios, studying the behavior of different Modulation and Coding Scheme (MCS) profiles in the downlink (DL) or the uplink (UL), designing mobile LTE scenarios using the controlled robotic platform provided by the testbed and many more.
This paper describes an LTE demonstration scenario showcasing the DL throughput achieved using different MCS profiles, as well as how neighboring cells operating in the same frequency channel can interfere and reduce the throughput. This is a realistic scenario deserving attention by the research community, as it has to be addressed in the context of 5G dense and small cell setups.

2. DEMONSTRATION
2.1 Test setup description
The LTE experimental facility of the iMinds w-iLab.t testbed consists of both an EPC network and a Radio Access Network (RAN). The EPC software platform is provided by SiRRAN Communications and is compliant with the 8th release of the 3GPP specifications for LTE. It consists of MME, HSS, S-GW and P-GW modules and provides a web interface for monitoring and configuration. The RAN part of the LTE testbed is composed of two femtocells provided by ip.access that can operate in 3GPP

MobiHoc'15, June 22-25, 2015, Hangzhou, China
ACM 978-1-4503-3489-1/15/06.
http://dx.doi.org/10.1145/2746285.2764936

[1] Belgian Institute for Postal services and Telecommunications

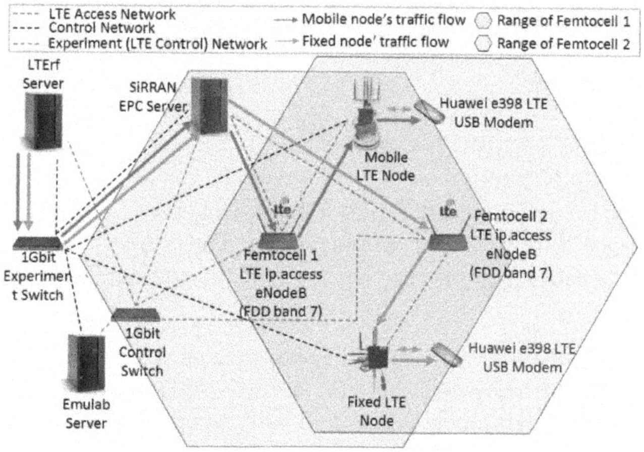

Figure 1: LTE Demo's architecture

bands 7 and 13, and 28 Huawei LTE USB dongles that can support 2x2 MIMO. Eight of these dongles are attached to fixed nodes distributed in the testbed, while the other 20 are mounted on mobile nodes. The different LTE software modules and femtocells provide an API that allows configuration of their parameters through scripts. Moreover, configuration can also be achieved via OMF [3], using the LTErf service [4] developed by the UTH team [5]. The configuration of LTE testbed resources with OMF aligns the LTE experimentation with the de facto testbeds' philosophy.

2.2 Experiment scenario

In our scenario, we examine the LTE DL throughput that can be achieved between the server hosting the LTErf service and a UE, using different MCS profiles. We further analyze how interference from a neighboring cell can affect this throughput. The UE is mounted on a mobile node that moves around following a predefined route. The interferer node is fixed. The LTE network consists of the EPC and 2 femtocells, while the LTErf server is used to configure the femtocells and initialize the traffic. Both femtocells are configured to operate in the same frequency and are placed closely together, so that their cell ranges overlap. Both nodes are in the range of the two femtocells, but are attached to a different femtocell. This way, transmission from/to the femtocells will interfere with each other. Figure 1 illustrates the described scenario.

2.3 Execution and results

The mobile LTE node is attached to femtocell 1 and the fixed (interferer) node to femtocell 2. Femtocell 1 is configured to use the 18th MCS DL profile and femtocell 2 is configured to use the 27th. When the experiment starts, the mobile node starts following the predefined route and the LTErf server initializes DL UDP traffic towards the mobile node using a data rate of 60 Mbps. As the node moves around, the received throughput is measured and is represented on a graph. Then, the traffic stops, femtocell 1 changes to the 27th MCS DL profile and the server hosting the LTErf service again sends LTE traffic. Meanwhile, the

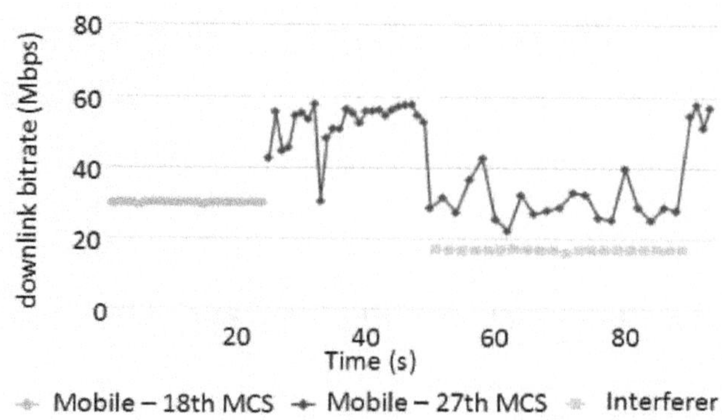

Figure 2: Downlink throughput using different MCS profiles and the degradation caused by interference

received throughput measurement continues. After a while, the LTErf server concurrently starts a second data stream to the fixed node. This causes interference leading to throughput degradation, as shown in Figure 2. The blue and black graphs denote the DL throughput using the 18th and the 27th MCS profile respectively. The graphs show that the higher MCS profile achieves higher throughput, but is more sensitive to the node's movement. As Figure 2 shows, after the first 50 seconds the controlled interference is introduced, resulting in a decreased throughput. Finally, the throughput increases again when the interference stops.

3. CONCLUSION

This paper presents the iMinds w-iLab.t LTE testbed and emphasizes its newest features offering LTE experimentation using commercial LTE equipment. We demonstrated a relevant scenario showcasing how an experimenter can use the LTE testbed with the standardized experimentation tool OMF to study the behavior of different MCS profiles and the impact of interference on the DL throughput.

ACKNOWLEDGMENTS

The research leading to these results has received funding from the European FP7 Program under grant agreement FP7-612050 (FLEX project).

REFERENCES

[1] P. Mogensen et.al. LTE Capacity compared to the Shannon Bound. In proc. of IEEE 65th VTC Spring, Apr. 2007

[2] iMinds w-iLab.t testbed. https://www.wilab2.ilabt.iminds.be

[3] T. Rakotoarivelo et.al. OMF: A Control and Management Framework for Networking Testbeds. In proc. of ACM SIGOPS Oper. Sys. Review, 2010

[4] N. Makris et.al. Enabling Open Access to LTE network components; the NITOS testbed paradigm. In proc. of IEEE NetSoft 2015

[5] NITOS Testbed. http://nitlab.inf.uth.gr/NITlab/

Demo: An Augmented Reality Based Social Networking System for Mobile Users Using Smartphones

Lien-Wu Chen
Department of Information Engineering and Computer Science, Feng Chia University, Taichung 407, Taiwan
lwuchen@fcu.edu.tw

Yu-Fan Ho
Department of Information Engineering and Computer Science, Feng Chia University, Taichung 407, Taiwan
d0163158@fcu.edu.tw

Yung-En Li
Department of Information Engineering and Computer Science, Feng Chia University, Taichung 407, Taiwan
d0107801@fcu.edu.tw

ABSTRACT

In this paper, we design an augmented reality based social networking system, called SocialYou, for mobile users using smartphones. The SocialYou system only needs a single-finger action that drags the icon of social networking websites to the target face on the screen of a smartphone. The target user webpage in a specific social networking website can be immediately displayed in the social media App or built-in web browser. Through SocialYou, mobile users do not need to know the target identifier in advance. In addition, mobile users do not need to input identifier information by themselves. Furthermore, mobile users can select a specific target among multiple candidates from the camera of a smartphone. SocialYou reveals an innovative user interface for social networking between mobile users. We have implemented an Android-based SocialYou system that outperforms existing methods in experimental results.

Categories and Subject Descriptors: C.2.1 [Network Architecture and Design]: Network communications

Keywords: Augmented Reality; Cloud Computing; Face Recognition; Mobile Device; Social Networking

1. INTRODUCTION

Growing popularity of smartphones with Wi-Fi/3G communications has made social networking without desktop or laptop computers possible. A specific user webpage in social networking websites can be immediately browsed by mobile users through smartphones. However, most of social networking systems for mobile devices have to obtain the target's identifier information in advance, such as Facebook, Twitter, Google+, etc. In addition, mobile users have to input it by hands before browsing the target's social webpage. The procedures of manual intervention may increase the time and inconvenience of social networking between mobile users.

For sharing files between mobile devices, we have developed an intelligent file transfer framework based on mobile cloud computing in our previous work [1]. Only single-finger action is required in the file transfer process, which is just dragging the file to the target face on the screen of a mobile device. Then, the dragged file is transmitted to the target receiver that can either get the file immediately as her/his mobile device is online or receive the file later after connecting to the Internet. Through the proposed framework, the total consumption time of file transfer between mobile devices can be reduced as much as possible.

Figure 1: System architecture of SocialYou.

To improve the convenience of social startups, we design and implement the SocialYou system for social networking between mobile users based on our file transfer framework. Mobile users just need to drag the icon of social networking websites to the target face on the screen of a smartphone through face detection [2, 3] and recognition [4, 5]. The contributions of SocialYou are four-fold. First, mobile users do not need to know the target identifier in advance. Second, mobile users do not need to input identifier information by themselves. Third, mobile users can select a specific target among multiple candidates from the camera of a smartphone. Finally, the total consumption time of social networking between mobile users can be significantly reduced.

2. SYSTEM DESIGN

Fig. 1 shows the system architecture of SocialYou. On the client side, mobile users use a smartphone with a dedicated SocialYou App to login the SocialYou server through Wi-Fi/3G communications. The user focuses the camera of the mobile device on the target of interest. Next, the user drags the icon of social networking websites to the target face on the screen and then the face photo of the target is sent to the SocialYou server. On the server side, the target's face photo is forwarded to the cloud of face recognition and then recognized by the cloud servers to obtain the registered ID of

MobiHoc'15, June 22–25, 2015, Hangzhou, China.
ACM 978-1-4503-3489-1/15/06.
http://dx.doi.org/10.1145/2746285.2764937.

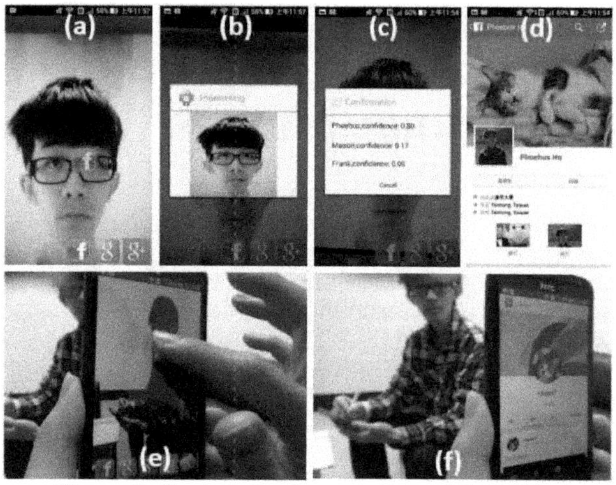

Figure 2: System implementation of SocialYou.

SocialYou. Next, the registered ID of SocialYou is mapped to the ID of the dragged website icon. The specific user webpage in the selected social networking website can be immediately browsed through smartphones.

Using the cloud of face recognition, SocialYou can prevent users from querying the target identifier and avoid keying identifier information by hands. Using the dedicated App, SocialYou can allow users to drag a website icon to the target's face on the screen in an augmented reality manner for social networking. Using the SocialYou server, the face photo can be forwarded from the user to the face recognition cloud for ID identification and the identified ID is mapped to the ID of the dragged website icon. The goal of SocialYou is to minimize the number of manual operations and total consumption time in social networking for mobile users.

In SocialYou, the social networking process between mobile devices is optimized as follows. First, the target face can be detected correctly as mobile users drag a website icon to a specific one among multiple candidates from the camera of a mobile device. Second, the target face can be transmitted rapidly and recognized successfully to obtain the target's identifier through the cloud servers of face recognition. Third, the target's identifier can be confirmed properly by mobile users as the identifier information is recognized by the cloud servers of face recognition. Finally, the target user webpage in a specific social networking website can be immediately displayed by the social media App or built-in web browser.

3. SYSTEM IMPLEMENTATION

We have developed an Android-based SocialYou system. The SocialYou App consists of website browsing and camera preview interfaces, as shown in Fig. 2. Users can use their fingers to press the website icon on the screen, drag it to a specific face from the camera, and release the dragged website on the target face, as shown in Fig. 2(a). To minimize the transmission and recognition time of the face photo, target face detection is implemented on the client side to upload the detected face photo instead of entire image, as shown in Fig. 2(b). For face recognition, the SocialYou server invokes the cloud APIs provided by Mashape [6] and Lambda Labs [7]. Using Mashape cloud APIs, the SocialYou server can send a photo for face recognition, and then receive three registrant IDs with highest face similarity. Then, the SocialYou server sends these registrant IDs returned by Mashape cloud APIs to the SocialYou App, as shown in Fig. 2(c). Once one of returned registrant IDs is confirmed as the target of interest, the target user webpage in the dragged website can be immediately browsed by the social media App or built-in web browser, as shown in Fig. 2(d). Fig. 2(e) and Fig. 2(f) show the system manipulation for Google+, where a demo video is provided online to show how social networking can be done by mobile users through SocialYou as fast as possible (see http://youtu.be/uYhDOlMpLbE).

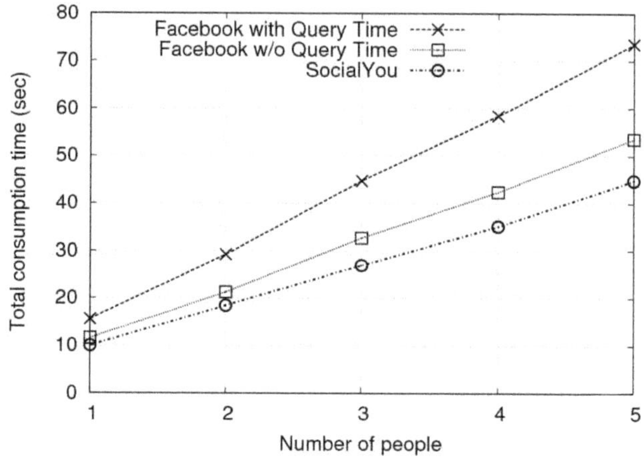

Figure 3: Comparison of Facebook App and SocialYou.

Fig. 3 shows comparisons of total consumption time using Fackbook App and SocialYou under different numbers of people for social startups. Each experimentation is repeated 10 times by realistic trial and we take the average value. For Facebook App, the durations to query and input the identifier information are set to 4 and 8 seconds, respectively. Specifically, the total consumption time using Facebook App is a lower bound without considering the query duration that could be tens of seconds, even minutes. From Fig. 3, we can observe that SocialYou has the lowest total consumption time with all numbers of social startup people. It is because SocialYou users do not need to know and input the target's identifier beforehand, which can save large amounts of time. In contrary, Fackbook App users need to take considerable time to obtain and input the target identifier.

4. ACKNOWLEDGMENT

This research is supported in part by NSC under Grant No. NSC102-2221-E-035-031-MY3 and by MOST under Grant No. 103-2815-C-035-056-E.

5. REFERENCES

[1] L.-W. Chen, Y.-F. Ho, W.-T. Kuo, and M.-F. Tsai. Intelligent File Transfer for Smart Handheld Devices Based on Mobile Cloud Computing. *WILEY International Journal of Communication Systems*, published online, Feb. 2015.

[2] S. Hayashi and O. Hasegawa. A Detection Technique for Degraded Face Images. In *IEEE Conference on Computer Vision and Pattern Recognition*, Vol. 2, pp. 1506-1512, 2006.

[3] J.-S. Jang and J.-H. Kim. Fast and robust face detection using evolutionary pruning. *IEEE Transactions on Evolutionary Computation*, Vol. 12, No. 5, pp. 562-571, 2008.

[4] R. Brunelli and T. Poggio. Face Recognition: Feature versus Templates. *IEEE Transactions on Pattern Analysis and Machine Intelligence*, Vol. 15, No. 10, 1993.

[5] W.-D. Yang. A simple approach to a small-scaled face recognition system. *Master Thesis, Department of Computer Science and Information Engineering, National Central University*, June 2007.

[6] Mashape - The Cloud API Hub. https://www.mashape.com/.

[7] Lambda Labs Face Recognition API. http://api.lambdal.com/.

Demo: xRadio: Development of Next Generation Machine-to-Machine (M2M) Radio Adopting Narrow Band OFDM

Weidong Xiang
University of Michigan
Dearborn
Dearborn,MI,USA, 48128
xwd@umich.edu

Fotios Sotiropoulos and
Sheng Liu
Odyssia Global
Communications
New York, NY. USA
arxaios@odyssia.com

ABSTRACT

In this demonstration, we present a software defined radio (SDR) prototype, xRadio, for next generation machine to machine (M2M) radio based on long term evolution (LTE) and/or smart utility network (SUN, the IEEE 802.15.4g standard), both adopting orthogonal frequency multiplexing division modulation (OFMD). The M2M radios occupy bandwidths of less than 1MHz offering data rates from several to hundreds of kilobits per second. The LTE and SUN baseband processing algorithms are all realized by C codes operating in the Linux operation system over a Raspberry Pi mini PC.

1. INTRODUCTION

The diagram of xRadio is illustrated in figure 1 where the mini PC, Raspberry Pi, integrates an ARM processor operating at clock rate of 700MHz. The RF module daughter board shown in figure 2 is designed as the RF front end for xRadio, including a dual channel ADC and DAC both connected with Raspberry Pi via the serial peripheral interface (SPI) interface. The RF module adopts the WiFi RF chip of MAX2829 from the maxim Company, which works in both 2.4/5.8GHz bands followed by a RF power amplifier, which further boosts the radiation power up to 20dBm. The MAX2829 chip is configured by the mini PC through the same SPI interface in the setup phase.

2. OFDM BASEBAND PROCESSING

The OFDM baseband processing for both transmitter and receiver are shown in figure 6 and figure 7. All modules are realized in C codes featuring with great flexibility. Both LTE M2M and SUN OFDM baseband processing can be realized by loading corresponding set of codes where LTE and SUN mainly distinguish each other with the fast Fourier transformation (FFT) size and coding. Other advanced baseband

MobiHoc'15, June 22–25, 2015, Hangzhou, China.
ACM 978-1-4503-3489-1/15/06.

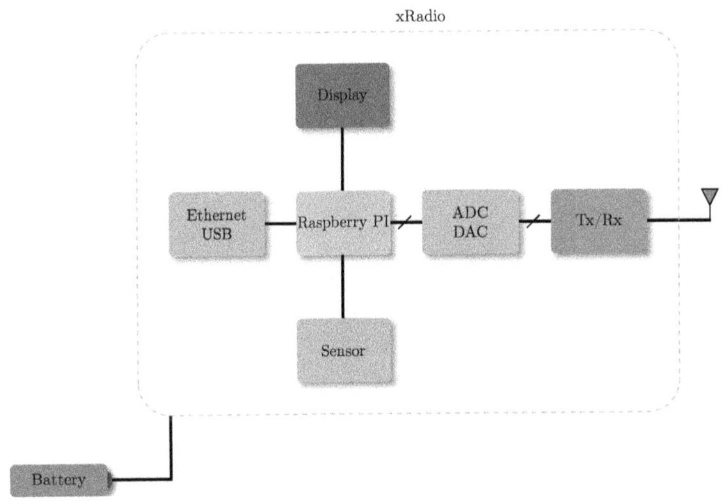

Figure 1: The diagram of xRadio

Figure 2: The picture of the RF module inserted on Raspberry Pi

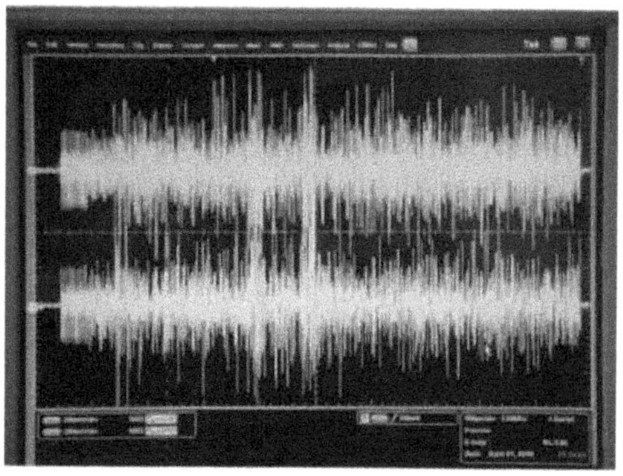

Figure 3: The snapshot of an OFDM symbol in I-channel and Q-channel

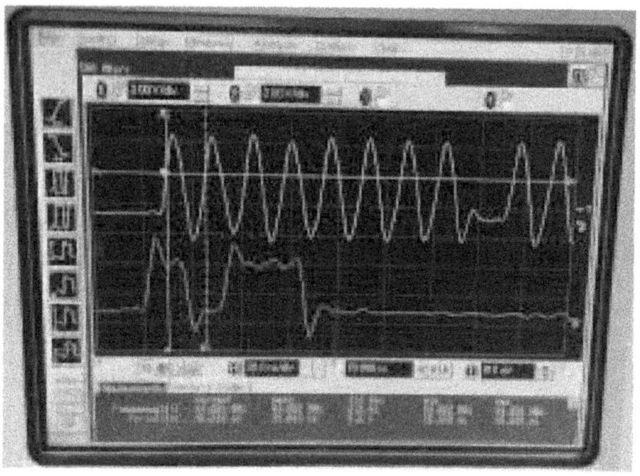

Figure 4: The data and clock of SPI high speed interface at 50MHz

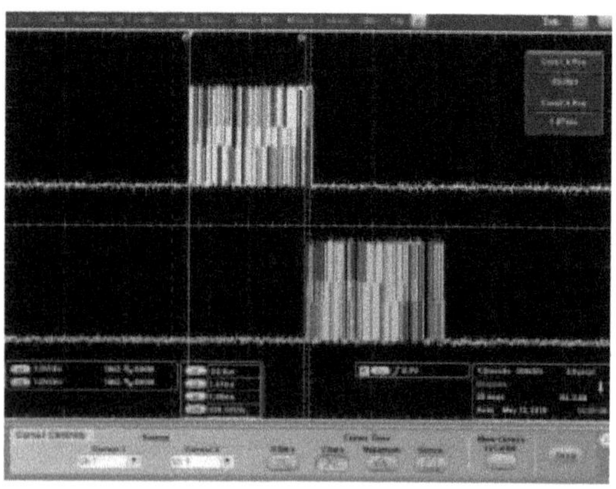

Figure 5: The transmitter and received bit stream within one OFDM symbol

algorithms, including robust and fast time synchronization, Doppler shift frequency estimate and compensation, channel estimate and advanced coding schemes, can be fully implemented and evaluated in a real-time mode for both low-speed event-driven message transmissions as well as high-speed periodic sensor data.

Moreover, two and more xRadio modules can be configured to realize advanced wireless schemes including multiple-input multiple-output (MIMO), beamforming, and spectrum awareness based channel selection, or cognitive radio.

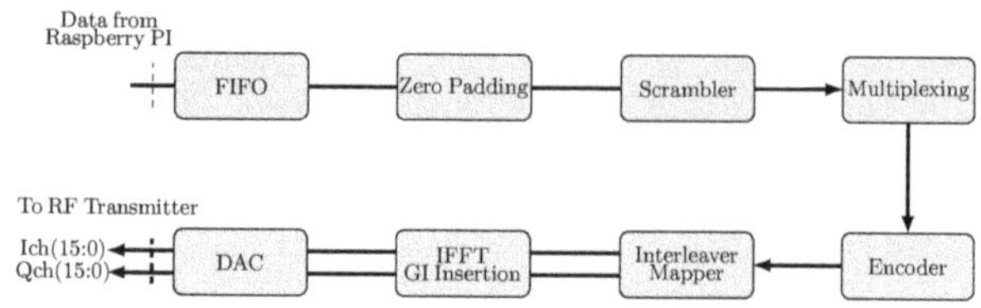

Figure 6: The diagram of transmitter

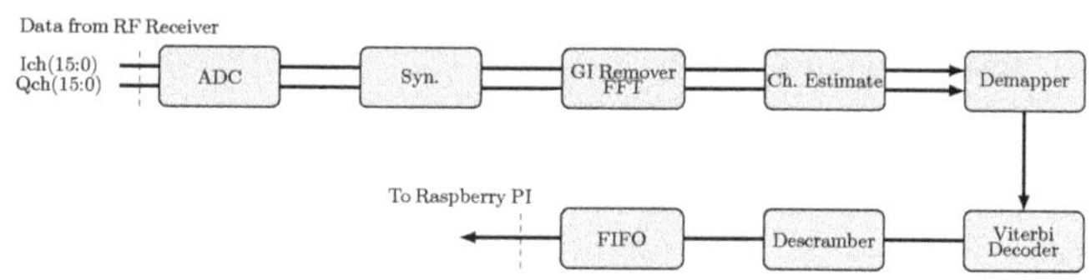

Figure 7: The diagram of receiver

3. EXPERIMENTS AND RESULTS

Due to the limitation of space, we illustrate some experiment results by pictures. A snapshot of one OFDM frame is shown in figure 3. The high speed data through SPI interface, at up to 50MHZ, is shown in figure 4. xRadio works in the time division duplex mode (TDD) and the SPI interface is used to deliver digital data between RF module and Raspberry Pi.

4. CONCLUSION

Compared to other SDR platforms [1, 2, 3], xRadio is a powerful SDR platform for rapidly prototyping a broad range of wireless communication systems at an affordable cost. The small factor of xRadio facilitates its applications while the baseband algorithms written in C make it easy to learn, develop and implement. At current, xRadio is being developed for the Mobility Transformation Center (MTC) Pillar Project, University of Michigan at the scale of up to thousands onboard unit (OBUs) in Ann Arbor, Michigan, USA.

5. REFERENCES

[1] Ettus Research. http://www.ettus.com/.
[2] GUN Radio, http://gnuradio.org/redmine/projects/gnuradio/wiki.
[3] WARP: Wireless Open-Access Research Platform. http://warp.rice.edu/.

Author Index

www.ingramcontent.com/pod-product-compliance
Ingram Content Group UK Ltd.
Pitfield, Milton Keynes, MK11 3LW, UK
UKHW051511290926
15471UKWH00008B/1557

9 781450 338769